Cork

0   200 yards

0   200 meters

Youghal Old Rd.

Cathedral Rd.
Cathedral Walk
John St. Upper
Wolfe Tone St.
Leitrim St.
Richmond
Audley Pl.
Park
Mary Aikenhead Pl.
Vincent's
St.
Glen Ryan Rd.
Fair St.
Shandon St.
John St.
Eason's Hill
Roman St.
John Redmond
Blarney St.
Old Market Pl.
Shandon Church
Dominick St.
Griffith Bridge
Pope's Quay (North Channel)
Christy Ring Bridge
Camden Pl.
North Lee
Mall
River
Bachelor's Quay
Kyrl's Quay
Coal Quay
Lavitt's Quay
Carroll's Quay
Oper
Grenville Pl.
Henry St.
Adelaide St.
Sheare's St.
Liberty St.
North Main St.
Cornmarket St.
St. Paul's Ave.
Crawford Art Gallery
Kyle St.
Coal Quay Market
Castle St.
Paul St.
English St.
Patri
Queens Old Castle
Triskel Arts Centre
Grand Parade
Prince's St.
Cook St.
Oliver
Morgan St.
Parnell Br.
Clonte
Albert
Victoria Rd.
Dyke Parade
Lancaster Quay
Washington St.
Hanover St.
Christ Church
Wandesford Quay
South Main
Marlborough St.
South Mall
Morrison's Quay (South Channel)
Union Quay
City Hall
Albert Rd.
South City Link Rd.
Gas Works Rd.
Sharman Crawford St.
Bishop St.
Nano Nagle Footbridge
Trinity Footbridge
St. Mathew Quay
River Lee (South Channel)
Copley St.
Angesea
St. Finbarr's Cathedral
Elizabethan Fort
Proby's Quay
Sullivan's Quay
George's Quay
Parliament Bridge
South Terr.
Hibernian Rd.
Gill Abbey
Cove St.
Mary
Dunbar
Rutland St.
Sawmill
Infirmary Rd.
Abbey St.
White St.
Langford Row
Southern
Barrack St.
Industry
Friar St.
Douglas St.
Nicholas St.
Old Blackrock Rd.
Bandon Rd.
Desmond Sq.
Keiln's Tower
Mount Carmel
Friars St.
Evergreen St.
Quaker Rd.
High St.

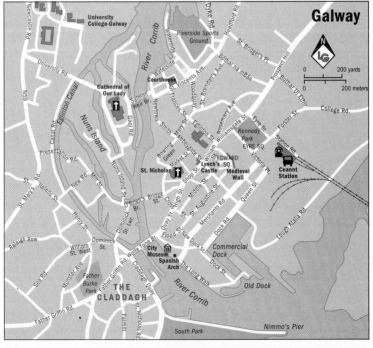

Galway

0   200 yards

0   200 meters

University College-Galway
Newcastle Rd.
River Corrib
Waterside
Dyke Rd.
Headford Rd.
St. Bridger's Pl.
Prospect Hill
Bothar Ui Eithir
Riverside Sports Ground
University Rd.
Eglinton Canal
Waterside
Courthouse
St. Vincents Ave.
Woodquay
St. Brendan's Ave.
Bothar na mBán
N59
Cathedral of Our Lady
Salmon Weir Br.
Newtown Smith
St. Frances St.
Abbeygate St.
Eglinton St.
Rosemary Ave.
Williamsgate St.
Eye St.
Forster St.
College Rd.
Nuns Island
Gaol Rd.
Bowling Green
Market St.
Shop
Lynch's Castle
EDWARD SQ
Kennedy Park
EYRE SQ
Station Rd.
Presentation Rd.
St. Nicholas
St. Helen St.
St. Augustine St.
Medieval Wall
Victoria Pl.
Ceannt Station
Canal Rd.
St. Mary's Rd.
Helens St.
Nuns Island St.
O'Brien's Bridge
Cross St.
Middle St.
Merchants Ave.
Queen St.
Lough Atalia Rd.
Henry St.
New Rd.
Mill St.
St. Bridge St. Lwr.
Flood St.
New Dock St.
Merchants Rd.
Dock Rd.
Raleigh Row
Dominick St.
Quay St.
Commercial Dock
William St. West
Wolfe Tone Br.
City Museum
Spanish Arch
Dock St.
Old Dock
Munster Ave.
Sea Rd.
Father Burke Park
Father Griffin Rd.
Claddagh Quay
The Long Walk
Father Griffin Rd.
THE CLADDAGH
St. Nicholas Rd.
Fairhill
River Corrib
South Park
Nimmo's Pier

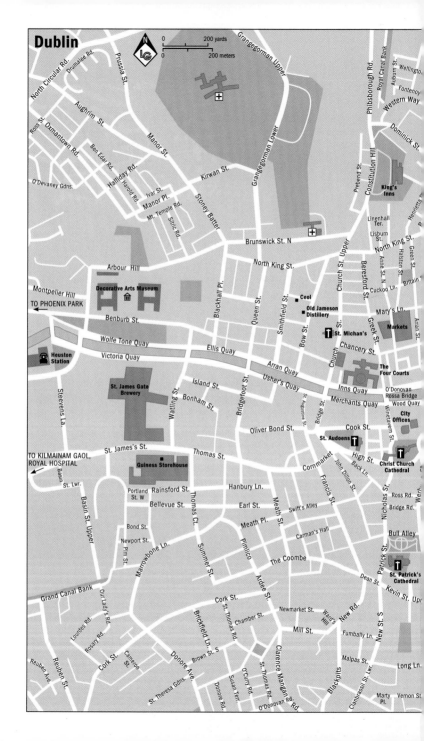

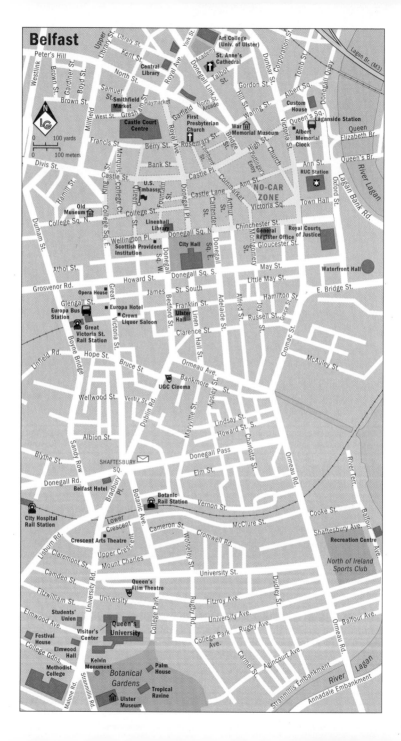

LET'S GO

■ THE RESOURCE FOR THE INDEPENDENT TRAVELER

"The guides are aimed not only at young budget travelers but at the indepedent traveler; a sort of streetwise cookbook for traveling alone."

—The New York Times

"Unbeatable; good sight-seeing advice; up-to-date info on restaurants, hotels, and inns; a commitment to money-saving travel; and a wry style that brightens nearly every page."

—The Washington Post

"Lighthearted and sophisticated, informative and fun to read. [Let's Go] helps the novice traveler navigate like a knowledgeable old hand."

—Atlanta Journal-Constitution

"A world-wise traveling companion—always ready with friendly advice and helpful hints, all sprinkled with a bit of wit."

—The Philadelphia Inquirer

■ THE BEST TRAVEL BARGAINS IN YOUR PRICE RANGE

"All the dirt, dirt cheap."

—People

"Anything you need to know about budget traveling is detailed in this book."

—The Chicago Sun-Times

"Let's Go follows the creed that you don't have to toss your life's savings to the wind to travel—unless you want to."

—The Salt Lake Tribune

■ REAL ADVICE FOR REAL EXPERIENCES

"The writers seem to have experienced every rooster-packed bus and lunar-surfaced mattress about which they write."

—The New York Times

"A guide should tell you what to expect from a destination. Here Let's Go shines."

—The Chicago Tribune

"[Let's Go's] devoted updaters really walk the walk (and thumb the ride, and trek the trail). Learn how to fish, haggle, find work—anywhere."

—Food & Wine

LET'S GO PUBLICATIONS

TRAVEL GUIDES

Alaska 1st edition **NEW TITLE**
Australia 2004
Austria & Switzerland 2004
Brazil 1st edition **NEW TITLE**
Britain & Ireland 2004
California 2004
Central America 8th edition
Chile 1st edition
China 4th edition
Costa Rica 1st edition
Eastern Europe 2004
Egypt 2nd edition
Europe 2004
France 2004
Germany 2004
Greece 2004
Hawaii 2004
India & Nepal 8th edition
Ireland 2004
Israel 4th edition
Italy 2004
Japan 1st edition **NEW TITLE**
Mexico 20th edition
Middle East 4th edition
New Zealand 6th edition
Pacific Northwest 1st edition **NEW TITLE**
Peru, Ecuador & Bolivia 3rd edition
Puerto Rico 1st edition **NEW TITLE**
South Africa 5th edition
Southeast Asia 8th edition
Southwest USA 3rd edition
Spain & Portugal 2004
Thailand 1st edition
Turkey 5th edition
USA 2004
Western Europe 2004

CITY GUIDES

Amsterdam 3rd edition
Barcelona 3rd edition
Boston 4th edition
London 2004
New York City 2004
Paris 2004
Rome 12th edition
San Francisco 4th edition
Washington, D.C. 13th edition

MAP GUIDES

Amsterdam
Berlin
Boston
Chicago
Dublin
Florence
Hong Kong
London
Los Angeles
Madrid
New Orleans
New York City
Paris
Prague
Rome
San Francisco
Seattle
Sydney
Venice
Washington, D.C.

COMING SOON:
Road Trip USA

IRELAND
2004

THERESA ANNE BOTELLO EDITOR
JANE CAFLISCH ASSOCIATE EDITOR

RESEARCH-WRITERS
Théa St. Clair Morton
Naomi Straus
Alex Cooley
Meaghan Casey

CHRISTINE PETERSON MAP EDITOR
JOANNA SHAWN BRIGID O'LEARY MANAGING EDITOR

MACMILLAN

HELPING LET'S GO If you want to share your discoveries, suggestions, or corrections, please drop us a line. We read every piece of correspondence, whether a postcard, a 10-page email, or a coconut. **Address mail to:**

Let's Go: Ireland
67 Mount Auburn Street
Cambridge, MA 02138
USA

Visit Let's Go at **http://www.letsgo.com,** or send email to:

feedback@letsgo.com
Subject: "Let's Go: Ireland"

In addition to the invaluable travel advice our readers share with us, many are kind enough to offer their services as researchers or editors. Unfortunately, our charter enables us to employ only currently enrolled Harvard students.

❧

Published in Great Britain 2004 by Macmillan, an imprint of Pan Macmillan Ltd.
20 New Wharf Road, London N1 9RR
Basingstoke and Oxford
Associated companies throughout the world
www.panmacmillan.com

Maps by David Lindroth copyright © 2004 by St. Martin's Press.

Published in the United States of America by St. Martin's Press.

ISBN: 1 4050 3309 6
First edition
10 9 8 7 6 5 4 3 2 1

Let's Go: Ireland is written by Let's Go Publications, 67 Mount Auburn Street, Cambridge, MA 02138, USA.

CONTENTS

MAPS

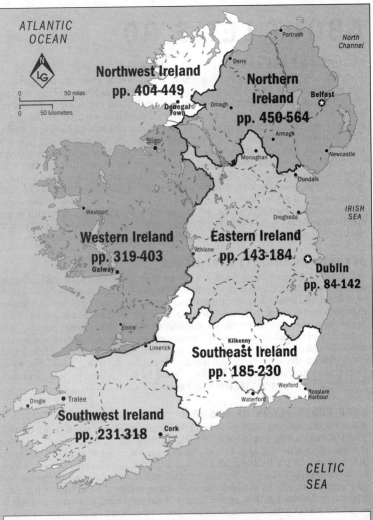

ATLANTIC OCEAN

North Channel

Northwest Ireland
pp. 404-449

Portrush

Derry

Donegal Town

Omagh

Northern Ireland
pp. 450-564

Belfast

Armagh

Sligo

Monaghan

Newcastle

Dundalk

IRISH SEA

Westport

Drogheda

Western Ireland
pp. 319-403

Athlone

Eastern Ireland
pp. 143-184

Galway

Dublin
pp. 84-142

Ennis

Kilkenny

Limerick

Southeast Ireland
pp. 185-230

Wexford

Dingle

Tralee

Waterford

Rosslare Harbour

Southwest Ireland
pp. 231-318

Cork

CELTIC SEA

0 50 miles

0 50 kilometers

ABOUT LET'S GO

GUIDES FOR THE INDEPENDENT TRAVELER

Budget travel is more than a vacation. At *Let's Go*, we see every trip as the chance of a lifetime. If your dream is to grab a knapsack and a machete and forge through the jungles of Brazil, we can take you there. Or, if you'd rather enjoy the Riviera sun at a beachside cafe, we'll set you a table. If you know what you're doing, you can have any experience you want—whether it's camping among lions or sampling Tuscan desserts—without maxing out your credit card. We'll show you just how far your coins can go, and prove that the greatest limitation on your adventure is not your wallet, but your imagination. That said, we understand that you may want the occasional indulgence after a week of hostels and kebab stands, so we've added "Big Splurges" to let you know which establishments are worth those extra euros, as well as price ranges to help you quickly determine whether an accommodation or restaurant will break the bank. While we may have diversified, our emphasis will always be on finding the best values for your budget, giving you all the info you need to spend six days in London or six months in Tasmania.

BEYOND THE TOURIST EXPERIENCE

We write for travelers who know there's more to a vacation than riding double-deckers with tourists. Our researchers give you the heads-up on both world-renowned and lesser-known attractions, on the best local eats and the hottest nightclub beats. In our travels, we talk to everybody; we provide a snapshot of real life in the places you visit with our sidebars on topics like regional cuisine, local festivals, and hot political issues. We've opened our pages to respected writers and scholars to show you their take on a given destination, and turned to lifelong residents to learn the little things that make their city worth calling home. And we've even given you Alternatives to Tourism—ideas for how to give back to local communities through responsible travel and volunteering.

OVER FORTY YEARS OF WISDOM

When we started, way back in 1960, Let's Go consisted of a small group of well-traveled friends who compiled their budget travel tips into a 20-page packet for students on charter flights to Europe. Since then, we've expanded to suit all kinds of travelers, now publishing guides to six continents, including our newest guides: *Let's Go: Japan* and *Let's Go: Brazil*. Our guides are still annually researched and written entirely by students on shoe-string budgets, adventurous travelers who know that train strikes, stolen luggage, food poisoning, and marriage proposals are all part of a day's work. Even as you read this, work on next year's editions is well underway. Whether you're reading one of our new titles, like *Let's Go: Puerto Rico* or *Let's Go Adventure Guide: Alaska*, or our original best-seller, *Let's Go: Europe*, you'll find the same spirit of adventure that has made *Let's Go* the guide of choice for travelers the world over since 1960.

GETTING IN TOUCH

The best discoveries are often those you make yourself; on the road, when you find something worth sharing, please drop us a line. We're Let's Go Publications, 67 Mt. Auburn St., Cambridge, MA 02138, USA (feedback@letsgo.com).

For more info, visit our website: www.letsgo.com.

PRICE RANGES >> IRELAND

Our researchers list establishments in order of value from best to worst; our favorites are denoted by the Let's Go thumbs-up (🏆). Since the best value is not always the cheapest price, we have incorporated a system of price ranges for quick reference. Our price ranges are based on a rough expectation of what visitors will spend. For **accommodations**, we base our price range off the cheapest price for a single traveler to stay for one night. For **restaurants** and other dining establishments, we estimate the average amount that visitors will spend in that restaurant. The table below tells what *typically* is available in Ireland at the corresponding price range; keep in mind that a particularly expensive ice cream stand may still only be marked a ❷, depending on what visitors will spend.

ACCOMMODATIONS	RANGE	WHAT YOU'RE *LIKELY* TO FIND
❶	under €17/ £14	Camping; most dorm rooms, such as HI, HINI, An Óige, other hostels or at university. Expect bunk beds and communal bath; may have to provide or rent towels and sheets.
❷	€17-26/ £14-21	Upper-end hostels or small hotels. May have a private bathroom, or there may be a sink in the room and communal shower in the hall.
❸	€27-41/ £22-31	Most B&B or a small room with private bath in a hotel. Should have decent amenities, such as phone and TV. Breakfast may be included in the price of the room.
❹	€42-56/ £32-46	Similar to 3, but may have more amenities or be in a more touristed area.
❺	above €57/£47	Large hotels or upscale chains. If it's a 5 and it is without the perks you want, you've paid too much.
FOOD		
❶	under €6/ £4	Mostly street-corner stands, pizza places, or fast-food joints. Rarely ever a sit-down meal.
❷	€6-10/£4-6	Sandwiches, bar appetizers, or low-priced entrees. May have the option of sitting down or takeaway.
❸	€11-15/ £7-10	Mid-priced entrees, possibly with soup or salad. Tip'll add some, since you'll probably have a waiter or waitress.
❹	€16-20/ £11-15	A somewhat fancy restaurant or castle. Either way, you'll have a special knife. Few restaurants in this range have a dress code, but some look down on t-shirt and jeans.
❺	above €21/£16	Food with foreign names and a decent wine list. Slacks and dress shirts may be expected.

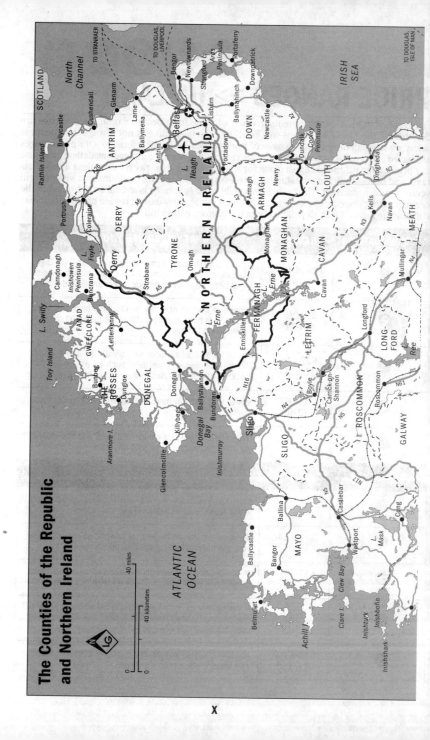

The Counties of the Republic and Northern Ireland

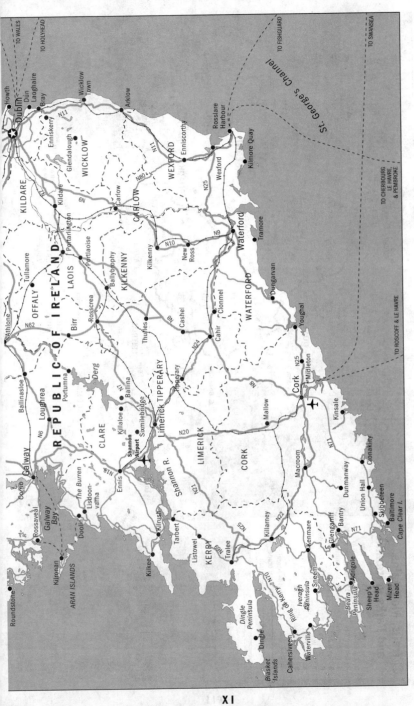

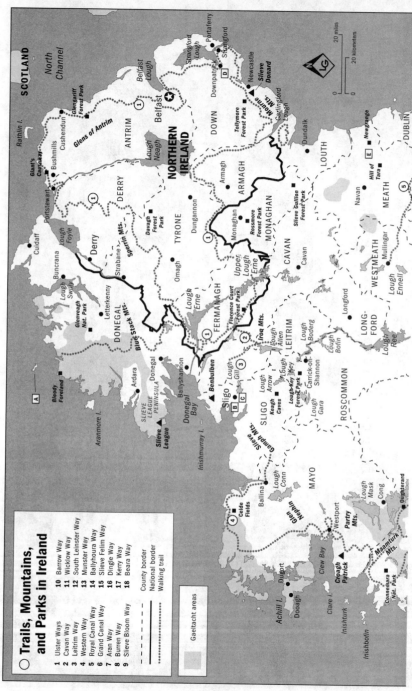

Trails, Mountains, and Parks in Ireland

1	Ulster Ways	10	Barrow Way
2	Cavan Way	11	Wicklow Way
3	Leitrim Way	12	South Leinster Way
4	Western Way	13	Munster Way
5	Royal Canal Way	14	Ballyhoura Way
6	Grand Canal Way	15	Slieve Felim Way
7	Aran Way	16	Dingle Way
8	Burren Way	17	Kerry Way
9	Slieve Bloom Way	18	Beara Way

County border
National border – – – –
Walking trail ••••••••

Gaeltacht areas

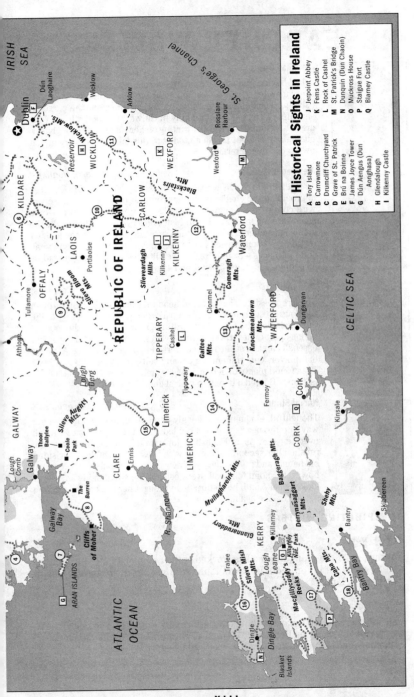

Historical Sights in Ireland

- A Tory Island
- B Carrowmore
- C Drumcliff Churchyard
- D Grave of St. Patrick
- E Brú na Bóinne
- F James Joyce Tower
- G Dún Aengus (Dun Aonghasa)
- H Glendalough
- I Kilkenny Castle
- J Jerpoint Abbey
- K Fems Castle
- L Rock of Cashel
- M St. Patrick's Bridge
- N Dunquin (Dun Chaoin)
- O Muckross House
- P Staigue Fort
- Q Blarney Castle

RESEARCHER-WRITERS

Meaghan Casey
West, Northwest, Midlands

A laid-back economics major, Meaghan stretched each penny and every minute to the max, sampling the surf on Ireland's West coast, catching a sailboat ride with locals, and driving along the gorgeous seacliffs of Donegal. With family in Galway, she had a hint of the green hills and friendly folk awaiting on her route, but through traveling alone she got reacquainted with this familiar country on her own *craic*-loving terms.

Alex Cooley
Belfast, Northern Ireland, Northwest

A veteran research-writer for *Let's Go Turkey 2002*, Alex approached the challenges of her route through Northern Ireland with confidence, perspicacity, and sincere respect for the people she met along the way. Her art-historian's eye helped her probe the meanings and bold beauty of the Derry and Belfast murals, and her outgoing personality led her to seek out *craic* and company in all sorts of places—from a Belfast wedding to an island populated by 40 people, 2 tractors, 3 jeeps, and 4 dogs.

Théa Morton
Southwest

The irrepressible Thea jumped head-first into her travels through the Southwest, from the peopled parks and pubs of Cork City to the intense isolation of the Beara. Although she lamented the gradual falling-apart of her travel attire, she never hesitated to throw on her baseball cap and strike up a conversation or go exploring. A volleyball player, government major, and self-proclaimed history buff, Thea found plenty of action, intrigue, and tales of times past on the Isle, and adopted a bunch of Irish slang along the way.

Naomi Straus
Dublin, East, Southeast

Thoughtful, eloquent, and keenly perceptive, Naomi charmed her way into the hearts of sweet old ladies and friendly bus drivers all over Leinster. As an English major with a fondness for Joyce, she relished her second encounter with "dear dirty Dublin," revisiting old haunts and finding plenty of new ones. Once outside the capital, however, Naomi fell head-over-heels for the countryside and never looked back...until her return flight brought her back to the city and she fell in love again.

CONTRIBUTING WRITERS

Brenna Powell

For the past three years, Brenna has worked at the Stanford Center on Conflict and Negotiation on projects in partnership with grassroots organizations in Northern Ireland.

Phillip Rankin

Phil is from Northern Ireland, although he is currently a nomad as he researches the Spirituality of Young People across the UK. He worked in conflict resolution, community development, and youth work for ten years.

ACKNOWLEDGMENTS

LET'S GO

SPECIAL THANKS TO our amazing, superb RWs, who never gave us less than their best despite a few snags in the road; Joanna, who answered every inane question with warmth and understanding; Christine for maps that are oh so pretty; Jessica for all the help and consultation; Brenna for all the words of wisdom; Phil for his advice.

THERESA THANKS my family for all the love: the Botellos for all the laughs, the Sullivans for the support and, of course, the heritage; my mom and dad for too many things to list; Grandma Anne because I miss you; Grandma Theresa porque siempre somos las dos Teresitas; the chicas for all the fun and support; Kathy, Leslie, and Brie for always lending a kind ear and sharing an amazing summer with me; my boys in the penthouse; Jessica for being truly amazing and never being too busy to talk or advise me; Cait for teaching me; Michael for making growing up fun; Tina because you make me smile; Joanna for all the caring; Jane for the hard work and patience.

JANE THANKS To my family, for introducing me to the storied landscape of Ireland, and to brown bread. To Jane, Kate, and Marie Morris, for playing Van Morrison in the car when I was little, and wearing Barbour coats. To "McNamara's Band," for providing me with a childhood nick-name. To unsettled weather. To Scott, for morning walks, late dinners, and understanding; for sharing your summer and your self with me. To Rebecca, for sunsets by the river and your brilliant company. To Ping, for being a kindred spirit. To Teri, for your devotion to this project, and to Joanna, for your unflagging support. Finally, to my mother, who cycled across Ireland when she was my age, and to whom I owe much inspiration and friendship.

CHRISTINE THANKS the whole Let's Go office and Mapland especially for being the greatest place to chill in the summer!

Editor
Theresa Anne Botello
Associate Editors
Jane Caflisch
Managing Editor
Joanna O'Leary
Map Editor
Christine Peterson
Typesetter
Abigail Burger

Publishing Director
Julie A. Stephens
Editor-in-Chief
Jeffrey Dubner
Production Manager
Dusty Lewis
Cartography Manager
Nathaniel Brooks
Design Manager
Caleb Beyers
Editorial Managers
Lauren Bonner, Ariel Fox,
Matthew K. Hudson, Emma Nothmann,
Joanna Shawn Brigid O'Leary,
Sarah Robinson
Financial Manager
Suzanne Siu
Marketing & Publicity Managers
Megan Brumagim, Nitin Shah
Personnel Manager
Jesse Reid Andrews
Researcher Manager
Jennifer O'Brien
Web Manager
Jesse Tov
Web Content Director
Abigail Burger
Production Associates
Thomas Bechtold, Jeffrey Hoffman Yip
IT Directors
Travis Good, E. Peyton Sherwood
Financial Assistant
R. Kirkie Maswoswe
Associate Web Manager
Robert Dubbin
Office Coordinators
Abigail Burger, Angelina L. Fryer,
Liz Glynn

Director of Advertising Sales
Daniel Ramsey
Senior Advertising Associates
Sara Barnett, Daniella Boston
Advertising Artwork Editor
Julia Davidson, Sandy Liu

President
Abhishek Gupta
General Manager
Robert B. Rombauer
Assistant General Manager
Anne E. Chisholm

HOW TO USE THIS BOOK

So, you want some of Ireland's famous brew? Well, we here at *Let's Go* think we've pulled the perfect pint to quench your thirst for the Emerald Isle. *Sláinte!*

THE HEAD. Now, what is a good stout without some creamy froth to ease you in? In *Let's Go Ireland 2004*, we have several sections to transition you into Ireland. **Discover Ireland** gives you highlights of the Republic and Northern Ireland and **Suggested Itineraries** for sojourns from a week to a month. For the details of trip planning, such as practical information and budget tips, we offer **Essentials**. To culturally acclimate you to the Emerald Isle, we feature two **Life and Times** sections: a larger one on the whole of Ireland and a smaller one on Northern Ireland. For quick reference, consult the **Appendix.**

THE BODY. After the gentle head, you're ready for the full body flavor of Ireland. To prevent the heartiness of Ireland from overwhelming you, we've divided the country into regional gulps and sudivided those into pleasant county sips. The chapters circle the island clockwise from **County Dublin,** devoted to the hub of Eastern Ireland. Next, is **Eastern Ireland.** Then, on to **Southeast Ireland** and its hub Kilkenny. From there the circle continues to **Southwest Ireland** and Cork, **Western Ireland** and Galway, and **Northwestern Ireland** and Donegal Town. The final chapter completes the cycle with **Northern Ireland** and cosmopolitan Belfast. Each chapter revolves around its hub city and the counties around their largest city. When planning an itinerary, look at the destination town or city for lines that run to it.

> ## STOUT OF HEART
> The classic Irish stout is secretly good for you. And so is *Let's Go*. The book features two **Scholarly Articles** by Brenna Powell on the Troubles and, for those who fall in love with Ireland, **Alternatives to Tourism** to help you explore the Isle more thoroughly.

THE GLASS. Of couse, we had to put your stout *in* something or the sweet nectar of Ireland would seep through your fingers. Our glass is a format system. Unless stated otherwise, all prices are for a solo traveler, and for transportation, a one-way, single ticket. Our transportation information is always listed as close to the beginning of a write-up as possible. After the destination city or town, the details of the route are listed in parentheticals: duration, departure time, and price. With establishments, the listings appear in order of optimum value, the bang for your buck. A 🍺 means superb quality. They are ranked solely by price through our price diversity chart (see p. ix). Now with a good pint, the glass is never clear at the end. The lighter foam clings to the interior. With such a rich country, it's nearly impossible to absorb all of the Isle. In the guide this foam appears as features and gray-boxes. Beyond the standard sights or history, these elements tell interesting tales of the town or area.

> ## A NOTE TO OUR READERS
> The information for this book was gathered by *Let's Go* researchers from May through August of 2003. Each listing is based on one researcher's opinion, formed during his or her visit at a particular time. Those traveling at other times may have different experiences since prices, dates, hours, and conditions are always subject to change. You are urged to check the facts presented in this book beforehand to avoid inconvenience and surprises.

DISCOVER IRELAND

Molann an obair an fear. The work praises the man. The old Irish proverb speaks wisdom in few words, like the Irish people. There is no shortage of conversation in Ireland, nor is there a dearth of literature. Ireland is a land of poets. Since its settlement, Ireland has created men of the word: bards, *fili*, novelists, playwrights, comedians, singers. The Irish have created a vast library of work over the centuries. Some of the world's oldest texts are Irish. The theme of all these works? Why, Ireland. The Irish are never tongue-tied about their island. There is little reason for them to be. Throughout the isle, the landscape calls out to be celebrated. She sings and her children listen. They write great epics of her, masterpieces. The work praises the man. The people praise their home.

FACTS AND FIGURES

Capitals: Dublin and Belfast

Number of female presidents: 2

Highest Point: 3415 ft.

Natural Resources: Zinc, lead, natural gas, *craic*, copper, gypsum, limestone, poets, peat, silver, stout

Literary Nobel Laureates: 4

Populations: 3,797,257 people live in the Republic. 1,663,200 people live in Northern Ireland

Population Distribution: More than 35% lives within 60 mi. of Dublin

Land Area: 32,589 sq. mi.

Population Under 25: 40.1%

Most Popular Names: Jack & Aoife

Daily Caloric Intake: 3638 calories

Annual Beer Consumption: 32.5 gallons per person

Number of Sheep per person: 2:1

WHEN TO GO

Off-season travel (mid-Sept. to May) brings cheaper airfares and accommodations and dodges the tourist hordes. On the flip side, many attractions, hostels, B&Bs, and tourist offices close in winter, and in some rural areas, local transportation dwindles to a trickle or shuts down altogether. Most of Ireland's best festivals also occur in the summer. The 'unsettled' Irish weather is subject to frequent changes but relatively constant temperatures. (See **Temperature and Climate,** p. 573.) The southeastern coast is the driest and sunniest, while western Ireland is considerably wetter and cloudier. July and August are the warmest months, but May and June see the most sunshine. December and January can be rather dismal, weather-wise. Year-round, take heart—clouded, foggy mornings usually clear by noon.

THINGS TO DO

WONDERS AND WANDERS

The tranquil, gorgeous **Beara Peninsula** (p. 265) and its 125 mi. of **Beara Way** don't know the meaning of tour buses. **Killarney National Park** (p. 279) is a hiking-biking-climbing paradise, and makes a good gateway to the understandably heavily touristed **Ring of Kerry** (p. 282). Trekkers along the **Kerry Way** (p. 282) traverse the same countryside without quite so much company. Several developed paths allow hikers to spend any number of days exploring Ireland's mountain chains—the **Wicklow Way** passes through the **Wicklow Mountains** (p. 149) in Dublin's backyard, while the new **Sperrin Way** treks through the **Sperrin Mountains** (p. 554). In remote Co. Donegal, the **Slieve League** (p. 416) mountains reach their dramatic end at the highest sea cliffs in Europe. The west coast is densely strewn with strange and beautiful geologic curiosities, including the limestone moonscape of **The Burren** (p. 336) and towering **Cliffs of Moher** (p. 336), which soar 700 ft. above the sea. The bizarre honeycomb columns of **Giant's Causeway** (p. 539) spill out from the **Antrim Coast,** a long strip of rocky crags and white beaches. Donegal's **Glenveagh National Park** (p. 429) contains salt-and-peppered **Mount Errigal.** Near Enniskillen, a series of underground caves carved the limestone earth into haunting **Marble Arch Caves** (p. 563).

LITERARY LANDMARKS

Natural beauty and urban grime have inspired centuries of superb literature. Dublin (p. 86) has promoted (and suffered) the caustic wit of **Jonathan Swift, Oscar Wilde, George Bernard Shaw, James Joyce, Sean O'Casey, Samuel Beckett, Brendan Behan, Eavan Boland, Flann O'Brien,** and **Roddy Doyle,** to name but a few. **W.B. Yeats** saw poetry all over the island, but chose Co. Sligo for his grave (p. 392). **John Millington Synge** found literary greatness depicting the domestic squabbles of Aran Islanders (p. 358). **Seamus Heaney** compared the bogland's fossilized remains of pre-Christian sacrifices to The Troubles. In Belfast (p. 462), **Brian Moore, Bernard MacLaverty,** and **Paul Muldoon** capture ordinary lives in a city known only for its extraordinary events. **Brian Friel's** plays bring to life the wilds of Co. Donegal (p. 404). Limerick (p. 309) has had a successful face-lift since the poverty-stricken childhood of **Frank McCourt.** Farther south, the dwindling *gaeltacht* of Co. Kerry is preserved through the autobiography of **Peig Sayers** and the poetry of **Nuala Ni Dhomhnaill.** Ancient **mythology** is the most pervasive of Ireland's literary forms—virtually every bump is accountable to fairies, giants, gods, and heroes.

BREWERIES AND DISTILLERIES

The Irish claim stout is blessed and whiskey is the "water of life": it follows that the island's breweries and distilleries are its holy wells. The **Guinness Storehouse** (p. 122) guards the secret of its black magic, but doles out ample samples at tour's end as consolation. Smaller, though as intoxicating, **Dublin Brewing Company** (p. 127) offers personal tours with plenty of hops to smell and beer to taste. **Smithwicks** (p. 192), the oldest brewery in Ireland, stores a blonder brew in a former monastery in Kilkenny. Back in Dublin, the **Old Jameson Distillery** (p. 127) makes a slightly sweeter whiskey than the hard stuff stored at **Bushmills Distillery** (p. 540) in Co. Antrim, but the folks at Bushmills provide more 'fulfilling' tours.

STONES AND THRONES

In Co. Meath, the 5000-year-old passage tombs of the **Boyne Valley** (p. 160) are architectural feats that stump modern engineers. Nearby **Hill of Tara** (p. 161) has been the symbolic Irish throne from Celtic chieftains to St. Patrick to 19th-century Nationalists. On the west coast, **Poulnebrane Dolmen** (p. 340) marks a group grave site with a 25-ton capstone atop two standing rocks. On the magnificent limestone **Rock of Cashel** (p. 198), a mish-mash of early Christian structures define the skyline. **Glendalough** (p. 149) is the picturesque home of St. Kevin's 6th-century monastery, a 100 ft. round tower, and the saint's small stone kitchen. In Donegal, near Derry, **Grianan Ailigh** (see p. 441) was first a Druidic temple, then the burial place for Aedh (divine king of the Túatha De Dannan), and finally a seat of power for the northern branch of the Uí Néill (O'Neill) Clan. The monastic ruins of **Clonmacnoise** (see p. 180), south of Ath-lone, keep watch over the River Shannon's boglands. St. Ciaran founded his monastery here in AD 548, and the gorgeous remains lure many a traveler to the otherwise untouristed midlands. The otherworldly **Skellig Rocks** (p. 289) astound visitors to the Iveragh Peninsula. The **Rock of Dunamase** (p. 183) rises in Portlaoise, a scar left by Cromwell.

THE ISLAND'S ISLANDS

The people of the **Aran Islands** (p. 358) live much like the rest of the country did at the turn of the century—speaking Irish, eking out their living fishing in *curraghs* at the mercy of the sea. Off the Dingle Peninsula, the now deserted **Blasket Islands** (p. 301) were once home to several impoverished memoirists. Now they hold only pensive walks through haunting village ruins. Electricity and tap water are recent introductions to Donegal's **Inishbofin Island** (p. 434), but serenity and camaraderie are not. **Sherkin Island** (p. 258) beckons visitors to its sandy, cliff-enclosed beaches, over-abundance of cows, and under-abundance of people. Nearby **Cape Clear Island** (p. 257) trades cows for goats, to make the best homemade goat's milk ice cream in all of Ireland.

FESTIVALS AND FESTIVITIES

The island loves to celebrate. Guinness runs freely during the island-wide frenzy of **St. Patrick's Day** (March 17th). Mid-May brings **Armagh's Apple Blossom Festival** (p. 519). James Joyce enthusiasts ramble for 18hr. through Dublin every year on June 16, **Bloomsday** (p. 133). In mid-July, the **Galway Arts Festival** (p. 358) hosts theater, trad, rock, and film for two weeks of vigorous revelry. Early August brings all types of musicians, artists, and merrymakers to Waterford's **Spraoi festival** (p. 230). He-goats compete for the title of alpha male in **Killorglin's Puck Fair** (p. 283) in mid-August. The **Connemara Pony Show** (p. 369) brings its colts to Clifden in late August. Around the same time, every set in Ireland tunes in to the nationally televised **Rose of Tralee Festival and Pageant** (p. 309). Cape Clear Island welcomes tale-spinners to the **International Storytelling Festival** (p. 257), also in late August. Many return home happy from the **Lisdoonvarna Matchmaking Festival** (p. 338) in early September. Fat ladies sing at the **Wexford Opera** (p. 214) in late October, and ghouls and goblins mob **Derry** for its carnivalesque **Halloween** celebration (Oct. 31). Ireland's largest arts festival, the **Belfast Festival** (p. 491) at Queen's College, is a three-week winter potluck of cultural events.

TOP TEN LIST

TOP 10 TRAD

Irish traditional music, in various incarnations, has become a worldwide phenomenon. To help sample the real thing at its best, *Let's Go* has compiled a list of festivals, pubs, and workshops where the *craic* is mighty, and you might even get to join in.

1. Tiny Milltown Malby, in Co. Clare, goes trad-mad for **Willie Week** with free sessions and music workshops.

2. The serious sessions at **McDermott's** show why Doolin is a trad pilgrimage site.

3. Rostrevor's **Fiddler's Green Festival** is an extravaganza of music, storytelling, and dancing in the streets.

4. Musicians flock nightly to **The Crane,** in Galway, for spontaneous jamming.

5. Musicians regale Achill Islanders with workshops and free concerts at the **Scoil Acla**.

6. Dublin cranks up the *craic* at **Cobblestones,** known for the best trad in the capital.

7. Kilrush's **Eigse Mrs. Crotty Festival** celebrates the feisty lady who helped revive trad in the 1950s.

8. **Matt Molloy's,** in Westport, is owned by the flautist of the Chieftains.

9. Cahersiveen, birthplace of patriot Daniel O'Connell, proudly showcases Irish musical heritage during its **Celtic Music Weekend.**

10. **An Droichead Beag** keeps Dingle tipsy and toe-tapping with constant trad sessions.

DISCOVER

BEST PUBS: Dublin's **Porter House** is one of Temple Bar's last bastions of local *craic*. Raise your spirits along the Wicklow Way at **Johnny Fox's**, the highest pub in all Ireland. Some of Ireland's biggest folk acts got started at **The Lobby**, in Cork City, and everyone (famous) and their brother has played Galway's legendary **Roisín Dubh**. With previous incarnations as a boxing venue and Communist printing press, **The Duke of York** now packs a punch with Belfast's largest selection of Irish whiskeys. The folks at **McCarthy's Hotel** in Fethard promise to "wine you, dine you, and bury you."

BEST VIEWS: Yeats admired the mile-high cliff views from **Drumcliffe** towards **Ben Bulben** (p. 400)—so will you. The finest views in two counties await you from high on **The Healy Pass** (p. 267). The sheer **Bunglass** (p. 416) cliffs near the Slieve League are Europe's highest coastal ledges. The views from **Slea Head** (p. 300) have brought many a filmmaker to the Isle. The towering heights of the cliffs around the **Giant's Causeway** (p. 539) both terrify and tantalize.

BEST ODDBALL COLLECTIONS: The **Irish National Stud**, Kildare, is an unforgettable Zen/equine experience (p. 158). **Fox's Lane Folk Museum** in Youghal has razor-sharp exhibits (p. 247). The medieval monks of **Greyabbey** (p. 503) cultivated herbs for all manner of maladies in their **"physick" garden**—there's even a remedy for breast-feeding. The doll house exhibit at the **Museum of Childhood** (p. 137), housed in Malahide Castle, inspires nostalgia for make-believe.

BEST AQUATIC FUN: Ride some of Europe's best waves at the sandy strands near **Tramore Bay Surf Centre** (p. 223), or hang ten up north in **Bundoran** (p. 411), where the North's best surfers strut their stuff. Snorkelers often see U-boat and galleon wrecks in the waters off **Baltimore** (p. 255). For windsurfing, canoeing, sailboating, motorboating, and anything else that can get you wet, head south to Co. Clare's **Killaloe** (p. 327). The folks at **Leeane's** Killary Adventure Company (p. 376) specialize in outfitting water-buffs.

BEST PLACES TO STAY: Snuggle in one of the three colorful gypsy trailers of Dunmanway's **Shiplake Mountain Hostel** (p. 249), surrounded by the Shehy mountains. Relax in the gentle embrace of the cushy, beachfront **Downhill Hostel** (p. 543). Abandon technology and get back to nature inside the gas-lamp-lit **Flax Mill Hostel** in the Sperrins (p. 555). Stay in **the Bastion** (p. 179) of cool in Athlone.

BEST LEGENDARY LANDSCAPES: The spurge is poisonous, so gaze but don't graze at the **Poison Glen,** Donegal (p. 427). Take in the lake views at **Glendalough,** which St. Kevin preferred to women (p. 149). Reveal in the sunsets on the **Bloody Foreland** (p. 430). **Navan Fort,** near Armagh, is not only home to men with childbirth pangs, but is a fascinating archaeological site as well (p. 524). Imagine the battle that wrestled the isle from the Formorian on tranquil **Lough Key** (p. 402).**The Cooley Peninsula** (p. 173) produced the greatest Irish hero Cuchulain amidst the majesty of the Mournes and Carlingford Lough.

BEST CASTLES AND FORTS: Eastern Ireland is filled with ancient castles and forts—**Trim Castle** (p. 163) is the granddaddy of them all. While the ruins at Trim stand untouched, **Kilkenny Castle** (p. 192) has been restored to its 17th-century splendor, to a temporally disorienting effect. On the Aran Islands, 7000-year-old **Dún Aengus** (p. 363) makes the 17th century seem not so cool anymore.

BEST CRITTERS: Eleven-pound **Lobzilla** was last spotted at the Seaworld and Leisure Centre in Lahinch (p. 332). Discover the **mummified cat and mouse** at Dublin's Christ Church (p. 122). Knocknarea's **bilingual sheep** beckon you in two different languages (p. 398). Check out Fota Island's very confused **Chilean flamingos** (p. 246). **Fungi** and his Ego await you in Dingle Bay (p. 295). And who could forget the **goats** of Cape Clear Island (p. 257)...or their ice cream?

THE BEST OF IRELAND

Giant's Causeway

NORTHERN IRELAND

Slieve League

Donegal Town

Belfast

Sligo

Galway

Athlone

Dublin

REPUBLIC OF IRELAND

Aran Islands

Doolin

Cliffs of Moher

Kilkenny

Ring of Kerry

Blarney Stone

Cork

Blarney Stone (p. 243). On your way back to Dublin, take a detour to medieval **Kilkenny** (p. 185), where a former monastery is now Ireland's oldest brewery.

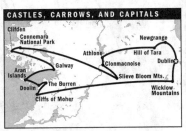

CASTLES, CARROWS, AND CAPITALS

Clifden

Connemara National Park

Newgrange

Athlone

Hill of Tara

Galway

Clonmacnoise

Dublin

Aran Islands

Slieve Bloom Mts.

Doolin

The Burren

Wicklow Mountains

Cliffs of Moher

THE BEST OF IRELAND (3½ WEEKS)

Spend a few days in **Dublin** (p. 86) exploring its many pubs. Drink a pint of the dark stuff at the Guinness Brewery and catch a football match at Croke Park before moving on to **Belfast** (p. 462). The complex history of this capital is spectacularly illustrated in the murals decorating its sectarian neighborhoods. Catch the bus to the **Giant's Causeway** (p. 539), a strange formation of octagonal rocks referred to as the earth's eighth natural wonder. Ride the bus back to the Republic and on to **Donegal Town** (p. 405). Get a good night's rest at one of Ireland's best hostels—tomorrow it's on to **Slieve League** (p. 414) to hike and view Europe's tallest sea cliffs. For nighttime entertainment, dip down to **Sligo** (p. 392), once the beloved home of W.B. Yeats. From there, head to **Athlone** (p. 178), everyone's favorite transportation hub and home to the monastic **Clonmacnoise** (p. 180). **Galway** (p. 342), a raging student center draws the best musicians on the island. Jump on a ferry to the desolate **Aran Islands** (p. 358) and relax for a few days. Return via **Doolin**, which rests right near the **Cliffs of Moher** (p. 336). Travel south and take a bus or bike ride around the **Ring of Kerry** (p. 282), a peninsula captured on Irish postcards worldwide. Return to civilization in **Cork** (p. 231), where you can daytrip out to see the

CASTLES, CARROWS, AND CAPITALS (3 WEEKS)

For a taste of both urban and rural Ireland, begin in **Dublin** (p. 86). Study up on Irish history and culture at the National Museums by day, and spend the evening on a literary pub crawl. From Dublin, take a daytrip to **Newgrange** (p. 160), a Neolithic burial site that's older than the pyramids; the nearby **Hill of Tara** (p. 161) was the seat of Irish kings from pre-Christian times up until just 400 years ago. Make for the Midlands and lively **Athlone** (p. 178), within close reach of the monastic ruins at **Clonmacnoise** (p. 180) and the lovely **Slieve Bloom Mountains** (p. 181). Keep those hiking boots laced while heading westward to the rugged peaks and boglands of **Connemara National Park** (p. 375). Connemara is an Irish-speaking region with **Clifden** (p. 369) as its welcoming capital. Wind along the breathtaking coastal road to the inviting and eminently walkable city of **Galway** (p. 342), home to thousands of students and one of Ireland's most energetic art scenes. Take a plane to the **Aran Islands** (p. 358) and cycle past ancient ring forts and contented seals sunning themselves on the rocky shore. Ferry back to join the trad-seeking pilgrims in **Doolin** (p. 334), a tiny, musical village snuggled into the rocky, starkly beautiful landscape of the **Burren** (p. 336). South of Doolin, waves smash against the looming **Cliffs of Moher** (p. 336). Return to Dublin via the **Wicklow Mountains** (p. 149), and spend two days hiking through "The Garden of Ireland" on the Wicklow Way.

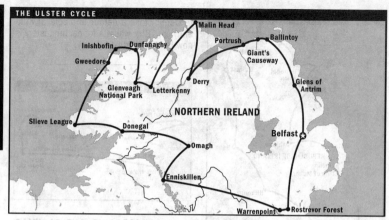

THE ULSTER CYCLE

THE ULSTER CYCLE (4 WEEKS)

Deplane in **Belfast** (p. 462) and tour this misunderstood city in a black cab. From the murals, University, and peace line, take the Antrim Coaster bus north along the waterfront past the glorious **Glens of Antrim** (p. 527). Farther north lies **Ballintory** (p. 536), a nearly Scottish village adjacent to **Carrick-a-rede Rope Bridge** (p. 536), a rickety fisherman bridge to a deserted island. The volcanic spillage of **Giant's Causeway** (p. 539) is the stuff of gigantic legend. From there, head to **Derry** (p. 544), the medieval maiden city that rivals Dublin in historical significance. It's a short jump over the border (emigration made easy) into Co. Donegal, the most remote, virgin area on the isle. Head up the Inishowen Peninsula to **Malin Head** (p. 447), Ireland's northernmost point. Inland, **Letterkenny** (p. 438) serves as a transportation hub to the rest of the county. To the west lies the mountainous **Glenveagh National Park** (p. 429) and the Irish-speaking, trad-loving **Gweedore** (p. 427). Neighboring **Dunfanaghy** (p. 435) is a quaint stop on the way to **Inishbofin Island** (p. 434), an untouched fishing island. Continue on to the infamous **Slieve League Peninsula** (p. 414), where soaring cliffs are a bus ride away from the conveniences of **Donegal Town** (p. 405). From there, cross the border and head to **Omagh** (p. 556), near gorgeous forests, the Sperrin Mountains, and replete with Ulster American history. To the south is the beautiful lake district and **Enniskillen** (p. 560), a base for exporation of the Mar-

ble Arch Caves and the lakes above. On the way back to Belfast, stop at **Warrenpoint** (p. 517), a pleasant loughside town and a skip away from the **Rostrevor Forest** (p. 519), one of the few unadulterated Irish oak forests. And that's the North folks!

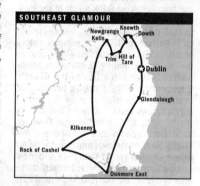

SOUTHEAST GLAMOUR

SOUTHEAST GLAMOUR (1½ WEEKS) The sunniest region of Ireland, and the most cinematic, has much to offer. From **Dublin** (p. 86), go to **Glendalough** (p. 149), St. Kevin's "Garden of Ireland" home. From there, trek south to the lovely village of **Dumore East** (p. 221) on beautiful Waterford Harbor. Head west to **The Rock of Cashel** (p. 197) and its namesake town for a dose of devilish fun. To the east is **Kilkenny** (p. 185) and its southeastern charm. To the North, **Kells** (p. 164) satisfies lovers of St. Colmcille and the thirsty. On the return to Dublin, visit **Trim** (p. 162), Ireland's largest castle of feature film fame, and the **Hill of Tara** (p. 161) home to Irish kings. Easy daytrips from Dublin ancient **Newgrange,** prehistoric **Knowth,** and mysterious **Dowth** (p. 160) offer one last taste of timeless Ireland before departure.

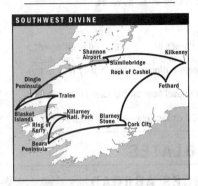

URBAN JOURNEY

SOUTHWEST DIVINE (3 WEEKS)

Land at **Shannon Airport,** stay overnight in **Sixmilebridge** (p. 326), and make your way quickly to the **Dingle Peninsula** (p. 295), where mountains, beaches, and Irish speakers abound. Don't leave before hitting the isolated *gaeltacht* in the **Blasket Islands** (p. 301). Move east through **Tralee** (p. 304), home of Ireland's most famous festival. Next, circle the **Ring of Kerry** (p. 282), southeast of Dingle. Home to magnificent **Killarney National Park** (p. 279), this highly touristed peninsula provides access to the usually bypassed **Valentia Island** (p. 285) and the **Skellig Rocks** (p. 289). Don't miss a third finger of land—the **Beara Peninsula** (p. 265), the most remote and splendid of the three. Stop in at **Cork City** (p. 231) for a taste of urbanania as you move inland. After a daytrip to the **Blarney Stone,** travel onward to the town of **Cashel** (p. 197), whose monolithic **Rock of Cashel** attracts thousands of visitors each year. Stop in at the small town of **Fethard** (p. 199) for some medieval porn before moving onward to **Kilkenny** (p. 185), where you can reacclimatize yourself to a busier way of life and raise a parting glass of Guinness before leaving the island.

URBAN JOURNEY (2½ WEEKS)

For the more cosmopolitan, spend a few days lounging about the tiny Irish metropolis of **Dublin** (p. 86). From there, journey southwest to "sunny" and sassy **Kilkenny** (p. 185), a base for exploring the Southeast and a fun city in its own right. Down South lies **Cork** (p. 231), rich in history and hub of the athletic and musical events on the isle. Go west to **Killarney** (p. 273), a pleasant city with a gorgeous national park and oh yeah, a tour bus away from the Ring of Kerry. To the North is hip **Galway** (p. 342), home to students, shoppers, and claddaghs. It's smaller neighbor to the north, **Sligo** (p. 392), offers easy access to Yeats Country and Co. Donegal. Cross the border and go farther north to **Derry** (p. 544), the maiden city. Then head to the northern capital **Belfast** (p. 462) to explore murals, black cabs, and the peace line.

ESSENTIALS

FACTS FOR THE TRAVELER

ENTRANCE REQUIREMENTS.
Driving Permit (p. 38). A valid foreign driver's license is required of all drivers; a driving permit is required only if you plan to drive for longer than 3 months.
Passport (p. 3). Required of all foreign nationals, though they may not be checked for EU citizens.
Visa (p. 10). Not required for short-term travel from the EU, Commonwealth, and North American countries.
Work Permit (p. 10). Required of non-EU citizens planning to work in Ireland.

EMBASSIES & CONSULATES

IRISH CONSULAR SERVICES ABROAD

For other Irish embassies, check the Worldwide Embassies and Consulates Search Engines at www.embassyworld.com and www.irelandemb.org.

Australia: Irish Embassy, 20 Arkana St., Yarralumla, **Canberra** ACT 2600 (☎062 73 3022).

Canada: Irish Embassy, Ste. 1105, 130 Albert St., **Ottawa,** ON K1P 5G4 (☎613-233-6281; embassyofireland@rogers.com).

New Zealand: Honorary Consulate-General, 6th fl., 18 Shortland St. 1001, **Auckland** 1 (☎09 302 2817; www.ireland.co.nz).

South Africa: Irish Embassy, 1st fl., Southern Life Plaza, 1059 Schoeman St., **Arcadia** 0083, Pret. (☎012 342 5062).

UK: Irish Embassy, 17 Grosvenor Pl., **London** SWIX 7HR (☎020 7235 2171). Consulates: 16 Randolph Crescent., **Edinburgh** EH3 7TT, Scotland (☎0131 226 7711); Brunel House, 2 Fitzalan Rd., **Cardiff** CF24 0EB (☎0207 225 7700).

US: Irish Embassy, 2234 Massachusetts Ave. NW, **Washington, D.C.** 20008 (☎202-462-3939). Consulates: 345 Park Ave., 17th fl., **New York,** NY 10154-0037 (☎212-319-2555); 400 N. Michigan Ave., **Chicago,** IL 60611 (☎312-337-1868); 100 Pine St., 33rd fl., **San Francisco,** CA 94111 (☎415-392-4214); 535 Boylston St., **Boston,** MA 02116 (☎617-267-9330).

UK CONSULAR SERVICES ABROAD

For embassies in countries not listed here, check the Foreign and Commonwealth Office website (www.fco.gov.uk/directory/posts.asp; ☎020 7270 1500).

Australia: British High Commission, Commonwealth Ave., Yarralumla, **Canberra** ACT 2606 (☎02 6270 6666; www.britain-in-canada.org). Consulate-General also in Brisbane, Melbourne, Perth, and Sydney; consulate in Adelaide.

Canada: British High Commission, 80 Elgin St., **Ottawa,** ON K1P 5K7 (☎613-237-1530; www.britain-in-canada.org). British Consulate-General, College Park, 777 Bay St., Ste. 2800, **Toronto,** ON M5G 2G2 (☎416-593-1290). Consulate-General also in Montreal and Vancouver.

France: British Embassy, 35 R. du Faubourg St. Honoré, 75383 Paris CEDEX 08 (☎331 44 51 31 00; www.amb-grandebretagne.fr). British Consulate-General, 18 bis R. d'Anjou, 75008 **Paris** (☎331 44 51 31 00). Consulates-general also in Bordeaux, Lille, Lyon, and Marseille.

Ireland: British Embassy, 29 Merrion Rd., Ballsbridge, **Dublin** 4 (☎01 205 3700; www.britishembassy.ie).

New Zealand: British High Commission, 44 Hill St., **Thorndon,** Wellington 1 (☎04 924 2888; www.britain.org.nz). Consulate-General, 17th fl., NZI House, 151 Queen St., **Auckland** 1 (☎09 303 2973).

South Africa: British High Commission, 255 Hill St., **Arcadia** 0002, Pret. (☎012 483 1400). Consulate-General, 15th fl., Southern Life Centre, 8 Riebeek St., **Cape Town** 8001 (☎021 405 2400). Other Consulates-General in Johannesburg and Cape Town; consulates in Port Elizabeth and Durban.

US: British Embassy, 3100 Massachusetts Ave. NW, **Washington, D.C.** 20008 (☎202-588-6500; www.britainusa.com). Consulate-General, 845 3rd Ave., **New York,** NY 10022 (☎212-745-0200). Other Consulates-General: Atlanta, Boston, Chicago, Houston, Los Angeles, and San Francisco. Consulates: Anchorage, Dallas, Kansas City, Miami, New Orleans, Salt Lake City, San Diego, Seattle, and Puerto Rico.

CONSULAR SERVICES IN IRELAND

Below is a list of the foreign embassies and consulates in Ireland. Should you run into any troubles along the way, contact your national branch immediately.

Australia: The Republic, 2nd fl., Fitzwilton House, Wilton Terr., Dublin 2 (☎01 664 5300). **UK,** Australia House, the Strand, London WC2B 4LA (☎020 7379 4334).

Canada: The Republic, Canadian Embassy, 65/68 St. Stephen's Green, 4th fl., Dublin 2 (☎01 478 1988). **Northern Ireland,** Consulate of Canada, 378 Stranmills Rd., Belfast, N.I., BT9 5 ED (☎028 660 212).

New Zealand: UK, New Zealand Embassy, New Zealand House, the Haymarket, London SW1Y 4TQ (☎0171 930 8422).

South Africa: The Republic, South Africa Embassy, Alexandra House, Earlsfort Terr., 2nd fl., Dublin 2 (☎01 661 5553). **UK,** South African High Commission, South Africa House, Trafalgar Sq., London WC2N 5DP (☎020 7451 7299).

United Kingdom: See **UK Consular Services Abroad,** p.1-2.

United States: The Republic, Embassy of the United States of America, 42 Elgin Rd., Dublin 4 (☎01 668 8777/7122). **Northern Ireland,** Consulate General, Queen's House, 14 Queen St., Belfast BT1 6EQ (☎028 9032 8239).

TOURIST OFFICES

Almost every town in Ireland has a tourist office. Their offerings, however, range from the useful (free local maps and pamphlets, transportation schedules, and accommodation booking services) to the partial (many tourist boards, especially in the Republic, will only list accommodations that have paid them a fee). All national tourist boards offer information on national hikes, parks, and trails.

Below are the main offices of the national tourist boards; for countries not listed here, check www.ireland.travel.ie and www.discovernorthernireland.com.

Irish Tourist Board (Bord Fáilte): Main office: Baggot Street Bridge, Baggot St., Dublin 2. (☎01 850 230 330 or 602 4000; www.ireland.travel.ie). **Tourism Ireland:** Bishops Sq., Redmonds Hill, Dublin 2 (☎01 476 3400; www.tourismireland.com). **Northern Ireland:** Beresford House, 2 Beresford Rd., Coleraine (☎028 7037 9300). **Australia:** Level 5, 36 Carrington St., Sydney NSW 2000 (☎02 9299 6177). **Canada:** 2 Bloor St. W., Ste. 1501, Toronto, ON M4W 3E2 (☎800-223-6470). **New Zealand:** 18 Shortland

St., 6th fl., Private Bag 92136, Auckland 1 (☎09 379 8720). **South Africa:** Everite House, 7th fl., 20 De Korte St., Braamfontein, 2001, Johannesburg (☎011 339 4865). **UK:** Ireland Desk, Britain Visitor Centre, 1 Regent St., London SW1Y 4XT (☎0800 039 7000; www.irelandholidays.co.uk). **US:** 345 Park Ave., New York, NY 10154 (☎800-223-6470 or 212-418-0800; www.irelandvacations.com).

Northern Ireland Tourist Board: Main Office: 59 North St., Belfast, BT1 1NB, Northern Ireland (☎028 9023 1221; fax 9024 0960; www.discovernorthernireland.com). **The Republic:** 16 Nassau St., Dublin 2 (☎01 679 1977; infodublin@nitb.com). **UK:** Ireland Desk, Britain Visitor Centre, 1 Regent St., London SW1Y 4XT (☎0800 039 7000). **Australia:** 36 Carrington St., 5th fl., Sydney NSW 2000 (☎02 9299 6177; info@tourismireland.com.au). **Canada:** 2 Bloor St., Ste. 1501, Toronto, ON, M4W 3E2 (☎800-223-6470). **New Zealand:** 18 Shortland St., Private Bag 92136, Auckland 1 (☎09 977 2255; fax 309 0725). **US:** 345 Park Ave., New York, NY 10154 (☎800 223 6470; info@shamrock.org). From elsewhere overseas, contact any British Tourist Office. Tourist boards should have free brochures, and sell a list of all B&Bs and campgrounds.

DOCUMENTS & FORMALITIES

PASSPORTS

REQUIREMENTS. Citizens of Australia, Canada, New Zealand, South Africa, the UK, and the US need valid passports to enter Ireland and to re-enter their home countries. You cannot enter Ireland if your passport expires in under six months; returning home with an expired passport is illegal and may result in a fine.

NEW PASSPORTS. Citizens of Australia, Canada, New Zealand, the UK, and the US can apply for a passport in their home countries at any post office, passport office, or court of law. Citizens of South Africa can apply for a passport at the nearest Home Affairs office. Any new passport or renewal applications must be filed well in advance of the departure date, although most passport offices offer rush services for a steep fee.

PASSPORT MAINTENANCE. Be sure to photocopy the page of your passport with your photo, as well as your visas and traveler's check serial numbers. Carry one set of copies in a safe place, apart from the originals, and leave another set at home. If you lose your passport, immediately notify the local police and the nearest embassy or consulate of your home government. To expedite its replacement you will need to know all information previously recorded and show ID and proof of citizenship. In some cases, a replacement may take weeks to process, and it may be valid only for a limited time. Any visas stamped in your old passport will be irretrievably lost. In an emergency, ask for immediate temporary traveling papers that will permit you to re-enter your home country.

VISAS & WORK PERMITS

VISAS. Citizens of most countries, including Australia, Canada, EU countries, New Zealand, South Africa, the UK, and the US, do not need visas for visits of less than 90 days in duration. For longer stays, contact the Irish Department of Justice (☎01 6028 202) to obtain official permission. If in doubt, or if your home country is not one of these, check with your embassy.

WORK & STUDY PERMITS. Admission as a visitor does not include the right to work, which is authorized only by a work permit. Students wishing to study in Ireland may enter the country without a visa, but must apply to the Aliens Office within seven days (Harcourt Sq., Dublin 2. ☎01 475 5555). Contact your own embassy for information. Also see **Alternatives to Tourism,** p. 46.

ONE EUROPE. The idea of European unity has come a long way since 1958, when the European Economic Community (EEC) was created to promote solidarity and cooperation. Since then, the EEC has become the European Union (EU), with political, legal, and economic institutions spanning 15 states: Austria, Belgium, Denmark, Finland, France, Germany, Greece, Ireland, Italy, Luxembourg, the Netherlands, Portugal, Spain, Sweden, and the UK.

What does this have to do with the average non-EU tourist? In 1999, the EU established **freedom of movement** across 14 European countries—the entire EU minus Ireland and the UK, but plus Iceland and Norway. This means that border controls between participating countries have been abolished, and visa policies harmonized. While you're still required to carry a passport (or government-issued ID card for EU citizens) when crossing an internal border, once you've been admitted into one country, you're free to travel to all participating states. Britain and Ireland have also formed a **common travel area,** abolishing passport controls between the UK and Ireland. This means that the only times you'll see a border guard within the EU are traveling between the British Isles and the Continent.

For more important consequences of the EU for travelers, see **The Euro** (p. 12) and **European Customs** and **EU customs regulations** (p. 12).

IDENTIFICATION

When you travel, always carry two or more forms of identification on your person, including at least one photo ID; a passport combined with a driver's license or birth certificate is usually adequate. Many establishments, especially banks, may require several IDs in order to cash traveler's checks. Never carry all your forms of ID together; split them up in case of theft or loss.

STUDENT, TEACHER & YOUTH IDENTIFICATION. The **International Student Identity Card (ISIC),** the most widely accepted form of student ID, provides discounts on sights, accommodations, food, and transport; access to 24hr. emergency helpline (in North America call ☎877-370-ISIC; elsewhere call US collect ☎ +1 715-345-0505); and insurance benefits for US cardholders (see **Insurance,** p. 20). The ISIC is preferable to an institution-specific card (such as a university ID) because it is more likely to be recognized and honored abroad. Applicants must be degree-seeking students of a secondary or post-secondary school and must be at least 12 years of age. Because of the proliferation of fake ISICs, some services (particularly airlines) require additional proof of student identity, such as a school ID or a letter attesting to your student status, signed by your registrar.

The **International Teacher Identity Card (ITIC)** offers teachers the same insurance coverage as well as similar but limited discounts. For non-student travelers who are 25 years old or younger, the **International Youth Travel Card (IYTC;** formerly the **GO 25** Card) also offers many of the same benefits as the ISIC.

Each of these identity cards costs US$22/€23. ISIC and ITIC cards are valid for one and a half academic years; IYTC cards are valid for one year from the date of issue. Many student travel agencies (see p. 31) issue the cards, including STA Travel in Australia and New Zealand; Travel CUTS in Canada; usit in the Republic of Ireland and Northern Ireland; SASTS in South Africa; Campus Travel and STA Travel in the UK; and Council Travel and STA Travel in the US. For a listing of issuing agencies and more information contact the **International Student Travel Confederation (ISTC),** Herengracht 479, 1017 BS Amsterdam, Netherlands (☎ +31 20 421 28 00; www.istc.org).

CUSTOMS IN THE EU. As well as freedom of movement of people within the EU (see p. 11), travelers in EU countries can also take advantage of the freedom of movement of goods. This means that there are no customs controls at internal EU borders (i.e., you can take the blue customs channel at the airport), and travelers are free to transport whatever legal substances they like, as long as it is for their own personal (non-commercial) use—up to 800 cigarettes, 10L of spirits, 90L of wine (60L of sparkling wine), and 110L of beer. You should also be aware that duty-free was abolished on June 30, 1999, for travel between EU states; however, travelers between the EU and the rest of the world still get a duty-free allowance when passing through customs.

CUSTOMS

ENTERING IRELAND. Upon entering Ireland, you must declare certain items from abroad and pay a duty on the value of those articles if they exceed the allowance established by Ireland's customs service. Note that goods purchased at **duty-free** shops abroad are not exempt from duty or sales tax; "duty-free" merely means you do not pay a tax in the country of purchase. (Also see **Customs in the EU,** above.)

LEAVING IRELAND. If you're leaving for a non-EU country, you can reclaim any **Value Added Tax (VAT).** Keeping receipts for purchases made abroad will help establish values when you return. Upon returning home, you must similarly declare all articles acquired abroad and pay a duty on the value of articles in excess of your home country's allowance. To expedite your return, make a list of any valuables brought from home, and be sure to keep receipts for all goods acquired abroad.

MONEY

CURRENCY & EXCHANGE

On February 9th, 2002, the Republic of Ireland's legal tender became the **euro,** denoted €. Euro coins come in denominations of 1, 2, 5, 10, 20, and 50 cents, and €1 and €2. Euro notes begin at €5. Legal tender in Northern Ireland is the **British pound.** Northern Ireland has its own bank notes, identical in value to English, Scottish, and Manx notes of the same denominations. Although all of these notes are accepted in Northern Ireland, Northern Ireland notes are not accepted across the water. UK coins come in denominations of 1p, 2p, 5p, 10p, 20p, 50p, and £1. Residents of both nations refer to pounds and euros as "**quid,**" as in "ten quid" (never "quids"). Also expect to hear the terms "**fiver**" (€5 or £5), and "**tener**" (€10 or £10).

 THE EURO. The official currency of 12 members of the European Union is now the euro. The currency has some important—and positive—consequences for travelers hitting more than one euro-zone country. For one thing, money-changers across the euro-zone are obliged to exchange money at the official, fixed rate (see below), and at no commission (though they may still charge a small service fee). Second, euro-denominated traveler's checks allow you to pay for goods and services across the euro-zone, again at the official rate and commission-free.

When changing money abroad, try to go only to banks or bureaux de change offices that have at most a 5% margin between their buy and sell prices. Since you lose money with every transaction, **convert large sums** (unless the currency is depreciating rapidly), **but no more than you'll need.**

If you use traveler's checks or bills, carry some in small denominations (the equivalent of US$50 or less) for times when you are forced to exchange money at disadvantageous rates, but bring a range of denominations since charges may be levied per check cashed. Store your money in a variety of forms; ideally, at any given time you will be carrying some cash, some traveler's checks, and an ATM and/or credit card. All travelers should also consider carrying some US dollars (about US$50), which may sometimes be accepted by local teller.

The currency chart below is based on August 2002 exchange rates between Euro currency and Australian dollars (AUS$), Canadian dollars (CDN$), New Zealand dollars (NZ$), South African Rand (ZAR), British pounds (UK£), US dollars (US$). Check the currency converter on financial websites such as www.bloomberg.com and www.xe.com for the latest exchange rates.

THE EURO		
AUS$1 = €0.55	€1 = AUS$1.81
CAD$1 = €0.65	€1 = CAD$1.53
NZ$1 = €0.48	€1 = NZ$2.10
ZAR1 = €0.10	€1 = ZAR10.14
US$1 = €1.03	€1 = US$0.97
UK£1 = €1.57	€1 = UK£0.64

As a general rule, it's cheaper to convert money in Ireland than at home. While currency exchange will probably be available in your arrival airport, it's wise to bring enough foreign currency to last for the first 24 to 72 hours of a trip.

TRAVELER'S CHECKS

Traveler's checks are one of the safest and least troublesome means of carrying funds. American Express, Travelex/Thomas Cook, and Visa are the most widely recognized brands in the UK. Many banks and agencies sell them for a small commission. Check issuers provide refunds if the checks are lost or stolen, and many provide additional services, such as toll-free refund hotlines abroad, emergency message services, and stolen credit card assistance.

While traveling, keep traveler's check receipts and a record of which ones you've cashed separate from the checks themselves. Also leave a list of check numbers with someone at home. Never countersign traveler's checks until you're ready to cash them, and always bring your passport with you to cash them. If your checks are lost or stolen, immediately contact a refund center (of the company that issued them) to be reimbursed; they may require a police report verifying the loss or theft. Ask about toll-free refund hotlines and the location of refund centers when purchasing checks, and always carry emergency cash.

CREDIT & DEBIT CARDS

Credit cards are generally accepted in urban and larger Irish establishments, but small businesses, B&Bs, and hostels often do not take them. Where they are accepted, credit cards often offer superior exchange rates—up to 5% better than the retail rate used by banks and bureaux de change. Credit cards may also offer services such as insurance or emergency help, and are sometimes required to reserve hotel rooms or rental cars. **MasterCard** and **Visa** are the most welcomed; **American Express** cards work at some ATMs and at AmEx offices and major airports. The **Discover Card** may not be readily accepted in Ireland.

Credit cards are also useful for **cash advances,** which allow you to withdraw Euros or Northern Irish pounds from associated banks and ATMs throughout Ireland instantly. However, transaction fees for all credit card advances (up to US$10 per advance, plus 2-3% extra on foreign transactions after conversion) tend to make credit cards a more costly way of withdrawing cash than ATMs or traveler's checks. In an emergency, however, the transaction fee may prove worth the cost.

Debit cards are a relatively new form of purchasing power. A debit card can be used wherever its associated credit card company (usually Mastercard or Visa) is accepted. The difference between a debit card and a credit card is that with a debit card purchase, money is withdrawn directly from the holder's checking account. Debit cards also function as ATM cards and can be used to withdraw cash from banks and ATMs throughout Ireland. Ask your local bank about obtaining one.

CASH CARDS (ATM CARDS)

Cash cards—popularly called ATM cards—are widespread in Ireland, though a few of the islands and smallest towns still do without. ATMs get the same wholesale exchange rate as credit cards, but there may be a limit on the amount of money you can withdraw per day (around US$500), and unfortunately computer networks sometimes fail. There is typically also a surcharge of US$1-5 per withdrawal.

The two major international money networks are **Cirrus** (US ☎ 800-424-7787) and **PLUS** (US ☎ 800-843-7587). **Ulster Bank Limited, AIB,** and **Bank of Ireland** typically accept Cirrus transactions. To locate ATMs around the world, call the above numbers, or consult www.visa.com/pd/atm or www.mastercard.com/atm.

Visa TravelMoney is a system allowing you to access money from any ATM that accepts Visa cards. (For local customer assistance in Ireland, call ☎ 800 559 345.) You deposit an amount before you travel (plus a small administration fee), and you can withdraw up to that sum. Obtain a card by either visiting a **Thomas Cook** or **Citicorp** office, by calling toll-free in the US ☎ 877-394-2247, or check with your local bank to see if it issues TravelMoney cards.

 PIN NUMBERS & ATMS. To use a cash or credit card to withdraw money from a cash machine (ATM) in Europe, you must have a 4-digit **Personal Identification Number (PIN).** If your PIN is longer than 4 digits, ask your bank whether you can just use the first four, or whether you'll need a new one. **Credit cards** don't usually come with PINs, so if you intend to hit up ATMs in Europe with a credit card to get cash advances, call your credit card company before leaving to request one.

People with alphabetic, rather than numeric, PINs may also be thrown off by the lack of letters on European cash machines. The following handy chart gives the corresponding numbers to use: 1=QZ; 2=ABC; 3=DEF; 4=GHI; 5=JKL; 6=MNO; 7=PRS; 8=TUV; and 9=WXY. Note that if you mistakenly punch the wrong code into the machine 3 times, it will swallow your card for good.

GETTING MONEY FROM HOME

If you run out of money while traveling, the easiest and cheapest solution is to have someone back home make a deposit to your credit card or cash (ATM) card. Failing that, consider one of the following options.

WIRING MONEY. It is possible to arrange a **bank money transfer,** which means asking a bank back home to wire money to a bank in Ireland. This is the cheapest way to transfer cash, but it's also the slowest, usually taking several days or more. Note that some banks may only release your funds in local currency, potentially sticking you with a poor exchange rate; inquire about this in advance. Money transfer services like **Western Union** are faster and more convenient than bank transfers—but also much pricier. Western Union has many locations worldwide. To find one, visit www.westernunion.com, or call in the US ☎800-325-6000, in Canada ☎800-235-0000, in the UK ☎0800 83 38 33, in Australia ☎800 501 500, in New Zealand ☎800 27 0000, in South Africa ☎0860 100031, or in Ireland ☎800 395 395. For the nearest Western Union location, consult www.westernunion.com. To wire money within the US using a credit card (Visa, MasterCard, Discover), call ☎800-225-5227. Rates for sending cash are US$10 cheaper than with a credit card, and the money is often available at the place you're sending it within an hour.

US STATE DEPARTMENT (US CITIZENS ONLY). In dire emergencies only, the US State Department will forward money within hours to the nearest consular office, which will then disburse it according to instructions for a US$15 fee. If you wish to use this service, you must contact the Overseas Citizens Service division of the US State Department (☎202-647-5225; nights, Sundays, and holidays ☎202-647-4000).

COSTS

The cost of your trip will vary considerably, depending on when you go, how you travel, and where you stay. The single biggest cost of your trip will probably be your round-trip (return) **airfare** (see **Getting There: By Plane**, p. 30). Before you go, spend some time calculating a reasonable per-day **budget** that will meet your needs. To give you a general idea, a day in Ireland would cost about €30 (US$36) if you were to camp or stay in hostels and cook your own food. Also, don't forget to factor in emergency reserve funds (at least €200) when planning how much money you'll need.

Considering that saving just a few dollars a day over the course of your trip might pay for days or weeks of additional travel, the art of penny-pinching is well worth learning. Bring a **sleepsack** (see p. 21) to save on sheet charges in some hostels, and do your **laundry** in the sink (unless you're prohibited from doing so). You can split **accommodations** costs (in hotels and some hostels) with trustworthy fellow travelers; multi-bed rooms almost always work out cheaper per person than singles. With that said, don't go overboard with your budget obsession. Though staying within your budget is important, don't do so at the expense of your sanity or health.

TIPPING

Some restaurants in Ireland figure a service charge into the bill; some even calculate it into the cost of the dishes themselves. The menu often indicates whether or not service is included. Most people working in restaurants, however, do not expect a tip, unless the restaurant is targeted exclusively toward tourists. In those incidences, consider leaving 10-15%, depending upon the quality of the service. Tipping is very uncommon for other services, such as taxis and hairdressers, especially in rural areas. In most cases, people are usually happy if you simply round off the bill to the nearest euro. Barmen at older or rural pubs may be surprised if you leave them a gratuity, while in cities or at bars with a younger clientele a tip may be expected—the trick is to watch and learn from other customers.

VALUE ADDED TAX

Both the Republic and Northern Ireland charge a **Value Added Tax (VAT),** a national sales tax on most goods and some services. In Ireland, the VAT does not apply to food and children's clothing but goes as high as 17% in restaurants and 21% on large consumer items. The VAT is almost always included in listed prices. The British rate, applicable to Northern Ireland, is 17.5% on many services (such as hairdressers, hotels, restaurants, and car rental agencies) and on all goods (except books, medicine, and food). Refunds are available only to non-EU citizens and only for goods taken out of the country, not services. In Ireland, **VAT refunds** are available on goods purchased in stores displaying a "Cashback" sticker (ask if you don't see one). Ask for a voucher with your purchase, which you must fill out and present at the Cashback service desk in Dublin or Shannon airports. Purchases greater than €250 must be approved at the customs desk first. Your money can also be refunded by mail, which takes six to eight weeks.

Visitors to Northern Ireland can get a **VAT refund** on goods taken out of the country through the **Retail Export Scheme.** Look for signs like "Tax Free Shopping" or "Tax Free for Tourists" and ask the shopkeeper about minimum purchases (usually €65-130) as well as for the appropriate form. Keep purchases in carry-on luggage so a customs officer can inspect the goods and validate refund forms. To receive a refund, mail the stamped forms back to the store in the envelope provided. Refunds can take up to three months to be processed. To use this scheme, you must export the goods within three months of purchase.

SAFETY & SECURITY

The **national emergency number** in Ireland for police, ambulance, fire, and (in appropriate areas) mountain rescue services is ☎ **999.**

PERSONAL SAFETY

Ireland's friendliness makes for a relatively safe country with a low rate of violent civilian crime, but there are incidents of petty crime by **muggers** and **pickpockets** (see **Financial Security,** p. 10). Certain areas of larger cities are particularly dangerous at night—don't walk alone, don't wear revealing clothing, and don't carry valuables. Check with the reception at hostels for more information on dangerous areas. When walking at night, stick to busy streets and avoid dark alleyways. If you feel uncomfortable, leave as quickly and directly as you can, but don't allow fear of the unknown to spoil your travels. If you're by yourself, be sure that someone at home knows your itinerary, and never admit that you're traveling alone.

SELF DEFENSE. There is no sure-fire way to avoid all the threatening situations you might encounter when you travel, but a good self-defense course will give you concrete ways to react to unwanted advances. Impact, Prepare, and Model Mugging can refer you to local self-defense courses in the US (☎ 800-345-5425). Visit the website at www.impactsafety.org/chapters for a list of nearby chapters. Workshops (2-3hr.) start at US$50; full courses run US$350-500.

TRANSPORTATION. The main concern for most drivers visiting the Republic or Northern Ireland is adjusting to driving on the left-hand side of the road (especially dealing with right turns). If you are using a **car,** learn local driving signals and wear a seatbelt. Study route maps before you hit the road, and if you plan on spending a lot of time on the road, you may want to bring spare parts. For long drives in desolate areas, consider a cellular phone and a roadside assistance program (see p. 38). Be sure to park your vehicle in a garage or well traveled area, and use a steering wheel locking device in larger cities. **Sleeping in your car** is one of the most dangerous (and often illegal) ways to get your rest.

If you're **cycling,** wear reflective clothing, drink plenty of water, and ride on the same side as the traffic. Learn the international signals for turns, and use them. Know how to fix a modern derailleur-equipped chain mount and change a tire, and practice on your own bike; a few simple tools and a good bike manual will be invaluable. Exercise caution when biking at night and on heavy-traffic roads.

Let's Go doesn't recommend **hitchhiking,** particularly not for women. For more information on the perils of traveling by thumb, see p. 40.

TERRORISM. Terrorism has become a serious international concern, but it is enormously difficult to predict where or when attacks will occur. Over the past several decades, Northern Ireland has combatted its own domestic terrorist organizations. Most of these terrorist organizations set out to cause maximum monetary damage but minimum casualties. Travelers are almost never targeted, and since the Good Friday Agreement in 1998, terrorism has ceased to be a major concern for most Irish, even in the North, though Troubles related violence still occurs especially during the summer Marching Season.

The most important thing for travelers is to gather as much information as possible before leaving and to **keep in contact** while overseas. The US Department of State website (travel.state.gov) is a good place to research the current situation anywhere you may be planning to travel. The U.K. Civil Contingencies Secretariat website at www.ukresilience.gov.uk features updates and warnings for citizens of and travelers to the UK. Depending on the circumstances, you may want to register with your home embassy or consulate when you arrive. The **Travel Advisories** box (below) lists offices to contact and webpages to visit for the most updated list of your home country's government traveling advisories.

TRAVEL ADVISORIES. The following government offices provide travel information and advisories by telephone, by fax, or via the web:

Australian Department of Foreign Affairs and Trade: ☎1300 555 135; www.dfat.gov.au.

Canadian Department of Foreign Affairs and International Trade (DFAIT): In Canada and the US call ☎800-267-8376, elsewhere call ☎613-944-4000; www.dfait-maeci.gc.ca. Call for their free booklet, *Bon Voyage...But.*

New Zealand Ministry of Foreign Affairs: ☎04 439 8000; fax 494 8506; www.mft.govt.nz/travel/index.html.

United Kingdom Foreign and Commonwealth Office: ☎020 7008 0232; fax 7008 0155; www.fco.gov.uk.

US Department of State: ☎202-647-5225; faxback service 202-647-3000; http://travel.state.gov. For *A Safe Trip Abroad,* call ☎202-512-1800.

FINANCIAL SECURITY

PROTECTING YOUR VALUABLES. There are a few steps you can take to minimize the financial risk associated with traveling. First, **bring as little with you as possible.** Second, buy a few combination **padlocks** to secure your belongings either in your pack—which you should **never leave unattended**—or in a hostel or train station locker. Third, **carry as little cash as possible;** instead carry traveler's checks and ATM/credit cards, keeping them in a **money belt**—not a "fanny pack"—along with your passport and ID cards. Fourth, **keep a small cash reserve separate from your primary stash,** along with your traveler's check numbers and important photocopies.

CON ARTISTS & PICKPOCKETS. Con artists often work in groups, and children are among the most effective. **Never let your passport or your bag out of your sight.** Beware of **pickpockets** in city crowds, especially on public transportation. Also, be alert in public telephone booths. If you must say your calling card number, do so quietly; if you punch it in, make sure no one looks over your shoulder.

ACCOMMODATIONS & TRANSPORTATION. Never leave belongings unattended; crime occurs in even the most demure-looking hostel or hotel. Bring your own **padlock** for hostel lockers, and don't ever store valuables in any locker. Be particularly careful on **buses** and **trains,** carry your backpack in front of you where you can see it, and try not to sleep on any public transportation. If traveling by **car,** don't leave valuables in it while you are away, and hide removable CD players in the trunk.

DRUGS & ALCOHOL

A meek "I didn't know it was illegal" will not suffice. Remember that you are subject to the laws of the country in which you travel, not to those of your home country. The Republic and the UK both regulate the possession of recreational drugs, with penalties ranging from a warning to lengthy prison sentences. Minor marijuana use generally results in a fine or warning, but harder substances are treated with severity. If you carry **prescription drugs** while you travel, it is vital to have a copy of the prescription and a note from a doctor readily accessible at country borders. The drinking age is 18 throughout Ireland and Northern Ireland.

HEALTH

Traveling in Ireland is not without its share of health risks, but many of these can be prevented with little more than common sense and a bit of foresight. Drink lots of fluids, wear sturdy, broken-in shoes and clean socks, and use talcum powder to keep your feet dry.

BEFORE YOU GO

In your **passport,** write the names of any people you wish to be contacted in case of a medical emergency, and also list any allergies or medical conditions of which you want doctors to be aware. Allergy sufferers might want to obtain a full supply of any necessary medication before the trip. Matching a prescription to a foreign equivalent is not always easy, safe, or possible. Carry up-to-date, legible prescriptions or a statement from your doctor stating the medication's trade name, manufacturer, chemical name, and dosage. While traveling, be sure to keep all medication with you in your carry-on luggage. For tips on packing a basic first aid kit or other health essentials, see p. 18.

USEFUL ORGANIZATIONS & PUBLICATIONS

US **Centers for Disease Control and Prevention (CDC;** ☎ 877-FYI-TRIP; toll-free fax 888 232 3299; www.cdc.gov/travel) maintains an international travelers' hotline and an informative website. CDC's comprehensive booklet *Health Information for International Travel,* an annual rundown of disease, immunization, and general health advice, is free online or for US$30 via Public Health Foundation (☎ 877-252-1200). Consult the appropriate government agency of your home country for consular information sheets on entry requirements and other issues for various countries (see the listings in **Travel Advisories,** p. 17). For quick information on health and travel warnings, call **Overseas Citizens Services** (☎ 202-647-5225; after-hours 202-647-4000), or contact a passport agency, embassy, or consulate abroad. For information on medical evacuation services and travel insurance firms, see the US government's website at http://travel.state.gov/medical.html or the **British Foreign and Commonwealth Office** (www.fco.gov.uk). For detailed information on travel health, including a country-by-country overview of diseases try the **International Travel Health Guide,** by Stuart Rose, MD (US$25; www.travmed.com). For general health information, contact the **American Red Cross** (☎ 800-564-1234; www.redcross.org).

MEDICAL ASSISTANCE ON THE ROAD

In the event of sudden illness or an accident, dial ☎ **999,** the general **emergency** number for the Republic and Northern Ireland. It's a free call from any pay phone to an operator who will connect you to the local police, hospital, or fire brigade.

EU citizens receive health care; others must have medical insurance or be prepared to pay, though emergency care is provided free of charge. Hospitals are plentiful and listed in the **Practical Information** sections.

If you are concerned about being able to access medical support while traveling, there are special support services you might employ. The *MedPass* from **Global-Care, Inc.,** 6875 Shiloh Rd. East, Alpharetta, GA 30005-8372, USA (☎800-860-1111; www.globalems.com), provides 24hr. international medical assistance, support, and medical evacuation resources.

Those with medical conditions (diabetes, allergies to antibiotics, epilepsy, heart conditions) may want to obtain a **Medic Alert** ID tag (first year US$35, annually thereafter US$20), which identifies the condition and gives a 24hr. collect-call number. Contact the Medic Alert Foundation, 2323 Colorado Ave, Turlock, CA 95382, USA (☎888-633-4298, outside US ☎209 668 3333; www.medicalert.org).

PREVENTING DISEASE

INSECT-BORNE DISEASES. Beware of insects—particularly mosquitoes, fleas, and lice—in wet or forested areas in Ireland (particularly in the northwest and near boglands). **Ticks**—responsible for Lyme and other diseases—can be particularly dangerous in rural and forested regions. Pause periodically while walking to brush off ticks using a fine-toothed comb on your neck and scalp. Do not try to remove ticks by burning them or coating them with nail polish remover or petroleum jelly. If you find a tick attached to your skin, grasp the head with tweezers as close to your skin as possible and apply slow, steady traction. Removing a tick within 24 hours greatly reduces the risk of infection.

FOOT AND MOUTH DISEASE. Although easily transmitted between cloven-hoofed animals (cows, pigs, sheep, goats and deer), Foot and Mouth Disease (FMD) does not pose a known health threat to humans. It is, however, devastating to livestock—causing severe depletions of milk and meat production—and can be transmitted by human traffic as well as animal contact. FMD is believed to be killed by heat, making cooked meats apparently safe for consumption. Fish, poultry, fruits and vegetables pose no FMD risk. In 2001, several European countries experienced a severe outbreak of FMD. Incidents in the Republic and Northern Ireland were relatively minor and contained. As of publication of this guide, general travel is not restricted in Ireland. For more information, contact the Republic's Department of Agriculture, Food, and Rural Development (☎01 607 2000; www.irlgov.ie/daff) or the North's Department of Agriculture and Rural Development (☎028 90 524 279 or 90 524 590; www.dardni.gov.uk).

MAD COW DISEASE. Bovine spongiform encephalopathy (BSE), better known as Mad Cow Disease, is a disease affecting the central nervous system of cattle. The human variant is called Creutzfeldt-Jakob disease (nvCJD), and both forms of the condition involve fatal brain diseases. Information on nvCJD is not conclusive, but the disease is supposedly caused by consuming infected beef; however, the risk is very small (around one case per 10 billion servings of meat). The US Centers for Disease Control has further information (www.cdc.gov/travel), as does the EU Commission on Food Safety (http://europa.eu.int/comm/food).

FOOD- AND WATER-BORNE DISEASES. Prevention is the best cure: be sure that everything you eat is cooked properly and that the water you drink is clean. **Parasites** hide in unsafe water and food. Symptoms of parasitic infection include swollen glands or lymph nodes, fever, digestive problems, and anemia. Tap water in

Ireland is generally safe, but river, streams, and lakes may carry bacteria, and water from them should always be purified. To purify your own water, bring it to a rolling boil or treat it with **iodine tablets,** available at any camping goods store.

HEPATITIS. Hepatitis B is a viral infection of the liver transmitted via bodily fluids or needle-sharing. Symptoms may not surface until years after infection. Vaccinations are recommended for health-care workers, sexually-active travelers, and anyone planning to seek medical treatment abroad. The three-shot vaccination series must begin six months before traveling. **Hepatitis C** is like Hep B, but the mode of transmission differs. IV drug users, those with occupational exposure to blood, hemodialysis patients, and recipients of blood transfusions are at the highest risk, but the disease can also be spread through sexual contact or sharing items like razors and toothbrushes that may have traces of blood on them.

AIDS, HIV, & STDS. For detailed information on Acquired Immune Deficiency Syndrome (AIDS) in Ireland, call the National AIDS Helpline Éire (☎ 01 872 4277); AIDS Ireland (☎ 800 232 320); or the Northern Ireland National AIDS Helpline (☎ 0800 137 437). You can also contact the US Centers for Disease Control's (☎ 800-342-2437), or the Joint United Nations Programme on HIV/AIDS (UNAIDS), 20, av. Appia, CH-1211 Geneva 27, Switzerland (☎ 22 791 36 66; fax 791 41 87). The Council on International Educational Exchange's pamphlet, *Travel Safe: AIDS and International Travel,* is posted on their website (www.ciee.org/travelsafe.cfm), along with links to other online and phone resources.

Sexually transmitted diseases (STDs) such as gonorrhea, chlamydia, genital warts, syphilis, and herpes are easier to catch than HIV and can be just as deadly. **Hepatitis** B and C can also be transmitted sexually (see above). Though condoms may protect you from some STDs, oral or even tactile contact can lead to transmission. If you think you may have contracted an STD, see a doctor immediately.

WOMEN'S HEALTH

Reliable **contraceptive devices** may be difficult to find, especially in rural areas. Women on birth-control should bring enough to allow for extended stays. Bring a prescription, since forms of the Pill vary. **Abortion** is illegal in Ireland, except when the life of the mother is in danger. Women who need an abortion while abroad should contact the **International Planned Parenthood Federation,** European Regional Office, Regent's Park, London NW1 4NS (☎ 020 7487 7900; www.ippf.org).

MEDICAL & TRAVEL INSURANCE

Travel insurance covers four basic areas: medical/health problems, property loss, trip cancellation/interruption, and emergency evacuation. Prices for travel insurance purchased separately run about US$50 per week for full coverage, while trip cancellation/interruption may be purchased separately at a rate of about US$5.50 per US$100 of coverage.

Medical insurance (especially university policies) often covers costs incurred abroad; check with your provider. **US Medicare** does not cover foreign travel. **Canadians** are protected by their home province's health insurance plan for up to 90 days after leaving the country; check with the Ministry of Health or Health Plan Headquarters. **Australians** traveling in the UK are entitled to many of the services that they would receive at home as part of the Reciprocal Health Care Agreement. **Homeowners' insurance** (or your family's coverage) often covers theft during travel and loss of travel documents (passport, plane ticket, railpass, etc.) up to US$500.

ISIC and **ITIC** (see p. 11) provide basic insurance benefits, including US$100 per day of in-hospital sickness for up to 60 days, US$3000 of accident-related medical reimbursement, and US$25,000 for emergency transport. Cardholders have access to a toll-free 24hr. helpline (run by **TravelGuard**) for medical, legal, and financial emergencies overseas (US and Canada ☎ 877-370-4742, elsewhere call US collect ☎ +1 715-345-0505). **American Express** (US ☎ 800-528-4800) grants most cardholders automatic car rental insurance (collision and theft, not liability) and ground travel accident coverage of US$100,000 on flight purchases made with the card.

INSURANCE PROVIDERS. Council and **STA** (see p. 31) offer plans that can supplement your basic coverage. Other private insurance providers in the US and Canada include: **Access America** (☎ 800-284-8300; www.accessamerica.com); **Berkely Group/ Carefree Travel Insurance** (☎ 800-323-3149; www.berkely.com); and **Travel Assistance International** (☎ 800-821-2828; www.europ-assistance.com). Providers in the **UK** include **Columbus Direct** (☎ 020 7375 0011; www.columbusdirect.net).

PACKING

Pack lightly. Lay out only what you absolutely need, then take half the clothes and twice the money. The less you have, the less you have to lose (or store, or carry on your back). Any extra space will be useful for souvenirs or items you might pick up along the way. If you plan to do a lot of hiking, see **Camping & the Outdoors** (p. 24).

CLOTHING. No matter when you're traveling, it's a good idea to bring a **warm jacket** or wool sweater, a **rain jacket,** sturdy shoes or **hiking boots,** and **thick socks.** Flip-flops or waterproof sandals are key for surviving grubby hostel showers. You may also want to add a nicer change of clothes for hitting the town at night. Remember to dress respectfully when visiting churches and cathedrals.

CONVERTERS & ADAPTERS. In Ireland, electricity is 220V AC, enough to fry any 120V North American appliance. 220/240V electrical appliances don't like 110V current, either. **Americans** and **Canadians** should buy an **adapter** (which changes the shape of the plug) and a **converter** (which changes the voltage; US$20). Don't make the mistake of using only an adapter (unless appliance instructions explicitly state otherwise). **New Zealanders** and **South Africans** (who both use 220V) as well as **Australians** (240/250V) won't need a converter but will need a set of adapters.

FILM. Film and developing in Ireland is expensive, so bring enough film for your entire trip and develop it at home. Less serious photographers should bring a **disposable camera** rather than an expensive permanent one.

FIRST-AID KIT. For a basic first-aid kit, pack: bandages, pain reliever, antibiotic cream, a thermometer, a Swiss Army knife, tweezers, moleskin, decongestant, motion-sickness remedy, diarrhea or upset-stomach medication (Pepto Bismol or Immodium), an antihistamine, sunscreen, insect repellent, burn ointment, and a syringe for emergencies (get an explanatory letter from your doctor).

IMPORTANT DOCUMENTS. Don't forget your passport, traveler's checks, ATM and/or credit cards, and adequate ID (see p. 11). Also check that you have any of the following that might apply to you: a hosteling membership card (see p. 23); driver's license (see p. 11); travel insurance forms; and rail/bus passes (see p. 35).

LUGGAGE. If you plan to cover most of your itinerary by foot, a sturdy **frame backpack** is unbeatable. (For the basics on buying a pack, see p. 25.) Toting a **suitcase** or **trunk** is fine if you plan to live in one or two cities and explore from there, but a very bad idea if you're going to be moving around a lot. In addition to your main piece of luggage, a **daypack** (a small backpack or courier bag) is a must.

SLEEPSACK. Some hostels require that you provide your own linen or rent sheets from them. Save cash by making your own sleepsack: fold a full-size sheet in half the long way, then sew it closed along the long side and one of the short sides.

OTHER USEFUL ITEMS. For safety purposes, you should bring a **money belt** and small **padlock.** Basic **outdoors equipment** (plastic water bottle, compass, waterproof matches, pocketknife, sunglasses, sunscreen, hat) may also prove useful. Quick repairs of torn garments can be done on the road with a **needle and thread;** also consider bringing electrical tape for patching tears. Doing your **laundry** by hand (where it is allowed) is both cheaper and more convenient than doing it at a laundromat. **Other things** you're liable to forget: an umbrella; sealable **plastic bags** (for damp clothes, soap, food, shampoo, and other spillables); an **alarm clock;** safety pins; rubber bands; a flashlight; earplugs; garbage bags; and a small **calculator.**

ACCOMMODATIONS

Bord Fáilte (bored FAHL-tshah; "welcome board") is the Republic of Ireland's tourism authority. Its system for approving accommodations involves a more-or-less frequent inspection and a fee. Those approved get to use Bord Fáilte's national booking system and display its icon, a green shamrock on a white field. Approved campgrounds and bed and breakfasts are listed with prices in *Caravan and Camping Ireland* and *Bed and Breakfast Ireland,* respectively, available from any Bord Fáilte office. Bord Fáilte's standards are very specific and, in some cases, far higher than what hostelers and other budget travelers expect or require. Unapproved accommodations can be a better value than their approved neighbors, though some unapproved places are, of course, real dumps. Most official tourist offices in Ireland will refer *only* to approved accommodations, and will book rooms for a €1-4 fee. **Credit card reservations** can be made through Dublin Tourism (☎800 6686 6866). Approval by the **Northern Ireland Tourist Board** is legally required of all accommodations in the North. Their tourist offices can provide all the contact information necessary to find lodging.

HOSTELS

Hostels are generally laid out dorm-style, often with large single-sex rooms and bunk beds, although some offer private rooms for families and couples. They sometimes have kitchens and utensils for your use, bike or moped rentals, storage areas, and laundry facilities. The Internet is becoming an increasingly common hostel amenity, though web access is often via mind-numbingly slow connections. There can be drawbacks to hostels: some close during daytime "lockout" hours, have a curfew, don't accept reservations, impose a maximum stay, or, less frequently, require that you do chores. In Ireland, a hostel bed will average €10-20.

In Ireland more than anywhere else, senior travelers and families are invariably welcome. Some hostels are strikingly beautiful (a few are even housed in castles), but others are little more than run-down barracks. You can expect every Irish hostel to provide blankets, although you may have to pay extra for sheets (see **Packing,** p. 21). Hostels listed are chosen based on location, price, quality, and facilities. In recent years, a number of Irish hostels have been turned into refugee houses and have closed their doors to the budget traveling scene—it is always a good idea to call ahead to hostels to ensure that they are open for business.

 A HOSTELER'S BILL OF RIGHTS. There are certain standard features that we do not include in our hostel listings. Unless we state otherwise, you can expect that every hostel has no lockout, no curfew, a kitchen, free hot showers, some system of secure luggage storage, and no key deposit.

HOSTELLING INTERNATIONAL

Joining the youth hostel association in your home country automatically grants you membership privileges in **Hostelling International (HI),** a federation of national hosteling organizations. This is rarely necessary in Ireland, although there are sometimes member discounts. Most HI hostels also honor **guest memberships** include: a blank card with space for six validation stamps, a nightly nonmember supplement (one-sixth the membership fee), and one guest stamp; get six stamps, and you're a member. Many HI hostels accept reservations via the **International Booking Network** (The Republic ☎01 830 1766; Northern Ireland ☎01 289 032 4733; Australia ☎295 651 699; Canada ☎800-663-5777; England and Wales ☎01 629 592 709; NZ ☎3379 9970; Scotland ☎0871 553 255; US ☎800-909-4776; www.hostelbooking.com). HI's umbrella organization's web page (www.iyhf.org) lists the web addresses and phone numbers of all national associations.

Travelers can apply for a HI card at most student travel agencies (see p. 31), or at the national hosteling organization of the country they are visiting. Listed below is **An Óige,** the national hosteling organization of Ireland, and **HINI,** the national hosteling organization of Northern Ireland. **Independent Holiday Hostels** offers similar and more extensive service in both the Republic and the North.

AN ÓIGE. In Ireland, **An Óige** (an OYJ), the **HI** affiliate, operates 32 hostels countrywide (61 Mountjoy St., Dublin 7. ☎01 830 4555; www.irelandyha.org; one-year membership €25, under 18 €10.50). Many An Óige hostels are in remote areas or small villages and were designed primarily to serve hikers, long-distance bicyclists, anglers, and others seeking nature, not noise. The North's HI affiliate is **HINI** (Hostelling International Northern Ireland; formerly known as **YHANI**). It operates only 8 hostels, all comfortable (22-32 Donegal Rd., Belfast BT12 5JN. ☎028 9031 5435; www.hini.org.uk; one-year membership UK£10, under 18 UK£6).

INDEPENDENT HOLIDAY HOSTELS. in Ireland a number of hostels belong to the Independent Holiday Hostels (IHH). Most of the 140 IHH hostels have no lockout or curfew, accept all ages, require no membership card, and have a comfortable atmosphere that generally feels less institutional than at An Óige hostels; all are Bord Fáilte-approved. Grab a free booklet with complete descriptions of each at any IHH hostel. Contact the IHH office at 57 Lower Gardiner St., Dublin 1 (☎01 836 4700; www.hostels-ireland.com).

BED & BREAKFASTS

For a cozy alternative to impersonal hostel dorms, B&Bs (private homes with rooms available to travelers) range from the tolerable to the sublime. Hosts will sometimes go out of their way to be accommodating, often accepting travelers with pets or giving personalized tours. "Full Irish breakfasts"—eggs, bacon, bread, sometimes black or white pudding, fried vegetables, cereal, orange juice, and coffee or tea—fill tummies until dinner. Singles run about €25-30, doubles €40-50. Many B&Bs do not provide phones, TVs, or private baths, but by and large, Irish B&Bs are excellent ways to meet locals who are laden with insights on their island. B&Bs displaying a shamrock are officially approved by Bord Fáilte. For accommodations in Northern Ireland, check the Northern Ireland Tourist Board's *Where to Stay in Northern Ireland* (UK£4), available at most tourist offices.

UNIVERSITY DORMS

Many **colleges and universities** open their residence halls to travelers when school is not in session; some do so even during term-time. These dorms are often close to student areas—typically areas of town chock-full of things to do and people to meet—and are usually very clean. Getting a room may take a couple of phone calls and require advanced planning, but rates tend to be low, and many offer free local calls. For appropriate cities, including **Dublin, Galway**, and **Belfast**, *Let's Go* lists colleges which rent dorm rooms in the Accommodations sections. **Cork** and **Limerick** are also big university towns with student housing available in summer.

GOING GREEN

ECEAT International (the European Centre for Eco Agro Tourism) publishes a *Green Holiday Guide to Ireland* ($14/€15), which lists hostels, B&Bs, campgrounds, and guest houses that are either organic farms or otherwise environmentally friendly. All ECEAT-listed accommodations are in beautiful, wild areas, and frequently beside protected parkland. Contact ECEAT-International at P.O. Box 10899, 1001 EW, Amsterdam (☎31 206 681 030; www.pz.nl/eceat). For more about work exchanges on Irish organic farms see **Alternatives to Tourism**, p. 44.

CAMPING AND THE OUTDOORS

Camping brings you closest to the land, the water, the insects, and continued financial solvency. Youth hostels often have camping facilities, which is fortunate for backpackers as many campsites are designed for people with caravans (RVs), not tents. Sites cost €5-13, depending on the level of luxury. It is legal to cross private land by **public rights of way;** any other use of private land without permission is considered trespassing. Remember, **bogs catch fire** extremely easily.

Camping in State Forests and National Parks is not allowed, nor is camping on public land if an official campsite is in the area. It is also illegal to start campfires within 2 mi. of these forests and parks. Caravan and camping parks provide all the accoutrements of bourgeois civilization: toilets, showers, and sometimes kitchens, laundry facilities, and game rooms. At many sites, caravans are available for hire. **Northern Ireland** treats its campers royally; there are well-equipped campsites throughout, and spectacular parks often house equally mouth-watering sites.

USEFUL PUBLICATIONS AND WEB RESOURCES. An excellent general resource for travelers planning on camping or spending time in the outdoors is the **Great Outdoor Recreation Pages** (www.gorp.com). For information about camping, hiking, and biking, call the publishers listed below for a free catalogue.

  Automobile Association, Contact Centre, Car Ellison House, William Armstrong Dr., Newcastle-upon-Tyne NE4 7YA, UK. (☎0870 600 0371; www.theaa.co.uk). Publishes Caravan and Camping: Europe (UK£9) and Britain & Ireland (UK£8).

  The Caravan Club, East Grinstead House, East Grinstead, West Sussex, RH19 1UA, UK (☎01342 32 69 44; www.caravanclub.co.uk). For UK£30, members receive equipment discounts, a 700-page directory and handbook, and a monthly magazine.

  The Mountaineers Books, 1001 SW Klickitat Way, #201, Seattle, WA 98134, USA (☎800-553-4453 or 206-223-6303; www.mountaineersbooks.org). Over 400 titles on hiking, biking, mountaineering, natural history, and conservation.

WILDERNESS SAFETY

THE GREAT OUTDOORS. Stay warm, stay dry, and stay hydrated. The vast majority of life-threatening wilderness situations can be avoided by following this simple advice. Prepare yourself for an emergency, however, by always packing raingear, a hat and mittens, a first-aid kit, a reflector, a whistle, high energy food, and extra water for any hike. Dress in wool or warm layers of synthetic materials designed for the outdoors; never rely on cotton for warmth, as it is useless when wet. Check **weather forecasts** and pay attention to the skies when hiking as weather patterns

ENVIRONMENTALLY RESPONSIBLE TOURISM. The idea behind responsible tourism is to leave no human trace. A campstove is a safer (and more efficient) way to cook than using vegetation, but if you must make a fire, keep it small and use only dead branches or brush rather than cutting vegetation. Make sure your campsite is at least 150 ft. (50m) from water supplies or bodies of water. If there are no toilet facilities, bury human waste (but not paper) at least 4 in. (10cm) deep and above the high-water line, and 150 ft. or more from any water supplies and campsites. Always pack your trash in a plastic bag and carry it with you until you reach the next trash can.

ESSENTIALS

can change suddenly. Whenever possible, let someone know when and where you are going hiking, and do not attempt a hike beyond your ability. See **Health,** p. 18, for information on outdoor ailments and basic medical concerns.

CAMPING AND HIKING EQUIPMENT

Backpack: Internal-frame packs mold better to your back, keep a lower center of gravity, and flex adequately to allow you to hike difficult trails. **External-frame packs** are more comfortable for long hikes over even terrain, as they keep weight higher and distribute it more evenly. Make sure your pack has a strong, padded hip-belt to transfer weight to your legs. Any serious backpacking requires a pack of at least 4000 in^3 (16,000cc), plus 500 in^3 for sleeping bags in internal-frame packs. Sturdy backpacks cost anywhere from US$125-420—this is one area where it doesn't pay to economize. Either buy a **waterproof backpack cover,** or store all of your belongings in plastic bags inside your pack. Also see **Packing,** p. 21.

Boots: Be sure to wear hiking boots with good **ankle support.** They should fit snugly and comfortably over 1-2 pairs of wool socks and thin liner socks. Break in boots over several weeks first in order to spare yourself painful and debilitating blisters.

Sleeping Bag: Most sleeping bags are rated by season ("summer" means 30-40°F at night; "four-season" or "winter" often means below 0°F). They are made either of **down** (warmer and lighter, but more expensive, and miserable when wet) or of **synthetic** material (heavier, more durable, and tolerable when wet). Prices range US$70-210 for a summer synthetic to US$250-300 for a good down winter bag. **Sleeping bag pads** include foam pads (US$10-30), air mattresses (US$15-50), and Therm-A-Rest self-inflating pads (US$45-120). Bring a **stuff sack** to store your bag and keep it dry.

Tent: The best tents are free-standing (with their own frames and suspension systems), set up quickly, and only require staking in high winds. Low-profile dome tents are the best all-around. Good 2-person tents start at US$90, 4-person at US$300. Seal the seams of your tent with waterproofer, and make sure it has a rain fly. Other tent accessories include a **battery-operated lantern,** a **plastic groundcloth,** and a **nylon tarp.**

Other Necessities: Synthetic layers and a **pile jacket** will keep you warm even when wet. A **"space blanket"** will help you to retain your body heat and doubles as a groundcloth (US$5-15). Plastic **water bottles** are virtually shatter- and leak-proof. Bring **water-purification tablets** for when you can't boil water. For those places that forbid fires or the gathering of firewood, you'll need a **camp stove** (the classic Coleman starts at US$40) and a propane-filled **fuel bottle** to operate it. Also don't forget a **first-aid kit, pocketknife, insect repellent, calamine lotion,** and **waterproof matches** or a **lighter.**

...AND WHERE TO BUY IT

Discount Camping, 880 Main North Rd., Pooraka, South Australia 5095, Australia (☎08 8262 3399; www.discountcamping.com.au).

Eastern Mountain Sports (EMS), 1 Vose Farm Rd., Peterborough, NH 03458, USA (☎888-463-6367; www.ems.com).

L.L. Bean, Freeport, ME 04033 (US and Canada ☎800-441-5713; UK ☎0800 891 297; www.llbean.com).

YHA Adventure Shop, 19 High St., Staines, Middlesex, TW18 4QY, UK (☎1784 458 625; fax 1784 464 573; www.yhaadventure.com). The main branch of one of Britain's largest outdoor equipment suppliers.

CAMPERS, CARAVANS, AND RVS

Renting an RV (called a "camper" or "caravan" in Ireland), will always be more expensive than tenting or hosteling, but the costs compare favorably with staying in hotels and renting a car. The convenience of bringing along your own bedroom, bathroom, and kitchen makes it an attractive option, especially for older travelers and families. Rates vary by region, season, and type of caravan. Rental prices for a standard caravan range from €750-1300 per week. It always pays to contact several different companies to compare vehicles and prices. **Motorhome Ireland** (www.motorhome-irl.co.uk), has offices in the North, in Co. Down (☎028 4062 1800), and the Republic, in Co. Meath (☎048 4062 1800).

ORGANIZED ADVENTURE TRIPS

Organized adventure tours offer another way of exploring the wild. Activities include hiking, biking, skiing, canoeing, kayaking, rafting, climbing, photo safaris, and archaeological digs. **Specialty Travel Index** (☎800-442-4922 or 415-459-4900; info@specialtytravel.com; www.specialtytravel.com) lists more than 500 adventure and specialty tour operators worldwide; tourist bureaus and outdoors organizations are also good sources of information.

KEEPING IN TOUCH

The Irish postal service is both reliable and speedy. Though Internet is readily available in the cities, it can often be hard to find in rural Donegal and Kerry.

BY MAIL

SENDING MAIL FROM IRELAND. Airmail from Ireland to the US averages five to six days; to Europe it averages three to four days. To Australia, NZ, or South Africa, it will take one to two weeks. Times are less predictable from small towns. To send a postcard or letter (up to 25g) to Britain costs €0.41; to Europe, €0.44; to other international destinations, €0.57. Add €3.40 for Swiftpost International. Domestic letter rate within Ireland is €0.41.

RECEIVING MAIL IN IRELAND. An Post is Ireland's national postal service (☎1850 57 58 59 or 01 459 11 33; www.anpost.ie). Dublin is the only place in the Republic with postal codes. Even-numbered codes are for areas south of the Liffey, odd-numbered are for the north. The North has number-and-letter postal codes like the rest of the UK. **Airmail** letters under 1 oz. between the US and Ireland take six to eight days and cost US$0.80. Letters under 20g from Canada are CDN$1.05. Allow at least five to seven days from Australia (postage AUS$1 for up to 20g) and three days from Britain (postage 36p for up to 20g). Make sure to write "air mail" or "par avion" on your envelope. There are several ways to arrange pickup of letters sent to you while you're abroad:

General Delivery: Mail can be sent to Ireland through **Poste Restante** (the international phrase for General Delivery) to almost any city or town with a post office. Address *Poste Restante* letters to (for example): "Robert BRIGHT, Poste Restante, Dunboyne, Co. Meath, Ireland." The mail will go to a special desk in the central post office, unless you specify a post office by street address or postal code. When picking up mail, bring a form of photo ID. There is generally no surcharge.

American Express: AmEx offices throughout the world offer a free **Client Letter Service** (mail held up to 30 days and forwarded upon request) for cardholders who contact them in advance. Address the letter in the same way shown above. Some offices will offer these services to non-cardholders (especially AmEx Travelers Cheque holders), but call ahead to make sure. *Let's Go* lists AmEx office locations for most large cities in **Practical Information** sections; for a complete, free list, call ☎ 800-528-4800.

If regular airmail is too slow, **Federal Express** can get a letter from New York to Dublin in two days for US$30; rates among non-US locations are prohibitively expensive (London to Dublin, for example, costs upwards of US$50). By **US Global Priority Mail,** a letter from New York would arrive in Dublin within four to six days and would cost US$5. From Australia, **EMS** can get a letter to Ireland in three to four working days for AUS$67. **Surface mail** is by far the cheapest and slowest way to send mail. It takes one to three months to cross the Atlantic and two to four to cross the Pacific.

BY TELEPHONE

CALLING IRELAND FROM HOME

To call Ireland from home, you must first dial the **international dialing prefix** of your home country. International access codes include: Australia 0011; NZ 00; South Africa 09; UK 00; US 011. After dialing the international code, dial the **country code** of the region you are calling. Country codes include: 353 to reach the **Republic of Ireland;** 44 to reach **Northern Ireland** and **Britain;** 048 to reach **Northern Ireland** from the Republic. Then dial the **city code.** City codes start with a 0 (e.g., Dublin is 01). This zero is dropped when dialing from overseas. *Let's Go* lists telephone codes opposite each city header (marked by a ☎ icon), except when covering rural areas where more than one telephone code may apply—here we list the area code before the number. **The city code is 028 throughout the North.** After dialing the area code, you must dial the **local number.** Regional telephone codes have recently been unified to 7 digits, below is a chart with the relevant new codes For example, to call the US embassy in Dublin from New York, dial ☎ 011 353 1 668 8777. To call the Irish embassy in New York from Dublin, dial ☎ 00 1 212 745 0200. .

LET'S GO PHONE HOME. Let's Go has recently partnered with **ekit.com** to provide a calling card that offers a number of services, including email and voice messaging. Before purchasing any calling card, always compare rates with other cards, and make sure it serves your needs (a local phonecard is generally better for local calls). For more info, visit www.letsgo.ekit.com.

Current code or county	new code	These 2 digits go before 5 digit numbers
046-Kells	no change	92
046-Trim	no change	94
0405-Edenderry, Rhode	046	97
056-Kilkenny	no change	77
0507-all areas	059	86
0508-all areas	059	64

ESSENTIALS

Current code or county	new code	These 2 digits go before 5 digit numbers
071-all areas	no change	91
072-all areas	071	98
073-all areas	074	97
074-all areas	no change	91
077-all areas	074	93
078 or 079-all areas	071	96
092-all areas	094	95
094Kilkelly, Knock	no change	93
0902-all areas	094	95
0902-all areas	090	64
0903-all areas	090	66
0905-all areas	090	96

CALLING HOME FROM IRELAND

A **calling card** is your cheapest option. Calls are billed collect or to your account. You can often call collect without possessing a company's calling card just by calling their access number and following the instructions. **To obtain a calling card** from your national telecommunications service before leaving home, contact the appropriate company listed below (using the numbers in the first column). To **call home with a calling card,** contact the operator for your service provider in Ireland by dialing the appropriate toll-free access number (listed below in the second column).

Where available, prepaid Irish phone cards and occasionally major credit cards can be used for direct international calls. **Swiftcall** phone cards or other prepaid Irish phone cards (available at post offices and newsagents) can score you great rates after 9pm, Irish time—often as low as €0.20-€0.30 per minute.

If you do dial direct, dial ☎ 00 (the international access code in both the Republic and Northern Ireland), and then dial the country code and number of your home. **Country codes** include: Australia 61; New Zealand 64; South Africa 27; UK 44; US and Canada 1. Alternatively, you can access an Irish international operator at ☎ 114. Note that to call the North from the Republic, you dial ☎ 048 plus the number. Phone rates tend to be highest in the morning, lower in the evening, and lowest on Sunday and late at night. International calls from the Republic are cheapest during **economy periods.** The low-rate period to North America is Monday through Friday 10pm-8am and Saturday and Sunday all day; to EU countries it's Monday

COMPANY	TO OBTAIN A CARD, DIAL:	TO CALL ABROAD, DIAL:
AT&T (US)	800-288-4685	800 550 000 (Republic) 0800 013 0011 (Northern Ireland)
British Telecom Direct	800 34 51 44	800 55 01 44 (Republic)
Canada Direct	800-668-6878	800 555 001 (Republic) 0800 89 00 16 (Northern Ireland)
MCI (US)	800-444-3333	800 55 1001 (Republic and Northern Ireland)
New Zealand Direct	0800 00 00 00	800 55 00 64 (Republic) 0800 89 00 64 (Northern Ireland)
Sprint (US)	800-877-4646	800552 011 (Republic) 0800 890 877 (Northern Ireland)
Telkom South Africa	10 219	800 550 027 (Republic) 0800 890 027 (Northern Ireland)
Telstra Australia	13 22 00	800 55 00 61 (Republic) 0800 856 6161 (Northern Ireland)

through Friday 6pm-8am and Saturday and Sunday all day; to Australia and New Zealand call Monday through Friday 2-8pm and midnight-8am, and Saturday and Sunday all day. There are no economy rates to the rest of the world.

Placing a **collect call** through an international operator is even more expensive, but may be necessary in case of emergency. You can place collect calls through the service providers listed above even if you don't have one of their phone cards.

CALLING WITHIN IRELAND

The simplest way to call within the country is to use a coin-operated phone. Using Irish pay phones can be tricky. Public phones come in two varieties: **coin phones** and **card phones.** Public coin phones will give you back unused coins (but not fractions of coins; don't insert a €1 coin for a 20 cent call) but private pay phones (called "one-armed bandits") in hostels and restaurants do not—once you plunk in your change, kiss it good-bye. In any pay phone, do not insert money until asked to, or until the call goes through. The pip-pip noise that the phone makes as you wait for it to start ringing is normal and can last up to 10 seconds. Local calls cost 40 cents on public phones; "one-armed bandits" charge more. Local calls are not unlimited—one unit pays for 4min.

CALLING FROM THE REPUBLIC OF IRELAND.
Operator: ☎ 10 (not available from card phones).
Directory inquiries: ☎ 11 850 or 11 811 (for the Republic and the North).
International access code: ☎ 00.
International operator: ☎ 114.
International directory inquiries: ☎ 11 818.

The smart option for non-local calls is buying a **prepaid phone card,** which carries a certain amount of phone time depending on the card's denomination. The time is measured in minutes or talk units (e.g. one unit/one minute), and the card usually has a toll-free access telephone number and a personal identification number (PIN). News agents sell phone cards in denominations of €2, €5, €10, or €20. Card phones have a digital display that ticks off the perilous plunge your units are taking. When the unit number starts flashing, you may push the eject button on the card phone; you can then pull out your expired calling card and replace it with a fresh one. If you try to wait until your card's units fall to zero, you'll be disconnected. Eject your card early and use the remaining unit or two for a local call.

CALLING FROM NORTHERN IRELAND AND LONDON.
Operator: ☎ 100.
Directory inquiries: ☎ 192.
International access code: ☎ 00.
International operator: ☎ 155.
International directory assistance: ☎ 153.

Pay phones in Northern Ireland initially charge 10p for local calls; most calls cost 20p. A series of harsh beeps warns you to insert more money when your time is up. The digital display ticks off your credit in 1p increments so you can watch your pence in suspense. Only unused coins are returned. You may use all remaining credit on a second call by pressing the "follow on call" button (often marked "FC"). Phones don't accept 1p, 2p, or 5p coins. The dial tone is a continuous purring sound; a repeated double-purr means the line is ringing. Northern **British Telecom Phonecards,** in denominations of UK£2, £5, £10, and £20, are sold at post offices and newsstands, and are accepted at most public phones.

TIME DIFFERENCES

Britain and Ireland are on **Greenwich Mean Time (GMT)**. GMT is 5hr. ahead of New York, 8hr. ahead of Vancouver and San Francisco, 2hr. behind Johannesburg, 10hr. behind Sydney, and 12hr. behind Auckland, although the actual time differences depend on daylight savings time. Both Britain and Ireland observe **daylight savings time** between the last Sunday of March and the last Sunday of October.

BY INTERNET

The **Internet**, delightful plague that it is, has infected even the Emerald Isle. **Electronic mail (email)** is a wonderful way to stay in touch, though slow connections in Ireland may make the experience more trying than you're accustomed to. Free, web-based email providers include **Hotmail** (www.hotmail.com), **Yahoo! Mail** (www.yahoo.com) and, in Ireland, **Ireland.com.** Internet access is available in Irish cities in cafes, hostels, and usually in libraries. One hour of webtime costs about €4-6 (an ISIC card may win you a discount). Look into a county library membership in the Republic (€2.50-3), which will give you unlimited access to participating libraries, and their Internet. Such membership is particularly useful in counties where Internet cafes are sparse, like Donegal, Mayo, and Kerry.

GETTING TO IRELAND

Ireland is best visited in July and August, when the climate becomes something near summery. There are a wealth of travel options available—if you want to get to Ireland cheaply, fly into London, and take a ferry from Wales.

BY PLANE

A little effort can save you a bundle. If your plans are flexible enough, courier fares are cheapest. Tickets bought from consolidators and standby seating are also good deals, but last-minute specials, airfare wars, and charter flights often beat these fares. The key is to hunt around, to be flexible, and to ask persistently about discounts. Students, seniors, and those under 26 should never pay full price.

AIRFARES

Airfares to Ireland peak between early June and late August; holidays are also expensive. The cheapest times to travel are in October and February. Midweek (M-Th morning) round-trip flights run US$40-50 cheaper than weekend flights, but they are more crowded and less likely to permit frequent-flier upgrades. Traveling with an "open return" ticket can be pricier than fixing a return date when buying the ticket. Round-trip flights are by far the cheapest; "open-jaw" (arriving in and departing from different cities) tickets tend to dent the wallet. Patching one-way flights together is the most expensive way to travel. Flights between capitals or regional hubs will usually be cheaper.

  Fares for round-trip flights to Dublin from the US or the Canadian east coast cost roughly US$700/$450 (summer/off season); from the US or Canadian west coast US$850/$600; from London UK£70/£35; from Australia AUS$2700/$2000. Flying into Shannon can be cheaper, while flights into Belfast cost about the same but arrive directly only from major cities such as New York and Paris. The cheapest way to enter Ireland is by flying into London and buying a return ticket that takes you from London to Dublin.

BUDGET & STUDENT TRAVEL AGENCIES

Travelers with **ISIC and IYTC cards** (see p. 11) qualify for big discounts from student travel agencies.

STA Travel, 7890 S. Hardy Dr., Ste. 110, Tempe AZ 85284, USA (24hr. reservations and info ☎800-781-4040; www.sta-travel.com). A student and youth travel organization with over 150 offices worldwide (check their website for a listing of offices), including US offices in Boston, Chicago, L.A., New York, San Francisco, Seattle, and Washington, D.C. Ticket booking, travel insurance, railpasses, and more. In the **UK**, walk-in office 11 Goodge St., London W1T 2PF (☎0207-436-7779). In **New Zealand**, Shop 2B, 182 Queen St., Auckland (☎09 309 0458). In **Australia**, 366 Lygon St., Carlton Vic 3053 (☎03 9349 4344).

Travel CUTS (Canadian Universities Travel Services Limited), 187 College St., **Toronto**, ON M5T 1P7 (☎416-979-2406; fax 979-8167; www.travelcuts.com). Offices across Canada and the United States in Seattle, San Francisco, Los Angeles, New York and elsewhere. Also in the UK, 295-A Regent St., **London** W1B 2H9 (☎020 7255 2191).

usit world (www.usitworld.com). Nearly 20 **usit NOW** offices in Ireland, including 19-21 Aston Quay, O'Connell Bridge, **Dublin** 2 (☎01 602 1600; www.usitworld.com), and Fountain Centre, College Street, **Belfast** (☎028 9032 7111; www.usitnow.com). Over 50 **usit campus** branches in the UK (www.usitcampus.co.uk), including 52 Grosvenor Gardens, **London** SW1W 0AG (☎0870 240 1010); **Manchester** (☎0161 273 1880); and **Edinburgh** (☎0131 668 3303). Offices also in Athens, Auckland, Brussels, Frankfurt, Johannesburg, Lisbon, Luxembourg, Madrid, Paris, Sofia, and Warsaw.

Wasteels, Skoubogade 6, 1158 Copenhagen K. (☎3314 4633; fax 7630 0865; www.wasteels.com). A huge chain with 180 locations across Europe. Sells Wasteels BIJ tickets discounted 30-45% off regular fare, 2nd-class international point-to-point train tickets with unlimited stopovers for those under 26 (sold only in Europe).

COMMERCIAL AIRLINES

The commercial airlines' lowest regular offer is the **APEX** (Advance Purchase Excursion) fare, which provides confirmed reservations and allows "open-jaw" tickets. Generally, reservations must be made seven to 21 days ahead of departure, with seven- to 14-day minimum-stay and up to 90-day maximum-stay restrictions. Book peak-season APEX fares early; by May you will have a hard time getting your desired departure date.

Specials advertised in newspapers may be cheaper but have more restrictions. A popular carrier to Ireland is its national airline, **Aer Lingus** (☎081 836 5000; UK 0845 084 4444; US ☎800-IRISHAIR; www.aerlingus.ie), which has direct flights to the US, London, and Paris. **Ryanair** (☎081 830 3030; www.ryanair.ie) is a smaller airline that offers a "lowest-fare guarantee"; check the website for details. The web-based phenom **easyJet** (UK☎08706 000 000; www.easyjet.com) has recently begun flying from England and Scotland to Belfast. If another airline doesn't fly directly to one of Ireland's airports, it can almost certainly get you to London.

FLIGHTS FROM NORTH AMERICA

Round-trip fares range from US$450-700. Standard commercial carriers like **American** (☎800-433-7300; www.aa.com) and **United** (☎800-241-6522; www.ual.com) offer the most convenient flights, but they may not be the cheapest. Foreign carriers often offer better deals. **Icelandair** (☎800-223-5500; www.icelandair.com) offers free stopovers in Iceland and flies from the east coast of the US to London, after which you can buy a ticket taking you from London to Dublin and back again.

ESSENTIALS

 SHE'S GOT AN E-TICKET TO RIDE. Most airline sites offer special last-minute deals on the Web. Other sites do the legwork and compile the deals for you—try www.bestfares.com,www.onetravel.com, and www.travelzoo.com.

■ **Student Universe** (www.studentuniverse.com), **STA** (www.sta-travel.com), and **Orbitz.com** provide quotes on student tickets, while **Expedia** (www.expedia.com) and **Travelocity** (www.travelocity.com) offer full travel services. **Priceline** (www.priceline.com) allows you to specify a price, and obligates you to buy any ticket that meets it; be prepared for antisocial hours and odd routes. **Skyauction** (www.skyauction.com) allows you to bid on last-minute and advance-purchase tickets. An indispensable resource on the Internet is the *Air Traveler's Handbook* (www.cs.cmu.edu/afs/cs/user/mkant/Public/Travel/airfare.html), with links to everything you need to know before you board a plane.

FLIGHTS FROM BRITAIN

Flying to London and connecting to Ireland is often easiest and cheapest. Aer Lingus (see p. 31) and several other carriers offer service on these routes. **British Midland Airways** (UK ☎ 0870 607 0555; from abroad 1332 854 854; www.flybmi.com) flies about seven times per day to London Heathrow. **British Airways** (UK ☎ 0845 773 3377; Republic ☎ 800 626 747; US ☎ 800 AIRWAYS; www.british-airways.com) flies into most Irish airports daily and into some Irish airports many, many times a day. Prices range from UK£60-225 round-trip but can drop from time to time. Check their website for specials. **Ryanair** (UK ☎ 0871 246 0000, Republic ☎ 0818 30 30 30; www.ryanair.com) connects Kerry, Cork, and Knock to London and more than nine other destinations in England and Scotland.

FLIGHTS FROM AUSTRALIA & NEW ZEALAND

Expect to pay somewhere between AUS$2000 (off season) and AUS$2700 (peak-season) for a basic round-trip fare to Ireland. Commercial carriers like Quantas (Australia ☎ 13 13 13, New Zealand ☎ 0800 808 767; www.qantas.com.au) will take you from major cities in Australia and New Zealand to London, where you will have to purchase a return-ticket taking you from London to Ireland. Others, such as Thai Airways (Australia ☎ 1300 65 19 60, New Zealand ☎ 09 377 02 68; www.thaiair.com), will take you directly to Dublin. Other commercial carriers include Air New Zealand (☎ 0800 73 70 00; www.airnz.co.nz.) and Singapore Air (Australia ☎ 13 10 11, New Zealand ☎ 0800 808 909; www.singaporeair.com.)

STANDBY FLIGHTS

Traveling standby requires considerable flexibility in arrival and departure dates and cities. Companies dealing in standby flights sell vouchers rather than tickets, along with the promise to get to your destination within a certain window of time (typically 1-5 days). You call in before your specific window of time to hear your flight options and the probability that you will be able to board each flight. You can then decide which flights you want to try to make, show up at the appropriate airport at the appropriate time, present your voucher, and board if space is available.

Carefully read agreements with any company offering standby flights, as tricky fine print can leave you in a lurch. To check on a company's service record in the US, call the **Better Business Bureau** (☎ 212-533-6200). It is difficult to receive refunds, and clients' vouchers will not be honored when an airline fails to receive payment in time.

TICKET CONSOLIDATORS

Ticket consolidators, or **"bucket shops,"** buy unsold tickets in bulk from commercial airlines and sell them at discounted rates. The best place to look for their ads is in the Sunday travel section of any major newspaper. Call quickly, as availability is typically limited. Not all bucket shops are reliable, so insist on a detailed receipt and pay by credit card (in spite of the 2-5% fee) so you can stop payment if you never receive your tickets. For more information, see www.travel-library.com/airtravel/consolidators.html.

Numerous ticket consolidators are based in North America. **Travel Avenue** (☎800-333-3335; www.travelavenue.com) searches for best available fares and then uses several consolidators to attempt to beat that fare. Other consolidators worth trying are **Cheap Tickets** (☎800-377-1000; www.cheaptickets.com); **Interworld** (☎305-443-4929); **Pennsylvania Travel** (☎800-331-0947); **Rebel** (☎800-227-3235; www.rebeltours.com); and **Travac** (☎800-872-8800). Yet more consolidators on the web include the **Internet Travel Network** (www.itn.com); **Travel Information Services** (www.tiss.com); **TravelHUB** (www.travelhub.com); and **The Travel Site** (www.thetravelsite.com). Keep in mind that these are just suggestions to get you started in your research; *Let's Go* does not endorse any of these agencies. As always, be cautious, and research companies before giving out your credit card number.

CHARTER FLIGHTS

Charters are flights a tour operator contracts with an airline to fly extra loads of passengers during peak season. Flights are often fully booked, and schedules and itineraries may change or be cancelled at the last moment (as late as 48 hours before the trip, and without a full refund), and check-in, boarding, and baggage claim are often much slower. However, they can also be cheaper.

Discount clubs and **fare brokers** offer members savings on last-minute charter and tour deals. Study contracts closely; you don't want to end up with an unwanted overnight layover. Discount travel to Ireland is the specialty of **O'Connors Fairways Travel,** located in the USA at 342 Madison Ave., Suite 437, New York, NY, 10173 (☎212-661-0550; reservations ☎800-662-0550; www.oconnors.com).

BY FERRY

Ferries are popular and usually a more economical, albeit considerably more time-consuming, form of transportation than airplanes. Almost all sailings in June, July, and August are "controlled sailings," which means that you must book the crossing ahead of time (a few days in advance is usually sufficient).

Fares vary tremendously depending on time of year, time of day, and type of boat. Traveling mid-week, during the night, in spring, fall, or winter, promises the cheapest fares. Adult single tickets usually range from UK£18 to £35 (€28-55), and there are many discount rates available. Some people tag along with car drivers who are allowed four free passengers. Bikes can usually be brought on for no extra charge. Students, seniors, families, and youth traveling alone typically receive discounts; **An Óige (HI) members** receive up to a 20% discount on fares from Irish Ferries and Stena Sealink, while **ISIC cardholders** with the **TravelSave Stamp** (€10; available at **usit NOW,** see p. 31) receive a 15% discount from Irish Ferries and an average 17% discount (variable among four routes) on Stena Line ferries. Ferry passengers from the Republic are taxed an additional €6.50 when traveling home from England.

BRITAIN AND FRANCE TO IRELAND

Assorted bus and train tickets that include ferry connections between Britain and Ireland are also available as package deals through ferry companies, travel agents, and usit offices. Contact Bus Éireann for information (see **By Bus**, p. 35).

Brittany Ferries: UK ☎08703 665 333; France ☎08 25 82 88 28; www.brittany-ferries.com. **Cork** to **Roscoff** (13½hr., Apr.-Sept. 1 per week, €52-99).

Irish Ferries: France ☎01 44 88 54 50; Ireland ☎1890 31 31 31; UK ☎08705 17 17 17; www.irishferries.ie. **Rosslare** to **Cherbourg** and **Roscoff** (17-18hr., Apr.-Sept. 1-9 per week, €60-120, students €48); and **Pembroke, UK** (3¾hr., €25-39, students €19). **Holyhead, UK** to **Dublin** (2-3hr., £20-31 return, students £15).

Stena Line: UK ☎1233 64 68 26; www.stenaline.co.uk. **Harwich** to **Hook of Holland** (5hr., UK£26). **Fishguard** to **Rosslare** (1-3½hr., UK£18-21, students £14-17). **Holyhead** to **Dublin** (4hr., UK£23-27, students £19-23) and **Dún Laoghaire** (1-3½hr., £23-27, students £19-23). **Stranraer** to **Belfast** (1¾-3¼hr., UK£14-36, students £10).

Cork-Swansea Ferries: Ireland (☎021 427 1166; www.swansea-cork.ie). Between **Swansea, South Wales,** and **Ringaskiddy** in Co. Cork (10hr., UK£24-34/€38-53).

Steam Packet Company: UK ☎08705 523 523; www.steam-packet.com. Sends SeaCats between **Belfast** and **Heysham** (4hr.; UK£34/€38, under 16 UK£20/€32) and **Troon** (2½hr.; UK£17-31/€27-49, under 16 UK£9-17/€14-27), also between **Liverpool** and **Dublin** (4hr.; UK£29-39/€49-61, under 16 UK£15-20/€24-32). SeaCat trips are faster than ferries but considerably pricier.

Stena Line: Charter House, Park St., Ashford, Kent TN24 8EX, England (☎08705 707 070). **Cork** ☎021 272 965; **Dún Laoghaire** ☎08705 755 755 has 24hr. recorded info; Tourist Office, Arthurs Quay, **Limerick** ☎061 316 259. **Rosslare Harbour** ☎053 33115; **UK,** ☎1233 64 68 26; www.stenaline.co.uk. Ferries from **Holyhead,** North Wales, to **Dún Laoghaire** (3½hr. on the Superferry, UK£23-29/€35-45); from **Fishguard,** South Wales, and **Pembroke,** Wales to **Rosslare Harbour** (3½-3¾hr., UK£18-23/€28-35); and from **Stanraer,** Scotland, to **Belfast** (90min. on the Stena Line, 3hr. on the SeaCat, UK£14-36/€22-56). Package deals include train service from London.

BY BUS

Bus Éireann (the Irish national bus company) reaches Britain and even the continent by working in conjunction with ferry services and the bus company **Eurolines** (Republic ☎01 836 6111, UK ☎990 143 219; www.eurolines.com). Most buses leave from Victoria Station in London (to **Belfast:** 15hr., €49/UK£74, return €79/UK£51; **Dublin:** 12hr., €42/UK£27, return €69/UK£45), but other major city stops include Birmingham, Bristol, Cardiff, Glasgow, and Liverpool. Services run to Cork, Derry, Galway, Limerick, Waterford, and Tralee, among others. The immense Eurolines network connects with many European destinations (Dublin-Paris 9hr., €90/UK£58, return €143/UK£92). Prices given are for adult fares during the summer—cheaper fares are available in the off season, as well as for children (under 13), young people (under 26), and seniors (60+). Tickets can be booked through usit, any Bus Éireann office, Irish Ferries, Stena Line, any Eurolines office, or **National Express** office in Britain (☎08705 808 080). You might also contact the Bus Éireann General Inquiries desk in Dublin (☎01 836 6111) or a travel agent for further information.

ESSENTIALS

ONCE IN IRELAND

Public transportation is, for the most part, regular and extensive. Most travel is done via buses, as the train system can only effectively be used to travel between urban centers. Travel in Co. Clare, Kerry, and Donegal, can be particularly spotty.

GETTING AROUND

Fares on all modes of transportation are either **single** (one-way) or **return** (round-trip). "Period returns" require you to return within a specific number of days; "day return" means you must return on the same day. Unless stated otherwise, *Let's Go* lists single fares. Round-trip fares are generally 30% above the one-way fare.

Roads between Irish cities and towns have official letters and numbers ("N" and "R" in the Republic; "M," "A," and "B" in the North), but most locals refer to them by destination ("the Kerry road"). Signs and printed directions sometimes give only the numbered and lettered designations, sometimes only the destination. Most signs are in English and Irish; destination signs in outlying *gaeltacht* are most often only in Irish. Old black-and-white road signs give distances in miles; new green and white signs are in kilometers. Speed limit signs are in miles.

BY BUS

Buses in the Republic of Ireland reach many more destinations and are less expensive than trains. Bus drivers are often very accommodating in where they will pick you up and drop you off. The national bus company, **Bus Éireann** (Dublin general helpline ☎ 01 836 6111; www.buseireann.ie), operates both long-distance Expressway buses, which link larger cities, and local buses, which serve the countryside and smaller towns. The invaluable bus timetable book is hugely difficult to obtain for personal ownership, though you may find one at Busáras Central Bus Station in Dublin. In Donegal, **private bus providers** take the place of Bus Éireann's nearly-nonexistent local service. *Let's Go* lists these providers when appropriate.

Bus Éireann's **Rambler** ticket offers unlimited bus travel within Ireland for three of eight consecutive days (€50; under 16 €25), eight of 15 consecutive days (€110; under 16 €70), or 15 of 30 consecutive days (€160; under 16 €100), but is generally less cost-effective than buying individual tickets. A combined **Irish Explorer Rail/Bus** ticket allows unlimited travel on trains and buses for eight of 15 consecutive days (€160; under 16 €80). Tickets can be purchased at any Bus Éireann big-city terminal.

Ulsterbus, (☎ 028 9033 3000, Belfast office 028 9032 0011; www.ulsterbus.co.uk), the North's version of Bus Éireann, runs extensive and reliable routes throughout Northern Ireland, where there are no private bus services. Coverage expands in summer, when several buses run a purely coastal route and full- and half-day tours leave from Belfast for key tourist spots. Pick up a free regional timetable at any station. There are excellent discounts for students (with ISIC cards) and families.

The **Irish Rover** pass covers both Bus Éireann and Ulsterbus services. It sounds ideal for visitors intending to travel in both the Republic and Northern Ireland, but unless you plan to travel extensively on the bus, its true value is debatable (unlimited travel for three of eight days €60/UK£90, children €33/UK£50; for eight of 15 days €135/UK£200, children €75/UK£113; for 15 of 30 €195/UK£293, children €110/UK£165). The **Emerald Card** offers unlimited travel on: Ulsterbus; Northern Ireland Railways; Bus Éireann Expressway, Local, and City services in Cork, Dublin, Galway, Limerick, and Waterford; and intercity, DART, and suburban rail Iarnród Éireann services. The card works for eight out of 15 consecutive days (€180/UK£129, under 16 €90/UK£65) or 15 out of 30 consecutive days (€310/UK£223, under 16 €155/UK£111).

BUS TOURS. Though some find that they limit a traveler's independence, bus tours often free a traveler from agonizing over the minutia of your trip while exposing you to a knowledgeable tour leader. Tours cost around €45 per day, with longer tours costing less per day. **Tír na nÓg Tours** (☎01 836 4684; www.tirnanog-tours.com) offers three- to six-day tours which include breakfast, hostels, and entrance to sights. **Paddywagon Tours** (☎01 672 6007; 0800 783 4191 from the UK; www.paddywagontours.com) has one-, three-, and six-day packages, including breakfast, hostels, and sights. The **Stray Travel Network** in London (☎0171 373 7737; www.straytravel.com) provides flexible tours of Ireland, minus accommodation or food provisions so you can choose where to spend your money. **Contiki Travel** (☎1-888-CONTIKI; www.contiki.com) runs comprehensive bus tours starting at $849. Tours include accommodation, transportation and some meals.

BY TRAIN

Iarnród Éireann (Irish Rail), is useful only for travel to urban areas, from which you'll need to find another form of transportation to reach Ireland's picturesque villages and wilds. Trains from Dublin's Heuston Station chug toward Cork, Ennis, Galway, Limerick, Tralee, Waterford, and Westport; others leave from Dublin's Connolly Station to head for Belfast (express), Rosslare (express), Sligo, and Wexford. For schedule information, pick up an InterCity Rail Travelers Guide (€1.20), available at most train stations. The **TravelSave** stamp, available for €10 at any **usit** agency if you have an ISIC card, cuts fares by 30-50% on national rail. (It also provides up to 30% discounts on bus fares above €1.30.) A **Faircard** (€10.15) can get anyone age 16 to 26 up to 50% off the price of any InterCity trip. Those over 26 can get the less potent **Weekender card** (€8; up to a third off, valid F-Tu only). Both are valid through the end of the year. The **Rambler** rail ticket allows unlimited train travel on five days within a 15-day travel period (€122). For combined bus-and-train travel passes, see **By Bus**, p. 35. Information is available from the Irish Rail information office, 35 Lower Abbey St., Dublin (☎01 836 3333; www.irishrail.ie). Unlike bus tickets, train tickets sometimes allow travelers to break a journey in stages yet still pay the price of a single-phase trip. Bikes may be carried on trains for a fee of €8; check at the station for specific restrictions.

While the **Eurailpass** is not accepted in Northern Ireland, it *is* accepted on trains in the Republic. Youth and family passes are also available but are cost-effective only if you plan to travel to the Continent as well. The BritRail pass does not cover travel in Northern Ireland, but the month-long **BritRail+Ireland** works in both the North and the Republic with rail options and round-trip ferry service between Britain and Ireland (5 days US$359; 10 days US$545). A traveler under 26 should look into a youth pass. You'll find it easiest to buy a Eurailpass before you arrive in Europe; contact Council Travel, Travel CUTS (see p. 31), or another travel agent. **Rail Europe Group** (US ☎877-456-RAIL 7245, UK ☎08705 848 848; www.raileurope.com), also sells point-to-point tickets.

Northern Ireland Railways (☎028 9066 6630; www.nirailways.co.uk) is not extensive but covers the northeastern coastal region well. The major line connects Dublin to Belfast. When it reaches Belfast, this line splits, with one branch ending at Bangor and one at Larne. There is also rail service from Belfast and Lisburn west to Derry and Portrush, stopping at three towns between Antrim and the coast. British Rail passes are not valid here, but Northern Ireland Railways offers its own discounts. A valid **Translink Student Discount Card** (UK£6) will get you up to 33% off all trains and 15% discounts on bus fares over UK£1.45 within Northern Ireland.

FROM THE ROAD

AROUND IRELAND WITHOUT CAR OR THUMB

As a 20-year-old American, traveling in Ireland has its perks—being able to walk into any pub and order a pint is fantastic. But there are still limitations as transportation is concerned; renting a car is out of the question, and I've always been hesitant to hitch alone. To truly see Ireland, everyone says, you have to get out of the cities, but my vehicular limitations seemed to make this well-nigh impossible. However, I set out for Dublin determined to reach the remote corners of the Southeast, with no clear plan of how to get there.

My journey began easily enough, as Iarnrod Eireann regularly runs down the coast from Dublin. Train travel is easy and comfortable, and gazing through the window at the seashore and countryside is its own reward.

Eventually the lines ran out, so I turned to buses. Many small towns receive Bus Eireann service only once a week, but independent bus companies have sprung up to fill the gaps. With a bit of asking around, I managed to figure out when and where these buses ran.

As my destinations became still more remote and even the bus lines ran out, I began to recognize the power of casual conversation. One morning, I hopped onto a bus to a small beach town, and found that I was the only passenger. Resisting the urge to grab a seat in the back, I sat down right in front, and started

(cont. on next page)

The **Freedom of Northern Ireland** ticket allows unlimited travel by train and Ulsterbus and can be purchased for seven consecutive days (UK£45), three out of eight days (UK£30), or a single day (UK£12).

BY CAR

Traveling by car has obvious advantages: speed, freedom, and direct access to the countryside. Unfortunately, disadvantages include gas (petrol) prices, unfamiliar automobile laws, and, for many travelers, the switch to **driving on the left side of the road.** Be particularly cautious at roundabouts (rotary interchanges): remember to **give way to traffic from the right.** For an informal primer on European road signs and conventions, check www.travlang.com/signs. Additionally, the **Association for Safe International Road Travel (ASIRT),** 11769 Gainsborough Rd., Potomac, MD 20854 (US ☎ 301-983-5252; www.asirt.org), can provide specific information on road conditions.

INTERNATIONAL DRIVING PERMIT (IDP). If you plan to drive a car while in Ireland for longer than a three-month period, you must have an International Driving Permit (IDP). If you intend to drive for longer than one year, you'll need to get an Irish driver's license. Your IDP, valid for one year, must be issued in your own country before you depart. An application for an IDP usually needs to include one or two photos, a current local license, an additional form of identification, and a fee. To apply, contact your home country's Automobile Association.

CAR INSURANCE. Most credit cards cover standard insurance. If you rent, lease, or borrow a car, you will need a **green card,** or **International Insurance Certificate,** to certify that you have liability insurance and that it applies abroad. Green cards can be obtained at car rental agencies, car dealers (for those leasing cars), some travel agents, and some border crossings. Rental agencies may require you to purchase theft insurance in countries that they consider to have a high risk of auto theft.

RENTING A CAR. Renting (hiring) an automobile is the cheapest option if you plan to drive for a month or less, but the initial cost of renting a car and the price of gas will astound you in Ireland. Prices range €150-370 (plus VAT) per week with insurance and unlimited mileage. Automatics are 40% more expensive to rent than manuals (stick-shifts). For insurance reasons, most companies require renters to be over 23 and under 70. **Dan Dooley** (☎ 062 53103; UK ☎ 0181 995 4551; US ☎ 800-331-9301; www.dandooley.com) is the only company in Ireland that will rent to drivers between 21 and 24, though such drivers incur an added daily surcharge. Major rental agencies convenient to major airports are **Budget Rent-A-Car** (Central Office ☎903 27711; Shannon Airport ☎061 471 361; Dublin Airport ☎01 844 5150; www.budgetcarrental.ie, and **Thrifty** (Freephone in Ireland ☎800 515 800; Dublin Airport ☎01 840 0800; Shannon Airport ☎061 471 770; www.thrifty.ie). It is always significantly less expensive to reserve a car from the US than from Europe.

BY BICYCLE

Many insist that cycling is *the* way to see Ireland and Northern Ireland. Much of the Island's countryside is well suited for pedaling by daylight, as many roads are not heavily traveled. Single-digit "N" roads in the Republic, and "M" roads in the North, are more busily trafficked; try to avoid these. Begin your trip in the south or west to take advantage of prevailing winds.

Many **airlines** will count your bike as your second free piece of luggage, but some charge extra. Check with the individual company for any special packaging procedures. Most ferries let you take your bike for free or for a nominal fee. You can ship your bike on some **trains,** but the cost varies; inquire at the information desk. You'll have better luck getting your bike on a **bus** if you depart from a terminal, not a wayside stop. Bikes are allowed on Bus Éireann at the driver's discretion for a fee of €10 (not always enforced).

Riding a bike with a frame pack strapped on it or your back is about as safe as pedaling blindfolded over a sheet of ice; **panniers** are essential. The first thing to buy, however, is a suitable **bike helmet** (US$25-50). U-shaped **locks** are expensive (starting at US$30), but most companies insure their locks against theft.

Raleigh Rent-A-Bike (☎01 465 9659; www.raleigh.ie) has rental shops across Ireland. You can hire a bike for €20 per day, €80 per week, plus deposit (usually €80). The shops will equip you with locks, patch kits, pumps, and, for longer journeys, pannier bags (€10 per week). The **One-Way Rental** plan allows you to rent a bike at one shop and drop it off at another for a fee of €20. **Celtic Cycling** (☎0503 75282; www.celtic-cycling.com) serves the Southeast, including Carlow, Kilkenny, Waterford and Wexford. Bikes are €10 per day, €60 per week, and require a credit card deposit. They also offer cycling tour packages of varing length, that include accommodations and pickup at the airport (€535 for 7 days).

Many small local dealers and hostels also rent bikes. Rates are about €8-16 per day and €40-70 per week. Tourist offices can direct you to bike rental

chatting with the driver. As we were swapping travel stories, I mentioned my next destination, a tiny town in the mountains. After running through the bus schedules in his head, the driver regretfully informed me that I wouldn't be able to get there for another three days. Just as I was resigning myself to this news, however, he realized that he would pass the town in the evening, on his way back from a driving route through the mountains. When he offered to give me a lift, off-duty, I gratefully accepted. The bus ride turned out to be fantastic. We spent the afternoon driving along gorgeous mountain roads, and talked the whole way about our travel experiences. By the time we arrived in the town that night, it was hard for me to get off the bus and leave my new friend. I was almost glad to be car-less.

Since then, I have taken ferries, tramped down little known short-cuts, and gotten a ride from a trio of fellow hostelers who I met over dinner. I have rented a bike and pedalled my way to a town, which gave me plenty of time to appreciate the countryside and the benefits of regular exercise. When the bike chain came inextricably loose, I met a friendly publican/undertaker/*Let's Go* reader who gave me a lift in his big, black, possibly-used-for-transporting-corpses van.

All in all, I've found that there's always a way to get to the out-of-the-way places, and things I've seen and people I've met getting there (wherever *there* is) are often more exciting than the places themselves. My advice—don't worry about how you'll get there, just GO!

-Naomi Straus

establishments and distribute leaflets on local biking routes, as well as providing the extensive *Cycle Touring Ireland* (€9). Adequate **maps** are a necessity; *Ordnance Survey* maps (€7) or Bartholomew maps are available in most bookstores.

BY FOOT

Ireland's mountains, fields, and heather-covered hills make walking and hiking an arduous joy. The **Wicklow Way,** a popular trail through mountainous Co. Wicklow, has hostels designed for hikers within a day's walk of each other. The best hill-walking maps are the *Ordnance Survey Discovery Series* (€6.60 each). Other remarkable trails include the **Kerry Way** (see p. 282), the **Burren Way** (p. 336), the **Western Way** (p. 368), and the **Fore Trail.** There are a multitude of other trails all over the island; consult Bord Fáilte (see p. 9) for more information and free pamphlets. *Let's Go* lists many of these longer hikes in the **Sights** sections, as well as a plethora of shorter strolls in virtually every Irish town.

The 560 mi. Ulster Way no longer exists, but is in the process of being split into new regional **Waymarked ways.** Contact any local tourist information office in Northern Ireland for more information.

WALKING TOURS. For those looking to avoid some of the pitfalls of hiking, **guided tours** may be the solution. Though expensive (upwards of €80 per day), an area expert will guide hiking greenhorns over the green hills as a bus transports their luggage, meals are served, and accommodations await. Less expensive and more independent, **self-guided tours** include the luggage transport and accommodations but usually do away with meals (and, of course, the guide). For a list of tours, see www.kerna.ie/wci/walking or www.walking.travel.ie. **Tír na nÓg Tours** (57 Lower Gardiner St., Dublin 1; ☎ 01 836 684), is a reputable and acclaimed choice.

BY THUMB

No one should hitch without careful consideration of the risks involved. Hitching means entrusting your life to a random person, risking theft, assault, sexual harassment, and unsafe driving. Although hitching in Ireland is probably safer than most places in the world, the risks of such travel have increased over recent years. Locals do not recommend hitchhiking in Northern Ireland; some caution against it in Co. Dublin, as well as the Midlands.

For women traveling alone, hitching is just too dangerous. A man and a woman are a safer combination, two men will have a harder time, and three will go nowhere. In all cases, **safety** should be the first concern. Safety-minded hitchers avoid getting in the back of a two-door car (or any car they wouldn't be able to get out of in a hurry) and never let go of their backpacks. If they ever feel threatened, they insist on being let off immediately. Acting as if they are going to open the car door or vomit will usually get a driver to stop.

In the **Practical Information** section of many cities, *Let's Go* lists the tram or bus lines that take travelers to strategic hitching points. Success will depend on appearance. Placement is crucial—experienced hitchers stand where drivers can stop, have time to look over potential passengers, and return to the road without causing an accident. Hitching on hills or curves is hazardous and usually fruitless; roundabouts and access roads to highways are better. You can get a sense of the amount of traffic a road sees by its letter and number: in the Republic, single-digit N-roads (A-roads in the North) are as close as Ireland gets to highways, double-digit N-roads see some intercity traffic, R-roads (B-roads in the North) generally only carry local traffic but are easy hitches, and non-lettered roads are a **hitcher's purgatory.** In Northern Ireland, hitching (or even standing) on motorways (M-roads) is illegal: you may only thumb at the entrance ramps—*in front* of the blue-and-white superhighway pictograph (a bridge over a road).

Let's Go strongly urges you to consider the risks before you choose to hitch. We do not recommend hitching as a safe means of transportation.

SPECIFIC CONCERNS

Let's Go has compiled some information below that should help answer many of the questions that those with special needs or specific concerns might have.

DIETARY CONCERNS

Let's Go lists restaurants with vegetarian options when we find them. You're not likely to find much pub grub without meat, but in almost every town at least one restaurant will have something for vegetarians. Eating in larger cities, particularly Dublin and Belfast, should pose no problems. Vegans will have more of a challenge and may need to cook for themselves.

The travel section of the **The Vegetarian Resource Group's** website, at www.vrg.org/travel, has a comprehensive list of organizations and websites that are geared toward helping vegetarians and vegans traveling abroad. The website www.vegdining.com has an excellent database of vegetarian and vegan restaurants worldwide. The **North American Vegetarian Society,** P.O. Box 72, Dolgeville, NY 13329 (☎518-568-7970; www.navs-online.org) also publishes information on veggie-happy travel. For more information, visit your local bookstore or health food store, or consult *The Vegetarian Traveler: Where to Stay if You're Vegetarian,* by Jed and Susan Civic (Larson Publications; US$16).

Travelers who keep kosher should contact synagogues in larger cities for information on kosher restaurants. Your own synagogue or college Hillel should have access to lists of Jewish institutions across the nation. Kosher is not a common term or practice in Ireland; if you are strict in your observance, you may have to prepare your own food. A good resource is the *Jewish Travel Guide,* by Michael Zaidner (Vallentine Mitchell; US$17).

TRAVELING ALONE

There are many benefits to traveling alone, including independence and greater interaction with locals. On the other hand, any solo traveler is a more vulnerable target of harassment and street theft. Lone travelers need to be friendly, well-organized, and confident at all times. If questioned, never admit that you are traveling alone. Maintain regular contact with someone at home who knows your itinerary. For more tips, pick up *Traveling Solo* by Eleanor Berman (Globe Pequot Press, US$17) or subscribe to **Connecting: Solo Travel Network,** 689 Park Road, Unit 6, Gibsons, BC V0N 1V7 (☎604-886-9099; www.cstn.org; membership US$35).

Several services link solo travelers with companions who have similar travel habits and interests; for a bi-monthly newsletter for single travelers seeking a travel partner (subscription US$48), contact the **Travel Companion Exchange,** P.O. Box 833, Amityville, NY 11701 (☎631-454-0880, or in the US ☎800-392-1256; www.whytravelalone.com).

WOMEN TRAVELERS

Though Ireland is an extremely safe place in which to travel, women exploring on their own will inevitably face additional safety issues. If you are concerned, consider staying in **centrally located accommodations.** Stay in places that offer single

ESSENTIALS

> **HEY, LADIES...** The world isn't half as big and bad as the women who wrote the books listed below—let them show you around.
> *A Journey of One's Own: Uncommon Advice for the Independent Woman Traveler*, by Thalia Zepatos. Eighth Mountain Press (US$17).
> *A Foxy Old Woman's Guide to Traveling Alone*, by Jay Ben-Lesser. The Crossing Press (US$11).
> *Travel Alone & Love It: A Flight Attendant's Guide to Solo Travel*, by Sharon B. Wingler. Chicago Spectrum Press, (US$15).

rooms that lock from the inside, avoid solitary late-night treks, and always choose train compartments occupied by other women or couples. **Hitchhiking** is never safe for lone women, or even for two women traveling together.

Carry a **whistle** on your key chain or a **rape alarm** (about €10), and don't hesitate to use them in an emergency. Mace and pepper sprays are illegal in Ireland. The national **emergency** number is ☎999, and the EU number is ☎112. The **Dublin Rape Crisis Centre** helpline is ☎1 800 778 888. *Let's Go* lists other hotlines in the **Practical Information** section of our city write-ups. An **IMPACT Model Mugging** self-defense course can prepare you for a potential attack, as well as raise your level of awareness of your surroundings and your confidence (see **Self Defense**, p. 16).

WOMEN'S HEALTH. Women who need an **abortion** or **emergency contraception** while in Northern Ireland should call the **fpa** (formerly the Family Planning Association) helpline (UK ☎0845 310 1334. Open M-F 9am-7pm), visit their website (www.fpa.org.uk/), or contact the London office, 2-12 Pentonville Rd., N1 9PF (☎020 7837 5432), for more information. Abortions are illegal in the Republic of Ireland; call the London office if you need help.

OLDER TRAVELERS

Senior citizens are eligible for a wide range of discounts on transportation, museums, movies, theaters, concerts, restaurants, and accommodations. If you don't see a senior citizen price listed, ask, and you may be delightfully surprised. **Age and Opportunity** (☎01 837 0570; http://indigo.ie/~ageandop/) promotes the participation of the elderly in all aspects of Irish society. The books *No Problem! Worldwise Tips for Mature Adventurers*, by Janice Kenyon (Orca Book Publishers; US$16) and *Unbelievably Good Deals and Great Adventures That You Absolutely Can't Get Unless You're Over 50*, by Joan Rattner Heilman (NTC/Contemporary Publishing; US$13) are both excellent resources. For more information, contact:

ElderTreks, 597 Markham St., Toronto, ON M6G 2L7 (☎800-741-7956; www.elder-treks.com). Adventure travel programs for the 50+ traveler in Ireland.

Elderhostel, 11 Ave. de Lafayette, Boston, MA 02111 (☎877-426-8056; www.elderhostel.org). Organizes 1- to 4-week "educational adventures" in Ireland for those over 55.

The Mature Traveler, P.O. Box 15791, Sacramento, CA 95852 (☎800-460-6676). Deals, discounts, and travel packages for the 50+ traveler. Subscription US$30.

BISEXUAL, GAY & LESBIAN TRAVELERS

Ireland is more tolerant of homosexuality than one might expect, but less tolerant than one might hope. People in rural areas may not have progressed as far as those in cities have since homosexuality was decriminalized in the Republic in 1993. Dublin now supports a small gay community, with growing student societies at Trinity and UCD and a growing array of pubs and clubs. Belfast and, to a lesser degree, Cork and Galway, also have growing gay communities. *Gay Community News* covers Irish gay-related news, and its listings page covers gay locales in all of Ireland. *Let's Go: Ireland* has gay pub and nightlife listings as well as phone numbers for gay information in Dublin, Belfast, Cork, and elsewhere (see the **Practical Information** sections). Listed below are contact organizations, mail-order bookstores, and publishers that offer materials addressing some specific concerns. **Out and About** (www.planetout.com) offers a bi-weekly newsletter and a comprehensive site addressing gay travel concerns. **Gay Ireland** (www.gay-ireland.com) provides information on gay locales and events in Ireland and offers a personals/chat services. Other useful websites include www.gcn.ie; www.timeout.com/dublin/; and www.esatclear.ie/~gay-hiking/.

Gay and Lesbian Youth in Northern Ireland (GYLNI), Cathedral Buildings, 64 Donegall Street, Belfast, BT1 2GT (☎028 9027 8636; www.glyni.org.uk). Offers a forum for meeting gay men and lesbians (ages 16-25), and info on gay locales in the North.

Ireland's Pink Pages (www.pink-pages.org). Ireland's web-based bisexual, gay, and lesbian directory. Extensive urban and regional info for both the Republic and the North.

International Lesbian and Gay Association (ILGA), 81 rue Marché-au-Charbon, B-1000 Brussels, Belgium (☎2 502 2471; www.ilga.org). Provides political information, such as homosexuality laws of individual countries.

TRAVELERS WITH DISABILITIES

Ireland is not particularly wheelchair-friendly. Ramps, wide doors, and accessible bathrooms are less common than in the US, even in cities like Dublin. *Let's Go* lists and indexes **wheelchair-accessible facilities. Guide dogs** are always conveyed free, but until recently both the UK and Ireland imposed a six-month quarantine on all animals entering the country and require that the owner obtain an import license. For more information, call the PETS Helpline in the UK at ☎870 241 1710 (pets@ahvg.maff.gsi.gov.uk). For general information and free guides on disability access, write to the British Tourist Authority or Bord Fáilte.

Those with disabilities should inform airlines and hostels of their disabilities when making reservations; some time may be needed to prepare special accommodations. Call ahead to restaurants, museums, and other facilities to find out about ramps, door widths, elevator dimensions, etc. **Rail** is probably the most convenient form of travel for disabled travelers in Ireland. Not all train stations are wheelchair-accessible. On the web, *Global Access* (www.geocities.com/Paris/1502/disabilitylinks.html) has links for disabled travelers in Ireland.

Mobility International USA, P.O. Box 10767, Eugene, OR 97440 (☎541 343 1284, voice and TDD; www.miusa.org). Provides a variety of books and other publications containing information for travelers with disabilities.

Society for Accessible Travel and Hospitality (SATH), 347 Fifth Ave., #610, New York, NY 10016 (☎212-447-7284; www.sath.org). An advocacy group that publishes free online travel info and the travel magazine *OPEN WORLD* (US$18, free for members). Annual membership US$45, students and seniors US$30.

Directions Unlimited, 123 Green Ln., Bedford Hills, NY 10507 (☎800-533-5343). Books individual and group vacations for the physically disabled; not an info service.

The Guided Tour Inc., 7900 Old York Rd., #114B, Elkins Park, PA 19027 (☎800-783-5841; www.guidedtour.com). Organizes travel programs for persons with developmental and physical challenges in countries including Ireland.

MINORITY TRAVELERS

Most of Ireland's five million people are white and Christian (largely Catholic in the Republic, mixed Catholic and Protestant in the North). Until recently, the Irish have never had to address racial diversity on a large scale. Recent influxes of non-European immigrants (drawn by Ireland's present economic boom) and a growing Malaysian, Indian, and Pakistani population in Dublin has changed this, however.

Darker-skinned travelers are common subjects of attention, especially in rural areas. Minority travelers may be subject to racial comments and refused service in more certain establishments. In a 2002 survey of minority travelers in Ireland, Sinead O'Casey and Michael O'Connelly found that over 64% of the people had experienced racial insults and 16% suffered physical attacks of some sort. Most uncomfortable experiences occur in public places, like pubs, B&Bs, and shops. For more statistical information, check www.amnesty.ie/act/racism/a-experience.shtml, and for community resources, consult www.nicem.org.uk.

That said, most of the time comments and stares are motivated by curiosity, rather than ill will. The Irish are a very welcoming and friendly people, but as in any place else, what is different, stands out.

TRAVELERS WITH CHILDREN

Family vacations often require that you slow your pace, and always that you plan ahead. When deciding where to stay, remember the special needs of young children; call ahead to hostels and B&Bs to make sure they are child-friendly. If you rent a car, make sure the rental company provides a car seat for younger children. Consider using a papoose-style device to carry a baby on walking trips. **Be sure that your child carries some sort of ID** in case of an emergency or if he or she gets lost, and arrange a reunion spot in case of separation when sight-seeing.

Virtually all museums and tourist attractions also have a children's rate. Children under two generally fly for 10% of the adult airfare on international flights (this does not necessarily include a seat). International fares are usually discounted 25% for children from two to 11.

 TEACH YOUR CHILDREN WELL. Travel is an invaluable learning experience, for kids from one to ninety-two; the books listed below will help you research for the perfect family vacation.
Backpacking with Babies and Small Children, by Goldie Silverman. Wilderness Press (US$10).
Take Your Kids to Europe, by Cynthia W. Harriman. Cardogan Books (US$18).
Adventuring with Children: An Inspirational Guide to World Travel and the Outdoors, by Nan Jeffrey. Avalon House Publishing (US$15).
Trouble Free Travel with Children, by Vicki Lansky. Book Peddlers (US$9).

OTHER RESOURCES

Listed below are books and websites useful for independent research.

TRAVEL PUBLISHERS & BOOKSTORES

Hunter Publishing, 470 W. Broadway, Fl. 2, South Boston, MA 02127, USA (☎ 617-269-0700; www.hunterpublishing.com). Has an extensive catalog of travel guides and diving and adventure travel books.

Rand McNally, P.O. Box 7600, Chicago, IL 60680, USA (☎847-329-8100; www.randm-cnally.com), publishes road atlases.

Adventurous Traveler Bookstore, P.O. Box 2221, Williston, VT 05495, USA (☎800-282-3963; www.adventuroustraveler.com).

Travel Books & Language Center, Inc., 4437 Wisconsin Ave. NW, Washington, D.C. 20016 (☎800-220-2665; www.bookweb.org/bookstore/travelbks/). Over 60,000 titles from around the world.

USEFUL PUBLICATIONS

Ireland: An Encyclopedia for the Bewildered, K.S. Daly. Ten Speed Press (US$8).

Dublin Pub Life and Lore: An Oral History, Kevin C. Kearns. Roberts Rinehart (US$16).

A Pocket History of Irish Traditional Music, Gearóid Ó hAllmhuráin. O'Brien Press (US$8).

Teach Yourself Irish, Diarmuid Ó Sé & Joseph Sheils. Hodder & Stoughton (US$10).

WORLD WIDE WEB

Listed here are some budget travel sites to start off your surfing; other relevant websites are listed throughout the book. Because website turnover is high, use search engines (such as www.google.com) to strike out on your own.

THE ART OF BUDGET TRAVEL

Backpacker's Ultimate Guide: www.bugeurope.com. Tips on packing, transportation, and where to go. Also tons of country-specific travel info.

Backpack Europe: www.backpackeurope.com. Helpful tips, a bulletin board, and links.

How to See the World: www.artoftravel.com. A compendium of great travel tips, from cheap flights to self defense to interacting with local culture.

Lycos: cityguide.lycos.com. General introductions to cities and regions throughout Ireland, accompanied by links to applicable histories, news, and local tourism sites.

Rec. Travel Library: www.travel-library.com. Fantastic links for personal travelogues.

INFORMATION ON IRELAND

CIA World Factbook: www.odci.gov/cia/publications/factbook/index.html.

The Irish Times: www.ireland.com. The Republic's major daily newspaper online.

MyTravelGuide: www.mytravelguide.com. Country overviews, with everything from history to transportation to live web cam coverage of Ireland.

World Travel Guide: www.travel-guides.com/country.asp. Helpful practical info.

 WWW.LETSGO.COM Our website, www.letsgo.com, now includes introductory content from all of our guides and a wealth of information on a monthly featured destination. As always, our website also has info about our books, a travel forum buzzing with stories and tips, and additional links that will help you make the most of a trip to Ireland.

ALTERNATIVES TO TOURISM

According to an old old Irish proverb, *Bíonn siúlach scéalach*, travelers are full of tales. For most visitors to the Emerald Isle, these tales include the amazing ancient ruins, lovely countrysides, gorgeous coasts, or quaint villages, visited briefly on worldwind bus tours or leisurely backpacking trips. Just as tourists taste the rich Irish heritage, a prior commitment draws them home, never seeing beyond the gloss of charming Ireland. For some, this morsel is satiating, but for those travelers left unsatisfied, Ireland offers a bounty of chances to explore the island more thoroughly.

With its diverse landscape and growing economy, Ireland allows visitors to engage in a broad range of activities. Students may take courses at campuses around the country, from urban universities to rural colleges. For the ambitious admirer of Irish, language courses are taught in several schools and cultural centers in the North and South. Amidst the economic boom of the Celtic Tiger, more and more employment opportunities—and job placement agencies—are springing up in cities. With hundreds of urban and rural sites of activism, volunteering in Ireland offers some of the best immersions into both the history and future of Ireland. Whether studying at Trinity in Dublin or working alongside Protestants and Catholics for a lasting peace in Belfast, taking advantage of the alternatives to tourism available in Ireland fills the traveler with tales of the Irish, behind the sights.

 FIND THE PATH. To read more on specific organizations that are working to better their communities, look for our **Giving Back** features throughout the book. We recommend **Oideas Gael,** in Co. Donegal (see Rare *Craic,* p. 417).

For those who seek more active involvement, Earthwatch International, Operation Crossroads Africa, and Habitat for Humanity offer fulfilling volunteer opportunities all over the world. For more on volunteering, studying, and working in Ireland and beyond, consult Let's Go's alternatives to tourism website, **www.beyondtourism.com.**

VOLUNTEERING IN IRELAND

Unlike some Western European countries, the opportunities for volunteerism in Ireland and Northern Ireland are endless. Most people choose to go through a parent organization that handles logistical details and provides a group environment and support system. There are two main types of organizations—religious (often Catholic) and non-sectarian—although there are rarely restrictions on participation for either. Some volunteer services charge a surprisingly hefty fee to participate (although they frequently cover airfare and most, if not all, living expenses).

A NEW PHILOSOPHY OF TRAVEL

We at *Let's Go* have watched the growth of the "ignorant tourist" stereotype with dismay, knowing that the majority of travelers care passionately about the state of the communities and environments they explore—but also knowing that even conscientious tourists can inadvertently damage natural wonders, rich cultures, and impoverished communities. We believe the philosophy of **sustainable travel** is among the most important travel tips we could impart to our readers, to help guide fellow backpackers and on-the-road philanthropists. By staying aware of the needs and troubles of local communities, today's travelers can be a powerful force in preserving and restoring this fragile world.

Working against the negative consequences of irresponsible tourism is much simpler than it might seem; it is often self-awareness, rather than self-sacrifice, that makes the biggest difference. Simply by trying to spend responsibly and conserve local resources, all travelers can positively impact the places they visit. Let's Go has partnered with **BEST** (**Business Enterprises for Sustainable Travel,** an affiliate of the Conference Board; see www.sustainabletravel.org), which recognizes businesses that operate based on the principles of sustainable travel. Below, they provide advice on how ordinary visitors can practice this philosophy in their daily travels, no matter where they are.

TIPS FOR CIVIC TRAVEL: HOW TO MAKE A DIFFERENCE

Travel by train when feasible. Rail travel requires only half the energy per passenger mile that planes do. On average, each of the 40,000 daily domestic air flights releases more than 1700 pounds of greenhouse gas emissions.

Use public mass transportation whenever possible; outside of cities, take advantage of group taxis or vans. Bicycles are an attractive way of seeing a community firsthand. And enjoy walking—purchase good maps of your destination and ask about on-foot touring opportunities.

When renting a car, ask whether fuel-efficient vehicles are available. Honda and Toyota produce cars that use hybrid engines powered by electricity and gasoline, thus reducing emissions of carbon dioxide. Ford Motor Company plans to introduce a hybrid fuel model by the end of 2004.

Reduce, reuse, recycle—use electronic tickets, recycle papers and bottles wherever possible, and avoid using containers made of styrofoam. Refillable water bottles and rechargable batteries both efficiently conserve expendable resources.

Be thoughtful in your purchases. Take care not to buy souvenir objects made from trees in old-growth or endangered forests, such as teak, or items made from endangered species, like ivory or tortoise jewelry. Ask whether products are made from renewable resources.

Buy from local enterprises, such as casual street vendors. In developing countries and low-income neighborhoods, many people depend on the "informal economy" to make a living.

Be on-the-road-philanthropists. If you are inspired by the natural environment of a destination or enriched by its culture, join in preserving their integrity by making a charitable contribution to a local organization.

Spread the word. Upon your return home, tell friends and colleagues about places to visit that will benefit greatly from their tourist dollars, and reward sustainable enterprises by recommending their services. Travelers can not only introduce friends to particular vendors but also to local causes and charities that they might choose to support when they travel.

Research a program before committing—talk to previous participants and find out exactly what you're getting into, as living and working conditions can vary greatly. Different programs are geared toward different ages and experience levels, so be sure the program doesn't demand too much or too little. Realistic expectations and informed decisions make for more enjoyable programs.

Volunteer jobs are readily available in the Republic and Northern Ireland. Sometimes, contacting individual sites and workcamps directly avoids high application fees. Northern Ireland's **FREEPHONE** connects callers to local volunteer bureaus (☎0800 052 2212). Two worldwide service databases with plenty of listings in Northern Ireland and the Republic are **Idealist** (www.idealist.org) and **ServeNet** (www.servenet.org).

COMMUNITY DEVELOPMENT

Though Ireland is a fully modernized, first world nation, community development will always be needed. Whether it is building homes or helping with childcare, volunteers in this field will be welcomed with open arms. If hands-on volunteering is not appealing, many organizations need volunteers for fundraising efforts.

Christian Aid, The Republic: 17 Clanwilliam Terr., Grand Canal Dock, Dublin 2, Ireland (☎01 611 0801). **Northern Ireland:** 30 Wellington Park, Belfast, BT9 6DL (☎028 9038 1204; www.christian-aid.org.uk). Individuals or groups of volunteers work in various fundraising and administrative roles, occasionally for a small stipend.

Elderhostel, Inc., 11 Avenue de Lafayette, Boston, MA 02111, USA (☎877-426-8056; www.elderhostel.org). Sends volunteers ages 55+ to work in construction, research, teaching, and many other projects. Costs average US$100 per day plus airfare.

Focus Ireland, 1 Lord Edward Court, Bride St., Dublin 8, Ireland (☎01 475 1955; www.focusireland.ie). Offers volunteers the opportunity to become involved in advocacy, fundraising, and assistance efforts for the homeless of Ireland.

Foróige, The Health Advice Cafe, 14 Francis St., Galway, Ireland (☎91 535 375; www.bbbsi.org), is the Irish branch of **Big Brothers Big Sisters International,** a mentoring program for young kids in need of guidance on a long-term basis.

Habitat for Humanity International, 121 Habitat St., Americus, GA 31709, USA (☎229-924-6935; www.habitat.org). Volunteers bui5ld houses in over 83 countries, including Northern Ireland, for anywhere from 2 wk. to 3 yr. Costs start at US$1200. 18+; under 18 must be accompanied by guardian.

Mental Health Ireland, Mensana House, 6 Adelaide St., Dun Laoghaire, Co. Dublin, Ireland (☎01 284 1166; www.mentalhealthireland.ie). Volunteer activities include fundraising, housing, "befriending," and promoting mental health in various regions of Ireland. Opportunities listed in their newsletter, *Mensana News,* available online.

Service Civil International Voluntary Service (SCI-IVS), 5474 Walnut Level Rd., Crozet, VA 22932, USA (☎434 823 9003; www.sci-ivs.org). Arranges placement in several types of camps in Dublin and Northern Ireland for those 18+. Registration US$175.

Volunteering Ireland, Carmichael Centre for Voluntary Groups, Coleraine House, Coleraine St., Dublin 7, Ireland (☎01 872 2622; www.volunteeringireland.com). Opportunities for individuals or groups in various volunteering and advocacy settings. Options listed online and placement service is free.

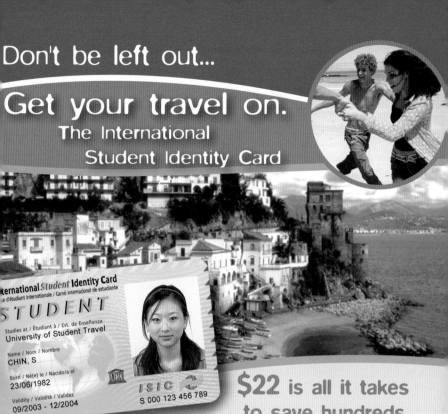

PEACE PROCESS

The conflict in Northern Ireland has raged for centuries. It has resulted in violence from both sides, and its roots run deep. The peace process has been in the works for over 30 years now, and has attracted international attention. In 1998, Catholic John Hume and Protestant David Trimble were awarded the Nobel Peace Prize for their work on the Good Friday Peace Agreement earlier that year. Violence is still very much a concern, however, and the peace process remains a high priority. Volunteering for these organizations is a good opportunity for foreigners whose primary objective is peace, not the furthering of one side.

Corrymeela Community, Corrymeela Centre, 5 Drumaroan Rd., Ballycastle BT54 6QU, Northern Ireland (☎028 2076 2626; www.corrymeela.org). A residential community committed to bringing Protestants and Catholics together to work for peace. Volunteer opportunities range from 1 wk. to 1 yr. Ages 18-30 preferred for long-term positions.

Global Volunteers, 375 East Little Canada Rd., St. Paul, MN 55117, USA (☎800 487 1074; www.globalvolunteers.org). Some opportunities at Glencree Centre for Reconciliation in Ireland. US$2155 for 1 wk., US$2355 for 2 wk.; US$100 student discount.

Harmony Community Trust, Glebe House, Bishopscourt Rd., Strangford BT30 7NZ, Northern Ireland (☎028 4488 1374; fax 4488 1620). Encourages cross-community interaction through social and educational programs for all ages. Volunteer opportunities range from 1 wk. to 2 yr. Short-term volunteers 18+, long-term volunteers 21+.

Kilcranny House, 21 Cranagh Rd., Coleraine BT51 3NN, Northern Ireland (☎028 7032 1816; www.kilcrannyhouse.org). A residential, educational, and resource center provides a safe space for both sides to interact and explore issues of non-violence, prejudice awareness, and conflict resolution. Volunteer opportunities range from 6 mo. to 2 yr. UK£20 per wk. for room and board. Drivers (25+) preferred.

Northern Ireland Volunteer Development Agency, 4th fl., 58 Howard St., Belfast BT1 6PG, Northern Ireland (☎028 9023 6100; www.volunteering-ni.org). Helps arrange individual and group volunteer efforts in Northern Ireland. Membership fees US$25 yr.; groups US$50-67 per yr.

Ulster Quaker Service Committe, 541 Lisburn Rd., Belfast BT9 7GQ, Northern Ireland (☎028 9020 1444; uqsc@btinternet.com). Runs programs for Protestant and Catholic children from inner-city Belfast. 6-week posts and 1- to 2-year posts available. Short-term volunteers 18+, long-term volunteers 21+.

Volunteers for Peace, 1034 Tiffany Rd., Belmont., VT 05730, USA (☎802-259-2759; www.vfp.org). Volunteers in work camps in Ireland. Spaces are limited. Membership required for registration (US$20). Programs average US$200 for 2-3 wk.

FARMING AND CONSERVATION

If inspired by the gorgeous countryside of the Emerald Isle, volunteering for a conservation project or working on an environmentally conscious organic farm may offer the perfect alternative to tourism.

Archaeological Institute of America, Boston University, 656 Beacon St., Boston, MA 02215, USA (☎617-353-9361; www.archaeological.org). *Archaeological Fieldwork Opportunities Bulletin,* on their website, lists field sites throughout Europe.

Conservation Volunteers Northern Ireland, Beech House, 159 Ravenhill Rd., Belfast BT6 0BP, Northern Ireland (☎028 9064 5169; www.bctv.org.uk/cvni). Involves volunteers in short-term practical conservation work, from tree planting to trail building. The Belfast office also welcomes long-term volunteers (6 month min. commitment). 18+.

The Donegal Organic Farm, Doorian, Glenties, Donegal, Ireland (☎075 51 286; www.esatclear.ie/~tbecht), in Northwest Ireland. Offers camps and programs for organic-oriented individuals.

Earthwatch, 3 Clocktower Pl., Ste. 100, Box 75, Maynard, MA 01754, USA (☎800-776-0188 or 978-461-0081; www.earthwatch.org). Arranges 1- to 3-week programs in Ireland to promote conservation of natural resources. Programs average US$1700. 16+.

Willing Workers on Organic Farms (WWOOF), P.O. Box 2075, Lewes BN7 1RB, England, UK (www.wwoof.org). Provides room and board at a variety of organic farms in Ireland in exchange for help on the farm. Membership costs US$25, UK£15.

STUDYING IN IRELAND

It's easy to spend a summer, a term, or even a year studying in Ireland or Northern Ireland. Each of the major cities is home to several universities, and smaller *gaeltacht* communities support many Irish language and cultural programs. Choosing a program requires research to weigh all options before making a decision—determining costs and duration, what kind of students participate in the program and what sort of accommodations are provided. For full cultural immersion, try to arrange housing with an Irish family through the university.

EU students will find it easier to gain acceptance to an Irish university than most other students. The standards for admission are much lower for those who have attended an EU secondary school, and while other students will have to pay between €15,000-30,000 a year, educational programs are free of charge for EU students. American students seeking to enroll in an Irish university will find it cheaper to enroll directly in the university from abroad, though gaining admission and college credit may prove more difficult. For all students, spots in Irish schools are scarce, especially in history and English departments.

A good resource for finding programs that cater to particular interests is **www.studyabroad.com,** which has links to various semester-abroad programs based on a variety of criteria, including desired location and focus of study. Also try **www.goabroad.com.** The following is a list of other organizations that can help place students in university programs in Ireland.

AMERICAN PROGRAMS

The following is a list of American organizations that help arrange study abroad.

Academic Programs International, 107 E. Hopkins, San Marcos, TX 78666, USA (☎800-844-4124; www.academicintl.com). Arranges placement in Galway and Limerick. Fees range from US$3900 (summer) to US$19,700 (full-year).

VISA AND PERMIT INFORMATION

Citzens of the EU and most western countries need only a passport to enter Ireland. To remain for longer than 90 days, visitors must obtain permission from the Alien's Registration Office in Dublin, or the local *Garda* (police) station.

To **study in Ireland,** students need to submit a copy of their acceptance letter from an educational institution in Ireland, verifying the duration and nature of the course and that requisite fees have been paid, to the Department of Foreign Affairs Visa Office in St. Stephen's Green.

American Institute for Foreign Study, College Division, River Plaza, 9 West Broad St., Stamford, CT 06902, USA (☎800-727-2437, ext. 5163; www.aifsabroad.com). Organizes programs for study at the University of Limerick. Costs range from US$10,995 (semester) to US$20,990 (full-year); scholarships available.

Arcadia University, Center for Education Abroad, 450 S. Easton Rd., Glenside, PA 19038, USA (☎866-927-2234; www.arcadia.edu/cea). Operates programs throughout Ireland. Costs range from $3490 (summer) to $20,190 (full-year).

College Consortium for International Studies, Truman State University, 120 Kirk Building, Kirksville, MO 63501, USA (☎660-785-4076; www.ccisabroad.org). Term-time programs from US$4860, summer courses in the Republic US$1530-2260.

Institute for the International Education of Students (IES), 33 N. LaSalle St., 15th fl., Chicago, IL 60602, USA (☎800-995-2300; www.IESabroad.org). Offers year-long, semester, and summer programs for college study in Dublin. Internship opportunities. US$50 application fee. Scholarships available.

Institute for Study Abroad, Butler University, 1100 W. 42nd St., Ste. 305, Indianapolis, IN 46208, USA (☎317-940-9704; www.ifsa-butler.org). Arranges study abroad at a variety of universities in the Republic and the North in several fields (fees vary by school; check website for details).

North American Institute for Study Abroad, 129 Mill St., Danville, PA 17821, USA (☎570-275-5099; www.naisa.com). Arranges placement in universities throughout the Republic and Northern Ireland (fees vary by school; check website for details).

University Studies Abroad Consortium, USAC/323, Reno, NV 89557, USA (☎775-784-6569; www.usac.unr.edu). Offers a full curriculum of study for a semester or a year in Cork from US$5190 (semester) to US$9680 (full-year).

UNIVERSITY PROGRAMS IN IRELAND

Most American undergraduates enroll in programs sponsored by US universities. Local universities can be much cheaper, though it may be more difficult to receive academic credit. Some schools that offer study abroad programs to international students are listed below.

Irish Studies Summer School, usit NOW, 19-21 Aston Quay, O'Connell Bridge, Dublin 2, Ireland (☎01 602 1630; www.usitnow.ie). 7-week-long program (US$5500) offering courses in Irish history and contemporary culture. usit also administrates the summer program **Ireland in Europe,** a 2-week course focusing on Irish civilization.

National University of Ireland, Galway, University Rd., Galway, Ireland (☎091 524 411; www.nuigalway.ie). Offers half- or full-year opportunities, from €4375 to €11,450, for junior-year students who meet the college's entry requirements. Summer school courses include Irish Studies, Education, and Creative Writing. Fees vary by field.

Queen's University Belfast, International Office, Belfast BT7 1NN, Northern Ireland (☎028 9033 5088; www.qub.ac.uk). Study in Belfast for a semester (UK£6485) or a full year (UK£18,725).

Trinity College Dublin, Office of International Student Affairs, East Theatre, Trinity College, Dublin 2, Ireland (☎01 608 3150; www.tcd.ie/isa). Offers semester or year programs of undergraduate courses for visiting students. Fees €4200-20,300.

University College Cork, International Education Office, West Wing, University College, Cork, Ireland (☎021-490-2543; www.ucc.ie). Students who enroll directly in the college can choose from a wide array of subjects and classes.

University College Dublin, International Summer School, Newman House, 86 St. Stephen's Green, Dublin 2, Ireland (☎01 475 2004; www.ucd.ie/summerschool). A 2½ wk. international summer course examining Irish culture and tradition. Fees €650.

University of Ulster, Shore Rd., Newtownabbey, Co. Antrim BT37 0QB, Northern Ireland (☎028 9036 6151; www.ulst.ac.uk). Offers semester- or year-long programs for visiting international students. Fees UK£2575-8830.

LANGUAGE SCHOOL

Although most university courses in Ireland are conducted in English, Irish (or *Gaeilge*) language classes and schools offer intensive training for beginners to advanced Irish-speakers. These language schools, often independently run international or local organizations, or divisions of foreign universities, rarely offer college credit. Language schools are a good alternative to university study for a deeper focus on Irish or a slightly less-rigorous courseload.

Daltaí na Gaeilge (www.daltai.com). Irish for "Students of the Irish Language," this non-profit corporation runs language programs throughout Australia, Europe, and the US. Website includes an extensive list of course offerings (check for individual contacts and fees), as well as online grammar and language games and exercises.

Donegal Gaeltacht Cultural Centre, Loughanure, Annagry, Co. Donegal, Ireland (☎075 48081; www.lochgael.com). In addition to offering accommodations and weekends of dance, song, and literature, the center offers week-long Irish language courses (€130), and cultural weekends (€40).

Taisce Árainn Teoranta, Árainn Mór Island, Co. Donegal, Ireland (☎075 21593; www.foghlaim.com). On secluded Árainn Mór Island in the Donegal *Galtacht,* Taisce offers week-long language courses (€165) and culture classes (€165), and hosts a range of outdoor activities.

Teach na hÉigse (The Poets' House), Clonbarra, Falcarragh, Co. Donegal, Ireland (www.poetshouse.ie). Offers one-year MA program in Creative Writing through Lancaster University, and two 10-day seminars in July and Aug. MA €12,000 non-EU, €4500 EU.

WORKING IN IRELAND

Despite the country's recent economic boom and growing job market, unemployment in Ireland remains high for an EU country. Travelers are most likely to find work in touristed urban centers such as Dublin, Galway, Belfast, or Cork. European Union citizens can work in any EU country, and if your parents were born in an EU country, you may be able to claim dual citizenship with Ireland, or at least the right to a **work permit.** Commonwealth residents with a parent or grandparent born in the UK do not need a work permit to work in Northern Ireland. Contact your British Consulate or High Commission (see p. 8) for details before departure and the **Department of Employment** (☎01 631 2121; www.entemp.ie) upon arrival. Outside these catagories, a **work permit** is necessary to be considered for paid employment in the Republic or Northern Ireland. The permit takes approximately four weeks to process, is valid for between one month and one year, and can be renewed upon expiration. Prospective employers must obtain this document.

There are two main schools of thought when it comes to working abroad. Some travelers want long-term jobs that allow them to get to know another part of the world in depth (e.g. teaching or working in the tourist industry). Other sojourners seek out short-term jobs to finance their future travel. They often seek employment in the service sector or in agriculture, working for a few weeks at a time to finance the next leg of their journey. This section discusses both short-term and long-term opportunities for working in Ireland.

LONG-TERM WORK

To spend a substantial amount of time (i.e., more than three months) working in Ireland, it is best to search for a job well in advance. International placement agencies are often the easiest way to find employment abroad, especially if you wish to teach, but be wary of advertisements or companies that claim to get a job abroad for a fee—often the same jobs are freely listed online or in newspapers. One useful database with job listings all over Europe is **www.stepstone.com.**

For US college students, recent graduates, and young adults, the simplest way to get legal permission to work abroad is through **Council on International Educational Exchange's Work Abroad Programs** (☎800-40-STUDY, students 207-553-7699; www.ciee.org). Council Exchanges can help obtain a three- to six-month work permit/visa and also provide assistance finding jobs and housing. Fees average around US$375. Internships, for college students, are a good way to segue into working abroad. Though they are often unpaid or poorly paid, many say the overall experience is well worth the financial inconvenience. **Association for International Practical Training** also helps obtain visas and work permits for students and professionals who have found their own internships. (☎410 997 2886, or 410 997 3068 for students; www.aipt.org. US$250 for professionals, US$75 for students.) **Search Associates** (www.search-associates.com) recruits for internships abroad. To obtain work through an organization, **Working Ireland,** 26 Eustace St., Templebar, Dublin 2, Ireland (☎01 677 0300; www.workingireland.ie) is the place to go. This multi-tasking agency arranges short- and long-term job placement throughout the country and assists visitors in finding accommodation. When it's time to leave Ireland, they help collect tax refunds and arrange travel home. In the South, the **Job Options Bureau,** Tourist House, 40-41 Grand Parade, Cork, Ireland (☎21 427 5369; www.joboptionbureau.com), is another good resource.

TEACHING

Teaching jobs abroad are rarely well paid, though some private American schools in Ireland pay relatively competitive salaries. In most cases, you must have a bachelors degree to work as a full-time teacher. College undergraduates lacking these degrees can often get summer positions teaching or tutoring. To teach in an American school overseas requires an American teaching certification.

A popular option for many is to volunteer as a teacher. While most fund their own way, some volunteers get free accommodations; others manage to obtain a daily stipend from their college. Those interested are encouraged to inquire at colleges and secondary schools for school specfic information.

The International Educator (☎508-362-1414; www.tieonline.com) lists overseas teaching vacancies and offers job search and resume posting online. A good teacher-job website specific to Ireland, complete with a tutorial on the Irish education system and first-hand accounts from student teachers, is **Americans in Ireland** (www.geocities.com/teachingirish). Also see **www.teachabroad.com** for a comprehensive list of paid and volunteer teaching opportunities in Ireland. Other programs that may arrange placement for teaching jobs in Ireland include:

European Council of International Schools, 105 Tuxford Terr., Basking Ridge, NJ 07920, USA (☎908-903-0552; www.ecis.org).

Institute of International Education, 809 United Nations Plaza, New York, NY 10017, USA (☎212-883-8200; www.iie.org).

North American Institute of Study Abroad, 129 Mill St., Danville, PA 17821, USA (☎570-275-5099; www.naisa.com).

AU PAIR WORK

Au pairs are typically females (ages 18-30) who work as live-in nannies, caring for children and doing light housework in exchange for room, board, and a small stipend. The average weekly pocket money allowance is between €60-70. All agencies stress that an au pair must have a strong love of children.

Though most au pairs speak favorably of their experience, drawbacks often include long hours of on-duty call, and severely decrepit pay. Much of the experience depends on the family with which you are placed. The agencies below are a good starting point for looking for employment as an au pair.

Accord Cultural Exchange, 750 La Playa, San Francisco, CA 94121, USA (☎415-386-6203; www.cognitext.com/accord).

Au Pair in Europe, P.O. Box 68056, Blakely Postal Outlet, Hamilton, ON, L8M 3M7, Canada (☎905-545-6305; www.princeent.com).

Douglas Au Pair Agency Ltd., 28 Frankfield, Douglas, Co. Cork, Ireland (☎21 489 1489; www.aupairhere.com).

Dublin Childcare Recruitment Agency, Newcourt House, Strandville Ave., Clontarf, Dublin 3, Ireland (☎01 833 2281; www.childcare-recruitment.com).

Shamrock Au Pair Agency, Magheree, Kilmorony, Athy, Co. Kildare, Ireland (☎50 725 533; www.aupairireland.com).

SHORT-TERM WORK

Roaming for long periods of time can get expensive; many travelers try their hand at odd jobs for a few weeks at a time to make some extra cash. Some of the most common forms of short-term work in Ireland include hostessing, waitressing, bartending, temping, childcare, farm work, and volunteering. Another popular option is to work several hours a day at a hostel for free or discounted room and/or board. Most often, these short-term jobs are found by word of mouth, or by talking to the owners of hostels and restaurants. Due to the high turnover in the tourism industry, many establishments are eager for help, even if only temporary. Ireland does not issue work permits for short-term manual or domestic labor, but depending on the employer, it may not be needed. *Let's Go* tries to list temporary jobs like these whenever possible; check under the **practical information** sections of all towns and cities for **work opportunities** listings.

FOR FURTHER READING ON ALTERNATIVES TO TOURISM

Alternatives to the Peace Corps: A Directory of Third World and U.S. Volunteer Opportunities, by Joan Powell. Food First Books, 2000 (US$10).

How to Get a Job in Europe, by Sanborn and Matherly. Surrey Books, 1999 ($US22).

How to Live Your Dream of Volunteering Oversees, by Collins, DeZerega, and Heckscher. Penguin Books, 2002 (US$17).

International Directory of Voluntary Work, by Whetter and Pybus. Peterson's Guides and Vacation Work, 2000 (US$16).

International Jobs, by Kocher and Segal. Perseus Books, 1999 (US$18).

Overseas Summer Jobs 2002, by Collier and Woodworth. Peterson's Guides and Vacation Work, 2002 (US$18).

Work Abroad: The Complete Guide to Finding a Job Overseas, by Hubbs, Griffith, and Nolting. Transitions Abroad Publishing, 2000 ($16).

Work Your Way Around the World, by Susan Griffith. Worldview Publishing Services, 2001 (US$18).

Invest Yourself: The Catalogue of Volunteer Opportunities, published by the Commission on Voluntary Service and Action (☎ 718-638-8487).

ALTERNATIVES TO
TOURISM

LIFE AND TIMES

Jagged coastal cliffs, thatch-roofed cottages, clouded, misty days, and the green rolling hills—poetic images of Ireland dominate the tourist's mind. Most travelers don't realize, however, that Ireland is a country on the rise. Poverty and unemployment have historically been widespread, but the EU has brought new life; impressed by the island's recent economic boom, the international media has christened Ireland the "Celtic Tiger." Under an influx of new faces—recent refugees and emigrants have brought Ireland its first population increase—the country's conservatism is slowly cracking. The short-term result is a growing generation gap and disparity between rural and urban areas. Amid the necessary grime of modernization, the lifestyle of the Irish continues unsullied, centering itself around music, sports, and The Pub.

Six of Ulster's nine counties make up Northern Ireland (see p. 450), officially a territory of the United Kingdom. Under the 1998 Northern Ireland Peace Agreement, residents of Northern Ireland may choose whether to individually identify themselves as Irish or British, but word choice can still be tricky, as some identify with neither. "Ulster" is a term used exclusively by Protestants in the North. It's best to refer to "Northern Ireland" or "the North" and "the Republic" or "the South." "Southern Ireland" is not a viable term.

HISTORY

IMPORTANT EVENTS

circa 7000 BC
Ireland's first settlers arrive from Britain. Ireland is one of the last areas in Europe to be colonized by human populations.

circa 3000 BC
Mound-builders build their mounds. The Hill of Tara is established.

2000 BC
Bronze becomes the latest craze.

History may seem, as it did to Joyce's Stephen Daedalus, a nightmare from which we're trying to awake, but visitors to Ireland unfamiliar with historical conflicts will pass by some of the island's most worthwhile attractions—namely, the character of its people and their cultural productions—with little sense of what lies beyond their surface charm. The following should provide you with a taste of the complexities underlying modern Ireland.

ANCIENT IRELAND (TO AD 350)

Our fragmented knowledge of ancient Irish culture comes from the scant remains of its stone structures and metalwork. From these we have learned that Ireland's first settlers quickly founded an agrarian civilization upon arriving from Britain in around 7000 BC. This civilization created and left behind many structures still prominent in the Irish landscape. Among them were **dolmens,** arrangements of huge stones in table-like forms, which were created as tombs and shrines for the recently dead (see **Poulnabrane Dolmen,** p. 340). **Passage tombs** were less common; these underground stone hallways and chambers often contained corpses and cinerary urns (see **Newgrange,** p. 160). **Stone circles** were rings of pint-sized gravestones that likely marked spots of religious significance.

Bronze poured into Ireland circa 2000 BC, and the agrarian society was slowly retooled into a warrior aristocracy. By 900 BC, the **Irish Golden Age** brought about an evolution from the simpler stone structures of the past to more impressive projects: **ring forts** (see **Dún Aengus**, p. 363), protective walls that circled encampments and villages; **souterrains,** underground hideouts for storing loot and escaping from various marauders; and **clochans,** mortarless beehiveshaped stone huts.

Although a few groups of **Celts** may have arrived as early as 2000 BC, their real migration didn't start until 600 BC. First referred to by the Greeks as the *Keltoi* (hidden people), an allusion to their vast but unwritten stores of scholarship and knowledge, the Celts quickly settled down to their new western outpost. (Their pan-European movement had already brought them as far east as Asia Minor.) At the time, the Romans were too busy conquering Germanic tribes to set their greedy sights on Ireland.

The Celts prospered on the peaceful isle, speaking a hybrid of Celtic and indigenous languages (called Old Irish) and living in small farming communities. Under their system, regional chieftains ruled territories called *tuath*, while provincial kings controlled several *tuatha*. The **Uliad of Ulster,** a northern kingdom of chariot warriors, dominated the La Tène culture from their capital near Armagh (see **Navan Fort,** p. 524). These kings organized raids on Britain, established settlements in Scotland and Wales, and set themselves up for a long and brutal comeuppance. Their valor and relative success inspired tales of mythic heroism prominent in the *Táin Bó Cuailnge* and other Irish epics (see **Legends and Folktales,** p. 73).

CHRISTIANS AND VIKINGS AND PIRATES, OH MY! (350-1200)

Starting in the 5th century with **St. Patrick,** Ireland was shown the light, Christian-style, by a series of hopeful missionaries. According to legend, Patrick was born in Scotland and kidnapped by Irish pirates. Enslaved, hungry, and forced to work in isolation as a shephard, he turned to Christianity for strength. He eventually escaped back home, but at the command of a prophetic vision, he returned to Ireland to spread the Gospel to the Celts.

The missionaries and monks that followed St. Patrick recorded observations of the unfamiliar Celtic culture, describing, among other things, the system of writing found on **ogham stones.** These large obelisks, which recorded lineages in a script of dots and slashes, are still present in the **Burren** (see p. 336), at the **Hill of Tara** (see p. 161), and at **Brú na Bóinne** in Co. Meath (see p. 160). Missionaries also introduced the Viking-inspired **round tower** to the architectural lexicon. These towers were built as fortifications against invaders, and their sturdy forms still rise from dozens of fields across the island. As Christianity spread through Ireland, melding with indigenous Celtic beliefs, **high crosses,** or Celtic crosses, sprung up throughout the landscape. These stone crucifixes, which combine the Christian cross with the Celtic circle, can be large enough to dwarf bystanders and sometimes feature elaborate carvings illustrating Bible stories or saintly legends.

900 BC-700 BC
The Irish Golden Age (bronze is SO last millennium).

600 BC–AD 0
The Celts migrate from central Europe.

200 BC
La Tène culture arrives.

AD 200
High Kingship begins in Tara.

circa AD 379
More southern (Co. Meath) Uí Néill clan gains prominence.

AD 350
The first Christians arrive in Ireland and begin their missionary work.

AD 432
St. Patrick's estimated time of arrival in Ireland.

AD 563
St. Colmcille sails to Iona.

circa AD 600
Monks illuminate the Book of Durrow.

LIFE AND TIMES

AD 500-700
Huge monastic
cities flourish.

AD 795
Full-scale Viking
invasions begin.

early AD 800s
Monks ignore
Vikings and
instead spend time
illuminating the
Book of Kells.

914-919
Vikings found
Waterford, Dublin,
and Limerick.

999
King Brian Ború
defeats Vikings.

1000-1100
Irish chieftains
fight amongst
themselves.

1002
Dal Cais clan of
Co. Clare captures
Armagh.

1014
Battle of Clontarf:
Vikings get
trounced once and
for all.

1171
Strongbow grovels
before English
crown.

1172
Pope decrees that
Henry II of England
is feudal lord of Ire-
land.

In the 5th century, Barbarians took their pillaging on the continent a bit too far, and asylum-seeking monks began arriving in Ireland. These events predated the policy of converting hostels into asylums (see **Wexford,** p. 210); instead, monks erected enormous **monastic cities,** which during the 6th through 8th centuries earned Ireland its reputation as the "land of saints and scholars." At their bases in **Glendalough** (see p. 149), **Clonmacnois** (see p. 180), and elsewhere, the monastics of the Early Irish Church recorded the old epics and composed long religious poems in both Latin and Old Irish. The monks also shed some of their Divine Light on the classics through illuminating manuscripts. The 7th-century **Book of Durrow** is the earliest surviving such manuscript; it is now exhibited at Trinity College (see p. 117) with the early 9th-century **Book of Kells.** Rather than bowing to Rome, monastic cities allied themselves with up-and-coming Irish chieftains. Armagh, an important religious center, owed its prominence in part to the **Uí Néill** (O'Neill) clan, whose jurisdiction gradually spread from Meath to central Ulster.

Before we get too much further along, we should explain that Ireland of yore was divided into four counties: **Leinster** (east and southeast), **Munster** (southwest), **Connacht** (west), and **Ulster** (north). Very well, then—proceed.

The Golden Age of Irish Scholasticism (not to be confused with the Irish Golden Age) was interrupted by **Viking** invasions in the 9th and 10th centuries. Their raids were most frequent along the southern coast, where they founded permanent settlements at Limerick, Waterford, and Dublin. The horned ones built Ireland's first castles, allied themselves with equally fierce chieftains, and littered the southeast with Norse-derived place names (Smerwick and Fota being choice examples).

In 1002, High King **Brian Ború** and his militant **Dal Cais** clan set off a period of bitter inter-*tuath* strife by capturing Armagh and challenging the Uí Néills for control of Ireland. The Dal Cais won a heroic victory but lost Brian Ború in the epic **Battle of Clontarf,** fought against the Vikings near Dublin in 1014. The island was then divided between chieftains **Rory O'Connor** and **Dermot MacMurrough,** who continued to duke it out for the crown. Dermot ill-advisedly sought the assistance of English Norman nobles—Richard de Clare (a.k.a. **Strongbow**) was all too willing to help. Strongbow and his Anglo-Normans arrived in 1169 and cut a bloody swath through south Leinster. Strongbow married Dermot's daughter **Aoife** after Dermot's death in 1171 and for a time seemed ready to proclaim an independent Norman kingdom in Ireland. Instead, he affirmed his loyalty to King Henry II and with characteristic generosity offered to govern Leinster on England's behalf.

FEUDALISM AND ITS DISCONTENTS (1200-1607)

Thus, the English came to Ireland and settled down for a nice, long occupation. The subsequent feudal period saw constant bickering between Gaelic and Norman-descended English lords. While the Norman strongholds in Leinster had more towns—including the **Pale,** a fortified domain around

Dublin—and more trade, Gaelic Connacht and Ulster remained intimidatingly agrarian. The two sides were of surprisingly unified culture: English and Irish fiefdoms built similar castles, ate similar foods, enjoyed the same poets, and hired the same mercenaries. The Crown fretted over this cultural cross-pollination and sponsored the notorious **Statutes of Kilkenny** in 1366. These decrees banned English colonists from speaking, dressing, or marrying Irish and forbade the Irish from entering walled cities like Derry. But the Gaelic lords went on reclaiming their territorial inheritance, and the new laws did little to alleviate English trepidation.

Feudal skirmishes and economic decline plagued the English lords until the rise of the "Geraldine Earls," two branches of the FitzGerald family who initially fought for control of south Leinster. The victors, the **Earls of Kildare,** ruled Ireland with panache from 1470 to 1534; their reign was marked with such gusto that the English crown quickly grew wary, fearing a threat to Royal supremacy. In 1494, **Poynings' Law** limited the Earls' authority, declaring the Irish Parliament could convene only with English consent and could not pass laws that did not meet with the Crown's approval. The Irish people were divided: half were not surprised, while the other half clung to an increasingly illusory belief in their own sovereignty.

The English Crown increased its control over Ireland throughout the next century, and the latter group finally began to catch on. When Henry VIII created the Church of England, the Dublin Parliament passed the 1537 **Irish Supremacy Act,** declaring Henry head of the Protestant **Church of Ireland** and effectively making the island property of the Crown. The Church of Ireland held a privileged position over Irish Catholicism, even though the English neither articulated any difference between the two religious outlooks nor attempted to convert the Irish masses. The lords of Ireland wished to remain loyal both to Catholicism and to the Crown—a daunting proposition even by 16th-century standards. Bold **Thomas FitzGerald** sent a missive to Henry VIII stating his position. In response, Henry denied his aristocratic title. FitzGerald, not to be easily silenced, sponsored an uprising in Munster in 1579, thus planting in the English imagination the idea that a loyal Ireland could only be achieved under direct Protestant control.

Not to be outdone by Leinster, the equally defiant Ulster Earl **Hugh O'Neill** led a rebellion in the late 1590s. The King of Spain promised naval assistance; his Armada arrived in Kinsale Harbour in 1601 but did little to stop the English army from demolishing Irish forces. Relieved of their power, O'Neill and the rest of the major Gaelic lords soared out of Ireland in 1607 in what came to be known as the **Flight of the Earls.** Though they aimed to return with assistance from the forces of Catholic rulers on the mainland continent, few ever returned to Ireland. While the world looked on in feigned astonishment, the English took control of the land and parceled it out to Protestants.

1361
Pure-bloods banned from positions of power.

1366
Statutes of Kilkenny passed.

1470-1534
Anglo-Irish Earls of Kildare bring relative stability to Irish politics.

1494
The Fretful Crown attempts to limit the Earls' power through Poynings' Law.

1537
Henry VIII claims Ireland for his own. Yoink.

1579
Catholic-minded FitzGerald uprising against the English.

1595-1601
Another uprising: Hugh O'Neill vs. English Crown.

1601
The Armada sits passive in Kinsale Harbour.

1607
The Flying Earls. Irish land is systematically parceled out to Protestants.

LIFE AND TIMES

1607-41
Under James I, Protestants from the Scotland lowlands are settled in the northern counties of Ireland

1641
Landless Irish revolt in Ulster.

1642
Confederation of Kilkenny is formed between the Church, Irish Lords, and English Earls.

1649
Cromwell arrives in Ireland.

1654-1655
Cromwell's policy of Plantation implemented.

1665
Act of Explanation passed under English Restorers: Catholics receive some meagre compensation for losses.

1688
Deposed King James II flees to Ireland.

1689
The Siege of Derry: Apprentice Boys do their trick with the gates.

1690
Battle of the Boyne: James is defeated.

1695
Penal Laws make life miserable for Catholics.

CROMWELL (1607-1688)

The English project of dispossessing Catholics of their land and replacing them with Protestants was most successful in Ulster. In a project known as the **Ulster Plantation,** Scottish tenants and laborers, themselves displaced by the English, joined the rag-tag mix of adventurers, ne'er-do-wells, and ex-soldiers bent on resettling the North. In 1641, a loose-knit group of Gaelic-Irish chiefs led the now landless Irish in a revolt in Ulster.

Owen Roe O'Neill returned from the Continent to lead the insurrection, Rome's blessing in hand. The rebels advanced south and in 1642 formed the **Confederation of Kilkenny,** an uneasy alliance between the Church and Irish and Old English lords. Some English lords believed they were rebelling against a treasonous viceroy but remaining loyal to the King, and the concurrent English Civil War complicated matters even further. **Oliver Cromwell's** victory in England made the negotiations between King and Confederation something of a moot point. After a celebratory glass of sparkling white wine, Cromwell's army turned to Ireland.

Following standard Cromwellian procedure, the Lord Protectorate destroyed anything he did not occupy, and then some. Catholics were massacred and whole towns razed. Entire tracts of land were confiscated, gift-wrapped, and handed out to soldiers and Protestant vagabonds. Native Irish landowners were presented with the option of going **"to Hell or to Connacht"**—both desolate and infertile, one with a slightly more tropical climate. By 1660, the vast majority of Irish land was owned, maintained, and policed by Protestant immigrants. After Cromwell's death in 1658, Restored King Charles II passed the 1665 **Act of Explanation.** The Act required Protestants to relinquish one-third of their land to the "innocent papists." The Catholics did not hold their breath for this to happen.

THE ASCENDANCY (1688-1801)

Thirty years after the Civil War, English political disruption again resulted in Irish bloodshed. In 1688, Catholic **James II,** driven from England by Protestant William of Orange and his Glorious Revolution, came to Ireland to gather military support and reclaim his throne. Irish Jacobites began bashing Williamites whenever the opportunity presented itself. This was fine with the Williamites, who had made their own decision to beat up Jacobites any chance they got. James tried to take Derry in 1689, but a rascally band of **Apprentice Boys** closed the gates on him and started the 105-day **Siege of Derry** (see p. 544). William ended the war and sent his rival into exile on July 12, 1690, at the **Battle of the Boyne.** Northern Protestants still celebrate the victory on July 12 (called **Orange Day** in honor of King Billy; for more on **"the silly season,"** see **Northern Ireland,** p. 450). The war was concluded with the **Treaty of Limerick,** which ambiguously guaranteed the defeated their civil rights. "Ambiguously" meaning that, at the turn of the 18th century, a set of **Penal Laws** were enacted for the purposes of further oppression, banning (among other things) the practice of Catholicism.

In Dublin and the Pale, the bourgeouis Anglo-Irish garden-partied, gossiped, and engineered their way to create a second London. **"Ascendancy"** was coined for them; it described a social elite whose elitehood depended upon Anglicanism. **Trinity College** was the quintessential institution of Ascended Protestants. Cultural ties notwithstanding, many aristocrats felt little political allegiance to England. **Jonathan Swift** pamphleteered on behalf of the Protestant Church and the Irish masses. Meanwhile, displaced peasants filled Dublin's poor quarters, creating the horrific slums that led to Swift's "Modest Proposal" (see **Wit & Resistance**, p. 74).

Away from the Protestants and their Ascended nonsense, the Catholic merchant class grew in cites like Galway and Tralee. Early 18th-century Catholics practiced their religion furtively, using large, flat rocks (dubbed **Mass rocks**) when they couldn't get their hands on an altar. Denied official education, Gaelic teens learned literature and religion in secret **hedge schools,** whose teachers who were often fugitive priests. Meanwhile, secret agrarian societies, like the **Defenders,** formed to protect peasants against Protestant landlords and their brutal rents.

REBELLION & UNION (1775-1848)

The Irish were not immune to the bold notions of independence that emerged from the American and French Revolutions. The *liberté*-fever was particularly strong among the **United Irishmen,** which had begun as a radical Protestant Ulster debating society with the nerve to challenge English rule. Although outlawed, the United Irishmen reorganized themselves as a secret society. Their leader, **Theobald Wolfe Tone,** hoped that a general rebellion would create an independent, non-sectarian Ireland. To this end, he admitted Catholics among the ranks of the United Irishmen. The bloody **Rebellion of 1798** erupted with a furious band of peasants and priests, and ended with their last stand at **Vinegar Hill,** near Enniscorthy in Co. Wexford (see p. 208). Always looking for an excuse to tussle with the Brits, French troops arrived and managed to hold their ground for about a month before being utterly destroyed. Noble Wolfe Tone committed suicide in captivity, and other United Irishmen escaped to France.

Any hopes England had held of making Irish society less volatile by relaxing anti-Catholic laws were canceled by such rebellious misbehavior. With the 1800 **Act of Union,** the Crown abolished Irish "self-government" altogether. The Dublin Parliament died and "The United Kingdom of Great Britain and Ireland" was born. The Church of Ireland entered into an unequal arranged marriage, changing her name to the "United Church of England and Ireland."

The carnage continued. Dublin's mad gaiety vanished, the Anglo-Irish gentry collapsed, and agrarian violence and poverty escalated. Meanwhile, the Napoleonic Wars raged in Europe, and many feared that Monsieur Bonaparte would notice the little green island in the Atlantic. Paranoid generals constructed squatty structures along the coast called **Martello towers.**

1713
Jonathan Swift becomes Dean of St. Patrick's Cathedral in Dublin.

1744
Edmund Burke, the son of a Protestant Dublin solicitor and a Roman Catholic mother, enters Trinity College.

Early 1700s
Catholics practice their religion in hiding on Mass rocks. Catholic youngsters educated in underground "hedge schools."

1775-1789
The American and French Revolutions foment Irish unrest.

1798
The bloody, unsuccessful, but very heroic Rebellion of 1798.

1801
The Act of Union: British dissolve the Irish Parliament and create "the United Kingdom of Great Britain and Ireland."

1803
Robert Emmett is hanged for organizing a rising against the British.

1829
Daniel "The Liberator" O'Connell is elected and Catholics finally allowed to sit in Parliament.

1841
Population of Ireland over 8 million.

1845-1847
Potato and other crops fall prey to a fungal disease.

1847-1851
The Great Famine: 2 to 3 million people die, another million emigrate. Social structure of Ireland completely revamped.

1849-1899
The British began to remove the Irish landlords from their properties.

1858
Irish Republican Brotherhood (IRB), a.k.a the Fenians, founded.

1868
William Gladstone elected as British Prime Minister; continues land reform

1870
Isaac Butt founds the Irish Home Rule Party and seeks to disrupt parliamentary procedure.

Union meant Irish representatives now held seats in the British Parliament. Thanks to a long-awaited set of electoral reforms, Catholic farmers found that they too could go to the polls. With their newfound suffrage they elected Catholic **Daniel O'Connell** in 1829, forcing Westminster to repeal the remaining anti-Catholic laws that would have barred him from taking his seat. "The Liberator" promptly forced Parliament to allot money for improving Irish living conditions, health care, and trade. When unsympathetic Tories took power, O'Connell convened huge rallies in Ireland, showing popular support for repealing the Act of Union. From this political enthusiasm arose unprecedented social reform.

THE FAMINE (1845-1870)

During the first half of the 19th century, the potato was the wondercrop of the rapidly growing Irish population. This reliance had devastating effects when these tubers fell victim to an evil fungal disease. During the years of the **Great Famine** (1847-51), an estimated two to three million people died and another million immigrated to Liverpool, London, Australia, and America on overcrowded boats known as **coffin ships** (see **New Ross**, p. 218). British authorities often forcibly traded inedible grain for what few potatoes peasants could find. The Irish, whose diet was supplemented by delicacies like grass, had little choice but to accept. Hungry Catholics converted to Protestantism in exchange for British soup, earning for themselves and their descendants the disdainful title "Soupers."

After the Famine, the societal structure of surviving Irish peasants was completely reorganized. The bottom layer of truly penniless farmers had been eliminated. Eldest sons inherited the family farm, while unskilled younger sons often had little choice but to leave the Emerald Isle for pastures perhaps-not-so-green. Depopulation continued, and **emigration** became an Irish way of life. Fifty years of land legislation converted Ireland, with the exception of Dublin and industrial northeast Ulster, into a nation of conservative, culturally uniform smallholders.

English injustice, like a splash of British Petrol, fueled the formation of more angry young Nationalist groups. In 1858, crusaders for a violent removal of their oppressors founded the Irish Republican Brotherhood (IRB), a secret society known as the **Fenians.** Encouraged by a purportedly sympathetic Parliament, agrarian thinkers and republican Fenians created the **Land League** of the 1870s and pushed for further reforms.

PARNELL AND IRISH NATIONALISM (1870-1914)

In 1870, Member of Parliament **Isaac Butt** founded the **Irish Home Rule Party.** Its several dozen members adopted obstructionist tactics—they made long speeches, introduced amendments, and generally kept the opposing MPs so angry, bored, and ineffective that they would have little choice but to grant Ireland its autonomy. Home Ruler **Charles Stewart Parnell** was a charismatic Protestant aristocrat with a hatred for everything English. Backed by Parnell's invigorated Irish party, British

Prime Minister **William Gladstone** introduced an ill-fated **Home Rule Bill**. Despite surviving implication in the **Phoenix Park murders** (see p. 127; more reason not to camp there), Parnell couldn't beat an adultery rap. In 1890, allegations that he was having an extra-marital affair were confirmed. The scandal split Ireland into Parnellites and anti-Parnellites.

While politicians, engrossed by the scandal, let their ideals fall by the wayside, civil society waxed ambitious. Following their British and American sisters, the fairer sex established the **Irish Women's Suffrage Federation** in 1911. Marxist **James Connolly** led strikes in Belfast, and Dubliner **James Larkin** spearheaded an enormous general strike in 1913. Conservatives, attempting to "kill Home Rule by kindness," pushed for (well, vaguely in the direction of) social reform.

Meanwhile, various groups tried to revive an essential "Gaelic" culture, unpolluted by foreign influence. The **Gaelic Athletic Association** (see **Sports**, p. 80) attempted to replace English sports with hurling, camogie, and Gaelic football. The **Gaelic League** spread the use of the Irish language (see **The Revival**, p. 73). Culture was not only trendy, but a politically viable weapon—the Fenians seized the opportunity to disseminate their ideas and became the movers and shakers in Gaelic organizations. Arthur Griffith began a tiny movement and a little-read newspaper advocating Irish abstention from British politics, both of which went by the name **Sinn Féin** (SHIN FAYN, "Ourselves Alone"). Equal and opposite reactions led thousands of Northern Protestants who opposed Home Rule to join mass rallies, sign a covenant, and organize a quasi-militia called the **Ulster Volunteer Force (UVF),** (see **UVF** p. 455; **Northern Political Groups** p. 573). Nationalists led by **Eoin MacNeill** in Dublin responded by creating the **Irish Volunteers,** which the Fenians correctly saw as a potentially revolutionary force.

THE EASTER RISING (1914-1918)

Summer 1914: Irish Home Rule seemed imminent, and Ulster was ready to go up in flames. As it turned out, someone shot an archduke, and the world went up in flames. British Prime Minister Henry Asquith passed a **Home Rule Bill** in return for some Irish bodies to fill trenches for the British army. A **Suspensory Act** followed, delaying home rule until peace returned to Ulster; meanwhile, 670,000 Irishmen signed up to fight the Kaiser.

An 11,000-member armed guard, the remnants of the Volunteers, remained at home. They were officially led by Eoin MacNeill, who knew nothing of the revolt that the Fenians were brewing. If an architect could be ascribed to the ensuing mayhem, it would be poet and schoolteacher **Padraig Pearse,** who won his co-conspirators over to an ideology of "blood sacrifice"—the notion that if a small cache of committed men died public martyrs' deaths, the island's entire population would join in the struggle for independence.

The Volunteers conducted a series of unarmed maneuvers and parades in an effort to convince the Dublin government of their harmlessness. Meanwhile, Fenian leaders were plotting to

1880
Gladstone and Parnell's Home Rule Bill is defeated

1884
The Gaelic Athletic Association founded.

1890
Parnell scandal divides the Home Rule contingent.

1893
Gaelic League founded to reinvigorate the Irish language.

1905
Arthur Griffith forms Sinn Féin

1911
Women's Suffrage movement established

1910-1913
Northern Protestants commence mass rallies to protest Home Rule.

1913
Dublin general strike. Nationalist Irish Volunteers founded. Unionist Ulster Volunteers founded.

1914
Home Rule Bill passed with an amendment excluding Ulster. 770,000 Irishmen enlist to fight with the Allies in WWI.

1915-1916
The Irish Volunteers and the Fenians prepare for the Easter Rising.

1916
Easter Rising begins a day late in Dublin. The insurrection fails and its leaders are executed right into martyrdom.

1917
Sinn Féin is reorganized under Éamon de Valera as a national movement fighting for Irish independence

1917
The Irish Volunteers reorganize under Fenian Michael Collins.

1918
The Irish public turns to Sinn Féin to resist British plans for Irish conscription.

1919
Ireland fights for its Independence.

1920
The first Black and Tans recruited. Government of Ireland Act is passed, dividing Northern Ireland from the rest of the island.

1921
The Anglo-Irish Treaty produces the 26-county Free State of Ireland. The British retain control of the six Northern counties.

receive a shipment of German arms for use in a nationwide revolt on **Easter Sunday 1916.** However, the arms arrived early (chalk it up to German efficiency) and were never picked up. Unsuspecting Fenian leaders continued planning their rebellion; they attempted to coerce MacNeill, who gave orders for Volunteer mobilization on Easter Sunday. On that Saturday he learned that he had been manipulated by a weaponless bunch of brigands. Putting his trust in mass media, he inserted a plea into the Sunday papers asking all Volunteers to forego the rebellion and stay home.

Although MacNeill and most Fenian leaders had been thinking in terms of military success, Pearse's followers wanted martyrdom. On Sunday, the group met and rescheduled their uprising shindig for the following Monday, April 24. Pearse, James Connolly, and about a thousand of their closest friends seized the **General Post Office** on O'Connell St. (see p. 124), read aloud a "Proclamation of the Republic of Ireland," and hunkered down for five days of brawling in the streets of Dublin. As their only tangible accomplishment was massive property damage, the rebels were initially seen as criminals in the eyes of most Dubliners.

The Crown retaliated with swift, vindictive punishments—in May, 15 "ringleaders" received the death sentence. Among the executed were Pearse, Pearse's brother (whose primary crime was being Pearse's brother), and James Connolly, who was shot while tied to a chair because his wounds prevented him from standing. **Éamon de Valera** was spared when the Crown discovered he was American.

The British, with their hasty martial law, proved Pearse a true prophet—the public grew increasingly anti-British and sympathetic to the rebels. Wicklow's **Kilmainham Gaol** (see p. 123), the site of the executions, became a shrine of martyrdom. Everything was falling together: the Volunteers reorganized under master spy and Fenian bigwig **Michael Collins,** and the Sinn Féin party became the political voice of military Nationalism. Collins brought the Volunteers to Sinn Féin, and Éamon "Don't Call Me Yankee" de Valera became the party president. In 1918, misjudging popular sentiment yet again, the British tried to introduce a military draft in Ireland and the Irish lost what little complacency they had left.

INDEPENDENCE AND CIVIL WAR (1919-1922)

Extremist Irish Volunteers became Sinn Féin's military might and started calling themselves the **Irish Republican Army (IRA).** Thus, the British saw another, though not their last, **War for Independence.** The Crown reinforced its police with brutal **Black and Tans**—demobilized soldiers nicknamed for their patched-together uniforms. In 1920, British Prime Minister **David Lloyd George** passed the **Government of Ireland Act,** which divided the island into Northern Ireland and Southern Ireland, two partially self-governing areas within the United Kingdom. Pressed by a newly elected Parliament, George conducted hurried negotiations with Collins and produced the **Anglo-Irish Treaty,** creating a

26-county Irish Free State but recognizing British rule over the northern counties. For a more in-depth history of Northern Ireland see **A Divided Island** p. 454. The treaty imposed on Irish officials an oath of allegiance to the Crown, but not to the British government. Resourceful Lloyd George pushed the treaty through with the threat of war.

Sinn Féin, the IRA, and the population split on whether to accept the treaty. Collins said yes; de Valera said no. Parliament said yes, and de Valera said "Fine, then I don't wanna be President anymore." Arthur Griffith said he'd assume the position. Amid this and other sayings, the capable Collins government began the business of setting up a nation. A portion of the IRA, led by **General Rory O'Connor,** opposed the treaty; these nay-sayers occupied the Four Courts in Dublin, took a pro-treaty army general hostage, and were attacked by the forces of Collins's government. Two years of **civil war** followed. Skipping all the ugly details: the pro-treaty government won, Griffith died from the strain of the struggle, Collins was assassinated (see **Clonakilty,** p. 251), and the dwindling minority of anti-treaty IRA officers went into hiding. Sinn Féin denied the legitimacy of the Free State government and expressed their disapproval by referring to the Republic as "the 26-county state" or "the Dublin Government," rather than the official "Éire."

THE ERA DE VALERA (1922-1960)

Éire emerged from its civil war looking quite a bit worse for the wear—it had lost its most prominent leaders and frankly felt a little underdressed without them. The Anglo-Irish Treaty required a constitution by December 6, 1922. With time running out, **W.T. Cosgrave** was elected prime minister and passed a hasty preliminary constitution. Under the guidance of **Éamon de Valera,** the government ended armed resistance by Republican insurgents, executed 77 of them, and imprisoned several more. Cosgrave and his party **Cumann na nGaedheal** (which evolved into today's **Fine Gael**) headed the first stable Free State administration. His government restored civil order, granted suffrage to women in 1923, and brought **electrical power** to much of western Ireland. In the Republic's first elections, the anti-treaty voters supported abstentionist Sinn Féin. Then, in 1927, de Valera broke with Sinn Féin and the IRA and founded his own political party, **Fianna Fáil,** in order to both participate in government and oppose the treaty non-violently. Fianna Fáil won the 1932 election, and de Valera held power for much of the next 20 years. In line with the vision of Ireland as a small nation of small farmers, Fianna Fáil broke up the remaining large landholdings and imposed high tariffs, instigating a trade war with Britain that battered the Irish economy until 1938. Meanwhile, IRA hard-liners trickled out of jails, resumed violence, and saw their party outlawed in 1936.

In 1937 and "in the name of the most Holy Trinity," de Valera and the voters approved the permanent Irish Constitution. It declared the state's name to be Éire and established the country's legislative structure, consisting of two chambers. The **Dáil** (DAHL), or big, bad lower house, is composed of 166 seats

1922
Arthur Griffith is elected President and begins makin' a nation.

1922-1923
The Irish Civil War.

Dec. 1922
A first constitution is framed for the Irish Free State.

1923
de Valera's government squelches Republican insurgents and ends armed resistance to the Irish State.

1923-1932
Cosgrave rules, granting women's suffrage and bringing electricity to the West.

1927
de Valera splits with Sinn Féin and establishes Fianna Fáil.

1936
The IRA is outlawed.

1937
The Irish Constitution is ratified. The official name of the country is changed to Éire.

1939
The IRA begin its bombing campaign in England.

LIFE AND TIMES

1939
Britain enters
WWII; Ireland
maintains "neutral-
ity" throughout
"The Emergency."

1948
An intermittently
Fine Gael govern-
ment declares the
Republic of Ireland
and ends Irish
membership in the
British Common-
wealth. Hoo-ah!

1949
Britain recognizes
the Republic but
decides to main-
tain control over
Northern Ireland.

1955
The Republic is
admitted to the
United Nations.

1969
"Troubles" and
clashes intensify in
Northern Ireland.
Protestants launch
siege of Catholic
Bogside neighbor-
hood in Derry. For
more information
on Northern Ire-
land, see p. 450

1973
Ireland enters the
European Eco-
nomic Community.
Secularization of
Irish society
marches forward.

1983
Abortion is reaf-
firmed as national
policy by way of
public referendum

1985
The Republic gains
an official place in
Northern Ireland
negotiations.

directly elected in proportional representation. The second-banana upper house, or **Seanad** (SHA-nud), has 60 members chosen by electoral colleges. The Prime Minister, called the **Taoiseach** (TEE-shuch), and his deputy the **Tánaiste** (tah-NESH-tuh) lead a Cabinet. The **President** is the ceremonial head of state, elected to a seven-year term.

Ireland stayed neutral during WWII (known as **The Emergency**), though many Irish citizens identified with the Allies and around 50,000 served in the British army. This may have had something to do with the fact that Hitler was bombing Dublin, though we don't want to jump to any conclusions. While the young government lacked the monetary and military strength to make much difference on the Front, Éire's brand of neutrality didn't exactly hinder the Allies. For example, downed American or British airmen were shipped north to non-neutral Belfast; German pilots were detained in P.O.W. camps.

In 1948, a Fine Gael government under **John Costello** had the honor of officially proclaiming "the Republic of Ireland" free, thus ending British Commonwealth membership altogether. Britain, who didn't quite catch all that, recognized the Republic a year later. They declared that the UK would maintain control over Ulster until the Parliament of Northern Ireland consented to join the Republic.

The last de Valera government (1951-59), and its successor, under **Sean Lemass,** boosted the Irish economy by ditching protectionism in favor of attracting foreign investment. Instead of the verbal and military skirmishes over constitutional issues that dominated the 20s, Irish politics became a contest between the ideologically similar Fianna Fáil and Fine Gael parties.

THE REPUBLIC TODAY

Ireland's post-war boom, ushered in with the efforts of Lemass, didn't arrive until the early 1960s. Economic mismanagement and poor governmental policies kept the boom short. By the early 1970s, Ireland was on its way back down again. In an effort to revitalize the nation, Ireland entered the European Economic Community, now the European Union (EU), in 1973. EU membership and an increased number of international visitors spurred by the creation of Bord Fáilte helped introduce the slow, painful process of secularization. Garret FitzGerald revamped Fine Gael under a secular banner and alternated Prime Ministership with Fianna Fáil's Charlie Haughey throughout the late 70s and early 80s. EU funds proved crucial to helping Ireland out of a severe mid-80s recession and reducing its dependence on the UK. In 1985, FitzGerald signed the Anglo-Irish agreement, which let Éire stick an official nose into Northern negotiations.

The Irish broke progressive social and political ground in 1990 by choosing **Mary Robinson,** a woman, as their President. Formerly a progressive barrister who had championed the rights of single mothers and gays, Robinson fought vigorously to overcome international (and local) evaluations of the Irish as conservative cronies. In 1993, the age of consent between gay men was lowered to 17, and in 1995, a national referendum finally made divorce legal in the Republic. When Mary was appointed the United Nation's High Commissioner for Human Rights in 1997, she was replaced by **Mary McAleese.**

Robinson's small, leftist **Labour Party** enjoyed enormous, unexpected success, paving the way for further, social reform. In 1993, Taoiseach **Albert Reynolds** made his top priority ending violence in Northern Ireland. A year later he announced a cease-fire agreement between Sinn Féin and the IRA. Despite his miracle-working in the North, Reynolds was forced to resign following a scandal involving his appointee for President of the High Court. His choice, Attorney General **Harry Whelehan,** was heavily criticized for his lack of action in a case involving a pedophilic priest, **Father Brendan Smyth.** The week following Whelehan's appointment, Fine Gael, led by **John Bruton,** introduced a no-confidence motion against the government. After Reynold's resignation, the Labour Party formed a coalition with Fine Gael, with Bruton as Taoiseach.

In June 1997, Fianna Fáil won the general election, making **Bertie Ahern,** at 45, the youngest Taoiseach in Irish history. Ahern joined the peace talks that produced the **Good Friday Peace Agreement** in April of 1998 (see p. 459). On May 22, 1998, in the first island-wide election since 1918, an overwhelming 94% of voters in the Republic voted for the enactment of the Agreement. (For the recent status of the Good Friday Agreement, see p. 461.)

In the summer of 2001, the Irish populace trickled out to the polls and defeated the **Nice Treaty.** The Treaty was the first step in the addition of 12 eastern European nations to the European Union. The result of the referendum shocked Ireland's pro-Treaty government and caused quite a stir on the continent. The government began a campaign to clarify the details of the treaty, as opinion polls found the Irish public pro-expansion but wary of union collapse. The treaty was eventually passed, welcoming Poland and 11 other eastern European countries. On May 11, 2004, Bertie Ahern will welcome the new countries into the union as president of the European Council.

With the money Ireland has garnered from the European Union over the years (in 1992 alone they received **six million dollars** for agreeing to sign onto the Maastrict Treaty); with increased foreign investment and the establishing of Ireland as a center for computer software development; and with a thriving tourism industry bringing millions of dollars into Ireland yearly, the Irish economy is thriving like never before. Such wealth has lead the nation to increase its commitment to education, leading Europe in the number of adults with higher education. In turn this educated, flexible work force has invited foreign investment. According to a 1999 report, the unemployment rate should be reduced to three percent by the year 2005. With the stability of the euro (see **The Euro,** p.12) dependent on a waning international market, however, the Irish may prove reluctant to take financial risks during their presidency of the European Union.

1990
Mary Robinson is elected President.

1993
Conservative Ireland goes liberal and lowers the age of consent for gay men to just 17.

1994
Peace-minded President Reynolds is forced to step down over Church scandals.

1995
Divorce is legalized in Ireland.

1997
Bertie Ahern is Prime Minister—the youngest ever.

1998
The Good Friday Peace begins in the North.

2002
The Euro is introduced to Ireland and the punt is phased out.

2004
Bertie Ahern becomes president of the European Council.

LIFE AND TIMES

THE IRISH

FROM THE ROAD

FOR THE *CRAIC* OF IT

Craic. The book sprinkles it wherever possible. Stay here long enough and you'll use it for anything from "what's up" (what's the craic?"), "etc." ("and all that *craic.*"), or "rockin'!" ("the *craic* was mighty!"). The phrase least appreciated as a cultural rallying cry, however, is doing something "for the *craic.*"

I realized quickly that Irish, British, and American English have their disparities, and ditched Yankee terms the minute I landed in Belfast. Getting info from personnel, I might casually throw in "what's the *craic* with" some business detail to gain respect for my cultural awareness.

Yet, chatting with new friends at the pub, my tongue was tied. Blame it on the loud *craic*, but I'm pretty sure they were telling me of ridiculous deeds done all "for the *craic.*" Singles traveled across the island to an unknown town to meet their mate, "for the *craic.*" Someone joined a band of Englishmen to play Irish trad, also "for the *craic.*" The best I could muster was paragliding "for kicks."

But my attempt didn't have the same effect. Doing something for the *craic* involves a wee risk: daring for a chance at love, fame, friendship, not just fun. Less frivolous than other meanings, it's something innately Irish that I had to learn. By the end of my stay, I made it to a stag party in Dunfanaghy, a wedding in Belfast, and a stay with one of Northern Ireland's premier skateboarders in Enniskillen. I assure you, each time, the *craic* was mighty.

-Alex Cooley, 2004

DEMOGRAPHICS

Recent estimates put the Republic of Ireland's population at around 3.8 million—with over 35% living within 60 mi. of Dublin—and Northern Ireland's at approximately 1.7 million. Over 50% of Ireland's population is under 25; indeed, the birthrate in Ireland is one of the highest in Europe, with 14.6 births per thousand in 2000. However, rates are expected to drop slightly as Irish couples have begun to wait longer before having children.

The demographic composition of Ireland is generally described as mono-racial, but the recent economic growth and prosperity of the "Celtic Tiger" have inspired unprecedented immigration to Ireland. This influx, a happy reverse of the historic emigration of the Irish people, includes, among others, the return of Irish citizens, foreigners in search of jobs, and refugees seeking asylum. Because of the limited diversity at present, racial strife remains negligible, especially compared to the more diverse urban areas of the United Kingdom.

Though Britain itself may boast a multi-racial population, the demographic make-up of Northern Ireland more closely resembles that of the Republic. Historically and presently, the most pervading cultural distinctions and disagreements in the Republic, and especially in Northern Ireland, have been between people of different creeds (Protestants and Catholics, Republicans and Loyalists), not color.

RELIGION

The Republic of Ireland is blessed with a population over 92% Catholic, making it one of the most Christian countries in the world. But the emergence of Catholicism didn't begin until St. Patrick's arrival some 1500 years ago. Before then, the island belonged to the Celts, a pagan people who worshipped a number of natural gods. When Christian missionaries arrived in the 5th century, they incorporated many Celtic beliefs into Christian practice (for example, Halloween is an old pagan Irish holiday), easing Ireland's transformation into a devoutly Catholic land.

Since the days of St. Patrick, Catholicism has been tightly woven into the everyday life of the island. Until recently, church and state were one and the same. Though divorce has since been legalized, abortion is still outlawed in the Republic. Public schools have mandatory religion classes and Sunday mass is a family event (often followed by a pint in the pub), enjoyed, not mourned, by parishioners. The importance of Catholicism to the lives of the Irish is further demonstrated by the respect garnered by the local parish priests (who often spring for parishioners in the pub after services). Though Catholicism is certainly the predominate religion on the isle, small Jewish and Buddhist populations can be found in the cities.

The ties between religion, politics, and culture, are more intertwined in the North. Northern Ireland's primary religions are Catholicism and Protestantism. Though Protestants have a slightly larger population, it is predicted that due to the higher birth rates of Catholics in the country, Catholics will outnumber Protestants within a couple of decades.

Though the troubles in the North are often attributed to religious disagreement, the contemporary problem is more an issue of nationalism, not religion. Fighting in the North often erupts between Catholics and Protestants, especially during the summer months, but religion is not the cause. Rather, Protestants, descended from the English imported to Ireland over the years, more often than not claim loyalty to England (Loyalists), while Catholics, more likely to be descended from the Irish masses abused by the English over the years, claim loyalty to the Republic (Republicans). Fighting usually erupts over one's loyalty to country, not savior. For a complete history of the **Troubles,** see p. 458.

LANGUAGE

The English language came to Ireland with the Normans in the 12th Century. Since this time it has become the primary language spoken in Ireland, but like many things British, the Irish have molded the language to make it their own. The Irish accent, or "lilt", differs from county to county. In the southern and western counties, bring a notebook for communication, as the accent is often so thick and guttural that visitors may find it hard to understand conversations. In Dublin and in the North, expect clearer pronunciation and a sing-song style of conversing, though with different lilts: Northerns bear the mark of Scottish settlement, whereas Dubliners bear the taint of globalization.

Because English is so commonly spoken in Ireland, the strong linguistic history of the Irish language is often unknown or unseen by the average traveler. Though the constitution declares Irish the national language of the Republic, there are only 86,000 individuals in the exclusively Irish-speaking communities, or **gaeltacht** (GAYL-tacht). The larger *gaeltacht* is composed of small settlements scattered about the most remote regions of the island. The most prominent of these are located in Connemara (see p. 375), in patches of Co. Donegal (p. 404), on the Dingle Peninsula (p. 295), Cape Clear Island (p. 257), and in the Aran Islands (p. 358). These geographically disparate communities are further divided by three different dialects: Ulster, Connacht, and Munster Irish.

The Irish government continues efforts to preserve and promote modern Irish; Irish citizens are required to take *Gaelige* throughout their educational experience. A Connemara-based Irish radio station and a new Irish language television station, *Telifís na Gaelige* (T na G [TEE NUH JEE] to locals), expand Irish-hearing opportunities. Peruse the **Glossary** (p. 573) for useful Irish words and phrases.

IRISH CULTURE

MEAT AND POTATOES

Irish food can be fairly expensive, especially in cities and in restaurants. The basics—and that's what you'll get—are simple and filling. The restaurant business is a fairly recent phenomenon in Ireland; up until the economy took off

ON THE MENU

RISE AND SHINE...

The Emerald Isle is a land of B&Bs, and in each of these homey establishments, the breakfast is just as important as the bed. If you want to be full until the sun goes down, ask for a "full fry." Here's a detailed list of what exactly you'll be eating—not for the squeamish!

Fried Egg: Traditionally fried on one side only, and cooked until the yolk is slightly runny.

Sausages: Pork scraps squeezed into a tube and tied into small links.

Bacon or Rashers: Thin slices of fried pork. Not as crispy as American bacon, and cured differently. Bacon comes from the pig's belly, rashers from its back.

Black & White Pudding: Unique to Irish Breakfasts, these are slices of thick sausage made from pork, barley, oatmeal, and spices. Black pudding gets its special color and flavor from pig's blood. Every butcher has his own recipe, and flavors vary based on the spices used.

Toast: Slices of white "pan," served with tea.

Brown Bread: Hearty, whole-grain bread, often home-made and seasoned with Guinness, served sliced but not toasted.

Waffles: Criss-cut potatoes, deep-fried. Closer to hash-browns than pancakes; using syrup on these is probably a mistake.

Tomatoes: Pronounced to-MAH-tos. Halved and fried, served with eggs.

Mushrooms: Sliced and sauteed. Most proprietors use these as a vegetarian substitute for all that meat.

about 20 years ago, only a few restaurants graced even the streets of Dublin. Today, eateries clutter Ireland's mini-metropoli, many specializing in international fare. The rural byways of the island remain limited in their culinary offerings. Quick and greasy staples are **chippers** (fish n' chip shops) and **takeaways** (takeout joints). At chippers, "fish" is a whitefish, usually cod, and chips are served with salt and vinegar; ketchup sometimes costs extra. Fried food delicacies include chips with gravy, potato cakes (pancakes made of potato flakes), or the infamous spiceburger (fried patty of spiced breadcrumbs). Most pubs serve food, and **pub grub** is a good option for a cheap but substantial meal. Typical pub grub includes Irish stew (meat, potatoes, carrots, and onions), burgers, soup, and sandwiches.

Most Irish meals are based on a simple formula: meat, potatoes, greens, and more meat. *Colcannon* (a potato, onion, and cabbage dish), Irish stew, and "ploughman's lunch" are Irish specialties. Loud and long will Irish bards sing the praises of the Clonakilty man who first concocted **black pudding.** This delicacy was invented during a shortage and makes the most of the bits of the pig not usually eaten. Black pudding is, as one local butcher put it, "some pork, a good deal of blood, and grains and things—all wrapped up in a tube." White pudding is a similar dish that uses milk instead of blood. **Irish breakfasts,** or **Ulster Fries** in the North, include eggs, sausage, white or black pudding, **rashers** (similar to thick American bacon), a fried tomato, brown bread, and toast, and are often served all day and a given at any B&B.

The true culinary strength of the Irish is their bread. Most famous is **soda bread:** heavy, white, sweetened by raisins, and especially yummy when fried. Most common are **brown bread** and **batch loaves.** The brown stuff is thick and grainy, while batch loaves are square-shaped, white, and ideal for sandwiches. Another indigenous bread is **barm brack;** perfect for holidays, it is a spicy mixture of dried fruits and molasses mixed to a lead-like density. Sandwiches are often served on a **bap,** a round, white bun. All of these breads are excellent in combination with locally produced cheeses.

Seafood can be a bargain in smaller towns; mussels and oysters are delectable, as is anything marinated in Guinness. In addition to the widespread fried fish, smoked mackerel is splendid year-round, and Atlantic salmon is freshest in July. Regional specialties include **crubeen** (pigs' feet) in

Cork, **coddle** (sausages and bacon with potatoes) in Dublin, and **blaa** (sausage rolls) in Waterford. **Coffee** is gaining ground as a rival to **tea** for the standard washer-down of unwanted cabbage. Aside from terminology, Northern food is much the same as in the Republic.

GUINNESS AND CRAIC

A 1998 study found that Irish students spend roughly €100 a month on drinks, which is no wonder considering the centrality of pubs in Irish culture. The pub is, in a sense, the living room of the Irish household. Locals of all ages from every social milieu head to the public house for conversation, food, singing, and *craic* (crack), an Irish word meaning "a good time." In the evening, some pubs host traditional music. Local and traveling musicians toting fiddles, guitars, and *bodhráns* drop in about 9:30pm to start impromptu sessions (see **Music**, p. 76). In rural pubs, a *seanachaí* (SHAN-ukh-ee, a storyteller) might make an appearance. Before hitting the street, you should learn the ground rules (see **Pub Ground Rules,** below).

Cocktails are an oddity found mainly in American-style bars and discos. In Ireland, expect **beer,** and not much else. Beer comes in two basic varieties, **lagers** (blond, fizzy brews served cold, a bit weaker than ales or stouts) and **ales** (slightly darker, more bitter, and sometimes served warmer than lagers). **Stout,** a type of ale, is thick, dark-ruby colored, and made from roasted barley to impart an almost meaty flavor. **Guinness** stout inspires a reverence otherwise reserved for the Holy Trinity. Known variously as "the dark stuff," "the blonde in the black skirt," or simply "I'll have a pint, please," it's a rich, dark brew with a head thick enough to stand a match in. For a sweeter taste, try it with blackcurrant or cider. **Murphy's,** brewed in Cork, is a similar, slightly creamier stout. Cork also produces **Beamish,** a tasty "economy" stout (read: cheap date drink). Stout takes a while to pour properly (usually 3-4min.); it should be drunk in slow measure as well, and never before it settles. **Smithwicks** is a hoppy, English-style bitter commonly perceived as an old man's drink. Two more popular domestic lagers are **Kilkenny** and **Harp.** You may be surprised by the many pubs serving Budweiser or Heineken and by the number of young people quaffing such imported lagers. In general, the indigenous brews are far worthier. Beer is served in **pint glasses** (20 oz.) or half-pints

PUB GROUND RULES **Pubs in the Republic** are generally open Monday through Saturday from 10:30am-11:30pm (11pm in winter) and Sunday from 12:30-2pm and 4-11pm (closed 2-4pm for the Holy hour). Late-hours licenses, becoming increasingly common in Dublin, allow some pubs to stay open until somewhere between midnight and 2am. Some pubs, especially ones catering to a clientele of fishermen, have been granted special "early" licenses, requiring an act of Parliament to revoke, which allow them to open at 7:30am. Pubs almost never charge a cover or require a drink minimum. **Pubs in the North** tend to be open Monday through Saturday from 11:30am-11pm (or recently, since the Troubles have calmed, until 1 or 2am on the weekends) and Sunday from 12:30-2:30pm and 7-10pm. Some rural pubs close for a few hours on weekday afternoons as well. Pub lunches are usually served Monday to Saturday from 12:30-2:30pm, while soup, soda bread, and sandwiches are served all day. Children are often not allowed in pubs after 7pm. The legal drinking age in Ireland and Northern Ireland is 18.

FROM THE ROAD

LOCALS SALUTE

Driving in rural Ireland, with its narrow, one-lane "highways" and omnipresent sheep crossing the road, can be a challenge for the uninitiated. Beyond the patience it requires, Irish driving also has its own etiquette, which can take some getting used to.

People often honk at each other here, though rarely is it to be an aggressive driving beast. Instead, it's a friendly greeting. As an American city-dweller, I rarely associate honking with the word "friendly." Usually when I hear a car horn, I look up anticipating the finger.

And let me say, often I do get flipped off. But instead of the oh-so-classy angry middle fingers that disgruntled American drivers wave, Irish drivers stick up their index finger in a nonchalant fashion as a way to say hello, not to start a fight.

A woman who gave me a lift into Killorglin one day explained this baffling phenomenon. "It's known as the one-finger salute. It's the way that drivers say hello to each other without waving their hands." As she told me this, a passing car honked and held a finger up. "I think it's only the one finger because we're too lazy to stick up our entire hand," she jokingly added.

Huh. So people honking their horns and making gestures to each other out of chumminess. What a novel concept. At times, I find myself doing the one-finger salute as I leisurely cycle down the street and for a moment, I feel like a local.

-Thea Morton, 2004

(called a "glass"). Ordering a beer by name will bring you a full pint, so be loud and clear if you can only stay for a half (or just take the pint and drink faster). A pint of Guinness usually costs about €4 in the Republic and about UK£3 in the North, with prices rising in urban settings.

Life in Ireland is tough. Luckily, when beer doesn't cut it, there's always the hard stuff for support. **Irish whiskey,** which Queen Elizabeth once claimed was her only true Irish friend, is sweeter than its Scotch counterpart, spelled "whisky" (see p. 245). In Ireland, whiskey is served in larger measures than in warmer climes. **Jameson** is popular everywhere. Dubliners are partial to **Powers and Sons. Bushmills,** distilled near Portstewart, is the favorite in the North, which takes pride in producing the world's oldest whiskey. Drinkers in Cork enjoy **Paddy's. Irish coffee** is sweetened with brown sugar and whipped cream and laced with whiskey. It's been more popular with the tourists than the natives ever since its alleged invention at Shannon Airport by a desperate bartender looking to appease cranky travelers on a layover. **Hot whiskey** (spiced up with lemon, cloves, and brown sugar) can provide a cozy buzz. In the west, you may hear some locals praise "mountain dew," a euphemism for *poitín* (put-CHEEN), an illegal distillation sometimes given to cows in labor that ranges in strength from 115 to 140 proof (see *Love Poitín #9*, p. 418). *Poitín* makes after-hour appearances in pubs throughout the island, but be warned that *poitín* is a highly toxic substance. While most alcoholic drinks are based on ethanol, *poitín* uses lethal methanol. *Let's Go* generally does not recommend drinking methanol.

CUSTOMS AND ETIQUETTE

Like in any other country, a set of culturally specific customs dictate how the Irish interact with one another. Those unfamiliar with these customs run the risk of accidently insulting locals. Some important customs include the following:

JUMPING THE QUEUE. In Ireland, when the occasion calls, people usually form orderly lines, or 'queues.' When people line up to get on a bus, enter a theater, or what have you, the 'queue' that forms is usually considered quite sacred. To 'jump the queue'—to ignore the order of the line and push your way to the front—will earn you disapproving stares, and often, verbal confrontations.

FLIPPING THE BIRD(S). Another easy way to anger the locals is to flip someone the fingers. Yes, fingers. While people in other countries usually flip only their middle finger when letting friends know what they really think, the Irish flip both their middle finger and their index finger, forming a V shape. Flipping the birds is only insulting when you position your hand so that the palm is facing inward; if the palm is facing outward, you've just said 'peace'—you damned hippy.

BUYING THE ROUND. Ordering at an Irish pub can become a complex affair. Rather than buying individual drinks, when in a small group, one individual will usually approach the bar and buy a round of drinks for everyone. Once those drinks are downed, another individual will buy the next round. This continues until everyone has bought a round. Don't order a whiskey when someone else is buying a round and order a half-pint of something cheap when you're buying. And don't think no one will notice if you forget to buy a round. Though they might not comment on it, everybody notices everything and nobody forgets anything. It's also considered extremely poor form to refuse someone's offer to buy you a drink.

CHASING THE RAINBOW. What may be funny in one culture can be terribly annoying in another. Try to avoid jokes or references to leprechauns, Lucky Charms, pots of gold, and the 'wee' people. Such comments will not earn you any friends at the local pub. Abortion, divorce, gay marriages, and the Troubles up North, likewise, do not make for casual conversation; these topics are largely avoided in pubs and public places. Discussing these subjects is likely to bring you serious troubles of your own—restrict questions and curiosity for another time.

IRISH LITERARY TRADITIONS

THE IRISH LANGUAGE

The oldest vernacular literature, and the largest collection of folklore in all of Europe, lies within the Irish language. Irish is a Celtic language that shares its Indo-European origin with Scottish Gaelic and Manx, and more distantly with Breton, Welsh, and Cornish. The Irish language is called *Gaeilge* (GALE-ga) by its speakers; the English word "Gaelic" (GAL-lik) refers to the Scottish language. In 1600, there were as many speakers of Irish worldwide as of English. The Anglophones, however, had more money and better armies; over the next 250 years, Irish became the language of the disenfranchised.

Irish re-entered the lives of the privileged classes with the advent of the Gaelic Revival. In 1893, **Douglas Hyde** (Éire's first President) founded the **Gaelic League** to inspire enthusiasm for Irish among those who didn't speak it. The League aimed to spread the everyday use of Irish as part of a larger project of de-Anglicization. W.B. Yeats and Lady Gregory count among Hyde's admirers; to help the cause, they founded the Abbey Theatre in Dublin for the promotion of Irish playwrights.

LEGENDS AND FOLKTALES

In early Irish society, what the bard (from the Irish *baird*) sang about battles, valor, and lineage was the only record a chieftain had by which to make decisions. Poetry and politics of the Druidic tradition were so intertwined that the *fili*, trained poets, and *breitheamh* (BREH-huv), judges of the Brehon Laws, were often the same people. The poet-patron relationship was as symbiotic in Ireland as anywhere else—the poet bought his lord's favor (and food and shelter) by selling his poetic soul in long praise poems.

In later years, legendary tales were written down for prosperity. The famous **Book of Invasions** (*Leabhar Gabhála*; LOWR GA-vah-lah) is a long-winded record of the pre-Christian cultures and armies that have invaded Ireland. The **Ulster Cycle,** a collection of old Irish folktales, includes the adventures of King Conchobar (Conor) of Ulster and his clan, the **Ulaid.** Conor's archenemy is his ex-wife Queen Medbh (MAVE) of Connacht. Ulster's champion is **Cúchulainn** (coo HOO-lin), the king's nephew and an athlete extraordinare known as the "Hound of Ulster." The central tale of the Ulster Cycle is the **Táin Bó Cuailnge** (Cattle Raid of Cooley), in which Queen Medbh decides first to borrow, and then to steal, the most famous bull in the country, the Donn of Cooley.

WIT AND RESISTANCE

After the English dispossessed the Irish chieftains at the Battle of Kinsale (see p. 58), most Irish writers predicted the imminent collapse of Irish language and culture. As the bards of the Irish courts lost their high status, they carried on their work among the peasant classes, so that Ireland developed a vernacular literary culture. Most of the authors writing in Irish at this time lamented their home as a land under cultural attack; a common theme in their poetry is the metaphor of Ireland as a captive woman, like the dark and beautiful "Roisin Dubh" (black rose).

By the 17th century, wit and satire began to characterize the emerging modern Irish literature. In Dublin, **Jonathan Swift** (1667-1745), Dean of St. Patrick's Cathedral, wrote some of the most sophisticated, misanthropic, and marvelous satire in the English language. Like writers throughout the island, Swift felt compelled to address the sad condition of starving Irish peasants. Besides his masterpiece *Gulliver's Travels*, Swift's razor-sharp pamphlets and essays took pot-shots at cruel English lords but still managed to defend the Protestant Church of Ireland.

In the mid-19th century, the Famine hit, and folk culture fell by the wayside in the face of destitution; while the peasants starved, the Industrial Revolution passed Ireland by. Cosmopolitan Dublin managed to breed talent, but gifted young writers traded the Liffey for the Thames in order to make their names. **Oscar Wilde** (1856-1900) moved to, or perhaps created, the high aesthetic culture of London. He wrote many vicious and delightful works, including his best-known play, *The Importance of Being Earnest* (1895). His work critiqued society and propriety while fetishizing it; he challenged Irish clichés and Victorian determinism by perfecting a pithy style whose absurd truths still stand today. Prolific playwright **George Bernard Shaw** (1856-1950) was also born in Dublin but moved to London in 1876, where he became an active socialist. His work *John Bull's Other Island* (1904) depicts the increasing hardships of the Irish peasant laborer.

THE REVIVAL

Toward the end of the 19th century, a portion of Ireland's crop of young writers no longer turned to London to cultivate their talent. Rather, a vigorous and enduring effort known today as the **Irish Literary Revival** took over the scene. Members of this movement turned to Irish culture, from its ancient mythology to contemporary folktales, for inspiration. The memoirs of Irish speakers were discovered and embraced. The most famous of them is *Peig*, the mournful autobiography of **Peig Sayers,** a girl growing up on the Blaskets (see p. 301). This memoir, and others like it, led readers to mourn the decline of Irish culture and language.

The Irish Literary Revival was hardly a nostalgic movement; it recognized the Anglo-Irish perspective as a practical reality. Many authors continued to write in English, which was, after all, the most commonly understood language on the island. **Lady Augusta Gregory** (1852-1932) wrote 40 plays and a number of translations, poems, and essays. She began her career collecting the folktales and legends of Galway's poor residents and later discovered her own skill as a writer of dialogue, cooking up comedic plays with staunch nationalist flavor. The early poems of **William Butler Yeats** (1865-1939) create a dreamily rural island of loss and legend. His early work, with its appealing mystic vision of a picturesque Ireland, won him worldwide fame. His 1923 Nobel Prize was the first ever awarded to an Irishman.

In 1904, Yeats and Lady Gregory founded the **Abbey Theatre** in Dublin (see p. 130), in order to "build up a Celtic and Irish school of dramatic literature." But conflict almost immediately arose between various contributors. Was this new body of drama to be written in verse or prose, in the realistic or the fantastic and heroic mode? In theory, the plays would be written in Irish, but in practice they needed to be written in English. A sort of compromise was found in the work of **John Millington Synge** (1871-1909), whose English plays were perfectly Irish in essence. A multifaceted man who "wished to be at once Shakespeare, Beethoven, and Darwin," he spent much of his early years traveling and living in Paris. His experiences with locals in bucolic Ireland gave him the subject matter for writing his black comedy *The Playboy of the Western World* (1907), which destroys the pastoral myth of Irish peasantry and portrays a rural society divided into classes. The play's first production was received with open civil disobedience. **Sean O'Casey** (1880-1964) also caused riots at the Abbey with the 1926 premiere of *The Plough and Star*, which depicted the Easter Rebellion without mythologizing its leaders. For a history of literature in the North, see p. 451.

MODERNISM: JOYCE AND BECKETT

Many authors still found Ireland too small and insular an island to suit their literary aspirations. **James Joyce** (1882-1941) headlines the cast of inky Irish expatriates. Joyce was born and educated in Dublin, but he left forever in 1904: "How sick, sick, sick, I am of Dublin! It is the city of failure, of rancour and of unhappiness. I long to be out of it." His writing, however, never escaped Ireland—his novels and stories exclusively describe the lives of the dear, dirty denizens of Dublin. Joyce's most accesible writing is a collection of short stories titled *Dubliners* (1914). His first novel, *A Portrait of the Artist as a Young Man* (1914), uses the protagonist Stephen Daedalus to describe Joyce's own youth, and his decision to leave his country, religion, and family behind him. Stephen reappears in *Ulysses* (1922), Joyce's ground-breaking Modernist (mock) epic. The novel's structure loosely resembles Homer's *Odyssey*—hence the title—but rather than tackling ten years and half the known world, Joyce deals with a single day in 1904 Dublin. This epic day is marked by Joyce-lovers each June 16 by "Bloomsday" festivities of the literary and inebriate kind.

Samuel Beckett (1906-89), a postmodern writer before there was such a term, concerned himself with the absurd and with the pain, loneliness, and minutiae many of his characters mistook for living. Beckett's poems, novels, and plays, including the absurdist masterpiece *Waiting for Godot*, earned him an honored place in the canon alongside his mentor Joyce. But unlike Joyce, Beckett sought to rid his prose of Irishness. By writing much of his work in French, then translating it into English, he eliminated the colloquialisms and speech patterns that might work against his universal subject matter.

POEMS, PLAYS, AND PLOTS

After the 1940s, Irish poetry once again commanded widespread appreciation. Living in the backwash of the Revival and the Civil War, these new Irish poets questioned their cultural inheritance, finding a new version of Ireland to complicate the old one. **Patrick Kavanaugh** (1906-67) debunked a mythical Ireland in such poems as "The Great Hunger" (1945), which was banned for its obscenities, prompting the Irish police to visit Kavanaugh's house and seize the manuscript. The works of **Thomas Kinsella** and **John Montague** display a keen awareness of the history of Irish poetry with a sensitivity to mid-19th-century civil strife. Although some poets are directly political and almost propagandistic, much of contemporary poetry is intensely private. Many poets treat the political issue from a removed, everyday perspective. For example, the contemporary poet **Eavan Boland** has received public recognition for her portrayal of middle-class Irish women. Perhaps the most famous contemporary Irish poet is **Seamus Heaney** (aka "Famous Seamus"), winner of the 1995 Nobel Prize in Literature. Born in rural County Derry, Heany become a controversial figure after leaving the North for the Republic and the release of his fourth book, *North* (1975), which tackles the Troubles head-on. For more on Heany, see **Literature** in Northern Ireland **p. 462.**

The dirt of Dublin continues to provide fodder for generations of writers. Notorious wit, playwright, poet, and terrorist **Brendan Behan** created semi-autobiographical works about delinquent life, such as his play *The Quare Fellow* (1954). Mild-mannered schoolteacher **Roddy Doyle** wrote the well-known Barrytown trilogy about family good times in down-and-out Dublin (see **Film,** p. 78), as well as the acclaimed *The Woman Who Walked Into Doors* (1996). Doyle won the Booker Prize in 1994 for *Paddy Clarke Ha Ha Ha.*

Noteworthy Irish playwrights include politically conscious **Frank McGuinness** and **Brian Friel.** Friel's *Dancing at Lughnasa* (1990) became a Broadway hit and a Meryl Streep-blessed movie, and McGuinness' war drama *Observe the Sons of Ulster Marching Towards the Somme* has seen international success. **Conor McPherson's** *The Weir* won the 1998 Olivier Award for "Best New Play" and captivated sold-out Broadway audiences with comic and poignant tales told in a rural Irish pub. Important critics and essayists include **Conor Cruise O'Brien,** a former diplomat who writes about most everything—history, literature, culture, politics; **Denis Donoghue** and his vigorous, skeptical *We Irish*; and the provocative **Declan Kiberd,** whose Ireland is a postcolonial society more like India than like England.

A pair of brothers who grew up in Limerick immigrated to New York and caught the next train to best-sellerdom. **Frank McCourt** won the Pulitzer Prize for his 1996 memoir about his poverty-stricken childhood, *Angela's Ashes* (1996), and followed up with the sequel *'Tis* (2000). Not to be outdone, **Malachy** "the brother of Frank" **McCourt** recently published his own memoir, *A Monk Swimming* (1999).

MUSIC

TRADITIONAL FOLK MUSIC AND DANCE

Despite Queen Elizabeth's best efforts to extinguish it, Irish traditional music has kept rollicking through the centuries. "Trad" is the array of dance rhythms, cyclic melodies, and embellishments that has been passed down through countless generations of musicians. These tunes can be written down, but that's not their primary means of transmission. Indeed, a traditional musician's training consists largely of listening to and innovating from the work of others. A typical pub session will sample from a variety of types, including reels, jigs, hornpipes, and slow airs. The same tune will produce a different result each time it's played.

Trad may be heard in two ways: studio-canned and pub-impromptu. Best-selling recording artists include **Altan, De Danann,** and the **Chieftains.** Equally excellent groups include the **Bothy Band** and **Planxty** of the 1970s, and, more recently, **Nomos, Solas, Dervish,** and **Deanta.** These bands have brought Irish music into international prominence, starting with the early recordings of the Chieftains and their mentor **Sean O'Riada,** who fostered the resurrection of trad from near-extinction to a national art form. While recording bands perform regularly at concerts, most traditional musicians are accustomed to playing before smaller, more intimate audiences of locals at a pub. A session takes place when independent musicians gather at the pub to play together; sessions are an excellent way to witness the real, amorphous identity of Irish traditional tunes. *Let's Go* lists many pubs with regular live music, but you'll find the best music by asking local enthusiasts. Pubs in Counties Clare, Kerry, Galway, Sligo, and Donegal have a deservedly good reputation. For the best trad, in quantity and quality, find a **fleadh** (FLAH), a musical festival at which musicians' officially scheduled sessions often spill over into nearby pubs. **Comhaltas Ceoltóirí Éireann,** the national Trad music association, organizes *fleadhs.* (☎01 280 0295; www.comhaltas.com.)

Purists get in heated arguments about what constitutes "traditional" singing. A style of unaccompanied vocals called *sean-nós* ("old-time") is definitely the oldest form on the island. This style of nasal singing descends from keening, an ancient practice of wailing lamentation. It requires the vocalist to sing each verse of a song differently, by peppering the tune with syllabic embellishments and tonal variations. More common than *sean-nós* is folk singing, which refers to guitar- or mandolin-accompanied ballads. Sessions in pubs typically alternate between fast-paced traditional instrumental music and folk songs. Ireland's favorite traditional songsters include **Dominick Behan, The Dubliners, Christy Moore,** and **Sean Tyrell.**

Hard-shoe dancing involves creating a percussion accompaniment by pounding the floor with foot-loose fury. Individual **step-dancing** and group **set-dancing** are centuries-old practices, but the spontaneous and innovative streak in each is fading fast. Today, traditional dancing follows the regimentation of formal competitions, where traditional dancers compete according to rote standards of perfection. *Céilís* (KAY-lees), at which attendants participate in traditional Irish set-dancing, still take place in most towns. The televised, pyrotechnic-accompanied spectacles *Riverdance* and *Lord of the Dance* offer loose interpretations—don't expect any of that Michael Flatley nonsense at the local pub.

IRISH ROCK, PUNK, AND POP

Along with their vastly successful exportation of trad, the Irish have developed a taste for adapting outside forms of music. The first commercially successful artist to cross-pollinate trad and imported forms was **John McCormack** of Athlone, one of the finest tenors of the early 20th century. While he was known internationally for opera, he endeared audiences to the Irish folk songs he included in his recitals. Bridging the gap between traditional folk ballads and contemporary Ireland to great popular acclaim is **Christy Moore,** who has been called the Bob Dylan of Ireland. The ballads and anthems that he made popular now form something of a pub sing-along canon—hardly a late-night session goes by without someone's moving rendition of "Ride On," "City of Chicago," or the lament "Irish Ways and Irish Laws." **Van Morrison's** early inspirations included American soul and blues, which he submerged into Celtic "soul." **Horslips** became hugely popular in the 70s by trying to merge trad and rock forms, but wound up shuffling uneasily between the two. The London-based **Pogues** also felt the desire to fuse rock and trad, to far different effect. In albums such as *Rum, Sodomy, and the Lash,* they whipped out reels and jigs of drunken, punk-damaged revelry, accompanied by poetic descriptions of Irish immigrant sorrows and the horrors of sectarian violence. Another outlet for modern trad is the synthesizer. **Enya** used Irish lyricism and electronics to create a haunting (and popular) sound. More recently, **Afro-Celt Sound System** achieved popular and critical success through their fusion of traditional Celtic and African sounds with manic rhythms of drum 'n bass.

Irish musicians have dabbled in practically every genre of purebred rock. In the 70s, **Thin Lizzy** produced early heavy metal laced with a sensitivity to Irish literary greatness. Dublin nurtured a thriving punk scene in the late 70s and 80s, with names like **Bob Geldoff** (of Live Aid fame) and **Gavin Friday.** The worldwide punk rock explosion spawned brilliance in Belfast, where **Stiff Little Fingers** spat forth three years of excellent anthems. Throughout the North, punk became an outlet for the younger generation trying to escape the conflicts and bigotries of the elder. **Ash** heralded a 90s revival of the Belfast punk aesthetic; their album *1977* reached

LIFE AND TIMES

number one on the UK charts. The presently defunct **My Bloody Valentine** weaved shimmering distortions that landed them in the outskirts of grunge.

Ireland's musicians have also set their sights on mainstream superstardom—embodied in **U2,** Ireland's biggest rock export. From the adrenaline-soaked promise of 1980's *Boy,* the band ascended into the stratosphere, culminating in worldwide fame with *The Joshua Tree* (1987). After a brief turn to funky techno dance tunes (1997's *Pop*), the recent *All That You Can't Leave Behind* (2000) has been heralded as a rock band's triumphant return to its senses. **Sinéad O'Connor** developed her 'rock star with attitude' style in 1980s Ireland, long before she became a phenomenon in 1990s America. The lowercase **cranberries** and the sibling-based **Corrs** cornered the international soft rock market in the early 1990s. The boy-group **Boyzone** has recently conquered the UK charts and the hearts of millions of pre-adolescent girls; similar black magic is practiced on the opposite sex by the girl-group **B*witched**.

POPULAR MEDIA

FILM: THE GREEN SCREEN

The deceivingly luscious green turf that devastated the lives of the native Irish for centuries is finally turning a profit thanks to Ireland's burgeoning movie industry. The island's expanses of green, its picturesque villages, and comparatively low labor costs are a filmmaker's dream. Hollywood discovered Ireland in John Wayne's 1952 film **The Quiet Man,** giving an international audience of millions their first view of the island's beauty, albeit through a stereotypical lens Irish film has long struggled to change. Aside from the garish green of Hollywood technicolor vision, art-filmmakers have also tried to capture Ireland. Robert Flaherty created cinematic Realism in his classic documentary about coastal fishermen, **Man of Aran** (1934). Alfred Hitchcock filmed Sean O'Casey's **Juno and the Paycock** with the Abbey Theatre Players in 1930. American director John Huston, who eventually made Ireland his home, made many films there; his last work, **The Dead** (1987), is the film version of the closing masterpiece from Joyce's *Dubliners.*

In the last ten-odd years, the Irish government has encouraged a truly Irish film industry. An excellent art cinema opened in Temple Bar in Dublin, and an office two blocks away lends its support to budding moviemakers. These recent efforts have resulted in a less idealistic but, most times, equally loving vision of Ireland. **Jim Sheridan** helped kick off the Irish cinematic renaissance with his universally acclaimed adaptation of Christy Brown's autobiography, **My Left Foot** (1991). More recently, Sheridan has worked with actor Daniel Day-Lewis in two films that take a humanitarian approach to the lives of Catholics and Protestants during the Troubles with **In the Name of the Father** (1993) and **The Boxer** (1997). In true Irish fashion, Sheridan's latest film **In America** (2002) is a personal tale of emigration and loss. Based on Roddy Doyle's Barrytown Trilogy, **The Commitments** (1991), **The Snapper** (1993), and **The Van** (1996) follow a family from the depressed North Side of Dublin as its members variously form a soul band, have a kid, and get off the dole by running a chipper. Another Dublin saga, **The General** (1998; see p. 155), by the English director John Boorman, describes the true rise and fall of one of the most notorious criminals in recent Irish history, Martin Cahill. Dublin native **Neil Jordan** has become a much-sought-after director thanks to the success of **The Crying Game** (1992), **Michael Collins** (1996), and **The Butcher Boy** (1998). The Ireland of fairytales is captured with exquisite cinematography in **The Secret of Roan Inish** (1995) and **Into the West** (1993). The darkly comic **I Went Down** (1997) demonstrated the growing overseas popularity of Irish independent film. **An Everlasting Piece** (2000), about wig salesman in Belfast, found international success for its comedic portrayal of the complicated everyday interactions of Protestants and Catholics. In the closing years of the 90s, the appeal of Irish scenery and accents was demonstrated in the profitable production of two highly Irish sounding and looking films by non-Irish filmmakers: Hollywood produced a film version of Donegal playwright Brian Friel's *Dancing at Lughnasa* (1998), the government of the Isle of Man sponsored *Waking Ned Devine* (1998), which describes the antics of a village of rustic eccentrics. The upcoming *Veronica Guerin* (2002) is Joel Schumacher and Disney's version of the assasination of Dublin's daring journalist.

The **Galway Film Fleadh** is Ireland's version of Cannes, appropriately reduced in scale but still featuring a week's worth of quality films. The **Dublin Film Festival** runs for a week in the middle of April. The month-long **Dublin Lesbian and Gay Film Festival** occupies all of August. Dublin also hosts the **Junior Dublin Film Festival** during the last week of November and the first week of December, showing the world's best children's films. In Northern Ireland, the **Foyle Film Festival** takes place in Derry during the last week in April.

NEWSPAPERS AND OTHER MEDIA

The Republic and Northern Ireland together support eight national **dailies** with a combined circulation of around 1.5 million. The largest of these papers in the Republic are the *Irish Times* and the *Irish Independent* [www.ireland.com and www.independent.ie]. The *Times* takes a liberal voice and is renowned worldwide for its coverage of international affairs. The *Independent* is more internally focused and often maintains a chatty writing style. *The Herald* is an evening daily that hovers somewhere in the middle. Neither the *Times* nor the *Independent* comes out with a Sunday paper, but their readership is generally satisfied with an Irish version of *The London Times*. The best-selling paper in the North is the *Belfast Telegraph* (www.belfasttelegraph.co.uk). The sectarian community is represented by two mainstream newspapers: Unionists read the *Belfast Newsletter* (www.nletter.com), while Nationalists turn to the *Irish News* (www.irish-news.com). **Tabloids** like the *Daily Mirror*, the *Irish Sun*, the *Irish Star*, and the *Sporting News* offer low-level coverage with an emphasis on stars, scandals, and sports, and the occasional topless picture. A large number of regional papers offer more in-depth local news; the largest is the *The Cork Examiner*. British papers are sold throughout the Republic and Northern Ireland.

BBC brought radio to the Irish island when it established a station in Belfast in 1924; two years later, the Irish Free State started the radio station 2RN in Dublin. The television began its invasion on Ireland in 1953, when the BBC started TV broadcasts from Belfast. Ulster Television, the island's first independent channel, was established in 1959. In 1961, the Republic's national radio service made its first television broadcast, renaming itself **Radio Telefís Éireann (RTE)**. Most of the island now has cable service with access to the BBC and other independent British channels. The Irish government's most recent developments include the start of Irish language radio and TV stations, called Telifis na Gaelige (see **The Irish Language**, p. 73). These efforts aim at combating the contribution of modern media forms to the deterioration of the Irish language.

Computers, with their viruses and email spam, have infected Ireland. Most major international hardware manufacturers have factories in Ireland, and local companies make personalized computers (some, such as **Celtic®computer,** are even proud of their heritage). Software is a huge industry—Ireland is one of the world's largest exporters of the stuff. While email has yet to overrun college campuses, web-ready cafes and hostels are fairly easy to find. The tourism industry is also becoming savvy in Internet commerce; many towns and accommodations now have their own websites and email accounts.

SPORTS & RECREATION

The Irish take enormous pride in their two native sports: **hurling** and **Gaelic football**. For many Irish, these games are the reason that spring changes into summer. Regional divisions are most obvious in county allegiances. Take notice of the hysteria of any Irish sporting event, when hordes of fans bedecked in their county colors bring bedlam to Irish city streets. Attending a pub the day of that county's game will leave you happy, deaf, drunk, and counting down to the next round.

Most traditional Irish sports are modern developments of contests fought between whole clans or parishes across expanses of countryside. In 1884, the **Gaelic Athletic Association (GAA)** was founded to establish official rules and regulations for hurling, Gaelic football, and other ancient Irish recreations. A secondary function of their efforts was to promote a non-British identity on the island. The organization's first patron was Archbishop Croke of Cashel and Emly; his name later came to adorn Croke Park in Dublin, Ireland's biggest Gaelic-games stadium. The GAA divided the island on a club-county-province level, in which the club teams are organized mostly according to parish lines. Arranged according to the four provinces Connacht, Munster, Leinster, and Ulster, all 32 counties of the island compete in the knockout rounds of the two sports' "All Ireland" Championships, but only two make it to the finals in September. Despite the fervent nationalism of its beginnings, the GAA has always included the Northern Ireland teams in these leagues. Sectarian politics plague today's GAA, but that doesn't stop them from running an amazingly comprehensive website (www.gaa.ie).

RULES OF THE GAME

According to the GAA, "played well, **Gaelic football** is a fast, skillful game striking to the eye. Played badly, it is an unimpressive spectacle of dragging and pulling!" Although it may seem like the love-child of American football and British rugby, Gaelic football is older than both. The ball is shorter and fatter than a rugby ball. Players may run holding the ball for no more than four paces, after which they must bounce, kick, or punch it in any direction. At each end of the field is a set of goalposts, and below the crossbar there is a net resembling a soccer net. One point is scored for putting the goal over the crossbar between the posts, three for netting it. The game is played by both men and women in teams of 15 for two 30-minute periods. Charging is within the rules, and often encouraged.

MUSCLE OVER DISTANCE

As fans like to say, if football is a game, then **hurling** is an art. This fast and dangerous-looking sport was first played in the 13th century. Perhaps best imagined as a blend of lacrosse and field hockey, the game is named after the stick with which it is played, the *caman* or "hurley." The hurley—like a hockey stick with a shorter and wider blade—is used to hit the ball along the ground or overhead. Players may also kick the ball, or hit it with the flat of their hands. The *sliothar* (ball) is leather-covered and can be caught for hitting, or carried along on the stick. Teams of 15 players each try to score a point by hitting the ball over the eight-foot-high crossbar of the goalposts. A "goal" is worth three points and is scored by hitting the ball under the crossbar. The female version of hurling is called **camogie,** which permits only 12 team members and considerably more protective-wear.

AND THEN THERE'S...

Road bowling. In County Antrim the wacky sport of road bowling is enjoying a bit of a revival. Imagine a game of golf. Make the fairway a nice winding stretch of Irish asphalt, about 2½ mi. long, lined with screaming fans. Replace that cute little white dimpled ball with 28 oz. of solid iron. Now you've got something like road bowling.

Oh—and clubs are for wimps. Just wind up and fling that sucker. (Check for cars first.) The sport, which probably arrived on William of Orange's glorious ships back in 1688, enjoys its most enthusiastic following in the North but can also be found on the twisty roads down in County Cork.

FOOTBALL AND OTHERS

Imported to Ireland in 1878, **football** (or soccer, to Americans) enjoys an equally fanatical, if less patriotic, following as hurling and Gaelic football. The Irish came close to realizing their dreams of international stardom in this sport when they reached the quarterfinals of the 1994 World Cup and tied Germany in the 2002 games. The Irish are also fiercely devoted to the football clubs of England, with Liverpool and Manchester United as the local favorites. **Rugby** achieves a strong fan base in both the Republic and Northern Ireland; when Ireland's not playing, expect people to cheer for the English team. **Horse racing** maintains a devoted following in the Republic, thanks to Co. Kildare's well-appreciated place as a breeding ground for champion racehorses. Water sports like **surfing** and **sailing** are popular hobbies, particularly along the Western and Northwestern coasts. And world-renowned **golf** links are available in towns across the country.

2004 HOLIDAYS AND FESTIVALS

For more information, contact the appropriate regional tourist office, or the national tourist boards for the Republic and Northern Ireland. Starred dates are national holidays—expect businesses to be closed or operating on Sunday hours.

DATE	CITY OR REGION	FESTIVAL
WINTER		
*December 25	Republic and UK	Christmas Day
*December 26	Republic and UK	St. Stephen's Day/Boxing Day
*December 27	Republic and UK	Bank Holiday
January 1	Republic and UK	New Year's Day
Mid-February	Dungarvan	Dungarvan Jazz Festival
*March 17	Republic and Northern Ireland	St. Patrick's Day
SPRING		
*April 9	Republic and UK	Good Friday
*April 12	Republic and UK	Easter Monday
March-April	Dublin	Dublin Film Festival
Late April	Galway	Cúirt International Literary Festival
May	Wicklow	Wicklow Mountains Spring Walking Festival
*May 3	Republic and UK	May Day, bank holiday
Mid-May	Bantry	Bantry Regatta
*May 31	United Kingdom	Bank holiday
Late May	Republic of Ireland	Fleadh Cheoil na hÉireann
*June 3	Republic of Ireland	Bank holiday
*June 3-4	United Kingdom	Jubilee Celebration
Early June	Kinsale	Kinsale Blues Festival
June 9-17	Dublin	Yeats' Bloomsday Festivities
SUMMER		
Late June	The Curragh, Co. Kildare	Irish Derby
Mid-Late June	Cork	Cork Midsummer Festival
Mid-Late June	Dublin	Dublin Gay Pride Festival
Late June-Early July	Kells	Kells Heritage Festival

Early July	Bangor	Bangor Regatta
Early July	Bray	Bray Seaside Festival
Early July	Glencolmcille	Folk Festival
Early July	Mullingar	International Bachelor Festival
*July 12	Northern Ireland	Orange Day
Early to Mid-July	Galway	Galway Film Fleadh
Mid-July	Galway	Galway Arts Festival
Mid-July	Drogheda	Samba Festival
Mid-July	Killarney	Killarney Races
Mid-July	Ballina	Ballina Street Festival
Mid-July	Tipperary	Pride of Tipperary
Late July	Belfast	Belfast Gay Pride Festival
Late July	Buncrana, Co. Donegal	Buncrana Music Festival
Late July	Galway	Galway Races
Late July–Early August	Dungloe	Mary from Dungloe International Festival
Late July–Early August	Wicklow	Regatta Festival
*August 5	Republic of Ireland	Bank holiday
Early August	Waterford	Spraoi and Rhythm Fest
Early August	Kinsale	Regatta and Welcome Home Festival
Early August	Glencolmcille	Fiddle Week
Early August	Dingle	Dingle Races
Early to Mid-August	Kilkenny	Arts Week
Mid-August	Armagh	All-Ireland Road Bowls Finals
Mid-August	Warrenpoint	Maiden of the Mournes Festival
Mid-August	Cobh	Cobh People's Regatta
Mid-August	Cushendall	Heart of the Glens Festival
August 15	Clifden	Connemara Pony Show
August 21	Knock	Feast of Our Lady of Knock
Late August	Tralee	Rose of Tralee International Festival
Late August	Derry	Feile An Chreagain
Late August	Cape Clear Island	International Storytelling Festival
*August 30	United Kingdom	Bank holiday
September	Monaghan	Jazz and Blues Festival
September	Dublin	All-Ireland Hurling and Football Finals
September	Cork	Folk Festival
September	Lisdoonvarna	Lisdoonvarna Matchmaking Festival
AUTUMN		
Late September	Westport	Arts Festival
Late September	Clifden	Community Arts Festival
October	Ennis	October Arts Festival
October	Dublin	Dublin Fringe Festival
October	Armagh	Arts Festival
Early October	Glenties	Fiddlers' Weekend
Early to Mid-October	Cork	Murphy's Film Festival
Mid-October	Kinsale	Kinsale Gourmet Festival
October 26	Dublin	Samhain Halloween Parade
*October 28	Republic of Ireland	Bank holiday
Late October	Cork	Guinness Jazz Festival

Late October-November	Belfast	Belfast Festival at Queen's
November	Ennis	November Trad Festival

ADDITIONAL RESOURCES

GENERAL HISTORY

A History of Ireland, by Mike Cronin. St. Martin's Press, 2001.

Ancestral Voices: Religion and Nationalism in Ireland, by Conor Cruise O'Brien. University of Chicago Press, 1995.

Hope Against History: The Course of Conflict in Northern Ireland, by Jack Holland. Henry Holt, 1999.

Reinventing Ireland: Culture and the Celtic Tiger, by Cronin, Kirby, and Gibbons. Pluto Press, 2002.

The IRA, by Tim Pat Coogan. St. Martin's Press, 2001.

The Irish Famine, by Gray and Burns. Abrams, Harry N Inc., 1995.

The Keeper's Recital: Music and Cultural History in Ireland, 1770-1970, by Harry White. University of Notre Dame Press, 1998.

FICTION AND NON-FICTION

How the Irish Saved Civilization: The Untold Story of Ireland's Heroic Role from the Fall of Rome to the Rise of Medieval Europe, by Thomas Cahill. Doubleday, 1995.

Killing Rage, by Eamon Collins. Granta Books, 1999.

My Celtic Soul: Our Year in the West of Ireland, by Patricia O'Brien. iUniverse, 2000.

Round Ireland With a Fridge, by Tony Hawks. St. Martin's Press, 2000.

The Truth About the Irish, by Terry Eagleton. St. Martin's Press, 2001.

FILM

For Irish films, search the websites www.filmboard.ie and www.irishfilm.net.

Contemporary Irish Cinema: From the Quiet Man to Dancing at Lughnasa, James MacKillop. Syracuse University Press, 1999

Irish Film: The Emergence of a Contemporary Cinema, by Martin McLoone. University of California Press, 2001.

On Location: The Film Fan's Guide to Britain and Ireland, by Brian Pendreigh. Mainstream, 1996.

Screening Ireland: Film and Television Representation, Lance Pettitt. Manchester University Press, 2000.

TRAVEL BOOKS

Bed and Breakfast Ireland: A Trusted Guide to Over 400 of Ireland's Best Bed and Breakfasts, by Dillard and Causin. Chronicle Books, 2002.

Daytrips Ireland: 55 One-Day Adventures by Car, Rail, or Bus, by Patricia Tunison Preston. Hastings House Daytrips, 2000.

Frommer's Ireland's Best-Loved Driving Tours, by Poole and Gallagher. Wiley, 2000.

Most Beautiful Villages of Ireland, by Fitz-Simon and Palmer. Thames & Hudson, 2000.

COUNTY DUBLIN

Dublin and its suburbs form a single economic and commercial unit, linked by a web of mass transit: the electric DART, suburban rail, and Dublin buses. The city teems with weekending suburbanites, tourists, and international hipsters on the prowl; despite the homogenizing effects of a booming economy and sprawling development, the suburbs offer a less polluted alternative (though the mobs they attract preclude any notions of romantic Irish villages). While the county overflows with beautiful beaches, literary landmarks, castles, and monastic ruins, the chief impression of most visitors is that this jet-setting metropolis has long forgotten the relaxed, agricultural lifestyle found in the rest of the island.

⌷ TRANSPORTATION

Rail lines, bus routes, and the national highway system radiate from the capital; transport between the country's major cities is so Dublin-centric that visitors often find it more convenient to arrange travel to other parts of Ireland while in the city. Students may wish to get **TravelSave** stamps for bus and rail discounts (see **Practical Information,** p. 93). For more information on transportation, see **Essentials,** p. 30.

BY BUS

Lime-green **Dublin Buses** (☎873 4222; www.dublinbus.ie) service the entire county. The buses, which come in a variety of shapes and sizes—all sporting "db" logos—run 6am-11:30pm and cover the city and its suburbs quite comprehensively: north to **Howth, Donabate,** and **Malahide;** west to **Rathcoole, Maynooth,** and **Celbridge;** and south to **Blessington, Enniskerry, Dún Laoghaire,** and **Bray.** Buses are cheap (€0.80-3; prices rise according to distance), and most frequent between 8am and 6pm (generally every 8-20min., off-peak hours every 30-45min.).

Most bus routes terminate in the city center, at stops located near Christ Church, the Trinity College facade, St. Stephen's Green, O'Connell St., and Parnell St. Bus stands along the quays post timetables detailing routes around the city center. The most important pamphlet for the bustling traveler is the free *Main Guide to Dublin Bus Services.* Along with the *Map of Greater Dublin* and the Dublin Bus Timetable, this handy guide includes a map of all the Dublin Bus routes and details every variety of special ticket and student discount available. All are available from newsagents and the **Dublin Bus Office** at 59 Upper O'Connell St. (Open M 8:30am-5:30pm, Tu-F 9am-5:30pm, Sa 9am-1pm.) Also see **Transportation,** p. 86.

The Dublin buses run fairly regularly within the city, especially the smaller **City Imp** buses (every 8-15min.). Suburban routes often have 1hr. between scheduled stops. Dublin Bus runs the **NiteLink** service to the suburbs. (M-W 12:30am and 2am, Th-Sa every 20min. 12:30-4:30am. €4; Celbridge/Maynooth €6. No passes valid.) Tickets for the NiteLink are sold at the Dublin Bus Office, by Nitelink bus drivers, and from "ticket buses" on the corner of Westmoreland and Fleet St. or on D'Olier St. next to Trinity College. NiteLink leaves for the northern suburbs from D'Olier St., the southern suburbs from College St., and the western suburbs from Westmoreland. The **Airlink** service (#747 and 748; €5) connects **Dublin Airport** to the Central Bus Station (Busaras) and Heuston Station, stopping on O'Connell St. and the quays along the way.

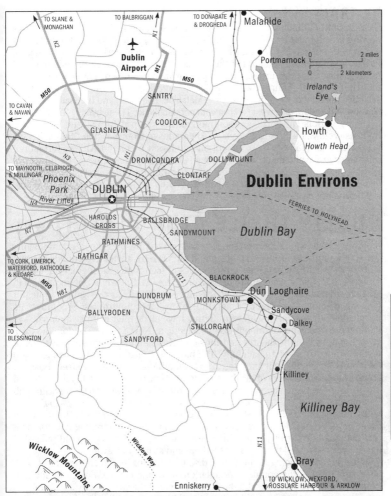

(Every 10-15min. 5:45am-11pm.) **Wheelchair-accessible buses** are ever more prevalent, with 35% of Dublin Buses now accessible. Check with the Bus Office or online (www.dublinbus.ie) for fully accessible routes.

Travel passes, called "Ramblers," are designed for people planning to travel a *lot;* each pass has a time limit that requires several trips a day to be worthwhile. **Rambler** and **Travel Wide** passes offer unlimited rides (1 day €5, 1 wk. €17.50; students €14.50). A **TravelSave** stamp purchased at a **usit** office saves a few euros (see **Practical Information,** p. 93). Other tickets allow for both bus and suburban rail/DART travel (1-day **short hop** €7.70, weekly €26, monthly €98, students €69). Be warned that a Dublin Bus week runs from Sunday to Saturday inclusive, no matter when the pass is purchased, so a weekly pass bought Friday expires the next day. Dublin Bus months, similarly, are calendar months. Discount tickets are available at the bus office and from city newsagents; ISIC cards are required for student rates.

BY TRAIN

Electric **DART** (Dublin Area Rapid Transit) trains run up and down the coast, connecting the city and its suburbs. The DART puts buses to shame in terms of cost and speed, but reaches a more limited number of destinations. From **Connolly, Pearse,** and **Tara Street Stations** in the city center, trains shoot south past **Bray** and north to **Howth.** Tickets are sold in the station and must be presented at the end of the trip (every 10-15min. 6:30am-11:30pm, €0.75-1.70). The orange trains of the **suburban rail** network continue north to **Malahide, Donabate,** and **Drogheda;** south to **Wicklow** and **Arklow;** and west to **Maynooth** and **Mullingar.** These trains all leave from Connolly Station. The north- and south-bound lines stop at Tara St. and Pearse Stations as well. Suburban rail trains to **Kildare** leave from **Heuston Station.** Trains leave frequently (30 per day), except on Sundays. Complete DART/suburban rail timetables are available at many stations (€0.65). **Bicycles** are never permitted on DART trains, sometimes allowed on suburban rail lines (ask first), and generally loaded onto mainline trains for a small fee (€7.60 one way). Special rail and bus/rail tickets are cost-effective only for travelers addicted to mass transit.

DUBLIN (BAILE ÁTHA CLIATH) ☎01

In a country known for its rural sanctity and relaxed lifestyle, the international flavor and boundless energy of Dublin stand out. The Irish who live outside the city worry that it has acquired the characteristics of metropoli elsewhere: crime, rapid social change, and susceptibility to short-lived trends. But while Dublin may seem gritty by Irish standards, it's still as friendly a major city as they come: though it may not resemble the rustic "Emerald Isle" promoted on tourist brochures, its people embody the charm and warmth that have made their country famous.

Not quite as cosmopolitan but just as eclectic as New York or London, the capital is home to vibrant theater and music enclaves, and multiple generations of pubs learning to coexist peacefully. The blend of cultures in Dublin has fostered extraordinary intellectual and literary communities—nearly every street boasts a literary landmark. The local drinking-holes continue to house much public life and a world-renowned music scene. Presently, the formerly wonderful nightlife hub Temple Bar has been discovered by hordes of tourists, but good new pubs and clubs are popping up farther south, along Great Georges St. towards Harcourt and Camden St. Smithfields, west across the River Liffey, is undergoing development that may make it the city's next big cultural center. And, the good old pubs that have always speckled the city are still there and as lively as ever.

With Ireland changing at an almost disconcerting pace, the city environs, with close to a third of the country's population, leads the charge. Fueled by international and rural emigration, and the deep pockets of the EU, the city's cultural and economic growth has been all but unstoppable. With modernity comes a price: traffic is thick, and although it seems that nearly everyone has a cell phone growing out of his ear, few young Dubliners can afford to buy a house in their own city.

✈ INTERCITY TRANSPORTATION

For more on national and international transportation, see **Essentials,** p. 30.

Airport: Dublin Airport (☎814 1111; www.aer-rianta.ie). **Dublin buses** #41, 41B, and 41C run from the airport to Eden Quay in the city center (40-45min., every 20min., €1.60). **Airlink shuttle** runs non-stop to Busáras Central Bus Station and O'Connell St. (☎844 4265; 20-25min., every 10min. 5:15am-11:30pm, €5), and to Heuston Station (50min., €4.50). **Taxis** to the city center cost €15-20. Wheelchair-accessible cabs available by calling ahead; see **Local Transportation,** p. 92.

Trains: Irish Rail Travel Centre, Iarnród Éireann (EER-ann-road AIR-ann), 35 Lower Abbey St. (☎836 6222; www.irishrail.ie; Open M-Sa 9am-6pm, Su 10am-6pm). Or book by credit card over the phone (☎703 4070.) Info desks and booking windows at Dublin's 3 major stations may have long lines. Purchase a ticket in advance at the Travel Centre, or at the station 20min. before departure. The Travel Centre has info on DART, suburban rail, international train tickets, and cross-channel ferries. Timetables for trains to: **Belfast** (☎805 4277); **Cork** (☎805 4200); **Galway** (☎805 4222); **Westport** (☎805 4244); **Killarney/Tralee** (☎805 4266); **Limerick** (☎805 4211); **Sligo** (☎805 4255); **Waterford** (☎805 4233); **Wexford/Rosslare** (☎805 4288). Bus #90 circuits Connolly, Heuston, and Pearse Stations, as well as Busáras. Connolly and Pearse are also **DART** stations serving the north and south coasts (see **Transportation, p. 84**).

Connolly Station, Amiens St. (☎703 2358 or 703 2359), north of the Liffey, close to Busáras. Buses #20, 20A, and 90 head south of the river, and the DART runs to Tara Station on the south quay. Ticketing open M-Su 7am-11pm. Trains to: **Belfast** (2hr., M-Sa 8 per day, Su 5 per day; €27); **Sligo** (3hr., 3-4 per day, €19); **Wexford** and **Rosslare** (3hr., 3 per day, €16.50).

Heuston Station (☎703 2132, night ☎703 2131), south of Victoria Quay and west of the city center, a 25min. walk from Trinity College. Buses #26, 51, 90, and 79 run from Heuston to the city center. Ticketing open daily 6:30am-10:30pm. Trains to: **Cork** (3hr., M-Th and Sa 8 per day, F 11 per day, Su 6 per day; €43); **Galway** (2½hr., 4-5 per day; €21, F and Su €28); **Kilkenny** (2hr.; M-Th and Sa 5 per day, F 1 per day, Su 4 per day; €15.80); **Limerick** (2½hr., 9 per day, €34); **Tralee** (4hr., 4-5 per day, €44); **Waterford** (2½hr., 3-4 per day, €16.50).

Pearse Station (☎703 3634), just east of Trinity College on Pearse St. and Westland Row. Ticketing open M-Sa 7:30am-10pm, Su 9am-10pm. Receives southbound trains from Connolly Station.

Buses: Intercity buses to Dublin arrive at **Busáras Central Bus Station,** Store St. (☎836 6111), directly behind the Customs House and next to Connolly Station. Info available at **Dublin Bus Office,** 59 O'Connell St. (☎872 0000; www.dublinbus.ie). The **Bus Éireann** (www.buseireann.ie) window is open M-F 9am-5pm and Sa 10:30am-2pm. Buses to: **Belfast** (3hr., 6-7 per day, €18); **Cork** (4½hr., 6 per day, €20); **Derry** (4¼hr., 5-6 per day, €17.50); **Donegal** (4¼hr., 5-6 per day, €14.50); **Galway** (3½hr., 13 per day, €13); **Kilkenny** (2hr., 6 per day, €10); **Killarney** (6hr., 5 per day, €20); **Limerick** (3½hr.; M-Sa 13 per day, Su 7 per day; €14.50); **Rosslare** (3hr.; M-Sa 10 per day, Su 7 per day; €14); **Shannon Airport** (4½hr., 13 per day, €14.50); **Sligo** (4hr., 4-5 per day, €14); **Tralee** (6hr., 6 per day, €20); **Waterford** (3hr., 10 per day, €10); **Westport** (5hr., 2-3 per day, €15); **Wexford** (2¾hr.; M-Sa 10 per day, Su 7 per day; €10). **PAMBO** (Private Association of Motor Bus Owners), 32 Lower Abbey St. (☎878 8422), provides names and numbers of private operators presently in service. Open M-F 10am-5pm. For more info on all manner of buses, see **By Bus, p. 84**.

Ferries: Bookings online (www.dublinport.ie/Ferries.html), in the Irish Rail office (see **Trains,** p. 86), or over the phone (☎855 0888.) **Irish Ferries** has an office off St. Stephen's Green at 2-4 Merrion Row. (☎638 3333 or 1890 313 131; www.irishferries.com. Open M-F 9am-5pm, Sa 9:15am-12:45pm.) **Stena Line** ferries arrive from Holyhead at the **Dún Laoghaire** ferry terminal (☎204 7777; www.stenaline.com); from there the **DART** shuttles passengers into central Dublin (€1.80). **Buses** #7, 7A, and 8 go from Georges St. in Dún Laoghaire to Eden Quay (€1), but the DART is easier. Irish Ferries arrive from Holyhead at the **Dublin Port** (☎607 5665). From here, buses #53 and 53A run to Busáras in the city (€1; 1 per hr.); **Dublin Bus** also runs buses tailored to ferry schedules (€2.50-3.20). **Norse Merchant Ferries** (☎855 0888) docks at Dublin port and goes to **Liverpool** (7½hr., 1-2 per day; €25-40, with car €105-170); booking available only from **Gerry Feeney,** 19 Eden Quay (☎819 2999). **Isle of Man Steam Packet Company** (UK ☎1800 551 743) docks at Dublin Port and sends 1 boat per day to the small isle; rates depend on dates and term of stay (from about €50).

COUNTY DUBLIN

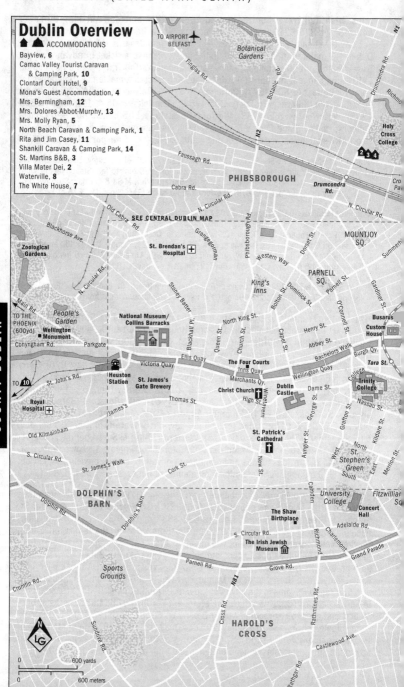

Dublin Overview

▲ ▲ ACCOMMODATIONS

Bayview, **6**
Camac Valley Tourist Caravan
  & Camping Park, **10**
Clontarf Court Hotel, **9**
Mona's Guest Accommodation, **4**
Mrs. Bermingham, **12**
Mrs. Dolores Abbot-Murphy, **13**
Mrs. Molly Ryan, **5**
North Beach Caravan & Camping Park, **1**
Rita and Jim Casey, **11**
Shankill Caravan & Camping Park, **14**
St. Martins B&B, **3**
Villa Mater Dei, **2**
Waterville, **8**
The White House, **7**

COUNTY DUBLIN

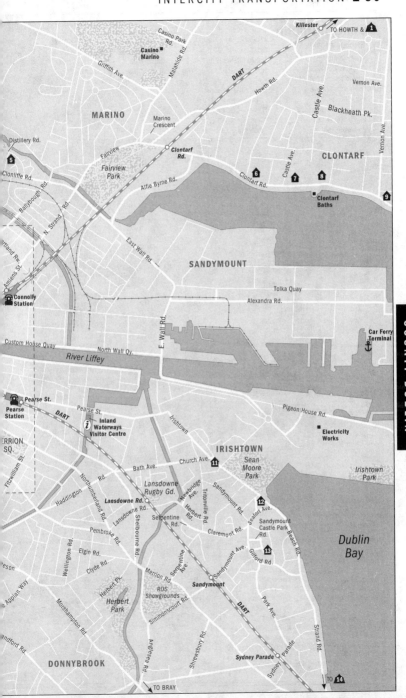

COUNTY DUBLIN

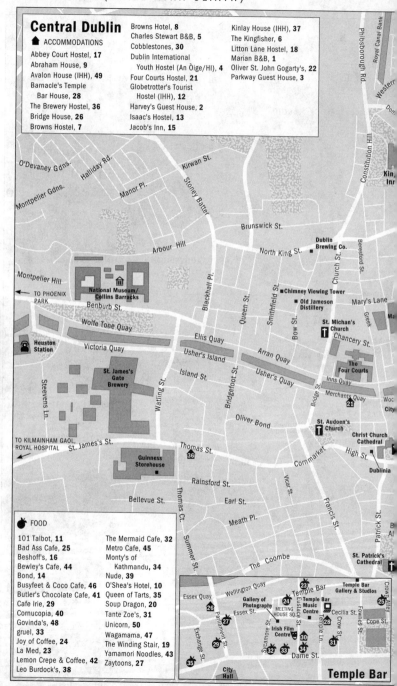

Central Dublin

🏠 **ACCOMMODATIONS**

Abbey Court Hostel, **17**
Abraham House, **9**
Avalon House (IHH), **49**
Barnacle's Temple
  Bar House, **28**
The Brewery Hostel, **36**
Bridge House, **26**
Browns Hostel, **7**

Browns Hotel, **8**
Charles Stewart B&B, **5**
Cobblestones, **30**
Dublin International
  Youth Hostel (An Óige/HI), **4**
Four Courts Hostel, **21**
Globetrotter's Tourist
  Hostel (IHH), **12**
Harvey's Guest House, **2**
Isaac's Hostel, **13**
Jacob's Inn, **15**

Kinlay House (IHH), **37**
The Kingfisher, **6**
Litton Lane Hostel, **18**
Marian B&B, **1**
Oliver St. John Gogarty's, **22**
Parkway Guest House, **3**

🍎 **FOOD**

101 Talbot, **11**
Bad Ass Cafe, **25**
Beshoff's, **16**
Bewley's Cafe, **44**
Bond, **14**
Busyfeet & Coco Cafe, **46**
Butler's Chocolate Cafe, **41**
Cafe Irie, **29**
Cornucopia, **40**
Govinda's, **48**
gruel, **33**
Joy of Coffee, **24**
La Med, **23**
Lemon Crepe & Coffee, **42**
Leo Burdock's, **38**

The Mermaid Cafe, **32**
Metro Cafe, **45**
Monty's of
  Kathmandu, **34**
Nude, **39**
O'Shea's Hotel, **10**
Queen of Tarts, **35**
Soup Dragon, **20**
Tante Zoe's, **31**
Unicorn, **50**
Wagamama, **47**
The Winding Stair, **19**
Yamamori Noodles, **43**
Zaytoons, **27**

Temple Bar

✈ ORIENTATION

In general, Dublin is refreshingly compact, though navigation is complicated by the ridiculous number of names a street adopts along its way; street names are usually posted on the side of buildings at most intersections and never on street-level signs. Buying a map with a street index is a smart idea. Collins publishes the invaluable *Handy Map of Dublin* (€6.50), available at the tourist office and most book stores. Less compact, but more detailed, the *Ordnance Survey Dublin Street Map* (€6) also has a hefty street index booklet. The most compact is *The Dublin Popout* (€4), which fits easily in a pocket and has excellent detail.

The **River Liffey** forms a natural boundary between Dublin's North and South Sides. The preponderance of famous sights, fancy stores, and fabulous restaurants are on the **South Side.** The **North Side** claims most of the hostels, the bus station, and Connolly Station. The streets running alongside the Liffey are called **quays** (KEYS); the name of the street changes each block as it reaches a new quay. A helpful Dubliner is more likely to direct by quays, not by street name or address. If a street is split into "Upper" and "Lower," then the "Lower" is the part of the street closer to the Liffey. The core of Dublin is ringed by **North** and **South Circular Roads,** which enjoy their own assortment of name changes. Most of the city's major sights are located within this area; the walk from one end to the other should take about 40min. **O'Connell Street,** three blocks west of Busáras Central Bus Station, is the primary link between north and south Dublin.

South of the Liffey, O'Connell St. becomes **Westmoreland Street,** passes **Fleet Street** on the right, curves around Trinity College on the left, and then becomes **Grafton Street.** One block south of the Liffey, Fleet Street becomes **Temple Bar.** While Temple Bar is the name of a street, it usually applies to the area bordered by the Liffey, Dame St., Westmoreland St., and Parliament St. as a whole, which is invaded nightly by battalions of pub-seeking students and tourists. By day, Temple's array of funky restaurants, art museums, and workshops attract slightly better-heeled crowds. **Dame Street,** which runs parallel to Temple Bar and terminates at Trinity College, defines the southern edge of the district. **Trinity College** is the nerve center of Dublin's cultural activity, drawing many bookshops and student-oriented pubs into its orbit. The college touches the northern end of **Grafton Street,** where street entertainers brush elbows with world-class shoppers. Grafton's southern end opens onto **St. Stephen's Green,** a sizable and famous public park.

Merchants on the North Side hawk merchandise for cheaper prices than those in the more touristed South. **Henry Street** and **Mary Street** comprise a pedestrian shopping zone that intersects with O'Connell just after the **General Post Office (GPO),** two blocks from the Liffey. The North Side has the reputation of being a rougher area, especially after dark. This reputation may not be wholly deserved, but tourists should avoid walking in unfamiliar areas on either side of the Liffey at night, especially when alone. It is wise to steer clear of Phoenix Park after dark.

▐ LOCAL TRANSPORTATION

Dublin Bus, 59 O'Connell St. (☎873 4222; www.dublinbus.ie). Open M 8:30am-5:30pm, Tu-F 9am-5:30pm, Sa 9am-1pm. (See **By Bus,** p. 84.)

Taxis: Blue Cabs (☎676 1111), **ABC** (☎285 5444), and **City Group Taxi** (☎872 7272) have wheelchair-accessible cabs (call in advance). Another option is **National Radio Cabs,** 40 James St. (☎677 2222). All available 24hr. €2.75 plus €1.35 per mi. before 10pm, €1.80 after; €1.50 call-in charge. Taxi stands outside Trinity College, behind the Bank of Ireland, on Lower Abbey St. at the bus station (Busáras), and on Parnell St.

Car Rental: Alamo, Dublin Airport (☎844 4162). Economy €75-89 per day, €220-250 per wk. Ages 25-74. **Argus,** 59 Terenure Rd. East (☎490 4444; www.argus-rental-car.com), also in the tourist office on Suffolk St., and the airport. Economy €50 per day, €220 per wk. Ages 25-70. **Budget,** 151 Lower Drumcondra Rd. (☎837 9611; www.budget.ie), and at the airport. Economy €33-40 per day, €165-200 per wk. Ages 23-75. Be warned that Dublin traffic is heavy, and parking spaces are scarce.

Bike Rental: Raleigh Rent-A-Bike, Kylemore Rd. (☎626 1333). Arranges 1-way rentals: pickup in Dublin and drop-off in another city. €19 surcharge. **Cycle Ways,** 185-6 Parnell St. (☎873 4748). Rents quality bikes, but no helmets. €20 per day, €200 per wk. Deposit €80. Open M-W and F-Sa 10am-6pm, Th 10am-8pm. (See **By Bicycle,** p. 39.)

Bike Repair and Storage: Square Wheel Cycleworks, Temple Ln. South (☎679 0838), off Dame St. Expert repair and excellent advice on bike touring. Storage available. Open M-F 8:30am-6:30pm. **Cycle Ways** does same-day repairs. (See **Bike Rental,** above.)

Hitchhiking: Since Dublin is well served by bus and rail, there is no good reason to thumb it. Still, those who choose to hitch from Dublin usually take buses to the outskirts where the motorways begin. Buses #25, 25A, 66, 66A, 67, and 67A from Wellington Quay go to Lucan Rd., which turns into N4 (to Galway and the West). For a ride to Cork, Limerick, and Waterford (N7), hitchers usually take bus #51, 51B, 68, or 69 from Fleet St. to Aston Quay to Naas ("nace") Rd. N11 (to Wicklow, Wexford, and Rosslare) can be reached by bus #84 from Eden Quay, or #46A from Fleet St. toward Stillorgan Rd. Bus #38 from George Quay or #39 from Burgh Quay to Navan Rd. goes to N3 (to Donegal and Sligo). Buses #33, 41, and 41A from Eden Quay toward Swords send hitchers on their way to N1 (Belfast and Dundalk). *Let's Go* does not recommend hitchhiking.

⁊ PRACTICAL INFORMATION

TOURIST AND FINANCIAL SERVICES

Tourist Information: Main Office, Suffolk St. (☎1850 230 330 or 605 7700; UK ☎0171 493 3201; international ☎669 792 083; www.visitdublin.com). From Connolly Station, walk left down Amiens St., take a right onto Lower Abbey St., pass Busáras, and continue until O'Connell St. Turn left, cross the bridge, and walk past Trinity College; the office is on the right, down Suffolk St., in a converted church. Books accommodations for €4, contracting with **Gulliver Ireland** travel agency for credit card bookings by phone (☎800 6686 6866). **American Express** branch office provides **currency exchange,** money transfers, Traveler's Cheques, and member services. (☎605 7709. Open M-Sa 9am-5pm.) **Bus Éireann** has representatives to provide info and tickets. **Argus Rent a Car** has a desk here. (☎605 7701 or 490 4444. Open M-F 9am-5pm, Sa 9am-1pm.) A list of car rental agencies and other goodies are available at **Bord Fáilte,** which also books tours, concerts, plays, and most anything else in Dublin that requires a ticket (through **TicketMaster**); booking fee €2. Main Office open M-Sa 9am-5:30pm, July-Aug. also Su 10:30am-3pm. Reservation desks close 30min. early.

Branch Offices: Dublin Airport. Open daily 8am-10pm. **Dún Laoghaire Harbour,** Ferry Terminal Building. Open M-Sa 10am-1pm and 2-6pm. **Tallaght,** the Square. Open M-Sa 9:30am-noon and 12:30-5pm. **Baggot St.** Open M-F 9:30am-5pm. **13 Upper O'Connell St.** Open M-Sa 9am-5pm. The latter 4 branches are well stocked and less crowded than the airport and main branches. All telephone inquiries handled by the central office (☎1850 230 330).

Northern Ireland Tourist Board: 16 Nassau St. (☎679 1977 or 1850 230 230). Books accommodations up North. Open M-F 9:15am-5:30pm, Sa 10am-5pm.

Community and Youth Information Centre: Sackville Pl. (☎878 6844), at Marlborough St., east of O'Connell St. Library of resources on youth and special-needs groups, careers, outings, travel, hostels (no bookings), sports, counseling, and referrals. Comprehensive **work opportunities** listing board and **free Internet** (call ahead). Open M-W 9:30am-1pm and 2-6pm, Th-Sa 9:30am-1pm and 2-5pm.

Budget Travel: usit NOW, 19-21 Aston Quay (☎602 1777), near O'Connell Bridge. The place for Irish travel discounts. ISIC, HI, and EYC cards; **TravelSave** stamps €10 (see **Student Travel Agencies,** p. 31). Photo booths €6. Big discounts, especially for ISIC cardholders and people under 26. **Internet** with ISIC card €1 per 15min., €2.50 per 45min. Open M-W and F 9:30am-6:30pm, Th 9:30am-8pm, Sa 9:30am-5pm. **Dust Travel** (☎677 5076), located on the Trinity College campus, also specializes in student travel. Turn left inside the main gate. Open M-F 9am-5:15pm.

Hosteling Organization: An Óige Head Office (Irish Youth Hostel Association/HI), 61 Mountjoy St. (☎830 4555; www.irelandyha.org), at Wellington St. Follow O'Connell St. north, ignoring its name changes. Mountjoy St. is on the left, 20min. from O'Connell Bridge. Book/pay for HI hostels here. Also sells bike and rail package tours. The *An Óige Handbook* lists all HI hostels in Ireland and Northern Ireland. Hugely beneficial membership card €15, under 18 €7.50. Open M-F 9:30am-5:30pm. (Also see **Hostels,** p. 22.)

Embassies: For an extensive list of embassies and consulates, see **Essentials,** p. 8.

Banks: Bank of Ireland, AIB, and **TSB** branches with **bureaux de change** and **24hr. ATMs** cluster on Lower O'Connell St., Grafton St., and in the Suffolk and Dame St. areas. Most banks are open M-W and F 10am-4pm, Th 10am-5pm. Bureaux de change also found in the General Post Office and in the tourist office main branch.

American Express: Suffolk St., in the tourist office main office (☎605 7709.) Traveler's Cheques, money transfers, bureau de change, card payments. Open M-Sa 9am-5pm.

Work Opportunities: Check out the helpful job listing board at the **Community and Youth Information Center** (see **Tourist and Financial Services,** above). To obtain work through an organization, **Working Ireland,** 26 Eustace St. (☎01 677 0300; www.workingireland.ie), is a multi-tasking agency that arranges short- and long-term job placement throughout Ireland. **The Job Shop,** 50 Grafton St. (☎672 7755) can also help.

LOCAL SERVICES

Luggage Storage: Connolly Station. €2.50 per item per day. Open M-Sa 7:40am-9:20pm, Su 9:10am-9:45pm. **Heuston Station.** €2-5 per item, depending on size. Open daily 6:30am-10:30pm. **Busáras.** €3 per item, lockers €4-9. Open M-Sa 8am-7:45pm, Su 10am-5:45pm.

Lost Property: Connolly Station (☎703 2363), **Heuston Station** (☎703 2102), **Busáras** (☎703 2489), and **Dublin Bus** (☎703 3055).

Library: Dublin Corporation Central Library, Henry and Moore St. (☎873 4333), in the ILAC Centre. Video facilities, a kids library, EU telephone directories, and **free Internet** (call ahead) are all available. To check out books requires proof of residence in Dublin. Tourists may apply for a reference ticket, which allows use of library facilities, minus check-out privileges. Open M-Th 10am-8pm, F-Sa 10am-5pm.

Women's Resources: Women's Aid Helpline (☎1800 341 900) offers info on legal matters and support groups (10am-10pm). **Dublin Rape Crisis Centre** (24hr. hotline ☎1800 778 888). **Dublin Well Woman Centre,** 35 Lower Liffey St. (☎872 8051), is a private health center for women. It also runs a clinic (☎660 9860) at 67 Pembroke Rd.

Ticket Agencies: HMV (☎679 5334) record stores and **TicketMaster** (www.ticketmaster.ie) are linked at the hip; try HMV on Grafton St. or the TicketMaster ticket desk at the Suffolk St. tourist office. Additional TicketMaster desk at Celtic Note, 14-15 Suffolk St.

Laundry: Laundry Shop, 191 Parnell St. (☎872 3541), near Busáras. Wash and dry €8-12. Open M-F 8am-7pm, Sa 9am-6pm, Su 11am-5pm. **All-American Launderette,** 40 South Great Georges St. (☎677 2779). Wash and dry €7; full service €8. Open M-Sa 8:30am-7pm, Su 10am-6pm.

EMERGENCY AND COMMUNICATIONS

Emergency: ☎999 or 112; no coins required.

Police *(Garda):* Dublin Metro Headquarters, Harcourt Terr. (☎666 9500); Store St. Station (☎666 8000); Fitzgibbon St. Station (☎666 8400); Pearse St. (☎666 9000). **Police Confidential Report Line:** ☎1800 666 111.

Counseling and Support: Tourist Victim Support, Harcourt Sq. (☎478 5295; 24hr. free phone ☎1800 661 771; www.victimsupport.ie). Helps robbery victims find accommodations and contact embassies or families; a loss or crime report must first be filed with the police. Also offers telephone, email, assistance with language difficulties, emergency meals and shelter, and can help with re-issuing travel tickets and canceling credit cards. Open M-Sa 10am-6pm, Su noon-6pm. **Samaritans,** 112 Marlborough St. (☎1850 609 090 or 872 7700), for anything and everything. **Rape Crisis Centre,** 70 Lower Leeson St. (☎661 4911; 24hr. hotline ☎1800 778 888). Office open M-F 8am-7pm and Sa 9am-4pm. **Cura,** 30 South Anne St. (☎1850 622 626; Dublin office ☎671 0598), is a Catholic-funded support organization for women with unplanned pregnancies. Open M and W 10:30am-6:30pm, Tu and Th 10:30am-8:30pm, F-Sa 10:30am-2:30pm. **AIDS Helpline** (☎1800 459 459). Open daily 10am-5pm.

Pharmacy: O'Connell's, 56 Lower O'Connell St. (☎873 0427). Convenient to city bus routes. Open M-Sa 7:30am-10pm and Su 10am-10pm. Other branches are scattered about the city, including 2 on Grafton St. **Dowling's,** 6 Baggot St. (☎678 5612), near the Shelbourne Hotel and St. Stephen's Green. Also on Church St. (☎674 0204), by the Four Courts. Both open M-W and F 8am-7pm, Th 8am-8pm, Sa 9am-7pm.

Hospital: St. James's Hospital, James St. (☎453 7941). Take bus #123. **Mater Misericordiae Hospital,** Eccles St. (☎830 1122), off Lower Dorset St. Buses #10, 11, 13, 16, 121, and 122. **Beaumont Hospital,** Beaumont Rd. (☎837 7755 or 809 3000). Buses #27B, 51A, 101, 103, and 300. **Tallaght Hospital** (☎414 2000), farther south, is served by buses #49, 49A, 50, 54A, 65, 65B, 75, 76, 77, 77A, 201, and 202.

Phones: Telecom Éireann (inquiries ☎1901; phonecard refunds ☎1850 337 337). Public pay phones are on almost every corner. Recent privatization of Ireland's phone industry means other companies are putting up their own pay phones; pay careful attention to varying rates for local calls. (Also see **Telephones,** p. 27.)

Directory Inquiries: ☎11850 (€0.59 per min.) or ☎11811 (3 inquiries €0.50); international ☎11818 (€0.58 for the 1st 30sec., €0.02 per sec. after).

Internet: Free Internet is available at the **central library** (see **Local Services,** p. 94) and at the **Community and Youth Information Centre** (book ahead by phone in both cases). Chains abound, the best being **The Internet Exchange,** with branches at 146 Parnell St. (☎670 3000) and Fownes St. in Temple Bar (☎635 1680). €4 per hr., members €2.50 per hr. Membership €5. Open daily 9am-10:30pm. **Global Internet Cafe,** 8 Lower O'Connell St. (☎878 0295), a block north of the Liffey, on the right. Wide array of services, excellent coffee and smoothies. €6 per hr., students €5, members €3. Membership €5. Open M-F 8am-11pm, Sa 9am-11pm, Su 10am-11pm. **The Planet Cyber Cafe,** 13 St. Andrews St. (☎670 5182). Science-fiction theme, with tasty nibbles. €6 per hr., students €5. Open M-W and Su 10am-10pm, Th-Sa 10am-11pm.

Post Office: General Post Office (GPO), O'Connell St. (☎705 7000). *Poste Restante* pickup at the **Post Restante** window (see **Mail,** p. 26). Open M-Sa 8am-8pm, Su 10am-6:30pm. Smaller post offices, including one on Suffolk St. across from the tourist office, open M-F 8:45am-5:30pm. **Postal code:** Dublin 1. Dublin is the only place in the Republic with postal codes. Even-numbered codes are for areas south of the Liffey, odd-numbered are for the north.

ACCOMMODATIONS

Reserve at least a week in advance, particularly around Easter weekend, bank holiday weekends, sporting weekends, St. Patrick's Day, New Year's, and the peak summer season (June-Aug.). The tourist office books local accommodations for a fee of €4, but they only deal in Bord Fáilte-approved B&Bs and hostels, which aren't necessarily better than unapproved ones (though they do tend to be cleaner). Phoenix Park may tempt the desperate, but camping there is a terrible idea, not to mention illegal—if the *Garda* or park rangers don't deter you, the threat of thieves and other unsavories should. If the accommodations below are full, consult Dublin Tourism's annually updated and incredibly helpful *Dublin Accommodation Guide* (€3.80), or ask hostel and B&B staff for referrals.

Hostels in **Dún Laoghaire** (see p. 138), only a DART ride away, offer an alternative to city life. In addition to hostels, a blanket of high-quality B&Bs warms Dublin and its suburbs. Those with a green shamrock sign out front are registered, occasionally checked, and approved by Bord Fáilte. B&Bs without the shamrock haven't been inspected but may be cheaper and better located—popular establishments often find that Bord Fáilte's advertising is unnecessary. Rooms rane from €15 at the very lowest to upwards of €38 per person sharing. On the North Side, B&Bs cluster along **Upper** and **Lower Gardiner Street,** on **Sheriff Street,** and near **Parnell Square.** Exercise caution when walking home through the inner-city yarea at night.

CV Camac Valley **CT** Clontarf **CR** Clonliffe Road **GC** Gardiner St. and Customs House **NB** North Beach **NOS** North of O'Connell St. **SK** Shankill **SM** Sandymount **TB** Temple Bar/the Quays **WTB** West of Temple Bar

UNDER €17 (❶)	
Barnacle's Temple Bar House (97)	TB
Browns Hostel (97)	GC
Isaac's Hostel (98)	GC
Camac Valley Caravan & Camping (101)	CV
North Beach Caravan & Camping (101)	NB
Shankill Caravan & Camping (101)	SK

€17-€26 (❷)	
Abbey Court Hostel (99)	NOS
Abraham House (98)	GC
Avalon House (IHH) (99)	WTB
The Brewery Hostel (99)	WTB
Cobblestones (97)	TB
Dublin Youth Hostel (An Óige/HI) (99)	NOS
▨ Four Courts Hostel (98)	WTB
▨ Globetrotter's Tourist Hostel (IHH) (97)	GC
Jacob's Inn (98)	GC
Kinlay House (IHH) (99)	WTB
Litton Lane Hostel(97)	TB
Mrs. Molly Ryan (100)	CR
Oliver St. John Gogarty's (97)	TB
Rita and Jim Casey (100)	SM

€27-€41(❸)	
Bayview (101)	CT
Bridge House(97)	TB
Marian B&B (99)	NOS
▨ Mona's Guest Accommodation (100)	CR
Mrs. Bermingham(100)	SM
Mrs. Dolores Abbot-Murphy (100)	SM
▨ Parkway Guest House (99)	NOS
Villa Mater Dei & St. Martin's B&B (100)	CR
The White House (101)	CT

€42-€56 (❹)	
Charles Stewart B&B (100)	NOS
Harvey's Guest House (99)	NOS
The Kingfisher (100)	NOS
Waterville (101)	CT

OVER €57(❺)	
Browns Hotel (98)	GC
Clontarf Court Hotel (101)	CT

Clonliffe Road, Sandymount, and Clontarf are no more than a 15min. bus ride from Eden Quay. Chances for decent B&Bs are greater farther out, especially without a reservation. *Dublin Accommodation Guide* lists all approved B&Bs

INSIDE THE CITY CENTER

TEMPLE BAR AND THE QUAYS

Chic cafes and ethnic restaurants crowd the cobblestone streets of Temple Bar. Unfortunately, so do throngs of tourists and drunken revelers. Located blissfully close to all the major sights and pubs, accommodations in Temple Bar are convenient and generally safe, but often quite noisy, especially on the weekends.

Cobblestones, 29 Eustace St. (☎677 5614). A breath of fresh air from the more industrial hostels, in the middle of Temple Bar. Snug rooms with large windows and a well-appointed kitchen. Book before Feb. and watch the St. Patrick's Day parade from the patio roof. Continental breakfast included. Dorms €15-21; doubles €48. Discounts mid-week, and for stays 1 wk. or longer. Student and group discounts available. ❷

Bridge House, corner of Parliament and Essex St. (☎672 5811; reservation@dublinhotelsfinder.com). Clean, comfortable, ensuite rooms in a fine old Georgian mansion across from The Porter House. Continental breakfast in beautiful dining room. Doubles €65-130; triples €80-178. ❸

Barnacle's Temple Bar House, 19 Temple Ln. (☎671 6277). "The burning hot center of everything." So close to the hopping (and noisy) heart of Dublin that patrons can crawl home from the Temple Bar pubs. Excellent lounge with open fire and TV, and a colorful, well-kept kitchen. All rooms with bath and indulgent water pressure. Continental breakfast included. Free luggage storage. Laundry €6.50. 12-bed dorms €13.50-17; 10-bed €16-20; 6-bed €19-23; 4-bed €22-25. Doubles €64-77. ❶

Oliver St. John Gogarty's Temple Bar Hostel, 18-21 Anglesea St. (☎671 1822). Fine dorms in an old, well-maintained building above a popular pub. A good location for partiers. Laundry €4. Dorms €13-30; doubles €56-80; triples €87-105. ❷

Litton Lane Hostel, 2-4 Litton Ln. (☎872 8389), off Bachelors Walk. Former studio for the likes of U2, Van Morrison, and Sinead O'Connor; Warhol-esque silk screens keep things hip. In addition to standard dorms, the hostel has shining new apartments, complete with separate lounge area, kitchen, bathroom, TV, and laundry facilities. Laundry €5. Key deposit €1. Dorms €15-25; doubles €70-80. 1-bedroom apartments sleep up to 4, €80-120; 2-bedroom apartments also sleep up to 4, €130-150. ❷

GARDINER ST. AND CUSTOMS HOUSE

The area near the train and bus station holds some of Dublin's best hostels in one of its less desirable neighborhoods. These are fine places to stay for late arrivals or early departures, or for those who don't mind a walk to good food and nightlife. **Gardiner St.** runs north from the **Custom House** and parallel to **O'Connell Street; Parnell Square** sits at the top of **Upper Gardiner Street.** Both Lower and Upper Gardiner St. are within walking distance of **Busáras** and **Connolly station;** buses #41, 41B, and 41C from Eden Quay travel to the end of the road.

▨ Globetrotter's Tourist Hostel (IHH), 46-7 Lower Gardiner St. (☎873 5893; www.iol.ie/globetrotters). A dose of luxury for the weary. Trendy pop-art, tropical fish, lush courtyard, and all-you-can-eat Irish breakfast make this Georgian mansion more like a posh B&B than a hostel. Real hotel rooms in the Townhouse next door. Free luggage storage. Towels €1. Dorms €19; singles €66.50-70; doubles €110-125. ❷

Browns Hostel, 89-90 Lower Gardiner St. (☎855 0034; www.brownshostelireland.com). Many long-term residents cook together in the cavernous wine-cellar-turned-kitchen of this friendly, spic-and-span hostel. TVs, closets, and A/C in every room. Large, clean, single-sex baths in the basement. For cool sky-lights, ask for the Shannon room. Break-

fast included. Lockers €1. Blankets €2. Towels €1. 20-bed dorm €12.50-15; 10- to 14-bed €15-20; 4- to 6-bed €20-25. Long-term bargains available. ❶

Browns Hotel, 90 Lower Gardiner St. (☎855 0034; www.brownshotelireland.com). Elegant Georgian building with newly refurbished rooms and professional, hospitable staff. Full breakfast. Connected to **Browns Hostel.** Doubles €65-145; triples €99-190. ❺

Jacob's Inn, 21-28 Talbot Pl. (☎855 5660; www.isaacs.ie). 2 blocks north of the Custom House. Huge new hostel stretches from the back of the bus station to Talbot St. Rooms, all with bath, are spacious, clean, and cheery. Gigantic luggage room with individual cages. Bike storage. Wheelchair-accessible. Light breakfast included. Lockers €1.50 per night. Towels €1.50. Laundry service €10. Lockout 11am-3pm. Dorms €13-26; doubles €60-65; triples €78-84. Weekend prices €2 higher. ❷

Abraham House, 82-3 Lower Gardiner St. (☎855 0600). Large, lived-in dorms with small ensuite baths. Comfortable private bedrooms sleep up to 4 and have TVs and kettles. Free parking, luggage and bike storage. Bureau de change. Light breakfast included. **Internet** €1 per 20min. Laundry service €5. 12-bed dorms €10-17; 8-bed €13-22; 6-bed €15-25; 4-bed €15-32. Private room €50-105. ❷

Isaac's Hostel, 2-5 Frenchman's Ln. (☎855 6215), off end of Lower Gardiner St., next to the DART. Attracts young, international backpackers. Bustling cafe, lobby, and courtyard, with fair-weather barbeques. Bike storage. **Internet** €1 per 15min. Towels €1.50. Laundry €10. Lockout 11:30am-2:30pm. 12- to 16-bed dorms €10.75-14.50; 8- to 10-bed €12.50-16.75; 4-bed €17.50-22.50; singles €29.50-34.50; doubles €58-60. ❶

WEST OF TEMPLE BAR

More industrial than the city center and farther from the nightlife action, but closer to the city's main sights (and the Guinness Brewery), the area west of Temple Bar has several star accommodations.

▨ **Four Courts Hostel,** 15-17 Merchants Quay (☎672 5839). South side of the river, near O'Donovan Rossa Bridge. The #748 bus from the airport stops next door. If arriving late without a place to stay, try here first. The friendly staff and relaxed atmosphere of this 250-bed, first-rate mega-hostel compensate for its non-central location. Beautifully renovated old building, a 10min. walk from Temple Bar. Clean rooms (most with showers), kitchen, laundry (€5), carpark facilities, and long-term stays available. **Internet** €1 per 10min. Continental breakfast. 12-16-bed dorms €15-16.50; 10-bed €16-17.50, 8-bed €17.50-19; 4- to 6-bed €20-23. Doubles €56-66; family room €23-25. ❷

Avalon House (IHH), 55 Aungier St. (☎475 0001; www.avalon-house.ie). Turn off Dame St. onto Great Georges St.; the hostel is a 5min. walk down on the right, a stumble away from Temple Bar or the clubs and pubs of Camden and Harcourt St. Avalon hums with the energy of transcontinental travelers. Dorms provide some privacy with a split-level setup connected by spiral staircases. Wheelchair-accessible. Swipe cards and lockers make this hostel feel secure. **Internet** available. Continental breakfast included. Storage cages €1 per day. Towels €2, deposit €8. Large dorms €10-20; 6-bed €23-30. Singles €30-37; doubles €56-70. ❷

Kinlay House (IHH), 2-12 Lord Edward St. (☎679 6644). Slide down oak banisters in the lofty entrance hall, snuggle on soft couches in the TV room, or gaze at Christ Church Cathedral from the window. Great location a few blocks from Temple Bar. **Internet** €1 per 15min. Continental breakfast. Free luggage storage. Lockers €2, deposit €5. Laundry €5. 15- to 24-bed dorms €15-18; 20-bed with 4-bed nooks €16-20; 4- to 6-bed €20-24, with bath €22-27. Singles €40-50; doubles €50-56, with bath €54-66. ❷

The Brewery Hostel, 22-23 Thomas St. (☎453 8600). Follow Dame St. past Christ Church through its name changes, or take bus #123. So close to the Guinness Brewery it smells of hops, and a 15-20min. walk from Temple Bar. Accommodating staff, and picnic area out back with barbeque for spontaneous cook-outs. Continental breakfast included. All rooms with bath. Free luggage storage. Free carpark. 1 key per room. 10-bed dorms €15-20; 8-bed €16-22; 4-bed €18-25. Doubles €60-78. ❷

NORTH OF O'CONNELL ST.

While Temple Bar has Dublin's small and eclectic museums and theaters, the big boys reside north of O'Connell St., around Parnell Sq.: Gate Theatre, the Dublin Writers Museum, and the National Wax Museum are all in the area.

▨ **Parkway Guest House,** 5 Gardiner Pl. (☎874 0469). High-ceilinged, tidy rooms in a central location. Run by a mother-and-son team. The son, a hurling veteran, offers discerning advice on the city's restaurants and pubs and can talk for hours about sports. Full Irish breakfast. Singles €35; doubles €52-62, with bath €60-75. ❸

Abbey Court Hostel, 29 Bachelor's Walk, O'Connell Bridge (☎878 0700; www.abbey-court.com). From O'Connell Bridge, turn left and it's up the street. Clean, narrow, smoke-free rooms overlook the Liffey. Great location. Free luggage storage; security box €1. Continental breakfast included. Full service laundry €8. 12-bed dorms €18-21; 6-bed €23-26; 4-bed €26-29. Doubles €76-88. ❷

Harvey's Guest House, 11 Upper Gardiner St. (☎874 8384; www.harveysguest-house.com.) In 2 lovely old townhouses near Mountjoy Sq. Smoke-free bedrooms with fine wooden sleighbeds, brilliant white coverlets, and sparkling bathrooms. Full breakfast. Singles €45-60; doubles €90-140; quads €150-200. ❹

Marian B&B, 21 Upper Gardiner St. (☎874 4129). Brendan and Catherine McElroy provide fine rooms for noteworthy prices. Singles €30-32; doubles €54. ❸

Dublin International Youth Hostel (An Óige/HI), 61 Mountjoy St. (☎830 4555; www.irelandyha.org), in a converted convent. O'Connell St. changes names 3 times before the left turn onto Mountjoy St. Calling home from the confessional-turned-phone-booths may cause regrettable admissions. Wheelchair-accessible. Bureau de Change.

Internet €1 per 15min. Don't forget to say grace during the free breakfast, served in the chapel. Carpark and buses to Temple Bar. Towels €1. Laundry €5. Dorms €20; doubles €51-57; triples €75-82; quads €92-99. €2 less for An Óige members. ❷

The Kingfisher, 166 Parnell St. (☎872 8732; www.clubi.ie/kingfisher/). Combined B&B, restaurant, and Internet cafe. Clean, modern rooms, uncomplicated food (fish and chips €8), and a full Irish breakfast, served until noon for the truly lazy. Cheap **Internet**. TV/VCR in each room, kitchenettes in some. Singles €45-60; doubles €80-110; triples €165. Prices drop in winter. ❹

Charles Stewart B&B, 5-6 Parnell Sq. E. (☎878 0350). Up O'Connell St. past Parnell St. More hotel than B&B. Birthplace of the infamous Oliver St. John Gogarty, close enough to Dublin Writer's Museum to feel properly literary. Full Irish breakfast. Singles €50-63.50; doubles €76-89; triples €120; quads €140. Tiny private room. €31.75. ❹

OUTSIDE THE CITY CENTER

CLONLIFFE ROAD

This is an ideal place to stay if planning to attend (or eavesdrop on) events at **Croke Park.** To make the 20min. walk from the city center, go up O'Connell St., turn right on Dorset St., head across the Royal Canal, then turn right onto Clonliffe Rd. Bus #11A runs to the city center; #41A, 41B, and 41C service the area from the airport.

🏠 **Mona's Guest Accommodation,** 148 Clonliffe Rd. (☎837 6723). Happy guests return year after year to this charming house run for 37 years (and probably 37 more) by Ireland's loveliest proprietress. Homemade brown bread accompanies the full Irish breakfast. Open May-Oct. Singles €35; doubles €66. ❸

Mrs. Molly Ryan, 10 Distillery Rd. (☎837 4147), off Clonliffe Rd. On the left, coming from the city center, in a yellow house attached to #11. The unsinkable Molly Ryan, in her countless years, has never marked the B&B with a sign. Small rooms, small prices, no breakfast. As honest as they come. Singles €15; doubles €30. ❷

Villa Mater Dei, 208 Clonliffe Rd., and **St. Martins B&B,** 186 Clonliffe Rd. (☎857 0920). Dedicated owner renovated 2 beautiful Victorian houses with modern amenities and lovely gardens. All rooms with TVs and baths. €35. ❸

SANDYMOUNT

Sandymount is a peaceful neighborhood near **Dublin Port,** 2 mi. south of the city and famous for its Joycean associations. Take bus #3 from Clery's Department Store on O'Connell St. or the DART to Lansdowne Rd. or Sandymount (10min.).

Mrs. Bermingham, 8 Dromard Terr. (☎668 3861), on Dromard Ave. Take #2 or 3 bus, get off at Tesco and make the next left. Down the street, the road forks; go left on Dromard Terr. Colorful Mrs. Bermingham resides in the ivy-covered, red brick house, amidst soft beds with fluffy comforters. Open Feb.-Nov. Singles €28; doubles with bath €52. ❸

Rita and Jim Casey, Villa Jude, 2 Church Ave. (☎668 4982), off Beach Rd. Bus #3 to first stop on Tritonville Rd.; Church Ave. is back a few yards. Call for directions from Lansdowne Rd. DART stop. Mr. Casey is the former mayor of Sandymount, and he and lovely Rita treat guests to clean rooms, big breakfasts, and good company. €25. ❷

Mrs. Dolores Abbot-Murphy, 14 Castle Park (☎269 8413). Ask the #3 bus driver to stop at Sandymount Green. Continue past Browne's Deli and take the 1st left; at the end of the road look right. A 5min. walk from Sandymount DART stop. Cheerful rooms in a charming cul-de-sac. Open May-Oct. €28, with bath €32. ❸

CLONTARF

Clontarf Rd. runs north along Dublin Bay to the neighborhood that bears its name. Sea breezes are more pleasant than the harbor traffic; but such are the problems of all swanky suburbs. Many B&Bs in Clontarf are unmarked; call ahead. Bus #130 goes from Lower Abbey St. to Clontarf Rd. (15min.).

Waterville, 154 Clontarf Rd. (☎833 0238). Wood floors, modern decor, and a dining room overlooking the bay. All rooms with baths, TVs, and phones. **Internet** hookup available. Doubles €70. ❹

The White House, 125 Clontarf Rd. (☎833 3196). Sink into bed and gaze out at pristine rose gardens and a roomy backyard. Full Irish breakfast. Singles €35; doubles €64. ❸

Bayview, 98 Clontarf Rd. (☎833 3950). The Barry family provides fresh, airy rooms and a friendly spot of tea on arrival. Lucky travelers are serenaded with Irish piano tunes in the evening. Singles €35; doubles with bath €70-74. ❸

Clontarf Court Hotel, 225 Clontarf Rd. (☎833 2680). Family owned hotel/restaurant/ pub overlooking a sailboat harbor. Room 104 has best views. Golf courses close by. W trad in the pub, Su features two locals banging out Irish tunes on the piano. Full Irish breakfast. Singles €65; doubles €95; family room €130. ❺

CAMPING

Most campsites are far from the city center, but camping equipment is available in the heart of the city. **The Great Outdoors,** on Chatham St. off the top of Grafton St., has an excellent selection of tents, backpacks, and cookware. (☎679 4293. 10% discount for An Óige/HI members. Open M-W and F-Sa 9:30am-6pm, Th 9:30am-8pm.) **O'Meara's Camping,** 4-6 Bridgefoot St., off Thomas St. near the Guinness Brewery, sells camping equipment and rents tents. (☎670 8639. 3-person tents €40 to buy; 3-room tents €150 to rent per wk. Open year-round M-Sa 10am-6pm, Su 2:30-5:30pm.) It is illegal and unsafe to camp in Phoenix Park.

Camac Valley Tourist Caravan and Camping Park, Naas Rd., Clondalkin (☎464 0644), near Corkagh Park. Take bus #69 (35min. from city center, €1.50). Food shop and kitchen facilities. Wheelchair-accessible. Dogs welcome. Laundry €4.50. €7 per person; €14 per 2 people with car; €17 with caravan; €15 with camper. Showers €1. ❶

Shankill Caravan and Camping Park (☎282 0011). The DART and buses #45 and 84 from Eden Quay run to Shankill, as does bus #45A from the Dún Laoghaire ferryport. Welcomes all ages. €9 per tent plus €2 per adult, €1 per child. Showers €1. ❶

North Beach Caravan and Camping Park, in Rush (☎843 7131; www.northbeach.ie). Accessible by bus #33 from Eden Quay (1hr., 25 per day) and suburban rail. Peaceful, beach-side location in a quiet town outside Dublin's urban jumble. Kitchen for washing dishes. Open Mar.-Oct. €6.50 per person, child €3. Electricity €3. Showers €0.50. ❶

LONG-TERM STAYS

Visitors expecting to spend several weeks in Dublin may want to consider a bedsit or a sublet. Longer stays are often most economical when sharing the cost of rent with others. Many hostels give special rates for long-termers, especially in the winter; ask at individual hostels for details. Rooms in locations outside the city center, like Marino and Rathmines, go for about €70-110 per week (ask whether electricity, phone, and water are included). B&Bs sometimes offer reduced rates for long-term stays but are reluctant to do so in the high season.

There are a number of sources for finding roommates and possible sublets; Dublin's countless university students are often looking for them, usually for the summer but also on a weekly basis. The most up-to-date and comprehensive postings of vacancies are at **usit NOW,** 19-21 Aston Quay (see **Practical Information,** p. 93).

Supermarket notice boards are another source. **Trinity College** has two spots worth checking out: one notice board is near the guard's desk in the Student Union and the other is on the main gate. Also check out the tourist office's *Dublin Accommodation Guide* (€3.80), or classified ads in the *Irish Independent*, the *Irish Times*, and particularly the *Evening Herald.* For someone else to do the legwork, try **Dublin Central Reservations,** 3 Sandholes, Castleknock, which arranges short or long stays in locations both humble and snazzy. (☎820 0394; www.dublinreservations.com. From €250 per wk. No finder's fee. Open M-F 9am-7pm, Sa noon-5pm.) **Working Ireland,** 26 Eustace St. (☎01 677 0300; www.workingireland.ie; Open M-F noon-6pm), also assists travelers in finding long-term accommodations.

Another reasonable option is **university housing,** available during the summer holiday—roughly mid-June to mid-September. Don't expect anything fancy, but prices are only a fraction more expensive than those of hostels. **Trinity College** is as central as possible, and offers single and shared rooms, some with bath. (☎608 1177; reservations@tcd.ie. €39-61.) The **Mercer Court Campus,** lower Mercer St., near Grafton St. and St. Steven's Green has single and double rooms, all with bath and TV. (☎478 0328; www.mercercourt.ie. €41-52.) **Dublin City University,** Glasnevin, can be reached on bus #11, 11A, 11B, 13, or 19A from the city center. (☎700 5736. Free morning breakfast. Singles with bath €47; doubles with bath €77.) Other options are available through **usit** (see **Practical Information, p. 93**), which operates **University College Dublin** dorms in Belfield. (☎269 7111. Take bus #3. Single private room in an apartment of 4 €33.)

❏ FOOD

Dublin's many **open-air markets** sell fixin's fresh and cheap. Vendors hawk fruit, fresh strawberries, flowers, and fish from their pushcarts. The later in the week, the livelier the market. Actors might head to **Moore Street Market** to perfect their Dublin accent, and get fresh veggies at the same time. (Between Henry and Parnell St. Open M-Sa 7am-5pm.) The **Thomas Street Market,** along the continuation of Dame St., is a calmer alternative for fruit and veggie shopping. (Open M-Sa 9am-5pm.) On Saturdays, **Temple Bar's** gourmet open-air market takes over Meeting House Sq. The cheapest **supermarkets** around Dublin are in the **Dunnes Stores** chain, with full branches at St. Stephen's Green (☎478 0188; open M-W and F-Sa 8:30am-7pm, Th 8:30am-9pm, Su noon-6pm), the ILAC Centre off Henry St., on N. Earl St. off O'Connell, and a small convenience version on Georges St. The **Runner Bean,** 4 Nassau St., vends whole foods, homemade breads, veggies, fruits, and nuts. (☎679 4833. Open M-F 7:30am-6pm, Sa 7:30am-3pm.) **Down to Earth,** 73 S. Great Georges St., stocks health foods, herbal medicines, and a dozen granolas. (☎671 9702. Open M-Sa 8:30am-6:30pm.) Health food is also available around the city at various branches of **Nature's Way;** the biggest is at the St. Stephen's Green shopping center. (☎478 0165. Open M-W and F-Sa 9am-6pm, Th 9am-8pm.)

TEMPLE BAR

This neighborhood is bursting with creative eateries catering to every budget. Temple Bar has more ethnic diversity in its restaurants than counties Louth, Meath, Wicklow, and Longford combined. (And probably Offaly, too.)

■ **Queen of Tarts,** 4 Cork Hill (☎670 7499). This little red gem offers homemade pastries, scones, cakes, and coffee. Excellent granola and fresh fruit (€6). Succulent sandwiches (€5). Breakfast €4-6. Open M-F 7:30am-6pm, Sa 9am-6pm, Su 10am-6pm. ❷

ASIAN

Wagamama (104)	GGS ❸
Yamamori Noodles (104)	GGS ❸

CAFES

Bewley's Cafes (105)	GGS ❷
Butler's Chocolate Cafe (105)	GGS ❶
Joy of Coffee (104)	NL ❶
Metro Cafe (105)	GGS ❶
🖼 Queen of Tart (102)	TB ❷
The Winding Stair (105)	NL ❷
Bookshop and Cafe	

CONTINENTAL

Bad Ass Cafe (104)	NL ❸
Bendini & Shaw (105)	GGS ❷
Bond (105)	NL ❺
Busy Feet & Coco Cafe (104)	GGS ❷
Lemon Crepe & Coffee Co. (104)	GGS ❶
The Mermaid Cafe (103)	TB ❺
O'Shea's Hotel (105)	NL ❷
Tante Zoe's	NL ❹

FISH AND CHIPS

Beschoff's (105)	NL ❷
🖼 Leo Burdock's (104)	GGS ❶

MEDITERRANEAN

🖼 101 Talbot (105)	NL ❹
La Med (103)	NL ❸
🖼 Unicorn Cafe Restaurant (104)	GGS ❹
Unicorn Market and Cafe (104)	GGS ❷

ORGANIC/VEGETARIAN

Cafe Irie (103)	NL ❶
Cornupia (104)	GGS ❷
gruel (103)	TB ❷
Nude (104)	GGS ❷
Soup Dragon (105)	NL ❷

SOUTH ASIAN/MIDDLE EASTERN

Govinda's (104)	GGS ❷
Monty's of Kathmandu (103)	TB ❹
Zaytoon's (103)	NL ❷

TB Temple Bar **GGS** Grafton and South Great Georges Streets **NL** North of the Liffey

---

The Mermaid Cafe, 69-70 Dame St. (☎670 8236), near S. Great Georges St. Modern art fills this comfortably gourmet cafe. Outstanding Su brunch. Grilled bass with crab risotto €21.50. Open M-Sa 12:30-2:30pm, 6-11pm; Su 12:30-3:30pm, 6-9pm. ❺

gruel, 68 Dame St. (☎670 7119). Keep your eye out for the lowercase "g" sign. Come in for quality organic home cooking. Their motto: "We gruel, you drool." Heavenly brownies €2.40. Lunch is on a weekly rotation; go F for roast lamb with apricot chutney (€6). Huge dinners €6-12. Coffee €1. Open M-Sa 8am-4:30pm, Su 10am-4pm. ❷

Monty's of Kathmandu, (☎670 4911), just off Dame St. on the right. Nepalese food with decor to match. Mains €13-18; try the Sekuwa Chatpate Chicken or the spicy Begum Bahar with an unorthodox mix of chicken and lamb (both €14). Open M-Sa noon-2:30pm and 6-11:30pm, Su 6-11:30pm. ❹

Tante Zoe's, 1 Crowe St. (☎679 4407), across from the back entrance of the Foggy Dew pub. New Orleans Creole food in an elegantly casual setting. Staff help get just the right spiciness. Mains €14-22. Open daily noon-4pm and 6:30pm-midnight. ❹

Cafe Irie, 11 Fownes St. (☎672 5090). Head up Fownes St. from Temple; it's on the left above the clothing store Sé Sí Progressive. Small, hidden eatery with impressive selection of lip-smacking sandwiches (€4-6). Vegan-friendly. Open M-Sa 9am-8:30pm. ❶

La Med, 22 East Essex St. (670 7358. www.lamed.ie). Mediterranean food in a pretty little restaurant overlooking the Liffey. Known for their seafood; start a meal with Mussels Provencale or Mariniere €9. Early Bird special (€13.65) of appetizer and entree served 5-7pm. Mains €11-22. Open M-F 5pm-11pm, Th-Su noon-4pm and 5-11pm. ❸

Zaytoons, 14-15 Parliament St. (☎677 3595). Serves good Persian food until late, on big platters of fresh warm bread. A cheap lunch or a healthy way to satisfy the post-pub munchies. Excellent chicken kebab €6.50. Open M-Sa noon-4am. ❷

COUNTY DUBLIN

Bad Ass Cafe, Crown Alley. (671 2596. www.badasscafe.com) A big, low-key pizza parlor with huge windows overlooking Temple Bar. Locals and tourists chow down at red tables. Large pizza €13-14. Other entrees € 10-18. Open M-Su 11:30am-late. ❸

Joy of Coffee, 25 Essex St. (☎679 3393). Communal feeling and happy tunes. Large tables and huge windows overlooking the action in Temple Bar encourage conversation mergers. A good place to meet people before pubbing. Coffee from €2. Open M-Th 9am-10pm, F-Sa 9am-11pm, Su 10am-10pm. ❶

GRAFTON AND SOUTH GREAT GEORGES STREETS

The power-shoppers of streets Grafton and South Great Georges are kept on their feet by the excellent, if trendy, eateries that proliferate in the area.

🏮**Unicorn Cafe Restaurant,** 12B Merrion Court (☎676 2182). Left off Merrion Row, behind Unicorn Market and Cafe. Legendary Italian restaurant serves classic dishes with panache. Mains €16-25. Open M-Th noon-4pm and 6-11pm, F-Sa noon-4pm and 6-11:30pm. ❹ For those with less time or less money, **Unicorn Market and Cafe,** (☎678 8588) Merrion Row, offers food from the same kitchen for a fraction of the price. Eat-in or takeaway (St. Stephen's Green, down the block, is perfect for a picnic.) Sandwiches and panini €4-6, pastas €3.50-5. Open daily 8am-7pm. ❷

🏮**Leo Burdock's,** 2 Werburgh St. (☎454 0306), up from Christ Church Cathedral, behind The Lord Edward pub. Real-deal fish and chips, served in brown paper. A holy ritual for many Dubliners. Takeaway only. Fish €4; chips €1.50. Open daily noon-midnight. ❶

Lemon Crepe & Coffee Co., 66 S. William St. (☎672 9004.) Squeeze into this tiny, trendy joint for crepes made on the spot. Eat them standing, or grab one of the highly prized tables outside. Savory and sweet crepes €3-6. Open M-W and F 8am-7:30pm, Th 8am-9:30pm, Sa 9am-7:30pm, Su 10am-6:30pm. ❶

Yamamori Noodles, 71-72 S. Great Georges St. (☎475 5001). Exceptional, reasonably priced Japanese cuisine. Traditional decor on one side, voguish paintings on the other. Mains €11-15. Maki roll €7.50. Open Su-W 12:30-11pm, Th-Sa noon-11:30pm. ❸

Cornucopia, 19 Wicklow St. (☎677 7583). If there's space, sit down for a rich meal (€8.50) or snack (€2). Organic vegetarian horn o' plenty spills huge portions onto plates. Open M-W and F-Sa 8:30am-8pm, Th 8:30am-9pm, Su noon-7pm. ❷

Busyfeet & Coco Cafe, 41-2 S. William St. (☎671 9514.) Grass-green facade announces this airy, calm cafe. Start the day with an Irish breakfast (€5.71) or fruit salad with yogurt (€3.65), or replenish with a sandwich on organic rye (€4.63-6.85). Outdoor seating. Open M-W and F 7:30-8pm, Th 7:30am-9pm, Sa-Su 9am-8pm. ❷

Govinda's, 4 Aungier St. (☎475 0309). Fabulous Indian veggie fare in an airy oasis with a soothing Hare Krishna sensibility. Dinner special €7.50. Open M-Sa noon-9pm. ❷

Wagamama, S. King St. (☎478 2152; www.wagamama.com). Sate noodle lust at this London-based chain. Service is efficient at long, communal tables. Ramen €9-12. Open M-Sa noon-11pm, Su noon-10pm; last orders 15min. before closing. ❸

Nude, 21 Suffolk St. Organic, fresh, free-range/free-trade food and modern design. Stroll down the astro-turfed floor to pick up fresh squeezed juices (€2-3.50), salads (€4), or hot panini (€4.50). Picnic bench seating. Great, quick, healthy lunch of which any mother (nature, that is) would be proud. Open daily 10am-7pm. ❷

Butler's Chocolate Cafe, 24 Wicklow St. (☎671 0591). Sinning never felt so good. In this luxury sweet shop, with branches throughout the city, lattes start at €2.20 and their signature hot chocolate is just €2.80. Open M-W and F 8am-7:30pm, Th 8am-9pm. ❶

Metro Cafe, 43 S. William St. (☎679 4515). Parisian-style cafe with fresh coffee, homemade breads, and outdoor seating. Simple but scrumptious. Sandwiches €4-5. Open M-Tu and F 8am-8pm, W 8am-9pm, Th 8am-10pm, Sa 9am-7pm, Su 10:30am-7pm. ❶

Bendini & Shaw. "Gourmet" sandwich shop with locations around Dublin. Irish smoked salmon, avocado, and ham salad on a baguette €3.80. Hot dog arrives in a fancy braided pastry bun. Delivery available for orders over €15. Five branches: 4 **St. Stephen's Green** (☎671 8651); 20 **Upper Baggot Street** (☎660 0131); 1A **Lower Pembroke Street** (☎678 0800); 2A **Upper Fownes Street** (☎671 0800); 4 **Lower Mayor Street** (☎829 0275). All open M-F 7am-5pm, Sa 8am-6pm, Su 9am-5pm. ❷

Bewley's Cafes. A Dublin institution, though some locals claim it ain't what it used to be. Dark wood paneling and marble table tops. Meals are plain but affordable. Decadent pastries €1.60. Many branches: 78 **Grafton St.,** with a room honoring its most famous patron, James Joyce (☎635 5470. Open daily 7:30am-11pm, later on weekends). 12 **Westmoreland St.** (☎677 6761. Open M-Sa 7:30am-7:30pm, Su 9:30am-8pm). 13 **South Great Georges St.** (Open M-Sa 7:45am-6pm). **Mary St.** past Henry St. (Open M-W 7am-9pm, Th-Sa 7am-2am, Su 10am-10pm). ❷

NORTH OF THE LIFFEY

Eateries here are less interesting than their counterparts on the South Side. **O'Connell Street** sports blocks of neon fast-food chains, while side streets overflow with chippers between newsagents hawking overpriced groceries.

▨ **101 Talbot,** 101 Talbot St., (874 5011) between Marlborough and Gardiner St. Through red doors and upstairs. Casual, airy restaurant serves excellent Italian-Mediterranean food and caters to Abbey Theatre goers. Handwritten menu changes frequently, but always has veggie specialties. Early Bird €20. Mains €12-19. Open Tu-Sa 5-11pm. ❹

The Winding Stair Bookshop and Cafe, 40 Lower Ormond Quay (☎873 3292), near the Ha'penny Bridge. A relaxed cafe overlooking the river shares space with an independent bookshop (see p. 132). Flowerboxes and red checkered tablecloths lend a country feel. Crepes €6-8; sandwiches €3-5.50. Open M-Sa 9:30am-6pm, Su 1-6pm. ❷

O'Shea's Hotel, 19 Talbot St. (☎836 5670), at Lower Gardiner St. Good bar vittles and a high window for peeking on pedestrians. Convenient to the North Side accommodations. Mains €10-20, sandwiches €6. Open daily 7:30am-10pm. ❷

Beshoff's, 6 Lower O'Connell St. (☎872 4400). Named for the cook in the 1925 Russian film *Battleship Potemkin.* Takeaway counter with a touch of class. Lots of seats, various levels, and loads of fish specials. Open daily 10am-10pm. Another branch at 14 Westmoreland St. Open daily 11am-11pm. ❷

Soup Dragon, 168 Capel St. (☎872 3277). A dozen soups (€4-11.35) by kitchen wizards, plus healthy juices, fruits, and breads. Open M-F 8am-5:30pm, Sa 11am-5pm. ❷

Bond, Beresford Pl. (☎855 9249). Minimalist design accented by bright blue chairs. Young professionals power-lunch on exquisitely prepared French cuisine. Choose a wine from the cellar downstairs. 8 oz. fillet of beef with Cajun-herbed mozzarella potatoes (€22). Open for lunch M-F noon-2:30pm; dinner M-W 6-9pm, Th-Sa 6-10pm. ❺

THE LOCAL STORY

THE PERFECT PINT

Bartender Glenn, of a local Dublin Pub, helps Let's Go resolve the most elusive question of all...

LG: Tell us, what's the most important thing about pouring a pint?

BG: The most important thing is to have the keg as close to the tap as possible. The closer, the better.

LG: And why's that?

BG: Well, you don't want the Guinness sitting in a long tube while you wait to pour the next pint. You want to pull it straight out of the keg, without any muck getting in between.

LG: Does stopping to let the Guinness settle make a big difference?

BG: Well, you can top it straight off if you want, but you might get too big a head with that. You don't want too small or big a head, so if you stop ¾ of the way, you can adjust the pint until the head is perfect. A true Guinness lover will taste the difference.

LG: Because of the head?

BG: No, because of the gas. If you pull the Guinness straight from the tap and get a big head, it means you've gotten too much gas. It kills the taste. That's why you have to tilt the glass.

LG: Anything else to look for?

BG: Well what you don't want is a window-clean glass; you don't want a glass that you can see through when you're done. Good Guinness leaves a healthy film on the glass. If it doesn't, you didn't get a good Guinness.

LG: Well, Glenn, you sure make pouring pints sound like an art form.

☒ PUBLIN

James Joyce proposed that a "good puzzle would be to cross Dublin without passing a pub." When a local radio station once offered £100 to the first person to solve the puzzle, the winner explained that any route worked—you'd just have to stop in each one along the way. Dublin's pubs come in all shapes, sizes, specialties, and subcultures. This is the place to hear country-and-western, Irish rock, and, on occasion, trad. Ask around or check *In Dublin*, *Hot Press*, or *Event Guide* for music listings. Normal pub hours in Ireland end at 11:30pm Sunday through Wednesday and 12:30am Thursday through Saturday, but the laws that dictate these hours are changing—often patrons get about a half-hour after "closing" to kill their drinks. An increasing number of pubs have permits for late hours, at least on some nights; drink prices tend to rise around 11pm to cover the permit's cost (or so they claim). Bars post their closing time as "late," meaning after midnight and, sometimes, after their legal limit. ID-checking almost always happens at the door rather than at the bar, and is more often enforced in Dublin than in other parts of Ireland. Note that a growing number of places are blurring the distinction between pubs and clubs, with rooms or dance floors opening after certain hours. So pay attention, and hit two birds with one pint.

The *Let's Go* **Dublin Pub Crawl** will aide in discovering the city while researching the perfect pint. We recommend beginning the expedition at Trinity gates, strolling up Grafton St., teetering to Camden St., stumbling to South Great Georges St., then triumphantly dragging your soused and sorry self to Temple Bar. Start early—say, noon. In the search for the best Guinness along the way, try three classic pubs: **Mulligan's, The Stag's Head,** and **Brogan's Bar;** each claim to pour the best pint. Of course, some might say this title goes to the new kid on the old block, the **Gravity Bar** at the top of the **Guinness Storehouse**...to judge for yourself, try them all.

GRAFTON STREET AND TRINITY COLLEGE AREA

McDaid's, 3 Harry St. (☎679 4395), off Grafton St. across from Anne St. Center of Ireland's literary scene in the 50s. Incredibly high ceiling, summer patio, and gregarious crowd. Open M-W 10:30am-11:30pm, Th-Sa 10:30am-12:30am, Su 10:30am-11pm.

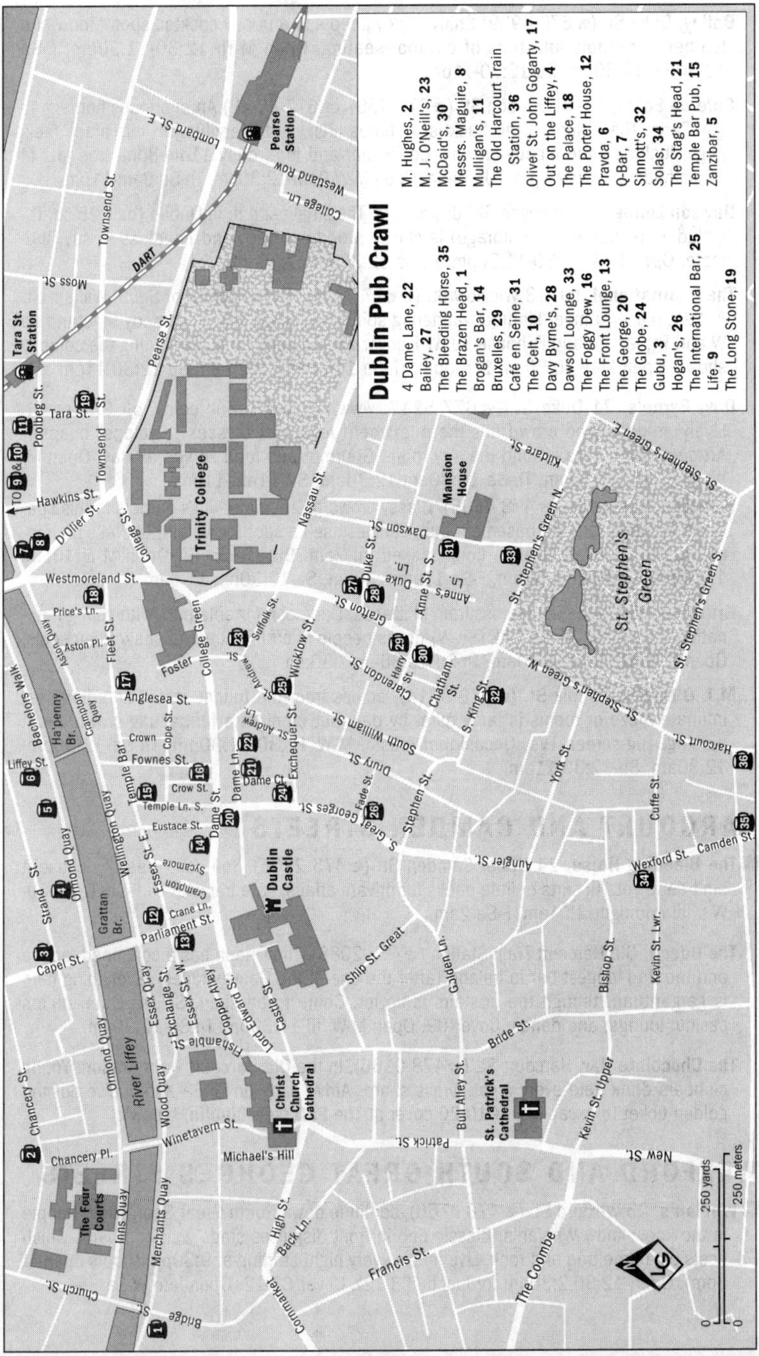

Dublin Pub Crawl
4 Dame Lane, 22
Bailey, 27
The Bleeding Horse, 35
The Brazen Head, 1
Brogan's Bar, 14
Bruxelles, 29
Café en Seine, 31
The Celt, 10
Davy Byrne's, 28
Dawson Lounge, 33
The Foggy Dew, 16
The Front Lounge, 13
The George, 20
The Globe, 24
Gubu, 3
Hogan's, 26
The International Bar, 25
Life, 9
The Long Stone, 19
M. Hughes, 2
M. J. O'Neill's, 23
McDaid's, 30
Messrs. Maguire, 8
Mulligan's, 11
The Old Harcourt Train Station, 36
Oliver St. John Gogarty, 17
Out on the Liffey, 4
The Palace, 18
The Porter House, 12
Pravda, 6
Q-Bar, 7
Sinnott's, 32
Solas, 34
The Stag's Head, 21
Temple Bar Pub, 15
Zanzibar, 5
Trinity College
St. Stephen's Green
Dublin Castle
Christ Church Cathedral
St. Patrick's Cathedral
The Four Courts
Mansion House
Pearse Station
Tara St. Station
River Liffey
Ha'penny Br.
Grattan Br.
DART
250 yards
250 meters

COUNTY DUBLIN

Bailey, Duke St. (☎670 4939) Shiny happy people in a trendy cocktail spot. Mod white leather bar stools and tons of outdoor seating. Open M-Th 12:30-11:30pm, F-Sa 12:30pm-12:30am, Su 12:30-11pm.

Cafe en Seine, 39-40 Dawson St. (☎677 4567 or 677 4549.) An enormous homage to gay Paris. The atrium in the back is 4 stories high, and everything in this place feels huge—including the nightly crowds. Coffee bar and food daily 11am-8pm. Live jazz M 10pm-midnight, Su 2-4pm. DJs Th-Sa. Open M-W 9am-12:30am, Th-Sa 9am-11pm.

Dawson Lounge, 25 Dawson St., downstairs. The smallest pub in Dublin (only 25 sq. ft., including restrooms and storage) is classy, wood-paneled, and needless to say, intimate. Open M-W 12:30-11:30pm, Th-Sa 12:30pm-12:30am.

The International Bar, 23 Wicklow St. (☎677 9250), on the corner of South William St. A great place to meet kindred wandering spirits. Excellent improv comedy M; stand-up W and Th; jazz Tu and F; house Su. W-F cover €8. Go early for a seat during the comedy shows. Open M-W 10:30am-11:30pm, Th-Sa 10:30am-12:30am, Su 12:30-11pm.

Davy Byrne's, 21 Duke St. (☎677 5217; www.davybyrnespub.com), off Grafton St. Lively, middle-aged crowd fills the pub where Joyce set *Ulysses'* "Cyclops" chapter. Art-deco bar curves around the airy room. Gourmet pub food served all day. Open M-W 10:30am-11:30pm, Th-Sa 10:30am-12:30am, Su 11am-11pm.

Sinnott's, S. King St. (☎478 4698). Classy crowd of 20-somethings gathers in this spacious, wooden-raftered basement pub. Fancies itself a spot for writers, but let's be honest: it's for drinkers. Dance floor packed 'til 2am. Big-screen TV. Open M-W 10am-11:30pm, Th 10am-2:30am, F-Sa 11am-2:45am, Su 12:30pm-1:30am.

Bruxelles (☎677 5362), across from McDaid's. Dark, comfortable pub, with young international clientele. Blues funk (Su-W) draws people in off the street to shake their souls. Open M-W 10:30am-1:30am, Th-Su 10:30am-2:30am.

M.J. O'Neill's, Suffolk St. (☎679 3614), across from the tourist office. Enormous yet intimate maze of rooms is fairly quiet by day, but by night a fun, young crowd has it pulsing. Big-screen TVs. Occasional music. M-W 12:30-11:30pm, Th-Sa 12:30pm-12:30am, Su 12:30-11pm.

HARCOURT AND CAMDEN STREETS

▨ **The Bleeding Horse,** 24 Upper Camden St. (☎475 2705). You can't beat it, 'cause it ain't dead yet. All sorts of little nooks for private affairs. Late bar with DJ F-Sa. Open Su-W until midnight, Th 1am, F-Sa 2am.

The Odeon, Old Harcourt Train Station (☎478 2088). The Odeon has a columned facade and the 2nd-longest bar in Ireland (after the one at the Galway races). Everything here is gargantuan, though the upstairs is cozier. Come to be seen. Sa DJ. Other nights casino, lounge, and dance. Cover €9. Open M-W 'til 11:30pm, Th-Su 12:30am.

The Chocolate Bar, Harcourt St. (☎478 0166), in the Old Harcourt Train Station. Young clubbers drink here every night. Dress sharp. Arrive early on Th-Sa and you've got the golden ticket to escape the €10-20 cover at **The PoD** (see **Clublin,** below).

WEXFORD AND SOUTH GREAT GEORGES STREETS

▨ **Whelan's,** 25 Wexford St. (☎478 0766), continue down South Great Georges St. People in the know know Whelan's. Classic pub in front disguises stage venue in back, which hosts big-name trad and rock. Live music every night starting at 9:30pm (doors open at 8pm). Open 12:30-2:30pm for lunch (€8-12). Cover €7-12. Open late W-Sa.

■ **The Stag's Head,** 1 Dame Ct. (☎ 679 3701). Beautiful Victorian pub with stained glass, mirrors, and evidence of deer decapitation. The student crowd dons everything from t-shirts to tuxes and spills into the alleys. Excellent pub grub; mains €10. Food served M-F noon-3:30pm. Bar open M-F 10:30am-11:30pm, Sa-Su 11am-12:30am.

Hogan's, 35 S. Great Georges St. (☎ 677 5904). Draws an attractive, voguish crowd, despite its no-frills name and minimalist decor. Self-proclaimed "surly bar staff" (not really). Su DJ from 4pm. Open M-W 12:30pm-11:30pm, Th 12:30pm-12:30am, F-Sa 12:30pm-2:30am, Su 4-11:30pm.

The Globe, 11 S. Great Georges St. (☎ 671 1220). Frequented by a laid-back, hip young crowd. Fine spot to relax with a Guinness or a frothy cappuccino. Open M-Sa noon-3am, Su 4pm-1am. **Rí Rá** nightclub attached (see **Clublin**, p.19).

4 Dame Lane, 4 Dame Ln. (☎ 679 2901). Look for the two flaming torches behind the Stag's Head. Well dressed crowd descends late at night on this brick warehouse to see and be seen. Live DJs nightly. Open M-Sa 5pm-3am, Su 11pm-1am.

Solas, 31 Wexford St. (☎ 478 0583) Live DJs spin pop music for local trendsters. Sidle into one of the huge velvet booths and check out the circular fishtank on the stairs. Open M-W noon-11:30pm, Th-Sa noon-12:30am, Su 4-11pm.

TEMPLE BAR

■ **The Porter House,** 16-18 Parliament St. (☎ 679 8847). Way, way, way more than 99 bottles of beer on the wall. The largest selection of world beers in the country plus 9 self-brewed porters, stouts, and ales. Excellent sampler tray includes a stout made with oysters (€9). Fills with a great crowd nightly for trad, blues, and rock. Open M, Tu, Th 11:30am-11:30pm, W 11:30am-midnight, F-Sa 11:30am-2am, Su 11:30am-11pm.

Brogan's Bar, 75 Dame St. (☎ 671 1844). Unassuming little spot ignored by tourists despite its location. Spend a night on an internal pub crawl marveling at their impressive collection of Guinness paraphernalia, or just enjoy pint after pint of the "black magic." Open M-W 4-11:30pm, Th 4pm-12:30am, F-Sa 1pm-12:30am, Su 1-11:30pm.

The Foggy Dew, Fownes St. (☎ 677 9328). Like a friendly village pub but twice as big and loud. Great spot for a pint without the flash of other Temple Bar pubs. Live rock Su nights. M-W 11am-11:30pm, Th 11am-12:30am, F-Sa 11am-1:30am, Su 12:30-11pm.

The Palace, 21 Fleet St. (☎ 677 9290), behind Aston Quay. Classic, neighborly pub has old-fashioned wood paneling and close quarters; head for comfy seats in the stained-glass, sky-lit back room. Favorite of many a Dubliner and the only true Irish Pub in Temple Bar. Open M-W 10:30am-11:30pm, Th-Sa 10:30am-12:30am, Su 12:30-11pm.

Messrs. Maguire, Burgh Quay (☎ 670 5777). Explore this classy watering hole under the spell of homemade microbrews. Sampler tray of 9 beers €10.50. Trad Su-Tu 9:30-11:30pm. Late bar W-Sa. Food served all day. Open M-Tu 10:30am-12:30am, W 11am-1:30am, Th 10:30am-2am, F-Sa 11am-2:30am, Su 12:30pm-12:30am.

Oliver St. John Gogarty, Fleet and Anglesea St. (☎ 671 1822). Lively, convivial atmosphere in a traditional but touristed pub. Named for Joyce's nemesis and onetime roommate, who appears in *Ulysses* as Buck Mulligan (see p. 140). Much-sought-after trad daily from 2:30pm. Open daily 10:30am-2am.

Q-Bar, Burgh Quay (☎ 677 7435), at O'Connell bridge. Modernistic and funky, with chrome pillars, bright red airline chairs, and a young, hip crowd. Dance floor opens with pop and chart at 10pm. Open Su-Tu 11:30-2am, W 11:30am-2:30am, Th-Sa 11:30am-2:45am.

Temple Bar Pub, Temple Ln. S. (☎ 672 5286). Sprawling, wheelchair-accessible pub with outdoor beer garden for balmy summer nights. Music daily at 12:30, 5:30, and 8:30pm. Open Su-Th 10:30am-12:30am, F-Sa 10:30am-1:30am.

THE BEST OF THE REST

⧉ Mulligan's, 8 Poolbeg St. (☎677 5582), behind Burgh Quay off Tara St. Upholds its reputation as one of the best pint-pourers in Dublin. A taste of the typical Irish pub: low-key and nothing fancy. People of all ages gather around the large tables to toast each other. Open M-W 10:30am-11:30pm, Th-Sa 10:30am-12:30am, Su noon-11pm.

Zanzibar (☎878 7212), at the Ha'penny Bridge. Mix of Oriental/Arab decor and pop culture. Quite the hot spot, but well air-conditioned. Bust out on the way from the fabulous high-ceilinged bar to the dance floor in back. Live DJ nightly. Open daily 4pm-2:30am.

M. Hughes, 19 Chancery St. (☎872 6540), behind Four Courts. Attracts the prosecution and the defense, and is loaded with *Garda* at lunch. Delightful neighborhood venue for authentic nightly trad and set dancing M and W-Th around 9:30pm. Join the Monday Morning Club and be the first in Dublin to down a Guinness; pub opens at 7am (woo hoo!), closes M-W at 11:30pm, Th-Sa at 12:30am, Su at 11pm.

Pravda (☎874 0090), 35 Lower Liffey St. on the north side of the Ha'penny Bridge. The Russian late bar and Russian DJ action goes Russian Th-Sa. Actually, there's nothing Russian about the place, other than Cyrillic on the wall murals. Trendy, popular, gay-friendly, and crowded. Late bar F-Sa until 2:30am.

Life, Lower Abbey St. (☎878 1032), next to the Irish Life Centre—to the left of the large "Chariot of Life" fountain and sculpture. The young and the beautiful head here after work to talk about important things like image. Cool aquarium in the middle of the bar. Pink-tinted skylights on upper level. Mediterranean-ish lunch €8-12. DJ Th-Sa.

The Celt, 81-82 Talbot St. (☎878 8655). Step out of the city and into Olde Ireland. Small, comfortably worn, and genuinely welcoming. Nightly trad. Open 10:30am-late.

The Long Stone, 10-11 Townsend St. (☎671 8102). Old books and handcarved banisters lend a rustic medieval feel. Carvery lunches (€8-9) M-F noon-2:30pm. Open M-W noon-11:30pm, Th-F noon-12:30am, Sa 4pm-12:30am, Su 4-11pm.

The Brazen Head, 20 North Bridge St. (☎679 5186), off Merchant's Quay. Dublin's oldest and one of its liveliest pubs, established in 1198 as the first stop after the bridge on the way into the city. The courtyard, with its beer barrel tables, is quite the pickup scene on summer nights. The United Irishmen once met here to plan their attacks on the British (see **Rebellion,** p. 61). Carvery and pub grub menu served 12:30-9pm. Nightly trad. Open M-W 10:30am-11:30pm, Th-Sa 10:30am-12:30am, Su 12:30pm-12:30am.

⧉ CLUBLIN

In Dublin's nightlife war, clubs were beginning to overtake pub rock venues, but the pubs are fighting back with later hours. As a rule, clubs open at 10:30 or 11pm, but the action heats up after the 11:30pm pub closings. Clubbing is an expensive end the evening, since covers run €7-20 and pints are a steep €5. Find a club with an expensive cover but cheap drink prices and stay all night. **Concessions** provide discounts with varying restrictions. Stag's Head (see **Publin,** p. 109) offers them around 11pm, but any nightclub attached to a pub distributes them in its home bar. There are a handful of smaller clubs on **Harcourt** and **Leeson Street** that can be fun, if a bit austere. Most clubs close between 1:30 and 3am, but a few have been known to last until daybreak. To get home after 11:30pm, when Dublin Bus stops running, dancing queens take the **NiteLink bus** (M-W

12:30am and 2am, Th-Sa every 20min. from 12:30am-4:30am; €4), which runs designated routes from the corner of Westmoreland and College St. to Dublin's suburbs. **Taxi** stands are located in front of Trinity, at the top of Grafton St. by St. Stephen's Green, and on Lower Abbey St. Be prepared to wait 30-45min. on weekend nights. For the most up-to-date information on clubs, check the **Event Guide's** "clubbing night by night" page.

▨ **The PoD,** 35 Harcourt St. (☎478 0225; www.pod.ie). Corner of Hatch St., in an old train station. Spanish-style decor meets hard-core dance music. The truly brave venture upstairs to **The Red Box** (☎478 0225), a separate, more intense club with warehouse atmosphere, brain-crushing music, and an 8-deep crowd at the bar designed to winnow out the weak. Often hosts big-name DJs—cover charges skyrocket. Cover €10-20; ladies free before midnight; Th and Sa €7 with ISIC card. Open until 3am. Start the evening at **The Odeon** or **Chocolate Bar,** which share the building (see **Publin,** p. 108).

Rí-Rá, 1 Exchequer St. (☎677 4835), behind the Globe (see **Publin,** p. 109). Generally good music steers clear of pop and house extremes. 2 floors, several bars, more crannies than a crumpet, and a womb-like downstairs. Open daily 11pm-2am. Cover €7-10.

Gaiety, S. King St. (☎679 5622; www.gaietytheatre.com), off Grafton St. Elegant theater shows late-night wild side midnight-4am every F-Sa. 4 bar areas. Best of all worlds with salsa, jazz, swing, latin, and soul. Cover about €10. Open F-Sa 11:15pm-4:15am.

Club M, Blooms Hotel, Cope St. (☎671 5622), in Temple Bar, in the big orange building. One of Dublin's largest clubs, attracting a crowd of all ages and styles, with multiple stairways and a few bars in back. If at first you don't succeed, grind, grind again. Cover Su-Th €7, ladies free before midnight; F-Sa €12-15. Free tickets often distributed in Temple Bar. Open M-Th 11pm-2:30am, F-Sa 10pm-2:30am, Su 10:30pm-1am.

Tomato, 60 Harcourt St. (☎476 4900). Smaller venue, usually blasting house and glam-girly sounds. College-age crowd during the school year. Very cheap drinks. Cover W-Th student night €4 or free; F-Sa €10. Open nightly.

Club Aquarium (Fibber's), 80-82 Parnell St. (☎872 2575). No charts here; mostly indie. Houses Ireland's only metal club. Occasional Goth nights. If the darkness, heat, or doom gets to be too much, head outside to the deck to finish things up (drinks, that is). Weekend cover €7. Open daily until 2am, later Th-Sa.

Switch, 21-25 Eustace St. (☎670 7655). Only 18+ club in Temple Bar, so younger crowd flocks here. M gay night, F drum and bass, Sa techno, Su funky groove, otherwise a lot of deep house. Cover Su-Th €7, F €10, Sa €13.

The Palace Niteclub, Camden St. (☎478 0808), in Camden de Luxe Hotel. Meat market for mostly young-20s crowd. Pop faves blast under barrel-vaulted ceiling. Cover M-Th €5.50 with €2 drinks, Sa free until 10pm. Open M-Sa until 2:30am.

The Village, 26 Wexford St. (☎475 8555). Newly renovated 2-floor glittering pub/club. Bands play Th-Sa from 7-10:30pm (cover €5-15), then DJs come in for chill-out, jungle, and house downstairs. Cover €10 after 11pm. Open Th-Sa until 3am.

The Turk's Head, Parliament St. (☎679 2606), beneath the pub. Think Istanbul in a jar. 70s-80s classics. F-Sa cover €5, free in early evening.

GAY AND LESBIAN NIGHTLIFE

The gay nightclub scene is alive and well, with gay venues (usually rented-out clubs) just about every night. Keep up-to-date by checking out the various entertainment publications around town (see **Gay and Lesbian Dublin,** p. 112).

▨ **The George,** 89 S. Great Georges St. (☎478 2983; www.capitalbars.com). This throbbing, purple man o' war is Dublin's first and most prominent gay bar. A mixed-age crowd gathers throughout the day to chat and sip. The attached nightclub opens W-Su until 2am. Frequent theme nights. Su night drag Bingo is accompanied by so much entertainment that sometimes the Bingo never happens. Look spiffy—no effort, no entry. Cover €8-10 after 10pm. Open M-Tu 12:30-11:30pm, W-Su 12:30pm-2:30am.

▨ **The Front Lounge,** Parliament St. (☎670-4112). The velvet seats of this gay-friendly bar are popular with a very mixed, very trendy crowd. Open M and W noon-11:30pm, Tu noon-12:30am, F-Sa noon-1:30am, Su 4-11:30pm.

Out on the Liffey, 27 Upper Ormond Quay (☎872 2480). Ireland's 2nd gay bar; its name plays on the more traditional, but still gay, Inn on the Liffey a few doors down. Lots of dark nooks in which to chat and drink. The short hike from the city center ensures a local crowd most nights. Tu game show, F-Sa DJ. No cover. Open M-Tu noon-11:30pm, W-Th noon-12:30am, F-Sa noon-2:30am, Su noon-midnight.

Gubu, 7-8 Capel St. (☎874 0710). Modern with small dance floor. Pleasant oasis in Dublin's working class neighborhood. Everything from disco to jazz to comedy during the week. Ask about origin of bar's name. Open Su-W 5-11:30pm, Th-Sa 5pm-12:30am.

⚞ TOURS

SELF-GUIDED WALKING TOURS

Dublin is definitely a walking city, as most major sights lie within 1 mi. of O'Connell Bridge. The tourist office sells *Dublin's Top Visitor Attractions*, which lists the main attractions, essential information, and directions. The first three walking tours listed below are in *Heritage Trails: Signpost Walking Tours of Dublin*. Individual trail pamphlets can be purchased for the Ulysses Trail and the Rock 'N' Stroll Trail. All guides are available at the tourist office (€1.50-3.50). New for 2004, *Let's Go* now features its own **Dublin Walking Tour.**

THE CULTURAL TRAIL. Starring James Joyce and Sean O'Casey, this route zips past the North Side's important sights: the Four Courts, the Custom House and King's Inns, the Municipal Gallery, and the Dublin Writers Museum.

THE OLD CITY TRAIL. This walk begins on College Green and weaves its way through the Liberties and the markets, ending in Temple Bar. Ironically, the Old City trail hits some of the city's newest, most garish exhibits, including Dublinia.

GEORGIAN HERITAGE TRAIL. No visitors to Dublin should deny themselves the pleasure of viewing the best-preserved Georgian streets, terraces, and public buildings south of the Liffey.

ULYSSES MAP OF DUBLIN. Charts Poldy's haunts and retraces his heroic actions, beginning with kidneys for breakfast. The walk takes a full 18hr. (including drinking and debauching), but it's faster than reading *Ulysses*. Take your pick.

ROCK 'N' STROLL TRAIL. Circuits the significant sights in Dublin's recent musical history. It covers U2's Windmill Lane Studios and provides the grim details of Sinead O'Connor's waitressing job at the Bad Ass Cafe.

GUIDED WALKING TOURS

For the more social type who enjoys big groups and doesn't mind the idea of a tour guide saying "Come on, move on, we can't let the rest of the group down," there are several tours to try. Most tours are about 2hr. long, but entertaining anecdotes and continuous movement keep boredom at bay.

HISTORICAL WALKING TOUR. Provides a crash course in Dublin and Irish history, stopping at a variety of Dublin sights. Guides seamlessly transition from one era to another and one street to another, protecting tourers from ignorance and Dublin's maniac drivers. (*Meet at Trinity's front gate.* ☎ *878 0227. Apr.-Sept. daily 11am and 3pm; May-Aug. also special themed tours at noon, Oct.-Mar. F-Su noon. €10, students €8.*)

TRINITY COLLEGE WALKING TOUR. Moderately irreverent and enormously pretentious, this student-led tour concentrates on University lore, with glimpses of Dublin history. All that pretension *does* skip tourers to the front at the Book of Kells. (☎ *608 1000. Wheelchair-accessible. 30min. Tours June-Sept. 10:15am-3:40pm leave every 40min. from the info booth inside the front gate; Mar.-May weekends only. €9; includes admission to the Old Library and the Book of Kells.; tour only €4. Children under 13 free.*)

DUBLIN FOOTSTEPS. This tour treads the beaten and offbeat paths of Irish literary greats past the Georgian architecture that housed them. (*Meet upstairs in the James Joyce room at the Grafton St. Bewley's.* ☎ *496 0641 or 269 7021. Tour lasts 2hr. M, W, and F-Sa 10:30am. €9.*)

1916 REBELLION WALKING TOUR. The creation of the Republic arguably began with the 1916 Rebellion (see p. 63), which took place solely in Dublin. See the scars it left and the state it created. (*Meet at the International Bar, 23 Wicklow St.* ☎ *473 4986. Tour lasts 2hr. Apr.-Sept. M-Sa 11:30am and 2:30pm, Su 1pm. Mar. and Oct. M-Sa 11:30am, Su 1pm. €10.*)

AUDIO WALKING TOUR OF DUBLIN. A comprehensive if somewhat mechanical guide for those who aren't into asking questions. Available in several languages. (*Aston Quay.* ☎ *670 5266. Open daily 10am-5pm. Half-day €8, students €6; full-day €11.*)

GUIDED PUB CRAWLS

THE DUBLIN LITERARY PUB CRAWL. The tour traces Dublin's liquid history in reference to its literary history, spewing informative factoids between entrancing monologues. (*Meet at The Duke, 2 Duke St.* ☎ *670 5602; www.dublinpubcrawl.com. Apr.-Oct. M-Sa 7:30pm, Su noon and 7:30pm; Nov.-Mar. Th-Sa 7:30pm, Su noon and 7:30pm. €10, students €8. Suffolk St. tourist office takes bookings.*)

MUSICAL PUB CRAWL. An enjoyable jaunt led by two musicians (and their instruments), who teach aspiring trad-heads how to differentiate between one session and another. (*Arrive a little early upstairs at Oliver St. John Gogarty's, on the corner of Fleet and Anglesea St.* ☎ *478 0193; www.musicalpubcrawl.com. Apr.-Oct. daily 7:30pm; Oct.-Mar. F-Sa 7:30pm. €10, students and seniors €8.*)

BUS TOURS

Dublin Bus runs a number of tours through and around the city, including the first two listings below. Both depart from the Dublin Bus office, at 59 O'Connell St. (☎ *873 4222. Open M-Sa 9am-7pm.*)

DUBLIN WALKING TOUR

Dublin is a compact city, and walking around is the best (maybe the only) way to learn to love it, in all of its bustling, mismatched glory. *Let's Go's* new walking tour leads you through the city to special places that avoid the lines but pack at least as much punch as what you'll get hopping on or off a bus. Best of all, nearly all the sites are free! Starting at 10:30am, and visiting all the sites we list,

Time: 8hr.

Distance: 3 mi.

Season: Year-round.

you'll have a full and definitely fulfilling day in the city. Or tailor the tour to your own desires stopping to enjoy whatever strikes your fancy.

1 MULLIGAN'S PUB: Begin in Mulligan's Pub, with possibly the best pint of Guinness you' ever drink. Journalists, writers, and JFK have all crowded into this classic Victorian pub.

2 TRINITY COLLEGE: Wind your way down to Trinity College's front gates, and wande through the quadrangles marvelling at the impressive stone buildings and the pristine grass—stays so green because nobody is allowed to walk on it—stick to the cobblestone pathways!

3 MERRION SQUARE: Exit onto Lincoln Pl. and jig down to Merrion Square, a wonderfu enclosed garden where a colorful statue of **Oscar Wilde** reclines on a rock. When you've soake up enough greenery, exit onto Merrion Sq. Rd., where you will pass by the imposing **Govern ment Buildings** and **Natural History Museum.**

4 UNICORN FOOD STORE: At the end of the street, turn right onto Merrion Row, and mak sure to stop at Unicorn Food Store to grab picnic supplies before heading to **St. Stephen' Green,** Dublin's most bustling and exciting park, for a relaxed lunch on the lawn.

5 DUBLIN CIVIC MUSEUM: Exit at the Northwest corner, where St. Stephen's Shopping Cer ter attracts crowds. Pass the poor fools by, head down William St. South, and stop in the Dubli Civic Museum for a free taste of old Dublin or go to **Powerscourt House** for chi-chi shopping.

6 BUTLER'S CHOCOLATE CAFE: By now you might be a bit tired, so hop into Butler's Cho olate Cafe and jolt yourself awake with a cup of their stunning hot chocolate. From there stro down Exchequer St. and onto South Great George's St. before hitting Dame St. for a few blocks

7 DUBLIN CASTLE: Turn left and pass by **City Hall** before entering the gates of Dublin Castl If the 20th-century wing doesn't impress you (it won't), go to the **circular lawn** behind the Stat Apartments. This large lawn, with a celtic knot path running through it, covers the spot wher the "black pool" from which Dublin derives its name used to stand. This is a good place t lounge, look at your map, and marvel at the funny and colorful turrets of Dublin Castle.

8 CHESTER BEATTY LIBRARY: Next to the lawn is the Chester Beatty Library. With no charg and no lines, this building houses beautiful old manuscripts, including some of the oldes extant pages of the Bible, written on fraying papyrus, and gorgeous illuminated manuscripts.

9 ST. AUDOEN'S GATE: Exit the Castle Grounds the way you came, and turn left to hea down Dame St., passing the grand **Christ Church,** and turning right on Winetavern St., to se St. Audoen's Gate, one of the few remaining pieces of the Old City walls. Cross O'Donova Rossa Bridge, and turn left in front of the **Four Courts,** a masterpiece of Georgian architecture

10 ST. MICHAN'S CHURCH: From here, if you look across the Liffey, is a great view of **Chris Church** and its flying buttresses. Turn right onto Church St. to find St. Michan's Church, and it nightmare-inducing **vaults.**

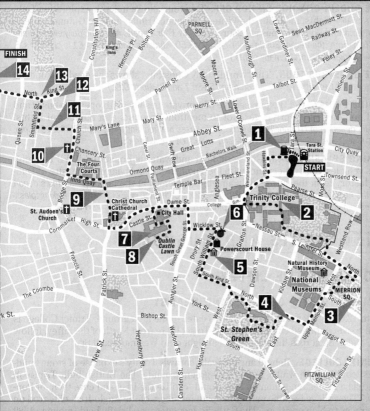

OLD JAMESON DISTILLERY: After all the coffins and cobwebs, you might want a drink, follow the signs to the Old Jameson Distillery and sample some firewater.

DULIN BREWING COMPANY: If you're not into the hard stuff or hordes of tourists, opt the Dublin Brewing Company tour instead, and see how beer really gets made. If you're dying for a spectacular view of the city, climb to the **Chimney Viewing Tower** for your to-ops.

CHIEF O'NEILL'S: Dinner is traditional Irish food at Chief O'Neill's, just below the er, or, for those on a budget, walk down King St. to **Stoneybatter Road,** where takeaway nters abound.

COBBLESTONE: To round out the night in grand fashion, grab a stool and a pint at Cob-stone and settle in for a night of trad (sessions start at 7pm). When you're finally ready for or, more likely, when the lights have been dimmed and the musicians sent home, walk two blocks down to Arran Quay to catch any bus heading back towards O'Connell St.

norrow: sleep late, and go eat a big Irish breakfast–you deserve it!

THE DUBLIN CITY HOP-ON HOP-OFF. This tour allows indepth exploration Dublin's major sights, including the Writers Museum, Trinity, and the Guinness Brewery. Exit and board the bus at leisure. (*Roughly 1¼hr. Departs Apr.-Sept. daily every 10min. 9:30am-5pm, then every 30min. until 7pm. €12.50, students and seniors €11, children €6. Ticket brings discounts at many sights.*)

THE GHOSTBUS TOUR. The "world's only Ghostbus" shows the dead and undead aspects of the city. (*2¼hr. M-F 8pm and Sa-Su 7 and 9:30pm. €22.*)

GUIDE FRIDAY. Get the perspective of a private bus line with open-top buses and full hop-on/hop-off privileges, not to mention discounts at a number of sights. (*Tours depart from O'Connell St. ☎676 5377. Buses run frequently Apr.-Sept. 9:40am-5:30pm, Oct.-Mar. 9:30am-4pm. €14, students and seniors €12, children €5.*)

VIKING SPLASH TOURS. Cruise on land and water in converted WWII amphibious vehicles. Razz other tours with the Viking Roar, and hear diverse tales of Dublin history from the surprisingly amiable Norsemen at the helm. (*1¼hr. Tours depart on the hour from Bull Alley St. behind St. Patrick's Cathedral. ☎453 9185; www.vikingsplashtours.com. M-Sa 10am-6pm, Su 11am-6pm. €15.95, children €8.85.*)

👁 🏛 SIGHTS AND MUSEUMS

SOUTH OF THE LIFFEY

WITHIN TRINITY COLLEGE AND NEARBY

With 12,000 students and 1200 staff to cater to the area around, Trinity College is like a self-contained city within a city. To get there from North of the Liffey, follow O'Connell St. across the river and bear right onto Westmoreland St.

TRINITY COLLEGE. Behind ancient walls sprawls Trinity's expanse of stone buildings, cobblestone walks, and grassy-green grounds. The British built Trinity in 1592 as a Protestant seminary that would "civilize the Irish and cure them of Popery." The college became part of the path members of the Anglo-Irish elite trod on their way to high positions. The Catholic Jacobites who briefly held Dublin in 1689 used the campus as a barracks and a prison (see The Ascendancy, p. 60). Jonathan Swift, Robert Emmett, Thomas Moore, Edmund Burke, Oscar Wilde, and Samuel Beckett are just a few of the famous Irishmen who studied here. Bullet holes from Easter 1916 mar the stone entrance. Until the 1960s, the Catholic church deemed it a cardinal sin to attend Trinity; once the church lifted the ban, the size of the student body more than tripled. (*Hard to miss—between Westmoreland and Grafton St., in the very center of South Dublin. The main entrance fronts the block-long traffic circle now called College Green. Pearse St. runs along the north edge of the college, Nassau St. to the south. ☎608 1000; www.tcd.ie. Grounds always open. Free.*)

THE OLD LIBRARY. This 1712 chamber holds an invaluable collection of ancient manuscripts, including the renowned **Book of Kells.** Around AD 800, four Irish monks squeezed multicolored ink from bugs and plants to illustrate this four-volume edition of the Gospels. Each page holds an intricate latticework of Celtic designs, interwoven with images of animals and Latin text. In 1007 the books were unearthed at Kells (see p. 164), where thieves had apparently buried them. For preservation purposes, the display is limited to two volumes, of which one page is turned each month. A new exhibit elegantly details the history of the book's illustration, and also describes the library's other prize holdings. The **Book**

of Durrow, Ireland's oldest manuscript (see **Christians and Vikings,** p. 57), is also on display periodically. Upstairs, the library's **Long Room** contains Ireland's oldest harp—the **Brian Ború Harp,** used as the design model for Irish coins—and one of the few remaining **1916 proclamations** of the Republic of Ireland. The room seethes with scholarship, although the catalogue system (smallest books on the top shelf, largest on the bottom) seems to be more for practical reasons than academic. *(From the main gate, the library is on the south side of Library Sq. ☎ 608 2320; www.tcd.ie/library. Open June-Sept. M-Sa 9:30am-5pm, Su noon-4:30pm; Oct.-May M-Sa 9:30am-5pm, Su noon-4:30pm. €7, students and seniors €6.)*

BANK OF IRELAND. Staring down Trinity from across College Green is the monolithic Bank of Ireland. Built in 1729, the building originally housed the **Irish Parliament,** a body that represented only the Anglo-Irish landowner class. After the Act of Union (see **Rebellion,** p. 61), the Brits sold the building to the bank on the condition that it destroy all material evidence of the parliament's previous existence. Despite the bank's effort, tourists can still visit the former chamber of the **House of Lords,** which contains a huge 1780s chandelier and Maundy Money—special coins once given to the poor on the Thursday before Easter and legal tender only for that day. *(☎ 677 6801. Open M-W and F 10am-4pm, Th 10am-5pm. 45min. guided talks Tu 10:30, 11:30am, and 1:45pm. Free.)*

GRAFTON STREET. The few blocks south of College Green are off-limits to cars and a playground for pedestrians. Grafton's **street performers** range from string octets to jive limboists. Upstairs at the Grafton St. branch of Bewley's and inside the chain's former chocolate factory is the **Bewley's Museum.** Tea-tasting machines, corporate history, and a Bewley's Quaker heritage display number among the marvels. *(Open daily 7:30am-11pm. Free.)*

THE DUBLIN CIVIC MUSEUM. This pint-sized, two-story townhouse holds photos, antiquities, and knick-knacks relating to the whole range of Dublin life, from the accessories of the Vikings to the shoes of Patrick Cotter, the 8½ ft. "Giant of Ireland." *(58 South William St., next to Powerscourt Townhouse Shopping Center. ☎ 679 4260. Open Tu-Sa 10am-6pm, Su 11am-2pm. Free.)*

KILDARE STREET

The block bordered by Kildare St., Merrion St. (continuation of Nassau St.), and St. Stephen's Green is loaded with impressive buildings and the major museums.

THE NATIONAL GALLERY. This collection of over 2500 canvases includes paintings by Brueghel, Goya, Carravaggio, Vermeer, Rembrandt, and El Greco. Works by 19th-century Irish artists comprise a major part of the collection. The works of **Jack Yeats,** brother of W.B., are of particular interest. Portraits of Lady Gregory, James Joyce, and George Bernard Shaw complete the display. The new **Millennium Wing** houses a 20th-Century Irish Art exhibit, a Yeats archive, and computer stations that give "virtual tours" of the museum, but the real thing is in the next room, so go see it! Summertime brings concerts, lectures, and art classes; inquire at the front desk for schedules. *(Merrion Sq. W. ☎ 661 5133. Open M-W and F-Sa 9:30am-5:30pm, Th 9:30am-8:30pm, Su noon-5pm. Free guided tours Sa 3pm; Su 2, 3, and 4pm. July-Aug. daily 3pm. Admission free. Concerts and art classes €6-20.)*

LEINSTER HOUSE. The Duke of Leinster made his home on Kildare St. back in 1745, when most of the urban upper-crust lived north of the Liffey. By building his house so far south, where land was cheaper, he could afford an enormous front lawn. Today, Leinster House provides chambers for the **Irish Parliament,** or **An tOireachtas** (on tir-OCH-tas). It holds both the **Dáil** (DOIL), which does most of the government work, and the **Seanad** (SHAN-ad), the less powerful upper house (see p. 65). The Dáil meets, very roughly and with lots of breaks, from October to Easter, Tuesday and Wednesday 3-9pm, and Thursday 10am-3pm. When the Dáil is in session, visitors can view the proceedings by contacting the Captain of the Guard, who conducts **tours** of the galleries. *(☎678 9911. Passport necessary. Tours leave from the adjacent National Gallery Sa on the hour.)*

■**THE NATURAL HISTORY MUSEUM.** This "museum of a museum" showcases Victorian taxidermy at its strangest, with exotic stuffed animals from the world over. Three creepy skeletons of giant Irish deer greet visitors at the front, and the museum is stocked with many more beautiful and fascinating examples of classic taxidermy, all displayed in old Victorian cabinets. The dodo skeleton draws crowds away from the Irish parasitic worms exhibit, and red tarps cover scary insect exhibits—lift them only if brave. *(Upper Merrion St. ☎677 7444. Open Tu-Sa 10am-5pm and Su 2-5pm. Free.)*

THE NATIONAL MUSEUM OF ARCHAEOLOGY AND HISTORY. The largest of Dublin's museums has extraordinary artifacts spanning the last two millennia. One room gleams with the **Tara Brooch,** the **Ardagh Hoard,** and other Celtic goldwork. Another section is devoted to the Republic's founding years and flaunts the bloody vest of nationalist hero **James Connolly.** *(Kildare St., next to Leinster House. ☎677 7444. Open Tu-Sa 10am-5pm and Su 2-5pm. Guided tours €1.50; call for times. Museum free.)*

THE NATIONAL LIBRARY. Chronicles Irish history and exhibits literary goodies in its entrance room. A genealogical research room helps visitors trace even the thinnest twiglets of their Irish family trees. The reading room is quite elegant, with an airy, domed-bridged ceiling. *(Kildare St., adjacent to Leinster House. ☎603 0200. Open M-W 10am-9pm, Th-F 10am-5pm, Sa 10am-1pm. Free. Academic reason required to obtain a library card and entrance to the reading room; just "being a student" is usually enough.)*

ST. STEPHEN'S GREEN AND MERRION SQUARE

Home to Ireland's trendiest shops and most expensive city homes, Merrion Sq. draws shoppers and gawkers, while chill-seekers relax nearby on the grass of Dublin's finest park.

ST. STEPHEN'S GREEN. This 22 acre park was a private estate until the Guinness clan bequeathed it to the city. Today, the grounds are teeming with public life: punks, couples, gardens, fountains, gazebos, strollers, swans, an artificial lake, a waterfall, a statue of Henry Moore, and a partridge in a pear tree. During the summer, musical and theatrical productions are given near the old bandstand. *(Kildare, Dawson, and Grafton St. all lead to it. ☎475 7826. Open M-Sa 8am-dusk, Su 10am-dusk.)*

MERRION SQUARE. The Georgian buildings and elaborate doorways of Merrion Sq. and adjacent Fitzwilliam St. feed any architectural longings. After leaving 18 Fitzwilliam St., Yeats took up residence at 82 Merrion Sq. Farther south on Harcourt St., playwright George Bernard Shaw and Dracula's creator, Bram Stoker, were neighbors at #61 and #16, respectively. At one point the Electricity Supply Board tore down a row of the townhouses to build a monstrous new office. Irate Dubliners had a row of a different sort, and to compensate, the ESB now funds #29 Lower Fitzwilliam St., a completely restored townhouse-turned-museum demonstrating the lifestyle of the 18th-century Anglo-Irish elite. *(☎702 6165. Open Tu-Sa 10am-5pm, Su 2-5pm. A short audiovisual show leads to a 25min. tour of the house. €3.50, students and seniors €1.50.)* The prim Georgians continue up Dawson St., which connects St. Stephen's Green to Trinity College one block west of Leinster House. Dawson St. has the honor of bestowing an address on the Mansion House, home to the Lord Mayors of Dublin since 1715. The house's eclectic facade exhibits evidence of several aesthetic eras. The Irish state declared its independence here in 1919, and the Anglo-Irish truce was signed in the mansion two years later. *(Not open to the public, but feel free to gawk outside.)*

NEWMAN HOUSE. This fully restored building was once the seat of **University College Dublin,** the Catholic answer to Trinity. *A Portrait of the Artist as a Young Man* chronicles Joyce's time here. The poet Gerard Manley Hopkins spent the last years of his life teaching classics at the college. The cursory tour is geared to the architectural and the literary. *(85-86 St. Stephen's Green S. ☎716 7422. Admission by guided tour. Open to individuals only in June-Aug. Tu-F at noon, 2, 3, and 4pm. Groups admitted throughout the year with advance booking. €4, concessions €3.)*

THE SHAW BIRTHPLACE. Suitable as either a period piece or a glimpse into G.B. Shaw's childhood. Mrs. Shaw held recitals here, sparking little George's interest in music; her lovely Victorian garden inspired his fascination with landscape painting. *(33 Synge St. Stroll down Camden, make a right on Harrington, and turn left onto Synge St. Convenient to buses #16, 19, or 122 from O'Connell St. ☎475 0854 or 872 2077. Open May-Sept. M-Sa 10am-5pm, Su 11am-5pm; no tours 1-2pm. Open for groups outside hours by request. €6, concessions €5, children €3.50.)* Nearby is the **Grand Canal,** where a stony version of the poet **Patrick Kavanagh** sits on his favorite bench by the water.

THE IRISH JEWISH MUSEUM. This museum resides in a restored former synagogue and houses a large collection of artifacts, documents, and photographs chronicling the history of the Jewish community in Ireland from 1079 (five arrived and were soon sent packing) through later waves of European migration (things didn't get much better). The most famous Jewish Dubliner covered is, predictably, Leopold Bloom of *Ulysses* fame. *(3-4 Walworth Rd., off Victoria St. S. Circular Rd. runs to Victoria St.; from there the museum is signposted. Any bus to S. Circular Rd., including #16 and 20, goes there. ☎490 1857. Open May-Sept. Tu, Th, and Su 11am-3:30pm; Oct.-Apr. Su 10:30am-2:30pm. Groups may call to arrange an alternate visiting time.)*

TEMPLE BAR

West of Trinity, between Dame St. and the Liffey, the Temple Bar neighborhood writhes with activity. Narrow neo-cobblestone streets link cheap cafes, hole-in-the-wall theaters, rock venues, and used clothing and record stores. In the early 1980s, the Irish transport authority intended to replace the neighborhood with a seven-acre transportation center. The artists and nomads who lived here raised a row about being forced into homelessness. In 1985, they circulated petitions and saved their homes and businesses from the heartless corporate interests of the transit project. Temple Bar immediately grew into one of Europe's hottest spots for nightlife, forcing the artists and nomads into homelessness. (Ah, the sweet irony of life.) To steer the growth to ends more cultural than alcoholic, the government-sponsored Temple Bar Properties has spent over €40 million to build a flock of arts-related tourist attractions, with independent coattail-riders springing up as well. Even so, weekend nights tend to be wild, with stag and hen (bachelor and bachelorette) parties pub-hopping with the largely tourist crowd.

▨THE IRISH FILM CENTRE. Centered around a covered courtyard, the IFC shows a continual program of new releases, festivals, and special retrospectives, and plays home to a film-centered bookshop, a memorabilia-filled restaurant, and a lively bar. Three screens show art-house and foreign films. The **Irish Film Archive** and a library can be seen upon request. *(6 Eustace St. ☎679 3497; www.fii.ie. Open M-F 9:30am-11:30pm. See Cinema, p.34.)*

TEMPLE BAR MUSIC CENTRE. The Centre holds terrific musical events virtually every night of the week, and has its own pub and cafe. (*Curved St.* ☎*670 9202; www.tbmc.ie. Open daily 9am-2am.*)

GALLERY OF PHOTOGRAPHY. Above an extensive photography bookstore lies Ireland's only photo studio. The walls of this four-story gallery are lined with contemporary photographs by Irish and some international photographers. The gallery also runs workshops and an advanced photography course, and has black-and-white and color darkrooms available for hire. (*Meeting House Sq.* ☎*671 4654. 6-session B&W photography course €150-170. 3hr. darkroom rental €15. Open Tu-Sa 11am-6pm.*)

TEMPLE BAR GALLERY & STUDIOS. One of Europe's largest studio complexes, the gallery draws artists from all over Ireland. Though the studio has a couple dozen live-in artists, each working on a variety of visual arts, the gallery is open, and free, to the public. (*5-9 Temple Bar.* ☎*671 0073; www.templebargallery.com.*)

DAME STREET AND THE CATHEDRALS

If in search of medieval castles, religious ruins, and tales of Vikings and past Irish warriors, look no farther.

DUBLIN CASTLE. Norman King John built the castle in 1204 on top of the Viking settlement *Dubh Linn;* more recently, a series of structures from various eras (mostly the 18th and 19th centuries) has covered the site, culminating in an uninspired 20th-century office complex. For the best view of the castle, and a nice picnic, head to the Irish knot lawn in the back of the complex, next to the **Chester Beatty Library.** For the 700 years after its construction, Dublin Castle was the seat of British rule in Ireland. Fifty insurgents died at the castle's walls on Easter Monday, 1916 (see **The Easter Rising,** p. 63). Since 1938, every Irish president has been inaugurated here. Next door, the intricate inner dome of **Dublin City Hall** (designed as the Royal Exchange in 1779) shelters statues of national heroes like Daniel O'Connell. (*Dame St., at the intersection of Parliament and Castle St.* ☎*677 7129. State Apartments open M-F 10am-5pm, Sa-Su and holidays 2-5pm; closed during official functions. €4.25, students and seniors €3.25, child €1.75. Grounds free.*)

■ **CHESTER BEATTY LIBRARY.** Honorary Irish citizen Alfred Chester Beatty was an American rags-to-riches mining engineer who amassed an incredibly beautiful collection of Asian art, sacred scriptures, and illustrated texts. He donated this collection to Ireland upon his death, and a new library behind Dublin Castle houses and exhibits his cultural wonderland. An illustrated book by Matisse and a collection of Chinese snuff bottles are just two highlights of the eclectic displays. The roof-top garden was specially designed for relaxation. Special exhibits and public lectures complete the academic environment. (*Behind Dublin Castle.* ☎*407 0750. Open May-Sept. M-F 10am-5pm, Sa 11am-5pm, Su 1pm-5pm; Oct-Apr. Tu-F 10am-5pm, Sa 11am-5pm, Su 1pm-5pm. Free.*)

CHRIST CHURCH CATHEDRAL. Originally built in the name of Catholicism, Irish cathedrals were forced to convert to the Church of Ireland in the 16th century. Sitric Silkenbeard, King of the Dublin Norsemen, built a wooden church on this site around 1038; Strongbow rebuilt it in stone in 1169. Further additions were made in the following century and again in the 1870s. Stained glass sparkles above the raised crypts, one of which supposedly belongs to Mr. Strongbow and his favorite lutefisk. In merrier times the cavernous crypt held shops and drinking houses, but nowadays cobwebs hang from the ceiling, fragments of ancient pillars lie about like bleached bones, and a mummified cat chases a mummified mouse. It's an extra €3 to view the new exhibit "Treasures of Christ Church," which drips with silver and gold. *(At the end of Dame St., uphill and across from the Castle. A 10min. walk from O'Connell Bride, or take bus #50 from Eden Quay or 78A from Aston Quay. ☎677 8099. Open daily 9:45am-5pm except during services. Donation of €3 strongly encouraged.)*

ST. PATRICK'S CATHEDRAL. The body of this church dates to the 12th century, although Sir Benjamin Guinness remodeled much of the building in 1864. Measuring 300 ft. from bow to stern, it's Ireland's largest cathedral. Jonathan Swift spent his last years as Dean of St. Patrick's, and his crypt is above the south nave. *(From Christ Church, Nicholas St. runs south and downhill, eventually becoming Patrick St. Take bus #49, 49A, 50, 54A, 56A, 65, 65B, 77, or 77A from Eden Quay. ☎475 4817; www.stpatrickscathedral.ie. Open Mar.-Oct. daily 9am-6pm; Nov.-Feb. Sa 9am-5pm and Su 9am-3pm. €4; students, seniors, and children free.)* **Marsh's Library**, beside the cathedral, is Ireland's oldest public library. A peek inside reveals elegant wire alcoves, an extensive collection of early maps, and occasionally a special exhibit. *(☎454 3511. Open M and W-F 10am-12:45pm and 2-5pm, Sa 10:30am-12:45pm. €3, students and seniors €1.50.)*

ST. AUDOEN'S CHURCH. The Normans founded this, Dublin's oldest parish church. Please do not confuse it with the more modern (more Catholic) St. Audoen's. *(High St. ☎677 0088. Open June-Sept. 9:30am-5:30pm. €2, students and children €1, seniors €1.25.)* **St. Audoen's Arch,** built in 1215 and now obscured by a narrow alley, is the only surviving gate from Dublin's medieval **city walls.** During the 16th century, the walls ran from Parliament St. to the castle, then to Little Ship St., along Francis St. to Bridge St., and then along the Liffey.

GUINNESS BREWERY AND KILMAINHAM

Within walking distance of Dublin central, it's best to take a bus west along the quays, or to hop on a train to nearby Heuston Station. The walk from O'Connell St. passes industrial buildings and vacant factories, and feels longer than it actually is.

GUINNESS STOREHOUSE. Discover how the storehouse brews its black magic and creates the world's best stout. The admirably farsighted Arthur Guinness signed a 9000-year lease on the original 1759 brewery. The lease is displayed on the floor of the atrium, an architectural triumph that rises seven floors and has a center shaped like a pint glass. The Storehouse offers a self-guided tour with multimedia eye-candy and hyper-technical fun. Learn about ingredients, brewing, the histories of advertising and transportation, and cooperage (the science of making beer barrels). Unfortunately, no brewing goes on here, but after walking through

---

GUINNESS IS AS GUINNESS DOES.

The numbers emblazoned on the thick side of every pint of Irish Guinness are no mystery. The "1759" marked between the golden harp must refer to the year that Arthur Guinness opened his legendary brewery in Dublin, right? Right...sort of.

While it is true that 1759 was the beer's birth year, some argue that the numbers are actually the exact time that Mr. Guinness poured the first pint of his eponymous black brew. However, one minute into the 5:59pm (17:59) pour, the 6pm Catholic *angelus* prayer sounded over Dublin, freezing any God-fearing soul into momentary reflection and requisite crossing... giving birth to the two part pour. The minute and odd seconds the frustrated pour was left sitting while its creator paid respects to his Creator serendipitously brought out the beer's now-famous body.

huge copper brewing tanks and under a roaring man-made waterfall, visitors feel like they've been transformed from a measly grain of barley to a dark, foamy pint. The pilgrimage concludes on the top floor, overlooking 64 acres of Guinness, with pints of dark and creamy goodness for all. *Sláinte. (St. James's Gate. From Christ Church Cathedral, follow High St. west through its name changes—Cornmarket, Thomas, and James. Take bus #51B or 78A from Aston Quay or #123 from O'Connell St. ☎453 8364; www.guinness-storehouse.com. Open daily 9:30am-5pm. €13.50; students over 18 €9; seniors and students under 18 €6.50; children 6-12—start them young!—€3.)*

KILMAINHAM GAOL. A place of bondage and a symbol of freedom—almost all the rebels who fought in Ireland's struggle for independence between 1792 and 1921 spent time here. "The cause for which I die has been rebaptized during this past week by the blood of as good men as ever trod God's earth," wrote Sean Mac-Diarmada in a letter to his family while he awaited execution for participation in the 1916 Easter Rising (see p. 63). The jail's last occupant was **Éamon de Valera**, the future leader of Éire. Today, Kilmainham is a museum that traces the history of penal practices over the last two centuries. Lengthy tours wander through the chilly limestone corridors of the prison and end in the haunting wasteland of the execution yard. *(Inchicore Rd. Take bus #51 from Aston Quay, #51A from Lower Abbey St., or #79 from Aston Quay. ☎453 5984. Open Apr.-Sept. daily 9:30am-4:45pm, Oct.-Mar. M-F 9:30am-4pm and Su 10am-4:45pm. Tours every 35min. €5, students €2, seniors €3.50.)*

THE ROYAL HOSPITAL KILMAINHAM. Built in 1679 as a hospice for retired and disabled soldiers, today the compound houses the **Irish Museum of Modern Art.** The hospital's facade and courtyard mimic Les Invalides in Paris; the Baroque chapel is also stunning. Museum curators have taken some heat over the avant-garde use of this historic space. Modern Irish artists share wall space with others as the gallery builds up its permanent collection. *(Military Rd. Bus #90 or 91 from Heuston Station, #78A or 79 from the city center. ☎612 9900. Open Tu-Sa 10am-5:30pm, Su noon-5:30pm. Guided tours W and F 2:30pm, Su 12:15pm. Free. Call for events.)*

THE COLLINS BARRACKS. The barracks are home to the **National Museum of Decorative Arts and History.** The most sophisticated of Dublin's three national museums, the barracks gleam with exhibits that range from the deeply traditional to the subversively multi-disciplinary. The Curator's Choice room displays a range of objects in light of their artistic importance, cultural context, and historical signifi-

---

DUBLINESE Mastering the Dublin dialect has been a persistent challenge to writers and thespians of the 20th century. James Joyce, Brendan Behan, and Roddy Doyle are just a few ambitious scribes who have tried to capture the nuances of this gritty, witty city. The following is a short introduction to Dubliners' favorite phrases. **Names for Outsiders:** The rivalry between Dubliners and their country cousins is fierce. For Dubliners, all counties outside their own blur into one indiscriminate wasteland populated with "culchies," "plonkers," "turf-gobblers," and "muck-savages." **In Times of Difficulty:** Dublinese is expeditious in keeping others in line. Idiots are rebuked as "eejits" or "gobshites." Total exasperation calls for "shite and onions." When all is restored to order, "the job's oxo and the ship's name is Murphy." **Affectionate Nicknames for Civic Landmarks:** Over the past couple of decades, the government has graced the city with several public artworks that personify the Irish spirit in the female form. Dubliners have responded with poetic rhetoric. Off Grafton St., the statue of the fetching fishmongress Molly Malone is commonly referred to as "the dish with the fish" and "the tart with the cart."

cance. (Benburb St., off Wolfe Tone Quay. Take the Museum Link bus which leaves from the adjacent Natural History and Archaeology museums once per hr. All-day pass €2.50; one-way €1. Or hop on buses #25, 66, or 67 from Middle Abbey St., or the #90 from Aston Quay, which goes to Heuston Station and stops across the street from the museum. ☎ 677 7444. Open Tu-Sa 10am-5pm and Su 2-5pm. Guided tours €1.30; call for times. Museum free.)

NORTH OF THE LIFFEY

O'CONNELL ST. AND PARNELL SQUARE

While tourists flock to the south, locals congregate and converse in the North. Less trendy than its southern partner, the area is flooded with street vendors and performers. The elusive "Real" Dublin lies just a dart off onto one of the area's many side streets, where fresh fruit and fish markets reside.

O'CONNELL STREET. Dublin's biggest shopping thoroughfare starts at the Liffey and leads to **Parnell Square**. At 150 ft., it was once the widest street in Europe. In its pre-Joycean heyday, it was known as Sackville St.; later the name was changed in honor of "The Liberator" (see **Rebellion,** p. 61). The central traffic islands contain monuments to Irish leaders O'Connell, Parnell, and James Larkin, who organized the heroic Dublin general strike of 1913 (see **Parnell,** p. 62). **O'Connell's statue** faces the Liffey and O'Connell Bridge; the winged women aren't angels but Winged Victories, although one has a bullet hole from 1916 in a rather inglorious place. At the other end of the street, **Parnell's statue** points toward nearby Mooney's pub, while the engraved words at his feet proclaim "Thus far and no further." In front of the GPO stands the recently erected **Dublin Spire,** towering 120m above most everything else in the city. Originally planned as a Millenium Spire, it wasn't actually completed until early 2003. It's the first step in the planned reconstruction of O'Connell St., which, when finished, will return the street to its tree-lined heyday. For now, however, O'Connell St. remains seriously under construction, causing traffic congestion and generally making a big mess. One monument visitors won't see is **Nelson's Pillar,** a freestanding column that remembered Trafalgar and stood outside the General Post Office for 150 years. In 1966 the IRA commemorated the 50th anniversary of the Easter Rising by blowing the Admiral out of the water.

THE GENERAL POST OFFICE. Not just a fine place to send a letter, the Post Office was the nerve center of the 1916 Easter Rising (see **The Easter Rising,** p. 63); Padraig Pearse read the Proclamation of Irish Independence from its steps. When British troops closed in, mailbags became barricades. Outside, a number of bullet nicks are still visible. *(O'Connell St. ☎ 705 7000. Open M-Sa 8am-8pm, Su 10am-6:30pm.)*

HUGH LANE MUNICIPAL GALLERY OF MODERN ART. A small but impressive collection hangs in Georgian **Charlemont House.** When American painter Lane offered to donate his collection of French Impressionist paintings to the city, he did so on the condition that the people of Dublin contribute to this gallery's construction. Because his collection and the architect chosen were foreign, Dubliners refused to lend their support; Yeats then lamented their provincial attitudes in a string of poems. Lane's death aboard the *Lusitania* in 1915 raised decades of disputes over his will, eventually resolved by a plan to share the collection between Dublin and London's Tate Gallery. *(Parnell Sq. N. Buses #3, 10, 11, 13, 16, and 19 all stop near Parnell Sq. ☎ 874 1903; www.hughlane.ie. Open Tu-Th 9:30am-6pm, F-Sa 9:30am-5pm, Su 11am-5pm. Free.)*

THE DUBLIN WRITERS MUSEUM. Read through placard after placard describing the city's rich literary heritage, and its role in shaping Irish history, or listen to it all on an audio headset tour. Manuscripts, rare editions, and memorabilia of

THE HIDDEN DEAL

THE EMERALD ISLE'S GOLDEN EGG

Many of Ireland's most touristed sights—its national parks, museums, monuments and gardens—are owned and operated by the Irish Department of Arts and Heritage. While this government-run department keeps the price of admission to these sights quite low, the accumulated cost of visiting each can grow too high for the ordinary budget traveler to afford.

Recently, the Department of Heritage has started to offer discount cards to those wishing to visit multiple sights. Their **Dúchas Heritage Discount Card** may just be Ireland's greatest hidden deal. Not only does the ticket give you access to all of the sights owned and operated by the Department of Heritage, it also gives you one full year of access so that you can return again and again to refresh your memory on why it is you bought the card in the first place.

There are ten sights in Dublin alone, including the Casino, Kilmainham Gaol, St. Audeon's Church, and the Royal Hospital Kilmainham. Other sights around Ireland include a slew of castles and ruins. The average price to visit one sight is between €2.50-5, so this card—at €19—is Ireland's best steal.

The Irish Heritage Discount Card. €19.05, students and children €7.62, seniors €12.70, families €45.72. For more info call ☎01 647 2461; or within Ireland ☎1850 600 601; www.heritageireland.ie/en/HeritageCard.

Swift, Shaw, Wilde, Yeats, Beckett, Brendan Behan, Patrick Kavanagh, and Sean O'Casey blend with caricatures, paintings, a great bookstore, and an incongruous Zen Garden. *(18 Parnell Sq. N. ☎872 2077. Open June-Aug. M-F 10am-6pm, Sa 10am-5pm, Su 11am-5pm; Sept.-May M-Sa 10am-5pm. €6, students and seniors €5. Combined ticket with either Shaw birthplace or James Joyce Centre €8.)* Adjacent to the museum, the **Irish Writers Centre** is the hub of Ireland's living community of writers, providing for today's aspiring penwrights and sponsoring frequent fiction and poetry readings. The Centre is not a museum, but provides information about Dublin's literary happenings. *(19 Parnell Sq. N. ☎872 1302; www.writerscentre.ie. Open M-F 9:30am-6pm.)*

JAMES JOYCE CULTURAL CENTRE. The museum features Joyceana ranging from portraits of individuals who inspired his characters to the more arcane fancies of the writer's nephew, who runs the place. The original door to 7 Eccles St. and guided walking tours of Joycean Dublin help bring *Ulysses* to life. Feel free to mull over Joyce's works in the library or the tearoom. Call for information on lectures and Bloomsday events. *(35 N. Great Georges St. Up Marlborough St. and past Parnell St. ☎878 8547; www.jamesjoyce.ie. Open Sept.-June M-Sa 9:30am-5pm, Su 12:30-5pm; July-Aug. extra Su hours 11am-5pm. €4.50, students and seniors €3.50.)*

OTHER SIGHTS. Just past Parnell Sq., the **Garden of Remembrance** eulogizes the martyrs who took and lost the General Post Office (see **The Easter Rising,** p. 63). A cross-shaped pool is anchored at one end by a statue representing the mythical Children of Lir, who turned from humans into swans. They proclaim their faith in freedom (in Irish): "In the winter of bondage we saw a vision. We melted the snows of lethargy and the river of resurrection flowed from it." *(Open until dusk.)* Turn right on Cathedral St. to find the inconspicuous **Dublin Pro-Cathedral,** the city's center of Catholic worship where tens of thousands gathered for Daniel O'Connell's memorial service. "Pro" means "provisional"—many Dublin Catholics still want Christ Church Cathedral returned (see p. 122). On Granby Row, to the Northwest of Parnell Sq., the **National Wax Museum** features life-size replicas of everyone from Hitler to the Teletubbies, including the Pope, complete with Popemobile. *(☎872 6340. Open M-Sa 10am-5:30pm, Su noon-5:30pm. €6, students €5.)*

ALONG THE QUAYS

Though it's not quite the Seine, a walk along the River Liffey can be pleasant enough, especially when broken up by quick visits to the following sights.

THE CUSTOM HOUSE. Dublin's greatest architectural triumph, the Custom House was designed and built in the 1780s by James Gandon, who gave up the chance to be Russia's state architect and settled in Dublin. The Roman and Venetian columns and domes hint at what the city's 18th-century Anglo-Irish highbrows wanted Dublin to become. Carved heads along the frieze represent the rivers of Ireland; Liffey is the only lady. *(East of O'Connell St. at Custom House Quay, where Gardiner St. meets the river. ☎888 2538. Visitors center open mid-Mar. to Nov. M-F 10am-12:30pm, Sa-Su 2-5pm; Nov. to mid-Mar. W-F 10am–12:30pm and Su 2-5pm. €1.)*

FOUR COURTS. Another of Gandon's works, this building appears monumentally impressive from the front, but the back and sides reveal 20th-century ballast. On April 14, 1922, General Rory O'Connor seized the Four Courts on behalf of the anti-Treaty IRA; two months later, the Free State government of Griffith and Collins attacked the Four Courts garrison, starting the Irish Civil War (see **Independence,** p. 64). The building now houses Ireland's highest court. Visitors can wander into the grand front room and marvel at the impressive domed ceiling or the displays of court cases on the docket. *(Inn's Quay, several quays to the west of the Custom House. ☎872 5555. Open M-F 9am-4:30pm. No scheduled tours. Free.)*

▨ ST. MICHAN'S CHURCH. This modest church, dating to 1095, is best visited for its creepy vaults, which may have inspired Bram Stoker's *Dracula*. Everything in here is real, from the mummified corpses in open caskets to the grisly execution notice of two 1798 rebels to the dusty cobwebs that drip from the ceiling. It's perfectly safe though...we think. *(Church St. ☎872 4154. Open Mar.-Oct. M-F 10am-12:45pm and 2-4:45pm, Sa 10am-12:45pm; Nov.-Feb. M-F 12:30-3:30pm, Sa 10am-12:45pm. Crypt tours €3.50, students and seniors €3, under 16 €2.50. Church of Ireland services Su 10am.)*

SMITHFIELD

With the government pouring thousands of euros into local development, this area is on its way to becoming the next Temple Bar. Don't rush here yet though, as true progress won't be seen for another few years. In the meantime, drink up.

OLD JAMESON DISTILLERY. Learn how science, grain, and tradition come together to form liquid gold—whiskey, that is. A film recounts Ireland's spirit-ual rise, fall, and renaissance; the subsequent tour walks through the creation of the drink, although the stuff's really distilled down the street. The experience ends with a glass of the Irish firewater; be quick to volunteer in the beginning and get to sample a whole tray of different whiskeys. *(Bow St. From O'Connell St., turn onto Henry St. and continue straight as the street dwindles to Mary St., then Mary Ln., then May Ln.; the warehouse is on a cobblestone street on the left. Buses #67, 68, 69, and 79 run from city centre to Merchant's Quay. ☎807 2355. Tours daily 9:30am-5:30pm. €7, students and seniors €5.75.)*

THE CHIMNEY VIEWING TOWER. Smithfield's answer to the Guinness Gravity Bar, the Old Jameson Distillery Chimney (185 ft.), with its glass viewing platform, offers another 360-degree urban panorama. *(Behind the Old Jameson Distillery, next to Chief O'Neill's pub. ☎817 3800. Open M-Sa 10am-5:30pm, Su 11am-5:30pm. €5, students and seniors €3.50.)*

DUBLIN BREWING COMPANY. For people wanting to see how beer is *actually* made, this microbrewery runs fun, personal tours with plenty of hops to smell and beer to taste. The tour takes visitors step by step through the brewing process. They also give more beer than at the *other* brewery, and more often than not, the tour guide partakes as well. Top off the night with more of their all natural beer and excellent trad at **Cobblestone** pub, down the street, see p. 110. *(144-146 N. King St. From Old Jameson, go up to N. King St., turn left, and it's on the left. ☎872 8622; www.dublinbrewing.com. Tours every hr. M-F noon-6pm, and by appointment. €9, students €7.)*

DISTANT SIGHTS

Far removed from the hustle and bustle of Dublin's main center, several attractions tempt on the outskirts.

PHOENIX PARK AND DUBLIN ZOO. Europe's largest enclosed public park is most famous for the "Phoenix Park murders" of 1882. The Invincibles, a Republican splinter group, stabbed Lord Cavendish, Chief Secretary of Ireland, and his trusty Under-Secretary 200 yd. from the **Phoenix Column.** A Unionist journalist forged a series of letters linking Parnell to the murderers (see **Parnell,** p. 62). The Phoenix Column, capped with a phoenix rising from flames, is something of a pun—the park's name actually comes from the Irish *Fionn Uisce,* "clean water." The 1760 acres incorporate the **President's residence** *(Áras an Uachtaráin),* the US Ambassador's residence, cricket pitches, polo grounds, and red deer. The deer are quite tame and beautiful to watch; they often graze in the thickets near Castleknock Gate. The park is peaceful during daylight hours but unsafe at night. *(Take bus #10 from O'Connell St. or #25 or 26 from Middle Abbey St. west along the river.)* **Dublin Zoo,** one of the world's oldest and Europe's largest, is in the park. It contains 700 critters and the **world's biggest egg.** For an urban zoo, the habitats are large and the animals tend to move around a bit, except for the lions, who feel it is their royal prerogative to sleep over 20 hours a day. *(Bus #10 from O'Connell St., #25 or 26 from Wellington Quay. ☎474 8900. Open M-Sa 9:30am-6:30pm, Su 10:30am-6pm. Last admission at 5pm. Zoo closes at dusk in winter. €10.10, students €7.70, children and seniors €6.30.)*

CASINO MARINO. This is an architectural gem and house of tricks. People certainly gamble here, but forget the slot machines—this is a casino only in the sense of "small house," built for the Earl of Charlemont in 1758 as a seaside villa. Funeral urns on the roof are actually chimneys, and hollow columns serve as drains. The casino has secret tunnels, trick doors, and stone lions standing guard. *(Off Malahide Rd. Take bus #123 from O'Connell St.; #27 or 42 from the quays by Busáras. ☎833 1618. Open June-Sept. daily 10am-6pm, May and Oct. daily 10am-5pm, Nov.-Mar. Sa-Su noon-4pm. Admission by tour only. €2.75, seniors €2, students and children €1.25.)*

GAELIC ATHLETIC ASSOCIATION MUSEUM AND CROKE PARK. Those intrigued and/or mystified by the world of Irish athletics—hurling, camogie, Gaelic football, and handball—appreciate the museum at **Croke Park Stadium.** The GAA museum spells out the rules and history of every Gaelic sport, with the help of touchscreens and audio-visual displays, while a 1hr. tour of the stadium brings visitors up close to the fields on which games are played. *(☎855 8176. Museum open M-Sa 9:30am-5pm, Su noon-5pm. Game days open to Cusack Stand ticket holders only. Last admission 4:30pm. €5, students and seniors €3.50, children €3. Stadium tour plus museum €2-4 more.)*

INLAND WATERWAYS VISITOR CENTRE. Known as the "box on the docks" in Dublinese, this floating museum educates those ignorant of the significance of the inland waterway. The canals don't get their proper respect, it seems—this takes visitors back to school. *(Take bus #3 to the Grand Canal. Open June-Sept. 9:30am-5:30pm, Oct.-May W-Su 12:30-5pm. €2.50, students and children €1.20, seniors €1.90, family €6.35.)*

♫ ARTS AND ENTERTAINMENT

Whether you're seeking poetry or punk, Dublin is well equipped to entertain. The *Event Guide* (free) is available at the tourist office, Temple Bar restaurants, and the Temple Bar Info Center. It comes out every other Friday, and has ads in the back, fawning reviews in the front, and reasonably complete listings of museums and literary, musical, and theatrical events in between. The glossier *In Dublin* (€2.50) comes out every two weeks with feature articles and listings for music, theater, art exhibitions, comedy shows, clubs, museums, gay venues, and movie theaters. *Events of the Week*—a much smaller, free booklet—is jammed with ads, but also has good info buried in it. Hostel staffers are often reliable, if opinionated, sources of information. Click to www.visitdublin.com for hot spots updated daily.

MUSIC

Dublin's music scene attracts performers from the world over. Pubs see a lot of musical action, as they provide musicians with free beer and a venue. There is often a cover charge (€4-7) for better-known acts. *Hot Press* (€1.90) has the most up-to-date listings, particularly for rock. Its commentaries on the musical scene are insightful, and its left-leaning editorials give a clear impression of what the Dublin artistic community is thinking. **Tower Records** on Wicklow St. has reams of leaflets, and bills posted across the city broadcast coming attractions. Scheduled concerts tend to start at 9pm; impromptu ones start later.

Traditional music (trad) is not only a tourist gimmick, but a vibrant and important element of Dublin's music world. Some pubs in the city center have trad sessions nightly, others nearly so: **Hughes, Slattery's, Oliver St. John Gogarty,** and **McDaid's** are all good choices (see **Publin,** p. 106). The best pub for trad in the entire city is ▨**Cobblestones,** King St. N. (☎872 1799), in Smithfield. No rock here, but live shows every night, a session in the basement, and real spontaneity. (Open M-W 4-11:30pm, Th-F 1pm-12:30am, Sa 4pm-12:30am, Su 1-11pm. Sessions Th-Sa at 7 and 9pm, Su at 1, 4, 7 and 9pm.) Another great small venue for live music is ▨**Whelan's,** at 25 Wexford St., the continuation of S. Great Georges St. (☎478 0766. Live music nightly. Cover €7-12.) Big-deal bands frequent the **Baggot Inn,** 143 Baggot St. (☎676 1430). U2 played here in the early 80s; some people are still talking about it.

The Temple Bar Music Centre, Curved St. (☎670 9202), has events and concerts every night. The **National Concert Hall,** Earlsfort Terr., provides a venue for classical concerts and performances. They have nightly shows in July and August, and their summer lunchtime series makes a nice break on occasional Tuesdays and Fridays. (☎671 1533. Tickets €8-16, students half-price; summer lunchtime tickets €4-8.) Programs for the **National Symphony** and smaller local groups are available at classical music stores and the tourist office. **Isaac Butt** on Store St. and the **Life** bar (see **Publin,** p. 106) have periodic jazz. Big acts play **Olympia,** 72 Dame St. (☎677 7744), and at **Vicar St.,** 99 Vicar St., off Thomas St. (☎454 6656). The stars also perform for huge crowds at the **Tivoli Theatre,** 135-138 Francis St. (☎454 4472); at **Croke Park,** Clonliffe Rd. (☎836 3152); and at the **R.D.S.** (☎668 0866), in Ballsbridge.

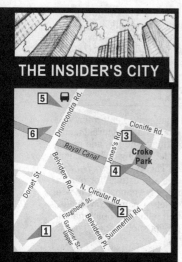

THE INSIDER'S CITY

A DAY AT CROKE PARK

Before you can brag about having "done" Dublin, you have to first experience what it's like to participate as a spectator at one of the city's raucous Gaelic Football Matches.

1 Spend Saturday night at **Parkway B&B** (see p. 99) so you can get to the park early the next morning. Follow North St. to Gardner Place.

2 Push and shove and bite and pinch—whatever it takes to get to the **ticket booth.** On Fitzgibbon St.

3 Run into the **GAA museum** inside the stadium to learn what you will need to know about the game.

4 Watch the game from the stadium's best seats at **Hill 16** or **Hogan's Stand,** where you'll find local Dubliners sitting and drinking.

5 Celebrate the victory or mourn the loss with the rest of the locals at Quinn's Pub (42 Lower Drumcondra Rd; ☎830 4973).

THEATER

Dublin has a long history of theatrical experimentation, and one of the world's premier national theatres. Check the *Event Guide* and look for flyers for the shows in any given week. Websites (except for the Abbey's) tend to be out of date. Dublin's curtains rise on a range of mainstream and experimental theater. There is no true "Theatre District," but smaller theater companies thrive off Dame St. and Temple Bar. Box office hours are usually for phone reservations; box offices stay open until curtain on performance nights. Showtime is generally 8pm.

☒ **Abbey Theatre,** 26 Lower Abbey St. (☎878 7222; www.abbeytheatre.ie). Founded by Yeats and his collaborator Lady Gregory in 1904 to promote the Irish cultural revival and modernist theater, which turned out to be a bit like promoting corned beef and soy burgers. Synge's *Playboy of the Western World* was first performed here in 1907. The production occasioned storms of protest and yet another of Yeats's hard-hitting political poems (see **The Revival,** p. 74). Today, the Abbey (like Synge) has gained respectability; it is now Ireland's National Theatre and on the cutting edge of international drama. Tickets €12-25; Sa matinees 2:30pm, €10; M-Th student rate €7:50. Box office open M-Sa 10:30am-7pm.

Peacock Theatre, 26 Lower Abbey St. (☎878 7222). The Abbey's experimental downstairs studio theater. Evening shows, plus occasional lunchtime plays, concerts, and poetry. Tickets €17, Sa 2:45pm matinees €12.50. Box office open M-Sa at 7:30pm.

Gate Theatre, 1 Cavendish Row (☎874 4045). Another classic Dublin theatre, with contemporary Irish and classic international dramas. Tickets €16-24; M-Th student discount with ID at curtain €10, subject to availability. Box office open M-Sa 10am-8pm.

Project Arts Centre, 39 E. Essex St. (☎881 9613). Sets its sights on the avant-garde and presents every imaginable sort of artistic production. Tickets under €15; student concessions available. Box office open M-Sa 11am-7pm. The **gallery** hosts rotating visual arts exhibits. Open same time as box office. Free.

Gaiety, South King St. (☎677 1717; www.gaietytheatre.com), just off Grafton St. Provides space for modern drama, ballet, music, and the Opera Ireland Society. Tickets €15-25. Box office open M-Sa 10am-7pm. Also see **Clublin,** p. 110.

Andrews Lane Theatre, Andrews Ln. (☎ 679 5720), off Dame St. Dramas of every sort (but usually comedic) presented on 2 stages; the studio stage tends toward the experimental. Mainstage tickets €17-24, studio €15. Box office open daily 10:30am-7pm.

City Arts Centre, 23-25 Moss St. (☎ 677 0643), parallel to Tara St. off Georges Quay. Avant-garde exploration of significant contemporary issues. Tickets €8, students €5. Box office open daily 9:15am-5pm.

Samuel Beckett Theatre, Trinity College (☎ 608 2461), inside the campus. Hosts anything it happens upon, including scores of student shows. Tickets €18, students €14.

Olympia Theatre, 72 Dame St. (☎ 679 3323). Specializes in commercial musical theater, plus midnight revues and tributes to the likes of ABBA and pivotal Northern European pop bands. Tickets €11-45. Box office open daily 10:30am-6:30pm.

The New Theatre, 43 E. Essex St. (☎ 670 3361), in the Temple Bar district. Opposite the Clarence Hotel, inside Connolly Books. Brand new avant-garde plays, usually quite well done. Small and intimate. Shows M-Sa 8pm. Tickets €12.50, students €10.

Crypt Arts Centre, Chapel Royal, inside Dublin Castle (☎ 671 3383.) This small venue inside the castle hosts various independent theatre troupes getting their start. Tickets €10-15. Box office open daily noon-8pm.

CINEMA

Ireland's well-subsidized film industry reeled with the arrival of the **Irish Film Centre,** 6 Eustace St., in Temple Bar. The IFC mounts tributes and festivals, including a French film festival in October and a **gay and lesbian film festival** in early August. A variety of classic and European art house films appear throughout the year. Must be a "member" to buy most tickets. (☎ 679 3477; www.fii.ie. Weekly membership €1.30; yearly membership €14, students €10. Membership must be purchased at least 15min. before show. Matinees €5; after 5pm €6.30.) **The Screen,** D'Olier St. (☎ 672 5500), also rolls artsy reels. First-run movie houses cluster on O'Connell St., the quays, and Middle Abbey St. The **Savoy,** O'Connell St. (☎ 874 6000), and **Virgin,** Parnell St. (☎ 872 8400), screen major releases for about €7.50.

SPORTS AND RECREATION

Dubliners aren't as sports-crazed as their country cousins, but that's not saying much. Games are still a serious business, especially since most tournament finals take place here. The season for **Gaelic football** and **hurling** (see **Sports,** p. 80) runs from mid-February to November. Action-packed and often brutal, these contests are entertaining for any sports-lover. Provincial finals take place in July, national semifinals on Sundays in August (hurling the first week, football the second and third), and **All-Ireland Finals** in either late August or early September. Games are played on **Phibsborough Road** and in **Croke Park.** (Clonliffe Rd., a 15min. walk from Connolly station. Bus routes #3, 11, 11A, 16, 16A, 51A, and 123. ☎ 836 3222; www.gaa.ie. Tickets €15-40.) Tickets are theoretically available at the turnstiles, but they tend to sell out quickly; All-Ireland Finals sell out immediately. The best bet is to hit the Dublin pubs on game day and see who's selling. Home games of the Irish **rugby** team are played in **Lansdowne Road Stadium;** the peak season runs from February to early April. **Camogie** (women's hurling) finals also occur in September. For more sports information, check the Friday papers or contact the **Gaelic Athletic Association** (☎ 836 3232; www.gaa.ie). **Greyhounds** race all year. (W-Th and Sa at 8pm at Shelbourne Park; ☎ 668 3502. M-Tu and F at 8pm at Harold's Cross; ☎ 497 1081.)

COUNTY DUBLIN

Horse racing and its attendant gambling are at Leopardstown Racetrack in Foxrock (☎289 2888). At the beginning of August, the **Royal Dublin Horse Show** comes to the RDS in Ballsbridge (see **Music**, p. 128).

▐ SHOPPING

Dublin is hardly a center for international trade, and consumer goods here are generally expensive—time maybe better spent in pubs and castles. That said, if an item is made anywhere in Ireland, it is probably sold in Dublin. Stores are usually open Monday through Saturday from 9am to 6pm, with later hours on Thursdays (until 7-8pm). Tiny shops pop up everywhere along the streets both north and south of the Liffey, but Dublin's serious shopping is on **Grafton** and **Henry Streets.** On pedestrianized Grafton St., well-dressed consumers crowd into boutiques and restaurants while sidewalk buskers lay down their caps for money. Most of the stores on Grafton St. are international chains, but the sides streets between Grafton and South Great Georges St. are full of interesting, often independent, boutiques. Teens and barely-twenties buy used clothes and punk discs in **Temple Bar.** Across the river, **Henry Street** and **Talbot Street** have the goods for those on a tighter budget. On **Moore Street,** vendors sell fresh produce at very low prices. (Open M-Sa 7am-5pm.) **Clery's,** Upper O'Connell St., is Dublin's principal department store. (☎878 6000. Open M-W and Sa 9am-6:30pm, Th 9am-9pm, F 9am-8pm.)

At the top of Grafton St., **St. Stephen's Green Shopping Centre** awaits shoppers. Lord Powerscourt's 200-year-old townhouse on Clarendon St. has been converted into the **Powerscourt Townhouse Centre**—a string of chic boutiques carrying Irish crafts. Gen-Xers and hippie-holdouts head to **Georges St. Market Arcade,** on South Great Georges St. near Dame St., home to a fortune teller and many vintage clothing and used-record stalls. (Open M-W and F-Sa 10am-6pm, Th 8am-7pm.)

DUBLIN'S LITERARY SHOPPING

Dawson St. houses many of Dublin's bookstores, with coffee shops sprinkled amongst them.

▨ **Books Upstairs,** 36 College Green (☎679 6687), across from Trinity Gate. Wonderful new and discounted books with excellent Irish and Humanities sections. Stocks several obscure Irish Literary magazines. Extensive sections on **gay literature** and women's studies. The principal distributor for *Gay Community News.* Open M-F 10am-7pm, Sa 10am-6pm, Su 1-6pm.

Winding Stair Bookstore, 40 Ormond Quay (☎873 3292), on the North Side. 3 floors of good tunes, great views, and cheap food. New and used books, contemporary Irish lit, and literary periodicals. Open M-W 9:30am-6pm, Th-Sa 9:30am-10pm, Su 1-6pm.

Eason Hanna's, 27-29 Nassau St. (☎677 1255), across from Trinity College at Dawson St. Knowledgeable staff answers all questions about contemporary Irish writing. Open M-W and F-Sa 8:30am-6:15pm, Th 8:30am-7:45pm, Su 1-5:15pm.

Eason, 80 Middle Abbey St. (☎873 3811), off O'Connell St. A floor-space behemoth. Lots of serious tomes and an extensive "Irish interest" section. Wide selection of local and foreign magazines and newspapers. Their bargain shelves are in the cleverly named **Bargain Books,** residing diagonally across Abbey St. Open M-W and Sa 8:30am-6:45pm, Th 8:30am-8:45pm, F 8:30am-7:45pm.

Chapters, 108-109 Middle Abbey St., (☎872 3297). Vast collection of new and used books. Come here to jettison the weight in a pack from those finished paperbacks—they'll buy or trade almost any used book imaginable. Open M-W and F-Sa 9:30am-6:30pm, Th 9:30am-8:30pm, Su noon-6:30pm.

RECORDS, TAPES, AND CDS

Freebird Records, 1 Eden Quay (☎873 1250), the North Side facing the river, downstairs under a convenience store. Crowded basement has perhaps Dublin's best selection of indie rock, plenty of vinyl, and used CDs. Proprietors can recommend local bands. Open M-F 10:30am-7pm, Sa 10:30am-6pm.

Claddagh Records, 2 Cecilia St. (☎677 0262; www.claddaghrecords.com), in Temple Bar between Temple Ln. and Crow St. Has a good selection of trad and a variety of international music. Open M-F 10:30am-5:30pm, Sa noon-5:30pm.

City Disks, Temple Ln. (☎633 0066.) Good selection of new and used indie rock, hip-hop, and blues, on disks or vinyl. Also sells concert tickets. Open M-W and F 11am-7pm, Sa 11am-6pm, Su noon-6pm.

Celtic Note, 14-15 Nassau St. (☎670 4157). Specializes in traditional Irish music. Also a Ticketmaster outlet. Open M-W and F-Sa 9am-6:30pm, Th 9am-8pm, Su 11am-7pm.

❀ FESTIVALS

The tourist office's annual *Calendar of Events* (€1.30) offers info on events throughout Ireland, including Dublin's many festivals, antique and craft fairs, flower marts, horse shows, and the like. The biweekly *Events Guide* or *In Dublin* (€2.50) are also good sources.

BLOOMSDAY. Dublin returns to 1904 each year on June 16, the day of Leopold Bloom's 18hr. journey, which frames the narrative (or lack thereof) of Joyce's *Ulysses*. Festivities are held all week long, starting before the big day and, to a lesser extent, continuing after it. The James Joyce Cultural Centre (see p. 125) sponsors a reenactment of the funeral and wake, a lunch at Davy Byrne's, and a Guinness breakfast. *(Call ☎878 8547 for info.)*

MUSIC FESTIVALS. The **Festival of Music in Great Irish Houses,** held during mid-June, organizes concerts of period music in 18th-century homes across the country, including some in the city. *(☎278 1528.)* The **Feis Ceoil** music festival goes trad in mid-March. *(☎676 7365.)* The **Dublin International Organ and Choral Festival** lifts every voice in Christ Church Cathedral. *(☎677 3066.)* The **Guinness Blues Festival,** a three-day extravaganza in mid-July, gets bigger and broader each year. *(☎497 0381; www.guinnessbluesfest.com.)* Ask at the tourist office about *fleadhs* (FLAHS), day-long trad festivals that pop up periodically.

ST. PATRICK'S DAY. The half-week leading up to March 17 occasions a city-wide carnival of concerts, fireworks, street theater, and intoxicated madness, celebrating one of Ireland's lesser-known saints. Many pubs offer special promotions, contests, and extended hours. *(☎676 3205; www.paddyfest.ie.)*

THE DUBLIN THEATRE FESTIVAL. This premier cultural event, held the first two weeks of October, showcases about 20 works from Ireland and around the world. Tickets may be purchased all year at participating theaters, and, as the festival draws near, at the Festival Booking Office. *(47 Nassau St. ☎677 8434. Tickets €13-20, student discounts vary by venue.)*

THE DUBLIN FILM FESTIVAL. Nearly two weeks of Irish and international movies with a panoply of seminars in tow. *(Early to mid-Mar. ☎679 2937; www.iol.ie/dff.)*

⚠ ACTIVITIES

Drinking stout and/or watching sporting events take precedence in Dublin, so finding activities can be tricky. Most outdoor activities take place beyond the city limits, but fishing is allowed on certain sections of the Liffey, bikes can be rented for whirls around town, and various parks have public tennis courts. While Dublin is not a big adventure activity city, hang gliding provides thrills for the daring.

BICYCLING. Cycle Ways rents bikes cheap. Remember to bring a helmet, as the shop doesn't provide any for their customers. (185-6 Parnell St. ☎873 4748. €20 per day, €80 per wk.; deposit €200. Open M-W and F-Sa 10am-6pm, Th 10am-8pm.)

FISHING. Fish the Liffey for perch, salmon, trout, and other scaled swimmers. Tackle shops can direct to the best spots to fish. Few places in town hire out fishing equipment, so buy gear or hire from out of town. For more information, contact **Cleere Patk & Son.** (5 Bedford Row, ☎677 7406, off Aston Quay. Open M-F 9:30am-5:30pm, Sa 9:30am-5pm.) Or, **Rory's Fishing Tackle.** (17A Temple Bar, ☎677 2351.)

GO-CARTS. There are two places around Dublin to get behind the small wheel, and both have indoor tracks. Be sure to book ahead at **Kart City,** Old Airport Rd. (☎842 6322. €20 per 15min., €26 per 20min, €38 per 30min. Open Tu-Su noon-10pm.) Also at **Kylemore Karting Centre,** Killeen Rd. (☎626 1444; www.kyle-karting.com. €15 per 10min., €20 per 15min., €25 per 20 min., €30 per 25min. Open daily 11am till late.)

GOLF. Most of the golf clubs around Dublin are private, but some allow visitors, usually on weekdays. There are also municipal courses, par-3, and pitch and putt courses around the city. For more info, pick up a copy of Dublin Tourism's free Golf visitor's guide, or contact the **Clontarf Golf Club,** Malahide Rd. (☎833 1892, in Clontarf), **Royal Dublin Golf Course** (☎833 6346); **Glencullen Golf** (☎294 0898); **Open Golf Centre** (☎864 0324); **Dublin City Golf Club,** Ballinascorney (☎451 6430; www.dublincitygolf.com); **Portmarnock Hotel and Golf Links** (☎846 0611; www.portmarnock.com); and **Edmondstown Golf Club,** Rathfarnham (☎493 1082; www.edmondstowngolfclub.ie).

HANG GLIDING. For greater thrills, **Adventure Ireland** plans activities for singles or groups, including hang gliding lessons (☎490 0246). **Amazing Days** offers paragliding lessons (☎045 630 3046, in Kildare).

TENNIS. Public courts are available in **Bushy Park** in Terenure (☎490 0320), **Herbert Park** in Ballsbridge (☎668 4364), and **St. Anne's Park** in Raheny. Call the **Dublin Parks Administration** for prices and information on all parks (☎833 8711).

▼ GAY AND LESBIAN DUBLIN

Dublin's less-retrograde-than-often-feared (but more than hoped) thinking allows the celebration of **PRIDE,** an annual, week-long festival in July celebrating gay identity (www.dublinpride.org.) While the BGLTQ community in Dublin is quite active, don't expect to see a bunch of rainbow flags happily fluttering in the breeze. To find where the action is this month, check the **Gay Community News (GCN),** Unit 2 Scarlet Row, W. Essex St. (☎671 9076; www.gcn.ie), which is free and comes out monthly, offering the most comprehensive and up-to-date information possible on gay life and nightlife in Dublin and beyond. *GCN* is available at Books Upstairs, The Winding Stair (see **Literary Shopping,** p. 132), Cornucopia, the George, and venues around Temple Bar. It has extensive listings of support groups and other organizations. *Sceneout* magazine is a periodic supplement to *GCN* that focuses on nightlife and prints classifieds. The queer pages of *In Dublin* list gay-friendly pubs, dance clubs, restaurants, bookshops, hotlines, and organizations. Since gay

Dublin seems to be consistent in its rapid rate of change, the listings are comprehensive but often outdated. ☒**The George, Gubu, Out on the Liffey,** and ☒**The Front Lounge** (see **Gay and Lesbian Nightlife,** p. 109) are always safe bets. If nothing is happening at night, **Books Upstairs** was Dublin's first bookstore to have a gay literature shelf, and it's still got the best selection of reading material around.

Gay Switchboard Dublin, a good resource for events and updates, sponsors a hotline (☎872 1055; Su-F 8-10pm, Sa 3:30-6pm). **The National Gay and Lesbian Federation,** Hirschfield Centre, 10 Fownes St. (☎671 0939), in Temple Bar, offers legal counseling. **OUThouse,** 105 Capel St. (☎873 4932), is a queer community resource center, offering a library and cafe along with information and advice. OUThouse organizes all sorts of social groups, support groups, seminars, and information sessions for gays, lesbians, teenagers, alcoholics, various permutations of the above, and everyone else. Drop-in hours M-F noon-6pm. **Gay Information Ireland** has a website at www.geocities.com/WestHollywood/9105. Tune into local radio for gay community talk shows: **Innuendo** is broadcast on 104.9FM (Tu 2-3pm); 103.8FM has **Out in the Open** (Tu 9-10pm); and **Equality** airs on 101.6FM (Th 4:30pm).

DUBLIN'S SUBURBS

Strung along the Irish Sea from Donabate in the north to Bray in the south, Dublin's suburbs offer harried travelers an easily accessible and calm alternative to the voracious human tide swarming about the Liffey. Castles and factories are surrounded by housing developments, all clamoring for a view of the rocky shore. Natural beauty combined with small-village streets help two regions stand out from the sprawl: tranquil Howth Peninsula to the north and the cluster of suburbs around Dún Laoghaire to the south. Howth, in particular, offers splendid views of the water and Dublin city. Bragging rights for Dublin's best beach go to the Velvet Strand, a plush stretch of rock and water between Malahide and Portmarnock (see p. 137). Dublin's southern suburbs tend to be tidy and fairly well-off—the coastal yuppie towns form a chain of snazzy houses and bright surf. The DART, suburban rail, and local buses make the area accessible for afternoon jaunts.

HOWTH (BINN EADAIR)   ☎01

Maud Gonne, winner of Yeats's unyielding devotion, described her childhood in Howth in *A Servant of the Queen:* "After I was grown up I have often slept all night in that friendly heather... From deep down in it one looks up at the stars in a wonderful security and falls asleep to wake up only with the call of the sea birds looking for their breakfasts." Favored by Ireland's literary lasses, Howth is also the location of Molly Malone's chapter in Ulysses. Their secret is out. Howth (rhymes with "both"), an affluent Eden dangling from the mainland, is becoming an increasingly popular destination. If the sun is shining on a weekend, expect crowds. And who could blame them? Less than 10 mi. from Dublin, Howth plays like a highlight reel of Ireland: rolling hills, pubs, a literary landscape, fantastic sailing, and a castle. The town's buildings are densest near the harbor and up in the village between the abbey and the church. Man-made structures from various millennia pepper the area, connected by quiet paths around hills of heather and stunning cliffs.

🗐 🛿 TRANSPORTATION AND PRACTICAL INFORMATION

The easiest way to reach Howth is by **DART.** Take a northbound train to the Howth end of the line. (30min., 6 per hr., €1.70.) Pay attention when boarding, as the same line splits to serve Malahide as well. **Buses** leave from Dublin's Lower Abbey St.: #31 runs every hour to the center of Howth, near the DART station, and #31B adds a loop that climbs Howth Summit. To get into town, turn left out of the DART station and walk toward the harbor on aptly-named Harbour Rd. The community-center-cum-**tourist office** is on the right in the Old Courthouse. (☎844 5976. Open occasional mornings.) In the likely event that the tourist office is closed, a hand-drawn map of the peninsula is posted at the harbor entrance. There is an **ATM** in the **Mace** on Harbour Rd. Fill the tank at Texaco, on Harbour Rd. across from the West Pier. Abbey St. leads to the village center from Harbour Rd. After Abbey St. runs into Main St., **McDermott's Pharmacy,** 6 Main St. (☎832 2069. Open M-Sa 9am-6pm, Su 10am-1pm.) is across from the library, which has free **Internet.** Call ahead to ensure a time slot (☎832 2130. Open M, W 2pm-8:30pm; Tu, Th 10am-1pm and 2pm-5:15pm; F, Sa 10am-1pm and 2pm-5pm). The **post office** (☎832 0899. Open M-F 9am-1pm and 2:15-5:30pm, Sa 9am-1pm) is at 26 Abbey St.

◪ ACCOMMODATIONS

The B&B's in Howth do their job perfectly, providing guests with full Irish Breakfasts and ensuite bathrooms. **Ann's Guest Accommodations,** a brand new B&B, is situated where East Pier meets Harbour Rd. Bessie, the owners' friendly Blue Kerry dog, leads guests to immaculate modern rooms, and her human companions happily share Howth knowledge their family has accumulated since 1956 (☎832 3197; www.annsofhowth.com. €40-60). Other B&Bs are quite a climb or a short bus ride up Thormanby Rd., but most proprietors will pick visitors up at the DART stop. Bus #31B makes regular stops running up Thormanby Rd. **Gleann na Smól ❸** ("The Valley of the Thrush"), on the left at the end of Nashville Rd. off Thormanby Rd., is an affordable option closest to the harbor. They have firm beds for the weary, in-room TVs, and a generous supply of reading matter to suit bookwormier guests. (☎832 2936; www.irish-bnb.com/glennasmol. Singles €40; doubles €62.) Rosaleen Hobbs welcomes guests into her grand suburban house, **Hazelwood ❸,** 1 mi. up Thormanby Rd., in the Thormanby Woods estate, at the end of the first cul-de-sac on the left (☎839 1391; www.hazelwood.net. Doubles €66; children 12 and under staying with parents €33.) **Highfield ❸,** farther up Thormanby Rd., is on the left and up a windy driveway. When the weather cooperates, a lovely view of the harbor complements the front bedrooms and the antique-laden traditional dining room. (☎832 3936. All rooms with showers and TVs. Doubles €65.) On the side of a hill lies smoke-free **Inisradharc ❸,** with brilliant views of **Ireland's Eye** from its sunny conservatory. Go up Thormanby Rd. and turn right onto Balkill Rd. at **The Summit;** it's down the windy road, on the left. (☎832 2306. Two night minimum stay. €36.)

◪ ▥ FOOD AND PUBS

Hungry shoppers head to **Mace,** on Harbour Rd. (Open M-F 7am-11pm, Sa-Su 8am-11pm.) Fish is the thing to eat in Howth, since it comes straight from the harbor and is super-fresh, but finding it at reasonable prices can be difficult. **Caffe Caira ❷,** on the corner of Harbour Rd. and Abbey St., is an above-average chipper. The takeaway window serves the same food at a breakneck pace for a fraction of the price. (☎832 3699. Open daily noon-9:30pm; takeaway noon-1am.) Follow the stairs right after the Abbey on Abbey Rd. to the **Big Blue** and **Cafe Blue,** 30 Church St., for a tasty "Leek and Hake Bake" (€13) and other seafood, steak, and pasta dishes. Housed in a friendly lodge overlooking the Abbey and the harbor, the cafe is also a nice place for an afternoon cappuccino. Call ahead for dinner reservations. (☎832 0565. Open Tu-Sa 1:30pm-11pm, Su 12:30pm-2:30pm. Cafe Tu-Sa 11am-6pm.) **The Country Kitchen,** on Main St. to the right of the Church, will pack up fresh sandwiches (€2.50-3) for hungry hikers. (☎839 5450. Open M-Sa 8:30am-6pm, Su 9am-1pm.) **Maud's ❶,** Harbour Rd., is a casual cafe with sandwiches and award-winning ice cream. (☎839 5450. Ice cream €1-

4.50; try their signature "Pooh Bear Delight," €4.50. Open 10am-6pm.) Top off your cliff walk with a pint and an incredible view of North Howth at **The Summit,** at the top of Thornby Rd., and groove at its adjoining nightclub **K2.** (☎832 4615. Open M-W 11am-11:30pm, Tu-Sa 11am-12:30am. Club open F-Su. Cover €3 before 11pm, €9 after.) On Main St., **Kruger's** ❸ offers bar bites and Irish entrees (€8-11) along with nightly trad. (☎832 2229. Food 12:30-8pm daily.) Join the fishermen at the **Lighthouse,** Church St., for lively trad sessions. Take Harbour St. from the train station, then right at El Paso and up the hill to Church. (☎832 2827. Sessions M and F from 9pm, Su afternoons.)

SIGHTS AND ACTIVITIES

A great way to experience Maude Gonne's heather and seabird nests is on the well-trod but narrow **cliff walk** (3hr.), which rings the Howth peninsula. The best section is a 1hr. hike between the harbor and the lighthouse at the southeast tip of the peninsula. At the harbor's end, **Puck's Rock** marks the spot where the devil fell when St. Nessan shook a Bible at him (it was that easy). The nearby **lighthouse,** surrounded by tremendous cliffs, housed Salman Rushdie for a night during the height of the *fatwa* against him. To get to the trailhead from town, turn left at the DART and bus station and follow Harbour Rd. around the coast for about 20min. From the lighthouse, to avoid the long trek back over the cliff walk, climb the path to the Summit Carpark and either hop the #31B back down to the heart of town or walk down Thormanby Rd. Take a moment in the parking lot to admire the magnificent view: on a clear day the Mourne Mountains in Northern Ireland are visible.

Several sights are clustered in the middle of the peninsula; go right as you exit the DART station and then left after ¼ mi. at the entrance to the Deer Park Hotel. Up that road lies the private **Howth Castle,** a charmingly awkward patchwork of materials, styles, and degrees of upkeep. Unfortunately, the castle's denizens prefer to keep to themselves and don't open their house to public rabble. Such rabble can instead ramble in the bloomin' **Rhododendron Gardens,** where Molly remembers romance (and such) at the end of *Ulysses.* Follow the signs up the road and past the golf course. (Always open. Free.) Turn right at the gardens' entrance for views of a collapsed **portal dolmen** with a 90-ton capstone, marking the grave of someone who was more important in 2500 BC than he is now. For a picturesque day of golf, play one of the glorious courses at **Deer Park Golf Club,** above the castle. (☎832 3487. €16 per 18-hole round. Open M-F 8am to dusk, Sa-Su 6:30am to dusk.) Train and car enthusiasts should stop behind Howth Castle at the **National Transport Museum,** an old tin warehouse packed with restored trains, trams, tanks, and ambulances from the 1880's to the 1970's. (☎848 0831. www.nationaltransportmuseum.org. June-Aug. daily 10am-5pm, Sept.-May Sa-Su and bank holidays 2pm-5pm. €3, children €1.50.) Just offshore, **Ireland's Eye,** a small island, once provided religious sanctuary for monks, whose former presence is visible in the ruins of **St. Nessan's Church,** and a military outlook from one of the coast's many **Martello towers** (see **Rebellion,** p. 61), which opened for visitors in 2001. The monks abandoned their

AMAZING GRACE Howth Castle is the private residence of the St. Lawrence family, which has occupied it for four centuries, but try knocking if your surname is O'Malley. In 1575, pirate queen Grace O'Malley (see **Clare Island,** p. 383) paid a social call but was refused entrance because the family was eating. Not one to take an insult lightly, Grace abducted the St. Lawrence heir and refused to return him until she had word that the gate would always be open to all O'Malleys at mealtimes.

island refuge when they tired of marauding pirates, and the island's long beach is now primarily a bird haven. **Ireland's Eye Boat Trips** jets across the water from the East Pier, near the lighthouse. (☎831 4200 or 087 267 8211. 15min., every 30min. 11am-6pm, weather permitting. €8 return, students and children €4.)

MALAHIDE (MULLACH ÍDE)   ☎01

Eight miles north of Dublin, Malahide presides over its little bay with quiet suburban hauteur. Rows of shops line the main street, smiling with smug satisfaction. The town's pride stems from its flowerboxes, sparkling ocean and, most of all, **Malahide Castle** and its gorgeous parklands. To complement the perfectly groomed grounds, the National Gallery has stocked the interior with furnishings and portraits from various periods between the 14th and 19th centuries. The dark-paneled oak room and the great hall are magnificent. (☎846 2184. Park open dawn to dusk. Castle open Apr.-Oct. M-Sa 10am-5pm, Su 11am-6pm; Nov.-Mar. M-Sa 10am-5pm, Su 11am-5pm. Admission by tour only. Tours last 35min. €6, students and seniors €5, children €3.50.) Next to the castle, track over to the Fry Model Railway, a 2500 sq. ft. working model with detailed miniatures of favorite Dublin landmarks. The 20min. tour gives the surprisingly interesting history of railroads and other transport throughout Ireland. (☎846 3779. Open Apr.-Sept. M-Sa 10am-1pm and 2-5pm, Su 2-6pm. Admission by tour only; tours every 30min. €6, students and seniors €5, children €3.50.) A live peacock welcomes those who discover the best secret in the castle complex: the incongruous ▨Museum of Childhood, a veritable antiques roadshow of 18th-century dollhouses and toys. This charity trust can't afford to advertise, so few know of the world's oldest known dollhouse (circa 1700) that lies in its midst. Upstairs is the spectacular Tara's Palace, a huge model mansion that fills an entire room. (M-Sa 10:45am-5:45pm, Su 1:30-5:30pm. €2 donation for charity requested.) In town, make sure to hit Malahide's gorgeous **beach.** Closer to neighboring Portmarnock is the even softer, more luxurious **Velvet Strand.**

Getting here from Dublin is easy, since the **DART** and **suburban rail** serve Malahide station (☎845 0422). Alternatively, take **bus** #42, 32A, or 230. All forms of transport to Dublin (except #32A) run at least once per hr. and cost around €1.50. From the DART/ train station on Main St., turn right for the nearby castle (cross the bridge and turn left into the parking lot), or left to reach the town center. Rent wheels at **Malahide Cycles,** downstairs in the Malahide Shopping Centre, across from the library. (☎845 0945. Open M-Sa 10am-1pm and 2-6pm, Sa 10am-6pm. €15 per day.) Coming from the DART station, the **library** is a large brick building on the right side of Main St. (☎845 2026. Open M, W, and F-Sa 10am-1pm and 2pm; Tu and Th 2-8:30pm.) The **Citizens Information Centre,** Main St., in the parking lot behind the library, has free maps and info. (Open M-F 10am-noon and 2:30-4pm.) **Malahide Internet Cafe,** 8 St. James Terrace, in a Georgian building off Main St., is the place for an e-fix. (☎845 7343. €4 per hr., €3 per hr. for students. Open 11am-10pm.) The **post office,** a few doors down in the shopping Centre, shares space with a locksmith and shoe-repair store. (Open M-F 9am-1pm and 2:15-5:30pm, Sa 9am-1pm.)

Continue on Main St. for 15min. as it becomes Coast Rd., to reach **Pegasus ❸,** 56 Biscayne, home to friendly Betty O'Brien and her lovely Irish or veggie breakfasts. (☎845 1506. Open Mar.-Oct. Doubles €60, with bathroom €62.) Closer to town on Grove Rd. is **Maud Plunkett's ❺,** a traditional pub/hotel decorated like a 19th-century apothecary. Turn right off of Main St. at the Grand Hotel. Named for an unfortunate local resident who was a maiden, bride, and widow in the same day—she married a soldier during WWI who was killed in battle the evening of their wedding day. Her luck improved when she married into the Talbot family and moved to Malahide Castle. Cozy but comfortable rooms with full hotel accommodations are available. (☎845 2208. Breakfast included. Singles €57; doubles €100.) Malahidean restaurants tend to cater to heavy purses, but budget options can be found. **Cafe la Marina,** 12 Townyard Ln., serves large breakfasts (€7), Asian-influenced salads (€9), and classic sandwiches (€4.25-5.50) in an unpretentious setting. (☎ 845 6278. Open daily 10am-6pm.) Otherwise, grab supplies for castle or beach-side picnics at **SuperValue,** in the shopping center on Main St. (☎ 845 0233. Open M-W 8am-8pm, Th-Sa 8am-9pm, Su 9:30am-6pm.)

DÚN LAOGHAIRE ☎ 01

As one of Co. Dublin's major ferryports, Dún Laoghaire (dun-LEER-ee) is many tourists' first peek at Ireland. Fortunately, this is as good a place as any to begin rambles along the coast. The surrounding towns, from north to south, are Black-rock, Monkstown, Dalkey, and Killiney; getting from one town to the next is quick and simple if staying within a few blocks of the sea. An entertaining jaunt would begin with a ride on bus #59 from the Dún Laoghaire DART station to the top of Killiney Hill and continue along the path through the park and down into Dalkey. Or, disembark at the Dalkey DART and ramble over the hills to Killiney's wonder-ful beach. On summer evenings, couples stroll down the Dún Laoghaire water-front, and the whole town turns out for weekly sailboat races.

ORIENTATION AND PRACTICAL INFORMATION

Dún Laoghaire is easily reachable on the **DART** from Dublin (€1.40), or on south-bound **buses** #7, 7A, 8, or (a longer, inland route) #46A from Eden Quay. For those who want to party downtown by night, the 7N **nightbus** departs for Dún Laoghaire from College St. in Dublin. (M-W 12:30 and 2am, Th-Sa every 20min. 12:30-4:30am.) From the ferryport, **Marine Rd.** climbs up to the center of town. **George's St.,** at the top of Marine Rd., holds most of Dún Laoghaire's shops; many are right at the intersection in the 70's-style **Dún Laoghaire Shopping Centre.** The section of the street to the right of Marine Rd. is Upper George's St., and to the left is Lower George's St. To reach **Bloomfield Shopping Centre,** head up Marine Rd. from the har-bor, take a right on George's St., and then take the third left. **Patrick Street,** the con-tinuation of Marine Rd., has some good, cheap eateries.

Danae and her comrades keep the **tourist office** humming at the ferry termi-nal and outfit visitors with maps and pamphlets. Ask for the series of six walks on the Dun Laoghaire Way. The pamphlets cover easy-to-miss sights, and pro-vide the maps needed to find them. (Open M-Sa 10am-1pm and 2-6pm.) Exchange money at the ferry terminal's **bureau de change.** (Usually open M-Sa 9am-4pm, Su 10am-4pm.) Banks, their ATMs, and **bureaux de change** cluster around the intersection of Marine Rd. and George's St. **Bank of Ireland** and its **ATM** are at 101 Upper George's St. (☎ 280 0273. Open M-F 10am-4pm, Th until 5pm.) The **post office** is beyond the bank on Upper George's St. (Open M and W-F 9am-6pm, Tu 9:30am-6pm, Sa 9am-1pm.) **Grafton Recruitment,** on Upper George's St. (☎ 284 1818), helps find **work opportunities,** as can **Dun Laoghaire Youth Info Centre,** in the church on Marine Rd. (☎ 280 9363. Open M-F 9:30am-5pm, Sa 10am-4pm.) Free **Internet** is also available at the Centre, and for a fee at **Net House,** 28 Upper George's St. (☎ 230 3085. €5 per hr. Open 24hr.) **U-Surf,** 88 Lower George's St., is blissfully smoke-free, but has fewer hours. (☎ 231 1186. €4 per hr., €2 min. Open daily 10am-10pm.)

ACCOMMODATIONS

Dún Laoghaire is prime ground for B&Bs, few of which are modestly priced. Two hostels are also within walking distance, the best being ■**Belgrave Hall** ❷ at 34 Bel-grave Sq. From the Seapoint DART station, head left down the coast, right on Bel-grave Rd., left on Eaton Pl., right across from the blue and yellow doors, and left again across from Belgrave House. In a splendid, well-maintained old mansion, this top-tier hostel has front rooms with bay views, and blissful showers. Frolic with lovable Irish wolfhounds in a family-friendly setting. (☎284 2106. Continental breakfast included. Laundry €7. Free parking. M-Th 10-bed dorm €20, F-Su €25.) Head left out of the Salthill and Monkstown DART station to **Marina House ❷**, at 7 Old Dunleary Rd., next to Purty Kitchen (see **Food and Pubs**, p. 139). Young, energetic owners mingle nightly with guests in this beat-up stone beach house. (☎284 1633 or 284 1524; www.marinahouse.com. Non-smoking bedrooms. Terrace BBQ. 6-bed dorms €16-19; 4-bed €18-21; doubles €51.) Fall off the DART or ferry into bed at **Marleen ❸**, 9 Marine Rd. Its convenient location attracts those in need of catching an early morning ferry. (☎280 2456. TV and tea facilities. Full breakfast. Singles €35; doubles €60.) **Avondale ❸**, 3 Northumberland Ave., off Upper George's St., is around the corner from Dunnes Stores. A crimson carpet and darling cocker spaniel (Oscar) lead guests to their big beds. (☎280 9628. €30.)

🔲🔳 FOOD AND PUBS

Tesco sells groceries downstairs in the Dún Laoghaire Shopping Centre. (☎280 0668. Open M-W, Sa 8:30am-7pm; Th-F 8:30am-9pm.) Fast-food restaurants and inexpensive coffee shops line George's St. The huge glass facade of **40 Foot,** above the harbor on Marine Rd., stretches trendiness across the horizon. The bar, with its patio and low leather benches, is *the* place to drink, and the restaurant serves savory steaks and seafood. (☎284 2982; www.40foot.info. Mains €14-25. Open M-W noon-11:30pm, Th noon-12:30am, F-Sa noon-1:30am, Su noon-11:30pm.) The sidewalk below the patio has several new cafes, perfect for a relaxing drink after a long ferry ride. The best family restaurant in town is **Bits and Pizzas ❷**, 15 Patrick St. Go early or be prepared to wait. (☎284 2411. Pizzas and pasta €6-10; homemade ice cream €1.40. Open daily noon-midnight.) Adults head to **Mia Cucina ❸**, 107 Lower George's St., for simple Italian meals featuring fresh seafood. (☎280 5318. Pizzas and pasta €8.50-13. Open M-Th noon-11:30pm, F-Su noon-midnight.) For home-baked Mediterranean-vegetarian fare, travel to bohemian **World Cafe ❷**, 56 Lower George's St. (☎284 1024. Open M-Sa 9am-5pm.) Across the street at **Weir's ❸**, 88 Lower George's St., mahogany and brass elegance and a wrought-iron spiral staircase add style to the classic pub meal. (☎230 4654. Open M-Th 10:30am-11:30pm, Sa 10:30am-midnight.) Next to the Marina Hostel, stylish 🔲**Purty Kitchen** pub transforms its loft into a nightclub with trad Tuesday and Thursday, and pop and jazz Friday through Sunday. They do dinner, too, and the specials are a steal at €8-11. (☎214 7666. Cover €10-12.) **Scott's Bar,** 17 Upper George's St., has music Wednesday through Sunday. (☎280 2657. F karaoke; Su trad. Open M-Sa 10am-12:30am, Su 12:30pm-12:30am.) Across the way, locals tear up the dance floor at **Nemo.** On Thursdays, the €10 cover is steep, but the €2 drinks are cheap. (☎280 2293. F-Sa €7 cover after 11pm. Open Su-W 9am-11:30pm, Th-Sa 9am-2:30am.)

👁🔺 SIGHTS AND ACTIVITIES

To get to 🔲**James Joyce Tower** from the Sandycove DART station, turn left onto Islington Ave., go down to the coast, turn right, and continue to the Martello tower in Sandycove; or take bus #8 from Burgh Quay in Dublin to Sandycove Ave. In September 1904, a young James Joyce stayed here for six tense days as a guest of Oliver St. John Gogarty, the surgeon, poetic wit, man-about-town, and first civilian tenant of the tower. Joyce later infamized Gogarty in the first chapter of *Ulysses*. The novel opens in and around the tower on the "snotgreen" sea, with Buck Mulligan playing Gogarty. The tower's museum is a motherlode of Joycenalia: his death mask, love letters to Nora Barnacle, a draft manuscript page from *Finnegan's Wake*, and many editions of *Ulysses*. The **Round Room** upstairs reconstructs the author's bedroom. Joyce novices enjoy views from the gun platform of "many crests, every ninth, breaking, plashing, from far, from farther out, waves and waves." (☎ 280 9265. Open Apr.-Oct. M-Sa 10am-1pm and 2-5pm, Su 2-6pm; Nov.-Mar. by appointment. €6, students €5.) At the base of the tower lies another Joyce-blessed spot, the 40 ft. **men's bathing place.** A wholesome crowd with a bevy of tod-dlers splashes in the shallow pool facing the road, but behind a wall, on the rocks below the battery and adjacent to the tower, men skinny-dip year-round.

The Dún Laoghaire harbor is a sight, full of boat tours, car ferries, fishermen, and yachts cruising in and out of the **new marina.** Frequent summer-evening **boat races,** usu-ally on Mondays and Thursdays, draw much of the town. On a clear day, head to the piers—the setting for Samuel Beckett's *Krapp's Last Tape*—to soak up the sun or brood with extended alienated pauses. A number of outdoor and water activities are available in town. The **Irish National Sailing School & Club,** on the West Pier, offers begin-ner weekend and week-long sailing courses. (☎ 284 4195; www.inss.ie. €215 per course.) The **Irish Canoe Union** has summer kayaking courses on area rivers (☎ 450 9838 or 087 245 7620. €150 for 4 evening courses and a daytrip). **Dublin Adventures** offers canoeing, kayaking trips, and rock climbing (☎ 087 287 3287; www.adventure-activi-ties-ireland.com). For indoor fun and dance, Dún Laoghaire's best *craic* is at ⬛**Comhal-tas Ceoltoiri Éireann** (COLE-tus KEE-ole-tori AIR-run), next door to Belgrave Hall hostel. This is the national headquarters of a huge international organization for Irish traditional music; it houses bona fide, non-tourist trad sessions *(seisiuns)* and *céilí* dancing. Of course, pints are available. (☎ 280 0295. Year-round F night *céilí* €6. July to mid-Aug. sessions M-Th at 9pm, with informal jam session after. €8-10.)

◼ DAYTRIPS FROM DÚN LAOGHAIRE

DALKEY AND DALKEY ISLAND. A medieval heritage town with its own castle, island, and exceptional restaurants, Dalkey walks a fine line between ritzy and quaint. Budget options are scarce. Most shops and restaurants are on or around Castle St. At the far end of Castle St. (from the DART station) is **Dalkey Castle** (a.k.a. Goat Castle, after a local medieval family's coat of arms) and its **Heritage Centre.** (☎ 285 8366. Open Apr.-Dec. M-F 9:30am-5pm, Sa-Su 11am-5pm; Jan.-Mar. Sa-Su 11am-5pm. Tour at 3pm €4.) If an overnight stay is in the cards, indulge at **Tudor House ❺**, off Castle St. This stately, yellow mansion has an elegant pond out back and secluded grounds. (☎ 285 1528. Singles €70; doubles €98-116.) Excellent but expen-sive dishes are at **The Guinea Pig ❺**, Railroad St. (☎ 285 9055. Early-bird special Su-F 6-7pm, Sa 6-7:30pm €20; mains begin at €22. Open daily 6pm-late.) **P.D. Woodhouse ❺**, at 1 Coliemore Rd., off Castle St. near the DART, cooks its dishes on an oak charcoal grill. Kebabs and barbeque mains are a pricey €20-29. (☎ 284 9399. Open Tu-F 6-11pm, Sa 5:30-11pm, Su 4-9:30pm.) For a change of scenery and pace, boat trips to **Dalkey Island** are available. (☎ 087 672 5647; talk to Aidan. €8.) The island's **Martello Tower Number Nine** was one of the many towers built in anticipation of Napoleon's impending but unfulfilled invasion of the coast.

KILLINEY. Farther south from Dún Laoghaire, Killiney (kill-EYE-nee), Dublin's poshest suburb, may have the most gorgeous beach around. Pick up the Heritage map of Dún Laoghaire for details on seven Killiney-area walks, or the Killiney Walk pamphlet of the Dun Laoghaire Way series. From the top of **Killiney Hill Park,** the views are breathtaking—the dark smudge on the horizon is called Wales. *(To reach the park from Castle St., turn left on Dalkey Ave. and climb Dalkey Hill, then take Burmah Rd. into the park.)* Before hitting the park, slip down to Torca Rd., where **Shaw's Cot-tage,** up the road on the left, once played home to young G. B. This is a private home; Shaw enthusiasts have to make do with visiting his birthplace on 33 Synge St. in Dublin (see **Merrion Square,** p. 119). Among Killiney's scattered B&Bs, the best views, both inside and outside the house, are found at **Druid Lodge ❺**, on Killiney Rd. Follow the road to Dalkey and look for white boulders on the right; the lodge is on the left. (☎ 285 1632. Singles €65; doubles €90.)

BRAY (BRÍ CHUALAIN) ☎01

Although officially located in Co. Wicklow, Bray functions as a suburb of Dublin: the DART and Dublin Bus trundle through the town regularly, bringing flocks of city folk to its beach. Well-tended gardens set against a commercialized, cotton candy- and arcade-laden seafront exemplify Bray's compromise between beach town and Victorian Ireland. However, the town clearly benefits from its mixed identities, stimulating tourists without sacrificing its small-town charm.

TRANSPORTATION AND PRACTICAL INFORMATION. Bray is a 40min. **DART** ride from Dublin's Connolly Station (€3.30 return). **Buses #45 and 84** arrive from Eden Quay. Bray has good connections to Enniskerry, in Co. Wicklow: from the Bray DART station, bus #185 runs to Enniskerry (€2), as does **Alpine Coaches,** which also runs to Powerscourt Gardens, Powerscourt Waterfall, and Glencree. (☎286 2547. 20min., 5-8 per day., €1.80. See tourist office for schedule.) **St. Kevin's Bus Service** shuttles from the town hall on Main St. to Glendalough. (☎281 8119. 1hr., 2 per day, €10 return.) Maps are posted in the DART station. To reach **Main Street** from the DART station, take **Quinsborough Road** or **Florence Road,** which run uphill, perpendicular to the tracks. Quinsborough Rd. has shops and inexpensive restaurants. **The Strand,** which holds the nicer restaurants and the cotton candy stands, runs along the beach, parallel to **Meath Rd. The Bike Rack,** in the Boulevard Centre on Quinsborough Rd., **rents bikes,** and does quick repairs. (Open M-Sa 9am-6pm; €15 per day, €80 per wk.) Bray's **tourist office** is the first stop south of Dublin for Wicklow info. Sharing a building with the **heritage center,** the office is downhill on Main St. (☎286 7128. Open June-Sept. M-F 9am-5pm, Sa 10am-4pm; Oct.-May M-F 9:30am-4:30pm, Sa 10am-3pm. Closed M-F for lunch 1-2pm.) **AIB** has an **ATM** on Main St., near Quinsborough. (Open M-Tu, F 10am-4pm; W 10:30am-4pm; Th 10am-5pm.) There's also an **ATM** at the DART station, and at several banks on Quinsborough and Main St. Call ahead to snag a seat at one of the popular, free **Internet** computers in the **library,** on the corner of Florence Rd. and Eglinton Rd. (☎286 2600. Open Tu,Th 10am-5pm, 6-8:30pm; W, F-Sa 10am-5pm.) The **post office** is at 18 Quinsborough Rd. (☎286 2554. Open M-F 9am-5:30pm, Sa 9am-1pm.)

ACCOMMODATIONS, FOOD, AND PUBS. B&Bs line the Strand, but cheaper ones are on Meath St. closer to the town center. Anne and Pat Duffy welcome guests to ◪**Moytura ❸,** 2 Herbert Rd. Herbert Rd. is the continuation of Quinsborough Rd. after Main St. The B&B is on the right before the fork with King Edward Rd. The Duffys offer superb homemade bread, freshly squeezed orange juice, and chats on Irish history and literature. (☎282 9827. All rooms with bath. Singles €40; doubles €60.) **Bayview ❸,** on Meath Rd., is a small B&B with soaring ceilings. The owner, a master craftsman, has installed beautiful wood floors in the dining room. (☎286 0887. Singles €30; doubles €55.) **Ulysses ❹,** a green house in the middle of the Strand, is a 200-year-old house once operated as a B&B by Joyce's niece. (☎286 3860. Free car park. Singles €40; doubles €76.)

SuperQuinn shelves groceries on Castle St., the continuation of Main St. downhill and across the bridge from the tourist office (☎286 7779; open M-Tu 8:30am-8pm, W-F 8:30am-9pm, Sa 8:30am-7pm), and **Dunnes** does the same at 7 Quinsborough Rd., across from the Bike Rack (open M-Tu 9am-6pm, W 9am-7pm, Th-F 9am-9pm, Sa 9am-6:30pm). The best meal in town is at ◪**Escape ❹,** Albert Ave., at the intersection with the Strand. A creative, vegetarian-friendly menu appears daily; the early-bird special shaves €3 off the price of any entree from 5-7pm. (☎286 6755. Mains €15-20. Open M-F 5-11pm, Sa-Su 12:30-11pm.) For lunch during the week try Escape's sister cafe, **Escapade ❷.** Continue down Albert Ave., go under the bridge, go left on Meath Rd., and it's on the left. (☎276 4647. Lunch €9 and under.)

For classic Irish meals of the carnivorous persuasion, head to **Seanchara ❹,** on the Strand between Convent Ave. and Sidmonton Ave. (☎286 0913. Mains €15-22. Open Tu-Su 5:30-10:30pm.) Back that up into **Weary Ass Coffee Shop ❷,** 5 Quinsborough Rd., for omelets and sandwiches. (☎286 2144 Open M-Sa 9am-5pm.) For nights out, try **Clancy's,** across Quinsborough Rd. from the Coffee Shop. It's a dark, old-time pub with wooden plank tables, and trad on Tuesdays, Thursdays, and Fridays (☎286 2362). Or, hit one of the pubs on the Strand. **The Porterhouse,** in an offshoot of the Dublin brew-pub, gathers a young crowd into its outside beer-garden in summer, and inside all year (☎286 0668).

◪ **SIGHTS.** Along the beachfront, couples stroll by the blue-fenced promenade, and predictable arcade palaces cater to a crowd of Dublin beachgoers. The **National Sea Life Centre,** on the Strand, marks the dawning of the age of aquariums. (☎286 6939. Open M-F 10am-5pm, Sa-Su 10am-5:30pm. €8.50, students and seniors €7, children €5.50.) For gorgeous views of the Wicklow Mountains and Bray Bay, hike to the summit of **Bray Head,** high above the south end of the Strand and away from the neon lights. The trail begins after the short paved pedestrian walkway begins to curve up the hill. On the right, past the picnicking area, a set of steps launches one of several winding trails to the top. The 30min. hike is very steep and requires some climbing over rocks, but rewards with a breathtaking panorama at the top. Just outside of town, **Killruddery House and Gardens** has gardens as beautiful as those of the not-too-distant Powerscourt Estate. Its Elizabethan-Revival house with fancy-dancy rooms and a unique 20 ft. pendulum clock await. Finnegan's Bus departs for the house twice hourly from the DART. (☎286 2777. Gardens open Apr.-Sept. 1-5pm. House open May-June and Sept. 1-5pm. Call for tour times. House and Gardens €6.50, students and seniors €4.50, children €2.50.)

🖈 **DAYTRIPS FROM BRAY**

POWERSCOURT ESTATE. Lordly Powerscourt Estate sits near **Enniskerry** in Co. Wicklow, 5 mi. east of Bray. Built in the 1730s, the house has become an architectural landmark. Powerscourt was gutted by flames in 1974, but work has recently begun to repair the lost interior. Outside, the terraced gardens—displaying everything from Italian opulence to Japanese elegance—justify the high admission. Pointed Sugar Loaf Mountain admires from the distance, and four-legged companions rest in peace under the headstones of the pet cemetery in back. Make time for the "long walk," which takes roughly 1hr., but can last considerably longer for the botanical explorer. (From Bray, take an Alpine bus to the garden entrance or #185 to Enniskerry; #44 runs direct from Dublin. Facing the town clock, take the left fork; the house and gardens are a few hundred yards beyond the gatehouse. ☎01 204 6000. Open daily 9:30am-5:30pm. Gardens and house €8, students and seniors €6.50; gardens only €6/€5.50.)

POWERSCOURT WATERFALL. The 398 ft. plunge makes Powerscourt Ireland's tallest (permanent) waterfall—a record challenged by the temporary falls on Hungry Hill, in Co. Kerry (see **Adrigole,** p. 267). Although they're worth the visit during any season, the falls are by far most impressive in late spring and after heavy rains. A 40min. nature walk begins at their base and rambles through quiet, untended woods. (The falls are 3½ mi. outside Enniskerry. Take a bus to Enniskerry and follow the somewhat cryptic signs from town, or catch one of the Apine buses that stops at the falls. Open June-Aug. 9:30am-7pm; Sept.-May 10:30am to dusk. €4, students €3.50.)

EASTERN IRELAND

Woe betides the unfortunate soul whose exposure to eastern Ireland is limited to what he sees from inside a bus headed west from Dublin—the untouristed towns of the east hold many a marvel. The monastic city at Clonmacnoise and the passage tombs (older than the pyramids) in Co. Meath continue to mystify archaeologists. The Wicklow Mountains offer spectacular views, and those too tired to continue hiking can head downhill to relax on the beautiful beaches. Farther north, the tiny lakeland towns of Co. Monaghan (actually a part of the Fermanagh Lake District in the North, see p. 560) harbor the warmest waters in the northern half of Ireland. And where else but Kildare (see p. 157) would host a bog-centric theme park? The comprehensive delights of Co. Wicklow, Kildare, Meath, and Louth, certainly deserve a closer look than daytrips from Dublin ever allow.

COUNTY WICKLOW

Ladies and gentlemen, welcome to the glorious "Garden of Ireland." Exhausted of its gold in the Bronze Age, sacked by Vikings in the 9th century, and then crushed under the English thumb after the fracas of 1798 (see **Rebellion**, p. 61), Wicklow Town has a long-standing reputation of desirability. These days, the lush and mountainous county offers outdoor enthusiasts deserted back roads and seesawing ridges for bicycling. Wild as parts of it are, Wicklow is right in the capital's backyard; its major sights are accessible by bus from downtown Dublin, though moving about within the county is best accomplished by bike or car. Visitors flock to Wicklow's Historical Gaol, the monastic ruins at Glendalough, and the birthplace of political leader Charles Parnell near Rathdrum. The Wicklow Way, the first of Ireland's waymarked trails, is an excellent invitation to rough it for a week, and Brittas Bay's golden beaches validate the fine art of lounging in the sun.

WICKLOW COAST

The sparsely populated towns of the Wicklow coast seem a world away from jet-setting Dublin, although the fingers of the capital have spread to catch commuters from as far away as Wicklow Town. The area lacks the heavy-hitting historical sights of the inland route through Glendalough and Kilkenny, but it also avoids the tourist glut. Those interested in exploring Dublin find towns like Wicklow or Arklow aren't too far to make a decent, cheaper base of operations.

WICKLOW TOWN (CILL MHANTÁIN) ☎0404

Touted both for its seaside pleasures and as a base camp for aspiring Wicklow mountaineers, Wicklow Town has a wide selection of restaurants and plenty of accommodations within walking distance of its pubs. An eager traveler can exhaust the sightseeing potential in the town itself fairly swiftly, but there are many afternoons' worth of hiking and cycling excursions lie within the hills.

EASTERN IRELAND

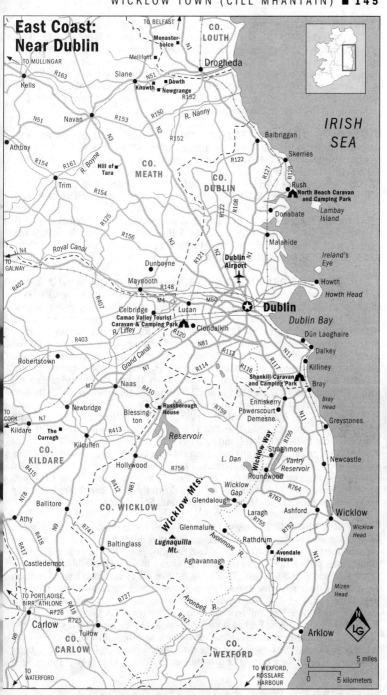

**East Coast:
Near Dublin**

EASTERN IRELAND

⌨ TRANSPORTATION. Trains run to Dublin's Connolly Station (1¼hr.; M-Sa 4 per day, Su 3 per day; €12.70 return) and to Rosslare Harbour via Wexford (2hr., 3 per day, €19 return). The station is a 15min. walk east of town on Church St.; head out Main St. past the Grand Hotel and turn right, then follow the signs. **Bus Éireann** leaves for Dublin near the gaol at the other end of Main St. (1½hr.; M-Sa 9 per day, Su 6 per day; €6.50). A **guided driving tour** of Glendalough and the Wicklow mountains leaves daily at 10am (returning at 6:30pm). The tour goes through Sally Gap to Rathnew, Glenealy, Rathdrum, and Glendalough. (☎45152. €15.)

▉▪ ORIENTATION AND PRACTICAL INFORMATION. Long, narrow **Abbey St.** snakes past Grand Hotel to the grassy triangle of **Fitzwilliam Square,** then continues as **Main Street,** ending in **Market Square.** The historic **gaol** sits up the hill from Market Sq. The **tourist office,** in Fitzwilliam Sq., provides free town maps and a wealth of information on the Wicklow Way. (☎69117. Open June-Sept. M-F 9am-6pm, Sa 9:30am-5:30pm; Oct.-May M-F 9:30am-1pm and 2-5:30pm.) **AIB,** with its 24hr. **ATM,** is on the left entering town from the train station. (Open M 10am-5pm, Tu-F 10am-4pm.) **Wicklow IT Access Centre,** on Main St. across from AIB, has **Internet**. (Open M-Sa 10am-1pm, 2-6pm; open Sept.-June M-F 7-10pm. €6.50 per hr.) From the town center, walk down Main St. toward Market Sq.; the **post office** is on the right. (☎67474. Open M-F 9am-5:30pm, Sa 9:30am-1pm.)

⌂ ACCOMMODATIONS AND CAMPING. Lovely ▉**Wicklow Bay Hostel ❶** garners *Let's Go's* most enthusiastic recommendation. From Fitzwilliam Sq., walk toward the river, cross the bridge, and head left until a big, yellow building called "Marine House." Call for pick-up from the train station, or look for a gravel path that begins between two boulders on the left leaving the station; the path crosses the river next to the railroad tracks and back up towards town. Marine House is on the right. The incredibly helpful, friendly family who runs the hostel treats guests to good beds, clean rooms, and amazing views. (☎69213; www.wicklowbayhostel.com. Ask about work opportunities. Closed Jan. Dorms €12-14; private rooms €16.) **Kilmantin B&B ❸,** next to the gaol, is decidedly un-prisonlike with its new sunroom and bright bedrooms, all with bath and TV. (☎67373 or 25081. Singles €45; doubles €60.) **Evergreen B&B ❸,** Friarsfield Rd., is a lovely large home with comfy beds, plenty of parking, and tasty breakfasts. Turn onto Friar's Hill Rd., downhill from the Grand Hotel, and then right onto Friarsfield Rd. (☎68347. €33.) Several campgrounds are scattered around the area. **Webster's Caravan and Camping Park ❶** at Silver Strand (see **Sights,** p. 147), 2½ mi. south of town on the coastal road, lets visitors pitch a tent. (☎67615. Open June-Sept. 1-person tent €6; 2-person €10. Showers €1.) In **Redcross ❶,** 7 mi. down the N11, **River Valley** has cushy campsites. (☎41647. Open Mar.-Sept. €8 per tent. Showers €0.50.)

◨▉ FOOD AND PUBS. Greasy takeaways and fresh produce shops glare at each other across Main St. **SuperValu,** on Wentworth Pl. off Church St., offers a grand selection. (☎61888. Open M-W and Sa 9am-8pm, Th-F 9am-9pm, Su 10am-7pm.) **Tesco,** out on the Dublin road, has an even wider range of edibles. (☎69250. Open M-W and Sa 8:30am-8pm; Th-F 8:30am-10pm; Su 10am-6pm.) Expect nothing short of fine dining at ▉**The Bakery Cafe ❸.** Come before 7pm and indulge with two delectable courses (€24). The menu changes every month but maintains its vegetarian options. (☎66770. Full Irish breakfast €7; lunch €7-9. Mains €20-23. Open M-Th 10am-3pm, 6-10pm; F 10am-3pm, 6-11pm; Sa 6-11pm; Su 6-10pm.) A little less posh, but equally elegant, **Rugantino's River Cafe ❺** offers a tranquil view of the water and an early-bird special Monday through Thursday (6-7:30pm; €17). Later diners pay €18-22 for a variety of fishy mains. (☎61900. Open M-Sa 6-10pm; Su 1-

3:30pm, 6-10pm.) **Casapepe ❸** serves no-frills Italian fare: pizzas €8-13; pastas, poultry, and fish €11-20. (☎67075. Open daily noon-midnight.) The super-friendly and accommodating staff at **Ping's Chinese Restaurant ❸**, on Main St., by the post office, serve honestly good Chinese food. (Mains €10-13. Open Su-Th 5:30-11:30pm, F-Sa 5:30pm-midnight.) Spice up your life, or just your palate, at **Jamuna Indian Restaurant ❸**, 1 Lower Mall, next to Casapepe. Traditional Indian cuisine, white linen, and sparkling glasses. (☎64628. Mains €11-13. Open daily noon-2:30pm, 6-11:30pm.) **Philip Healy's ❷**, Fitzwilliam Sq., serves food all day and doubles as a lively nocturnal hot spot on weekends. (☎67380. Open Su-W noon-11:30pm, Th-Sa noon-12:30am.) **The Bridge Tavern,** Bridge St., reverberates with the sweet sounds of trad, local chatter, and clinking pints. (☎67718. Tunes nightly at 10pm. Open M-Sa noon-12:30am, Su noon-11:30.)

◑ ▓ SIGHTS AND FESTIVALS. Wicklow's premier attraction is **Wicklow's Historic Gaol.** The museum fills nearly 40 cells with audio clips, displays, and interactive activities relating to the gaol, its history, and the messy business of shipping convicts off to Australia. The canned wailing and moaning may seem a bit overblown, but the live actors keep it real. The walls of several cells are covered with the graffiti prisoners scrawled to pass the time when they weren't in the prison yard doing hard labor. (☎61599. Tours every 10min. Open daily 10am-6pm; last admission 5pm. €5.70, students and seniors €4.40, children €3.50.) The first left past Market Sq. leads to what remains of **Black Castle.** The Normans built the castle in 1178, and the local Irish lords began attacking it almost immediately, finally destroying it in 1301. Since then, many assaults and changes in ownership have left only a few wind-worn stones, but the promontory offers a great vantage point over meadows and waves. At the other end of Main St., the ruins of a **Franciscan friary** hide behind a small gate and a run-down hut. The friary was built at the same time as the Black Castle and fell right along with it. It was subsequently rebuilt and became a place of retirement for both Normans and the native Irish, who considered it neutral ground. Now wildflowers grow in its remaining arches.

A cliff trail provides smashing views while en route to ▓**St. Bride's Head** (a.k.a. **Wicklow Head**), where St. Patrick landed on Travilahawk Strand in AD 432. The townspeople greeted him by knocking the teeth out of his sidekick, Mantan ("the toothless one" or "gubby"), who was later assigned to convert the same local hooligans. Either cut through the golf course from the Black Castle or head out the coastal road past the clubhouse and find the trailhead in the parking lot on the left. Hiking to St. Bride's Head takes over 1hr. Adventurous walkers continue for 30 min. to reach the isolated **lighthouse** at Wicklow Head. At Market Sq., Main St. becomes Summer Hill and then Dunbur Rd., the coastal road, from which beaches extend south to **Arklow.** From Wicklow, the closest strips of sun and sand are **Silver Strand** and **Jack's Hole,** though most people head to the larger ▓**Brittas Bay,** halfway to Arklow. Those who venture farther to the town of Arklow should bring fishing gear to take advantage of the excellent **angling opportunities** along the sea on both sides of the town. Arklow is also home to the **longest stone bridge in Ireland** and its 19 very impressive arches (only 17½ of which are visible today).

Beginning the last week of July, Wicklow hosts its annual **Regatta Festival,** the oldest such celebration in Ireland. The two-week festivities feature hard-core skiff racing and a parade of whimsical homemade barges; join the spectators on the bridge and let loose with eggs and tomatoes! At night, amicable pub rivalries foster singing competitions and general revelry. The **Wicklow Gaol Arts Festival** livens up mid-July nights with plays and concerts. (☎69117; www.wicklowartsweek.com. Tickets €10-15.) Contact the tourist office for more information.

THE LOCAL LEGEND

SO YOU THOUGHT HOLLYWOOD WAS IN CALIFORNIA....

Wandering in the Wicklow Mountains might evoke images of knights in shining armor, damsels in distress, and thousands of warriors mooning their enemies. Yes, you've found it–Hollywood's vision of "ye olden times." From the beginning of the silver screen, directors have come to the "Garden of Ireland" to shoot their versions of 13th-century Scotland, Arthurian England, post-apocalyptic landscapes, and sometimes even small-town Ireland. The lakes, taverns, mountains, and Wicklow Bay Hostel have hosted Oscar-winning actors Liam Neeson, Daniel Day Lewis, Mel Gibson, Julia Roberts, and Meryl Streep. Pierce Brosnan dashed around Enniskerry, Wicklow Town, and Roundwood, but there was no international spying being filmed–just a love story called *The Nephew*. Recently, Matthew McConnaughy and Christian Bale battled through Wicklow Gap's lead mines and the Black Castle on Wicklow Head in the dragon movie *Reign of Fire*...and you thought it was shot on blue-screen.

County Wicklow takes great pride in its connection with the movies; the countryside is scattered with signs to "The Michael Collins Drive," the "Braveheart Trail," and even to Hollywood. It might seem that naming a town after the business is going a bit far, but ask a resident and you'll get another side of the story.

According to Hollywood (Ireland, that is) town legend, Mr. McGuirk, whose descendents still live in Hollywood and run the town's post office,

(cont. on next page)

NEAR WICKLOW: AVONDALE HOUSE & RATHDRUM   ☎0404

The birthplace and main residence of political leader Charles Stewart Parnell, **Avondale House** is now a museum devoted to the charismatic, ill-fated hero and a fine look at how the upper-class of early 19th century Ireland lived. The Parnell family study contains framed love letters from Charles to his mistress Kitty O'Shea, and the small pantry is bedecked with political cartoons from the late 19th century. A 20min. video provides a celluloid glimpse into Parnell's life and his role in the development of Irish independence (see **Parnell**, p. 62). If hunger for liberty turns out to be merely a craving for sausage rolls, the small **cafe** downstairs can help out. (☎46111. House open mid-Mar. to Oct. daily 11am-6pm; Mar.-Apr., Sept.-Oct. closed M. €5, students and seniors €4.50.) Floraphiles and hikers fawn over the hundreds of acres of **forest** and **parklands** surrounding the house and spreading along the west bank of **Avonmore River.** Avondale House sells guides (€2.50) to the grounds, with maps and extensive information on four walks of varying length: the Pine Trail, Exotic Tree Trail, and River Walk.

Avondale House is on the road from Wicklow Town to **Avoca,** 1 mi. after **Rathdrum** and before the **Meeting of the Waters.** From Rathdrum, take Main St. heading toward Avoca (downhill) and follow the signs. **Buses** arrive in Rathdrum from Dublin (2¾hr.; M-Sa 2 per day, Su 1 per day), as do **trains** (1hr., M-F 4 per day). Rathdrum is not easily visible from the train station; after exiting the station's driveway, turn left at the *Garda* station and stroll 200 yd. uphill to a path on the right—the path cuts through the Parnell National Memorial Park and up to Main St. Avondale House is to the right; the town center is to the left. **T. McGrath,** on main St., rents **bicycles.** (☎46172. €10 per day, €50 per wk.) The **tourist office,** in the Square at the center of town, offers pamphlets on hikes and area attractions. (☎46262. Open July-Aug. M-F 9am-5:30pm; Sa-Su 1-6pm; Sept.-May M-F 9am-5:30pm. Sometimes closed 1-2pm.) The **Bank of Ireland,** its 24hr. **ATM,** and the **post office** (☎46211) are concealed within Smith's Fancy Goods on the Square.

In the center of town, ▨**Stirabout Lane B&B ❸**, Main St., has beautifully decorated, doll-themed rooms and a lovely back garden. Ask the owner about the best local fishing areas. (☎43142. Off-street parking. Singles €40; doubles €60; family rooms €30 per person.) Also in town, **Old Presbytery Hostel (IHH) ❶** has many fine beds and a plethora of bathrooms. To find it, continue past the tourist office, turn left after the grocery store, and then right at the top of the hill. (☎46930. Dorms €13; private rooms €16.) Among the many B&Bs outside Rathdrum is the family-run **Woodland B&B** ❹, on the left when heading towards Avondale. (☎46011. Irish breakfast included. Singles €40; doubles €56.) Fish & chips, grilled fish, fish fillet, and yes, some veggie and meat options await consumption at the **Avondale Restaurant** ❸ on Main St. (☎46137. Mains €10-17.) For nightly refreshment and daily dinner, check out **Woolpacker Pub** ❸ in the Square. Hollywood geeks may recognize the upstairs from the film *Michael Collins*. Live music on weekend nights. (☎46574. Main courses €7-19. Open M-Th 10:30am-11:30pm, F-Sa 10:30am-12:30am, Su 12:30-11pm.) **Cartoon Inn** on Main St. is a pub with suitably wacky walls and lively, mixed clientele. (☎46774. Open M-W 10:30am-11:30pm, Th-Sa 10:30am-12:30am, Su 12:30-11:30pm.)

WICKLOW MOUNTAINS

Over 2000 ft. high, carpeted in fragrant heather and rushing with sparkling water, the Wicklow summits provide a happy home to grazing sheep and scattered villages alike. This region epitomizes the romantic image of pristine rural Ireland. Glendalough, a verdant, blessed valley renowned as a medieval, monastic village, draws a stream of coach tours from Dublin. Visitors also make it a point to see Ireland's tallest waterfall, near **Bray** (see p. 141). Public transportation is limited in this region, so driving is the easiest way to connect the scattered sights and towns. Those behind the wheel should be careful on the narrow and winding roads and expect to maneuver around hikers, bikers, tour buses, and the occasional flock of oblivious sheep. Everyone except hardcore wilderness demigods find portions of the Wicklow Way challenging, but the effort is rewarded by the best-maintained trailpath in Ireland and its charming hostels. Stop by the tourist offices in Bray, Wicklow Town, Arklow, and Rathdrum for advice and colorful maps.

GLENDALOUGH (GLEANN DÁ LOCH) ☎0404

In the 6th century, a vision inspired St. Kevin to give up his life of ascetic isolation and set up a monastery. He offset the workaday austerity of monastic life by choosing one of the most spectacular valleys in Ireland in which to found Glendalough ("glen of two lakes"; glen-DA-lock). More recently, the valley has become known for ruins, excellent hikes, and the swarms of tourists that accompany so many of Ireland's best sights. Glendalough, no longer a true town,

immigrated to America in the 1800s. After crossing the country and settling in Southern California, McGuirk became homesick for the green mountains of Wicklow. Instead of returning home (it would have been a long, dank boat ride), he named the hillside near Los Angeles where he had set up camp after his dear hills at home. It is, we are led to believe, mere coincidence that over a hundred years later directors choose this spot for most of the filming in Ireland.

For detailed info on Wicklow movie history, and self-led driving tours to various film locations in the county, ask at any Co. Wicklow tourist office for the brochure "Film Action in County Wicklow."

PRIESTLY PROGRAMS

It was inevitable that in a country as Catholic as Ireland, someone would eventually produce a television comedy starring priests. In fact, two tremendously popular shows have appeared in the last decade, with slightly different takes on the lives of the holy brethren.

Ballykissangel is filmed in the green hills of **Avoca**. The show stars Father Damien Daly, a young British priest who alights in a small Irish town to minister to its parishioners. For six seasons this detective-drama-comedy kept viewers across the world wondering whether Father Daly was going to forsake his vows and finally jump into the sack with the lovely local barmaid.

Father Ted, a darker comedy (blasphemy be damned), features an anxious housekeeper and a set of three nun-hating, dysfunctional, Irish priests creating trouble on a fictional Craggy Island. The final episode makes a jab at its rival priestly program "Killybashangles."

consists of St. Kevin's habitat, a hostel, hotel, and roads barely wide enough for the convoy of tour buses that frequent the valley. However, the area's numerous hiking trails make it possible to avoid crowds and to explore the beautiful scenery in relative solitude. One mile up the road, the village of **Laragh** has groceries, food options, and plenty of B&Bs.

TRANSPORTATION. If not arriving on one of the countless charter bus tours, pilgrims come by **car** on R756, on **foot** along the Wicklow Way, or in **buses** run by **St. Kevin's Bus Service.** (☎01 281 8119. Buses leave from St. Stephen's Green in Dublin M-Sa 11:30am and 6pm, Su 11:30am and 7pm; €13 return.) Buses also leave from Bray, past the Town Hall on the right hand side, in front of Onyx Boutique. (M-Sa 12:10 and 6:30pm, Su 12:10 and 7:30pm; €12 return.) **Bus Éireann** (☎01 836 6111; www.buseireann.ie) also runs **day tours** from Dublin's Busáras Station to Glendalough and through the mountains. (Apr.-Oct. daily 10:30am, return 5:45pm. €25, students and seniors €23, children €12.50.) Hitching to Glendalough is fairly easy from Co. Wicklow towns, but most Glendalough-bound traffic from Dublin is bus tours. Hitchers at the beginning of N11 in southwest Dublin hop to the juncture of N11 with Glendalough's R755.

PRACTICAL INFORMATION. Little Glendalough sits on a tributary of **R756,** where **Glenealo River** pools into its **Upper and Lower Lakes.** Bike rental is available at Glendaloch Hostel. (See **Accommodations,** p. 154; €10.20 for under 5hr., €15.25 per day. No deposit for hostel guests.) Road signs lead to the Bord Failté **tourist office,** located in a small trailer in the parking lot behind the Glendalough Hotel. (☎45688. Open from mid-June to Sept. M-Sa 10am-1pm, 2-5:30pm.) The considerably more glamorous **Glendalough Visitor Centre** (see **Sights,** p. 151) is a wealth of both information and parking spaces. The **National Park Information Office,** between the lakes, is the best source for hiking information in the region. (☎45425. Open May-Aug. daily 10am-6pm, Apr.-Sept. Sa-Su 10am to dusk.) When the park office is closed, call the **ranger office,** located in nearby Trooperstown Wood (☎45800). **Laragh IT,** in the parking lot next to Lynham's pub, has **Internet.** (☎45600. €6 per hr. Open M-F 9:30am-4:30pm, 7-10pm.) The Glendalough and Laragh **post office** is tucked into a row of B&Bs between **Wicklow Heather** and **Lynham's** (see **Accommodations,** p. 151).

ACCOMMODATIONS, FOOD, AND PUBS. ⓦThe Glendaloch Hostel (An Óige/HI) ❷, a 5min. walk up the road past the Glendalough Visitor Centre, on the left. Verges on the institutional, but good beds, excellent security, and an in-house cafe make it by far the best option in the area. The comparatively cramped Dublin hostels can't compete with the grandeur of this establishment or the inspiring Wicklow Mountains backdrop. As with all the accommodations in the area, book well in advance in the summertime. (☎45342. **Internet** available. Wheelchair-accessible. Picnic lunch €5.50; full Irish breakfast €6.50; dinners €11. Towels €1.30. Laundry €5. All rooms with private baths. Dorms €20-22; private rooms €22.50-24. off season€3 less.) A little farther down the road to the lakes, **Luganure B&B ❸** is the vision of a quaint cottage, complete with flowers growing up its stone walls. It was once less cozy, when it housed the Glendalough Police station, but now it's all scones and forest views, so snuggle in. (☎45563. Singles €35; doubles €60.)

B&Bs abound in neighboring Laragh. Tucked into the forest on the road up to St. Kevin's Church, **Pinewood Lodge ❸** offers excellent rooms furnished with, appropriately, pinewood. Full breakfast, with options to please even the pickiest eaters. Non-smoking. (☎45437. All rooms with bath. Singles €50; doubles €60-66.) At nearby **Oakview B&B ❸,** elegant rooms are the rule. (☎45453. Open Mar.-Oct. Singles €35; doubles €46, with bath €50.) Hotel options include the established and stately **Glendalough Hotel ❺** (☎45135 or 45391) and brand-new **Lynham's Hotel ❺** (☎45345 or 45398). Both offer similar facilities, including in-house restaurants, at premium, near-identical prices. (Singles €87-107; doubles €130-170.)

Laragh's **Wicklow Heather ❸** is family- and vegetarian-friendly and about the only place in the area open for breakfast. (☎45157. Breakfast €5-10; mains €10-18; Su 3-course lunch €17.95. Open M-Th 8am-9:30pm, F-Sa 8am-10pm, Su 8am-9pm.) **Lynham's ❸** also piles plates high; the Guinness beef stew (€11.50) is tasty and filling. (☎45345. Mains €11-15. Open daily 12:30-3:30pm, 6-9pm.) The attached **Lynham's Pub** lures travelers with siren-like cover bands and rock sessions every Wednesday, Thursday, and Saturday. (☎45345. Open daily until 11:30pm.)

◧ SIGHTS. The amiable staff at **Glendalough Visitors Centre** presents ample information on the valley's intriguing past. The admission fee covers an exhibition, a 17min. audio-visual show on the history of Irish monasteries and St. Kevin's in particular, and occasionally a tour of the ruins. Visitors learn, among other interesting tidbits, that St. Kevin, in keeping with his ascetic image, would sometimes stand in one of the frigid lakes long enough for birds to make nests in his outstretched hands—before, of course, returning home to pray. (☎45325. Open daily mid-Mar. to mid-Oct. 8:30am-6pm; mid-Oct. to mid-Mar. 9:30am-5pm. Group tours by request; individuals free to jone one in progress. €2.75, students €1.25.)

The well-preserved ruins are free and always open. The present remains reflect only a small part of what the monastery looked like in its heyday, but they're still pretty impressive. A tiny 3 ft. base supports the 100 ft. **Round Tower** of Glendalough, one of the best-preserved in all of Ireland (see **Christians and Vikings**, p. 57) and the centerpiece of the monastery. It was built in the 10th century, primarily as a belltower, but also served as a watchtower and retreat in tumultuous times. The entrance is 12ft. above ground; when Vikings threatened, the monks would climb the inside of the tower floor by floor and draw up the ladders behind them. The **cathedral**, constructed in a combination of Romanesque architectural styles, was once the largest in the country. In its shadow stands **St. Kevin's Cross,** an unadorned high cross that was carved before the monks had tools to cut holes clean through stone. The 11th-century **St. Kevin's Church,** whose stone roof remains intact, acquired the misnomer "St. Kevin's Kitchen" because of its chimney-like tower. After 500 years of worshipful use, it has laid derelict except for a brief revival in the 19th century. To peek inside, join one of the Visitor's Centre's tours.

The **Upper and Lower Lakes** are a rewarding digression from the monastic site. Cross the bridge at the far side of the monastery and head right on the paved path for 5min. to reach the serene Lower Lake. Twenty minutes later, the path hits the National Park Information Office (see **Practical Information**, p. 150) and the magnificent Upper Lake. Drivers should continue past the hotel and park (€3) in the lot by the Upper Lake. The trail continues along the lakeside, passing **St. Kevin's Bed,** the cave where he prayed. Legend has it that when St. Kevin went there, his words ascended in a vortex of flame and light that burned over the Upper Lake's dark waters with such intensity that none but the most righteous monks could witness it without going blind. Before reaching the cave, look for the **burial grounds** at Reefert Church, where local chieftains found their eternal resting places.

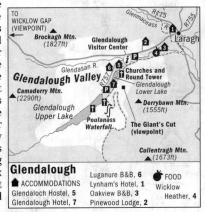

Glendalough

TO WICKLOW GAP (VIEWPOINT)

Glenmacnass · R115

R115 · R755

Laragh

Brockagh Mtn. (1827ft)

Glendalough Visitor Center

Glendasan R.

Glendalough Valley

Camaderry Mtn. (2290ft)

Glendalough Upper Lake

R757

Churches and Round Tower

Glendalough Lower Lake

Derrybawn Mtn. (1555ft)

Poulanass Waterfall

The Giant's Cut (viewpoint)

Cullentragh Mtn. (1673ft)

🏠 ACCOMMODATIONS
Glendaloch Hostel, 5
Glendalough Hotel, 7

Luganure B&B, 6
Lynham's Hotel, 1
Oakview B&B, 3
Pinewood Lodge, 2

🍴 FOOD
Wicklow Heather, 4

EASTERN IRELAND

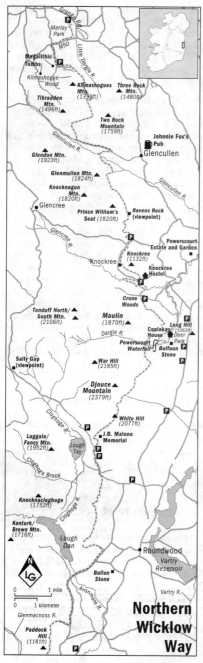

Northern Wicklow Way

For further walking inspiration, Duchas publishes a pamphlet *The Walking Trails of Glendalough* (€0.80; available at the Visitor Centre or the National Park Information Office). These nine well-marked trails range from easy hikes to a boggy, mountainous "Hill Walk," and take 45min. to 4hr. The "Poulanass and St. Kevin's Cell" path—a quick jaunt up the waterfall, stopping at St. Kevin's Cell and Reefert Church on the way down—is the perfect way to top off a day at the ruins.

THE WICKLOW WAY

Ireland's oldest marked hiking trail (est. 1981) is also its most spectacular. Stretching from **Marlay Park** at the border of Dublin to **Clonegal** in Co. Carlow, the 76 mi. Wicklow Way meanders north to south through Ireland's largest highland expanse. As hikers weave over heathered summits and through steep glacial valleys, yellow arrows and signs mark the Way's various footpaths, dirt tracks, and even paved roads. Civilization is rarely more than 2 mi. away, but appropriate wilderness precautions should still be taken: bring warm, windproof layers and raingear for the exposed hills, and, although the terrain never gets frighteningly rugged, sturdy footwear is a must (see **Wilderness Safety**, p. 24). Water is best taken from farmhouses (with permission), not streams. Open fires should be carefully monitored, and are illegal within a mile of the forest.

▣ TRANSPORTATION

Several bus companies drop happy packers at various spots along the trail. **Dublin Bus** (☎01 873 4222) runs frequently to Marlay Park in Rathfarnham (#47B or 47A from Trinity College) and Enniskerry (#44 or 185 from Bray), and less frequently to Glencullen (#44B). **Bus Éireann**

(☎01 836 6111) comes somewhat near the Way farther south, with infrequent service from Busáras in Dublin to Tinahely and Shillelagh. **St. Kevin's** runs two shuttles daily between Dublin's St. Stephen's Green West, Bray, Roundwood, Laraugh. and Glendalough. (☎01 281 8119. €15 return.) To combat trail erosion, **bikes** are allowed only on forest tracks and paved sections, but many off-Way roads are equally stunning. For a particularly scenic route, take R759 to **Sally Gap**, west of the trail near Lough Tay, then head south on R115 past **Glenmacnass Waterfall** (roughly 15 mi.).

✦ ⁊ ORIENTATION AND PRACTICAL INFORMATION

Most tourist offices in the county sell the *Wicklow Way Map Guide* (€5.50), which is the best source of information on the trail and its sights—don't let the unconventional compass confuse you; the map *is* oriented with North pointing down. Hiking 7-8hr. each day for six days carries backpackers from one end to the other, though there are plenty of attractive abbreviated routes. Numerous side trails make excellent day hikes; *Wicklow Way Walks* (€6.50) outlines several of these loops. The northern 44 mi. of the Way—from Dublin to Aghavannagh—is the older section and, since it has the best scenery and all the hostels, attracts more people. An Óige publishes a pamphlet detailing 4-5hr. hostel-to-hostel walks (available at An Óige hostels in Co. Wicklow and Dublin). A trip touching on the highlights of the Way runs the 20 mi. from Powerscourt Waterfall near Enniskerry (see p. 144) to Glendalough, passing stupendous **Lough Dan** and gorgeous **Lough Tay,** and offering views as far away as Wales. For more information, contact the **National Park Information Office** (☎45425), between Glendalough's lakes (see p. 151). For-

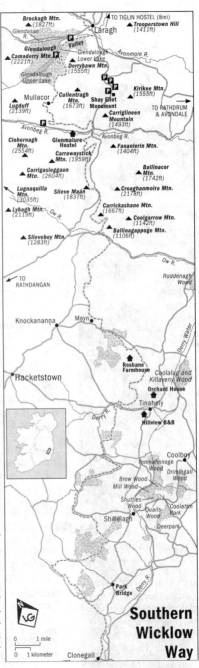

Southern Wicklow Way

EASTERN IRELAND

THE HIDDEN DEAL

THE CHEAP AND EASY **WICKLOW WAY**

Rolling hills, craggy ravines, misty waterfalls, rocky summits...appealing? Yes. Easily accessed...Yes! If the Wicklow Way calls you, but haven't the time (or energy) to hike it, can't rent a car due to those silly age restrictions or would simply prefer to let someone else do the mountain driving, Christopher Stacey is your man.

Mr. Stacey, who has led tours all over Europe, leads some each summer featuring the Wicklow Way. In a small (6-person) van, the tour is more like driving around with an old, well-informed friend than the typical bus tour. The drive begins in Wicklow Town, moves into the mountains to Rathdrum and the lovely Avondale House, and through the Vale of Clara to the monastic ruins of Glendalough. Once in Glendalough, you receive tips on the best hiking trails, and are left to explore the area. A few hours later, pile back into the car, head up past the Glenmacnass waterfall to Sally Gap, and then head back down towards Wicklow Town via Lough Tay, a beautiful lake where scenes in *Braveheart* were shot. The trip ends with the Mount Usher Gardens and, by dinner, returns to town, where there are actually restaurants to eat in!

Call Christopher Stacey ☎ 0404 45152 to ensure a spot. Trip runs July-Aug. 10am-6:30pm. At only €15 per person, this is truly a hidden deal--a bus ride to Glendalough costs as much.

estry lands are governed by **Coillte** (KWEEL-chuh; ☎ 01 201 1111), but much of the Way is simply on a right-of-way through private lands.

ACCOMMODATIONS

The splendor of the Wicklow Way isn't exactly a well-kept secret—many accommodations take advantage of the endless stream of bodies that trek the hike. **Camping** is feasible along the Way but requires planning ahead. Many local farmhouses allow tents on their land; ask permission first. National Park lands are fine for low-impact camping, but pitching a tent in state plantations is prohibited.

HOSTELS

An Óige runs a cluster of hostels close to the Way. All hostels include self-catering facilities, but only Glendaloch sells meals and boxed lunches; bring food along or expect to walk a few miles to a grocery store. Except for the Glendaloch Hostel, all bookings are handled through the An Óige Head Office (☎ 01 830 4555; www.irelandyha.org). Hostels run from north to south in the following order:

Knockree (An Óige/HI), Lacken House, Enniskerry (☎ 01 286 4036), right on the Way. A reconstructed farmhouse 4 mi. from the village and 2 mi. from Powerscourt Waterfall. From Enniskerry, take the right fork of the road leading uphill from the village green and follow the signs to the hostel. Sheets €1.25. Lockout 10am-5pm. Dorms €11-12. ❶

Tiglin (An Óige/HI), a.k.a. **Devil's Glen,** Ashford (☎ 0404 49049), by the Tiglin Adventure Centre, 5 mi. from the main trail and a hilly 8 mi. from Powerscourt. From Ashford, take the Roundwood road for 3 mi., then follow the signs for the Tiglin turnoff and R763 on the right. Recent renovations on the courtyard of this former farm brought a barbecue to the grassy front lawn. Basic, single-sex dorms. Curfew 11pm. Dorms €11-12. ❶

Glendaloch (An Óige/HI), a stone's throw from the Way (☎ 0404 45342), by the monastic ruins. An absolutely fabulous hostel, well worth a 2-3 day break from the Wicklow Way. Dorms €20-22; doubles €45-48. See **Glendalough,** p. 150. ❷

Glenmalure (An Óige/HI), Glenmalure. At the end of a dead end road 7½ mi. along the Way south from Glendalough. By road, head from Glendalough to Laragh and take every major right turn. Back-to-nature lodging; doesn't even have a telephone or electricity (but they do have beds). Open July-Aug. Dorms €11-12. ❶

BED AND BREAKFASTS

Approved accommodations along the Way can be booked with a credit card through the **All-Ireland Room Reservation** service. (Freephone ☎00 800 668 668 66; www.ireland.travel.ie.) A number of B&Bs offer **camping** and pickup if called ahead; the *Wicklow Way Map Guide* comes with a sheet that lists about 20. The following few will pick up hikers and allow camping.

Coolakay House (☎01 286 2423), 2½ mi. outside Enniskerry, next to the Powerscourt Waterfall. Small cafe and nice rooms bordering on hotel-esque. Doubles €70. ❸

Hillview B&B, Tinahely in Knockananna (☎0508 71195). Sits 1 measly mile away. Singles €25; doubles €40. **Camping** €5-7 per person. ❸

Rosbane Farmhouse, Rosbane (☎0402 38100). A 7min. walk from the Way, near the summit of Garryhoe. €30. **Camping** €7 per tent. ❸

Orchard House, Tinahely (☎0402 38264). Within earshot of the main trail. Relax by picking apples from the backyard orchard. **Internet** available. Singles €25-30. ❸

◨◧ FOOD AND PUBS

All hikers should carry enough food to last through the length of the journey (5-6 days), as restaurants and groceries are only found in towns located off the Way (Glendalough and Laragh excepted). Water can be replenished at hostels and B&Bs along the Way; it is very important for hikers to drink plenty of water during the strenuous hike as many people fall ill from dehydration. With few opportunities for *alcoholic* rehydration, hikers who reach Glencullen or Enniskerry should make an extra effort to climb to ◪**Johnnie Fox's**, Ireland's highest pub. Established in 1798, Johnnie's is 1200 ft. above sea level. Here, Wicklow Way walkers drink and dine while enjoying the pub's excellent *craic*. The nightly trad sessions and delicious food (mains €9-18) make the journey worthwhile. Locals usually crowd into the back room. (☎01 295 5647. Open M-Sa 10am-11:45pm, Su noon-11pm.)

WESTERN WICKLOW

Squatter, lumpier, and less traveled than the rest of the county, western Wicklow offers lovely scenic walks for misanthropic travelers looking to avoid the picnicking families elsewhere. It's possible to hike between western Wicklow and the Wicklow Way, but turn around at red flags; the Irish Army maintains a few shooting ranges in the region. Hiking is safe in un-flagged areas. Lungnaquilla Mountain, the highest peak in Co. Wicklow, has stunning views and challenging hiking trails.

BLESSINGTON (BAILE COIMÍN)   ☎045

Blessington lies beside the reservoir of the Liffey, close to the intersection of N81 from Dublin (30min. by car) and R410 from Naas (15min.). Hikers come here to rest their tired, Wicklow Mountain-exploring feet. Cultured types make the daytrip from Dublin for the world-class art inside the Palladian grandeur of **Russborough House**, sprawling amidst its vast parkland 2 mi. south of Blessington on N81 toward Baltinglass. Richard Cassells, who also designed Dublin's Leinster House and much of Trinity College, built the house in 1741 for Joseph Leeson, an Anglo-Irish man-about-Parliament. Russborough now houses an impressive collection of paintings, sculpture, furniture, and Baroque plaster-work. In 1986, the Dublin mobster "The General" orchestrated the theft of the 17 most valuable paintings, including works by Goya, Vermeer, and Velasquez; all but one have been recovered. The best pieces are now in the National Gallery in Dublin (see p. 118), but a few excel-

EASTERN IRELAND

lent ones remain here in Wicklow. Unfortunately for 2004 travelers, the paintings have been removed for conservation, but eventually the house will be spiffier than ever. For the time being, tours visit upstairs rooms to make up for the missing paintings. On summer Sundays, a **life-size maze** lets explorers get lost in the garden. (☎865 239. Open May-Sept. daily 10am-5pm; Easter-Apr. and Oct. Su 10am-5pm. Admission by hourly 45min. tours only. €6, students and seniors €4.50, children €3. Maze open June-Aug. Su 12:30-5pm.) Although swimming is technically prohibited in the reservoir, many activities take place on its waters. **Blessington Sports Centre** is activity central. From town, heading away from Dublin, take the first left before the roundabout; it's on the left, ½ mi. down the road. The center offers kayak trips, fishing, windsurfing, and sailing. Quad biking, mountain biking, and hillwalk expeditions are also available. (☎865 092; www.blessingtonsports.com. Open Mar-Oct. daily 9am-6pm. Most activities €16 per hr., children €11. Multi-activity half days €55/€23; full day €90/€40.)

The easiest way to reach Blessington is by the #65 **bus** from Eden Quay in Dublin. Some buses continue on to Ballynmore; those that do stop at the entrance to Russborough House on request. (M-Sa 14 per day, Sa 8 per day, Su 17 per day; €3). Turn to the **tourist office,** in the town square, for ideas on outdoor pursuits. (☎865 850. Open M-F 10am-5pm, also June-Aug. Su 11am-4pm.) **Ulster Bank,** on Main St., has a **bureau de change** and an **ATM.** (☎865 125. Open M-F 10am-4pm, Th until 5pm.) **Hayland's House B&B** ❸, less than a 10min. walk out of town on the N81 to Dublin, across the road from the #65 bus stop, offers super-clean baths and a relaxed smoke-free environment. (☎865 183. Singles €35, with bath €37; doubles €54/€58.) On the other side of town, 1 mi. out on the road to Naas, the friendly owners of **Fairhill B&B** ❸ provide excellent rooms for weary walkers of the Wicklow Way. (☎865 692. Singles €35; doubles €55.) Four miles down the road to Valleymount, **Baltyboys (An Óige/HI)** ❶, also known as the Blessington Lake Hostel, has excellent views and affordable rooms. (☎867 894; call ahead. Sheets €2. Lockout 10am-5pm. Open Mar.-Nov. daily; Dec.-Feb. F-Su. June-Sept. dorms €12; Oct.-May €11.) For a quick bite to eat, **The Courtyard Restaurant** ❷ right next to the tourist office, serves large Irish breakfasts (€5.20) in the morning and tasty food throughout the day. (☎865 850. Open M-Sa 8:30am-6pm, Su 10am-6pm..

COUNTY KILDARE

The towns immediately west of Dublin in Co. Kildare are still well within the city's orbit; the best sights—Kildare's horses and Lullymore Heritage Park—make easy day-trips. From the 13th to 16th century, the FitzGerald Earls of Kildare controlled all of eastern Ireland. Today, mansions and the big-money Irish Derby evoke Kildare's former prominence. The Irish National Stud rears horses that win the world's great derbies while the Curragh Racecourse, a few miles outside of Kildare town, hosts them. Farmhouse B&Bs are still the area's greatest attraction.

MAYNOOTH (MHAIGH NUAD)   ☎01

Maynooth (ma-NOOTH) is a town of the erudite and religious. In 1795, St. Patrick's College, the first Catholic seminary in Ireland, opened with George III's permission—he was concerned priests educated in Revolutionary France would acquire dangerous notions of independence. Priests are still ordained here, but the 120 clerical students are far outnumbered these days by their 5000 peers in other disciplines at what is now NUI Maynooth. The serenely beautiful campus includes A.W. Pugin's Gothic **St. Mary's Square, College Chapel,** and **Bicentenary Garden.** The **National Science Museum** displays scientific and ecclesiastical artifacts. (Open June-Aug. M-F 2-4pm, Su 3-5pm. €1.30.) The **Visitor Centre,** under the arch of the large building directly in front of the Main

St. entrance, provides an info-packed map (€4) and tours of the college. (☎708 3576. Open daily 8:30am-11pm. Tours €3 per person for groups of 15 or less, €2.50 for larger groups, students and seniors €1.) The FitzGerald family controlled its vast domain from **Maynooth Castle,** near the college but built in 1176. The castle's exhibition room is lined with attractive comic-book-style panels explaining the history of the castle and the Fitzgerald family; guided tours pass through the remnants of the fortress. (☎628 6744. Open June-Sept. M-F 10am-6pm, Sa-Su 1-6pm; Oct. Su 1-5pm. €1.50, students €0.75.)

Maynooth is 15 mi. west of Dublin on the M4. The **suburban rail** runs from Connolly Station in Dublin; **bus** #66 goes directly to Maynooth, and #67A runs via Celbridge, with both departing from Wellington Quay (€2). The **Citizens Information Centre,** around the corner on the end of Main St. farthest from St. Patrick's, is a volunteer staffed center with information and maps to spare. (☎628 5477. Open M-F 10am-4:30pm.) **usit** has an office on Mill St., which runs perpendicular to Main. (☎628 9289. Open M-F 9:30am-5:30pm, Sa 10am-1pm.) **Internet** is at **Nikita Solutions Ireland** on Leinster St., off Main St. one block from St. Patrick's. (☎610 6454. Open M-F 10am-10pm, Sa 11am-9pm. €4.50 per hr.)

St. Patrick's College ❸ rents student apartments during the summer and a small number of rooms during the year; the fee includes access to the college swimming pool, weight room, tennis courts, and playing fields. The housing office shares space with the Visitor Centre. (Contact Bill Tinley, ☎708 6200; info@maynooth-campus.com. All rooms available early June to mid-Sept., limited quantity Oct.-May. Singles €24.50-54, with breakfast €31.20-60.70; doubles from €40/€54.40.) For food on a student budget, enjoy light fare and baked goods (€1.20-3.80) at **Elite Confectionery ❶,** Main St. (☎628 5581. Open M-Sa 8:30am-6pm.)

CELBRIDGE. Pretty little Celbridge lies 5 mi. south of Maynooth on Celbridge Rd. At the end of a long, lime-tree-lined road is **Castletown House,** magnificent home of William Connolly. The richest man in 1720s Ireland, Connolly built this grandiose mansion and sparked a nationwide penchant for Palladian architecture. Comprehensive tours cover the origin of each painting, wall hanging, and piece of furniture. (☎628 8252. Open Apr.-Sept. M-F 10am-6pm, Sa-Su 1-6pm; Oct. M-F 10am-5pm, Su 1-5pm; Nov. Su 1-5pm. Admission by guided tour only. €3.50, seniors €2.50, students and children €1.25, family €9.50.) Connolly's "philanthropic" widow built an obelisk 2 mi. behind the estate to employ Famine-starved locals in 1740. Known as **Connolly's Folly,** its unruly stack of arches was used for the original plans of the Washington Monument. At the other end of Main St., the family-friendly grounds of **Celbridge Abbey** offer a small playground, model railway, and elegant gardens. (☎627 5508. Open M-Sa 10am-6pm, Su noon-6pm. €4, seniors and children €3.) The Abbey's **Tea Room ❷** (admission not required) serves sandwiches, salads, and pastries from €1.10-5.70. If the weather is fair, eat those treats in the gardens or put together a picnic at **Centra** on Main St. (☎628 8337. Open daily 7am-11pm.) **Buses** #67 and 67A run to Celbridge from Dublin. The **suburban rail** arrives roughly every hour at the Hazelhatch & Celbridge stop. A shuttle bus runs between the station and town during peak hours; otherwise it's a €5 taxi.

KILDARE (CILL DARA)   ☎045

Kildare is Ireland's horse-racing holy land. Carefully bred, raised, and raced here, purebloods are the lifeblood of the town. The town's past is somewhat less equine-centric; it grew around a church founded in AD 480 by St. Brigid. The sacred lass chose a site next to an oak tree she saw in a vision, hence the town's Irish name, meaning "Church of the Oak." The center of town is a triangular Square, which is scarred, unlike its calmer periphery, by ceaseless traffic from the N7.

🖪🖪 TRANSPORTATION AND PRACTICAL INFORMATION. Kildare straddles busy, harrowing N7 (Dublin-Limerick) and is connected to Heuston Station by **suburban rail** (40min., M-Sa every 30min. 6am-10:30pm). **Bus Éireann** heads for Dublin en route from Limerick (1½hr., 15 per day, €10). **Rapid Express Coaches** (☎01 679 1549) offers a cheaper service between Dublin's Middle Abbey St. and Kildare (4-6 per day, €6). The **tourist office** is in the Market House, on the Square. (☎530 672. Open May-Oct. M-Sa 9:30am-1pm and 2-5:30pm; Apr.-Sept. M-F 9:30am-1pm and 2-5pm.) The same building houses the brand-new **heritage center,** which screens a short video about the town, hosted by the ghost of a monk from the local monastery. (☎530 672. Open same hours as tourist office. €3, students €2.50, children €1.50.) The **Bank of Ireland,** the Square, has a 24hr. **ATM.** (☎521 276. Open M 10am-5pm, Tu-F 10am-4pm.) For **work opportunities,** inquire at the Castleview Farm B&B (see p. 158). **Internet** is available at the **library,** in the Square. (☎520 235. Open Tu 2:30-5pm and 6:30-8:30pm, Th 6:30-8:30pm, F 2:30-5pm, Sa 11am-1pm and 3-5pm.) The **post office** is in a brick building on Dublin St., near the Square. (☎521 349. Open M and W-F 9am-5:30pm, Tu 9:30am-5:30pm, Sa 10am-1pm and 2:30-4pm.)

🖪🖪🖾 ACCOMMODATIONS, FOOD, AND PUBS. The only B&B in town is **Singleton's ❸,** 1 Dara Park. From the heritage center, follow the road to the right; it's before the Esso station and on the right. (☎521 964. All rooms with bath and TV. Doubles €55.) Breakfastless but right in town, **Lord Edward Guest House ❸,** behind the Silken Thomas pub and under the same ownership, has spacious rooms with varying levels of elegance, all with tea, coffee, TVs, and baths. (☎522 389 or 521 695. Singles €30; doubles €50-60.) Five miles from town, on a working poultry farm, Julie and Colm Keane run the **Eagle Hill B&B ❸.** Call for pickup or take Tully Rd. out of town following the signs to top-notch rooms, all with bath. (☎526 097. **Bike rental** €10 per day. Singles €27-35; doubles €54.) Three miles from town toward Monasterevin, the 50 cows at **Castleview Farm and B&B ❸** produce milk for Bailey's Irish Creme. Ask farmer Ned about **work opportunities,** but be prepared to work long, hard dairy days. (☎521 816. Singles €38; doubles €56.)

If you're hungry enough to eat a horse...don't. Not in this town, mister. However, **Kristianna's Bistro ❹,** Main St., serves other upscale Irish meals. (☎522 895. Dinner mains €18-24. Lunch served F and Su 12:30-2:30pm; dinner Su and Tu-Sa 6-10pm.) Pubs are plentiful in Kildare, and most serve good grub. **The Silken Thomas ❷,** the Square (☎522 232), has locally renowned meals ranging from sandwiches (€4-5) to huge, tasty carvery lunches (€7.50-8.50), with pricier dinner mains (€10-20) from 6-10pm. The pub's name refers to "Silken Thomas" FitzGerald, who raised Dublin in revolt against the British in 1534. **Li'l Flanagan's,** behind Silken Thomas, is a delightfully scruffy old-time pub with low ceilings, open peat fires, and an impressive matchbox collection hanging from the ceiling. (☎521 695. Live music most nights.) **Nolan's,** the Square, is a low-key joint—frequent trad sessions have replaced the hammers and handsaws in this former hardware store. (☎521 528.)

🖸 SIGHTS. The **🖾Irish National Stud and Japanese Gardens,** 1 mi. from the Square on Tully Rd., was founded by the eq-centric Colonel William Hall-Walker in 1900. The mystical son of a Scottish brewer, he cast each foal's horoscope at its birth—if the stars weren't lined up favorably, the foal would be sold, regardless of its lineage. These days, the Irish National Stud facilitates the rearing of thoroughbred racehorses; mating season kicks off on Valentine's Day, naturally. The Stud's small **Irish Horse Museum** tells the history of the horse through a few displays and the skeleton of Arkle, a bygone champion. **Tours** leave every hour to educate the ignorant about the world of stud farms and horseracing.

The **Japanese Gardens** allegorize the "life of man" through a beautiful, if phallo-centric, semi-narrative trail. From the cave of birth to the hill of mourning, visitors experience learning, disappointment, and marriage in the media of caves, hills, and bridges. Choose the "rugged path" after the Gate of Oblivion, and the path of life is much more difficult to follow than expected. The newest addition to the Stud is the 4-acre **St. Fiachra's Garden,** opened for the new millennium. Peaceful St. Fiachra's blandly evokes "monastic spirituality" with quiet lakes, waterfalls, and a pit of Waterford Crystal. (☎521 617; www.irish-national-stud.ie. Open mid-Feb. to mid-Nov. daily 9:30am-6pm; last admission 5pm. 35min. tours of the National Stud leave on the hour beginning at 11am. €8.50, students and seniors €6.50.) In town, the 10th-century **round tower,** off the Square, is one of the few in Ireland that visitors can enter and climb; most others lack floors. (Open M-Sa 10am-1pm and 2-5pm, Su 2-5pm. €3, children €1.50.) Recently restored **St. Brigid's,** a Church of Ireland cathedral that lay derelict for over 200 years, lies in the shadow of the tower. The cathedral dates from the 12th century and sits on the site of a church founded by St. Brigid in AD 480. Brigid, one of the first and only powerful women in the Catholic Church, was accidentally ordained bishop by scatter-brained Mel of Ardagh. Her monastery was one of the few ever to accept both women and men. The site seems to attract untraditional bishops; a sheela-na-gig (erotic female figure carving) spreads her legs under the lid of Bishop Wellesley's tomb. (Open May-Oct. M-Sa 10am-1pm, 2-5pm; Su 2-5pm. Su services noon. Strongly suggested donation €1.50.) Next to the church is **St. Brigid's Fire Temple,** a pagan ritual site that St. Brigid repossessed for Christianity. Only female virgins were allowed to tend the fire, which burned continuously for 1000 years. Archbishop George Browne of Dublin ended this nonsense—by extinguishing the flames, not the virginity.

▶ DAYTRIPS FROM KILDARE

THE CURRAGH. Between Newbridge and Kildare on the N7 lies the Curragh—5000 acres of perhaps the greenest fields in Ireland. Thoroughbred horses graze and train, hoping to one day earn fame and fortune at the **Curragh Racecourse,** host of the **Irish Derby** (DAR-bee) each year. The Derby is Ireland's premier sporting and social event and one of the most prestigious races in the world. Hit the Curragh as early as 7:30am and watch scores of horses take their daily training run on one of the five gallops, each 1-1½ mi. long. (☎441 205; www.curragh.ie. Races every other weekend late Mar.-Oct. Sa-Su 2:15 or 2:30pm. Tickets generally start at €15, but run from €45 for the Derby. Train €20 from Heuston Station, includes admission. Bus Éireann serves the Curragh on race days, leaving from Busáras in Dublin.)

PEATLAND WORLD AND LULLYMORE. The boglanders know whom to turn to in times of need: their friend Peat. Ten miles from Kildare in Lullymore, **Peatland World** explains this phenomenal flammable material. On a mineral island in the immense Bog of Allen, Peatland World features a museum and natural history gallery. It displays bog-preserved prehistoric artifacts, a model of an Irish cottage with turf fire, and trophies from turf-cutting competitions. (☎860 133. Open Apr.-Oct. M-F 9:30am-6pm, Su 2-6pm, Sa by appointment; Nov.-Mar. M-F 9:30am-5pm. €5, students €4, family €12.) Two miles toward Allenwood, the **Lullymore Heritage and Discovery Park** explores life in the boglands from the Mesolithic era through the Famine. Visitors also climb out onto the peat bog and watch peat mining in action. (To reach Lullymore from Kildare, take R401 to Rathangan and then R414 toward Allenwood. Buses go to Allenwood from Dublin roughly 8 times per day. ☎870 238. Open Apr.-Oct. M-F 9:30am-6pm, Sa-Su noon-6pm; Nov.-Mar. M-F 9:30am-4:30pm. Open other times by appointment. €5, family €12.)

COUNTY MEATH

Meath is a hushed county, with a heavy blanket of history on its shoulders and ancient crypts lurking deep in its hills. The Hill of Tara was Ireland's political and spiritual center in prehistoric times and retains an air of solemn mystery for today's visitors. The countryside, with its winding roads, rolling hills, and castle-laden towns, provides the perfect backdrop for a Sunday drive or bike ride.

BOYNE VALLEY

The thinly-populated Boyne Valley hides Ireland's greatest archaeological treasures. Massive passage tombs create subtle bumps in the landscape that belie their cavernous underground chambers. These wonders are older than the pyramids and at least as puzzling. Celtic High Kings once ruled from atop the Hill of Tara, leaving a dose of mysterious folklore in their wake. The Hill's enduring symbolic significance and incredible views attract visitors aplenty, as do the well-preserved Norman fortifications in Trim. According to legend, St. Patrick lit a flame atop the Hill of Slane that brought Christianity to Ireland. Every so often, farmers plow up artifacts from the 1690 Battle of the Boyne (see **The Ascendancy,** p. 60).

NEWGRANGE, KNOWTH, AND DOWTH ☎ 041

Along the curves of the River Boyne, between Slane and Drogheda, sprawls Brú na Bóinne ("homestead of the Boyne"). The Boyne Valley may not have all the passage tombs in the world—just the biggest and best. In this 2500-acre region there are some 40 passage tombs, all with more than five millennia of history behind them. Neolithic engineers constructed Newgrange, Dowth, and Knowth within walking distance of each other, possibly with future lazy travelers in mind.

No one really knows why the ancient settlers took on these immense projects, but the standard assumption is improvements in farming allowed more time for other pursuits, so locals naturally decided to build mega-structures that would remain intact and waterproof for some 5000 years. Using a log-rolling mechanism, the builders imported enormous kerbstones from miles away. The work was sluggish (it took 80 men 10 days to move one kerbstone), and the larger mounds took a half-century to build, when a decent lifespan was 30 years.

Most impressive of the three main sights, for archaeologists if not for visitors, is **Knowth** (rhymes with "mouth"). Apparently, there was a hunter-gatherer settlement here in 4000 BC, followed by an extraordinary number of subsequent dwellers: the Stone Age brainiacs who built the mound visible today; mysterious Bronze Age "beaker people," named for their distinctive urns; Iron Age Celts, whose many burials include two headless men with their gaming dice; and Christians as late as the 12th century. The enormous passage tomb, quite unusually, houses *two* burial chambers, back to back, with separate east and west entrances—possibly a nod to the Sun's movement across the horizon. The tomb is surrounded by an incredible 127 of the aforementioned kerbstones, decorated and undecorated. Knowth's carvings are well preserved as prehistoric art goes, with unexplained spirals and etchings adorning the passage. Long-term excavations prevent the general public from entering, but the visitors center **tour** (see below) offers a peek.

🖾**Newgrange** offers tourists the best glimpse at the structure and innards of a spectacular passage tomb. After about 1000 years of peaceful existence, the front of this one-acre circular mound collapsed and fell into disrepair. It stayed that way for 4000 years before it was rediscovered by landowner Charles Campbell in 1699; he originally planned to quarry the stones. Unfortunately, Campbell left the tomb open and unsupervised, and so it remained for the next two and a half centuries, gathering uncreative Renaissance graffiti (still visible) and succumbing to vandalism. In 1962, archaeologists began a fantastic real-life jigsaw puzzle to piece the outer wall back together, one rock at a time. During the reconstruction, archaeologists discovered a roof box over the passage entrance. At dawn on the shortest day of the year (Dec. 21), 17 gilded minutes of sunlight shine through the box, reach straight to the back of the 60 ft. passageway, and irradiate the burial chamber. The tour provides a brilliant simulation of this experience, leaving visitors in awe. Those wishing to see the real event must sign up for a lottery, held every October. Unfortunately, the soft Irish weather may cloud those 17min. of sun. Ongoing excavations have kept **Dowth** (rhymes with "Knowth") closed to the public for several years. To gain admission, get a Ph.D. in archaeology.

Access to Knowth and Newgrange requires admission to ◪**Brú na Bóinne Visitors Centre,** located near Donore on the south side of the River Boyne, across from the tombs themselves. Do not try to go directly to the sites—a guard minds the gate. Instead, head to the visitors center and immediately book a tour. The place is mobbed every day of the summer, and Sundays are especially manic. While awaiting a tour, check out the center's excellent exhibit on the lives of the gifted and talented Stone-Agers. Remember to dress appropriately when visiting—Neolithic tombs lack central heating. (☎988 0300. Open June to mid-Sept. 9am-7pm; May 9am-6:30pm; late Sept. 9am-6:30pm; Mar.-Apr., Oct. 9:30am-5:30pm; Nov.-Feb. 9:30am-5pm. Admission to the visitors center only €3.50, seniors €2.50, students and children €2.25, family €8; center and Newgrange tour €6/€4.50/€3.50/€15; center and Knowth €4.50/€3/€2.25/€12.75; center, Newgrange, and Knowth €10/€7.50/€5.25/€24. Last tour 1½hr. before closing. Last admission to center 45min. before closing.) Downstairs a **tourist office** distributes a free area map. (☎980 305. Open daily 9am-7pm.) To reach the visitors center from Drogheda, turn left by the bus station and head straight on the uphill road. It's a pleasant 5 mi. bike ride, and hitchers report successful journeys. **Bus Éireann** (☎836 6111) sends shuttles to the visitors center from Dublin (1½hr., every hr., €12.70 return), stopping at **Drogheda** (10min., €3.80 return). Several **bus tours** from Dublin include admission to the sights, including Bus Éireann's (Sa-Th, €24.20).

NEWGRANGE FARM. Down the road from Newgrange, **Newgrange Farm** has a coffee shop and a children's petting zoo. Farmer Bill charms tykes and their parents with his tractor tour of the farm, including a small passage tomb and a bit of wildlife. There are usually scavenger hunts on Sundays, Teddy Bear Picnics on the June bank holiday, and Cadbury Easter-Egg Hunts on Easter weekend. (☎24119. Open Easter-Aug. daily 10am-6pm; last admission 5pm. 30min. tour leaves Su 3 and 4pm, or when there's enough interest. Access to farm €4, invest another €2 for a tractor ride.)

HILL OF TARA ☎046

Tara, deeply marked by a long, enigmatic history, awaits visitors with the serenity of ages. From prehistoric times until the 10th century, **Tara** was the social, political, and cultural heart of Ireland. Home to 142 former Irish Kings, the largest collection of Celtic monuments in the world, and a sacred site for ancient Irish religion, Tara beckons visitors to its flourishing green expanse. Many secrets are buried under the 100 acres of grassy mounds called Tara. The grounds are free and open to the public for casual perusal. Seeking secrets is allowed, but don't bring a shovel—in the early part of the 20th century, a misguided cult on a hunt for the Arc of the Covenant damaged the Mound of the Synods. Though the Arc remained elusive, they did manage to find a few ancient Roman coins. Located at Tara is the sacred *Lia Fail* ("Stone of Destiny"), an ancient phallic rock once used as a coronation stone; the rock was said to roar when the rightful king of Tara placed his hands upon it. The **Mound of Hostages,** the resident burial mound, dates to 2500 BC.

The enormous site is about 5 mi. east of Navan on the N3. Take any **local bus** from Dublin to **Navan** (1hr.; M-Sa 37 per day, Su 15 per day; €7) and ask to stop at the turn-off, on the left and marked by a small brown sign; then it's 1 mi. of uphill legwork. The actual buildings—largely wattle, wood, and earth—have long been buried or destroyed; what remains are concentric rings of grassy, windswept dunes. They are always open for exploration; to make sense of them, hit the **visitors center** in the old church. The center displays aerial photos and an audio enhanced slideshow on Tara's history. After the film, a ticket includes an excellent **guided tour** (35min., by request only; call ahead). The tour covers only the sights at the top of the hill, though Tara actually encompasses 100 acres of smaller mounds and ring forts. (☎046 25903. Center open mid-May to mid-June daily 10am-6pm. €2, seniors €1.25, students €1.)

TRIM (BAILE ATHÁ TROIM) ☎046

Jaded travelers looking for a break from Dublin should treat themselves to Trim, a little town lying an hour outside of the capital. Ireland's largest Norman castle (and occasional Hollywood backdrop and set), surrounded by flocks of fat and happy sheep, overlooks this jewel of a heritage town located on the River Boyne.

🖃 🔃 TRANSPORTATION AND PRACTICAL INFORMATION. Bus Éireann stops in front of Trim Castle on its way to and from Dublin (1hr.; M-Sa roughly 1 per hr., Su 3 per day; €7). **Castle Street** intersects the central **Market Street,** which has most of the town's shops, then crosses the **River Boyne** under the alias **Bridge Street.** The first left crossing the bridge is **Mill Street.** Bridge St. curves uphill on the far side, turning into **High Street** before splitting. The left fork becomes **Haggard Street** and the right becomes **Navan Gate Street,** the road to the nearby Newtown ruins. The **visitors center** and **tourist office** share a building on Castle St., below the castle and next to the bus stop; they distribute a useful map of Trim's sights, sell souvenirs, and give an audio-visual tour of the town's history. (☎37111. Tourist office desk open June-Aug. M-Sa 10am-1pm and 2-5:30pm; mid-Apr. to May and Sept. M-F 9:30am-1pm and 2-5:30pm. Visitors center open May-Aug. daily 10am-6pm; Sept.-Apr. closed on Th.) **Bank of Ireland,** replete with an **ATM,** is on Market St. (☎31230. Open M 10am-5pm, Tu-F 10am-4pm.) The **library,** on High St., has **free Internet.** (Open Tu 1:30-5pm and 7-8:30pm, W and F 10am-1pm and 2-5pm, Th 10am-1pm and 6-8pm, Sa 10am-12:30pm.) The **post office** is at the intersection of Market and Emmet St. (☎31268. Open M-F 9am-12:30pm and 1:30-5:30pm, Sa 9am-12:30pm.)

🖪 🖾 🖾 ACCOMMODATIONS, FOOD, AND PUBS. The **Bridge House Tourist Hostel ❷,** tucked down a driveway from either High St. or the bridge onto Mill St., offers a mixed bag of co-ed rooms ranging from cramped to luxurious. The TV lounge is a funky converted medieval wine cellar. (☎31848. 4-bed dorms €15; doubles with bath €36.) Trim's B&B options are, on the whole, excellent. **◪Highfield House ❸,** a spectacular stone building overlooking Trim Castle and the river, used to be a maternity hospital, but now offers a fine maternal welcome and the most luxurious stay in town at reasonable prices. From the bus station, walk away from the bridge; it's on the right before the roundabout. (☎36386. Singles €40-44; doubles €66-68.) The folks at sunny, spacious, and fastidiously clean **White Lodge ❹** retrieve guests with reservations at the bus stop. Otherwise, from the roundabout, cross the bridge onto High St., walk right onto Navan Gate St., walk between the posts; it's on the other side of the cross street. (☎36549; www.whitelodget-rim.com. Breakfast included. Singles €44; doubles €60, with bath €56, without breakfast €50.) In the heart of town, **Brogan's ❹,** High St., offers top-notch rooms with TVs, showers, coffee- and tea-making facilities, and telephones. At the in-house pub and beer garden are good eats and frequent live music. (☎31237. Breakfast included. Singles €42-48; doubles €68-76.) The Bounty Bar (see below) also has a **B&B ❷** for those who like their breakfast, and pints, in bed.

Get **SuperValu**-able groceries at the top of Haggard St. (☎31505. Open M-F 8am-9pm, Sa 8am-7:30pm, Su 9am-6:30pm.) **Watson's Elementary Café ❷**, Market St., serves an adequate, inexpensive breakfast and is the only eatery open Sundays at 8am. (☎38575. Filled baguettes €2.75. Breakfast €5-7. Open M-Sa 7:45am-5:30pm, Su 8am-4pm.) Local families flock to **The Boyne Bistro & Bakery ❶**, Market St., for fresh sandwiches (€3-5), wraps, and bakery treats. (Open M-Sa 9am-6pm, Su noon-6pm; closes at 3pm in winter). Cheerful **Bennini's ❷**, in the carpark next to Trim Castle, is known for creative salads and homemade baked goods. (☎31002. Lunch mains €7.50-8.60; dinner €12-18. M-F 9:30am-5pm, 6-10pm; Sa-Su 10am-5:30pm, 6-10pm.) One door down, under the same ownership, bright and welcoming **Franzini O'Brien's ❸** blends Irish, Italian, Asian, and other culinary influences. (☎31002. Mains €11-20. Open May-Sept. M-Sa 6:30-9:30pm, Su 5-8:30pm, Oct.-Apr. closed M.) **Emmet Tavern,** Emmet St., left facing the post office, has boisterous, mostly local customers and a popular pub lunch. (☎31378. Generally serves until 11:30pm.) Bring a fiddle to old-fashioned, antique-laden **The Bounty,** on High St., where open mic participation is encouraged. The bar also has rooms upstairs, but no breakfast. (☎31640. Singles €35; doubles €45. M-F 5pm-1am, Sa-Su 1pm-1am.)

◑⚑ SIGHTS AND ACTIVITIES. ▨Trim Castle, built by Norman invader Hugh de Lacy in 1172 and now open to the public after a regal £3 million face-lift, presides over Trim. The castle was the hub of social life during the Middle Ages, when the town was powerful and populous, and supported seven monasteries. When Norman power collapsed, the castle lost nearly all its strategic importance and thus survived the centuries relatively untouched. The keep costs a little extra to see, but the renovations inside are extraordinarily well done, and the views from the top are fabulous. If the household doesn't inspire, try to recognize scenes from *Braveheart*. (☎38619. Open Easter-Oct. daily 10am-6pm; Nov.-Easter Sa-Su 10am-6pm, last tour 5:15pm. Admission with 35-45min. guided tour only. Tours every 45min.; sign up upon arrival in Trim. No tour needed for the grounds. Tour and grounds €3.50, students €1.25; grounds only €1.50/€0.75.)

Across the river stands the remains of the 12th-century **Yellow Steeple,** a belltower named for its twilight gleam; the gleam, however, left with the lichen that was removed during restoration. In its shadow, **Talbot's Castle,** adapted from the steeple's original abbey, was home to Jonathan Swift and the undefeated Duke of Wellington. Despite the "private house" sign, the current owner often provides tours of its motley interior upon request. To get there, take the first right after crossing the bridge; a right-of-way through the driveway leads to the Yellow Steeple and **Sheep Gate,** the only surviving piece of the town's medieval walls. Ten minutes out on the Dublin road in the direction opposite the castle, halloo your name to the reverberating ruins of **St. Peter and St. Paul's Cathedral,** across the river from **Echo Gate.** The cathedral grounds contain a tomb with two figures mistakenly called the **Jealous Man and Woman.** The sword between them conventionally signified chastity, not resentment. Put a pin between the two figures; when the pin rusts, your warts should disappear.

Trim Visitors Centre, in the tourist office, educates and frightens with a multimedia presentation and dramatic slideshow. Displays describe decapitations, the lecherous behavior of sinewy Hugh de Lacy, and hideous plague rats—so much for prim and proper Trim. (☎37227. Open daily 10am-5pm. Admission for the 30min. show every 30min. €3.20, students and seniors €2.20.) Green thumbs enjoy **Butterstream Gardens,** 15min. past the SuperValu. The several serene acres are especially beautiful in June. (☎36017. Open May-Sept. daily 11am-6pm. €6, students €3.)

EASTERN IRELAND

Each June, the **Scurlogstown Olympiad Town Festival** fills Trim with animal shows, carnival rides, haymaking, trad, and the evening High Nellie Rally, in which men and women wear absurd costumes and ride black bikes around town. For the daytime festival, locals dress up in 19th-century period attire, move into thatched huts on the outskirts of town, and show off traditional artifacts. During the rest of the year, **fishing** on the Boyne is quite excellent. Diligent **kayakers** should also try their paddles at the notoriously tricky river. Join up with one of the many local **canoeing** clubs to rent transportation. If paddles aren't appealing, what about stirrups? Contact **Bachelors Lodge** in Navan (☎ 046 21736) and **Borallion Riding Centre** in Balreesk (☎ 046 23800) for horse-riding options near Trim. For more information on all activities in the Boyne Valley, contact the Trim tourist office or David Byrne at the **Navan Tourist Centre** (☎ 046 73426).

BEYOND THE VALLEY OF THE BOYNE

KELLS (CEANANNAS MÓR)   ☎ 046

Kells has two main attractions: ruins and artifacts of the religious persuasion, and shrines to the devil's nectar. The latter appear about every other door; the former fill visitors with ancient tales of religious infighting and thievery. In 559 St. Colmcille (colm-KILL) founded a monastery here before going to establish the more significant settlement on Iona, an island west of Scotland. At Iona, the famous *Book of Kells*, an elaborately decorated version of the Gospels, was begun. It came to Kells at some stage of completion in 804, when the Columbans fled Iona. In 1007, the book was stolen, its gold cover ripped off and its pages buried in a bog. The book was rescued two months later and remained in Kells until 1661, when it was carted off to Trinity College, where it is now recovering. Like the rest of Ireland, Kells is sick of Dublin hoarding all the loot and is desperately trying to retrieve it. Trinity finds this infinitely amusing.

🖃 🔟 TRANSPORTATION AND PRACTICAL INFORMATION. Bus Éireann runs frequently from Dublin (1hr.; M-Sa 2-4 per hr., Su 15 per day; €8.50) and stops in front of Headfort Arms Hotel. With Headfort behind, the outstanding **tourist office** and **heritage center** are to the left, in the former courthouse at the fork in the road. Get free town maps and heritage booklets, explore a collection of replicated relics, and enjoy an audio-visual presentation for €4; or spend hours learning Book of Kells minutiae from an interactive computer terminal. (☎ 49336. Open M-Sa 10am-6pm, Su 1:30-6pm.) Take advantage of **free Internet** at the **library**, on Maudlin St. **AIB**, on John St., has a 24hr. **ATM** (☎ 40610. Open M 10am-12:30pm, 1:30-5pm; Tu-F 10am-4pm.) So does **Bank of Ireland**, by Headfort. (Open M-F 10am-12:30pm, 1:30-4pm). The **post office** is on Farrel St. (☎ 40127. Open M-Sa 9am-5:30pm.)

📭 ACCOMMODATIONS AND CAMPING. Kells Hostel ❷ sports a newly renovated kitchen, a pool table, two **bikes to rent** (€10 each per day), and decent facilities. A giant hand-painted map in the common room is helpful, pointing out sights, restaurants, and pubs. From the center of town, wind uphill on Carrick St. When SuperValu is on the left, look right (beside Carrick House) for the big blue letters. The bus from Dublin will stop across the street. (☎ 49995. Laundry €8. Reception 9am-noon, 5-10pm. Access code needed after hours. 15-bed dorms €15; private 2- to 4-bed rooms with baths €20. **Camping** €8.) B&Bs in town are pricey but worth it. Unbeatable **White Gables ❹**, Headfort Pl., sits across from the tourist office. Enjoy exceptionally clean rooms, white linen beds, abundant flowers, and food prepared by the owner, a former chef. (☎40322. Singles €40; doubles €60.) Down the road is **Avalon B&B ❹**, 5 Headfort Park, offering homestyle luxury, including TVs and exceptionally comfy beds. (☎41536. Singles €40; doubles €58.)

🔲🔳 FOOD AND PUBS. SuperValu grocery store lies across from the hostel. (Open M-W, Sa 8am-7:30pm; Th-F 8am-10pm; Su 8am-6:30pm.) Many places in Kells shut down for lunch from 12:30-1:30pm—be a follower and eat then too. Get one hell of a meal at **Dante's ❷**, Market St. Specialty pizza, pasta, and chicken are €10-14, fish and steak a sinful €15-19. (☎41630. Lunch €6.35-9. Open M-Th noon-11pm, F-Sa noon-midnight, Su 1-11pm; closed daily 3-6pm.) Dishin' out vegetarian-friendly delights, carnivorous fare, and pumpin' 70s funk, **The Ground Floor ❹**, Bective Sq., manages to serve a triple-layer chocolate cake called "R.I.P." *and* be endorsed by the Irish Heart Association. (☎49688. Mains €15-22. Open M-Sa 5:30-11pm, Su 5:30-10pm.) **Vanilla Pod ❹**, next to Headfort Arms Hotel, pleases all palates with fresh ingredients and an eclectic world menu. (☎40084. 3-course early-bird special €16. Reservations recommended. Open M-F 5:30-10pm, Sa-Su 5:30-11pm.) **Pebbles ❷**, Newmarket St., is a popular coffee shop, serving salads, shepherds pie, and the like. (☎49229. Lunch €7-9. Open M-Sa 8am-5:30pm.) **Tower Grille ❷**, Farrell St., is the place for takeaway grease: fried chicken, kebabs, burgers, and spring rolls are €3-6. (☎40314. Open M-Tu, Th-Sa noon-1am; Sa open until 2am.)

O'Shaughnessy's, on Market St., has pub grub by day (€8.50-12.50), raucous locals celebrating or seething over the most recent soccer game by night, and live trad on weekends. (☎41110. Food served noon-3pm.) At **The Blackwater Inn**, Farrell St. (☎40386), get more one-man-band trad on Wednesday and Friday. No food, so stick to the black water—Guinness, that is. Join the drunk, loud, and smoky crowd at **Chasers**, Cross St. (☎49293), where students play pool and read quotes on the walls until 12:30am. A pair of nightlife winners are **The Kelltic Bar** and **Vibe**. The Kelltic rocks with trad on Tuesday, DJ on Thursday, karaoke on Friday, and live bands every Sunday. (☎40063. Open M-F 4pm-midnight, Sa-Su noon-12:30am.) Vibe is the only dance club in Kells; it's fairly small but modern, attracting a young crowd. Occasional bands start around 11pm, otherwise don't bother showing up before midnight. (☎40063. 18+, ID required. €8-10. Ladies free Su before 12:30am. Open F-Sa until 2:30am, Su until 2am.)

◧ SIGHTS. Thanks to its position as a center of Christian learning, the **monastery** at Kells was a favorite target for monkish rivalries. With the exception of the 12th-century bell tower, the current structure dates back to the 1700s. Most points of interest lie up the street from the new tourist office and **heritage center**, where there's a replica *Book of Kells*, with enlarged copies of selected pages. The grounds of **St. Columba's Church** hosts four **high crosses** covered with Biblical scenes; the west cross is little more than a stump, but the south cross, with its instructional depictions of crucifix-making, remains intact. Go upstairs inside the church for detailed explanations of each drawing and for more *Book of Kells* information and photos. A 12th-century wall encircled the church until 1997, when the County Council decided to build a path alongside it, undermining its foundations (and the walls came tumbling down). The nearby 100 ft. **round tower** never succeeded in protecting anything: its monks were torched, its book and saintly relics stolen, and would-be High King Murchadh Mac Flainn was murdered there in 1076. (Church grounds open to dusk. Church open M-Sa 10am-1pm, 2-5pm; Su for services only at 11:30am.)

Time has been kinder to **St. Colmcille's House**, across Church Ln., an awe-inspiring oratory where the *Book of Kells* may have been completed. Pick up the key from amiable and retired Mrs. Carpenter, who often escorts visitors up the hill (groups preferred). Visit her brown house at 10 Church View, or ask the tourist office to phone her; then head up 600 ft. to the unmistakably oratory-like structure. The place looks almost exactly as it would have in St. Colmcille's day, except the current doorway enters into the basement, which was originally connected by a secret tunnel to the church. The daring can climb the extremely steep staircase to walk around the tiny attic (those over four feet tall must crouch).

Two miles down Oldcastle Rd., within People's Park, is the **Spire of Loyd,** a 150 ft. mock-lighthouse viewing tower erected by the old Headfort landlords at the end of the 18th century. (☎47840. Group bookings of 10 or more only.) Coupling the adorable and morbid, the spire is flanked by a public playground and recently restored **Pauper's Graveyard,** where during Famine the area's impoverished were buried.

COUNTY LOUTH

On its way between the pulsing capitals of Dublin and Belfast, N1 shoots through Lough, a county filled with smaller towns, crumbling ruins, and soaring mountains. History buffs appreciate Drogheda, which lies 3 mi. east of where William and James battled on the Boyne and 5 mi. south of Monasterboice and Mellifont Abbey. Dundalk is not only a convenient place to cross into the North, but it's also responsible for brewing Harp. The hills and seacoasts of the Cooley Peninsula, meanwhile, command the affections of hikers, bikers, and ancient bards.

DROGHEDA (DROICHEAD ÁTHA)   ☎041

The description perhaps best suited to this mid-sized industrial town is 'potential.' Convenient to Newgrange, Dowth, and Knowth, as well as Monasterboice, Mellifont, and Slane, Drogheda (DRAW-head-ah) is an ideal jumping-off point for many of eastern Ireland's historic sights. With a skeleton of crumbling medieval walls and gates, there is considerable history to be explored. For the less morbid of curiosities, plenty of friendly pubs line the streets in this expanding town.

■ TRANSPORTATION

Trains: Station on the Dublin Rd. east of town (☎983 8749). Follow John St. south of the river. To: **Belfast** (2hr.; M-Sa 7 per day, Su 4 per day; €26.60) and **Dublin** (1hr., express 30min.; M-Sa 20 per day, Su 7 per day; €12.40).

Buses: John St. at Donore Rd. (☎983 5023). Inquiries desk and **luggage storage** open M-F 9am-6pm, Sa 8:30am-5:30pm. To: **Athlone** (2½hr., 2 per day, €10.70); **Belfast** (2hr.; M-Sa 7 per day, Su 6 per day; €11.30); **Dublin** (1hr.; M-Sa every 30min., Sun every hr.; €8.70); **Galway** (4hr., 1 per day, €25); **Mullingar** (2hr., 1 per day, €17.10).

Bike Rental: Quay Cycles, 11 North Quay (☎983 4526). €12 per day; ID deposit. Open M-Sa 9am-6pm.

🛈 PRACTICAL INFORMATION

Tourist Offices: Main branch in bus station (☎983 7070). Offers a regional and Drogheda town map. Open M-Sa 9:30am-5:30pm. Equally helpful is **Information Point** at Millmount Museum (☎984 5684); head to the hilltop Martello tower. Open M-F 9:30am-1pm, 2-5pm.

Banks: Cross St. Mary's Bridge and take the 2nd left to find numerous banks lining West St. **AIB** (☎983 6523; Open M-F 9:30am-5pm, Th until 7pm) and **Permanent TSB** (☎983 8703; M-F 10am-5pm, Th until 7pm) both have **ATMs.**

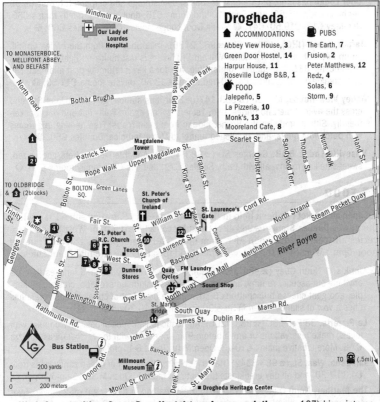

Drogheda

⌂ ACCOMMODATIONS

Abbey View House, **3**
Green Door Hostel, **14**
Harpur House, **11**
Roseville Lodge B&B, **1**

🍴 FOOD

Jalepeño, **5**
La Pizzeria, **10**
Monk's, **13**
Mooreland Cafe, **8**

🍺 PUBS

The Earth, **7**
Fusion, **2**
Peter Matthews, **12**
Redz, **4**
Solas, **6**
Storm, **9**

EASTERN IRELAND

Work Opportunities: Green Door Hostel (see **Accommodations,** p. 167) hires international staff to work at the hostel, bar, and adventure center. Min. stay of 2 months is preferred. Contact owner Gavin in advance for availabilies.

Laundromat: FM Laundry, 13 North Quay (☎983 6837). Turn right across St. Mary's Bridge. Self-service €6.50. Open M-Sa 9am-6pm.

Emergency: ☎999; no coins required. **Police** (*Garda*): West Gate (☎983 8777).

Pharmacy: Hickey's, West St. (☎983 8657), has everything. Open M-W 8:30am-6:30pm; Th, F 8:30am-9pm; Sa 9am-6pm; Su 11am-6pm.

Hospital: Our Lady of Lourdes, Cross Lanes (☎983 7601).

Internet: Surf at **Write Access,** West St. (☎980 1533). Open M-Sa 10am-9pm, Su 2-7pm. €4 per hour.

Post Office: West St. (☎983 8157). Open Tu-Sa 9am-5:30pm, W open 9:30am.

🏠 ACCOMMODATIONS

🛏 **Green Door Hostel,** 47 John St. (☎983 4422; www.greendoorhostel.com), 1 block from bus station. Friendly young staff, convenient location, joyously clean baths, and **Green Room Bar** more than outweigh small kitchen and common area. Next to hostel, **Green**

Door Lodge has more private ensuite rooms. Bike storage and carpark. **Internet** €6.50 per hr. Laundry €5.50. June-Sept. 10-bed dorms €15; doubles €45; family rooms €60. Oct.-May €12/€19.50/€47. ❶ Green Door Lodge singles €40; doubles €60. ❹

Harpur House (IHO), William St. (☎983 2736). Take Shop St. from the bridge up hill, go up Peter St. and go right onto William St.; hostel is last house on right. Drogheda's older hostel/B&B, but equally comfortable. Ask for a key if returning past midnight. Full Irish breakfast €5. Laundry €4. 10-bed dorms €13.50; private rooms €17.50. ❶

Abbey View House, Mill Ln. (☎983 1470). From bus station, go left on John St., and cross the river at the 2nd bridge; take 1st left; go left again. Well-kept and backpacker-friendly. Sitting pretty on the Boyne, hidden from main roads. Free parking, big rooms with patchwork quilts, and an alleged tunnel to Monasterboice. Doubles €50. ❹

Roseville Lodge B&B, Georges St. (☎983 4046). Amiable Denis offers good-sized, sweet-smelling rooms, all with bath. Singles €32; doubles €55; family rooms €70. ❸

🍴 FOOD

An **open-air market** has been held in Bolton Square every Saturday since 1317, while the newer **Dunnes Stores** (☎983 4211) and **Tesco** (☎983 7063) on West St. sell groceries all week. (Both open M-W 9am-6pm, Th-F 9am-9pm, Sa 8:30am-7pm, Su noon-6pm.) West St. is the place for fast food to satisfy the late-night munchies.

🏅**Monk's,** 1 North Quay (☎984 5630). Shiny cafe with breakfasts and lunches that are anything but ascetic. Yummy, unusual sandwiches include an avocado, crushed pineapple, and goat cheese bruschetta (€6.30), while a breakfast of chunky French toast justifies a vow of silence. Open M-Sa 8:30am-6pm, Su 10:30am-5pm. ❷

La Pizzeria, 38 Peter St. (☎983 4208). Authentic Italian specialities. Very popular with locals; make reservations or arrive before 9pm—or earlier with the *famiglia*. Pasta, pizza €7-8. More creative mains €10-13. Open M-Tu, Th-Su 6-11pm. ❷

Jalepeño, West St. (☎983 8342). Heats it up with all manner of grilled sandwiches from €4.30-7.30, and all-day breakfasts that sate for the day. Open M-Sa 11am-6:30pm. ❷

The Mariner, North Quay. (☎983 7401). Best seafood in town, right off the river. Try it fried, poached, grilled, or any other way imaginable. Mains €8-12. Open M-Sa noon-10pm, Su 12-6pm. ❷

Moorland Cafe, West St. (☎983 3951). Tasty sandwiches and soups can be had in the cafe or taken away. Sandwiches €3.50. Open M-Sa 10am-6pm. ❶

🎭🎵 PUBS AND CLUBS

As the largest town in the area, Drogheda has an active and ever-expanding nightlife. Hours of operation are slightly longer in the summer and on Friday and Saturday nights, but in general, assume that places close by midnight (i.e., expect to be kicked out by 12:30am). After the pubs close, Drogheda's clubs start rocking.

🏅**Peter Matthews,** 9 Laurence St. (☎983 7371), better known as **McPhail's.** Old likeable pub hosts the best *craic* in town. Live rock, blues, jazz, and Latin M, Th-Sa nights. €2 cover F-Sa. Open M-W 1-11:30pm, Th-Sa 1pm-12:30am.

Redz, 79 West St. (☎983 5331). Deceptively narrow facade conceals huge, traditional bar, quiet lounge area, and clubby back room. DJs and live bands Th-Su. Open M-W 10:30am-11:30pm, Th-Su 10:30am-12:30am.

Solas, Old Abbey Ln., tucked off West St. Downstairs is for the young and trendy. Open daily 6pm-12:30am.

EASTERN IRELAND

The Earth, Stockwell Ln. (☎983 0969), in back of Westcourt Hotel. Exhibitionists groove on the lowered dance floor as the rhythmically challenged look on from 3 packed bars above. Geological theme played out in rock-textured bathrooms and rough, crooked walls. Cover Sa €10, otherwise €6. Open Th-Su 11:30pm-3am.

Storm, Stockwell (☎987 5170), across from Earth. Futuristic, flashy, this new club plays on the weather theme with fluorescent columns of bubbling water and lightning. Circular booths provide relative obscurity. Open Th-Su 11:30pm-2am.

Fusion, Georges St. (☎983 0088), upstairs from McGuinness pub. Funky alternative style, good cover bands, and a beer garden. Draws the pub crowd after hours.

🔘 SIGHTS

ST. PETER'S CHURCHES. Drogheda has two St. Peter's Churches, and both could satisfy even the most morbid of curiosities. Come face-to-face with the blackened, shriveled head of St. Oliver in the imposing, neo-Gothic St. Peter's Church on West St. Built in the 1880s, this St. Peter's safeguards what's left of the martyr Oliver Plunkett. A handful of his bones are on display, as is the door of his London prison cell. *(Open daily 8:30am-8:30pm. Free.)* The other St. Peter's Church (Church of Ireland) hoards bad luck at the top of Peter St. The tower of the original timber structure was destroyed in a 1548 storm. Another wooden structure replaced it, only to be torched (with refugees inside) by Cromwell. The present church was built in 1752 and is being renovated after falling victim to another more recent fire. Mounted on the wall of the cemetery's far left corner are cadaver tombs, with brutally realistic carvings of the half-decayed bodies of a man and woman. Dating from 1520, they are two of only 19 such tombs in the world

BATTLE OF THE BOYNE. The Battle of the Boyne raged at **Oldbridge,** 3 mi. west of Drogheda on Slane Rd. In 1690, William of Orange's victory over James II secured for Protestants the English Crown and far more than the eastern half of Ireland (see **The Ascendancy,** p. 60). For the slightly more ambitious traveler, the not-for-profit **Obelisk Centre** (located in a small trailer) offers visitors a view of the battle site. *(Head 1½ mi. down Slane Rd. to the Obelisk Bridge; it's on the right. ☎984 1644. Open M-*

YOU CAN'T KEEP A HARDMAN DOWN

In the town of Drogheda a wild story surrounds the affluent Anne Hardman, of Hardman Gardens, who died in 1844 after living a respectable 71 years. Legend has it that she was buried according to the customs of the day, in a tomb rather than a grave. Unfortunately—or fortunately, as it turns out—Mrs. Hardman had a selfish servant who went to her tomb to plunder her jewelry the night of her burial. "Why should the old hag get to rot with all those pounds?" he reasoned. After eagerly helping himself to her necklaces, earrings, and bracelets, he couldn't resist going for the prized rings. So impassioned was he that when he couldn't pull the rings off her swollen hands he resolved to take them anyway, fingers and all. Much to his surprise, after a few successful hacks, Mrs. Hardman began to move! Understandably frantic, the servant ran straight down the hill to St. Mary's Bridge and promptly boarded the next vessel for Liverpool. (Upon arrival his hair was completely white.) Meanwhile, poor rich Mrs. Hardman awakened to find herself in a cold tomb, wrapped in shrouds. She was, well, a little upset. The situation became more distressing when she returned home and her superstitious family refused to admit her "ghost." Finally, her husband—the bravest and most cool-headed of the lot—realized that a ghost wouldn't be bleeding and allowed her inside. She died again 20 years later. This time, her condition was terminal.

Th 9am-1pm, 2-5pm; F 9am-1pm, 2-4pm.) Those with little imagination should stay home, since there's not much to see anymore. No car? Get up and walk the 45min. from town. Dúchas runs the **Battle of the Boyne Oldbridge Estate Center,** offering an informative 30min. tour recreating the Battle on the old battlefield. On Sundays it hosts a **living history program,** complete with cannons and live cavalry. *(2 mi. north of Donore Village, on the right. ☎988 4343. Open daily 9:30am-5:30pm. Free.)*

MILLMOUNT MUSEUM. The recently reconstructed Martello tower dominates the Drogheda skyline. Inside, **Millmount Museum** displays antique household appliances, a rock collection, and artifacts from the Civil War period (see **Independence and Civil War,** p. 64), including grenades with names etched in (for that personal touch). The museum also offers tours of the tower, shelled during the Civil War but repaired at long last. *(☎983 3097. Tours 25min. Open M-Sa 10am-6pm, Su 2:30-5:30pm. Museum €3, students €2.50, seniors and children €2, family €7. Tower only €2.50/ €2/€1.50/€5. Museum and tower tour €4.50/€3/€2.50/€11.50.)*

TOURS AND OTHER SIGHTS. For entertaining history that's at least 98% true, try the **Walking Tours of Historical Drogheda.** Or, complete the walk solo with the guidance of the *Drogheda Heritage Route* pamphlet or the *Local Story* booklet, both free at the Millmount Information Point and the tourist office. *(☎984 5684. Tours 1½hr. Tours leave Tu-Sa at 10:20am and 2:20pm from the bus station tourist office. €1.90, seniors €1.30.)* At the end of West St. are the four-story towers of 13th century **St. Laurence's Gate.** At the top of the hill on Peter St., the 14th-century **Magdalen Tower** is all that remains of the Dominican Friary that once stood on the spot.

■ DAYTRIPS FROM DROGHEDA

MONASTERBOICE AND MELLIFONT ABBEY

Both ruins are signposted off the Drogheda-Collon Rd. Cyclists head 5 mi. north on N1 until the Dunleer exit. At the bottom of the ramp, turn left and follow the Monasterboice signs. When that road ends, turn right and veer left when meeting the larger Drogheda-Collon Rd. to get to Mellifont. By taxi, establish a charge at the start—it should cost no more than €20. Monasterboice Information Office is open July-Aug. M-Sa 10am-6pm. Mellifont Abbey Information Office (☎982 6459; open daily 10am-6pm) offers tours for €2; seniors €1.20, students €1. The site is free after hours.

What were once two of the most important monasteries in Ireland stand crumbling 5 mi. north of Drogheda. The grounds of **Monasterboice** (MON-uh-ster-boyce) include a round tower and some of the most detailed high crosses in existence, and also serve as the oldest working cemetery in Europe. The monastery was one of Ireland's most wealthy from its founding around AD 520 until the Vikings sacked it in 1097. An **information office** is on site, offering impromptu tours and information on the crosses. **Muireadach's Cross,** the first visible upon entering the grounds, is possibly the best preserved cross in the country, sporting an array of Biblical scenes and Celtic designs. On one side, Satan pulls down his side of the Judgment scales and kicks 14 souls to hell. At a height of nearly 21 ft., the **West Cross** is the tallest high cross on the whole island, and it's covered head to toe with wonderfully intricate work. And, while it is an impressive religious monument, it's not without zanier touches—note the two old men trying to pluck out each other's beards. For more fun, go to the cross at the northeast corner of the graveyard—the nook below the sundial was purportedly used as a wart remover. *Let's Go* does not recommend rubbing your warts on crosses (at least not around other tourists). Another cross, in front of the tower, was chipped away at by emigrants who wanted to take a piece of the Old Country with them during the Famine.

As the monastery at Monasterboice fell, the Cistercians planted their first foothold for Rome a few miles away. **Mellifont Abbey,** founded in 1142, quickly became one of Ireland's wealthiest monasteries, hosting a number of tragedies in the process. The 1152 Senate of Mellifont weakened the independent Irish monastic system and sent their traditions of scholarship into decline. Three years later, Cistercian Pope Adrian IV granted the English King authority to "correct" Ireland, thereby putting his seal of approval on the Norman invasion of the 1170s. In 1603, the last of the proud O'Neills surrendered to the English at Mellifont and fled Ireland for the Continent (see **Feudalism,** p. 58). Most of the ruins now lack both grandeur and basic substance, since the site's stones were plundered between 1727 and 1880 for use in nearby buildings. The delicate Romanesque octagon of the **lavabo,** where monks once cleansed themselves of sins and grime, retains a sense of the original structure's impressiveness and intricacy of detail. The **visitors center** houses a small exhibition, provides a hand-drawn map of the area, and leads tours.

THE HILL OF SLANE, SLANE CASTLE, AND THE SLANE CONCERT

To get to the town of Slane, take bus #183, 70, or 188 from Drogheda (1 every hr.), or bus #32 or 33 to Letterkenny from Dublin (1 every 2hr.). Entrance to Hill of Slane is free. Admission to Slane Castle (☎ 988 4400; www.slanecastle.ie) by tour only. Tours 30min. €7, students and seniors €4. For info and tickets to Slane Concert, call The Soundshop (☎ 983 1078), in town. Concert takes place on the last Sa in Aug. Tickets €50-200. Slane Farm Hostel (☎ 982 4390) has rooms for €15.

The tiny town of Slane, which hosts a riotous **Samba Festival** the second week of July, lies about 10 mi. northwest of Newgrange. For truly spectacular views of County Meath, climb the **Hill of Slane,** where, in AD 433, St. Patrick lit a large celebration fire to oppose the druid fires on hills nearby. He was brought before the druid king Laoghaire, who refused to be converted but spared St. Patrick's life and allowed him to preach in his kingdom. Buses go into town, unless the driver agrees to stop next to the hill. Otherwise, take a left at the town intersection and walk up the road until the hill and tower are visible on the left. At the peak, climb the ancient and diminutive stone spiral staircase in the **tower** to see why St. Patrick thought it was such a magical location.

Ouside of town is **Slane Castle,** recently reopened to the public after renovations following the horrific 1991 fire that burned down half of the castle. Built in 1785, it is a spectacular example of the Gothic Revival style. The 1hr. castle tour details the minutiae of over 20 rooms, including the dining room and its amazing neo-Gothic ceiling, saved during the fire by two firemen who doused the room with water for over eight hours. Each August, the castle opens its doors to the likes of U2 and the Red Hot Chili Peppers for the annual **Slane Concert.** The concert is one of Ireland's most magnificent and popular, drawing crowds nearing 100,000. Tickets usually go on sale in March or April, and sell out at the beginning of summer. If the accommodations at the castle prove too expensive, inquire at nearby **Slane Farm Hostel ❷,** where Paddy Macken welcomes music lovers into spacious, comfortable dorm rooms, complemented by a modern kitchen and sitting room with good books. To find the hostel, take the road that intersects the main road across from the castle and look for **Slane Farm Cottages.**

DUNDALK TOWN (DÚN DEALGAN) ☎ 042

Dundalk, home of the Harp Brewery and the Corrs, sits at the mouth of Dundalk Bay, halfway between Dublin and Belfast. Recently, the town has tried to establish itself in the tourism industry as an information source on the history and mythology of the Cooley Peninsula. Unfortunately, the criss-crossing streets of this mid-size town suffer from big-city congestion during the day, so visitors should not expect the carefree pace or locals of other Irish towns. At night, Harp flows freely at Dundalk's 141 pubs, though the brewery is closed to visitors. Dundalk's streets are unsafe at night and utmost caution is necessary when maneuvering them.

▣ **TRANSPORTATION.** The N1 zips south to Dublin and north to Belfast, becoming A1 at the border. The **train station** (☎933 5521; www.irishrail.ie) is on Carrickmacross Road. From Clanbrassil St., bordering the main square in front of the post office, turn right on Park St., then right again on Anne St., which becomes Carrickmacross. Service to: Belfast (70min.; M-Sa 10 per day, Su 4 per day; €10, students with ISIC card and CIE stamp €7.50, daytrip €15) and Dublin (express 55min., regular 1½hr.; M-F 13 per day, Sa 9 per day, Su 4 per day; €16, students €9.50, 5-day return €21). **Buses** stop at the Bus Éireann station (☎933 4075) on Long Walk and run to: Belfast via Newry (1½hr.; M-Sa 7 per day, Su 4 per day; €11.50) and Dublin (1½hr.; M-F 15 per day, Sa 13 per day, Su 7 per day; €9).

▣▨ **ORIENTATION AND PRACTICAL INFORMATION.** Dundalk's main street is **Clanbrassil Street; Park Street** is the runner-up. Dundalk's streets change names often; Clanbrassil becomes **Market Square,** moving from north to south past the post office and courthouse, and changes again to **Earl Street** before intersecting **Park Street.** Left of this intersection, Park turns into **Francis Street,** then **Roden Place,** then **Jocelyn Street** as it moves east toward the waterfront. To the right, Park St. becomes **Dublin Street.** It's worth grabbing free maps and brochures of the city's sights from the **tourist office.** From the bus stop, walk down Long Walk, turn right onto Crowe St., passing the main square on the left, and continue until it becomes Jocelyn St.; the office is on the right after the cathedral. (☎933 5484; www.ecoast-midlands.travel.ie. Open June to mid-Sept. M-F 9am-6pm, Sa 9:30am-1pm and 2-5:30pm; mid-Sept. to May M-F 9:30am-1pm and 2-5:30pm.) **Tommy the Bike Outdoor World,** 11 Earl St., past the courthouse, sells **camping equipment.** (☎933 3399. Open M-F 9am-1pm and 2-6pm, Sa 9am-6pm.) **Jock's,** 1-2 Park St., carries a variety of watersport gear, packs, army surplus accesories, and sleeping bags at reasonable prices. (☎933 9368. Open M-Sa 9am-6pm.) Many **banks** (including **AIB** and **Bank of Ireland**) with 24hr. **ATMs** cluster on Clanbrassil St. **A1 Cabs,** Crowe St. (☎932 6666), runs cabs day and night. Additionally, many taxis wait in the Square. **Datastore,** 58 Dublin St., provides a daily dose of **Internet.** (☎933 1212. €4 per 30min., €6 per hr. Open M-F 10am-10pm, Sa noon-8pm, Su 2-8pm.) The **post office** is on Clanbrassil St. (☎933 4444. Open M and W-Sa 9am-5:30pm, Tu 9:30am-5:30pm.)

▣▨▨ **ACCOMMODATIONS, FOOD, AND PUBS.** Dundalk's B&Bs are extensive, but most lie outside the town center. If not traveling by car, ask carefully about locations. ▨**Glen Gat House ❸,** 18-19 The Crescent, a left off Anne St. before the train station, has the air of an ancient curio shop. (☎933 7938; gelnga@eircom.net. Wheelchair-friendly bathrooms on first floor. Singles €35-40; doubles €60-70.) For those with cars, **Krakow ❸,** at 190 Ard Easmuinn, signposted from the train station, is a good but distant option, with TVs, hair dryers, and hot-pots in tidy rooms. A pedestrian shortcut goes to the city center, but taking it after dark is not recommended. (☎933 7535. Singles €39; doubles €54.) In town, **Oriel House ❷,** 63 Dublin St., has basic rooms, but is conveniently located and inexpensive. (☎933 1347. Singles €25; doubles €40; triples €60.)

Restaurants and late-night fast-food joints clutter the main streets of town. **La Cantina ❷,** 1 River Ln., a left off Park St. and a block after the Imperial Hotel heading away from the water, is a local favorite for its quality Italian eats and quaint decorations. (☎932 7970. Open Tu-Su 6:15-10:45pm.) The sign in the window of **Deli Lites ❶,** 20 Clanbrassil St., challenges the passerby: "Try our delicious sandwiches, no one likes a coward." The healthy breakfasts and sandwiches (€3.50-6) hardly inspire fear. (☎932 9555. Open M-Sa 8:30am-6pm.)

With 141 pubs lining the streets, Dundalk has a ready pint at every turn, but as in every busy town caution is advised at night. **Courtney's** interior resembles a Gothic church. A huge projection screen, instead of a pulpit, announces the gospel of Beckham during soccer season (Sept.-May). (☎932 6652; courtney@goodpubguide.com. Open M-W noon-11:30pm, Th-Sa noon-12:30am, Su 12:30-11pm.) **The Spirit Store,** Georges Quay on the waterfront, is a new favorite worth the long walk down Jocelyn, though a cab (€5) may be a better bet. Live music upstairs every night, from trad to alternative rock, and international beers from local Harp to Zimbabwe's finest brew draw crowds from 18-80. The **Windsor Bar ❶,** 36-37 Dublin St., across from Oriel House, serves "good drinks and bad manners" alongside particularly tasty cheap pub eats. (☎933 8146; windsorbar@eircom.ie. Sandwiches €3.50; mains €7-8. Food served noon-3pm and 6-10pm. Bar open 10:30am-midnight.) On Saturdays, those over 21 soothe their lonely hearts at the **Imperial Hotel,** home of **Sgt. Peppers,** a late-night club for the young at heart. (☎933 2241. Bar open M-W 11:30am-11:30pm, Th-Sa until 12:30am, Su until 11pm. Club open Sa 11:30pm-2:30am.)

◨ **SIGHTS.** Grab a free brochure on the *Dundalk Heritage Trail* at the tourist office. It outlines the town's historical, non-Corrs, sites. Gothic **St. Patrick's Cathedral,** Francis St., was modeled after King's College Chapel in Cambridge. The warm, more interior makes it a source of comfort and solace. (☎933 4648. Open daily 7:30am-5pm.) Next to the tourist office, the award-winning **County Museum,** Jocelyn St., tells the story of County Louth, from the Bronze Age to the present, with interactive activities that make pre-history and early Christianity engaging. Even those short on time and money can see its most fun exhibit: the ◪**Heinkel Bubble Car.** This Dundalk-made, 60s-era vehicle was the only car manufactured in the Republic by the German Heinkel company, famous for engineering the Heinkel 1-11 fighter bomber that was expelled from Germany post-WWII. It looks like a cockpit on wheels. (☎932 7056; dlkmuseum1@eircom.net. Open June-Aug. M-Sa 10:30am-5:30pm, Su 2-6pm; Sept.-Apr. closed M. €3.80, students and seniors €2.50, children €1.25, family €10.15.) Past the far northwest corner of town, about 3 mi. out Castletown Rd. (N51), and a left after St. Louis Secondary School, the 12th-century **Cúchulainn's Castle** supposedly stands on the birthplace of the Ulster Cycle's most famous hero (see **Legends and Folktales,** p. 73). The seven-story **Seatown Windmill,** on Seatown Place, was once the largest in Ireland, but the wind was taken out of its sails when they were removed in 1890. When weather permits, nice beaches and restaurants beckon from **Blackrock,** 3 mi. south on R172.

COOLEY PENINSULA

The numerous trails in the mountains surrounding the Cooley Peninsula are a hiker's paradise, and Carlingford Lough has the warmest waters in the northern half of the island. Several ancient Irish myths are set in this dramatic landscape, among them the epic *Táin bo Cuailnge,* "The Cattle Raid of Cooley" (see **Legends and Folktales,** p. 73). Remarkably well-preserved stone remnants of medieval settlements are scattered across the peninsula.

CARLINGFORD (CARLINN)   ☎042

The fresh, earthy scent of the mountains mingles with the salty breeze rising off the lough in the quiet village of Carlingford. While Slieve Foy, the nearest and highest of the Cooley Mountains, affords rewarding hiking, many never leave the narrow medieval cobblestone alleys, tidy buildings, and the calming sea vistas that surround it. The sleepy little shire wakes up to rage on Friday and Saturday nights, and groggily retreats to the quiet cafes and dusty bars during the week.

CATTLE RAID OF COOLEY Like any good story, many versions exist, and as with any good Irish story, each is more exaggerated than the next. Chronicled here is only one permutation:

In ancient times, King Conchobar (Conor) of Ulster hosted a neighboring king. A banquet was laid out for the two kings' men and the wine was a-flowin' when the two hatched an excellent bet: the foreign king put up his fastest man to challenge Conor's best runner. With common sense erased by sweet wine, Conor put up his wife, Queen Medbh (Maeve), who, though admittedly a fast footman, was also quite pregnant. Dragged out of bed and into the race, Maeve won swiftly but collapsed in pain at the end of the race, cursing Ulster with the promise that in its greatest moment of need, all its warriors would collapse in the pangs of childbirth.

Years passed before the moment of greatest peril arrived. Queen Maeve, embittered and estranged from her husband, decided to steal the most beautiful and famous bull in Ulster, the Donn of Cooley. Her efforts were realized by the convenient fruition of her prophecy. The Donn of Cooley followed her forces placidly as Ulster's greatest warriors collapsed in birthing pains. It was Cúchulainn (cuh HUL an), the king's nephew who had mercifully been born just outside of Ulster, who came to the rescue and single-handedly retrieved the bull, who wandered home, only to die in his master's field.

Cúchulainn performed many other feats worthy of poets' praise, but is most often remembered for his dying wish, to die standing up. He is thus often depicted, blonde locks waving in the wind, tied to a rock.

⊟⊉ TRANSPORTATION AND PRACTICAL INFORMATION. Buses (☎ 933 4075) stop at the waterfront en route to: Dundalk (50min., M-Sa 6 per day, €4.25) and Newry (20min., M-Sa 5 per day, €3.10). The **tourist office** is by the bus stop. (☎ 937 3033. Open Apr.-Sept. M-F 10am-5:30pm, Sa-Su 11am-5:30pm; Oct.-Mar. daily 11am-5pm.) A 24hr. **ATM** is on Newry St. For **taxis**, call **Gally Cabs** (☎ 937 3777). Those with solid aquatic or outdoors experience may find **work opportunities** among the international staff of **Carlingford Adventure Center** (see **Accommodations**, p. 174). A minimum two-month stay is requested; contact ☎ 937 3100 for more info. **Murphy's Laundry** (☎ 938 3812; open M-Sa 9am-6pm; €9) is next to the **post office** on Dundalk St. (☎ 937 3171. Open M-F 9am-1pm and 2-5:30pm, Sa 9am-1pm.)

⊞⊡⊠ ACCOMMODATIONS, FOOD, AND PUBS. On Tholsel St., one block inland toward King John's castle ruins and left into town, **Carlingford Adventure Centre and Hostel (IHH) ❷** provides small dorms on the first floor, while the new second floor has much nicer rooms with bath for just €5 more. Daylight hours are quickly crammed by the conveniently attached adventure center, based at reception. It offers over 20 land- and water-based activities. Unfortunately, none of them involve cattle herding. The hostel often fills with school groups; call ahead in May and June. (☎ 937 3100; www.carlingfordadventure.com. Hostel: www.hostels-ireland.com. Open Feb.-Nov., all year for groups. **Internet** €1 per 16min. Downstairs: 8-bed dorms €15; 4-bed €17; bunked doubles €18; singles €20, with bath €20-24.)

Carlingford seems to have as many B&Bs as people, and nearly all are posh and pricey; most outside the village center advertise lough views. Savvy travelers will *hora* to the ⊠**Shalom B&B ❸**, Ghan Rd., well-signposted from the waterfront. The palm trees and manicured lawn resemble a tropical oasis, but the reality of the Irish coast does not disapoint. Tastefully eclectic decorations, free chocolate in every room, and **Internet** upon request, make this one of Carlingford's nicest places to stay. (☎937 3151; www.jackiewoods.com. Singles €34; doubles €54; apartments for four €95. MC/V.) In the center of town, **Belvedere House ❹** on Newry St., a right at the ruins of King John's Castle on the left, has stimulatingly decorated, themed rooms, all related to the legend of Cúchulainn. Who knew Queen Maeve was a motif? Rejoice in double-powered showers. (☎937 3731; www.belvederehouse.ie. €40-45. MC/V.) Next to Beaufort's Guest House on Ghan Rd., **Barnave House ❺** claims private baths, tea- and coffee-making facilities, and satellite TV. (☎937 3742; barnavave@eircom.net. Singles €48; doubles €65. MC/V.)

Though Carlingford contains only a handful of pubs and eateries, these offer up everything from traditional Irish hospitality to supernatural phenomena. Particularly strong *craic* is on tap at **PJ O'Hare's,** otherwise known as **The Anchor Bar;** entering town, turn left at King John's Castle. The bar was once only slightly bigger than a breadbox, but popularity forced a makeover that more than doubled the bar area. The backyard provides an alternative setting for slurping oysters (€6.50 for 6) and drinking with locals. (☎937 3106. 18+. Open Su-Th 11am-11:30pm, F-Sa 11am-12:30am.) Vegetarians are far better off next door at **Captain Corelli's Mandolin ❹,** where the Italian chef prepares fine pastas (€10-11), seafood (€13-17.50), and meats. (☎938 3848. Open M and W-Su 6-9:30pm.) For daytime fare, follow the signs to **Georgina's Bakehouse ❶,** where tasty sweets and light lunches are consumed in a homey atmosphere. (☎937 3346. Soups, salads, sandwiches, and desserts about €3 each. Open daily 10:30am-6pm.)

■ **SIGHTS.** The **Holy Trinity Heritage Centre** is housed in a renovated medieval church squeezed among several more recent buildings. The center's staff and a small exhibition educates visitors on the history and local lore of Carlingford from the 9th century to the present. (☎937 3454. Open M-F 10am-12:30pm and 2-4:30pm. €2, children €1.) The nearby ruins of the **Dominican Friary** have retained some of their high walls and dramatic arches and are open for exploration. Carlingford's three other surviving pre-Renaissance buildings provide interesting scenery for a stroll through town, but their interiors are closed to visitors. **King John's Castle,** by the waterfront, is the largest and most foreboding of Carlingford's medieval remains. It was built in the 1190s and named for King John, who visited briefly in 1210. **Taaffe's Castle,** along the quay, was built during the 16th century as a merchant house and contains classic Norman defensive features. In a tiny alley off Market Sq., the turret-laden 16th-century **Mint** is notable for its ornate limestone windows. At the end of the street, one of the old 15th-century town gates, the **Tholsel** (TAH-sehl), creates a narrow passageway for cars entering town. Although Carlingford is normally known for its serenity, a weekend-long **folk festival** in September draws lively musicians from all over the Republic.

THE MIDLANDS

The Irish Midlands are traditionally composed of six counties: Cavan, Monaghan, Laois, Offaly, Longford, and Westmeath. These central counties are often passageways rather than destinations. Co. Monaghan and Cavan's friendly wee villages beckon calmer travelers seeking a convenient rest-stop on their way to the Northwest. The 19 lakes of Co. Westmeath have earned it the buttery nickname "Land of Lakes and Legends." Farther south in famously soggy Co. Offaly, small towns and the impressive ruins of Clonmacnoise civilize the peatland. The Slieve Bloom Mountains, shared between Offaly and Laois, are splendid and under-appreciated. Co. Longford is calm and collected, but hardly exciting.

MONAGHAN TOWN (MUINEACHÁN)   ☎047

Like many Midlands towns, Monaghan has undergone dramatic changes in recent years. The administrative center of its county, Monaghan has been the major beneficiary of the booming EU's euros. The effect on the fabric of the community is striking—chic boutiques and trendy bars now lie behind deteriorating limestone facades. With new names and glammed-up interiors, pubs and restaurants are trying with all their might to cater to the newly affluent populace.

⚏ TRANSPORTATION AND PRACTICAL INFORMATION. The **bus depot** is 5min. north of Market Sq. To reach the center of town from the station, walk against traffic up North Rd. (☎82377. Open M-Sa 8:30am-8pm.) **Buses** run to: Belfast (1½hr.; M-Sa 5 per day, Su 2 per day; €8.25) and Dublin (2hr.; M-Sa 7 per day, Su 3 per day; €8.90). **ABC** (☎71500) runs 24hr. **taxis.** The roads in Monaghan are organized in a loop around the old courthouse and the enormous modern shopping center. From **the Diamond** in the northeast, **Dublin Street** heads south to **Broad Street,** which heads west to **Park Street,** which heads north to **Market Square.** The **tourist office,** Broad St., at the edge of the shopping center containing Tesco, books accommodations and sells stamps, guidebooks, and maps. (☎81122; 1800 668 668 for after-hours hotel reservations. Open June-Sept. M-F 9am-1pm, and 2-5:30pm; call for off seasonhours.) **AIB** has an **ATM** on the Diamond. Book ahead for 45min. of **free Internet** at the **library,** North Rd. (☎81830. Open M-F 11am-1pm and 2-5pm; M, W, and F also 6-8pm.) The **post office** lies just north of Church Sq. on Mill St. (☎81342. Open M-F 9am-5:30pm, Sa 9am-1pm.)

⚏⚏⚏ ACCOMMODATIONS, FOOD, AND PUBS. The narrow, winding hallways of central **Ashleigh House ❸,** 37 Dublin St., recall an M.C. Escher painting. However, at the end of each twist lies a bright sunny room, each with bath and tea- and coffee-making facilities. The airy garden beside the house provides another escape. (☎81227. Singles €35; doubles €60.) **Hildene House ❸,** Canal St., the second right off the Dublin Road out of town, houses plain, cozily worn rooms. Breakfast served in knick-knack heaven. (☎83297. From €30.) **Tesco,** in the shopping center on the corner of Broad and Dawson St., is a well-lit warehouse disguised as a grocery store. (☎71525. Open M-W and Sa 8:30am-8pm, Th-F 8:30am-10pm, Su noon-6pm). Across Dawson St. lurks competitor and two-for-one grocery/clothing store, **Dunnes Stores.** (Open M-Tu 9am-7pm, W and F 9am-9pm, Sa 9am-7pm, Su noon-6pm.) **Pizza D'Or ❷,** 23 Market St. in Market Sq. behind the tourist office, is a late-night town institution adorned with magic eye posters. Never fear, the prices aren't an illusion. (☎84777. Pizzas from €6.70. Open M-F 5pm-1am, Sa-Su 5pm-3am.) **Mediterraneo ❸,** on Dublin St., makes decadent pasta and gourmet pizza in a fluorescent room. (Pastas and pizza €10-12; meat dishes €16-25. Open M and W-Sa 5:30-10:30pm, Su 4:30-10pm.) **Paramount Restaurant ❺,** affiliated with **Cooper's Bar,** Market St., serves delicious seafood, meat, and vegetable dishes in a spare and elegant setting. (☎72877. Prix-fixe dinner €35; a la carte dishes €20-22. Open daily 5-10pm.) For good *craic*, Monaghan town has plenty of pubs to quench any thirst. Overactive drinkers head to **The Squealing Pig,** the Diamond on Dublin St., for two huge flat-screen TVs. With so much going on, don't forget the pints. (☎84562. Bar food around €6, served daily noon-10pm.) **Jimmy's,** on Mill St. off North Rd. across from the post office, is a sliver of a bar with a big sound. Thursday and Saturday nights and Sunday afternoons feature enthusiastic live bands. Just follow the

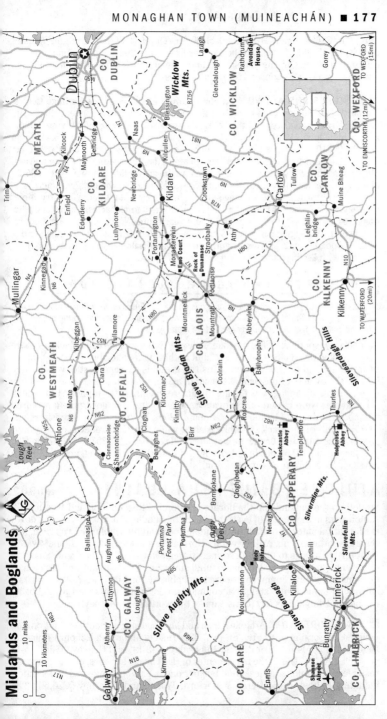

Midlands and Boglands

EASTERN IRELAND

music. (☎81694. Open M-W 12:30-11:30pm, Th-Su 12:30pm-midnight.) **Master Deery's,** on Market St. next to the Cooper Bar, is another neophyte on the scene offering class and dancing to residents and roamers. Wooden booths, nice lighting, and flowing alcohol bode well for future success.

SIGHTS AND ACTIVITIES. The comprehensive **St. Louis Heritage Centre,** Market Rd., occupies a red-brick building on the grounds of a convent school. Its exhibits trace the history of the St. Louis Order of nuns. (☎83529. Wheelchair-accessible. Open M-Tu and Th-F 10am-noon and 2:30-4:30pm, Sa-Su 2:30-4:30pm. €1.30.) On Hill St. across from the tourist office, the **Monaghan County Museum** chronicles the county's history. (☎82928. Open Tu-Sa 11am-1pm and 2-5pm. Free.) Monaghan's most impressive building lies on the south side of town—the 1895 **St. Macartan's Cathedral** features stunning views. Monaghan abounds with activities for the adventurous. Perfect riding skills or just enjoy a jaunt in the countryside at the **Greystones Equestian Centre** (☎047 88100) or the **Carrickmacross School of Equitation** (☎042 966 1017), which are both open year-round. Work on that chip shot on the several challenging **golf** courses in the area, including **Rossmore Golf Club** (☎047 71222). Dodge friends and peg enemies in a game of **paintball** in the Rossmore Forest Park with **Escarmouche Paintball** (☎0044 7774 or 636 254).

DAYTRIP FROM MONAGHAN: LOUGH MUCKNO

In Castleblaney, 20 mi. southeast of Monaghan on the N2. ***Buses*** *on their Dublin route run 4-5 times per day. To get to the park from town, follow the main street north to the bottom of the hill, make a right, and head through the tall metal gates.*

Castleblaney, southeast of Monaghan, is home to the lovely **Lough Muckno Leisure Park.** Muckno means "Swimming Pig," but nothing is squalid about these 900 acres of forest and lake. The park contains the grounds of **Hope Castle,** which once housed the owners of the **Hope Diamond.** In a Marxian turn of events, the castle is now over-run by immigrants fleeing the environmental catastrophe at Chernobyl. All activities were closed for renovations in 2003 after the government acquired the land. They should be fully operational in 2004. Hydrophobic park visitors can tour the trails of the **Black** and **White Islands,** while aquatic daredevils enjoy watersports at the **Adventure Centre,** next to the castle. (☎087 249 1305. Windsurfing €25 per 4hr.; tennis €2.50 per hr. Also sailing, horse-riding, bowling, and golf. Open Mar.-Oct. Tu-F 2-7pm, Sa-Su noon-7pm.)

EASTERN IRELAND

ATHLONE (BAILE ÁTHA LUAIN) ☎0902

Settled on the flatlands on the border of counties Roscommon and Westmeath, Athlone sits in the center of everything and the middle of nowhere. Holding down the fort at the intersection of the Shannon River and the Dublin-Galway road, it is *the* transportation hub. A 13th-century Norman castle dominating Athlone's waterfront further attests to the city's former strategic importance. The scenic Shannon offers enough fishing and boating to fulfill any waterlover's dream, and the monastic ruins of nearby Clonmacnoise are reachable by road or boat. Athlone hosts a surprising number of standout accommodations, restaurants, and pubs, but its remote location means few tourists make the worthwhile journey.

TRANSPORTATION. Athlone's **train** and **bus depot** are on Southern Station Rd., which runs parallel to Church St. (☎73322. Tickets M-Sa 9am-5:30pm.) **Trains** to: Dublin (1¾hr.; M-Sa 12 per day, Su 15 per day; €13-19) and Galway (1¼hr.; 16-18 per day; €10-15). This is the nerve center of **Bus Éireann** services; on their map, all roads lead to Athlone. At least one bus per day departs to almost all major cities, including Belfast, Cork, Derry, Waterford, Tralee, and Killarney (€14.60). The main route from Dublin to Galway trundles through frequently (14-15 per day; Dublin €9.50, Galway €10). **Nestor Buses** (☎ 091 797 244) also serves the region; for their routes and schedules, call or stop by the Royal Hotel on Church St.

⚡ 🔢 ORIENTATION AND PRACTICAL INFORMATION. The River Shannon splits Athlone into the **left bank** and **right bank.** The former is hipper and claims the castle, but the latter holds the shops and eateries. **Church Street** cuts through the right bank, while most of the action on the left bank happens on **High Street.** The besieged **tourist office,** in the castle, counterattacks with an arsenal of orientation ammunition; ask for the *Athlone and District Visitors Guide.* (☎ 94630. Open Easter-Oct. M-Sa 9am-6pm, Su 10am-5pm.) **Bank of Ireland** (☎ 92747) and **AIB** (☎ 75810), on Church St., have **ATMs.** (Both open M 10am-5pm, Tu-F 10am-4pm.) **Internet** is splendid and cheap at **Techstore.ie,** Paynes Ln., a bit away from the river off Church St. (☎ 78888. €5 per hr., students €4. Open daily 9am-10pm.) The **post office** is by the castle on Barrack St. (☎ 83544. Open M-Sa 9:30am-5:30pm.)

🏠 ACCOMMODATIONS AND CAMPING. For a lively locale, look to 🔲**The Bastion ❸,** 2 Bastion St., a spectacular B&B in the middle of the Shannon's funkier left bank. An eclectic blend of art and tapestries adds a touch of chic. (☎ 94954. Fantastic continental breakfast. Singles €35-45; doubles €50-55.) The **Lough Ree Lodge ❷,** 25min. from the town center on the Dublin road, is Athlone's lone hostel. To get there, walk out Church St. past the shopping center, take the right fork, cross the bridge, and keep going until the Athlone Institute of Technology. Bus Éireann shuttles between the hostel and the Golden Island shopping mall (5min., every 15-20min., 9am-6pm; €1). A cut above the typical hostel, the biggest dorms at Lough Ree have four beds and all rooms have TVs, but the boob tube does not hold sway here. Instead, visitors mingle in the superbly clean kitchen or shoot pool in the common area. (☎ 76738. Wheelchair-accessible. Continental breakfast. Internet. Laundry €10. Dorms €15.50; singles €25; doubles €40.) **The Riverside Inn ❸,** a bar and hotel opposite the castle, has palatial, amenity-happy rooms and plenty of noise from the bars below; quieter rooms are pricier, but have bathtubs. (☎ 94981. Singles €35; doubles €54-70.) **Higgins' ❹,** 2 Pearse St., on the left bank, has friendly, down-to-earth owners and decent rooms at the top of a steep staircase. (☎ 92519. Singles €38-42; doubles €60.) Over on the right bank, three cozy rooms await at the petite and sufficient **Shannon View ❸,** 3 Shannon Villas, a few blocks up Church St. from the church. (☎ 78411. €30.) **Lough Ree East Caravan and Camping Park ❶** stakes tents 3 mi. northeast on N55 (the Longford road) by a pleasant inlet on Lough Ree. Follow signs for the lough. (☎ 78561 or 74414. Open Apr.-Sept. Laundry €7. Tents €2.50; caravans and cars €7; motorhomes €5.)

🍴 FOOD. The first floor of **Dunnes,** Irishtown Rd., fulfills all grocery needs. (☎ 75212. Open M-W and Sa 9am-7pm, Th-F 9am-9pm, Su noon-6m.) 🔲**Manifesto ❹,** Church St., after the bridge on the right bank, is relaxed but elegant, and the fantastic food is served on giant plates. (☎ 73241. Mains €14-20. Open W-Su 12:30-9:30pm, Tu 12:30-4:30pm.) **The Left Bank Bistro ❹,** Bastion St., was named one of the 100 best restaurants in Ireland. The lunches are affordable and filling; the steak sandwich with potatoes and salad satisfies for €8-10. (☎ 94446. Lunch noon-5pm; dinner 5:30pm-"late".) Three cheers for local favorite **Tribeca ❸,** hidden off High St. on the left bank and in one of Athlone's oldest buildings, modernized by bright purple paint. Excellent pasta and pizzas are the order of the day. (☎ 98805. Mains €9-16. Open M-W 5-10pm, Th-F 5-11pm, Sa 4-11pm, Su 2-10pm.) The **Bonne Bouche ❷,** 21 Church St., upstairs in Rick's Bar, serves a small variety of plate-filling, palate-pleasing meals in an atmosphere cluttered with Emerald Isle memorabilia. (☎ 72112. Mains €9. Open daily 10am-7pm.)

📺📻 PUBS AND CLUBS. No one likes to be all Athlone when the sun goes down—look to the town's lively pubs for companionship and music. The Weekend *Westmeath Independent* has entertainment listings, as does the *B-Scene* magazine that appears biweekly in local cafes. Sawdust lines the floor and fishing rods decorate the ceiling at **Sean's Bar** (☎92358), behind the castle on Main St. It claims to be Ireland's oldest inn, established in AD 900, but the building holds up well despite raucous school-night trad. **Gertie Brown's Costume Place,** formerly The Hooker, now entertains more regulars than ever. (☎74848. M trad.) Check crowns at the door of **The Palace,** Market Sq. (☎92229), for intergenerational mingling and occasional live music. No clowning around permitted at **BoZo's,** in the basement of Conlon's on Dublingate St.—just the usual boogying to chart-topping music. (☎74376. Cover €8. Open Th-Sa 11:30pm-2:30am.) At **Club Ginkel's,** above Manifesto, the crowd spiffs up to match the leopard-skin decor and purple roof. (Cover W-Sa €8. Open Th-Sa 11:30pm-2:30am, M and W 11:30pm-2am.)

◐🌾 SIGHTS AND FESTIVALS. Athlone's historical fame can be traced to a single, crushing defeat. Orange Williamite forces besieged **Athlone Castle** in 1691, and, with the help of 12,000 cannonballs, they easily crossed the river and swept up. The defending Jacobites, unskilled soldiers at best, suffered countless casualties; the attackers lost fewer than 100 of their 25,000 (see **The Ascendancy,** p. 60). The castle is free for all to wander, and provides some grand Shannon views. (Open May-Sept. daily 9:30am-6pm.) Inside, the **visitors center** tells a 45min. audio-visual tale of the battle, and marches on (without the slightest hint of transition) through Athlone history to relate the stories of home-grown tenor **John McCormack** and the river Shannon. The **museum** inside the visitors center features, among other things, gramophones and uniforms from the Irish Civil War. (☎92912. Open May-Sept. daily 10am-4:30pm. €4.55, students and seniors €2.65. Museum only €3/€1.50.) The two master crafters at **Athlone Crystal Factory,** 29-31 Pearse St., invite all to discover the fascinating details of crystal-making, and covet their final products. (☎92867. Open M-Sa 10am-1pm and 2-6pm. Free.) **Viking Tours** supplies helmets and swords for an authentic Viking experience on a replica Viking ship that sails up the Shannon to Lough Ree and, depending on demand, to Clonmacnoise. The Clonmacnoise ride includes a guided tour of the monastic ruins. (☎73383 or 086 262 1136. 1½-4hr. voyages depart from the Strand across the river from the castle. 2 or more per day. €8, students and children €5. Clonmacnoise tour €13/€8.) Not up for marauding? The **Jolly Mariner Marina rents cruisers** that berth up to eight people, perfect for a self-guided float down the Shannon. (☎72892 or 72113. Rates vary by season. 3-berth cruiser €435-890 per wk.; 8-berth €1015-2390.) They also hire **outboards** (€65 per wk.; €65 deposit) and **bicycles** (€40 per wk.).

The last week in June brings the **Athlone Festival** with all its parades, exhibitions, and free concerts. Athlone hosts the **John McCormack Golden Voice Conference,** named for the town's famous songbird (see **Music,** p. 76), in late autumn. The town also celebrates the Irish novelist **John Broderick** the first weekend in May, replete with guest speakers, poetry readings, and a general to-do about the man. Contact the tourist office (☎94630) or the Athlone Chamber of Commerce (☎73173) for further information on this and other summertime merriment.

CLONMACNOISE (CLUAIN MHIC NÓIS)   ☎0905

Fourteen isolated miles southwest of Athlone, the monastic ruins of Clonmacnoise (clon-muk-NOYS) keep watch over Shannon's boglands. St. Ciaran (KEER-on) founded his monastery here in AD 548; the settlement grew into an important center for religion and brainiactivity. Monks wrote the precious **Book of the Dun Cow** here around 1100, on vellum supposedly from St. Ciaran's cow. The holy heifer traveled everywhere with the saint, and miraculously produced enough milk for the whole monastery. The cows munching their way across the landscape today have ordinary udders, but the grandiosity of the sight still incites the imagination. The ruin's **cathedral** has seen its share of attacks over the course of its thousand years. One of its doorways is known as the **whispering arch;** quiet sounds travel up one side over to the other. **O'Connor's Church,** built in the 12th century, has Church of Ireland services from June through August on Sundays at 4pm. Peaceful **Nun's Church** lies beyond the modern graveyard behind the main site, about ¼ mi. down the path. Its finely detailed doorways are some of the most impressive Romanesque architecture in Ireland.

By car, the easiest way to reach Clonmacnoise from Athlone or Birr is to take N62 to **Ballynahown** and follow the signs from there. The town is accessible by bike, but cycling involves a 14 mi. gauntlet of hilly terrain. Access to the monastery is through the **visitors center** and their displays, which include a 23min. audio-visual show. (☎74195. The center, unlike the sites, is wheelchair-accessible. Open June to mid-Sept. daily 9am-7pm; mid-Mar. to May and mid-Sept. to Oct. 10am-6pm; Nov. to mid-Mar. 10am-5pm. €4.40, students €1.90, seniors €3.10.) The **tourist office,** at the entrance to the Clonmacnoise carpark, sells various guides to the city. (☎74134. Open Mar.-Nov. daily 10am-6pm.) **Paddy Kavanagh** runs a **minibus tour** that hits the monastery, a local pub, and the **West Offaly Railway,** which runs through a peat bog. Paddy accommodates almost all schedules and connects with incoming buses and trains. He will pick up sightseers from their accommodations if they're eager enough to call ahead. The tour is engaging and offers several "surprises," as Paddy shows off his Ireland with heart and charm. (☎0902 74839 or 087 240 7706. Clonmacnoise €17; Clonmacnoise and West Offaly Railway €22. Site admission fees an additional €14.) Without Paddy, trains run through the bog every hr. between 10am and 5pm. (☎74114, 74172, or 74121.)

One outstanding B&B is ⚑**Kajon House ❸,** on Shannonbridge Rd. near the ruins. Mrs. Kate Harte is a lovely ball of fire, and gladly retrieves guests in Athlone if they call ahead. She and her husband, a chef, also make a fabulous dinner (€17-19) or snack (€7-10), and greet guests with delicious homemade scones. (☎74191; www.kajonhouse.cjb.net. Singles €35-39; doubles €46, with bath €51. Stuffed animals included.) **Meadow View B&B,** half a mile in the other direction from Clonmacnoise, has modern rooms, a sunny dining room, and friendly, welcoming owners. (☎74257. Singles €33; doubles €46-50, half-price if under 12.) The area's camping is 3 mi. east, at the **Glebe Touring Caravan and Camping Park ❶.** (☎0902 30277. Open Easter-Oct. Laundry €5. €2 per person. €5 per tent.)

THE SLIEVE BLOOM MOUNTAINS

Though less than 2000 ft. at their highest point, the Slieve Bloom Mountains burst lustily from the rolling plains between **Birr, Roscrea, Portlaoise,** and **Tullamore.** The mountain terrain is a combination of forest and energy-rich bogland. The 43 mi. circular **Slieve Bloom Way** takes hikers through and around the mountains. For all the necessary details, pick up the *Slieve Bloom Way Map Guide* (€5) from the Portlaoise tourist office. The mountains' greatest asset, contrary to what a tourist office might advertise, is their lack of tourist-oriented activity—there's nothing to do but relax. The towns surrounding the mountains, bastions of rural Ireland's small-town lifestyle, aid wanderers in the quest for peace and quiet.

Transportation can be tricky. Two of the best towns for entry to the mountains are **Kinnitty,** to the northwest, and **Mountrath,** to the south; getting from one to the other should pose no problems for the automotive-blessed. Travelers reliant on public transportation, however, are considerably handicapped; ask locals how to get places, where to go, and who else to talk to. The **tourist offices** of the surrounding towns are good starting points; the **Portlaoise** branch (☎0502 121 178) provides a handy list of Co. Laois residents who have been trained as tour guides. Noreen Murphy, for instance, is a mountain specialist and owns **Conlán House ❸,** one of the few B&Bs near the mountains. This cozy lodge sits atop a small hill and overlooks part of the walk 1¼ mi. away. (☎0502 32727. Singles €40; doubles €30-40; children half-price.) **Roundwood House ❺,** a gorgeous 16th-century house with two resident peacocks, is also fairly near the mountains: 3 mi. out R440 from Mountrath. (☎0502 32120. Singles €95; doubles €140.) The owners of the modern **Farren House Hostel ❶** gives guests lifts from **Ballacolla,** a town reached twice a day by bus from Portlaoise. The hostel rooms are large and comfy, and the old farm junk sculptures in the driveway force a smile. (☎0502 34032. Wheelchair-accessible. Continental breakfast €4.50; Irish breakfast €6.50. Laundry €6. Dorms €14. **Camping** €6.)

The *craic* can be mighty in Slieve Bloom villages, but it's all about the timing. When the pubs have trad sessions, they're not looking to impress the shamrock-seeking hordes. On Thursday nights, the **Thatched Village Inn** (☎0502 35277) in **Coolrain** gets the locals together for some infectiously fun set dancing. The **Irish Music and Set Dancing Festival** jigs into Coolrain on the first weekend in May. Contact Micheál Lalor (☎086 260 7658) for information on either festival.

BIRR (BIORRA)   ☎0509

William Petty named Birr *"Umbilicus Hiberniae,"* the belly button of Ireland, though the town's non-too-central location leads *Let's Go* to suspect that old Will may have been speaking from behind a pint glass. Mislabeling aside, Birr's castle at least is well worth a visit. The rest of town is pleasant if unremarkable, and does a good job packing visitors off to the Slieve Bloom Mountains. The peaks don't start until **Kinnitty,** 9 mi. east, so those without cars should bike; a dearth of cars makes thumb-travel as impractical as it is risky.

⬛ TRANSPORTATION. Buses stop at the post office in Emmet Sq. **Bus Éireann** runs to: Athlone (50min.; M-Sa 3-5 per day, Su 1 per day; €7); Cahir (2hr., 1 per day, €11.10); Dublin (2½hr.; M-Sa 4 per day, Su 2 per day; €9); and Limerick (M-F 4-5 per day, Su 1 per day; €11.90). **Kearns Coaches** (☎0509 20124; www.kearnstransport.com) offers better fares to Dublin and Galway; pick up a schedule at Square News in Emmet Sq.

⬛🖪 ORIENTATION AND PRACTICAL INFORMATION. The *umbilicus* of Birr is **Emmet Square.** Most shops and pubs are in the Square, or south down **O'Connell Street.** The areas to the north and west, down **Emmet** and **Green Streets,** are primarily residential. The **tourist office** is in a business park on Chapel Ln., the continuation of Castle St. after it crosses Main St. (☎20110. Open May-Sept. daily 9:30am-1pm and 2-5:30pm.) They have a free heritage map of town and maps of the Slieve Blooms, and connect travelers with the Slieve Bloom Rural Development Society (☎37299). **P.L. Dolan,** Main St., **rents bikes.** (☎20006. €9 per day, €40 per wk.; deposit €50.80. Open M-W and F-Sa 9:30am-1pm and 2-6pm.) The **Bank of Ireland** in Emmet Sq. has an **ATM.** (☎20092. Open M 10am-5pm, Tu-F 10am-4pm.) The **post office** posts from Emmet Sq. (☎20062. Open M-F 9am-5:30pm, Sa 9am-1pm.)

⬛⬛🖪 ACCOMMODATIONS, FOOD, AND PUBS. It would appear that Birr's navel-status, albeit dubious, is enough to hike up the price of a night's stay. Luckily, the town's B&Bs seem to justify the splurgitude. **Spinner's Town House ❸,** Castle St., is the epitome of country elegance, with crisp decor and roomy rooms; framed documents from Birr's past deck the walls. A charming **bistro** downstairs offers breakfast options like scrambled eggs with smoked salmon; dinner might cost as much as a room. (☎21673. Singles €35-45; doubles €65; "Gothic wing" doubles €90, but the castle view isn't worth the mark-up.) If Spinner's is full, head across the road to **Maltings Guest House** ❹ on Castle St., part of a large hotel/restaurant/craftshop complex with impersonal but comfortable rooms, many overlooking the river. (☎21345. Singles €40; doubles €64-70.) The attached **restaurant** ❷, one of the few in town, serves decent vegetarian-friendly meals for €10-18.

A **SuperValu** hawks grocer-goods on O'Connell St. (☎20015; open M-W and Sa 8am-7:30pm, Th-F 8am-9pm, Su 9am-6pm.) **Londis** (☎21250), in the other direction from Emmet Sq., stays open daily until 9pm. Locals point to **Kong Lam** ❷, Main St., for cheap Chinese takeaway or sit-down. (☎21253. Mains €7-10. Open Su-M and W-Th 5pm-12:30am, F-Sa 5pm-1:30am.) Spend a few more pence on lunch and eat *al fresco* in the beer garden at the **Coachhouse Lounge** ❸, in Dooly's Hotel on the Square. (☎20032. Lunch €4-7, dinner €13-16.) **Melba's** is Dooly's nightclub. (Cover €7. Open until 2am F-Su.) **Whelehan's**, on Connaught St., off Main St. (☎21349), owned by members of the Offaly hurling team, is the liveliest place in town.

◙ **SIGHTS.** Visitors are welcome (for a fee) to tread on the Earl of Rosse's turf at **Birr Castle**, which remains his private home. The 120-acre demesne has babbling brooks, the tallest box hedges in the world, and paths perfect for aimless wandering. The gardens have been constantly improved over the past 300 years, and represent a living history of the evolution of gardening style. For those who like their romanticism without all the walking, **Declan Cleare** offers 30min. carriage rides through the gardens, accompanied by lively commentary. (☎21753 or 087 6693 237. €8 per person, min. 4 people; 8 students €30.) The ◙**Historic Science Centre,** inside the castle, showcases the noteworthy astronomy and photography that took place in the castle in the 19th century. The Third Earl of Rosse discovered the Whirlpool Nebula with the **Leviathan,** an immense telescope whose 72 in. mirror was the world's largest for 72 years. In order to build the telescope he had to invent metal alloys strong and shiny enough to give his mirrors a clear surface. The starry-eyed can still observe the Leviathan (outside in a stone enclosure) in action today, but only if the weather is cooperating. The newly opened **Birds of Prey Centre** features feathered predators and their human trainers. (☎20336. Castle open Mar.-Oct. daily 9am-6pm; Nov.-Feb. daily 10am-6pm. Leviathan tours 5 days per wk., around noon and 1pm. Wheelchair-accessible. €9.50, students €7.50.)

PORTLAOISE (PORT LAOISE)   ☎0502

Travelers who ask the folks at the tourist office what there is to do in Portlaoise (port-LEESH) are likely to be pointed outwards. The one worthwhile sight in close range is the **Rock of Dunamase.** To get there, take the Stradbally Rd. east for 4 mi. and follow the sign at the big red church to Athy/Carlow; the Rock is on the left. This ancient fortress was the very model of impregnability until Cromwell cannonballed onto the scene some 400 years ago. Modern visitors can scramble among its ruins and nab great photos of the Slieve Bloom Mountains.

James Fintan Lawlor Avenue runs parallel to **Main Street.** Lawlor Ave. is a four-lane highway that opens onto Portlaoise's several shopping centers, the most prominent of which is **Lyster Square.** To get to Main St., turn into any of the shopping centers and head behind the stores. The **train station** is at the curve on **Railway Street,** which follows **Church Street** from Main St. (☎21303. Open daily 6am-11pm.) **Trains** run to Dublin and most points south (1hr.; 11-13 per day, Su 6 per day; €16). **Bus Éireann** stops on Lawlor Ave. on its way to Dublin (1½hr., 13 per day, €7.80). **Rapid Express** (☎067 26266) also serves Carlow (2 per day) and Dublin (5-6 per day) from Lawlor Ave. The **tourist office** in Lyster Sq., on Lawlor Ave., has plentiful info. (☎21178. Open June-Sept. M-Sa 10am-5:30pm; Oct.-May 9:30am-5pm.) **AIB** (☎21349) graces Lawlor Ave. with an **ATM**, as does the **Bank of Ireland.** (☎21414. Open M 10am-5pm, Tu-F 10am-4pm.) The **library** has **Internet**. (☎22333. €2.50 per 30min. Open Tu and F 10am-5pm, W-Th 10am-7pm, Sa 10am-1pm.) The regional **post office** is inside the shopping center on Lawlor Ave. (☎74220. Open M and W-F 9am-5:30pm, Tu 9:30am-5:30pm, Sa 9am-1pm.)

Affordable accommodations in Portlaoise are limited. The stark white facade of **Oakville ❸,** Mountrath Rd., a 5min. walk from Main St., on the left after the train tracks, belies its cozy rooms and friendly proprietors. Morris Murphy is a trained tour-guide, and sits guests down for a briefing on Laois over tea in the conservatory on arrival. (☎61970; oakvillebandb@eircom.net. Singles €36-40; doubles €56-60.) **Donoghue's B&B ❸,** 1 Kellyville Park, on the roundabout at the end of Lawlor Ave., is in a well-kept house with colorful flower gardens. (☎21353. Singles €35-45; doubles €65, with bath €70.) Those who've had enough with affordability and want a bit of luxury try to book a room at **Ivyleigh ❺,** on Bank Pl. near the train station. Chandeliers glisten in the dining and sitting rooms in this historic house that dates back to 1850, and the fresh-squeezed orange juice at breakfast is served in Waterford glasses. (☎22081. Singles €58-70; doubles €110.) For groceries, try **Tesco,** inside the mall on Lawlor Ave., opposite Main St. (☎21730. Open M-Tu and Sa 9am-7pm, W-F 9am-9pm, Su noon-6pm.) Dinner options are limited, but competing Indian and Chinese restaurants on Main St. offer ethnic flavor. Local favorite **Jim's Kitchen** (aka **The Kitchen**) ❷, in Hynes Sq. off Main St., serves the best meals in town; too bad it's only open until 5:30pm. A great selection of salads complements the mains, which start at €8.25. (☎62061. Open M-Sa 9am-5:30pm.) As the evening wears on and the pocketbook opens, try **The Kingfisher ❹,** in the old brick AIB building on Main St., an upscale Indian restaurant that specializes in baltis and raitas. (☎62500; www.kingfisherrestaurant.com. Mains €14-19. Open Su-Tu 5:30-11:30pm, W-F noon-2pm and 5:30-11:30pm.) In addition to plentiful pubbly-grubbly options on Main St., brilliant coffee and a touch of class percolate at the **Cafe Latte ❷** branch in the sparkling, fabulous **Dunamaise Arts Centre,** the large orange building on the corner of Main St. and Church St. The cafe offers delectable lunches; the Arts Centre holds a well-designed 250-seat theater. (☎63355. **Internet** €2.50 per 30min. Cafe open M-Sa 8:30am-5:30pm.)

⚡ DAYTRIP FROM PORTLAOISE: EMO COURT AND GARDEN. With panoramic views of the **Slieve Bloom Mountains** and beautiful gardens out back, **Emo Court** is one of James Gandon's finer creations. Famous for his work on the Four Courts and Custom House in Dublin, Gandon designed the house in the 1780s for the first Earl of Portarlington. Work progressed somewhat slowly, however, and Emo Court wasn't completed for nearly 84 years. Gandon's obsession with perfection and fetish for symmetry can be seen throughout the house—in the foyer, two of the four stately doors are for decoration only. The house was originally set on 11,500 acres of land, but the Irish Land Commission bought it in 1920 and divvied it up, selling the house to the Jesuits in 1929 for use as a seminary. After dismantling several of the rooms, including the spectacular rotunda with its extremely detailed carved wood floor, the Jesuits sold the house to the government in 1969; in the mid-1990s the Heritage Foundation dutifully re-built the floor and patched together the rest of the house for visitors to enjoy. (*About 4 mi. out the N7 toward Dublin.* ☎*0502 26573. Open mid-June to mid-Sept. Tu-Su noon-6:30pm. Gardens open during daylight hours for free; tours given July-Aug. Su at 3pm. Court admission by guided tour only. Tours every hr. €2.75, students and seniors €2.*)

SOUTHEAST IRELAND

Miles of coastline and acres of fertile soil, mountains dotted with wildflowers and wide tidal harbors have drawn visitors to the Southeast, from Vikings to Normans to modern-day travelers. Excellent sandy beaches and a greater likelihood of sunshine draw Irish families to the coastal towns of Wexford, Dunmore East, and Ardmore. Tiny Kilmore Quay has a beach, incredibly fresh fish, and achingly quaint thatched-roof cottages, while Tramore draws the young and noisy to its excellent surf. The region is famous for its strawberries and oysters, whose aphrodisiacal powers may account for the gaggles of children playing on its beaches. Round towers abound; St. Caince's in Kilkenny affords an aerial view of this well-preserved medieval city, and the tower perched on the Rock of Cashel is the oldest structure to conquer the heights. Inland, the fields are green and the mountains stunning, and mellow sheep graze at the base of the enormous Rock of Cashel, with its superbly preserved castle and cathedral complex. Trad and rock thump in the pubs of Waterford, Kilkenny, Carlow, and Wexford. The region is most easily seen by automobile and best seen by bicycle, but buses and trains make most of the cities and towns reachable for the wheel-less.

COUNTIES KILKENNY AND CARLOW

Northwest of Counties Wexford and Waterford and southwest of Dublinopolis, Co. Kilkenny and Carlow consist of lightly populated hills, small farming villages, and scattered medieval ruins. The medieval city of Kilkenny, a popular destination for international tourists and the young Irish, is the bustling exception to the seemingly endless string of provincial towns. The town of Carlow, though much smaller, manages to produce a fair buzz on weekend nights.

KILKENNY CITY (CILL CHAINNIGH)   ☎056

Kilkenny is a perfect destination for travelers in search of the classic Irish city. In proud Irish fashion, it has a renowned medieval namesake castle, bright-colored storefronts, excellent shopping, a tremendous selection of pubs, and its own brewery. While Dublin seems to be increasingly international and full of traffic, Kilkenny staunchly clings to its roots; it's much easier to find a smoky pub filled with the sounds of an illin pipe than a trendy gastro-pub serving Asian-fusion food.

The city cemented itself in the history books in 1172 when Strongbow built the first rendition of Kilkenny Castle to command the crossing of the River Nore. His son-in-law later replaced the original structure with sturdier stone and incorporated the town in 1204. The town wall, part of which still stands today, once designated the border between "English Town," inside the gates and governed by the

Southeast Ireland

Normans, and "Irish Town," governed by the local bishop. The two governments were apt to quarrel, and Kilkenny's nickname, "the fighting cats," is garnered from their behavior (see **Entertainment,** p. 193). Today, a casual walk down its handsome streets reveals Kilkenny's attempt to recreate its 15th-century charm. The city's buildings glint with polished limestone, and storefronts have eliminated tacky neon—even fast-food joints have hand-painted facades. These efforts are reaping their touristic reward: the city has twice earned the coveted title of Tidy Town, and its population doubles during high season.

⌐ TRANSPORTATION

Trains: Kilkenny MacDonagh Station, Dublin Rd. (☎22024). Open M-Sa 7am-8:15pm, Su 9am-1pm and 2:45-9pm. Always staffed, though the ticket window is open only at departure time. Kilkenny is on the main **Dublin-Waterford** rail route (3-5 per day). To: **Dublin** (2hr.); **Thomastown** (15min.); **Waterford** (45min.). Connections to the west can be made at **Kildare Station,** 1hr. north on the Dublin-Waterford line.

Buses: Kilkenny Station, Dublin Rd. (☎64933 or 051 879 000), as well as a stop in the city center at **The Tea Shop,** Patrick St.; buy tickets at either location. To: **Clonmel** (1¼hr., 6 per day, €6); **Cork** (3hr.; M-Sa 3 per day, Su 2 per day; €16); **Dublin** (2hr.,

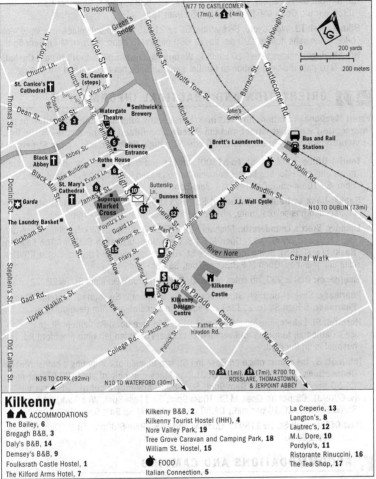

Kilkenny

⌂▲ ACCOMMODATIONS
The Bailey, **6**
Bregagh B&B, **3**
Daly's B&B, **14**
Demsey's B&B, **9**
Foulksrath Castle Hostel, **1**
The Kilford Arms Hotel, **7**

Kilkenny B&B, **2**
Kilkenny Tourist Hostel (IHH), **4**
Nore Valley Park, **19**
Tree Grove Caravan and Camping Park, **18**
William St. Hostel, **15**

● FOOD
Italian Connection, **5**

La Creperie, **13**
Langton's, **8**
Lautrec's, **12**
M.L. Dore, **10**
Pordylo's, **11**
Ristorante Rinuccini, **16**
The Tea Shop, **17**

5-6 per day, €10); **Galway** via **Athlone** or **Clonmel** (5hr.; M-Sa 6 per day, Su 3 per day; €19); **Limerick** via **Clonmel** (2½hr.; M-Sa 4 per day, Su 2 per day; €13.30); **Rosslare Harbour** via **Waterford** (2hr.; M-Sa 2 per day, Su 3 per day; €7); **Waterford** (1½hr.; M-Sa 2 per day, Su 3 per day; €6.35). **Buggy's Coaches** (☎41264) run from **Kilkenny** to **Ballyragget** (30min., M-Sa 6 per day) and **Castlecomer** (15min., M-Sa 6 per day, €2.50) with stops at the **An Óige hostel** (15min.) and **Dunmore Cave** (20min.). Buggy's also runs **local bus tours. J.J. Kavanagh's Rapid Express** (☎31106) has prices that beat Bus Éireann's to **Dublin** (M-Sa 4 per day, Su 2 per day; €6).

Taxis: All companies have a €5.10 min. charge, plus an additional €1.50 per mi. after 3-4 mi. **Paul Butler** (☎087 222 6077); **Frank O'Neill** (☎086 633 4777); **Grab a Cab** (☎086 250 3475); **Ken Kelly** (☎62622 or 087 242 299). **Castle Cabs** (☎61188) also **stores luggage** for €1.30 per day.

Car Rental: Barry Pender, Dublin Rd. (☎65777 or 63839). 25+. Compact €55 per day, €330 per wk. Open M-F 9am-5:30pm, Sa 9am-1pm.

Bike Rental: J.J. Wall Cycle, 88 Maudlin St. (☎21236), is the only place in town to rent bikes. Bike sans helmet €20 per day or €80 per wk. ID deposit. Open M-Sa 9am-6pm.

Hitchhiking: Hitchers take N10 south to **Waterford,** Freshford Rd. to N8 toward **Cashel,** and N10 past the train station to **Dublin.** *Let's Go* does not recommend hitchhiking.

✈🛈 ORIENTATION AND PRACTICAL INFORMATION

From **MacDonagh Station,** turn left onto burgeoning **John Street** and downhill to the intersection with **High Street** and **the Parade,** dominated by the castle on the left. Most activity occurs in the triangle formed by **High, Rose Inn,** and **Kieran Streets.**

Tourist Office: Rose Inn St. (☎51500), on the 2nd fl. of a 1525 pauper house. Free maps and bus info; bus tickets can also be purchased here. Open Mar.-Sept. M-F 9am-6pm, Sa 10am-6pm; Oct.-Feb. M-F 9am-5pm.

Banks: Bank of Ireland, Parliament St. (☎21155), has an **ATM;** the High St./Parade intersection has several more. All open M 10am-5pm, Tu-F 10am-4pm.

Laundry: Brett's Launderette, Michael St. (☎63200). Soap €1.30. No self-service drying. Wash and dry €10-12. Open M-Sa 8:30am-8pm; last wash 6:30pm. **The Laundry Basket** (☎70355), at the top of James St. Full-service wash and dry starting at €5. Dry-cleaning facilities. Open M-F 8:30am-7pm, Sa 9am-6pm.

Emergency: Dial ☎999; no coins required. **Police** (*Garda*): Dominic St. (☎22222).

Pharmacy: Several on High St. All open M-Sa 9am-6pm; Su rotation system. **White's Pharmacy,** 5 High St. (☎21328) specializes in cameras and film development.

Hospital: St. Luke's, Freshford Rd. (☎51133). Continue down Parliament St. to St. Canice's Cathedral, turn right and veer left onto Vicars St., then left onto Freshford Rd. The hospital is on the right.

Internet: By the tourist office on Rose Inn St. is a triangle of competing e-cafes: **Mobile Connections,** Rose Inn St. (☎23000), has Macs and helpful staff. €0.08 per min., €4.50 per hr. Open M-Sa 9am-9pm, Su 2-8pm. **Kilkenny e.centre,** 26 Rose Inn St. (☎60093). €5 per hr. Open M-Sa 10am-9pm, Su 11am-8pm. **Web Talk,** 24 Rose Inn St. (☎50355). €0.10 per min., €4.50 per hr. Open M-Sa 9am-9pm, Su 2-8pm.

Post Office: High St. (☎21891). Open M and W-Sa 9am-5:30pm, Tu 9:30am-5:30pm, Sa closed 1-2pm.

⌂ ACCOMMODATIONS AND CAMPING

The average Kilkenny B&B costs around €30 sharing, but some places hike prices up to €40 on weekends. B&Bs tend toward the institutional here; hostels step in as the bastions of hominess. Call ahead in the summer or on weekends to avoid bedless headaches. The Waterford Rd. and more remote Castlecomer Rd. have the highest concentration of sleeps-and-eats.

▨ **Kilkenny Tourist Hostel (IHH),** 35 Parliament St. (☎63541). Near the popular pubs and next to Smithwick's Brewery. Bright rooms brim with activity: people bustle about in the kitchen and dining room, lounge on couches, and sip Guinness on the front steps. Tons of town info posted in the front hall. Non-smoking. Kitchen open 7am-11pm. Laundry €5. Check-out 10am. 6- to 8-bed dorms €13-14; 4-bed €15-16. Doubles €34-36. ❶

▨ **Foulksrath Castle (An Óige/HI),** Jenkinstown (☎67674; call ahead, leave a message 10am-5pm). On the N77 (Durrow Rd.), 8 mi. north of town, but fine for those with cars. Turn right at signs for Connahy; the hostel is ¼ mi. down on the left. Buggy's Buses run from the Parade M-Sa twice a day (20min., call hostel for times, €2). Housed in a 15th-century castle, Foulksrath is literally a royal accommodation. Grand rooftop views, a common room with a fireplace, and paintings by the wonderful, artistic warden compensate for mediocre bathrooms. Lock-out 10am-5pm. Dorms €11-12; under 16 €9-10. ❶

William St. Hostel (☎56726), in the Methodist Church complex at the end of William St., off High St. Centrally located, with adequate beds and a small kitchen. Call here if the other hostels are full. Non-Christians may be put off by the religious signs in the sitting room, but the friendly staff puts guests at ease. €14; 2 nights €24. ❶

Demsey's B&B, 26 James St. (☎21954). A little old house by the Superquinn supermarket, off High St. Delightful proprietors rent out simple, clean, TV-blessed rooms. Parking €1 per night. Singles €35; doubles with bath €60-64. ❸

Daly's B&B, 82 John's St. (☎62866). Ferns and other hanging plants greet guests in the sky-lit entrance hall; immaculate, spacious rooms and a large breakfast area await farther on. Singles €35-38; doubles €64. Slightly reduced rates in the off season. ❸

The Bailey, 13 Parliament St. (☎64337). Excellent B&B rooms conveniently located above Bailey's Pub (see **Pubs,** p. 190). Relish breakfast in the delightfully whimsical dining room. Singles €40-45; doubles €70-100. ❸

Bregagh House B&B, Dean St. (☎22315), the 1st B&B on the left turning off High St. Clean rooms, all with small baths, handsome wood furniture, and firm beds. Singles €40; doubles €70-76. ❸

The Kilford Arms Hotel, John St. (☎61018; www.travel-ireland.com/irl/kilford.htm). New hotel between Ó'Faoláin's bar and the White Oak restaurant (see **Food** and **Pubs,** p. 189). Nice, large rooms, all with bathtub and shower. Check out the Bengal tiger in the lobby. Breakfast, and entrance to the nightclub, included. F-Sa €65, Su-Th €45. ❺

Kilkenny B&B, Dean St. (☎64040). In operation for 33 years with an eccentric owner and basic, old-fashioned rooms. Rates vary; higher on weekends and bank holidays. Singles €30-35; shared rooms €20-40. ❸

Nore Valley Park (☎27229 or 27748). 7 mi. south of Kilkenny between Bennetsbridge and Stonyford, marked from town. Take the New Ross Rd. (R700) to Bennetsbridge, and the signposted right before the bridge. A class act, with hot showers, TV room, and a children's play-area. Mini-golf (€2), peddle go-carts (€1.50), picnic and barbeque areas. Wheelchair-accessible. Open Mar.-Oct. Backpackers €5; 2-person tent €11. Laundry €5.70. ❶

Tree Grove Caravan and Camping Park (☎70302). 1 mi. past the castle on the New Ross road (R700). 2-person tent €12. Free showers. ❶

🄵 FOOD

Dunnes Supermarket, Kieran St., sells housewares and food. (☎61655. Open M-Tu and Sa 8:30am-7pm, W-F 8:30am-10pm, Su 10am-6pm.) **Superquinn,** in the Market Cross shopping center off High St., has an equally huge selection, and free samples. (☎52444. Open M-Tu and Sa 8:30am-7pm, W-F 8:30am-9pm.) Everything in Kilkenny's restaurants is great except the prices, which hover somewhere in the lower stratosphere. Below are some reasonable options; otherwise, hit the pubs.

▧ Pordylo's, Butterslip Ln. (☎70660), between Kieran and High St. One of the best eateries on the island. Zesty dinners (€17-23) from across the globe, with plentiful veggie options. Reservations recommended. Open daily 6-11pm. ❹

La Creperie, 80 John St. Sweet and savory crepes and sandwiches (€2.45-5), fresh salads, and fruit smoothies, all for a great price. Open M-W and Sa 10am-6pm, Th-F 10am-7pm, Su 11am-5pm. ❶

Langton's, 69 John St. (☎65123). This ever-changing highbrow restaurant occupies a classy leather lounge where James Bond might dine and a conservatory dining room that seems lifted from the Titanic. Full lunch menu with an Irish twist (€8) served daily

12:30-3:30pm; sophisticated dinner menu (2-course €25, 3-course €30) 6-10:30pm. bar menu (€9-20) served 12:30-9:30pm. ❹

Ristorante Rinuccini, 1 the Parade (☎61575), opposite the castle. Couples enjoy authentic Italian delights and romantic music in this glittering first-rate establishment. Lunch (€8-12) served daily noon-2:30pm; dinner (€13-25) served M-F 6-10:30pm, Sa 5:30-10:30pm, Su 5:30-9:30pm. ❹

The Tea Shop, Patrick St. (☎70051). Excellent little cafe in the city center where travelers grab tasty breakfasts (€6) or sip herbal teas (€1.40) before catching the bus outside. Open M-F 8:30am-6pm, Sa 10am-5pm, Su 10:30am-3pm. ❷

Italian Connection, 38 Parliament St. (☎64225). Decked out in mahogany and carnations, but not too fancy-shmancy. Lunch specials (€7.50-8.25) served noon-3pm. Dinner €9.50-23. Open daily noon-11pm. ❸

Lautrec's, 9 Kieran St. (☎62720). Glorious Italian food in a jazzy wine-cellar ambience. Pizza and pasta €8.50-14, mains €17-25. Open daily 5-11pm. ❸

M.L. Dore, High St. (☎63374). Entrance on High and Kieran St. Large, fresh deli case lures passers-by into this "nostalgia cafe", with 4 floors of old posters and wooden statues for sale. Sandwiches €3.50, light mains €7-15. Open daily 8am-11pm. ❷

PUBS

Kilkenny, "The Marble City," is also known as the "Oasis of Ireland"—its watering holes have a range of live music on most nights, especially in summer. John St. is where local youths shake their thangs, while Parliament St. offers a seemless string of traditional pubs. *Let's Go* has picked 14 of the best for an unmatchable **Kilkenny Pub Crawl.** We suggest starting the crawl at either the top of John St. or the end of Parliament St.—the former for pubbers who want to wind the night down slowly, the latter for pubbers who need a late-night fix and want to keep throwing down the Smithwick's well into the night. Alternatively, start at 3pm in the **Smithwick's Brewery** and begin the buzz on the house (tickets required, see **Sights** p. 192).

The Pump House, 26 Parliament St. (☎63924). Remains a favorite among locals and hostelers. Loud, conveniently located, and packed. Downstairs is fairly low-key; ultra-hip upstairs enclave makes you wish you packed some Prada. Pool table upstairs €1. M-Th summer trad, Su rock and blues.

Tynan's Bridge House Bar (☎21291), around the corner from the tourist office, on the river. 300 years old and still Kilkenny's most original bar. Small, with terrific atmosphere, stained glass, and old spice drawers behind the bar.

Ryan's, Friary St.(☎62281), off High St. No frills, just a good crowd and a beer garden past the rude bathroom signs. The place to be on Th for trad; Sa mongrel mix of trad, blues, and sweet, sweet soul.

Anna Conda, Parliament St. (☎71657), near Cleere's. Outstanding trad fills the pub from the low ceilings in front to the high rafters in back. Tall wooden booths and dripping candles in wine bottles add to the atmosphere. New beer garden overlooks the ducks on the Suir. W and F-Su music. No cover.

Ó'Faoláin's, John St. (☎61018). Throbbing new bar with 3 floors, a 25 ft. ceiling, and a stunning rebuilt Welsh church crafted into the walls. Late bar (W-Sa until 2:30am, Su-M until 2am) and dance club (cover €5-10) make for a great place to end the night.

Paris, Texas, High St. (☎61822). Not as cheesy as the name. Cool Parisians pack in like cattle at this popular bar; hipster cowpokes shimmy and smoke themselves a good time. Trad Tu, W, Su. Blues Th. Steaks and Tex-Mex food (€12-17) served noon-10pm.

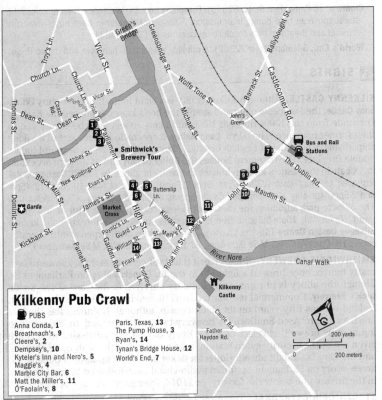

Kilkenny Pub Crawl

PUBS

Anna Conda, 1
Breathnach's, 9
Cleere's, 2
Dempsey's, 10
Kyteler's Inn and Nero's, 5
Maggie's, 4
Marble City Bar, 6
Matt the Miller's, 11
Ó'Faolaín's, 8

Paris, Texas, 13
The Pump House, 3
Ryan's, 14
Tynan's Bridge House, 12
World's End, 7

Marble City Bar, 66 High St. (☎61143). Modern pub tucked between High and Kieran St. Glowing marble countertop and occasional jazz make this an elegantly hip night-spot. Excellent meals including Asian-inspired dishes and the "joint of the day" (usually stews or roasts) for €8.

Dempsey's, 61 John St. (☎21543). Examine the musty tomes in the big bookcase. As traditional as it gets, with great €8 carvery lunches served daily noon-2:30pm.

Maggie's, Kieran St. (☎62273). Crowds bury themselves in this smoky, vaguely Gothic wine cellar. Lunch (€7.30) served noon-2:30pm. Dinner €13-20. M-Th and Sa trad, rock on summer weekends. Cover €5-7.

Matt the Miller's, 1 John St. (☎61696), at the bridge. Huge, thronged, and magnetic. Pilgrims are sucked in and forced to dance to silly Europop or a bizarre trad/reggae mix. M rock music; cover €5. Th and Sa DJ; Tu and F bands. M, W, F late bar until 2:30am.

Breathnach's Steak and Ale House, John St. (☎841 5237). New and old blend in this multi-level, multi-bar pub with a terrific grill (steaks €12.60-16). Occasional live music.

Kyteler's Inn, Kieran St. (☎21064). The oldest pub in Kilkenny and the 1324 house of Alice Kyteler, Kilkenny's witch, whose husbands (all 4) had a knack for poisoning them-selves on their 1st anniversaries. The food and drink have since become safer. Trad fills the air twice a week. F-Su fiddle away the evening at **Nero's,** a nightclub that burns down the house. Cover €8-12. Open 11pm-2am.

Cleere's, 28 Parliament St. (☎62573). Thespians from the Watergate Theatre across the street converge here during intermission. A black-box theater in back hosts vivacious musical and theatrical acts (occasional cover up to €20). Trad M.

World's End, 34 John St. (☎22302). A drinking man's pub, hardcore with music Th-Su.

☺ SIGHTS

KILKENNY CASTLE. Although Kilkenny city is a sight in itself, 13th-century ■**Kilkenny Castle,** the Parade, is plain and simply the bee's knees. It housed the Earls of Ormonde from the 1300s through 1935, and many rooms have been restored to their former opulence. The 50 yd. **Long Galley,** a spectacle reminiscent of a Viking ship, displays portraits of English bigwigs, giant tapestries, and a beautiful Italian double fireplace. The basement houses the **Butler Gallery** and its modern art exhibits. A **cafe** in the castle's kitchen houses the resident ghost. (☎21450. Castle and gallery open June-Aug. daily 9:30am-7pm; Sept. 10am-6:30pm; Oct.-Mar. 10:30am-12:45pm and 2-5pm; Apr.-May 10:30am-5pm. Castle access by guided tour only. €5, students €2.) The 52-acre **park** adjoining the castle provides excellent scenery for an afternoon jaunt. (Open daily 10am-8:30pm. Free.) Across the street, the internationally known **Kilkenny Design Centre** fills the castle's former stables with expensive Irish crafts. (☎22118. Open Apr.-Dec. M-Sa 9am-6pm, Su 10am-6pm; Jan.-Mar. M-Sa 9am-6pm.)

SMITHWICK'S BREWERY. Rumor has it that 14th-century monks, known to be a crafty bunch, once brewed a light ale in the **St. Francis Abbey** on Parliament St. Though the abbey is in ruins, their industry survives in the yard at the **Smithwick's Brewery.** Commercial use started in 1710, making it the oldest brewery in Ireland—it has fifty years on its black cousin, although Guinness has the last laugh as it purchased Smithwick's Brewery two years ago (and, to add insult to injury, now brews Budweiser on-site). Every day 50 free admission tickets are given out at the security guard station; take a right after the Watergate Theatre, and the gate is straight ahead. Collect a ticket and show up at 3pm outside the green doors on Parliament St. for an audio-visual tour, followed by **two free pints** in the private pub below the factory. (☎21014. Tours given July-Aug. M-F.)

ST. CANICE'S CATHEDRAL. Thirteenth-century St. Canice's sits up the hill off Dean St. The name "Kilkenny" itself is derived from the Irish *Cill Chainnigh,* meaning "Church of St. Canice." With an impressive wooden ceiling and expertly carved tombs, the cathedral holds out plenty of eye-candy for the wanderer. The 100 ft. **round tower** next to the cathedral was built in pre-Norman, pre-scaffolding times, and still stands tall on its 3 ft. foundation. With €2 and a bit of faith, the non-acrophobic can climb the six steep ladders to a panoramic view of the town and its surroundings. (☎64971. Open Easter-Sept. M-Sa 9am-1pm and 2-6pm, Su 2-6pm; Oct.-Easter M-Sa 10am-1pm and 2-4pm, Su 2-4pm. Cathedral entrance €3, students €1.50; round tower €2/€1.50; combined ticket €4.)

THE BLACK ABBEY. Just off Abbey St., Black Abbey was founded in 1225 and named for the habits of its Dominican friars—a row of coffins used to contain bodies struck by the Plague lie outside. Artifacts are routinely found buried around the grounds, most of which were originally hidden for fear of invaders. The heavy silence inside is probably due to the awe-inspiring, wall-sized stained-glass window depicting the 15 mysteries of the rosary. Gaze on the dark heights of nearby **St. Mary's Cathedral,** constructed during the Famine.

ROTHE HOUSE. Rothe House, Parliament St., was a Tudor merchant house when it was built in 1594, and now it's a small museum of local archaeological finds and Kilkennian curiosities, including 1850-1990 period costumes. The 15min. introductory video seems to take 15 painful hours; thankfully, it's skippable, and the museum and house are worth the visit. (☎22893. Open Apr-Oct. M-Sa 10:30am-5pm, Su 3-5pm; Nov.-Mar. Sa-Su 3-5pm. €3, students €2, children €1.)

WALKING TOUR. Travelers interested in Kilkennalia, including the down-and-dirty on folkloric tradition, take a **Tynan Walking Tour.** Besides spinning some animated yarns, the tour is the only way to see the **old city gaol.** Tours depart from the tourist office on Rose Inn St. *(☎ 087 265 1745; www.tynantours.com. 1hr. tours Apr.-Oct. M-Sa 6 per day, Su 4 per day; Nov.-Mar. Tu-Sa 3 per day. €6, students and seniors €5.)*

ENTERTAINMENT

The Kilkenny People (€1.30) is a good newsstand source for arts and music listings. **The Watergate Theatre,** Parliament St., stages drama, dance, and opera year-round. (☎ 61674. Tickets €10-20, student discounts available. Box office open M-F 10am-7pm, Sa 2-6pm, Su 1hr. before curtain.) Each August, Kilkenny holds its **Arts Festival,** which has a daily program of theater, concerts, and readings by famous European and Irish artists. (☎ 52175; www.kilkennyarts.ie. Festival Aug. 6-15, 2004. Event tickets free-€20; student and senior discounts vary by venue. Sold at the box office on the Parade next to the castle, by phone, or online. Box office open M-F 10am-6pm.) The city's population increases by more than 10,000 when the **Cat Laughs** (☎ 63837); this **festival,** held the first weekend in June, features international comedy acts. The cat in question is the Kilkenny mascot of limerick fame: "There once were two cats from Kilkenny / Each thought there was one cat too many/ So they fought and they fit / And they scratched and they bit / 'Til excepting their nails and the tips of their tails / Instead of two cats there weren't any."

SPORTS AND ACTIVITIES

Activities in and around Kilkenny are plentiful, especially for outdoors enthusiasts. The **Kilkenny Anglers Club** (☎ 65220) sets up **fishing** on the Nore and sells permits to make it legal. To **kayak** on the river Barrow, call **Go with the Flow River Adventures** (☎ 087 252 9700). Those with equestrian aspirations choose from **Grange Equine Centre** (☎ 56205) for "half-day adventure trail blazing," **Kilkenny Top Flight Equestrian Centre** (☎ 22682) to ride along the banks of the Nore, or pricier **Mount Juliet** (☎ 73044) for trail rides on a country estate. For a petrol-powered trip through the hills, call **Country ATVs** (☎ 33328) to hire a quad bike. The **Kilkenny Golf Course** (☎ 65400), out Castlecomer Rd., is an 18-hole championship course open to non-members. To watch rather than participate, see the "Fighting Cats" in a **hurling match** in Nowlan Park, near the train station (ticket info ☎ 65119; kilkenny.gaa.ie). **Horseracing** thrills fans in **Gowran Park** (☎ 26225), on the N9.

DAYTRIPS FROM KILKENNY

THOMASTOWN AND JERPOINT ABBEY

Bus Éireann stops at Jerpoint Inn in Thomastown on its way from Waterford to Kilkenny (4-7per day). The folks at the Inn have a schedule for Rapid Express (☎ 31106), a private bus running between Dublin and Tramore. Trains run through Thomastown desperately seeking Dublin (M-Sa 5 per day, Su 3 per day) and Waterford (4-5 per day). The train station is a 10min. walk out of town on Marshes Rd. Jerpoint Abbey: ☎ 24623. Open June-Sept. daily 9:30am-6:30pm; Oct. and Mar.-May 10am-5pm; Nov. 10am-4pm. €2.75.

Thomastown, a tiny community on the Nore River south of Kilkenny, is the gateway to impressive ▦**Jerpoint Abbey,** 1½ mi. away and a great afternoon trip from town. The strict Cistercian order founded Jerpoint in 1158. Though they stressed simplicity, at some point the monks cut loose and decorated their home with beautiful stone carvings of their favorite saints. The artistic trend caught on, and it seems that if it was made of stone, someone carved on it; virtually every pillar and wall is decorated with a figure. Tours discuss the life of medieval monks and give insights into the meanings behind the stonework and paintings. In town, at one end of Market St., rest the 13th-century remains of **Thomastown Church.** A trilogy of curiosities lie amongst the church's gravestones: an ancient ogham stone, a Celtic cross, and a weathered 13th-century effigy.

DUNMORE CAVE

Buggy's Coaches (☎41264) stops at the cave between Kilkenny and Castlecomer. From the drop-off point, the route is well signposted. (20min., M-Sa 8 per day, €2.50.) By car, take N78 (the Dublin-Castlecomer Rd.) from Kilkenny; the turnoff for Dunmore is on the right after the split with N77 (Durrow Rd.). ☎67726. Open June-Sept. 9:30am-7:30pm; Oct.-Nov. and Mar.-May daily 9:30am-5:30pm; Dec.-Feb. Sa-Su and holidays 9:30am-5:30pm. Last admission 1hr. before closing. €2.75, students €1.25.

Six miles north of Kilkenny on the road to **Castlecomer,** the massive, eerie **Dunmore Cave** sulks underfoot. Known affectionately as "the darkest place in Ireland," the cave has a strange history. Human bones recently unearthed from its limestone entrails show that 100 people died underground here in AD 928; whether the Vikings were involved is anyone's guess. A few years back, a couple of tourists who strayed outside the marked boundaries discovered a Viking stash of silver thread, coins, and other spoils, further confounding archeologists. Tours (35min.) available by request, point out the important stalactites and stalagmites in the caves and accompany visitors up and down all 352 steps.

CARLOW TOWN (CEATHARLACH)   ☎0503

The small, busy town of Carlow adorns the eastern side of the River Barrow on the N9 between Dublin and Waterford. Although visitors would never guess it from the town's placid demeanor, in past centuries Carlow hosted several stunningly gruesome battles between Gael and Pale. During the 1798 Rebellion, 640 Irish insurgents were ambushed in the streets; a part of the gallows from which they were hanged is on display in the county museum. The rebels were buried across the River Barrow in the gravel pits of Graiguecullen (greg-KULL-en). Today's crowds have less of the insurgent flavor about them, in part, perhaps, because Carlow's surprisingly good nightlife offerings, led by the benevolent monarchy of Dinn Ri, keep morale high.

▐ **TRANSPORTATION. Trains** run through Carlow from Dublin's Heuston Station on their way to Waterford (☎31633; 1¼hr.; M-Sa 5 per day, Su 3 per day; €15.20). The cheapest **buses** to Dublin depart from Doyle's, by the Shamrock D.I.Y.—it goes to the Custom House and back for as little as €5. **Bus Éireann** leaves from the corner of Barrack and Kennedy, in a little bus turnabout. Buses go to Athlone (2¼hr., 1 per day, €12.70); Dublin (1¾hr.; M-Sa 7 per day, Su 4 per day; €7.60); and Waterford (1¼hr.; M-Sa 7 per day, Su 6 per day; €7.60). **Rapid Express Coaches,** Barrack St. (☎43081 or 056 31106), run a Tramore-Waterford-Carlow-Dublin route (M-Sa 8-10 per day, Su 7-8 per day); they have timetables to a variety of Midland destinations at their office. For a **taxi,** call **Carlow Cab** (☎40000).

▐ ▐ **ORIENTATION AND PRACTICAL INFORMATION.** From the train station, it's a 15min. walk to the center of town; head straight down **Railway Road,** turn left onto the **Dublin Road,** and make another left at the Court House onto **College Street.** The **tourist office** is on College St., off Tullow St. behind the library. (☎31554. Open M-F 9am-1pm and 2-5pm, June-Aug. also Sa 10am-1pm and 2-5:30pm.) The **AIB** on

Tullow St. has a 24hr. **ATM** and **bureau de change**. (☎31758. Open M 10am-5pm, Tu-F 10am-4pm.) For 'net-heads, **Carlow Internet Cafe**, 3 Castle St., off Dublin St., connects for €1.50 per 15min. The **post office** officiates from the corner of Kennedy Ave. and Burrin St. (☎31773. Open M-Sa 9am-5:30pm, Tu open 9:30am.)

⌐ ◻ ☒ ACCOMMODATIONS, FOOD, AND PUBS. The **Redsetter Guesthouse ❸**, 14 Dublin St., is next to the Royal Hotel in the center of town. Look no farther for the plush sitting room and spacious, pedigreed bedrooms of a B&Ber's dreams. (☎41848. Parking available. Singles €35, with bath €40; doubles €65.) The 200-year-old Georgian **Otterholt Riverside Lodge ❶**, a hostel near the banks of the Barrow, is beginning to show its age. It's half a mile from the town center on the Kilkenny Rd.; the Kilkenny bus stops there on request. Saturday nights are popular; reserve ahead. (☎30404. Laundry €5. Dorms €15; doubles €36. **Camping** €7 per person.) For the entire entertainment experience, **Dinn Rí ❹** has nice hotel rooms above its pub and restaurant complex; a stay ensures free admission to the **nightclub**. (☎33111. Singles €48, not available F-Sa; doubles €96-120; triples €120-160.)

It's a bird, it's a plane...it's **Superquinn**, in the Carlow Shopping Centre between Tullow and Kennedy St. (☎30077. Open M-Tu and Sa 8:30am-7pm, W 8:30am-8pm, Th-F 8:30am-9pm, Su 11:30am-6pm.) Quinn faces off with **Super-Valu** on Tullow St. for grocery supremacy. (☎31263. Open M-W 9am-7pm, Th-F 9am-9pm, Sa 9am-6pm, Su 10am-6pm.) **La Napoletana ❷**, 63 Tullow St., serves piles of pasta (€8-12) at delicious prices. (☎40951. Open daily 6-11pm.) **Strada ❷**, 144 Tullow St., has a lush atmosphere and lively music to complement its exotic "world cuisine," which includes such delicacies as kangaroo (€22) alongside more traditional foodstuffs. (☎40366. Lunch €5-8, dinner mains €15-22. Open Tu-Su noon-4:30pm and W-Su 6-10pm.) The folks at **Sambodino's ❶**, on Tullow St., call themselves "the sandwich specialists," and they're not kidding—five bread choices and lots of fillings make the difference. (☎34389. Sandwiches €2-5. Open M-F 8am-5pm, Sa 9am-5pm.) **Teach Dolmain ❷** (CHOCK DOL-men), 76 Tullow St., has plates *teach*-full of award-winning grub. (☎30911. Lunch €7, dinner €9-17. Open daily noon-9pm.)

Pleasure seekers from all over Ireland come to Carlow to visit the **Dinn Rí**, an über-pub spanning the entire block between Tullow St. and Kennedy Ave., attached to the eponymous hotel (see **Accommodations**, above). It's been named Black and White Pub of the Year three of the past four years, and has plenty of seats to go around for the Sunday trad sessions. Its two nightclubs combine on Saturday nights, admitting a crowd larger than the populations of most Irish towns. Of the two, **The Foundry** is rumored to be the coolest, but **The Towers** has live music. (☎33111. Carvery lunch €6.65-7.75, served noon-2:30pm. Nightclub open F-Su until 2:30am. Cover F and Su €5, Sa €10.) The local hipsters in Carlow groove to live rock and tributes at the surprisingly large and fun ▧**Scragg's Alley**, 12 Tullow St. (☎42233. Music Su.) On Saturday nights, and summer Tuesdays and Thursdays, the music continues upstairs at the **Nexus** nightclub. **Tully's**, 149 Tullow St., pulls in the young and stylish. (☎31862. Lunch served daily 10:30am-2pm. F-Sa DJ).

◧ ▨ SIGHTS AND FESTIVALS. In the middle of a field 2½ mi. from Carlow lies the **Brownshill Dolmen.** Marking a 6000-year-old burial site, the granite capstone is the largest of its kind in Europe, tipping the scales at no fewer than 150 tons. No one has a clue how those brawny neolithic lads managed to heft it up there, though *Let's Go* is not ruling out the possibility of intergalactic assistance. Dolmen-seekers: follow Tullow St. through the traffic light and keep going straight until the roundabout pointing to Dublin. Go left, then right at the next roundabout and follow the signs. **Carlow Castle** hunkers down behind the storefronts on Castle St.; it's in serious disrepair but visitors can still walk

SOUTHEAST IRELAND

around its base and peer at the rubble. The castle's current condition can be blamed on one Dr. Middleton, who required larger windows and thinner walls. To make his modifications, he used the delicate touch of Acme dynamite. The good doctor, incidentally, was trying to make the castle into an insane asylum.

The best time to visit Carlow is during the first half of June, when the town hosts **Éigse** (AIG-sha, "gathering"), a 10-day festival of the arts. The gifted and talented from all over Ireland gather to present visual, musical, and theatrical works; only some events require tickets. For more information, check with the festival office on College St. (☎40491; www.itc-carlow.ie/eigse).

COUNTY TIPPERARY

In southern Tipperary, the towns of Clonmel, Cahir, and Cashel rest amid a sprawl of idyllic countryside and medieval ruins. The north of the county is far from the beaten tourist track, and for good reason: this fertile region has more spud farmers than visitors centers. South of the Cahir-Cashel-Tipperary triangle stretch the Comeragh, Galty, and Knockmealdown Mountains. Lismore, though located in Co. Waterford, is covered here in Co. Tipperary with the Knockmealdowns.

TIPPERARY TOWN (THIOBRAID ARANN)   ☎062

"Tipp Town," as it's affectionately known, is primarily a market town for the fertile Golden Vale farming region. Compared with the surrounding hills and the **Glen of Aherlow** to the south, Tipp Town doesn't have a particularly star-studded collection of sights. However, this doesn't stop happy Tippers from singing its praises each July during the **Pride of Tipperary Festival,** which features bands, sporting events, and old-fashioned fun.

Buses go from Tipp's **Abbey Street** to Limerick (M-Th and Sa 7 per day, F 8 per day, Su 6 per day). The **tourist office,** on Mitchell St. in the Excel Centre—a large orange building that also houses the **Interpretive Centre,** a **Family Historical Research Centre,** and a cineplex—is a useful resource for trips into the Glen and the nearby mountains. Glen of Aherlow trail maps go for €0.50. (☎51457; www.tipperary.ie. **Internet** €1 per 15min. Entrance to the Interpretive Centre €3. Open M-Sa 9:30am-5:30pm, Su 2-6pm.) **AIB** is on Main St., along with its arch-rival **Bank of Ireland.** Each has an **ATM.** (Both open M-F 10am-4pm, Th until 5pm.) The **library** on Davis St. provides **Internet**—call or stop by in advance to get on the waiting list. (☎51761. 1hr. per day €2. Open Tu and F-Sa 10am-1pm and 2-5:30pm, W 2-5:30pm and 6:30-8:30pm, Th 11am-1pm and 2-5:30pm.) The **post office** is on Davis St. (☎51190. Open M and W-F 9am-5:30pm, Tu 9:30am-5:30pm, Sa 9am-1pm.)

The Royal Hotel ❸, on Bridge St. next to the bus stop, has adequate hotel rooms at a reasonable price, all with phones, TVs, and baths. (☎33244. €40.) The attached disco, **Hunters,** fires on until 2am Friday and Saturday nights (cover €8). The aptly named **Central House B&B ❸,** 45 Main St., has a welcoming owner and free bike lockup. (☎51117. Singles €30; doubles €58.) Other B&Bs are on **Emly Road,** about ½ mi. west of town off Main St. Tipp features a **SuperValu** with entrances on Main St. (☎52930. Open M-W and Sa 8am-8pm, Th-F 8am-10pm, Su 10am-6pm.) For those seeking simple bistro fare, the bright, colorful **Shamrog ❸,** Davis St., dishes out everything from sandwiches to steaks. (☎82847. Lunch €7, dinner €9-15. Open M-Th 9am-5:30pm, F-Su 9am-8:30pm.) For a bit more elegance, try the **The Brown Trout ❸** on Bridge St., one block down from Main St., where a framed fish tank on the wall entertains diners. (☎51912. Lunch €7.50, dinner €12-17. Open daily 12:30-3pm and W-Su 6-9pm.) Enjoy how sweet it is to watch others sweat and grunt while you sit back with a Guinness and watch the game on the big screen at **Tony Lowry's**, 46 Main St., next to Central House B&B. (☎52774. Lunch served noon-3pm. Live music Th nights.) Pubbers who think they're better athletes than any up on the telly stumble across the road to **T.C. Ryan's** to prove it with a game of pool or darts. (☎52774. Su live country-western music.)

CASHEL (CAISEAL MUMHAN)   ☎062

The town of Cashel lords over green fields tucked between a series of mountain ranges on the N8, 12 mi. east of Tipp Town. Legend has it that the devil furiously hurled a rock from high above the Tipperary plains when he discovered a church was being built there. The assault failed to thwart the plucky citizens, and today the town sprawls defiantly at the base of the 300 ft. Rock of Cashel. With a splendid hostel and convenient location, Cashel is as fitting a base for the backpacker as it was for the medieval religious orders that scattered the region with ruins.

🖪🖪 TRANSPORTATION AND PRACTICAL INFORMATION. All but one of Cashel's **buses** leave from the Bake House on Main St., across from the tourist office; the Dublin bus departs from Rafferty's Travel a few doors down. **Bus Éireann** (☎061 33333) serves: Cahir (15min., 6 per day, €3.35); Cork (1½hr., 6 per day, €12); Dublin (3hr., 6 per day, €15); Limerick (1hr., 5 per day, €12). **Main Street** is where it's at—all of it except the Rock, which is up a hill and very well signposted from Main St. Cashel's **tourist office** splits rent with the **heritage center** in the City Hall on Main St. (☎61333. Open June-Sept. M-F 9am-6pm, Su 10am-6pm.) **McInerney's**, three doors from the SuperValu, **rents bikes.** (☎61225. €10 per day, €60 per wk. Open M-Sa 9:30am-6pm.) The **AIB** has an **ATM.** (Open M-F 10am-12:30pm and 1:30-4pm, Th until 5pm.) The **post office** rocks the Cashel on Main St. (☎61418. Open M-F 9am-1pm and 2-5:30pm, Sa 9am-1pm.)

🖪 ACCOMMODATIONS AND CAMPING. A 5min. walk from Cashel on Dundrum Rd., a few hundred yards from the ruins of Hore Abbey, lies the incredible 🖪**O'Brien's Farm House Hostel ❶.** O'Brien's deserves several gold stars for its incredible view of the Rock, cheerful rooms, and extremely courteous hosts. (☎61003. Full-service laundry €8-10. Dorms €15; doubles €50. Camping €7.50 per person. Free showers.) Just steps from the Rock in a quiet residential neighborhood on Dominic St., the sunny rooms of **Rockville House ❸** are a great bargain. (☎61760. Singles €35; shared rooms €25.) **Rahard Lodge ❸**, ¾ mi. up Dualla Rd. (from Main St., turn onto Friar Rd.

THE BIG SPLURGE

GLUTTONY IS NOT A SIN IN THIS CHURCH

Descend from the Rock of Cashel and dine like a corrupt bishop under the neo-Gothic ceiling of **Chez Hans.** This top-notch restaurant occupies an 1850s church, and plenty of strange history and excellent artwork seasons the award-winning food.

Unlike its famous neighbor, this church was not built by a saint, but by an irate member of the Church of Ireland who, after a serious tiff with his bishop, decided to erect a rival Methodist church in town. As an added insult, he funded his project from Church coffers, only announcing his heretical intent after the place was built. His congregation never materialized. The church was eventually sold to a local family, who used it as a bingo parlor and disco bar.

The church finally found its calling in 1968 when Hans-Peter Matthiu, a German chef, converted the building into a sanctuary for the culinary and visual arts. An eclectic mix of classical and contemporary, Irish and international, the original paintings that grace the walls rival most galleries'. The cuisine thrives on the same eclecticism, blending Italian, French, and Irish influences. Hans and his son Jason craft succulent dishes from local ingredients—meats, fresh fish, organic produce, and artisinal cheeses—with a reverence that fits the setting.

Chez Hans (☎61177), Moore Ln., Cashel. 2-course early-bird menu (€22) served Tu-F 6-7:30pm. Starters €8-15, mains €18-30. Open Tu-Sa 6-10pm.

and then left onto Dualla), is a modern farmhouse with tourist-attracting gardens and Rockin' views. (☎61052; www.rahardlodge.com. Singles €35; doubles €60-64.) **Thornbrook House ❸,** less than 1 mi. up Dualla Rd., shimmers with elegant chandeliers and sparkling bathrooms. Caring hostess Mary Kennedy has been ensuring that her guests' tea stays warm for the past 24 years. (☎62388. Singles €40, with bath €50; doubles €54-66.) If O'Brien's Hostel is booked, bunk-beds abound at the **Cashel Holiday Hostel (IHH) ❸,** on John St., just off Main St. The vertically-blessed should ask for the "Big Fellows" room, which has extra-long beds. (☎62330; www.cashelhostel.com. Laundry €7.50. Dorms €13; 4-bed ensuite rooms €16; singles €20; doubles €36.)

🝙🝙 FOOD AND PUBS. SuperValu has a large selection of groceries at its Main St. location. (☎61555. Open M-Sa 9am-9pm, Su 8am-6pm.) While waiting for the bus, enjoy decadent sweets at **The Bake House ❶,** across from the tourist office. Coffee and light meals are served in pseudo-elegance upstairs. (☎61680. Mains €4-6. Open M-Sa 8:30am-5:30pm, Su 10am-5:30pm.) The superior €8 pubmunch at **Ó'Suil-leabáin ❷** (O'Sullivan's), Main St., makes it the local lunchtime haunt. (☎61858. Food served M-F 11am-2:30pm.) Relish inexpensive soup and sandwiches at **Spearman ❶,** behind Main St., near the tourist office. (☎61143. Open M-Sa 9am-6pm.) **Pasta Milano ❸,** on Lady's Well St., has loads of affordable cuisine and flavorful wines to complement the outgoing Italian vibe and offset the garish facade. (☎62729. Pasta and pizza €8-15. Open daily noon-10:30pm.)

Cashel's pub crawl is a straight shot down Main St. Start the night at **Feehan's** (☎61929), where the atmosphere is timeless. Head left out the back door to get to **Moor Lane Tavern,** where pubbers can shoot some darts, play snooker, or bust a move. (☎62080. DJ Th-Su.) If the stars are out, move next door to the multi-level beer garden at wheelchair-accessible **Mikey Ryan's** (☎61431). Cross over Main St. for some singing, joke-telling *craic* at **Davern's** (☎61121; music M and W), and finally, end the night down the street at **Dowling's,** where bartenders make it their business to pour the best pint in town.

◙ SIGHTS. Smart visitors head to the **Heritage Center,** in the same building as the tourist office on Main St., before making the trek to **The Rock of Cashel** (see p. 198). The center features temporary exhibits and permanent installations such as "The Rock: From the 4th to 11th Century" and its much-anticipated sequel, "The Rock: 12th-18th Century." (☎62511. Open Mar.-Sept. daily 9:30am-5:30pm; Oct.-Feb. M-F 9:30am-5:30pm. Free.) The **GPA-Bolton Library,** John St., displays a musty collection of books and silver that once belonged to Theophilus Bolton, an Anglican archbishop of Cashel. The library harbors ecclesiastical texts and rare manuscripts, including a 1550 edition of Machiavelli's *Il Principe,* the first English translation of *Don Quixote,* and what is (locally) reputed to be the **smallest book in the world.** Inquire at the Heritage Center for tours. The internationally-acclaimed **◪Brú Ború Heritage Centre,** at the base of the Rock, hosts wonderful traditional music and dance. Afterwards, the musicians invite the audience to the bar for a round of informal trad. Before the show, visit the new **Sounds of History** audio-visual museum for a crash course in Irish song and dance. (☎61122. Performances mid-June to mid-Sept. Tu-Sa at 9pm. €15, with dinner €35. Center open M-F 9am-11:30pm, Sa 10:30am-11:30pm. Sounds of History display €3, students €1.) In the town of **Golden,** 5 mi. west of Cashel on the Tipperary Rd., stand the ruins of lovely **Althassel Abbey,** a 12th-century Augustinian priory founded by the Red Earl of Dunster.

◪ THE ROCK OF CASHEL. Welcome to the Rock. It looms on the horizon from miles away—that huge limestone outcropping topped with medieval buildings is the **◪Rock of Cashel,** sometimes called **St. Patrick's Rock.** The Rock is attached to a number of legends, some historically substantiated, others more dubious. St. Patrick almost certainly baptized the king of Munster here around AD 450; whether or not he accidentally stabbed the king's feet in the process is debatable. Periodic guided tours are informative, if a bit dry; exploring the buildings while in earshot of the guide is a more attractive option. The bi-steepled **Cormac's Chapel,** consecrated in 1134, holds semi-restored Romanesque paintings, disintegrating stone arches, and an ornately carved sarcophagus once thought to be the tomb of King Cormac. The 1495 burning of the **Cashel Cathedral** by the Earl of Kildare was a highlight of Cashel's illustrious history. When Henry VII demanded an explanation, Kildare replied, "I thought the Archbishop was in it." As any Brit worth his blue blood would, the King made him Lord Deputy. However, the 13th-century cathedral survived the Earl, and today's visitors wander beneath its vaulted Gothic arches. Next to the cathedral, a 90 ft. **round tower,** built circa 1101, is the oldest part of the Rock. The **museum** at the entrance to the castle complex preserves the 12th-century **St. Patrick's Cross.** A stirring film on medieval religious structures is shown every hour or so. (Rock open mid-June to mid-Sept. daily 9am-7pm; mid-Mar. to mid-June and mid-Sept. to Oct. 9am-5:30pm; Nov. to mid-Mar. 9am-4:30pm. Last admission 45min. before closing. €5, students €2, seniors €3.50.) As impressive as the Rock is during the day, it's truly inspiring by night, flooded by thousands of watts of light. The best view is from the cow path leading down from the Rock. On the other end of the path lies the wreck of **Hore Abbey,** built by Cistercian monks who were fond of arches, and presently inhabited by nonchalant sheep. The intact ceiling is quite impressive, and there are far fewer tourists to elbow out of the way. Jogging down the hill next to the Rock is the fastest route to the abbey masonry.

NEAR CASHEL: FETHARD (FIODH ARD)   ☎052

Within cycling distance from Cashel and Clonmel, and built on the River Clashawley, the tiny medieval town of Fethard is protected by an impressive intact stone wall dating from the 13th to 15th centuries. Behind the wall, the medieval **Holy Trinity Church** (not to be confused with the modern Holy Trinity Church at the opposite end of Main St.) looms over the surrounding graveyard. Pick up the key to the churchyard from the XL Stop & Shop on Main St.; the church is a block down on the left. For a peek into the church itself, talk to someone in the **Community Office** on Barrack St. (☎31000; www.fethardon-line.com), and pick up general **tourist information** and a guide to the town's sights. Another architectural sight of note is the **Town Hall** building, next to the churchyard's entrance. This nondescript building dates to the 17th century and is one of the oldest urban buildings of its type in Ireland. For those seeking medieval erotica, Fethard is also host to two **Sheela-na-gig,** bizarre 15th-century exhibitionist stone carvings of nude women doing very un-Irish things. One of the two is adjacent to the Watergate Bridge; the other is next to the **Augustine Friary,** past the gate on the far end of town. Just outside town, toward Cashel, the **Fethard Folk Museum** holds thousands of items from the 19th and early 20th centuries, including farm tools, cooking utensils, bicycles, and a horse-drawn carriage. On Sundays, hundreds of people flock to the grounds for the biggest **car boot sale** in Ireland. (☎31516. Museum and boot sale Su 11am-5pm. Museum open other times by request. €1.50, children €1.)

Just 2 mi. up the Killenuale Rd. from Fethard lie the immaculately groomed and insanely high-security grounds of **Coolmore,** the world's leading **stud farm.** Breeders from all over the world pay up to €100,000 a pop for these stellar stallions to "cover" their mares. While the grounds are not usually open to the public, those who call in advance and sound interested enough can usually get a tour of the

SOUTHEAST IRELAND

THE BIG SPLURGE

MCCARTHY'S...HOTEL?

The outrageously unique **McCarthy's Hotel** in **Fethard** was established by Richard McCarthy in the 1850's as a hotel, restaurant, liquor store, grocer, draper, hackney service, undertaker, and china shop. To the delight of many a weary traveler, the treasure behind the yellow and green facade still offers at least three of those original services. Indeed, the good folks at McCarthy's promise to "wine you, dine you, and bury you," all with the same warm, family care.

The Pub. Perhaps the biggest draw to McCarthy's (though the competition from its other services is quite deadly) is its historic Irish pub, which has served the likes of Éamon de Valera and Michael Collins. Andrew Lloyd Weber, whose castle is nearby, is a regular, and is rumored to have written an episode for the British sitcom *Blackadder* while sitting at the bar. The pub was recently featured favorably in Pete McCarthy's pub-guide, *The Road to McCarthy.*

The Restaurant(s). The surprisingly upscale but extremely popular J's Restaurant offers fresh, classic cuisine, including baked fillet of salmon with cucumber hollandaise, and a vegetarian stir-fry. (☎052 31176. Mains €16-22. Open W-Sa 6-10pm, Su 12:30-2:30pm and 6-9pm.) McCarthy's also runs G&T's Restaurant, next door, which offers tasty and reasonably priced

(cont. on next page)

grounds and marvel at the beautiful stables that would make any Manhattan studio apartment dweller weep. (☎052 31289; www.coolmore.com. Or check at McCarthy's pub—someone from the farm is almost guaranteed to be sipping a pint.)

Travelers usually flock to the **Gateway B&B ❷**, Rocklow Rd., for its sunny breakfast room, soft, welcoming beds, and gregarious owner, Paddy. (☎31701; www.gatewaybandb.com. €25-28.) For a cold pint, head down Coleen St. around the corner from the main square to the **Wishing Well** ("the Well"; ☎31053), the town's resident provider of Guinness and good cheer. **McCarthy's**, on Main St., meets all needs **(See Feature)**. **Centra**, on the continuation of Main St., sells groceries and sandwiches, and has the only **ATM** in town. (☎31383. Open daily 8am-9pm.)

CAHIR (AN CATHAIR)   ☎052

The small town of Cahir (CARE) sits on the edge of the Galty Mountains and offers the hiker decent accommodations and pub choices that make up for the limited food options. As the crossroads of the Waterford-Limerick and Dublin-Cork roads, it's a good base for the bus-reliant. Visitors enjoy the well-preserved castle and the seemingly misplaced Swiss Cottage, a nice walk from town down the River Suir.

▐ TRANSPORTATION. Trains leave from the station off the Cashel road just past the church, heading out to Limerick and Waterford (M-Sa 2 per day). **Bus Éireann** is the way to go, and runs from the tourist office to: Cashel (15min., 6-7 per day, €3.20); Cork (1½hr., 7 per day, €11.70); Dublin (3hr., 6-7 per day, €15.90); Limerick via Tipperary (1hr., 5-7 per day, €9.30); Waterford (1¼hr., 6-7 per day, €10.30). Hitchers to Dublin or Cork position themselves on N8, a 20min. hike from the center of town. Those hitching to Limerick or Waterford wait outside of town on N24, which passes through the town square. *Let's Go* does not recommend hitchhiking.

▐ PRACTICAL INFORMATION. The **tourist office** on Castle St. offers many goodies: the free *Southeast Guide*, which includes a map; *Discovery Maps* #74 and 75, which cover fantastic hill walks in the area (€7.10); *Galty Mountains Walks* (€0.50-1); and one of Ireland's best collections of postcards, not to mention a helpful staff. (☎41453. Open Mar.-Oct. M-Sa 9:30am-1pm and 2-6pm.) **AIB**, up the street (☎41735), has an **ATM;** a bit farther down, across from the Cahir House Hotel, is **Bank of Ireland.** (☎41299. Both open M-F 10am-4pm, W until 5pm.) Backpackers can take advantage of the free **luggage storage** available at the **Crock O' Gold,** across from the tourist office. The **post office** is on Church St. (☎41275. Open M-F 9:30am-1pm and 2-5:30pm, Sa 9:30am-1pm.)

ACCOMMODATIONS, FOOD, AND PUBS.

The Rectory ❸, on the Cashel road just behind the rail station, provides old-fashioned rooms in a stately manor. A family as outstanding as the one that runs these heavenly accommodations would be hard to find. (☎41406. Open May-Sept. Singles €40; doubles €55-60.) On the town square, the modest exterior of **Tinsley House B&B ❸** is a gateway into splendid, spacious, TV- and bath-equipped rooms. The elegant sitting room has an incongruous foosball table. Proprietor Liam Roche is an encyclopedia of local history. (☎41947. Singles €40; doubles €60.) There are two hostels relatively close to Cahir. **Lisakyle Hostel (IHH) ❶,** 1 mi. south on Ardfinnan Rd., is the more accessible; from the bus station, walk up the hill and make a right at Cahir House Hotel. The exterior is bedecked with flowers, and the rooms are rustic but adequate. Gregarious owner Morris does pick-up service from the bus or train. (☎41963. 6- to 8-bed dorms €12. Private rooms €16-17. **Camping** €7.) **The Kilcoran Farm Hostel (IHH) ❶** offers an education in rural living, hosted by a garrulous chorus of sheep. From Cahir, either call for pickup or take the Cork road for 4 mi., turn left at the Top Petrol Station, and after ¼ mi., make a right at the T-shaped junction. This 25-acre organic farm at the foot of the mountains has no bunk beds and no breakfast, but there is a playground for the kids. Ask about **work opportunities.** (☎41906 or 086 344 9406; call ahead. €13.)

For groceries, try **SuperValu,** on Bridge St. across the bridge from the castle. (☎41515. Open M-W 8:30am-6:30pm, Th 8:30am-8pm, F 8:30am-9pm, Sa 8:30am-7pm, Su 9am-1pm.) The **Galtee Inn ❸,** the Square, is a local favorite. Lunches are small and cheap (€8.50), but dinners swell in size and price, up to €11-23. (☎41247. Food served M-Sa until 10pm, Su until 9:30pm.) **La Serenata ❷,** Church St., invites hungry travelers into its stone walls with the delicious smell of fresh pizza and pasta. (☎45689. Mains €8-10. Open M-F noon-10pm, Su 1-10pm.) The **Castle Arms ❷,** Castle St., serves cheap chow in an atmosphere that could only be called "pub." Expect an older crowd at night. (☎42506. Mains around €8. Food served daily 10:30am-3pm.) Next door, **Irwin's,** an old fashioned pint-puller, has cheap sandwiches (€4) and a rowdier crowd during the day than at night. Cannons once aimed toward the castle from the site of **J. Morrissey's,** Castle St.—these days sieges are staged around the bar. (☎42120. W trad.)

SIGHTS.

Cahir's most famous landmark is **Cahir Castle.** It's exactly what every romantic envisions a castle to be—heavy on the battlements and decked out in a vibrant palette of grays. Perhaps this is why it was deemed the ideal site for the 1981 flick *Excalibur*. Built in the 13th century to

sandwiches, pastries, and full meals. (☎052 32050. Mains €5-12. Open M-Sa 9am-6pm.)

The Undertaker. Perfect for when you've had just a little too much to eat and drink. Services provided by the undertaker include the funeral home, hearse and casket, coordination with the clergy, arrangement of death notices, preparation of the deceased for viewing, cremation, grave site preparation, repatriation to or from Ireland, and catering. Contact Annette McCarthy or Vincent Murphy ☎052 31149.

The multi-talented owners are also world-class **jockeys,** and horse-racing fans the likes of George Foreman have stopped in for a pint to chat with the owners. Not surprisingly, with all the drunk and dead people floating around, McCarthy's also supposedly houses one or two resident **ghosts**— talk about *hidden* deal. Strangely enough, we still haven't figured out where the *hotel* part of McCarthy's Hotel comes in. Either way, it's a fabulous deal, though you hopefully won't have to take advantage of *all* their services any time soon.

McCarthy's Hotel, 2 Main St., Fethard (mccarthyshotel.com).

be all but impregnable to military attack, the castle's defenses couldn't hold out after the implementation of gunpowder. In 1599, the Earl of Essex forced its surrender by lobbing a few cannonballs its way, one of which is still visibly stuck in the wall. Note the 11,000-year-old preserved head of the long-extinct Irish Elk; the noble beast's antlers span just about the whole wall. (☎41011. Open mid-June to mid-Sept. daily 9am-7pm; mid-Sept. to mid-Oct. and Apr. to mid-June 9:30am-5:30pm; mid-Oct. to Mar. 9:30am-4:30pm. Last admission 30min. before closing. 30min. tours and 15min. audio-visual presentation. €2.75, students €1.25.)

The broad **River Suir** that flows into Waterford Harbour is but a wee stream in Cahir. A wild, verdant **river walk** starts at the tourist office and leads past the 19th-century **Swiss Cottage,** a ½ mi. walk from town. A charming jumble of architectural styles, the cottage was built so that occupants of Cahir Castle could fish, hunt, and pretend to be peasants. Gorgeously restored, with an incredibly thick, undulating thatched roof, it is a delight for anyone who fancies building, decorating, or being fabulously rich. (☎41944. Open mid-Apr. to mid-Oct. daily 10am-6pm; mid-Mar. to mid-Apr. Tu-Su 10am-1pm and 2-6pm; mid-Oct. to mid-Nov. Tu-Su 10am-1pm and 2-4:30pm. Last admission 45min. before closing. €2.50, students €1.30, seniors €1.90.) **Fishing** opportunities line the river walk past the Swiss Cottage. Fishing licenses (€20 per day) are the first step, and can be obtained at the Heritage Cornerstone on Church St., right on the town square. (☎42730. Open daily 7am-11pm.)

The **Mitchelstown Caves** are 8 mi. off the Cork road, halfway between Cahir and Mitchelstown in the hamlet of **Burncourt.** Ask the bus driver on the Cork bus to stop at the caves; it's a 2 mi. walk from the N8. A 30min. tour journeys deep into a series of rippled subterranean chambers filled with fantastic mineral formations. (☎67246. Open daily 10am-6pm; last tour 5:30pm. €4.50.)

NEAR CAHIR: GALTY MOUNTAINS AND GLEN OF AHERLOW

South of Tipperary Town, the river **Aherlow** cuts through a richly scenic valley called the Glen of Aherlow. West of Cahir, the **Galty Mountains** rise abruptly along the southern edge of the Glen. The purple-tinted, lake-studded range boasts **Galty-more Mountain** (3018 ft.), Ireland's third-highest peak. The Glen and mountains are ideal settings for both picnicking and full-fledged trekking. Serious hikers should invest in #66 and 74 of the *Ordnance Survey Discovery Series*, available at tourist offices and bookstores in Tipperary and Cahir (€6.60). The Tipp Town tourist office sells a series of trail maps of varying difficulty (€1). **Glenbarra** is also a popular base camp, reached by driving west from Cahir toward Mitchelstown. Call the **Glen of Aherlow Info Point** (☎062 56331) for detailed information on the area.

Dedicated hikers make the 10 mi. sojourn across the mountains to the **Mountain Lodge (An Óige/HI) ❶** in Burncourt, a gas-lit, Georgian hunting lodge in the middle of the woods. From Cahir, follow the Mitchelstown road (N8) for 8 mi., turn right at the sign, and continue another 2 mi. on the unpaved path. (☎052 67277. June-Sept. €12, under 18 €10.) The **Kilcoran Farm Hostel** is a convenient stop on the hike back. (☎052 41906. See **Cahir,** p. 200.) The staff of the **Ballinacourty House ❶,** an excellent campsite in the Aherlow valley, provides detailed information on the Glen. (☎062 56230. Meals and cooking facilities available. Open Easter to Sept. €2 per adult, €1 per child. €10-11.50 per tent.) They also operate a pricey **restaurant** and a pleasant **B&B ❹.** (Dinners €30. Singles €40; doubles with bath €56-60.) To reach Ballinacourty House, take R663 off the Cahir-Tipperary road (N24) in **Ban-sha** and follow it for 8 mi. to the signposted turnoff. Newly opened **Glen of Aherlow Caravan and Camping Park,** on R663 between Bansha and Lisvernane, lets the weary traveler pitch a tent and do some laundry. (☎062 56555; www.tipperarycamp-ing.com. €3 per adult. €10 per tent. Electricity €2. Free showers.)

CLONMEL (CLUAIN MEALA) ☎052

This medieval town on the banks of the River Suir (SURE) sweetens in the fall, when locally-produced Bulmer's Cider infuses the air with hints of apple. As Co. Tipperary's economic hub, Clonmel offers visitors returning from a day in the Comeragh Mountains all the comforts of modern life.

▐ TRANSPORTATION

Trains: Prior Park Rd. (☎21982), less than 1 mi. north of the town center. Trains chug to: **Limerick** (50min., M-Sa 2 per day, €12) and **Waterford** en route to **Rosslare Harbour** (1¼hr., M-Sa 1 per day, €8.20).

Buses: Bus info is available at the tourist office and train station. Coaches leave from in front of the train station to: **Cork** (2hr., 3-4 per day, €12.10); **Dublin** (3¼hr., 4-6 per day, €10.50); **Galway** (3¾hr., 4-6 per day, €15.80); **Kilkenny** via **Carrick-on-Suir** (5 per day, €6); **Limerick** via **Tipperary** (5-7 per day, €7.35); **Rosslare** (3½hr., 2-3 per day, €13.30); **Waterford** (1hr., 6-8 per day, €7.85). **Rapid Express** (☎29292) also runs their own bus to **Dublin** via **Kilkenny** (3hr.; M-Sa 3-4 per day, Su 2 per day; €8).

◄▮ ▐ ORIENTATION AND PRACTICAL INFORMATION

Clonmel's central street runs parallel to the **Suir River.** From the station, follow **Prior Park Road** straight into town. Prior Park Rd. becomes businesslike **Gladstone Street,** which intersects the main drag, known successively as **O'Connell, Mitchell,** and **Parnell Street,** and then **Irishtown. Sarsfield Street** is the continuation of Gladstone St., and **Abbey Street** runs off the main street toward the riverside quays.

Tourist Office: Sarsfield St. (☎22960), across from Clonmel Arms Hostel. Pick up the 6 self-guided walking tours of the Knockmealdown Mountains (€1) or the free Heritage Trail map. Open M-F 9:30am-5:30pm.

Banks: AIB (☎22500) and **Bank of Ireland** (☎21425) are neighbors on O'Connell St. Both have **ATMs** and are open M 10am-5pm, Tu-F 10am-4pm.

Pharmacy: Joy's, Market Pl. (☎29202). Open M-W and Sa 9am-6pm, Th-F 9am-9pm.

Emergency: ☎999; no coins required. **Police** (*Garda*): Emmet St. (☎22222).

Hospital: St. Joseph's and St. Michael's, Western Rd. (☎21900).

Internet: Circles, 16 Market St. (☎23315). Snooker club (€6 per hr.) and Internet cafe (€0.1 per min., €5.70 per hr.) all in one. Open daily 11am-11pm. The **library,** Emmet St. (☎24545), provides web access in 50min. slots (€2). Open M-Tu 10am-5pm, W-Th 10am-8:30pm, F-Sa 10am-1pm and 2-5pm.

Post Office: Emmet St. (☎21164), by the library. Open M-F 9am-5:30pm, Sa 9am-1pm.

Work Opportunities: Employment Services, 2-3 Emmett St. (☎23486), has listings for work opportunities and training. Open M-F 9am-1pm and 2-5pm, closes F at 4:45pm.

▐ ACCOMMODATIONS AND CAMPING

Clonmel caters to the hotel and B&B crowd, and is not the most backpacker-friendly town. The area along the Cahir road past Irishtown is dotted with B&Bs, which run about €28-45. Budget options multiply a mile or two from town.

Brighton House, 1 Brighton Pl. (☎23665; www.tipp.ie/brighton.htm). From the train/bus station, walk toward town—it's on the left at the 1st set of lights. From town, walk out Gladstone St. This elegant 1823 Georgian guest house has beautiful rooms and a garden with a working well. Singles €35-40; doubles €70-100. ❸

Riverside House, New Quay (☎25781). Close to downtown, guests watch swans swim by from the large windows of their expansive rooms. This stately house has been overlooking the Suir for more than a century. TVs in every room. €25. ❸

Trasses (☎41459; www.theapplefarm.com). An apple farm turned campsite halfway between Clonmel and Cahir on the N24. Mid-June to Sept. €5 per person, €3 per child; May to mid-June €4.50/2.50. Electricity for caravans €2. Free showers. ❶

Powers-the-Pot Camping & Caravan Park, Harney's Cross (☎23085). Well outside town. Follow Parnell St. east out of town, turn right at the 1st traffic light (not N24), cross the Suir, and continue for 5½ mi. of arduous mountain road to the signposted turnoff. Only camping is available while renovations are under way on their hostel. Owners Niall and Jo can answer all hillwalking questions and provide maps and guides for the Munster Way. 2-person tent €11; each additional adult €3, child €1.50. ❶

FOOD

Massive **SuperQuinn** lords over Market Pl., basking in supermarket glory. (☎27222. Open M-Tu and Sa 8:30am-7pm, W 8:30am-8pm, Th-F 8:30am-9pm, Su 11am-6pm.) ▓**The Honey Pot,** 14 Abbey St., avoids all that plastic packaging and sells health foods, bulk grains, organic veggies, and exquisite "free-trade" crafts from co-ops in India and Nepal. (☎21457. Open M-F 9:30am-6pm, Sa 9am-6pm.)

▓ **Niamh's** (NEEVS), Mitchell St. (☎25698), at Gladstone St. Specialty coffees, hot lunches, sandwiches, and all-day brekkie (delicious meatless sausage option available) in a bustling deli-style restaurant. Menu also caters to specific diets. Breakfast €4-6.70, sandwiches €3.55-6.50. Open M-F 9am-5:45pm, Sa 9am-5pm. ❷

Angela's Restaurant and Coffee Emporium, Abbey St. (☎26899), off Mitchell St. Remarkably fresh and boldly creative. Fruit smoothies are an unexpected treat. Sandwiches and specials €5-7.60. Open M-Sa 9am-5:30pm. ❷

O Tuamas Cafe, 5-6 Market Pl. (☎27170). A filling meal, hot or cold (under €9), in a brightly-colored, upbeat environment. Finish with a mouthwatering dessert. Open M-Th 8:30am-5:30pm, F 8:30am-8pm, Sa 9am-5:30pm. ❷

Catalpa, Sarsfield St. (☎26821), next to the tourist office. Italian feasts in a former bank vault. Popular with the locals; call ahead. Pizza and pasta €6-10, meat dishes €9.50-18. Open Tu-Su 12:30-2:30pm and 6:30-11:30pm. ❸

Tom Skinny's Pizza Parlor, Market St. (☎26006). Specializes in the very un-skinny delicacies of pizza—made fresh before your eyes—and ice-cream. Glorious aromas, a shiny jukebox, and a portrait of Marilyn Monroe make this a scrumdiddlyumptious stop. Pizzas €4.50-13.50. Open M-W 12:30-11pm, Th-Su 12:30pm-12:30am. ❷

PUBS

For entertainment listings, check the *Nationalist* (€1.30) at newsagents or pick up a free copy of *South*, which lists local events, including pub happenings.

John Allen's (☎21261), next to St. Mary's in Irishtown. Surprisingly spacious and bright; lures a jolly all-ages crowd. Full meals (€8.50) served M-Sa noon-6pm. Sa trad.

Mulcahy's, 47 Gladstone (☎25054). Enormous and elaborate, with a curious combination of decorative themes and a whole lotta snooker tables. W night trad. Th-Su hosts **Danno's,** an 18+ disco. Cover €4-8.

Barry's, O'Connell St. (☎25505). A classic, popular hangout. Check out Tom Ryan's framed jersey from the 1962 All-Ireland hurling championship. Tom still stops by sometimes for a pint. **Cosmo,** the disco upstairs, rocks Th-Su 11pm-3am. Cover €7-10.

⊙ SIGHTS

The Heritage Trail map, free at the tourist office, point pedestrians to a good time in Clonmel. Stops along the way include the **West Gate** (at the western end of O'Connell St.), an 1831 reproduction of the medieval gate that separated Irishtown from the more prosperous Anglo-Norman area. The 84 ft. octagonal tower of **Old St. Mary's Church**, Mary St., stands near the remnants of the town wall that failed to resist Cromwell's advances in 1650. Just inside the door of the **Franciscan Friary** on Abbey St. are the 15th-century tomb effigies of a knight and lady of the Butler family. Clonmel's history as a transport hub is celebrated at the ⊠**Museum of Transport,** off Emmett St., in a converted mill packed to the ceiling with antique cars and classic road signs. (☎29727. Open June-Aug. M-Sa 10am-6pm, Su 2:30-6pm; Oct.-May closed Su. €3.50, children €2.) The **Tipperary S.R. County Museum,** the Borstan, behind the library, tells of the county's history since the Stone Age and hosts small traveling exhibitions. (☎25399. Open Tu-Sa 10am-5pm. Free.) The tourist office's glossy leaflets *Clonmel Walk* #1 and 2 describe several **walks** in the area and nearby **Nire Valley.** See **Comeragh Mountains** (below) for day hike info.

THE EAST MUNSTER WAY

The East Munster Way begins as a gentle footpath through the lowland hills of **Carrick-on-Suir, Kilsheelan,** and **Clonmel,** and extends to a perch on the **Comeragh Mountains,** then runs full-force into the **Knockmealdowns,** ending 43 mi. later in **Clogheen.** Walkers pass a variety of tranquil scenes along the way, including the **Kilsheelan Woods,** the glistening River Suir, and the impressive vistas in the Comeragh Mountains. In Clogheen, ambitious hikers can follow the **Druhallow Way,** which connects with the **Kerry Way** (see p. 282), or take **Blackwater Way** into isolated Araglin Valley.

The best maps to use are #74 and 75 of the *Ordnance Survey Discovery Series.* The *East Munster Way Map Guide* (€6.20), available at the tourist office in Clonmel, provides a written guide and an accurate but less detailed map—though it does point out all the pubs along the way. For specific information on the East Munster Way, contact the Tipperary Co. Council in Clonmel (☎052 25399); **Powers-the-Pot Campground** (see p. 203) is the best bet for information on hikes in the Comeragh and Knockmealdown Mountains.

◪ THE COMERAGH MOUNTAINS

The only sierra mountains in Ireland, the Comeraghs are distinctly wave-shaped, which means that they vary greatly in difficulty depending on the direction of approach. The terrain ranges from perpetually soft and wet to exciting and difficult areas like the rocky *coums.* Irish for "mountain hollows," *coums* often house lakes. (The Welsh equivalent is *cwms,* which Scrabble buffs will recognize as the only word in the English language without a vowel.)

The Comeragh terrain includes marshy plateaus that are manageable for city folk in sneakers. *Nire Valley Walks* #1 through 12 (€1 each, at the Clonmel tourist office and Powers-the-Pot) are excellent waterproof maps illustrating fairly easy 2-4hr. day hikes from Clonmel. More challenging treks can also be found in this region. One such option begins from Powers-the-Pot, ½ mi. off the Munster Way (see **Clonmel,** p. 203). With the *Ordnance Survey #75* in hand, head east from the campsite and follow the ridges south. The land is mostly open and it's relatively hard to get lost in good weather, but be sure someone knows you're out there. Guided walking is also available; ask Niall at Powers-the-Pot (☎052 23085).

⚑ THE KNOCKMEALDOWN MOUNTAINS

The Knockmealdown Mountains are a stunning collection of roughly contoured summits straddling the Tipperary-Waterford border 12 mi. south of Cahir. *Knockmealdown Walks* #1-4 (€1 each) are available at local tourist offices, including those in Clonmel and Clogheen. All four start at Clogheen; walks #2 and 4 leave from the nearby carparks. Many hikers prefer to begin in the town of **Newcastle,** where tiny but locally renowned **Nugent's Pub** stands. For guided **tours,** contact Helen McGrath—her tours depart at noon on Sundays from the Newcastle Carpark. (☎052 36359. €5-8. M-Sa tours available by request.) One sight of particular interest is the spectacular **Vee Road,** which runs south from Clogheen to the **Knockmealdown Gap,** erupting with purple rhododendrons in May and June. Just before the Vee Rd., in the town of **Graigue,** thirsty pilgrims can stop in at thatch-roofed **Ryan's Pub,** a charming little building in the middle of a farmyard. At the mountain pass about two-thirds of the way up the Gap, pines give way to heather and bracken, and a parking lot marks the path up **Sugarloaf Hill.** This walk, roughly 1hr. long, challenges hikers to describe the landscape without using the words "patchwork" or "quilt." From there, you can continue on to the **Knockmealdown Peak,** the highest in the range (2609 ft.). The road back down to Lismore passes the beautiful (and supposedly bottomless) **Bay Loch.**

The affable and decidedly unofficious **tourist office** in Clogheen, across from the turnoff for the Vee Road, serves generous portions of maps with a side of local lore. (☎052 65258. Open M-Sa 9am-5pm.) **Parsons Green,** 5min. from the village on the Cahir road, is a garden-campsite-activity center medley, offering **river walks, boating trips,** and **pony rides.** (☎052 65290; www.clogheen.com. Pony rides €1 per person. **Camping** €2.60 per person, €1.30 per child; €5 per small tent, €6.50 per family tent. Laundry €6. Free showers.)

LISMORE (LIOS MÓR)   ☎058

Lismore's incongruously grand castle and glorious cathedral remind visitors that the sleepy little town was once a thriving monastic center. Although it sits next to the Blackwater River in Co. Waterford, Lismore is included here because it makes a convenient base for exploring Co. Tipperary's Knockmealdown Mountains.

⬛⬛ TRANSPORTATION AND PRACTICAL INFORMATION. Bus Éireann stops across from the tourist office and runs to Cork (1¼hr., F 1 per day, €9.30) and Waterford via Dungarvan (1¼hr., M-Sa 1 per day, €10.20). A particularly nice way to reach Lismore from Clogheen is via the Vee Road. Hitchers wishing to get to Cork ride east to **Fermoy,** then south on N8. Hitching to Dungarvan is also common, but never recommended by *Let's Go.* The eager-to-please **tourist office** and the **heritage center** share the old courthouse building. (☎54975. Both open June-Aug. M-F 9am-5pm, Sa 10am-5:30pm, Su noon-5:30pm; Apr.-May and Sept.-Oct. M-F 9:30am-5:30pm.) **Free Internet** is available at the **library** on Main St. (Open M, W, and F 11:30am-1pm and 2-6pm, Tu and F 1-4:30pm and 5:30-8pm.) The **post office** is located on E. Main St. (☎54220. Open M-F 9am-1pm and 2-5:30pm, Sa 9am-1pm.)

⬛⬛⬛ ACCOMMODATIONS, FOOD, AND PUBS. Accommodations in Lismore are sparse, but warm B&Bs can be found on either side of the town with a little insider information from the tourist office. From the tourist office, take a right at the statue and head up Main St. out of town to reach **Beechcroft ❸** (☎54273) and **Silver Birches ❸** (☎53405), both with gorgeous wood floors and electric blankets, part of the friendly Power family's ever-expanding accommodations estate. (Singles €30-35; doubles €60.) On the other side of town (head left from the tourist office and left at the fork in the road), **Pine Tree House ❸** is run by a welcoming family and has an expansive front lawn and a horse in the attached paddock. Oh, and rooms for rent. (☎53282. Singles €33-36; doubles €55-57.)

Food in Lismore is tasty, but not exactly plentiful. **Roches** on E. Main St. has groceries. (☎54122. Open M-W 9am-6pm, Th 9am-7:30pm, F 9am-8pm, Sa 9am-8:30pm, Su 10am-6pm.) ▧**Eamonn's Place ❸**, E. Main St., is *the* place to be, serving tasty meals in a gorgeous beer garden. Try the chicken Maryland with banana and pineapple (€10) or the fish specials snagged right out of the Blackwater. (☎54025. Lunch from €7, served Th-Tu 12:30-2:30pm; dinners €10-14, served Th-Tu 6-9pm.) **Madden's Bar,** E. Main St., serves soup and sandwiches at reasonable prices, and many a pint, accompanied by the refined Mr. Billy Hogan on the piano. (☎54148. Lunch €3.50, served M-F 12:30-2:30pm.)

▣ **SIGHTS.** Stunning **Lismore Castle** looms over the Blackwater River, swathed in foliage and aristocratic grandeur. Once a medieval fort, then a bishop's residence, the building was also home to Sir Walter Raleigh and the birthplace of 17th-century science guy Robert Boyle (of PV=nRT fame). Remodeled with great imagination in the 19th century, the castle is now privately owned by the English Duke of Devonshire, who sometimes takes in guests for an estimated €25,000 per week (yeah, that's a ❺). In 1814, the Lismore Crozier and the *Book of Lismore*, priceless artifacts thought to have been lost forever, were found hidden in the castle walls. Visitors can tour the **gardens,** or just scamper across the bridge for a free peek. (☎54424. Open mid-Apr. to Sept. daily 11am-4:45pm. Garden tours €5, children under 16 €2.50.) The bridge is also the starting point for peaceful **Lady Louisa's Walk** which runs along the tree-lined Blackwater.

Locals claim that a secret passage connects the castle to **St. Carthage's Cathedral,** on Deanery Hill. A number of tombs in the cathedral's ancient graveyard are sealed with heavy stone slabs, relics of Lismore's past as a hotspot for body-snatching. The cathedral did a better job of retaining historical markers—a collection of 9th- and 10th-century engraved commemorative stones are set into one of its walls. Lismore's **heritage center,** housed with the tourist office in the town square, includes a 30min. video presentation and a cursory exhibit highlighting the 1000-year-old *Book of Lismore.* A new science room is dedicated to the life and works of Robert Boyle. (☎54975. Open June-Aug. M-F 9am-6pm, Sa 10am-5:30pm, Su noon-5:30pm; Apr.-May and Sept.-Oct. M-Sa 9:30am-5:30pm. €4, seniors and students €3.50.) The center also runs **guided tours** of town (€6) and sells self-guided tour booklets (€2). Two miles from Lismore is a carpark for the **Towerswalk,** beloved by many a local. From the castle, cross the bridge and turn left; Towerswalk will be on the right after 3 mi. Keily-Ussher, a local landlord in the mid-1800s, began the tower and entrance gate to what was to be a grand castle; today the woodsy, 1hr. walk runs to "the Folly."

COUNTIES WEXFORD AND WATERFORD

Wexford and Waterford may be a little too welcoming for their own good—Ireland's invaders, from Vikings to Christians to modern backpackers, have all tended to begin their island-conquering here. Away from the salty pubs and crowded streets of Wexford Town, beaches stretch thin in dismal, highly trafficked Rosslare and pop up again at the county's southwest edge, along idyllic Waterford Harbour. Waterford City is the commercial and cultural core of the

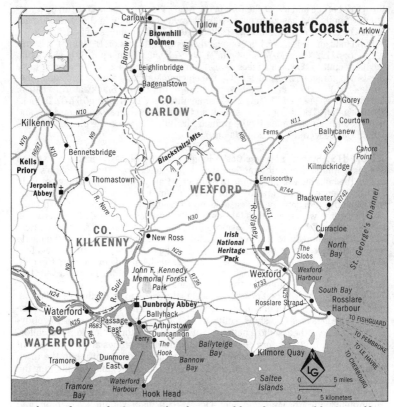

southeast, famous for its crystal and seasoned by a long, proud heritage. New Ross, with its fine hostels and urban amenities, is a good base for exploring the southeast. **Slí Charman** (SHLEE KAR-man), usually referred to as "An Slí," is a pathway that runs 135 mi. along Co. Wexford's coast, from the Co. Wicklow border, through Wexford and Rosslare, all the way to Waterford Harbour. Major roads in the region are the east-west N25 (Rosslare-Waterford), the north-south N11 (Wexford-Dublin), and the N79 (Enniscorthy-New Ross).

ENNISCORTHY (INIS COIRTHAIDTH) ☎054

Fourteen miles north of Wexford, the handsome town of Enniscorthy lies among the hills that surround the River Slaney. The town takes great pride in its part in the nationalist struggle—mention the year '98 to locals, and they'll think of the Rebellion of 1798, when a local priest led an uprising at nearby Vinegar Hill and held the British at bay for 12 days (see **Rebellion,** p. 61). A sparkling new museum has been built specifically to chronicle the events of 1798. Hot-headed Enniscorthy was also one of the only towns to join Dublin in the 1916 Easter Rising, and it was the last to surrender (see p. 63). Nowadays, modern Enniscortians channel their rebellious natures into more musical pursuits, filling pubs with raucous music during their two largest festivals, the Strawberry Festival and the Blues Festival, and whenever the mood strikes during the year.

TRANSPORTATION. N11 passes through Enniscorthy, heading south to Wexford and north to Arklow, Wicklow, and Dublin. **Trains** run to: Dublin (2½hr., 3 per day, €15.50) and Rosslare (50min., 3 per day, €10). **Buses** stop outside the Bus Stop Shop on Shannon Quay (between the 2 bridges and across the river from the Squares) on their way north to Dublin via Ferns (5-7 per day, €12.70), and south to Waterford (8-10 per day, €12.70) and Wexford (9-12 per day, €4.70). For **taxis,** call ☎37222, 33975, 36666, or 37888.

ORIENTATION AND PRACTICAL INFORMATION. From the railway station, take Templeshannon and cross the River Slaney into the center of town; turn left for **Abbey Square,** one of the main shopping areas, or continue uphill to bustling **Market Square.** A few brochures in the **Wexford County Museum** in the castle are all that remain of the **tourist office.** For further Enniscorthian lore, and a free monthly *Events Guide*, see the divine Maura Flannery in **Castle Hill Crafts,** 4 Castle Hill. (☎36800.) Several banks have 24hr. **ATMs,** among them **AIB** (☎33163; open M 10am-5pm, Tu-F 10am-4pm) and **Irish Permanent Bank,** Market Sq. (☎35700; open M-F 9:30am-5pm, W open 10:15am). A **post office** is by the Abbey Sq. roundabout (☎33226; Open M-F 9am-5pm, Sa 9am-1pm.). Next to the post office is **Enniscorthy Cleaners,** for all laundry needs. (☎36466. Open M-Sa 8am-6pm.) The **Afrocorthy Centre,** Temple Shannon, next to the movie theater, has **Internet** for €2.50 per hr. and African foodstaples. (☎37675. Open M-F 10am-11pm, Sa-Su 11am-11pm.)

ACCOMMODATIONS. Valeview Farmhouse ❸, adjacent to Ringwood Park, is a delightful, modern farm bungalow 1½ mi. out of town on Slaney Dr. Tea or coffee, homemade treats by the chef/owner (who also make dinner for €25-30), and snuggly electric blankets await in winter. (☎35262. €25-30.) At **Adelmar ❷,** Summerhill, Mrs. Agnes Barry's hospitality and delightful company do the trick. Take the N11 toward Dublin, take a left at the Shell station, and follow the signs. (☎33668. Open June-Oct. €23.) Between Market Sq. and the cathedral is **Mrs. Maura Murphy's B&B ❸,** 9 Main St., directly above P.J. Murphy's Pub. The rooms are cozy and the guest sitting-room is full of plump cushions. (☎33522. €25 per person sharing; singles €26.) The **Old Bridge House ❹** is well located, next to the Old Bridge on Slaney Place. Large, eclectically furnished rooms, friendly proprietors, and a river view compensate for occasionally noisy traffic. (☎34222. €30.)

FOOD AND PUBS. Caulfield's SuperValu, in the shopping center on Mill Park Rd. at the Abbey St. Roundabout, sells groceries and small edibles. (☎34541. Open M-W and Sa 8am-8pm, Th 8am-9pm, F 8am-10pm, Su 10am-6pm.) Universally known as the best place in town, **Galo Chargrill ❸,** 19 Main St., across from P.J. Murphy's Pub, serves fresh and exquisitely grilled meats and veggies. The relaxed, unpretentious atmosphere of this Portuguese restaurant makes it incredibly popular; reservations are essential on the weekends. Corn on the cob appetizer (€4.50) is grilled to perfection, and kebabs hang tantalizingly over the plates. (☎38077. Mains €11-17. Open Tu-Su noon-3pm and 5:30-10pm.) For delicious meals and piping-hot homemade baked goods, head to **Cozy Kitchen ❷,** at 11 Rafter St., where hot scones and tea make cheap and filling starts to the morning. (☎36488. Bakery items around €2; most mains €4-6. Open M-Sa 9am-6pm.) Just down the hill from the castle, **Argh Tandoori ❸** launches a taste revolution with its authentic and reasonably priced Indian food. (☎43922. Mains €12-15. Open Su-W 5-11:30pm, Th-Sa 5pm-midnight.) **The Antique Tavern,** 14 Slaney St., lives up to its name, with Enniscorthy artifacts

SOUTHEAST IRELAND

and worldwide antiques, gifts from devoted patrons. (☎33428. Open M-W 10:30am-11:30pm, Th-Sa 10:30am-12:30am, Su noon-11:30pm; bar menu noon-3:30pm.) With more room and live music on Wednesdays, **Rackards,** 23 Rafter St., is among the hippest spots in town. A zesty, vegetarian-friendly lunch is served from noon to 3pm. (☎33747. Open M-W 10am-11:30pm, Th-Sa 10:30am-12:30am, Su 10am-11pm.) **Shenanigan's** is the mischievous youngster in Market Sq. Munch grub and check out the mosaics. (Late bar Th-Sa; disco Th-F.)

🖸 🎿 **SIGHTS AND FESTIVALS.** The **National 1798 Visitor Centre,** a 5min. walk from town on Mill Park Rd., is an impressive multimedia barrage examining the Rebellion of 1798 and the Battle of Vinegar Hill. One room presents the conflict as a chess problem with larger-than-life pieces. There's also a 14min. film with all the battle violence one could want. (☎37596; www.1798centre.com. Open M-Sa 9:30am-6pm, Su 11am-6pm.) If you're up for a 2½ mi. walk (or drive), head across the river to the summit of **Vinegar Hill** itself—the site offers a fantastic battle's-eye view of the town below. For a more intimate perspective, Maura Flannery's **Walking Tour of Enniscorthy** can't be beat. The 1hr. trek reveals the dirty little secrets of the town's past. Find out about the time, in 1649, when Enniscorthy women got Cromwell's soldiers drunk and killed them; or learn why, after flagrantly kissing up to Queen Elizabeth with *The Faerie Queene,* poet Edmund Spenser declined her offer of the local castle. (☎36800. Call a day ahead to reserve a tour. Offered in English or French; check to see if tours are already scheduled. €4, children €2.)

The **Wexford County Museum** fills the bulk of the **Norman Castle** on Castle Hill, chronicling Wexford's collective stream of consciousness and exhibiting oddities donated by various county citizens. The rooms display the original letters and belongings of principal players in the Rebellions, both 1798 and 1916. Since the museum's sad days as a 13-object display back in 1960, the curators have stuffed it from dungeon to eaves with odd bits like ship figureheads and a collection of international police patches. Don't miss the bicycle display on the third floor or the circa 1585 graffiti made by an unfortunate inmate. (☎35926. Open M-Sa 10am-6pm, Su 2-6pm. €4, seniors and students €3.50, children €1.)

St. Aiden's Cathedral, on Cathedral St. uphill from Murphy's Hotel, was lovingly restored up to its star-spangled roof. Original construction began in 1843 under the close supervision of architect Augustus Pugin, who scattered the whole of Britain with his neo-Gothic creations. Something of a wunderkind, Pugin also made jewelry, textiles, and metalworks, and at the ripe old age of 14 he designed all of the furniture in Windsor Castle. In Market Sq., a statue commemorates **Father Murphy,** who fanned the flames of rebellion in 1798. (Got an afternoon to kill? Try walking around town and counting the number of times the word "Murphy" appears.) The priest had been something of a Loyalist before an angry mob threatened to burn down his church. He promptly installed himself at the head of the United Irishmen (see **Rebellion and Union,** p. 61) and led the pikemen of Enniscorthy into battle.

If you're around in late June, check out the annual **Strawberry Fair's** long weekend of festivities and fructose. Pubs host literati-laden theater performances, and roots and rock music plays on into the night. (www.wexlive.com has info on the music, for exact dates contact Maura Flannery ☎36800, who puts out the *Enniscorthy Events Guide.*) The **Blues Festival** in mid-September brings three days of entertainment by locally and internationally renowned musicians.

WEXFORD (LOUGH GARMAN)   ☎053

Incessant fighting between Gaels, Vikings, and Normans gave birth to Wexford's labyrinth of narrow, winding streets; sidewalks here are so small that cars along Main St. must yield to a convoy of baby carriages that march down its middle. Park the car and pound the pavement to visit Wexford's main attractions—its quality

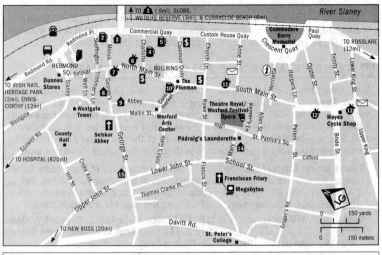

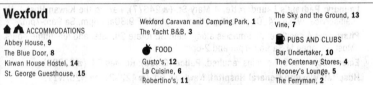

Wexford

♠ ⌂ ACCOMMODATIONS

Abbey House, **9**
The Blue Door, **8**
Kirwan House Hostel, **14**
St. George Guesthouse, **15**

Wexford Caravan and Camping Park, **1**
The Yacht B&B, **3**

🍴 FOOD

Gusto's, **12**
La Cuisine, **6**
Robertino's, **11**

The Sky and the Ground, **13**
Vine, **7**

🍺 PUBS AND CLUBS

Bar Undertaker, **10**
The Centenary Stores, **4**
Mooney's Lounge, **5**
The Ferryman, **2**

pubs and restaurants. These line the stone passageways that were built in the 12th century when the Normans conquered the Viking settlement of Waesfjord. Today, fishing trawlers line the harbor, and a newly constructed promenade encourages leisurely strolling by the waterside. One street back, crowds filter down Main St. and enjoy the many shops, restaurants, and traffic-dodging opportunities that give this unique, historical town its down-home charm.

▛ TRANSPORTATION

Trains: O'Hanranhan (North) Station, Redmond Sq. (☎22522). Facing away from the water at Crescent Quay, turn right, and walk for 5min. If office is closed, buy tickets onboard. Info available from 7am until about 7:40pm. Trains to: Connolly Station in **Dublin** (2¾hr., 3 per day, €21 return) and to **Rosslare** (15min., 3 per day, €3.50).

Buses: Buses stop at the train station. The Station Cafe (☎24056) across the street has info and sells tickets. Buses run to **Dublin** (2¾hr., 8-10 per day, €10) and **Rosslare** (20min., 9-12 per day, €3.50). Buses to and from **Limerick** (4 per day, €16) connect with **Irish Ferries** and **Stena-Sealink** sailings.

Taxis: Walsh Cabs (☎41449 or 087 256 7489); **Noel Ryan** (☎24056); **Wexford taxis** (☎46666). A list of additional taxi companies is posted in the train station.

Bike Rental: Hayes Cycle Shop, 108 S. Main St. (☎22462). Rents touring bikes. 1-way rentals possible. €15 per day, €75 per wk. €75 or ID deposit. Open M-Sa 9am-6pm; bikes available by arrangement on Su.

Hitchhiking: The odds of getting a ride are highest around noon or from 5-7pm when the boats come in and traffic is heavier. Hitchers to Dublin (via N11) stand by the Wexford Bridge off the quays; those bound for Rosslare head south along the quays to Trinity St., just past the Talbot Hotel. For Cork, New Ross, or Waterford, thumbers continue down Westgate and turn left onto Hill St. then right onto Newtown Rd. (N25). N11 and N25 merge near the city; savvy hitchers specify either the Dublin road (N11) or the Waterford road (N25). *Let's Go* doesn't recommend hitching, with savvy or otherwise.

✦ 🛈 ORIENTATION AND PRACTICAL INFORMATION

Most of the town's action takes place one block inland, along the twists and turns of **Main Street**. A plaza called the **Bullring** is near the center of town, a few blocks from where North Main St. changes to South. Another plaza, **Redmond Square,** sits at the northern end of the quays near the station. Two steeples and a number of other towers—including the Franciscan Friary at the top of the hill—define the town's skyline but are less prominent to pedestrians navigating its narrow streets.

Tourist Office: Crescent Quay (☎23111), facing the backside of Commodore Barry's statue. Scars on the windowsills attest to centuries of knife-sharpening sailors. Pick up *Discover Wexford* (€2), *Front Door to Ireland* (free map), or *Welcome to Wexford* (free). Open Apr.-Sept. M-Sa 9am-6pm, Su 10am-6pm; Nov.-Mar. M-F 9:30am-5:30pm.

Banks: 24hr. **ATMs** are available at **TSB,** 73-75 Main St. (☎41922; Open M-F 9:30am-5pm, Th until 7pm); **AIB,** S. Main St. (☎22444); and **Bank of Ireland,** at the Bullring (☎21365; Both open M 10am-5pm, Tu-F 10am-4pm).

Laundry: Pádraig's Launderette, 4 Mary St. (☎24677), next to the Kirwan Hostel. No self-service. Wash €4. Dry €0.75 per 5min. Open M-F 9:30am-6pm, Sa 9am-7pm.

Pharmacy: A gaggle of pharmacies along Main St. rotate Su, late, and lunchtime hours. Most are open M-Sa 9am-1pm and 2-6pm.

Emergency: ☎999; no coins required. **Police** (*Garda*): Roches Rd. (☎22333).

Hospital: Wexford General Hospital, Newtown Rd. (☎42233), on N25/N11.

Internet: Wexford Library (☎21637), Redmond Sq. In a parking lot—enter through the drugstore on Slaney St. or lot entrance on Wellinton Pl. Call to reserve a **free** 1hr. slot. Open Tu 1-5:30pm, W-F 10am-5:30pm. **Megabytes,** in the Franciscan Friary, has computers and coffee. €5 per hr. Open M-Th 9am-9:30pm, F 9am-5:30pm, Sa 10am-4pm.

Post Office: Anne St. (☎22587). Open M-Sa 9am-5:30pm, Tu open 9:30am. Smaller offices on S. Main St. and in The Station Cafe at Redmond Sq.

🏠 ACCOMMODATIONS AND CAMPING

If the hostels and B&Bs below are full, ask the proprietors for recommendations or look along N25 (the Rosslare road or New Town Rd.). If you plan to be in town during the opera festival (see **Entertainment,** p. 214), book as far in advance as possible; rooms are often reserved up to a year ahead of time.

▨ **The Blue Door,** 18 Lower Georges St. (☎21047). Well-kept building with flower baskets and, of course, a blue door. View the castle from immaculate rooms, or head downstairs for veggie-friendly breakfasts and fresh-squeezed OJ. Smoke-free. €32-35. ❸

▨ **Kirwan House Hostel (IHH),** 3 Mary St. (☎21208). A refurbished 200-year-old Georgian house right in the heart of town. Some slants and creaks in its wooden floors, a BBQ-friendly patio out back, and loads of local info from the staff. Impromptu pub-crawls led by Chris. Laundry available next door. Dorms €12-12.50; doubles €32; triples €48. ❶

Abbey House, 34 Abbey St. (☎24408). This family-run B&B flaunts a central location, comfy quarters with large baths, and a dining room with an electric fireplace. Singles €35-40; doubles with bath €56-62. ❸

St. George Guesthouse, Georges St. (☎24814). 4min. uphill from North Main St. in a sprawling yellow and white house. More like a hotel than a B&B, with bright, clean rooms. Free parking. TVs and phones in rooms. No smoking in rooms. €35. ❸

The Yacht B&B, 2 Monck St. (☎22338). Above Yacht Pub, ideal for those who like their stumbles short. Relaxed atmosphere in an old house. Call ahead. €25. ❸

Wexford Caravan and Camping Park (☎44378). On the eastern edge of town; cross the bridge and go straight. Clean sites with striking ocean views, convenient to town. Open May-Oct. 1-person tent €7.60; 2-person €11.50. Showers €2. Laundry €3. ❶

🃏 FOOD

Dunnes Store on Redmond Sq. has everything from groceries to clothes to lampshades. (☎45688. Open M-Tu 9am-8pm, W 9am-9pm, Th-F 9am-10pm, Sa 9am-7pm, Su 10am-7pm.) Find **Tesco** in Lowney's Mall on Main St. (☎24788. Open M-Tu and Sa 9am-7pm, W-F 9am-9pm, Su 11am-6pm.)

The Sky and the Ground, 112 S. Main St. (☎21273). Lots of Guinness ads and old-time memorabilia make this a good stop for lunch. Scaled-down versions of the pricier fare served by the late-night restaurant upstairs (**Heavens Above;** mains €14-21) are served here until 6pm. Lunch is so good they occasionally sell out the entire menu. Most main courses €8.50-10. Su-Th live music, typically trad. ❸

Vine, 109 N. Main St. (☎22388), upstairs in the old YMCA. Twinkling candles, high ceilings, and whimsical bronze sculptures create a romantic atmosphere in this excellent Thai restaurant. Plenty of veggie options. Mains €12-17. Open daily 6:30pm til late. ❸

Gusto's, 106 S. Main St. (☎24336). Gusto's is to be relished. Its small, cafe-like appearance belies high-quality breakfasts, sandwiches, and soups, and a slightly artysophisticate vibe. The panini are a warm treat (€5.50). Breakfast €4-6. Open M-F 8:30am-5:30pm, Sa 8:30am-5pm, Su 10am-2pm. ❶

Robertino's, 19 S. Main St. (☎23334). Excellent pizzas outweigh reluctant service at this classic and popular Italian restaurant. Pizzas and pastas €10-15. Mains €14-23. Open M-Sa 10am-11pm, Su noon-11pm. ❸

La Cuisine, 80 N. Main St. (☎24986.) Down-home bakery with snug seating area behind the busy takeaway counter. Good sandwiches (€3) and amazing desserts (€2.75)—the apple sponge-cake can be addictive. Open M-Sa 8am-5:30pm. ❶

📺🎧 PUBS AND CLUBS

Mooney's Lounge, Commercial Quay (☎21128), by the bridge. Wexford's hot late-night venue. One side hosts a disco bar after 9:30pm while the other keeps pubbing. Carvery lunch and bar menu until 8pm daily. Live music Th-Su. Impressive TV. 18+. Occasional cover (€7) for larger gigs. Open M-W 10:30am-11:30pm, Th-Su until 2:30am.

The Centenary Stores, Charlotte St. (☎24424), off Commercial Quay. A classy crowd flocks to this stylish pub/cafe/dance club situated in a former warehouse. Patio for those sunny afternoon pints. Asian-inspired pub food (€6-8) served M-Sa noon-6pm. Excellent trad Su mornings, M and W nights. DJ spins techno and top-40 on a black-lit dance floor Tu-Su 10:30pm-2am. Nightclub cover €8.

The Ferryman, 12 Monck St. (☎23877), on the corner of Redmond Pl. facing the water. Large and bright, with ample skylights and faux torches. Carvery lunch served 12:30-3pm. Occasional live music. Open M-W 10:30am-11:30pm, Th-Sa 10:30am-12:30am, Su 10:30am-11pm.

Bar Undertaker, next to the Pikeman in the Bullring (☎22949). As the evening wears on at this little pub, drinkers morph into serious jazz fans. Music Th, Sa, and Su until 1am.

👁 🚶 SIGHTS AND ACTIVITIES

The remains of the Norman **city walls** run the length of High St. **Westgate Tower,** near the intersection of Abbey and Slaney St., is the only one of the wall's six gates still standing. The tower gate now holds the **Westgate Heritage Centre,** where an excellent 30min. audio-visual show (€2) recounts the town's history. (☎46506. Open May-Sept. M-Sa 10am-5pm, Su noon-6pm; Oct.-Apr. Tu-Sa 10am-5pm, Su noon-6pm.) Next door, the peaceful ruins of **Selskar Abbey**—site of Henry II's penance for his role in Thomas Beckett's murder—act as flower-bed for glorious weeds. (Enter through the wicket gate by the Centre. Open M-F 10am-4pm. Free.)

An open area between North and South Main St. marks the **Bullring.** In 1621, the town's butcher guild inaugurated bull baiting as a promotional device—the mayor got the hide and the poor got the meat. In the ring stands **The Pikeman,** a statue of a stalwart peasant fearlessly brandishing his homemade weaponry, which commemorates the 1798 uprising (see **Rebellion,** p. 61). On Crescent Quay, a statue of dashing **Commodore John Barry,** native son and founder of the US Navy, faces the sea. The **Friary Church,** in the Franciscan Friary on School St. (☎22758), houses the "Little Saint" in the back corner of the nave. The wax effigy of young St. Adjutor shows the gash inflicted by the martyr's Roman father. The order of Franciscan monks who live and pray has called Wexford home since 1230. If you're seeking company, the **historical society** (☎52900 or 46506) runs evening **walking tours** (free), depending on weather and interest—call ☎22663 after 5pm. If not, *Welcome to Wexford* (free at the tourist office) details a self-guided "Magical History" tour.

Wexford's hilly countryside and beaches make for excellent horseback riding. **Shelmalier Riding Stables,** 4 mi. away at Forth Mountain, has riding for novices and experts (☎39251; booking essential). **Boat trips** from Wexford Harbour are another way to explore the area and are perfect for those seeking close-up pictures of the **seals** at Raven Point. (☎40564. 30min. tour €7.)

🎵 ENTERTAINMENT

For detailed information on events throughout the county, pick up *The Wexford People* (€1.50) from any local newsstand or pub. The funky **Wexford Arts Centre,** Cornmarket, presents free visual arts and crafts exhibitions. Evening performances of music, dance, and drama take place here throughout the year. (☎23764. Tickets generally €9-10. Center open M-Sa 9am-6pm.) The **Theatre Royal,** High St., produces shows throughout the year, culminating in the internationally acclaimed **Wexford Opera Festival,** held in late October and early November. The festival rescues three obscure but deserving operas from the artistic attic and performs them in an intimate setting. (☎22400, box office ☎22144; www.wexfordopera.com. Box office open May-Sept. M-F 11am-1pm and 2-5pm; Oct.-Nov. M-F 9:30am-5:30pm.)

🔆 DAYTRIPS FROM WEXFORD

THE SLOBS AND CURRACLOE BEACH

The Wildfowl Reserve is on the North Slob, 2 mi. north of Wexford. Take Castlebridge/ Gorey Rd. to well-signposted Ardcavan Ln. (a €5 cab ride), or hike through the Ferrybank caravan park and along the increasingly sandy beach for 40min. Viking Bus departs from the Supervalu parking lot M-F at 10:45am, ask the driver to stop off at Curracloe or Ballinesker, and arrange to be picked up on the return trip, usually at 3:30pm. Reserve Centre, ☎23129. Open mid-Apr. to Sept. daily 9am-6pm, Oct.-Apr. 10am-5pm. Free.

Wexford worked hard to get its Slobs, and it was worth it—they're now quite a sight to behold. Originally boglands, in the late 1840s the Slobs were filled to create more land for agriculture. Today, 420 of these acres are reserved for **The Wexford Wildfowl Reserve,** a safe haven for rare birds from around the world. Ten thousand of Greenland's white-fronted geese (one-third of the entire species) descend on the Sloblands between October and April, cohabiting with other honkers from as far away as Siberia and Iceland. Resident Irish birds arrive in the summer to mate along the channels. The **Reserve Centre** has a new wing that details the creation of the Slobs, highlights wildlife, and displays a water-based cannon formerly used to take out dozens of birds at a time.

Six more miles down the coast lies broad **Curracloe Beach,** and beyond it **Ballinesker Beach,** where Spielberg filmed the D-Day landings in *Saving Private Ryan.* Curracloe makes a fabulous cycling or walking daytrip; the beach is lined with dune bluffs whose stature rivals the steeples on the far side of the Slaney. To get there by bike, follow Castlebridge/Gorey Rd. beyond the turnoff for the Slobs to a signposted right turn for Curracloe Town. Cycle past fields of sheep, and turn right in Curracloe Town at the post office (35min. from the bridge; 10min. by car).

THE IRISH NATIONAL HERITAGE PARK

The park is 3 mi. outside Wexford on the N11; cabs cost about €7. ☎20733. Open daily 9:30am-6:30pm, last admission 5pm; €7, students €5.50.

The Irish National Heritage Park allows visitors to stroll through a Stone Age campsite, an early Norman tower, old Irish homesteads, tombs, and fortifications that archaeologists discovered across Ireland—over 9000 years of Irish history, packed into a park that dates all the way back to the late 1980s. The guided tours, included in the price of admission, are an excellent way to explore the park. If you get hungry afterwards, hop over to the park's restaurant, **Fulacht Faidh,** which serves carvery food and excellent chips. (Open daily 12:30-5:30pm. Mains €7-8.)

ROSSLARE HARBOUR (ROS LÁIR)   ☎053

Rosslare Harbour, best viewed from the deck of a departing ship, is a decidedly pragmatic seaside village whose primary function is welcoming voyagers and bidding them *bon voyage* as they depart for France or Wales. Unlike the seaports of popular imagination, Rosslare does not play host to international intrigue, spies, or casinos; it doesn't even have many good pubs or restaurants.

⎗ TRANSPORTATION. Trains run from the ferryport to: Dublin (3hr., 3 per day, €18.50); Limerick (2½hr., 1-2 per day, €16.50) via Waterford (1¼hr., €8.50); and Wexford (15min., 3 per day, €3.50). The rail office (☎33592) is open daily from 6am-10pm. The same office houses the bus station (☎33595). Most **buses** stop at the ferry terminal, by the Kilrane Church and the Catholic church, and go to: Dublin (3hr., 10-12 per day, €14); Galway via Waterford (4 per day, €23); Killarney (M-Sa 5 per day, Su 3 per day; €22) via Cork (€18.50) and Waterford (€12); Limerick (M-Sa 5 per day, Su 3 per day; €18.50); Tralee (M-Sa 4 per day, Su 2 per day; €23); Wexford (20min., 13-17 per day, €3.70). **Stena Line** (☎61560; 24hr. info ☎61505) and **Irish Ferries** (☎33158) serve the port. **Ferries** shove off for Wales (summer 5-6 per day, winter 2 per day); Britain (2 per day); and France (1 every other day). For further info see **By Ferry,** p. 33. Trains and buses often connect with the ferries; **Irish Rail** (☎33114) and **Bus Éireann** (☎051 879 000) have desks in the terminal. An office in the ferry terminal offers **Europcar** (☎33634), **Hertz** (☎33238 or 33511), and **Budget** (☎33318) rentals. Prices hover around €100 for 1-2 days. Only Europcar rents to drivers under 24. For a **taxi** out of town, check for phone numbers at the blue information board to the left of the bureau de change, or try Michael Browne (☎ 087 294 7883), Jimmy Ferguson (☎ 087 232 4618), or Strand Cabs (☎ 087 223 0543).

⚑ ▨ ORIENTATION AND PRACTICAL INFORMATION. To get from the ferryport into town, climb the ramp or walk the steps up the cliff; the path goes to the N25 which cuts through town. The Rosslare-Kilrane **tourist office** is 1 mi. from the waterfront on the Wexford road in Kilrane. (☎ 33622 or 33232. Open daily 11am-6pm) For help in the ferry terminal, head to the **port authority desk** (☎ 33114). Exchange currency at the **Bank of Ireland,** on St. Martin Rd. (☎ 33304. Open M-F 10am-12:30pm and 1:30-4pm. 24hr. **ATM.**) The **post office,** in the **pharmacy** in the new SuperValu shopping center, has a **bureau de change.** (☎ 33201. Open M-F 9am-1pm and 2-5:30pm, Sa 9am-1pm. Pharmacy open M-Sa 9am-6pm.)

▟ ▙▨ ACCOMMODATIONS, FOOD, AND PUBS. Exhausted ferry passengers often take what they can get in town, while good B&Bs and accommodations in Wexford and Kilmore Quay are often overlooked. B&Bs swamp N25 just outside of Rosslare. **▨Mrs. O'Leary's Farmhouse ❷**, off N25 in Kilrane, a 15min. drive from town, stands high above the rest of the rabble. Open since 1955 and set on a glorious 100 acre farm right by the seaside, Mrs. O'Leary's well-kept home is a holiday unto itself. On fine days, stroll down to the quiet beach. If the weather threatens, stay inside by the fireplace with tea and scones. Breakfasts please all, with vegan and vegetarian options, and homemade bread and jam. Call for pickup from town. (☎ 33134. €30, low season €26.50.) Old-fashioned grandeur, and a four-poster bed in some rooms, await at **St. Martin's B&B ❹**, on St. Martin's Rd. near the bank. (☎ 33133. €39, low season €30.) If the ferry ride calls for a more luxurious rest, the modern amenities of the **Tuskar House Hotel ❹** on St. Martins Rd. should more than suffice. (☎ 33363. B&B shared rooms €42-52; 2 nights plus breakfast and 1 dinner €109-130.) To get to the **Rosslare Harbour Youth Hostel (An Óige/HI) ❶**, Goulding St., take a right at the top of the cliff stairs, then head left around the far corner of the Hotel Rosslare; the hostel is past the convenience store to the left. Not the most luxurious accommodations in town, though they do have brand new mattresses. The cinder-block walls are compensated for by the courtyard out back. (☎ 33399. Luggage storage €1 per day. Check-in 5pm. Dorms €11.50-14.50.)

The restaurants in Rosslare Harbour tend to be expensive and uninteresting—the best bet is to grab some groceries and cook. The **SuperValu,** on N25l, has a substantial selection. (☎ 33107. Open M-W and Sa 8am-7pm, Th 8am-8pm, F 8am-9pm, Su 9am-5pm.) For chipper lovers, there is no better place than Rosslare, land of quick fried fish. **Tuskar House Hotel ❸**, on St. Martins Rd. overlooking the ferryport, hosts a Chinese restaurant and a carvery in a conservatory overlooking the sea. (☎ 33363. Mains €8-15.) The Tuskar also houses a small hotel bar and the larger, residential **Punters Bar.** The best pub in Rosslare, however, is **Mac Faddens,** on the N25 about 1 mi. out of town. The *craic* here is as good as it gets in Rosslare, so it's worth the walk. (☎ 33590. Open Su-W 10:30am-11:30pm, Th-Sa 10:30am-12:30am.) The **Kilrane Inn,** on N25 in Kilrane, is so good that a man known as "The Resident" has been coming here every night for the past 60 years. Sit in his seat, marked with a plaque, at your own peril. (☎ 33661. Trad sessions F and Su. Pub food from 5:30-10pm. Open M-W 11am-11:30pm, Th-Sa 11am-12:30am, Su 11am-11pm.)

◑ ◭ SIGHTS AND ACTIVITIES. On the way off or onto a boat, you'll walk across the gangplank over the waters of Rosslare Harbour. Look down while crossing, as the **Harbour** is Rosslare's only sight. Though a transportation hub for thousands of visitors each year, the town has yet to invest in tourist attractions of any sort. For entertainment of any kind, head to the Tuskar House Hotel, which arranges **golf** outings and **sea angling** trips for guests of the hotel.

NEAR ROSSLARE HARBOUR

KILMORE QUAY AND THE SALTEE ISLANDS   ☎053

Thirteen miles southwest of Rosslare Harbour on Forlorn Point, the small fishing village of Kilmore Quay (pop. 550) sings a siren song of thatched roofs and white-washed seaside cottages. In early July the entire town is on *craic* for the annual family-oriented Seafood Festival, but during the rest of the year, the salty air keeps everything moving at a slow, dreamy pace. Kilmore Quay provides the ideal escape destination—it's where people come to get away from it all and write a novel on a romance with the sea. No, really, it is.

■▮ **ORIENTATION AND PRACTICAL INFORMATION.** To reach Kilmore Quay from Rosslare Harbour, take the Wexford road to Tagoat and turn left; from Wexford, take the Rosslare road, turn right on R739 near Piercetown, and continue for 4 mi. **Viking Buses** runs between Wexford, across from Dunnes Supermarket, and Kilmore Quay (☎086 308 8465. M-Sa 3 per day, €5). **Doyle's Hackney & Bus Hire** (☎29624 or 087 472 959) shuttles a bus into Wexford on Tuesdays, Thursdays, and Fridays, leaving at 11am and returning at 2pm. Doyle's is also available for 24hr. hackney ("taxi") service. In town, two streets diverge from the harbor: **Wexford Road** and "**the back road.**" A small beach lies to the left of the harbor, and the 7 mi. **Ballyteigue Beach,** to the right of the harbor. **Tourist information** is available at **Stella Maris Community Centre** on the Wexford road, which also has private showers for €2 and **Internet** for €4 per hr. (☎29922. Center open M-Sa 8am-8pm, Su 9am-8pm.) There are **no banks** or **ATMs** in town, so make sure to bring enough cash to last through a stay. The **post office** is on the Wexford road, just beyond the church. (☎29641. Open M-F 9am-12:30pm and 1:30-5:30pm, Sa 9am-12:30pm.)

▮▮▮ **ACCOMMODATIONS, FOOD, AND PUBS.** After months of renovations, thrifty and rustic lodging is available at the **Kilturk Independent Hostel ❷.** The hostel, which used to be an old schoolhouse, is located 1½ mi. from town on the Wexford road between Kilmore Quay and Kilmore Town. The buses between Wexford and Kilmore Quay will stop at the hostel by request; otherwise call the hostel for pickup. (☎29883. Dorms €15.) Among the town's many B&Bs is **The Haven ❸,** 100 yd. down from the first right after the post office. Visitors delight in the ocean view, tea and coffee, and the elegant and friendly Betty Walsh. (☎29979. Singles €30; doubles €50.) May Bates's **Harborlights B&B ❸,** New Ross Rd., has a good view of the Saltee Islands, plenty of free parking, and insider's advice on the restaurants in town. It's in the middle of town across from the Silver Fox restaurant, just to the left of the driveway. (Singles €32-35; doubles €56.)

Bird's Rock ❷ coffee shop, housed in the Stella Maris Community Centre (see above), is the place for affordable food. It serves huge dishes for €4-6, including breakfast all day. (☎29922. Open M-F 9:30am-5pm, Sa-Su 9am-1pm.) Reel in the best meal around at the ▧**Silver Fox ❹,** across from the Maritime Museum. The super-fresh seafood is served in morbidly ironic fish-shaped dishes. Everyone knows it's good, so call ahead for reservations. (☎29888. Mains €15-22, vegetarian mains €15. Open M-Sa 5-9:30pm.) **The Wooden House ❷,** on the Wexford Road to the left heading up from the Maritime Museum, serves pub food (€7-8) and sates thirsty fishermen in a cozy thatched roof cottage. (☎29804. Trad sessions nightly.

Open M-W until 11:30pm, Th-Sa until 12:30am, Su until 11pm.) Head to **James Kehoe's Pub,** on the Wexford road directly across from St. Peter's Church, for a fill of swills and gills. Check out the handy pamphlets on Kilmore Quay lore. (☎29830. Mains €13-14. Food served until 8:30pm. Live music every Sa and Su night. Open M-W 11am-11:30pm, Th-Sa 11-12:30am, Su 11am-11pm.)

◑ ❀ **SIGHTS AND FESTIVALS.** Kilmore Quay runs daily boat trips to the **Saltee Islands,** formerly a pagan pilgrimage site and now Ireland's largest **bird sanctuary.** The winged population numbers near 50,000, and sings loudly on the rocks and in every crevice of the cliff banks. Little more than salt and feathers fill this refuge for puffins, razorbills, and grey seals, but it's an ideal place for a long picnic. Prominent granite monuments and a throne in the middle of one of the islands provide reminders that the Saltees once belonged to absentee landlord Prince Michael Salteens. A narrow ridge of rock is thought to have connected the smaller island to the mainland in ancient times. This land bridge, called **St. Patrick's Causeway,** was used for driving cattle to pasture on the islands. The beginning of St. Pat's bridge is visible at low tide. To get there, take the road to Kilmore town and turn right at the signpost, roughly 1 mi. from town; or scramble over rocks and tide-pools on the beach—turn left, it's a 20min. walk from the harbor. **Boats** leave the mainland each morning, weather permitting. **Declan Bates** makes the 30min. trip daily at around 11am and returns at 4pm. (☎29684 or 087 252 9736. €14, children €4.) **Dick Hayes** brings visitors aboard for **deep-sea angling** and **reef-fishing;** call ahead to arrange a time or to ask about renting equipment. (☎29704 or 087 254 9111. Full-day boat rental €300; evening rental 4:30-8pm €200. Rods €10.)

The village floats its **Maritime Museum** in the lightship *Guillemot*, once anchored near the harbor and now cemented into it. Climb into the hold and view Irish naval artifacts and marine accessories, then learn the tragic stories of local shipwrecks. Wall speakers give short audio explanations of the room's contents, available in French, German, or English. (☎29655. Open June-Aug. daily noon-6pm; May and Sept. Sa-Su noon-6pm. €4; students, seniors, and children €2.) Through town and just around the corner, the **Millennium Memorial Hiking Trail** winds along Forlorn Point. A stone ship overlooking the majestic ocean pays tribute to local sailors lost at sea, and a giant rib-bone from a fin whale that recently washed ashore is on display nearby. The **Kilmore Seafood Festival** hauls in seafood, music, and games for 10 raucous days in mid-July. Call the **Stella Maris Centre** (☎29922) for information.

NEW ROSS (ROS MHIC TREOIN) ☎051

New Ross makes an ideal rest from a tour of Ireland's southeast corner; Waterford, the Hook, Wexford, and Kilkenny lie within easy reach of this fair hamlet. The town has a tidy little list of sights, most involving the Irish exodus and its beloved great-grandson John F. Kennedy. The *Dunbrody*, a coffin ship replica from the Famine era, is a powerful must-see.

◢ ⊓ **ORIENTATION AND PRACTICAL INFORMATION.** Most events in New Ross occur on a strip of waterfront known as **the Quay.** Other major thoroughfares are **Mary Street,** which extends uphill from the bridge, and **South Street,** which runs parallel to the Quay one block inland and later changes its name to **North Street** as it crosses Mary St. New Ross is on N25 (to Wexford and Waterford) and N30 (to Enniscorthy); hitchers find plenty of rides on either, especially in the morning and late afternoon. *Let's Go* does not recommend hitching at any time of day. **Bus Éireann** runs from the Mariners Inn on the Quay to Dublin (3hr., 3 per day, €10); Rosslare Harbour (1hr.; M-Sa 4 per day, Su 3 per day; €9); and Waterford (25min.; M-Sa 8 per day, Su 4 per day; €5.50). **Donovan's Taxi** (☎425 100) drives the exhausted up the hill to the hostel. The New Ross **tourist office,** in **Dunbrody Centre** next to the famine ship, has useful maps in the free *New Ross Town and Area Guide* and

Talk of the Town. (☎ 421 857; www.newrosschamber.ie. Open daily 9am-6pm.) Banks with 24hr. **ATMs** abound: **Bank of Ireland,** the Quay (☎ 421 267), is steps away from the bus stop and tourist office; **AIB** (☎ 421 319) and **TSB** (☎ 422 060) are across from each other on South St. The **post office** signs, seals, and delivers on Charles St., off the Quay. (☎ 421 261. Open M-Sa 9am-5:30pm.)

▓▊▨ ACCOMMODATIONS, FOOD, AND PUBS. ▓**Mac Murrough Farm Hostel ❶** is reason enough to visit New Ross. Follow Quay St. to Mary St. uphill to its end, turn left, then right, then left at the traffic lights (the SuperValu is on the left) onto the Ring Rd. Take a right at Statoil Station; the remaining mile to the hostel is signposted. Confused? Call for pickup. The sheep give a rowdy greeting joined by a chorus of dogs and cats, and down-to-earth owners. (☎ 421 383; www.macmurrough.com. Dorms €12-14; doubles €28-32.) For a bed in town and a bigger dent in the wallet, try **Riversdale House ❸,** William St. Follow South St. to William St. and turn left up the hill. The owners take pride in their snazzy rooms and commanding view of town. (☎ 422 515. Singles €50; doubles €64.) **Inishross House ❷,** 96 Mary St., is a good deal cheaper and far more eccentric. (☎ 421 335. Singles €25.)

L&N SuperValu, generic grocer is on the Quay. (☎ 421 392. Open M-Tu 8am-7pm, W 8am-8pm, Th 8am-9pm, F 8am-10pm, Sa 8am-7:30pm, Su 9am-6pm.) On South St., the friendly staff at **Il Primo ❸,** 18-21 South St., dishes out large portions of Italian fare late into the night. (☎ 425 262. Mains €11-20. Open daily noon-11pm.) Behind a bakery counter and gourmet health food store is **Cafe Nutshell ❷,** 8 South St., which serves breakfasts, sandwiches, and excellent coffee in a lovely seating area. (☎ 422 777. Breakfast €2.50-4, sandwiches €3.50. Open M-Sa 9am-5pm.) Dine in transit aboard **The Galley** (☎ 421 723), which runs restaurant cruises from New Ross into Waterford Harbour. Choose a meal: lunch (2hr.; 12:30pm; €20, cruise only €10), tea (2hr.; 3pm; €10/€8), or dinner (2-3hr.; 6 or 7pm; €30/€15).

◢ SIGHTS. During the **Great Famine,** thousands of emigrants seeking a better life stepped into the dank, dreary, and crowded holds of wooden sailboats to make the torturous 52-day journey to America. Many left from New Ross, and one of the ships that carried the hopeful souls was called *The Dunbrody.* The original ship sank off the coast of Canada after her days as a famine ship were complete, but a brand new 410-ton, 176 ft. oak replica sits at the New Ross Docks, inviting visitors to see the conditions both first class and "steerage" passengers had to endure. Tours start with a 10min. video highlighting the making of the new ▓**Dunbrody;** then actors lead ticket-holders into the ship to relive the ordeal. The ship also has a computerized database for researching coffin ship passengers. (☎ 425 239; www.dunbrody.com. Open daily April-Oct. 9am-6pm; Nov.-Mar. 10am-5pm. €6.50, students and children €4.) For landlubbers, there's 13th-century **St. Mary's Church,** off Mary St. Mrs. Culleton, four doors down at 6 Church St., provides the key and a booklet on the significance of the stone structures inside. Protestant masses are held in a new annex on Sundays. The roots of Camelot run deep in Co. Wexford— the **John F. Kennedy Arboretum** lies 7 mi. south of New Ross on the Ballyhack Rd. (R783). Stroll around 623 gorgeous acres and nearly 6000 species dedicated to Ireland's favorite Yankee Prez. The small **cafe** doubles as a gift shop. (☎ 388 171. Open daily May-Aug. 10am-8pm; Apr. and Sept. 10am-6:30pm; Oct.-Mar. 10am-5pm. Last admission 45min. before closing. €2.50, seniors €1.90, children €1.20.)

THE HOOK PENINSULA

Southeast of New Ross, the Hook is a peaceful peninsula noted for its historic abbeys, forts, and lighthouses. Sunny coastlines draw deep-sea anglers to Waterford Harbour and Tramore Bay, while the pubs on the oceanfront keep the midnight oil burning long past midnight. Unfortunately, public transportation does not reach this burgeoning vacation region, so itinerant travelers must depend on cars or bikes. The peninsula is accessible by an inland route from New Ross, or by crossing Waterford Harbour on the Ballyhack-Passage East ferry (every 20min., pedestrians €2). Hitchers find short rides fairly easily, although *Let's Go* doesn't recommend it. Those who make it here are rewarded with a quiet, relaxed place for enjoying the sanctity of solitude. Plan ahead at www.thehook-wexford.com.

BALLYHACK AND ARTHURSTOWN ☎051

Ten miles south of New Ross, **Ballyhack** threatens its cross-channel neighbor, Passage East, with a profile dominated by 15th-century **Ballyhack Castle**. Although the Castle fails to strike fear into the hearts of current invaders, it was built around 1450 by William Marshall (Strongbow's heir; see **Christians and Vikings**, p. 57) to protect his precious port at New Ross. To make sure the job was done right, Marshall hired the Crusading Order of the Knights Hospitallers, who were known for their valor in battle and compassion for the sick. Tours lead visitors up the castle tower and take special delight in displaying the ghastly methods of self-defense employed by the "charitable" knights. The 500-year-old intact barrelvaulted wicker ceilings inspire new faith in patio furniture. (☎389 468. Open mid-June to Sept. daily 9:30am-6:30pm. €1.50, students €0.75.)

Two miles north of Ballyhack on the New Ross Rd. lurks **Dunbrody Abbey**, a magnificent ruin that originally housed a late 12th-century Cistercian monastic order. The abbey is almost wholly intact, and visitors wander through its rooms with considerable freedom. Across the road, a **visitors center** and **cafe** sit among the rubble of a **castle** associated with the abbey. The center features a fully-furnished dollhouse replica of the castle. An impressive **hedge-row maze**, planted in 1992, began with 2 ft. yew trees that once confounded only Lilliputians. They're now strapping 6 ft. adolescents, and will eventually reach 15 ft. (☎388 603. Center open July-Aug. 10am-7pm; May-June and Sept. 10am-6pm. Abbey €4. Castle and maze €5.)

The Ballyhack-bound find lodgings in **Arthurstown**, where the Hook's budget accommodations are at their best and brightest. Take a right from the Ballyhack ferryport's landing area and follow the **Slí Charman** (SHLEE KAR-man) coastal path; the village lies half a mile up the trail. Arthurstown has a pub and opulent views of water, water everywhere, but nary a bite to eat, so cook or head to Ducannon, a few miles away. There are no large grocery stores in the area, so aspiring chefs must grab supplies in one of the larger towns (Wexford, New Ross, or Waterford) before heading to the Hook. Back in Ballyhack, the only edibles are found at **Byrne's ❷**, a small food store and pub by the ferryport. The pub serves sandwiches (€3.50); the store has a limited grocery selection. (☎389 107. Open M-F 9:30am-9:30pm, Sa 9:30am-8pm, Su noon-7pm.) Coming from Ballyhack, the first left leads to **Arthurstown Youth Hostel (An Óige/ HI) ❶**, built 200 years ago to the uncompromising specifications of the English Coast Guard. The weathered interior hides a decent arrangement of dorms and a fantastic kitchen with broad pine tables, candles, and an upbeat communal air. (☎389 411. Lockout 10:30am-5pm. Dorms €12-14.50, private rooms €16.50.) To switch from rustic to elegant, try the B&B next to the hostel. **Marsh Mere Lodge ❹** has a spectacular view from the deck and superb artwork and antiques inside, including the sitting room's grand piano. (☎389 186 or 087 222 7303; www.marshmerelodge.com. Singles €40-50; shared rooms €30-40.) Alternatively, head to **Glendine Country House B&B ❹**, a Georgian manor up Duncannon Hill; look for the shetland cows on the lawn. The rooms are huge and beautifully decorated; the breakfasts feature homemade breads and organic produce. (☎389 258; www.glendinehouse.com. Singles €50-65; doubles €80-100.) Behind the house are two self-catering cottages, with plenty of room for children to romp. (Sleeps up to 5. €300-550 per wk.) An Italian-infused seafood restaurant is scheduled to open in November 2003 in a new annex off the back of the house.

HOOK HEAD

This tiny hamlet at the tip of the peninsula possesses the area's biggest attraction. A little under 5 mi. down the road from Templetown, a sign warns: "Great care must be taken near the water's edge: freak waves and slippery rocks." The **Hook Lighthouse,** a stout medieval tower founded by St. Dubhan, is the oldest operating beacon in the British Isles. Tours run up its 115 13th-century steps to reach panoramic views of the peninsula and neighboring Waterford Harbour. During the ascent, visitors are treated to a hearty dose of history and lighthouse lore. The top room is a recent addition—that is, it only dates back to 1800. (☎397 055. Open Mar.-Oct. daily 9:30am-5:30pm. Guided tours every 30min. €4.75, students and seniors €3.50.) On the eastern side of the peninsula is Ireland's own gloriously secluded **Tintern Abbey,** founded in the 13th century, and the perfect place for an early evening picnic. (☎562 650. Open June-Sept. 9:30am-6:30pm. Wander freely or take a tour for €2.) The abbey is 3 mi. from the Ballycullane stop on the Waterford-Rosslare rail line. Call the community office in nearby **Fethard** for more information on the Hook region. (☎31000; www.fethardonline.com.)

WATERFORD HARBOUR

Waterford Harbour straddles the Waterford-Wexford county line east of Waterford City. It is here that Oliver Cromwell coined the phrase "by hook or by crook": he had plotted to take Waterford City from either Hook Head or the opposite side of the harbor at Crooke. Both sides of the harbor host historic ruins, fishing villages, and stunning ocean views. In most of the region, travelers should expect peace and quiet, but not convenience. To cross the harbor, either drive up 37 mi. and around through New Ross or take the **Passage East Car Ferry** between Ballyhack and Passage East. (☎382 480 or 382 488. Continuous sailings Apr.-Sept. M-Sa 7am-10pm, Su and holidays 9:30am-10pm; Oct.-Mar. M-Sa 7am-8pm, Su and holidays 9:30am-8pm. Cars €6, cyclists €2.50, pedestrians €2.) **Suirway Coaches** runs a bus between Passage East and Waterford. (☎382 422. M-Sa 2 per day. €3.) Unless you're seeking total rest and relaxation, the town of **Passage East** is best passed through. The journey from Waterford to Passage East and then around the Hook Peninsula affords some spectacular views, but be advised that Waterford is the only place in the harbor to rent a bike. The roads outside Waterford are hilly and windy, and a long bike journey tests the stamina of even the most ferocious cyclist. From Wexford, follow the signs for Ballyhack to reach the ferry.

DUNMORE EAST (DÚN MÓR)   ☎051

Vacationing Irish families have made little Dunmore East their summertime mecca. In good weather, it's hard not to squash the children swarming underfoot on the beaches. When not watching for urchins, look out to sea—the calm harbor, stunning cliffs, and distant Hook make for spectacular views. Dunmore's **beaches** are great for swimming, especially at several points where trails descend into isolated coves. Kittiwakes (small gulls) throng the coastline, building their nests in cliff faces unusually close to human habitation—hundreds of them on the cliffs of

Badger's Cove. Wave after mesmerizing wave crashes onto the rocks at the less fowl precipices, which are accessible via the dirt road past Dock Rd. For offshore thrills, the friendly folks at **Dunmore East Adventure Centre** on the docks teach surfing, kayaking, canoeing, and rock-climbing. Bring a towel and swimsuit; they provide the rest. (☎383 783; www.dunmoreadventure.com. €30 per half-day activity. Pre-booking essential. Inquire about the excellent day-camps for children.)

The **Suirway** bus service (☎382 209; 24hr. timetable ☎382 422) runs the 9½ mi. from Waterford to Dunmore East (30min., M-Sa 4 per day, €3). Wait outside the Bay Cafe, or flag it down anywhere on its route. The town is spread along two areas: **the Strand,** and **Dock Road,** which leads uphill and to the docks. Ulster Bank has a 24hr. **ATM** outside the Londis Supermarket on Dock Rd.

🖺**Church Villa ❸,** across from the church between Dock Rd. and the Strand, is an immaculate B&B with bright rooms, conservatory dining room, and a sunny owner to match. For breakfast, ask for the french toast with real maple syrup. (☎383 390. Singles €35-38; doubles €58-62.) **Creaden View B&B ❸,** on Dock Rd., next to the post office, has a nice garden and rooms overlooking the bay, all with sparkling white bedspreads. (☎383 339. Open Mar.-Oct. Singles €38-40; doubles €56-62.) **Springfield B&B ❸,** a signposted 200 yd. from the beach, past the Anchor Pub, has clean modern rooms and a conservatory breakfast room. (☎383 448. Open Mar.-Nov. Doubles €56-64.) Past the Anchor pub on the hill from the beach lies **Queally's Caravan and Camping Park ❶,** where the assorted Queally's let guests squeeze a tent among their trailers. (☎383 001. Laundry €7. €15 per tent. Free showers.)

Groceries are plentiful at **Londis Supermarket,** Dock Rd., on the right after passing the Ocean Hotel. (☎383 471. Open summer daily 8:30am-9pm; shorter off season hours.) 🖺**The Melting Pot Cafe and Craft Shop ❸,** on Dock Rd. near the post office, simmers with yummy smells and fantastic bay views. Indulge in tasty mains, such as pan-fried cod in herb butter, chips, and salad for €11.50, or one of many veggie options. (☎383 271. Lunch €4.50-12.50; dinner €12-17. Open M-W noon-6pm, Th-Sa noon-4pm and 7-9:30pm, Su 11am-5pm.) **Bay Cafe ❷,** also on Dock Rd., has homemade food for sit-down or takeaway. (☎383 900. Sandwiches €3-6. Open daily 9am-6pm.) In the evening, denizens of Dunmore gather to enjoy live music at the **Anchor** (☎383 133) or **Power's Bar,** the favorite of local fishermen, on Dock Rd. across from the post office. (☎383 318. Open trad sessions Tu night.)

TRAMORE (TRÁ MHÓR)　　　　　　　　☎051

Those crazy Celts had an eye for the obvious—*Trá Mhór* is Irish for "big beach." Every summer, Tramore (Tra-MORE) draws vast numbers of tourists to its smooth 3 mi. strand, many of whom hope to take advantage of what is arguably the best surf in Europe. Despite the tacky amusements at seaside resorts the world over, Tramore retains something of its small-town character. The cliffs rising above the beach are great places to escape the seaside horde, roost, and gape at the views.

🚍 **TRANSPORTATION.** Many buses connect Tramore to Waterford. **Bus Éireann** runs two routes: around the beach (12-16 per day) and via the race course (6-9 per day); both cost €2 and take 40min. **Rapid Express Coaches** (☎872 149) sends buses from the station to Waterford every 2hr. (7 per day, €2.50), and to Dublin. Call **Tramore Cabs** for a taxi. (☎391 500).

🖼🗐 **ORIENTATION AND PRACTICAL INFORMATION.** Tramore is difficult to navigate, as few streets keep their names for more than a block and undulating hills confound even the most homesick homing pigeons. The bus station is on the **Waterford Road** (technically **Turkey Road**), a block from the intersection of **Strand Street** (which becomes **Main Street** then **Summer Hill**) and **Gallwey's Hill** (which joins **Church Road** up the cliff). The **tourist office** moves all over, and was last seen next to the bus station. (☎381 572. Open June-Aug. M-Sa 10am-1pm and 2-6pm.) **AIB** (☎381 216) is on Strand St., and the **Bank of Ireland** (☎386 611) lies farther up; both have 24hr. **ATMs.** Inquire at the **library,** on Market St. (☎381 479), about **free Internet.** (Open M-Tu 11am-1pm and 2-6pm, W-F 11am-1pm and 2-8pm.) The **post office** is on Main St. (☎390 196. M-F 9am-1pm and 2-5:30pm, Sa 9am-1pm.)

⌐ ACCOMMODATIONS AND CAMPING. Tramore is bursting with B&Bs—the cheapest are along the Waterford Rd., and the best are along Church Rd. The most competitive rates and best views in Tramore are at ◪**The Cliff ❸,** Church St., a first rate Christian Guest House owned by the YWCA. The Cliff provides beds, breakfast, parking, and, for a little extra, an evening meal. (☎381 363; www.iol.ie/~thecliff. Singles €28-35; doubles €50-56. Only Christian groups can book in winter; summer is non-denominational.) **Ard More House ❸,** Doneraile Dr., gazes at the water over town-house rooftops. The rooms are lovely and the hallways are filled with artifacts from the owners' international travels. Head up Church Rd. and take the first left. (☎381 716 or 086 379 943. Open Apr.-Sept. €28-35.) **Venezia ❸,** on Church Road Grove and signposted off Church Rd., is somewhat lacking in decor, but has TVs in every room. (☎381 412. Doubles €60.) Take a sharp right on Church Rd. at the top of Gallwey's Hill to find **Turret House ❹.** Its stylish, chic, spacious rooms with huge windows—some with ocean views—make the climb worthwhile. (☎386 342. Singles €45; doubles €60.) **Cloneen B&B ❹,** on Love Ln., lives up to its address with romantic rooms and a fantastic garden. (☎381 264. Open Mar.-Oct. Singles €50; doubles €60.) If all the B&Bs in town are full, try **Seacrest ❸,** at the top of a hill on the main road out to Waterford. (☎381 888. Singles €30, with bath €38; doubles €60.) A mile and a half out Dungarvan Coast Rd., between the golf course and the Metal Man monument to shipwreck victims, the family-style **Newtown Caravan and Camping Park ❶** is the best of several nearby campsites. (☎381 979 or 381 121. Open Easter-Sept. €6 per tent, plus €5 per person. Showers €1.)

◨◪ FOOD AND PUBS. Up Main St., **L&N SuperValu** awaits wandering taste buds. (☎386 036. Open M-W and Sa 8am-9pm, Th-F 8am-10pm, Su 9am-8pm.) Schools of frying fish are as ubiquitous in Tramore as in any other Irish sea town. **Apple Brown Betty ❶,** in a wee octagonal hut on the beach directly across from the lifeguard station, has splendid ocean fare. (☎391 680. Giant crepes €3-5.50. Open 10am-7pm.) Trot over to **The Sea Horse ❷** on Strand St. for pub chow, fancy coffee, and a friendly atmosphere. (☎386 091. Mains €7; "mixed grill" meat and veggies €11. Food served noon-9pm.) If craving "fancy" for dinner, head to **Asila ❸,** 2 Market St., but book ahead. (☎330 807. Lunches €7.50; dinner mains €17-22. Open Tu-F 10am-2pm, 6-9pm; Sa-Su 6-9pm.) For drinks and dance, the three floors of **The Victoria House ("The Vic"),** Queens St., get younger, louder, and more crowded as you descend. (☎390 338. Live music F nights. Open M-Th until 11:30pm, F-Sa 12:30am, Su 11pm.) A young set also fills **The Hibernian ("Hi B"),** or, as the late bar is dubbed, **The Cellar,** at the intersection of Gallwey's Hill and Strand St. (☎386 396. Carvery menu €8.50, served noon-7pm. Open M-W 11am-11:30pm, Th-Sa 11am-12:30am, Su 12:30-11pm.) After the nightly live music at the bar ends, hop next door to pop chart-happy **Hi B Disco,** where tunes blast across a packed floor. (Disco W-Su. Cover €6.35. Doors close at 1am.)

⚠ ACTIVITIES. Surfing? In Ireland? Dude. The Emerald Isle boasts some of the best surf in Europe, and ◪**Tramore Bay Surf Centre** provides top-of-the-line daytime and evening fun. The friendly staff rents surfboards, bodyboards, wetsuits, and other surfing accessories that could even make doggy-paddling look cool. They also offer individual and group lessons that help make you an Irish Big Kahuna. Call ahead to check the variable surf. (☎391 297; www.surfbay.com. Complete surf package €13 per hr. Open daily 9:30am-6:30pm; call ahead to book.) The waterfront promenade offers all sorts of entertainment including **Splashworld** indoor waterpark, an assortment of rides, pools, and screaming children. (☎390 176.

Open M-F 7am-10pm, Sa-Su 9am-9pm. €9, students €7.) Outside town the **cliffs** get *truly* spectacular; the tourist office provides a list of historic and scenic walks along them. The best is **Doneraile Walk**, a path that stems off Church Rd.—follow the little, red markers away from Tramore and into a land of cliff, ocean, and cloud. About 1 mi. out, give **Guillamene Cove** a swim. Ignore the "Men Only" sign— a smaller one underneath explains that it's been "retained merely as a relic of the past." *Let's Go* does not recommend foolish diving or other acts of machismo.

DUNGARVAN (DUN GARBHÁN)   ☎058

Filled with fishermen, market-goers, ocean breezes, and rollicking pubs, Dungarvan is far more endearing than most transportation hubs. Nestled a short distance from the Comeragh Mountains on a harbor with especially large tides, pub-goers on Davitt's Quay sip their pints while watching the harbor boats ground themselves as the water slowly ebbs. Shopping is plentiful in the active square, and those hankering for another castle tour delight in the well-used King John's Castle. **Dungarvan Castle,** presiding over Davitt's Quay, fell into disrepair a few years ago, at the beginning of the 14th century, after being under seige on and off for 100 years. The Provisional IRA didn't much help matters when they set the joint on fire in 1922. The *Garda* took control of the building and used it as barracks until 1987, when it was vacated for renovations. A short video and the tour take visitors through the castle's turbulent history and all of its reconstructions. (☎48144. 40min. tours, 7 per day. Open June-Sept. daily 10am-5pm.) The **deep-sea fishing** in Dungarvan is excellent, though nearby waters do have a reputation for sharks. Fishing licenses are distributed at the tourist office for €25. Capt. John Tynan leads expeditions on the *Avoca*. (☎42657 or 41327. €60 per day with rod and tackle.) **Baumann's Jewellers**, 6 St. Mary St. (☎41395), has semi-precious tackle and a wealth of free information. Dungarvan's **Féile na nDéise** (FAY-la nah ne-DAY-sya, "local area festival") packs the Square with free concerts and historical reenactments the first weekend in May. In early July, **Motorsport Weekend** pulls in vintage and race car enthusiasts.

   Buses (☎051 879 000) leave from Davitt's Quay. They run east to Waterford (1hr.; M-Sa 16-17 per day, Su 13 per day; €8.20), west to Cork (13 per day, €12.50), north to Ardmore (M-Sa 2 per day, €4.50), Dublin (M-Sa 5 per day, Su 6 per day; €12.50), and Lismore (M-Sa 1 per day, €4.70). Advance bus tickets are sold at the **John Lynch Vegetable Shop**, next to **Davitt's Pub. Main Street**, also called **O'Connell Street**, runs through the town's central square; **Emmet Street**, or **Mitchell Street**, runs parallel to Main St. one block uphill and is home to the hostel and several B&Bs. The **Cork Road** veers off Emmet St. at the *Garda* station. The **tourist office**, outside the Square in the Courthouse building, has free maps and music listings for area pubs. (☎41741. Open M-Sa 9am-6pm.) **Bank of Ireland,** the Square, has a 24hr. **ATM,** as does **AIB** on Meagher St. (Both open M 10am-5pm, Tu-F 10am-4pm.) **Free,** speedy **Internet** is available at the **library** on Davitt's Quay. (☎41231. Open Tu-Sa 10am-5pm, also W-Th 6-8pm.) The **post office** sits on Bridge St., outside the Square. (☎41176. Open M-F 9am-5:30pm, Sa 9am-1pm.)

   🛏Alwin House ❸, O'Connell St., a bit down and across from the movie theater, is run by an extremely friendly family and has spacious rooms in a well-renovated historic building. Admire the gorgeous roses on the path from the private carpark. (☎45994; www.alwinhouse.com. Singles €40; doubles €65.) Slightly pricier, **Mountain View House ❹**, off O'Connell St. down from the theater, has similar amenities, a gorgeous dining room, a stuffed deer head in the entryway, and great views. (☎42588; www.mountainviewhse.com. Singles €45-50; doubles €80-90.) The **Dungarvan Holiday Hostel (IHH) ❶,** on the Youghal Rd. (Rice St.) off Emmet St. opposite the *Garda* Station, is housed in a sprawling, simple former Christian Brothers friary. (☎44340. Wheelchair-accessible. Dorms €14; private rooms €16.)

SOUTHEAST IRELAND

The immense **SuperValu** is on Main St. (☎41754. Open M-F 8am-9pm, Sa 8am-8pm, Su 9am-6pm.) Laid-back **⬛Ormond's Cafe ❶**, on the Square, a few doors down from the tourist office, serves meals (€6-9) and outstanding desserts in a stone-walled, family-oriented, skylit cafe. (☎41153. Open M-Sa 9am-5pm.) At the far end of Darvitt's Quay, near the castle, **Moorings Bar and Restaurant ❹** has a nautical feel, tasty seafood-themed fare, and a spacious beer garden. (☎41461. Food served noon-9:30pm. Dinner mains €15-22.) **The Shamrock Restaurant ❶**, 4 O'Connell St., serves simple, homemade Irish food in a soothing, peach-walled, family-friendly diner. The €6.50 steak pie is a local favorite. (☎42242. Sandwiches €3-4, dinner mains €7.50-12. Open M-Sa 9am-9pm.) **Davitt's Pub,** Davitt's Quay, is huge, fabulous, and usually packed. A crowd of 18- to 80-year-olds finds everything from intimate booths and tranquil tables overlooking the river to a large dance floor that opens as the night wears on. An interesting mix of Mexican, Asian, and Irish food is served daily 12:30-2pm and 6-10pm. (☎44900. Club Th-Su 11:30pm-2:30am.) In true seaside form, Dungarvan has its own **Anchor Bar** (☎41249), on Davitt's Quay. Small but sprightly in hip primary colors, Anchor hosts rock and trad bands most weekends. **Bridie Dee's,** 18 Mary St. (☎44588), has trad on Thursday-Sunday nights.

ARDMORE (AIRD MHÓR)   ☎024

St. Declan Christianized Ardmore in the 4th century; the town's claim that it is the oldest Christian settlement in Ireland is well-supported by its ruins. These ruins, gorgeous cliffs, a sandy beach, and an excellent restaurant draw happy pilgrims back to Ardmore summer after summer. The town's must-do is the **cliffwalk,** a windy, 3 mi. path steeped in great ocean views and sprinkled with stops at all of the town's historic sights. A free map is available at the tourist office and at Paddymac's Pub. At one end of the walk is Ardmore's **cathedral,** built piecemeal on the site of St. Declan's monastery between 800 and 1400. The Deckster himself is said to be buried here, and the faithful swear that soil from the saint's grave cures diseases. In addition to its own collection of carvings, the cathedral houses two **ogham stones** (see **Ancient Ireland,** p. 56). Nearby stands a 97-foot **round tower** whose door is the standard 12 monk-protecting feet above ground (see **Glendalough,** p. 149). **St. Declan's Stone** is perched at the water's edge, on the right from Main St. along the shore. This intrepid lil' stone *floated* from Wales after the holy man visited. Past Cliff House hotel, at the other

THE LOCAL LEGEND

BARGING IN

A walk along the cliffs of Ardmore delights ramblers with fragrant wildflowers, ancient ruins, and a strange metal thing thrusting out of the ocean. This rusty tower was formerly the crane on the barge *Samson,* which took its place on the edge of the cliffs in December 1987, after a particularly violent storm.

Luckily, no-one was on board at the time of the wreck, but the crash did create a problem for the town's engineers. Due to the depth of the water and the sunken barge's proximity to the unforgiving cliffs, even the most skilled engineers could not figure out how to haul it safely away. The townspeople became resigned to this new addition to their coastline—all of them, that is, but one eccentric citizen. This enterprising man believed that if he took up residence on the barge for three weeks, he would establish salvage rights, and sell the parts for a tidy sum. So, he moved in among the seagulls precariously perched on the forlorn crane.

This went on for several days, until the authorities informed him that if he did manage to gain the rights he would be held responsible for removing the debris and, since this had proven nearly impossible, he would end up with a large fine instead of a free boat. With that news, he reluctantly returned to shore. Fifteen years later, the barge remains untouched, slowly rusting, settling among the crashing waves and flocks of birds.

end of the cliffwalk, is **St. Declan's Well,** which contains water rumored to cure all afflictions. Hardy hikers jump on the 56-mile **St. Declan's Way,** which starts in town and runs up to Cahir in Co. Tipperary.

Buses run to: Cork (1½hr.; M-Sa 3 per day, Su 1 per day; €10.10) and Waterford via Dungarvan (2hr.; M-Th and Sa 2 per day, F 3 per day; €10.30). Ardmore is a 3 mi. detour off the Cork-Waterford road (N25). Hitching from the junction can be slow, and is not recommended by *Let's Go.* The excellent **tourist office,** housed in what appears to be a demonic sandcastle in the carpark by the beach, has information about the local beaches and an excellent leaflet outlining a **walking tour** of town. (☎94444. Open June-Aug. M-Sa 11am-1pm and 2-5pm.) The **post office** is on Main St. (☎94191. Open M-F 9am-1pm and 2-5:30pm, Su 9am-1pm.)

The simple comforts of **Ardmore Beach Hostel ❷,** which include beach access, are at the bottom of Main St., a hop, skip, and jump away from the sand and surf. (☎94166. Dorms €14; private room €35 for 2, €8 for each additional person.) It's a steep walk up the hill from Main St. to reach **Duncrone B&B ❸** (turn right at the round tower and walk about 0.5 mi.; the driveway is signposted on the right), but incredible views of the round tower and ocean from spacious and colorful rooms make it worthwhile. (☎94860. Singles €45; doubles €60.) Those with a car and a tent camp at **Goat Island,** a secluded peninsula and beach near Ardmore. (Free. No showers.) Turn right at the round tower and head up the road to find it, or ask at the tourist office for more information. Ardmore's food offerings thrive on quality, not quantity. **Quinn's Foodstore** is at the top of Main St., and has a little bit of everything. (☎94250. Open M-Tu and Th-F 8am-7pm, W and Sa 8am-8pm, Su 8am-6pm.) Everyone and their children are drawn to **Wildhorses ❹** by the aroma of fresh fish and the case of outstanding desserts. Gourmet without being stuffy, this restaurant shouldn't be missed. Call for reservations, even for lunch. (☎94040. Lunch €5-15, dinner mains €18-25. Open Su noon-11pm, Tu-Sa 11am-11pm.) Less crowded, but still tasty, **Garden Cafe ❷,** Main St., has a delightful flower garden out back, a distinctive homemade goodness, and meals for €5-7. (☎087 268 2403. Open daily 10am-6pm.) Vast **Paddy Mac's,** Main St. (☎94166), has pub grub on reserve from 12:30-8:30pm and a variety of weekend music. **Keever's Bar,** Main St. (☎94141), where the only sustenance is liquid, is a favorite of the older Ardmore crowd.

WATERFORD (PORT LÁIRGE)   ☎051

A skyline of huge metal silos and harbor cranes greet the visitor to Waterford. Fortunately, behind this industrial facade lies a city with 10 centuries of fascinating history. The grandson of the Viking Ivor the Boneless founded Vadrafjord around AD 914 to harbor his longships, making it the oldest city in Ireland. Long considered mere brutes, the Vikings have recently gained recognition for their suave contributions to the development of this mercantile hub (see **Christians and Vikings,** p. 57). Traces of early Vadrafjord persist in Waterford's streets, and many more were unearthed during a massive archaeological dig in the 1980s, but massive freighters have long since replaced the longships in the river.

▐ TRANSPORTATION

Airport: ☎875 589. Served by **Euroceltic** (www.euroceltic.com). Follow the Quay, turn right at Reginald's Tower, then left at the sign. 20min. from town.

Trains: Plunkett Station, across the bridge from the Quay (call ☎317 889 M-F 9am-6pm; ☎876 243 for 24hr. timetable). Staffed M-Sa 9am-6pm, Su at departure times. To: **Dublin** (2½hr., M-F 5-6 per day, €17-21); **Kilkenny** (40min., 3–5 per day, €8); **Limerick** (2¼hr., M-Sa 2 per day, €15.50); **Rosslare Harbour** (1hr., M-Sa 2 per day, €10).

Buses: The station is on the Quay, across from the tourist office (☎879 000). Office open M-Sa 8:15am-6pm. To: **Cork** (2½hr., 10-13 per day, €14.50); **Dublin** (2¾hr.; M-Sa 10-12 per day, Su 6 per day; €10); **Galway** (4¾hr., 5-6 per day, €18.50); **Kilkenny** (1hr., 1

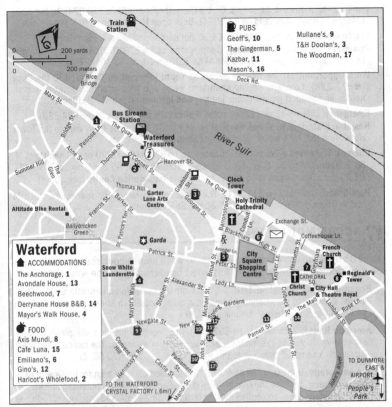

PUBS

Geoff's, **10**

The Gingerman, **5**

Kazbar, **11**

Mason's, **16**

Mullane's, **9**

T&H Doolan's, **3**

The Woodman, **17**

N9

Train Station

200 yards

200 meters

Rice Bridge

Mary St.

Summer Hill

The Glen

Bridge St.

Anne St.

Penrose Ln.

Thomas St.

Bus Eireann Station

The Quay

Waterford Treasures

O'Connell St.

Hanover St.

Gladstone St.

The Quay

Clock Tower

River Suir

Dock Rd.

Thomas Hill

Garter Lane Arts Centre

Georges St.

Holy Trinity Cathedral

Altitude Bike Rental

Francis St.

Barker St.

St. Patrick's Ter.

Barronstrand

Conduit Ln.

Exchange St.

Coffeehouse Ln.

Ballybricken Green

Blackfriars

High St.

Henrietta St.

Greyfriars Ln.

French Church

Garda

Patrick St.

Arundel Ln.

Peter St.

City Square Shopping Centre

Keyser Ln.

Waterford

⬆ ACCOMMODATIONS

The Anchorage, **1**

Avondale House, **13**

Beechwood, **7**

Derrynane House B&B, **14**

Mayor's Walk House, **4**

🍴 FOOD

Axis Mundi, **8**

Cafe Luna, **15**

Emiliano's, **6**

Gino's, **12**

Haricot's Wholefood, **2**

Snow White Launderette

Mayor's Walk

Stephen St.

St. Alexander St.

Broad St.

Lady Ln.

John St.

Spring Gardens

Michael St.

Colbeck St.

Christ Church

CATHEDRAL SQ.

City Hall & Theatre Royal

Reginald's Tower

The Mall

Lombard St.

Rose Ln.

Newgate St.

New St.

Parnell St.

Catherine St.

TO DUNMORE EAST & AIRPORT

Convent Hill

Hennessys Rd.

Castle St.

Parliament St.

Manor St.

John's River

People's Park

TO THE WATERFORD CRYSTAL FACTORY (.6mi)

per day, €8); **Limerick** (2½hr.; M-Th and Su 6 per day, F 7 per day; €14.50); **Rosslare Harbour** (1¼hr., 3-5 per day, €12.50). **City buses** leave from the Clock Tower on the Quay. €1.20 for most areas. **City Imp** minibuses (€1.20) also cruise the town.

Taxis: A piece of cake to find, 24hr. a day. Either go to the **cab stand** on Broad St. or try: **7 Cabs** (☎877 777); **Five-O Cabs** (☎850 000); **Rapid Cabs** (☎858 585).

Bike Rental: Altitude, 22 Ballybricken St. (☎870 356), past the *Garda* station on the far side of the green. €20 per day; includes helmet. Free delivery to local accommodations.

Hitching: Waterford's few hitchers place themselves on main routes, away from the tangled city center. To reach N24 (Cahir, Limerick), N10 (Kilkenny, Dublin), or N25 (New Ross, Wexford, Rosslare), they head over the bridge toward the train station. For N25 to Cork, they contnue down Parnell St.; others take city buses to the Crystal Factory before sticking out a thumb.

■✳🛈 ORIENTATION AND PRACTICAL INFORMATION

Modern Waterford sits on the ruins of the triangular Viking city. The horned ones must have had a knack for urban planning, because the area between **the Quay, Parnell Street (the Mall),** and **Barronstrand Street (Michael and Broad Street)** is still hopping, long after the sweet music of falsterpipes faded away.

Tourist Office: On the Quay (☎875 823), across from the bus station. From the train station, cross Rice Bridge and turn left. Open M-F 9am-6pm, Sa 10am-6pm.

Banks: 24hr. **ATMs** line the streets. On the Quay, they're at **AIB** (☎874 824), by the clock tower, and **Bank of Ireland** (☎872 074). Both open M 10am-5pm, Tu-F 10am-4pm.

Luggage Storage: Plunkett Station. €1.30 per item. Open M-Sa 7:15am-9pm.

Pharmacy: Gallagher's Pharmacy, Barronstrand St. (☎878 103). An oasis of pharmaceutical care in the city center. Open M-Sa 8:30am-10pm, Su 10am-7pm.

Work Opportunities: The friendly people at **Youth Information Centre,** 130 the Quay (☎877 328), help with finding short-term work, and also offer info on work, travel, health, and support groups (including **gay and lesbian**). Open M-F 9:30am-5:30pm.

Emergency: Dial ☎999 or 112; no coins. **Police** *(Garda)*: Patrick St. (☎874 888).

Hospital: Waterford Regional Hospital (☎848 000). Follow the Quay east to the Tower Hotel. Turn left, then follow signs straight ahead to the hospital.

Internet: Waterford e-Centre, 10 O'Connell St. (☎878 448). €1.20 per 10min. Open M-Sa 9:30am-10pm, Su 11am-8pm. **Voyager Internet Cafe,** 85 the Quay (☎843 843). €1.20 per 10min. Open M-Sa 10am-7pm. **Youth Information Centre** (see above).

Post Office: The Quay (☎874 321). The largest of several letter-dispensaries. Open M and W-F 9am-5:30pm, Tu 9:30am-5:30pm, Sa 9am-1pm.

⌐ ACCOMMODATIONS

Most B&Bs in the city center are nothing to write home about; those outside town on the Cork Rd. are better. All Waterford's hostels have gone the way of the dodo.

Beechwood, 7 Cathedral Sq. (☎876 677). From the Quay, go up Henrietta St. Mrs. Ryan invites guests into her charming home on a quiet pedestrian street. Windows look out on Christ Church Cathedral. Doubles €50. ❷

Avondale House, 2 Parnell St., (☎852 267). Old Georgian mansion with plenty of modern luxuries, including TVs, phones, and hairdryers in all rooms. The red-carpeted stairway lends a sense of grandeur to this guesthouse. Doubles €70-80. ❹

The Anchorage, 9 the Quay (☎854 302). The location can't be beat for those with early buses or trains, and the showers are incredible. Each room at this hotel-esque B&B has a TV, phone, and tea- and coffee-making facilities. Singles €40-45; doubles €70-80. ❸

Mayor's Walk House, 12 Mayor's Walk (☎855 427). A 15min. walk from the train station. Convenient to many pubs. Quiet, subdued rooms at simple prices. Open Feb.-Nov. Singles €25; doubles €44. ❸

Derrynane House, 19 the Mall (☎875 179). Clean but not sparkling, Derrynane is showing its age with out-dated rugs and ceiling lights. Great views of town hall and the Theatre Royal through the B&B's fantastic floor-to-ceiling windows. €25. ❸

⌂ FOOD

Satisfy cravings with some groceries at **Dunnes Stores** in the City Square Shopping Centre. (☎853 100. Open M-W 9am-7pm, Th-F 9am-9pm, Sa 9am-6pm, Su noon-6pm.) **Treacy's,** on the Quay between the Granville Hotel and the tourist office, has a small deli and a large variety of food-stuffs. (Open daily 8am-11pm.)

Haricot's Wholefood Restaurant, 11 O'Connell St. (☎841 299). Healthy, innovative, veggie-friendly dishes made from scratch. Come often to see what's new on the menu, or to visit with the sociable staff. Mains €8-10. Open M-F 10am-8pm, Sa 10am-6pm. ❷

Emiliano's, 21 High St., (☎820 333). Candle-lit tables and a well-dressed crowd set a romantic mood for truly authentic Italian food. Call ahead for reservations, or arrive before 7pm for a 3-course early-bird special (€18). Pasta €11-12, mains €17-24. Open Tu-F 10:30pm, Sa-Su 12:30pm and 5-10:30pm. ❸

Gino's, John St. (☎879 513). Busy, bright, family restaurant that prepares pizza before your eyes. Call for takeaway. Individual pizzas €4.30-7. Open daily 12:30-10:30pm. ❷

Cafe Luna, 53 John St. (☎834 539). Late-night cafe serves pasta, salads, and sandwiches in a vaguely pretentious, artsy environment. Homemade soup and half-sandwich €4.15. Most mains €6-9. Open M-W 8:30am-midnight, Th-Su 8:30am-3:30am. ❷

Axis Mundi, 2-3 the Mall (☎855 087), behind Reginald's Tower. Lean against a section of the Norman wall that defended 14th-century Waterford while imbibing. A bar/restaurant/night club with trendy food and a classy modern-meets-ancient environment. ❸

🔲🔳 PUBS AND CLUBS

The Quays are flooded with old-fashioned pubs, but the corner of John and Parnell St. is where local youngsters get their drink on. The good times continue past pub closings at 12:30am, when late bars and weekend discos kick it into high gear.

▨ **Geoff's,** 8 John St. (☎874 787). One of Waterford's most popular pubs for over 100 years, Geoff's still manages to feel young and friendly. Locals of all ages drop into this deceptively spacious wood-panelled pub for pints and laughs, but go elsewhere for matches—Geoff staunchly refuses to install a demon-box. Italian-style sandwiches (€4-7) served until 9pm. Open until 12:30am on weekends.

▨ **T&H Doolan's,** George's St. (☎841 504). Doolan's has been serving for a respectable 300 years, in an awe-inspiring building with low, low ceilings that has been standing for over 800. Sinead O'Connor crooned here during her college days. Crowd is split between natives and imports. Trad nightly at 9:30pm. Pub food €13-19 until 9pm.

Kazbar, John St. (☎843 729). Posh urbanites flock to the outdoor tables and indoor lanterns of this Middle-Eastern themed bar/cafe to pretend they're somewhere truly exotic. Live music Su nights. Open M-W noon-11:30pm, Th-Sa noon-12:30am, Su noon-11pm. Food served daily until 8pm.

The Gingerman, Arundel Ln. (☎879 522). Looks like a dark French bistro, but trad sessions jam on M nights, and the good times spill into the dramatic dark-wood-and-mirrors back room. Food served noon-6pm. Live music M and Th-Sa. Open M-W 10am-11:30pm, Th-Sa 10am-12:30am, Su 10am-11pm.

The Woodman, at Parnell and John St. (☎858 130). A small traditional pub. Shuts down at 12:30am on weekends, so click those heels and head to the adjoining **Ruby's Nightclub,** which throbs with chart hits until 2:30am. Th-Sa cover €8-10.

Mullane's, 15 Newgate St. (☎873 854), off New St. Sessions this intense aren't easy to find. Older regulars with a sprinkling of young and dash of tourist. Call ahead for session times (usually W-Th, Sa-Su 9:45pm-12:15am); pub is almost empty without one.

Mason's, at Parnell and John St. (☎875 881). Colored lights and flat-screen TVs merge with giant faux-stone chessmen and a huge Gothic arch over the huge bar in this clubby pub. Open M-W 5pm-11:30pm, Th-F 5pm-12:30am, Sa 3pm-12:30am, Su 3-11pm.

🔲 SIGHTS

To cover all of Waterford's sights in a day requires the swiftness of a Viking raider and the organization of a Norman invader. Buying the **City Pass** from **Waterford Tourism,** 1 Arundel St. (☎852 550), or at the Waterford Crystal Factory, Waterford Treasures, or Reginald's Tower, gets admission to all three for €9.20.

▨ **THE WATERFORD CRYSTAL FACTORY.** What links fancy dinner sets, the Times Square Millenium Ball, and all major glass sporting trophies? They were handcrafted at the spectacular Waterford Crystal Factory, 2 mi. from the city center on N25 (the Cork Rd.). Watch master craftsmen transform molten goo into sparkling crystal or admire the finished products (and their sky-high prices). The tour covers the refreshingly gritty and real factory and ends in the gallery's fantasy world. *(Catch the City Imp outside Dunnes on Michael St. and ask to stop at the factory. 10-15min., every 15-20min. €1.20. Or, take city bus #1, Kilbarry-Ballybeg, leaving across from the Clock Tower every 30min. Factory ☎ 332 500; www.waterfordvisitorcentre.com. Gallery open daily Mar.-Oct. 8:30am-6pm; Nov.-Feb. 9am-5pm. 1hr. tours every 15min.; audio-visual shows by request. Tours €6.50, students €3.50. Mar.-Oct. daily 8:30am-4pm; Nov.-Feb. M-F 9am-3:15pm.)*

※ WATERFORD TREASURES. To touch up on the 1000-year history of Waterford, head to Waterford Treasures at the Granary, connected to the tourist office. Named the **1999-2000 Ireland Museum of the Year,** the €4.5 million museum is well worth a visit. While the kids entertain themselves with the multimedia displays, parents can check out the amusing (and gory) cartoons that line the walls. An audio-visual handset details the historical oddities on display. The actual artifacts, including plenty of Viking goods and the only extant item of Henry VIII's clothing (a velvet hat) make quite an impressive show. *(☎ 304 500. Open June-Aug. M-F 9am-9pm, Sa 9am-6pm, Su 11am-5pm; May and Sept. M-Sa 9:30am-6pm; Oct.-Apr. M-Sa 10am-5pm, Su 11am-5pm. €6, students €4.50.)*

REGINALD'S TOWER. At the end of the Quay, Reginald's tower has guarded the city entrance since the 12th century. Its virtually impenetrable 10-foot thick walls have housed a prison, mint, and Strongbow and Aoife's wedding reception (see **Christians and Vikings,** p. 57). Tiny models illustrate the contributions of Vikings, Normans, and English kings to Waterford's growth. *(☎ 873 501. Tours by request. Open daily June-Sept. 9:30am-6:30pm; Oct.-May 10am-5pm. €2, seniors €1.25, students €1.)*

OTHER SIGHTS. Stellar tour-guide Jack Burtchaell leads **The Walking Tour of Historic Waterford** and helps sort out the city's mongrel lineage. The tour includes a visit to part of the original Viking walls. *(☎ 873 711 or 851 043. 1hr. tours depart from the Granville Hotel on the Quay and the Granary museum. Tours Mar.-Oct. daily at 11:45am and 1:45pm. €5.)* Many of the more recent buildings were the brainchildren of 18th-century architect John Roberts. The **Theatre Royal** and **City Hall,** both on the Mall, are his secular masterpieces. He's also responsible for Catholic **Holy Trinity Cathedral** on Barronstrand St. and Church of Ireland **Christ Church Cathedral** in Cathedral Sq. (up Henrietta St. from the Quay), making Waterford the only city in Europe where Catholics and Protestants worship in buildings designed by a common architect.

♪ ※ ENTERTAINMENT AND FESTIVALS

The tourist office provides an annual list of major events in town, and any local newspaper, including the free *Waterford Today*, should have more specific entertainment listings. Watch for posters as well. The summertime **Waterford Show** at City Hall presents a program of Irish music, stories, and dance. Ticket cost €7, and include a glass of Baileys or wine at the show. *(☎ 358 397 or 875 788; after 5pm try ☎ 381 020. Open July-Aug. Tu-Th and Sa 9pm; May-June and Sept. Tu, Th, Sa 9pm. Call for reservations or inquire at the tourist office.)* The **Garter Lane Arts Centre,** 22a O'Connell St., supports all different forms of art inside its old Georgian brick. Visual exhibits adorn the walls and are usually free. Concerts cost less than €15, and dance and theater productions grace its stage year-round. *(☎ 855 038. Center and box office open M-Sa 10am-6pm; performance nights until 9pm. Excellent films shown occasionally €7. Students and seniors discount €3-5.)* Waterford's largest festival is the **Spraoi** ("spree"), held during the August bank holiday weekend. A celebration of life that inundates the streets of the city, the Spraoi attracts street theater troupes and bands from around the globe and culminates in a sizeable parade. *(☎ 841 808; www.spraoi.com.)*

SOUTHWEST
IRELAND

With a dramatic landscape ranging from lush lakes and mountains to stark, ocean-battered cliffs, Southwest Ireland is rich in storytellers and history-makers. Out-laws and rebels once lurked in hidden coves and glens now frequented by visitors and lorded over by publicans. The urban activity of Cork City and the area's frantic pace of rebuilding and growth contrast with the ancient rhythm of nearby rural vil-lages. The Ring of Kerry draws huge numbers of visitors every year, and no place in Ireland has as many multilingual real estate signs as Killarney—the land in west Cork is steadily being snapped up by investors, the French, and the occasional movie star. If the tourist mayhem is too much for you, retreat to the placid stretches along the Beara Peninsula and Cork's southern coast.

EASTERN COUNTY CORK

Historically, the superb harbors along the eastern coast of Co. Cork have made the area into a prosperous trading center. Its distance from Dublin and the English Pale, however, saved the area from total domination during the 1600s, and afforded local Irishmen much freedom from the invasive British. Consequently, Cork was seething with patriotic activity during the 19th and 20th centuries. Head-quarters of the "Munster Republic" controlled by anti-Treaty forces during the Civil War, the county produced patriot Michael Collins, as well as his assassin (see **Independence and Civil War,** p. 64). Today, Cork City is a hotbed of industry and cul-ture, while the seaside towns of Kinsale and Cobh gaily entertain tall ships and stooped-over backpackers. Ireland's rich archaeological history is particularly accessible from Cork, with Celtic ring forts, mysterious stone circles, and long-ruined abbeys dotting the nearby sheep-speckled hills.

CORK CITY (AN CORCAIGH) ☎ 021

In its capacity as Ireland's second-largest city, Cork (pop. 150,000) hosts most of the athletic, musical, and artistic activities in the Southwest. The river quays and pub-lined streets display architecture both grand and grimy, evidence of "Rebel Cork's" history of resistance, ruin, and reconstruction. Indeed, what few pre-industrial charms smokestacks didn't blacken, the English blighted. The old city burned down in 1622, Cromwell expelled half its citizens in the 1640s, the Duke of Marlborough laid siege in 1690, and Cork was torched again in 1920 during the Irish War for Independence. Wise visitors will exploit the city's resources more politely: Cork is a base to eat, drink, shop, and sleep while exploring the exquisite scenery of the surrounding countryside. Within the city limits, time is best filled by reveling in the urban bustle and vibrant street life, or meandering across the cam-pus of University College Cork.

Southwest Ireland

◪ INTERCITY TRANSPORTATION

Airport: Cork Airport (☎431 3131), 5 mi. south of Cork on the Kinsale Rd. **Aer Lingus** (☎432 7155), **British Airways** (☎800 626 747), and **Ryanair** (☎01 609 7800) connect Cork to Dublin, Paris, and several English cities. A taxi (€15) or bus (16-18 per day, €3.15) will run from the airport to the bus station on Parnell Pl.

Trains: Kent Station, Lower Glanmire Rd. (☎450 6766; www.irishrail.ie), in the northeast part of town across the river from the city center. Open M-Sa 6:30am-8:00pm, Su 7:50am-8pm. Train connections to: **Dublin** (3hr.; M-Sa 7 per day, Su 5 per day; €51.50); **Killarney** (2hr.; M-Sa 4 per day; €25.50); **Limerick** (1½hr.; M-Sa 7 per day, Su 4 per day; €25.50); **Tralee** (2½hr., 3 per day, €30.50).

Buses: Parnell Pl. (☎450 8188), 2 blocks east of Patrick's Bridge on Merchant's Quay. Inquiries desk open daily 9am-6pm. **Bus Éireann** goes to all major cities: **Bantry** (2hr.; M-Sa 7 per day, Su 4 per day; €13); **Dublin** (4½hr.; M-Sa 6 per day, Su 5 per day; €20); **Galway** (4hr.; M-Sa 7 per day, Su 4 per day; €17); **Killarney** (2hr.; M-Sa 13 per day, Su 10 per day; €13); **Limerick** (2hr., 14 per day, €13.20); **Rosslare Harbour** (4hr., 3 per day, €18.50); **Sligo** (7hr., 5 per day, €23); **Tralee** (2½hr., 12 per day, €14); **Waterford** (2¼hr., M-Sa 13 per day, €14.50). Round-trip fares offer better deals.

Ferries: Ringaskiddy Terminal (☎427 5061), 8 mi. south of the city, sends ferries off to Roscoff, France (14hr., €46-96). Call **Brittany Ferries** (☎437 8401) or visit their office on the Grand Parade, by the tourist office. Bus Éireann (☎450 8188) makes the 30min. trip to the ferry, leaving from the Cork bus station. Buses leave 1¼hr. prior to ferry departure from bay #10. **Swansea-Cork Ferries** sends daily ferries on the 10hr. trip to Swansea, Wales. (☎427 1166; €29.) For more info, see **By Ferry,** p. 33.

◪ ORIENTATION

Cork's compact city center wasn't always an island. Before being diverted to create its modern moat, the River Lee's present north and south channels once ran straight through the city in grand Venetian fashion. The pavement of horseshoe-shaped **St. Patrick's Street** was laid directly over the waterflow, inspiring its unconventional U-shape. St. Patrick St. ends its horseshoe and becomes **Grand Parade** to the West; to the north it crosses **Merchant's Quay,** home of the bus station. North across St. Patrick's bridge, **McCurtain Street** runs east to **Lower Glanmire Road** and the train station, before becoming the **N8** to Dublin, Waterford, and Cobh. Downtown action concentrates on the vaguely parallel **Paul, St. Patrick's,** and **Oliver Plunkett Streets.** Their connecting north-south avenues are shop-lined and largely pedestrian. Heading west from Grand Parade, **Washington Street** becomes **Western Road** before reaching **University College Cork** and the **N22** to Killarney.

◪ LOCAL TRANSPORTATION

Bus: The main bus station (☎450 8188) at Parnell Pl. offers free timetables for the **city buses.** From downtown, catch the buses (and their schedules) at the bus station on Merchant's Quay, across from the Father Matthew statue. **Bus #8** runs down Western Rd. toward UCC and the An Óige hostel. Downtown buses run M-Sa every 10-30min., 7:30am-11:15pm, with reduced service Su 10am-11:15pm. Fares from €0.95.

Car Rental: Budget Rent-a-Car, Tourist Office, Grand Parade (☎427 4755). €56 per day, €279 per wk. 25+. **Great Island Car Rentals,** 47 McCurtain St. (☎481 1609). €70-75 per day, €250-340 per wk.; add €13 per day for drivers under 25. 23+.

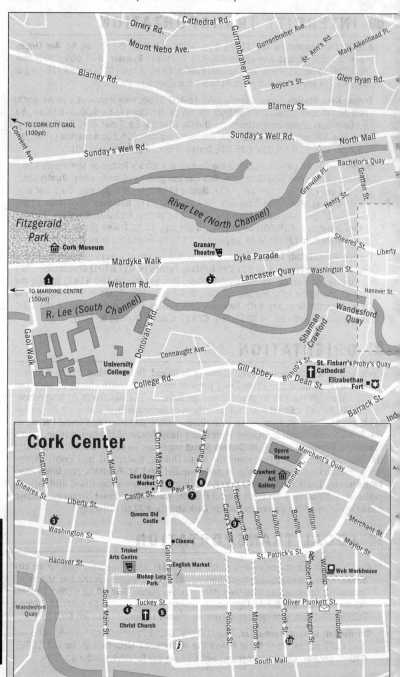

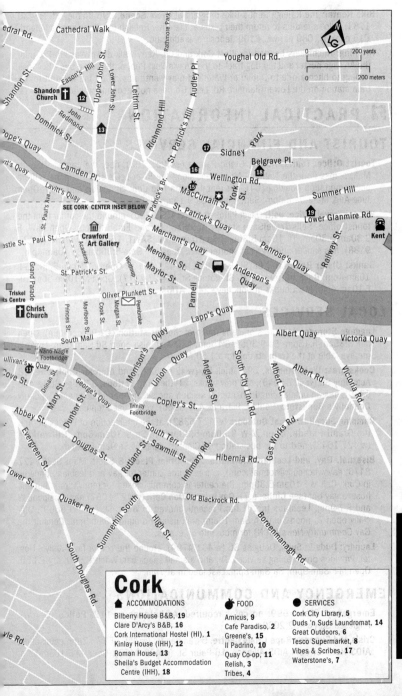

Cork

ACCOMMODATIONS

Bilberry House B&B, **19**
Clare D'Arcy's B&B, **16**
Cork International Hostel (HI), **1**
Kinlay House (IHH), **12**
Roman House, **13**
Sheila's Budget Accommodation
Centre (IHH), **18**

FOOD

Amicus, **9**
Cafe Paradiso, **2**
Greene's, **15**
Il Padrino, **10**
Quay Co-op, **11**
Relish, **3**
Tribes, **4**

SERVICES

Cork City Library, **5**
Duds 'n Suds Laundromat, **14**
Great Outdoors, **6**
Tesco Supermarket, **8**
Vibes & Scribes, **17**
Waterstone's, **7**

Bike Rental: The Raleigh Rent-a-Bike program at **Cycle Scene,** 396 Blarney St. (☎430 1183), allows renters to return their bikes at the other Raleigh locations across Ireland. €15 per day, €80 per wk. €100 deposit or credit card.

Hitching: Hitchhikers headed for West Cork and Co. Kerry walk down Western Rd. past the An Óige hostel and the dog track to the Crow's Nest Pub, or they take bus #8. Those hoping to hitch a ride to Dublin or Waterford may want to stand on the hill next to the train station on the Lower Glanmire Rd. Let's Go does not recommend hitchiking.

🛈 PRACTICAL INFORMATION

TOURIST AND FINANCIAL SERVICES

Tourist Office: Tourist House, Grand Parade (☎425 5100), near the corner of South Mall, across from the National Monument along the River Lee's south channel. Offers accommodation booking (€4), car rental, and a free Cork city guide and map. Open June-Aug. M-Sa 9am-6pm; Sept.-May M-Sa 9:15am-5:30pm.

Budget Travel Office: usit, Oliver Plunkett St. (☎427 0900), around the corner from the tourist office. Sells **TravelSave** stamps and Rambler and Eurail tickets. Open M-W, F 9:30am-5:30pm, Th 10am-5:30pm, Sa 10am-2pm. **SAYIT,** 76 Grand Parade (☎427 9188), has similar offerings but shorter lines. Open M-F 9am-5:30pm, Sa 10am-4pm.

Banks: Ulster Bank Ltd., 88 St. Patrick St. (☎427 0618). Open M 10am-5pm, Tu-F 10am-4pm. **Bank of Ireland,** 70 St. Patrick St. (☎427 7177). Open M 10am-5pm, Tu-F 10am-4pm. Most banks in Cork have 24hr. **ATMs.**

LOCAL SERVICES

Luggage Storage: Reliable storage is found at the **bus station** (€1.90 per item). Open M-F 8:35am-6:15pm, Sa 9:30am-6:15pm; June-Aug. also open Su 9am-6pm. Lockers are available at the **train station** for €1.50.

Bookstores: Waterstone's, 69 Patrick St. (☎427 6522), and **Mercier Bookstore,** 18 Academy St. (☎427 5040), sell new books. ▓**Vibes and Scribes,** 3 Bridge St. (☎450 5370), has an outstanding Irish-interest section and second-hand basement. Scholarly **Connolly's Bookstore,** Paul St. Plaza (☎427 5366), vends used tomes.

Camping Supplies: Great Outdoors (☎427 6382), at the intersection of Patrick St. and the Grand Parade. Open M-W 9:30am-5:30pm, Th-Sa 9:30am-6pm. **Hillwalking** (☎427 1643), next to the bus station on Clontarf. Open M-Sa 9am-5:30pm.

Bisexual, Gay, and Lesbian Information: The Other Place, 8 South Main St. (☎427 8470; gayswitchcork@hotmail.com), is a resource center for gay and lesbian concerns in Cork. Call M-F 10am-5:30pm. The center is currently closed for renovations, but still hosts a gay bar (see **Clubs,** p.7). **Gay Information Cork** (☎427 1087) has a helpline W and F 7-9pm. **Lesbians Inc. (L.Inc.)** recently moved to White St. (☎480 8600). Officially open Tu noon-3pm, Th 8am-10am; staff usually around 10am-5pm. Consult the *Gay Community News* (GCN) for more info on events.

Laundry: Duds 'n Suds, Douglas St. (☎431 4799), around the corner from Kelly's Hostel. Provides dry-cleaning services, TV, and a small snack bar. Wash €2.50, dry €3.50. Open M-F 8am-9pm, Sa 8am-8pm. Last load in at 7pm.

EMERGENCY AND COMMUNICATIONS

Emergency: Dial ☎999; no coins required. **Ambulance:** ☎112. **Police** *(Garda):* Anglesea St. (☎452 2000).

Crisis and Support: Rape Crisis Centre, 5 Camden Pl. (☎450 5577). 24hr. counseling. **AIDS Hotline,** Cork AIDS Alliance, 16 Peter St. (☎432 0450). Open M-F 10am-5pm.

Samaritans (☎ 427 1323 or 800 460 9090). 24hr. support line or follow signs to the Coach St. office.

Pharmacies: Regional Late Night Pharmacy, Wilton Rd. (☎ 434 4575), opposite the Regional Hospital on bus #8. Open M-F 9am-10pm, Sa-Su 10am-10pm. **Phelan's Late Night,** 9 Patrick St. (☎ 427 2511). Open M-Sa 9am-10pm, Su 10am-10pm.

Hospital: Mercy Hospital, Grenville Pl. (☎ 427 1971). €25 fee for emergency room access. **Cork Regional Hospital,** Wilton St. (☎ 454 6400), on the #8 bus route.

Internet: ▧Web Workhouse, Winthrop St. (☎ 427 3090), connecting Patrick and Oliver Plunkett St. Near the post office. Lofty, converted warehouse hums with high-speed computers. Smoking and non-smoking sections. Tea and coffee available. 8am-noon €3 per hr.; noon-5pm €4-5; 5pm-3am €2.50; 3am-8am €1.25. Open M-Su, 24hr. **Cork City Library** (☎ 427 7110), across from the tourist office. €1 per 30min. Open M-Sa 10am-5:30pm.

Post Office: Oliver Plunkett St. (☎ 427 2000). Open M-Sa 9am-5:30pm.

⚐ ACCOMMODATIONS

Cork's international youth hostels stand like student-populated fortresses at three ends of the city. All three are excellent, and popular, so call ahead. A few terrific B&Bs populate **Patrick's Hill;** the best ones congregate nearer **Glanmire Road. Western Road,** leading out toward University College, is knee-deep in pricier B&Bs.

▧ **Sheila's Budget Accommodation Centre (IHH),** 4 Belgrave Pl. (☎ 450 5562; www.sheilashostel.ie), at the intersection of Wellington Rd. and York Street Hill. Sheila's offers a central location, a roomy kitchen, and occasional summertime barbecues in a secluded backyard. All rooms non-smoking and with bath. The 24hr. reception desk doubles as a general store and has breakfast for €3.20. **Sauna** €2. **Bike rental** €12. **Internet** €1 per 20min. Free luggage storage. Check-out 10am. Dorms €15-16; singles €30; doubles €40-50. ❷

▧ **Clare D'Arcy B&B,** 7 Sidney Place, Wellington Rd. (☎ 450 4658; www.darcysguesthouse.com). From St. Patricks bridge, start up St. Patricks Hill, turning right onto Wellington road; look for the blue sign on the left. The most authentically luxurious guesthouse in Cork. Elegant Parisian-style interior, chandeliers and all. Rooms #5 and 6 have panoramic views of the city; the enormous arched window of room #7 overlooks the garden. Freshly squeezed OJ and smoked salmon for breakfast. Doubles €80; shared rooms €35-45 per person. ❹

Kinlay House (IHH), Bob and Joan Walk (☎ 450 8966; www.kinlayhouse.ie), down the alley to the right of Shandon Church. Kinlay House's bright colors and warm atmosphere offset its large, motel layout. Recent renovations brought wonderful family-sized rooms and a plush lounge area to the house. Video library and game room. Continental breakfast included. **Internet** €1 per 15min. Laundry €7. Free parking. 10- to 14-bed dorms €14; singles €25-30; doubles €40-45. Family-sized rooms €18 per person. ❷

Roman House, 3 St. John's Terr., Upper John St. (☎ 450 3606); www. interglobal.ie/ romanhouse), in a muted red building with a black door. Cross the North Channel by the opera house, make a left on John Redmond St., then bear right onto Upper John St. Located across from Kinlay House. Colorful Roman House is Cork's only B&B catering specifically to gay and lesbian travelers (though any and all are welcome). Walls display artist/proprietor's work. Bath, TV, oversized armchairs, and hot-pots in every room. Vegetarian breakfast option. Singles €40; doubles €60. ❷

Cork International Hostel (An Óige/HI), 1-2 Redclyffe, Western Rd. (☎ 454 3289), a 15min. walk from the Grand Parade. Bus #8 stops across the street. Turn left and walk about 2 blocks. Immaculate, spacious rooms with high ceilings compensate for the out-of-the-way location of this stately brick Victorian townhouse. All rooms with bath. Continental breakfast €3.50. **Internet** €1 per 10min. Check-in 10:30am-midnight. 10-bed and 6-bed dorms €17; 4-bed €19. Doubles €44. Reduced prices if under 18. ❷

Bilberry House B&B, 1 Patricks Terrace, on Lower Glanmire Rd. (☎435 3133). Rooms are spare, but several have wonderful views of the town. Singles €35; doubles €50. ❸

🚺 FOOD

Downtown Cork is blessed with an array of delicious restaurants and cafes; the lanes connecting Patrick St., Paul St., and Oliver Plunkett St. are particularly appealing. The **English Market**, accessible from Grand Parade, Patrick St., and Oliver Plunkett St., displays a wide variety of meats, fish, cheeses, and fruits fresh from the farms and fisheries of West Cork. Cork's local specialties include *crubeen* (pig's feet), *drisheen* (blood sausage; its texture is a hybrid of liver and Jell-O), and Clonakilty black pudding (an intriguing mix of blood, grain, and spice). The **Tesco** on Paul St. is the biggest grocery store in town. (☎427 0791. Open M-W and Sa 8:30am-8pm, Th-F 8:30am-10pm.)

🍴**Quay Co-op,** 24 Sullivan's Quay (☎431 7660). Large townhouse windows enliven the vibrant colors and youthful intellectual buzz. A vegetarian and vegan's delight, but no chore for carnivores either. Excellent soups and desserts. Apricot and yogurt flan €2.50. Specials €6.50. Open M-Sa 9am-9pm. Store open M-Sa 9am-6:15pm. ❷

🍴**Tribes,** Tuckey St. (☎427 6070). Continue past the fountain ending Oliver Plunkett St., keeping the Bishop Lucy park to your left. Late-night, low-light college java shop with south-islander theme. Serves full menu into the wee hours. Global spectrum of coffee blends (€1.65). Teas from blackcurrant to strawberry nettle (€1.80). Bronx burger or Hawaiian bagel sandwich €5.40. Open M-W noon-12:30am, Th-Sa noon-4:30am. ❶

Greene's, 48 MacCurtain St. (☎455 2279). Walk through the overhang toward a large fountain and it's on the right. Warm colors, grand skylights, stone and wood accents, and beautiful food. Ask for a seat by the window. Entrees €16-22. M-Th 6-10pm, F-Sa 6-10:30pm, Su 6-9pm. Early-bird 3-course menu €19.50, served nightly 6-7pm. ❹

Café Paradiso, 16 Lancaster Quay (☎427 7939). Award-winning vegetarian meals bordering on gourmet. Cool-colored Mediterranean feel; popular with breezy jet-setters. Watermelon, feta, and cucumber salad €7. Lunch €7-13; dinner €9-18. Open Tu-Sa 12:30-3pm and 6:30-10:30pm. ❸

Amicus, 14A French Church St. (☎427 6455). Artistic and elegant, from the paintings to the creative cuisine. Entrees €12-20. Open M-Sa 10am-10:30pm, Su 10am-10pm. ❹

Relish, 32 Washington St. (☎490 5986). Bright California bistro whisks travelers away from the Irish rain. Entrees €10-15. Great breakfasts. Open M-F 8am-10pm, Sa 9am-10pm, Su 10am-10pm. ❸

Il Padrino, 21 Cork St. (☎427 1544). Quality Italian fare in a relaxed atmosphere. Pizzas €12, salads €7. Open M-F 10:30, Sa-Su noon until late. ❷

🍺 PUBS

Cork's pub scene has the variety of music and atmosphere expected of Ireland's second-largest city. Pubs beyond counting crowd along Union Quay, Oliver Plunkett, and South Main St.; to guide you on your tipsy quest, *Let's Go* offers our very own Cork City Pub Crawl. The city is especially proud of its Murphy's, a thick, creamy stout that some say rivals Guinness. (Others say this boast is Cork-bred, misled rubbish.) A cheaper stout, Beamish, is also brewed here. Nearly all pubs stop serving at 11:30pm.

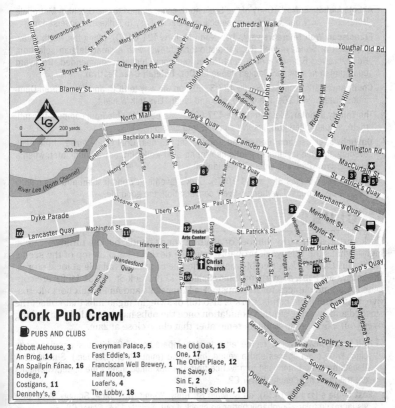

Cork Pub Crawl

🍺 PUBS AND CLUBS

Abbott Alehouse, 3	Everyman Palace, 5	The Old Oak, 15
An Brog, 14	Fast Eddie's, 13	One, 17
An Spailpín Fánac, 16	Franciscan Well Brewery, 1	The Other Place, 12
Bodega, 7	Half Moon, 8	The Savoy, 9
Costigans, 11	Loafer's, 4	Sin E, 2
Dennehy's, 6	The Lobby, 18	The Thirsty Scholar, 10

🍺 **The Lobby,** 1 Union Quay (☎431 9307). Arguably Cork's most famous venue; some of Ireland's biggest folk acts had their first shining moments here. Two floors overlook the river. Live music nightly, from trad to acid jazz. Come early for more popular acts. Occasional cover €2.50-6.35.

🍺 **An Spailpín Fánac** (on spal-PEEN FAW-nuhk), 28 South Main St. (☎427 7949), across from Beamish Brewery. One of Cork's favorite pubs, and one of its oldest (est. 1779). Visitors and locals come for live trad most nights; storytelling last Tu of every month.

An Brog, at the corner of Oliver Plunkett and Grand Parade. Ideal scene for those who crave good alternative rock, and want to sport their eyebrow rings. Mixed crowd.

Bodega, 46-49 Cornmarket St. (☎427 2878), off the northern end of Grand Parade and the western end of Paul St. Stone front, wood floors, stratospheric hall ceiling. An artsy cafe by day with a tasty selection of edibles, it transforms into a classy club at night. Great wine selection and an intimate balcony.

The Old Oak, Oliver Plunkett St. (☎427 6165), across from the General Post Office. Year after year it wins a "Best Traditional Pubs in Ireland" award. Packed and noisy; each section has its own vibe. Bar food served M-F noon-3pm. Bar closes F-Sa 1:45am.

Sin E, 8 Coburg St. (☎450 2266), just left of McCurtain St. after crossing St. Patrick's bridge. Mosaic glass exterior. Some of Cork's best live music, especially Th nights. Mixed crowd, mellow (though still noisy) atmosphere.

Abbott Alehouse, North Quay of the Lee's north channel, next to the Gresham Metropole Hotel. Tiny, cozy pub with a great selection of beers. Easy to strike up conversation.

Franciscan Well Microbrewery, 14b North Mall (☎421 0130), along the North Quay, just east of Sundays Well Rd. Fantastic local brews, with a great Belgian selection. Home-brewed Blarney Blonde and Rebel Red come highly recommended. Backyard beer garden in summer. Packed venue for **Oct. Belgian Beer Festival.**

Costigans, 11 Washington St. (☎427 3350), on the way to UCC, and across from Dominoes Pizza. Jovial 20s-30s crowd joke and laugh. Live folk W night.

The Thirsty Scholar, Western Rd. (☎427 6209). An easy stumble from campus, this intimate, student-filled pub has live summer trad sessions.

Dennehy's, across from Bodega on Cornmarket St., near Coal Quay. Arrive in the early evening and join jovial Irish gentlemen for an after-work pint, or wait until later, when a younger crowd rolls in. Open 3pm-midnight.

Loafer's, 26 Douglas St. (☎431 1612). Cork's favorite gay and lesbian pub fills nightly with all age groups. Live bands, lively conversation, the good life.

🎵 CLUBS

Cork nurtures a healthy number of aspiring young bands, but the turnover rate is high—what's hip this week probably won't be next. To keep on top of the scene, check out *List Cork*, a free bi-weekly schedule of music available at local stores. **The Lobby** (see **Pubs,** above) and **Nancy Spain's,** 48 Barrack St. (☎431 4452), are consistently sound choices for live music. **Fred Zeppelin's** and **An Phoenix** host alternative, punk, and indie bands. Cork is also full of swingin' nightclubs that collect the sloshed and swaying student population once the pubs have closed. When forking over your €5-10 cover, though, remember that clubs close at 2am.

🎵 Half Moon, Academy Ln., on the left side of the opera house. Cork's most popular dance club. Wide open spaces and a young, hip crowd (minus teeny-boppers). Strictly 18+. Tickets must be purchased in advance from the box office across the street. Su nights are the most happening. Cover €9.

Fast Eddie's (☎425 1438), off S. Main St. Busy. Young. Thumping. Shaggy. A bit of a visual marketplace—probably better go check it out. Strictly 18+. Cover €8.

The Savoy, Center of Patrick St. Hard to miss the grand entrance. High-brow. Turn to the left, now turn to the right, strike a pose, now vogue. Cover €6.

One, 1 Phoenix St. From Oliver Plunkett St., walk towards Parnell St., turn right onto Smith St., and turn right again onto Phoenix St. Trendy rave and techno music in one room, hip-hop in another. Cover €5-12.

The Other Place (☎427 8470), in a lane off South Main St. Cork's gay and lesbian disco rocks F and Sa 11:30pm-2am. Dance floor and bar/cafe upstairs (opens earlier). Highly appreciated by Cork's gay population, especially the younger set, on weekend nights. Cover F (€7.50) and Sa (€10).

Everyman Palace, 15 McCurtain St. (☎450 3077). Theater also houses a popular late-night blues and jazz club on weekends. Open F-Su 10pm-2am, as well as show nights.

🔍 SIGHTS

Cork's sights can be loosely sorted into three areas: the Old City, on the island in the center of town; the Shandon neighborhood, to the north of the River Lee; and the western part of the city, around the university. All can be reached on foot, a sensible approach in such a pedestrian-friendly city. For guidance, pick up *The Cork Area City Guide* at the tourist office (€1.90).

THE OLD CITY

TRISKEL ARTS CENTRE. The small but dynamic Triskel Arts Centre maintains two small galleries with rotating exhibits. It also organizes a wide variety of cultural events, including music, film, literature, theater, and the visual arts. *(Tobin St. ☎ 427 2022; triskel@iol.ie. Open M-Sa 10am-5:30pm. Gallery free; films €5.50-7.)*

ST. FINBARR'S CATHEDRAL. Looming over Proby's Quay, St. Fin's is a testament to the Victorian obsession with the neo-Gothic. Finbarr allegedly founded his "School of Cork" here in AD 606, but no trace of the early foundation remains. The present cathedral, built between 1735 and 1870, houses contemporary art exhibits in summer. *(Bishop St. ☎ 496 3387. Open M-Sa 10am-5:30pm. €2.50 requested donation.)*

KEYSER HILL. On a nice day, there's a decent view of Cork—and a dangerously good view of Beamish Brewery—from Keyser Hill. At the top of the stairs leading up the hill is the **Elizabethan Fort,** a star-shaped and ivy-covered remnant of English domination. To access the fort's impressive view, climb the stairs just inside the main gate. *(Follow S. Main St. away from the city center, cross the South Gate Bridge, turn right onto Proby's Quay then left onto Keyser Hill. Always open. Free.)*

CHRIST CHURCH. The area around steeple-less Christ Church provides a quiet spot to rest in a city center otherwise lacking green space. The site, scattered with eclectic statues, suffered Protestant torching three times between its 1270 consecration and the construction of the final version in 1729. *(Off the Grand Parade just north of Bishop Lucy Park. Walk down the Christ Church Ln., keeping the park on your left, until you emerge on S. Main St. To the right is the church. Always open. Free.)*

SHANDON AND EMMET PLACE

ST. ANNE'S CHURCH. Commonly called Shandon Church, St. Anne's sandstone-and limestone-striped steeple inspired the red and white "rebel" flag that still flies throughout the county. Like most of Cork, the original church was ravaged by 17th-century pyromaniacal English armies; construction of the current church began in 1722. Clocks grace the four sides of Shandon's tower. Notoriously out of sync and usually plain wrong, the clocks have been held responsible for many an Irishman's tardy arrival at work and earned the church its nickname, "the four-faced liar." *(Walk up Shandon St., take a right on unmarked Church St., and continue straight; the church overlooks Kinlay House. ☎ 450 5906. Open June-Sept. M-Th, Sa 10am-5:30pm, F 10am-5:30pm. €4, students and seniors €3.50, family €12. Group rates available.)*

OTHER SIGHTS. The monstrous cement **Opera House** was erected two decades ago after an older, more elegant opera house went down in flames. *(Emmet Pl. Over the hill from Shandon Church and across the north fork of the Lee. ☎ 427 0022. Gallery open M-Sa 10am-5pm. Free.)* **Cork Butter Museum** comes closer than one might think to making Cork's commerce history, and preserved butter, interesting. *(Church St. ☎ 430 0600. Open May-Sept. daily 10am-1pm and 2-5pm. €4, students and seniors €2.50.)* **Crawford Art Gallery** runs a program of temporary exhibitions, both Irish and international. The striking main gallery room is filled with marble ghosts of the Venus de Milo, Michelangelo, and others of artistic fame. *(Off Paul St. ☎ 427 3377. Open M-Sa 10am-5pm. Free.)* At the **Shandon Craft Centre,** potters, crystal-blowers, and other artisans display and sell their wares. *(Church St., across from the church.)*

WESTERN CORK CITY

▧ UNIVERSITY COLLEGE CORK (UCC). Built in 1845, UCC's campus is a collection of brooding Gothic buildings, manicured lawns, and sculpture-studded grounds, which make for a fine afternoon walk or picnic along the River Lee. One of the newer buildings, **Boole Library,** celebrates number-wizard George Boole, mastermind of Boolean logic and model for Sherlock Holmes's arch-nemesis Prof. James Moriarty. *(Main gate on Western Rd.* ☎ *490 3000; for more information on the college and college-related events, visit www.ucc.ie.)*

■ **FITZGERALD PARK.** Rose gardens, playgrounds, and a permanent parking spot for the ice cream man are all here. Also present are the befuddlingly esoteric exhibitions of the **Cork Public Museum,** which features such goodies as 18th-century toothbrushes and the clothes of James Dwyer, Sheriff of Cork. *(From the front gate of UCC, follow the signposted walkway across the street.* ☎ *427 0679. Museum open M-F 11am-1pm and 2:15-5pm, Su 3-5pm. M-F students and seniors free, family €3; Sa-Su €1.50.)*

CORK CITY GAOL. This not-to-be-missed museum is a reconstruction of the gaol as it appeared in the 1800s, complete with eerily life-like mannequins. Descriptions of Cork's social history accompany tidbits about miserable punishments, such as the "human treadmill" that was used to grind grain. The building also houses an intriguing radio museum. *(Sunday's Well Rd. From Fitzgerald Park, cross the white footbridge at the western end of the park, turn right onto Sunday's Well Rd., and follow the signs.* ☎ *430 5022. Open daily Mar.-Oct. 9:30am-6pm, Nov.-Feb. 10am-5pm. Last admission 1hr. before closing. €5, students and seniors €4, family €14. Admission includes audio tour.)*

🎭 ENTERTAINMENT

In the lively streets of Cork, amusement is easy to find. Those who tire of the pub scene can take advantage of the music venues, dance clubs, theaters, and sports arenas, or just explore the innumerable cafes and bookshops.

THEATER AND FILM

Everyman Palace, McCurtain St., hosts big-name musicals, plays, operas, and concerts. (☎ 450 1673. Tickets €10-23. Box office open M-Sa 10am-6pm, until 8pm on show nights.) The **Opera House,** Emmet Pl., next to the river, presents an extensive program of dance and performance art. (☎ 427 0022. Open M-Sa 9am-5:30pm.) The **Granary,** Mardyke Quay (☎ 490 4275), stages performances by local and visiting theater companies. **Triskel Arts Centre,** Tobin St. (☎ 427 2022), simmers with avant-garde theater and hosts regular concert and film series. **The Firken Crane Centre,** Shandon Court, houses two theaters dedicated to developing local dance talent. Performance dates vary throughout the year. (☎ 450 7487. Tickets €9. Call for details.) For Hollywood celluloid and the occasional art-house flick, head to **Capitol Cineplex** at Grand Parade and Washington St. (☎ 427 2216 or 427 8777; www.filminfo.net. €7, students €4.45; matinees €4/€3.81.)

SPORTS

Cork is sporting-mad. Its soccer, hurling, and Gaelic football teams are perennial contenders for national titles (see **Sports,** p. 80). From June through September, **hurling** and **Gaelic football** take place every Sunday afternoon at 3pm. For additional details contact the Gaelic Athletic Association (☎ 439 5368; www.gaa.ie) or consult *The Cork Examiner.* Be cautious when venturing into the streets on football game days, especially during championships—screaming, jubilant fans have been known to mow tourists down, or, far more dangerous, force them to join the revelry. Tickets to big games run €17-20 and are scarce, but Saturday, Sunday, and Wednesday evening matches are cheap (€1.50-5) or free. To buy tickets to these local games, visit **Pairc Uí Chaoimh** (park EE KWEEV), the GAA stadium. Take the #2 bus to Blackrock and ask the driver to stop at the stadium. The newly opened

Mardyke Arena provides a break from the Irish rain. The massive complex holds three training gyms, a lap pool, basketball courts, and climbing walls. (☎490 4751. Day passes €10, family €20. Open M-F 7am-10:30pm, Sa 10am-7pm. Call ahead.)

FESTIVALS

Big-name musicians play for free in local pubs and hotels during the three-day **Guinness Cork Jazz Festival** (☎427 8979) in late October. Book rooms well ahead if visiting that weekend. The week-long **International Film Festival** (☎427 1711), in early October at the Opera House and the Triskel Arts Centre, is another popular choice. The **Cork Midsummer Festival** (☎427 0022; www.corkfestival.ie) promises to enchant from mid-June through the beginning of July. In April, the **International Cork Choral Festival** (☎430 8308) fills city hall, churches, and outdoor venues with voices from across the globe. **The Irish Gay and Lesbian Film Festival** is in mid-October; call The Other Place (see **Clubs, p.7**) for details.

▣ DAYTRIP FROM CORK: BLARNEY

Bus Éireann runs buses from Cork to Blarney M-F 15 per day, Sa 16 per day, Su 10 per day; €4.50 return. Arrive at the castle by 9:30am (5min. wait), or wait for up to 3hr. when the tour buses arrive .

In the middle of the idyllic countryside stands Ireland's tourism epicenter, **Blarney Castle**, resting place of the celebrated **Blarney Stone.** The prevailing myth of the stone's origin holds that it is a chip of the Scottish Stone of Scone that was presented to the King of Munster in gratitude for support during a rebellion in 1314. (Any excuse to do battle with the Brits.) Today it stands as just another slab of limestone among so many others in the castle wall. Still, throngs of tourists literally bend over backwards each day to kiss the stone in hopes of acquiring the legendary eloquence—otherwise known as the "gift of the gab"—bestowed on the smoocher. The term "blarney" refers to the supposedly Irish talent of stretching, or even obstructing, the truth. Queen Elizabeth I allegedly coined it during her long and tiring negotiations for control of the castle. The owner, Cormac McCarthy, Earl of Blarney, followed the rules of 16th-century diplomacy, writing grandiose letters in praise of the Queen, but never relinquished the land. Ruffling her royal feathers, Her Majesty was heard to say, "This is all blarney—he never says what he means!" The Irish consider the whole thing a bunch of blarney; they're more concerned with the sanitary implications of so many people kissing the same hunk o' rock. Unless stone-smooching is a life-long ambition, roll over to the castle itself, built in 1446. Other stone-boycotters head left through the archway to explore the more authentic **Druid Gardens**—intrepid travelers will tag along with a passing tour group for an explanation of the garden's intriguing mythological history. (☎438 5252. Open June-Aug. M-Sa 9am-7pm, Su 9:30am-5:30pm; Sept. M-Sa 9am-6:30pm, Su 9:30am-sundown; Oct.-Apr. M-Sa 9am-6pm or sundown, Su 9:30am-5pm or sundown; May M-Sa 9am-6:30pm, Su 9:30am-5:30pm. Last admission 30min. before closing. Castle and grounds €4.50, seniors and students €3, children €1.50.)

NEAR CORK CITY: MIDLETON   ☎021

Sweet, sweet Jameson is distilled in Midleton (*Mainstir na Corann*), where visitors learn why Queen Elizabeth called Irish whiskey her one true Irish friend. Pilgrims in search of the "water of life" (a literal translation of the Irish *uisce beatha*) come to Midelton for the **Jameson Heritage Centre.** The center rolls visitors through a 1hr. tour that details the craft of whiskey production and includes a glass of the potent stuff at the end—for demonstration purposes only, of course. After all, "the

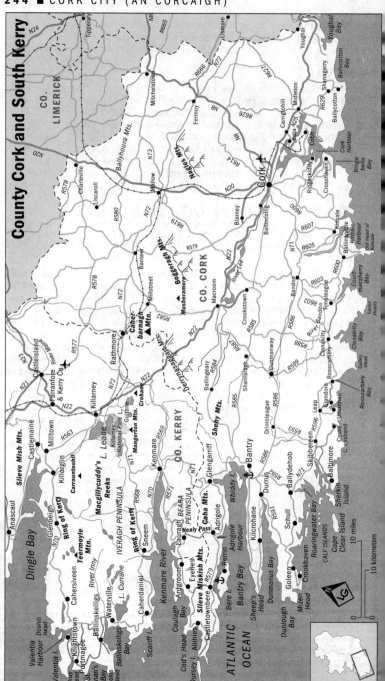

SOUTHWEST IRELAND

KNOW YOUR WHISKEY Anyone who drinks his or her whiskey as it's meant to be drank—"neat," or straight—can tell you that there's a huge difference between Scotch whiskys (without an e), American whiskeys, and Irish whiskeys (Bushmills, Jameson, Power and Son, and the like). But what makes an Irish whiskey *Irish?* The basic ingredients in whiskey—water, barley (which becomes malt once processed), and heat from a fuel source—are always the same. It's the quality of these ingredients, the way in which they're combined, and the means of storage, that gives each product its distinctive flavor: American whiskey is distilled once and is often stored in oak; bourbon is made only in Kentucky; scotch uses peat-smoked barley; Irish whiskey is triple distilled. After this basic breakdown, individual distilleries will claim that their further variations on the theme make their product the best of its class. The best way to understand the distinctions between brands is to taste the various labels in close succession to one another. Line up those shot glasses, sniff, and then taste each one (roll the whiskey in your mouth like a real pro), and have a sip of water between each brand.

story of whiskey is the story of Ireland." (☎461 3594. Wheelchair-accessible. Open Mar.-Oct. daily 10am-6pm. Tours every 30-45min., last tour 4:30pm. Open Nov.-Feb. by tour only, M-F at noon and 3pm, Sa-Su at 2 and 4pm. €6, students and seniors €5, children €2.50. Tours in French, German, and Italian by request.) **The Courtyard,** 8 Main St., offers beautiful paintings, sculptures, jewelry and other crafts for display and sale. Whisk away to Midleton on a **bus** from Cork (30min.; M-F 18 per day, Sa 13 per day, Su 4 per day; €4.88) or drive from Cork or Cobh on the main Cork-Waterford highway (N25).

Comfortable rooms and a warm welcome await at ◪**An Stór (IHH) ❶**. From Main St., turn onto Connolly St. and take the first left onto Drury's Ave. This hostel lives up to its Irish name ("the treasure") with cozy beds, a spacious kitchen, and a wealth of information from its incredibly friendly and helpful owners, Frank and Marie. (☎463 3106. Laundry €5. Dorms €13.50; doubles €19.50.) Delicious meals are cooked daily by Eleanor O'Sullivan at **The Granary Foodstore ❷** in Roxboro Mews, an alley off Main St. (☎461 3366. Meals €5-8. Open M-Sa 9am-6pm.) For scrumptious pastries and sandwiches at reasonable prices, **The Rendezvous Cafe ❶**, off Main St. in Roxburo Court, is an excellent choice (☎463 0691. Meals €3-6. Open M-Sa 7am-5pm). Get groceries at **Tesco** on Main St. (☎463 1530. Open M-W and Sa 9am-7pm, Th-F 9am-9pm, Su 12:30-6pm.) Otherwise, Main St. offers multiple options for pub grub or simple takeaway to soak up the whiskey. Head to **The Meeting Place** and the adjoining **Rory Gallagher's Bar,** Connolly St., for pints and excellent live music on most nights. (☎463 1928. Tu Irish Folk Club night. Occasional €3 cover.) **McDaid's,** towards the end of Main St., has a mixed crowd of elders and youngsters, but is sure to be a rowdy good time.

COBH (AN CÓBH)   ☎021

Little more than a slumbering harbor village today, Cobh (KOVE) was Ireland's main transatlantic port until the 1960s. For many of the emigrants who left between 1848 and 1950, the steep hillside and multicolored houses comprised their final glimpse of Ireland. In 1912, the city was the *Titanic's* last port of call before the "unsinkable" ship went down. Just a few years later, when the Germans torpedoed the *Lusitania* during World War I, most survivors and some dead were taken back to Cobh in lifeboats. Cobh commemorates its eminent but tragic history with class and style at ◪**The Queenstown Story,** a heritage center adjacent to the railway station. The museum's flashy multimedia exhibits trace the port's past, with sections devoted to emigration, the *Lusitania,* the *Titanic,* and the peak of transatlantic travel. Resolve confusion over the town's three names—the original

Cove, Victoria-inspired Queenstown, and finally the Irishized Cobh. (☎481 3591. Open daily 10am-6pm, last admission 5pm. €5, students €4.) The ornate Gothic spire of **St. Colman's Cathedral** dominates the town's architectural landscape, but is closed to visitors, who will have to content themselves with the view of the harbor from the hill. Completed in 1915, the cathedral boasts the largest carillon in Ireland, consisting of 47 bells weighing over 7700 lb. (Open daily 7am-8pm. Free.)

Visitors interested in creating their own ocean adventure can contact **International Sailing,** based on East Beach. Dinghy, windsurfing, and power boat lessons are available here (from €45), as are canoes for €7 per hr. (☎481 1237. Open M-Th 9:30am-9pm, F-Sa 9:30am-6pm, Su 10:30am-5:30pm.) Marine Transport Services, at the harbor, launches 1hr. **Harbour Cruises.** (☎481 1485. Tours leave daily at noon, 2, and 3pm, and also Su at 4 and 5pm. €5, children €3.) Those who've vowed to remain on dry land after learning of the town's sobering history can take a guided walking tour or minibus ride on the **Titanic Trail,** which offers interesting tidbits about the town's history. (☎481 5211. 1¼hr. walking tour daily at 11am from the Titanic Queenstown, afternoons by request. May-Sept. €7.50, includes a cup of coffee. 1hr. minibus tour daily at 3pm from the Waters Edge Hotel. May-Sept. €8.)

Cobh is an easy trip by **rail** from Cork (25min.; M-Sa 19 per day, Su 8 per day; €4 return). Drivers take N25, then R624. The **tourist office** occupies the restored site of the Royal Cork Yacht Club, built in 1854 and reputedly the **world's first yacht club.** Located on the water to the right coming out of the train station, the office gives out free maps, guides, and advice. (☎481 3301; www.cobhharbourchamber.ie. Open M-F 9:30am-5:30pm, Sa-Su 1-5pm.) The **library,** underneath the bridge across from the bus stop, has free **Internet** for members; the cost of membership is €2.50 (☎481 1130; Internet available Tu-Sa 11am-4pm).

If anchoring in Cobh, hurry over to **The Vega B&B** ❸, above Voyager pub. The rooms are brand new and sparkling, and the pancakes are a welcome change from greasy Irish breakfasts. (☎481 4161 or 086 230 4424. Singles €55; doubles €90.) Another option in town is the **Beechmont House Tourist Hostel** ❶. Pass the Cathedral's main doors and take a right at the Quarry Cock Pub; the house is atop the hill. Comfortable beds compensate for the slight griminess. (☎481 2177. Call ahead. Dorms €12.50.) A bit more removed, **Ardeen B&B** ❸, 3 Harbour Hill, offers comfortable rooms overlooking the harbor. On Westbourne Place, walk east to Harbour Row. Ardeen is on the left. (☎481 1803. Singles €39; doubles €60; triples €75.) Pubs, restaurants, and more B&Bs face Cobh's harbor from Beach St. **The River Room** ❷, on West Beach, grills large and tasty ciabatta sandwiches (€5.40), and lunchtime quiche. (☎481 5650. Open M-Sa 9am-5pm.) **SuperValu** earns its name on the same thoroughfare. (☎481 1586. Open M-Tu 9am-6pm, W-F 8am-9pm, Sa 9am-7pm.) Cobh holds its own in the pub count. The DJs and rock acts at **Voyager** pack in a young horde nightly. (☎481 4161. M-Tu 4-11:30pm, W-Sa noon-11:30pm, Su noon-2pm and 4-11pm.) **Maguire's,** across from Voyager, offers the young and the beautiful a chance to shine with pop music and a friendly atmosphere (M-Th until 11:30pm, F-Sa until 12:30am, Su until 11pm). **The Ship's Bell** (☎481 1122) attracts a more seasoned, local crowd for pub grub and live trad on weeknights.

▶ DAYTRIP FROM COBH: FOTA ISLAND.

Fota is an intermediate stop on the train from Cork to Cobh; if you buy a ticket from Cork to Cobh or vice versa, get off at Fota and re-board for free.

Ten minutes from Cobh by rail lies Fota Island, where penguins, peacocks, cheetahs, and giraffes roam, largely cages-free, in the ◪**Fota Wildlife Park.** The closest many ever come to a ring-tailed lemur or Chilean flamingo. The park has as many species as acres—70—with animals from South America, Africa, and Asia. (☎481 2678. Open Apr.-Oct. M-Sa 10am-6pm, Su 11am-6pm. Last admission 5pm. €8;

seniors, students, and children €5.) A **snack bar** in the park serves sandwiches and burgers (€2-4). The **Fota Arboretum,** next to the park but 1mi. from the station, cares for greenery as exotic as the beasts next door. (Gates close 5:30pm. Free.)

YOUGHAL (EOCHAILL)   ☎024

Thirty miles east of Cork on N25, beach-kissed Youghal (YAWL) has been basking in notoriety garnered after being chosen for the filming of *Moby Dick* starring Gregory Peck. A popular beach and remarkably narrow streets have kept Youghal interesting after its fifteen minutes of fame. The huge **Clockgate,** built in 1777, straddles crowded Main St. From here the old **city walls,** built on the hill sometime between the 13th and 17th centuries, are visible. The tower served as a prison and makeshift gallows (prisoners were hanged from the windows). On Church St., **St. Mary's Church** and **Myrtle Grove** stand side-by-side. The former may be the oldest operating church in Ireland, with parts from the original Danish-built structure, constructed in 1020. One corner of the church holds the elaborate grave of Robert Boyle, first Earl of Cork. Myrtle Grove was the residence of Sir Walter Raleigh when he served as mayor of Youghal in 1588-89. Though the house is privately owned, literary buffs can glimpse the window where Raleigh's buddy Edmund Spencer is said to have finished his hefty epic *The Faerie Queen.* For a condensed history of Youghal since the 9th century, drop by the tourist office's **heritage center.** (☎20170. Same hours as tourist office. €2.) Across the street from the center and up a little alley, ◪**Fox's Lane Folk Museum** is the place to discover the interesting history of razor blades and sewing machines. (Open Tu-Sa 10am-1pm and 2-6pm. Last admission 5:30pm. €3.) **Tynte's Castle,** the **Almshouses,** and a number of historical buildings throughout the city are worth viewing, if only from afar (they are not accessible for entry). Music, bowling, and other festivities fill the town for three days in late June during the **Youghal Summer Festival** (www.youghalfestivals.com).

Buses stop on Main St. in front of the public toilets and across from Dempsey's Bar. They travel to **Cork** (50min., 17-19 per day, €9) and **Waterford** via **Dungarvan** (1½-2hr., M-Su 14 per day, €15.20). Hitching to Cork or Waterford along N25 is possible, but hitchers should always consider the potential risk involved. The **tourist office,** Market Sq., on the waterfront behind the clocktower, distributes a useful "tourist trail" booklet (free). (☎20170. Open July-Aug. M-F 9am-6:30pm, Sa 9:30am-5pm, Su 9:30am-5pm; June and Sept. M-F 9am-5:30pm, Sa-Su 11am-5pm; Oct.-May M-F 9am-5:30pm.) The **library,** on Church St. off Main St., provides free **Internet** with a €2.50 membership to Cork County libraries. (☎93 459. Open Tu-Sa 10am-1pm and 2-5:30pm.)

Finding lodgings in Youghal might take a little legwork; the tourist office has a list of Bord Fáilte-approved accommodations. Try majestic **Avonmore House ❸**, South Abbey, where fully equipped rooms are kept tidy by a capable and helpful staff. (☎92 617. Singles €34-40; doubles €58-66.) Alternatively, many tourists are drawn to **Attracta ❸**, across the street, slightly closer to the beach. (☎92 062. Singles €32-38; doubles €56-62.) **Devon View B&B ❸**, in Pearse Sq., has basic rooms at reasonable prices. (☎92298. Groups €25; singles €30, without breakfast €20.)

The town's eateries tempt a wide range of taste buds and budgets. For huge scones, go to **The Red Stone Pub & Restaurant ❸**, 150-151 N. Main St. (Scone and coffee €3.20; mains €12-13. Breakfast 10:30am-12:30pm; carvery lunch until 2:30pm; dinner 5:30-9:30pm.) And as always, the foraging option: **Pasley's SuperValu** is in the town center on Main St., by the tourist office (☎92150; open M-W 9am-7pm, Th and Sa 9am-8pm, F 9am-9pm, Su 10am-6pm), and **L&N SuperValu** lies up the road on N. Main St. (☎92279; open M-W 9am-6pm, Th-Sa 9am-9pm, Su 9am-6pm).

Music fills each cranny twice a week at popular **Nook Pub,** which celebrated its 100th year under the ownership of the Treacy family in 2001. (☎92225. Open M-W 10:30am-11:30pm, Th-Sa 10:30am-12:30am, Su 12:30-11:30pm.) Young'uns head to

THE BIG SPLURGE

THE MUSTARD SEED AT ECHO LODGE

Once a hilltop convent, Ballingarry's charming **Echo Lodge** country hotel now houses 17 high-ceilinged rooms and suites, each exquisitely decorated to a unique cultural theme. Crisp white linen, well-fluffed pillows, and original pane glass windows mark each room, while bold, classic colors provide background for the house's museum art collection. Guests of the lodge also have access to a small fitness room, massage room, and a sauna.

Even more enticing, owner Daniel Mullane and head chef David Norris welcome guests and non-guests to the elegant dining room of the **Mustard Seed restaurant** downstairs. The award-winning gourmet food—made from fresh herbs and vegetables grown in the gardens out back—matches the tasteful decor and friendly staff. Splendid four-course dinner menu, from **grilled goat's cheese** to **steamed salmon**, costs around €47. The food can also be prepared to meet specific dietary requirements. This is an all-around world-class dining experience.

The Mustard Seed, Echo Lodge, Ballingarry (☎069 68508). From the top of Adare village, take the N21 toward Killarney for ½ mi., and turn left for Ballingarry. Follow signs for Rathkeale, then Ballingarry. Wheelchair-accessible. Restaurant open daily 7-9:45pm. Bed and breakfast open year-round. Doubles €165-254. AMEX/MC/V.

The Clock Tavern, S. Main St., where dark recesses echo with the tick-tock of rock six nights a week. (☎93 052. Cover for big-namers €5. Open M-W and Su noon-11:30pm, Th-Sa noon-12:30am.) Tourists have a whale of a time at **Moby Dick's,** in Market Sq., which flaunts its nautical motif. ☎92099. Ballads F.)

WESTERN COUNTY CORK

Western Cork, the southwestern third of the county, was once the "badlands" of Ireland; its ruggedness and isolation rendered it lawless and largely uninhabitable. Ex-hippies and antiquated fishermen have replaced the roving, cave-dwelling outlaws, and they do their best to make the villages hospitable to tourists. Roaringwater Bay and wave-whipped Mizen Head mark Ireland's land's end. The lonely beauty here is a stately solitude unmarred by the tourist-approved shamrocks planted elsewhere in Ireland. From Cork City there are two choices for westward rambles—an inland or a coastal route. A **coastal bus** runs from Cork to Skibbereen, stopping in Bandon, Clonakilty, and Rosscarbery (M-Sa 8 per day, Su 6 per day). An **inland bus** travels from Cork to Bantry, via Bandon and Dunmanway (M-Sa 7 per day, Su 4 per day). **Hitchers** are reported to have few problems finding a ride in these parts, but should always consider the dangers involved.

THE INLAND ROUTE

Those looking to avoid the tourist crowds should consider one of the scenic inland routes that move westward from Cork. Winding like the serpents that St. Paddy expelled years ago, these roads are not for saving time, but for savoring the scenery. Popular choices include Cork-Macroom-Killarney, Cork-Macroom-Ballingeary-Bantry/Glengarriff, and Cork-Dunmanway-Bantry/Skibbereen. The rocky faces of the Shehy Mountains, between Dunmanway and Ballingeary, have some of Ireland's most well-preserved wilds—best explored by foot or bike.

DUNMANWAY (DÚN MÁNMHAI)   ☎023

Located in relative isolation at the intersection of R586, R587, and R599, **Dunmanway** is a hidden treasure, one of few Irish towns that truly prizes tradition over tourism. No red carpets for visitors—Dunmanway lets its scenery speak for itself. Northwest, over the mountains, quiet **Ballingeary** (*Béal Athán Ghaorthaídh*) is the heart of one of West Cork's declining *gaeltachts*. Ballingeary lacks accommodations and restaurants, so visitors must base themselves in Dunmanaway and cycle over to take advantage of Ballingeary's scenic offerings. Seven miles beyond the Shiplake hostel turnoff lies soup-bowl **Lake Cullenagh**. Its pinelined paths and shaded picnic areas make for a lovely day; inquire at Shiplake Hostel for information on hiking and biking routes in the area. Closer to town, **Lake Coolkellure** hides its miniature beach and provides prime brown-trout **fishing**. Over in Ballingeary, the entrance to **Gougane Barra Forest** lies open. From the road through the forest, visitors can see the River Lee's pure source streams flow together. A **church** marks the site of **St. Finbarr's monastery** at the base of the mountains, next to a lake. Sweeping views reward those willing to climb the wooded trails to the ridgeline.

Bus Éireann voyages eastward from Cork to Dunmanway (M-Sa 6 per day, Su 4 per day; €8); buses depart from in front of Tom Twomey's jewelers on the main square. **Market Square** is home to a number of pubs and shops, and hosts the **library** (*'An Leabharlann'*), which offers the town's lone **Internet** to members. (☎55411. Membership €2.50. Open Tu 1-8pm, W-Sa 10am-5:30pm.) To reach Ballingeary from Dunmanway, take R587 northwest to R584. It's on the Macroom to Bantry/Glengariff road. A true *gaeltacht*, signs are posted in traditional script and only in Ballingeary's Irish name (*Béal athán Ghaorthaídh*).

Located in the hills 3 mi. from town, ▨**Shiplake Mountain Hostel (IHH)** ❶ is a perfect example of Dunmanway's unassuming dignity. Shiplake's luckiest guests stay in one of three colorful **gypsy caravans**, all with heat, electricity, and breath-taking views of the surrounding Shehy mountains. A wood stove cozifies the farmhouse common room and brownies (€0.80 each) ameliorate ailments. Call for a free ride from Dunmanway, or follow Castle St. from the corner of the main square (Gatsby's Nightclub) toward Coolkelure, turning right at the small hostel sign. (☎45750; www.shiplakemountainhostel.com. **Bike rental** €6 per day. Breakfasts €2.50-5; bag lunches €5; vegetarian mains €7-10. Singles €16-18; dorms €11; caravans €12.50-13.50 per person. **Camping** €6 per person, children €4; laundry €6.)

Central **Centra** stocks victuals. (☎45778; Open M-Sa 8am-9pm, Su 8:30am-6pm.) Overlooking the main square, newly converted **Upstairs at the Merchants** ❸ serves serious three-course lunches and delicious dinners. (☎55556. Wild salmon €15. Open daily 9am-6pm and 7-9pm.) Dunmanway's 8500 residents support 23 pubs, and most serve food. Owned and operated by a sixth-generation O'Donovan, ▨**The Shamrock** ❷ (☎45142), in Market Square, has a traditional atmosphere and rollicking Sunday afternoons. Enjoy a true Irish meal (€6.50-9) and discuss ancestors with owner Mike, whose forefathers adorn the walls. Main Street **An Toísín** serves a mellow meal by day and diverse music at night. (☎45076. DJ Sa.)

SOUTHERN COAST

From Cork, N71 runs its asphalt course all the way to Clonakilty via Bandon. Past Clonakilty, the population starts to thin. Mountains rise, craggy ridges replace smooth hills, and rocky shoals proliferate as Ireland's southern coast begins to look more like its western one. The islands on the stretch of ocean between Baltimore and Schull may be the fiercest, most outlandish places in all of southern Ireland. High cliffs plunge into the sea, earning the islands a legacy of shipwrecks. The intrepid O'Driscoll clan (of pirating fame) informally ruled the bay for centuries, sallying into the Atlantic for raids, off-loading brandy from Spanish galleons, then speeding home through secret channels among the islands. These days, crossroads along N71 link mellow tourist towns and hardworking fishing villages.

"Blow-ins," expatriates from America and Northern Europe, have settled in the area, replacing the dwindling native population. These kick-back expats are drawn to Western Cork's leisurely pace and extraordinary scenery, but are shaping its culture to their own tastes.

KINSALE (CIONN TSÁILE)   ☎021

Every summer the population of upscale Kinsale temporarily quintuples with a flood of tourists. Visitors come to swim, fish, and eat at Kinsale's 12 famed "Good Food Circle" restaurants. Connoisseurs of culture, dreamy beachcombers, and high-speed aquatic daredevils find their fix in Kinsale—as do the millionaires who helicopter onto the links at the Old Head for a quick nine holes. Kinsale's pleasant present barely recalls the grimmer roles the town has played in history: the victory of Elizabethan England at the 1601 Battle of Kinsale cleared the way for several centuries of colonialism (see **Feudalism,** p. 58); 80-odd years later, deposed Catholic King James II came here for a last failed attempt to claim his throne; and in 1915, the *Lusitania* was sunk just off Kinsale's Old Head. These days, boats from Britain come loaded with vacationers eager to fill the town's coffers.

⚍ 🛈 ORIENTATION AND PRACTICAL INFORMATION. Kinsale lies at the base of a U-shaped inlet, a 30min. drive southwest of Cork on R600. Facing the water, **Charles Fort** and the **Scilly Walk** (pronounced "silly") are to the left; the piers, **Compass Hill,** and **James Fort** are to the right; the town center is behind. **Buses** to and from Cork stop at the Esso station on the Pier. (40min.; M-Sa 10-11 per day, Su 5 per day; €6.50 return.) The **tourist office,** Emmet Pl., in the black-and-red building on the waterfront, distributes free maps. (☎477 2234. Open July-Aug. daily 9am-7pm, Mar.-Nov. M-Sa 9am-6pm.) The **Bank of Ireland,** Main St., has a 24hr. **ATM.** (☎477 2521. Open M 10am-5pm, Tu-F 10am-4pm.) At 8 Long Quay, **Mylie Murphy's** painted sign displays a plump fish riding a bicycle. (☎477 2703. **Bike rental** €12 per day, €65 per wk. **Fishing poles** €10 per day, €60 per wk. **Fresh bait** €2-6. Deposit or credit card required. Open M-Sa 9:30am-6pm, call ahead Su in summer.) Access the **Internet** at **Finishing Services,** also on Main St. (☎477 3571. €2.50 per 15min., €6 per hr. Open M-F 9am-5:30pm.)

⌐ ACCOMMODATIONS AND CAMPING. Kinsale's hotels and plush B&Bs cater to an affluent crowd—budget-oriented beds can be found at **Guardwell Lodge ❷,** Guardwell St., as can self-catering kitchens and modern, cheerful top-floor rooms. (☎477 4686. Dorms €15; private rooms €25. 10% discount with the mention of *Let's Go.*) Just up the road, **O'Donovan's B&B ❸** sports delightfully simple and comfortable rooms. (☎477 2428. Singles €60, larger rooms €35 per person.) The can't-miss-it canary yellow facade of **The Gallery ❸** speaks volumes for the quirkiness within. The proprietor is a jazz musician (hence the white baby grand), his wife is a painter, and the award-winning salmon breakfasts are occasionally joined by heaping scoops of ice cream—who knew? (☎477 4558. Singles €70; larger rooms €34-43.) For authentic Georgian elegance, **The Old Presbytery ❹** offers luxurious self-catering apartments. Each comes complete with a sitting room, fireplace, full kitchen, and claw-footed porcelain tub; some have a jacuzzi. The owners also rent bedrooms to more budget-minded travelers. (☎477 2027; www.oldpres.com. 4-5 person apartments €155 per night; 3-night minimum stay. 2- to 4-person bedrooms €95-140.) For those bringing their own accommodations, plots of land can be rented at the **Garrettstown House Holiday Park ❷,** 6 mi. west of Kinsale outside Ballinspittle on the R600. (☎477 8156. Open May-late Sept. One adult with tent €12.)

🖪 🍴 FOOD AND PUBS. If craving gourmet, look no farther—locals claim that Kinsale is the only town in Ireland with more restaurants than pubs, though good food often comes at a price. Budget visitors fill their baskets at the ever-affordable

SuperValu on Pearse St. (☎477 2843. Open M-Sa 8:30am-9pm, Su 10am-9pm.) At **Patsy's Corner ❶**, Market Sq., locals pack behind the wraparound corner window for light meals (€3-7) and homemade cakes. (☎086 865 8143. Open Sept.-July M-Sa 9am-5:30pm, Aug. daily 9am-5:30pm.) **Diva Cafe ❶**, an artsy, femme-themed coffee house, offers sip-worthy, affordable brews. (Open June-Sept. daily 9am-9pm, Oct.-May M-Sa 9am-8pm, Su 9am-7pm.) On Main St., **The Mad Monk ❶** supplies dependable pub grub and music most nights. (☎774 602. Meals €5-8.) The best of the best changes weekly; inquire at your B&B for the tastiest meal in town.

A proper pub crawl will take you well out of Kinsale's small maze of streets. ☒**The Spaniard** (☎477 2436), atop the hill on the Scilly Peninsula, is well worth the trip. With its thick stone walls, low-beamed ceilings, and dark wood paneling, this tiny pearl lures fishermen and other locals to foot-tapping trad sessions held several nights a week. To reach the pub, follow the signs to Charles Fort for ¼ mi. (☎477 2436. Mains €7-14.) Those who make the hike to Charles Fort are rewarded with a pint of Irish black gold at the picturesque **Bulman Bar** (☎477 2131). The long walk home is sobering. In town, locals and tourists gather for live trad at cozy **An Seanachaí**, 6 Market St. (☎477 7077; www.anseanachai.com.)

⚅ SIGHTS. A 30min. trek up **Compass Hill**, south of Main St., affords wide views of the town and its seascapes. Even more impressive is the vista from **Charles Fort,** the classic 17th-century star-shaped fort that was a British naval base until 1921. The battlements and buildings overlook the water and offer nearly limitless opportunities for climbing and exploration. To reach Charles Fort, follow **Scilly Walk** (30min.), a sylvan path along the coast that starts at the end of Pearse St. (☎477 2263. Open mid-Mar. to Oct. M-F 10am-6pm; Nov. to mid-Mar. Sa-Su 10am-5pm, M-F by appointment. €3.50, seniors €2.50, students and children €1.25.) Across the harbor from Charles Fort, the ruins of similarly-starry **James Fort** tempt explorers with secret passageways and panoramic views of Kinsale. To reach this fort, follow the pier away from town, cross the Duggan bridge, then turn left. After scrambling through the ruins and the rolling heath, descend to Castlepark's hidden arc of **beach** behind the hostel. (Always open. Free.)

Back in town, on Cork St., **Desmond Castle** broods over its rather gloomy history. The 15th-century customs house served as an arsenal during the 100-day Spanish occupation of 1601 and as a naval prison during the 17th century. Inside the castle, the **International Museum of Wine** douses visitors with the chronicle of Kinsale's history as a wine port. (☎477 4855. Open mid-June to early Oct. daily 10am-6pm; mid-Apr. to mid-June Tu-Sa 10am-6pm. Last admission 45min. before closing. €2.75, seniors €2, students and children €1.25.) In 1915, a trigger-happy German U-boat torpedoed the British ocean liner *Lusitania* off the Old Head, a promontory south of Kinsale. The fury provoked by over 1000 civilian deaths hastened the United States' entrance into WWI. Hearings on the *Lusitania* case took place in the **Kinsale Courthouse**, Market Sq., which now contains a regional **museum**. Up the hill from Market Sq. is the restored west tower of the 12th-century **Church of St. Multose,** the patron saint of Kinsale. The ancient graveyard is also worth a peek. (☎477 2220. Church open until dusk. Graveyard always open. Free.) Back in the 21st century, feast your eyes on the vibrant, impressionistic paintings on display at tiny **Gallery Catoire**, in Market Square (☎477 7395; www.gallerycatoire.com).

CLONAKILTY (CLOCH NA COILLTE) ☎023

Once a linen-making town with a workforce of over 10,000 people, Clonakilty ("Clon") lies between Bandon and Skibbereen on N71. Henry Ford was born nearby, but the favorite son is military leader, spy, organizational genius, and real Irish hero Michael Collins. The wily Collins returned home during the Civil War, for "they surely won't kill me in my own country." So much for nationalist bravado—he was ambushed and murdered 25 mi. from town. Most visitors, more interested in relaxation than revolution, head to nearby Inchydoney Beach. During the second week of July, there is much feasting at the Black and White Pudding Festival (see **Food and Drink**, p. 69); prizes are given for the best recipe and the most pudding consumed—not for the faint of heart, or stomach.

🖼🔃 ORIENTATION AND PRACTICAL INFORMATION. Clonakilty's main drag begins at the tourist office on **Ashe St.** and continues along the road, eventually turning into **Pearse St.** and finally **Western Rd.** A stone tribute to axe-wielding rebel Tadgh an Astna serves as a central point. To the statue's left, **Rossa St.** runs into **Connelly** near the Wheel of Fortune water pump. **Astna St.** angles off the statue toward the harbor and **Inchydoney Beach** (bear right.) **Buses** from Cork (3-4 per day, €8.50) and Skibbereen (M-Th and Sa-Su 2 per day, F 3 per day; €5.50) stop in front of Lehane's Supermarket on Pearse St. Walk the 3 mi. to Inchydoney or **rent a bike** at **MTM Cycles** on Ashe St. (☎33584. €10 per day, €45 per wk.) The **tourist office,** 25 Ashe St., hands out maps and advice. (☎33226. Open July-Aug. M-Sa 9am-7pm, Su 10am-6pm; June M-Sa 9am-6pm; Mar.-May and Sept.-Nov. M-Sa 9:30am-5:30pm.) **AIB** and **Bank of Ireland** cash in on Pearse St.; each has a 24hr. **ATM.** (Both open M 10am-5pm, Tu-F 10am-4pm.) With a membership to the Co. Cork **library** (€2.50), **Internet** is available at the Clon branch in the Old Mill on Kent St. (☎34275. Open Tu-Sa 10am-6pm.) The Gothic **post office** addresses town from Bridge St. (Open M-F 9am-5:30pm, Sa 10am-1pm.)

🛏🍴🎵 ACCOMMODATIONS, FOOD, AND PUBS. The **Old Brewery Hostel ❶**, Emmet Sq., also known as the Clonakilty Hostel, has a super kitchen area and comfortable beds. From Lehane's, head down Pearse St., make a left at the Roman Catholic church, and a right at the park in Emmet Sq. (☎33525. **Bike rental** €9 per day. Wheelchair-accessible. Dorms €12; doubles €30.) A 5min. walk from town and a right turn after the museum lead to **Nordav ❸**, 70 Western Rd. Removed from the road by a well-groomed lawn and splendid rose gardens, this family-style B&B features gloriously spacious suites and smaller but lovely doubles. (☎33655. €26-33.) **Desert House Camping Park ❶** is connected to a dairy farm half a mile southeast of town on the road to Ring Village. (☎33331. Open May-Sept. €1 per person; small tent €8; family tent €10. Showers €1.)

Clonakilty's culinary fame (and infamy) derives from its style of **black pudding**, a sausage-like concoction made from beef, blood, and grains. Those eager to try it, or its pasty **white pudding** sister (made with pork minus the blood), can head to the award-winning butcher at **Twomey's.** (☎33365. Open M-Sa 9am-6pm.) Most local restaurants also offer it, generally for breakfast. But fear ye not—Clon has many other options for daily sustenance. Zesty nouveau-cuisine is served with flair at 🖼**Richy's Bar and Bistro ❹**, Wolfetone St. Lounge in the colorful couches while waiting. (☎21852; www.richysbarandbistro.com. Mains €12-18. Open daily noon-10pm.) **Betty Brosnans ❶**, 58 Pearse St., cooks up the best cafe lunch in town. (☎034 011. Chicken and avocado baguette €4; fresh milkshakes €2.50. Breakfast all day. Open M-Sa 9am-6pm.) Under vine-covered arches lies **Gearoidins ❷**, 18 Pearse St., great for salad-and-sandwich values. (☎34444. Most meals €6-10. Open M-Th 9:30am-5:30pm, F 9:30am-7:30pm, Sa 9:30am-9pm, Su 11am-8pm.) Brown-bag it at **Lehane's Supermarket** on Pearse St. (☎33359. Open M-Th 8am-6:30pm, F 8am-8pm, Sa 8am-7pm, Su 9am-1:30pm.)

There's music aplenty in Clonakilty, the diamond in the rough of Western Cork's otherwise unremarkable trad scene. The hugely popular **De Barra's** on Pearse St. draws big-name acts with a superb sound system and ideal set-up. The nightly folk and trad can be enjoyed anywhere in the huge venue—in the main room, small nooks, beer garden, or upstairs on the balcony. (☎33381. Occasional €4 cover.) Around the corner, **Shanley's,** 11 Connolly St. (☎33790), does music every night of the summer, juggling folk, rock, and the occasional nationally-known star. Through the arched Recorders' Alley off Pearse St., **An Teach Beag** is Clonakilty's center for storytelling and set dancing.

◙ **SIGHTS.** To fill the hours before the pubs pick up, join the locals at ◙**Inchydoney,** one of the nicest beaches this side of Malibu. The Inchydoney Rd. passes the **West Cork Model Railway Village,** where the Kinsale, Bandon, and Clonakilty of 1940 are reborn in miniature. (☎33224. Open Feb.-Oct. daily 11am-5pm. €5.50, students €4.) Back in town, the **West Cork Museum,** Western Rd., displays an early 20th-century beer-pouring machine, the christening shawl of patriot O'Donovan Rossa, and other historical baubles, and lets visitors play dress-up with an antique silk cloak. (Open May-Oct. M-Sa 10am-6:30pm. €3, students €1.50, children free.) While in Clon, don't miss the opportunity to learn about the heroic **Michael Collins.** Tours of various sights relating to his life and death can be arranged through the tourist office or Timothy Crowley (☎46107). The Crowleys also operate the **Arigideen Valley Heritage Park,** a hilltop cottage with splendid views and a wealth of information on the area's traditions and folklore. (☎46107; www.reachireland.com. Open mid-June to mid-Sept. M-Sa 10:30am-5pm, Su by appointment only. Guided walking tours of surrounding countryside available. "Michael Collins Experience" slideshow M-Th 7:45pm, €5.) Two miles east is the **Lios na gCon Ring Fort,** which was "fully restored" based on excavators' guesses at its 10th-century form. It is the only ring fort in Ireland reconstructed on its original site.

UNION HALL (BREANTRA) ☎028

Between Clonakilty and Skibbereen, across the water from the tiny hamlet of **Glandore,** sits the fishing village of **Union Hall.** Set amidst rolling green pastures and forested land too rocky for farming, the town was once a hangout for **Jonathan Swift.** Travelers passing between Union Hall and Skibbereen often pause to picnic in the shady seaside groves of **Rennin Forest. Knockdrum Fort,** just west of town, demonstrates exactly what becomes of Iron Age Celtic forts over the centuries. Three miles out of town, tourists flock to the pterodactyl teeth, dinosaur droppings, stone-age calendars, and Easter Rising rifles of ◙**Ceim Hill Museum.** The museum's proprietress, possibly even more interesting than her collection, found all the artifacts in her backyard, and sells booklets (€8) detailing her life and discoveries. (☎36280. Open daily 10am-7pm. €4.) For more interactive distractions, consult the folks at ◙**Atlantic Sea Kayaking** (☎021 058), who provide guided waterborne transportation to the area's nearby islands and sea caves. They also run **overnight camping trips** to an uninhabited island and run a spectacular ◙**moonlight paddle.** (☎21058; atlanticseakayaking@eircon.net. Half-day trip €45, full day €60. Overnight camping trip leaves W and F, €100; contact in advance for a spot. Moonlight paddle €38.) For **fishing trips** and **whale-watching expeditions,** Capt. Colin Barnes (☎086 327 3226) has a blessed knack for spotting seals and whales.

The town is also home to legendary ◙**Maria's Schoolhouse Hostel (IHH) ❶.** To reach Maria's, turn right after the bridge into the village center, bear left at the church, then take the first right (marked by a small sign). Or take the Skibbereen-Clonakilty bus, ask to be let off in **Leap** (LEP), and call the hostel for a lift. Once the Union Hall National School, Maria's hostel has been redecorated in Brobdingnagian style—the huge common room was refitted with a cathedral ceiling and big skylights were installed in the dorm. This hostel is reason enough for a detour en route to Skibbereen. (☎33002. 3-course dinner with occasional musical accompaniment F-Sa €22. Laundry €7. Dorms €12; doubles €38-50; singles €27.) Back in town, centrally located **Seascape B&B** ❸ (☎33920) has gorgeous bay views. (Singles €30-35; larger rooms €27.) For the hungry, **Centra** stocks the basics (☎034 955. Open M-Sa 8am-9pm, Su 8am-2pm), and **Dinty's Bar** ❷ serves huge portions of ocean-centric victuals. (☎033 373. Mains €7-8. Food served 12:30-2:30pm and 6-9pm.) Fresh seafood or less expensive pub grub await at the waterside patio/beer garden of **Casey's Bar** ❷. (☎33590. Mains €6.50-12. Food served daily noon-8:30pm.) The jovial atmosphere and billiard tables at **Maloney's** (☎33610) draw a young crowd. **Nolan's Bar** (☎33758) supplies a few bites and spirited trad.

SKIBBEREEN (AN SCIOBAIRIN)   ☎028

The biggest town in Western Cork, Skibbereen ("Skib") is a convenient stop for travelers roaming the coastal wilds. Skib was established in 1631 by refugees fleeing Baltimore, which was being sacked by marauding Algerian pirates. In more recent times, Skib has evolved into a market town for local farmers, whose big-wheeled vehicles still rumble through town on a regular basis. Many stores in Skibbereen close on Thursdays around noon to recover between market days (W, F, and Sa). If joining the farm fun isn't appealing, the town is a good base for day-trips to seaside destinations like Baltimore, Schull, and Castletownshend.

■◪ **ORIENTATION AND PRACTICAL INFORMATION.** Skibbereen is laid out in an L-shape, with **North St.** as the base, supporting **Main St.** and **Bridge St.** (Main St. turns into Bridge St. at the small bridge). The clock tower, post office, and stately "Maid of Erin" statue are at the elbow. Hitchers typically stay on N71 to go east or west but switch to R595 to go south. **Buses** stop at Calahane's Bar on Bridge St. and run to Baltimore (year-round M-F 5 per day, June-Sept. also Sa 4 per day; €2.80); Clonakilty (M-Sa 8 per day, Su 3 per day; €5.65); Cork (7 per day, €11.30); and Killarney (2 per day, €14). **Roycroft Cycles,** on Ilen St. off Bridge St., participates in Raleigh's One-Way Rent-A-Bike program and provides an **airport pickup service;** call for details. (☎21235. €14.50 per day, including helmet. Deposit €65. Open M-Sa 9:15am-6pm.) The **tourist office** is next to the Town Hall on North St. (☎21766. Open July-Aug. daily 9am-7pm; June M-Sa 9am-6pm; Sept.-May M-F 9:15am-5:30pm.) **AIB** has an **ATM** at 9 Bridge St., and **Bank of Ireland** has one in front of the SuperValu on Main St; the bank itself is on Market St. (☎21388 and 21700. Both open Tu, Th, F 10am-4pm, W 10:30am-4pm.) There's an interesting **Fine & Rare Book Shop** across from the post office on Market St. (☎22115. Open June-Aug. daily 11am-5pm; Sept.-May by appointment.) **West Cork Dry Cleaners** is across from the bus stop on Bridge St. (☎021 627. €6.50 per load. Open M-F 10am-6pm, Sa 10am-5:30pm.) There are two affiliated **pharmacies** facing each other on Main St. (☎21543; after-hours emergency ☎086 858 8957. M-Sa 9am-6pm.) Two computers with **Internet** are available at the **library,** across from the Arts Centre on North St., which participates in the Co. Cork Library's one-time membership fee (€2.50) granting unlimited free access to their web connections. (☎22400. Open Tu-Sa 10am-5:30pm; Internet 10am-5pm) More computers with fast access are available at the **Flexible Learning IT Center,** on the 3rd floor of the Arts Centre building. (☎21011. €0.09 per min. Open M-F 9:30am-1pm and 2-5pm.) The **post office** is on Market St. (☎21002. Open M, W-F 9am-5pm, Tu 9:30am-5pm, Sa 9am-1pm.)

▐ **ACCOMMODATIONS AND CAMPING.** **Russagh Mill Hostel and Adventure Centre (IHH)** ❶, about 2 mi. out of town on the Castletownshend road, features a **climbing wall,** and runs adventure camps for children and adults, but also welcomes the simple hosteler. This renovated 200-year-old mill has basic dorms, but the glassed-in sunroom is a marvel. (☎22451. Check-out 11am. Open mid-Mar. to Nov. Dorms

€11; private rooms €15.) The proprietress of **Bridge House ❸,** Bridge St., could be a set designer for Victorian period films; as she puts it, "My house is my stage!" Each room is decorated with a theatrical sense of humor. (☎21273. €30.) **Dalton's ❷,** on North St., provides the most basic beds in town, with TV and bath, but no breakfast. Single, double, and family-sized rooms. (☎23881. €22.) The **Hideaway Campground ❶,** Castletownshend St., is the place for campers and caravaners. (☎22254. Kitchen facilities available. Tent €14; with car €14. Showers €1.)

◨ ◪ FOOD AND PUBS. The cafes along Main St. and North St. offer a number of inviting options. Field's **SuperValu,** Main St., struts its stuff as a supermarket and houses a cafe. (☎21400. Open M-Sa 9am-7pm.) **The Wine Vaults ❷,** on Bridge St., has tasty, freshly baked pizza, and typical pub standards. (☎023 112. Pizzas €6.50-11, mains €11.50. Food served mid-July to Aug. M-Sa noon-9pm; Sept. to mid-July M-Sa noon-7pm.) **Kalbo's Bistro ❸,** 48 North St., has a pleasant atmosphere and is a good option for dinner (☎21515. Lunch €6-9; dinner €11.50-18. Open M-Sa 11:30am-4:30pm and 6:30-9:30pm, Su noon-2:30pm and 6:30-9:30pm. Reserve ahead in July and Aug.) Scones and hearty breakfasts are served at **The Stove ❷,** on Main St. (☎22500. Meals €6-9. Open M-Sa 8am-6pm.) Find blues, folk, and a young crowd at **Wine Vaults** (see above), where locals and tourists crush a happy cup together. **Seán Óg's,** Market St. (☎21573), hosts contemporary folk and blues several nights a week, a Tuesday trad session, and nightly outdoor beer garden. **Kearney's Well,** 52-53 North St. (☎21350), attracts lively locals, while the more comfortable digs at **Bernard's,** off Main St., are all the better to converse in.

◨ ◪ SIGHTS AND ACTIVITIES. Newly opened in the old gasworks building on Upper Bridge St., the **Skibbereen Heritage Centre** leads visitors through interactive displays highlighting the natural beauty and biological wealth of **Lough Hyne** (also spelled Ine; see **Baltimore,** p. 255), and educates well-fed visitors about the devastation of the Famine. (☎40900; www.skibbheritage.com. €4, students and seniors €3, children €2, family €9. Open mid-May to mid-Sept. daily 10am-6pm; mid-Mar. to mid-May, mid-Sept. to Oct. Tu-Sa 10am-6pm. Last admission 5:15pm.) **Skibbereen Historical Walks** (☎40900) offers guided tours through the town with a hefty dose of history. (90min. tours leave from Skibbereen Heritage Centre; Tu, Sa at 6:30pm. Adults €4.50, children under 15yrs. €2.) The **West Cork Arts Centre,** North St., rotates exhibits of Irish modern art. (☎22090. Gallery open M-Sa 10am-6pm. Free.) Get wired into the local arts scene with *Art Beat,* free at the center. For a self-guided tour of the town's major sights, pick up a copy of the *The Skibbereen Trail* map at the tourist office (€1.75). Included on this tour is the **Abbeystrewery Cemetery,** where between 8000 and 10,000 Famine victims are buried. The gardens at **Liss Ard Experience,** down the Castletownshend road toward the hostel, promise to "induce new perceptions of light and sky." Created as a unique attempt at conservation, the Experience's 50 acres include a waterfall garden, a wildflower meadow with over 100 species of butterflies, and the surreal "Irish sky garden" designed by American artist James Turrell. (Open May-Sept.) Based about 8 mi. from Skib, Jim Kennedy at **Atlantic Sea Kayaking** offers paddle daytrips, and night paddles in Lough Hyne and Castlehaven Bay. (☎21058 or 086 606 5973. €38.) The **Atlantic Boating Services'** shack on Bridge St. sells wet suits, flippers, and other water accessories. (☎22145; www.atlanticboat.ie. Open M-Sa 9am-6pm.)

BALTIMORE (BAILE TAIGH MÓR) ☎028

The tiny fishing village of Baltimore (pop. 200) has traded its pirates for tourists and is becoming a center for aquatic sport and point of departure for the Sherkin and Cape Clear Islands. In the center of town is the stone wreckage of Dún na

Sead (The Fort of the Jewels), one of nine regional 16th-century castles belonging to the prolific O'Driscoll clan. O'Driscolls from near and far congregate here every June to elect a chieftain and stage a family gathering, complete with live music, jammed pubs, and convivial inebriation. Artists and tourists flock to Baltimore with almost equal enthusiasm to enjoy its bright, dramatic seascapes.

▣▨ TRANSPORTATION AND PRACTICAL INFORMATION. It's difficult to miss anything in Baltimore. The main road from Skibbereen passes along the water before running 1½ mi. out of town to the milk bottle **Beacon,** a cliff-top lighthouse that once guided ships between the mainland and Sherkin Island. Inside the small **General store** below O'Driscoll castle, the **post office** (☎20101; open M-F 9am-5:30pm, Sa 9am-1pm) displays a **Bus Éireann** schedule; buses run to **Skibbereen** regularly (M-Sa 3-4 per day, fewer in winter; €3). For information on ferries to Cape Clear or Sherkin, see p. 257. The small summer **tourist office** (☎20441), in the blue harbor-side craft center, is non-Bord Fáilte and keeps sporadic hours.

▮▣▨ ACCOMMODATIONS, FOOD, AND PUBS. Hallway candles light the way through the stone walls of ▧**Fastnet B&B ❸.** The secluded back double room has the best ocean views. The upstairs triple sports plum curtains and has room enough to do cartwheels. (☎20515. Doubles €72-80; singles €50. Children half-price.) A delightful German family runs the popular **Rolf's Hostel (IHH) ❶,** a 300-year-old complex of stone farmhouses just 10min. from the waterfront. From the pier, start back up the Skibbereen road, and turn left at the signposted turnoff. The comfortable pine beds (brass in private rooms) and stunning views are hard to resist. (☎20289. Laundry €5. Dorms €13-15; doubles €40; family rooms €55; holiday cottages €450-500 per wk.) On the waterfront, the Diving & Watersports Centre welcomes budget-seeking guests to the **Baltimore Holiday Hostel ❷.** Follow the signs downhill from the post office and look for the red sign that says "Le Bistro." (☎20300. **Bike rental** €10 per day. Laundry €7. Dorms €15.)

Provisions for extended island stays can be found at **Cotter's Gala,** on the main road facing the harbor. (☎20106. Open June-Aug. daily 9am-8pm; Sept.-May 9am-7:30pm.) **Cafe Art and Restaurant ❷,** at Rolf's Hostel (see above), is famous for its fresh Mediterranean salads. Candles and wine goblets separate the cafe from the restaurant. (☎20289. Open Tu-Su 8am-9pm. Sandwiches €4-5. Mains €12-14.) Front and center **La Jolie Brise ❸** peddles the tastiest pizzas (€6-10) in town. (☎020 600. Open 8:30am-11pm; closes 9pm in winter.) Shying away from the front-row hubbub, **Mews Restaurant ❺** is decked out in forest greens and glossed pinewood floors, and is known for the best food (Duck Confit €25) in town. (☎20390. Open June-Sept. M-Sa 6-10pm.) Baltimore's pub stride of ten to twelve paces begins at lively **McCarthy's,** famous for its trad and folk bands (F and Sa in summer), and its mid-May **Fiddle Fair** that attracts the likes of Christie Moore. (☎20159. Bar food noon-10pm. Occasional cover €3-13.) The maritime theme continues in **Bushe's Bar** (☎20125), and, around the corner, at the well-cushioned **Algiers Inn** (☎20145).

◨▨ SIGHTS AND ACTIVITIES. Most of Baltimore's best sights are found underwater; wrecked U-boats, galleons, and other subaquatic curiosities await more amphibious visitors. To arrange dives or equipment rentals, contact the **Baltimore Diving & Watersports Centre,** located in the Baltimore Holiday Hostel. (☎20300. 1hr. snorkel dive €12.50, including equipment; course and dive for the inexperienced €40.) **Atlantic Boating Service,** at the end of the pier, offers all manner of aquatic fun. (☎22145; www.atlanticboat.ie. **Boat rental** €19 per hr., €63 per day.) Explorers with wheels can head east to circular **Lough Ine** (sometimes spelled Hyne), Northern Europe's only saltwater lake, where clear rapids change direction with the tide. The lough, originally freshwater, was converted by rising sea levels following the last Ice Age. These days Ine is a stomping ground for marine biologists searching for its dozens of sub-tropical species. **Walking trails** wind through the woods around the lake, and steeper climbs lead to incredible views. A few miles back toward Skib, the well-groomed **Creagh Gardens** hold the surrounding woodlands at bay. (☎22121. Open daily 10am-5pm. €3.80, children €1.90.)

CAPE CLEAR ISLAND (OILEÁN CHLÉIRE)   ☎028

The scenery visible from the ferry landing is desolate and foreboding; the landscape of patchwork fields separated by low stone walls hasn't changed much since Spanish galleons stopped calling here hundreds of years ago. The main industry on this wild and beautiful island is farming—ask locals about the legendary banana plantation (but resist offers of employment as a harvester at all costs).

TRANSPORTATION AND PRACTICAL INFORMATION. Capt. Conchúr O'Driscoll runs ferries to and from **Baltimore**. (☎39135. 2-6 per day; €11.50, children €5.50). Capt. Molloy ferries directly to **Schull**. (☎28138. 45min.; June 1 per day, July-Aug. 3 per day.; €11.50 return.) Capt. Cierán O'Driscoll offers **ferry loops** from Cape Clear to Baltimore, Schull, and back. (☎28138. Daily departures from Cape Clear Island mid-June to mid-Sept. 9am and 12:15pm; single €8, full-loop, including lunch voucher €13.) Life here is leisurely and hours are approximate—for current opening hours and general island information consult the **information office** in the Pottery Shop, on the left just up from the pier. (☎39100. Open June-Aug. 11am-noon and 3-6pm; Sept. 3-5pm.) There are **no banks or ATMs** on the island, but the green box trailer on the far side of the pier houses a temporary **library**. (Open W-Sa 2-4pm, Th 2-4pm and 7-9pm.)

ACCOMMODATIONS, FOOD, AND PUBS. Cléire Lasmuigh (An Óige/HI) ❶, the Cape Clear Island Adventure Centre and Hostel, is a 10min. walk from the pier; follow the main road and keep left. In a picturesque stone building with killer views of the harbor, the hostel fills with Irish students in the summer, so call ahead. (☎39198. Dorms €11-13.) Opposite from **Ciarán Danny Mike's** (see p. 257), the **Cluain Mara B&B ❷** has sunny rooms with harbor views. (☎39153. €28-30; self-catering apartment €40.) Up the (very) steep hill past the hostel, flowered **Ard Na Gaoithe ❸** has spacious doubles, family rooms, and a filling breakfast buffet. (☎39160. €25.) **Cuas an Uisce Campsite ❶**, on the south pier, is a 5min. walk from the harbor. Start uphill from the harbor, bear right before colorful Ciarán Danny Mike's, and it's 400 yd. up on the left. Pete the warden takes to the sea by day—leave a note or check in at the pubs. (☎39136. Open June-Sept. €5 per person, under 16 €2.50, children free. Tent rental €5. Showers €1.)

An Siopa Beag (☎39099), on the pier, stocks basic groceries. The shop also has a small **coffee dock** that peddles takeaway pizzas on some summer evenings. (Open June F-Sa 5-7pm, July-Aug. daily 6-8:30pm.) Dinner options on Cape Clear are limited to the island's two pubs. Multi-generational **Ciarán Danny Mike's ❸** is Ireland's southernmost pub and restaurant. Ciarán (son), Danny (father), and Mike (grandfather) serve slurpalicious soups and tempting dinners. (☎39172. Soup €3, sandwiches €3, mains €8-15.) Closer to the pier, **Cotter's Cape Clear Bar** also serves bar necessities—pub grub and Guinness. (☎39102. Open daily 11am-9pm.) What Cape Clear's pub scene lacks in variety it makes up for in stamina; without a resident island *Garda* to regulate after-hours drinking, the fun often rolls on past 3am.

SIGHTS AND ACTIVITIES. A steep 25min. hike up the narrow hill above the harbor sits the Cape Clear **heritage center**, packed with everything from a family tree of the ubiquitous O'Driscolls to a waterlogged deck chair from the *Lusitania.* (Open June-Aug. M-Sa noon-5pm, Su 2pm-5pm. €2.50.) On the road to the center, after the hill, in the second house on the left, **Cléire Goats** (☎39126) is home to some of the best-bred furry beasts in Ireland. Test the owner's claim that his **goat's milk ice cream** (€1.50) is richer and more scrumptious than the generic bovine variety. Cléire Goats also runs half-day to week-long courses for those who want to blend the theory and practice of goat-keeping. (Bookable only through www.emara.com.) From many of the island's hills, the ruins of the **O'Driscoll castle** (near the North Harbour) and the **old lighthouse** (to the south, beyond the hostel) make a lovely panorama. Though the castle remains on private property, the lighthouse is open for exploration. On the northeast corner of the island, the **marriage stones** were visited throughout the centuries by young, intrepid lovebirds hoping to gain the gift of fertility. The **bird observatory,** a white farmhouse in the North Harbour, is one of the most important in Europe. (☎39189. Only die-hard ornithologists roost here; €14 per night.) Three miles off the east shore is **Fastnet Rock Lighthouse;** for a closer look contact Capt. Cierán O'Driscoll (☎39153; Tu, Th, Su. 7:30pm sailings in summer). Capt. Cierán also runs **whale and dolphin watching** excursions and **ocean bird watching** trips with resident experts like Pete the warden. (☎39172. €15.) For **sea-kayaking** and **diving** trips, contact the **Roaringwater Bay Centre.** (Kayaking €12 per hr., snorkeling €10 per hr.) Swallow a hefty dose of island lore in early September at Cape Clear's annual **International Storytelling Festival,** which features puppet workshops, music sessions, and a weekend of memorable tales. (☎39116; www.indig.ie/~stories. €7 per event, €30 all weekend events.)

SHERKIN ISLAND (INIS ARCAIN)   ☎028

Just 10min. across the water from Baltimore, Sherkin Island (pop. 100) lures visitors with its sandy, cliff-enclosed beaches, wind-swept heaths, over-abundance of cows, and absence of people. The first sight after the ferry is a ruined 15th-century **Franciscan abbey,** founded by the infamous Fineen O'Driscoll. Vengeful troops from Waterford sacked the abbey in 1537 to avenge the theft of their wine. **Dún-na-Long Castle** ("fort of the ships"), also built by the buccaneer clan and also sacked in the '37 raid, lies in a heap north of the abbey behind Islander's Rest. From the ferry dock the main road passes blue-green **Kinnish Harbour** and the Sherkin **Art Exhibition Community Hall.** The Hall was damaged in a recent fire, but is undergoing repairs and scheduled to reopen in 2004. (☎020 336. Open June-Sept. 9am-6pm.) To reach Sherkin's best beaches, continue down the main road to the east side of the island and the glorious **Silver Strand.** Nearby lie **Cow Strand** and **Trabawn,** which are more secluded and great for swimming. For particularly breathtaking views from the island's east side, turn left at the signs for **Horseshoe Harbour** and its defunct **lighthouse.** Sherkin is liveliest on the last Sunday of July during the annual **regatta.**

    Ferries arrive from Baltimore ten times a day in the summer and thrice in the winter (€7 return). Ferry schedules are posted outside the **Islands Craft Office** in Baltimore (see p. 255) and on the back of the ubiquitous Sherkin brochure; Capt. Vincent O'Driscoll (☎20125) can also provide information. Ferries run by Capt. Kieran Molloy depart from **Schull.** (☎28138. 1hr., June-Sept. 1-3 per day, €11.50 return). The friendly family at ⬛**Windhoek Cottages and B&B ❷** converted their old stone stables into cozy self-catering cottages, all equipped with kitchen, bath, and heating—a steal for families or groups of four to five. They also rent warm B&B rooms that fit up to three. Follow signs straight on from the ferry dock toward Silver Strand beach. (☎020 275 or 086 608 4428. Cottages €60, €380 per wk. B&B €50.) Another alternative is **The Islander's Rest ❹,** across the street from the Jolly Roger Pub, with lovely views and warm-toned basic bedrooms. (☎020 116; www.islandersrest.ie. €40-55, depending on season.) Central **Abbey Store,** on the main road and visible from the pier hill, stocks the basics and houses a small **post office.** (☎020 181. Open M-Sa 9am-1pm and 2-6pm, Su noon-6pm.) The amiable **Jolly Roger ❸** (☎020 379) has periodic trad sessions during the summer and serves dependable pub grub from noon to 7pm. Their heaping bowls of fresh-herbed ⬛**Sherkin mussels** (€6) are reason enough to visit the island. To eat closer to the beach, grab a sandwich (€2-3) at **Cuisin Snack Bar ❶** (☎086 238 4228), on the road between Silver and Cow Strands.

MIZEN HEAD AND SHEEP'S HEAD

The serene southwestern tip of Ireland is comprised of two narrow peninsulas. Sheep's Head, to the north, extends out into the ocean like a skinny finger along Bantry Bay. Across Dunmanus Bay to the south, Mizen Head reaches as far to the southwest as the borders of Ireland allow. Both make for excellent day-long cycling trips, perhaps best for the cycling-fit, but the endless isolated coves and windswept beaches along the coast may entice more careful exploration.

SCHULL (AN SCOIL)   ☎028

An ideal base for forays onto Mizen Head and ferry trips to nearby Cape Clear and the Sherkin Islands, the seaside town of Schull (pronounced "skull"; Irish for "school") is situated 4 mi. west of **Ballydehob,** on R592, off N71. Schull provides the last stronghold of culture and commerce before sheep society begins to edge out human society. With its first-rate hostel, surprisingly sophisticated eateries, and bike and boat rental options, it is the perfect spot for enjoying the rare Irish sunshine. Be warned that many other travelers are wise to Schull's charms; holiday cottages and B&Bs draw droves during the summer months, when the town's population explodes from 300 to 3000.

🖃�》 TRANSPORTATION AND PRACTICAL INFORMATION. Buses to Cork via Skibbereen (M-Sa 2-3 per day, Su 1-2 per day; €12.10) and Goleen (M-Sa 2 per day, Su 1-2 per day; €3.50) stop in front of the **AIB** on Main St. Check the schedule posted on the corner or call the Cork bus station (☎021 450 8188); Schull does not have a local **Bus Éireann** agent. **Ferries** connect Schull to **Cape Clear** and the **Sherkin Islands** (June 2 per day, July-Aug. 2-3 per day; €12 return; contact Capt. Molloy ☎28138 or inquire at the pier) and to Baltimore (June to mid-Sept. 3 per day; €8 return; contact Capt. O'Driscoll ☎39135). For lovely jaunts to Barley Cove Beach or along the Dunmanus road on the northern side of the peninsula, **rent bikes** at **Schull Backpackers' Lodge** (see **Accommodations,** p. 259). Pick up the detailed *Schull Guide*, which has good suggestions for walking and cycling in the area, in any store (free), or peruse one of the hostel's copies. Make money appear out of thin air at the 24hr. **ATM** at **AIB** on Upper Main St. (☎28132. Open M-F 10am-12:30pm and 1:30-4pm.) There's a **pharmacy** on Main St. (☎28108. Open M-Sa 9:30am-1:15pm and 2:15-6pm.) Restaurants up and down Main St., such as Adele's Bakery (☎28459; www.adelesrestaurant.com), occasionally offer travelers summer **work opportunities** waiting tables and in the kitchen. Pay is usually about €6 per hr., plus tips. The **post office** on Main St. doubles as a photography shop. (☎28110. Open M-F 9am-1pm and 2-5:30pm, Sa 9:30am-1pm.)

🚪🏠🖼 ACCOMMODATIONS, FOOD, AND PUBS. Schull's appeal to budget travelers can be traced to the ⬛**Schull Backpackers' Lodge (IHH) ❶** on Colla Rd. From the bus stop, walk up Main St. and bear left; walk past the old church and take a right down the marked and extremely long driveway. The wooden lodge is clean and friendly, with spacious dorms, fluffy comforters, and welcoming staff eager to share information on local walks and rides over hot cocoa. The in-house **English language school** keeps the hostel lively with long-term guests in summer, but beds are also booked by groups, so call ahead in July and August. The lodge **rents bikes** (€10 per day), has **Internet** (€1 per 15min.), and may offer short term **work opportunities** in the summer season. (☎28681; www.schullbackpackers.com. Laundry €4.50. Key deposit €2. June-Aug. dorms €12; singles €18; doubles €36, with bath €40; family room €56. Low season a bit less.) **Adele's B&B ❸**, Main St., above the eponymous restaurant, has three small but cozy doubles with dark wooden floors. (☎28459; www.adelesrestaurant.com. Tasty continental breakfast included. Shared bathroom. €25.50.) Three miles toward Goleen, **Jenny's Farmhouse ❷** is a quiet place to stable for the night. (☎28205. Call for pickup from Schull. €15, with breakfast €20-5.)

Those tiring of traditional Irish stew and fried chips will delight in the surprising variety of fine food available in Schull. For standard supplies, head to **Spar Market** (☎28236; open July-Sept. daily 8am-9pm, Oct.-June M-Sa 8am-7:30pm, Su 8am-8pm) or smaller **Hegarty's Centra** (☎28520; open daily 7am-10pm), across from each other on Main Street. **The Courtyard ❷**, also on Main St., caters to those with more discerning taste buds; its delicious fruit scones with currants, raisins, and lemon zest (€0.55) make for a lovely breakfast, while sandwiches (€7-9.50) such as ciabatta with bacon, smoked cheese, and tomato relish (€9.50) are superb for lunch. (☎28390. Open M-Sa 9:30am-6pm.) Just up the street, **Adele's ❷** bakes fresh breakfast treats and a variety of tea-time pastries. (☎28459. Sandwiches €6-9. Open Easter-Nov. W-Sa 9:30am-6pm, Su 11am-5pm; takeout available until 6pm.) Several Schull pubs have thrown off the culinary yoke of standard fried Irish fare in favor of much more creative offerings. **Hackett's Bar ❶**, on Main St., has a great range of affordable options on its lunch menu, from a hummus and salad plate (€5) to mussels in white wine and cream (€4.45). This joint also features live rock bands on weekends throughout the year. (☎28625. Food served daily noon-3pm.) Another spot for relatively inexpensive fine food is the classy **⬛Courtyard Pub & Restaurant ❷**, located behind its sister gourmet shop on Main St. The spicy salmon cakes with lemongrass and corriander dip (€12.50) are a favorite. The pub also features excellent live trad and folk several nights a week. (☎28390. Mains €9-12.50. Food served noon-9pm. See posters outside for music nights and hours.) The portions at **The Waterside Inn ❷** are sure to satisfy, with classic Irish and seafood standards served in the pub; live music follows on most nights. A much more upscale menu (mains €18-25) is available at the adjacent **restaurant ❺**. (☎28203. Pub meals €8-12, served daily 12:30-9:30pm in the summer; winter weekends only.) Cozy **An Tigín** (☎28830), at the top of Main St., caters to local Gaelic football fans, hosts live music by the hearth most Fridays, and has a small beer garden out back.

◨ ⚐ SIGHTS AND ACTIVITIES. The **Schull Planetarium**, Colla Rd., features extraterrestrial diversions for rainy days and occasional lecture series on such topics as "Creation." (☎28552. 45min. star shows usually at 4 or 8pm, but call ahead for schedule. €4.50.) Schull invites visitors to take a break from historical hype and explore the **walking** and **biking trails** snaking along the water and up into the hills. Inquire at the Backpacker's Lodge for maps and information or consult the Schull Visitor's Guide for a thorough walking map. While Schull's many shipwrecks belie the calm harbor and beckon the curious diver, there is sadly no full service dive shop. However, the **Watersports Centre** on the pier rents wetsuits, scuba tanks, and fishing gear, and offers **kayak** and **sailing courses**. (☎28554. Open Apr.-Oct. M-Sa 9:30am-6pm. Dinghies €40 per half-day. Motorboats €80 per day. Half-day kayak trip €50. 2½hr. sailing course €85.)

GOLEEN, CROOKHAVEN, AND MIZEN HEAD ☎028

The Mizen becomes more scenic and less populated west of Schull. The peninsula's native population thins out, but European house-buyers have answered the call for reinforcements. Thus, the Mizen is mobbed during peak-season weekends when sun-loving vacationers pack sandy beaches. The most reliable transit is **Betty Johnson's Bus Hire**, which gives tours of the Mizen via the scenic northern coast road. The tour includes bits of local history and runs to the **Mizen Vision** (see p. 261). Call Betty for her schedule; she will make a run any day when there are at least six people interested. (☎28410. About 3hr. €12.) **Bus Éireann** only goes as far as Goleen (2 per day on the Cork-West Cork line; inquire in Schull or Ballydehob for a detailed schedule). **Bantry Rural Transport** offers limited service from Schull to Goleen and Bantry. (☎027 52727. 2 per day; Tu, F). **Hitching**, while always risky, is possible in the peak-season, with hitchers often perching at the crossroads on the Goleen Rd. just outside of town. Confident **cyclists** can make a daytrip to Mizen Head (36 mi. return from Schull); less confident cyclists can tackle less taxing jaunts—the Backpackers' Lodge includes a good **bike map** with rental.

The block-long town of **Goleen** *(Goilín)* is a nice spot for ice cream on the way to more southwesterly points. **The Green Kettle** specializes in antiques and homemade scones served in its rear garden. (☎35033. Open June-Sept. daily 11am-6pm, Oct.-May Sa-Su 10am-5pm.) About a mile up the hill just outside of town is **The Ewe**, a wonderfully eccentric "art retreat" that offers pottery classes and zany gifts from its gallery/shop. For €3.50 (children €1.75), visitors stroll through the low-growing sculpture garden. (☎35492; www.theewe.com. Open daily 10am-6pm. Half-day pottery courses €40, "paint-a-bowl" €12.) Those seeking a quiet place for rest and relaxation can head to **Heron's Cove B&B ❸**, down the hill from Goleen on the water. (☎35225; www.heronscove.com. All rooms with bath and TV. €25-35; family room €70.) The **restaurant ❹** downstairs serves a delicious pan-fried lemon sole (€19.50), among other excellent seafood. (☎35225. Open June-Aug. daily 5:30-9:30pm. Booking required Sept.-May.)

Slightly longer than the main road, and tremendously worthwhile, is the coast road, which winds past **Barley Cove Beach** and continues to Mizen Head. Tiny **Crookhaven** *(An Cruachan;* pop. 37), a 1 mi. detour off this road, is perched at the end of its own peninsula. Meet half the population at **O'Sullivan's ❷**, which serves sandwiches, soups, and cold pints by the water's edge, and live music on occasional summer nights. (☎35319. Food served daily noon-8pm.) The other half goes to the **Crookhaven Inn ❷** for similar fare in a lovely outdoor cafe by the bay. (☎35309. Sandwiches €3, meals €7-10. Food served daily noon-8pm.) **Barley Cove Caravan Park ❶**, 1½ mi. from Crookhaven, offers **camping** near Mizen's most celebrated strand, and includes **tennis** and **pitch-and-putt** facilities. (☎35302. Open Easter-Sept. Mini-market and takeaway. **Bike rental** €15 per day; deposit €50. €13-15 per 2-person tent. Laundry €10.) Campers have a short walk to the warm, shallow waters of Barley Cove Beach, a sandy retreat for those not ready to brave the frigid sea.

Three miles past Barley Cove, Ireland comes to an abrupt end at spectacular **Mizen Head**, where cliffs rise 700 ft. above the waves. **Mizen Head Lighthouse**, built in 1909, was recently automated and electrified, while the nearby buildings were turned into a small museum, the **Mizen Vision**. To get there, visitors must cross a suspension bridge only slightly less harrowing than the virtual shipwreck that waits inside. The museum illuminates the solitary lives of lighthouse keepers and the lighthouses they keep. Its small, windy viewing platform is the most southwesterly point in Ireland. Return via the 99 steps (or take the ramp) to the newly opened **Visitor Centre**, to peruse more exhibits or indulge in pricey items from the **cafe.** (☎35115. Open June-Sept. daily 10am-6pm; mid-Mar. to May and Oct. 10:30am-5pm; Nov. to mid-Mar. Sa-Su 11am-

4pm. €4.50, students €3.50, under 12 €2.50, under 5 free.) Those on wheels can return to Schull via Dunmanus along the locally renowned coastal road, which runs the northern coast of the peninsula.

BANTRY (BEANNTRAI)   ☎ 027

According to the big *Book of Invasions*, Ireland's first human inhabitants landed just 1 mi. from Bantry (see **Legends and Folktales**, p. 73). In the grand tradition of British invasion, 17th-century English settlers arrived in the bay and drove the Irish out. In 1796, Wolfe Tone and a band of Irish patriots made an ill-fated attempt to return the favor with the help of the French Armada. These days, the invasion racket has died down considerably, but the town still has plenty to plunder for the eager explorer. Bantry's distinctly untouristed, working-town feel is refreshing, and its pubs and live music provide authentic *craic* every night. The town's main attraction is the incredibly elegant Bantry House and gardens, which should not be missed. For daytrips out onto the Sheep's Head peninsula or to Whiddy Island, this is the best place to anchor for the night.

█ TRANSPORTATION. Buses stop outside Julie's Takeaway in Wolfe Tone Sq. **Bus Éireann** heads to Cork via Bandon and Bantry (M-Sa 8 per day, Su 4 per day; €10) and to Glengarriff (M-Sa 3 per day, Su 2 per day; €3.50). From June to September, buses go to Killarney via Kenmare (2 per day) and Tralee (2 per day), and to Skibbereen (2 per day). **Berehaven Bus Service** (☎70007) also stops here en route to and from Cork. **Tinstar Cabs** offers basic transportation throughout the area and guided tours of Bantry, Sheep's Head, and the Standing Stones (☎028 31995. €50+ per person, min. 2 people. Half- and full-day tours available.) **Rent bikes** from **The Bicycle Shop,** formerly Kramer's, on Glengarriff Rd., Newtown, near the Independent Hostel. (☎52657. €12 per day, €50 per wk.; helmet included. ID or credit card deposit. Open June-Aug. M-Sa 10am-6pm; Sept.-May M-Tu and Th-Sa 10am-5pm.)

█▐ ORIENTATION AND PRACTICAL INFORMATION. Bantry lies at the eastern end of **Bantry Bay.** Facing away from the water, **New Street** leads straight into town, out of **Wolfe Tone Square,** while **William Street** branches off to the right. From the left corner of the Square, **Marino Street** splits into **Old Barrack Road** and **Glengarriff Road. Main Street** runs perpendicular to the Square, intersecting New St., which becomes **Bridge Street.** Sheep's Head lies due west; the Beara Peninsula is northwest. Cars, cyclists, and hitchers stay on N71 to get into or out of town. The **tourist office,** Wolfe Tone Sq., has a **bureau de change,** maps of Bantry and Sheep's Head, and helpful, patient staff. (☎50229. Open July-Aug. M-Sa 9am-6pm, Su 9:30am-5:30pm; Apr.-June and Sept.-Nov. M-Sa 9:30am-5:30pm.) **AIB,** Wolfe Tone Sq., has an **ATM,** as does the neighboring **Bank of Ireland.** (☎50008 and 51377. Both open M 10am-5pm, Tu, Th, F 10am-4pm, W 10:30am-4pm.) Travelers seeking short-term **work opportunities** in Bantry might find odd-jobs at **The West Cork Chamber Music Festival,** the last week of June and the first week of July. Inquire at Bantry House (☎50047) or at the box office (☎52788). **Coen's Pharmacy,** the Square, peddles potions. (☎50531. Open M-Sa 9:30am-1pm and 2-6pm.) The **police** (*Garda*) guards from the Square (☎50045). **St. Joseph's Bantry Hospital,** Dromleigh Rd. (☎50133), is a quarter mile past the library. The **library,** at the top of Bridge St., provides **Internet** to Cork library cardholders; purchase a card for €2.50 at any participating branch. (☎50460. Open Tu-W and F-Sa 10am-1pm and 2:30-6pm, Th 10am-6pm.) Internet can also be found at **fast.net business solutions** on Main St. (☎51624. €1 per 10min., €5 per hr. Open M-F 9am-6pm, Sa 10am-5pm.) The **post office** is at 2 William St. (☎50050. Open M-Sa 9am-5:30pm, Tu open 9:30am.)

⌐ ACCOMMODATIONS AND CAMPING. Bantry Independent Hostel (IHH) ❶, on the former Bishop Lucey Pl. in Newtown, provides clean, spacious rooms, formidable security, and a secluded setting. From the Square, head away from town on Glengarriff Rd.; take the left fork, walk up the slight hill, down the street, and around the far bend (about 8min.). If arriving by bus on Glengarriff Rd., skip the walk and ask the driver to stop at O'Mahoney's Quickpick Food Store. From there, walk up the hill across the road and turn right around the bend. (☎51050. Laundry €5. Open mid-Mar. to Oct. 6-bed dorms €11; doubles €24.) For more upscale rooms on the Square, check out the **Bantry Bay Hotel ❹**. Rooms with views of the Square are best. (☎50062. Live music nightly July-Aug. Singles €45-55; doubles with breakfast, TV, and bath €84-90.) On Main St. across from the hotel is **Atlanta Guest House ❸**. Don't be fooled by the retro entryway—the roomsare comfortable, clean, stocked with TVs and phones, and worth the money. (☎50 237; www.atlantaguesthouse.com. Breakfast included. €30; singles €40.) Four miles from town, on Glengarriff Rd. in Ballylickey, the **Eagle Point Camping and Caravan Park ❶** has a private beach, tennis courts, TV room, and free showers. (☎50630. Open May-Sept. Laundry €5. €8 or more per person; family €29.)

◨◪ FOOD AND PUBS. SuperValu, New St., stocks foodstuffs. (☎50001. Open M-Th 8:30am-7pm, F 8:30am-9pm, Sa 8:30am-6:30pm.) **Organico,** on the Glengarriff Rd., has a surprising variety of health and whole foods, including freshly baked organic bread. (☎51391. Open M-Sa 9:30am-6pm.) The Square is lined with touristy, pricey restaurants, but those off the Square, and most of the pubs, offer cheaper options. For delicious toasted sandwiches (€3-4) and a great choice of sweet treats, turn off New St. onto Main St. and follow your nose to **Floury Hands Cafe and Bakery ❶**. (☎52590. Open M-Sa 8am-5:30pm.) Family-owned and operated **O'Siochain ❷**, Bridge St., offers tasty homemade Irish standards in a comfy, kitschy coffeehouse. (☎51339. Mains from €9. Open June-Sept. daily 9am-10pm, Oct.-May 9am-6pm.) Vegetarians need not apply at **Peter's Steak House ❷**, a no frills diner-style joint on New St. (☎50025. Most mains €11-12, sirloin steak €16.50, omelettes €7. Open July-Aug. daily 10am-11pm; Sept.-May 10am-10pm.) **Chin Fong Chinese Restaurant & Takeaway ❶** fries up food late into the night on Main St. (☎52811. Mains €6.50-9, veggie dishes €5.50. Open Su-Th 5:30pm-1am, F-Sa 5:30pm-2am.)

Bantry's pubs have real homegrown spirit and character; the locals work hard during the week and drink hard on weekends. **Anchor Bar,** New St. (☎50012), is usually the liveliest, luring the locals with a pub/disco atmosphere on weekends and live music on summer Thursdays. **The Schooner,** Barrack St. (☎52115), features a cargo of mixed music on weekends. In the Square, ballad-lovers get their fill from frequent sessions at **J.J. Crowley's** (☎50027), and **Barry Murphy's (O Murchu)** blasts hip-hop for a younger crowd (☎50900). After the pubs shut, night-owls head to the **disco** (cover €7; open June-Aug. F-Sa midnight-2am) in the Bantry Bay Hotel (see **Accommodations,** p. 263).

◎◪ SIGHTS AND ENTERTAINMENT. Bantry's main tourist attractions lie a 10min. walk from town up a long, shady driveway off the Cork road. ⬛**Bantry House and Gardens,** a Georgian manor with magnificently restored grounds dramatically overlooking the Bay, is a lovely sight not to be missed. The former seat of the Earls of Bantry, the house was a hospital during Ireland's Civil War and again during "the Emergency" (neutral Éire's term for WWII). The house is currently under renovation, but is expected to reopen Easter 2004. Full admission allows visitors to wander freely around the manicured gardens and gain access to the house, with an ornate interior to match the elaborate grounds. A challenging ascent up the "Stairway to the Sky" rewards visitors with a gorgeous view of the manor and bay.

The Earls had to scramble a bit when Irish rebel **Theobald Wolfe Tone** harnessed a bit of France's anti-English sentiment for his own nationalist insurrection (see **Rebellion**, p. 61). Wolfe Tone's campaign and the 1980's discovery of an Armada ship once scuttles in the harbor are thoroughly documented in the **1796 Bantry French Armada Exhibition Centre.** Enjoy the irony of its location next to Bantry House, former residence of Richard White, the man who mobilized British resistance to Wolfe Tone's invasion. **Refreshments** (coffee and cakes €2-3) are available in the Armada center. (☎50047. House open mid-Mar. to Oct. daily 9am-6pm; exhibition 9am-5pm. Garden and exhibition €4. House, exhibition, and gardens €9.50, students and seniors €8. Accompanied children free.)

If doomed missions and grandiose nobles don't entice you, take a cruise on one of the **sea trips** that circumnavigate the harbor and stop at **Whiddy Island,** where quiet beaches attract birds and their watchers. (☎51739. Trips depart July-Sept. daily at 2:30, 4, and 6pm, as well as M, W, F at 9:30 and 11am. €7 return.) Bantry hosts the **West Cork Chamber Music Festival** during the last week of June and early July. The **RTE Vanburgh String Quartet** is joined by scores of other international performers. Performances take place in the elegant rooms of Bantry House. (☎52788. 1-show tickets from €8.50-30; daily passes €24-48; full-week tickets €165-365; workshops €5-20.) The Chamber Music Festival includes the spin-off **Literary Fringe,** which holds readings and workshops at the Bantry Library and Bantry House, and awards the prestigious Fish Short Story Prize. (Workshops €25-160; readings and discussions free.) Glut on seafood during the annual **Bantry Mussel Fair,** held the second weekend in May.

NEAR BANTRY: SHEEP'S HEAD (MUINTIR BHAIRE)

Although largely ignored by tourists passing through Skibbereen and Bantry en route to more publicized peninsulas, Sheep's Head is a pleasant alternative for those eager to evade the company of camera-toters and the exhaust of tour buses (which aren't allowed here). Visitors already impressed by the gentle southern coves and craggy northern cliffs also marvel at the prevalence of bovine beasts over the peninsula's woolly "namesake." (English-speaking cartographers flagrantly misinterpreted the Irish name for the peninsula, which actually meant "the people of Baire.") Hitchers may find it difficult to catch rides to or from this least populated part of West Cork. Many **walkers** and **cyclists** take advantage of the peaceful roads and the well-plotted **Sheep's Head Way.** Maps and guides of the Way are available in the Bantry tourist office (see **Bantry**, p. 262). Criss-crossing paths provide endless options for those on foot. The road circling Sheep's Head sticks to the coast, making for easy cycling with constant vistas. Aside from the climb connecting the village of **Kilcrohane** to the northern road, which rewards with stunning views from **Finn MacCool's Seat,** the counterclockwise route feels downhill most of the way.

Sheep's Head is a manageable cycling daytrip from Bantry for the extremely fit (40 mi. return), but those who prefer a more leisurely pace will find peaceful lodging at any of the B&Bs speckling the peninsula or at the tiny **Carbery's View Hostel ❶** in Kilcrohane. The hostel is conveniently signposted from the western end of town and is perfectly situated over the bay. (☎67035. €12.50.) If staying in Kilcrohane, pick up limited supplies at **O'Mahoney's Shop** on the main road (☎67001; open M-Sa 9am-9pm, Su 10:30am-1pm and 7-9pm), which also houses the **post office.** Head to **Fitzpatrick's ❶** (☎67057) for a pint, then wash it down with a sandwich or two (€2).

BEARA PENINSULA

Beara Peninsula's rugged and desolate landscape offers a haunting canvas for the lonely explorer. Fortunately, the tourist mobs circling the nearby Ring of Kerry usually skip the Beara altogether, but in doing so they ironically miss some of the best views of the Iveragh from across the bay. Thus, this is the place for unspoiled scenery and solitude; travelers seeking pubs, people, and other signs of civilization might be happier on the Iveragh or Dingle Peninsulas. The spectacular **Caha** and **Slieve Miskish Mountains** march down the center of the peninsula, separating the Beara's rocky south from its lush northern shore. West Beara remains remote—travelers wander treacherous single-track roads along the stark Atlantic coastline, picking their way though mountains, rocky outcrops, and the occasional herd of sheep. The dearth of cars west of Glengarriff makes **cycling** the 125 mi. of the **Beara Way** a joy, but for hitchhikers, the town marks the point west of which they'll find themselves admiring the views for longer than sanity can bear.

GLENGARRIFF (AN GLEANN GARBH)   ☎027

A midday stroll through Glengarriff may leave visitors wondering if anyone actually lives here full-time; the town's position as gateway to the Beara Peninsula and its prominence in the wool industry draw hordes of tourists in the summer months. But that shouldn't stop the solitude-minded from enjoying the lovely walks in the nearby nature reserve or the unusual gardens on Garinish Island.

▐ TRANSPORTATION. Bus Éireann stops in front of Casey's Hotel on Main St. Buses run to Glengarriff from Bantry (25min.; M-Sa 3-5 per day; Su 2-3 per day; €3.45), Castletownbere via Adrigole (45min., 2-3 per day, €3.10), and Cork (2hr., 3 per day). From June to mid-September, a route runs twice a day to: Kenmare (45min.), Killarney (1¾hr.), and Tralee (3hr.). **Berehaven Bus Service** (☎70007) also serves Bantry (M 2 per day, Tu and Th-Sa 1 per day; €4), Castletownbere (M-Tu and Th-Sa 2 per day, €5-6), and Cork (2hr., M-Tu and Th-Sa 3 per day, €11-12.) **Rent bikes** from **Jem Creations,** an art gallery just down from the main intersection on Main St. (☎63113. Open daily 9:30am-7pm. €10 per day, €50 per wk.)

▐ PRACTICAL INFORMATION. Glengarriff is graced with two friendly **tourist offices.** The **Bord Fáilte** office is on the Bantry road at the edge of town. (☎63084. Open May-Oct. M-Tu and Th-Sa 9:30am-1pm and 2-5:30pm.) The other, privately-run office is next to the public bathrooms on the main road, just down from the bus stop. (☎63201. Open daily July-Aug. 9am-9pm; Sept.-June 9am-6pm.) There are several **bureaux de change** (in tourist offices and B&Bs) but **no bank** or **ATM** in Glengarriff, so stock up on cash before visiting. The **post office** is inside O'Shea's Market on Main St. (☎63001. Open M-F 9am-1pm and 2-5:30pm, Sa 9am-1pm.)

▐▐▐ ACCOMMODATIONS, FOOD, AND PUBS. Comfortable, clean rooms and baked delectables await at **Murphy's Village Hostel ❶,** in the middle of town on Main St. (☎63555. **Internet** €6.50 per hr. Laundry €6.50. Dorms €12; doubles €32.) A friendly owner welcomes travelers to **O'Mahoney's Hostel ❶,** about 5 minutes from downtown Glengariff along the road to Bantry. (☎63033. Dorms €15; singles €20.) The **Hummingbird Rest ❶** (☎63195), a 10min. walk from town along the Kenmare road and right near the entrance to the nature reserve, offers small singles (€12.50) and doubles (€25), free laundry, and excellent **camping** (€5 per person). Two **campsites** are neighbors on the Castletownbere road 1½ mi. from town: **Dowling's** (☎63154; open Apr.-Oct.; €5 per person) and **O'Shea's** (☎63140; open mid-Mar. to Oct.; €6 per person with or without car).

Groceries can be had in town from **O'Shea's Market** on Main St. (☎63346. Open M-Sa 8am-9pm, Su 9am-7pm.) Restaurants in Glengarriff are touristy but decent. Abundant and affordable options await at **The Village Kitchen ❷,** attached to the Murphy's hostel, which serves a breakfast menu all day, including vegetarian sausage and pancakes with maple syrup (€7.60), and has **Internet** for €6.50 per hr. (☎63555. Vegetarian tortilla €7.25. Omelettes from €3.25. Open Mar.-Oct. 8am-6pm.) The best place in town for live trad and jovial pint-slurping is **Benjamin Harrington's** (☎63021), on Main St. **Johnny Barry's** (☎63315), and **The Maple Leaf** (☎63021), also on Main St., serve standard pub fare at standard prices daily until around 8:30pm. Both host live music on weekends through the year: everything from disco to country at Johnny Barry's; trad at the Maple Leaf.

◨⚑ **SIGHTS AND ACTIVITIES.** Hike through giant rhododendrons and moss-encrusted evergreens at the lush **Glengarriff National Nature Reserve and Ancient Oak Forest.** Trails range from pebbled paths for curious, scone-scarfing pedestrians to rugged climbs for serious, granola-munching hikers. *Walking Around Glengarriff* (€0.10), available at hostels in town and at the tourist office, outlines several walks in the park; for those with a good pair of boots and a yearning for hilly thrills, there are more detailed maps available. A popular walk with a panoramic view of water, mountain, and forest is the path leading to **Lady Bantry's Lookout** (45min. return). Glengarriff is also a good starting point for the Beara Way.

Bountiful lakes, rivers, and inlets around Glengarriff are perfect territory for the hook-wielding fisherman. Prounouncing **Lake Eekenohoolikeaghaun** (ISH-na-hoo-lick-a-gone) will twist the tongue, but fill the time waiting for fish to bite. Upper and Lower Lough Avaul are well-stocked with trout, but would-be anglers need a permit (available at the Maple Leaf Pub, €7.50 per day) to catch them. **Fishing** in Barley Lake, nearby rivers, and the ocean is permissible for the permitless. Fish fanatics can pick up *Fishing in Glengarriff* (€0.10) at the tourist office. (For more info, ask at the piers or call the regional Fisheries Board ☎026 41222.)

Gardening connoisseurs and picnic fans will delight in **Garinish Island,** an islet in Glengarriff Harbour. Garinish was a rocky outcrop inhabited by a thriving society of gorse bushes until 1900, when English financier Annan Bryce acquired the island from the War Office and dreamed up a fairyland for his family. A million hours of labor and countless boatloads of topsoil later, he had his elaborately designed exotic garden; plans for a mansion were completed but never put into action. Bryce's diplomat son bequeathed their blooming island to the Irish people in 1953, and it has been considered a national treasure ever since. (☎63040. Open July-Aug. M-Sa 9:30am-6pm, Su 11am-6pm; June M-Sa 10am-6pm, Su 11am-6pm; May and Sept. M-Sa 10am-6:30pm, Su noon-6:30pm; Apr. M-Sa 10am-6pm, Su 1-4:30pm; Mar. and Oct. M-Sa 10am-4:30pm, Su 1-5pm. Last landing 30min. before closing. Guidebook €2. €3.50, children and students with ID €1.25, seniors and groups €2.50, family €8.25.) Three boats run trips to the island. **Blue Pool Ferry** leaves from the pier in town, next to the public bathrooms; the other boats depart from the Eccles Hotel. (8min., about every 20min., €7 return with same boat. Blue Pool offers €1 discounts for Murphy's hostelers.) Watch for seals lounging on the seaweedy rocks along the way.

The exotic-garden tradition continues at the **Glengariff Bamboo Park,** built and operated by another wealthy family, the Thibaults. Head east from Glengariff on N71, and watch for signs and bamboo fences. Visitors wander through 13-acres of thoroughly un-Irish vegetation, trying to spot the 30 different species of bamboo and 12 distinct varieties of palm trees. (☎63570 or 63975; www.bamboo-park.com. Open daily 9am-7pm; closes at dusk in winter. €5, seniors €4, students €3, disabled €1, children free. Group rate €3.50.)

THE HEALY PASS

According to the proprietor of a Bantry pub, a patron once remarked in passing that "something ought to be done about the path from Adrigole to Lauragh." Tim Healy, the listener, must have remembered those words when he became Lord Governor of Ireland, and anyone who travels across the pass that bears his name will be grateful he did. R574 winds up between some of the highest peaks in the **Caha Mountains,** connecting the two tiny towns of Adrigole and Lauragh over the border between counties Cork and Kerry. Since the roads are narrow, steep and winding, the curvaceous pass is best explored by car. To enjoy the full effect of the breathtaking views it's wisest to travel from south to north. Begin in Adrigole near the Hungry Hill Hostel (see **Adrigole,** p. 267), and thread through rocky terrain and flocks of sheep to reach **Don's Mountain Cabin** and its excellent selection of local-interest books. The choice of frozen treats from Don's gas-powered fridge is less extensive, but still hits the spot. (Open daily 10am-6pm.) Fifty yards beyond, the verdant sweep of Co. Kerry opens like a dream. The ride down may be slightly harrowing, but the views of Glanmore Lake, Kenmare Bay, and the distant mountains of the Iveragh Peninsula are worth a racing pulse. Hit the pub in Lauragh for a few pints to quiet the mind. The challenge of **biking** the pass intimidates all except the most robust cyclists, but hitchers judge the panoramic payoff to be worth the wait for a lift, despite the risks involved.

ADRIGOLE (EADARGOIL)   ☎027

Before taking the pass north to Lauragh, spend a night in Adrigole. The spacious dorms and extensive facilities at the **Hungry Hill Hostel ❶,** along the Castletownbere road, make it a good base for outdoor expeditions. The hostel will outfit travelers for land or sea, and after a day of hiking or boating the attached **restaurant** is a nice spot to relax. (☎60228. **Bike rental** €8 per day. **Boat rental** €80 per day. Diving compressor available. **Internet** €0.65 per 6min. Laundry €2.50. Dorms €13; doubles €30; family rooms €45. **Camping** from €6.) Roughnecks can attempt to tackle 2245 ft. **Hungry Hill,** where a mountaintop lake overflows on rainy days to create Ireland's tallest (temporary) **waterfall.** (For the permanent record, see p. 144.) Also nearby, the **West Cork Sailing Centre** offers courses ranging from a 3hr. half-day lesson to a week-long course. (☎60132; www.westcorksailing.com. Half-day lesson July-Aug. 2-person group €110, off season €90. Week course July-Aug. €334, off season €265. **Kayak rental** €5 per hr. Open St. Paddy's Day through Oct.)

CASTLETOWNBERE (BAILE CHAISLEAIN BHEARRA)   ☎027

Castletownbere sits on the peninsula's southern edge west of Adrigole. One of Ireland's largest fishing ports, this commercial hub attracts rigs from as far as Spain. Cyclists often speed through en route to villages farther west and north, and the town occasionally fills with nirvana-seekers headed to the nearby Buddhist center. The town's energetic pubs and swimmingly fresh fish restaurants revitalize weary trekkers going around the rest of the peninsula, and entices travelers to linger.

▐ **TRANSPORTATION. Bus Éireann** offers a year-round service to Cork via Glengarriff (3hr., 1-2 per day, €19.20) and a summer route between Castletownbere and Killarney via Allihies, Ardgroom, and Kenmare (M-Sa 2 per day, €14.10 to Killarney). Two **minibuses** operate between Cork and Castletownbere via Bantry and Glengarriff; they will take interested groups on tours of the Beara. Phone **Harrington's** (☎74003) or **O'Donoghue's Berehaven** (☎70007) for reservations. (Leaves

Cork M-Tu and F-Sa 6pm; Castletownbere M-Tu and F-Sa 8am. To Cork €12, Glengarriff €5.30, Bantry €6.50. Tours €25-30.) **Hire bikes** at **Beara Cycles,** Main St., just up from the Square. (☎086 101 2026. Rental includes helmet, map, and lock. €9.50 per day, €55 per wk. Open M-F 9am-6pm, Su 10am-6pm.)

⊞ ❼ ORIENTATION AND PRACTICAL INFORMATION. Castletownbere centers around one main street—**Main Street.** The molehill-sized **tourist office** shares a frazzled office with **Beara Action** (see below) in the main square. (☎70054. Open June-Sept. M-F 10am-5pm.) The **AIB** across the Square has the **only ATM** on the peninsula. (☎70015. Open M 10am-5pm, Tu,Th-F 10am-4pm, W 10:30am-4pm.) For **laundry,** head to **O'Shea's Laundrette** on Main St. near the SuperValu. (☎70994. €8 per load. Open M-F 9am-6pm, Sa 9:30am-6pm.) The *Garda* toward the end of Main St. can be reached at ☎70002 or 50045. Free emergency numbers are ☎999 or 112. **Beara Action,** under the same roof as the tourist office, provides **Internet.** (☎70880. €1.50 per 15min., €5.50 per hr.; students €1.25/€4.50. Open M-F 9:30am-5:30pm, July-Aug. Sa 10am-6pm, Su noon-6pm.) The **library,** on Main St. near Beara Cycles, offers free **Internet** for members. (☎70233. Membership €2.50. Open Tu 6pm-8pm, W 2pm-6pm, Th 11am-1:30pm, F 10:30am-1:30pm and 2pm-6pm.)

❼ ❒ ❙ ACCOMMODATIONS, FOOD, AND PUBS. Castletown House ❷, on Main St. above the Old Bank Seafood Restaurant, offers fine rooms, all with bath and TV, and lots of advice. Be sure to brandish a *Let's Go* guide. (☎70252; www.irishwalking.com. **Internet** €2.50 per hr. for guests. Doubles €48-53; triples €70.) **Harbour Lodge Hostel ❶,** located behind the church in a former convent (head up the church steps and around to the right), provides a serene atmosphere and decent rooms, some with views of the convent garden. (☎71043. Wheelchair-accessible. Laundry €50. Doubles €26, with bath €40; family rooms €40.) Six miles west of town on the Allihies road is **Garranes Farmhouse Hostel (IHH) ❶.** The sea views from this intimate cottage are gorgeous. The €11 cab ride from Castletownbere is worthwhile for the car-less. Sometimes the attached Buddhist center (see **Sights,** below) occupies all the rooms, so phone ahead. (☎73147. Laundry €10. Dorms €12; family rooms €30 for 2, €14 for each additional person. Cottages available for weekly rental.)

Spar, the Square, supplies cheap, snacky options. (☎70057. Open M-Sa 8am-10pm, Su 9am-10pm.) Seafood lovers head to **The Lobster Bar ❸,** the Square, for its homemade bread, potato salad, and seafood platters (€10-12) practically large enough for two. Maria's secret-recipe banoffee pie is sensational. (☎70031. Main menu served June-Aug. only noon-9pm.) The vaulted ceilings and baked delectables at ◪**The Olde Bakery Cafe ❶,** at the fork of Main St., a 5min. walk from the entrance to town, are delightful. Decadent chocolate-covered pancakes (€3.50) satiate the sweet-tooth. (☎70869. Open M 9am-3pm, Tu-F 9am-9pm, Sa-Su 10am-9pm; closes in winter M-W at 3pm.) **Jack Patrick's ❷** gets meat fresh from the eponymous butcher next door. (☎70319. Lunches €7. Dinner mains €7-10. Open M-Sa 11am-9pm; July-Aug. also Su 1-9pm.) The less-epicurean **Cronin's Hideaway ❷** serves cheap food, fast and fresh. (☎70386. Mains €4.50-10. Open M-Sa 5-10pm, Su 12:30-10pm; takeaway open daily 5:30pm-midnight.) When the fishing boats are in, most of the pros spend their land time touring from pub to pub; the lucky might hear a tall tale from the sea. For a pint, repast, or provisions, join the locals at **MacCarthy's.** (☎70014. Sandwiches under €3. Food served 11am-7pm. Trad and ballads Tu and weekends.) **O'Donoghue's** (☎70007), the Square, lures a sporty crowd with big-screen TV, sunny (or starry) outdoor tables, and live bands most Saturdays. Trad on summer Fridays keeps feet tapping at **Twomey's Ivy Bar** (☎70114).

◙ ⚠ SIGHTS AND ACTIVITIES. A 5min. walk up North Rd. from the church, a brand new museum offers visitors a break from outdoor adventures, overgrown ruins, and the ubiquitous smell of fish. With interactive exhibits on two floors, **Call of the Sea: The Beara Experience** covers the main topics of the peninsula's history and illuminates the lesser-known exploits of smugglers and slavers. (☎ 70835. Open May to mid-Sept. M-Sa 10am-5pm, Su 1-5pm; last admission 4:15pm. €4, students and seniors €3, family €9. Call ahead in low season.) Six miles west of town, the **Dzogchen Buddhist Centre** (☎ 73032; phones answered Tu-Th 2:30-5:30pm, otherwise leave a message) is in the same cliff-perched compound as the Garranes Farmhouse Hostel (see **Accommodations,** above). The view from the meditation room is inspiration itself. A very respected Tibetan Buddhist teaching site, the center offers a daily program with meditation and compassion exercises.

Two miles southwest of Castletownbere on the Allihies road, a discretionary donation buys admission to the two-piece ruins of **Dunboy Castle.** Cows graze the grounds of the **19th-century mansion,** with its crumbling, Gothic halls. A quarter-mile past the mansion, the 14th-century fortress **O'Sullivan Bere** is in far worse shape. The original owner accidentally blew up the fort in 1594, and English armies finished the job eight years later. The road that runs by the castle becomes a shady trail and passes a number of sheltered coves. A small detour off the Allihies Road, bearing right at the fork on the way out of town, leads to a cluster of ancient structures typical of West Cork and Kerry. The first is a **stone circle,** at Derrintaggart West, with a dozen of the original 15 stones still standing. At Teernahillane, about 1 mi. farther along, lies a raised **ring fort** 30 yd. in diameter and 2 yd. high, beyond is a small **wedge grave.**

Castletownbere's seat at the foot of hefty **Hungry Hill** (2245 ft.) makes it a fine base for daytrips up the mountain. (Inquire at the tourist office; see **Adrigole,** p. 267.) For those who prefer to wile away the time splashing about in the harbor, Frank Conroy at **Beara Watersports** arranges **kayak** excursions and offers **sailing lessons.** (☎ 70692 or 086 309 8654; www.seakayakingwestcork.com. Kayak daytrip including small lunch €57. 3hr. morning sail instruction €40. Groups cheaper.)

▞ DAYTRIPS FROM CASTLETOWNBERE

BERE ISLAND

*Two ferries chug to Bere Island. **Murphy's Ferry Service** (☎ 027 75014; www.murphysferry.com) leaves from the pontoon 3 mi. east of Castletownbere off the Glengarriff road but lands much closer to the island's "center" at Rerrin Village. (30min.; June-Aug. 8 per day, Sept.-May 4 per day; €6 return, children free; with car €20 return including passengers.) The other company, **Bere Island Ferry** (☎ 027 75009), leaves from the center of Castletownbere and lands inconveniently on the western end of the island, near the walking paths, ruins, and the island's other pub. (June 21-Sept. M-Sa 7 per day, Su 5 per day; €4 return, with car €20 return. Phone ahead during the off season.)*

The spectacular ferry ride to the tiny fishing community of Bere Island makes for a lovely daytrip. Visit the friendly folks and take in the beautiful scenery and quirky run-down cars on the island—old autos now get transported from the mainland to Bere. There are no *Garda* on the island, so be aware that the absence of law enforcement leads to much drunk driving. The island used to be a British naval base—forts and military remnants are still scattered across it—and the Irish Army now uses it for training. Across the harbor from Rerrin, the masts of a fishing ship jut from the sea; the ship burned in 1982 under mysterious circumstances after her owner ran out of money to pay the crew.

Inviting common spaces, clean rooms, and enthusiastic, accommodating owners make the newly-opened ▨**Lawrence Cove Lodge** ❶ the best choice for quality hostel accommodations on the island. Located almost directly off the Murphy

Ferry. (☎75988; www.lawrencecovelodge.com. Wheelchair accessible. Breakfast €6. Laundry €6.50. Apr.-Sept. €18; family room €50; group rates €15. Oct.-Mar. €15; family room €40.) **The Admiral's House Hostel/B&B ❷,** a 7min. (well-signposted 300 yd.) walk from Rerrin, has basic but comfortable rooms and pleasant sea views. (☎027 75213 or 75064. 6-bed dorms with bath €15; singles €30; doubles €40.) **Kitty Murphy's Cafe ❷,** by the Murphy ferry landing in Rerrin, serves affordable food all day. (☎027 75996. Sandwiches €2.50, mains €6.50-12. Open Tu-Sa 12:30-4:30pm and 6:30-9pm.) The attached **shop** furnishes supplies. (☎027 75004. Open M-Sa 9am-4:30pm and 7-9pm.) Gaze at maps or chat with locals next door at **Desmond O'Sullivan's** pub. **The Hotel** pub is 3 mi. down the main road, about a 15min. walk from the Bere Island Ferry pier. (☎027 75018. Sandwiches €2-3.)

DURSEY ISLAND

Just off the tip of the Beara, accessible by Ireland's only cable car. The cables begin 5 mi. out from Allihies, off the Castletownbere road. Car runs M-Sa 9-10:30am, 2:30-4:30pm, and 7-7:30pm; Su hours vary depending on which church has Mass that day. €4 return, children €1. For cable car info, call the Windy Point House. (☎73017; see below.)

A copy of the 91st Psalm adorns the wall of the cable car out to Dursey—travelers have been known to call upon "the Lord my defender" while dangling above the Atlantic. The 10min. aerial trip out is the most thrilling aspect of the island, whose enchanting tranquility and sweeping panoramas may inspire poetic musings but are unlikely to set hearts racing. Walks around the island expose a stark combination of sea, sky, land, and sheep. The English army laid waste to **Dursey Fort** in 1602, but only after raiding the unarmed garrison and callously tossing soldiers over the cliffs to their doom. A trip to the western tip provides a stunning view over sea cliffs and a chance to observe the island's much-vaunted flocks of migrant birds, who have the edge in numbers over Dursey's seven human residents. Lunch at **Windy Point House ❷,** near the base of the cable car on the mainland, makes an overnight stay tempting. Windy Point provides a full midday menu, luxurious accommodations, and views of Dursey Sound. (☎027 73017. Food served 11am-6:30pm. B&B €27.50, with bath and sea view.) **Camping** on the island is legal.

NORTHERN BEARA PENINSULA

Past Castletownbere, the Beara Peninsula stretches out into the Atlantic, the landscape becoming rocky and harsh; yet sojourners find fulfillment in the lonely beauty of the cliff-lined coast and distant wee villages. The isolation of this part of the southwest both attracts and frustrates hitchers who report finding rides mainly during mid-afternoon beach traffic in July and August. Despite some steep hills and strong winds, **biking** is a beautiful, if occasionally thrilling, way to tour the area, with the road hugging the coastline for most of its route. The solitary adventurer can take to the hills along the **Beara Way.** And while the barren beauty of the Beara cannot be fully experienced from behind the glass of a car window, motoring around the peninsula has its own benefits.

ALLIHIES (NA HAILICNI)   ☎027

Set between the Slieve Miskish mountains and the rolling sea, Allihies's abandoned cottages nearly outnumber its inhabitants. Fenced-off mine shafts, empty buildings, and a carved-up hillside testify to what was once a booming copper-mining town. Even **Ballydonegan Strand** is a by-product of the mines: the sand is ground-up mountain extract. Although some might call Allihies desolate, visitors in a tranquil state of mind will delight in gorgeous sunsets over glistening beaches. More pristine and secluded are the white sands of **Garinish Strand,** which lies a few miles down the road toward Dursey; follow the signs to the right at the fork. At the turnoff to Dursey, look for the largest **wedge tomb** on the Beara peninsula—it consists of two sidestones and a single capstone. The road to the Dursey cable car, off the Castletownbere road, passes **Lehanmore Ring Fort,** which remains an impressive remnant even if its crumbling walls can barely keep the cows out these days.

Pamphlets and maps are available at the **tourist information** hut on Main St., which is open sporadically, mostly afternoons in summer. **O'Sullivan's** fills shopping bags and picnic baskets. (☎73004. Open M-Sa 9am-8pm.) After a long day of hiking, sink into a sofa in the cavernous sitting room of the recently-renovated **Village Hostel (IHH) ❶,** next to the very red O'Neill's pub on Main St. (☎73107. Open May-Oct. Dorms €13; singles €18; doubles €36; family room €55.) For those seeking breakfast with their beds, **The Sea View House ❸** has spacious, modern rooms (☎73004; www.seaviewallihies.com. Singles €40; doubles €50.) **Anthony's ❶** is well equipped for **camping** all year, with hot showers and scenery to spare. Take the road all the way to the beach, turn right, and look for signs that say "campground;" it's about a 10min. walk from town. (☎73002. 1 person with tent €4.50. Showers €1.) Allihies's five pubs cater mostly to locals. Usually one— seemingly chosen by tacit consensus among the villagers—is lively each night. **O'Neill's ❷** hosts trad and ballads on Wednesdays and Sundays in the summer; it's also the best bet for a meal, even for the veggie-minded. (☎73008. Sandwiches €2.50-6, evening menu from €9. Food served noon-9pm, with more options after 6pm.) Music fills **Jimmy's** (☎73110) and **O'Sullivan's** (☎73165) on weekend nights most of the year. **The Lighthouse** (☎73000) and the **Oak Bar** (☎73110) also see their share of action; both have occasional trad.

EYERIES AND ARDGROOM   ☎027

Venture across the craggy coast, home to none but the hardiest of sheep, to reach the hamlet of Eyeries *(Na Haorai)*. In summer, Bus Eireann provides service between **Castletownbere** and **Kenmare,** stopping in Eyeries and Ardgroom twice daily in each direction. Three miles outside of Eyeries, on the main road to Allihies, is the **Urhan Hostel ❶,** housed in an old schoolhouse along with a **post office** and a **general store.** This clean, no-frills hostel has been booked solid in July-Aug. for the next three years by Belgian schoolchildren, but is still available the rest of the rainy year. (☎74005. Dorms €10; private rooms €12 per person. Camping €5.) The affiliated **Urhan Inn Pub** (☎74088), right next door, makes for ridiculously easy stumbles home. Within Eyeries village, culinary options are limited. **O'Sullivan's** vends general provisions on Main St. (☎74016. Open daily 8:30am-9pm.) Several pubs, including **O'Neill's** (☎74009), **O'Shea's** (☎74025), and **Causkey's** (☎74161), serve sandwiches and grub. Causkey's might throw in some music on the side.

For fuller menus and lively *craic*, head down the road to the smaller village of **Ardgroom** (a-GROOM; *Dha Dhrom*). Basic, pleasant rooms are available at **O'Brien's B&B ❷.** (☎74019. Open May-Sept.; Singles €25; doubles €40), right by **The Village Inn Bar and Restaurant ❷,** which serves hearty meals from seafood to pasta. (☎74067. Lunch €3-8; dinner from €13. Food served daily noon-4:30pm and Tu-Su 6-9pm.) **The Holly Bar,** one door down, keeps patrons happy with frequent summertime trad. Around the corner at the gas station, **Harrington's General Store** stocks provisions. (☎74003. Open daily 8:30am-10pm.)

Several mysterious ancient sights lie along the much longer—and much hillier— scenic coastal route between Eyeries and Ardgroom. At **Ballycrovane,** the tallest *ogham* stone in Ireland recalls the Isle's ancient past (see **Christians and Vikings,** p. 57). This 17-foot stone is on private property, but it is well signposted; the landowners collect €1.50 from each visitor. Farther on in Kilcatherine sits the **Hag of**

Beara, a bizarre rock formation that, according to legend, is the petrified remains of an ancient woman. It's hard to see, but some say that the outline of the hag's face is on one side. Nearby, off the Allihies road, skulk around the 18th-century ruins of **Kilcatherine Church;** an unusual stone carving of a cat's head adorns the entrance door. Also look for the **Mass Rock,** which was used as an altar by Catholics forced to hide their religion. (See **The Ascendancy,** p. 60.)

COUNTIES LIMERICK AND KERRY

The imagined Ireland of wee villages, enchanted green mountains, and jagged coastal cliffs finds its inspiration in the landscape of Co. Kerry. Arguably the most beautiful region on the Emerald Isle, it's indisputably the most touristed; each summer, tiny towns open their doors to floods of visitors. The Iveragh Peninsula, home of the picturesque and well-traveled Ring of Kerry, is anchored at its base by the mountainous Killarney National Park, and extends all the way out to tranquil

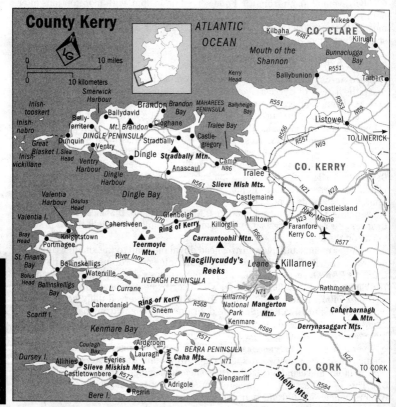

County Kerry

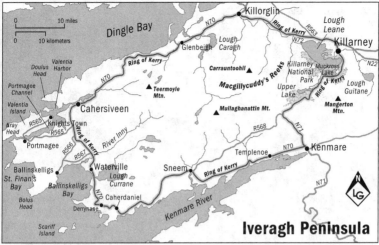

Iveragh Peninsula

Valentia Island at its tip and beyond to the mysterious monastic settlement on the Skellig Islands far off its western shore. The Dingle Peninsula's popularity is growing rapidly, but skinny roads help preserve the ancient sights and traditional feel of Slea Head, the West Dingle *gaeltacht*, and the haunting Blasket Islands. Farther North, in Co. Limerick, rich green pastures dotted with ancient castle ruins characterize the landscape. Now known for its dairy cattle and the gentle Galtee Mountains, the area once played host to a number of important monasteries. The historic poverty of Limerick City has been recently erased with the help of the EU and the raging Celtic Tiger. Convenient to Shannon Airport and pretty little Adare, the city at the foot of the Shannon now attracts visitors like pubbers at last call. In the summer, buses are readily available to most areas in these counties, but public transportation dries up in the off season.

IVERAGH PENINSULA

As the Southwest's most celebrated peninsula, the Iveragh's picturesque villages, fabled ancient forts, and rough romantic scenery often adorn the photographs and postcards handed around back home. The peninsula's majestic views rarely disappoint the droves of tourists that cruise through on private tour buses. The bus-bound tend to know the area only as "The Ring of Kerry," but travelers who take the time to explore the rugged landscape find much more than the views glimpsed through windows at 50mph. The Kerry Way walking trail, which sweeps its pilgrims up above the asphalt Ring and lays the best views at their feet, is one such detour; another is the Skellig Ring, which swings through Ballinskelligs and Portmagee along the westernmost tip of the peninsula.

KILLARNEY (CILL AIRNE)   ☎064

Only a short walk from some of Ireland's most extraordinary scenery, Killarney manages to celebrate its tourist-based economy without offending the leprechaun-loathing travelers out there. The town has all the essentials, and scads of not-so-essential trinkets to weigh down packs, but all that fades to dust in the face of the glorious national park only a few minutes away.

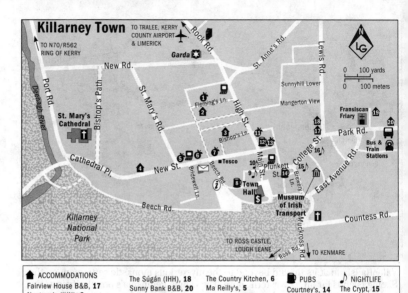

Killarney Town

ACCOMMODATIONS
Fairview House B&B, 17
Neptune's (IHH), 3
Orchard House B&B, 2
Paddy's Palace Hostel (IHH), 4
The Railway Hostel (IHH), 19

The Súgán (IHH), 18
Sunny Bank B&B, 20

FOOD
Busy B's Bistro, 7
Copperage, 13

The Country Kitchen, 6
Ma Reilly's, 5
Robertino's, 11
The Stonechat, 1

PUBS
Courtney's, 14
The Granary, 8
O'Connor's, 12

NIGHTLIFE
The Crypt, 15
The Grand, 9
McSorley's, 16
Mustang Sally's, 10

⌐ TRANSPORTATION

Airport: Kerry Airport, Farranfore (☎976 4644), halfway between Killarney and Tralee on the N22. 20min. from Killarney; cabs and buses go back and forth to town. **Ryanair** (☎01 609 7800; www.ryanair.com) flies to **London Stanstead** (2 per day); **Aer Arann Express** (☎1890 462 726; www.aerarannexpress.com) goes to **Dublin** (4 per day).

Trains: Killarney Station (☎31067, recorded info ☎1890 200 493, inquiries ☎1850 366 222). Off E. Avenue Rd. near the intersection with Park Rd. Open M-Sa 7am-12:30pm and 2-6pm, Su 30min. before departures. 4 trains per day to: **Cork** (2hr., €19.50); **Dublin** (3½hr., €51.50); **Limerick** (3hr.; €19.50).

Buses: Park Rd. (☎30011), connected to the outlet mall. Open mid-Sept. to June M-Sa 8:30am-5pm; July to mid-Sept. 8:30am-6pm. Buses to: **Belfast** (3-4 per day, Su 2 per day; €30); **Cork** (2hr., 10-14 per day, €13); **Derry**, via **Sligo** and **Donegal**, (7½hr., 2-3 per day, €24); **Dingle** (2hr.; M-Sa 7 per day, Su 4 per day; €12.50); **Dublin** (6hr., 5-6 per day, €20); **Farranfore/Kerry Airport** (10-17 per day, €3.10); **Galway**, via **Tarbert Ferry**, (6-7 per day, €18.50); **Kenmare** (40min., 2-3 per day, €6.35); **Kilkenny** (2-3 per day, €18.50); **Limerick** (2hr., 6-7 per day, €13.50); **Shannon Airport** (3hr., 6-7 per day, €15); **Skibbereen** (1 per day, €13.50); **Tralee** (10-17 per day, €6.50); **Waterford** (9-12 per day, €18.50). Buses leave June-Sept. daily on the **Ring of Kerry Circuit**, stopping in **Killorglin, Glenbeigh, Kells, Cahersiveen, Waterville, Caherdaniel, Sneem,** and **Moll's Gap.** (Book tickets at hostel; students €18.25 return with 1-night stop.) **Bus Éireann** runs a no-frills Ring of Kerry loop in the summer (2 per day; see **Ring of Kerry**, p. 282). The **Dingle/Slea Head** tour hits **Inch, Anascaul, Dingle, Ventry, Slea Head, Dunquin,** and **Ballyferriter** (June to mid-Sept. M-Sa 2 per day, €12.50).

Bike Rental: O'Sullivans, Bishop's Ln. (☎31282), next to Neptune's Hostel. Free panniers, locks, repair kits, and park maps. €12 per day, €70 per wk. Open daily 8:30am-6:30pm. Other locations on Beech Rd. across from the tourist office and on Brewery Ln. **Killarney Rent-a-Bike** (☎32578), with locations at the An Súgán hostel, Market Cross, Main St., and at the Flesk Campsite out on Muckross Rd. €12 per day, €60 per wk.

ORIENTATION AND PRACTICAL INFORMATION

Most of Killarney is packed into three crowded streets. **Main Street,** in the center of town, begins at the **Town Hall,** then becomes **High Street. New Street** and **Plunkett Street** both head in opposite directions from Main St.—New St. goes west toward Killorglin, and Plunkett becomes **College Street** then **Park Road** on its way east to the bus and train stations. **East Avenue Road** connects the train station back to town hall, meeting **Muckross Road,** which leads to the Muckross Estate and Kenmare.

Tourist Office: Beech Rd. (☎31633). Exceptionally helpful, deservedly popular. Open July-Aug. M-Sa 9am-8pm, Su 10am-1pm and 2:15-6pm; June and Sept. M-Sa 9am-6pm, Su 10am-1pm and 2:15-6pm; Oct.-May M-Sa 9:15am-1pm and 2:15-5:30pm.

Banks: AIB, Main St. (☎31922), next to the town hall. Open M-Tu and Th-F 10am-4pm, W 10am-5:30pm. **Permanent TSB,** 23-24 New St. (☎33761). Same hours as AIB. Both have **ATMs;** others are scattered throughout the town.

Laundry: J. Gleeson's Launderette (☎33877), on Brewery Ln. off College St. Self-service €6.90; full-service €8. Open M-Sa 9am-6pm.

Pharmacy: Sewell's Pharmacy, Main St. (☎31027), at New St. Open mid-July to mid-Aug. M-Sa 9am-9pm; mid-Aug. to mid-July M-Sa 9am-6:30pm.

Emergency: Dial ☎999; no coins required. **Police** (*Garda*): New Rd. (☎31222).

Hospital: District Hospital, St. Margaret's Rd. (☎31076). Follow High St. 1 mi. from the town center. Nearest emergency facilities are in Tralee.

Internet: Killarney library (☎32655), at the end of High St. towards New Rd., offers **free Internet.** Call ahead to reserve a time. ID required. Open M-Sa 10am-5pm and Tu, Th until 8pm. **Cafe Internet,** 18 New St. (☎30207), next to the Country Kitchen. €1 per 15min. Open June-Aug. daily 9:30am-11pm; Sept.-May M-Sa 9:30am-10pm, Su 10am-10pm. **Ri-Ra** (☎38279), on College St. towards the intersection with Main St. €0.08 per min.; pre-paid accounts available for 4hr. (€3.75 per hr.) and 10hr. (€3 per hr.). Open M-Sa 9am-11pm, Su noon-9pm. Hours vary in winter.

Post Office: New St. (☎31051). Open M and W-F 9am-5:30pm, Tu 9:30am-5:30pm, Sa 9am-1pm.

Outdoor Gear: Trailways Outdoor Centre, 9 Beech Rd., next to the tourist office (☎39929; www.trailwayskillarney.com). Outfits the fresh-air-minded with clothing, equipment, and **bikes** for rent. Open M-F 9am-8pm, Sa 9am-6pm, Su noon-6pm.

ACCOMMODATIONS AND CAMPING

With every other house a B&B, it's easy enough to find cushy digs in Killarney. Cheap digs, on the other hand, require more work—call ahead. Camping is not allowed in the National Park, but there are excellent campgrounds nearby.

IN TOWN

■ **Neptune's (IHH),** Bishop's Ln. (☎35255), first walkway off New St. on the right. Ideally located, immense, and immaculate, with superb showers and numerous amenities. Friendly, professional staff. A model hostel. **Tour booking:** Dingle €17.50, Ring of Kerry

€16.50, Gap of Dunloe €24. Wheelchair-accessible. Breakfast €2.50. Free luggage storage. Locker deposit €10. Laundry €7. Curfew 3am. 8-bed dorms €11-12.50; 6-bed €11.50-14; 3- to 4-bed €12-16.50. Doubles €31-38. 10% ISIC discount. ❶

The Railway Hostel (IHH), Park Rd. (☎35299). The first right as you head toward town from the bus station. Big, modern building with large beds and a pool table. Curfew 3am. Laundry €5. Dorms €13.50-16; doubles €36. ❶

Paddy's Palace Hostel (IHH), 31 New St. (☎35388), a block past the post office. Cramped bunks aren't as palatial as the name implies, but a relaxed atmosphere and proximity to the Park help offset the aesthetic offenses. Continental breakfast included. Free luggage storage. **Tour booking:** Dingle €19, Ring of Kerry €15. 4- to 6-bed dorms €14; doubles €35; family rooms €40. ❶

The Súgán (IHH), Lewis Rd. (☎33104), 2min. from the bus or train station. Make a left onto College St.; Lewis Rd. is the 1st right. Small, ship-like bunk rooms blur the distinction between intimacy and claustrophobia; exuberant staff and impromptu storytelling and music around the fire-lit common room provide a happy escape. **Bike rental** discount at Killarney Rent-a-Bike €10 per day. 4- to 8-bed dorms €12; singles €14. ❶

Orchard House B&B, Fleming's Ln. (☎31879), off High St. Down a quiet lane right in the center of town. An unbeatable bargain, with TV, tea, coffee, and hair dryer in each comfy, immaculate room. Consult with the proprietors about activities in the area. Individually-tailored breakfasts. Singles €25-30; doubles and triples €45-60. ❸

Sunny Bank B&B, Park Rd. (☎34109), across from the bus station. Cheerful and cushy; glassed-in breakfast room starts the day on a sunny note (should Ireland ever in fact be blessed by sun). €30-35. ❸

Fairview House B&B, College St. (☎34164), next to An Súgán. Hotel-equivalent luxury for B&B prices; be sure to mention *Let's Go,* as the proprietor discounts rooms for *LG* readers (discounted prices listed below). This plush establishment treats weary travellers like royalty, with fluffy beds, TVs, and an elegant dining and sitting room (wheelchair accessible; €35-45 per person). If that's not enough, rooms at the extra-luxurious annex, **The Copper Kettle** (€28-38), or **Rosslands** (€25-35), out near the Park, take pampering over the top. **Tours** can be arranged upon request. ❸

OUTSIDE TOWN

▨ **Peacock Farms Hostel (IHH),** Gortdromakiery (☎33557), 7 mi. from town. Take the Muckross Rd. out of town, turn left just before the Muckross post office, then go 2 mi. and follow the signposts up a steep hill; or call for a ride from the bus station. Brave rough and narrow roads for cheap, clean, cheerful digs with an unsurpassed view of Lough Guitane. Free daily buses to town at 9am and 6:30pm. Wheelchair-accessible. Organic breakfast €3.50. Open Apr.-Oct. Dorms €10-12; doubles €28. ❶

Killarney Hostel (An Óige/HI), Aghadoe (☎31240), 3 mi. west of town on the Killorglin road. Call for a ride from the bus or train station. Well-equipped hostel in a stone mansion. Kitchen, TV room, occasional barbecues. Tours: Ring of Kerry €16.50, Gap of Dunloe €25. Bike rental €10 per day; deposit €10. Internet €1 per 10min. Breakfast €4.50; lunch €5.50; dinner €12. Laundry €5. Reception 7am-midnight. Dorms €16, members €14; doubles €40, €34; quads €80, €60. Sept.-June €2 less. ❶

Black Valley Hostel (An Óige/HI), Beaufort (☎34712). 14 mi. from town on the Gap of Dunloe Rd., a few miles from Lord Brandon's Cottage. Conveniently located on the Kerry Way. Street signs are scarce, so call for directions in advance. Buses stop 6 mi. away in Beaufort Bridge. This spare but spotless hostel was one of the last buildings in Ireland to receive electricity. Friendly owners have a small shop that sells groceries. Sheets €1.30. Midnight curfew. Peak-season dorms with membership €12, without €14. off season €2 cheaper for members. ❶

Kiltrasna Farmhouse, Loughguittane Rd. (☎31643). Off Muckross Road. 2nd road on the left after Gleneagle Hotel, about 1.5 mi. uphill from the main road. Six ensuite bedrooms, including 1 wheelchair-accessible room, tastefully decorated with colorful bedspreads. Lounge in woodbacked, cushioned chairs in the elegant dining room, gazing at hills and sheep. In the visitors book, previous guests laud the peace and tranquility. Open Mar. to mid-Oct. €26; inquire about group rates. ❸

Fleming's White Bridge Caravan and Camping Park, on the Ballycasheen road (☎064 31590). A 2nd site is in Glenbeigh, near the beach. An award-winning site many times over, the campsite offers laundry, TV lounge, game room, a shop for essentials, and modern shower facilities. The enticing grassy stretches inspire impromptu football matches. €7 per person with tent; 2-person tent with car €17. ❶

▚ FOOD

Food in Killarney is affordable at lunchtime, but prices skyrocket when the sun sets. New St. is the best place to look for quality, cheap food around the clock. Also, a number of fast-food joints and takeaways stay open until 3-4am to satisfy the post-Guinness munchies. **Tesco,** in an arcade off New St., has groceries. (☎32866. Open M-W 8:30am-8pm, Th-F 8:30am-9pm, Sa 8:30am-7pm, Su 10am-6pm.) For organic foods, try **Horan's,** in Innisfallen Centre near the tourist office carpark. (☎35399. Open M-W and Sa 9am-6:30pm, Th 9am-7pm, F 9am-8pm.)

▨ **The Stonechat,** Fleming's Ln. (☎34295). Hanging plants, paintings, and swirls of incense adorn the inside of this tranquil, intimate cottage. The delicious cuisine leans toward the vegetarian, but chicken and fish dishes are also available. One of Killarney's best. Lunch €7-9, dinner €11-14. Open M-Sa 11am-5pm and 6-10pm. ❸

The Country Kitchen, 17 New St. (☎33778). Delicious odors waft onto the street. Glorious baked goods, sandwiches, and hot evening meals. Worth a visit just for dessert. Lunch (€5.10-6.35) served until 5pm; dinner €7.60-11.50. Open July-Aug. M-F 8am-8pm, Sa 9am-6pm; Sept.-June M-Sa 9am-5:30pm. ❷

Ma Reilly's, 20 New St. (☎39220). Irish stew and other hot treats in a popular little joint, filled with black and white photos of Killarney past. Open daily 9am-9:30pm. ❷

Robertino's, High St. (☎34966). Great date spot complete with Italian serenades and candlelight. Frescoes and statues add extra Roman flavor to savory pastas (€11.80-12.90), pizzas (€14.70-19.75), and meat dishes (€17-23). Open daily 4-10:30pm. ❹

The Copperage, Old Market Ln. (☎37716). With funky lighting and cool teal walls, the dining room's modern, eccentric decor can distract diners from their meals, but try to concentrate—the food deserves attention. Lunch €8-11, dinner €18-20. Open 12:30-2:45pm and 6-10pm. ❹

Busy B's Bistro, upstairs next to Cafe Internet on New St. (☎31972). Homey and packed with locals, Busy B's serves filling, affordable food all day—a rare occurrence in Killarney. Sandwiches €3.15-5.50, hot meals €6-8. Open daily 11am-9:30pm. ❷

▞ ▞ PUBS AND CLUBS

Trad is a staple in Killarney's pubs on summer nights, but herds of lumbering tourists seeking the next great jig make for a crowded, noisy drinking experience. Several nightclubs simmer from 10:30pm until 3am; most charge €6-8 cover but often offer discounts before 11pm.

▨ **The Grand,** High St. (☎31159). A mixed crowd starts the night early (open at 7pm) but stick around late for the fantastic live music. Extremely popular club for young tourists. Follow its nightly progression from trad (9-11pm) to Irish rock (11pm-1am) to a disco in the back (midnight-3am). Arrive before 11pm and dodge the €5-8 cover.

■ **O'Connor's Traditional Pub,** 7 High St. (☎31115). Patrons both foreign and domestic mingle in an upbeat, comfortable atmosphere. Traditional Irish food available from 12:30-5pm (try the Irish stew or the chowder). M-Tu and Th-F trad 9-11:30pm.

Courtney's Bar, Plunkett St. (☎32689). Join in with locals for Th and Su night open sessions, or just unwind in good company with hearty stout.

The Granary, across from the tourist office on Beech Rd. (☎20075; www.granary-pub.com). Quality live music satisfies tourist crowds nightly in this stylish, cavernous pub. Cover €5 after midnight.

Buckley's Bar, College St. (☎31037). Classy and traditional, with lots of dark wood and leather. Older crowd enjoys pints and conversation. Trad Th-Su in the summer.

The Crypt, College St. (☎31038), next to the Killarney Towers Hotel. Looks Gothic but attracts neatly-dressed trendy types. Mixed dance music. Cover €5-9.

McSorley's, College St. (☎39770). Locals and tourists get intimate on 2 dance floors to chart and hip hop hits. Pool table and comfy seats when things slow down. M pints €2.50. Nightly live band in summer. Su Ladies Night. DJs M and Th-Su. Cover €10.

Mustang Sally's, Main St. (☎35790). Blues Brothers blast, several TVs broadcast the match, and a largely tourist crowd boogies on the 2 dance floors of this massive pub. Huge menu variety. (Lunch 12:30-3pm; dinner 5-9pm. Mains €8.50-16.50. 4-course early-bird meal €12.95.) Cover €6; free on F. DJ spins the hits Th-Su 9pm-12:30am.

👁 🏔 SIGHTS AND ACTIVITIES

Congested with bureaux de change, souvenir shops, and disoriented foreigners, Killarney plays second fiddle to the glorious National Park just beyond the city limits. Still, the town has a charm of its own. The soaring, neo-Gothic **St. Mary's Cathedral** on New St. has three huge altars and can seat 1400 within its rough limestone walls, providing peaceful refuge from the tourist hoards and tempting pubs. (Always open. Free.) At the **Museum of Irish Transport,** located down a lane between College St. and East Avenue Rd., modern travelers contemplate the evolving art of getting from here to there. Turn-of-the-century cars and a horse-drawn fire engine from 1842 impress the nostalgic, but weary cyclists count their blessings at the sight of the 1820s hobby horse, an early pedal-less bicycle that could only be propelled a la Fred Flintstone. (☎34677. Open June-Aug. daily 10am-6pm; last admission 5:30pm. Open Apr.-May and Sept.-Oct. daily 11am-5pm; last admission 4:30pm. €5, students and seniors €3.50.) The Killarney area has excellent **salmon and trout fishing,** especially in August and September. Unrestricted trout-hunting is allowed in nearly all of Killarney's lakes, but fishing in rivers and Barfinnihy Lake requires a permit (€3.80 per day). Contact **O'Neill's Fishing Shop,** Plunkett St. (☎31970), for details. **Trailways,** College St. (☎39929), rents rods for €8 per day.

Trailways is also the one-stop shop for tours of the National Park. They'll book **boat and riding tours** free of charge and advise on how best to see the National Park. **O'Donoghue's** (☎35593) offers a **pony and cart trip** through the mountains to a picnic site, followed by a **boat tour** through the lake systems. The **Lily of Killarney Watercoach** (☎31068) has five daily sailings leaving from Ross Castle (€8; special group rates available). Tours cover the Park, accompanied by history- and folklore-infused commentary in the comfort of a heated vessel. Those unsure of their sea legs can try **Quad Safari** (☎066 947 4465). Tours are 3½-6hr. If 4-legged bikes don't seem appealing, 4-legged steeds are available from the **Killarney Riding Stables** (☎31686; €20-50 per person) and **Rocklands** (☎32592; €16.50 per hr.).

It's a stroke of luck to swing through town during one of Killarney's festivals; locals take them quite seriously and always make a great showing. In mid-May and mid-July, horses gallop in the **Killarney Races** at the race course on Ross Rd. (Tick-

SOUTHWEST IRELAND

ets available at gate, €3.80-6.35.) The **Killarney Regatta,** the oldest in Ireland, draws rowers and spectators to Lough Leane the first Sunday in July. From the last week in June through the first week in August, the town goes all out for **Killarney Summerfest,** when musicians, artists, and entertainers fill the streets and big-name bands draw crowds to evening concerts (☎064 71560; www.killarneysummerfest.com).

KILLARNEY NATIONAL PARK

During the Ice Age, glaciers sliced up the Killarney region, scooping out a series of lakes and glens and scattering silk-smooth rocks and precarious boulders across the terrain. As a result, Killarney National Park now makes for preternaturally dazzling hiking, biking, and climbing. The park, stretched across 37 sq. mi. of prime Kerry real estate, between Killarney to the northeast and Kenmare to the southwest, incorporates a string of forested mountains and the famous **Lakes of Killarney:** huge **Lough Leane (Lower Lake),** medium-sized **Muckross (Middle) Lake,** and the small **Upper Lake,** 2 mi. southwest of the other two and connected by a channel. An indigenous but elusive herd of 850 red deer inhabits the glens surrounding the lakes.

The Kenmare road curves along the southeastern shores of the lakes, passing the park sights but missing some of the woodland paths. With many more tourists than locals driving these sections, hitching can be difficult as well as risky. **Bikes**

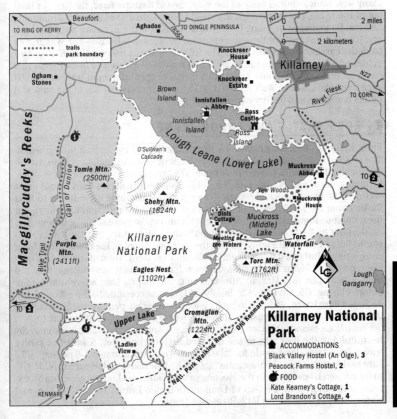

Killarney National Park map. Legend:
- •••••• trails
- – – – – park boundary

Labeled features: TO RING OF KERRY, Beaufort, Aghadoe, TO DINGLE PENINSULA, N22, Knockreer House, Killarney, Ogham Stones, Brown Island, Innisfallen Abbey, Knockreer Estate, River Flesk, TO CORK, Innisfallen Island, Ross Castle, Ross Island, Macgillycuddy's Reeks, O'Sullivan's Cascade, Lough Leane (Lower Lake), Muckross Abbey, TO 2, Tomie Mtn. (2500ft), Gap of Dunloe, Shehy Mtn. (1824ft), Yew Woods, Muckross House, Dinis Cottage, Muckross (Middle) Lake, Bike Trail, Purple Mtn. (2411ft), Killarney National Park, Meeting of the Waters, Torc Waterfall, Eagles Nest (1102ft), Torc Mtn. (1762ft), Lough Garagarry, TO 3, Upper Lake, Cromaglan Mtn. (1224ft), Old Kenmare Rd., Natl. Park Walking Route, Ladies View, N71, TO KENMARE.

Killarney National Park

▲ ACCOMMODATIONS
Black Valley Hostel (An Óige), **3**
Peacock Farms Hostel, **2**

🍴 FOOD
Kate Kearney's Cottage, **1**
Lord Brandon's Cottage, **4**

are a great means of exploring (see **Practical Information,** p. 275). Walkers can't cover as much ground, but they have more freedom to climb the off-road trails. Unfortunately for both bikers and hikers, many visitors choose to admire the woods from horse-drawn carriages (€20-30). Unlike bikers and hikers, horses leave behind *cac capall* (Irish for the substance whose smell is a constant companion). The park's size demands a map; as luck would have it, maps are available at the Killarney tourist office.

The park's most popular destinations are **Ross Castle** and **Lough Leane, Muckross House** on **Middle Lake,** and the **Gap of Dunloe,** just west of the park area and bordered on the southwest by **Macgillycuddy's Reeks,** Ireland's highest mountain range. Visits to most of these sights can be managed in several hours or stretched over a full day, depending on your mode of transport. Hikers and bikers should take the necessary precautions, and maybe a few unnecessary ones just for kicks (see **Camping,** p. 24). As always, watch out for both domestic and foreign crazy drivers.

For those on foot, the **Gap of Dunloe** (see p. 281) demands more than a casual day excursion. However, biking from Killarney—stopping to explore Muckross and Torc—is an enjoyable way to see a good chunk of the park in one day. If 14 mi. of cycling seems exhausting, there are several short, well-marked and well-paved walking trails closer to Killarney. The park is also a perfect starting point for those rugged few who plan to walk the 129 mi. **Kerry Way** (see p. 282). For the less rugged many who want a shorter taste of the Way, the **Old Kenmare Road,** the first (or last) leg of the route, passes through the spectacular Torc and Mangerton Mountains and can be managed in a day. From Killarney, follow the Kenmare road for 4 mi. and turn left just beyond the main entrance to Muckross House—the Way leaves from the carpark on this side road. The Killarney tourist office sells a *Kerry Way* guide, which has topographic maps. The *Ordnance Survey* (#78 and 83 in this case) includes minor roads, trails, and archaeological points of interest (€6.60 each). Or take a **Guided Walk** (☎ 064 33471) for €7 that covers 2hr. of the park and points out sights and history of the region.

⚑ ROSS CASTLE AND LOUGH LEANE

From Killarney, **Knockreer Estate** is a short walk down New St. past the cathedral. The original mansion housed the Catholic Earls of Kenmare and, later, the Grosvenor family of *National Geographic* fame. The current building, built in the 1950s, is unimpressive and not open to the public, but nearby **nature trails** afford great views of the mountains and roaming deer. Visitors can drive or walk out to **Ross Castle** (from the Muckross road turn right on Ross Rd. 2 mi. from Killarney), but the numerous footpaths from Knockreer (15min.) make more scenic journeys. The castle, built by the O'Donaghue chieftains in the 14th century, was the last in Munster to fall to Cromwell's army. During the past two decades, the building has been completely refurbished in 15th-century fashion. (☎35851. Guided tour only. Tours begin on the half-hour and last 40min. Open June-Aug. daily 9am-6:30pm; May and Sept. 10am-6pm; mid-Mar. to Apr. and Oct. 10am-5pm. Last admission 45min. before closing. €5, students €2, family €11.) Paths continue to the arboreal and secluded **Ross Island,** which is actually a lobster-claw shaped peninsula stretching into Lough Leane. Its greenish pools testify to the area's copper mining past.

From Ross island, the view of Lough Leane and its mountains is admittedly beautiful, but the best way to see the area is from the water. A **waterbus service** leaves from behind the castle for lake cruises. (☎31068. Summer 5-6 per day. €7.) Hire **rowboats** (☎32252) by the castle (€4 per hr.), or take a **motorboat trip** (☎34351) to Innisfallen Island (€4), to the Meeting of the Waters via Lough Leane and Muckross Lake (€7), or to the Gap of Dunloe via Lough Leane, Muckross Lake, and Upper Lake. (€9.50, return €12. Bikes ride free.)

On Innisfallen Island the remains of **Innisfallen Abbey** remain stoic and even graceful, despite the wear of time. The Abbey was founded around AD 600 by St. Finian the Leper; then in the Middle Ages it became a university and daringly opened its doors to students. The *Annals of Innisfallen*, now housed at Oxford, were written here by 39 monastic scribes, circa 1326; they recount the Abbey's take on Irish and world history in both Irish and Latin. At the Abbey's center is a yew tree; yew and oak groves were sacred to the Druids, and resolutely non-Druidic abbeys were often built among and around them. The separate **Augustinian Abbey** is so ruined that it might be a challenge to identify, but it's still worth a visit.

◪ MUCKROSS AND THE MEETING OF THE WATERS

The crumblings of **Muckross Abbey,** built in 1448, lie 3 mi. south of Killarney on the Kenmare road. The abbey's grounds contain a diligently maintained modern graveyard, and the remains of the abbey itself are haunting and serene. (Always open. Free.) From the abbey, signs point to **Muckross House,** a massive Victorian manor whose garden blooms brilliantly in early summer. The house, completed in 1843, oozes staid aristocracy and commands a regal view of the lakes and mountains. Its elaborate furnishings and decorations include justifiably angry-looking deer mounted on the walls. Upon first visiting Muckross House, the philosopher George Berkeley proclaimed: "Another Louis XIV may make another Versailles, but only the hand of the Deity can make another Muckross." Outside the house lie the **Muckross Traditional Farms,** a living history museum designed to depict rural life in early 20th-century Kerry. Help costumed demonstrators whip up traditional cuisine and crafts, or just lounge on the lawns. Surprisingly affordable sustenance (sandwiches €2.95, salads €4.25) can be had at the newly-opened **Garden Restaurant ❶,** for those willing to brave the swarm of hungry tourists. (☎31440; www.muckross-house.ie. House open daily July-Aug. 9am-7pm; Sept.-Oct. and mid-Mar. to June 9am-6pm; Nov. to mid-Mar. 9am-5:30pm. Farms open June-Oct. 10am-7pm; Mar.-May 10am-6pm. House or farms each €5.50, students €2.25, family €13.75. Joint ticket €8.25/€3.75/€21. Last admission 1hr. before closing.)

From Muckross House, a path leads along the water to the 60 ft. drop of **Torc Waterfall.** The waterfall is also the starting point for several short trails along **Torc Mountain.** Walking among the moss-jacketed trees affords some of the park's best views. It's a 2 mi. stroll in the opposite direction to the **Meeting of the Waters**—walk straight down the front lawn of Muckross House and follow the signs. The paved path is nice, but the dirt trail through the **Yew Woods** is more secluded and not accessible to bikes. The Meeting of the Waters is a quiet spot where channels from the Upper Lough introduce themselves into the Middle, which then offers its watery handshake to the Lower. The weary, however, may be more happy to meet sandwiches (€3.20) and cold drinks at **Dinis Cottage.** (☎31954. Open mid-May to Sept. daily 10:30am-6pm.) Park explorers should note that there's no direct route from the Muckross sights to Ross Castle; those wishing to conquer both in one day must return to Killarney, making for a total trip of 10 mi.

◪ GAP OF DUNLOE

A visit to the Gap of Dunloe is a many-splendored thing—pilgrims can expect both misty mountain vistas and a generous dose of physical exhertion. **Organized treks** to the Gap can be booked from area hostels or the Killarney tourist office. (☎31633; see **Practical Information,** p. 275. €25.) Such treks, which combine a guided walking tour with a boat trip, shuttle visitors to the foot of the Gap, eliminating the 7 mi. hike from town. Foresighted travelers pack their lunches, though after walking over the Gap and down to **Lord Brandon's Cottage ❶,** a warm meal or a cold pint may be hard to resist. (☎34730. Sandwiches €2.50 and soups €2.20. Open May-Oct. daily 10am-4pm.) From there, trekkers meet a boat that takes them across the lake to Ross Castle. (Open June-Sept. daily 9am-6pm.) A bus returns them, at long last, to Killarney. Attempting the Gap on foot using this route, however, is a trek up the long side of the mountain. It is far easier, and potentially less expensive, to attack by bike from the opposite direction. Bring your wheels on the scenic **motorboat** trip from Ross Castle to the head of the Dunloe Gap. (1½hr. €12 per person, €12 for the bike. Book ahead at the Killarney tourist office or hostels.) From Lord Brandon's Cottage, turn left over the stone bridge and continue for 2 mi. to the hostel and church. Hang a right onto a hairpin-turn-laden road that winds up to the top of the Gap (1½ mi.). What follows is a well-deserved 7 mi. downhill coast through the park's most magical scenery.

At the foot of the Gap is **Kate Kearney's Cottage** ❷. Kate was an independent mountain-dwelling woman famous for brewing and serving a near-poisonous *poitín* (see **Love Poitín #9**, p. 418). Her former home is now a pub and restaurant that sucks in droves of tourists. (☎44146. Sandwiches €2.30-7; hot dishes €6.35-7.60. Food served 12:30-9pm. Summertime trad W and F-Sa.) To return home to Killarney, "click your heels," bear right after Kate's, turn left on the road to Fossa, and turn right on the Killorglin Rd. The 8 mi. ride back to Killarney passes the entirely ruined **Dunloe Castle,** an Anglo-Norman stronghold demolished by Cromwell's army, and a set of *ogham* stones, circa AD 300.

RING OF KERRY AND THE KERRY WAY

The term **"Ring of Kerry"** is generally used to describe the entire Iveragh Peninsula, but more precisely, it refers to a particular set of roads: N71 from Kenmare to Killarney, R562 from Killarney to Killorglin, and the long loop of N70 west and back to Kenmare. If the captivity of the prepackaged private bus tours that run out of Killarney isn't appealing, **Bus Éireann** offers a regular summer circuit through the major towns on the Ring (☎064 30011; mid-June to Aug., 2 per day; entire ring in 1 day €18.50). Buses travel around the Ring counterclockwise, from Killarney to Killorglin, along Dingle Bay, east by the Kenmare River, and north from Sneem back to Killarney. Another bus runs year-round in the mornings, traveling clockwise from Waterville back to Killarney (1 per day). **Bikers** may find themselves jammed between buses and cliffs on the narrow, bumpy roads, though traffic can often be avoided by doing the Ring clockwise. Additionally, cycling clockwise faces the eye-candy, rather than leaving it behind. Signposts lead to a new bike route that avoids most main roads and has better views. Drivers must choose between lurching behind large tour buses and meeting them face-to-face on narrow roads.

Those wishing to avoid the tour bus superhighway that is the Ring of Kerry road need not write off the Iveragh Peninsula entirely; a step from the N70, solitude and superior scenery reward walkers along **The Kerry Way.** This well-planned route traverses a wide variety of terrain, from rugged inland expanses to soaring coastal cliffs. Described as an "inner" ring of Kerry, the Way brings walkers above the road, to higher ground and better views. Its 135 mi. route follows a smorgasbord of paths—from pastures to old "butter roads" to ancient thoroughfares between early Christian settlements—and crosses the main road often enough to make day-trips convenient from almost anywhere on the Ring. Look for the wooden posts marked with a yellow walking man. Those who like their landscapes stark and a little rough around the edges enjoy the dramatic stretch from Kenmare through Killarney and northwest to Glenbeigh. An especially inspiring stretch of the Way runs between Waterville and Caherdaniel, filled with views known to elicit a tear or two from even the gruffest pint-puller.

KILLORGLIN (CILL ORGLAN) ☎ 066

Killorglin lounges along the banks of the River Larne, 13 mi. west of Killarney in the shadow of Iveragh's mountainous spine. Tourists tend to pass through on their way west to the showier scenery, but what the town lacks in sights it more than makes up for with its annual festival dedicated to he-goats. In mid-August, the ancient **Puck Fair** transforms the town, as thousands of visitors flock in for three riotous days culminating in the coronation of a large mountain goat as King Puck. Pubs stay open until 3am, then close for an hour so publicans can rest their arms. Be aware that the town's hostel and B&Bs fill as early as a year in advance of the revelry; aspiring Pucksters should call ahead. If visiting Killorglin outside the three-day reign of King Puck, catch up on the spectacle at **The Basement Museum,** past the church down Mill Rd. Though the exhibits primarily focus on the festival, there is also a collection of circus posters. (☎976 1353. €2. Open noon-9pm, or thereabouts.) Five miles from town off the Killarney Rd., **Ballymalis Castle** rests on its 16th-century laurel, dozing on the banks of the Laune in view of Macgillycuddy's Reeks. **Cromane Beach** lies 4 mi. west of Killorglin; follow N70 (toward Glenbeigh) and branch to the right at the signs. More swimmer friendly, less rocky **Rossbeigh Beach** lies 8mi. west of Killorglin. **Cappanalea Outdoor Education Centre,** 7 mi. to the southwest off the Ring of Kerry road, offers canoeing, rock-climbing, windsurfing, sailing, hill-walking, and fishing. (☎976 9244; www.oec.ie. Open daily 10am-5pm. Day course with any 2 activities €40, teenagers €25; any 1 activity €20/€12. Individual booking July-Aug. only; year-round group booking for a min. of 6.)

The Ring of Kerry **bus** from Killarney (June-Sept. 2 per day, €4.40) stops in Killorglin on Mill Rd., down from the tourist office, and runs to Cahersiveen (50min., €7.50), Waterville (1¼hr., €7.50), and Sneem (3hr., €9.50). An eastbound Cahersiveen bus goes to Killarney (July-Aug. M-Sa 4-6 per day; Sept.-June M-Sa 2-4 per day). Killorglin's **Main Street** runs from the river and widens into **the Square.** To the right at the top of the Square, **Upper Bridge Street** climbs to the tourist office and intersects **Iveragh Road.** For a **taxi,** call **Killorglin Cabs** (☎087 274 0269). The **tourist office's** friendly staff distributes info. (☎976 1451. Open July-Aug. M-Sa 9am-1pm, 2-7pm; Sept.-June 9am-6pm.) **AIB,** on Main St., has an **ATM.** (☎976 1134. Open M-F 10am-4pm, Tu until 5pm.) **Laune Dry Cleaners and Launderette,** Upper Bridge St., cleans up. (€7 per load. Open M-Sa 9am-6pm; Oct.-June closes W at 1pm.) **Mulvihill Pharmacy** is halfway up Main St. (☎976 1115. Open M-Tu and Th-Sa 9am-6:30pm, W 9am-6pm. After hours call ☎976 1387.) Get 50min. of fast, **free Internet** at the **library,** set back from Iveragh Rd. near the tourist office. (☎976 1272. Open Tu-Sa 10am-1:30pm, 2:30-5pm.) The **post office** is a bit farther down on Iveragh Rd. (☎976 1101. Open M-Tu and Th-F 9am-1pm, 2-5:30pm; W 9am-1pm, 2-5pm; Sa 10am-1pm.)

Bright, bountiful **Laune Valley Farm Hostel (IHH) ❶,** 1¼ mi. from town off the Tralee Rd., beds guests alongside its cows, chickens, dogs, and ducks. Farm-fresh milk and eggs for sale make whipping up scrambled eggs irresistable. (☎976 1488. Wheelchair-accessible. Dorms €12-14; doubles €35-50. **Camping** €5 per person.) **Orglan House B&B ❸,** a 5min. walk from town on the Killarney Rd., has grand views from immaculate rooms and its individualized breakfasts relieve brown bread delirium—even the pancake (scarce in Ireland) is available. (☎976 1540. Oct.-June singles €37; doubles €43. July-Sept. €42.50/€60.) **Laune Bridge House B&B ❸** is a few doors closer to town than Orglan. (☎976 1161. Singles €30; doubles €55.) Tent up at **West's Caravan and Camping Park ❶,** 1 mi. east of town on the Killarney road in the shadow of **Carrantoohill,** Ireland's tallest peak. Fishing, table tennis, and a tennis court are available. (☎976 1240. Open Easter to mid-Oct. Laundry €3. Adult and tent €5; car, tent, and 2 adults €15. 2 night caravan rental €75. Showers €2.)

Eurospar serves deli sandwiches in the Square. (☎976 1117. Open M-Sa 9am-9pm.) Nearby, an organic cornucopia spills from **Broadbery's Irish Food Hall ❷,** a gourmet deli/restaurant. Enjoy delicious platters of local farm cheese, smoked salmon, homemade liver and pork pâté, and bread baked on the spot. (☎976 2888. Sandwiches €5; meals €7-9. Open M-Tu and Th-F 9am-10pm; W and Sa 9am-5pm.) **Bunker's ❷**, across from the tourist office, covers all bases—it's a restaurant and coffeeshop with a pub next door and takeaway across the street. (☎976 1381. Mains €8-13. Open daily 9:30am-10:30pm; takeaway until 9:30pm.) On Mill Rd., across from the carpark, **Natterjacks ❷** (☎979 0917) offers tasty meals and tempting pastries at reasonable prices. (Sandwiches €2.50-3.65, hot lunches €5.50-6.95. Open M-Sa 9am-5:30pm.) **Murray's Restaurant ❸**, the Square (☎979 0812), is a classier and more expensive alternative to typical Killorglin fare, and has vegetarian options. (Lunch €11-14, dinner €17-20. Open M-Sa 9am-3pm and 6-10pm, Su 12:30-4pm and 6-10pm.) Locals sate their Guinness needs at **Old Forge**, a lively stone pub on Main St. (☎976 1231. Trad Th nights in summer, disco F-Su.) An older, more subdued crowd watches football at **Laune Bar**, Lower Main St., on the water. The Laune Rangers football club began here in 1888. (☎976 1158. Trad Th.) DJs, cocktails, and Friday karaoke lure youngsters to **The Shamrock**, Main St. (☎976 2277).

CAHERSIVEEN (CATHAIR SAIDBHIN) ☎066

Best known in Ireland as the birthplace of patriot Daniel O'Connell (see **Rebellion**, p. 61), Cahersiveen (CAH-her-sah-veen) serves as a useful base for exploring nearby archaeological sites and for short trips to Valentia Island and the Skelligs. With a cozy hostel, excellent restaurant, Internet cafe, and plenty of local pub charm, this hamlet leads many to pause on their way around the Ring.

🚆🚌 TRANSPORTATION AND PRACTICAL INFORMATION. The Ring of Kerry **bus** stops in front of Banks Store on Main St. (mid-June to Aug., 2 per day) and continues on to Killarney (2½hr., €11.50) via Waterville (25min., €4), Caherdaniel (1hr., €4.25), and Sneem (1½hr., €8). Another bus heads directly east to Killarney (M-Sa 1 per day, in the morning, all year). The town revolves around one street, the N70 **Ring of Kerry Road**, which takes on the names **Church**, **Main**, **West Main**, and **New Street** as it passes through. **Casey's**, on Main St., **rents bikes**. (☎947 2474. €10 per day, €50 per week; helmet and lock included. Open July-Aug. M-Sa 9am-6pm, Su 10:30am-12:30pm; Sept.-June M-Sa 9am-6pm and by appointment.) Cahersiveen's **tourist office** is across from the bus stop, next to the post office. (☎947 2589. Open June to mid-Sept. M-F 9:15am-1:15pm and 2:15-5:15pm.) A map and walking guide to the **Heritage Trail** is sold for €1.50 at the Barracks Heritage Centre (see **Sights**, p. 285). Main St. is home to an **AIB** with an **ATM**. (☎947 2022. Open M 9am-5pm, Tu and Th-F 9am-4pm, W 10:30am-4pm.) **Internet** is **free** at the **library** on Main St. Anyone over 18 is allowed two 50min. sessions per week. (☎947 2287. Open Tu-Sa 10:30am-1:30pm and 2:30-5pm.) For those under 18 with a parent present, and even for those over 18, an extensive **video game collection** and high speed **Internet** are available at the island-themed **Java Cybercafe**, 11 Church St. (☎947 2116. €3 per 20min., €7 per hr. Open M-Sa 11am-8pm, Su 2-6pm.) The **post office** is on Main St. (☎947 2010. Open M-F 9:30am-1pm and 2-5:30pm, Sa 9:30am-1pm.)

🏠🍴🍺 ACCOMMODATIONS, FOOD, AND PUBS. Sive Hostel (IHH) ❶, 15 East End, Main St., has a welcoming, well-informed staff, comfortable beds, and a third-floor balcony. For those lacking the private transport necessary to reach Portmagee, where most of the ferries to the **Skellig Islands** set sail, the hostel also arranges boat trips to the Skelligs. (☎947 2717. Laundry €6. Dorms €13; doubles €31-35. Camping €7 per person.) Next to the post office, **O'Shea's B&B ❸** has comfortable rooms, some with impressive castle and mountain views. (☎947 2402. Vegetarian breakfast option. Singles €35; doubles €50.) Campers revel in **Mannix Point Caravan and Camping Park ❶**, at the west end of town. The site adjoins a nature reserve and faces the romantic ruins of Ballycarbery Castle across the water. The common area's turf fire and antique piano complete the mood. (☎947 2806. Open mid-Mar. to Oct. Laundry wash and dry €3 each. €6.50 per person. Showers €1.)

Centra sells colossal scones and other necessities. (☎947 2583. Open M-F 8am-10pm, Sa-Su 8am-9:30pm.) The freshest seafood available is at **QC's Chargrill Bar & Restaurant ❹**, Main St. The colorful, modern restaurant is a bit pricey, but the fish and steaks grilled on its unique Basque barbecue are worth the price. The delicious fresh crab claws, courtesy of the chef's father, owner of the local fish shop, are served with garlic and chilis. (☎947 2244. Mains €15-22. Food served 12:30-3pm and 6-9:30pm.) **Relish Cafe and Sandwich Bar ❷**, Main St., near the web cafe, has everything the hungry could want—delicious mains (€5-7) and even tastier desserts. (☎947 3499. Open M-F 9am-6pm, Sa 9am-4pm.) For classic dishes with international flair, try the **Red Rose ❸**, Church St. (☎947 2293. Day menu €6-9, served M and W-Su 12:30-6pm. Evening menu €11.50-16.50, served daily 6-9pm.)

The pubs on Main St. harken to the tradition of the early 20th century, when establishments served as both watering holes and the proprietor's "main" business, be it general store, blacksmith, or leather shop. Directly across from the hostel on East End, **The East End,** Main St. (☎947 2970), hosts live trad on Tuesday, Wednesday, and Thursday nights in summer. **Mike Murt's** (☎947 2396) brims with characters and ancient tools. Prepare to tell your life story to the pint-clutching ensemble. Modernity hit **Fertha Bar** (☎947 2023), where trendy rock bands sometimes appear on weekends—Fridays are a good bet. **The Shebeen** (☎947 2361) has trad and set dancing on Thursdays. Youth from around the Ring head to **The Harp Nightclub.** (☎947 2436. Cover €10. Open F-Sa midnight-3am.)

⚅ ❀ SIGHTS AND FESTIVALS. O'Connell's Church in Cahersiveen is the only house o' worship in Ireland named for a layperson. "The Liberator," other heroes, and high points of Irish history are celebrated at the **Old Barracks Heritage Centre,** a block down Bridge St. (☎947 2777. Open May to mid-Sept. M-Sa 10am-5pm, Su 1-5pm. €4, students and seniors €3.50, family €9.) Though the center's exhibits are well done and often have visitors reading all day about the rise and fall of the town's fishing industry, the building itself may be of more interest—its bizarre architecture has inspired a local rumor that confused officials accidentally built a colonial outpost, while a proper barracks was erected somewhere in India.

Past the barracks and across the bridge, a wealth of fortifications huddle together. Turn left past the bridge, and left again off the main road, about a 40min. walk, to reach the ruined 15th-century **Ballycarbery Castle,** once owned by O'Connell's ancestors. Two hundred yards past the castle turnoff stand a pair of Ireland's best-preserved stone forts. Walk atop the 10 ft. thick walls of **Cahergall Fort,** or visit the small stone dwellings of **Leacanabuaile Fort,** the best-preserved of Ireland's 40,000 ring forts. A few minutes' walk beyond the second fort is **Cuas Crom Beach,** known for its fine swimming. Continue past the turnoff to Cuas Crom and take the next left to arrive at **White Strand Beach,** another popular swimming area. Turn right after passing over the bridge to **Knocknadobar Mt.,** which holds 14 stations of the cross and a holy well at its base. The map and the manager at the Sive Hostel can help plot the way. During the first weekend in August, Cahersiveen hosts a **Celtic Music Weekend** (www.celticmusicfestival.com), which features street entertainment, fireworks, pub sessions, and numerous free concerts.

VALENTIA ISLAND (DAIRBHRE) ☎066

A welcome escape for travelers sick of the hustle and bustle of Irish life—if such a stressful existence be possible in this beautiful region—Valentia Island's removed location has stunning views of the mountains on the mainland. The island's tranquility was compromised over a century ago with the installation of the first trans-atlantic cable, which connected Valentia to Newfoundland; important characters from the world over, including Queen Victoria, came to test it. Things have since died down, and the island's tiny, winding roads are perfect for biking or hiking. The locals' reputation as amusingly off the mark keeps the *craic* flowing, despite its isolated locale. Bridge and ferry connections to the mainland are at opposite ends of the island. A summer shuttle is available through **Kerry Community Transport.** (☎ 1890 528 528 or 714 3100. €2. Call ahead to reserve a spot. From Cahersiveen to Valentia Island M-Sa 1 per day.) No public transportation is available on Valentia.

⚏⚏ TRANSPORTATION AND PRACTICAL INFORMATION. A comically short car ferry trip departs during the summer from **Reenard Point**, 3 mi. west of Caher-siveen, off the Ring of Kerry road. **Taxis** from Cahersiveen cost about €7. The ferry drops passengers at **Knightstown,** the island's population center. (☎ 947 6141. Ferries depart every 8min. April-Sept. M-Sa 8:15am-10pm, Su 9am-10pm. Cars €5 return, pedestrians €1.50, cyclists €2.50.) Most cars are headed for the pier, making thumbing it pretty easy. The bridge connecting Valentia to the mainland starts at **Portmagee**, 10 mi. west of Cahersiveen. To get to Portmagee, head south from Cahersiveen or north from Waterville, then west on R565. Hitching in this area is difficult and not recommended by *Let's Go*. Enthusiastic bikers can follow the gorgeous **Skellig Ring,** an offshoot of the Ring of Kerry that branches from Water-ville and runs along the coast through Ballinskelligs and Portmagee, rejoining the main Ring road at Cahersiveen. The **Kerry Community Transport** offers rides every Friday in the summer around this area to Cahersiveen. (☎ 1890 528 528 or 714 3100. Call ahead. €2.) For a **taxi** on the island, call Teddy (☎ 947 6183 or 087 264 8646).

⚏⚏ ACCOMMODATIONS AND FOOD. Valentia has a surprising variety of budget accommodations in and around Knightstown. The large **Royal Pier Hostel (IHH)** ❷ in Knightstown once hosted Queen Victoria. The rooms are clean but cramped; the more expensive dorms are extremely spacious and have enviable views of the bay. (☎ 947 6144. Wash and dry €8. Dorms €15-20; singles €25, with breakfast €30.) A 30min. walk down the main road from Knightstown lies tiny **Chapeltown,** home to the **Ring Lyne Hostel and B&B ❶,** which puts guest up in basic double and triple rooms above a **restaurant** and pub. (☎ 947 6103. Mains €6.50-10 served noon-8pm. Dorms €15; B&B €25.) Back in Knightstown, halfway up the main street and then down to the right on Peter St. (follow the brown signs depicting a hut and tree), the **Valentia Island Youth Hostel (An Óige/HI) ❶** is housed in an old coast guard station overlooking the bay. Don't be fooled by its rough exterior; the neat dorms are a bargain. Check in after 5pm. (☎ 947 6154. Sheets €1.50. Open June-Sept. Dorms €13.) **Altazamuth House ❸,** to the left on Peter St., has pretty bedrooms, a sunny breakfast room, and a brand-new sunroom—should the sun ever dare show its face in Ireland. (☎ 947 6300. Open Apr.-Oct. **Bike rental** €10 per day. €27.)

GREEN ROOTS It seems that *homo sapiens* aren't the only species with an ancestral stake in the Emerald Isle. In 1992, Swiss geologist Ivan Stossel discovered a track of small footprints on the rocky shore of Valentia Island. After analyzing layers of volcanic ash in the groove-like prints, scientists concluded that they were stamped out 385 million years ago, making them the oldest fossilized footprints in the Northern Hemisphere. They are believed to be those of a "Devonian tetrapod," a creature that predates the dinosaurs. The prints are currently unmarked and unprotected, but the government is taking steps to preserve this and other important archaeological sites. Until then, fossil fanatics can ask locals for directions.

Limited supplies are available at the **store** a block up from the water to the left along the main street. (Open M-Sa 9am-8pm, Su 9:30am-2pm.) ▨**Knightstown Coffee ❷**, on the right walking up the street, is a pleasant and cozy cafe with outdoor tables and excellent espresso, soup, and scrumptious desserts. (☎947 6373. Sandwiches €2.50-6.35; veggie or chicken tortillas €7.50. Open Easter-Sept. daily noon-6pm.) **Boston's,** on the main road out of Knightstown, serves quality pub dishes. (☎947 6140. Specials €7.70; sandwiches €2.50-6.50. Food served daily noon-8pm. Live music F-Su.) Enjoy fine dining with a twist at **Fuschia ❹.** Their Sirloin Steak Shakespeare is an 11 oz. prime beef cooked "As you like it" or "To be or not to be" for €18.95. (☎947 6051. Mains €15.50-18.95. Open W-Su 5:30-9pm.) The **pub** attached to the Royal Pier has pub grub, a pool table, and comfortable chairs that look out onto the harbor. (☎947 6144. Meals €7-15. Food served noon-9pm.)

◙⚑ SIGHTS AND ACTIVITIES. The road from town to the **old slate quarry,** runs past the turnoff to the Coombe Bank House and ends with Valentia's best views across Dingle Bay. Arrive at the quarry (a 1hr. hike from Knightstown) just before sunset. Slate from this massive dig roofed the British Parliament, and the hollowed-out cliffside now houses a "sacred grotto." At the opposite end of the island, hike up to **Bray Head,** where the ruins of a Napoleonic lookout tower afford a perfect vantage of the Skelligs. The way from Knightstown passes the turnoff for **Glanleam Subtropical Gardens,** with such attractions as the 50 ft. tall Chilean Fire Bush. (☎947 6176. Open daily 10am-7pm. €12.50, students €3.50, child €2.50.)

The Royal Pier Hostel arranges **sea angling.** (☎947 6144. Or call boatman Owen Walsh directly ☎947 6327 or 087 283 3522. Groups €25 per hr., individuals €250-300.) **Moriarty's Dive Center,** down from the pier, teaches a one-week certification course Easter to October, all equipment included. (☎947 6204. €380 per person.)

WATERVILLE (AN COIREAN) ☎066

Wedged between crashing Atlantic waves and the quiet waters of Lough Cussane, Waterville was built as a telecommunications portal by the English, who then flooded it every summer as they came to vacation on its scenic shores. Nowadays, Waterville's human traffic comes from the tour bus hordes who are released for a seaside lunch before rumbling on to Sneem for sweater shopping. Yet, Waterville still manages to be a serene, cheerful town. Those who remain might take a surf lesson or splurge on a meal at one of the peninsula's best restaurants. The meditative traveler is left to amble along the isolated shore, which Charlie Chaplin once treasured for the liberating anonymity it granted him.

▆⛯ TRANSPORTATION AND PRACTICAL INFORMATION. The Ring of Kerry **bus** stops in front of the Bay View Hotel on Main St. (June to mid-Sept. 2 per day), with service to Caherdaniel (20min., €3.20), Sneem (50min., €6.50), and Killarney (2hr., €12.20). Eastbound **Bus Éireann** goes to Cahersiveen in the morning once per day, year-round, en route to Killarney. The **tourist office,** on the beach, across from the Butler Arms Hotel, is armed with an extremely friendly staff to field all travel querries. (☎947 4646. Open late May-Sept. M-Sa 9:30am-5:30pm.) An **ATM** is inside Centra (☎947 4257) and the **Bank of Ireland** opens a sub-office facing the water once a week. (Open W 10:45am-1pm.) A small **pharmacy** resides in the town center. (☎947 4141. Open M-Sa 9:30am-6pm, Su 9am-1pm for newspaper and candy only.) **Web connections** are available at the new **Internet Cafe** on the southern end of town, next to the hostel. (☎947 4608. €1.50 per 10min., €5 per hr. Hostelers €1/€4. Open April-Oct. daily 8am-midnight or so.) **Skelligs Surf School** has an **Internet cafe** on Main St. within Bayview Hotel. (☎947 8992. €2 per 20min., €1 per every 10min. thereafter. Open

THE BIG SPLURGE

SHEILIN SEAFOOD RESTAURANT

The warm, family-run **Sheilin Seafood Restaurant** in **Waterville** serves unbelievably fresh fruits from the sea with exquisite taste and simplicity. Fresh local lobster, salmon, scallops, and crab are featured on the menu nightly, and are prepared in unpretentious fashion by owner/chef Marie Courtney. The perfect meal, as recommended by Ms. Courtney herself, would begin with the **avocado and crab starter** (€7), served hot or cold, followed by the inventive and tasty **fish o' soup**—chock full of mussels, salmon, squid, and cockles (€4). For a main, the **black sole,** simply grilled and buttered and served with fresh vegetables, is the house specialty (€17). Finally, the delectable **blackberry tart,** made from freshly picked berries (seasonal from Aug.-Nov.), makes for a scrumptious dessert. The fine seafood, friendly atmosphere, and creative menu at Sheilin's truly speaks for itself and is well worth the price. Believe us, your taste buds won't believe they're still in Ireland.

Sheilin's Seafood Restaurant and Wine Bar, Waterville (☎947 4231), just down from the Centra and P. Murphy's grocery store. Dinner nightly 6:30-9:30pm. Book in advance July-Aug., especially Th-Sa. Call ahead in winter. MC/V.

daily 9am-8pm or so.) The **post office** is just across from the tourist office. (☎947 4100. Open M-F 9am-5:30pm, Sa 9am-2pm.)

▮▮▮ ACCOMMODATIONS, FOOD, AND PUBS.

B&Bs line Main St. (prices run €25-32), but ▮**Peter's Place ❶** is the only hostel in Waterville. On the southern end of town facing the water, it exemplifies the ideal relaxed hostel atmosphere. Fascinating artwork includes an Australian dot-painting on the mantle. The friendly owner (Peter, naturally) purchased an acoustic guitar for guests to play when not listening to the excellent, eclectic tunes on the hostel's stereo. Inquire with Peter about **work opportunities** available between March and October. (☎947 4608. **Skellig boat trips** €35. Dorms €12.50; doubles €15. **Camping** €5.) Next to the tourist office, **The Huntsman ❷** rents deluxe apartments overlooking the sea, each with its own sauna, jacuzzi, and fireplace. If staying a few days with friends, this is the best option, though it is difficult to get a room. Be sure to contact them far in advance. Currently it is very booked from Easter to October 2004. (☎947 4124; www.rci.com. Sleeps 4 people. €150 per night, €700 per wk.)

Between **Centra** (☎947 4257; open May-Sept. daily 7am-11pm, Oct.-Apr. 8am-9:30pm) and neighboring **Curran's** (☎947 4253; open June-Sept. daily 7:30am-11pm; Oct.-May 7:30am-10pm), all grocery needs are met. **The Chédean ❷,** across from the Butler Arms Hotel, has small-town ambience, delicious homebaking, and a friendly hostess. Peruse the wacky selection of secondhand books on sale for charity (€2) and the Skellig-inspired puffin paintings (€20-65) over frosted coffee cake or fresh quiche. (☎947 4966. Food €2.50-8.50. Open late Apr.-Oct. 10am-6pm.) Across from the post office, choose from the takeaway selection at **Beach Cove Cafe ❶;** there are several tables inside, but the food tastes best by the water, weather-permitting. (☎947 4733. Pizza, burgers, and sandwiches €2-5. Open M-Th 10am-11pm, F-Su 9:30am-1am.) Gaelic football legend Mick O'Dwyer lends his name to **O'Dwyer's: The Villa Restaurant & Pub ❷,** at the corner of Main St. and the Ring of Kerry Rd. Enjoy a pint or some homemade cottage pie with the locals. (☎947 4248. Meals €6.50-10. Food served daily noon-4pm, 6-9pm.) Mick also runs the **Piper 2000** nightclub at the Strand Hotel down the road. (☎947 4436. Cover €7. Open June-Sept. W and Sa-Su.) **The Bay View Hotel** pours pints in two bars and throws a Friday night disco in July and August. (☎947 4122. Cover €7.) On Main St., the **Lobster Bar and Restaurant** attracts tourists with a Guinness-grasping lobster on its sign and a variety of live music and events including trad, karaoke, and theme nights—check with the tourist office. (☎947 4629 or 947 4183. Trad is typically Tu, F, Su. DJ W, Sa.) **The Fishermen's Bar** (☎947 4144) once poured pints for the Little Tramp. (No live music. Food served daily noon-3pm and 6-8:30pm.)

◎ 🎨 SIGHTS AND ACTIVITIES. Lough Currane's waters lie about 2 mi. inland from town. Keeping the ocean on the right, follow the lake road then turn left, or head inland along the smaller streets. Locals claim that a submerged castle can be seen in times of low water, but outsiders seem to have better luck with the ruins of a monastery on Church Island. **Quad Safari** on Main St. leads adventurers around the mountains and lakes on mountain bikes and all-terrain four-wheelers. (☎947 4465; www.actionadventurecentre.com. 3hr. guided bike trek €55.) These folks also book **horseback riding** (€25 per hr.), **Skellig jaunts** (€35), and "**war games**" (€55 per 3½hr.), operated with pseudo-military equipment, helmets with light sensors, and strategic plans. If craving **fishing**, head down Main St. to **O'Sullivan's Tackle Shop**, which outfits fishers with lures, rods, boots, and nets. (☎947 4433. Open May to late Sept. daily 9am-6pm; call for an appointment the rest of the year.) For lake and sea angling **boats for hire** and **salmon and seatrout fishing** opportunities, contact John Murphy (☎947 5257 or 086 399 1074). Perhaps the waves are calling; to learn how to catch one, try the **Surf School** next to Bayview Hotel, in the same spot as the new Internet cafe. They use a gentle break at the other end of Ballinskelligs Bay, on the sandy **Reena Rua Beach** (named for the red grass that grows along the dunes) to teach beginner lessons. (2hr. lesson €30. Open daily 9:30am-9pm.)

The Irish-speaking hamlet of **Ballinskelligs**, across the bay from Waterville, probably isn't worth a special trip. But if you're there to catch a Skellig-bound boat or passing through by bike or car on the scenic and bus-free **Skellig Ring**, check out the ruins of **Ballinskelligs Monastery**, near the pier. The monks of Skellig Michael (see **The Skelligs**, p. 263) retreated here after 11th-century storms made journeys to the island increasingly treacherous. **Prior House Youth Hostel (An Óige/HI) ❶** offers basic hostel accommodations, a convenient general store, and close proximity to **Ballinskelligs Beach.** (☎947 9229. Store open 9am-9pm. Open Apr.-Oct. Dorms €13.) Two miles south of Ballinskelligs, the dead-end road to **Bolus Head** affords great views of the Skelligs and St. Finan's Bay. As it heads around the bay through the lovely area known as **The Glen,** the Skellig Ring passes popular **surfing spots** and climbs to a summit with gorgeous vistas.

THE SKELLIG ROCKS   ☎066

About 8 mi. off the shore of the Iveragh Peninsula, the stunning Skellig Rocks rise abruptly from the sea. More than just masses of natural rubble, these islands awe visitors who, like George Bernard Shaw, often find them "not of this world, but a place you dream of." While the multitudes rush around the Ring of Kerry, those who detour to the Skelligs are rewarded with an encounter unforgettable for birdlovers and the ornithologically indifferent alike. As **Little Skellig** comes into view, the jagged rock pinnacles appear snow-capped; increased proximity reveals that they are actually covered with 24,000 pairs of crooning gannets—the largest such community in Europe. Boats dock at the larger **Skellig Michael,** where daytrippers have 2-3hr. to picnic, explore, and cavort with hundreds of peculiar puffins and nearby seals. Climb the vertigo-inducing 630 stone steps past kittiwakes, petrels, and many more gannets and puffins, to reach an ancient **monastic settlement.** Sixth-century Christian monks carved out an austere community along the craggy faces of the 714 ft. high rock to escape the secular scourges of the mainland. Their still-intact, beehive-like dwellings are fascinatingly explained by guides from *Dúchas,* the Irish Heritage service, though the dark interiors and stark surroundings alone speak eloquently of the monks' severe spiritual path. There is no toilet or shelter on the rock, and the Ministry of Tourism does not recommend the trip for young children, the elderly, or those who suffer from serious medical conditions.

The fantastic and sometimes soggy **ferry voyage** takes about 1hr. (depending on conditions, point of departure, and boat) and costs €35. Most boats depart around 10am from Portmagee, the straightest shot to the Skelligs, but some pick up passengers beforehand from Reenard Point and Valentia Island. Many boats return to the dock by around 3pm. The Sive Hostel and the campsite in **Cahersiveen** (see p. 284), and Peter's Place in **Waterville** (see p. 287), arrange trips that include a ride to the dock for no extra cost. Departing from **Ballinskelligs** are Joe Roddy and Sons (☎947 4268 or 087 284 4460; can collect passengers from Waterville) and Sean Feehan (☎947 9182). From **Portmagee** are Michael O'Sullivan (☎947 4255; can collect passengers from Waterville) and Mr. Casey (☎947 2437 or 087 239 5470; can collect passengers from Cahersiveen). Seanie Murphy picks up passengers in **Reenard** on Valentia Island and Portmagee (☎947 6214 or 087 236 2344). To arrive at a different town than you departed from, make arrangements with the captain. Ferries run from April to October, depending on weather; call ahead for reservations and to confirm departures.

The grass-roofed **Skellig Experience Visitors Centre** is across the Portmagee Bridge on Valentia Island. Videos and models engulf visitors in virtual Skellig; it's an extra (steep) charge to sail from the center to the islands themselves, although the boats do not dock. The video is a relaxing 15min. diversion, provided you ignore its dramatic rhetorical questions or, if you so desire, shout out the obvious answers, although *Let's Go* does not recommend irritating other museum-goers. (☎947 6306 or 947 9413. Open July-Aug. daily 10am-7pm; Apr.-June and Sept. 10am-6pm. €4.40, students with ID and seniors €3.80; with cruise €21.50/€19.40.)

CAHERDANIEL (CATHAIR DONAL) ☎066

There's little to attract the Ring's droves of travel coaches to Caherdaniel. However, the hamlet (that is, two pubs, a grocer, a restaurant, and a takeaway) does lie near **Derrynane National Park,** which contains the ancestral home of patriot Daniel O'Connell (see **Rebellion,** p. 61) and miles of beaches ringed by sparkling dunes.

📧📷 TRANSPORTATION AND PRACTICAL INFORMATION. Ring of Kerry **bus** stops in Caherdaniel twice a day at the junction of the Ring of Kerry Rd. and Main St., picking up passengers for Killarney (1½hr., June-Sept. 2 per day, €13) and Sneem (30min., June-Sept. 2 per day, €4.40). Eastbound buses come through once a day in the morning all year, heading to Waterville, Cahersiveen, and Killarney. The **tourist office** is 1 mi. east of town at the Wave Crest Camping Park. (☎947 5188. Open mid-Apr. to mid-Sept. daily 9am-8pm.) The **post office** is located in central Caherdaniel. (☎947 5101. Open M-F 9am-12:30pm and 1:30-5:30pm, Sa 9am-1pm.)

📷📧📱 ACCOMMODATIONS, FOOD, AND PUBS. Guests have the run of the house at **The Travelers Rest Hostel ❶,** across from the gas station near the crossroads. A relaxing sitting room with a fireplace and small dorms makes this hostel look and feel more like a B&B. (☎947 5175. Continental breakfast €4. Dorms €12.50; private rooms €16.) Just down from the Blind Piper Pub & Restaurant (see p. 291), roomy accommodation awaits weary trekkers at the **Kerry Way B&B ❸.** The managers can also arrange **diving trips** for €45.50. (☎947 5277. All rooms with baths. €25.) Campers perch over the beach 1 mi. east of town on the Ring of Kerry Rd. at **Wave Crest Camping Park ❶.** The well-stocked shop and self-service laundry are handy, even for non-campers. (☎947 5188. Laundry €4 per load. Shop open 8am-10pm. Site open mid-Mar. to Oct.; offseason by arrangement. €5.50 per person including tent, €15 per couple including car. Showers €1.)

Caherdaniel's grocery and pint needs are met at **Freddy's Bar and Grocery** on the main corner. (☎947 5400. Grocery open daily 8:30am-8:30pm or so; pub has standard hours.) The **Blind Piper Pub ❹** is a popular local hangout—outdoor tables by the stream are perfect for enjoying pub vittles. Music drowns out the babbling brook in July and August, with trad on Fridays and discos Saturday and Sunday. (☎947 5126. Pub food €5-10, served noon-10pm.)

◙ SIGHTS. A trip to Caherdaniel is incomplete without a visit to **Derrynane National Park,** 1½ mi. along the shore from the village and well signposted. The highlighted attraction, **Derrynane House,** was the residence of Irish patriot Daniel "The Liberator" O'Connell, whose election to Parliament and inability to take his seat as a Catholic inspired the movement that culminated in the Catholic Emancipation Act of 1829 (see **Rebellion,** p. 61). Inside the house are the dueling pistol that O'Connell used to kill challenger John d'Esterre and the black glove he wore to church for years afterwards to mourn his victim. The 30min. film on O'Connell presents an engrossing and refreshingly textured image of the acerbic barrister. (☎947 5113. Open May-Sept. M-Sa 9am-6pm, Su 11am-7pm; Apr. and Oct. Tu-Su 1-5pm; Nov.-Mar. Sa-Su 1-5pm. Last admission 45min. before closing. €2.75, students and children €1.25, family €7.) A few trails lead from the house through dunes and gardens down to the beach, about a 45min. walk from town. Worth the 15min. walk, **Abbey Island**—only a true island during exceptionally high tides—extends into the water to the southwest. There, the **Abbey of St. Finian** shows the wear and tear of 1300 years and enchants explorers with its creepy graveyard.

After a 6 mi. hike or pedal uphill, the pre-Christian **Staigue Fort,** west of town and marked with large signs, makes visitors feel tall and powerful. The largest stone fort in Ireland, Staigue surveys the sea from high on a hill and keeps an eye out for any pesky Pictish invaders. (☎947 5288. Fort always open. Free.) For a close look at the watery side of Caherdaniel, contact **Activity Ireland,** housed in the Kerry Way B&B. (☎947 5277. Diving €45.) They also help direct the interested to horse-riding options available at **Eagle Rock Equestrian Centre** (☎947 5145) and toward **Bealtra Boats** (☎947 5129) for fishing and Skelligs trips.

SNEEM (AN TSNAIDHM)   ☎064

The hordes tend to make Sneem their first or last stop along the Ring, and the town is well prepared to receive them. Canned Irish music rolls out of the shops on the South Sq. between the clutter of postcard stands. Two public squares and a unique sculpture collection made Sneem a browser's paradise. Charles de Gaulle visited Sneem in 1969. The town was so honored it erected a bronze bust of de Gaulle on a boulder of local stone. Thus, a tradition was born. Today, Sneem's **sculpture park** celebrates the late President Cearbhaill O'Dalaigh, Egyptian goddess Isis, wrestling champ "Crusher" Casey, and an odd set of cave buildings. Despite being known as a sculpture park, it is actually a conglomeration of various statues scattered about town. It's difficult to decide which is more bizarre, the sculptures themselves or their collective name, "The Way the Faeries Went." *Sneem Guide,* from the tourist office, contains a brief tour (€0.65).

The Ring of Kerry **bus** travels straight to Killarney (1hr., June-Sept. 2 per day, €13), and another bus connects to Kenmare (mid-June to Aug. M-Sa 2 per day, €16). The eastbound bus from Killarney stops once a day before continuing all the way around the Ring. The **tourist office** is housed in the Joli Coeur Craft Shop near the bus stop. (☎45270. Open late June-late Sept. daily 10:30am-6pm.) **M. Burns Bike**

Hire, in the North Sq., **rents bikes.** (☎45140. €12 per day, €60 per wk. Open M-Sa 9:30am-7pm.) **Internet** is available at **Goosey Island Campsite** (see below), but only for guests. Jockey for a position with postcard-wielding warriors at the **post office** a few doors down. (☎45110. Open M-F 9am-1pm and 2-5:30pm, Sa 9am-1pm.)

The **Harbour View Hostel ❶,** an 8min. walk on the Kenmare Rd., used to be a motel; with ranch-style units in a gravel lot, it's hard to forget. Basic dorms are smaller walk-throughs, but the more expensive dorms and doubles are quite roomy. (☎45276. Laundry €10. Dorms and singles €15; doubles €30. **Camping** €5 with tent.) Sneem's oldest and arguably nicest B&B is **The Bank House ❸,** North Sq., where the gregarious owner makes all feel right at home. (☎45226. Open Mar.-Nov. €26. Singles €40.) **Old Convent House ❸,** Pier Rd., a right off the South Sq. just after Erin Co. Knitwear, is an old stone house with magnificent views; redone rooms are comfy but lack soul. (☎45181. €25-30.) With its excellent location in the town center and enviable scenic views, **Goosey Island Campsite ❶** lets guests camp along the grassy river bank. Those in hotels suddenly wish they had a tent. (☎45577. **Internet** €6 per hr. Open Apr. to mid-Oct. €7 per person. Showers €1.)

North of the bridge, **The Village Kitchen ❷** serves seafood and sandwiches in a cafe setting. (☎45281. Sandwiches €3-4, house specials €5.50-9.75. Open June-Sept. daily 9:30am-6pm; Oct.-May 9am-5pm.) Throw on some dirty sneakers and gallop to **Hungry Knight ❶** for fish and chips or pool with young Sneemen. (☎45237. Burgers from €1.70. Open Easter-Oct. daily noon-1am or so.) Ditching hiking boots for fancy loafers is in order before entering **Sacre Coeur ❹,** above the North Sq. Steak, seafood, and chicken dishes (€12.50-18.50) are served in an imposing dining room. (☎45186. Su prix-fixe 3-course lunch €15, served 12:30-2:30pm. Open Easter-Oct. daily 6-10pm.) Massive pub meals await at **The Blue Bull** by the post office. Stick around for ballad sessions on Saturday nights in the summer. (☎45382; food daily noon-8pm.) At the **Fisherman's Knot** (☎45224), across the bridge on the Caherdaniel Rd., locals tap their toes to trad and catch disco fever a few nights a week in summer. **O'Shea's** (☎45515), in the North Sq., reverberates with old-fashioned summer sessions on Sundays and Wednesdays.

KENMARE (NEIDIN) ☎064

A bridge between the Ring of Kerry and the Beara Peninsula, Kenmare has adapted to a continuous stream of visitors. With colorful houses, misty mountains, and the like, it fits the image of the classic Irish town. Tourists fresh off the bus may dilute Kenmare's appeal, but pleasant surroundings overshadow the sweater stalls and postcard stands. Its convenient location along the Kerry Way makes Kenmare a common stop for trekkers.

▐ TRANSPORTATION

Buses: From Brennan's Pub on Main St. to **Castletownbere** via **Ardgroom** and **Eyeries** (40min., June-Aug. M-Sa 2 per day, €7-8); **Cork** via **Glengarrif** and **Skibbereen** (June-Sept. daily 2 per day, €13); **Killarney** (1hr.; M-Sa 3 per day, Su 2 per day; only 2 per day in winter, €7.20), where connections are available to **Tralee** and **Cork; Sneem** (35min., June-Aug. M-Sa 2 per day, €6.50), where connections are available to the **Ring of Kerry** bus during the summer (€18.50). Significantly fewer routes and times in the off season (Oct.-May); check with the tourist office for current schedules or call the bus station in Killarney (☎34777).

Taxis: Kenmare Koach & Kab (call Declan Finnegan ☎41491 or 087 248 0800). Also offers bus tours around the Rings of Beara and Kerry (€20 per person) and to Glengarrif and Killarney (€10 per person) during the summer.

Bike Rental: Finnegan's (☎41083), corner of Henry and Shelbourne St. €12 per day, €75 per wk. Open June-Sept. M-Sa 10am-8pm; Oct.-May M-Sa 10am-6:30pm.

✈ 🛈 ORIENTATION AND PRACTICAL INFORMATION

Kenmare's main streets form a triangle: **Henry Street** is the lively base, while **Main Street** and **Shelbourne Street** connect on either side. The intersection of Henry St. and Main St. forms **the Square**, which contains a small park and the tourist office. Main St. then becomes N71, heading toward **Moll's Gap** and **Killarney**; N70 to **Sneem** and the **Ring of Kerry** also branches off this road. From Kenmare, take N70 west (rather than N71 north) to navigate the Ring clockwise and avoid tour bus traffic.

Tourist Office: the Sq. (☎41233). Friendly staff hands out *Heritage Trails* maps and houses the free **Heritage Center** (see **Sights,** p. 295). Open May-June M-Sa 9am-1pm, 2-5:30pm; July-Oct. M-Sa 9am-6pm, Su 10am-5pm.

Bank: AIB, 9 Main St. (☎41010), on the corner of Henry St., and **Bank of Ireland,** the Square (☎41255). Both have **ATMs.** Banks open M 10am-5pm, Tu-F 10am-4pm.

Work Opportunities: Kenmare has plenty of restaurants hiring summer cooks and wait staff, such as **An Leath Phingin,** 35 Main St. (☎41559). Several sizable hotels will hire travelers, including the **Landsdowne Arms** (☎41368), at the top of Main St.

Bookstore: The Kenmare Bookstore, Main St. (☎41578). Bestsellers and Irish classics. Open June-Aug. M-Sa 9:30am-9pm, Su 11am-6pm; Sept.-May M-Sa 10am-6pm.

Laundry: O'Sheas, Main St. (☎41394). Wash €3, dry €1 per 10min. Also serves as a **photo shop** with film and development. Open M-F 8:30am-6pm, Sa 9:30am-6pm.

Pharmacy: Sheahan's, Main St. (☎41354). Open M-Sa 9am-6pm. **Brosnan's,** Henry St. (☎41318, same number after-hours). Open M-Sa 9am-6:30pm, Su 12:30-1:30pm.

Emergency: ☎999; no coins required. **Police** *(Garda)*: Shelbourne St. (☎41177).

Hospital: Old Killarney Rd. (☎41088). Follow the signs on Railway Rd.

Internet: The **library** (☎41416), on Shelbourne St. near its intersection with Main St., offers **free Internet,** but call ahead to reserve a time. Open Tu-Sa 10am-1:30pm and 2:30-5pm, Th 10am-8pm.

Post Office: Henry St. (☎41490), at the corner of Shelbourne St. Open June-Sept. M-F 9am-5:30pm, Sa 9am-1pm; Oct.-May M-F 9am-1pm and 2-5:30pm, Sa 9am-1pm. Also has **Internet**: €1 per 10min.; students €1 per 15min. Computers available June-Aug. 8am-8pm, Sept.-May 8am-6pm.

🏠 ACCOMMODATIONS AND CAMPING

▩ **Fáilte Hostel (IHH),** at the corner of Henry and Shelbourne St. (☎42333). Proprietress Maureen runs a tight ship at this excellent and immaculate hostel. The fully-equipped kitchen, TV room, and great location often persuade guests to stay another night. Curfew 1:30am. Open Apr.-Oct. Dorms €12; doubles €32-40; triples €42; quads €56. ❶

▩ **Kenmare Lodge Hostel,** 27 Main St. (☎40662; www.neidin.net/lodgehostel), toward the intersection with Shelbourne St. This hostel has immaculate rooms, a spacious kitchen, and an appreciation for art. Hungry guests receive a 20% discount at the cheap and delicious **Cafe Ice** (☎40808), downstairs. Dorms €12-15. ❶

Hawthorn House, Shelbourne St. (☎41035; www.hawthornhousekenmare.com). The delightful Mary O'Brien helps guests feel at home, as do her comfortable rooms. Open year-round. Book ahead July-Aug. All rooms with bath and TV. Doubles €60-70. ❸

Rose Cottage, the Sq. (☎41330), next door to Keal Na Gower House. A gracious stone house set back behind a lovely green garden. Enjoys very marginal historical signifi-cance as the temporary home of Abbess Mary O'Hagan, sister to Ireland's first Catholic Chancellor, Thom O'Hagan. June-Sept. €35; Oct.-May €30. ❸

Keal Na Gower House B&B, the Sq. (☎41202), near the tourist office. A small B&B with a lovely patio overlooking a babbling brook. The sound of rushing water and the brook views from 2 rooms make it easy to overlook the retro decor. €28-30. ❸

Ring of Kerry Caravan and Camping Park, Sneem Rd. (☎41648), 3 mi. west of town. Overlooks mountains and a bay. Kitchen, TV room, and small shop. Open Apr.-Sept. Laundry €3.50. 1 person with tent €7, 2 with car and tent €16.50. Showers €0.50. ❶

🏠 FOOD

Food is plentiful but pricey in Kenmare, especially for dinner. Try the smaller cafes for snacks, and check the pubs for cheap lunches. **SuperValu** is on Main St. (☎41307. Open M-Th 8am-8pm, F 8am-9pm, Sa 8am-7pm, Su 9am-5pm.) **The Pantry,** Henry St., has a limited selection of organic stock. (☎42233. Open M-Sa 9:30am-6pm.) Takeaway is always a cheap option; there are several on Main St., including the late-night **Wharton's Traditional Fish & Chips,** serving fried fish, burgers, and chicken for under €3. (☎42622. Open Su-F 12:30pm-midnight, Sa 12:30pm-4am.) **Ferrari,** serves the same stuff. (☎42045. Open June-Sept. daily 3pm-3am; Oct.-May Su-Th 3pm-1am, F-Sa 3pm-3am.)

🗺 An Leath Phingin, 35 Main St. (☎41559). Gaelic for "The Half Penny." Enjoy a taste of Italy in an old stone townhouse. Skylights illuminate the wonderful food, which ranges from king prawns (€8.50) and baked salmon (€17.90) to pizza and pasta (€13-16). Book ahead July-Aug. Open Mar.-Nov. M-Tu and Th-Su 6-9:30pm. ❹

Jam (☎41591). Kerchiefed town belles serve bakery and deli delights. Try a tomato and cheese scone topped with poppy seeds (€1) or construct an original toasted sandwich masterpiece (€3.30). Open M-Sa 8am-7pm. ❶

Cafe Mocha, on Main St. across from the park (☎41233). Delivers the baked goods for cheap (€2-4) in an artsy space, plush couches and all. Open M-F 9am-5:30pm, Sa 10am-5:30pm, Su 10am-4:30pm. ❶

The Purple Heather Pub, Henry St. (☎41016). Has served very tasty lunches and snacks transcending that of the average pub since 1964. Sample assorted local farm cheeses (€6.90) or the special potato, cheddar, onion, and thyme omelette served with organic greens (€7.10) in a cozy red leather booth. Open M-Sa 10:45am-7pm. ❷

Mickey Neds Bar & Restaurant (☎40200; www.mickeyneds.com), off the Square, across from the tourist office. Creative, experimental combinations, like grilled turbot with orange chive butter (€23). Slick, modern lounge for an after-dinner drink. Lunch €7-10, dinner €20-23. Food served Tu-Sa noon-3pm and 6-9pm, Su noon-6pm. ❹

The Coachman's Inn, Henry St. (☎41311). A popular wood-paneled pub that serves Irish standards like roast Kerry lamb with mint sauce (€8.25). Lunch menu (€6-8) served noon-5:30pm, dinner menu (€12.50-14) served 5:30-9:30pm. ❸

🍺 PUBS

Kenmare's pubs attract a hefty contingent of tourists, making live music easy to come by in summer. The locals still hold their own at most watering holes.

The Bold Thady Quill, in the Landsdowne Arms Hotel (☎41368), at the top of Main St. Wise visitors follow the locals here. Trad F-Su June-Sept.; varies the rest of the year.

Atlantic Bar, the Square (☎41094). Relaxed local joint with a lot of character. Serves breakfast 9:30-11:30am, lunch 12:30-2:30pm, dinner 5-9pm. Live trad Su. Disco Sa.

Crowley's, Henry St. (☎41472) Poses the question: "With frequent trad, why bother with interior decorating?" The crowds that pack this intimate pub each night give the answer.

The Square Pint, Main St. Decidedly un-square. Get down on the dance floor between pints. Open until 2:30am.

👁 SIGHTS

There are plenty of good hikes in the country around Kenmare, but few sights in the town itself. To reach the **Kerry Way,** walk along the street that runs past the tourist office and take the little stone bridge that crosses over the brook; brown signs will point the way to the Way, which heads up and over the surrounding green hills of farmland. Picnic among local herds of goat and cow while absorbing wonderful views of the peninsula and distant coastline. Closer to town, the ancient **stone circle,** a 2min. walk down Market St. from the Sq., is the largest of its kind (55 ft. diameter) in southwest Ireland. (Always open. €1.50.) The stone circle is one stop on Kenmare's **tourist trail** (maps at the tourist office), a well-marked route that leads visitors over historic bridges and past a small tower known as **Hutchin's Folly.** The new **Heritage Centre,** in the back of the tourist office, has a model of the stone circle and other historical exhibits, as well as puzzling attempts to connect the town to Margaret Thatcher and Confederate general P.G.T. Beauregard. (Open May-June M-Sa 9am-1pm and 2-5:30pm; July-Sept. M-Sa 9am-6pm, Su 10am-6pm. Free.) **The Kenmare Lace and Design Centre,** above the tourist office, has demonstrations of the Kenmare lace-making technique, invented in 1862 by local nuns and once on the cutting edge of lace technology. (☎42636. Open Mar.-Sept. M-Sa 10am-1pm and 2-5:30pm. Free.) **Seafari Cruises** explores Kenmare Bay's otter and seal colonies, with the off-chance of a whale sighting. (☎83171 for reservations; www.seafariireland.com. 2-3 per day. €20, students €15, teens €12.50, children €10, family €50-55.) The cruises depart from the pier. Take Henry St. out of town and follow the Glengarriff road; turn right just before the bridge. For fishing gear, permits, and info, head to **John O'Hare Fishing Tackle** on Main St. (☎41499. Day permit for fly fishing €5. Open M-W and F-Sa 9:30am-1pm and 2-6pm, Th 9:30am-1pm.)

The Summer Rhapsody Art Festival, in the first week of May, celebrates the visual arts with workshops and exhibitions. (Contact Miranda at ☎086 370 3482 or Fiona at ☎064 41753 for more information.) The performing arts have their day during **Fleadh Cheoil Chiarrai** in the third weekend in June, when traditional Irish music and dance fill the town and spill into the streets. In November, tale-spinners abound at Kenmare's **storytelling weekend.**

DINGLE TOWN (AN DAIGEAN) ☎066

Despite the hordes of tourists (hoping to catch a glimpse of Fungi the Dolphin) that flood the town, the *craic* in Dingle is still home-grown. With fantastic hostels and eateries, a swingin' music scene, and easy access to the most isolated highways of its namesake peninsula, this bayside town draws a mix of travelers, from the well-heeled to the backpack-laden.

▮ TRANSPORTATION

Buses: Buses stop by the harbor, on the Ring rd. behind Garvey's SuperValu. Information available from the Tralee bus station (☎712 3566). **Bus Éireann** runs to: **Ballydavid** (Tu and F 3 per day, €4.80 return); **Ballyferriter** (M-Sa 2 per day, €4.80); **Dunquin** (M-Sa 2 per day, €4.80); **Tralee** (1¼hr.; M-Sa 6 per day, Su 4 per day; €8.60).

Taxis: Kathleen Curran (☎087 254 9649), **Cooleen Cabs** (☎087 248 0008) and **Dingle Co-op Cabs** (☎087 222 5777).

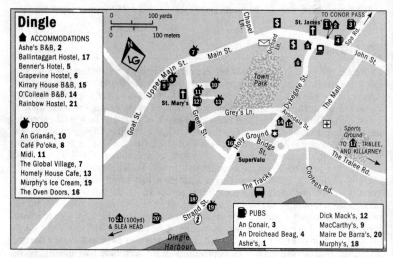

Bike Rental: Foxy John's, Main St. (☎915 1316). €8 per day, €40 per wk. Open M-Sa 9:15am-8pm, Su 11am-8pm. **Paddy's Bike Shop,** Dykegate St. (☎915 2311). €9 per day, €45 per wk.; students €8/€40. Panniers €2 per day. Open Mar.-Oct. 9am-7pm.

◼▪ 🛈 ORIENTATION AND PRACTICAL INFORMATION

The **R559** heads east to Killarney and Tralee, and west to Ventry, Dunquin, and Slea Head. A narrow road runs north through Conor Pass to Stradbally and Castlegregory. Downtown, **Strand Street** flanks the harbor along the marina, while **Main Street** runs parallel to it uphill. **The Mall, Dykegate Street,** and **Green Street** connect the two, running perpendicular to the water. In the eastern part of town, a roundabout splits Strand St. into **The Tracks,** which continue along the water, **The Holy Ground,** which curves up to meet Dykegate St., and the **Tralee Road.**

Tourist Office: Strand St. (☎915 1188). Tries to keep up with scores of dolphin-crazy tourists. Open mid-June to mid-Sept. M-Sa 9am-7pm, Su 10am-5pm; mid-Sept. to mid-June daily 9:30am-5:30pm.

Banks: AIB, Main St. (☎915 1400). Open M 10am-5pm, Tu-F 10am-4pm. **Bank of Ireland,** Main St. (☎915 1100). Same hours. Both have **ATMs.**

Camping Equipment: The Mountain Man, Strand St. (☎915 2400). Sells the informative *Guide to the Dingle Peninsula* (€5.50), which includes walking and cycling maps for specific regions of the peninsula. No tent rental. Open July-Aug. daily 9am-6pm and 7pm-9pm; Sept.-June 9am-6pm.

Laundry: Níolann an Daingin, Green St. (☎915 1837), behind Midi. Wash and dry €10 per load. Open M-Sa 9am-1pm and 2-5:30pm.

Work Opportunities: Dingle's many pubs, restaurants, and takeaways could all use a helping hand. Many restaurants on and around Strand St. hire travelers as short-term employees, especially during the summer. Technically, only EU residents are eligible to work in Ireland without a costly permit, but more informal arrangements are common.

Emergency: ☎999; no coins required. **Police** *(Garda)*: The Holy Ground (☎915 1522).

Pharmacy: O'Keefe's Pharmacy Ltd. (☎915 1310), on The Holy Ground next to the SuperValu. Open M-W and F-Sa 9:30am-6pm, Th 9:30am-1pm, Su 10:30am-12:30pm.

Internet: The **library** (☎915 1499). 50min. free, twice weekly. Call for a spot. Open July-Aug. M-Sa 10am-5pm; Sept.-June Tu-Sa 10am-5pm. **Dingle Internet Cafe,** Main St. (☎915 2478). Leather chairs and cyber space. €2.60 per 30min., €5 per hr. Open May-Sept. M-F 9am-10pm, Sa 10am-8pm, Su 1-6pm; Oct.-Apr. daily 10am-4pm.

Post Office: Upper Main St. (☎915 2091). Just the place for mailing Fungi postcards. Open M-F 9am-5:30pm, Sa 9am-1pm.

ACCOMMODATIONS AND CAMPING

Most of Dingle's hostels are great, but only some are close to town. Accommodations in town and along Dykegate and Strand St. fill up quickly—always call ahead.

Ballintaggart Hostel (IHH), on N86 (☎915 1454). A 25min. walk east of town on the Tralee rd.; the Tralee bus stops here on request. Built in 1703 as a hunting lodge and used as a soup kitchen during the Famine, this grand stone mansion witnessed the strangling of Mrs. Earl of Cork after a poisoning attempt went awry. Her ghost supposedly haunts the enormous bedchambers, enclosed cobblestone courtyard, and elegant, fire-heated common rooms. The stunning views of Dingle's fields and sparkling bay remain phantom-free. Free shuttle to town, 3-5 per day. Laundry €6 and ironing equipment available. 8- to 12-bed dorms €13; 4-bed €20; doubles €48; family rooms €65. **Camping** €11 per small tent. €13 per van. ❶

Cafe Po'oka, Main St. (☎915 0773). Two new hostel rooms above a chill, bohemian restaurant (see **Food,** p. 298). Stylish, immaculate, and blessed with superb showers, these digs rival many a hotel's, and guests can waltz down to the cafe in the morning for a free breakfast. Call the cafe for bookings. €20; singles €25. ❷

Grapevine Hostel, Dykegate St. (☎915 1434), off Main St. Smack in the middle of town and a brief stagger from Dingle's finest pubs. Friendly folks guide guests through the musical, cushy-chaired common room to close but comfy bunk rooms. The Dingle Internet Cafe is but a short stride away. 8-bed dorms €13; 4-bed €15. ❶

Rainbow Hostel (☎915 1044). Take Strand St. west out of town and continue straight through the roundabout for ¼ mi. Jackson Pollock-style interior and camaraderie to spare in the cavernous kitchen. Free lifts to and from town all day in the Rainbow-Mobile. **Bike rental** €6 per day. **Internet** €1 per 10min. Laundry €8. 5- to 12-bed dorms €13; private rooms €14. **Camping** €6.50 per person. ❶

O'Colleain B&B, Dykegate St. (☎915 1937), on the corner of Avondale St. At this ideal retreat in the center of town, the young proprietors and their wee helpers show guests to handsome rooms, all with bath and lovely hardwood floors. Tea and coffee facilities in the sitting room. **Bike rental** €8 per day. €30. ❸

Ashe's B&B, Lower Main St. (☎915 0989). Peer onto Main St., or choose to be creepy and gaze upon the old graveyard. The 4 rooms are tastefully decorated with soft cream colors and antique bureaus. All rooms with impressive baths and TVs. Closest B&B to the pub downstairs. €40; singles €60. ❸

Benner's Hotel, Lower Main St. (☎915 1638). Four-poster beds, antique wood furniture, and chandelier lighting await the weary traveler at this plush, centrally located hotel. Each room has a fireplace, phone, and coffee-making supplies. Baths are blessed with large tubs. Enjoy a meal at the connected restaurant or a drink at the bar. Wheelchair-accessible. Jan.-Mar. and Nov.-Dec. €55-60; Apr. and Oct. €60-67; May-June and Sept. €70-80; July-Aug. €85-102; special children's rates. ❺

Kirrary House B&B, Avondale St. (☎915 1606), off Dykegate St. With pride and good cheer, Mrs. Collins puts up guests in pleasant rooms. Book whirlwind **archaeological tours** with Sciúird Tours, operated by Mr. Collins (see **Sights,** below), or lounge in the garden with tea and cake. **Bike rental** €7.60 per day. €30, with bath €33.50. ❸

FOOD

Dingle is home to a wide range of eateries, from doughnut stands to gourmet seafood restaurants. **SuperValu,** The Holy Ground, stocks a SuperSelection of groceries and juicy tabloids. (☎915 1397. Open June-Aug. M-Sa 8am-10pm, Su 8am-9pm; Sept.-Apr. M-Sa 8am-9pm, Su 8am-7pm.) **An Grianán,** Green St., on the side street before El Toro and Dick Mack's, vends crunchy wholefoods and organic vegetables. (☎915 1910. Open M-F 9:30am-6pm, Sa 10am-6pm.)

🍴 **Cafe Po'oka,** Main St. (☎915 0773). Swish through the beaded curtain into a Bohemian wonderland. Feast like a local on crepes (€3.50-7), fruit with homemade yogurt (€3.50), or all-day breakfasts (€3.50-6.50). Listen to the cheerful staff clutter dishes and croon along to spicy Latin beats and funky down-home blues. Open M-F 10:30am-5pm, Sa-Su 11am-5pm or thereabouts. Luckily, happy diners can stay after the meal is done, thanks to 2 brand new **hostel rooms** upstairs (see **Accommodations,** p. 297). ❷

Midi, Green St., across from the cathedral. Self-described as "Mediterranean food with a touch of the orient," Midi serves veg-friendly fusion fare in a zesty upstairs dining room. Savor the Jamaican fish curry (€12.50) while gazing at the hills. Mains €9.90-14.50, pizzas with salad €7.50-12.50. Open M-Tu and Th-Sa 5:30pm until late. ❸

Murphy's Ice Cream, Strand St. (☎915 2644). American brothers Kieran and Sean scoop scrumptious homemade ice cream (from €2). Cappuccinos €2.50. Open June-Sept. 11am-6pm and 8-10:30pm; mid-Mar. to May 10:30am-6pm. ❶

Homely House Cafe, Green St. (☎915 2431), near the laundrette behind Midi. A perpetually busy cafe, with breezy outdoor seating in the courtyard. Menu divided into "Just a little hungry," "Pretty darn hungry," and "HUNGRY!!!". Mains €4-8.50, depending on hunger level. Open M-Sa noon-5:30pm. ❷

The Oven Doors, The Holy Ground (☎915 1056), across from SuperValu. Tasty pizzas (€6-9), spectacular sundaes (€4.80), and incredible cakes (€3.20) draw mobs to this art-bedecked cafe. Open June-Aug. daily 10am-10pm; Sept.-May 11am-6pm. ❸

The Global Village, Main St. (☎915 2325). A fantastic variety of meals from around the world, several of them veggie-oriented. Swap travel stories with the owner, who collected many of the recipes himself, or enjoy an intimate candlelit dinner with a date. Dinner €13.95-22. Open mid-Mar. to mid-Nov. 5-10pm. ❹

PUBS

Dingle has 52 pubs for 1500 people, and, not surprisingly, many of them cater to tourists. Don't fret—there's still plenty of *craic* to be found in town.

🍺 **Ashe's,** Lower Main St. (☎915 098). Young and old gather in this plush, intimate pub for a friendly evening of drinking, and heart-to-heart in the cozy, back lounge area. During the day, sample their delicious, non-traditional pub food (salads €7.50-9.90, sandwiches €5.20, and wraps €5.95) from 10am-6pm.

An Droichead Beag (The Small Bridge), Lower Main St. (☎915 1723). The most popular pub in town unleashes 363 sessions of trad a year—9:30pm every night and the odd afternoon as well. Numerous nooks nurture conversation. The pool table encourages pub-scale rivalries, while the big-screen TV raises cheers for those more established during the Su matches. Disco F-Sa.

An Conair, Spa Rd. (☎915 2011), off Main St. Word has it that music-minded An Conair hosts the most authentic sessions in town. Subdued local crowd enjoys exceptional trad and lusty ballads. July-Aug. M set dancing; W-Sa trad starting at 9:30pm, Su 5-7pm.

Maire De Barra's, Strand St. (☎915 1215). A mixed-age, largely tourist crowd looking to hear great folk and modern trad. Music nightly in summer, weekends in winter.

Dick Mack's, Green St. (☎915 1960), opposite the church. The proprietor leaps between the bar and leather-tooling bench at "Dick Mack's Bar, Boot Store, and Leather Shop." Shoeboxes and whiskey bottles line the walls. Though heavily touristed, frequent spontaneous sing-alongs indicate enduring local support.

Murphy's, Strand St. (☎915 1450). Ballads and trad resound from this classic pub by the marina. Listen or chat in cozy corners. Music Apr.-Oct. nightly; Nov.-Mar. Sa only.

MacCarthy's, Main St., next to Cafe Po'oka (☎915 1205; www.maccarthypub.com). Lounge area in back provides ample opportunity for spontaneous trad sessions, with locals and tourists mingling and tapping their feet.

🔆 🔼 SIGHTS AND ACTIVITIES

When **Fungi the Dolphin** was first spotted in 1983, the townspeople worried about his effect on the bay's fish population. To say he is now welcome is an understatement, as he single-fipperedly brings in droves of tourists and plenty of cash to his exploiters. **Dolphin Trips** leave to see him from the pier 10:30am-6pm in the summer. (☎915 2626. 1hr. €11, children 12-18 €10, children under 12 €5, free if Fungi gets the jitters and doesn't show.) Watching the antics from the shore east of town is a cheaper, squintier alternative. Walk 2min. down the Tralee road, turn right at the Skellig Hotel, and follow the strand away from town for about 10min. The small beach on the other side of a stone tower is often crowded with Fungi-fanatics. Anti-dolphinites can be coaxed along by the promise of great views on the walk. **Dingle Ocean World,** Strand St., has smaller critters yanked from the sea for your viewing pleasure. Observe fish in an underwater tunnel or pet the skates in the touch tank. (☎915 2111. Tours and feeding shows. Open July-Aug. daily 9am-8:30pm; May-June and Sept. 10am-6pm; Oct.-Apr. 10am-5pm; last admission 30min. before closing. €7.50, students €6, seniors €5.50, children €4.50.)

Acquatic explorers **rent wetsuits** from **Blasket Wetsuit Hire** on Cooleen Rd., just east of town off the Tralee rd. The company also runs **swim trips.** (☎915 1967. Wetsuits day rental €20; swim trips 8-10am, €15, weather permitting.) **Finn McCool's,** Green St., rents **surfboards** with their wetsuits for those who want to surf the nearby beaches (☎915 0833. €35 for adults. Open M-Sa 9am-7pm, Su 11am-5pm). **Dingle Marine Eco-Tours** offers two trips that head in opposite directions along the peninsular coast, granting insights on bay life and views of archeological sites (☎086 285 8802; tours 2-2½hr.). To check out the **Blasket Islands,** board the *Peig Sayers,* named for one of the island's most famous residents, at the Dingle pier. (☎915 1344 or 087 672 6100. 11am, 1, or 3pm; inquire at Dolphin Trips. €30.) The trip to the islands takes 40min., and visitors have a couple hours to hike before being evacuated like the islanders before them. Those willing to risk getting stranded on the island can purchase an overnight package, which includes the boat trip, lodging, dinner, and breakfast (€70). **Deep-sea angling** trips leave daily in summer. (☎915 9947. €30 per half-day, includes equipment and skippered boat.)

The Mountain Man camping store (see **Orientation and Practical Information,** p. 296) sells *The Easy Guide to the Dingle Peninsula* (€5.50), which includes walks, cycling tours, history, and a map. **Sciúird Archaeology Tours** leads a whirlwind bus tour of the area's ancient spots. (☎915 1606 or 915 1937. 3hr., 2 per day, €15. Book ahead.) There are several **Slea Head Tours,** minibus trips highlighting the peninsula's scenery and historic sights (2hr., €15). **Moran's Tours** (☎915 1155 or 086

275 3333) and **O'Connor's Tours** (☎ 087 248 0008) depart from the pier daily at 10am and 2pm. **Dingle Horse Riding** grants the chance to canter on mountain trails and gallop on local beaches. (☎ 915 2199; www.dinglehorseriding.com. 1-1½hr. ride €25; half-day beach ride 10am-2pm, €95; full-day Slea Head ride 10am-4pm, €130.) Summer festivals periodically set the town a-reelin'. A **Folk Concert Series** featuring local and international musicians runs from May to September in St. James Church. (Call Steve Coulter at ☎ 087 982 9728. Performances M, W, F at 7:30-9:30pm. €10 in advance, €12 at the door.) The **Dingle Regatta** hauls in salty dogs on the third Sunday in August. In mid-August, flirt with Lady Luck at the **Dingle Races.** In early September, the **Dingle Music Festival** lures big-name trad groups and other performers from across the musical spectrum. (☎ 915 1983; www.iol.ie/~dingmus.)

VENTRY, SLEA HEAD, AND DUNQUIN ☎ 066

Glorious Slea Head presents a face of jagged cliffs and a hemline of frothy waves. Green hills, interrupted by rough stone walls and occasional sheep, suddenly break off into the foam-flecked sea. Hollywood satisfied its craving for classic Irish beauty and filmed *Ryan's Daughter* and *Far and Away* here, successfully exploiting the scenery's tendency toward the highly dramatic. The most rewarding and unforgettable way to see Slea Head and Dunquin in a day or less is to bike along the predominantly flat Slea Head Drive (R559).

VENTRY (CEANN TRÁ). Less than 4 mi. past Dingle Town toward Slea Head on R559, the village of Ventry contains little more than a sandy beach and the hillside bric-a-brac of **Rahinnane Castle.** While this small ruin is hardly worth peeping into, the ▨**Celtic and Prehistoric Museum,** 2 mi. farther down the road, is a must-see. Trek over slabs of fossilized sea worms from the Cliffs of Moher and past a nest of dinosaur eggs to the main collection, illuminated by guidebooks in eight languages. The 50,000-year-old, fully restored skull and tusks of "Millie," recently recovered off the coast of Holland, make everyone grateful that the last woolly mammoth has shuffled off to that great glacial meadow in the sky. (☎ 915 9191. Open Mar.-Nov. daily 9:30am-5:30pm; other months call ahead. €5, students and seniors €3.50, children €3, family €14.) Near the old castle, ▨**Ballybeag Hostel's ❷** marvelous new facilities and secluded-yet-convenient location make it an ideal place to recharge before exploring the western end of the peninsula. To reach the hostel's massive beds and soothing sitting room, follow signs from the inland turn just past the beach, or hop one of seven free daily shuttles from Dingle Town. Ballybeag was built by an Italian tourist who never ended her vacation to Ventry—guests understand her decision completely. (☎ 915 9876; www.iol.ie/~ballybeag. **Bike rental** €7 per day. Wheelchair-accessible. Laundry €2. Dorms €10; singles €15.)

SLEA HEAD (CEANN SLÉIBHE). Slea Head Drive continues past several Iron Age and early Christian rocks and ruins. Clustered on hillsides over the cliffs, **Dunbeg Fort** and the **Fahan** oratories (beehive-shaped stone huts built by early monks) can be explored for €2, but are visible for free from the road. Slea Head looks out onto the resplendent **Blasket Islands** (see p. 301). Try to pick out the **Sleeping Giant's** profile from among the scattered group. For the best views, locals advise hiking to the top of **Mount Eagle,** which is an easy jaunt from the Ballybeag Hostel (see **Ventry,** above). If rough seas prevent a visit to the Blaskets, or even if they don't, check out the outstanding exhibits at the ▨**Great Blasket Centre,** just outside of Dunquin on the road to Ballyferriter. Thoughtfully designed, the museum evokes the islanders' lost way of life, bringing visitors physically and emotionally closer to the Great Blasket as they descend the long corridor to a glassed-in viewing point. There is also a **cafe**

(meals €6-9; open 10am-5pm) for sandwiches and light lunch. (☎915 6444. Open July-Aug. daily 10am-7pm; Easter-June and Sept.-Oct. 10am-6pm. Last admission 45min. before closing. €3.50, students €1.25, family €8.25.)

DUNQUIN (DÚN CHAOIN). North of Slea Head, the scattered settlement of Dunquin consists of stone houses, a pub, the guttural music of spoken Irish, and no grocery store—stock up in Dingle or in Ballyferriter. At the delightful **⊠Gleann Dearg B&B ❸**, try to tear your eyes away from the Great Blasket long enough to appreciate the homey, spacious rooms and conservatory dining room. Also serves up a splurge-worthy three-course lobster and crab dinner for €30 (weather permitting to bring in the catch). The four-person family suite is a rare find, and the sitting room has a guitar for strumming and a wonderful fireplace. (☎915 6188. Open Apr.-Oct. €28.50; singles €35.) Along the road to Ballyferriter across from the turnoff to the Blasket Centre and right on the **Dingle Way**, the **An Óige Hostel (HI) ❶** offers ocean views from the bunks and limited supplies from the mini-general store. Plan ahead, since reception hours are limited. (☎915 6121. Continental breakfast €3. Sheets €1.30. Reception 9-10am and 5-10pm. Lockout 10am-5pm. May-Oct. 8- to 10-bed dorms €12.50, €10.50 with An Óige membership; 4- to 6-bed €14-14.70/ €12.70; doubles €32/€28. Jan.-Apr. and Nov.-Dec. €1.30-2.50 cheaper.) **Kruger's ❸**, purportedly the westernmost pub in Europe, features pub grub, spontaneous music sessions, and superlative views. (☎915 6127. Mains €6.35-12.70. B&B €27.)

BLASKET ISLANDS (NA BLASCAODAÍ) ☎066

Whether bathed in glorious sunlight or shrouded in impenetrable mist, the islands' magical beauty and aching sense of eternity explain the disproportionately prolific literary output of the final generation to reside there. Six islands comprise the Blaskets: Beginish, Tearaght, Inishnabro, Inishvickillane, Inishtooskert, and Great Blasket. **⊠Great Blasket Island** once supported an austere but proud community of poet-fishermen and storytellers, peaking at 176 inhabitants during WWII. However, the collapse of the fish export market on which islanders depended resulted in a tide of emigration, and the village's future became bleak: as one resident reluctantly predicted, "After us, there will be no more." The islands were evacuated in 1953, after their population dropped below a safely sustainable level. Mainlanders attempted to preserve the dying tradition by sponsoring the autobiographies of Blasket storytellers. The resulting **memoirs** bemoaned the decline of *gaeltacht* life; among them are Maurice O'Sullivan's *Twenty Years A-Growing*, Thomas O'Crohan's *The Islander*, and Peig Sayers' *Peig*. Mists, seals, and occasional fishing boats continue to pass through the Blaskets, but the unique way of life that once thrived there has faded into an inky memory.

A day on Great Blasket cannot be spent better than in uninterrupted rumination. Wander along the white strand, follow grass paths across all four of the island's miles, explore silent stone skeletons of houses clustered in the village, and observe the puffins and seals that populate the shores. The isolated Blaskets have no public litter system; kindly pack out everything you bring here.

Blasket Island Ferries bridge the gap between the Blaskets and Dunquin. (☎915 6422. 20min. Apr.-Oct. daily every 30min. 10:30am-5:30pm, weather permitting; €20 return, students €18.) Keep in mind that if the weather is bad, the boats don't run; people have been stuck here for three weeks during gales. Of course, this may mean coordinating your trip to match a likely gale—we don't blame you. Another boat—the *Peig Sayers*—connects the **Dingle Marina** to Great Blasket Island. (☎915 1344 or 087 672 6100. 35min., every 2hr. €30, children €15.)

A warm bed and a hot drop are available at the **Blasket Island Hostel and Cafe ❶**, up the hill at the top of the old village. The cafe serves basic sandwiches (€3.80-5.10), soup, and sweets whenever the ferries run or guests are staying. Full meals can be had by prior arrangement. Hostelers should expect unparalleled tranquility and simplicity in the unaltered former home of Peig Sayers herself. (☎086 848 6687 or 086 852 2321; www.greatblasketisland.com. Sheets €2.50. Open Apr.-Oct. Dorms €12-18.) The rugged can **camp** on Great Blasket, but like the hostelers, they should come prepared for the rigors of island life as the settlers before did.

BALLYFERRITER (BAILE AN FHEIRTÉARAIGH)   ☎066

Ballyferriter is western Dingle's closest approximation to a town center. The surrounding settlement is an unpolluted *gaeltacht*—you ought to have memorized those Guinness signs by now. The **Chorca Dhuibhne Museum,** in the center of town, brims with photos and text relating to the area's wildlife, archaeology, and folklore. (☎915 6333. Open Apr.-Sept. daily 10am-5pm. €2.50, students €1.50.) The museum represents a noble attempt to make the area's history accessible, and it's a good starting point for visiting nearby ancient sights. From the hostel at the western end of Ballyferriter, signs point to the Iron Age **Dún An Óir** ("Fort of Gold"), where, in 1580, the English massacred over 600 Spanish, Italian, and Irish soldiers engaged in a rebellion against Queen Elizabeth. Many more sites lie along the main road back to Dingle. Closest to Ballyferriter is **Riasc,** a puzzling monastic sight with an engraved standing slab. Heading east, follow signs to **Gallarus Oratory,** a mortarless yet watertight masterpiece of 8th-century stonework that was used for worship. Continue straight on the dirt road to view the sight for free at any hour, or turn left at the signs for the **visitors center** to begin with the 15min. video tour of Dingle's ancient places. (☎915 5333. Oratory always open. Free. Visitors center open Apr. to mid-Oct. daily 9am-9pm. €2.50, students €2, children free.)

For grandeur uncorrupted by hype, take the longer route back to Dingle Town, which passes through **Murreagh** to **Kilmalkédar Church.** The church (*Cill Mhaoilchéadair*) is a remarkably intact 7th-century specimen with blended Romanesque and traditional Irish architectural features. Among the graves overlooking Smerwick Harbour, look for the **ogham stone** (see **Christians and Vikings, p. 57**) and a mysterious **sundial.** Local legend holds that even hapless sinners can ensure entrance to heaven by passing through the rear window of the old church three times consecutively. (Go all the way around, don't cut through the side window—God doesn't like a cheater.)

An Cat Dubh ❶ provides basic rooms 5min. outside town on the Dunquin rd., behind an eponymous shop. (☎915 6286. €12. **Camping** €4 per person.) There are several Ballyferriter B&Bs: next door to the hostel, quiet **An Spéice ❸** provides restful nights and varied breakfasts. (☎915 6254. All rooms with bath. €28.) For a more raucous time, try the **B&B ❸** at the Tigh'n tSaorsaigh Pub (see below). Many visitors head straight for **Tigh Pheig ❸** (Peig's Pub), on Main St. Frequent evening trad sessions in the summer, appetizing meals, and two pool tables keep the locals coming too. (☎915 6433. Daily lunch specials €7.50, dinner mains from €8.90.) Across the street, **Tigh Uí Mhurchú** (Murphy's), with its cushioned stools and attentive bartender, is a perfect place to watch the matches or hear music several times a week. (☎915 6224. Lunch 12:30-3pm. Dinner 6-9pm.) Locals also flock to **Tigh Uí Chathain** for lunch and return for lively banter in the evening. (☎915 6359. Mains €6-9.50. Lunch noon-2:30pm, dinner 6-8:30pm. Open M-Tu and Th-Su.) Stop for pints or a filling meal (mains €5.50-9) at **Tigh'n tSaorsaigh** and perhaps stay the night at the connected **B&B ❸.** (☎915 6344. Open daily 1-9pm. Doubles €50-60.)

NORTHERN DINGLE   ☎066

Hikers and beach junkies alike get their fix on the peninsula's northern shore, far from the tourist bonanza to the south and west. Jaw-dropping views from the mountains motivate casual ramblers to make the daytrip from Dingle Town, while the more serious packers following the Dingle Way enjoy the solitude. The seaside villages, though not destinations in themselves, are all pleasant places to get a meal, a pint, or a night's rest. On Fridays, **Bus Éireann** runs a bus from Tralee to Castlegregory and on to Cloghane. Hitchhiking over the Conor Pass is reportedly common during the tourist season, but always consider the risks.

From Dingle Town, a winding cliff road runs north through the **Conor Pass,** which at 1500 ft. is the highest mountain pass in Ireland. Buses won't fit on the narrow road, but cars squeeze through, and superstar bikers and walkers huff-and-puff it past valley views on 3 mi. of continuous incline. Bikers and hikers should be wary of inclement weather; low visibility and strong winds can make the trip hazardous. The road crests at **Brandon Ridge,** and transportation tribulations are rewarded with dazzling views. On clear days, visitors can gaze awestruck at lakes thousands of feet below, even at distant **Valentia Island** (see p. 285) off the south coast across the peninsula and the **Maharee Islands** to the north. As the road twists down, a small waterfall and a few picnic tables mark the base of **Pedlars Lake,** named in honor of a traveling tradesman who lost his wares (and his life) to a gang of brigands. These days, a pedlar is more likely to encounter geologists than bandits roaming the glacier-sliced lakes and boulder-pocked landscape.

CLOGHANE (AN CLOCHÁN) AND BRANDON (BRÉANAINN). Beyond the lake, the road heads downhill to the sea. Signs point out the westward fork to **Cloghane** (Claw-hane) and its even smaller northern neighbor, **Brandon.** These quiet hamlets are good starting points for hiking up the 3127 ft. **Mt. Brandon** or tackling the seldom-trod but magnificent region to the north that culminates in **Brandon Point.** Pick up maps of the area in the **tourist office** on the main road in Cloghane; the staff is a joy to converse with. (☎713 8277. Open June to mid-Sept. Hours limited and sporadic—usually daily 10am-2pm and 2-4pm, or thereabouts; call ahead or go to the post office down the street.) Each July 25, the devout head up the "Saint's Road" on Mt. Brandon, which was misnamed in honor of alleged trailblazer and Holy Wandering Spirit St. Brendan. The rest of the year, the **Pilgrim's Route,** which forks off the Dingle Way west of Ventry and rejoins it in Cloghane, attracts hikers who prefer ancient Christian sites and inland ridges to coastal rambles. The 4hr. hike passes glassy lakes, standing stones, and an alleged former sacrificial stone.

Whether you've just conquered the mountain, are preparing for the trek, or prefer to savor a good novel or film from a perch by the sea, ■**Mount Brandon House Walking Lodge ❶** leaves little (or nothing) to be desired. Stretch those weary legs in the glassed-in sitting room and watch the tide recede, or curl up on the massive couch and pop in a video from the small but excellent collection. (☎713 8299; www.mountbrandonhostel.com. Wheelchair-accessible. Laundry €4. Family rooms available. 3- to 6-bed dorms €15-16; singles €23-25; doubles €34-36.) The lively **Tigh Tomsi ❷** pub serves hot meals next door (☎713 8301. Open M-Sa noon-1am, Su noon-11pm; music Su in summer), while **The Coffee Shop ❶,** attached to the front of the hostel, dishes up delightful soups, sandwiches (€2.70-4), snacks (€3.50), and breakfast. (Open "9am-5ish.")

STRADBALLY (STRAID BAILE). Six miles east of Cloghane, Stradbally's quiet **Conor Pass Hostel (IHH) ❶** has a few small beds. (☎713 9179. Open mid-Mar. to mid-Oct. €13.) The hostel makes a good base for hikes in the **Slieve Mish Mountains** to the east. The 2713 ft. ascent to **Cáherconree** culminates in a lookout over the Shannon Estuary, the Iveragh, and the Atlantic. Stradbally is also an excellent starting point for the **Loch a'Duín** nature and archaeology walk. (Map guides available in area tourist offices and gift shops.) Stradballyans stock up at **Tomásin's Pub and Restaurant ❸,** across from the hostel. (☎713 9179. Lunch €5-9.25, served noon-4pm; dinner €10.75-17, served 6-9pm.) For a surprisingly varied selection of whole foods and organic produce, stop at **An Siopa** 100 yd. down the road to the west. (☎713 9483. Open mid-Mar. to mid-Oct. Tu-Su 10am-7pm.) Take picnics to Stradbally's **beach;** the strand beyond the dune is especially magnificent at low tide.

CASTLEGREGORY (CAISLEAN CHRIARE). In Castlegregory, 1½ mi. north of the main road, lies the only real grocery store in northern Dingle and more than a fair share of the excitement. Residents and visitors take advantage of the unrelenting winds along the narrow, sandy **Maharees Peninsula,** stretching into the sea north of the village, where wetsuited windsurfers show off for sunbathers. The conditions so pleased competitors in the 2000 **Windsurfing World Championships** that the event seems to have settled on Castlegregory as its permanent venue, returning each October. Strive to stay afloat with gear rented from **Jamie Knox** (☎713 9411) or **Waterworld** (☎713 9292), both located on the waterfront with similar services at similar prices. (Wetsuits €5 per hr.; kayaking and canoeing €6; windsurfing €20; snorkeling €5 per hr.; ski and wakeboarding €50 for 30 min.) Gallop on horseback through the surf of the Maharees beaches courtesy of **O'Connor's Trekking** (☎066 713 9216), or lower your handicap at **Castlegregory Golf and Fishing Club** (☎713 9444. €25 for 18 holes. Clubs €6.) The **Maharees Regatta** hits the waves in early July, and a week or two later the **Summer Festival** rouses the town with parades and dances.

A bus connects Castlegregory to Tralee six days a week (€5.40). The small but informative **tourist office** is next to Spar Market. (☎713 9422. Open M-F 9:30am-5pm, Sa-Su 1-5pm.) For a bare-bones night's rest (i.e. bring your own sheets), try **Fitzgerald's Euro-Hostel ❶,** above the pub at the junction between the main road and the route to Maharees—not to be confused with the town's other two eponymous pubs. (☎713 9133. Dorms €12; doubles €24.) For a more luxurious experience, feel like royalty at the spacious **Castle House B&B ❸,** 50 yd. down the Maharees rd. from the village. Soak in the bath or stroll down their private beach before choosing from the extensive breakfast menu. (☎713 9183. All rooms with bath and TV. €30.) Pitch a tent just steps from the popular watersports spots at **Sandy Bay Caravan Park ❶.** There's also a **restaurant** with barbeque fare and a shop stocked with basic necessities. (☎713 9338. Laundry €4. Restaurant open M-F 4pm-midnight, Sa-Su noon-midnight. Shop open daily 8:30-9pm. €8-10 per small tent.) **Spar Market** is an oasis in otherwise grocery-free terrain. (☎713 9433. Open daily 8:30am-9pm.) **Barry's Village Bistro ❷,** just before the Spar, is a great spot for burgers and pizza, topped off with homemade apple pie. (☎713 9214. Burgers €6.50, fish and chicken from €8.50.) **Ned Natterjack's,** named for the area's rare and vocal Natterjack toad, has a wide range of music and a hoppin' beer garden. (☎713 9491. Music F-Su.)

TRALEE (TRÁ LÍ)   ☎066

Tralee lacks true village charm. As the economic and residential capital (pop. 20,000) of Kerry, it offers little appeal to the long-term visitor. Still, large storefronts line the city's main streets, and quality pubs serve bar food and trad. Ireland's second-largest museum, detailing the history of Kerry, stands out, but no tourist development could possibly top the city's famed gardens. The annual **Rose of Tralee** is a centuries-old pageant that has Irish eyes glued to their TVs in August.

▐ TRANSPORTATION

Airport: Kerry Airport, in **Farranfore** (☎976 4966), off N22 halfway between Tralee and Killarney. (See **Killarney,** p. 273.)

Trains: Oakpark Rd. (☎712 3522). Ticket office open daily before departures. Trains to: **Cork** (2½hr.; M-Sa 5 per day, Su 3 per day; €25); **Dublin** (4hr.; M-Sa 4 per day, Su 3 per day; €51.50); **Galway** (5-6hr., 3 per day, €51.50); **Killarney** (40min., 4 per day, €7.50); **Rosslare Harbour** (5½hr., M-Sa 1 per day, €51.50); **Waterford** (4hr., M-Sa 1 per day, €40).

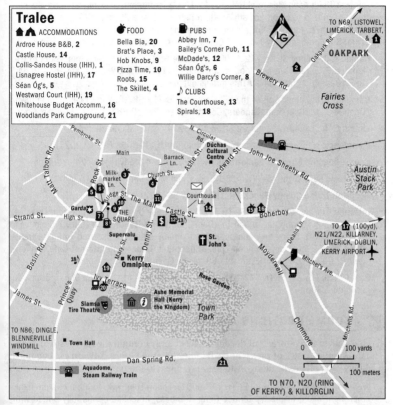

Tralee

⌂⌂ ACCOMMODATIONS
Ardroe House B&B, **2**
Castle House, **14**
Collis-Sandes House (IHH), **1**
Lisnagree Hostel (IHH), **17**
Séan Óg's, **5**
Westward Court (IHH), **19**
Whitehouse Budget Accomm., **16**
Woodlands Park Campground, **21**

🍅 FOOD
Bella Bia, **20**
Brat's Place, **3**
Hob Knobs, **9**
Pizza Time, **10**
Roots, **15**
The Skillet, **4**

🍺 PUBS
Abbey Inn, **7**
Bailey's Corner Pub, **11**
McDade's, **12**
Séan Óg's, **6**
Willie Darcy's Corner, **8**

♪ CLUBS
The Courthouse, **13**
Spirals, **18**

Buses: Oakpark Rd. (☎ 712 3566). Open June-Aug. M-Sa 8:30am-6pm, Su 8:30am-4pm; Sept.-May M-Sa 9am-5:15pm. To: **Bantry** (2½hr., June-Sept. 2 per day, €13.50); **Cork** (2½hr.; M-Sa 14 per day, Su 10 per day; €14); **Dingle** (1¼hr.; July-Aug. M-Sa 6 per day, Su 5 per day; Sept.-June M-Sa 4 per day, Su 2 per day; €8.60); **Galway**, via **Tarbert Ferry**, (M-Sa 11 per day, Su 9 per day; €17); **Killarney** (40min.; June-Sept. M-Sa 14 per day, Su 12 per day; Oct.-May M-Sa 5 per day, Su 6 per day; €5.85); **Limerick** (2¼hr., 9 per day, €13.20); **Skibbereen** (3hr., June-Sept. 2 per day, €16).

Taxis: Cabs park at the intersection of Denny St. and the Mall. Generally €1.30 per mi., less for long distances.

Bike Rental: O'Halloran, 83 Boherboy (☎ 712 2820). €10 per day, €50 per wk. Helmet €1.50 per day. Open M-Sa 9:30am-1pm and 2-6pm.

✳🛈 ORIENTATION AND PRACTICAL INFORMATION

Tralee's streets are hopelessly knotted; travelers should arm themselves with free maps from the tourist office. The main avenue—variously called **the Mall,** as it passes **the Square, Castle Street,** and **Boherboy**—has stores and restaurants along its roughly east-west path. **Edward Street** connects this main thoroughfare to the stations. Wide **Denny Street** runs south to the tourist office and park.

Tourist Office: Ashe Memorial Hall (☎712 1288), at the end of Denny St. From the station, head into town on Edward St., turn right on Castle St., then left onto Denny St. Well-informed, friendly staff provides free maps and such. Open July-Aug. M-Sa 9am-7pm, Su 9am-6pm; May-June and Oct. M-Sa 9am-6pm; Nov.-Apr. M-F 9am-5pm.

Banks: AIB, Denny St. (☎712 1100), at Castle St. Open daily 9am-6pm. **Bank of Ireland** (☎712 1177), a few doors down. Open M 10am-5pm, W 10:30am-4pm, Tu and Th-F 10am-4pm. Both have **ATMs** throughout town.

Camping Equipment: Call of the Wild, Ivy Terr. (☎712 3820). Widest selection in town. Open M-Sa 9:30am-6pm. **Landers,** Courthouse Ln. (☎712 6644). Open M-F 9am-6pm.

Laundry: The Laundry, Pembroke St. (☎712 3214). Open M-F 9am-6pm.

Emergency: ☎999; no coins required. **Police** *(Garda)*: High St. (☎712 2022).

Counseling and Support: Samaritans (☎712 2566), 44 Moyderwell. 24hr. hotline.

Pharmacy: Kelly's, the Mall (☎712 1302). Open M-Sa 9am-6pm.

Hospital: Tralee County General Hospital (☎712 6222), off the Killarney Rd.

Internet: Library, Moyderwell St. (☎712 1200). Book by phone or in person. Open M, W, F and Sa 10am-5pm; Tu and Th 10am-8pm. **White Rabbit Web Cafe,** 7 Church St. (☎719 4009). Shiny new computers and yummy edibles make web-surfing a treat. Open M-Sa 9am-10pm, Su noon-7pm. **Millennium Games and Internet Cafe,** Ivy Terr. (☎712 0020). €4 per hr., students €3 per hr. Open M-Sa 10am-6pm.

Post Office: Edward St. (☎712 1013), off Castle St. Open M and W-Sa 9am-5:30pm, Tu 9:30am-5:30pm.

⌂ ACCOMMODATIONS AND CAMPING

Tralee's several scattered but decent hostels barely contain the rosy festival-goers in late August. Rows of pleasant B&Bs line the area where Edward St. becomes Oakpark Rd.; others lie along Princes Quay, close to the park.

Westward Court (IHH), Mary St. (☎718 0081). Follow Denny St. to the park; turn right, then right again at the Ivy Terrace Diner. Spotless, hotel-like dorms fully armed with baths, bureaus, desks, and quality showers are a pleasant change from the average hostel. Wheelchair-accessible. Continental breakfast included. Laundry €6. Curfew 3am. 4-bed dorms €16.50; singles €24; doubles €44. ❷

The Whitehouse Budget Accommodation and B&B, Boherboy St. (☎710 2780; www.whitehousetralee.com). Though slightly pricier than the average hostel, the incredibly clean rooms, hardwood floors, TVs, and quality showers stretch a few extra euros to the extreme. Spacious pub downstairs with wicked pool tables, big-screen TV, and trad Th night. Wheelchair-accessible. Dorms €19; singles €30; doubles €50. ❷

Ardroe House B&B, Oakpark Rd. (☎712 6050). The ivy facade of this delightful B&B hints at the charm inside. Great amenities and care to detail make it worth the price. Open mid-May to mid-Sept. €25; singles €40. ❷

Collis-Sandes House (IHH), Oakpark Rd. (☎712 8658). Near-perfect, but far from town and sometimes booked solid. Follow Oakpark Rd. (N69) 1 mi. from town, take the 1st left after Spar, and follow signs another ½ mi. to the right; or call for pickup. Magnificent high ceilings and Moorish arches lend grandeur to this ex-convent. Free rides to town, 5 per day. Wheelchair-accessible. Laundry €5 wash, €5 dry. 8- to 14-bed dorms €12; 4- to 6-bed €14. Singles €25; doubles €38. **Camping** €6.50 per person. ❶

Seán Óg's, 41 Bridge St. (☎712 8822). This centrally located B&B has 14 rooms above a traditional pub. Friendly service and an easy crawl to bed after several pints. €25. ❸

Castle House, 27 Upper Castle St. (☎712 5167). Watch satellite TV in a fully-loaded room and listen to the traffic pass. Ideally located for pub crawls; morning pancakes ease even the worst hangovers. €20-25. ❹

Lisnagree Hostel (IHH), Ballinorig Rd. (☎712 7133). 1 mi. from town, near the train station. Follow Boherboy St. out of town—it's on the left fork after the traffic circle. Great for couples and kids, but remote for those hitting the pubs at night. Dorms €13; singles €20; doubles €32; family room €12 per person. ❶

Woodlands Park Campground, Dan Spring Rd. (☎712 1235), a ¼ mi. past the Aquadome. National award-winner. Game room and shop. Wash €4.50, dry €4.50. Open Apr.-Sept. €15 for 2 people in a tent with car, €13 without car. Showers €1. ❶

◖ FOOD

True gourmands may be disappointed with the culinary landscape of Tralee, but pub grub and fast food are readily available, and the massive **Tesco** in the Square is a boon for cooks and snack-seekers. (☎712 1110. Open M-Sa 8am-10pm, Su 10am-8pm.) Across the street, **Seancar** peddles wholefoods and organic produce. (☎712 2644. Open M-W and Sa 9am-6pm, Th 9am-8pm, F 9am-9pm.)

The Skillet, Barrack Ln. (☎712 4561), off the Mall. Red walls and traditional decor match the tasty regional specialties at this welcoming restaurant. Lunch €7.50-9.50; steak dinner from €14.50. Open M-Sa 10:30am-10pm; Apr.-Sept. also Su 1-10pm. ❸

Hob Knobs, the Square (☎712 1846). This low-key cafeteria brushes elbows with tasty breakfasts (large Irish €5) and shoots the breeze with decent lunches (€4.45-6). Open M-Sa 8am-5pm; July-Aug. until 9pm. ❷

Roots, 76 Boherboy (☎712 2665). A limited but ever-changing menu of gargantuan vegetarian dishes. Watch them prepare your meal or relax at one of 5 tables in this cozy establishment. Open M-Sa 11am-3:30pm. ❷

Brat's Place, 18 Milk Market Ln., down a pedestrian walkway off the Mall. A veg-head's dream. Lunch on local and organic ingredients in a pleasant, private setting. Soup €3, mains €7, desserts €3.50. Open M-Sa 12:30-2:30pm, later if the food lasts. ❷

My Mo, the Square (☎718 5388). This friendly, centrally located cafe is a pleasant and economical retreat from the hubbub of Tralee. Sandwiches €2.80-4, house specials €4.20-5. Open June-Sept. M-Sa 8:30am-6pm; Oct.-May until 5pm. ❶

Bella Bia, Ivy Terr. (☎714 4896). A taste of Italy, with 3 courses for only €12.90. 12" pizzas €9-14. Open daily 5pm until late. ❸

Pizza Time, the Square (☎712 6317). No pretense, just high quality eats at low prices. Pizzas €7-10, pasta €8-9, burgers €5.75. Delivery available 6pm-midnight. Open M-Th and Su 1pm-midnight, F noon-1am, Sa noon-1am. ❷

◪◪ PUBS AND CLUBS

Seán Óg's, 41 Bridge St. (☎712 8822). Plenty of room to chat up other patrons in this classic pub. Mike and JP serve as drinking consultants and pass out toasted sandwiches and snacks between pints. Impressive fireplace (hand-built by the owner) keeps pubbers and snugglers warm on long winter nights. Trad Tu, W, F, and Su. Comfy **B&B** beds upstairs facilitate long nights at the bar (see **Accommodations,** p. 306).

Abbey Inn, Bridge St. (☎712 3390), across from Seán Óg's. Edgy crowd comes to hear live rock most weekends. Bono swept here—when U2 played the Abbey in the late 70s, the manager made them sweep up to pay for their drinks because he thought they were so bad. Young late-nighters spend more time scoping than drinking or dancing. Live music Th, Su; DJ other nights. Open M-Sa until 2:30am, Su 1am. Food 9am-9:30pm.

Willie Darcy's Corner, the Square (☎712 4343). Just over 2 years old and pure class. All ages meet here over candlelit tables. Genial conversation takes the place of music. Soups and sandwiches served 12:30-2:30pm.

Bailey's Corner Pub (☎712 6230), at Ashe and the Mall. Kerry's rugby legacy adorns the walls. Current players join an older crowd at the bar. Munch on sandwiches and a variety of hot food (€3-6.50) while watching matches. Trad M-W and Su.

McDade's, Upper Castle St. (☎712 1877). Part of the Quality Tralee Hotel, this immense, polished pub attracts a slightly older, touristy crowd. Fills late when folks come to grind in the club **The Courthouse** (see below).

Spirals, Princes Quay (☎712 3333), located in the Brandon Hotel. One of Tralee's two nightclubs, Spirals spins the disco ball every F and Sa night. Cover €8.

The Courthouse, Upper Castle St. (☎712 1877), behind McDade's Pub. The 2nd of Tralee's 2 nightclubs, the Courthouse keeps the crowds groovin' F-Sa. Cover €10-12.

👁 🌿 SIGHTS AND FESTIVALS

Tralee is home to Ireland's second-largest museum, **⊠Kerry the Kingdom,** in Ashe Memorial Hall on Denny St. One of the perennial favorites for museum awards, the Kingdom marshals all the resources of display technology to narrate the county's history from 8000 BC to the present. Vivid dioramas and videos on everything from Kerry's castles to her greatest Gaelic football victories captivate budding historians. Downstairs, "Geraldine Tralee" leads visitors through a superb recreation of medieval city streets. Enjoy the shouts and clamor of yesteryear as life-sized townspeople go about their daily activities. The museum hosts a special exhibition each year with contributions from museums around the world, exploring topics from the wilds of Antarctica to the French Revolution. (☎712 7777. Open mid-Mar. to Oct. daily 9:30am-6pm; Nov. noon-4:30pm. Free audio tours in French and German; last admission for tour 4:30pm. €8, students €6.50, children €5, family €22.) Across from the museum, another of Ireland's "second-largests"—the **Town Park**—blooms in summer with the **Roses of Tralee.** Nearby, the stained glass at **St. John's Church,** Castle St., is worth a peek, though gray carpeting dampens the echo and Gothic mood.

Just down the Dingle road is the **Blenneville Windmill and Visitors Centre,** the largest operating windmill in the British Isles. The small museum recalls Blenneville during the Famine, when it was Kerry's main port of emigration, focusing on the "coffin ships" that carried Ireland's sons and daughters to distant shores. A 10min. audio-visual presentation covers the region's history and the windmill's restoration. For €10, visitors can search databases to discover when their ancestors migrated on those infamous "coffin ships." (☎712 1064. Open Apr.-Oct. daily 10am-6pm. €5, students €4, children €2.50, family €12.50.) The building on the Princes Quay traffic circle looks like a hybrid Gothic castle and space-age solarium, but it's actually Tralee's €6-million **Aquadome,** complete with whirlpools, steam room, sauna, and gym. Waterslides and a mini-golf course entertain even the most demanding wee ones. (☎712 8899; www.discoverkerry.com/aquadome. Open daily 10am-10pm. June-Sept. €9, children €8; Oct.-May €8/€7. Aquagolf €4.50/€3.50.) **Tralee & Dingle Railway,** restored to its days of wine and roses, runs the 2 mi. between the Aquadome and the Blenneville complex. (☎712 1064. Trains leave July-Aug. from the Aquadome every hour on the hour and the windmill on the half-hour 10:30-4:30pm; May-June and Sept. 11am-3:30pm. Call in advance. Closed M. €5, students €4, children €3, family €15.)

The **Siamsa Tíre Theatre,** at the end of Denny St. next to the museum, is Ireland's national folk theater. Its brilliant summer programs depict traditional Irish life through mime, music, and dance. Various touring productions come through from

October to April. (☎712 3055; www.siamsatire.com. Performances July-Aug. M-Sa; May-June and Sept. M-Th and Sa. May-Sept. shows start at 8:30pm; Oct.-Apr. 6pm. Box office open M-Sa 9am-8pm. Tickets from €17; group rate from €14.)

Lovely lasses of Irish descent flood the town during the last week of August for the beloved **Rose of Tralee Festival.** A maelstrom of entertainment surrounds the main event, culminating in a "personality" contest to earn the coveted title "Rose of Tralee." Rose-hopefuls or spectators can call the Rose Office in Ashe Memorial Hall (☎712 1322; www.roseoftralee.com). As if the live music on every street corner and a four-day party weren't enough, the festival is followed by the **Tralee Races,** and another four days of revelry.

TARBERT (TAIRBEART)   ☎068

A tiny, peaceful seaside spot on N69 in Kerry, Tarbert is home to an incredible hostel and convenient ferry between Co. Kerry and Clare. The boat ride avoids an 85 mi. coastal drive through Limerick. **Bus Éireann** stops outside the hostel on its way from Tralee to Doolin and Galway (5hr.; mid-June to Sept. M-Sa 3 per day, Su 2 per day; Galway to Tralee €19). During the rest of the year, the nearest stop to Tarbert is in Kilrush. **Shannon Ferry Ltd.** makes the Shannon crossing from the port a mile between Tarbert and Killimer. (☎065 905 3124. June-Aug. every 30min., Apr.-Sept. 7:30am-9:30pm, Oct.-Mar. 7am-7:30pm.; 20min.; every hour on the half-hour from Tarbert and on the hour from Killimer; Su year-round from 10am; €12.50 per carload, €3 per pedestrian or biker.) A **bus** leaves from the Tarbert ferry terminal and goes to Kilrush; check at the hostel for a schedule (☎036 500; M-Sa 2-3 per day, Su 2 per day). The **tourist office** is in the carefully restored 1831 Bridewell Jail and Courthouse; walk down the street from the hostel and turn right onto the road toward the ferry. (Open Apr.-Oct. daily 10am-6pm. Tours €5, students €3.50.) Be sure to get cash before visiting; the nearest **ATM** is 15 mi. away in Listowel.

A few hundred yards from the ferry stands **Tarbert House,** which has been home to the family of Signeur Leslie of Tarbert since 1690. The recently restored exterior rivals the period pieces and priceless art it protects. (☎036 198. Open daily 10am-noon and 2-4pm. €2. Tours given by Mrs. Leslie herself.) The 1hr. **Tarbert House Woodland Walk** takes ramblers through Leslie's Wood, with views of the River Shannon, Tarbert Old Pier, and Tarbert Bay. The path is marked and begins next to the tourist office. The ▓**Ferry House Hostel ❶** is the central, 4-year-old occupant of a 200-year-old building, located at the intersection of the town's two roads. The friendly owners spent a year traveling and taking detailed notes on the best and worst of the world's hostels before opening their own. The success of their study is evident in the cushy bedding, excellent showers, and cafe. (☎36555. Wheelchair-accessible. Sheets €1.30. Laundry €5.10. Open year-round. Cafe open June-Sept. Reception May-Sept. 8am-7pm. Dorms €8.90; doubles €25-33.) **Coolahan's** is the most notable of Tarbert's five pubs, a little establishment with regulars speaking English and Irish at the bar. Drop down to **The Anchor,** half a block up the hill from the hostel, for a light seafood chowder and live music Saturday nights.

LIMERICK (LUIMNEACH)   ☎061

Despite a thriving trade in off-color poems, Limerick City has long endured a bad reputation. Its 18th-century Georgian streets and parks are both regal and elegant, but 20th-century industrial and commercial developments cursed the city with a featureless urban feel. During much of the 20th century, economic hardship spawned poverty and crime, earning the city the nickname "Stab Town." The little attention Limerick received seemed to focus on squalor—exemplified in Irish-

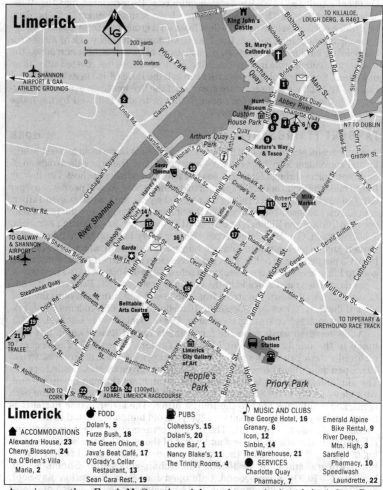

Limerick

TO KILLALOE, LOUGH DERG, & R463

King John's Castle

St. Mary's Cathedral

0   200 yards
0   200 meters

Thomond Br.

Priory Park

TO SHANNON AIRPORT & GAA ATHLETIC GROUNDS

Ennis Rd.

Clancy's Strand

Merchant's Quay

Abbey River

Georges Quay

N7 TO DUBLIN

Hunt Museum

Custom House Park

Arthurs Quay Park

Nature's Way & Tesco

Savoy Cinema

TO GALWAY & SHANNON AIRPORT – N18

N. Circular Rd.

River Shannon

The Shannon Bridge

Milk Market

TAXI

Garda

Steamboat Quay

Dock Rd.

Belltable Arts Centre

TO TRALEE

Limerick City Gallery of Art

Colbert Station

TO TIPPERARY & GREYHOUND RACE TRACK

People's Park

Priory Park

N20 TO CORK

St. Alphonsus

TO 23 & 24 (100yd), ADARE, LIMERICK RACECOURSE

Limerick

ACCOMMODATIONS
Alexandra House, **23**
Cherry Blossom, **24**
Ita O'Brien's Villa Maria, **2**

FOOD
Dolan's, **5**
Furze Bush, **18**
The Green Onion, **8**
Java's Beat Café, **17**
O'Grady's Cellar Restaurant, **13**
Sean Cara Rest., **19**

PUBS
Clohessy's, **15**
Dolan's, **20**
Locke Bar, **1**
Nancy Blake's, **11**
The Trinity Rooms, **4**

MUSIC AND CLUBS
The George Hotel, **16**
Granary, **6**
Icon, **12**
Sinbin, **14**
The Warehouse, **21**

SERVICES
Charlotte Quay Pharmacy, **7**

Emerald Alpine Bike Rental, **9**
River Deep, Mtn. High, **3**
Sarsfield Pharmacy, **10**
Speediwash Laundrette, **22**

American author Frank McCourt's celebrated memoir *Angela's Ashes*. But despite the historical and literary stigma, Limerick is now a city on the rise. A large student population fosters a strong arts scene, adding to a wealth of long unnoticed cultural treasures. Additionally, the Republic's third largest city boasts top quality museums and a well-preserved 12th-century cathedral.

▐ TRANSPORTATION

Trains: (☎315 555). Help desk open M-Sa 9am-5:30pm. Trains to: **Cork** (2½hr.; M-Sa 6 per day, Su 5 per day; €19.50); **Dublin** (2hr.; M-Sa 10 per day, Su 7 per day; €36.50); **Ennis** (M-Sa 2 per day, €7.50); **Killarney** (2½hr.; M-Sa 5 per day, Su 3 per day; €21.50); **Rosslare** (3½hr., M-Sa 1 per day, €17.50); **Tralee** (3hr.; M-Sa 5 per day, Su 3 per day; €21.50); **Waterford** (2hr.; summer M-Sa 2 per day, winter 1 per day; €15).

Buses: Colbert Station, off Parnell St. (☎313 333). Open June-Sept. M-F 8:10am-6pm, Su 9am-6pm; Oct.-May M-Sa 8:10am-6pm, Su 3-7pm. **Bus Éireann** sends buses to: **Cork** (2hr., 14 per day, €13.20); **Derry** (6½hr., 3 per day, €24); **Donegal** (6hr., 4 per day, €22); **Dublin** (3½hr., 13 per day, €14.50); **Ennis** (45min., 14 per day, €7.50); **Galway** (2hr., 14 per day, €13.20); **Kilkenny** (1½hr., 3 per day, €14.50); **Killarney** (2½hr.; M-Sa 6 per day, Su 3 per day; €13.50); **Tralee** (2hr., 8 per day, €13.20); **Waterford** (2½hr., 7 per day, €14.50); **Wexford** and **Rosslare Harbour** with some buses to meet departing ferries (4hr., 3-4 per day, €18.50). **Local buses** run to the suburbs from the city center (M-Sa 2 per hr. 7:30am-11pm, Su 1 per hr. 10:30am-11:20pm; €1.10); #2 and 8 access the university; #6 and 305 follow the Ennis rd.

Taxis: Top Cabs (☎417 417). Most city destinations under €3.80; to airport about €20.

Bike Rental: Emerald Alpine, 1 Patrick St. (☎416 983). €70-100 per wk. Credit card number as security deposit. Return to any participating Raleigh location for an additional €25. Open M-F 9:15am-1pm and 2-5:30pm, Sa 9:15am-5:30pm.

ORIENTATION

Limerick's streets form a grid, bounded by the **Shannon River** to the west and the **Abbey River** to the north. The city's most active area lies in the blocks around **O'Connell Street,** which becomes **Patrick Street,** then **Rutland Street** to the north, and **the Crescent** to the south. Follow O'Connell St. north past Hunt Museum and cross the Abbey River to reach **King's Island,** where St. Mary's Cathedral and King John's Castle loom over the landscape. The city itself is easily navigable on foot, but the preponderance of one-way streets makes it a nightmare for drivers.

🛈 PRACTICAL INFORMATION

Tourist Office: Arthurs Quay (☎361 555; www.shannonregiontourism.ie), in the space-age glass building. From the station, follow Davis St. as it becomes Glentworth; turn right on O'Connell St., then left at Arthurs Quay Mall. Free city maps and info on the region. Open July-Aug. M-F 9am-6pm, Sa-Su 9:30am-5:30pm; May-June and Sept. M-Sa 9:30am-5:30pm; Nov.-Apr. M-F 9:30am-5:30pm, Sa 9:30am-1pm.

Budget Travel Office: usit (☎415 064), O'Connell St. at Glentworth St., issues ISICs and **TravelSave** stamps. Open M-W and F 9:30am-6:30pm, Th 9:30am-8pm, Sa 9:30am-5pm. **Budget Travel,** 2 Sarsfield St. (☎414 666). Open M-F 9am-6pm.

Banks: Bank of Ireland (☎415 055) and **AIB** (☎414 388) are among the many banks on O'Connell St. Both have **ATMs** and are open M 10am-5pm, Tu-F 10am-4pm.

Camping Equipment: River Deep, Mountain High, 7 Rutland St. (☎400 944). O'Connell St. becomes Rutland St. as it approaches the Abbey River. Open M-Sa 9:30am-6pm.

Luggage Storage: Bus/Train Station (☎217 331). €2.50 per item per day. 24hr. limit. Open M-F 8am-6pm and 6:30-8:30pm, Sa 8am-6pm, Su 10am-6pm.

Laundry: Speediwash (☎319 380), 11 Gerard St. Full service from €8. Open M-F 10am-6pm, Sa 10am-4pm. **Launderette** (☎312 712), on Mallow St. Full service from €9. Open M-F 9am-6pm, Sa 9am-5pm. No self-service launderettes in town.

Emergency: ☎999; no coins required. **Police** *(Garda)*: Henry St. (☎414 222).

Pharmacy: Charlotte Quay Pharmacy, Charlotte Quay (☎400 722). Open daily 9am-9:30pm. **Sarsfield Pharmacy** (☎413 808), at the corner of Sarsfield and Liddy St., around the corner from tourist office, has later hours.

Hospital: Regional (☎ 301 111). Follow O'Connell St. south past the Crescent.

Internet: Euro@Surf, Todds Bow (☎ 404 040), off Cruise St. Ridiculously low rates. €1 per hr., €2 per 3hr. Open M-Sa 10am-10pm, Su noon-8pm. **White Rabbit Web Cafe,** 15 Thomas St. (☎ 310 407). Delicious food alone justifies a visit. €1.50 per 15min., €4 per hr. 10% student discount. Open M-Sa 9am-10pm, Su noon-7pm. **Surfers Cafe,** 1 Upper William St. (☎ 440 122), uphill from O'Connell St. Tea and coffee available. Internet €5 per hr., students €3. Calls to Australia, Canada, Europe, UK, and US €0.10 per min. Open M-Sa 9am-10pm, Su noon-9pm.

Post Office: Lower Cecil St. (☎ 315 777), off O'Connell St. Open M-Sa 9am-5:30pm, Tu open 9:30am.

ACCOMMODATIONS

Limerick suffered from a series of hostel closures in 2002. Lured by government funding, many of those still operating fill their rooms with long-term residents (most political asylum seekers), and permanent "no vacancies" signs hang on their doors; others house university students for the majority of the year. Smaller private budget accommodations are beginning to fill the gap, including a promising row of mid-market B&Bs on southern O'Connell St. and some more rural options lining Ennis road (over Sarsfield bridge).

Alexandra House B&B, O'Connell St. (☎ 318 472), several blocks south of the Daniel O'Connell statue. Red brick townhouse with a pleasantly pastel interior and sun-lit upstairs bedrooms. One of the better B&B values in the city center. All rooms with TVs and tea-making facilities. Full Irish breakfast. Great deals for families. Student concessions. Singles €26; shared rooms €24-32 per person. ❸

Cherry Blossom Budget Accommodation, O'Connell St. (☎ 469 449), next to Alexandra House. Limerick's newest kid on the block. Agnes, the energetic proprietress, aims to fill the gap created when the city's hostels fled town. She welcomes guests with comfortable, spacious rooms, quality baths, and scrumptious breakfasts. €20. ❶

Ita O'Brien's Villa Maria, 27 Belfield Park (☎ 455 101), up Ennis Rd. from Sarsfield Bridge, opposite Jury's Hotel. Charmingly old-fashioned rooms animated by vivid color schemes. No smoking. Singles €30; doubles €46; triples available (negotiable). ❷

FOOD

Inexpensive, top-notch cafes around Limerick's center provide refreshing alternatives to fast food and pub grub; O'Connell and Catherine St. are full of good budget bets. Forage for groceries at **Tesco** in Arthurs Quay Mall. (☎ 412 399. Open M-W and Sa 8:30am-8pm; Th-F 8:30am-10pm; Su noon-6pm.) **Nature's Way,** also in the mall, has a limited selection of natural foods and veggie basics. (☎ 310 466. Open M, W, Sa 9am-6pm; Th 9am-7pm; F 9am-7pm.)

▧ Furze Bush Cafe Bistro, the corner of Catherine and Glentworth St. (☎ 411 733). If the delicious crepes (€11.50) and "succulent crab meat" sandwiches (€6.95) don't impress, perhaps the eccentric, Mary-Poppins-esque interior will. Open June-Aug. M-Sa 10:30am-5pm; Sept.-May M-W 10:30am-5pm, Th-Sa 10:30am-5pm and 7-10pm. ❷

Dolan's, 4 Dock Rd. (☎ 314 483). Friendly little pub doubles as a spirited restaurant out back. Limerick's best choice for an evening pre-pub meal. Next stop: here, of course. Lunch menu €6-10 all day, pub hours. ❷

The Green Onion, Rutland St. (☎400 710). In a converted library building with a loft and high molded ceilings. International fare to match the bold, dramatic interior and jazz soundscape. After 6pm, dinner prices fly high (€13.70-21.50), but the "all-day" lunch menu has simpler, cheaper options (€7.65-13.70). Open M-Sa noon-10pm. ❸

Sean Cara Restaurant, 3 Dock Rd., next to Dolan's. Intimate and candlelit, with stone masonry walls and plank wood floors. Harpist on weekends. Vegetarian options and an excellent wine selection. Oven-baked wild Shannon Salmon (€15.20); chargrilled sirloin prime Irish beef (€17.70). Most dishes enough for 2. Open Th-Sa 6-10pm. ❹

O'Grady's Cellar Restaurant, O'Connell St. (☎418 286). Look for the green awning. This subterranean spot serves as a midday refuge from the bustling streets. Irish cuisine anchors the menu. Meals €6.50-9. Open M-F 9am-10pm, Sa-Su until 10:30pm. ❷

Java's Beat Cafe, 5 Catherine St. (☎418 077). Flavored coffees and herbal teas combat Limerick's drear. Enjoy a salad, sandwich, or bagel (€2.50-7) upstairs in the hearth- side hammock. Open M-Sa 9am-10pm, Su 11am-8pm. ❶

PUBS

A variety of musical options cater to Limerick's diverse pub crowd and immense student population. Young *craic*-seekers head towards Denmark St. and Cornmarket Row. Trad-seekers can certainly get their nightly fix, though the chase may be more challenging than in other Irish cities. After weeks of "Wild Rover," however, Limerick is the perfect spot to sample some accordion-free tunes.

Dolan's, 4 Dock Rd. (☎314 483; www.dolanspub.com). Worth a Shannon-side walk from the city center to join rambunctious locals for nightly trad. Live rock bands and comedians also frequent the **Warehouse** nightclub, in the same building (see **Clubs,** below).

Nancy Blake's, Denmark St. (☎416 443). The best of both worlds—an older crowd huddles in the sawdust-floored interior for trad M-W nights, while boisterous students take in nightly rock in the open-air "outback."

Clohessy's, on Howley's Quay (☎468 100). Classy and cavernous, with sleek hardwood floors and intimate nooks. Live jazz on Su afternoons and evenings. The attached **Sinbin Nightclub** (see **Clubs,** below) keeps people dancing through the night.

IN RECENT NEWS

AT LEAST THEY HAVEN'T TRIED TO BAN GUINNESS

Following the lead of American cities like New York and Boston, the Irish government has decided to ban smoking in all pubs and restaurants come January 1, 2004. Considering that it's difficult to escape cigarette smoke anywhere in the country, the idea of a total ban on smoking is a bold step, possibly in the direction of folly.

Restaurant and bar managers are outraged, assuming that they will lose their puffing customers, and are trying to convince the government to ease the ban by creating special non-smoking areas or raising ventilation requirements, instead of banning smoking completely.

Many civilians, even those who smoke, seem remarkably calm about the matter—they just assume that even if the ban goes into effect, it will be impossible to enforce. They feel that the *Garda* presence is so limited, and publicans so jolly, that smoking in pubs will continue as it has for hundreds of years. Considering the routine disregard for speed limits, they're probably right.

Smoking may not disappear as quickly as the government would like, but the ban does show an increased awareness that many people dislike eating and drinking amidst clouds of smoke, and clean-lunged visitors are likely to find more and more establishments that cater to their needs.

The Trinity Rooms, Michael St. (☎417 266), at Charlotte's Quay in the Granary. The outdoor beer garden, complete with palm trees and a waterfall, banishes the Irish drizzle. College bands often play during term, and DJs bust out chart-toppers most weekend nights. **The Granary** nightclub (see **Clubs,** below) shares the building.

Locke Bar and Restaurant, Georges Quay (☎413 733). Join the classy crowd on the quay-side patio, or head inside where owner Richard Costello, a former member of Ireland's national rugby team, joins in trad sessions several nights a week.

ⓒ CLUBS

Limerick's insatiable army of students keeps dozens of nightclubs thumping nightly from 11:30pm until 2am. Cover charges can be steep (€8-12); keep an eye out for "Ladies' Night" and other promotions.

The Warehouse (☎314 483), behind Dolan's on Dock Rd. Draws big-name bands and rising stars, with something for all ages. Cover €7-12, higher for well-known acts.

The Granary, inside The Trinity Rooms, on Michael St. (☎417 266). Get down to hip-hop, funk, and soul. Cover €7-9.

Icon, Cornmarket Row, Denmark St. Currently *the* hotspot for 20-somethings. Central dance floor suits groovers and onlookers. Cover €7-9.

The George Hotel, O'Connell St. (☎414 566). Pick a decade: Th for 70s, F for 80s, and Sa for 90s. Circular dance floor and balcony are always packed. Cover €10.

The Sinbin, inside Connehy's on Howley's Quay (☎468 100). Mid-20s crowd dances the night away, "Elvis-style." Cover about €12. Open Th-Sa.

⊙ SIGHTS

▧ THE HUNT MUSEUM. This fascinating museum houses Ireland's largest collection of art and artifacts outside the National Museum in Dublin, spanning from the Stone Age to the 20th century. The collection includes one of Leonardo da Vinci's four "Rearing Horse" sculptures, a gold crucifix given by Mary Queen of Scots to her executioner, and a coin reputed to be one of the infamous 30 pieces of silver paid to Judas by the Romans. When browsing, open any drawer to find surprises like one of the **world's smallest jade monkeys,** or call ahead for a guided tour if hungry for details. The just plain hungry are satisfied by the sandwiches and delectable deserts at the museum **cafe.** *(Custom House, Rutland St. extension of O'Connell. ☎312 833; www.huntmuseum.com. Open M-Sa 10am-5pm, Su 2-5pm. €6, seniors and students €4.75, children €3, family €14.70.)* The nearby **Limerick City Gallery of Art,** Perry Sq., contains a densely packed collection of Irish paintings and international exhibits. *(☎310 633. Open M-W and F 10am-6pm, Th 10am-7pm, Sa 10am-5pm, Su 2-5pm. Free.)* Abstract and experimental pieces fill the small **Belltable Arts Centre,** O'Connell St. *(☎319 866. Open M-F 9am-6pm, Sa 10am-6pm. Free.)*

KING JOHN'S CASTLE. The visitors center has vivid exhibits and a video on the castle's gruesome past. Outside, the **mangonel** is a convincing testament to perverse military tactics: repopularized by *Monty Python's Quest for the Holy Grail,* the mangonel was used to catapult pestilent animal corpses into enemy cities and castles. *(Nicholas St. Walk across the Abbey River and take the 1st left after St. Mary's Cathedral. ☎411 201. Open Mar.-Oct. daily 9:30am-5:30pm; Nov.-Feb. 10:30am-4:30pm. Last admission 4:30pm. €7, students and seniors €5.60, children €4.20, family €17.50.)*

ST. MARY'S CATHEDRAL. The rough exterior of St. Mary's, near King John's Castle, was built in 1172 on the site of a Viking meeting place. The fold-down shelves built into the wall by the altar display elaborate carvings depicting the struggle between good and evil. These carvings are called *misericordia*, Latin for "acts of mercy," and were used by choir members for relief during long services when sitting was prohibited. (☎ 416 238. Open daily 9:15am-5pm. Suggested donation €2.)

THE LIMERICK MUSEUM. With a huge collection of artifacts dating from the Bronze Age to the present, this award-winning museum lets visitors explore the past of Limerick City and the surrounding area. (☎ 417 826; www.limerickcity.ie. Open Tu-Sa 10am-1pm and 2:15-5pm. Free.)

THE GEORGIAN HOUSE AND GARDENS. Considered one of the best examples of Georgian architecture in Limerick, this historic house currently casts an eye to the city's less elegant past, hosting an exhibit on Frank McCourt's *Angela's Ashes* in its restored coach house. (2 Perry Sq. ☎ 314 130. Open M-F 10am-4:30pm, last admission 4:30pm; Sa-Su by appointment only.)

WALKING TOURS. Tours cover either the northern, sight-filled King's Island region or the more downtrodden locations described in Frank McCourt's *Angela's Ashes*. (☎ 318 106. King's Island tour daily at 11am and 2:30pm; Angela's Ashes tour M-F at 2:30pm, Sa-Su by appointment. Both depart from the tourist office. €8.)

ACTIVITIES AND ENTERTAINMENT

The **Belltable Arts Centre**, 69 O'Connell St. (☎ 319 866), stages big-name productions year-round. (Tickets €15-18. Box office open M-Sa 9am-6pm and prior to performances.) The **Theatre Royal**, Upper Cecil St. (☎ 414 224), hosts the town's largest concerts. The **University Concert Hall**, on the UL campus, showcases opera and classical music. (☎ 331 549. Tickets €9-40.) For a more casual evening, catch a film at **Savoy** on Bedford Row. (☎ 411 611. €8, before 6pm €5.50, M-F before 6pm students €4). Or play billiards or snooker at **Stix** on King's Island, 28 Nicholas St. (☎ 410 170. Open M-Su 9am-10pm. Pool €5 per hr., snooker €6 per hr.)

DAYTRIPS FROM LIMERICK

BUNRATTY CASTLE AND FOLK PARK

Buses running between Limerick and Ennis stop outside the Fitzpatrick Hotel in Bunratty, 8 mi. northwest of Limerick along the Ennis rd. (16 per day; from Limerick €3.50, from Ennis €5.35). Avoid the fanny-packed crowds by arriving early and heading straight for the castle. An ATM is across from the hotel in the Village Mills shopping complex.

Up the road to the right of the four-star Fitzpatrick Hotel, **Bunratty Castle and Folk Park** has a jumbled collection of historical attractions from all over Ireland. Built in 1425 by the MacNamara clan, the castle shines amidst its surroundings in the otherwise forgettable park. It is allegedly the most complete medieval castle in Ireland, and impresses even jaded tourists with superbly restored furniture, tapestries, and stained-glass windows. Don't miss the **Earl's bedroom,** where the ornate, enormous posts and canopy dwarf the pathetically tiny bed, bringing new meaning to the term "king size." Crowds of visitors clog the castle's narrow stairways during summer months, but the view from the battlement may be worth the spiraling climb. **The Great Hall** of the castle comes to life twice nightly with **medieval feasts** for deep-pocketed tourists, as local damsels in full wench-regalia serve meals and bottomless glasses of wine. (☎ 360 788; www.shannonheritage.com. 4-course meal with wine €50.25. Book 1wk. in advance.) The **folk park** originated in the 60s, when builders at Shannon Airport couldn't bear to destroy a quaint cottage for a new runway. Instead, they moved the cottage, now labeled the **Shannon Farmhouse,** to Bunratty, and since then, reconstructions of turn-of-the-century houses and stores from all over Ireland have been added. Peat fires blaze in the cottages, lit each morning by inhabitants in period attire. In some of the buildings, period tasks and crafts are demonstrated on a rotating basis. Most appealing is the baking that goes on in **Golden Vale Farmhouse,** where hungry visitors watch apple pies (€3) and biscuits made the old-fashioned way before following the finished products to the **Tea Rooms** for a taste test. (Open June-Aug. 9am-5:30pm, last admission 4:30pm; Sept.-May 9:30am-4pm. May-Sept. €10, children under 18 €5.60, family €26.60; Oct.-Jan. €8.40/€5/€23.) The weary head back to the main road for oysters (€8.50) or a sandwich (€3-8.50) on the balcony at **Durty Nelly's** (☎364 861). The original proprietress earned her name in 1620 by serving Bunratty's soldiers more than just beer, if you know what we mean.

NEAR LIMERICK: ADARE (AN DARE)   ☎061

The well-preserved medieval architecture and meticulous rows of tiny thatched cottages have earned Adare a reputation as one of the prettiest towns in Ireland. With that distinction comes a legion of tourists, who infiltrate the town's pricey restaurants and fancy hotels daily. The four major historical sights of note are the 13th-century **Trinitarian Abbey** on Main St., the 14th-century **Augustinian Priory,** the **Franciscan Friary,** and **Desmond Castle.** Though it's officially private, visitors who ask are often granted permission to explore the grounds of ▨**Adare Manor.** Formal French gardens, the wandering Maigue river, and magnificent mature trees (some over 300 years old) cover the sprawling 840-acre estate. Stay for **afternoon tea,** or move on to polish your polo skills at the **Clonshire Equestrian Centre** (☎396 770), on the A21; alternatively, come in October for the **International Horse Show.**

  Buses arrive in Adare from Limerick (25min., 8 per day, €5) and Tralee (1¾hr., 8 per day, €12). From the bus stop, head down Main St. to the sky-lit **heritage centre** complex, home of the **tourist office.** (☎396 255; www.adaretouristoffice.ie. Open June-Aug. M-F 9am-7pm, Sa-Su 9am-6pm; Sept. M-F 9am-6pm; May M-Sa 9am-6pm; Nov.-Dec. and Feb.-Apr. M-Sa 9am-5pm. Heritage Centre €5, students €3.50, family €15; group rates available.) **AIB,** near Texaco, has an **ATM.** (☎396 544. Open M-F 10am-4pm.) The **police** watch from Main St. (☎396 216). The **library** by the tourist office provides **free Internet** by appointment. (☎396 822. Open Tu and F 10am-1pm, 2-5:30pm, and 6:30-8:30pm; W-Th and Sa 10am-1pm and 2-5:30pm.)The **post office,** Main St., handles mail (☎396 120. Open M-F 9am-1pm and 2-5:30pm, Sa 9am-1pm.)

  Although it has no hostel, Adare offers several reasonably priced accommodations. Station Rd., the street to the right of the heritage center, is lined with B&Bs that cost around €30. Just 250 yd. up N21 to Killarney, **Ardmore House B&B ❸** has freshly linened rooms with plenty of light and pinewood floors smooth enough to glide across. (☎396 167. Doubles €50.) A 5-7min. trek to Manorcourt, **Riversdale's ❸** tastefully decorated rooms are modern and tidy. (☎396 751. €30.) To reach **Adare Camping and Caravan Park ❶,** bear left onto N21 at the uptown fork, turn left at Ivy Cottage toward Ballingeary, and follow the signs. A family of horses welcomes visitors to this grassy site. (☎395 376. Laundry €8. Hot tub €5. €15.50 per tent; €20 per caravan.) Twelve miles out of town on N69, nature trails wind through **Curraghchase Forest Park.** Extensive grounds include an arboretum and the former home of 18th-century poet Aubrey DeVere. The more intrepid camp in summer (May-Sept.) at **Curraghchase Caravan Park ❶.** (☎396 349. Open field tent spot. Showers, kitchen, groceries. Laundry €6. €10 per tent; €15 per caravan.)

Picnic-makings are sold at **Centra** on Main St. (☎ 396 211. Open M-F 8am-9pm, Sa 8am-8pm, Su 9am-6pm.) **The Blue Door ❷,** a 200-year-old thatch-roofed, rose-fronted cottage, serves reasonable lunches and pricey dinners. (☎ 396 481. Lunches €7-10, dinners €15-21.55. Open daily 11am-3pm and 6-10pm.) **The Arches Restaurant ❸** has similar lunchtime values. (☎ 396 246. Lunches €6.50-9.50, dinners €14-18. Open M-Sa noon-3pm and 5-9:30pm, Su 5-8:30pm.) Whatever sort of pub you're seeking, Adare has a Collins for you: **Pat Collins Bar** (☎ 396 143), next to the post office on Main St., opens early and serves cheap grub in a relaxed atmosphere, while around the corner, **Sean Collins Bar** (☎ 396 400) rollicks with trad on Sunday evenings from 8:30-11:30pm. On the Killarney/Rathkeale rd., **Bill Chawke's** (☎ 396 160)—of innovative name choice—hosts live trad on Thursdays at 9:30pm and live rock bands Saturday nights and Sunday afternoons.

WESTERN IRELAND

Ask any publican—he will probably agree that the West is the "most Irish" part of Ireland. Yeats (perhaps perched on a barstool) once said, "For me, Ireland is Connacht." For less privileged Irish in recent centuries, it was mostly poor soil and emigration. When Cromwell uprooted the native Irish landowners in Leinster and Munster and resettled them west of the Shannon, the popular phrase for their plight became "To Hell or Connacht." The Potato Famine (see p. 62) that plagued the entire island was most devastating in the West—entire villages emigrated or died. Today, every western county has less than half its 1841 population. Though wretched for farming, the land from Connemara north to Ballina is a boon for hikers, cyclists, and hitchhikers who enjoy the isolation of boggy, rocky, or strikingly mountainous landscapes. Western Ireland's gorgeous desolation and enclaves of traditional culture are now its biggest attractions.

Galway is a different story: the city has long been a successful port and is currently a haven for young ramblers and music lovers of every ilk. Farther south, the Cliffs of Moher, the mesmerizing moonscape of the Burren, and a reputation as the center of the trad music scene attract travelers to Co. Clare. The Shannon River, the longest in all of Britain and Ireland (214 mi.), pools into holiday-haven Lough Derg and runs south through the city of Limerick, sketching the eastern boundary of the rugged, rocky west. To the north, the farmland of the upper Shannon spills into Co. Sligo's mountains, lakes, and ancient monuments.

COUNTY CLARE

Wedged between the tourist metropoli of Galway and Kerry, Co. Clare is largely free of the traveling hordes. What tourists do venture into the county, flock to the area's premier attraction, the Cliffs of Moher. As they rise 700 ft. from the ocean's surface, waves crash upon the rocks and seagulls circle below its skyscraper-high ledges. Elsewhere, Co. Clare unfurls other geologic wonders: fine sands glisten on the beaches of Kilkee, and 100 sq. mi. of exposed limestone form Ireland's most peculiarly alluring landscape, the Burren. On the coast, charmismatic seaside villages line the strands while farming communities dot the stark and empty inland.

ENNIS (INIS)   ☎ 065

Growing fast, but slow to lose its charm, the capital of Clare combines city-calibre nightlife and shopping with the familiarity of a small town. Quaint, overlapping streets belie the Ennis that, by winning the title "Information Age Town," earned each of its households a free computer a few years back. The constantly dividing River Fergus flows around much of Ennis, fully enclosing a large area just north of today's town center—this is the "island" from which Ennis draws its name. The town is best experienced on a Saturday, when the pubs and clubs are hopping and a makeshift produce market springs up in Market Square. The town does not lack charm the rest of the week, though, and Ennis's proximity to Shannon Airport and the Burren make it a common stopover for tourists, who can enjoy a day of shopping followed by a night at the musical pubs.

WESTERN IRELAND

Western Ireland

0   20 miles
0   20 kilometers

ATLANTIC OCEAN

CO. DONEGAL

CO. TYRONE

N15

N56

Donegal Town

Donegal Bay

Ballyshannon
Bundoran

Lower Lough Erne

A47
A46

CO. FERMANAGH

A35

N15

Lough Melvin

Drumcliff
Manor-hamilton

Enniskillen

A4

A32
A509

Ceide Fields

Killala Bay

Easky
Irishcrone (Enniscrone)

Sligo Bay

Sligo
Dromahair

CO. CAVAN

Belmullet

Ballycastle

Killala

N59

Ballina

N26

Ballysadare
Colooney

Riverstown

CO. SLIGO

N16

N4

N17

Tobercurry

Ballymote

Lough Allen

Drumshanbo

Bangor

Blacksod Bay

CO. MAYO

Lough Conn

N59

N26

N58

N5

N17

Boyle

Carrick-on-Shannon

CO. LEITRIM

Keel
Achill Island

Clare Island

Clew Bay

Roonagh Quay
Louisburgh

Westport

Castlebar

N84

N60

Knock

Castlerea

CO. ROSCOMMON

N5

N61

Longford

N4

Inishturk

CONNACHT

Claremorris

N60

Roscommon

N60

CO. LONGFORD

N63

Inishbofin

Leenane

Lough Mask

Ballinrose

WESTMEATH

Lough Ree

N55

Inishshark

Letterfrack

Cong

Tuam

N63

Athlone

N6

Cleggan

Connemara National Park

Lough Corrib

N84

CO. GALWAY

N61

Clifden

CONNEMARA

N59

Oughterard

N17

Ballinasloe

N6

Roundstone

Rossaveal
Inveran

Barna

Galway

N6

N65

CO. OFFALY

N62

N52

Carraroe

Spiddal

Galway Bay

N59

N18

Loughrea

Portumna

Birr

ARAN ISLANDS

Inishmore

Kinvara
Gort

N52

Rosscrea

N7

Inishmaan
Inisheer

Ballyvaughan

Lisdoonvarna

N67

Corofin

Lough Derg

N52

N62

CO. LAOIS

Doolin

Cliffs of Moher

N18

N7

Nenagh

Lahinch

N85

CO. CLARE

Ennis

R. Shannon

CO. TIPPERARY

Milltown Malbay

Sixmilebridge

Thurles

N75

Kilkee

Shannon Airport

N18

N18

Kilrush

N68

N19

Limerick

N24

N62

Killimer

N69

Tarbert

Mouth of the Shannon

N69

MUNSTER

Rathkeale

CO. LIMERICK

N24

Cashel

Listowel

N21

Newcastle West

N20

Kilmallock

Tipperary

N74

N8

Clonmel

Tralee Bay

Abbeyfeale

N21

N24

DINGLE PENINSULA

Tralee

N22

N23

N73

CO. WATERFORD

Dingle Bay

N70

Killarney

Kanturk

N72

Mallow

Fermoy

N72

Dungarvan

WESTERN IRELAND

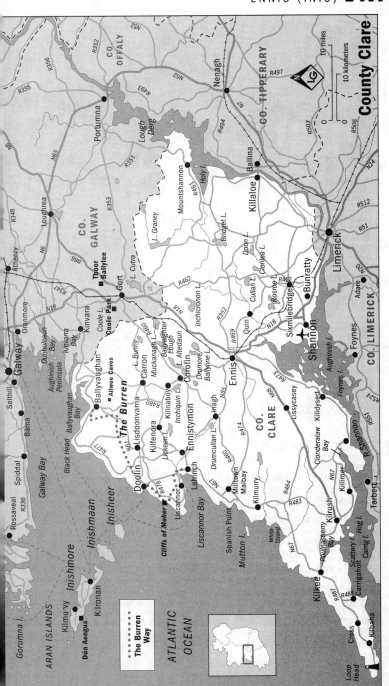

County Clare

10 miles

10 kilometers

CO. OFFALY

CO. GALWAY

CO. TIPPERARY

CO. CLARE

CO. LIMERICK

ARAN ISLANDS

ATLANTIC OCEAN

The Burren Way

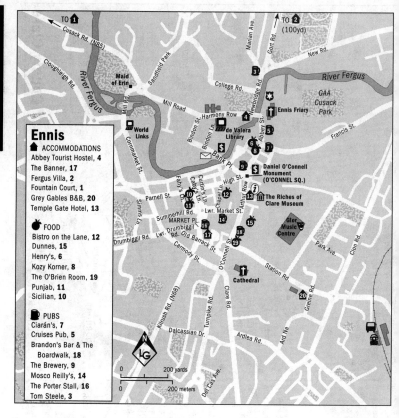

Ennis

🏠 **ACCOMMODATIONS**
Abbey Tourist Hostel, **4**
The Banner, **17**
Fergus Villa, **2**
Fountain Court, **1**
Grey Gables B&B, **20**
Temple Gate Hotel, **13**

🍎 **FOOD**
Bistro on the Lane, **12**
Dunnes, **15**
Henry's, **6**
Kozy Korner, **8**
The O'Brien Room, **19**
Punjab, **11**
Sicilian, **10**

🍷 **PUBS**
Ciarán's, **7**
Cruises Pub, **5**
Brandon's Bar & The
    Boardwalk, **18**
The Brewery, **9**
Mosco Reilly's, **14**
The Porter Stall, **16**
Tom Steele, **3**

🔲 TRANSPORTATION

Trains: The station (☎ 684 0444) is a 10min. walk from the town center on Station Rd. Open M-Sa 6:15am-5:30pm, Su 15min. before departures. Trains leave for **Dublin** via **Limerick** (M-Sa 2 per day, Su 1 per day in the evening; €26.60).

Buses: The bus station (☎ 682 4177) is beside the train station. Open M-Sa 7am-5:15pm. Between 7:20am and 7:20pm, hourly departures head to: **Cork** (3hr., €13.90); **Dublin** via **Limerick** (4hr., €13.30); **Galway** (1 hr., €9.95); **Limerick** (40min., €6.70); **Shannon Airport** (40min.). Buses head less regularly to **Doolin** (1hr., 2 per day, €4.70) and **Kilkee** (1hr.; M-Sa 3 per day, Su 2 per day; €9.20). The West Clare line (4-7 per day) goes to combinations of **Doolin, Ennistymon, Kilkee, Kilrush, Lahinch,** and **Lisdoonvarna.** The crowded post bus runs from the post office to **Liscannor** and **Doolin** (M-Sa 2 per day, €3.50); arrive early to get a seat.

Bike Rental: Michael Tierney Cycles and Fishing, 17 Abbey St. (☎ 682 9433, after 6pm ☎ 682 1293). Dispenses info on bike routes and fishing expeditions. Bikes €10 per afternoon, €20 per day, €80 per wk. Deposit €50. Open M-Sa 9:30am-6pm.

🔁🔂 ORIENTATION AND PRACTICAL INFORMATION

Ennis' crisscrossing layout can be confusing, and while locals are happy to give directions, they often become just as perplexed as visitors when trying to explain how to get from point A to point B. Luckily, most streets curve back into the town center at some point, so the lost eventually find what they need. **O'Connell Square** marks the center of town; to reach it from the bus and train stations, head left down **Station Road.** At the cathedral, turn right on **O'Connell Street** and go down to the end of the street. A soaring statue of Daniel O'Connell stares down a from high atop a column in the Square. From O'Connell Sq., **Abbey Street** and **Bank Place** lead across the river and into the suburbs. **High Street** (which becomes **Parnell Street**) runs almost perpendicular to O'Connell St. through the center of town. **Market Street,** running between O'Connell and High St., leads to **Market Place.**

Tourist Office: A friendly tourist office (☎028 366), off O'Connell Sq. on Arthur's Row. Also has a **bureau de change.** Open July-Sept. daily 9am-1pm and 2-6pm; Apr.-June and Oct. M-Sa 9:30am-1pm and 2-6pm; Nov.-Mar. M-F 9:30am-1pm and 2-6pm.

Banks: Bank of Ireland, O'Connell Sq. (☎682 8777). **AIB,** Bank Pl. (☎682 8089). Both have **ATMs** and are open M-F 9:30am-5pm.

Luggage Storage: At the bus station. Lockers €2. Open M-Sa 7am-7pm, Su 10am-7pm.

Laundry: Parnell's, High St. (☎682 9075). Wash and dry €8-12. Open M-Sa 9am-6pm.

Pharmacy: O'Connell Chemist, Abbey St. (☎682 0373). Open M-Sa 9am-6pm. **Michael McLoughlin,** O'Connell St. (☎682 9511), in Dunnes Shopping Centre. Open M-W and Sa 9am-6pm, Th-F 9am-9pm.

Emergency: ☎999; no coins required. **Police** *(Garda):* ☎682 8205.

Internet: de Valera Library (☎682 1616), down Abbey St. and over the bridge. The library is 2 blocks from the bridge on the left. 5 terminals for public use; arrive early. Open M, W, and Th 10am-5:30pm; Tu and F 10am-8pm, Sa 10am-2pm. **World Links,** Mill Rd. (☎684 9759. €3 per 1hr. Open M-Sa 10am-11pm, Su 11am-11pm.)

Post Office: Bank Pl. (☎682 1054). Open M-F 9am-5:30pm, Sa 9:30am-2pm.

🛏 ACCOMMODATIONS

Abbey Tourist Hostel, Harmony Row (☎682 2620; www.abbeytouristhostel.com). A freshly painted exterior overflows with flowers, and clean, comfortable rooms welcome guests inside. Friendly, young owners give advice on town and Burren exploration, and run **minibus trips** to Doolin and the Cliffs of Moher. Curfew Su-W 1:30am, Th 2:30am, F-Sa 3am. Dorms €12-15; singles €25; private rooms €19. ❶

The Banner (☎682 4224), at Old Barrack St. and Market Pl. Hotel-esque accommodations atop a pub for reasonable prices. All with bath and TV; most with telephone and windows overlooking the town. Breakfast included. €24-28, singles €40. ❸

Fergus Villa, Gort Rd. (☎682 4981 or 086 211 0085), 2min. north of the town center. A sparklingly clean B&B run by an incredibly energetic family of athletes and musicians. All rooms with TV and hairdryer. Singles €40; shared rooms €30 per person. ❸

Fountain Court, the Lahinch rd. (☎682 9845), 2 mi. out of town. Comfortable, if a little pricey. All rooms include bath, TV, and CD player. Guests lounge in the big sitting room and enjoy a generous breakfast menu. €32.50-45. ❸

The Grey Gables, Station Rd. (☎682 4487), a short walk from the bus station toward town. Great rooms with private baths. Full Irish Breakfast. Singles €35; doubles €60. ❸

Temple Gate Hotel, O'Connell Sq. (☎682 3300) More luxurious accommodations in a quiet corner amidst all the action. Rooms start at €70. ❺

FOOD

Enormous **Dunnes,** on O'Connell St., offers enough inexpensive food and beverages to feed all of Clare. (☎684 0700. Open M-Tu and Sa 9am-7pm, W 9am-9pm, Th-F 9am-10pm, Su 11am-7pm.)

■ **Henry's** (☎682 2848), by the Abbey St. carpark. Scrumptious, overfilled baps and salads bring locals in the know to this hidden gem tucked between the carpark and the river. Ham, salami, provolone, green olives, and olive oil on a plump bap €4.70. For dinner, try one of the huge pizzas (€10). All-natural, homemade ice cream is the Ennis dieter's menace (one scoop €1.30). ❶

Kozy Korner (☎682 4214), across the carpark from Henry's. In this corner cafe, cozy up to a traditional Irish Breakfast (€4) or their sandwiches and baps (€3.25). A popular place for students to grab a cup of coffee or tea (€1.25). Open daily 8am-5pm. ❶

Punjab, Parnell St. (☎684 4655). Excellent Balti and tandoori meals at good prices, especially as most suffice for dinner tonight and lunch tomorrow. A group of 4 can enjoy a complete meal for €44, while 2 vegetarians can have it all for €25. Takeaway prices about €1 less. Delivery within a 3 mi. radius €2.50. Open daily 5-11pm. ❸

Sicilian, the corner of Cabey's Ln. and Parnell St. (☎684 3873). Surprisingly bright and cheerful behind the Venetian blinds. One of the biggest bangs per euro, with pizza (from €6.35) and pasta (€10), portions big enough to feed twice. Open daily 5-11pm. ❷

Bistro on the Lane, Chapel Ln. (☎684 0622), off Lower Market St. Gourmands will find this little stone bistro worth the splurge—the well-traveled chef combines local produce to create a small but inventive and delightful menu. Salad with mozzarella, bacon, and peaches €7; noissettes of lamb €18. Cheaper veggie options. Open daily 6-10pm. ❸

The O'Brien Room, O'Connell St. (☎682 8127), in the Old Ground hotel. Fantastic array of seafood dishes, along with the chef's specialty, Burren lamb. Vegetarians taken care of with other tasty options. Dinner mains €20-24. Open 12:30pm-9:15pm.❸

 PUBS

With over 60 pubs to its name, Ennis has no shortage of nightlife. Most host trad sessions that help uphold Clare's reputation for musical excellence. Good pubs line the streets—just stop and listen for a moment. For music listings, get *The Clare Champion* (€1.35) in about any shop.

■ **Cruises Pub,** Abbey St. (☎682 1800), next to the Friary. A high-class restaurant fills the back, and quality Mediterranean grub sneaks through into the lively front pub until session time (9:30pm). Built in 1658, it is one of the oldest buildings in Co. Clare, and much of the original interior remains intact. International music star Maura O'Connell once lived upstairs. Now, local music stars appear nightly for cozy sessions.

Ciarán's, off O'Connell St., opposite the Queen's Hotel (☎684 0180). Traditional music in a contemporary space. Locals turn out in droves when owner Ciarán takes his bodhrán and joins the top-notch sessions twice weekly. Trad with or without the drummer boy W-Su.

Brandon's Bar, O'Connell St. (☎682 8133). Regulars gobble up huge plates of spuds, meat, and veggies (mains €7-8) with their pints. M trad, Su open mic, F-Sa live rock. On weekends, a popular nightclub opens upstairs. Sing-a-long club nights every alternate W. Cover Th-Sa €6-8.

Tom Steele, Newbridge Rd. (☎682 1238). Fewer tourists make it to this side of the river, where the young and chic congregate for frequent live jazz and acoustic sets. Weekends bring DJs to the clubbier 2nd fl.

The Brewery, 2 Abbey St. (☎684 4172). Packed with people slurping their pints and distilling conversation. Especially popular on weekends, when locals crowd the small bar-room floor.

Mosco Reilly's, Market St. (☎682 9413). Upright drinkers on stools lean their elbows on upright beer barrels. Two airy rooms leave ample space for open mic on Th, live bands on weekends, and raucous Gaelic football watching Su afternoons.

The Porter Stall, Market Pl. (☎087 682 1322). DJs and drink promos draw a rowdy young crowd of 20-somethings to this impressively sized bar.

◎ ❀ SIGHTS AND FESTIVALS

The Riches of Clare Museum, attached to the tourist office, traces the history of Co. Clare from the Bronze Age to its present state through concise explanations and audio-visual exhibits. The uppermost floor focuses on the recent achievements of Clare's residents, displaying such gems as James Devine's recent world record for tap dancing speed—a searing 38 taps per second. (☎682 3382. Open M-Sa 9:30am-5:30pm. €3.50, students €2.50, children €1.50.) Two blocks along Abbey St. away from O'Connell Sq. rest the ruins of the 13th-century **Ennis Friary,** second only to the Clare hurling team in the local esteem it commands. In 1375 the seminary became one of Ireland's most important theological schools. In the entrance to the south transept, a small inset depicts the crucifixion of Christ. Legend has it that Judas's wife, while cooking chicken soup, attempted to comfort her husband by telling him that Christ was as likely to rise from the grave as the chicken she was cooking was to rise from its pot. Well, the cock rose, as seen in the lower right corner of the inset. Another unusual feature is the ecclesiastical **jail cell** behind the gate in the sacristy. Here young scholars who engaged in wine-induced revelry were sent to think about what they'd done. (☎682 9100. Open June to mid-Sept. daily 10am-6pm; Apr.-May and mid-Sept. to Oct. Tu-Su 10am-5pm. Last admission 45min. before closing. €1.50, students €0.75.) Across from the Friary, a block of sandstone is inscribed with part of Yeats's "Easter 1916" (see **Easter Rising,** p. 63).

Perched nobly on his monument in his central square, **Daniel O'Connell** watches over today's town. A 10min. walk from the town center on Harmony Row, which becomes Mill Rd., leads to the **Maid of Erin,** a life-sized statue remembering one of the **"Manchester Martyrs,"** three nationalists hung in Manchester in 1867 (see also **Kilrush,** p. 328). She stands proudly with her left hand on a Celtic cross; an Irish wolfhound to her side looks up for guidance. Saturday is **Market Day** in Market Sq., where all conceivable wares are sold beneath a statue of crafty Daedalus. A 30min. walk winds along the trout-filled **River Fergus;** directions (and lists of varmints to watch for) are posted in the parking lot between the river and Abbey St. **Cusack Park,** where Ennis's much beloved **hurling** team stages matches most weekends, lies along the Fergus in the easterly direction. Check local papers or local fanatics for game times and buy tickets at the park (most tickets €3-10). Several miles out of town lies **Dromore Wood,** a beautiful nature reserve around a lake where the stillness is broken only by the occasional youngster reveling in the delicious freedom of a bicycle or summertime. (Open daily until 9pm. Free.)

While most locals enjoy the free music at pubs, tired tourists head to the new, state-of-the-art **Glor Music Centre** to hear their fill earlier in the evening. The venue is not solely for tourists, though; it serves as a regional arts center and has expanded its repertoire to incorporate a diverse mixture of contemporary film, theater, and music, along with the more tourist-oriented performances of traditional music and dance. Pick up a schedule of performances in the tourist office, or almost anywhere in town. (☎684 3103; www.glor.ie. Box office open M-Sa 9:30am-5:30pm. Traditional performances Su-Th. Tickets €12-22, student concessions often available.) The last weekend in May, Ennis takes its musical inclinations for the full ride during the **Fleadh Nua Music and Culture Festival,** when sessions and other festivities spill into the streets.

THE SHANNON VALLEY AND LOUGH DERG

Northeast of Limerick, the River Shannon widens into the lake region of Lough Derg. Affluent middle-aged tourists powerboat between the small towns of Killaloe, Ballina, Mountshannon, and Portumna; younger, vehicle-free travelers are rarer here than in regions to the south and west. Lough Derg's summer watersport culture provides a good workout but little in the way of archaeological interest. Travelers lured into the deceptively sleepy Sixmilebridge on their way to and from the airport are in danger of falling in love and never leaving.

SIXMILEBRIDGE
(DROICHEAD ABHANN Ó GCEARNAIGH) ☎061

Halfway between Shannon and Limerick, this sleepy town has a spectacular hostel and makes a perfect stop on the way to or from the airport. **Buses** hit Sixmilebridge twice daily coming from Shannon Airport and four times from Limerick. There is a **bureau de change** at the **Credit Union** on Main St., but **no ATM** in town. The **pharmacy** is on the corner when entering town. (Open M-F 9:15am-1:30pm and 2:30-6:15pm, Sa 9:30am-1:30pm.) On the first street on the right heading up Main St., enjoy **free Internet** for up to 1hr. at the gorgeous **Kilfinaghty Public Library,** housed in an 18th-century stone church recently refurbished with the financial support of poet laureate Seamus Heaney. (☎369 678. Open Tu-F 10am-1pm and 2-5:30pm, Tu and Th also from 6-8pm, and Sa 10am-2pm.)

After a night in Sixmilebridge's hostel, ▧**The Jamaica Inn ❶,** visitors often extend their travel plans. Head downhill from the bus stop at the center of town and cross the bridge, which, at a distance of exactly six old Irish miles from Limerick, gave the town its name. Take the first left and follow the signs—it's a short walk from town past the Duck Inn near the old mill pond. This spotless hostel provides every possible amenity in the most serene of settings. The courtyard is a wonderful lounging spot for rare sunny afternoons, and the hostel staff cheerfully supplies guidance to explorers. (☎369 220. **Bike rental** €10, with notice. Laundry €10. Dorms €14-15; singles €28-30; doubles €22-24.) The Inn also serves breakfast in its **restaurant ❶.** (Open 8:30am-noon.) Sixmilebridge doesn't offer much else in the restaurant department, but **John and Seppie Crowe's Supermarket** on Main St. satisfies cooks, and has a small coffee shop. (☎369 176. Open M-Sa 7:30am-9:30pm, Su 8am-8:30pm.) **Tasty Fry's ❷,** on Main St., is a good spot for breakfast, burgers, and chips. Take food outside to gaze at the sea god statue by the bridge. An adjoining wine bar is an anticipated addition. (☎369 825. Open daily noon-midnight.) The town's six pubs quench the thirst worked up by a long day of hiking. **The Mill Bar** (☎369 145) serves snacks with their drinks, and has live trad on Fridays. Hurling enthusiasts populate **Casey's** (☎369 215).

The beauty of the Shannon Valley begs for exploration. Hostel co-owner Michael is a wealth of information on scenic walks, the most rewarding leading to the breathtaking views atop **Gallows** and **Woodcock Hills.** Icthyophiles might pass the time trying to hook dinner 2 mi. north of town at **Castle Lake.**

KILLALOE AND BALLINA ☎061

A flowery bridge connects twin towns Killaloe (Kill-a-LOO; Cill Dalua) and Ballina (Beal an Átha) across the base of Lough Derg, 15 mi. northeast of Limerick City. Residents celebrate the rich history of King Brian Ború's old residence, though weary city-dwelling visitors seem more interested in the area's present tranquility, broken only by the purr of powerboats and trailing waterskiers.

🖻🖬 TRANSPORTATION AND PRACTICAL INFORMATION. Transportation to one town serves for both. Local buses run between Killaloe and Limerick (4 per day; €8.20), depositing riders 150 yd. outside town. **Bikes** are available for rent from **Mountshannon Harbour.** (☎927 950. Delivery available, with €10 surcharge depending on distance. €30 per wk.) The **tourist office,** in the former Lock House on the Killaloe side of the medieval bridge, provides information on walks in the area, including the brochure *Walks in the Killaloe District.* (☎376 866. Open May-Sept. daily 10am-6pm.) The tourist office also houses a **heritage centre,** purveyor of knowledge of all things Ború. (☎376 866. Open daily 10am-5:30pm. €2.10, students and seniors €1.60, children €1.15, family €6.) An **ATM**-blessed **AIB** sits on Main St. (☎376 115. Open M-F 10am-4pm, Tu until 5pm.) **Grogan's Pharmacy,** on Main St. in Killaloe, heals pains. (☎376 118. Open M-Sa 9:15am-6:30pm.) The **library,** in the same building as the tourist office, provides **free Internet.** (☎376 062.) The **post office** is up the hill on Main St. (☎376 111. Open M-F 9am-12:30pm and 1:30-5:30pm, Sa 9am-12:30pm.)

🖍🖸🖬 ACCOMMODATIONS, FOOD, AND PUBS. Killaloe is a manageable daytrip from Limerick, but several nice B&Bs near town make it a pleasant stopover. The Kellys of 🖬**Mount Bernagh ❸,** 1¼ mi. north along the Killaloe side of the river, are quite possibly two of the nicest people in Ireland. Their warmth and hospitality renew faith in humanity, while their comfortable rooms and electric blankets maintain the warm fuzzy feeling through the night. (☎375 461. Singles €32; shared rooms €27.) In town, the well-appointed rooms at **Derg House B&B ❸** have soothing, sea-green bedspreads, baths, TVs, and river views. (☎375 599. Singles €40; shared rooms €32-35.) The hospitable **Kincora House ❸,** Main St., across from Crotty's Pub, is filled with antiques and serves a healthy breakfast with vegetarian options. (☎376 149. Singles €40; shared rooms €35.)

Purchase basic groceries at **McKeogh's,** on Main St. in Ballina. (☎376 249. Open M-W 8am-7:45pm, Th 8am-7:30pm, F 8am-9pm, Sa 8am-8:30pm, Su 8am-1:30pm.) On the Killaloe side of the river, the new-born, buzzing **Coffee Pot & Deli ❷** whips up breakfasts, sandwiches, and other hot specials. (☎325 599. Sandwiches €3-6.50. Breakfast 8am-11:30am, specials 11am-6pm.) **Crotty's Courtyard Bar ❸** serves hearty grub on a patio decorated with antique ads. (☎376 965. Lunch €6, served noon-3pm; dinner €8-12, served 5-10pm.) The mini-grocery and **butcher shop** next door also fall under Crotty's jurisdiction. Crossing over into Ballina yields more tasty options. To the immediate left is **Galloping Hogan's ❹,** where diners choose to sit outdoors or almost outdoors, in the glassed-in front room. Typical mains run €13-20; pastas and veggie options are slightly cheaper. (☎376 162. Call ahead for dinner. Lunch served daily noon-6pm, dinner 6-10pm.) Straight up from the bridge, **Molly's** serves quality pub grub with lake views and rooftop seating for fine-weathered days. (☎376 632. Mains €8-12. Food served 11am-10pm.)

🖸🖳 SIGHTS AND ACTIVITIES. At the base of the town on Royal Parade lies **St. Flannan's Cathedral,** built around 1200 and still in use today. Inside, the **Thorgrim Stone** is inscribed with a prayer for the conversion of the Viking Thorgrim to Christianity, in both Scandinavian runes and the monks' *ogham* script (for those whose

Old Norse is a bit rusty). Market Sq. may have once held the **Kincora palace** of legendary Irish High King Brian Ború, granddaddy of the O'Brien clan, who ruled here in 1002. The other candidate for the site of Ború's palace is the abandoned fort known as **Beal Ború** (now a subtle circular mound in a quiet forest glade), 1½ mi. out of town toward Mountshannon. **St. Lua's Oratory** was built on Friar's Island in the 9th century. When the Shannon hydroelectric scheme required total submersion of the island, the oratory was moved to its present location at the top of Church St. In mid-July, the **Féile Brian Ború** celebrates Killaloe's most famous resident with four days of music, watersports, and various Ború-ish activities. The final night brings pageantry and banquets—raid your pack for that perfect Viking t-shirt. Immediately following is the **Killaloe Music Festival** (☎202 620; tickets €10-30), featuring the **Irish Chamber Orchestra.**

The **Lough** has been drawing people to Killaloe and Ballina for centuries. An option for today's visitor is a relaxing, 1hr. cruise on the *Derg Princess*, leaving from Molly's daily at 2:30pm. (☎376 159. €7.50, children €4, family €20.) **Whelan's** also runs a cruise with historical narration on its *Spirit of Killaloe* twice daily. (☎086 814 0559. €7.50, children €4.) The same company rents **motorboats** for fishing or cruising; boats hold four, and include life-jackets. (☎376 159. €15 first hr., €10 second hr., €5 per hr. thereafter. Call for fishing rod availabilities. Open daily 9am-9pm.) A boat, and a bit of navigational prowess, grants access to the eminently picnicable **Holy Island** (a.k.a. **Iniscealtra**), the remains of five **churches** dating to the 6th century, and a **round tower.** For more guidance, try the **Holy Island Boat Trip,** which departs from Mountshannon Harbour. (☎921 615. €8, children €4. Call for times; trips based on demand.) A few miles north of Killaloe, indulge in an afternoon of watersports at the **University of Limerick Activity and Sailing Centre.** Those interested in sailing must have experience and be able to prove it to staff before setting sail. (☎376 622. Windsurfing €25 per hr., sailboats €15-25 per hr., 2-day kayaking or sailing course €175. Call ahead.) Get out of the water and into the saddle at **Carrowbaun Farm Trekking Centre.** (☎376 754. €13 per hr.)

CLARE COAST

The Cliffs of Moher form the most famous part of the Clare coastline, where limestone walls soar 700 ft. over the Atlantic. However, the spectacular scenery is not limited to this single tourist-laden spot; the majority of the western coastline of Clare is composed of similarly thrilling cliffs, and scenic walks and drives delight the travelers who trek past the typical tour bus route to discover their own favorite ledges, islands, and coves. At several places, the cliffs seem to have lost the battle with the Atlantic, and sandy beaches at Lahinch and Kilkee sit low within the rocky landscape. The southern border of Clare looks across the River Shannon at Kerry from small maritime towns. Those traveling between Co. Clare and Co. Kerry may want to take the 20min. **Tarbert-Killimer car ferry** across the Shannon estuary, avoiding the 85 mi. inland drive by way of Limerick. (☎905 3124. €11.50 per car, €2.50 for pedestrians and bikers.)

KILRUSH (CILL ROIS) ☎065

In spite of its size, tiny Kilrush is home to the coast's principal marina. The first permanent settlement here began in the 12th century, when monks from nearby Scattery Island built a church in a mainland meadow. Seven hundred years later, Famine-stricken tenants banded together to withhold rent from their absentee landlords; "Boycott" was the name of the debt collector who was the first to be refused. Today, music, boating, and the opportunity to see dolphins bring small but steady numbers of travelers to town.

WESTERN IRELAND

⌨ ⚐ TRANSPORTATION AND PRACTICAL INFORMATION. Bus Éireann (☎682 4177) stops in Market Sq. on its way to Ennis (1hr., 2-5 per day, €7.80) and Kilkee (20min., 1-4 per day, €2.55). Pricey **bike rental** is available at **Gleesons,** Henry St., through the Raleigh Rent-A-Bike program. (☎905 1127. €20 per day, €80 per wk. Deposit €80.) The **tourist office,** with its **bureau de change,** is currently on Moore St., but moves frequently; call for the latest location. (☎905 1577. Open May-Sept. M-Sa 10am-6pm.) **AIB** on Frances St. has an **ATM.** (☎905 1012. Open M 10am-5pm, Tu-F 10am-4pm.) **Anthony Malone's pharmacy,** on the right side of Frances St., has everything for a quick fix. (☎905 2552. Open M-Sa 9am-6pm, Su 11am-1pm.) One hour of **free Internet** comes compliments of **Kilrush Library,** on O'Gorman St. (☎905 1504. Open M-Tu and Th 10am-1:30pm and 2:30-5:30pm; W and F 10am-1:40pm and 2:30-8pm; Su 10am-2pm.) The **Internet Bureau,** beside the marina, also provides access. (☎905 1061. €4 per 20min. Open daily; call for hours.) The **post office** is on Frances St. (☎905 1077. Open M-F 9am-5:30pm, Sa 10am-4:30pm.)

▞ ⚑ ⚎ ACCOMMODATIONS, FOOD, AND PUBS. Katie O'Connor's Holiday Hostel (IHH) ❶, on Frances St. next to the AIB, provides clean quarters in rooms that date back to 1797. Hostelers enjoy an open hearth and the warmest of welcomes from kindly owners Mary and Joe. (☎905 1133. Self-serve kitchen open all night. Check in at the store next to the sign for the hostel. Dorms €11; doubles €25; quads €46.) **The Kilrush Creek Lodge ❸,** in the blue and red building across from the marina and next to the Activity Centre, is art deco and popular with youth and business groups. (☎905 2595. Some rooms with balconies. Wheelchair-accessible. Laundry €4. Singles €39; shared rooms €30-35 per person.) Irish, American, and Canadian flags fly high by **The Grove ❸** on Francis St. Inside this guesthouse are spacious rooms with tables and desks for dashing out those long-neglected postcards; out back, guests volley on the tennis courts. (☎905 1451. Singles €35; doubles €50.) Across the street a friendly family awaits at **Iveragh House B&B ❷.** Enjoy your own company in the comfy rooms, with baths, or enjoy the company of others in the downstairs living room. (☎905 1176. Singles €24-26; doubles €50.)

A gargantuan **SuperValu** sells groceries at the marina end of Frances St. (☎905 1885. Open M-W and Sa 8:30am-7pm, Th-F 8:30am-9pm, Su 9am-6pm.) The incredible aroma of bread floating down Frances St. comes from **Cosidines ❶.** (☎905 1095. Soda loaf €1.30. Open M-Sa 8am-6pm.) For a quick lunch, the **Quayside ❶** restaurant and coffee shop offers soups and sandwiches from behind baskets of homemade scones. (☎905 1927. Toasted sandwich €3. Open M-Sa 9:30am-6pm.) For dinner there are three choices: pub grub, fast food, or Chinese. **Chan's Chinese ❷,** the Square, is the most elegant of the bunch; the house special is Szechaun is €10. (☎905 1200. Open daily 4pm-midnight. Takeaway €1-2 less.) Of Kilrush's 15 or so pubs, at least one is sure to have music on any given night. **▓Crotty's Pub,** Market Sq., is where concertina player Mrs. Crotty helped repopularize trad in the 1950s, as evinced by the pub's inspirational tributes to the legendary lady. Today, cozy Crotty's is the place for the hottest trad in town and even crazier *craic*. (☎905 2470. Trad Tu-Th, Sa.) **Charlie Martin's,** next to the hostel, reopened in 2002 after a 10-year hiatus. Older locals reminisce about its older days, while the younger crowd celebrates the contemporary entertainment. (Trad Sa-Su.)

◎ ⚐ SIGHTS AND ACTIVITIES. Kilrush's real attractions lie offshore, and most visitors head straight for the marina. The Shannon Estuary is home to Ireland's only known resident population of **bottlenose dolphins.** Climb aboard the *M.V. Dolphin Discovery* for a 98% chance of cruising alongside the playful swimmers. (☎905 1327. 2-2½ hr. May-Sept. 3 per day; sailings based on weather and demand, so call ahead. €14; children €7.) The eco-cruise passes by **Scattery Island,** the site of a 6th-century monastic settlement. The island's resident population took off for the mainland back in the 70s, leaving behind the rubble of monastic ruins, church-yards, and a 120 ft. circular tower. **Scattery Island Ferries** sails regularly in summer from the marina (May-Sept. 3-4 per day; €8 return, children €6) and irregularly in other seasons. Transportation can be arranged with Gerald Griffins (☎905 1327) or at the marina. More active aquatic exploration starts at the **Kilrush Creek Adventure Centre,** in the red and blue building at the end of Francis St. Instructors lead 1hr. sessions of **sailing, kayaking, canoeing, archery,** and **windsurfing** for €15, and half- or full-day multiactivity sessions for €30 and €50, respectively. Call ahead for sched-ules. (☎905 2855; www.kcac.nav.to. Open Apr.-Sept. daily.) On the mainland, the small but interesting **Scattery Island Centre,** Merchant's Quay, gives oodles of insights on the island's natural and cultural history, and includes a dolphin and marine wildlife display. (☎905 2139. Open mid-June to mid-Sept. daily 10am-6pm. Free.) In the center of town, a monument facing the town hall remembers the Manchester Martyrs of 1867 (see **Ennis,** p. 319). Just outside town on the ferry road, the dirt paths of the 420 acre **Kilrush Forest Park** lead to the **Vandeleur Walled Garden,** where small patches of flowers shine between stretches of serene lawn. Many find the free park more beautiful than the gardens. Follow signs from the ferry road for the walled garden; it's a 20min. walk from town. (Open summer 10am-6pm; winter 10am-4pm. €4, children €2.)

The **Éigse Mrs. Crotty Festival** ("Rise up, Mrs. Crotty!") celebrates the glory of the concertina (see **Music,** p. 76) with lessons, lectures, and non-stop trad in the pubs and on the streets for a weekend in mid-August. (Contact Rebecca Brew of Crotty's Pub ☎905 2470 for more info, or check out the website, www.eigsemrs-crotty.com.) In late July, Kilrush celebrates its finned friends with the new, family-oriented **Shannon Dolphin Festival,** which includes live music in the Square, kiddie rides and dolphin fun-facts by the marina, and an aquatic-themed parade. (Contact the Festival Office ☎905 2522 for more information.)

KILKEE (CILL CHAOI)   ☎065

From the first weekend in June through the first weeks of September, Kilkee is an Irish holiday town. Families fill the pastel summer homes, teens working resort jobs party until early morning, and beach bums fill the swimming holes along the shore. But the crescent-shaped town overlooking a half-circle of soft sand has a quieter side that emerges when the holiday-makers leave, the population drops from 25,000 back down to 2300, and the countryside is again green and quiet.

🖥🗋 TRANSPORTATION AND PRACTICAL INFORMATION. Bus Éireann (☎682 4177 in Ennis) leaves from the corner of Grattin St. and Erin St. Leaving the tourist office, take an immediate right, and walk to the very end of the street. Buses head to Galway with a stop at the Cliffs of Moher (4hr., summer 2 per day) and to Lim-erick (2hr., 3-4 per day) via Ennis (1hr.). The **tourist office** is next to the Stella Maris Hotel in the central square. (☎056 112. Open June-Sept. daily 10am-6pm.) The **ATM** at the **Bank of Ireland,** O'Curry St., dishes cash. (☎056 053. Open M-F 10am-12:30pm and 1:30-4pm, M until 5pm.) **William's,** a hardware store and **pharmacy** that happens to **rent bikes,** is located on Circular Rd., just left of the round-about at the end of O'Curry St. (☎056 041. Open M-Sa 9am-6pm. Bikes €9 per day, €45 per wk. Deposit €40.) **Internet,** limited to one golden hour per day, happens at the pink **Kil-kee Library,** on O'Connell St. (Open M and W 1:30-5:30pm, Tu and Th-F 10am-1pm and 2-5:30pm. Free.) After hours, head to **The Myles Creek Pub,** where use of the **Internet** terminal costs €1 per 8min. (☎905 6771). Go **postal** on O'Connell St. (☎056 001. Open M-F 9am-5:30pm, Sa 9am-12:30pm.)

ACCOMMODATIONS, FOOD, AND PUBS. Halfway down O'Curry St., the **Kilkee Hostel ❷** has clean rooms and a self-serve kitchen. (☎905 6209. Laundry €7. Dorms €13.) The friendly folk at **Dunearn ❸**, a 10min. walk out of town up the left coastal road, welcome backpackers with open arms. (☎905 6545. Open June-Sept. Singles €33; shared rooms €26 per person.) Neighboring **Duggerna B&B ❸** has the same spectacular views of cliffs and sea, and similarly comfortable rooms. (☎905 6152. Open May-Sept. Singles €38; shared rooms €26.) With more fantastic views, plush rooms, and Vittles Restaurant is **Halpins Hotel ❹** on Strand Line, practically on the beach. (☎905 6032. Rooms start at €80.) Planning on staying a while? Inquire about summer rentals at **Diamond Rocks Holiday Homes ❹** (☎905 6565.)

Along the beach in the summer, vendors sell a Kilkee delicacy, winkles and dillisk. Winkles are sea snails and dillisk is sea grass, all collected from the tide pools that form during low tide. Both are cooked and salted, and sold in bags for about €1.50. If this is not appealing, try these other options. **Gala** vends victuals on the corner of O'Curry St. and O'Connell St. (☎905 6446. Open summer M-F 9am-11pm, Sa 9am-10pm, Su 9am-9pm.) **The Pantry ❷**, O'Curry St., is a culinary oasis in a desert of fast food. Because "Life's too short to drink bad wine," they stock a large selection, with gourmet food to further please the palate. (☎905 6576. Lunches €8. Open May-Sept. daily 9:30am-6:30pm.) The **Country Cooking Shop ❶**, in the alley behind its parent Pantry, bags the same quality fare for considerably cheaper takeaway and makes desserts for the decadent traveler. (Carrot cake €6.) At night, grab some tasty lo mein (€6) from **Gold Sea ❷** and picnic beneath the stars. (☎908 3847. Open M-Sa 1pm-1am, Su 1pm-1:30am.) The **Old Bistro ❸** is a rough-hewn gem rebuilt several years ago by a handy Limerick chef and his wife. Serving a delicious sea-inspired menu, the restaurant draws weekend crowds, so call ahead. (☎905 6898. Mains €15-20.) Fancier diners head to **Croker's Restaurant ❸**, in the Kilkee Bay Hotel on O'Connell St. Meals for everyone: those who love the sea, those who love the land, and those who love animals too much to eat them. (Call the hotel for reservations, ☎906 0060. Open 6:30pm-10pm. Mains €17-20.)

After a day spent frolicking or snoring on the beach, fritter away still more time by drinking through the dense strip of pubs along O'Curry St. **Naughton's** is a pretty pub that gets packed—get there early for a seat, or join the jumble of locals and vacationers flooding the floor. **The Myles Creek Pub** (☎905 6771) features a different live band each summer night to accompany its 18-25 crowd. The **Central Bar** (☎905 6103) has plenty of seating, pool tables, and dark wood to go with the dark pints. It's also a good bet for weekday music, with trad, folk, and country bands performing M-Th. The **Strand Bar** (☎905 6177) is a great place to end the crawl—a high-heel's throw from the beach, the Strand has live music and dancing on most nights.

SIGHTS AND ACTIVITIES. The spectacular **Westend Cliff Walk** begins at the end of the road left of the seacoast and gently climbs along the tops of the cliffs, which are nearly as impressive as those of Moher, and far less touristed. The Cliff Walk intersects with the similarly scenic **Loop Head Drive** after passing the Diamond rocks, where bits of *Ryan's Daughter* were filmed. The drive passes unusual islands just off the cliffs, which rise straight out of the water with near perfect verticality, and sport flat, grassy tops. To the right, the photogenic drive runs through small villages, ruined farmhouses, hippie enclaves, and plenty of pasture to the **Loop Head Lighthouse**, at the tip of Co. Clare. On the way, it passes through **Carrigaholt**, a village 7 mi. south of Kilkee on the Shannon Estuary. The Loop Head Drive can be biked (30 mi.), though the return trip has some steep moments. To the left, the road leads back to Kilkee.

THE HIDDEN DEAL

WILLIE WEEK

For the better part of the year, the quiet town of **Milltown Malbay** (*Scraid Na Catharach*), 10 mi. south of Lahinch, doesn't have much to offer the ordinary traveler. Accommodations and transportation are scarce; the main street has a few pubs and lots of cars puttin' it in reverse when they realize they've missed the turnoff to the Cliffs of Moher. But beginning the first Saturday in July, the town lights up with the excitement of **Willie Week,** a huge—and affordable—music festival hosted by the **Willie Clancy School of Traditional Music** (☎065 708 4148). Throughout the week, thousands of musicians, instrument-makers, fans, tourists, and *craic*-heads flock here from all corners of the globe to celebrate the famous Irish piper and Milltown's native son. Participants pay only **€90 for an entire week** of lectures, lessons, and recitals (the trad sessions in the town's packed pubs are free). On the final Saturday a monster concert of international artists closes out the festivities; an event not be missed.

Accommodations in Milltown— including the sprawling Station House (☎065 708 4008) and the conveniently located O'Loughlin's Ocean View B&B (☎065 708 4249; both around €25)—are usually booked months in advance, but the trip to Milltown can be easily made from Lahinch. In town, marvelous sandwiches can be had at Baker's Cafe (☎065 708 4411); Cleary's, Clancy's, and O'Malley's are the most happening pubs.

If the tide is out, scramble out onto the rock formations in front of the carpark of the Cliff Walk— the three **Pollock Holes** should be exposed. The first and easiest to reach is traditionally called the Children's Hole, the second, the Women's Hole, and the third, the Men's Hole (where women are now allowed, but men still dip nude). Dry off over a relaxed game of **pitch-and-putt;** the 18-hole course starts on the other side of the carpark. (☎906 6152. Open daily in the summer 10am-8:30pm. €6.) Those in search of über-relaxation can lounge at the ▨**Kilkee Thalassotherapy Centre,** across from the bus stop. Seaweed baths in the 160-year-old porcelain tub (€16 per 25min.) are the center's specialty. (☎905 6742. Open mid-June to mid-Sept. M-Sa 10am-7pm, Su noon-6pm; shorter hours mid-Sept. to Jan. and Mar. to mid-June.) For a change of locomotion, commandeer a set of hooves at the **Kilkee Pony Trekking & Riding Centre.** (☎906 0071. €15 per hr.) More into underwater exploration— what luck—Kilkee is famous for its **diving.** Jump in at the **Kilkee Diving Centre,** a 5min. walk down the shore road from town. The center also rents **kayaks** for €5 per 30min. (☎905 6707. Open daily June-Sept.; call for off season hours. 2hr. beginner lesson €65. Experienced divers can rent equipment; €52 per dive.)

LAHINCH (LEACHT UI CHONCHUIR) ☎065

In the 1880s, small, lively Lahinch became a summer haven for the well-to-do; the arcades and fast-food spots that now outnumber establishments of fine dining are evidence of the town's wider appeal today. While the moneyed still come to Lahinch for its championship-level golfing and mile-long beach, surfers and teens are the more visible contingent of the summer population, descending on the town to ride the waves by day and dance their remaining energy away come nightfall.

⊟⊡ TRANSPORTATION AND PRACTICAL INFORMATION. Buses stop near the golf course 2-3 times a day during the summer, coming from Cork, Doolin, Dublin, Galway via Ennis, and Limerick. Gerard Hartigan runs a **taxi** service (☎086 278 3937); see below for his Burren tours. The nearest **bike rental** is **Griffin's,** in Ennistymon. (☎707 1009. €10 per day, €50 per wk. ID deposit. Opens at 9am; bikes can be returned any time to the bar next door.) The **Lahinch Fáilte** tourist office, at the bottom of Main St., organizes tours and books accommodations. (☎708 2082. Open summer 9am-9pm; winter 9am-6pm.) An **ATM** is next door. **Medicare,** on Main St., is the only **pharmacy**

in town, and takes advantage of its monopoly with hiked-up sunblock prices. (☎708 1999. Open M-Sa 9:30am-1:30pm and 2-5:30pm.) **Mrs. O'Brien's Kitchen and Bar,** Main St., has **Internet** until late. (☎708 1020. €9 per hr. Open daily 9am-11pm.) A **bureau de change** is at the bottom of Main St. (☎708 1743; open M-Su 9am-10pm), and the **post office,** Main St., also changes money (☎708 1001; open M-F 9am-1pm and 2-5:30pm, Sa 9am-1pm).

⌐ ☐ ☒ ACCOMMODATIONS, FOOD, AND PUBS. B&Bs abound in Lahinch; the weary will find rest on almost any road off Main St. **St. Mildred's B&B ❸,** next to the hostel on Church St., is not just the oldest B&B in Lahinch, it's also the oldest house; wear isn't evident though, as the delightfully friendly and hospitable owners keep it in top condition. The sitting room, and most of the bedrooms, have sweeping beach views. (☎708 1489. Singles €25; shared rooms with bath €25.) The **Lahinch Hostel (IHH) ❷,** on Church St., at the end of Main St. away from the tourist office, has good-sized 4-bed dorms, and somewhat tight 6-bedders. Luckily, all are immaculate and remarkably free of surfers' sand tracks. (☎708 1040. Laundry €6. Dorms €15; private rooms €17.) Walk 10min. up N67, past the campground sign, to **Cois Farraige B&B ❸.** This serene house has beautiful rooms with light wood paneling and views of the sea and the family's horses. Ask for an upstairs room. (☎708 1580. June-Sept. Singles €35; doubles €53. off season €30/ €50.) **Lahinch Caravan & Camping Park ❶,** also on N67, makes space for campers amidst a well-entrenched set of caravans. (☎708 1424. Open Easter-Sept. Reception summer daily 9am-9pm; off season 9am-5pm. Laundry €5. €6 per person.)

Lahinch's dining options are less than tantalizing, making the shelved food of the **Centra,** Main St., particularly appealing. (☎708 1636. Open June-Sept. daily 8am-10pm, Oct.-May 8am-8pm.) **The Spinnaker Restaurant and Bar ❷,** next to Lahinch Fáilte, has a spacious purple and blue Chinese restaurant upstairs and a denser pub/club below. (☎708 1893. Meals €5-10. Live music weeknights; Sa DJ. No cover.) **O'Looney's,** on the Promenade, features a perfectly located deck to survey the waves from while filling up on grub o' th' pub. Party with the surfing crowd on weekends—this is one of the town's hottest nightclubs. (☎708 1414. Food served until 9:30pm. 18+. Cover €8. Nightclub open May-Aug. Th-Sa.) **Flanagan's,** Main St. (☎708 1161), is a popular pub that hooks people of all ages with its eclectic mix of live music—everything from reggae to jazz, acoustic, trad, and pop gets a turn within these cozy confines. Sharply dressed clubbers pack into the modern space of **Coast** on weekends; during the week cool cats sip their cocktails in the front bar before a brilliant backlit fishtank (F-Sa cover €8).

⚑ ACTIVITIES. Visitors to **Lahinch Seaworld & Leisure Centre,** at the far end of the promenade, can watch baby lobsters take their first unsure steps, bringing to mind the miraculous cycle of life, death, and butter sauce. The last laugh, however, goes to ▧**"Lobzilla"**—this 11 lb. behemoth eluded lobster nets for approximately 50 years before Thomas Galvin pulled him from the depths. (☎708 1900. Open M-F 10am-10pm, Sa-Su 10am-8pm. Aquarium or pool only €5.90, students €4.90; combined admission €9.90/€7.90.) Catch fish in their natural habitat with **O'Callaghan Angling.** (☎682 1374. Boats run June-Sept. Evening trips 6-9:30pm €30; full-day trips 9am-6pm €70.) Lahinch, sometimes referred to as the St. Andrews of Ireland, is world-renowned for its **golfing.** But fame costs: a trip to the links starts at €50 for the **Castle course** and a whopping €110 for the **Championship course,** and reservations should be made three months in advance (☎708 1003). John McCarthy, of **Lahinch Surf School,** seeks out the breakers. A 2hr. lesson with all equipment costs those over 16 €25 and youngsters €18, while a weekend **surf "camp"** (€55) gives a more comprehensive start. Solo surfers can also rent equipment for fairly cheap. (☎960 9667.

2hr. surfboard rental €8; bodyboard €5; wetsuit €8.) Surf's up? Call the **Surf Report** to find out (☎081 836 5180). **Arcades** along the beach are mostly glutted with those in the 7-16 age. Gerard Hartigan offers entertaining minibus **tours** of the Burren and Cliffs of Moher. Please take the proper precautions—his enthusiasm is infectious. (☎086 278 3937. 4½hr. €14.)

DOOLIN (DUBH LINN) ☎065

Something of a national shrine to Irish traditional music, the little village of Doolin draws thousands of visitors every year to its three pubs for nights of *craic* that go straight from tappin' toes to Guinness-soaked heads. Walk 15min. up Fisher St. to see crashing waves or a few minutes out of town for rolling hills crisscrossed with stone walls. However, be back in time for dinner—several of Doolin's restaurants won the coveted Bridgestone award for the best food in Ireland. Most of Doolin's 200-odd permanent residents run its four hostels, countless B&Bs, and pubs. The remaining locals farm the land and, in their spare time, wonder how so many backpackers end up in their small corner of the world.

▐ TRANSPORTATION

Buses: Stop at the Doolin Hostel and Nagle's Camping Ground; advance tickets can be purchased at the hostel. Route #15 to **Kilkee** or to **Dublin** via **Ennis** and **Limerick** (2 per day). #50 to the **Cliffs of Moher** (15min.) and to **Galway** (1½hr.) via other towns in the Burren (summer M-Sa 5 per day, Su 2 per day; off season M-Sa 1 per day).

Ferries: Boats to the **Aran Islands** leave from the town's pier, about 1 mi. from the town center along the main road, but those from Galway and Rossaveal are cheaper under almost all circumstances. See **Aran Islands,** p. 342.

Bike Rental: The **Doolin Bike Store** (☎707 4260), outside the Aille River Hostel. €10 per day. Open daily 9am-8pm.

◢ ▐ ORIENTATION AND PRACTICAL INFORMATION

Doolin can be divided into two villages about a mile apart from each other, though many locals ignore such distinctions. Close to the shore is the **Lower Village,** with **Fisher Street** running through it from the pier. Fisher St. traverses a stretch of farmland and B&Bs on its way to the **Upper Village,** where it turns into **Roadford.** Virtually all of Doolin's human and commercial life resides on this main road. The 8 mi. paved and bicycle-friendly segment of the **Burren Way** links Doolin to the **Cliffs of Moher.** Pedestrians find the route an exhausting but manageable half-day trip; the steep climb along the road from Doolin to the Cliffs lets cyclists coast the whole way back, saving energy for a night of foot-stomping fun at the pubs.

Banks: A traveling bank comes to the Doolin Hostel every Thursday at 10:30am. The nearest **ATM** is in Ennistymon, 5 mi. southeast.

Internet: Available at the Aille River Hostel. Nonresidential rate is €8 per hr.

Post Office: Nearest post office is in Ennistymon, but stamps are sold at Doolin Hostel.

▐ ACCOMMODATIONS AND CAMPING

Tourists pack Doolin in the summer, so book early. Locals know where the money is: almost every house on the main road is a B&B.

Aille River Hostel (HIH), Main St. (☎ 707 4260), halfway between the villages. Friendly, laid-back atmosphere in a gorgeous location. Out front, the Aille River gurgles around a tiny island overflowing with wildflowers; an unofficial beer garden sets up on the island before hostelers head to the pubs for the nightly session. Musicians often stop by Aille to warm up before gigs. **Internet** €6 per hr. for guests. Washer and detergent free, dryer €2. Dorms €11-11.50; private rooms €13.50. **Camping** €6. ❶

Westwind B&B (☎ 707 4227), Upper Village, behind McGann's, in the same driveway as the Lazy Lobster. The rooms are sunny and immaculate, and the french toast is breakfast bliss. The owners give helpful advice to spelunkers and other explorers. €25. ❸

Doolin Cottage (☎ 707 4762), next to the Aille. Friendly young proprietress keeps rooms spotless and bright. Vegetarians savor yogurt and honey for breakfast; meat-eaters can, too, but the full fry is also available. Open Mar.-Nov. All rooms with bath. €22. ❷

Doolin Hostel (IHH), Fisher St. (☎ 707 4006; www.doolinhostel.ie), Lower Village. This, the oldest hostel in town, is also Doolin's bus station, occasional bank, and unofficial town hall; bright-faced owner Paddy is the kind overseer. Hostel includes a small shop, **bureau de change, Western Union** office, and bus ticket sales. Laundry €4. Reception 7:30am-9pm. Large-ish dorms €11.50; 4-bed with bath €12.50. Doubles €33. ❶

Rainbow Hostel (IHH), Toomullin (☎ 707 4415), Upper Village. Steps from pubs-of-legend McGann's and McDermott's. Ship-like wooden interior, with cheery and comfy pastel rooms. Free guided **Burren walking tours; Burren slideshows** upon request. Laundry €4. Dorms €11; doubles €26. ❶

Flanagan's Village Hostel (IHH), Toomullin (☎ 707 4564), a 5min. walk from the Upper Village (away from Lower Village). Spacious, sunny rooms, leather couches, and a back garden with farm creatures. Laundry €6. 6-bed dorms €11; doubles €25. ❶

▣ ▨ FOOD AND PUBS

Doolin's few restaurants are excellent though pricey; first prize (and perhaps a small fortune!) goes to the entrepreneur who opens an affordable restaurant in this four-hostel town. Until then, be grateful that all three pubs serve quality grub.

The Doolin Deli (☎ 707 4633), Lower Village. The only place to go for food under €8. Packs overstuffed sandwiches (€2.50), bakes scones (€0.90), and stocks groceries. Take-out only. Open June-Sept. M-Sa 8:30am-9pm, Su 9:30am-8pm. ❶

The Doolin Cafe (☎ 707 4795), Upper Village, just past McDermott's. The "cafe" part refers to the comfortably casual atmosphere, not the excellent, upscale food. The early-bird special (5:30-7pm) is still pricey but nonetheless an outstanding value, with 4 gourmet courses for €22. Dover sole with fennel and crab sauce €19. Vegetarian options. Open for dinner daily 5:30-10pm, lunch Sa-Su noon-3pm. ❹

Bruach na hAille (☎ 707 4120), Upper Village, has as a working antique phonograph and delicious, creative, home-grown dishes. Lunchtime panini (served with salad) are tasty, if somewhat overpriced (€8.95). Arrive before 7pm to score the 3-course early-bird special €18.50. Open daily noon-4pm and 5:30-11pm. ❸

McDermott's (☎ 707 4328), Upper Village. Local foot-traffic heads this way around 9:30pm nightly, and remains at a standstill 'til closing; a 9:20pm arrival may win a seat (not to mention smirking rights). Serious sessions prove that Doolin's trad is more than a tourist trap. Grub until 9:30pm.

O'Connor's (☎ 707 4168), Lower Village. The busiest and most touristed of the three, O'Connor's serves above-average pub grub 'til 9:30pm (mains €10), when the music and Guinness take over.

McGann's (☎ 707 4133), Upper Village. Music nightly at 9:30pm in the summer and Th-Su at 9:30pm in the winter.

▓ DAYTRIP FROM DOOLIN: THE CLIFFS OF MOHER

The cliffs are 6 mi. south of Doolin on R478. **Bus Éireann** *clangs by on the summer-only Gal-way-Cork route, sometimes cooling her heels at the Cliffs for 30min. (2-3 per day), while the local Doolin-Limerick bus rounds out the public transport options with an additional 3 buses per day. In winter, a bus originating in Galway leaves Doolin at noon and deposits riders at the Cliffs for 1hr. before retracing its route. The well-signposted 20 mi. Burren Way and several trails weave through limestone and wildflowers from Doolin and Liscannor. Hitchers report some difficulty finding rides here. Parking €4.*

The ▓**Cliffs of Moher,** members of an elite group of Ireland's über-touristy attractions, draw more gawkers on a good July day than many counties see all year. Although cliffs compose much of Clare's coast, this stretch has been targeted for tourism because the cliffs are at their highest here, where 700 ft. of sheer verticality are battered by Atlantic waves. Touristy they may be, but with good reason—the views are breathtaking, and unquestionably among Ireland's most dramatic. To the north, the **Twelve Pins of Connemara** form dark and mysterious silhouettes against the skyline; to the west lie the limestone stitched Aran Islands; to the south more cliffs jut from the sea along the route to Loop Head, while the Kerry Mountains peak across the River Shannon. Finally, the view straight down is exhilarating—gulls whirl several hundred feet below the edge, and farther down still the overmatched waves explode against unrelenting limestone. **O'Brien's Tower** is a viewing point just up from the carpark; don't fall for its illusion of medieval grandeur—it was built in 1835 as a tourist-trap-tower by Cornelius O'Brien, an early tour-promoter. The ground view is just as striking—what's another dozen feet compared to the several hundred provided by Mother Nature? (Tower open Apr.-Oct. daily 9am-7:30pm. €1.50, students €0.80.) Most tour groups cluster around the tower, experiencing the exhilaration of the drop through telephoto lenses and binoculars. The more adventurous climb over the stone walls and head left, trekking along a clifftop path (officially closed) for more spectacular views and a greater intimacy with the possibility of falling. (**Warning:** Winds can be extremely strong at the top of the Cliffs, and blow a few tourists off every year; *Let's Go* does not recommend falling off a Cliff as it would hurt, greatly.) The seasonal **tourist office** beside the parking lot houses a **bureau de change** and a **tea shop** amidst hundreds of postcards. (☎065 708 1171. Open May-Sept. daily 9:30am-5:30pm.) **Liscannor Ferries** operates a fantastic cruise from Liscannor that sails directly under the cliffs. (☎065 708 6060. 1¾hr., 2-3per day, €20.)

THE BURREN

Entering the Burren's magical 100 sq. mi. landscape is like happening upon an enchanted fairyland. Lunar limestone stretches end in secluded coves, where dolphins rest after a long day of cavorting with locals. Mediterranean, alpine, and Arctic wildflowers peek brightly from cracks in mile-long rock planes, while 28 of Ireland's 33 species of butterfly flutter by. Geologists are baffled by the huge variety of animalian and botanic species that coexist in the area; their best guess points vaguely to the end of the Ice Age. Disappearing lakes and proud prehistoric tombs—including the 5500-year-old **Poulnabrone Dolmen,** one of Ireland's most touristed and photographed sights—add to the mystery and the expectation that witches, fairies, or ogres might come ambling across the rocks at any moment.

The best way to see the Burren is to **walk** or **cycle,** but be warned that the dramatic landscape makes for exhausting climbs and thrilling descents. Check your brakes before setting out. Tim Robinson's meticulous maps (€6.35) detail the **Bur-**

ren Way, a 26 mi. hiking trail from Liscannor to Ballyvaughan; *The Burren Rambler* maps (€2.55) are also extremely detailed. For bikers, the Shannon Cycleways guide (€3.80) illustrates several bike trails in County Clare, including two in the Burren. Burren **bus** service is some of the worst in the Republic. Bus Éireann (☎065 682 4177) connects **Galway** to towns in and near the Burren a few times daily in summer but infrequently in winter. Every summer weekday (June-Oct.) some of those buses continue to **Killimer** and the Shannon Car Ferry (to Killarney and Cork). **Buses stop at:** the Doolin Hostel in **Doolin** (p. 334), Burke's Garage in **Lisdoonvarna** (p. 338), Linnane's in **Ballyvaughan** (p. 337), and Winkle's in **Kinvara** (p. 340). Other infrequent but year-round buses run from individual Burren towns to **Ennis**. **Full-day bus tours** from Galway are another popular way to see the area (see p. 342). Based in Lahinch, Gerard Hartigan gives a more thorough **minibus tour** (see p. 332). Hitching in these parts requires patience and, as always, entails some risk.

BALLYVAUGHAN(BAILE UÍ BHEACHÁIN)   ☎065

Along the jagged edge of Galway Bay, about 8 mi. northeast of Lisdoonvarna on N67, the Burren's desolation is suddenly interrupted by the little oasis of Ballyvaughan. The town center is minutes from caves and castles, making it a frequent stopover for spelunkers and old-bone fiends, and a popular starting point for trips into the burren. ■**Burren eXposure,** a mile out on N67 toward Kinvara, gives a soaring audio-visual introduction to the Burren landscape. (☎707 7277. €5, children €2.50. Open daily 10am-6pm.) Also on N67 is the turnoff for **Newtown Castle and Trail,** where the restored 16th-century home of the O'Loghlens, Princes of the Burren, awaits. A 1hr. **guided tour** covers about half a mile of beautiful hillside terrain, discusses the geology of the Burren, and visits a Victorian folly "gazebo" (a miniature children's castle), and an 18th-century military waterworks system. (☎77216. Open Easter to early Oct. daily 10am-6pm. Castle free but donations appreciated. Trail tour €2.50.) Beside Newtown Castle, the **Burren College of Art** (☎707 7200; www.burrencollege.com), offers year-long and summer courses. Several weekend workshops are offered in the summer, focusing on painting the Burren landscape or learning about the area's botany. On the way to Ballyvaughan, find peace and solitude interrupted only by the birds chirping at **Corcomroe Abbey.** Founded in 1194 as a monastery by the Cistercian Order, the foundation actually dates back to 1182. The impressive walls and arches house centuries-old graves, while the cemetery outside is still in use. Prehistoric bears once inhabited the two million-year-old **Aillwee Cave** (EYEL-wee), 2 mi. south of Ballyvaughan and almost a mile into the mountain. Since caves are the same temperature year-round, bears felt their way inside and scratched out cozy beds. Anyone scared of the dark should avoid the tour, as should experienced spelunkers. (☎707 7036. Open July-Aug. daily 10am-7pm; mid-Mar.-June and Sept.-early Nov. 10am-4pm. Parking €2. €7.50.) Those itching to do serious **spelunking** should contact the **Speleological Union of Ireland** (SUI; www.cavingireland.org) or **Burren Outdoor Education Centre** (☎707 8066).

Buses come to Ballyvaughan from Galway, Doolin, and the Cliffs of Moher (M-Sa 4 per day, Su 2 per day). The **tourist office,** inside Spar on Main St., stores a healthy collection of pamphlets and gives information on walks and accommodations. (☎707 7077. Open June-Sept. daily 9am-9pm; Oct.-May 9am-5pm.) **Bike rental** and **laundry** services are found at **Connoles,** up the road toward N67. (☎707 7061. Open M-Sa 9am-6pm. Bikes €12.70 per day, €50 per wk. Deposit €20 and ID. Laundry €10.) The cafe next -door serves java and **Internet.** (☎707 900. €5 per hr. Open M-Sa 10am-7pm.)

B&Bs rule the roost in Ballyvaughan—several line the road into town, and almost every other door *in* town seems to be one as well. **O'Brien's B&B ❸,** above the pub/restaurant on Main St., has pleasing rooms, a constellation of cozy fireplaces, and a hearty Irish breakfast. (☎707 7292. Doubles €40.) Popular **Seaside**

THE LOCAL STORY

An interview with Willie Daly, the Lisdoonvarna "matchmaker."

LG: How long have you been with the matchmaking festival?

WD: I've been with the festival since I was 24. My father was in it and me grandfather was in it. Farmers would come to them about getting married. I had no curiosity in it and didn't expect to fall into it, but I think it's an important service.

LG: So people fill out a form and then they receive phone numbers?

WD: Aye, they do. They give us the form and we give them the names of people we think would be suitable.

A few minutes into the interview the phone rings...

WD (into phone): ... yes, I'll take the details. I'll send you a form and you can put in a little bit about yourself. And write down the sorts of things that you desire in a woman. And we put that in a file, and it's very confidential, it's just me daughter and meself, and we're very private. Ah, you will. I'll send you off a list of names. Yeah. When did you get the last one, John, when did you get the last one? And was there not anything in it that was suitable for you, then? Hmmm. Have you got a pen with you, and I'll give you the name of a some nice girl I have now. What age are you John?...*the phone cuts off.*

LG: So how do you decide which people are good for one another?

WD: I give each person a questionnaire to fill out, explaining about themselves and what they look for in a mate. Then they call

(cont. on next page)

Oceanville ❺, next to Monk's Pub on the pier, has gorgeous views and beautiful rooms for families and couples. (☎707 7051. Open Mar.-Oct. €54-57.) About 2 mi. from the city center on N67, friendly owners welcome guests to **Burren Dale B&B ❸** with cozy rooms and stories of Jacko McGann, proprietor's grandfather and discoverer of the famed Aillwee Caves. (☎707 7137. Singles €30, doubles €50.)

Spar sells foodstuffs. (☎77077. Open M-Sa 8:30am-8pm, Su 9:30am-5:30pm.) **The Tea and Garden Rooms ❷** (aka **An Féar Gorta**) serves tea and tasty cakes in a garden setting to enchant. (☎707 7157. Sandwiches €6-7. Open June-Sept. M-Sa 11am-5:30pm.) Sunny **Tea Junction Cafe ❷** has sandwiches and vegetarian mains, but it's tempting to go straight for their rhubarb pie. (☎707 7289. Vegetarian chili €6. Open June-Sept. daily 9am-6pm; Oct.-May 10am-5pm.) **Monk's Pub and Restaurant ❷** holds its Guinness seminary by the sea; try mussels outside on a sunny day. Tourists crowd around the huge stone fireplace for trad, while locals gravitate toward the bar. (☎707 7059. Famous seafood chowder €5. Music 2 nights a week.) Back in town, **Greene's** is a small, card-playing locals' pub frequented by an older crowd who knows where the Guinness runs best. (☎707 7147. Open M-Sa 6pm-midnight.)

LISDOONVARNA (LIOS DÚN BHEARNA) ☎065

The locals call it "Lis-doon," but for everyone else in Ireland, its name is synonymous with its **Matchmaking Festival.** September's month-long *craic*-and-snogging fest has drawn the likes of Jackson Browne and Van Morrison to its all-day music stages. Amidst the hullabaloo, farm boys and girls of all ages—their crops safely harvested, but with wild oats yet to sow—gather together to pick their mates. Local celebrity and professional matchmaker Willie Daley from Ennistymon presides over the event. No one really talks about how successful the festival is at making matches that last longer than a six-pint hangover, but as one Lisdoon local puts it, "Everything works if you want it to." For more info on the festival, or on matchmaking in general, contact the **Hydro Hotel** and stay for their nightly music. (☎707 4005. Wheelchair-accessible. Open Mar.-Oct.) In the 1700s, Lisdoon saw carriage upon carriage of therapy-seekers rolling in to try the curative wonders of sulfur and copper. You can still give it a whirl at the **Spa Wells Health Centre,** Sulfur Hill Rd., at the bottom of the hill south of town. Loosen up with a massage or sulfur bath before the big evening at Ireland's only operational spa. (☎707 4023. Sulfur bath €25; full massage €35. Open June-Sept. M-F 10am-6pm, Sa 10am-2pm.)

Buses travel 4 mi. to Doolin and on to Lahinch daily from the main square during the summer (1-3 per day). **Rent a bike** at the Esso filling station. (☎707 4022. €8 per day, €45 per wk. Deposit €60 or ID. Open M-Sa 9am-7pm, Su 10am-6pm.) Peter Mooney's **cab hire** is a welcome relief from the Burren's dismal public transportation system. (☎707 4663 or mobile ☎087 206 9019.) A **tourist office**, next to the Spa, provides ample information on the town and region. (☎707 48011. Open June-Sept. M-F 10am-6pm, Sa 10am-2pm.) There is no hostel in Lisdoonvarna, but the B&Bs are more than accommodating. Dermot of ◼**Dooley's Caherleigh House ❷**, right up the hill from the Spa, pampers every guest with tea and cookies, crackling fires, and superb breakfasts. (☎707 4543. All rooms with bath. €23.) Those staying at **Mrs. O'Connor's Roncalli B&B ❸** can visit the lovingly kept garden or bathe in the natural light that floods the rooms. It's a 7min. walk from the town center; pass the Esso station, the Smokehouse, and the next filling station. (☎707 4115. All rooms with bath. Open Apr.-Oct. €25.) Enjoy the perks and comforts of a three-star hotel at the **Carrigann Hotel ❹**. Owner and chef Mary Howard leads visitors to cozy rooms with beautiful garden views, and cooks up bar food or a delightful dinner to suit their taste. (☎707 4036. Open Mar.-Oct. €40-60.) Guests can book **Burren Walking Holidays,** 3-6hr. walks with Shane Connolly, a charming in-house guide who brings the Burren to life through his stories.

The smoked trout salad (€9) from the **Roadside Tavern and Restaurant ❷,** on the Doolin Rd., is enough to feed two. The pub itself is dimly lit and decorated with shellacked postcards from around the world. Ghostly old photos of trad sessions past form a backdrop to their living versions. (☎707 4084. Food served daily 12:30-9pm. Trad Mar.-Sept. nightly at 9:30pm, Oct.-Feb. Sa only.) The **Smokehouse** next door is a one-stop shop for the salmon of knowledge, the trout of truth, and the eel of eternity. (☎707 4432. Tours €2.60, students €2. Open M-Su 9am-6pm.)

KILFENORA (CILL FHIONNÚRACH) ☎065

The village of Kilfenora lies 5 mi. southeast of Lisdoonvarna on R478. Its **Burren Centre** and several grocers make it an ideal departure point for trekkers and bicyclists heading into the limestone wonderland (that is, if they already have a bike: there are no rental agencies in town). However, visitors would be wise not to miss the non-geological sights—seven **high crosses,** numerous **wedge tombs,** and a **cathedral.** The town also has one of the most overlooked trad scenes in the county.

up and I give them names and numbers of people in my file for them to call and meet.

LG: Have any marriages resulted?

WD: Well, I get invited to some but I don't attend in case it embarrasses them, since people know what I do.

LG: So, what is the most important advice you have for people looking to get married?

WD: A woman needs to be treated with respect. She needs be made to feel important and wanted. You can't take her for granted. That's the key.

The phone rings again...

WD (into phone): Hello? Sorry, okay John. Now this is the name of a very nice woman. She's somewhere around 60, she's just 60. Her name is Kathleen.* She has her own house. What? No, I can't give out her last name, she only wants her first name given out. Now there's another girl. Now what age are you again John? Ah, you're not that well on. But that girl I was going to say, Mona,* is in her 70s. So here's another number for you John... Best of luck with you now. They're both nice women. Oh now you're right. You have a very good attitude, now. Now there is another girl, who doesn't want to see anyone young. Her name is Eileen.* Now, she is somewhere in her 50s now and she doesn't want a young fella. Now don't be afraid of that now. You've got a good attitude, you'll be fine. Well you have the number now, so you have no excuse. Now try those three now, and if it doesn't work out, don't worry, we have thousands of others. Okay John, good luck. Good luck. You're welcome. It's not a problem, I do this all the time. It's me job.

The **Burren Centre** provides a comprehensive guide to the nearby stony stretches, featuring a 3D model of the relatively flat Burren, lectures, and a film on the natural history of the region. (☎708 8030. Open daily Mar.-May 10am-5pm; June-Aug. 9:30am-6pm; Sept.-Oct. 10am-5pm. €5, children €3.) Next to the Burren Centre, Church of Ireland services are still held in the nave of the **Kilfenora Cathedral.** (1st and 3rd Su of the month at 9:45am.) Although the structure itself dates from 1190 AD, the site has hosted a church since the 6th century. West of the church is the elaborate 12th-century **Doorty Cross,** one of the "seven crosses of Kilfenora." Although time and erosion have taken their toll, carved scenes of Christ's entry into Jerusalem remain visible among odd birds and menacing heads.

In the yellow house across from the Burren Centre, **Mary Murphy ❷** greets arriving guests with tea and coffee. Rooms are basic but include bath; prices also include a sizzling morning fry. (☎708 8040. Open Feb.-Oct. Singles €30; doubles €44.) Kilfenora's pub trifecta hums with so much music and dancing it could make travelers miss the bus…if Kilfenora had buses, that is. **Vaughan's ❶** offers trad sessions nightly, set dancing in the adjacent thatched cottage on Thursday and Sunday nights, and weekend barbeques, weather permitting. (☎708 8004. Sandwiches €3-4.50, superb seafood chowder €4. Food served 9am-9pm.) Kitty Linnane and her *céilí* band of '54 put Kilfenora on the musical map; **Linnane's,** affectionately called "Kitty's Corner," still hosts lively trad sessions in a familial environment and has won various awards for food and music. (☎708 8157. Sessions nightly in summer, weekends in off season; year-round W supersession.)

CARRON (AN CARN) ☎065

A pub, a hostel, and a mile-wide, 5 yd. deep puddle in the midst of a limestone landscape is the sum total of Carron. Sure enough, its dimensions constitute a mind-boggling figure; this is **Europe's largest disappearing lake.** Four miles northwest of Carron stands the ▧**Poulnabrone Dolmen,** Ireland's second-most popular and photogenic rock group. About 5000 years ago, over 25 people were put to rest with their pots and jewels under the five-ton capstone, only to be dug up by intrepid archaeologists in 1989. Two miles east of the village, Ireland's only **perfumery** creates scents from the Burren's moss and lichens; the wildflowers are now protected and can no longer be distilled for their aromas. (☎89102. Open daily Mar.-June and Sept.-Oct. 9:30am-5pm; July-Aug. 9am-7pm.)

The village lies a few miles east of the R477, off a small road connecting Bellharbor to Killnaboy; to get there, **drive** (8min.) or **hike** (1½hr.) south from Bellharbor. It's also possible to **bike** from Kilfenora, but the climbs on the small roads are exhausting. Hitching odds approach nil, which is how much *Let's Go* recommends this form of transport. A single magnificent hostel overlooking the giant lough houses half the town's population: **Clare's Rock Hostel ❶,** on the main road, has comfortable dorms with baths, tasteful decor, and cheerful management. (☎89129. Laundry €7. Reception 5-10pm. Open June-Oct. Dorms €10.50; singles €13; doubles €30.) Across the way, **Croide Na Boirne ❷** offers gorgeous views, a crackling fire, a pool table, and **goat burgers.** (☎89109. Mint-embalmed kidburger €6.40. Food served Apr.-Dec. noon-9pm.)

KINVARA (CINN MHARA) ☎091

Across the bay from the tourist hordes of Galway, this small harbor town of floating swans and passing hookers (boats!) gets surprisingly lively on weekends. **Dunguaire Castle,** 10min. from town on the Galway Rd., is actually a tower house—a popular type of dwelling for 16th-century country gentlemen. The narrow, winding staircase leads to expansive views of town, sea, and countryside. (☎637 108. Last admission 4:30pm. Open May-Sept. daily 9:30am-5pm. €4, students €3.50.) The first weekend in May, Kinvarans go crazy at the **Cuckoo Fleadh,** welcoming over 200 musicians to their town (check www.kinvara.com for more information). In mid-August they celebrate the **Cruinn Iú Na mBád,** "the gathering of the boats." **Galway Hooker Trips** (☎087 231 1779) gathers boats all year; for a cheap hooker ride, set sail with skipper Mehall on the *An Traonach*. Alongside Kinvara, **Doorus Peninsula** reaches out into Galway Bay. For those not enamored with nature, it's probably best to stay in Kinvara, but for hikers, bikers, or families with cars, Doorus is a worthwhile trip. Many of its sights are detailed in *Kinvara: A Rambler's Map and Guide*, available throughout town.

Buses connect Kinvara to Galway City and nearby Doolin (€5) three times a day from Flatley's Pub (see **Pubs,** below). **Bike rental** can be found at McMahon's Hardware on Main St. The **post office** is off Main St. (☎637 101. Open M-F 9am-5:30pm, Sa 9am-12:30pm.) There are no laundry, Internet, or banking facilities in town.

All visitors to Kinvara should hit **Fallon's B&B ❸,** in the center of town on Main St. Sweetheart Maura Fallon and family offer lovely rooms ranging from spacious singles to doubles and family rooms. (☎637 483. All rooms with bath, TV, and snacks. Irish breakfast €8-10. Singles €35; doubles €60.) Located on the Quay, **Cois Cuain B&B ❸** is a quaint B&B with clean, bright rooms perhaps best suited to couples. (☎637 119. Open Apr.-Nov. Doubles €54, all with bath.) The more upscale **Merriman Hotel ❺,** across from Fallon's, has 32 rooms, each with a bath, TV, and phone. Two rooms accommodate disabled travelers, and the hotel has its own restaurant, **The Quilty Room,** with 3-course meals for €30, and bar, **M'Asal Beag Dubh,** to boot. (☎638 222. June-Sept. singles €75; doubles €115; Oct.-May €60/€90.)

Food of the supermarket variety can be had at the **Londis** on the main road (☎637 250). The wood floors and blue tablecloths at **Rosaleen's ❶** provide a cafe-like atmosphere for intimate conversation over coffee and sandwiches. (☎637 503. Open mid-June to Sept. daily 5:30-9:30pm, lunch on weekends; Mar. to mid-June Th-M 5:30-9:30pm.) Inside **Keogh's ❷,** a restaurant that doubles as a bar, a humorous sign requests: "If you're drinking to forget, please pay in advance." (☎637 162. Breakfast €5-6.50, sandwiches €7-9.)

Kinvara's pub scene is the most active thing in town—all are located within seconds of each other on Main St., making for a very convenient pub crawl. A 20-something crowd flocks to **The Ould Plaid Shawl,** named after the Frances Fahy poem (Fahy was born in this very building in 1854). Tuesday nights are devoted to dart competitions (€2 to enter), but patrons can take advantage of the jukebox and pool table anytime. (Th trad. Open Th-Sa 5pm-12:30am, M-W 5-11:30pm, Su 5-11pm.) The older set of locals heads to **Greene's** for Guinness and spontaneous trad sessions. Reportedly the place to be for music on Monday nights, tiny Greene's has been passed down through generations of daughters and remains one of the few Irish bars owned and run by females. (☎637 110. Th-Sa 10:30pm-1am, M-W 10:30pm-midnight, Su 10:30-11:30pm.)

COOLE PARK AND THOOR BALLYLEE   ☎091

Two of W. B. Yeats's favorite retreats, both of which he eulogized, lie about 20 mi. south of Galway near **Gort,** where N18 meets N66. **Coole Park** is now a ruin and a national park; **Thoor Ballylee** has been restored to appear as it did when Yeats lived there. The sights are best accessed by car, but biking is another option. Be warned, though—high winds can make biking the 4 mi. from Kinvara a painful struggle.

The **Coole Park** nature reserve was once the estate of Lady Gregory, a playwright and friend of Yeats (see **The Irish Literary Revival,** p. 74). To Yeats, Coole Park represented the aristocratic order being destroyed in the 1920s by industrialism and war. Although the house was ruined in the 1922 Civil War (see p. 64), the yew walk and garden have survived. In the picnic area, a great copper beech known as the

"autograph tree" bears the initials of several important historic figures, including George Bernard Shaw, Sean O'Casey, Douglas Hyde (the first president of Ireland), and Yeats himself. The **Coole Park Visitors Centre** offers a 30min. film on the park and the poet, as well as an ample book collection on local rocks, trees, and wildlife. The best guide to Coole Park is *The 7 Woods Trail and Family Trail* (€1.20), available at the visitors center. (☎631 804. Open mid-Apr. to mid-June Tu-Su 10am-5pm; Easter to Aug. daily 9:30am-6:30pm; Sept. daily 10am-5pm. Last admission 1hr. before closing for the audio program and 15min. for the Centre. €2.50, students €1.20.) A mile from the garden, **Coole Lake** is where Yeats watched "nine-and-fifty swans... all suddenly mount/ And scatter wheeling in great broken rings/ Upon their clamorous wings." **Whooper** and **mute swans** still gather here in winter; in summer, they are replaced by cows lumbering down to the beach.

Three miles north of Coole Park, a mile-long stretch of road runs from the Galway road to **Thoor Ballylee,** a tower built in the 13th and 14th centuries. In 1916, Yeats bought it for £35 (€44.50!) and renovated it; he lived here with his family off and on from 1922 to 1928. While cloistered here to write his "Meditations in Time of Civil War," Republican forces blew up the bridge next to the tower. In Yeats's account, they "forbade us to leave the house, but were otherwise polite, even saying at last 'Good-night, thank you.'" The **visitors center** plays a 30min. film on Yeats's life and boasts a nice gift shop and rather extensive book selection. (☎631 436. Open Easter-Sept. M-Sa 10am-6pm. €5, students €4.50.)

The **Kilartan Gregory Museum** greets visitors in a large stone house situated on the road from Kinvara at the turnoff to N18. The building was once the national school where Lady Augusta Gregory started one of the first branches of the **Gaelic League** (see p. 60). It now houses a charming reproduction of a traditional Irish schoolroom, complete with actual posters and books from the turn of the century. (☎631 069 or 632 346. Open June-Aug. daily 10:30am-5:30pm; Sept.-May Su 1-5pm. €2.50, students €1, family €6.)

COUNTY GALWAY

The third-largest county in Ireland, Galway is also its most varied. The day and night, never-ending *craic* of Galway City draws more musicians and travelers than any other city outside Dublin. Twenty miles offshore lies the ancient silence of the Aran Islands' stacked limestone walls. The rugged mountain landscape of the county's coastline offers daytripping hikers the opportunity to commune with grazing cattle, and provides shade for the exquisite beaches that lie in between each ridge. Connemara is a largely Irish-speaking region with a harsh rocky interior and hardy locals to match; Clifden, its largest city, has abandoned the native tongue in favor of tourism. Nearby, Inishboffin and Inishturk provide intense doses of island isolation.

GALWAY CITY (GAILLIMH)   ☎091

In the past few years, Co. Galway's reputation as Ireland's cultural capital has brought flocks of young Celtophiles to Galway City (pop. 70,000). Mix the over 13,000 students from Galway's two major universities, a large transient population of twenty-something Europeans, and waves of international backpackers, and you

Galway

ACCOMMODATIONS
Adria House, **40**
Archview Hostel, **38**
Ashford Manor, **8**
Atlantic View, **41**
Barnacle's Quay St. Hostel, **33**
The Galway Hostel, **20**
Kinlay House (IHH), **22**
St. Joseph's, **28**
Salmon Weir Hostel, **3**
San Antonio, **1**

Sleepzone, **2**
St. Martins B&B, **29**
The Western, **4**
Woodquay Hostel, **5**

FOOD
Anton's, **39**
Brasserie Eleven, **25**
Bueno Appetito, **16**
Cafe Star, **14**
Couch Potatas, **15**

Conlon's Seafood Rest., **13**
Cougar's Organic Bistro, **35**
Da Tang, **30**
The Home Plate, **12**
Java's, **17**
McDonagh's, **37**
Mocha Mania, **24**
Pierre's, **36**
Tulsi, **26**
Vina Mara, **27**

SERVICES
The Bubbles Launderette, **10**
Celtel e.centre, **19**
Charlie Byrne's Bookshop, **31**
FAS, **9**
Fun World, **18**
Galway Peoples' Resource Ctr., **21**
Kenny's Bookshop, **34**
Neatsurf, **6**
Net@ccess, **23**
Prospect Hill Launderette, **7**
River Deep Mountain High, **32**
usit now, **11**

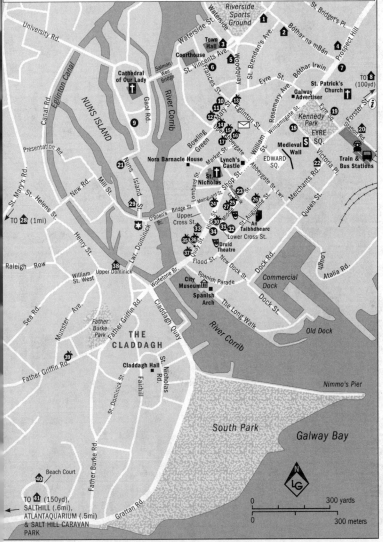

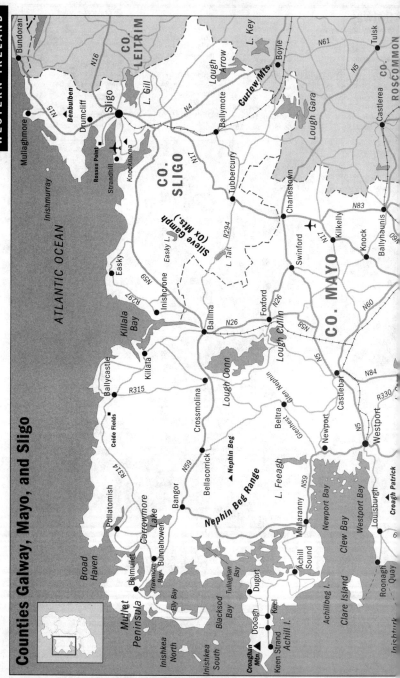

Counties Galway, Mayo, and Sligo

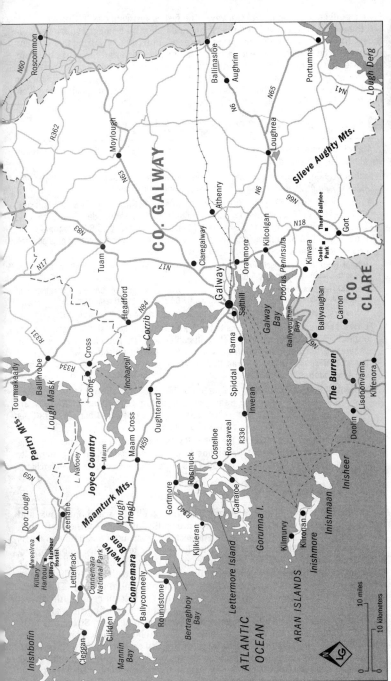

have a college town on *craic*. Galway is the fastest-growing city in Europe, and it has the energy to prove it. Street performers dazzle with homegrown tricks while locals, tourists, and wandering spirits lounge in outdoor cafes during that contemplative stretch of time between the *craic* that's been had and the *craic* to come. Fast-walking hipsters dish out flyers, entrance keys to the night's most exuberant live music. Follow them down the rabbit hole and become another strange face in Galway's mesmerizing pub universe. In the summer, a series of excellent festivals quickens the city's already frenetic pace.

✈ INTERCITY TRANSPORTATION

Airport: Carnmore (☎ 755 569), about 3 mi. from the city center. 5 small **Aer Éireann** planes jet to **Dublin** daily.

Trains: Eyre Sq. (☎ 561 444). Open M-Sa 9am-6pm. Trains to **Dublin** (3hr., 4-5 per day, €21-30) via **Athlone** (€11-14); transfer at Athlone for all other lines.

Buses: Eyre Sq. (☎ 562 000). **Bus Éireann** heads to: **Belfast** (7hr., M-Su 2-3 per day, €27.50); the **Cliffs of Moher** (late May to mid-Sept. M-Sa 3-4 per day, Su 1-2 per day; €11.40) via **Ballyvaughan** (€7.80); **Cork** (4½hr., 13 per day, €15.80); **Donegal** (4hr., 4 per day, €15.20); **Dublin** (4hr., 14 per day, €12). Private coach companies specialize in **Dublin**-bound busery.

Citylink (☎ 564 163) leaves from Supermac's, Eyre Sq. (14 per day, last bus 5:45pm; €14). Also runs to Shannon Airport (9 per day, €14).

Michael Nee Coaches (☎ 095 51082) drives from Forster St. through **Clifden** to **Cleggan**, and meets the **Inishboffin** ferry (M-Sa 2-4 per day; €7.80 single, €11.20 return).

P. Nestor Coaches (☎ 797 144) leaves from the Forster St. carpark (5-7 per day, €10).

Ferries: Three companies ferry folks to the **Aran Islands;** in general, the best prices are at the ticket booths in the tourist office. It can be tough to get info about the Doolin-based **O'Brien Shipping/Doolin Ferries** in Galway, but the other two companies, **Island Ferries** and **Queen of Aran II,** have ticket booths all over town. For more info, see **Aran Islands,** p. 358.

Car Rental: Budget Rent-a-Car, 12 Eyre Sq. (☎ 566 376). 23+. Economy class €55 per day, €379 per wk. Open M-F 8am-6pm, Sa-Su 9am-6pm. **Windsor Rent-A-Car,** Monivea Rd. (☎ 770 707). Free pickup. 23+. Economy class €58 per day, €286 per wk. Frequent weekend deals. Open M-Sa 9am-4pm.

Hitching: Hitchers usually wait on the Dublin Rd. (N6) scouting rides to Dublin, Limerick, or Kinvara. Most catch bus #2, 5, or 6 from Eyre Sq. to this main thumb-stop. University Rd. leads drivers to Connemara via N59. *Let's Go* recommends caution when hitching.

⚑ ORIENTATION

Buses and trains stop near **Eyre Square,** a central block of lawn, monuments, and lounging tourists; the train and bus station are up the hill on its southeastern side. To the northeast of the Square, along **Prospect Hill,** a string of small, cheap B&Bs await, while **Forster Street,** to the southeast, leads to the **tourist office** before turning into **College Avenue** where larger and more plush B&Bs are clustered. The town's commercial zone spreads out in the other direction. Northwest of the Square, **Woodquay** is an area of quiet(er) commercial and residential activity. The northwest corner of the square is the gateway to the pedestrian center, filled with hoards of shoppers and coffee-sippers by day and throngs of partiers and pint-chuggers by night. **Shop Street** becomes **High Street** becomes **Quay Street,** but without the passing traffic it feels like a single, long stretch of street-carnival fun. The few pubs along **the docks** in the southeast of the city are largely fishermen hangouts that close up and clear out early in the night. When weather permits, guitar players and lusty paramours lay on the lawn by the river along the **Long Walk.**

Fewer tourists venture over the bridges into the more bohemian **left bank** of the Corrib, where great music and some of Galway's best pubs await, largely untapped. Just south of the left bank is the **Claddagh**, Galway's original fishing village. A road stretches west past the quays to **Salthill**, a tacky beachfront resort with row-houses and skyrocketing property values. To the north of the west bank are the university areas of **Newcastle** and **Shantallow**, quiet suburbs where students and families live. Galway's Regional Technical College is a mile east of the city center in suburban **Renmare**, which dozes peacefully by its bird sanctuary.

⌨ LOCAL TRANSPORTATION

With its many pedestrian-only and one-way streets, little Galway lends itself best to walking. Other forms of transport are of use mostly to those staying out of the city center or planning excursions from the city.

Buses: City buses (☎562 000) leave from the top of Eyre Sq. (every 20min., €0.95). Buses to every neighborhood: #1 to **Salthill**, #2 to **Knocknacarra** (west) or **Renmare** (east), #3 to **Ballybrit**, #4 to **Newcastle**, and #5 **Rahoon.** Service M-Sa 8am-11pm, Su 11am-11pm. Commuter tickets €12 per wk., €40 per month. Students €10/€32.

Taxis: The biggest companies are **Big O Taxis**, 21 Upper Dominick St. (☎585 858), and **Cara Cabs,** Eyre Sq. (☎563 939). 24hr. taxis can usually be found around Eyre Sq. and near the tourist office. **Black Cabs** are considerably cheaper than taxis due to differences in licensing and fixed-price service, but they can't be hailed on the street; they are run by **MGM** (☎757 888), **Claddagh** (☎589 000), and **Eyre Square** (☎569 444).

Bike Rental: Europa Cycles, Hunter Buildings, Earls Island (☎563 355), opposite the cathedral. €9 per day, €40 per wk. Deposit €40. Open M-Sa 9am-6pm, Su 9am-noon and 4-6pm. **Mountain Trail Bike Shop**, Middle St. (☎569 888). €9 per day, €75 per wk. €40 deposit. Open daily 9:30am-5:45pm.

⊉ PRACTICAL INFORMATION

TOURIST AND FINANCIAL SERVICES

Tourist Office: Forster St. (☎537 700). A block south of Eyre Sq. Big, busy office where little is free; ask for free *Galway Tourist Guide* to avoid paying for info. **Bureau de change** available. Books accommodations upstairs for €4 fee. Open July-Aug. daily 9:30am-7:45pm; May-June, Sept. daily 9am-5:45pm; Oct.-Apr. M-F, Su 9am-5:45pm; Sa 9am-12:45pm. **Salthill** office (☎520 500) in an odd, round, metallic building next to the aquarium, visible from the main beach. Open May-Sept. daily 9am-5:45pm.

Travel Agency: usit now, Mary St. (☎565 177). Sells the ever-important **TravelSave** stamps (a well-spent €10). Also books student and youth-rate flights. Open May-Sept. M-F 9:30am-5:30pm, Sa 10am-3pm; Oct.-Apr. M-F 9:30am-5:30pm, Sa 10am-1pm.

Banks: Bank of Ireland, 19 Eyre Sq. (☎563 181), and **AIB**, Lynch's Castle, Shop St. (☎567 041), both have 24hr. **ATMs** and are open M-F 10am-4pm, Th until 5pm.

LOCAL SERVICES

Camping Equipment: Forget raingear? Visit **River Deep Mountain High,** Middle St. (☎563 968). Open M-Th and Sa 9:30am-6pm, F 9:30am-7:30pm.

Bookstores: Charlie Byrne's Bookshop, Middle St. (☎561 776). Massive stock of secondhand and discounted books, neatly organized by subject. Open July-Aug. M-Th, Sa 9am-6pm; F 9am-8pm; Su noon-6pm. Sept.-June M-Th, Sa 9am-5pm; F 9am-8pm. **Kenny's** (☎562 739), between High and Middle St., has an enormous collection of Irish interest books and an art gallery. Open M-Sa 9am-6pm.

Library: St. Augustine St. (☎561 666). Open M 2-5pm, Tu-Th 11am-8pm, F-Sa 11am-1pm and 2-5pm. Don't expect an oasis of calm—the children's wing can be quite noisy.

Bisexual, Gay, and Lesbian Information: Galway Gay Helpline, Eglinton St., P.O. Box 45 (☎566 134). The line is open 8am-6pm; afterwards a recorded message gives info on meetings and events. The *Gay Community News* is available at Charlie Byrne's Bookshop (see above), and in Stano's and Zulu's (see **Pubs,** p. 351).

Laundry: The Bubbles Laundrette, 18 Mary St. (☎563 434). Wash and dry €8. Open M-Sa 9am-6pm. **Prospect Hill Launderette,** Prospect Hill (☎568 343). Self-service wash and dry €6. Open M-Sa 8:30am-6pm; last wash 4:45pm.

Work Opportunities: See **Long-Term Stays,** p. 349.

EMERGENCY AND COMMUNICATIONS

Emergency: ☎999; no coins required. **Police** *(Garda):* Mill St. (☎538 000).

Counseling and Support: Samaritans, 14 Nun's Island (☎561 222). 24hr. phones. **Rape Crisis Centre,** 3 St. Augustine St. (☎1850 355 355). Limited hours.

Pharmacies: Pharmacies abound in the city; all keep similar hours. **Flanagan's,** Shop St. (☎562 924). Open M-Sa 9am-6pm. **Matt O'Flaherty's,** Shop St. (☎566 670).

Hospital: University College Hospital, Newcastle Rd. (☎524 222).

Internet: Celtel e.centre, Eyre Sq., conveniently located. €4.80 per hr., students 10% off. Open daily 8am-10pm. **Fun World,** Eyre Sq. (☎561 415), above Supermac's, can be noisy but great night deals. €5 per hr.; 8-11pm €3 per hr. Open M-Sa 10am-11pm, Su 11am-11pm. **Net@ccess,** Olde Malt Arcade, off High St., great morning and weekend prices. Open M-Sa 10am-10pm, Su 12-6pm. **Neatsurf,** 7 St. Francis St. (☎533 976). Fastest, cheapest at €0.75 per 10min. Open M-Sa 9am-11pm, Su 11am-11pm.

Post Office: Eglinton St. (☎562 051). Open M, W-Sa 9am-5:30pm; Tu 9:30am-5:30pm.

▮ ACCOMMODATIONS

In the last few years, the number of accommodations in Galway has tripled; it now approaches one thousand. Nevertheless, it is wise to call at least a day ahead in July and August and on weekends. Hostels are spread throughout the city and come in all shapes and sizes; almost all are well run and conscientious. Most B&Bs can be found in Salthill, but there are also a few closer to the city center.

HOSTELS AND CAMPING

▨ **Salmon Weir Hostel,** 3 St. Vincent's Ave. (☎561 133). Not as impressively stacked or spacious as some of its brethren, but extremely homey, with a friendly, laid-back vibe. Don't be surprised to find members of the staff strumming away in the stairwell, or travelers communing out back over their beverages of choice. Free tea and coffee. Laundry €6. Curfew 3am. 12-bed dorms €9-10; 6-bed €13-14; 4-bed €14-15. Doubles €35. ❶

▨ **Sleepzone,** Bóthar na mBán (☎566 999; www.sleepzone.ie), northwest of Eyre Sq. So accommodating it takes the "s" out of "hostel." Beautiful, new, fully loaded—huge kitchen, common room with flatscreen TV, carpark, **Internet** (guests free 8pm-10am), calm terrace. Wheelchair-accessible. 8- to 10-bed dorms €16.50; 6-bed €18; 4-bed €20. Singles €40; doubles €54. Weekends €1.50-10 more, Nov.-Apr. €2-17 less. ❷

Kinlay House (IHH), Merchants Rd. (☎565 244), half a block off Eyre Sq. Surprisingly huge, well-located hostel with plethora of rooms and services, including a foosball table. **Aran Island Ferry bus** departs from out front. Discounts for booking with their other locations in Cork and Dublin. **Bureau de change.** Wheelchair-accessible. Small breakfast included. Laundry €7. 8-bed dorms €15; 4-bed €16, with bath €19. Singles €27; doubles €40, with bath €48. Oct.-June €0.50-1.50 less. ❷

The Galway Hostel, Eyre Sq. (☎566 959), right across from the station. Burren Shale tiles lead up past soft yellow walls to tight dorms and clean bathrooms. Busy and hospitable. Light breakfast included. **Internet** €5 per hr. 24hr. reception. Large dorms €15; 4-bed €19, with bath €22. Doubles €45-50. ❷

Barnacle's Quay Street Hostel (IHH), Quay St. (☎568 644). Bright, spacious rooms in the eye of the Quay St. storm. Super-convenient for post-pub-crawl returns, but that same convenience can make front rooms quite noisy. Light breakfast included. No alcohol allowed on premises. Excellent security. Big dorms €15; 8-bed €16.50; 6-bed €19; 4-bed €20. Singles €50; private rooms €25 per person. Rates lower in off season. ❷

Archview Hostel, Dominick St. (☎586 661). Tucked away before the bridge, laid-back Archview welcomes travelers passing through and long-termers inclined to hang around. The hostel's location near some of the best music-spots in Galway compensates for the longer walk from the station (about 15min.). A bit worn, but at these prices, who cares. **Internet** €5 per hr. Dorms €10. Long-term stays €45 per wk. ❶

Woodquay Hostel, Woodquay (☎562 618). An oasis of calm and comfort just outside the busy center. Sheets €1; towels €2; laundry €8. Dorms €15. ❷

Salthill Caravan and Camping Park (☎523 972). Beautiful bayside location, about ½ mi. west of Salthill. A good hour walk along the shore from Galway. Open Apr.-Oct. €6 per hiker or cyclist. ❶

BED AND BREAKFASTS

St. Martin's, 2 Nun's Island Rd. (☎568 286), on the west bank of the river at the end of O'Brien's Bridge. The gorgeous back garden spills into the river. Located near Galway's best pubs, and just across the river from the main commercial district. All rooms with bath. Singles €32; doubles €60. Large family room €25. ❸

Adria House, 34 Beach Court (☎589 444; www.adriaguesthouse.com). On a quiet cul-de-sac off Grattan Rd., between the city center and Salthill. Home to a dynamic duo of owners—one is a former chef and the other a former member of the tourist board. €20-55, with prices highest July-Aug. ❹

Ashford Manor, 7 College Rd. (☎563 941), by Lynfield House. Classy, if pricey, B&B with TVs, direct dial phones, and hair dryers in each room. Ample parking. Big breakfast selection. €45-48. ❹

San Antonio, 5 Headford Rd. (☎564 934), a few blocks north of Eyre Sq. Dorms with single beds are backpacker-friendly, as are the owners. €25; without breakfast €20. ❷

The Western, 33 Prospect Hill (☎562 834; www.thewestern.ie), just past Eyre Sq. A large B&B that is well priced and convenient to the stations, Eyre Sq., and the pub downstairs. Rooms are simple but have cable TV and hotpots. Free parking. July-Aug. singles €40; shared rooms €35. Oct.-May €30-32.50. ❸

Atlantic View, 4 Ocean Wave (☎582 109), off Grattan Rd. Fully loaded B&B with relatively easy access to both Salthill and Galway City. Some 2nd fl. rooms open onto a balcony with great ocean views. Luxurious room 3 features a double, single, and jacuzzi. Some rooms wheelchair-accessible. Late July-Aug. €45-75; June to mid-July and Sept. €35-50; Oct.-May €35. ❹

St. Joseph's, 24 Glenard Ave. (☎522 147), Salthill. Small B&B with the lowest prices around. €17 with continental breakfast, €20 with full Irish breakfast. ❷

LONG-TERM STAYS

Galway has a large population of youthful transients who visit, fall in love, find jobs, stay for a few months, and move on. Most share apartments in and around the city, where rents run €50-75 per week. Those staying for less than a month are best off at one of the hostels, such as the Archview (see above), that have cheap weekly rates (€45). The best place to look is the *Galway Advertiser*. Apartment hunters line up outside the *Advertiser*'s office at the top of Eyre Sq. at around 2pm on Wednesdays; when the classified section is released at 3pm they high-tail it to the nearest phone box (in Eyre Sq.). Announcement boards in hostels also fill up with roommate-seekers. An ideal time to start looking for housing or jobs is just before the university lets out, in the second or third week of May.

Jobs are also relatively attainable in Galway, with most **short-term work** found in the service industry—simply ask around at local pubs and restaurants. A four-month student visa or other work permit helps a great deal by making one legal, although the situation isn't entirely hopeless without it. The Thursday morning *Galway Advertiser* has a long list of various job vacancies. Galway also has two centers which aid the introduction to productive society. **FAS,** in Island House to the left of the cathedral, posts vacancies for everything from service to managerial to research positions, and link with recruiters. (☎534 400; www.fas.ie. Open M-F 9am-5pm.) The friendly folk at the **Galway Peoples' Resource Centre,** in Canavan House on Nun's Island Rd., provide free guidance services through all aspects of the job search. (☎564 822 or 562 688. Open M-F 9am-5pm.) For those who want to secure something before arrival, **Alternatives to Tourism,** p. 46, lists other job-placement services in and around Ireland.

◖ FOOD

The east bank has the greatest concentration of restaurants; the short blocks around Quay, High, and Shop St. are filled with good values, especially at the cafes and pubs. **SuperValu,** in the Eyre Sq. mall, is for those who want to cook or stock up on fruit and cereal. (☎567 833. Open M-W and Sa 9am-6:30pm, Th-F 9am-9pm, Su noon-6pm.) **Evergreen Health Food,** 1 Mainguard St., has all the healthy stuff. (☎564 215. Open M-Sa 9am-6:30pm. Additional location in the Galway Shopping Centre on Headford Rd. is open W-F until 9pm.) On Saturday mornings, an ▨**open market** sets up cheap pastries, ethnic foods, and fresh fruit, as well as jewelry and art-work, in front of St. Nicholas Church on Market St. The crepes are a steal—€3.50 for Belgian chocolate, banana, and Bailey's. (Open 8am-5pm.)

▨ **Anton's** (☎582 067). Just over the bridge near the Spanish Arch and a 3min. walk up Father Griffin Rd. Self-consciously hip eateries on the other side of the river could learn a lot from this hidden treasure where they let the food do all the talking. Scrambled eggs with smoked salmon €5. Open M-F 8am-6pm, Sa 10am-5pm. ❶

▨ **Java's,** Abbeygate St. (☎567 400). Hip, dimly lit cafe. The craving and the raving flock here at all hours to satisfy hunger and various other pangs. The New York-style bagels are excellent (€4.75), as are the brownies. As reliable as Irish rain—only closes early Christmas Eve. Open daily 10:30am-3am. ❶

▨ **McDonagh's,** 22 Quay St. (☎565 001). Fish and chips madness—locals and tourists alike line up and salivate at this century-old institution. Takeaway fish fillet and chips €5.65. Open daily noon-midnight; takeaway M-Sa noon-midnight, Su 5-11pm. ❷

The Home Plate, Mary St. (☎561 475). Diners enjoy massive helpings on tiny wooden tables. Quaint and vegetarian-friendly, with curry dishes and sandwich variations big enough to share (but good enough to inspire hoarding). The vegetarian wrap (€8.85) is fantastic. Mains €7-10. Open M-Sa noon-9:30pm. ❷

Tulsi, Buttermilk Walk (☎564 831), between Middle and High St. This award-winning restaurant serves Ireland's best Indian food. The lunch (€6.95) is better and almost as cheap as the fast food joints around the corner. Open daily noon-3pm and 6-10pm. ❷

Cougar's Organic Bistro, Quay St. (☎569 600). A chance for vegans to leave the kitchen and let someone else cater to their diet; meat-eaters won't mind joining them—there are many diverse and tasty options for everyone. Roasted pumpkin paella €8.20; goat-cheese ravioli €8.50. After 6pm head upstairs to the **Claddagh Loft,** where similarly inventive meals are excellent, if more expensive. Open daily noon-10pm. ❸

Cafe Star, 3 Mary St. More than just a cafe, Star serves full meals that are both filling and delicious. Pasta dishes (€8) are enough to feed two, and the Funghi Pizza (€8) is eight little slices of heaven. Open M-Sa 8am-8pm, Su 12-8pm. ❷

Da Tang, Middle St. (☎561 443). Businessmen and hipsters crowd together in this busy Chinese noodle house. Some of the best food in town. Pickled mustard mixes with shredded pork in broth (€9). Takeaway available. Open M-Th 12:30-3pm and 5:30-10pm; F-Sa 12:30-3pm and 6-11pm; Su 6-10:30pm. ❷

Couch Potatas, Upper Abbeygate St. (☎561 664). Locals eat huge portions until dizzy. Try the Sir Walter Raleigh—potato with chicken breast and curry—€8.55; not even the staff knows where that name came from. Open M-Sa noon-10pm, Su 1-10pm. ❷

Bueno Appetito, Upper Abbeygate St. (☎538 166). The rarely found pizza-by-the-slice is available here for those who don't want a whole pie (meat or veggie €2.50). Pastas (€6.30) are about the cheapest in town. Open daily 10:30am-10:30pm. ❷

Pierre's, 8 Quay St. (☎566 066). Breaking the bank ought to happen at this oasis of quiet amidst the din of Quay St. Save room for dessert—the raspberry mousse floating in a chocolate cup is divine. 3-course meal €21. Open 6-10:30pm. ❹

Brasserie Eleven, 19 Middle St. (☎561 610). A good spot for an upscale, pre-theater meal, with an enticing range of meat, seafood, and vegetarian options. Tomato and basil lamb with salad and garlic bread €14.50. Open daily 12:30-10:30pm. ❸

Mocha Mania, Mainguard St. (☎566 146). Smokeless craic. A bright, friendly, cigarette-free coffee shop with dozens of coffee concoctions. Lovely apple tarts. Tasty panini (€5). Espresso €1.70; desserts €3.50. Open M-Sa 8am-6pm, Su noon-5pm. ❶

Conlon's Seafood Restaurant, 3 Eglinton St. (☎562 268). If waiting in line at McDonagh's isn't appealing, this friendly, casual spot is a good alternative. Choose from some 20 varieties of fish and chips (€7.50), or feast on the seafood salad bar (€14.50). Dozen oysters €15.75. Open M-Sa 11am-11:30pm. ❸

Vina Mara, 19 Middle St. (☎561 610). This wine bar and restaurant caters to all types of appetites with its lovely seafood, meat, and even vegan dishes. Order from their extensive wine list to complete the gourmet meal. Lunch €12; dinner mains €22. Open M-Sa 12-2:30pm and 6pm until late. ❹

☑ PUBS

With approximately 650 pubs and 70,000 people, Galway maintains a healthily low person-to-pub ratio (100:1, roughly). Indeed, the city's intricate constellation of pubs is its number one attraction. Music is alive and well every night, whether as the latest alternative rock, live trip-hop, or some of the best trad in the country. Very broadly speaking, Quay St. and Eyre Sq. pubs cater more to tourists, while locals stick to the more trad-oriented Dominick St. pubs; *Let's Go's* **Galway Pub Crawl** caters to all sorts. Look for flyers for specific dates, or check the *Galway Advertiser,* freely available at their office at the top of Eyre Sq.

DOMINICK STREET

◙ Roisín Dubh ("The Black Rose"), Dominick St. (☎586 540). Intimate, bookshelved front hides one of Galway's hottest live music scenes. Largely rock and singer-songwriters, but folk and blues put in appearances, and sessions are quite frequent. Marvel at the musicians pictured on the walls—they've all played the Roisín. Cover usually €5-20.

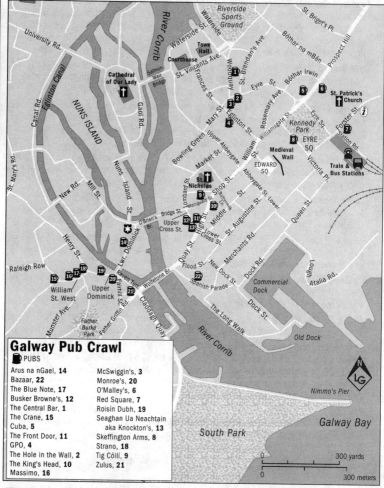

Galway Pub Crawl

🍺 PUBS

Arus na nGael, **14**	McSwiggin's, **3**
Bazaar, **22**	Monroe's, **20**
The Blue Note, **17**	O'Malley's, **6**
Busker Browne's, **12**	Red Square, **7**
The Central Bar, **1**	Roisín Dubh, **19**
The Crane, **15**	Seaghan Ua Neachtain
Cuba, **5**	aka Knockton's, **13**
The Front Door, **11**	Skeffington Arms, **8**
GPO, **4**	Strano, **18**
The Hole in the Wall, **2**	Tig Cóilí, **9**
The King's Head, **10**	Zulus, **21**
Massimo, **16**	

🞐 **Zulus,** Dominick St. (☎581 204). Galway's first gay bar. Approximately 95% male, but all are welcome to join in the fun at this friendly little place. Lively local banter and laughter ricochet off the walls until late into the night.

🞐 **The Blue Note,** William St. West (☎589 116). Where all the cool kids go. Twenty-something hipsters amass on lush couches, getting up to mingle or dance. Galway's best bet for turntable music, with top-notch guest DJs. Occasional indie films in the winter.

🞐 **The Crane,** 2 Sea Rd. (☎587 419), a bit beyond the Blue Note. A friendly, musical pub that is well known as the place to hear trad in Galway. Enter through the side door and hop up to the 2nd fl. loft. 2 musicians quickly become 6, 6 become 10, 10 become 20. Trad every night and all day Su. Set dancing Tu.

Strano, William St. West (☎588 219). A mixed lesbian and gay bar/club/meeting house with a pool room on the 3rd fl. Frequent theme nights; check out the GCN at Charlie Byrne's for current listings. DJs Th.

Monroe's, Dominick St. (☎583 397). Trad in a veritable *craic* warehouse. One of Galway's finest for Irish music. Nightly sessions from 9:30pm weekdays. Tu Irish dancing. Cheap pizzas from the joint next door are served until midnight.

Massimo, William St. West (☎588 239). Modern, sleek bar with comfy couches and a young crowd. Nightly DJs have a jazzy slant.

Arus Na nGael, Dominick St. (☎526 509). A bar for Irish speakers, this club nonetheless welcomes all sorts (well, kind of). On F or Sa night absorb the rhythms of the Irish language and music while quietly nursing a Guinness.

THE QUAY

▨ **The King's Head,** High St. (☎566 630). Like visitors to the city itself, pubbers come into King's Head expecting to spend the night, but fall in love and end up living there instead. There's certainly enough room for it, with 3 floors and a huge stage devoted to nightly rock. Upstairs music varies from trad to rock. Su jazz brunch 1-3pm.

Busker Browne's (☎563 377), between Cross St. and Kirwin's Ln. in an old nunnery. Get thee to this upscale, 20-something bar that packs a professional crowd onto wall-to-wall couches. If the first 2 floors seem unimpressive, head to the fantastic 3rd floor ▨ **"Hall of the Tribes,"** easily the most spectacular lounge in Galway. Su morning excellent live jazz downstairs.

Seaghan Ua Neachtain (a.k.a. **Knockton's**), Quay St. (☎568 820). The oldest pub in Galway, dating back to 1894. Afternoon pint-sippers munch sandwiches and study the streams of pedestrians from street-corner tables. Nightly trad.

Tig Cóilí, Mainguard St. This is the place to be for trad on this side of the river. Nightly sessions at 6pm and 9:30pm. When good weather rolls around, grab a seat outside to watch the street performers who make this particular street-corner their stage.

The Front Door, Cross St. (☎563 757). Beams of light criss-cross the dark interior of this pub. More rooms open as it gets busier, filling 3 maze-like stories. Get lost with that special someone, but don't expect any privacy—rowdy young pubbers fill in quickly.

Bazaar (☎534 496), across from the Arch and lit with purple lights. A lush, Moroccan-themed bar popular with the smartly dressed. No trad here, but jazz on W and DJs F-Sa.

EYRE SQUARE

▨ **The Hole in the Wall,** Eyre St. (☎565 593). This surprisingly large pub fills up fast with college-age singletons year-round. An ideal meat-market with booths for intimate groups, 3 bars for mingling, and tables to dance on. Flirtation spills into the small beer garden. Quality of music varies, but *craic* is a constant.

Cuba, Prospect Hill (☎565 991). Conveniently located under the club and live music venue (see **Clubs,** below), this colorful bar liberates itself on weekends and becomes an independent rogue club. Ask the bartender for Cuban cigars. M wonderful 20-piece jazz band, F disco, Sa ballads, Su stand-up comedy. Cover €5-10 most nights.

McSwiggin's, Eyre St. (☎568 917), near Eglinton St. A sprawling mess of small rooms and stairwells spanning 3 stories, McSwiggin's holds hundreds at a time, with room to spare. As the music rolls, so too does the food, which is served until 10pm on the 3rd fl.

Skeffington Arms (☎563 173), across from Kennedy Park. "The Skeff" is a splendid, multi-storied hotel pub with 6 different bars to wander between. Suspended walkways overlook the rear. A well-touristed, multi-generational pub crawl unto itself. DJs F-Sa.

The Central Bar, 32 Woodquay St. A refreshingly small pub—a rarity among Galway's labyrinthine giants.

Red Square, 11 Forster St. (☎569 633). Monolithic pub with enough space and taps to intoxicate Mao's army. The crowd is generally of the 30-40 variety, with many descending from the hotels above and on both sides. Frequent live rock; DJs on weekends.

▨ CLUBS

Between midnight and 12:30am, the pubs drain out and the tireless go dancing. Unfortunately, most of Galway's few clubs lag slightly behind its pubs in the fun factor. The place to be often rotates at disco-ball speed; a good way to find out what's hot is to simply follow the herd after last call.

▨ **Cuba,** on Prospect Hill, right past Eyre Sq. Far and away the best club, though the top fl. live-music venue is superior to the 2nd fl. standard dance club, which fills up quickly. Upstairs provides a little more room, a little less flash, and wonderfully varied but danceable live music. Cover varies (€5-10).

GPO, Eglinton St. (☎563 073). A student favorite during term; the inescapable yellow smiley faces try to convince summer clubbers that it should be theirs as well. Bank holiday M "Sheight Night" gives the chance to dress the sheightiest and dance to Abba's greatest hits. Tu 70s night, W comedy club. Cover €6.

O'Malley's, Prospect St. (☎564 595). Don't be deceived by its traditional appearance, this club/pub blasts thoroughly modern music. W Tribal Club, F drum and bass, Sa funk/house, Su live rock. Cover €3 midweek, weekends €6.

Karma, Eyre Sq. (☎563 173). The Skeff's swank little sister, Karma invites those dressed to impress (so leave the sneakers behind). A great place to get down with fellow-tourists. Open Th-Su at 11pm.

◪ TOURS

If pressed for time, half- or full-day group tours may be the best way to see the sights of Galway, the Burren, and Connemara. Some offer excellent values, with lower prices than bus tickets. Hour-long tours in and around the city seem largely unnecessary, as Galway is central and walkable, but they might be a good option on a rainy day. These hop on, hop off **buses** line up outside the tourist office (most €9, students €8). Several lines depart from the tourist office, bus station, and Merchant's Rd. (by Kinlay House) once a day for both Connemara and the Burren (€20-25, students €15-20): **Bus Éireann** (☎562 000), **Healy Tours** (☎770 066), **Lally Tours** (☎562 905), and **O'Neachtain Tours** (☎553 188). The *Corrib Princess* (☎592 447) sails from Galway's Woodquay and tours north-lying Lough Corrib (1½hr., June-Aug. daily 2:30 and 4:30pm, €9).

◉ SIGHTS

EYRE SQUARE. If traveling by bus or train, Eyre Square will undoubtably be the first sight stumbled upon. Visitors and locals gather on this centrally located square of grass for picnics, sunbathing, and downtime. Although the park was rededicated with officially as **John F. Kennedy Park,** referring to it as anything but Eyre Square tends to draw confused looks. Around its grassy commons, a collection of monuments speak to various interests. **The Browne Doorway** was transferred from the ruins of an ornate 17th-century home to serve as the Square's gate in 1904; it now looks strangely out of place without the fence that enclosed the park until 1965. The big rusty sculpture in **Quincentennial Fountain** celebrates the **Galway Hooker;** while the nearby statue portrays the Irish-speaking poet **Pádraig Ó'Cónaire.** On the south side of the Square is **Eyre Square Shopping Centre,** a large indoor mall that encloses a major section of Galway's 13th-century **medieval town wall.**

CLADDAGH. Until the 1930s, this area was an Irish-speaking, thatch-roofed fishing village. Stone bungalows replaced the cottages, but a bit of the small-town atmosphere persists in this predominantly residential area. The famous **Claddagh rings,** traditionally used as wedding bands, are today's mass-produced reminders. The rings depict the thumb and forefingers of two hands holding a crown-topped heart. The heart should be turned outward until marriage; once the heart is turned inward, the wearer's heart is no longer available. *(Across the river, south of Dominick St.)*

LYNCH'S CASTLE. The Lynch family ruled Galway from the 13th to the 18th century. Their elegant 1320 mansion now houses the Allied Irish Bank. The bank's small displays relate a dubious family legend: in the late 1400s, Lynch Jr. killed a Spaniard whom he suspected of eyeing his girl. Lynch Jr., sentenced to hang, was so beloved by the populace that no one would agree to be the hangman. Lynch Sr., the lord of the castle, was so determined to administer justice that he hanged his own son before a horrified yet admiring public. As various versions of the episode passed along, the term **Lynch's Law** came to refer to execution without legal authority—strange, since this execution was carried out for the purpose of following the law. *(Exhibit room open M-F 10am-4pm, Th until 5pm. Free.)*

NORA BARNACLE HOUSE. The little home of James Joyce's life-long companion has hardly changed since its famous-by-association inhabitant left. Original love letters and the table where Joyce composed a few lines arouse followers of the literary great. *(8 Bowling Green; the house with the maroon split-door. ☎ 564 743. Open mid-May to mid-Sept. W-F 10am-1pm and 2-5pm. Times vary; call ahead. Mid-Sept. to mid-May by appointment only. €2.50.)*

CHURCH OF ST. NICHOLAS. St. Nicholas is the patron saint of travelers, so bring some prayers along. A stone marks the spot where Columbus supposedly stopped to pray before sailing the ocean blue. Note the three-faced clock on the exterior; local folklore claims that the residents on the fourth side neglected to pay their church taxes. Glorious stained glass and relics from the Connacht Rangers provide further distraction. Don't miss the **farmer's market** outside on Saturdays. *(Market St., behind the castle. Open May-Sept. daily 9am-5:45pm. Free.)*

CATHEDRAL OF OUR LADY ASSUMED INTO HEAVEN AND ST. NICHOLAS. The enormous yet dull exterior of Galway's Catholic cathedral provides no hint of the controversy that assailed its eclectic design a quarter-century ago: the interior consists of dark and imposing Connemara stone walls decorated with elaborate mosaics, as well as green Connemara marble floors. *(Beside the Salmon Weir Bridge at the intersection of Gaol and University Rd. Open M-F 9am-6pm. Organ practice most weekdays 3:30-5:30pm. Open for mass M-F and Su at 9, 11am, and 6pm.)*

MENLO CASTLE. Depending on the amount of *craic*-induced adrenaline in the system, **hire a boat** and drift, row, or zoom up Lough Corrib to visit the ruined seat of the Blake family. **Frank Dolan's** fleet of boats sail away from the crowd and up Galway's gorgeous stretch. *(13 Riverside, Woodquay. ☎ 565 841. €4 per hr.)*

GALWAY CITY MUSEUM. Old photographs of the Claddagh, a knife-sharpener by a peat fire, and some fishy statistics form the bulk of this small exhibit, which could benefit from fuller, clearer labeling. The patio area above the Spanish Arch provides a nice view of the sea, river, and the plebs stretched out below. *(In the tower house next to the Spanish Arch. ☎ 567 641. Open May-Oct. daily 10am-1pm and 2:15-5pm; check at the tourist office for Nov.-Apr. opening times. €2, students €1.)*

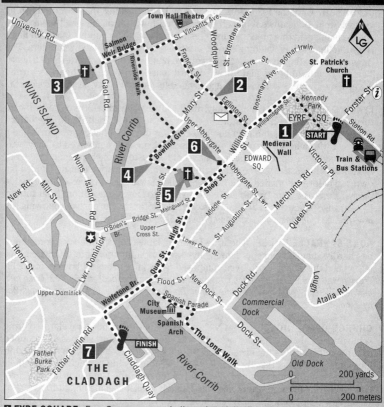

1 EYRE SQUARE: Eyre Square was rededicated as John F. Kennedy Park, but the name won't stick.

2 ELINGTON STREET: Walking south along Prospect Hill leads to Elington St. A stroll up Elington St. brings you to the **Town Hall Theater** on the corner of Elington and St. Vincent's Ave.

Time: 8hr.

Distance: 5 mi.

Season: Year-round.

3 CATHEDRAL OF OUR LADY: Across the **Salmon Weir Bridge** lies the **Cathedral of Our Lady Assumed into Heaven,** erected on the old Galway Jail, and made from Galway limestone and Connemara Marble.

4 NORA BARNACLE'S: Crossing back over the bridge leads to the **Riverside Walk,** down the Corrib. At Bridge St., turn right, heading up Leonard St. to Bowling Green and Nora Barnacle's house, a museum dedicated to her and her husband, **James Joyce.**

5 ST. NICHOLAS CHURCH: On the other side of Market St. is the **Lynch Memorial Window** and St. Nicholas Church. The southern exit goes to **Church Lane,** filled each Sunday with merchants selling everything from horse-shoe wine racks to various fried goodies.

6 LYNCH'S CASTLE: Head up Shop St. and then continue up William St. to the Edward Square Shopping Center. A passage inside the Center leads to **Galway's Medieval Wall.** From the Center, take **Shop Street** toward Lynch's castle to reach **High Street** and **Quay Street,** Galway's hub of shops, restaurants, and pubs.

7 CLADDAGH: Before the river, turn left toward the **Spanish Arch** and the **City Museum.** Continue past the Arch for the scenic **Long Walk.** Across the **Wolfe Tone Bridge** is Claddagh, an ancient fishing village and the birthplace of the famous Claddagh Rings.

ATLANTAQUARIA. Recently opened as the National Aquarium of Ireland, the museum features all things aquatic, with a particularly interesting tank filled with rays and ridiculous-looking "dabs." Like big eyes? A wax paper-covered jar upstairs holds the gigantic peeper of a fin whale. (☎585 100. Open 10am-8pm.)

OTHER SIGHTS. Across the University Rd. bridge from the cathedral is the **National University of Ireland at Galway.** The university was built 157 years ago, during the Famine, as the Tudor-style Queen's College Galway. Today, the university enrolls some 12,000 students each year. The **Long Walk,** by the river, makes for a pleasant stroll that leads to the **Spanish Arch,** which was built in 1584 as a defensive bastion and is now one of the city's finest surviving medieval structures.

🏃 ACTIVITIES

From the Claddagh, the waterfront road leads west to **Salthill,** where the coast alternates between pebbles and sand; when the ocean turns sunset red, it's time for some serious beach frolicking. Casinos, swimming pools, and a mini amusement park join the unappealing facades of new hotels that dominate the esplanade. (**Leisureland swimming pool** ☎521 455. Open daily 8am-10:30pm. Call for lane times. €7, children €4.80. **Summer carnival** open daily noon-11pm. Most rides €2-3.) A 15min. walk along the coast from Salthill leads to **Rusheen Riding Centre,** where the foot-weary can gallop on horseback over the beach or countryside. (Barna Rd. ☎521 285. Call for reservations. Most rides €20-25 per hr., 10% student discount.) The nearest **golf course** to the city is **Galway Bay Golf and Country Club,** which is beautifully surrounded by the ocean on three sides (☎790 500; €55-60 per person). There is also a **GAA Stadium** in Salthill (Pearse Stadium; Dr. Manix Rd.).

🎭 ENTERTAINMENT

ARTS, THEATER, AND FILM

The free *Galway Advertiser* provides listings of events and is available at the Galway Advertiser office at the top of Eyre Sq. **Zhivago** on Shop St. sells tickets to big concerts and events throughout Ireland. (Ticket hotline ☎509 960. Open June-Sept. M-Sa 9am-9pm, Su 10am-6pm; Oct.-May M-W and Sa 9am-6pm, Th-F 9am-9pm, Su noon-6pm. €1.90 booking fee.)

SIAMSA NA GAILLIMHE. At Claddah Hall, dancers, singers, musicians, and actors stun audiences with their showcase of traditional Irish performances. *(On Nimmos Pier, off Claddagh Quay. ☎755 479; www.homepage.eircom.net/~siamsa. Performances July-Aug. M-F 8:45 pm. Tickets €10-18.)*

TOWN HALL THEATRE. Presents everything from Irish-themed plays and original Irish films to international hit musicals. Responsible for the summer **Film Fleadh** and **Arts Festival.** *(Courthouse Sq. ☎569 777. Programs daily in summer; most performances 8pm. Tickets €6.50-20; student discounts often available.)*

AN TAIBHDHEARC. An Taibhdhearc (an TIVE-yark), Galways's oldest and mostly Irish-language theater, was founded in 1928 by a group of academics from Galway University, and has launched quite a few Irish actors into the limelight. Poetry readings and musicals alternate with full-blown plays. *(Middle St. ☎562 024. Box office open M-F 10am-6pm, Sa 1-6pm. Tickets €8-12, student discounts often available.)*

DRUID THEATRE. Internationally renowned performances of contemporary Irish plays, all in English. *(Chapel Ln., between Quay and Flood St. Performances nightly 8pm. Tickets €15-20, students €12-15.)*

GALWAY ARTS CENTRE. Hosts rotating art and photography exhibits and frequent workshops on dance, printing, and painting, as well as occasional poetry readings. *(47 Dominick St. ☎ 565 886; www.galwayartscentre.ie. Open M-Sa 10am-6pm. Free.)*

FESTIVALS AND EVENTS

Festivals rotate through Galway all year long, with the greatest concentration during the summer months. Reservations for accommodations during these weeks, especially Race week, are key.

GALWAY RACES. The gates go up at the end of July. The attending masses celebrate horses, money, and stout, not necessarily in that order. The grandstand bar at the 23,000-seat-capacity **Ballybrit track** measures over 70 yd., making it the **longest bar in Europe.** The major social event is Ladies' Day, when those with the best hats and overall dress are officially recognized. Hotels in the area can get booked up to a year in advance, so plan ahead. *(☎ 753 870; www.iol.ie/galway-races. Tickets €15-20 at the gate or by advance purchase.)*

GALWAY ARTS FESTIVAL. For two crazed weeks in mid-July, the largest arts festival in Ireland reels in famous trad musicians, rock groups, theater troupes, and filmmakers. Unofficial performers flock to the streets, which are only cleared for parades. *(General information ☎ 583 800; www.galwayartsfestival.ie. Box Office, Victoria Pl. ☎ 566 577. Open M-Sa 9:30am-5:30pm.)*

GALWAY POETRY AND LITERATURE FESTIVAL. Also known as the Cúirt, this festival gathers the very highest of the nation's brows in the last week of April. Past guests have included Caribbean poet and Nobel Prize winner Derek Walcott and reggae star Linton Johnston. Performances take place all over the city, but the main events are held in Town Hall. *(☎ 565 886.)*

GALWAY FILM FLEADH. Filmmania. Ireland's biggest film festival is a jumble of films, lectures, and workshops. The Fleadh happens in early July, right before the Arts Festival, and features independent Irish and international filmmakers. *(☎ 569 777; www.galwayfilmfleadh.com.)*

GALWAY INTERNATIONAL OYSTER FESTIVAL. Galway's last big festival of the year takes place in late September. Street theater, parades, and free concerts surround this 49-year-old Galway tradition, which culminates in the **Guinness World Oyster Opening Championship.** *(☎ 527 282; www.galwayoysterfest.com.)*

ARAN ISLANDS ☎ 099

On the westernmost edge of Co. Galway, isolated from the mainland by 20 mi. of swelling Atlantic, lie the spectacular Aran Islands *(Oileán Árann)*. The green fields of Inishmore, Inishmaan, and Inisheer are hatched with a maze of limestone walls—the result of centuries of farmers piling the stone that covered the islands to clear the fields for cultivation. The landscape is as moody as the Irish weather and tends to adopt its disposition, from placid blue calms to windy torments. The majestic, mythical Arans have continually sparked the imaginations of both Irishmen and foreigners. Little is known of the earliest islanders, whose tremendous but mysterious cliff-peering forts seem to have been constructed by the secret designs of the limestone itself. Early Christians flocked here seeking seclusion; the ruins of their churches and monasteries now pepper the islands.

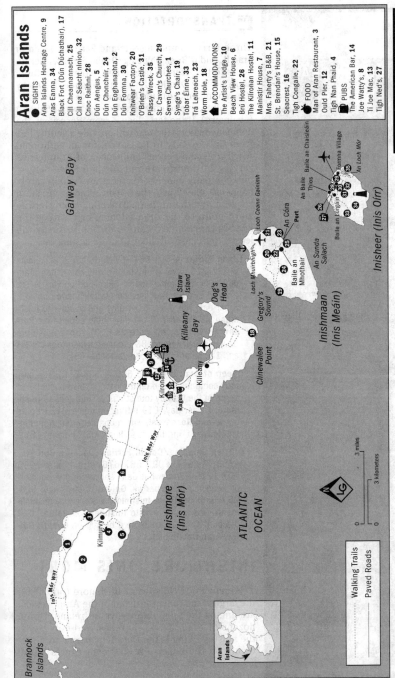

Aran Islands

● SIGHTS
Aran Islands Heritage Centre, 9
Aras Eanna, 34
Black Fort (Dún Dúchathair), 17
Cill Cheannannach, 25
Cill na Seacht nInion, 32
Choc Raithni, 28
Dún Aengus, 5
Dún Chonchúir, 24
Dún Eoghanachta, 2
Dún Formna, 30
Knitwear Factory, 20
O'Brien's Castle, 31
Plassy Wreck, 35
St. Cavan's Church, 29
Seven Churches, 1
Synge's Chair, 19
Tobar Éinne, 33
Trá Leitreach, 23
Worm Hole, 18

▲ ACCOMMODATIONS
The Artist's Lodge, 10
Beach View House, 6
Brú Hostel, 26
The Kilronan Hostel, 11
Mainistir House, 7
Mrs. Faherty's B&B, 21
St. Brendan's House, 15
Seacrest, 16
Tigh Congaile, 22

● FOOD
Man of Aran Restaurant, 3
Ould Pier, 12
Tigh Nan Phaid, 4

🍺 PUBS
The American Bar, 14
Joe Watty's, 8
Tí Joe Mac, 13
Tigh Ned's, 27

THE HIDDEN DEAL

AER ÁRANN

Have you ever noticed how expensive it can be to travel to an island? Because islands' secluded yet inconvenient locations blatantly preclude all notions of driving, walking, or biking, enterprising ferry companies develop veritable monopolies on the island-transit business, and therefore charge whatever they please. The three ferries that travel to the islands charge between €19-35 round-trip—a high price for budget travlers to pay. At these prices however, the €44 round-trip air-journey offered by Aer Árann, suddenly becomes a hidden deal. For only €9-24 extra, travelers can enjoy the luxury of flying to and from the magnificent isles. It's double the fun and takes just a fraction of the time, and it's especially attractive considering how unreliably the ferries run. And you know there's nothing like seeing an island from the sky! Better yet, a combined flight/sail option (€37) satisfies those who can't decide on one mode of locomotion.

Aer Árran (☎01 814 1458; within Ireland ☎1890 46 27 26; www.aerarran.ie). Flights to all three islands leave from the small airport in Inverin, 19 mi. west of Galway, and can be booked over the phone or at the Galway tourist office. To Inishmore: 10min.; 8 per day; €44 return, students €37. Shuttle bus to the Airport leaves from Kinlay House in Galway 1hr. before departure, €6.

TRANSPORTATION

Three ferry companies—**Island Ferries, Queen of Aran II,** and **O'Brien Shipping/Doolin Ferries,** operate boats to the Aran Islands. They depart from three main points: **Doolin** (40min. to Inisheer), **Galway** (2hr. to Inishmore), and **Rossaveal,** the main departure point, several miles west of Galway (40min. to Inishmore). If the ferry leaves from Rossaveal, the company making the trip will provide a shuttle bus from Galway City to Rossaveal for an additional fee. The Island Ferries and Queen of Aran ferries serving Inishmore are reliable and leave daily—one company cancels for weather (which rarely happens), check with the others, as some are more trepidatious than others. Traveling from Galway and Doolin to the Aran Islands, or between the islands themselves, can be difficult, to say the least— purchase all tickets before setting sail.

Island Ferries (☎091 561 767 or 568 903, after-hours ☎572 273; www.aranislandferries.com), has main offices in the Galway tourist office and on Forster St., close to Eyre Sq. One ferry sails to **Inishmore** (Apr.-Oct. 3 per day, Nov.-Mar. 2 per day) and another to **Inishmaan** via **Inisheer** (2 per day); both depart from **Rossaveal** (€16 return, students €10). A bus runs from Galway's Kinlay House B&B to the ferryport (departs 1½ and 1hr. before sailings; €6, students €5).

Queen of Aran II (☎566 535 or 534 553). The only ferry company based on the islands; also has a ticket booth in the Galway tourist office. Only goes to **Inishmore.** (4 per day. €19 return, students €12.) Boats leave from **Rossaveal,** with a bus departing from Kinlay House (1¼hr. before sailings; €6, students €5).

O'Brien Shipping/Doolin Ferries (Doolin ☎065 707 4455; Galway ☎091 567 676; after-hours ☎065 707 1710). Somewhat daily service in the summer, off season 3 times per wk. **Galway** to any island €20-25 return. **Doolin** to **Inishmore** €32 return, to **Inishmaan** €28 return, and to **Inisheer** €25 return. ISIC discount €5 (not available if bought on board). **Galway-Aran-Doolin** about €35.

INISHMORE (INIS MÓR)

The archaeological sites of Inishmore (pop. 900), the largest and most touristed of the Aran Islands, are among the most impressive in Ireland. Of the dozens of ruins, forts, churches, and holy wells, the most dazzling is the Dún Aengus ring fort, teetering on the edge of a cliff over the Atlantic.

Crowds disembark at Kilronan Pier at the center of the island, spread out to lose themselves amidst stone walls and stark cliffs, then coalesce again around major sights. Minivans and "pony traps" traverse the island, encouraging waery pedestrians to climb aboard and pay up, though bikes are the most scenic way to get around. Exactly 437 types of wildflowers rise from the rocky terrain and over 7000 mi. of stone walls divide the land.

▛ TRANSPORTATION

Ferries: Boats arrive in **Kilronan** from **Galway** and **Doolin**. See **Transportation, p. 360**.

Minibus: Minibuses at the pier stepping off the boat offer identical tours. 2hr. €10.

Pony Traps: Ponies and their carts also hover by the gangplanks, offering more picturesque, if bumpier, rides around the island. 2-2½hr. 4 adults €60.

Bike Rental: Aran Bicycle Hire (☎61132). €10 per day. Deposit €10. Open daily 9am-5pm. **B&M Bicycle Hire** (☎61402), next to the tourist office. €10 per day, €60 per wk. Deposit €10. Open Mar.-May 9am-5pm; June-Sept. 9am-7pm. Bike theft is a problem after dark—either lock it up or don't leave it.

▟ ▛ ORIENTATION AND PRACTICAL INFORMATION

The majority of human life hangs out in **Kilronan** *(Cill Rónáin)*, a cluster of buildings that makes up the island's main village, although houses and a few restaurants also huddle below Dún Aengus. Kilronan is the only place on the island to buy supplies, so stock up. The **airstrip** is on Inishmore's east end, while Kilmurvey, Dún Aengus, and most of the major sights are on the west. Anyone spending a few days on the Arans should invest in the Robinson map (€6.35), which meticulously documents every rock on all three islands, though a free map from one of the bike rentals might suffice for basic exploration.

Tourist Office: Kilronan (☎61263). Changes money, helps find accommodations, and has limited **luggage storage** (€1) during the day. Also sells the *Inis Mór Way* (€1.90). Open daily July-Sept. 10am-6:45pm; Oct. 10am-5pm; Nov.-Mar. 10am-4pm.

Banks: Bank of Ireland, up the hill before the post office. Open July-Aug. W-Th 10am-12:30pm and 1:30-3pm. Plastic-dependent travelers beware: there are **no ATMs on any of the Islands.**

Work Opportunities: The American Bar (☎61130) has been known to hire travelers for short-term work in the summer. 1-month minimum. Minimum wage plus tips.

Internet: At the **heritage center** M-F 9am-1pm and 2-5pm. €6.50 per hr.

Post Office: (☎61101), up the hill from the pier, past the Spar Market. Also has a **bureau de change.** Open M-F 9am-1pm and 2-5pm, Sa 9am-1pm.

▛ ACCOMMODATIONS

Many minibuses make stops at hostels and B&Bs that are farther away; call the individual accommodations or ask at the tourist office for more information.

▨ **The Kilronan Hostel** (☎61255), visible from the pier and adjacent to Tí Joe Mac's. 4-bed dorms are small, but bright and immaculate. Central location near all important liquids—a 2min. walk from the pier and close to the taps of Joe Mac's pub. Helpful, knowledgeable staff direct guests toward the island's wonders. €1 sheets are essential to avoid sleeping on plastic mattresses. **Bike rental** €10. Dorms €13, all with bath. ❶

Mainistir House (IHH), Main Rd. (☎61169), 1 mi. from "town" on the road that begins between the American Bar and the sweater stores. Once a haven for musicians and writers, this sprawling hostel still attracts expats to its magazine-filled sitting room, where big windows look onto the sea. Cook Joel prepares legendary dinner (see **Food,** p. 362) and tasty breakfast biscuits. **Bike rental** €10 per day. Laundry €6. Dorms €12; singles €20; private rooms €16 per person. ❶

The Artist's Lodge (☎61457). Take the turnoff across from Joe Watty's pub on the main road, continue straight down the path, and look right at the end. Cozy and inviting, with 3 good-sized, 4-bed dorms. Lodgers sip free tea and peruse the hostel's video collection by a crackling fire, or head out to the picnic table in the yard. Dorms €10. ❶

St. Brendan's House (☎61149). Take an immediate left off the entrance to the main road. An ivy-covered house with character across the street from the ocean. Full Irish breakfast included. Apr.-Oct. €20 per person, with bath €25; Nov.-Mar. €18/€20. €2 less with continental breakfast. ❷

Beach View House (☎61141), 3½ mi. west of Kilronan, on the main road near Kilmurvey. A great base for hiking. Some rooms have inspiring views of Dún Aengus, and all have beautifully warm quilts. Open May-Sept. Singles €36; doubles €48.50. ❸

Seacrest (☎61292), before St. Brendan's. A bright, spacious B&B close to the pier. **Jetski hire** can be arranged for €20 per 15min. with Amanda (☎087 298 6114). All B&B rooms with bath. Shared rooms €28 per person. ❸

🔥🍺 FOOD AND PUBS

The **Spar Market,** up the main road, functions as an unofficial community center. (☎61203. Open summer M-Sa 9am-8pm, Su 10am-6pm; winter M-Sa 9am-8pm, Su 10am-5pm.)

🍴 **Mainistir House** (see **Accommodations,** above). Dinner here is far and away the best deal on the island. Fill up for days on magnificent, mostly vegetarian buffets. 8-person tables are arranged to encourage conversation with fellow travelers or locals in search of epicurean bliss. BYO-wine. Dinner 8pm, reserve beforehand. €12. ❸

Tigh Nan Phaid (☎61330), in a thatched building at the turnoff to Dún Aengus. A nice resting spot after a morning of trekking. Specializes in home-cooked bread with home-smoked fish. Whiskey-cured Aran smoked salmon €5.95. Open daily 11am-5pm. ❷

The Ould Pier (☎61228), up the hill from the town center. Serves up fresh fish-and-chip configurations, burgers, and sandwiches. Eat inside or outside on sturdy picnic benches adorned with fresh flowers. Fish and chips €8.70. Open June-Sept. daily until 7pm. ❷

The Man of Aran Restaurant (☎61301), just past Kilmurvey Beach to the right. Wonderfully fresh, organic lunches in a historic setting. Toasties €3.20. Lunch daily 12:30-3:30pm; dinners in summer. ❷

Tí Joe Mac (☎61248), overlooking the pier. A popular beginning for the evening. Locals and hostelers savor pints on the terrace and their music in the back room. Sessions W.

The American Bar (☎61130). Despite the name, an Irish pub true and true. The 2 sides of the bar attract different clientele—young islanders and tourists stick to the left by the pool table, while older locals chew the fat on the right. Music most summer nights.

Joe Watty's (☎61155), west of the harbor on the main road. You've used it for orientation, why not use it for intoxication? Weekends usually bring bands and trad.

⊙ ♪ SIGHTS AND ENTERTAINMENT

The time-frozen island, with its labyrinthine stone wall constructions, rewards the wandering visitors who take the day to cycle or walk around its hilly contours. The **Inis Mór Way** is a mostly paved route that makes a great bike ride, circling past a majority of the island's sights. The graveled portion of the path leading from Dún Árran to Kilmurvy offers exhilarating views and bumpy, but fun, riding. The tourist office's maps of the Inis Mór Way (€2) purportedly correspond to yellow arrows that mark the trails, but the markings are frustratingly infrequent and can vanish in fog; it's best to invest in a Robinson map for serious exploring, or follow the crowds and hope for the best.

If time is scarce, high-tail it to the island's deservedly most famous monument, **Dún Aengus**, 4 mi. west of the pier at Kilronan. The **Visitors Center** below guards the stone path leading up to the fort. (☎61008. Open May-Sept. 10am-6pm, Oct.-Apr. 10am-4pm. €2.50; students €1.20.) One of the best-preserved prehistoric forts in Europe, Dún Aengus opens its 4000-year-old concentric stone circles onto the seacliff's 300 ft. drop, leaving the modern visitor awed and thoroughly humbled. Controversy continues as to whether it was built for defensive or ceremonial reasons. Many visitors are fooled by the occasional appearance of an island on the horizon—a vision so realistic that it appeared on maps until the 20th century. **Be very careful:** strong winds have been known to blow tourists off the cliffs.

The road to Gort na gCapall, toward the cliffs, leads to a small freshwater stream. If the wind and light are just right, glinting droplets of water suspended in air form an upside-down waterfall. A few minutes beyond the stream is a view of the **Worm Hole,** named for a sea serpent once believed to dwell in this saltwater lake. The bases of the surrounding cliffs have been hollowed by mighty waves to look like pirate caves. For a closer look at the caves, follow the cliffs to the left of Dún Aengus for about 1 mi., climb down into the tidal pool and walk back beneath the cliffs to the Worm Hole. The walk is thrilling at high tide, but more accessible at low tide. The sound of waves crashing under the rock is worth the 30min. trek.

The road leading to the fort from Kilronan splits near Dún Árann. Either way leads to Dún Aengus; turning left up the big hill goes to Dún Árann, and then down through a windy, gravel path to Kilmurvey, where it rejoins the flatter, paved coastal route. Most tourists decide that **Dún Árann Heritage Park,** at the top of the hill, is not worth the €3.50 admission fee. With sights such as cow dung and edible seaweed, they're probably right, though the lighthouse does provide a nice view from high atop the island. Inishmore's best beach is at **Kilmurvey,** with a sandy stretch and cold, cold water. Half a mile past the beach, a left turn leads to **Dún Eoghanachta,** a huge circular fort with 16 ft. walls. To the right past Eoghanachta are the misleadingly named **Seven Churches**—there were never more than two; the other buildings were likely monks' residences.

Uphill from the pier in Kilronan, the new, expertly designed ◪**Aran Islands Heritage Centre** provides a fascinating introduction to the islands' monuments, geography, history, and peoples. The center also screens *Man of Aran* several times a day. (☎61355. Open June-Aug. 10am-7pm; Apr.-May, Sept.-Oct. 11am-4pm. Exhibit or film only €3.50, students €3. Combined admission €5.) **Black Fort** (*Dún Dúchathair*), 1 mi. south of Kilronan across eerie terrain, is larger than Dún Aengus, a millennium older, and greatly underappreciated. Finish off the day on Inishmore with ◪**Ragus,** performed at the Halla Rónáin (down the street from the Aran Fisherman Restaurant)—an hour-long jaw-droppingly energetic display of traditional Irish music, song, and dance that receives rave reviews and costs almost twice as much in Dublin. (Tickets available at the door or from **Aran Fisherman Restaurant,** ☎61104. Shows at 2:45, 5, and 9pm. €13.) On summer Saturday nights, the first steps of a *céilí* begin at midnight at the dance hall (cover €6).

INISHMAAN (INIS MEÁIN)

Seagulls circle the cliffs and goats chew their cud, but there's little human activity to observe in the limestone fields of Inishmaan (pop. 300). With the rapid and dramatic changes that occured on the other two islands over the last few years, Inishmaan remains a fortress, quietly avoiding the hordes of barbarians invading from the east via Doolin and Galway. Even residents of Inishmore report that stepping onto Inishmaan is like stepping twenty years into the past.

For those who find beauty in solitude, a walk along the rocky clifftop is sheer bliss. The *Inishmaan Way* brochure (€2) describes a 5 mi. walking route that passes all of the island's sights. The thatched cottage where John Synge wrote much of his Aran-inspired work is a mile into the island on the main road. Across the road and a bit farther down is **Dún Chonchúir** (Connor Fort), an impressive 7th-century ring fort. At the western end of the road sits **Synge's Chair,** where the writer came to think and compose. The view of splashing waves and open seas is remarkable, but an even more dramatic landscape awaits a bit farther down the path where the coastline comes into view. To the left of the pier, the 8th-century **Cill Cheannannach** church left its rubble on the shore; islanders were buried here until the mid-20th century under stone slabs. A mile north of the pier, **Trá Leitreach** is Inishmaan's safest, most sheltered beach. Entering the **Knitwear Factory,** near the center of the island, is uncannily like stepping into a Madison Ave. boutique. The company sells its sweaters internationally to upscale clothiers, but visitors get them here right off the sheep's back at nearly half the price—expect to pay €90 for an Aran sweater. (☎73009. Open M-Sa 10am-5pm, Su 10am-4pm.)

For **tourist information,** as well as the chance to buy a variety of local crafts, try the **Inishmaan Co-op** (☎73010; open M-F 8:30am-5pm). Take the turnoff for the knitwear factory, continue straight, then make a right turn after the factory. The **post office** (☎73001) is in **Moore Village,** Inishmaan's tiny population center. **Mrs. Faherty** runs a B&B ❸, signposted from the pier, and stuffs guests with an enormous dinner. (☎73012. Open mid-Mar. to Nov. Dinner €12. Singles €30; doubles €50.) **Tigh Congaile ❸,** on the right-hand side of the first steep hill from the pier, is a gorgeous B&B. (☎73085. Singles €35; shared rooms €30.) Its **restaurant ❸** concentrates on perfecting seafood. (Lunch under €6.80, dinner from €16. Open June-Sept. daily 10am-7pm.) The **An Dún Shop** (☎73067) sells food at the entrance to Dún Chonchúir. **Padraic Faherty's** thatched pub is the center of life on the island and serves a small selection of grub until 6:30pm.

INISHEER (INIS OÍRR)

The Arans have been described as "quietness without loneliness," but Inishmaan can get pretty lonely, and Inishmore isn't always quiet. Inisheer (pop. 300), the smallest Aran, is the perfect compromise. On clear days, when the island settles into an otherworldly peacefulness, visitors wonder if these few square miles don't hold the key to the pleasures of a simpler life. The sights of the island can be explored alone by foot or bike, or with guidance on a **Wanderly Wagon** (☎75078) or **pony cart tour** (☎75092; both €7 per 45min.). **Inis Oírr Way** covers the island's major attractions on a 4 mi. path. The first stop is in town, at **Cnoc Raithní,** a bronze-age tumulus (stone burial mound) that is 2000 years older than Christianity. Walking along **An Trá** shore leads to the romantic overgrown graveyard of **St. Cavan's Church** *(Teampall Chaomhain)*. On June 14, islanders hold mass in the church's ruins in memory of their saint; a festival has recently been added. Cavan's nearby grave is said to have great healing powers. Below the church, a sandy beach stretches back to the edge of town. Farther east along the water, a grassy track leads to majestic **An Loch Mór,** a 16-acre inland lake brimming with wildfowl. The stone ring fort **Dún Formna** is above the lake. Continuing past the lake and back onto the seashore is the **Plassy Wreck,** a ship that sank offshore and washed up on Inisheer in 1960. The wreck has been taken over by buttercups, crows' nests, and graffiti. Ironically enough, the **lighthouse** is quite visible from the wreck. The walk back to the island's center leads through **Formna Village** and on out to **Cill na Seacht nIníon,** a small monastery with a stone fort. Remains of the 14th-century **O'Brien Castle,** razed by Cromwell in 1652, sit atop a nearby knoll. On the west side of the island, **Tobar Einne,** St. Enda's Holy Well, is believed to have curative powers, and is still a place of pilgrimage for the islanders. ◪**Aras Eanna** is a huge, double-winged building sitting atop one of the island's highest points as peacefully as the nearby clouds. The left wing of the building houses visiting artists, whose Aran-inspired work is then displayed in the right wing. The center also screens films on Inisheer and runs **Irish language courses** (beginner, intermediate, and advanced; week-long course €150). Its cafe serves up delectable scones for €1. One night a week, the center's theater becomes Aran's only **cinema,** while other nights see the occasional concert. (☎75150. Films €3, concerts €7. Gallery free. Open 10am-5pm.)

Rothair Inis Oírr rents **bikes.** (☎75033. €8 per day, €50 per wk.) Free **Internet** is available at **Inisheer Co-op Library,** a nondescript beige building up the road from the pier, past the beach. (☎75008. Open Tu, Th, Sa 2:30-5pm.) The **post office** is farther up to the left of the pier, in a turquoise house. (☎75001. Open M-F 9am-1pm, 2-5:30pm; Sa 9am-1pm.) **Brú Hostel (IHH) ❶,** visible from the pier, is spacious and promises great views. The upper rooms have skylights for star-gazing, but lower rooms have bigger windows. Call ahead in July and August. (☎75024. Continental breakfast €4, Irish breakfast €6.50. Laundry €5. 4- to 6-bed dorms €12; private rooms €16 per person.) **The Mermaid's Garden ❷,** signposted from the airstrip, on the other side of the beach, rents lovely, big rooms in their family home and serves a wonderful selection of breakfasts. (☎75062. €25 per person; €60 per family.) **Sharry's B&B ❸,** behind Brú Hostel, promises views and high ceilings. (☎75024. Singles with bath €32, without €25; shared rooms €25 per person.) For campers who don't mind chilly ocean winds, **Ionad Campála Campground ❶** stretches its tarps near the beach. (☎75008. Open July-Aug. €5 per tent, showers included.)

Tigh Ruairí, an unmarked pub and shop in a white building up the road running perpendicular to the beach, is the best bet for groceries. (☎75002. Shop open July-Aug. daily 9am-8pm; Sept.-June M-Sa 10am-6pm, Su 10:30am-2pm.) **Fisherman's Cottage ❷** serves amazing, organic, mostly island-grown meals. They've also been known to offer "Food for Healing" courses in April, May, and September. (☎75053. Soup and bread €2.50, dinners €12.70. Open daily 11am-4pm, 7-9:30pm.) **The Mermaid's Garden ❷** (see **Accommodations,** above), pleases steak lovers and tree-huggers with its impressive menu. (Vegan sandwich with hummus, roasted peppers, aubergine, and olives, €8.50.) **Cafe na Trá ❷** ("Cafe on the Beach") is, as its name implies, just off the sand. The decor is summery with Mediterranean hues, and the fish is fresh and tasty. (Cod and chips €7.50. Open June-Aug. 10:30am-6pm.) **Tigh Ned's** pub, next to the hostel, caters to a young crowd. The dim pub at **Ostan Hotel** (☎75020), up from the pier, is as crowded as a place on Inisheer can get.

WESTERN IRELAND

LOUGH CORRIB

Three hundred and sixty-five islands dot Lough Corrib, one for every day of the year. The lough, Ireland's largest, has enough elbow room for all of them. The eastern shores of Lough Corrib and Lough Mask stretch quietly into fertile farmland. The West slips into bog, quartzite scree, and the famously rough Connemara country. The island of Inchagoill, in the middle of the lough, contains the site of the second-oldest existing Christian monuments in Europe, while nearby Inisheanbó's luxurious and secluded digs have delighted Bob Hope and two of the Rolling Stones. Lough Corrib is considered one of Europe's best spots for salmon and trout angling, the principal activity on shore and boat.

OUGHTERARD (UACHTAR ÁRD)   ☎091

A small population center along the N59 between Galway and Clifden, Oughterard (OOK-ter-rard) watches most touring vehicles blink briefly in its direction before heading to bigger and better-known attractions. But this little town draws Galway natives to its quiet shores for weekend respite, and the city-weary traveler might do well to follow their lead. Hikers use Oughterard as a base for hikes into the Maamturk Mountains, while the less energetic prefer to angle in Lough Corrib's salmon-rich waters. Aughnanure Castle, a few miles from town, is worth a visit even for those just passing through.

⊞⊠ TRANSPORTATION AND PRACTICAL INFORMATION. Bus Éireann stops on Main St. in Oughterard (July-Aug. M-Sa 6-9 per day, Su 2 per day; Sept.-June 1 per day) on their way from Galway via Clifden. Hitchers report easy going in summer between Galway and anywhere west. *Let's Go*, as you well know, does not recommend hitchhiking. A helpful independent **tourist office,** on Main St., sells the useful *Oughterard Walking & Cycling Routes* handbook for around €3. (☎552 808. Open May-Aug. M-F 9:30am-5:30pm, Sa-Su 10am-5pm; Sept.-Apr. M-F 9:30am-5pm.) The **Bank of Ireland** on Main St. has an **ATM.** (☎552 123. Open M-F 10am-12:30pm and 1:30-4pm, Th until 5pm.) **Flaherty's Pharmacy** mends from Main St. (☎552 348. Open M-Sa 9:30am-1pm and 2-6pm.) Also on Main St. is the **post office.** (☎552 201. Open M-F 9am-1pm and 2-5:30pm, Sa 9am-1pm.)

⊞⊠⊠ ACCOMMODATIONS, FOOD, AND PUBS. Cranrawer House (IHH) ❶, a 10min. walk down Station Rd. off Main St., is a beautiful hostel with big windows looking out on its generous expanse of land. The owner is a professional casting instructor and guides day expeditions to the lough, at a cost. (☎552 388. **Bike rental** €10 per half-day, €15 per day, €70 per wk. Fishing trips €25 per hr., full-day €100. Laundry €8. Common room lockout midnight-8am. Open Feb.-Nov. 8-to 12-bed dorms €11; 5-bed family room with bath €13; private rooms with bath €15.) The large lawn of **Corrib View House ❸,** about 6 mi. down the Aughnanure Castle road off N59, descends to the lake's edge, where angling can be arranged. Guests also have full use of the tennis court. (☎552 345. All rooms with bath. €32.) B&Bs are easily found on Camp St. and the Glann Road. **Abhainn Ruibe ❷,** on Camp St., is the big yellow house on the right. The rooms are just as cheery, and the owners just as sunny. (☎552 144. Singles €30; doubles €25.) ❸

  Keogh's Grocery, a.k.a. **Spar,** sells food and fishing tackle from its location at the bend in Main St. The photo of Bob Hope buying snacks is not for sale. (☎552 583. Open summer M-Sa 8am-10pm; winter M-Sa 8am-8pm, Su 9am-9pm.) The "Full Monty Breakfast" (€6) at **Louise's Diner ❷,** on Camp St., is what the morning fry was meant to be; it's sure to keep you going all day. (☎557 685. Lunches €6-7, dinner €9-10. Open M-F 8:30am-8pm, Sa 8:30am-4pm, Su noon-4pm.) Great pub grub and brilliant *craic* flow from **The Boat Inn ❷,** across from Spar, and spill onto the tables that line the sidewalk. (☎552 196. Sandwiches and stews €4-7. Food served 11:30am-10pm. Live music F-Su.) Thatched **Power's Bar,** a few doors down, is the local Guinness tap. (☎557 222. Music Th and Su. Sa disco.) Across the street at **Keogh's Bar,** try your unsteady hand at drunk emailing. (☎552 222. Th disco, summer Sa-Su live rock or trad. **Internet** €6.35 per hr.)

🄖 🄐 **SIGHTS AND ACTIVITIES.** A mile south of town, a turnoff from N59 leads to Oughterard's top attraction, 16th-century **Aughnanure Castle.** Here a river, red with peat, curves around the impressively preserved fortified tower that was once home to the O'Flaherty clan, but is now home to a family of bats. The secret chamber and murder hole are highlights of the optional 40min. tour. Be careful—the O'Flaherty's were not a tall people, and they intentionally built their spiral staircases imperfectly in the hopes that ascending attackers would be tripped up. (☎82214. Open mid-June to mid-Sept. daily 9:30am-6:30pm. €2.50, students €1.20.) The 19th-century silver- and lead-yielding caverns of **Glengowla Mines,** 2 mi. west of town off N59, are the only show mines in Ireland. (☎552 360. Open Mar.-Nov. daily 9:30am-6pm. Call for off season hours.) Glann Rd. covers the 9 mi. from Oughterard to the infamous **Hill of Doon,** where the pre-Celtic Glann people annually sacrificed a virgin to the panther goddess Taryn. The 16 mi. **Western Way Walk** begins where Glann Rd. ends and threads through mountains, loughs, and Connemara coastline affording gorgeous views of the **Twelve Bens** and **Maamturks.**

Closer to home than many of the town's other sights, local sports enthusiasts swarm the **Gaelic pitch,** near the intersection of Pier Rd. and Main St., where they cheer on the local boys for €5 in the spring, though prices approach €20 as September's championships near. **Angling** on Lough Corrib is easily the most popular activity in Oughterard, and is arranged for visitors almost entirely through the town's accommodations. Private companies **Corrib Wave House** (☎552 147) and **Lakelands** (☎552 121) also lead angling expeditions. Surprisingly enough, golfing is generally less expensive than fishing; the **Oughterard Golf Club,** at the turnoff to Aughnanure Castle, is a beautiful 18-hole course with fine facilities. (☎552 131. €25 per person.)

Following the hatch of the mayfly, a myriad of **angling competitions** tangle Lough Corrib with lines in May, while competitors from all over Ireland assemble in June for the **Currach Racing Championships.** A family-oriented festival atmosphere accompanies the **Oughterard Pony Show** in late August.

🄑 **DAYTRIP FROM OUGHTERARD: INCHAGOILL.**

The Corrib Queen (☎092 46029) sails daily from Lisloughrea Quay on Cong's Quay Rd. (see p. 377), Ashford Castle, and the Quay road in Oughterard; it offers a brief but enlightening tour of the island (1½hr., June-Aug. 4 per day, €12-14 return). Those interested in more extensive exploration should take a morning ferry out and return in the afternoon.

Inchagoill (INCH-a-gill), reputed to mean "the Island of the Stranger," has been uninhabited since the 1950s. Aside from a few ancient monastic ruins and some toppled gravestones, there's little to see on the island. Still, at the right time of day, Inchagoill's eerie beauty and solitude make it as captivating as any of its more touristed island cousins. Two churches, about which very little is known, lie just down the right-hand path from the pier. **St. Patrick's Church,** built in the 5th century, has crumbled almost beyond recognition. The famous **Stone of Lugna,** which supposedly marks the gravesite of St. Patrick's nephew and navigator, is 3 ft. tall and stands among the other stones surrounding the church. Its inscription means "stone of Luguaedon, the son of Menueh." (Good thing we cleared *that* up.) This is the earliest known example of the Irish language written in Roman script, and the second-oldest known inscribed Christian monument in Europe (the oldest are the catacombs of Rome). The second Church, the **Church of the Saint,** only dates back to the 12th century and therefore bears less discussion.

WESTERN IRELAND

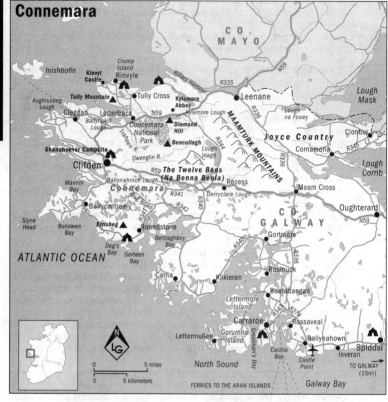

Connemara

Inishbofin

Crump Island

Kinvyl Castle

Rinvyle

Killary Harbour

CO. MAYO

R335

N59

Lough Mask

Aughrusbeg Lough

Tully Mountain

Tully Cross

Kylemore Abbey

Leenane

Lough na Fooey

R336

Cleggan

Letterfrack

N59

Kylemore Lough

MAAMTURK MOUNTAINS

Clonbur

Ballynakill Lough

Connemara National Park

Diamond Hill

Joyce Country

R345

Shanaheever Campsite

Benccullagh

R344

Cornamona

Lough Corrib

Clifden

Owenglin R.

Traheen R.

Lough Inagh

N59 The Twelve Bens (Na Benna Beola)

Recess

Maam Cross

Oughterard

Mannin Bay

Ballynahinch Lough

Connemara

R341

Derryclare Lough

N59

Bog Road

R340

CO GALWAY

Ballyconneely

R342

Slyne Head

Bunowen Bay

Errisbeg

Roundstone

R340

Gortmore

R336

Oughterard

N59

Dog's Bay

Bertraghboy Bay

ATLANTIC OCEAN

Gorteen Bay

Carna

Kilkieran

Rosmuck

Bealadangan

Lettermore Island

R343

R374

Carraroe

Rossaveal

Lettermullen

Gorumna Island

Greatman's Bay

Ballynahown

Spiddal

Inveran

Cashla Bay

Castle Point

TO GALWAY (15mi)

0   5 miles

0   5 kilometers

North Sound

FERRIES TO THE ARAN ISLANDS

Galway Bay

CONNEMARA (CONAMARA)

Connemara, a thinly populated region of northwest Co. Galway, extends a lacy net of inlets and islands into the Atlantic Ocean. The rough gang of inland mountains, desolate stretches of bog, and rocky offshore islands are among Ireland's most arresting and peculiar scenery. Driving west from Galway City, the relatively tame and developed coastal strip stretching to Rossaveal suddenly gives way to the pretty fishing villages of Roundstone and Kilkieran. Farther west, Clifden, Connemara's largest town, draws the largest crowds and offers the most tourist services. Ancient bogs spread between the coast and the rock-studded green slopes of the two major mountain ranges, the **Twelve Bens** and the **Maamturks.** Northeast of the Maamturks is **Joyce Country,** named for a long-settled Connemara clan. Ireland's largest *gaeltacht* also stretches along the Connemara coastline, and Irish-language radio (Radio na Gaeltachta) broadcasts from Costelloe.

Cycling is a particularly rewarding way to absorb the region. The 60 mi. routes from Galway to Clifden (via Cong) and Galway to Letterfrack are popular despite fairly challenging dips and curves toward their ends. The seaside route through Inverin and Roundstone to Galway is another option. In general, the dozens of loops and backroads in north Connemara make for beautiful and worthwhile riding. **Hiking** through the boglands and along the coastal routes is also popular—the **Western Way** footpath offers dazzling views as it winds 31 mi. from Oughterard to Leenane through the Maamturks. One word of caution for those traveling outdoors: **beware** the midges. These mayflies are out in full force during the summer months. **Buses** serve the main road from Galway to Westport, stopping in Clifden, Oughterard, Cong, and Leenane. N59 from Galway to Clifden is the main thoroughfare; R336, R340, and R341 make more elaborate coastal loops. **Hitchers** report that locals are likely to stop; *Let's Go* does not recommend taking advantage of locals' generosity. If all else fails, Connemara through the tinted windows of a tour bus (see **Galway,** p. 354) is better than no Connemara at all.

ROUNDSTONE (CLOCH NA RÓN) ☎095

Roundstone is a one-street fishing village that, like many of its neighbors along the Coast road, could do well in a quaint little Irish town contest. That withstanding, the striking surroundings and surprising variety of cultural offerings make Roundstone worthy of a brief visit. In the distance beyond the bay, a few prominent Bens rise into the clouds. The 2hr. hike up **Errisbeg Mountain,** which overlooks Roundstone's main street, culminates in a panoramic view of the entire region. Two miles along the coast beyond Roundstone, the beaches between Dog's Bay and Gorteen Bay fan out to a small knobby island.

The town is home to the famed **Roundstone Musical Instruments,** the only full-time *bodhrán* maker in the world (see **Traditional Music,** p. 76). Instruments built here are used across the world by famous Irish musicians, including the Chieftains. The owners have taken advantage of this fame and its attendant attendance by opening a veritable trad megastore with attached Irish kitsch warehouse. (☎35875. Open daily 9am-6pm.) Roundstone's primary cultural event is its annual **arts festival,** held in July. For information on the festival, check with the town's ever-informative **Information Centre.** (☎35815. Open M-F 10am-1pm and 2-3pm.)

The ever-attentive proprietress of ◼**Wit's End B&B ❸** maintains cozy and immaculately coordinated rooms. (☎35951. Open June-Sept. €28.) Travelers more interested in thrift than comfort seek out the **Gorteen Bay Caravan and Camping Park ❶,** 6 mi. west of Roundstone on the R341. (☎35882. No kitchen. Hot showers €1. Plots of land €6 per person.) After (or before) drumming up a frenzy, head to **Espresso Stop ❶** for coffee and cafe fare at the cheapest prices in town. (€4-7. Open daily 10am-6pm.) Vegetarians might prefer to venture a few doors down to **O'Dowd's ❸,** where mains are more expensive (€9-15) but explicitly non-carnivorous options are readily available. Explicitly alcoholic options are available at the attached pub.

CLIFDEN (AN CLOCHÁN) ☎095

The town proper is a cluster of touristically directed buildings resting between a small cliff and a pair of modest peaks. Socially, Clifden serves as a buffer between the built-up southern half of Co. Galway and pristine northern Connemara. In the off season (Sept.-May), the town is relatively quiet, but tourists flood in during the summer months. Outdoors outfitters and other upscale amenities cater to this crowd; budget accommodations have become increasingly scarce in recent years.

☐ TRANSPORTATION

Buses: Bus Éireann (☎091 56200) rolls from the library on Market St. to: **Galway** via **Oughterard** (2hr.; mid-June to Aug. M-Sa 6 per day, Su 2 per day; Sept.-May 1-3 per day; €9) and **Westport** via **Leenane** (1½hr., late June-Aug. M-Sa 1 per day). **Michael Nee** (☎51082) runs a private bus from the courthouse to: **Cleggan** (mid-June to Aug. 3 per day, Sept.-May 3 per wk.; €6) and **Galway** (2hr., 2 per day, €11).

Taxis: C&P Hackney Service (☎21309 or 086 859 3939). **Shannon Cabs** (☎51123 or 087 667 1738). **Joyce's** (☎21076 or 22082) is based out of the Clifden Town Hostel.

Bike Rental: Mannion's, Bridge St. (☎21160, after-hours 21155). €9 per day, €60 per wk. Deposit €20. Open M-Sa 9:30am-6:30pm, Su 10am-1pm and 5-7pm.

Boat Rental: John Ryan, Sky Rd. (☎21069). Fishing trips and excursions. €50 per day. Open year-round. Call anytime.

✦☐ ORIENTATION AND PRACTICAL INFORMATION

Most local traffic comes in on N59 from Galway (1½hr. to the southeast), which curves at the Esso Station and heads northeast to Letterfrack, Connemara National Park, Westport, and all other points north. **Market Street,** where the bus stops, runs parallel to **Main Street,** and the two meet at **the Square; Bridge Street** connects these main arteries near the Esso station. **Church Hill** runs up steeply from the Sq., and **Sky Road** and **Clifden Beach** are on the far side of town. Reportedly, hitchers find rides at the Esso station on N59. It's also been reported that *Let's Go* doesn't recommend hitching.

Tourist Office: Galway Rd. (☎21163). Extensive info on Connemara, including transportation schedules and lists of restaurants and activities in the area. Open June M-Sa 10am-6pm; July-Aug. M-Sa 9am-6pm and Su noon-4pm; Sept.-Oct. M-Sa 10am-5pm; Mar.-May M-Sa 10am-5pm.

Banks: AIB, the Sq. (☎21129). **Bank of Ireland,** Sea View (☎21111). Both have **ATMs;** both open M-F 10am-12:30pm and 1:30-4pm, W until 5pm.

Laundry: The Shamrock Washeteria, the Sq. (☎21348). Wash and dry €6 per load. Open M-Sa 9:30am-6pm. **Hillview Laundrette** (☎21836). Wash and dry €6.20 per load. Open M-Sa 9am-6pm.

Pharmacy: Clifden Pharmacy, Main St. (☎21821), just off the Sq. Open M-F 9:30am-6:30pm, Sa 9:30am-6pm.

Emergency: ☎999; no coins required. **Police** *(Garda):* ☎21021.

Hospital: ☎21301 or 21302. On the right entering Clifden from Galway.

Internet: Two Dog Cafe, Church Hill (☎22186). Cafe amenities run the gamut from creative, organic bistro fare and tasty sandwiches (€6.50) to weekly poetry readings (Su 8-10pm), discount international calls, and speedy computers. €1.30 per 15min. Food served M-Sa 10:30am-5pm. Internet available M-Sa 10:30am-7pm.

Post Office: Main St. (☎21156). **Currency exchange** at just 1.5% commission. Open M-F 9:30am-5:30pm, Sa 9:30am-1pm.

⌂ ACCOMMODATIONS & CAMPING

B&Bs are as plentiful as the wildflowers, especially in the center of town and along the Westport road. The going rates are €25 per person and up. Reservations are necessary in July and August.

Clifden Town Hostel (IHH), Market St. (☎21076). Great facilities, spotless rooms, helpful owner, quiet atmosphere, and vicinity to the pubs will endear guests to this hostel. Behind the modern decor, stone walls remind guests that the house is 180 years old. Open year-round, but in Nov.-Feb. call ahead. Dorms €12-15; doubles €32-34; triples €32; quads €56-60. ❶

Brookside Hostel (IHH), Hulk St. (☎21812), at the bottom of Market St. Clean, roomy dorms look over fat, innocuous sheep loitering in the backyard. Super-knowledgeable owner will painstakingly plot a hiking route for outdoorsy types. Wheelchair-accessible. Laundry €6. Open Mar.-Oct. Dorms €11.50; doubles €30. ❶

White Heather House, the Sq. (☎21655). Great location, with panoramic views from most rooms. Full Irish breakfast included. Singles €25-30; doubles €50. ❸

Foyles Clifden Bay Hotel, Main St. (☎21801). Pretty rooms right in the center of town. All with bath and breakfast. July-Aug. doubles €55-60; Sept.-June €37-45. ❸

Shanaheever Campsite, Westport Rd. (☎21018 or 22150), a little over 1 mi. outside Clifden. The tranquility of this spot compensates for its distance from the pubs. Game room and hot showers included. Laundry €6. Open year-round, but May-Sept. call ahead. €12 per person for tent or trailer. ❶

◪ FOOD

Clifden has a surprising variety of culinary options, ranging from family-run kitchens to pub fare to aspiring gourmet cooking to Chinese and fast food. For those who prefer cooking for themselves, **O'Connor's SuperValu,** Market St., provides supermarket standards. (Open M-F 9am-8pm, Sa 10am-7pm, Su 10am-6pm.)

Cullen's Bistro & Coffee Shop, Market St. (☎21983). Family-run establishment that cooks hearty meals (thick Irish stew €12.50) and home-bakes temptingly delicious desserts (rhubarb crisp with fresh cream €3.90). Open daily 11am-10pm. ❸

Walsh's, Market St. (☎21283). A busy bakery with a large seating area, Walsh's serves soups and sandwiches, baps, fresh pastries, and other morsels, all for €2-5. Open June-Sept. M-F 8:30am-6pm, Sa-Su 9am-6pm; Oct.-May M-Sa 8:30am-6pm. ❶

High Moors Restaurant, off the Ballyconneely road (☎21342). Up a tiny road from the center of town, this is Clifden's hidden pot of gold. The view of the bay from the restaurant's huge windows is almost as exquisite as the food. This luxury comes with a price—the 3-course offering costs a hefty €35—but dining here is an experience to savor long after the meal is done. Open daily from 7pm. Call for reservations. ❺

Connemara Diner, the Sq. Burgers (beef, fish, or bean) and other takeaway tasties served hot, fast, and late. Burger and chips €5. Open daily 6pm-1am. ❷

E.J. King's, the Sq. (☎21330). Crowded pub serves excellent food amidst exceptionally old wood furniture. Fish and chips €9. Food served daily noon-9pm. The official restaurant upstairs serves the same food at higher prices until 10pm. ❷

Mitchell's, Market St. (☎21867). The ambience here may be casual, but the food is elegant. Locals and tourists flock to their gourmet dishes, sampling roast duckling (€17) and chicken with bleu cheese sauce (€15). Gets crowded, so call ahead. Open mid-Mar. to mid-Nov. daily noon-10pm. ❸

Jasmine Garden, Church Hill (☎21174). Walk up the steep hill from the Square and bear to the right. Standard Chinese selections with plenty of veggie options. Mains €6.50-10. Open M-F 5:30-11:30pm, Sa-Su 5:30pm-midnight. ❷

PUBS

Malarkey's, Church Hill (☎21801). Pool table, poetry readings, open mic nights, and good impromptu music. Revelers sit on the floor when the chairs and pool table fill up. As the sign out front proclaims: "The *Craic* Begins at 6pm!"

Mannion's Bar and Lounge, Market St. (☎21780). Bring an instrument, or just pick up some spoons once there. Music nightly in summer, F-Sa in winter.

E.J. King's, the Sq. (☎21330). Edgar Allen Poe lighting with a spacious interior. Live music in the summer starts at 10pm. Opens at 10am.

King's, the Sq. (☎21900). A quiet pub with an older (masculine) local crowd. The town's best pint by consensus. Open daily from 10:30am.

O'Toole's, Bridge St. (☎21222), offers a pub disco some F-Sa nights for the dancing types and local young'uns. Open year-round from noon.

👁 🎭 SIGHTS AND ACTIVITIES

The 10 mi. long **Sky Road** provides a lovely route for hiking, biking, or a scenic drive. Starting just past the Square, it loops around the little peninsula to the west of town, paving the way to beautiful views of green hills and some legitimately dizzying coastline cliffs. Although good for bicycling, there are a few strenuous climbs to reach the highest vistas. The whole loop takes about 4-5hr. to hike. A mile down Sky Rd. stands what's left of **Clifden Castle,** once home to Clifden's founder, John D'Arcy. Farther out, a peek at the bay reveals the site where US pilots John Alcock and Arthur Brown landed the first nonstop trans-Atlantic flight in 1919, on a bog near Ballyconneely. One of the nicer ways to get acquainted with Connemara is to hike south to the **Alcock and Brown monument,** situated just off the Ballyconnelly road 3 mi. past Salt Lake and Lough Fadda. Those with wheels (of any kind), or the energy for a hike, should travel down the Galway road for about 6 mi. to **Ballyhinch Castle.** Formerly housing the likes of the O'Flaherty chieftains, Grace O'Malley, and Maharajah Ranjitsinji, the castle has been converted into a luxury hotel and restaurant. Daytime visitors are welcome for lunch (€4-9) or dinner (€17-20), or to stroll the grounds. The hotel boasts a river stocked with wild salmon, and displays the catch of the day each evening. After visiting the castle, head back to town via the Bog road, which leads to Clifden through a meandering 8 mi. stretch of beautiful and flat bogland, inhabited only by the occasional sheep.

Open up to the magic of the bog by joining one of the inspiring tours led by Michael Gibbons, the critically acclaimed archaeologist-raconteur of the **Connemara Walking Centre** on Market St. The tours explore the history, folklore, geology, and archaeology of the region, and investigate bogs, mountains, and the Inishbofin and Omey islands. The center also sells wonderful maps and guidebooks. Though closed for renovation for the 2003 season, it should be reopened for 2004. (☎21379 or 22278; www.walkingireland.com. Open Mar.-Oct. M-Sa 10am-6pm. Call ahead. Full-day or 2 half-day boat tours Easter-Oct. daily; call for a schedule. €19-32.)

Clifden Town Hall, at the base of the Sq. on Seaview Rd., erupts with performances of trad, dance, and song every Tuesday in July and August at 9pm. In late September, during the annual **Clifden Arts Week** (☎21295), dozens of free concerts, poetry readings, and storytellings summon even larger hordes of well-heeled tourists. Famous guests have included the Nobel Prize-winning Irish poet Seamus Heaney. On the third Thursday of August, attractive and talented equine contenders come to Clifden from miles around to compete for top awards at the **Connemara Pony Show,** held in the backyard of the Brookside Hostel.

INISHBOFIN ISLAND (INISH BÓ FINNE)   ☎095

Inishbofin, the "island of the white cow," has gently sloping hills (flat enough for pleasant cycling) scattered with rugged rocks, an excellent hostel, and near-deserted sandy beaches. Seven miles from the western tip of Connemara, the 200 rough-and-tumble islanders keep time according to the ferry, the tides, and the sun; visitors can easily adapt to their system. There's not much to do on the island except scramble up the craggy hills, sunbathe on the sand, commune with the seals, watch birds fish among the coves, and sleep under a blanket of bright stars. It's a rough life, but somebody has to live it.

▣⊁ TRANSPORTATION AND PRACTICAL INFORMATION. Ferries leave for Inishbofin from **Cleggan,** a tiny village with stunning beaches 10 mi. northwest of Clifden. Two ferry companies serve the island. Malachy King operates the *Island Discovery* and *Galway Bay,* which comprise the larger, steadier, and faster of the two fleets. (☎44642. 45min.; July-Aug. 3 per day, Apr.-June and Sept.-Oct. 2 per day; €15 return, children €7.50. Tickets available at the pier or on the boat.) The *M.V. Dún Aengus/Queen of Aran* is operated by Paddy O'Halloran. (☎45806. 45min.; July-Aug. 3 per day, Apr.-June and Sept.-Oct. 2 per day, Nov.-Apr. 1 per day; €12.70 return. Purchase tickets onboard.) Stock up at the **Spar** before going, especially if taking a later ferry. (☎44750. Open daily 9am-10pm.) **Bike rental** is available at the Inishbofin pier (☎45833) for €8 per day, but the island's hills and narrow roads are best explored on foot. To sort out a stay, call ahead or visit the **Community Resource Centre** (☎45909) to the left of the pier on the main road. The pleasant staff provides information, maps (€1.20-4.50), and limited **Internet.**

▌◪▣ ACCOMMODATIONS, FOOD, AND PUBS. Kieran Day's excellent ▥**Inishbofin Island Hostel (IHH) ❶** is a 15min. walk from the ferry landing. Take a right at the pier, bear left at the bottom of the hill, and ascend; the hostel is in the unmistakably yellow building. Visitors enjoy a large conservatory, swell views, and poetic tidbits. (☎45855. Sheets €1. Laundry €5 for wash and dry, €2.50 for wash. Dorms €10. **Camping** €5 per person.) The **Emerald Cottage ❷,** a 10min. walk west from the pier to the left, greets guests with home-baked goodies. (☎45865. Singles €20; doubles €40.) **Horseshoe Bay B&B ❷,** on the east end of the island, is still famed for a visit from Nicholas Cage (or a reasonable facsimile thereof) several years back; somehow, the place remains pleasantly isolated. (☎45812. Doubles €42.) Mary Day-Louvel of the **Lapwing House B&B ❸,** up the road behind the Community Center, feeds guests through the winter (☎45996. Doubles €30.)

Cloonan's Store, in front of the community center, sells picnic items year-round. (☎45829. Open M-Sa 11am-1pm and 3-5pm, Su noon-3pm.) **The Dolphin Restaurant ❹,** next to the Island Hostel, gets rave reviews from locals for its high cuisine. (☎45992. Mains €16-19. Open June-Aug. 7-9pm.) The island's nightlife is surprisingly vibrant, with frequent summertime trad. Near the pier, **Day's Pub** (☎45829) serves food from noon to 5pm, and stays open for pool playing, drinking, and occasional evenings of music. Smaller, more sedate **Murray's Pub,** a hotel-bar 15min. west of the pier, fills around 2pm for good grub and gab, slurred or otherwise.

◙ SIGHTS. Days on Inishbofin are best spent meandering through the rocks and wildflowers of the island's four peninsulas. Paths are scarce, but rambling through the hills is rewarding. Each peninsula warrants about a 3hr. walk. Most items of historic interest are on the southeast peninsula. East of the hostel lie the ruins of the 15th-century **Augustinian Abbey,** built on the site of a monastery founded by St. Colman in 667. A **well** and a few **gravestones** remain from the 7th-century structure. East of the Abbey, a conservation area encompasses pristine beaches and a small village. Spectacular views reward those who scramble up nearby **Knock Hill. Bishop's Rock,** a short distance off the mainland, becomes visible at low tide. On the other side of the island, to the west of the pier, is the **Cromwellian Fort,** which was used to hold prisoners before transporting them to the West Indies.

The ragged northeast peninsula is fantastic for **bird watchers:** gulls, cormets, shags, and a pair of peregrine falcons fish among the cliffs and coves. Inishbofin provides a perfect climate for vegetation hospitable to the corncrake, a bird that's near extinction everywhere except in Seamus Heaney's poems; two pairs of corncrakes presently call Inishbofin home. Fish swim in the clear water off two massive blowholes, while small land masses called **The Stags** tower offshore. The tidal causeway that connects The Stags to the mainland during low tide is extremely dangerous—stick to the shore proper. **Trá Gheal** (Silvery Beach) stretches along the northwest peninsula, but swimming there is dangerous. Off to the west is Inishark, an island inhabited by sheep and seals; the seals are most visible during their date-and-mate season in September and October. Inspirational archaeologist Michael Gibbons, of the **Connemara Walking Centre** in Clifden, offers tours focusing on Inishbofin's history, archaeology, and ecology. Leo Hallissey's fantastic **Connemara Summer School** (☎43443) studies the island's archaeology and ecology.

INISHTURK ISLAND (INIS TOIRC)   ☎098

Inishturk (pop. 90), a small, rounded peak rising 600 ft. out of the ocean between Inishbofin and Clare Island, has more spectacular walks and views than either of its more populated neighbors. Consult locals for directions to the ◙**Sea Cliffs,** a 30min. hike that will not disappoint. You'd never guess it now, but before the Famine, the island teemed with a population of nearly 800. These days, Inishturk seems virtually undiscovered. John Heanue's two **boats,** the *Caher Star* and the *Lady Marlyn,* make the bumpy passage to the island twice a day. (☎45541 or 086 202 9670. Departures from **Cleggan** Tu-Th; from **Roonah Quay** daily. Call ahead for times. €20 return; buy tickets on the boat.) For transport to and from Roonah Quay, check with **Port Cabs** (☎087 220 2123). Those attempting an expedition to Inishturk should treat it as such: bring adequate supplies and a good book. There are no budget restaurants on the island, but the three B&Bs serve ginormous home-cooked meals. **Concannon's B&B ❷** is a colorful house just off the pier with vibrant rooms and a flower garden. (☎45610. Dinner upon request €25. Doubles €50.) **Teach Abhainn ❸** lies far from the pier but close to the most striking scenery on the island. (☎45510. Dinner €25. Singles €30; doubles €50.) Guests at the Heanue's **Ocean View ❷,** up the road from Concannon's, heartily applaud fantastic meals and decadent rooms. (☎45520. Doubles €25.) A 15min. walk up from the pier, **The Community Centre** (☎45655) serves as the town **pub** and hosts traditional dancing, singing, and music sessions. It also houses the island's **Annual Trad Festival,** featuring nationally known musicians, every second weekend of June. For **tourist information,** call island manager Danny Kirrane (☎45778 or 45862).

LETTERFRACK (LEITIR FRAIC)   ☎095

Perched at the crossroads of N59 and the Rinvyle road, Letterfrack boasts three pubs and a legendary hostel, but little else. The **Galway-Clifden** bus (mid-June to Aug. M-Sa 11 per wk.; Sept. to mid-June M-Sa 4 per wk.) and the summertime **Clifden-Westport** bus (M and Th 2 per day, Tu-W and F-Sa 1 per day) stop at Letterfrack. **Hitchers** report short waits on N59.

The ■**Old Monastery Hostel ❶**, a sharp right and up the hill from the crossroads, is one of Ireland's finest. Sturdy pine bunks, desks, and couches fill the spacious high-ceilinged rooms, a peat fire burns in the lounge, and framed photos of jazz greats hang in the cozy basement cafe. Owner Steve Gannon cooks buffet dinners of the vegetarian and (mostly) organic style during the summer (buffet €9, plate €7; call by 5pm); he also serves fresh scones and porridge for breakfast. **Work opportunities** are sometimes available; inquire with Steve. (☎41132. Breakfast included. **Bike rental** €9 per day. **Free Internet** for residents. Laundry €5. 6- and 8-bed dorms €10; 4-bed €12. Doubles €15. **Camping** €6.) Fine pub grub, gourmet groceries, and friendly locals are all in evidence at **Veldon's ❷**, which fills at 10:30am and empties late, sometimes after a trad session. (☎41046. Open June-Aug. daily 9:30am-9pm; Sept.-May 9am-7pm.)

Visitors in the mood for a morsel of fishy camp should head to Derryinver's **Ocean's Alive**, 1½ mi. north of Letterfrack on the Rinvyle road. If touch tanks leave you cold—or if they just leave you hungry for more fishy fun—head to the dock. Ocean's Alive's own *Connemara Queen* cruises seven times a day for a 1hr. **seal and deserted island-viewing expedition.** According to local legend, the ship's captain can be persuaded to play his accordion. **Fishing trips** also arranged on demand. (☎43473. Open May-Sept. 10am-6pm; Oct.-Apr. 10am-4pm. Museum €5, students €4. *Queeny* cruise €13/€10. Fishing trip €32/€28.) During **Bog Week** (the last week in Oct.) and **Sea Week** (the first week in May), respected environmentalists gather to discuss bog- and sea-related issues while musicians jam amongst the peat. (Check www.connemara.net for more information.)

The road from Letterfrack to Leenane passes **Kylemore Abbey,** a castle in the dramatic shadow of a rocky outcropping. Built in 1867 by an English industrialist, the castle was sold to some Benedictine nuns in 1920 to pay the Duke of Manchester's gambling debts. The same Benedictine sisters have lived there ever since, and they cheerfully chat with interested tourists. The small neo-Gothic **church** a few hundred feet down from the Abbey is a tranquil glimpse of the past. A ledge above the castle, reachable by clammering up a rocky path, affords an exquisite view of the lake. (☎41146. Abbey open Apr.-Oct. 9am-6pm; Nov.-Mar. 10am-4pm; Jan.-Feb. 10am-5pm. €5, students €3.50.) The restored 6-acre **Victorian Walled Garden** delights those with nature-taming fantasies and fans of *The Secret Garden*. The immaculately trimmed plot of local and tropical plants is a lovely anachronism amidst the looming, nearby mountains. (Open Easter-Nov. Garden €6.50, students €4. Garden and Abbey €6.50/€5.)

CONNEMARA NATIONAL PARK   ☎095

Connemara National Park occupies 8 sq. mi. of mountainous countryside and is home to a number of curiosities, including hare runs, orchids, and roseroot. The far-from-solid terrain of the park is composed of bogs thinly covered by a screen of grass and flowers. Be prepared for muddy legs and a raised pulse. Guides lead free walks through the bogs (July-Aug. M and F at 10:30am) and offer several children's programs on Tuesdays and Thursdays. The ■**Visitors Centre** and its adjoining museum team up with perversely funny anthropomorphic peat and moss creatures to teach visitors the differences between hollows, hummocks, and tussocks. Follow this with the dramatic 25min. slide show about the park, which elevates the battle against opportunistic rhodo-dendrons to epic scope. (☎41054. Open June daily 10am-6:30pm; July-Aug. 9:30am-6:30pm; May and Sept. 10am-5:30pm. €2.50, students €1.25.)

The **Snuffaunboy Nature** and **Ellis Wood Trails** are easy 20min. hikes. The Snuffaunboy features alpine views while the Ellis wood submerges walkers in an ancient forest; both teem with wildflowers. A guidebook mapping out 30min. walks (€0.60) is available at the visitors center. For the more adventurous, trails lead from the back of the Ellis Wood Trail and 10min. along the **Bog Road** onto ▥**Diamond Hill,** a 2hr. hike that rewards climbers with views of bog, harbor, and forest, or, depending on the weather, impenetrable mist. (Diamond Hill has been closed for the past two years for erosion control; call ahead to confirm opening.) More experienced hikers may head for the **Twelve Bens,** a rugged range that stretches to heights of 2400 ft. There are no proper trails, and the range is not recommended for novice hikers, but Jos Lynam's guidebook, available at the visitors center (€6.35), meticulously plots 18 short hikes through the Twelve Bens and the Maamturks. Hikers often base themselves at the **Ben Lettery Hostel (An Óige/HI) ❶,** which overlooks postcard-quality stretches of scenery in Ballinafad. The turnoff from N59 is 8 mi. east of Clifden. (☎51136. Dorms €10-12.) A hike from this remote but friendly hostel through the park to the Letterfrack hostel can be made in a day. A tour of all 12 Bens takes hardy walkers 10hr. **Cycling** the 40 mi. loop through Clifden, Letterfrack, and Inagh valley is breathtaking, but only appropriate for strong bikers.

LEENANE (AN LÍONÁN) ☎095

Farther east along N59, **Killary Harbour,** Ireland's only fjord, slices through coastal mountains and continues inland to the wilderness outpost of Leenane (pop. 47). Wrapped in the skirts of the **Devilsmother Mountains,** this once-populous region was reduced to a barren hinterland during the Famine. Today, the crumbled remnants of farms cover surrounding hills. *The Field* was filmed here in 1989 and no one in town will ever forget it. Those who rank among the legions of *Field* enthusiasts will be the only people excited to learn that Aasleagh Falls served as the backdrop for the murder scene. At the **Leenane Cultural Centre,** on the Clifden-Westport Rd., spinning and weaving demonstrations expose the grisly fate of wool. (☎42323. Open Apr.-Oct. daily 10am-6pm. €2.35, students €1, family €7.) The **coffee shop ❶** in the Cultural Centre has cheap lunches. (Sandwiches and sweets €2-5.)

For a dose of excitement, head to ▥**Killary Adventure Company,** a few miles outside Leenane. It's Ireland's leading adventure company, offering everything from rock climbing to water skiing, windsurfing to helicopter rides. Archery, clay-pigeon shooting, and kayaking are other options. They also have accommodations for adventurers too tired to walk into town. (☎43411; www.killary.com. Half-day of activities starts at €32, full day €58.)

Killary Harbour Hostel (An Óige/HI) ❶ perches on the fjord's edge 7 mi. west of Leenane; the turnoff from N59 is marked. Aside from its unbeatable waterfront location, this hostel's claim to fame seems to be that Ludwig Wittgenstein (he of logical positivism fame) lived there for several months back in 1947. The building's hall windows and front door are no match for harsh Harbour winds, so pack warm clothes and supplies. (☎43417. Lockout 10am-5pm. Curfew 11:30pm. Sheets €1.25. Open on weekends Mar.-May; all week June-Sept. Dorms €12-13.) If the hostel-*craic* has become a bit much, cloister yourself in **The Convent B&B ❸,** on the northern side of town along N59. The dining room retains stunning stained windows from its previous life as a chapel. (☎42240. Open Easter-Nov. Doubles €50.)

COUNTY MAYO

Ancient, boggy plains and isolated settlements typify the dramatic countryside of Co. Mayo, but its enormous inland loughs and curved coastline also provide a wealth of memorable scenery, including multitudes of majestic islands and quaint harbor towns. Westport is lively and popular; these days, Ballina is as famous for nightlife as it is for its salmon fishing; and intriguing former sea resorts, such as Achill Island and Enniscrone, call out to travelers from the seaboard. In 1798, "The Year of the French," a certain General Humbert landed at Kilcummin. The good general ill-advisedly formed a combined force of French soldiers, Irish revolutionaries, and rural secret societies, and launched an attack, only to be foiled at Ballina and Ballinamuck by the wily Brits.

SOUTHERN MAYO

Southern Mayo is not oft-overlooked, like many of Ireland's most beautiful areas, nor is it offensively touristy, like many others. Cong can draw crowds, but overall the area seems like a destination between destinations, a place for in-the-know backpackers to recharge (Westport) and explore (Achill Island) before trekking on. The area itself is rural and quiet, except for the brief moments of summer tourism insanity, and public transport tends to be difficult year-round.

CONG (CONGA)   ☎092

Just over the border from County Galway is little, deep-green Cong (pop. 300). Bubbling streams and shady footpaths criss-cross the forests surrounding the town, and a ruined abbey crumbles at their edge. Nearby, majestic Ashford Castle towers over the choppy waters of Lough Corrib. In the past century, main roads were built to bypass this little hamlet; were it not for two recent events, Cong might have slumbered into obscurity. In 1939, Ashford Castle was turned into a zillion-euro-per-night luxury hotel, bringing the rich and famous to Cong from around the world. And, in 1951, John Wayne and Maureen O'Hara shot *The Quiet Man* here. Thousands of fans come each year to find the location of every scene, providing locals with a popular combination of bemusement and profit.

▐▀█ TRANSPORTATION AND PRACTICAL INFORMATION. Buses leave for Clifden from Ryan's Hotel (M-Sa 1 per day), Westport from Ashford gates (M-Sa 1-2 per day), and Galway from both locations (M-Sa 2-3 per day; all are €8-9). Because of infrequent transportation, some hitchhikers find rides at the nearby bus stop at Ballinrobe. **O'Connor's Garage,** Main St., **rents bikes.** (☎46008. Open daily 7am-9pm. €10 per day, ID deposit.) The town's **tourist office,** Abbey St., points visitors toward Cong's wonders, listed in *The Cong Heritage Trail* (€2.35). *Cong: Walks, Sights, Stories* (€3.59) describes good hiking and biking routes and, unlike hitchhiking, is highly recommended. (☎46542. Open Mar.-Nov. daily 10am-1pm and 2-6pm.) Across from the tourist office are **pay phones** and public toilets. Pick up meds at **Daly's Pharmacy,** Abbey St., by the tourist office. (☎46119. Open M-F 10am-6pm.) Got mail? The **post office** is on Main St. (☎46001. Open M-Tu and Th-Sa 9am-1pm and 2-5:30pm, W 9am-1pm.)

▐▘ ACCOMMODATIONS AND CAMPING. The **▨Cong Hostel (IHH) ❶,** on Quay Rd., 1 mi. down the Galway road near the entrance to Ashford Castle, is an immaculate compound with every imaginable facility. The playground, picnic area, game room, and huge TV room are sure to keep guests entertained. The tremendous camping area sprouts its own little village every summer. (☎46089. Continental breakfast €3.50, full Irish breakfast €6. Sheets €1. 14-bed dorms €10; 4-bed €13.50. Doubles with bath €32. **Camping** with facilities €6. Showers €0.70.) Other options provided by the family that runs the Cong Hostel include **Mary Kate B&B ❷**, offering rooms with bath and TV, and 4-person **cottages** in town. For more information, inquire with the owners at Cong Hostel. (☎46089. €20.) The **Courtyard Hostel (IHH) ❶**, on Cross St. in the small village of **Cross,** east of Cong, provides peace of mind several miles off the beaten track. Although its exterior may have seen better days, the hostel maintains the rustic charm of a farmhouse, with ducks and chickens roaming the yard. (☎46203. Dorms €10; doubles €30. **Camping** €5.) Within town, B&Bs are mostly of the above-pub variety. For more peaceful roosts, look along the main road between Cong and Cross. The star of this stretch is **Ballywarren Country House ❺**. Two of the three rooms come equipped with VCR and bidet; all have large baths, telephones, flower-topped beds, and complimentary sherry and chocolates. (☎46989; www.ballywarrenhouse.com. Award-winning candlelit dinners €35. Doubles €112-136.) **Inchagoill Island** has a free, eerie **camping** venue, though it costs a bit to get there (see p. 367).

◨▨▨ FOOD, PUBS, AND CLUBS. Cooks can go crazy at **O'Connor's Supermarket.** (☎46485. Open M-Sa 8am-9pm, Su 9am-8pm.) At **Danagher's Hotel and Restaurant ❷,** on Abbey St., young locals and Ashford Castle staffers down mammoth meals and countless pints. (☎46028. Mains around €9.25; toasties €3.50. Sa rock, Su DJ; occasional karaoke.) **The Quiet Man Coffee Shop ❶**, Main St., is obviously obsessed. A bright, cheery street-front counter rides in tandem with a dark dining room overlooking a river; both are freckled with black- and white- film memorabilia. (☎46034. Sandwiches €2.80. Open mid-Mar. to Nov. daily 10am-6pm.) **Lydon's** Main St. (☎46053), across the street and around the corner from the Spar, is the place to attend trad sessions; they begin at around 10pm on Wednesdays, Fridays, and Saturdays. The nearest nightclub, **The Valkenburg,** is in Ballinrobe; a bus picks groups up outside Danagher's on weekend nights around 11:30pm and drops them back at 3am. (Bus €2; varying cover around €10.)

◸ SIGHTS. Lord and Lady Ardilaun, former heirs to the Guinness fortune, were more interested in the scenery of Mayo than the brewing of beer; accordingly, they spurned Dublin for **Ashford Castle,** where they lived from 1852 to 1939. Much of *The Quiet Man* was shot on its grounds, though the castle itself was used as cast housing, not scenery. The castle is only open to guests, but visitors can gape at and stroll through the **gardens** for €5. Oscar Wilde once informed Lady Ardilaun that she could improve what he called her "dull" gardens by planting petunias in the shape of a pig, the family crest. Sadly, she never complied. A walk from the castle along Lough Corrib leads to a public **swimming beach.**

The sculpted head of its last abbot keeps watch over the ruins of the 12th-century **Royal Abbey of Cong,** near Danagher's Hotel. (Always open. Free.) Ruairi ("Rory") O'Connor, the last High King of a united Ireland, retired to the abbey for his final 15 years of life, after multiple losses to Norman troops. At the other end of the abbey grounds, a footbridge spans the **River Cong.** To the left is the **Monk's Fishing House,** a 12th-century structure with a hole in the floor through which the monks held a net to catch fish swimming downstream. After the fishing house, the path becomes pocked with caves, including **Pigeon Hole; Teach Aille,** a 4000-year-old burial chamber; **Giant's Grave;** and the **Ballymaglancy caves.** (Hostels lend out detailed cave maps.) The caves are often wet and slippery, and are obviously not

WEBB-DEFEAT Of the many caves in Cong Forest, none has as sinister a history as Captain Webb's. In the 18th century, a deformed and mentally disturbed Captain "Webb" Fitzgerald led 12 women to the cave, forced them to strip, and pushed them over the abyss to their deaths. The 13th victim fared better: she asked Webb to turn around in the name of decency while she disrobed, and once he did, the wily woman gave him a taste of his own medicine. When any woman in Cong is done harm, it is said Webb's cry can be heard from his resting place deep underground.

for the claustrophobic. Spelunkers, however, should enjoy exploring the dark depths. Essential spelunking safety gear consists of waterproof clothing, at least one flashlight, and a friend who knows where to expect you back.

The Quiet Man Heritage Cottage, Cong's thatch-roofed replica of Hollywood's studio replica of a Cong thatch-roofed cottage, provides a dose of fun for postmodernists and *Quiet Man* enthusiasts. Upstairs, there is a brief yet thorough timeline of the pre-John Wayne Cong and a 6min. video on the film. (☎46089. Open daily 10am-5pm. €3.75, students €3.) **Lough Corrib Cruises** runs a nightly cruise on the Lough with on-board live trad. (☎46029. €13, students €10.)

WESTPORT (CATHAIR NA MART) ☎098

In the lovely town of Westport, palm trees and steep hills lead down to quaint, busy streets, where tourists and residents duck into brightly-colored pubs, cafes, and shops. Small arched bridges span the still, mirror-like Carrowbeg River, which spills out into Westport Harbor. Visitors would be well-advised to follow the river's lead and head to the Quay, have a pint outside, and watch the wide, blue water become red, then blue again, as the sun sets. Hustle back to Bridge St. for pure, unadulterated *craic*. Book accommodations in advance to avoid trouble; tourists flock to Westport like hungry seagulls to harbor feed.

▐ TRANSPORTATION

Trains: Trains arrive at the **Altamount St. Station** (☎25253 or 25329), a 5min. walk up the North Mall. Open M-Sa 9:30am-6pm, Su 2:15-6pm. Train service to **Dublin** via **Athlone** (M-Th and Sa-Su 3 per day, F 2 per day; €21-23).

Buses: The **Bus Éireann** counter is housed in the tourist office. Buses leave from Mill St. and head to: **Achill** (2hr., 1-3 per day, €7.35); **Ballina** (1hr., 2-6 per day, €8.50); **Castlebar** (20min.; M-Sa 11-15 per day, Su 6 per day; €3.35); **Galway** (2hr.; M-Sa 7-8 per day, Su 4 per day; €11.60); **Louisburgh** (40min., M-Sa 2-3 per day, €4.25).

Taxis: Brendan McGing, Lower Peter St. (☎25529).

Bike Rental: Sean Sammon, James St. (☎25471). €8 per day; includes lock and pump on request. Open M-Sa 10am-6pm, Su by prior arrangement.

◪ ▐ ORIENTATION AND PRACTICAL INFORMATION

Bridge Street and **James Street** are the town's parallel main drags. At one end the streets are linked by **The Mall** and the **Carrowbeg River.** At the other end, **Shop Street** connects **the Octagon,** at the end of James St., to the **Town Clock** at the end of Bridge St. **High Street** and **Mill Street** lead out from the town clock, the latter into **Altamount Street,** where the Railway Station lies beyond a long stretch of B&Bs. Westport

House is on **Westport Quay**, a 45min. walk west of town along **Quay Road.** The original site of the town before it expanded down the river, the Quay is now a miniature Westport. The N60 passes through Clifden, Galway, and Sligo in addition to Westport. Hitchers report finding rides easily, although there is always risk involved.

Tourist Office: James St. (☎25711). Free town maps. Open daily 9am-5:45pm.

Banks: Bank of Ireland, North Mall (☎25522), and **AIB,** Shop St. (☎25466), both have **ATMs** and are open M-F 10am-4pm, Th until 5pm.

Work Opportunities: Several of the accommodations in town (see below) will hire travelers for short-term work, usually for 2-3 months min. Most offer free housing and stipend in exchange for reception, cleaning, or pub duties, and some prefer prior experience. Specifically, inquire at: **Old Mill Holiday Hostel** (contact Aoife Carr, ☎27045; oldmill@iol.ie); **Club Atlantic** (contact Anne McGovern and Oliver Hughes, ☎26644 or 26717); **Dunning's Pub and B&B** (contact Mary, ☎25161).

Laundry: Westport Washeteria, Mill St. (☎25261), near the clock tower. Full-service €6; self-service including detergent €5. Open M-Sa 9:30am-6pm.

Emergency: ☎999; no coins required. **Police** (Garda): Fair Green (☎25555).

Pharmacy: O'Donnell's, Bridge St. (☎25163). Open M-Sa 9am-6:30pm, Su 12:30-2pm.

Internet: Dunning's Cyberpub, the Octagon (☎25161). Guinness and email? €1.30 per 10min., €7.60 per hr. Guinness €3.30. Open daily 9am-11:30pm. **Gavin's Video and Internet Cafe,** Bridge St. (☎26461). Not much of a cafe (no food or drink), but cheaper than Dunning's. €1 per 10min. Open M-F 10am-10pm, Sa-Su noon-10pm. **Staunton's Music and Games,** Bridge St. (☎28431), boasts fastest connection in Westport. €1.30 per 10min., €6 per hr. Open daily 9:30am-6pm, later in summer.

Post Office: North Mall (☎25475). Open M-Sa 9am-5:30pm.

■ ACCOMMODATIONS AND CAMPING

Westport has hostels to suit every taste; its B&Bs cluster on Altamount Rd. off the North Mall, with more farther off near the Quay. Most charge €25-32 .

▨ **The Granary Hostel** (☎25903), a 25min. walk from town, at the 2nd fork in Quay Rd., on the left. Converted granary with a conservatory and serenely removed garden. Amenities are basic, with showers and toilets a few steps outdoors, but lovingly placed stones and a tree pushing through the wall of the conservatory lend an otherworldly calm. Cooking facilities and showers 8am-10:30pm. Open Apr.-Sept. Dorms €10. ❶

▨ **Altamont House,** Altamont St. (☎25226). Award-winning Irish breakfasts and hospitality have kept travelers coming back for 36 years. Cheerful owner Mary acts as a mother-away-from-home, but don't worry, she's more likely to light guests a fire and make a cup of tea than ask them to do dishes and keep curfew. €25, with bath €27. ❸

Old Mill Holiday Hostel (IHH), James St. (☎27045), through an archway next to the tourist office. Character, comfort, and convenience in a renovated mill and brewery. Sheets €1.50. Laundry €6. Kitchen/common room lockout 11pm-8am. Dorms €12. ❶

Club Atlantic (IHH), Altamont St. (☎26644 or 26717), across from train station and a 5min. walk up from the Mall. Popular with youth organizations, this massive complex has a game room, shop, and elephantine kitchen. Dorms are quiet and comfortable. **Camping** space beside a forest and bubbling river. **Sauna** and **pool** use at the nearby Westport Hotel €6. 4- to 6-bed dorms €10-11.50; doubles €26-31. Camping €6. ❶

Roscaoin House, Altamont St. (☎28519). Chandeliers in the foyer are the first indication of the luxury level at this B&B, which features well-appointed rooms with bath, a beautiful back garden, and **free Internet.** Doubles €60-75. ❸

Dunning's Pub and B&B, the Octagon (☎25161). Centrally yet quietly located above a bustling pub and convenient Internet cafe. Guests lounge with pints and pizzas at sidewalk tables, surveying the Westport action. €30. ❸

▣ FOOD

The **country market,** by the town hall at the Octagon, vends farm-fresh vegetables, eggs, baked-goods, rugs, and crafts. (Open Th 9am-1pm.) The **SuperValu** on Shop St., by contrast, has abundant supplies of processed goodies. (☎27000. Open M-Sa 8:30am-9pm, Su 10am-6pm.) Restaurants, which primarily cluster around Bridge St. and the Octagon, cater to yuppie tourists, and are generally crowded and expensive; book ahead for tables after 6:30pm on weekends.

■ **McCormack's,** Bridge St. (☎25619). An upstairs hideaway with creative dishes and local art adorning the walls. Ravenous locals and tourists feast on huge sandwiches, salads, and hot specials. Several veggie options, not including warm brie and bacon salad (€6.30). Hot breakfast baguette €3.80. Open M-Tu, Th-Sa 10am-5pm. ❷

Sol Rio, Bridge St. (☎28944). Romantically lit, lovingly prepared Italian. Tempting dinner mains set eaters back a few thousand *lira* (or €15), but delicious lunches are reasonably priced (€4-8). Appetizers, available as main courses upon request, are the most interesting of several vegetarian options—Mushroom Ripinne makes an excellent meal. Open daily noon-3pm and 6-10pm. ❸

Antica Roma, Bridge St. (☎28778). Striking a compromise between fast food and finer dining, this Italian restaurant/burger joint may not have the fanciest decor in town but does serve the cheapest meals available after the 6pm cafe closing time. Pizzas €7-9, burger and chips €5-7. Open Tu-Sa noon-10pm, Su 4-10pm. ❶

Gavin's Cafe, Bridge St. (☎087 932 8463). Emerald-green everything. Cheap sandwiches (€3) and tasty pastries (€1). Open M-Sa 9am-6pm; takeaway after 5:30pm. ❶

The Lemon Peel (☎26929), just off the Octagon, quietly located off the main restaurant glut. Rolls tide over hungry diners as they peruse the short but impressive menu, which includes veggie options. Barbary duck (€18) is highly recommended. Open June-Aug. daily 6-9:30pm; Sept.-May Tu-Sa 6-9:30pm. ❹

The Cove, Bridge St. (☎27096). Seafood takes priority at this local favorite, though a sirloin steak (€17.50) should please those who prefer their meat land-side. Open daily for breakfast (10am-noon); lunch (noon-3:30pm); dinner (M-Sa 6-9:30pm). ❸

The Urchin, Bridge St. (☎27532). Modern cuisine and sunny, yellow walls. Specializes in fresh seafood, but serves interesting, filling meals to resident vegetarians as well. Vegetarian crepes €12.90, seafood-stuffed sole €17.80. Open daily 6-10pm. ❹

◩◪ PUBS AND CLUBS

Westport's excellent pub scene tends to be overrun by tourists seeking great local *craic;* lucky for them, their cravings are often fulfilled.

■ **Matt Molloy's,** Bridge St. (☎26655). Owned by the flutist of the Chieftains. All the cool people (and apparently everyone else) go here. Officially, trad sessions occur nightly at 9:30pm; in reality, any time of day is deemed appropriate. Go early to get a seat. Open M-W 12:30-11:30pm, Th-Sa 12:30pm-12:30am, Su 12:30-11pm.

Henehan's Bar, Bridge St. (☎25561). A run-down exterior hides a vibrant pub. Beer garden in back is ripe for people-watching; 20-somethings fight 80-somethings for space at the bar. Music nightly in summer, weekends only in winter.

Cosy Joe's, Bridge St. (☎28004). Despite its 3 floors and 2 bars, the place still manages to live up to its name. Tightly packed with the young and happy. DJ Th-Sa. Open M-W and Su 10:30am-11:30pm, Th-Sa 10:30am-1am.

McHale's, up Quay Rd. from the Octagon (☎25121). Its excellent sessions are often overlooked by tourists, but not by friendly locals. Slightly older crowd. Trad W, F, and Sa, country Su. Open Su-W noon-11:30pm, Th-Sa noon-12:30am.

Hoban's, the Octagon (☎27249). A cozy local fave, with handshakes at every turn. Mature crowd. Trad Th-Sa. Open M-Sa 12:30-11:30pm, Su 12:30-11pm.

Kelly's, Castlebar St. (☎28834), off the Mall. An alternative pub where an eclectic set of young locals lounge and listen to frequent live music. DJs Sa. Open "late."

The Jester, Bridge St. (☎29255), trendy coffee house by day, but when the sun goes down the young and hip make their way here. From here, follow crowd to the club of the night. Open Su-Th 12:30-11:30pm, F-Sa 12:30pm-12:30am.

The West, Bridge St. (☎25886). Young, old, locals, tourists—everyone lounges on the purple couches, especially for weekend DJs. Open noon 'til they're forced to close.

Wits, Mill St., in the Westport Inn. Upscale bar becomes Westport's #1 down-and-dirty nightclub on weekends. 18+. Cover €8. Open F-Su midnight-2:30am.

Castlecourt Hotel, Castlebar St. Multi-leveled dance club with inspired lighting effects and a younger crowd than Wits. 18+. Cover €8. Open Th-Su midnight-2:30am.

👁 🏔 SIGHTS AND ACTIVITIES

Westport House's current state of commercial exploitation must be a bitter pill to swallow for Lord Altamont, its elite inhabitant and 13th great-grandson of Grace O'Malley. The small **zoo, train ride, paddle swan boats,** and **log flume** may entertain younger children, but the overcrowded and slightly faded house struggles to hold the attention of older visitors, especially as most rooms are closed off. The **grounds,** on the other hand, are beautiful and free. All this supposed fun is a 45min. stroll from town along the main roads—from the Octagon, ascend the hill and bear right, then follow the signs to the Quay. (☎25430 or 27766. Open July-Aug. M-F 11:30am-5:30pm, Sa-Su 1:30-5:30pm; June house and zoo only M-Sa 1:30-5:30pm, everything Su 1:30-5:30pm; Apr.-May house and rides only Su 2-5pm; Sept. house only daily 2-5pm. Full admission €19, house only €9; students €13/€6; children €12/€6.) More interesting is the **Clew Bay Heritage Centre** at the end of the Quay. A veritable garage sale of history, this charmingly crammed center brims with scraps from the past, including a pair of James Connolly's gloves, a sash belonging to John MacBride, and a stunning original photograph of the not-so-stunning Maud Gonne. The Centre also provides a **genealogical service.** (☎26852. Open July-Sept. M-F 10am-5pm, Su 2:30-5pm; Oct.-June M-F 10am-2pm. €3, students €1.50, under 15 free.) The manager of the Heritage Centre also leads **historical walks** from the town clock in July and August (1½hr.; Tu and Th at 8pm; €5, children free). In town is the more basic **Westport Heritage Centre,** housed in the tourist office (see **Orientation and Practical Information,** p. 379). The Centre details the history of the town's development and has an **interactive scale model** of Westport as precious as the real thing (€3).

Conveniently located behind the tourist office is **Westport Leisure Park,** with a **fitness suite** to work off the pints, large **pool** for laps, and for a reward, the **sauna** or **jacuzzi.** (☎29160. Open M-F 8:30am-10pm, Sa-Su 10am-8pm. Pool and spa facilities €5.20, students €4; fitness suite €6.40/€5; combined €7.50/€6.) Just outside town, **Carrowholly Stables & Trekking Centre,** leads trots to the banks of Clew Bay. (☎27057. €20 per hr.) In late August, celebrate **Westport Arts Festival** (☎66502), a week of free concerts, poetry readings, and plays, or enjoy all things equine at **Westport Horse and Pony Fair Competitions** in late September (☎25616).

▶ DAYTRIP FROM WESTPORT: CROAGH PATRICK

Murrisk Abbey is several mi. west of Westport on R395 toward Louisburgh. Buses go to Murrisk (July-Aug. M-F 2-3 per day; Sept.-June M-Sa 1-2 per day), but if traveling with a friend, a cab (☎ 27171) is cheaper and more convenient. Biking is another option, but not palatable to those climbing the mountain. Ballintubber Abbey (☎ 094 30709) is about 6 mi. south of Castlebar on N84, and 22 mi. from Croagh Patrick. The Croagh Patrick Information Centre (☎ 64114) foots the mountain on the Pilgrim's Path off R395, and has shower and locker facilities.

Conical **Croagh Patrick** rises 2510 ft. over Clew Bay. The summit has been revered as a holy site for thousands of years; it was considered most sacred to Lug, the Sun God, and one-time ruler of the Túatha de Danann (see **Legends and Folktales,** p. 73). After arriving here in AD 441, St. Patrick prayed and fasted for the standard 40 days and 40 nights, argued with angels, and then banished the snakes from Ireland. Another tale holds that the pagan Celtic god Crom Dubh resided at Croagh Patrick until St. Paddy himself threw him into a hollow at the mountain's base. Faithful Christians have climbed the mountain in honor of St. Paddy for nearly 1400 years. The barefoot pilgrimage to the summit originally ended on St. Patrick's feast day, March 17th, but the death-by-thunderstorm (an act of God, no doubt) of 30 pilgrims in AD 1113 moved the holy trek to Lughnasa—**Lug's holy night** on the last Sunday in July—when the weather is slightly more forgiving. Others climb the mountain for the sheer exhilaration and incredible views. The hike takes 4hr. round-trip, but be forewarned: the terrain can be quite steep, and the footing unsure. Well-shod climbers start their excursion from the 15th-century **Murrisk Abbey;** pilgrims and hikers also set out for Croagh Patrick along the Tóchar Phádraig, a path from **Ballintubber Abbey.** The new and useful **Croagh Patrick Information Centre** offers tours, showers, luggage storage, food, and directions to the summit.

NEAR WESTPORT: CLARE ISLAND   ☎ 098

Although only a ferry ride away, Clare Island occupies a world entirely different from bustling, heavily touristed Westport. Sheep calmly rule this desolate but beautiful island, intently grazing and wholly indifferent to the dramatic green climbs and rugged cliff descents of their kingdom. Grace O'Malley, known locally as Granuaile, ruled the 16th-century seas west of Ireland from her castle above Clare's little but lovely Blue Flag **beach.** Granuaile died in 1603; supposedly, she was laid to rest under the ruins of the **Clare Island Abbey,** near the shop. Granuaile's legacy is maintained by the island's residents, at least half of whom are O'Malleys.

The main activity on the island is **hiking,** with paths, appropriate for both walking and biking, running to all of the major sights, and mountains that provide more challenging terrain. A leaflet detailing five walks is available at the hotel or at the ferry ticket counters. The cliffs of **Knockmore Mountain** (1550 ft.) rise from the sea on the western coast, where the ruins of a Napoleonic **signal tower** stand crumbling. A 2hr. walk runs along the east side of the island to the **lighthouse.** Ten minutes. before the lighthouse is the **Ballytougheny Loom Shop and Demonstration Centre,** a short walk up a path to the left of the road. The family of weavers that resides here spin their own wool and dye it using lichens and onions; sometimes they even let visitors try a hand at the spinning wheel. For those who want a full introduction to the trade, longer workshops are offered. (☎ 25800. Open Apr.-Oct. M-Sa 11am-5pm, Su noon-4pm; Nov.-Mar. call ahead.) **Andrew O'Leary,** of bike hire fame (see below), gives **minibus tours** of the island. (Inquire at bike shop. 1¼hr. €30 flat rate.) After a few hours of trekking, relax on the harbor's pristine sandy beach and contemplate becoming the island's 155th inhabitant.

To get on and off the island, take either **O'Malley's Ferry** (☎25045; July-Aug. 8 per day, May-June and Sept. 3 per day, Oct.-Apr. call ahead; bikes free; €15 return, students €10, children €7.50) or the **Clare Island Ferry** (☎26307; 20min. July-Aug. 5 per day, May-June and Sept. 3-5 per day, Oct.-Apr. call ahead; bikes free; €15 return, students €12), which both offer free tea and coffee on board. Both leave from **Roonah Pier**, 4 mi. beyond Louisburgh and 18 mi. from Westport. Those without wheels can take the Bus Éireann/Clare Island Ferry **day-trip**, which departs from the tourist office at 10am and returns by 6pm (bus and ferry combined €25). Once island-side, take advantage of **O'Leary's Bike Hire**, near the harbor (€10 per day); if no one's there, knock at **Beachside B&B ❸** (☎25640), where the same family rents out clean rooms (with baths) for €25. Just past the beach, the hospitable **Sea Breeze B&B ❸** (☎26746) offers comfortable rooms for the same price. Those who want to get to know Clare's natural charms can pitch their tents at the **Clare Island Camp Site ❶** on the beach. (☎26525. Showers and toilet facilities across the road at the Community Center. €4 per person.) Two miles along the west road from the harbor, **O'Malley's Store** has food staples. (☎26987. Open daily 11am-6pm.) A little before O'Malley's is the ◼**Wavecrest Restaurant ❸**, an in-home restaurant that serves scones so moist and flavorful, butter and jam get ignored. (☎26546. Scones €1.30, crab salad sandwiches €10. Open daily 11am-5:30pm and 7:30-9:30pm for €22 set menu dinner.) To the right along the coast from the harbor, the **Bay View Hotel** (☎26307) houses Clare's only pub and alcohol source.

ACHILL ISLAND (ACAILL OILÉAN)

Two decades ago, Achill (AK-ill) Island was Co. Mayo's most popular holiday destination. Its popularity has inexplicably dwindled, but Ireland's biggest little isle remains one of its most beautiful and personable. Ringed by glorious beaches and cliffs, Achill's interior consists of some mountains and more than a few bogs. **Cycling** the Atlantic drive is another great way to see the island. During the first two weeks of August, Achill hosts the **Scoil Acla** (☎45284), a festival of trad and art where local musicians return to the island and offer music lessons and free concerts to all. The **Achill Seafood Festival** goes down the second week in July—mussels, oysters, and fish, oh my!

Buses run infrequently over the bridge linking Achill Sound, Dugort, Keel, and Dooagh to Westport, Galway, and Cork (June-Aug. M-Sa 5 per day; Sept.-May M-Sa 2 per day), and to Sligo, Enniskillen, and Belfast (June-Aug. 3 per day; Sept.-May 2 per day). If the buses are too infrequent, call for a **taxi**, "no matter how short the trip" (☎087 243 7686). Hitchhiking is relatively common during July and August, as is cycling. The island's **tourist office** is beside the Esso station in Cashel, on the main road from Achill Sound to Keel. (☎098 47353. Open M-F 10am-5pm.) There is an **ATM** in Achill Sound but no bank on the island, though **currency exchange** is available at Achill Sound's post office.

ACHILL SOUND (GOB A CHOIRE)   ☎098

Achill Sound's strategic location at the island's entrance accounts for the high concentration of shops and services, but practicality isn't the only reason to stop here; come for the **ATM** and stay for the internationally famous stigmatic and faith healer who holds services at **Our Lady's House of Prayer.** The OLHOP is about 20 yd. up the hill from the town's main church and is open for services daily 9:30am-6pm. The healer draws thousands to the attention-starved town each year, but local opinions remain polarized—some profess a great deal of faith, while others express only skepticism. (This latter feeling no doubt subverts the entire premise of faith healing; what a conundrum.) About 6 mi. south of Achill Sound—turn left at the first crossroads—two ruined buildings stand in close proximity. The ancient **Church of Kildavnet** was founded by St. Dympna after she fled to Achill to escape her father's incestuous intentions. Nearby, a crumbling 16th-century tower house with memories of better days calls itself the remains of **Kildavnet Castle.** Grace O'Malley, Ireland's favorite medieval pirate lass, once owned the castle.

Achill Sound has a **post office** with a **bureau de change** (☎45141; open M-F 9:30am-12:30pm and 1:30-5:30pm); a **SuperValu** (Open M-Sa 9am-7pm); a **Bank of Ireland ATM;** and a **pharmacy.** (☎45248; Open July-Aug. M-Sa 9:30am-6pm; Sept.-June M-Sa 9:30am-6pm.) **Bike rental** is available at the **Achill Sound Hotel.** (☎45245. €9 per day, €40 per wk. Deposit €50. Open daily 9am-9pm.) **The Wild Haven Hostel ❶,** a block past the church on the left, positively glows with polished wood floors and antique furniture. The sunny conservatory doubles as a swank ivy-walled dining room. (☎45392. Sheets €1.30. Laundry €2.50, dry €3. Dorms €13; private rooms €17-19. **Camping** €5.) If that doesn't work out, try the **Railway Hostel ❶,** just before the bridge to town. The hostel is housed in a former rail station—the last train pulled out about 70 years ago—and is bursting with recently renovated dorm-style rooms. Look for the proprietors at the **Mace Supermarket** in town, or call for pick-up. (☎45187. Laundry €3. Dorms €10; doubles €25.) Opposite the Railway Hostel, **Alice's Harbour Bar** flaunts gorgeous views, a stonework homage to the deserted village, a boat-shaped bar, and a brand-new disco that spins top-40 hits on summer weekends. (☎45138. Bar food €5-8; served noon-8pm. Cover for disco €7.)

KEEL (CAOL)   ☎098

Keel is an old-fashioned resort town at the bottom of a wide, flat valley. The sandy and cliff-flanked **Trawmore Strand** sweeps eastward for 3 mi. Stimulated by a government tax scheme, hundreds of holiday developments have sprung up like subsidized mushrooms over the past three years. To the relief of locals who prefer their hills green, that pro-development plan has now ended. Two miles north of Keel on the road that loops back toward Dugort sits **Slievemore Deserted Village,** which (being deserted) is now populated only by the stone houses cattle ranchers used until the late 1930s. Resist the temptation to crawl up and around the existing structures: not only are many of them dangerously unstable, but doing so incurs the wrath of **blood-thirsty archaeologists** who wander the site between June and September searching for ancient artifacts when the **Archaeological Summer School** hits town. (Call Theresa McDonald at the Achill Folklife Centre for details: ☎43569 or 087 677 2045; www.achill-fieldschool.com.) Along the same road as the abandoned village is **Giant's Grave,** a megalithic multichambered tomb.

O'Malley's Island Sports sells groceries, fishing tackle, and ammunition, and **rents bikes.** (☎43125. Bikes €12 per day, €65 per wk. Open M-Sa 9am-7pm, Su 10am-2pm.) Guests at the **Wayfarer Hostel (IHH) ❶,** on the outskirts of town near the caravan park, take in Keel Strand from comfy rooms. (☎43266. Laundry €4. Open mid-Mar. to mid-Oct. Dorms €10; private rooms €9-10.) Opulent vistas abound at the **Richview Hostel ❶,** at the far end of Keel, which offers a taste of the laid-back, friendly, and slightly disheveled life. (☎43462. Dorms €10; private rooms €13.) Everyone deserves some extravagance now and then—Mrs. Joyce's **Marian Villa ❹** is a 20-room hotel/B&B with thoughtfully decorated rooms and a veranda overlooking the sea. (☎43134. Singles €44.50; doubles €63.50.) Directly on the beach, **Keel Sandybanks Caravan and Camping Park ❶** provides a sandy spot to pound tent stakes, conveniently located near the pubs. (☎43211. Laundry €4. July-Aug. €8.25 per tent; late May-June and Sept. €6.50. Electricity €1.50.)

Price Cutters Market sells crisps and biscuits. (☎43125. Open M-Su 9am-8pm.) Keel has numerous chippers; more nutritious food and (less nutritious) sweaters are available at **Beehive Handcrafts and Coffee Shop ❶**. Their salads, sandwiches, and home-baked goodies delight; the apple-rhubarb pie is a slice of heaven. (☎43134 or 43018. Open daily 11am-6:30pm.) **Calvey's ❸**, next to Price Cutters, whips up hearty meals. (☎43158. Catch of the day €12.50. Open daily 11:30am-4:30pm and 5:30-9:30pm.) Inspired drinking is encouraged and music is applauded at the very vinyl **Annexe Inn**. (☎43268. Nightly sessions July-Aug.) On weekends, thangs are shaken and grooves gotten on at the **Achill Head Hotel**, the randiest party in Achill. (☎43108. 18+. Su cover €8.) The **Shark's Head Bar** in the hotel serves pints until 12:30am, after which people retire to the back-room nightclub to dance until the cows come home (assuming the cows come home around 2am).

DOOAGH (DUMHACH)   ☎098

Corrymore House, 2 mi. up the road from Keel in Dooagh (DOO-ah), was one of several Co. Mayo estates owned by Captain Boycott, whose mid-19th-century tenants went on an extended rent strike that verbified his surname. **The Pub**, Main St. (☎43109), serves soup and sandwiches and is lovingly maintained by the mistress of the house. Across the street is a monument to Don Allum, the first man to row across the Atlantic in both directions. A similarly grueling bike ride over the cliffs to the west of Dooagh leads to **Keem Bay** beach, the most beautiful spot on the island. Wedged between the sea and woolly, green walls of weed, rock, and sheep, the Bay was once a prime fishing hole for Basking sharks.

A river of amethyst runs under the Atlantic and comes up for air in **Croaghaun Mountain**, west of Keem Bay. Most of the accessible crystals have been plundered, but local old-timer Frank McNamara still digs out the deeper veins with a pick and shovel and sells the haul at his store in Dooagh (☎43581). The mountains, climbable from Keem Bay, provide bone-chilling views of the **Croaghaun Cliffs**, hot contenders in the ongoing intra-Ireland competition for the title "highest sea cliffs in Europe" (see **Slieve League, p. 416**). Dooagh is also home to the **Achill Folklife Centre** (☎43564), which hosts lectures and rotating exhibitions and runs the Archaeological Summer School. (€2.50. **Weekend archaeological course**, with accommodation, €314. Open June-Sept. M-Sa 9:30am-5:30pm.)

NORTHERN MAYO

Northern Mayo's twin claims to fame could not look more different. The Mullet Peninsula is one of the most remote and sublime destinations outside of Donegal and Northern Ireland; Ballina is a magnetic commercial and social center that draws crowds from the farthest reaches of this expansive, rural region.

BELMULLET (BÉAL AN MHUIRTHEAD) AND THE MULLET PENINSULA   ☎097

On the isthmus between Broad Haven and Blacksod Bays at the beginning of the Mullet Peninsula, Belmullet withstands cold Atlantic winds and the constant threat of rain, providing a sheltered base for the intrepid traveler. Not many tourists make it to the Mullet; peak-season crowds consist mostly of youths attending Irish-language summer schools farther down the peninsula. Travelers who do journey here seek cultural immersion and solitude. The beaches are mostly empty, as is the soggy moorland covering the peninsula's western half. Nevertheless, fishing holes and friendly pubs abound. Some might find this less than thrilling, but for those set on authenticity and rustic relaxation, the Mullet can't be beat.

⬛🔁 TRANSPORTATION AND PRACTICAL INFORMATION. An infrequent **bus** service departs from Ballina and runs the length of the peninsula (July-Aug. M-Sa 2 per day; Sept.-June 1 per day; €9.55). The **Erris Tourist Information Centre** on Barrack St. is amazingly helpful. (☎81500. Open for walk-ins July-Aug. M-Sa 10am-6pm; phones open year-round M-F 9am-4pm.) **Bank of Ireland** has an **ATM.** (☎81311. Open M-F 10am-12:30pm and 1:30-4pm, Th until 5pm.) **Belmullet Cycle Centre,** 2 mi. outside Belmullet in Binghamstown, **rents bikes.** (☎086 237 7069. €10 per day. Open M-Sa 10:30am-6pm.) **The Computer Store,** the Square, has **Internet.** (☎88878. €2 per 15min., €3 per 30min. Open M-Sa 10am-6pm.) The **post office** is at the end of Main St. (☎81032. Open M and W-Sa 9am-2pm, 3-5:30pm; Tu 9:30am-5:30pm.)

🏠🍴🍺 ACCOMMODATIONS, FOOD, AND PUBS. The Mullet itself lacks budget accommodations. Fortunately, the village of **Pollatomish** (PO-lah-to-MUS), 15 mi. northeast on the coast road, features two high-quality hostels. Vegetarians and meatlovers enjoy the fresh, organic home-cooking at clean and cozy **Kilcommon Lodge Hostel ❶.** Ducks and rabbits wander about while the owners help guests plot hiking routes. (☎84621. Breakfast €5, dinner €10. Dorms €9.50; private rooms €1. **Camping** €6.50 per person.) **⬛The Old Rectory Holiday Hostel ❶** welcomes wanderers with a peat fire, incredibly comfortable rooms, and an eclectic book collection. (☎84115. Open Apr.-Oct. Dorms €15.) For a bed *in* Belmullet, try the centrally located **Western Strands Hotel ❸,** Main St., with breakfast and bath for all. (☎81096. Singles €32-38; shared rooms €26-31. Discounts for families and children.)

Erris Superstore, the Square, peddles groceries somewhat late into the night. (Open daily 9am-10pm.) **The Appetizer ❷** posits several solutions to the potato problem—the lunch specials here feature copious helpings of fried, mashed, and saladed spuds. Potatoes with a side of meat costs €9. (☎82222. Open M-F 9:30am-2pm.) Impromptu good cheer abounds at **McDonnell's,** Barrack St. (☎81194), any early evening of the week. A more restrained time awaits at **Lavelle's** (☎81372), where crowds come for Belmullet's best pints and stay for the weekend karaoke sessions. **Lenehan's** (☎81098) and **Clan Lir** (☎82360), both on Main St., are popular with patriarchs and football rowdies, respectively.

◼🔱 SIGHTS AND ACTIVITIES. The **Ionad Deirbhle Heritage Centre,** at the end of the peninsula in Aughleam, explores local history, from the whaling industry to the Inishkey *(Inis Gé)* islands. The guides also provide info on day hikes and boat rides in the area. (☎85728. Open Easter-Oct. 10am-6pm. €3.) Josephine and Matt Geraghty run **sea angling** excursions and **boat trips** to the islands off the peninsula's southern coast. (☎85741. Open May-Sept. Call ahead. Island junket €20 per person; 6-person min. Fishing trips €215 for the whole boat.) Nearby **Cross Lake** is a popular spot for **fly-fishing** from shore or boat; for details, contact **George Geraghty** (☎81492) or the **Fishing Supply Store** on American St. (☎82093). The **Belmullet Sea Angling Competition** (☎81076), in mid-July, awards €2.55 per lb. for the heaviest halibut. The **Feille Iorras** (FAY-la ER-is), a peninsula-wide music festival, is held during the last weekend in July (☎81500; www.belmullet.net).

BALLYCASTLE, KILLALA, AND THE CEIDE FIELDS ☎096

Along R314 north of Ballina lies a series of towns and sights, the grandest of which is Ballycastle *(Baile an Chaisil)*, a strip of shops and pubs surrounded by holiday cottages and rolling hills of rugged bog. Ballycastle's main attraction is the **Ballinglen Arts Foundation,** which provides grants for international artists to spend five- to six-week periods of residency in Ballycastle. In return, each artist leaves behind a work for the Foundation's archive. Each set of paintings reveals a distinct experience of Northern Mayo; together, they comprise a diverse and thought-provoking collection. (☎43189. Only open to the public July-Aug. Call ahead for hours.) **Bus Éireann** runs a service from Ballycastle to **Ballina** and **Killala** (M-Sa 1 per day, €6.35). Obtain funds at **Ulster Bank.** (Open Tu 10am-noon.)

The **Ballycastle Resource Centre** sells a small brochure (€0.25) outlining pleasant walks in the area. (☎43407. Open July-Sept. M-W 10am-4pm, Th-Sa 11am-3:30pm, Su 11:30am-4pm.) One walk makes its charming way along the coast road down to the ocean, the **Dun Briste** sea stack, and stoic **Downpatrick Head** (see below). Five miles west of Ballycastle on R314, the **Ceide Fields** (KAYJ-uh feeldz) excavation site has finally opened to the public. A futuristic four-story glass, steel, and peat ziggurat built around a 5000-year-old pine tree, the center elegantly articulates—through exhibits, tours, and an audio-visual presentation—the dynamic relationship between Northern Mayo's first settlers and the environment. (☎43325. Open daily June-Aug. 10am-6pm; Sept. 9:30am-5:30pm; Oct. and Mar.-May 10am-5pm; Nov. 10am-4:30pm. Tours every hr.; film every 30min. €3.10.) If the peat is boggin' you down, the 350-million-year-old **Ceide Cliffs** rear up nearby, and are dramatically visible from the center's observation deck.

Eight miles south of Ballycastle, along the Ballina Rd., is **Killala** *(Cill Alaidh)*, a charming seaport best known as the site of the French Invasion of 1798 (see **Rebellion,** p. 61). That year, at the peak of international revolutionary fervor, 1067 French soldiers landed at Killala to join the United Irishmen under Wolfe Tone in a revolt against the English (see **Bantry,** p. 262). Instead of a well-armed band of revolutionaries, the French found a rag tag band of pure-of-heart (as well as impoverished, Irish-speaking, and poorly equipped) peasants. Undeterred, the combined forces pressed on, winning a significant victory at Castlebar before being soundly hammered by British forces at Ballnamuck. Aside from the Ballina Rd., Killala and Ballycastle are also connected by the **Coast Road,** a scenic expanse of (Irish-style) highway with views of dramatic blowholes and unique geological formations such as **Downpatrick Head,** an isolated spire separated from the sea cliffs by erosion. This multilayered rock formation supposedly broke off from the mainland during a dispute between St. Patrick and a pagan king.

A 25min. walk away from town on R314 leads to the **Keadyville B&B ❸,** where spacious accommodations and a glass-walled dining room encourage afternoons of exquisite loafing. (☎43288. Singles €33; doubles €47.) **McNamee's Supermarket** sells the essentials. (☎43057. Open daily 8am-9pm.) **Mary's Bakery and Cottage Kitchen ❷** whips up authentic baked goods and scrumptious lunch specials complete with Mayo, naturally. (☎43361. Open June-Oct. daily 10am-6pm; Nov.-Dec. and Feb.-May M-Sa 10am-6pm.)

BALLINA (BÉAL AN ÁTHA) ☎096

Ballina (bah-lin-AH) is a fisherman's mecca. Armies in olive-green waders invade the town each year during salmon season (Feb.-Sept.), and wade waist-deep in the river to wait for a bite. Ballina holds at least one non-ichthyological attraction, though: on Saturday nights, everyone within a 50 mi. radius, from sheep farmers to students, descends on the town seeking city-style *craic*. These weekly influxes shake up the humble hub, leaving it slightly hipper for the wear. Many pubs forsake trad for rock and blues; restaurants supplement pub grub with stir-fry, fajitas, and calzones. These developments turn a layover in Ballina into an incongruous cross-cultural experience. Former Irish President Mary Robinson grew up here and refined her political skills in the town's pubs (see **Current Issues,** p. 66).

TRANSPORTATION

Trains: Station Rd. (☎71818), near the bus station. Open M-Sa 6:45am-6pm, Su 10am-6pm. To: **Dublin** via **Athlone** (M-Su 3 per day, €25). From the station, go left, bear right, and walk 4 blocks to the town center; several signs point the way.

Buses: Kevin Barry St. (☎71800). Open M-Sa 7:30am-9:30pm. To: **Athlone** (1 per day, €15.20); **Donegal** (M-Sa 3 per day, Su 1 per day; €14); **Dublin** via **Mullingar** (4hr., 6 per day, €12.10); **Galway** via **Westport** (2hr.; M-Sa 6 per day, Su 5 per day; €11.50); **Sligo** (2hr., M-Sa 3-4 per day, €10.75).

Taxis: Call **Lynott's Cabs** (☎087 295 8787 or 086 295 8787), or wait at the **taxi stand** in the town center on O'Rahily St., near the post office.

Bike Rental: Michael Hopkins, Lower Pearse St. (☎21609). €10 per day, €45 per wk. Deposit €40. Open Apr.-Sept. M-Sa 9am-6pm.

ORIENTATION AND PRACTICAL INFORMATION

On the east bank of the **River Moy** stand the cathedral and tourist office. A bridge crosses to the west bank, where the commerical center is located; the bridge connects to **Tone Street,** which turns into **Tolan Street.** This main strip intersects **Pearse** and **O'Rahily Streets,** which run parallel to the river, to form Ballina's center.

Tourist Office: Cathedral Rd. (☎70848), on the river past St. Muredach's Cathedral. Open June-Aug. daily 10am-5:30pm; May and Sept. M-Sa 10am-1pm and 2-5:30pm. **Fishing Permits and Licenses** (€4-32) are available at the **Northwest Regional Fisheries Board** (☎22788). Open daily 9:30-11:30am.

Banks: Bank of Ireland, Pearse St. (☎21144). Open M and Th-F 10am-4pm, Tu 10am-5pm, W 10:30am-4pm. **Ulster Bank,** Pearse St. (☎21077). Open M-F 10am-4pm, Tu until 5pm. Both have **ATMs.**

Laundry: Gerry's Laundrette, Tone St. (☎22793). Laundry €8. Open M-Sa 9am-6pm.

Pharmacy: Molloy's, Garden St. (☎21375). Open M-Sa 9am-6pm.

Emergency: ☎999; no coins required. **Police** *(Garda):* Walsh St. (☎21422).

Internet: Surf 'N' Train Internet Cafe, Hill St. (☎70562). Walking down Tolan St. toward the river, turn right on James Connolly St., which becomes Hill St.; it's 2 blocks down on the right. €1.50 per 10min. Open May-Aug. M-F noon-9pm, Sa noon-7pm; Sept.-Apr. M-F noon-7pm, Sa 1-7pm. **Moy Valley Resources** (☎70905), in the tourist office. Open M-Th 9am-1pm and 2-5:30pm, F 9am-1pm and 2-5pm. €8 per hr.

Post Office: Corner of Bury St. and O'Rahilly St. (☎21309). Open M-Sa 9am-5:30pm.

ACCOMMODATIONS AND CAMPING

B&Bs line the main roads into town, charging €27-35.

Lismoyne House, Kevin Barry St. (☎70582), near the bus station. Newly renovated, stately rooms with high ceilings and big bathtubs perfect for soaking away long hours of fishing or pubbing. The owner gives expert angling tips. €35. ❸

Ms. Corrigan's Greenhill, Cathedral Close (☎22767). Behind the tourist office and a cast away from river, lake, and sea fishing. Bright, spacious rooms look onto rose gardens. Singles €33-39. €3-4 reduction with Continental instead of full Irish breakfast. ❸

Breda Walsh's Suncraft (☎21573), 2 doors down from Greenhill B&B. Another fine option, with bright rooms and a cheery, helpful owner. Singles €35; doubles €54. ❸

Belleek Camping and Caravan Park, Killala Rd. (☎71533). 2 mi. from Ballina toward Killala on R314, behind the Belleek Woods. Laundry €4. Open Mar.-Oct. €5 per person with tent; 2 people in camper €13. ❶

🍴 FOOD

Aspiring gourmets prepare for a feast at the **Quinnsworth** supermarket on Market Rd. (☎21056. Open M-W and Sa 8:30am-7pm, Th-F 8:30am-9pm, Su noon-6pm.) Lard-soaked takeaway may be cheap and plentiful, but it's not always a welcome treat. Fortunately, most Ballinalian restaurants are attached to pubs and serve similar menus in the pub at a cheaper price. (See **Pubs and Clubs,** p. 390.)

Cafolla's (☎21029), up from the upper bridge. One of the town's 2 unique Irish diners, serving everything from eggs and toast to curry burgers to tongue-tingling milkshakes. Takeaway counter and restaurant open daily 10am-midnight. ❷

Chungs at Tullio's, Pearse St. (☎70815). Chinese and Italian cuisine preside on different sides of the restaurant. Mains €9-14. Open daily noon-2:30pm and 6-10pm. ❸

Dillon's, Dillon Terr. (☎72230). Head down Pearse St. until it curves into Dillon Terr. It's through a stone archway on the left. Creative pizza and pasta dishes capitalize on local ingredients—salmon, smoked salmon, grilled salmon, fried salmon, and dill (€8-11). Trad on W nights. Pub serves food M-Sa 3-9pm, Su 1-9pm; restaurant serves M-Sa 6-10pm, Su 1-10pm. ❸

The Bard, Garden St. (☎21894 or 21324), above Tone St. The haute cuisine option in Ballina, with Mexican and Thai selections, warm goat cheese salad (€3.60), and a variety of pasta dishes (€12-14). Open M-Sa 5-9:30pm, Su noon-9pm. ❸

Padraic's Restaurant, Tone St. (☎22383). A friendly greasy-spoon with all-day breakfasts (€8) and diner fare (€5-12). Open M-Sa 10am-8pm, Su noon-8pm. ❷

The Stuffed Sandwich Company, Tone St. (☎72268). A treat for vegetarians and lunchtime gourmets; brie on toast, anyone? Sandwiches €4-8. Open M-Sa noon-6pm. ❷

🏠🍺 PUBS AND CLUBS

Gaughan's, O'Rahilly St. (☎70096). Pulling the best pint in town since 1936. No trad or TV—just great grub, homemade snuff, and lively chat over the black brew.

The Parting Glass, Tolan St. (☎72714). Jolly, musical drinkers raise this glass over and over again. Trad sessions weekly and live music most nights; call ahead for schedule.

Murphy Bros., Clare St. (☎22702), across the river, 3 blocks past the tourist office. The Brothers Murphy pour pints for 20-somethings amidst dark wood furnishings. They also serve good if typical pubmunch from noon to 8:30pm.

Emmett's Treffpunkt, Tolan St. (☎21608). An appreciably funkier crowd packs into this deceptively tiny pub, downing pints beneath a mural of venerable rock legends; live alternative and hardrock bands draw legions of fans each weekend.

The Music Box (☎72379), in the rear of the Broken Jug, at the top of Reilly St. Top 40-lovin' folks arrive in herds when Ballina's most popular nightclub opens its doors. Cover €7-9. Open W and F-Su 11:30pm-2:30am.

The Loft, Pearse St. (☎21881). Young and old mix like oil and water within the dark confines of this energetic club. Three floors. Live music Su and Tu-F.

👁 🗲 SIGHTS AND HIKING

Walking through the idyllic, bird-rich **Belleek Woods** surrounding **Belleek Castle,** visitors often find it difficult to resist nostalgia for Narnia, Sherwood, and the Forbidden Forest. For a return to child-like wonderment, cross the lower bridge from the tourist office, take the second right, and follow Nelly St. (which becomes Castle Rd.) for 1 mi. To dull the pain of returning to the grown-up world, stop in at the castle for a drink. At the back of the railway station is the **Dolmen of the Four Maols,** a.k.a. the "Table of the Giants." The dolmen, which dates to 2000 BC, is said to be the burial site of four Maols who murdered Ceallach, a 7th-century bishop.

The lonely **Ox Mountains** east of Ballina are eminently cyclable, with scads of dirt and asphalt trails criss-crossing the slopes. The 44-mile **Ox Mountain drive** traces the scenic perimeter of the mountains and is well signposted from **Tobercurry** (21 mi. south of Sligo on the N17). The **Western Way** footpath begins in the Ox Mountains and winds past Ballina through Newport and Westport, ending in Connemara. The Western then meets the **Sligo Way,** which continues toward Sligo. Tourist offices sell complete guides to both trails. The **Ardchuan Lodge,** 5 mi. north of Ballina on the Sligo road, hires out horses for group treks through the woods. (☎45084. €15 per person. Open M-Sa 8am-6pm.) The annual 10-day █**Ballina Street Festival** (☎79814), has been swinging through mid-July since 1964. Much of Co. Mayo turns out for the festival's **Heritage Day,** when the streets are closed and life reverts to the year 1910, greased pig contests and all. Other highlights include **International Day,** when the town tries on costumes and cuisine from all over the world, and **Mardi Gras,** which tops off the revelry.

NEAR BALLINA: ENNISCRONE (INISHCRONE) ☎096

The strikingly gorgeous Enniscrone Strand stretches along the eastern shore of Killala Bay, 8 mi. northeast of Ballina on scenic Quay Rd. (R297). Sunny days see droves of Irish weekenders vying for towel space; therefore, the miles of sand generally remain unpopulated. Across from the beach, the family-run █**Kilcullen's Bath House** simmers—steam baths in cedar wood cabinets and cool seaweed baths relax even the tensest travelers. (☎36238. Seaweed bath €15, plus steam bath €17.50. 30min. massage by appointment €22.50. Open May-Oct. daily 10am-9pm; mid-Mar. to Apr. M-F noon-8pm and Sa-Su 10am-8pm; Nov. to mid-Mar. M-F noon-8pm and Sa-Su 10am-8pm.) The **tourist office** closed in 2001 but is rumored to be reopening soon; contact the Ballina tourist office (☎70848) in the meantime.

Gowan House B&B ❸, Pier Rd., set back from the sea, has spacious bedrooms decorated in bright colors and finished with Baltic pine. (☎36396. Singles €34; doubles €56.) The biggest draw of Maura O'Dowd's **Point View House ❸,** Main St., may be its central location, but that doesn't eclipse Ms. O'Dowd's 50 years' experience running the place and its kitchen. (☎36312. All rooms with bath. €25.50.) The **Atlantic Caravan Park ❶,** on Main St. at the edge of town, has grass for tents of all sizes. (☎36132. Laundry €7. €6.50 per tent. Showers €0.65.) For victuals, head to **Tracey's ❶** on Main St. (☎087 682 3745). Run by Tracey herself, this cafe specializes in all-day breakfasts and other simple treats. (Open June-Aug. daily 9:30am-8pm; Sept.-May M-F 9:30am-5pm and Sa-Su 9:30am-7pm.) **Walsh's Pub,** also on Main St. near the bus stop at the top of the hill, serves great pub food and hosts weekly music sessions. Inquire about **Internet.** (☎36110. Lunch served 1-2:30pm.)

COUNTY SLIGO

Known best as the birthplace and poetic inspiration of William Butler Yeats, County Sligo is one of Ireland's most magical and least frequented treasures. The near-symmetrical peaks of Knocknarea and "bare Ben Bulben" dominate the fairy-haunted landscape, which besides being a geographical map of Yeats's verse—hides the country's oldest megalithic tombs in its hills. Sligo's Strandhill beach is renowned for its top-notch waves and attracts crowds of wetsuited surfers. The commercial center of the county, Sligo Town has the bustle of a city and the intimate, narrow passages of a hamlet. A fleet of high-quality hostels and a lively pub culture make it a good base for daytripping.

SLIGO TOWN (SLIGEACH)   ☎ 071

A cozy town with the sophistication of a city, present-day Sligo often gets lost in a haze of Yeats nostalgia; the Yeats Memorial Building and countless other landmarks look wistfully to the wordsmith's bygone days. On Rockwood Parade, street fiddlers serenade swans along the Garavogue River, while locals nibble their lunches under restaurant canopies. Toward the city center, the pace quickens, as drivers and pedestrians wait at congested intersections and shoppers dart in and out of the many clothing and book stores. Later on, the town's thriving nightlife is as diverse as any in Ireland, from traditional bars that relish their silence, to musical pubs that showcase nightly trad sessions, to modern, trendy clubs.

▐ TRANSPORTATION

Airport: Sligo Airport, Strandhill Rd. (☎68280). Open daily 9:30am-5:30pm. To: **Dublin** (35min., 3-5 per day).

Trains: McDiarmada Station, Lord Edward St. (☎69888). Open M-Sa 7am-6:30pm, Su 20min. before departures. To: **Dublin** via **Carrick-on-Shannon** and **Mullingar** (3hr., 4 per day, €22).

Buses: McDiarmada Station, Lord Edward St. (☎60066). Open M-F 9:15am-6pm, Sa 9:30am-5pm. To: **Belfast** (4hr., 2-3 per day, €22); **Derry** (3hr., 4-7 per day, €14.50); **Donegal** (1hr., 3-7 per day, €11.25); **Dublin** (3-4hr., 4-5 per day, €13.70); **Galway** (2½hr., 4-6 per day, €11.40); **Westport** (2½hr., 1-4 per day, €12.70).

Local Transportation: Frequent **buses** to Strandhill and Rosses Point (€4 return).

Taxis: Cab 55 (☎42333); **Finnegan's** (☎77777 or 41111). €5 for first 2½ mi.

Bike Rental: Flanagan's Cycles, Market Sq. (☎44477; after hours ☎62633). Rental and repairs. €15 per day, €60 per wk.; deposit €50. Open M-Sa 9am-6pm.

▐ ▐ ORIENTATION AND PRACTICAL INFORMATION

Trains and buses pull into **McDiarmada Station** on **Lord Edward Street.** To reach the main drag from the station, turn left onto Lord Edward and continue straight onto **Wine Street,** then turn right onto **O'Connell Street** at the post office. More shops, pubs, and eateries beckon from **Grattan Street,** a left off O'Connell St. To get to the river, continue down Wine St. and turn right after the Yeats Building onto idyllic **Rockwood Parade,** a waterside pedestrian walkway where plenty of swans and locals take their feed. From here, the bridge over the river leads to **Bridge Street,** while a right turn on **the Mall** leads to the **Model Arts Centre and Niland Gallery.**

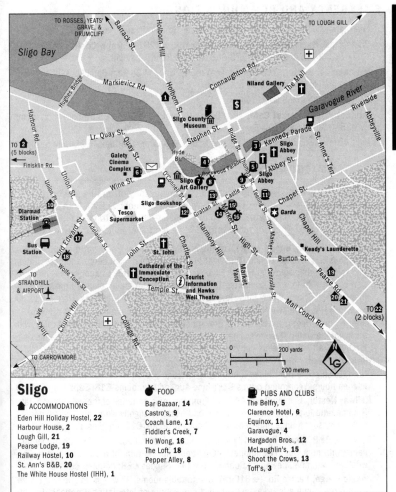

Sligo

♠ ACCOMMODATIONS

Eden Hill Holiday Hostel, **22**
Harbour House, **2**
Lough Gill, **21**
Pearse Lodge, **19**
Railway Hostel, **10**
St. Ann's B&B, **20**
The White House Hostel (IHH), **1**

♦ FOOD

Bar Bazaar, **14**
Castro's, **9**
Coach Lane, **17**
Fiddler's Creek, **7**
Ho Wong, **16**
The Loft, **18**
Pepper Alley, **8**

⬤ PUBS AND CLUBS

The Belfry, **5**
Clarence Hotel, **6**
Equinox, **11**
Garavogue, **4**
Hargadon Bros., **12**
McLaughlin's, **15**
Shoot the Crows, **13**
Toff's, **3**

TOURIST, FINANCIAL, AND LOCAL SERVICES

Tourist Office: Northwest Regional Office, Temple St. (☎61201), at Charles St. From the station, turn left along Lord Edward St. and follow the signs right onto Adelaide St. and around the corner to Temple St. Provides info on the whole of the Northwest. Open June-Aug. M-Sa 9am-7pm, Su 10am-6pm; Oct.-May M-F 9am-5pm.

Bank: AIB, the Mall (☎42157). 24hr. **ATM.** Open M-W, F 10am-4pm, Th 10am-5pm.

Luggage Storage: Bus station. Open M-F 9:30am-1:30pm and 2:45-6pm. €2.

Bookstore: The Sligo Bookshop, O'Connell St. (☎47277). Fiction, Irish, travel, and the requisite Yeats, sometimes at discounted prices. Open M-Sa 9am-6pm.

Laundry: Keady's, Pearse Rd. Full-service from €8. Open M-Sa 9am-6pm, Th until 8pm.

Camping Supplies: Call of the Wild, Stephen St. (☎46905). Supplies and info on camping, hiking, and surfing. Open M-F 9:30am-6pm, Sa 9am-6pm.

WESTERN IRELAND

EMERGENCY AND COMMUNICATIONS

Emergency: ☎999; no coins required. **Police** *(Garda):* Pearse Rd. (☎42031).

Crisis Line: Samaritans, 11 Chapel St. (**24hr.** ☎42011). **Rape Crisis Line** (☎1800 750 780; **24hr.** line ☎1800 778 888) M-F 10:30am-midnight.

Pharmacy: T. Hunter, O'Connell St. (☎42696). Open M-Sa 9am-6pm. Local pharmacies post schedules of rotating Su openings.

Hospital: On the Mall (☎71111).

Internet: Cygo Internet Cafe, 19 O'Connell Street (☎40082). €6.50 per hr., students €5.25. Open M-Sa 10am-7pm.

Post Office: Wine St. (☎59266). Open M and W-Sa 9am-5:30pm, Tu 9:30am-5:30pm.

▶ ACCOMMODATIONS

There are plenty of high-quality hostels in Sligo, but they often fill quickly, particularly in mid-August when the Yeats International Summer School is in session. If you're staying a few days with a group of people, getting a cottage can be cheaper; contact the tourist office for more info. B&B-seekers get lucky on Pearse Rd./ N4.

▨**Eden Hill Holiday Hostel (IHH),** off Pearse Rd. A 20min. trek from the bus station, though hikers shouldn't mind. Turn right at the Marymount sign before the Esso station and take another quick right after 1 block. Recently renovated to supplement its Victorian charm with modern comforts, this clean, airy hostel grants respite from the clamor of town. Showers only hot a few hours each day. Laundry facilities. Dorms €11. ❶

The White House Hostel (IHH), Markievicz Rd. (☎45160). Take the first left off Wine St. after Hyde Bridge; reception in the brown house. Convenient to the heart of town, with a view of the water. Despite the name, the *brown* house (not the neighboring white one) is where staff and travelers congregate. Key deposit €3. Dorms €10. ❶

Harbour House, Finisklin Rd. (☎71547). A 10min. walk from the bus station, away from town. Plain stone front hides a luxurious, TV-laden hostel. All rooms with bath. Limited kitchen hours. Year-round dorms €16; June-Aug. private rooms €18; Sept.-May €17. ❷

Railway Hostel, 1 Union Pl. (☎44530). From the main entrance of the train station, take 3 immediate lefts. The exterior of this 8-bed hostel is slightly worn, but it's still homey, with a pleasant lounge and free tea and coffee. Dorms €10; doubles €26. ❶

St. Ann's B&B, Pearse Rd. (☎43118), 1½ blocks past the *Garda* station. Charming bungalow with spacious, TV-equipped rooms and unusual perk of a swimming pool. Fair-weather swimmers, beware the unheated water. Singles €38; doubles €58. ❸

Pearse Lodge, Pearse Rd. (☎61090). Comfortable rooms, all with bath and hair dryers. Even more exciting is breakfast, when a cornucopia of international options delights every palate. French toast and bananas, bagels with cream cheese, and the omnipresent full Irish are but a few of the enticing choices. Singles €35-44. ❹

Lough Gill, Pearse Rd. (☎50045). Ivy-laced exterior leads to small but tastefully decorated rooms. A basket of toiletries, digestives, and tissues for the Irish cold are thoughtful additions to every room. Singles €38; shared rooms €28. ❸

◉ FOOD

Tesco Supermarket, O'Connell St., stocks comestibles. (☎62788. Open M-Tu and Sa 8:30am-7pm, W-F 8:30am-9pm, Su 10am-6pm.) **Kate's Kitchen,** Castle St., has *pâté* and other deli-cacies. (☎43022. Open M-Sa 9am-6:30pm.) The demands of international visitors have inspired culinary d2evelopment; grab *Discover Sligo's Good Food,* free at most hostels and bookstores, for new listings.

■ **Bar Bazaar,** 34 Market St. (☎44749). An alternative spot to sip fantastic coffee concoctions. The Honey Bee (mocha, almond syrup, and honey; €2.65) is most popular, but the Irish Cream milkshake (€2.80) is true bliss. Chill in the cozy back room, with funky lanterns and board games. Open M-Th 9:30am-6pm, F 9:30am-8pm, Sa 10am-8pm. ❶

Coach Lane, 1-2 Lord Edward St. (☎62417). Winner 2000's "Newcomer of the Year" award. Excellent service and amazing food blend local sensibilities with international flair. A meal might start with a goat cheese purse (€6), followed by monkfish sauteed in Chardonnay (€23), tiramisu (€5.50), and a hefty bill. Open nightly 5:30-10pm. ❹

Castro's, 10-11 Castle St. (☎48290). A painting of Fidel graces the cheery walls of this Cuban-Irish cafe. Spicy tortilla wraps (with salad, €6) are a welcome break from standard sandwich fare. Open M-Sa 9am-6pm. ❷

Fiddler's Creek, Rockwell Parade (☎41866). New and popular 'pubstaurant.' Dinners are pricey (veggie menu €11, meats €14-20), but a casual atmosphere prevails. Lunch noon-3pm; dinner 6-9:30pm. Pub 21+. Open daily noon-1am. ❹

The Loft, Lord Edward St. (☎46770), across from the bus station. Mexican meals sizzle but don't come cheap at this oft-recommended spot. Chicken fajitas €15.30. Veggie options. Open nightly 6-10:30pm, Su lunch 12:30-4pm. ❸

Ho Wong, Market St. (☎45718). Centrally located Cantonese and Szechuan takeaway. Mains €5-9. Open M-Th 5pm-12:30am, F-Sa 5pm-1:30am, Su 5pm-1am. ❷

Pepper Alley, Rockwood Parade (☎70720), along the river. Popular for its prices and location. Huge selection of sandwiches (€2.55-4.20). Weekends bring more upscale Mexican dinners. Open M-W 8am-6pm, Th-Sa 8am-10pm. ❶

PUBS

Over 70 pubs crowd Sligo's main streets, filling the town with live music during the summer. Events and venues are listed in *The Sligo Champion* (€1.50). Many pubs post signs restricting their clientele to 21+, but that often means over 18—those without proof won't be given the time of day.

■ **Shoot the Crows,** Grattan St. Owner Ronin holds court at the hippest destination for Sligo pint-seekers. Dark faery-folk dangle from the ceiling as weird skulls and crazy murals look on in amusement; the welcoming atmosphere banishes any potential creepiness. No phone to interrupt weekend revelry. Music Tu, Th 9:30pm.

■ **McLaughlin's Bar,** 9 Market St. (☎44209). A true musician's pub, where all manner of song may break out in an evening, from trad to folk and grunge. Open M-W 4-11:30pm, Th-Sa 4pm-12:30am, Su 7am-11pm.

McLynn's, Old Market St. (☎60743). Three generations in the making, with a 4th up and coming, McLynn's is an excellent spot for weekend trad, with owner-cum-fiddler Donal leading the music Th-Su. Lord of the Dance Michael Flatley's favorite pub. Open M-W 4-11:30pm, Th-Sa 4pm-12:30am, Su 7-11pm.

Hargadon Bros., O'Connell St. (☎70933). A pub worth spending the day in. Open fires, old Guinness bottles, and *poitín* jugs in a maze of dark and intimate nooks. Pints unfettered by modern audio-visual distractions; no music but for muffled sips and the clinking of glasses. Open M-W 10:30am-11:30pm, Th-Sa 10:30am-12:30am, Su 5-11pm.

Garavogue (☎40100), across the river from the footbridge. Spacious, modern pub with a 20-something crowd and palm trees beneath skylights. Dress to impress. DJs Th and Sa. Occasional trad. Open M-Sa 10:30am-midnight, Su 11:30am-11pm.

The Belfry, Thomas St. (☎62150), off the bridge. Modern-medieval decor, with a big bell and bigger chandelier. 2 floors, 3 bars, 30 Irish whiskeys. Live bands F; DJ Sa. Open M-W 10:30am-11:30pm, Th-F 10:30am-12:30am, Sa 4pm-1am.

WESTERN IRELAND

The Clarence Hotel, Wine St. DJs spin cutting-edge melodies in the club and international jazz in the front bar—a welcome alternative to MTV remixes. Not as big or popular as others, but draws a faithful and appreciative crowd. Cover €4.50-8, with early birds catching discounts. Club Tu and Sa. Bar open Su-Th until 12:30am, F-Sa 'til late.

Equinox, Teeling St. (☎44721). Modern, pulsating club. Navigate its dark bar rooms, shake it on the dance floor, or retreat to the bathrooms to watch music videos on flat-screen TVs. 18+. Cover €5-10. Open M and W-Su 11pm-2:30am.

Toff's, Kennedy Parade (☎62150), on the river behind the Belfry. Well-lit, crowded dance floor reveals that young local club-goers drink better than they dance. Th-Su disco. 18+. Cover €7-10; €2 discount with card from the Belfry. Open 11pm-2:30am.

👁 🏔 SIGHTS AND ACTIVITIES

In town stands the well-preserved, Yeats-free 13th-century **Sligo Abbey,** on Abbey St. The former Dominican friary contains cloisters and ornate coupled pillars that, though old, can hardly be called ruined. Look for the love-knot carved onto onesuch pillar. Most of the walls and many of the ceilings are intact, and visitors are free to duck in and out of the little rooms. Those who enjoy preaching to the (imaginary) choir mount the stairs to the Reader's Desk to send forth their words of wisdom. (☎46406. Open Apr.-Oct. daily 10am-6pm; Nov.-Mar. call for weekend openings. Last admission 45min. before closing. Tours available on request. €1.90, students and children €0.70.) The 69 stained-glass windows of the 1874 **Cathedral of the Immaculate Conception,** John St., are best visited at dawn or dusk when the sun streams through. Farther down John St., the **Cathedral of St. John the Baptist,** built in 1730, has a tablet dedicated to Susan Mary, Yeats's mother. The fanciful **courthouse** on Teeling St. was built in 1878 on the site of its predecessor.

■**The Model Arts Centre and Niland Gallery,** on the Mall, holds an impressive collection in an elegant and airy space. On wide, white walls hangs one of the country's—and thus, presumably, the world's—finest collections of modern Irish art, including a number of works by Jack Yeats, William's brother, and the contemporaneous Nora McGuinness and Michael Healy. The gallery also hosts frequent exhibitions of recent works. (☎41405. Open Tu-Sa 10am-5:30pm; June-Oct. also Su noon-5:30pm. Free.) The **Sligo County Museum** preserves small reminders of Yeats, including pictures of his funeral. The collection's highlights include first editions by the man himself, a few illustrated broadside collaborations between Papa Yeats and Baby Yeats, cartoons by Jack Yeats, and Countess Markievicz's prison apron. (Open June-Sept. Tu-Sa 10:30am-12:30pm and 2:30-4:50pm; Oct.-May 10:30am-12:30pm. Free.) The **Sligo Art Gallery,** in the Y[ou-know-who]eats Memorial Building on Hyde Bridge, has innovative exhibits of contemporary Irish art and mounts an annual exhibition on northwest Ireland every October. (☎45847. Open M-Sa 10am-5:30pm, except bank holidays.) Also in the **Yeats Memorial Building** is a small exhibit by the Yeats Society on their main man. Photos, writing snippets, and a brief history of Yeats complement a brief film matching images of nearby countryside with his poetic descriptions. (☎42693. Open daily 10am-4:30pm. Free.)

For a break from Yeats-worshipping, head to **Sligo Riding Centre** in Carrowmore, only 2 mi. from Sligo Town, to gallop over beach and mountain. (☎61353. €18 per hr. Open daily 10am-10pm.) Swelter in the sauna or dip in the pool at the **Regional Sports Centre** (☎60539), near Doorly Park. Or dive deeper with **Sligo Sub Aqua Club.** (Contact Stuart Barker at ☎42241. Dives on W evenings and Su afternoons; small donation requested.)

WESTERN IRELAND

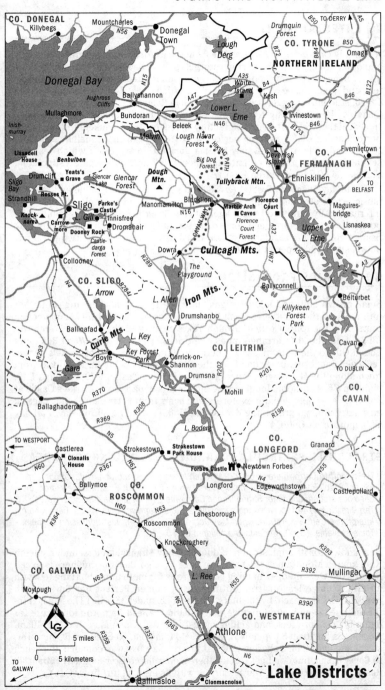

Lake Districts

♫ ENTERTAINMENT

A monthly *Calendar of Events*, free from the tourist office, describes festivals and other goings-on in the northwestern Republic. **Hawk's Well Theatre**, on Temple St. beneath the tourist office, presents modern and traditional dramas, ballets, and musicals. (☎61526 or 61518. Box office open M-Sa 10am-6pm. Tickets €8-20, students and children €5-8.) The **Blue Raincoat Theatre Company,** Lower Quay St., is a traveling troupe that spends 16 weeks each year performing "physical theatre" in its Quay St. factory space. (☎70431. Tickets for lunchtime performances €6.50, evening performances €10.) For more mainstream fare, Hollywood-style, try the **Gaiety Cinema Complex** on Wine St., which features seven screens of trad-free entertainment. (☎74002; www.gaietysligo.com. Tickets €4.50-6.50, children €4-5.)

The 10-day **Sligo Arts Festival** (☎69802) takes place in early June and features music, art, theater, and children's events. During the first two weeks of August, the internationally renowned **Yeats International Summer School** opens some of its poetry readings, lectures, and concerts to the public. International luminaries like Seamus Heaney are regular guests. (☎42693; www.yeats-sligo.com. Applications on website. Office open M-F 9:30am-5:30pm.)

▚ DAYTRIPS FROM SLIGO

Small brown quill and inkwell signs mark the **Yeats trail,** a driving route that hits most of the must-sees. **John Howe's** bus company (☎42747) runs coach tours from the tourist office through Yeats country (3½hr.) and to Lough Gill (3hr.). Call ahead to arrange times and prices. The **Wild Rose Water-Bus** tours Lough Gill to the tune of Yeats' poetry, and includes a stop at **Parke's Castle.** (☎64266. June-Aug. 2 per day from the Blue Lagoon, a 10min. walk east from town along the Garavogue; 5 per day from Parke's Castle. €12, students €10, children €6. Additional lough cruise on F nights departs from Parke's Castle at 9pm.) Independent aquatic explorers **rent boats** from **Peter Henry's Blue Lagoon;** alas, nary a poem graces the decks. (☎42530. Rowboat €30 full day, half-day €20; motorboat €60/€40.)

STRANDHILL PENINSULA, CARROWMORE, AND KNOCKNAREA

The turnoff to Carrowmore is on R292, which loops around the peninsula, about 1 mi. west of Sligo. From town, follow the signs west from John St. Bus Éireann departs from the Sligo bus station, bound for Strandhill and Carrowmore (M-F 7 per day, Sa 5 per day; €3). Taxi Direct (☎41444) services the peninsula; a taxi to Carrowmore costs €5. Carrowmore Interpretive Centre ☎61534. Open May-Oct. daily 10am-6pm; last admission 5:15pm. Tours available. €1.90, students and children €0.70.

Best known for its 2 mi. stretch of dunes, windy **Strandhill** ducks under solemn Knocknarea Mountain at the southern edge of Sligo Bay. Surfing here is excellent for the wetsuited; swimming is dangerous for mere mortals. Hang ten with an all-inclusive lesson from optimistically named **Perfect Day Surf School.** (☎68464. On the beach, by the bus stop. 2hr. €25, under 18 €15.) Those who prefer their seaweed heated indulge in a ▨**Celtic Seaweed Bath,** the ideal cure for damp bones, sore feet, and aching backs. (☎68686. Open May-Oct. M-F 10am-9:30pm, Sa-Su 10am-8:30pm; Nov.-Apr. M-F 11am-9pm, Sa-Su 10am-6:30pm. 1hr. steam and bath €14; 2 sharing €20.) At low tide, a causeway connects the beach to **Coney Island,** but don't get stuck—there's no rollercoaster out there. **Strandhill Hostel,** on the shore road, warms surfers with its evening turf fires (€15).

An assortment of passage graves spooks visitors at **Carrowmore**, 3 mi. south-west of Sligo. The site had over 100 tombs and stone circles before modern folks quarried and cleared many away, but it's still the largest megalithic cemetery in Ireland. About 30 of the 70 remaining tombs are open to the public, some dating from 5400 BC. Ongoing excavation uncovers one or two new formations each year. The small but interesting **Interpretive Center** does its best to explain their meaning based on the scant information available, as do the **guided tours** that lead through the site. (€3, students €2. Open daily 9am-5pm. Tours every 40min.)

The 1078 ft. ■**Knocknarea** ("hill of the moon") perches above the southwest-ern shore of Sligo Bay. The 30min. climb to the summit rewards pilgrims with stunning views of misty bays, heathered hills, and the mighty Benbulben Mountain. Queen Mebdh (or Maeve), the villain of the *Táin bo Cuailnge* (see **Legends and Folktales, p. 73**), is reputedly interred in the 30 ft. high, 160 ft. wide **cairn** on the summit; she stands upright, facing her Ulsterside enemies. Sheep bleat mere yards away while layers of peat reluctantly give way underfoot. The **forested park** on Knocknarea's eastern slopes is criss-crossed by trails; there are several ways up, but on rainy days it's best to stick with the graveled paths, as it can get quite slick otherwise.

LOUGH GILL

The forested 24 mi. road around Lough Gill, southeast of Sligo, runs past woody nature trails, Yeatsian haunts, a castle, and several small towns. It's flat enough for a wonderful bike trip from Sligo, but start early. Take Pearse Rd. and turn left at Lough Gill signs. The Wild Rose Water Bus (see Daytrips from Sligo, p. 398) is another popular way to tour the lough. Parke's Castle (☎64149) open mid-Mar. to Oct. daily 10am-6pm; last admission 5:15pm. 25min. tours on request. €2.75, students and children €1.25, family €6.30.

Beautiful Lough Gill, dotted with some 80 tiny islands, is bordered on one side by gnarled mountains, while thickly wooded hills cut through farmlands on the other. The striking outline of Benbulben Mountain, rising from beyond, com-pletes the scene. Legend has it that the bell from Sligo Abbey is buried in its depths; only the chosen (or delusional) can hear it ring from below the waves.

The first stop on the round-lough route is **Holywell**, a leafy, flower-strewn shrine resting near a well and waterfall; Catholics held mass here in secret dur-ing Penal times. The main road then reaches **Dooney Rock,** on the south shore near Cottage Island. Here, Yeats's "Fiddler of Dooney" made "folk dance like a wave of the sea." Nature trails around the rock and through the woods lead to views of **Innisfree,** a perfectly round island that the young Yeats wistfully wrote about from the hustle-bustle of 1893 London: "I shall have some peace there, for peace comes dropping slow, / Dropping from the veils of the morning to where the cricket sings."

The next town past the Inisfree turnoff is **Dromahair,** which still shelters the **Creevelea Friary.** Founded in 1508 as the Friary of Killanummery, its frying days ended in 1650 when Oliver Cromwell expelled the monks and confiscated their home. Since 1721, it has been used as a burial site. Dromahair is the farthest point on the route; from here, turn left onto R286 to head back to Sligo Town.

On the road back stands **Parke's Castle,** a recently renovated 17th-century manor -cum-fortress. Built by Anglo Captain Robert Parke in 1609 to protect himself from dispossessed Irish landowners, the castle stands on the still-visi-ble foundation of an earlier O'Rourke family stronghold. The remains of a moat are also still visible, though it was filled in long ago. The main part of the house now hosts an exhibit on traditional Irish dwellings and shows a film about area sites. Two miles from town, a left turn leads to **Hazelwood,** the park where Aengus wandered "among long dappled grass" in "The Song of Wander-ing Aengus." Its **sculpture trail** makes for an artistic ramble and a perfect picnic.

DRUMCLIFFE AND BENBULBEN: YEATS, YEATS, YEATS

Buses from Sligo to Derry stop at Drumcliffe (10min. Summer M-Sa 7per day, Su 3 per day; winter M-Sa 3 per day). Returns require flagging down the bus, as it is a request-only stop (€4 return). Hitching is reportedly painless, but Let's Go doesn't recommend it. Glencar Lake is signposted 1 mi. north of Drumcliffe on N15. Drumcliffe Church Visitors Centre has turned to commerce: sandwiches and Guinness magnets predominate, but a free pamplet is available. Lissadell House ☎63150. Open June to mid-Sept. M-Sa 10:30am-1pm and 2-5pm; last tour 45min. before closing. €5, children €2.50. Grounds free.

Yeats composed the epitaph that was to be placed on his gravestone a year before his 1939 death in France; "Under bare Ben Bulben's head / In Drumcliffe churchyard Yeats is laid... / By his command these words are cut: / Cast a cold eye / On life, on death / Horseman pass by!" Georgia, his wife, didn't get around to carrying out his dying wish (to be buried in France, disinterred a year later, and then buried next to Benbulben) until nine years later, which is sort of creepy, but not nearly so creepy as the dying wish itself. (Another fun fact: When the two married, he was a venerable 52 years, while she was an innocent 15.) The road Yeats refers to is now N15, where noisy trucks and motorcycles pass by daily; his grave is in **Drumcliffe's** churchyard, 4 mi. northwest of Sligo, to the left of the church door. The church also projects an informative animated feature on Drumcliffe's pre-Yeatsian significance as a 6th-century Christian site, of which the **ancient cross** and **round tower** across N15 are remnants (☎63125; call ahead for film). A few miles northeast of Drumcliffe, **Glencar Lake** and its majestic **waterfall,** mentioned in Yeats's "The Stolen Child," provide a venue for further excursions.

Farther north of Drumcliffe, myth-infused **Benbulben Mountain** protrudes from the landscape like the keel of a foundered boat. St. Colmcille founded a monastery on the peak in AD 547, and it remained a major religious center until the 16th century. The 1729 ft. climb is inevitably windy, and the summit can be extremely gusty. If you can avoid being blown away, standing at the 5000 ft. drop at the mountain's edge can be a humbling and beautiful experience. (*Let's Go* does not recommend the overzealous pursuit of humbling experiences, especially when the weather is bad.) Signs on Drumcliffe Rd. guide travelers to Benbulben; for detailed directions to the trails, ask at the Drumcliffe gas station.

Eva Gore-Booth and her sister Constance Markievicz entertained Yeats and his friends 4 mi. northwest of Drumcliffe at **Lissadell House.** Countess Connie was the first woman elected to the *Dáil* and was second in command for the Easter Rising (see p. 63). The house's current restoration reflects an attempt to return the house to the grandeur of those heady times. Former man of the manor Henry Gore-Booth was an avid hunter, but the real trophy on display— a formerly ferocious and presently dead brown bear—was actually shot by the butler. To reach the house from Drumcliffe Rd., take the first left after Yeats Tavern Hostel and follow the signs.

COUNTIES ROSCOMMON AND LEITRIM

Rivers and lakes (and a significant number of fast-moving highways) meander through untouristed Roscommon and Leitrim, which span a diamond-shaped area between Sligo and Centre O'Ireland. Carrick-on-Shannon teems with pubs but remains relaxed, while Boyle is an excellent festival hostess with a soaring abbey.

Motor vehicle is the transportation of choice in this region. Because of traffic that is predominantly fly-by and non-local, Roscommon and Leitrim don't always make for easy hitching. **Parke's Castle, Dromahair,** and **Crevelea Abbey** are over the border in Co. Leitrim, but covered in Sligo (see p. 392).

CARRICK-ON-SHANNON (CORA DROMA RÚISC)   ☎078

Coursing slowly through the green hills of Leitrim on its way to the sea, the Shannon River pauses when it reaches the rows of white yachts moored at Carrick-on-Shannon's marina. Life is low-key in this proud seat of Ireland's least populous county—anglers fish for pike during the day, and in the evening merry drinkers fill the pubs with song. The town's few sights won't sustain an energetic visitor, but the parks and lakes nearby make good daytrips. A bridge over the Shannon crosses into town from Co. Roscommon, leading to the clock tower and Main St.

🖪🔃 TRANSPORTATION AND PRACTICAL INFORMATION. Elphin Road Station (☎20036) is a 10min. walk southwest of town. **Trains** go to: Dublin (2¼hr., 3-4 per day, €19) and Sligo (1hr., 3-4 per day, €11.75). **Buses** (☎071 60066) run from Coffey's Pastry Case to: Boyle (12min., 3-4 per day, €4.20); Dublin (3hr., 3-4 per day, €11.45); and Sligo (1hr., 3-4 per day, €8.70). For a **taxi,** call Michael Flynn (☎086 831 5566). **Geraghty's** on Main St. **rents bikes.** (☎21316. Weekly rentals only. €30 per wk. Open daily 9:30am-7pm.) Amazingly friendly, accommodating staff await at the 🖪**tourist office,** on the Marina. (☎20170. Open June-Aug. M-Sa 9am-6pm, Su 10am-2pm; Apr.-May, Sept. M-F 9am-1pm, 2-5pm. Contact Northwestern Tourism in Sligo the rest of the year ☎071 61201.) **AIB** on Main St. has an **ATM.** (☎20055. Open M 10am-5pm; Tu, Th-F 10am-4pm; W 10:30am-4pm.) Also on Bridge St. are **Cox's pharmacy** (☎20158; open M-Th 9:30am-6pm, F-Sa until 6:30pm) and **Gartlan's Cyber Cafe,** with **Internet.** (☎21735. €6 per hr. Open M-Sa 9:30am-5:30pm.) The **post office** is on St. George's Terr. (☎20020. Open M-Sa 9am-5:30pm.)

🖪🔃🖪 ACCOMMODATIONS, FOOD, AND PUBS. Lough Key Campground ❶, 4 mi. northwest of town on the road to the lake, supplies earth to pitch a tent, clean facilities, and piping hot showers. (☎079 62212. €12 per tent, €14 per vehicle.) **An Oiche Hostel ❷** ("The Night"), Bridge St., is sparklingly tidy, but small. It's convenient for going out, but unfortunate if sleeping when others come back. (☎21848. Dorms €20.) **The Four Seasons B&B ❸,** conveniently located on Main St. in the hub of town, has large ensuite rooms. (☎21333. €30.) Other B&Bs line the Dublin Rd., Station Rd., and the manicured lawns of St. Mary's Close.

Cheap dinners are hard to come by; **Londi's Supermarket,** Bridge St., is a good place to stock up on raw materials. (Open M-Sa 8am-10pm, Su 8am-8pm.) Popular **Chung's Chinese Restaurant ❷,** Main St., cooks up a storm. Book dinner well in advance to avoid long waits, or save by ordering takeaway. (☎21888. Takeaway around €7.60; sit-down €10. Open daily 6-11pm.) Intimate eatery, **La Belle Vita ❸,** Main St., serves top-notch pizza, pasta, meat, and fish à la italiana. (☎20333. Most pastas €8.50; meat or fish around €15. Open Tu-Su noon-3pm, 5-10:30pm.) **Coffey's Pastry Case ❶,** Bridge St., has sandwiches (€3), but the wealth of pastries—served with a dollop of rich cream—truly require a taste; the meringues (€1.50) are lighter than air. (☎20929. Open M-Sa 8:30am-7:30pm, Su 9:30am-7pm.)

The Anchorage, on Bridge St., is the town's most popular and venerable pub, with a traditional feel and mixed crowd. (☎20416. Open Su-W noon-11:30pm, Th-Sa noon-12:30am.) Across the town bridge, the glorious, grassy beer garden at **Ging's** entices tourists to sit, relax with a glass, and watch the yachts pass. (☎21054. Open

Su-W 1-11:30pm, Th-Sa 1pm-12:30am.) Carrick's nearest nightclub, **Rockin' Robbins**, 1 mi. from the town center, pulls in 21+ partiers from the whole county. Minibuses (€2) leave from The Anchorage on weekends. (Cover €5-9. Open F-Su.)

SIGHTS AND ACTIVITIES. At the intersection of Main St. and Bridge St., tiny **Costello Memorial Chapel** is, at 16x12 ft., reputedly the second-smallest church in the world, though no one in town seems to know what's first. Edward Costello had the chapel built as a monument to his wife after she died in 1877; the loving couple's coffins are on display beneath fogged plexiglass on either side of the aisle. The **Angling and Tourism Association** (☎20489) gives the line on rentals, sights, and fishing. Licenses aren't necessary to fish on the river. To really go native, head to the 12,000-seat **football pitch** outside town on a Sunday afternoon and watch Leitrim battle other counties in Gaelic football. (Tickets €20, students €8; pay at the field.) Pick up the *Leitrim Observer* at any newsagent for other local listings.

Four miles northwest of Carrick-on-Shannon on the road to Boyle, the 850 acres and 33 forested islands of **Lough Key Forest Park** burst with rhododendrons in spring, but are worth exploring any time of year. The park was once the center of **Rockingham Estate,** which covered most of the surrounding area. The estate's classical mansion burned down in 1957, though the less impressive stables, church, and icehouse were spared the fire's wrath. Numerous signposts point to the **round tower, faery bridge,** and **wishing chair;** all are on the Green Walk. (☎079 62363. Map and brochure available from the Carrick-on-Shannon tourist office. Park always open. Admission €2.55 per car 10am-6pm.) **Lough Key** and the diminutive castle-topped **Castle Island** offshore can be explored in group fashion on a **Lough Key Boat Tour** (☎20252). The same company also rents boats to those prefering to chart their own routes. Also nearby is **Lough Key Campground** (see **Accommodations,** p. 401). North of the lough lies the site of Ireland's most important pre-human battle, in which the Túatha De Danann defeated Ireland's indigenous demons, the Formorians (see **Legends and Folktales,** p. 73).

BOYLE (MAINISTIR NA BÚILLE)   ☎079

Settled on a river and squeezed between two lakes, hilly Boyle was once used by clans and troops as a strategic base. The modern explorer would do well to follow their example—Boyle contains numerous historical sights and offers convenient access to nearby mountains, lakes, and parks. At the bottom of Main St.'s hill, Gothic arches curve over the green lawns of magnificent **Boyle Abbey.** Although the Abbey was built by Cistercian monks, its high arches and intricate Celtic carvings impress anyone. (☎62604. Open Apr.-Oct. daily 10am-6pm. Tours every hour. €1.20. Key available from Mrs. Mitchell at Abbey House B&B.) In the early 1990s, the Roscommon Council voted to raze **King House,** Main St., to make room for a carpark. Luckily for visitors, the pavement-happy were thwarted by the building's sturdy architectural base—and so it remains, a tribute to its own history. Built by Sir Henry King circa 1730 to impress his young bride, the Georgian mansion has served as a family home for 40 years and an army barracks for 140 years. Within the mansion, the **Boyle Civic Art Collection** houses contemporary Irish sculpture and paintings. (☎63242. Open Apr.-Sept. daily 10am-6pm; last admission 5pm. €4.) **Frybrook House,** a 5min. walk from the bridge, was built in 1752 and restored to shininess in 1994. Although it is now a family home, most of the house's furniture is Georgian or Victorian. (☎63513. Appointment only, call a few days ahead.)

For a lesson in musical culture, pick up the tin whistle at early July's **Dr. Douglas Hyde Summer School of Traditional Irish Music and Dance** in nearby Ballaghaderreen. (Contact Paddy McGray ☎086 850 8605; www.ballaghaderreen.com. €55, under 18

€40.) The month's final week rings in the **Boyle Arts Festival,** and with it a series of recitals, workshops, and exhibitions that render art aficionados delirious. (☎ 63085 or 64069; www.boylearts.com. Tickets free-€8.)

Trains (☎ 62027) run from Boyle to Dublin (3hr., 3-4 per day, €19) and Sligo (30min., 3-4 per day, €6.30). **Buses** stop outside the Royal Hotel on Bridge St. and go to Dublin (3½hr., 3-4 per day, €12) and Sligo (30min., 3-4 per day, €7.35). The **tourist office,** inside the gates of King House on Main St., welcomes visitors with open arms. (☎ 62145. Open May-Sept. daily 10am-1pm, 2-6pm.) **National Irish Bank,** at the intersection of Bridge St. and Patrick St., has an **ATM.** (☎ 62058. Open M 10am-5pm, Tu-F 10am-4pm; closed 12:30-1:30pm.) **Ryan's pharmacy** is at the intersection of Patrick St. and Main St. (☎ 62003. Open M-Sa 9am-6pm.) **Internet** is at the **library,** in King House. (☎ 62800. "Free" with €3.80 membership fee. Open Tu, Th 1-8pm; W, F-Sa 10am-1pm, 2-5pm.) The **post office** is on the Carrick Rd. (☎ 62029. Open M, W-F 9am-5:30pm; Tu 9:30am-5:30pm; Sa 9am-1pm, 2-5:30pm.)

The nearest budget digs are found at the hostel in Carrick-on-Shannon (see p. 401). More lavish beds, however, abound in Boyle's B&Bs. Every visitor to the 170-year-old **Abbey House ❸,** on Abbeytown Rd., is housed in an elegant, antique-laden room. The spacious sitting areas have views of an authentic, dyed-in-the-wool babbling brook, while some of the rooms look onto Boyle Abbey. Self-catering family cottages for four are also available. (☎ 62385. All rooms with bath. €28; cottage prices available on request.) Cheery **Cesh Corran ❸,** across from the Abbey, welcomes visitors into bright, comfy rooms with hair dryers and chocolates, in addition to the usual amenities. (☎ 62247. Singles €35; shared rooms €30.)

Londi's Supermarket, Bridge St., stocks sundries. (☎ 62112. Open M-F 8am-8pm, Sa 8am-7pm, Su 8am-2pm.) **Stone House Cafe ❶,** on Bridge St., is an old stone tower turned intimate cafe. (☎ 64861. Veggie options. Sandwiches from €2. Open M-F 9am-6pm, Sa 10am-6pm.) **King House Restaurant ❷,** within the gates of King House (see **Sights,** below), offers tasty, convenient breakfasts (€6) and lunches (€8). (☎ 64805. Open daily 9am-6pm.) An excellent view of the river accompanies the Asian-Irish meals at **Chung's Restaurant ❸,** at the Royal Hotel on Bridge St. (☎ 62390. Dinners €9-18.) For perfect pints and rousing trad most nights, everyone heads to **Kate Lavin's** (☎ 62855) on Patrick St.

NORTHWEST IRELAND

Northwest Ireland is comprised entirely of Co. Donegal. Among Ireland's counties, Donegal (DUN-ee-gahl) is second to Cork in size and second to none in glorious wilderness. The landscape here contrasts sharply with that of Southern Ireland, replacing lush, smooth hillsides with jagged rock and bald, windy cliffs. Cottage industries, fishing boats, and tweed factories occupy locals' days, while a pure form of trad keeps them packed in the pubs at night. Donegal's *gaeltacht* is a storehouse of genuine, unadulterated Irish tradition, left largely untouched by the Irish tourism machine. In its 13th year, the **Earagail Arts Festival** in Co. Donegal distinguishes itself from other Irish arts festivals in its scope and remarkable selection of artists, musicians, and performers. Hitchhikers report that Donegal drivers provide the most rides in Ireland, though *Let's Go* doesn't recommend it.

COUNTY DONEGAL

Although its name means "fort of the foreigner," Donegal is in fact the least touristed, least Anglicized, and most remote of Ireland's "scenic" provinces. Donegal escaped Ireland's widespread deforestation, and vast wooded areas engulf many of the county's mountain chains. The coastline alternates between beautiful beaches and craggy cliffs; Europe's tallest are near Slieve League. Driving or cycling along the coast of remote Inishowen Peninsula is unforgettable. And, the county's distance from all things English has preserved Ireland's largest *gaeltacht*.

◧ TRANSPORTATION

Donegal has public transportation, but only for those willing to wait. There is **no train** service in the county, and **buses** tend to hit smaller towns only once or twice per day, often in the early morning or late at night. Only major towns like Letterkenny, Donegal Town, and Dungloe—and a few smaller towns—**rent bikes.** Hitchers report short waits and friendly drivers on major roads, particularly those north of Donegal Town. Byways are largely devoid of drivers.

When hopping on a bus, ask if student, child, or senior fares are available. Tourist offices and bus depots have schedules for **Bus Éireann** (Dublin ☎ 01 836 6111; Letterkenny ☎ 074 912 1309; Sligo ☎ 071 60066; Strabane ☎ 074 31008; www.buseireann.ie), which connects Donegal Town to Dublin (4¼hr.) and Galway (4hr.); Letterkenny to Galway (4¾hr.); Donegal Town (4hr.); and some of the smaller villages in the southern half of the region. **Private buses** replace Bus Éireann for most of the major routes in Donegal. Their prices are reasonable and their drivers more open to persuasion if you hope to be let off on the doorstep of a remote hostel. The flexibility of their routes also means that the buses aren't always on time. **Lough Swilly Buses** (Derry ☎ 028 7126 2017; Letterkenny ☎ 074 912 2873) cover the northern area, connecting Letterkenny, Derry, Inishowen Peninsula, Fanad Peninsula, and western coastal villages as far south as Dungloe (€5.85-11.45). **McGeehan's Bus Co.** runs daily between Donegal, Dublin, and most intervening towns. (☎074 954 6150. Donegal Town to Dublin; route serves Burtonport, Dungloe, Mountcharles, Glenties, Glencolmcille, Carrick, Kilcar, Killybegs, Ardara, Ardaghey, Pettigo, and Cavan.) **Feda O'Donnell** (☎075 48114; Galway ☎091 761 656; www.fedodonnell.com) runs along the Donegal coast, connecting the northwest with Galway and Sligo (from Donegal Town via Letterkenny to Dunfanaghy, Gweedore, and Crolly; €7.60), and carries bikes for free.

SOUTHERN DONEGAL

With infrequent buses running between Donegal town and most other Irish cities, and no local train service to speak of, many visitors travel by way of Sligo. Some take a direct bus (1hr.) to Donegal Town, while others stop to relax in the surfing town of Bundoran before continuing northward.

DONEGAL TOWN (DÚN NA NGALL)   ☎073

A gateway for travelers heading to more isolated destinations to the north and northwest, this sometimes sleepy town ignites on weekends, and everything awakens when festivals arrive. The town swells with tourism in July and August, but manages to do so without losing its charm—somehow this "fort of the foreigner" keeps a full invasion at bay while still providing splendid scenery, and a smile.

▐ TRANSPORTATION

Buses: Bus Éireann (☎21101; www.buseireann.ie) to: **Derry** (M-Sa 6 per day, Su 3 per day; €10.30) via **Letterkenny** (€6.35); **Dublin** (M-Th and Sa 5 per day, F 7 per day, Su 6 per day; €13.35); **Enniskillen** (M-Sa 5 per day, Su 4 per day; €7.90); **Galway** (M-Sa 4 per day, Su 3 per day; €13.35); **Sligo** (3-7 per day, €9.80). **McGeehan's Coaches** (☎075 46150) go to **Dublin** via **Enniskillen** and **Cavan;** also to: **Killybegs, Ardara, Glenties, Glencolmcille,** and **Dungloe** (3 per day). Bus Éireann and McGeehan stop outside the Abbey Hotel on the Diamond; timetables posted in the lobby. **Feda O'Donnell** (☎075 48114) leaves for **Galway** from the tourist office (M-Sa 9:45am and 5:15pm; additional times F at 1:15pm, Su 9:45am, 4:15, and 8:15pm) and also goes to **Dunfanaghy** via **Crolly** and **Gweedore.**

Taxis: McCallister (☎087 277 1777) and **McBrearty Quinn's** (☎087 762 0670).

Bike Rental: The Bike Shop, Waterloo Pl. (☎22515), first left off the Killybegs Rd. from the Diamond. Bikes €10 per day, €60 per wk. Open M-Sa 10am-6pm.

✳ ▐ ORIENTATION AND PRACTICAL INFORMATION

The center of town is called **the Diamond,** a triangle bordered by Donegal's main shopping streets. Three roads extend from the Diamond: the **Killybegs Road, Main Street,** and **Quay Street** (the **Ballyshannon Road**).

Tourist Office: Quay St. (☎21148; www.donegaltown.ie). Facing away from the Abbey Hotel, turn right; the tourist office is outside the Diamond on the Ballyshannon/Sligo Rd., next to the quay. Brochures galore on Co. Donegal, a free town map, and accommodations bookings throughout the Republic. There are few tourist offices in the county; it's wise to stop here before heading north. Open July-Aug. M-Sa 9am-6pm, Su noon-4pm; Sept.-Oct. and Easter-June M-F 9am-5pm, Sa 10am-2pm.

Banks: In the Diamond are an **AIB** (☎21016), **Bank of Ireland** (☎21079), and **Ulster Bank** (☎21064); each with 24hr. **ATMs.** All open M-F 10am-4pm, Th until 5pm.

County Donegal

0 ___ 5 miles
0 ___ 5 kilometers

Tory Island

Tory Sound

Inishbeg

Horn Head

Inishdooey

Inishbofin

Dunfanaghy

Shee

Bloody Foreland

Magheraorty

Cloghaneely

Falcarragh

Gortahork

Creeslou

Muckish Mtn.

Derrybeg

Bunbeg

Gweedore

Owey Island

Donegal Airport

Dunlewy

Errigal Mtn.

Derryveagh Mountains

Lough Beag

Cruit Island

Crolly

Annagry

Rosses Bay

The Rosses

Aranmore Island

Burtonport

Slieve Snaght

Glenveagh National Park

Glendowan Mts.

Rutland Island

Dungloe

Crohy Head

R252

Fintown

R250

C   O   .   D

Gweebara Bay

Lough Finn

Dunmore Head

Portnoo

Aghla Mtn.

Dawros Head

Rosbeg

Maas

Gaugin Mtn.

R261

Glenties

N56

Tormore Island

Shevetooey

Glengesh Pass

Ardara

Blue Stack Mountains

Glen Head

Mulmosog Mtn.

SLIEVE LEAGUE PENINSULA

Letterbarrow

Lough Eske

Rossan Point

Glencolmcille

N15

Malin Beg

Slieve League

Donegal

Rathlin O'Birne Island

Carrick

Killybegs

Bruckless

Mountcharles

N56

Kilcar

R256

Dunkineely

Carrigan Head

Teelin

Muckros Head

Drumanoo Head

Killybegs Harbour

Doorin Point

Ballintra

T35

St. John's Point

Donegal Bay

Ballyshannon

Bundoran

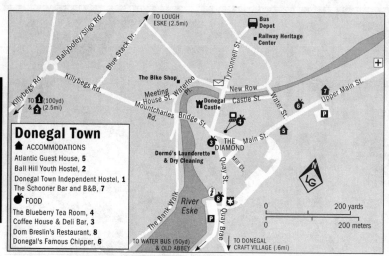

Donegal Town

⌂ ACCOMMODATIONS

Atlantic Guest House, **5**
Ball Hill Youth Hostel, **2**
Donegal Town Independent Hostel, **1**
The Schooner Bar and B&B, **7**

🍴 FOOD

The Blueberry Tea Room, **4**
Coffee House & Deli Bar, **3**
Dom Breslin's Restaurant, **8**
Donegal's Famous Chipper, **6**

Laundry: Dermó's Launderette & Dry Cleaning, Millcourt Suite 8, the Diamond (☎22255). Large wash and dry €13, small load €10. Open M-Sa 9am-7pm.

Emergency: ☎999; no coins required. **Police** *(Garda):* ☎21021.

Pharmacy: Begley's Chemist, the Diamond (☎21232). 1hr. photo processing. Open M-Sa 9:15am-6pm.

Hospital: Donegal Hospital, Main St. (☎21019).

Internet Access: The Blueberry Tea Room has a cyber-cafe on its 2nd fl. (see **Food,** below). €3.50 per 30min. €6 per hr. Open M-Sa 9am-7pm.

Post Office: Tyrconnell St. (☎21007), past Donegal Castle and over the bridge. Open M-Sa 9am-5:30pm.

🏠 ACCOMMODATIONS AND CAMPING

Donegal Town has some of the most welcoming hostels in the country. The tourist office provides a list of B&B options for travelers hooked on the full fry. During the high season, beds are in demand, so plan and call ahead.

📧 **Donegal Town Independent Hostel (IHH/IHO),** Killybegs Rd. (☎972 2805), a 10min. walk from town. Family-run hostel makes siblings of road-weary backpackers. Linda and her daughters greet guests with smiles, and make home feel not so far away. Murals grace the walls of some rooms. Call for possible pickup. Popular with savvy travelers, so call ahead. Open June-Aug. Dorms €10.50; doubles €22. **Camping** €6 per person. ❶

Ball Hill Youth Hostel (An Óige/HI), Ball Hill (☎972 1174), 3 mi. from town. Go 1½ mi. from town on the Killybegs Rd., turn left at the sign, and continue toward the sea. Buses from Abbey Hotel (€1.30) often go as far as the Killybegs road. Hospitable owner leads an "archaelogical tour" around the building, and offers a host of activities, including horseback riding, swimming, hiking, boating, and bonfires. Dorms €10.50. ❶

Atlantic Guest House, Main St. (☎972 1187). Unbeatable location. Despite being on a busy street, this 16-room guest house offers the privacy of a fancy hotel. Each room has plush carpets, TVs, phones, and sinks. Singles €30-35; doubles €45-60. ❸

Schooner Bar and B&B, Upper Main St. (☎972 1671). Tastefully decorated period-style rooms with an award-winning pub downstairs. Most rooms with bath. €35. ❸

FOOD

A good selection of cafes and takeaways occupy the Diamond and nearby streets. For groceries, head to **SuperValu**, minutes from the Diamond down the Ballyshannon Rd. (☎972 2977. Open M-W and Sa 9am-7pm, Th-F 9am-9pm, Su 10am-6pm.) **Simple Simon's**, the Diamond, sells fresh baked goods, local cheeses, and homeopathic remedies. (☎972 2687. Open M-Sa 9:30am-6pm.)

▨ **The Blueberry Tea Room,** Castle St. (☎972 2933), on the corner of the Diamond toward the Killybegs Rd. Justifiably popular home-made sandwiches, daily specials, and all-day breakfasts. Cyber-cafe upstairs. Mains around €6.50. Open M-Sa 9am-7pm. ❷

Dom Breslin's Restaurant and Bar, Quay St. (☎972 2719), next to the tourist office. Mariner theme—food arrives from "The Galley," but "Third Class" and "Steerage" receive first-class meals. Steak and seafood specialties (€12-19). Lunch 12:30-4pm; dinner 4-9:30pm. Trad nightly July-Aug.; Sept.-June F-Sa. Nightclub open July-Aug. W and Sa. ❹

Donegal's Famous Chipper, Main St. (☎972 1428). The quintessential takeaway. €4 for the day's catch and its potato partner. Open M-Tu and Th-Su 4:30-11:30pm. ❶

The Coffee House and Deli Bar, the Diamond (☎972 1014), attached to the Abbey Hotel. Try a sandwich (€3.25-5) or the satisfying 2-course "Plate of the Day" with veggies and potatoes (€6.35). Open daily 9am-5:30pm. ❷

PUBS AND CLUBS

Donegal's pubs are well-equipped to deal with a town's worth of thirsty visitors. To help make the most of these watering holes, *Let's Go* presents the ultimate **Donegal Town Pub Crawl**. If it's on the map, you want to be there.

The Schooner Bar and B&B, Upper Main St. (☎9721671). Great mix of hostelers and locals gather in this lantern-lit James Joyce Award-winning pub. Best trad and contemporary sessions in town on weekends from June-Aug. Sa nights summon trendy DJs.

The Olde Castle Bar and Restaurant, Castle St. (☎972 1062). Stone walls and corbel windows, for that recently renovated medieval feel. Low-key place for soulful conversation with a lovely lad or lass. Bar food noon-3pm. Open June-Aug. M-Th until 11:30pm, F-Su 'til 12:30am; Sept.-May until 11pm.

Charlie's Star Bar, Main St. (☎972 1158). Well-lit and spacious. Sip Guinness around the huge horseshoe shaped bar. Folks gather for GAA games and ballads.

Donegal Town Pub Crawl

0 — 100 yards
0 — 100 meters

Tyrconnell St.
New Row
Meeting House St.
Waterloo Pl.
Castle St.
Donegal Castle
Water St.
Upper Main St.
Mountcharles Rd.
Bridge St.
THE DIAMOND
Main St.
Mill St.
Quay St.
The Bank Walk
River Eske
Quay Brae

PUBS
Charlie's Star Bar, 4
The Coach House, 5
McGroarty's Lounge Bar, 3
Olde Castle Bar, 2
Schooner Bar, 6
The Voyage, 1

McGroarty's, the Diamond (☎972 1049). The biggest bar in town packs in a well-mannered crew of locals and tourists for blues and ballads on weekends. Food M-F noon-4pm.

The Voyage Bar, the Diamond (☎972 1201). This pub keeps its patrons happy, but ask the jovial proprietor about its name and a tear glints in his eye: "Everyone has a voyage to make in life." Younger crowd. Rock music on weekends.

The Coach House, Upper Main St. (☎972 2855). Spontaneous sing-alongs are standard at this wood-beamed local. Downstairs **Cellar Bar** opens nightly at 9:15pm for trad and ballads. Confident musicians and singers are encouraged to join. Cover €2.

◉ ▓ SIGHTS AND FESTIVALS

▓**DONEGAL CRAFT VILLAGE.** Six craftspeople open their workshops to the public in Donegal's craft village. The innovative work of a potter, a jeweler, a painter, an ironsmith, and two sculptors make great gift alternatives to the legions of mass-produced leprechauns sold elsewhere. *(About 1 mi. south of town on the Ballyshannon Rd. ☎972 2225. Open July-Aug. M-Sa 10am-6pm, Su noon-6pm; Sept.-June call ahead.)*

DONEGAL CASTLE. Originally the seat of several chieftains, Donegal was torn apart by Irish-English conflict during the 17th century. Evidence of this turmoil remains at Donegal Castle, former residence of the O'Donnell clan and, later, various English nobles. The recently refurbished ruins of the O'Donnell clan's castle of 1474 stand beside the manor built by English rulers in 1623. *(Castle St. ☎972 2405. Open Mar.-Oct. daily 10am-5:15pm; Nov.-Feb. Sa-Su 10am-5:15pm. Guided tours on the hour. €3.80, students and children €1.50, seniors €2.50, family €9.50.)*

OLD ABBEY AND ST. PATRICK'S CHURCH. The stones and doorways of Donegal Castle's grand manor were taken from this ruined 15th-century Franciscan Friary. The remains of the original building—stairways and wall fragments—mingle with those of humans, evidence of the site's later incarnation as a cemetery. The abbey was destroyed in an explosion in 1601; a quartet of dispossessed monks went on to write the *Annals of the Four Masters*, the first narrative history of Ireland and the source of many still-extant myths. An **obelisk** built on the Diamond in 1937 pays homage to the holy men, as does **St. Patrick's Church of the Four Masters,** a stolid Romanesque church about half a mile up Main St. *(Old Abbey is a short walk from the tourist office along the south side of town. St. Patrick's open M-F 9am-5pm. Free.)*

WATERBUS. A new addition to Donegal Town's tourism machine, the Waterbus shuttle provides aquatic tours of Donegal Bay. The tour is at once scenic and morbid, as it encompasses many sights associated with the Famine-era "coffin ship" industry. Among the tour's highlights are a colony of seals, a shoreside castle, and an oyster farm. *(Ferry leaves from the quay next to the tourist office. ☎972 3666. Departures depend on tides; call ahead. €10; students, seniors, and children €5.)*

ACTIVITIES. Donegal Guided Town and Country Walks exercise the mind and the legs, educating walkers about the town's history and delighting them with rambles through the surrounding countryside. Experienced guides are also available year-round to plan attacks on the Slieve League, Bluestacks, Errigal, and Derryveagh

---

STATION ISLAND Station Island in County Donegal's **Lough Derg** is the site of one of Ireland's most arcane and interesting Christian rituals. In AD 554, the priest soon to be known as St. Patrick arrived on Station Island and shut himself in a cave for 15 days. According to legend, he experienced a series of hellish visions during his cavely meditations. Every summer since, hosts of pilgrims have come to Station Island to emulate the Original Paddy's saintly lifestyle. The pilgrimage, undertaken in June or July, is a three-day orgy of fasting, praying, and circling the island barefoot. It begins with 24 hours of uninterrupted meditation known as The Vigil, immediately followed by the Celtic-Chrisitan ritual of "Stations." The one daily meal consists of dry toast and tea. Recently, an expurgated version of the ritual that forgoes all the fasting and shoeless wandering has gained popularity. Some old-schoolers scoff at this "softer" pilgrimage, forgetting that the modern three-day ceremony is a mere shadow of its original 15 days, which involved none of this namby-pamby toast-eating. Whichever path the contemporary pilgrim chooses, he need bring no more than warm clothes and a repentant heart. *(Contact the Prior of St. Patrick's Purgatory ☎072 61518; www.loughderg.org.)*

Mountains. (☎973 5967; info@northwestwalkingguides.com.) Those less inclined to explore on their own two feet rent four from **Deane's Open Farm.** The farm has horse trekking and pony rides. Kids can feed and nurse a variety of animals. (☎973 7160. *From Donegal Town, drive 12 mi. on N56 toward Killybegs and follow the signs.*)

FESTIVALS. During the last weekend in June, the **Donegal Summer Festival** fills the town with craft and antiques fairs, air-sea rescue displays, clay-pigeon shoots, the Bonny Baby show, and plenty of live bands and trad sessions. To join the three-day party, call ahead for a room—the town doubles in size that weekend. *(Contact the tourist office at ☎972 1148.)* For two weeks in July, the **Earagail Arts Festival** rages throughout County Donegal. Twenty towns and over 40 venues host 100 events, from music, dance, and theater to special children's performances. Tickets free-€25. Info and schedules available at the tourist office. *(Ticket hotline ☎074 29186. Info ☎074 912 0777. www.donegalculture.com.)*

◪ DAYTRIP FROM DONEGAL TOWN: LOUGH ESKE

The hike to the lough and back takes 2hr. Follow signs for "Harvey's Point" (marked from the Killybegs Rd.). About 3 mi. down the path is a stone pillar. Turn right and follow the path to the remains of Lough Eske Castle. Drivers can reach the 15 mi. loop around the lough by following signs to Lough Eske from the Mountcharles Rd.

The most worthwhile of Donegal Town's sights actually lies a few miles outside of town at Lough Eske ("fish lake"), an idyllic pond among a fringe of trees and ruins. The crumbling but majestic **Lough Eske Castle,** built in 1861, stands loughside; its slightly overgrown grounds make a gorgeous site for picnics and afternoon rambles. Follow the path around front to a **Celtic high cross** (see **Christians and Vikings,** p. 57) surrounded by breathtaking gardens.

BUNDORAN (BUN DOBHRÁIN)   ☎071

At the mouth of the Dobhran River, Bundoran is the first stop in Donegal for visitors from Sligo or Leitrim. In 1777, Bundoran was the summer residence of Viscount Enniskillen, but it has since been appropriated by the plebeian masses. Beautiful beaches, fishing, and some of the best surf in Ireland make this a popular destination for tourists from across the Republic and Northern Ireland. In recent years, taxbreak-fueled development has been rapid and haphazard—the town's population swells from 2000 to 20,000 in summer. By day, tourists stroll the mile-long shore road; at night, youngsters party in the town's many pubs, saloons, and nightclubs. Bundoran's beach-town bustle, set to the rhythm of crashing waves, makes it a pleasant stop en route to Donegal.

◪◪ TRANSPORTATION AND PRACTICAL INFORMATION. Catch **Bus Éireann** (☎985 1101) at the Main St. depot for: Donegal (7 per day); Dublin (3 per day); and Galway via Sligo (M-Sa 4 per day, Su 3 per day). **Ulsterbus** runs to Enniskillen (summer M-Sa 7 per day, Su 3 per day; off season M-Sa 3 per day, Su 1 per day). **Feda O'Donnell** (☎075 48356) serves Galway and Letterkenny. **Goodwin's Hire and Sell** rents **bikes** and **fishing equipment** from the blue shed behind the Sand Dune B&B on Sea Rd. (☎984 1526. Bikes €10 per day, €35 per wk.; deposit €30. Fishing rods €8 per day. Open M-Sa 8:30am-6pm.) The **tourist office,** over the bridge on Main St., provides brochures on Donegal's attractions. (☎984 1350. Open June-Aug. M-Sa 9am-6pm, Su 10am-6pm; off season daily 9am-5pm.) **AIB,** on Main St., has an **ATM.** (☎984 1222. Open M 10am-5pm, Tu-F 10am-4pm.) **Donegal Adventure Centre** (see **Accommodations,** below) also **rents bikes.** Short-term **work opportunities** can be found at La Sabbia restaurant, attached to the Homefield Hostel (see **Accommodations,** below). Direct inquires to the owner/chef at the hostel (☎984 1977) or at the restaurant (☎984 1288). For **Internet** access, head to **CyberZone,** Station Rd., off Main St. near the Railway Bar. (☎982 9428. €1.60 per 15min.)

NORTHWEST IRELAND

ACCOMMODATIONS, FOOD, AND PUBS. Every third house in Bundoran seems to be of the B&B persuasion; the cheaper and quieter ones are farther down Main St., away from the bridge. There are two hostels in town, but they fill quickly in summer, so call ahead. **Homefield Hostel (IHH) ❷,** Bayview Ave., is off Main St.; head left up the hill between the Church of Ireland and Bay View Guest House. One wing of the huge building, former summer residence of that famous Viscount Enniskillen, connects to a surprisingly good Italian restaurant (see **La Sabbia,** below), while the other cradles a high-ceilinged parlor. The bunks are a bit creaky, but rooms are reasonably comfortable and well-maintained. (☎984 1977. Continental breakfast included. Dorms €16; doubles €25.) A few steps from the hostel, **Donegal Adventure Centre ❶** caters specifically to youth groups but also welcomes backpackers into its rooms and facilities, inviting them to join in **mountain biking, surf lessons,** and other adventure activities. The friendly manager Niamh (NEEV) is a font of information. (☎984 2418. Surf lessons from €20. Free laundry. Curfew 3am. Dorms €12; private rooms €20. Mar.-Oct. 3-day activity weekend over bank holidays, €150.) **Thalassa House ❷,** W. Main St., is an orange-red B&B with sunny, ensuite rooms. (☎984 1324 or 984 1685. Singles €25-35.)

The best restaurant in town is ▨**La Sabbia ❷,** an Italian bistro connected to the Homefield Hostel. Enjoy impeccable food in a cozy yet cosmopolitan atmosphere. (☎984 1977. Gourmet pizzas and pasta €7-11. Open June-Aug. Th-Tu 7-10pm; Sept.-May Th-Su 7-10pm, but call ahead.) **McGarrigle's Restaurant ❸** serves dishes with a bit more panache than its Main St. neighbors, often at lower prices. (☎984 2060. Breakfast all day. Mains €11-17. Open June-Sept. daily 10am-10pm; Oct.-May 10am-3pm and 6-10pm.) **Ould Bridge Bar,** Main St., over the bridge, is a cross between a local pub and a surfer bar; it's a favorite with hostelers. (☎984 2050. Food until 9pm; bar open 8am-late.) **Railway Bar** (☎984 1196), farther up the hill on Main St., pours fine pints to the local wisemen, including the mayor. Huge crowds of over a thousand have been reported at the edge of town in **The Dome,** Bundoran's superclub. (☎984 2430. Cover Sa €8, Su €7. Open Sa-Su nights.)

SIGHTS AND ACTIVITIES. A stroll past the Northern Hotel affords an impressive view of the mighty Atlantic waves. Curious sights include the **Faery Bridges, Wishing Chair,** and **Puffing Hole,** where water spouts through a bed of rocks. The **Aughross Cliffs** ("Headlands of the Steeds") were once a pasture for warhorses. At the western end of town, down the hill from Thalassa House, a bathing pool is built onto the smooth rock face. In the center of town is the small **Bundoran Beach,** which suffers terribly in comparison to the golden sand of its neighbor, **Tullan Strand.** To bathers' chagrin, the beaches in this area are better for **surfing** than for swimming. Several accessible breaks are adjacent to town, including a reef break called the Peak at Bundoran Beach and a shore break on the Tullan Strand. **Fitzgeralds Surfworld,** Main St. (☎984 1223; www.surfworldireland.com), reports conditions and serves as local surf oracle. Rentals and lessons are available from the **Donegal Adventure Centre** (see **Accommodations,** p. 412.) **Bundoran's Water World** provides a heated environment for summertime splashing, with a pool and two large water slides. (☎984 1172. Open summer daily 10am-6pm. €7, children and seniors €5.) Parents can retreat to the adjacent **Aqua Mara Spa** for a Seabath Steam (€15 per hr.) or a spin in the Relaxarium (€8), combining music, murals, artificial sunsets, and aromatherapy into a 15min. extravaganza. (☎984 1173. Open Su and W-Sa 10am-8pm; call ahead if possible.) **The Homefield Hostel's Equestrian Centre** encourages galloping across dunes and beaches. (☎984 1977. Open Apr.-Oct. Lessons €20 per hr.) The brand new six-screen **Cineplex** shows standard Hollywood fare nightly, and the occasional wee Irish film. Turn off Main St. away from the sea at the Railway Bar to reach it. (☎982 9999. €6.50. Weekly schedule posted around town.) The annual **Bundoran Music Festival,** held over October's bank holiday weekend, attracts big names in trad, bands, and the occasional hypnotist.

BALLYSHANNON (BÉAL ÁTHA SEANAIDH)   ☎072

Quainter and quieter than its touristically rowdy neighbor Bundoran, Ballyshannon twiddles its thumbs by the River Erne, which splashes over the Falls of Assaroe *(Ess Ruaid)* west of the bridge. The falls are one of Ireland's oldest pagan holy sites, but now they serve as a shrine for those who worship the fishing rod.

▐▐ **TRANSPORTATION AND PRACTICAL INFORMATION. Allingham's Bridge** connects the town's two halves and honors Ballyshannon poet William Allingham, who inspired Yeats to study the mythic traditions of Co. Sligo. Most of the town lies north of the river, where **Main Street** splits halfway up a hill. This hill, named **Mullach na Sidh** ("hill of the fairies"), is believed to be the burial site of legendary High King Hugh, who supposedly drowned in the Assaroe falls. **Buses** (☎074 31008) leave the depot beside the bridge for Donegal Town (25min., 8-10 per day, €4.55) and Sligo (1 hr.; M-Sa 8 per day, Su 4 per day; €7.25.) For quick cash, hit the **ATM** at **AIB,** Castle St. (☎985 1169; open M-F 10am-4pm, Th until 5pm), or the **Bank of Ireland** on Main St. (☎985 4153; open M-F 10am-4pm, Th until 5pm). The **post office** is in the main triangle where Market St. splits from Main St. (☎985 1111. Open M-F 9am-1pm and 2-5:30pm, Sa 9am-1pm.) **Internet** can be accessed at **The Engine Room,** in the rear of the shopping center across from the Cineplex. (☎985 2960. €4 per 30min. Open M-F 9am-2pm and 2:30-5:30pm.)

▐▐▐ **ACCOMMODATIONS, FOOD, AND PUBS. Duffy's Hostel (IHH) ❶** is a small bungalow-turned-hostel 5min. from town on the Donegal Rd. The gregarious owners maintain a wonderful second-hand bookshop. (☎985 1535. Open Mar.-Oct. Laundry €2. Dorms €10. **Camping** €5 per person.) Ten minutes down the Belleek Rd., **Assaroe Lake Side Caravan & Camping Park ❶** has a beautiful location and brand new facilities, including sports fields and a playground. (☎985 2822. Laundry €2. 2-person tent €10, 4- to 6-person tent €14.) **Shannon's Corner B&B ❸,** at the top of Main St., has sunny rooms. (☎985 1180. €25.) The **bistro ❷** downstairs is normally crowded with locals clawing for the €7 open prawn sandwich. (Open M-Sa 8am-5pm.) **Mace Supermarket** vends fruits and veggies. (☎985 8144. Open M-Tu 8:30am-7pm, W and Sa 8:30am-7:30pm, Th-F 8:30am-8pm, Su 9:30am-2pm.) **Finn McCool's,** on Main St., is the most popular pub in town and reputedly hosts the best trad sessions in Donegal. Get here early; the pub is tiny and Guinness glasses take up as much space as drinkers. (☎985 2677. Trad every other night in the summer at 10pm.) **The Cellar** (☎985 1452), 5min. down the Bundoran Rd. below Sweeny's White Horse, has live trad every Friday from 9:30pm.

▐▐ **SIGHTS AND FESTIVALS.** From the left fork of Main St., a left turn past the Imperial Hotel leads to **St. Anne's Church,** where William Allingham is buried with all his kit and kin. Around June, a fish ladder in the river near the power station allows tourists to marvel at salmon and trout struggling upstream to spawn. The 12th-century Cistercian **Abbey of Assaroe** sits peacefully by the river. From town, take the left fork of Main St. past Thatch Pub and take the second left. The Cistercians put a canal in the river, harnessing its hydraulic power for a still-operational water mill. A tiny path outside leads to the **Abbey Well,** blessed by St. Patrick. Pilgrims bless themselves with its water each August 15. To the right of the bridge and 120 yd. down the riverbank, a tiny cave harbors a **mass rock** from

Penal days and two hollow stones that once held holy water (see **The Ascendancy,** p. 60). Things heat up on the first weekend in August, when the annual **Ballyshannon Music Festival** (☎51088) brings a mix of Irish folk music and Irish folk to town.

SLIEVE LEAGUE PENINSULA

Just west of Donegal Town, the Slieve League Peninsula's rocky cliffs jut imposingly into the Atlantic. The cliffs and mountains of this sparsely-populated area harbor coastal hamlets, untouched beaches, and some of Ireland's most dramatic scenery. R263 extends along the peninsula's southern coast, linking each charming village to the next. Backpackers and cyclists navigating the hilly terrain are advised to work their way westward, then northward, toward Glencolmcille. Stunning coastal vistas, pleasant inland paths, and windy, cottage-speckled fields of heather are hidden along the bends and twists of this road, so it pays to take time. **Ardara** and **Glenties** make pleasant stops along the inland return and fine points of departure for a trek north, deeper into Donegal. Although most easily covered by **car,** the peninsula is spectacular for **cycling** (with bike walking on frequent, serious hills). Despite recent improvements in service, **buses** to area hostels remain infrequent. Hitchers report finding rides in and to Slieve, especially from Donegal.

SOUTHEASTERN SLIEVE LEAGUE   ☎074

A handful of single-street villages skitter along the coast road between Donegal Town and Slieve League. For those fierce, furious **cyclists** willing to endure such demanding grades, the route offers rewarding coastal views. **The Art Gallery,** on the coast road to Killybegs, features the work of local artists inspired by the incredible beauty around them. (☎973 5675. Open Mar.-Oct. W-Su 11am-7pm.) About 12 mi. outside of Donegal Town—10 mi. past the tiny village of **Mountcharles**—is *very* tiny **Dunkineely,** surrounded by megalithic tombs, holy wells, and small streams, all of which are accessible by round-trip walks of less than 4 mi. A detailed pamphlet describing these walks is available at ▓**Gallagher Farm Hostel (IHH) ❶,** which sits about quarter of a mile off the main road in the town of **Bruckless,** about 1½ mi. beyond Dunkineely. This original 17th-century barn has been converted into a wonderfully clean, well-equipped hostel, with lots of kitchen space for dormers and campers, a huge fireplace, and a ping-pong table. (☎973 7057. Sheets €1. Laundry €4. Dorms €12.50. **Camping** €6.50.) Between the hostel and Dunkineely, a turn-off leads to **St. John's Point,** which has views across to the Sligo coastline.

KILCAR (CILL CHARTHAIGH)   ☎073

A breathtaking 8 mi. down R263 from Killybegs is the village of Kilcar, the gateway to Donegal's *gaeltacht* and commercial base for many Donegal weavers. The main street, also known as the scenic coast road that runs east to Killybegs and north to Carrick, passes Kilcar's main attraction—its superlative accommodations.

▤Ⓝ TRANSPORTATION AND IMPRACTICAL INFORMATION. The **Bus Éireann** (☎972 1101) route from Donegal Town to Glencolmcille stops in Kilcar (July-Sept. M-Sa 3 per day, Su 1 per day; Oct.-June M-Sa 1 per day). **McGeehan's Coaches** (☎075 46150) also has service (July-Sept. 2 per day; Oct.-June M-Th 1 per day, F-Su 2 per day) to Donegal Town and Dublin from Dungloe, Ardara, Glenties, Glencolmcille, and other towns on the peninsula. The nearest **bank, pharmacy,** and **civilization** are in Killybegs. However, **Internet** is at the newly renovated **Áistan Cill Cartha** (see **Sights;** €6 per hr.) and money at the **ATM** next to the Mace store.

ACCOMMODATIONS AND CAMPING. Located 1½ mi. out the steep Carrick coast road from Kilcar and only 5min. from the beach, ⬛Derrylahan Hostel (IHH) **❶**, a 200-year-old former church, doubles as a hostel and working farm. Call for pickup from Kilcar or Carrick. Booking ahead in July and August is a good idea; visiting in the beginning of April, during lambing season, is an even better one. (☎973 8079. Laundry €7. Dorms €10; private rooms €14. **Camping** €6, with separate showers and kitchen.) Less then a mile from Kilcar, ⬛Dún Ulún House **❶** offers a remarkable range of luxurious accommodations. These options are dizzying, but they can't hold a candle to the *blitzkrieg* of information from the energetic owners. (☎973 8137. 6- to 10-bed cottage dorms around €10; B&B-style rooms €23.50, less without breakfast or bath. **Camping** €5 per person.)

On the scenic road from Killybegs to Kilcar that becomes Main St., ⬛Inishduff House B&B **❸** sits next to Blue Haven restaurant. Ethna welcomes guests with tea and biscuits before showing them to one of six luxurious en suite rooms. (☎973 8542. All rooms with TV and bath. €32.)

FOOD AND PUBS. **Spar Market** on Main St. sells groceries and fishing tackle. (Open M-Sa 9am-9:50pm; Su 9:30am-1:30pm, 7-10:30pm.) **The Rendezvous Coffee Shop ❷**, set behind a convenience store, serves sandwiches for €3.50 and lasagna for €6. (☎973 8344. Open M-Sa 9:30am-4:30pm.) Kilcar's best meal by far is at **Teach Barnai ❸** on Main St. Ann and Michael Carr's rustic restaurant serves fare from lamb to *colcannon*. (☎973 8160. Mains €10.15-16.50. Open 6-10pm.) Down the street, **John Joe's** (☎973 8015) hosts nightly trad that's as lively as it gets (in Kilcar). **Piper's Rest Pub,** Main St. (☎973 8205), has recently changed hands; the new hands stripped the stone walls of their musical instruments, so the *craic* has yet to be established by the mixed, younger crowd.

SIGHTS AND FESTIVALS. **Studio Donegal** sells handwoven tweeds fresh off the loom. Visitors are invited to watch yarn being spun, cloth being woven, and jackets being sewn. (☎973 8194. Open M-F 9am-5:30pm; June-Sept. also open Sa 9:30am-5pm.) In the same building, on the same floor, is **Áistan Cill Cartha** (ASHlahn kill KAR-ha). This community organization provides genealogical information, compendiums of residents' oral histories, and local history collections. The center also has a gym, a library, **Internet,** and films for children that show regularly during the summer. Locals can direct you to the **prehistoric and natural wonders** that surround Kilcar, including megalithic tombs, old graveyards, and the Spanish church. If interested in **deep-sea fishing,** inquire at a hostel or B&B for help in arranging an appropriate venture, or contact *Nuala Star* in Teelin (☎973 9365). Kilcar's **International Sea Angling Festival** casts off during the first weekend in August. (Contact Cara Boyle ☎973 8341.) It's directly followed by the **Kilcar Street Festival,** a week of sport, art, and tomfoolery. (Contact Joe McBrearty ☎973 8135.)

CARRICK AND TEELIN ☎073

From Kilcar, the coast road passes the villages of **Carrick** (*An Carraig*) and **Teelin** (*Teileann*). The two villages are about 2 mi. apart; take the left in the village of Carrick to continue on to Teelin and the **Slieve League Cliffs.** For most of the year, these mighty mites are but brief stopping points for travelers on their way to Slieve League Mountain (see p. 416) or the peninsula's larger villages. During the last bank holiday weekend in October, though, the village scene is transformed by the annual **Carrick Fleadh,** when the town fills to the brim with people seeking barrels of creamy, foaming refreshment accompanied by bushels of trad. **Fishing** is the other main attraction, and it manages to bait a goodly number of visitors each year. The *Nuala Star* in Teelin offers day-long, half-day, hourly, or evening trips, and **diving charters** (☎973 9365 or 087 628 4688). Dropping lines is especially rewarding around **Teelin Bay,** particularly in an area called **Salmon Leap.** Salmon fishing requires a permit (€15 per day), available in Teelin from Frank O'Donnell (☎973 9231) or at **Teelin Bay B&B ❸** across from the river. In addition to pescredentials, Kathleen and Patrick offer comfortable rooms and delicious breakfasts for fishermen and other travelers. (☎973 9043. Singles €25; doubles €45.) **Glen River** is best for trout; tackle can be bought at the **Spar** in Kilcar. For food that won't try to get away, head 3 mi. up the Ardara road to **Bialann Na Sean Scoile ❷** for homecookin' and mashed potatoes stacked as high as Slieve League. (☎973 9477. Mains €5-10, dinner specials €6. Open daily 10am-10pm.) To engage in the part of fishing that involves drinking, turn left off of Carrick's Main St. and head up the Teelin road to **Cúl A' Dúin** (☎973 9101). Formerly known as the Rusty Mackerel, this pub was recently purchased by international trad megastars and native Teelinites Altan. When not touring, they sometimes hold court here.

THE SLIEVE LEAGUE WAY   ☎073

🄼**Slieve League Mountain** lays claim to the hotly-contested title "highest sea cliffs in Europe." The face of its sheer, 2000 ft. drop really is spectacular—on a clear day, a hike over the cliffs inspires awe at the infinite expanse of the Atlantic and the compact hamlets along the inland portion of the peninsula. To reach the mountain, turn left halfway down Carrick's Main St. and follow the signs for Teelin. A right turn at the Cúl A' Dúin pub (see **Carrick and Teelin,** p. 415) leads to the inland route to Slieve League. The more popular route involves hanging a left at the pub and following the coastal route to **Bunglass** (a 1½hr. walk from Carrick), where there is a carpark at the head of the cliff path. From there, the trail heads north and then west along the coast. One hour along the path from the carpark, the mountaintop narrows to 2 ft., becoming the infamous **One Man's Pass.** On one side of this pass, the cliffs drop 1800 ft. to the ocean below. No worries, though—the rocky floor on the other side is only 1000 ft. down. There are no railings here, and those prone to vertigo generally opt to lower their centers of gravity by slithering across the 33 yd. platform. After near-certain death, the path continues along the cliffs all the way to **Rossarell Point,** 6 mi. southeast of Glencolmcille. While humans refuse to peer over the edge, herds of sheep calmly graze on the steep inclines. The entire hike from the Teelin carpark to Rossarrell Point takes about 4-6hr., depending on frequency of stops; length of legs; and sudden, life-threatening, and random weather conditions. Other, shorter routes involving loop-like figures can also be plotted. (For advice and in the interest of safety, discuss your plans with a hostel owner and carry the *Ordnance Survey Discovery Series #10.*)

One possible itinerary for backpackers starts in **Kilcar** at Derrylahan Hostel and devotes 6 or 7hr. to hiking over the Slieve League Way to Malinbeg Hostel in **Malinbeg.** Following a short jaunt across the Silver Strand (see **Glencolmcille,** p. 418), packer rats can continue north and east to Dooey Hostel in **Glencolmcille.** This route passes three great hostels and some of Ireland's most stunning scenery, but it's not obligatory; hostel owners often provide pickup.

> **⚠** **Never go to Slieve League in poor weather; in suboptimal weather, the cliffs at Bunglass are a safer option. People have died here in the past, and by all indications, they will continue to do so.**

Use extreme caution if planning to cross the pass; it is not a necessary part of the hike across Slieve League. (The inland face of the mountain also offers a steep climb.) Hikers are blown off the pass by gusts of wind which arise unexpectedly; people slip at moments of poor visibility. Bear in mind that weather at high elevations is *not* always the same as weather at low elevations; the former is given to rapid and drastic change. If it is a cloudy day, chances are the clouds will engulf the top of the mountain, and visibility will be nil. It's always a good idea to ask a local expert for advice and to tell someone reputable when you expect to return so that you will be missed. If you hike alone, *Let's Go* will scold you mercilessly.

GLENCOLMCILLE (GLEANN CHOLM CILLE) ☎073

Wedged between two sea-cliffs at the northwestern tip of the Slieve League peninsula, ◙Glencolmcille (glen-kaul-um-KEEL) is actually a parish—a collection of several tiny, *gaeltacht* villages that have come to be regarded as a single entity. "The Glen," as it is affectionately known, was named after St. Colmcille, who founded a monastery here. This sometime pilgrimage site centers around the street-long village of Cashel, off R236 along aptly-named Cashel St. The road leads past the village's several storefronts and down to the coast, where most of the area's accommodations and attractions lie. Buses of tourists roll in for the Folk Village (see Sights, p. 418), but few venture to the desolate, wind-battered cliffs beyond.

▣▨ TRANSPORTATION AND PRACTICAL INFORMATION.
Bus Éireann (☎972 1101; www.buseireann.ie) leaves from the village corner to Donegal Town, stopping in Killybegs and Kilcar (July-Sept. M-Sa 3 per day, Su 1 per day; Oct.-June M-Sa 1 per day). McGeehan's buses leave from Biddy's Bar for Carrick, Kilcar, Killybegs, Ardara, Glenties, Fintown, and Letterkenny (July-Sept. 2 per day; Oct.-June M-Th 1 per day, F-Su 2 per day). The tiny tourist office is on Cashel St. (☎973 0116. Open July-Aug. M-Sa 10am-7:30pm, Su 11am-6pm; Apr.-June, Sept. to mid-Nov. M-Sa 10am-6pm, Su 11am-1:30pm.) The nearest banks are in Killybegs and Ardara; the nearest ATM is in Kilcar. A bureau de change is at the Folk Village and the post office, east of village center. (☎30001. Open M-F 9am-1pm, 2-5:30pm; Sa 9am-1pm.)

▰▣▨ ACCOMMODATIONS, FOOD, AND PUBS.
A trip to Donegal, or even to Ireland, wouldn't be complete without a visit to ◙Dooey Hostel (IHO) ❶, the original Irish independent hostel. Owners Mary and her favorite son Leo could not be friendlier, funnier, or more helpful. To get there, turn left at the end of the village and follow the signs uphill for almost a mile. It's a hike, but the view is spectacular, and the building follows suit; it's built into the hillside overlooking the sea, and a garden's worth of flowers grows out of the rocky face that is the hostel's corridor. Simply put, don't miss this one—it has been the high-point of many a traveler's journey. (☎973 0130. Wheelchair-accessible. Dorms €9.50; doubles €21. Camping €5.50 per person.) Mrs. Ann Ward's Atlantic Scene ❸, the next house after the hostel, lives up to its name. The beds are soft, and the gorgeous view and tasty breakfasts are worth losing sleep over. (☎973 0186. Open May-Sept. €25-30.) More B&Bs surround the Folk Village (see Sights, below). Five miles southwest of Cashel lies Malinbeg, and the

GIVING BACK

RARE *CRAIC*

Under British rule, all things Irish were banned: dance, language, folklore, music. The goal was to Anglicize the Irish; the result was the slow death of the Irish language and a fierce, resistant pride in Irish heritage, which led to a revival at the turn of the century (see Revival, p. 74).

Now quite independent, the Republic tries to preserve its hard-won culture amidst a modern world. As mandatory Irish classes create disinterest in the young and hectic cosmopolitan life distances the adult, some Irish long for the purity of Irish tradition. Engaged visitors may also wish to leave the spectator's seat and educate themselves more deeply about the roots of the Isle's vibrant culture—and perhaps even participate a bit.

In coastal Glencolmcille in Co. Donegal, Oideas Gael provides a gateway to that tradition for the young and curious. In summer, they offer week-long courses for €140-170. Though primarily in language, they also have cultural courses ranging from hill-walking to dancing, pottery to whistle playing. The immersion doesn't end when class does. Various planned events further introduce students (and the welcome crasher) to Irish culture, including instructional *céilís* with set dancing. (Info ☎074 973 0248; www.oideas-gael.com.)

welcoming arms of **Malinbeg Hostel** ❶. Run by Frank and Kathleen, the hostel combines more bells and whistles than any hostel in the area, and offers superlative views of Raithlin O'Byrne Island's lighthouse. The hostel is a 5 mi. hike from Glencolmcille, but the owners picks up those who phone ahead—a good way to ensure a private room. (☎973 0006 or 973 0965. Dorms €10; doubles €24-28. Family rooms available.)

Byrne and Sons Food Store, Cashel St., supplies basic nutritive and printed matter, and, across the street, petrol. (☎973 0018. Open M-Sa 9am-10pm; Su 9am-1pm, 6-9pm.) **An Chistin** ❸ (AHN KEESHT-ahn; "The Kitchen"), at Foras Cultúir Uladh (see **Sights**), is especially affordable and tasty for lunch. (☎973 0213. Mains €6.50-15. Open May-Sept. daily 9am-9pm; Apr., Oct. noon-9pm.) The **teashop** ❶ in the Folk Village tempts with delicious sandwiches for €2.50 and even better Guinness cake for €1.40. (Open with Museum.) The town's three pubs have a dark 1950s Ireland feel: imagine spare rooms with plastic-covered snugs and, for once, a minimal amount of wood paneling. The pubs are primarily a haven for locals; regardless, they develop an affinity for visitors during July and August. Most famous among them is unassuming 120-year-old **Biddy's,** at the mouth of Carrick Rd. A favorite of the older crowd, this is the place to meet all those dreamy Irish speakers. (☎973 0016. Trad 3 times per week in summer.) **Roarty's** (☎973 0273), the next pub down Cashel St., welcomes guests with trad several times a week. Last on the road is **Glen Head Tavern** (☎973 0008), the largest of the pint-peddling trio. Practically the whole village fits into its recently redone lounge, host to legendary trad sessions.

⬛ **SIGHTS.** Glencolmcille's craft movement began in the 1950s under the direction of the omnipresent **Father James McDyer,** who was also responsible for bringing in electricity, founding the Folk Village, and building the local football field. Today, the town is renowned for its handmade products—particularly its sweaters, which are on sale at numerous "jumper shops" on the roads surrounding the town. Close to town is **Foras Cultúir Uladh** (FOR-us KULT-er UH-lah; "The Ulster Cultural Institute"), which runs the **Oideas Gael Institute** for the preservation of the Irish language and culture. Foras offers regular courses of varied lengths on such pursuits as hiking, painting, pottery, local archaeology, traditional music, and Irish language. They also have trad recordings and books on Ireland, concerts, performances, and frequently changing exhibitions on local history. (☎973 0248. Open June-Aug. daily 9am-6pm; Sept.-May M-F 9am-5pm.)

LOVE POITÍN #9 The county may be more famous for fiddling and tweed, but there is another, lesser-known craft that denizens of Donegal have practiced with similar single-mindedness and mythological resolve: the distillation of *poitín* (pah-CHEEN). Generation after generation, elusive bootleggers of hill and bog pass down the secret of bottling lightning. Despite years of legal persecution, bottles of powerful *poitín* are stashed under sinks and in broom closets all across Donegal. It is said that the poet Dylan Thomas moved to the valley next to Port in an attempt to isolate himself and cleanse the alcohol from his system, but that he was foiled by the availability of *poitín*. The drink is a part of the regional folklore, a symbol of the silent resistance to authority that is so central to the Donegal character.

Poitín is a 140-proof kick in the face. Culled from potatoes steeped in a mixture of apples, berries, and barley, then thrice-distilled in a gigantic copper worm, this gift of the gods arrives clear, with a bouquet reminiscent of paint thinner. The traditional method for determining the quality of a batch is to pour a bit into a saucer and set it ablaze. Like arsenic, the stuff should burn bright blue. If it doesn't, it may blind you. If it does, it may blind you. **Beware:** Because of its high alcohol content and über-dodgy mode of preparation, *poitín* is simultaneously illegal and dangerous. It is not served in pubs or brought out in polite company.

A bit past the village center is Father McDyer's **Folk Village Museum and Heritage Centre,** the town's attraction for non-hiking, non-Irish speakers. The museum is housed in thatch-roofed stone cottages, dating from 1700, 1850, and 1900; the 1850s schoolhouse is open to the public, and guided tours describe the furniture and tools from each of these eras in Irish history. A short nature trail from the village leads up a hill past various reconstructed remains, including a Mass rock, sweat house, and lime kiln. The **sheeben** (the old name for an illegal drinking establishment) sells whiskey marmalade. (☎973 0017. Open Easter-Sept. M-Sa 10am-6pm, Su noon-6pm. Tours July-Aug. every 30min.; Apr.-June, Sept. every hr. Tours €2.50.) The two-day **Glencolmcille Folk Festival,** a lively and occasionally raucous celebration, occurs the first or second weekend of August. (Contact Ellen McGinley ☎973 0053 or Gerry Gilespie ☎973 0111.)

Fine beaches and cliffs make for excellent hiking in all directions. A 5 mi. walk southwest from Cashel leads to **Malinbeg,** a winsome hamlet at the edge of a sandy cove that now has its own hostel (see **Accommodations,** p. 418). This coastal area was once notorious for smuggling *poitín* through tunnels (see **Love Poitín #9,** above), some of which may still be in use. When a sunny day happens to grace Donegal, a trip to the **Silver Strand** rewards with stunning views of the gorgeous beach and surrounding rocky cliffs. The strand starts a long-distance trek along the Slieve League coastline (see **Slieve League Way,** p. 416). A sandy beach links the cliffs on the north and south sides of Glencolmcille. An hour's walk north of town through land dotted with prehistoric ruins (including St. Colmcille's stations of the cross, his well, and church), **Glen Head** is easily identified by the Martello tower at its peak. The tourist office and the hostel have maps showing the locations of major sights. A third 3hr. walk from town begins at the Protestant church and climbs over a hill to the ruins of the ghostly "Famine villages" of ▣**Port** and **Glenloch,** in the valley on the other side. Supposedly haunted by crying babies, Port has been empty since its last, hunger-stricken inhabitants emigrated. The only current resident, according to local rumor, is an eccentric artist who lives by the isolated bay without electricity or water. The slightly less eerie Glenloch is the former home of painter Rockwell Kent, who wanted to return permanently, but was kept away by the US because of a trip to the Soviet Union. The gargantuan **phallic rock** sticking out of the sea is what it appears to be: the only part of the Devil still visible after St. Colmcille banished him into the ocean.

The road east from Glencolmcille to Ardara passes through the spectacular **Glengesh Pass.** Nine hundred feet above sea level, the road scales the surrounding mountains with hairpin turns. **Biking** is common in these parts, but be warned that the steep and winding pass makes a challenging ride suitable for only the most intrepid cyclists. Hitching is a tough task along this unfrequented road.

ARDARA (ARD AN RÁTHA)   ☎074

The historic center of the Donegal tweed industry, Ardara (ar-DRAH) now tends to attract tweed fiends with high credit limits. The town is one of the cheapest sources of locally-produced knit and woven articles, though better deals can often be found at small "craft centers" in surrounding villages. Today, Ardara's heritage center plays an important role in the movement to revive traditional hand-weaving and silversmithing techniques, and to raise local arts consciousness. During the first weekend of June's **Weavers' Fair,** weavers from all over Donegal congregate in Ardara to flaunt their weft, while musicians make their own contribution to the festivities. Visitors uninterested in merchandise and vexed by crowds escape to the spectacular scenery along the Maghera Caves Rd.

▣⦿ **TRANSPORTATION AND PRACTICAL INFORMATION.** Bus Éireann (☎912 1309) stops in Ardara in front of O'Donnell's on a circular route running from Donegal Town to Glenties (M, W, F 10:40am). **McGeehan's Coaches** (☎954 6150; www.mgbus.com) stops on the Diamond as part of the Dublin-Donegal Town-Dungloe route (July-Sept. 2 per day; Oct.-June M-Sa 2 per day). The town is also a stop on the

Letterkenny-Glencolmcille route, with pickup at the Nesbitt Arms Hotel. Also departing from the hotel, **Feda O'Donnell's** (☎075 48114) service between Donegal and Galway stops in Ardara once a day (Su and M only) with farther stops throughout the *gaeltacht.* A **tourist information point** resides on Main St. in **Triona Designs,** almost out of town down the Killybegs Rd. Reading materials and Triona employees are on hand, but they're likely to provide more information on their extensive collection of tweed than anything else. (☎954 1422. Open M-F 9am-8pm, Sa-Su 9am-6pm.) **Ulster Bank,** the Diamond, has a 24hr. **ATM.** (☎954 1121. Open M-F 10am-12:30pm and 1:30-4pm, Th until 5pm.) **Don Byrne's,** past the tourist information point on the Killybegs Rd., provides maps and new **rental bikes.** (☎954 1658 or 954 1156; donbyrne@indigo.ie. €15 per day, €70 per wk. Open June-Sept. M-Sa 9:30am-6pm, Su 10:30am-12:30pm. Call ahead in the winter.) The **Ardara Medical Hall,** Front St., next to the heritage center, is a glorified **pharmacy.** (☎954 1120. Open M-Sa 9am-1pm and 2-6pm.) The **post office** is on Main St. (☎954 1101. Open M-F 9am-1pm and 2-5:30pm, Sa 9am-1pm.)

📍 **ACCOMMODATIONS.** ▨**The Green Gate (An Geata Glás)** ❹, 1 mi. outside of town, is an idyllic respite from Ardara's tweed-hawking and late-night revelry. From the Diamond, go west on the Donegal Rd., ascend the hill to the north, and follow the discreet signs, or call for pickup. The owner, Paul Chatenoud, traded his musical bookshop and apartment overlooking Notre Dame for this trio of 200-year-old bayside cottages to write about "love, life, and death." The library, gardens, and spartan, white-washed rooms reflect his artistic vision. Ask for the room with a view. (☎954 1546. Book in advance. Singles €45; shared rooms €30.) If the Green Gate is full, try **Holly Brook B&B** ❸, on the Killybegs Rd. near the outskirts of town. The rooms are sunny and immaculate, but the owner's family makes this place special: Peter Oliver, a famed local musician, runs the Corner Bar (see **Food and Pubs,** p. 420), and his even more famous daughters won national prizes in Irish step-dancing—one currently stars in Riverdance. (☎954 1596. €25.) **Rossmore House** ❸, on the Donegal Rd., at the foot of the hill leading to Green Gate, is a simple B&B with an art studio next door, featuring the work of the artist son and his friends. Proximity to the town center (2min. walk) is a plus, as is its serenity and lack of curfew. (☎954 1126; dl31@familyhomes.ie. Singles €28; doubles €25.)

🍴🛏 **FOOD AND PUBS.** A **Spar** market sits on Main St. (☎41107. Open M-Sa 8:30am-9pm, Su 8:30am-1pm.) **L'Atlantique Restaurant** ❹, below the tourist information point on Main St., serves delicious French seafood in a classy dining room full of fishing nets. (☎954 1707. 4-course prix-fixe menu €17. Open nightly 6:30-9:30pm. Reservations recommended.) On Main St., the **Nesbitt Arms Hotel** ❷ serves locally renowned pub grub that bends convention with steak baguettes and beef and Guinness pie. (☎954 1103. Food €3-14. Open noon-9pm.) The attached restaurant serves snazzier fare. **Charlie's West End Cafe** ❷, halfway up Main St., lacks the trendy atmosphere its name suggests, but the service is quick and the quality food is cheap. (☎954 1656. Enormous lunch specials €4.75, sandwiches and pizzas €3.95. Open M-Sa 10am-11pm, Su 2-10pm.) Adjoining brick hovels are decked with bright copper kettles, comical mugs, and other relics from some fantastic grandfather's attic at ▨**Nancy's Bar,** Front St., before the Diamond. Come for the seafood or the weekend trad. (☎954 1187. Oysters €7. Food served noon-9pm.) Local musician Peter Oliver, of the Holly Brook B&B, returned to the publican business with his purchase of the **Corner Bar** (☎954 1736). The place is filled with tourists, but for good reason—the nightly summertime trad is worth the crowd.

📷 **SIGHTS.** The **Ardara Heritage Centre,** the Diamond, tells the story of the centuries-old Donegal tweed industry. Occasional hand-loom demonstrations show the dexterity required to create the richly varied textiles that are sold in mass quantities throughout the world. (☎954 1473. Open Jan.-Nov. daily 9:30am-6pm. Free.)

Next door in the same building, **The Loom House** has food for the weaving-weary. (Open Jan.-Nov. daily 9:30am-9:30pm.) Beautiful walks abound in the area surrounding Ardara. From town, head south toward Glencolmcille and turn right toward **Loughros Point** (LOW-crus) at the "Castle View" horse-riding sign. At the next horse-riding sign, either turn right for a beautiful view of Ardara Bay, or continue straight for stupendous views of the sea at the Point (1hr. walk). One mile from town on the Killybegs Rd., a sign points toward the coastal **Maghera Caves,** which housed weapons during the Irish War for Independence. The British eventually found the guns and, pursuant to their consistently successful revolution-crushing procedures, killed the rebel owners. After the caves turnoff, follow the signs several miles west on some of the most beautiful small roads in Ireland. The six caves vary in size, depth, and cohesion; all require a flashlight. Low tide opens up the Dark Cave, once the refuge of *poitín*-makers. The road past the caves continues across a mountain pass to Dungloe. Independent and guided **horse rides** start from **Castle View Ranch,** 2½ well-posted miles from Ardara off Loughros Point Rd. (☎954 1212. €20 per hr., €75 per day.)

Only the most steel-willed tourist resists buying a hand-knit sweater. Fortunately, Ardara has three shops with superior stock and relatively reasonable prices. The **John Molloy Factory Shop,** half a mile from town on the Killybegs Rd., has tons to choose from; if asked nicely, they'll show off the factory floor in back. The tour inspires new respect for the art of knitting and weaving, dispelling any notions of old women clustered together in rocking chairs. (☎954 1133. Open M-Th 9am-6pm, F 9am-5pm, Sa 10:30am-5pm, Su 1-5:30pm.) **Kennedy,** Front St. (☎954 1106), near the top of the hill, sells garments with more contemporary designs. The town's other manufacturers are **Bonner's** (☎954 1303), Front St., and **Triona Design** (☎954 1422), at the entrance of town on the Killybegs Rd., whose tourist information point keeps it packed during the day.

GLENTIES (NA GLEANNTA) ☎074

Glenties, repeatedly named "Ireland's Tidiest Town" in the mid-90s, has several welcome conveniences and short hikes that make it a pleasant stop on the route through northwest Donegal. Hikes are signposted from the crossroads next to the hostel. One of the most satisfying routes leads to **Inniskeel Island,** 8 mi. past Glenties toward Dungloe; signs point from the carpark to lovely, batheable **Narin Beach.** The island, where the ruins of **St. Connell's** 6th-century church lie, is accessible only when the tide is out; check the *Irish Independent* for tidal information, or ask a local. Another series of trails leads into the foothills south of town.

South of Glenties on N56, an uphill turnoff points to "Meenachallow" and, less clearly, "organic farm"; true to its word, 2 mi. up that road is Thomas Becht's **Donegal Organic Farm,** a hillside *mélange* of forestry plantation, hydroelectric power plant, and vegetable garden. In addition to peddling veggies, the farm has tree-sponsorship programs, ECO-Working camps for adolescents, and longer-term opportunities for individuals with serious interests in sustainable agriculture or forestry. (☎955 1286; www.esatclear.ie/~tbecht. Open M-Sa 9:30am-8pm.) A **nature trail** at the farm guides visitors through the forest and connects to the longer trail bound for **Lough Anney,** Glenties' reservoir. Farther uphill is a waterfall and Special Area for Conservation (SAC) that makes a nice picnic-spot. The entire walk is 8 mi. round-trip. A shorter option is the 2½ mi. walk along the **Owenrea River** leading to **Mullantayboyne;** from town, head down Main St. toward Glencolmcille and turn right at the Meenahall sign. The river lies ahead on the right side of the road. *Ordnance Survey Discovery Series #11* is the best map for walking the area.

September's **Harvest Fair** was once an annual celebration of local agriculture, industry, and beer; the former two have since fallen by the wayside to make more room for the latter. On the first weekend in October, **Fiddler's Weekend** draws musicians from across the globe. (Info on both festivals at www.glenties.ie.)

Bus Éireann (☎912 1309) stops in front of the post office on its way to Donegal Town via Ardara (M, W, F 11:15am). **McGeehan's** (☎954 6150; www.mgbus.com) summertime Letterkenny-Glencolmcille bus stops at most Slieve League Peninsula villages, including McGuinness' Pub in Glenties (M-Sa 9am, 1:20pm). **Feda O'Donnell's** (☎075 48114) service between Donegal and Galway stops at the Glenties Community Centre, across from St. Connell's Museum, once a day (Su 3:30pm, M-Sa 8:40am). In town, **Bank of Ireland,** Main St., has one of the area's few **ATMs.** (☎955 1124. Open M-F 10am-12:30pm and 1:30-4pm, Th until 5pm.) **Glenties Medical Hall,** Main St., provides pharmaceuticals. (☎955 1289. Open M-Tu and Th-F 9:30am-1pm and 2-6pm, W 9:30am-1pm.) Inquire at the Donegal Organic Farm (see **Accommodations,** below) about **work opportunities.** The **post office** is on Main St., snuggled inside a newsagent. (☎955 1101. Open M-F 9am-1pm and 2-5:30pm, Sa 9am-1pm.)

Campbell's Holiday Hostel (IHH) ❶, around the bend at the far end of Main St. toward Ardara, behind the St. Connell Museum, provides spare, clean rooms in primary colors. The common space has a fireplace, satellite TV, and two fully equipped kitchens. (☎955 1491; www.campbellireland.com. Wheelchair-accessible. Sheets €2. Laundry €4. Open Mar.-Oct. Dorms €12; private rooms €14.) The most convenient and best-priced B&Bs in the area are on the far side of town, at the western end of Main St. **Brennan's B&B ❸** has antique fireplaces, family rooms, and a video rental store. (☎955 1235. Singles €30; shared rooms €27.50.)

On Main St. is a wholefoods shop called **Good Earth** (☎955 1794; open M-Sa 9:30am-6pm). For a sit-down meal, the bar in **Highlands Hotel ❷** boasts the county's best steak (€17.50), and its vegetarian curry and stir fry (€11) keeps herbivores happy. (☎955 1111. Sandwiches €2.55, lunch €5.70, mains €6.70-11.10.)

Like everything else in town, the pubs are on Main St. **Keeney's Pub** (☎955 1920), on the opposite side of the street, dishes pub grub from 12:30-9pm, and Chinese from its adjoining restaurant **The Money Tree ❶** (☎955 1881). Three-course lunch specials shake your money tree for €6.50. (Lunch Tu-F 12:30-2:15pm, Su 1-3pm; dinner Tu-Su 5:30-11:30pm.) **Paddy's Bar** (☎955 1158), at the end of Main St. headed toward Ardara, draws youngish locals and hostelers with rock and trad performances every night during the summer. The big-screen TV broadcasts Sunday matches, and the fireplace keeps pubbers warmer than the pints do.

THE NORTHWEST GAELTACHT

The four parishes in Co. Donegal's northwest corner comprise the largest *gaeltacht* in the Republic. Though the Rosses, Gweedore, Gartan, and Cloghaneely all maintain distinct identities, they are united by their staunchly traditional Irish culture, which has flourished unperturbed in the *gaeltacht's* geographic isolation. Donegal's distinct dialect of Irish and the county's famous style of fiddling are championed in other parts of the country as cultural showpieces. In Northwest Donegal, they are living parts of daily routines, and locals often feign incredulity about their appeal for the few travelers who visit the area. Do not let them fool you—whether it be the solitude of Derryveagh Mountain rambles or the raucous *craic* of a great trad session, there is plenty to discover in the isolated North.

THE ROSSES

Extending northward from Dungloe, the Rosses are part of a linguistic buffer zone, the "broken" *gaeltacht;* locals here regularly employ both the English and Irish language in everyday conversation. While the N56 rides along the spectacular midwest coast from Glenties to Dungloe, expansive, sandy beaches lie isolated by the eerie stillness of the Derryveagh Mountains. A stay among the Rosses's bogs and hills is an excellent primer for journeys deeper into the *gaeltacht;* this is also the northernmost outpost for information and supplies.

DUNGLOE (AN CLOCHÁN LIATH) ☎ 074

The capital of the Rosses, Dungloe (dun-LO) is the last bastion of tourist information for visitors continuing northwest. It's also near Crohy Head, with a beautiful beach perfect for hiking and cycling. Party animals flock to Dungloe during the last week of July, when the population swells to 80,000 for the 10-day **Mary from Dungloe Festival.** The highlight of the festival is the coronation of the new "Mary from Dungloe," although most attendees argue that Daniel O'Donnell's three concerts really make the festival. Tickets for the songster go on sale in January and sell out almost immediately; interested parties should join in the madness with similar enthusiasm. For festival information and ticket bookings, call the **Festival Booking Office** next to the tourist office. (☎ 952 1254; www.maryfromdungloe.info. Open M-Sa 10am-6pm.) Traditional music greats throw down for the **Peader O'Donnell Weekend Festival** in October. For sea-angling and boat tours, visitors should contact Neil and Ann Gallagher at **West Donegal Sea-Angling Charters** (☎ 954 8403 or 087 833 2969; www.donegalseaangling.com). For information on inland fisheries or inland boat hire in the Rosses, the pertinent contact is **Rosses Anglers Association.** (☎ 952 1163 or 954 2167. Day permit €10; boat fee €15.) Or, march up to **C. Bonner and Sons** on Main St. to rap with Charlie Bonner, in charge of area fishing. Californian, Austrian, and Irish **surfers** have discovered the waves just west of Dungloe. Hanging ten is easy with ex-world champ and member of the Irish surf team, **Kevin Tobin.** (☎ 952 2468 or 086 886 8693; kevintobin@iol.ie. Lessons €25 per 2hr., €75 per wk.) Also surfing Dooey Beach is **NaRossa Surf School** (☎ 087 629 6912; www.narossasurf.com), which offers pick-up.

The town is a stop for **Bus Éireann** (☎ 912 1309) en route to Donegal Town (July-Aug. 3 per day). Private bus lines also serve Dungloe: **Doherty's** (☎ 087 571 348, or 075 21105) to Larne via Letterkenny and Derry (Sept.-June M, W, F-Sa; July-Aug. daily); **Feda O'Donnell** (☎ 075 48114) picks up at Greene's Garage and heads to Galway (Su 2:40pm, M 8:10pm) via Glenties, Ardara, Killybegs, Donegal Town, and Sligo; **McGeehan's** (☎ 954 6150) to Dublin via Glenties, Ardara, Donegal Town, and Enniskillen (July-Sept. 2 per day; Oct.-June M-Sa 2 per day); **Swilly** (☎ 912 2863) to Derry via Burtonport, Annagry, Crolly, Bloody Foreland, Falcarragh, and Letterkenny (M-F 3 per day). **Brennan** (☎ 086 261 0888) and **Joyce** (☎ 087 222 4967) provide **taxis.** Larger parties use **Frank Gallagher's Minibuses** (☎ 086 821 5936).

The Dungloe **tourist office,** on a well-marked side street off Main St. toward the shore, is the only such office in northern Donegal. (☎ 952 1297. Open May-Sept. M-Sa 10am-6pm; July-Aug. also Su noon-4pm.) Main St. has a **Bank of Ireland** with a 24hr. **ATM** (☎ 952 1077; open M-F 10am-12:30pm and 1:30-4pm, Th until 5pm), and **O'Donnell's Pharmacy.** (☎ 952 1386. Open M-Sa 9am-6pm.) The **library,** housed in the chapel on Chapel St., offers **Internet** access. (☎ 952 2500. €2.50 per 30min. Open Tu and Th 12:30-8pm, W and F 10:30am-5:30pm, Sa 10:30am-2pm.) The **post office** is on Quay Rd., off Main St. toward Crohy Head and the hostel. (☎ 952 1067. Open M-F 9am-1pm and 2-5:30pm, Sa 9am-1pm.)

Greene's Independent Holiday Hostel (IHH) ❶, Carnmore Rd., is a turn off Main St. across from the Bank of Ireland. It has a comfy common room and kitchen, but not much else in the way of bells and whistles. (☎ 952 1943. **Bike rental** €6.50 per day for guests; others €7.60. Dorms €11; private rooms €12-14.) **Dungloe Camping and Caravan Park ❶** is behind Greene's hostel. (☎ 952 1943. Laundry €5. €6 per person; €13 per car or caravan.) If it's full, call up the road to **Cois Na Mara** in neighboring Burtonport (see p. 425). A 10min. walk down the Burtonport road, **Ard Crone House ❸** welcomes guests into its curiously red halls and sunny, ensuite rooms. (☎ 951 153. Singles €38; shared rooms €26.)

Wandering cooks stock up at **Cope Supermarket,** Main St. (☎ 952 1022. Open M-Sa 9am-6pm, F until 7pm.) **SuperValu** is about half a mile down Carnmore Rd. (☎ 952 1006. Open M-Th 9am-6:30pm, F 9am-8pm, Sa 9am-7pm.) **Doherty's ❷,** at the mid-

NORTHWEST IRELAND

GAELTACHT PUBSPEAK *Let's Go,* ever by your side, has assembled a survival course on *gaeltacht* pub-speak. When you enter a pub, you will likely be greeted with a friendly *"Cen chaoi an bhfuil sibh?"* (ken QUEE on WILL shiv; "How's it going?") to which you would reply, *"Beidh mé go-brea ma tagann tu Guinness domsa!"* (BAY may GO-bra ma TA-gin to Guinness DUM-sa; "I'll be fine if you give me a Guinness!"). As the night proceeds you may need to use the facilities—just ask *"Cá bhfuil an leithreas le'dthoil?"* (ka WILL on le-RUSS le-the-HULL; "Where's the toilet?"). And if you're deep in the *gaeltacht,* you'll likely hear *"Amach ansin"* (a-MOCK on-SHIN; "Outside"). Later, when you spot a young lass or lad, steel yourself and ask *"Ar mhaith leat a bheith ag damsha?"* (err WA lat a VE-egg DOWSA-a; "Would you like to dance?"). When the time is right, and you and Seamus/Molly are staring soulfully at each other through your pint glasses, you might slip in a subtle *"Ar maith leat a beith ag dul a codladh liomsa?"* (err MA lat a VE-egg DULL-a COLL-ah LUM-sa; "Would you like to sleep with me?"). If you receive a *bos* in the *aghaidh,* blame it on pronunciation. For more fun with the mother tongue, see the **Glossary,** p. 573.

---

point of Main St., provides a variety of consistently cheap dishes in a voluminous cafeteria/takeaway. (☎952 1654. Pizza €5.50-7.60; mains from €4.50. Open M-Th 9am-11pm, F-Sa 9am-midnight, Su 1-9pm.) At the **Riverside Bistro ❸,** on Main St. toward the road to Burtonport, patrons can expect slightly snazzy versions of traditional cuisine, served at somewhat inflated prices under Parisian surrealist photographs. Vegetarian mains begin at €8.30 and meaty meals run €13-19. (☎952 1062. Lunch specials €6.30. Open daily 12:30-3pm and 6-10pm.) **Beedy's,** Main St. (☎952 1219), rocks out with local bands on weekends and has a beer garden perfect for those occasional sunny days. For the not-so-sunny days (welcome to Ireland), cultivate prowess at the pool table. **Patrick Johnny Sally's** (☎952 1479), up Main St. toward Glenties, has an impressive view from its backyard deck, an upscale but unpretentious dark wood interior, and enough *craic* to get away with no live music or TVs. Idle youngsters congregate across the street at the **Atlantic Bar** (☎22166) to watch live rock bands on weekends year-round. For trad fans, **Ostan na Rossan Hotel** rips it up olde Irish style on W nights.

The ◧**Crohy Head** (*Ceann na Cruaiche*) peninsula, 6 mi. southwest of Dungloe, is surrounded by a slew of oddly shaped rock formations that extend from its jagged coast. The **Crohy Head Youth Hostel (An Óige/HI) ❶,** in an old coast guard station, has stupendous views of these formations and the Atlantic beyond. Come prepared for wind and cold, as the building sits as it did 30 years ago. (☎952 1950. Call ahead; warden may be off-site. July-Sept. €10.) To reach Crohy Head from Dungloe, turn onto Quay Rd. (toward Maghery) halfway down Main St. and follow the bumpy road along the sea for 3½ mi., about 1 mi. past Maghery.

BURTONPORT AND ENVIRONS (AILT AN CHÓRRAIN)   ☎074

About 5 mi. north of Dungloe, the fishing village of Burtonport is less a town than a few pubs clustered around a pier. The ferry to Arranmore Island docks here, and the village also makes a good base for **fishing** and **boat trips** to the many uninhabited islands in the area. **Burtonport Sea Angling** (☎954 2077; mosh@eircom.net) is happy to oblige in that department. For **bus** travel, **Swilly** (☎952 1380) has 1-2 daily stops in Burtonport on its Derry-Letterkenny-Dungloe route.

More salmon land here than anywhere else in the British Isles. Intense **sea angling competitions** occur during July and August—call the Dungloe tourist office for details. **Sea anglers** book trips from the shop on Burtonport Pier. (☎42077 or 086 833 2969. Fishing trips €30; rod rental €6.50. Open daily 10am-5pm.) July's **Burtonport Festival** primes locals for the subsequent Mary from Dungloe Festival with trad, dance, and sport. The **post office** is at the start of town, about 200 yd. from the pier. (☎954 2001. Open M-F 9am-1pm and 2-5:30pm, Sa 9am-1pm.)

Call ahead from Dungloe to the big yellow ▧**Cois na Mara Hostel ❶** (cush Na-mara), about a 10min. walk from town on the main road. This former B&B ("Erin House") has now become a hostel-guesthouse, complete with high ceil-ings, custom bunk beds, wall murals, and breakfasts of scones and oatmeal. Owner Tim, a well-traveled trad fan, directs guests to the best local sessions and, by day, leads boat tours and fishing expeditions for kicks. Call for pickup. (☎954 2079. Breakfast included. Scrumptious sea-inspired dinners €8-18. **Inter-net** access €3 per hr. **Laundry** €4. Dorms €12; doubles €30.) The **Cope,** at the top of the town, is the largest **grocery** on either side of the water, so stock up before boarding the Arranmore ferry. (☎954 2004. Open M-Sa 9am-6pm.) The James Joyce Award-winning **Lobster Pot ❸,** on Main St. beside the harbor, attracts the biggest crowds in town. Make the Irish-built ship proud and tackle the €25.50 Titanic Seafood Platter. (☎954 2012. Sandwiches from €2.50; mains €6.35-14. Open daily 6-9:30pm; bar food 1-6pm.) All of Burtonport's pubs squat around the harbor, and most sport a maritime theme.

Five miles north of Burtonport on the coast road is the village of **Kincasslagh** (*Cionn Caslach*), birthplace of singer Daniel O'Donnell. A minor road heads west to the beaches and thatched cottages of **Cruit Island** (actually a peninsula). Farther north, the magnificent sandy stretch known as **Carrickfinn Strand** is marred only by the presence of tiny **Donegal Airport** (☎954 8284; www.donegalairport.ie). To find this beautiful beach, take the left leading to the airport and continue to the carpark at the edge of the beach; from here the strand is a stroll away. Due to strong cur-rents, swimming is restricted to the shallowest areas.

ARRANMORE ISLAND (ÁRAINN MHÓR)   ☎075

The Arranmore Way is the main attraction on this little island. This well-marked footpath runs the circumference of the island; hikers can choose from three possible routes. The longest of the three trails (about 6hr.) goes to the **lighthouse** at the far tip of the island, high above cliffs and crashing water. The trail passes **The Old Mill,** the **Old Coast-guard Station,** the inner-island **lakes,** a **mass rock,** and all the sights off the town's main road. Down steps near the lighthouse lies an intriguing **hidden cove.** The scramble down is slippery and steep and should be undertaken only with decent footwear, in good weather. Swimming is discouraged due to sudden rough currents. For those who have seen one lighthouse too many, the second walk (about 4hr.) passes the town's main sights, including the **craft shop** and **The Bridge,** with an amazing view of the islands and the Donegal coastline. The third hiking option, only 5 mi. (about 2hr.), sticks mainly to the southeastern part of the island, and leads to easily accessible views per-fect for the faint of heart or fatigued of foot. All three trails are detailed in the *Siúlóid Árainn Mhóir* (€1.05), available at Teac Phil Bán's (see **Food,** p. 426). Those who wish to devote their summers to self-edification run to the **Foglhaín.com Irish Language and Culture Center,** offering Gaelic-language courses on Arranmore Island. A typical day in this one-week summer program consists of classes in conversational and prac-tical Gaelic, workshops on various aspects of Irish culture, guided historical walks around the island, poetry readings, and set dancing. (☎952 1593. 1-week course €165.)

The **ferry office,** up the road from the pier in Bonner's Restaurant and Amusement Centre, sends boats to Burtonport. (☎952 0532; www.arainnmhor.com/ferry. Open daily 8:30am-8:30pm. 25min.; July-Aug. 7-8 per day, Sept.-June M-Sa 6 per day, Su 4 per day; €10, students €8, children €5, seniors free with ID; bicycles €3.) Although Arran-more has no official tourist office, **Tele Áráinn Teo,** commonly known as the co-op, serves as unofficial source of information; turn left at the end of the coastal road and pass Teach Phil Bán's. (☎952 0531; www.arainnmhor.com. Open M-F 9am-12:30pm and 1-4:30pm.) Maps of the island (€3) can be purchased at most off-shore stores and B&Bs. A guide to the Arranmore Way (€1) is available at Teac Phil Bán's store (see **Accommodations, Food, and Pubs,** below). By day, **O'Donnell's** (☎087 260 6833 or 952

0570) provides **taxis. Siob Teo,** a new **minibus service,** carts people all over the island (☎087 135 8028). The **post office** is across from Teach Phil Bán's. (☎952 0501. Open M-F 9am-1pm and 2-5:30pm, Sa 9am-1pm.)

Those with culinary aspirations should buy provisions off the island, as food in the shops can be pricey. Along the shore left of the ferryport stretches a string of pubs and houses. Down the street from the ferry lies the newly renovated ■**Arranmore Hostel ❶**, a clean, modern building in an excellent seaside location visible from the quay. Call ahead, especially on summer weekends, to tell the owners (who live off-site) when you're coming and to book the popular sea-view dorm. (☎952 0015 or 952 0515; www.arainmhor.com/hostel. Wheelchair-accessible. July-Aug. dorms €13; private rooms €14.50; family rooms €47. Rates reduced in Sept. and June.) A right up the road and the hill from the pier, **Grace Boyle's B&B ❷** treats guests to tea, fluffy beds, and comfortable rooms. (☎952 0758. €25.) Farther inland is **Ocean View B&B ❷**, a right at the end of the coastal road. Inside the small white house wait neat, compact rooms in soothing pastels. (☎952 0160. €25.)

Although one side of Arranmore Island (pop. 600) is primarily Irish-speaking and shows relatively little mainland influence, the other was once famous for its riotous partying into the wee hours. Alas, community complaints resulted in an increased *Garda* presence on the island during summer weekends. Some claim this development has forced revelers out onto the beach in search of *craic*, but the fact remains that every pub is now swept out at 1am. Plenty of fine, standard-hours pubs still thrive here, however. **Early's Bar** (☎952 0515), on the right 50 yd. up the hill from the landing, is where crooner Daniel O'Donnell got his start; he gives an annual concert on-island each August as a token of thanks. (☎952 0515. Trad on summer weekends.) To the left on the road from the ferry dock is **Teach Phil Bán's.** At high tide the ocean laps against the restaurant's foundations; crowds fill its musty interior bar on rainy days and wild nights. At the attached grocery store, visitors sample *dulce*, a local seaweed delicacy, and buy books on Arranmore genealogy for €6.35. (Bar ☎952 0908, store ☎952 0508. Store open M-Sa 9am-6pm, Su 11:30am-1:30pm.) A hike from the pier to **The Atlantic Bar ❷** rewards with a rich red interior and the best food in Arranmore. Turn right at the end of the road past Teach Phil Bán's, and continue for 10min. (☎952 0918. Fish €8.50.) **Neily's** (☎952 0509), ½ mi. to the right at the end of the coastal road, past the Ocean View B&B, is a local watering hole globalized by the installation of a satellite TV. Sunday night trad sessions draw up to 25 players.

RANAFAST AND ITS ANNAGRY (ANAGAIRE) ☎075

In the heart of the Donegal *gaeltacht,* the village of **Annagry,** about 6 mi. past Burton-port on R259, marks the beginning of the **Ranafast** area, famous for its storytelling tradition. Usually an eerily still coastal hamlet, Annagry is upended each summer by flocks of young people from across the island piling in to attend Irish-language camps. **Swilly buses** (☎074 912 873) run to Annagry (1 per day) and Crolly (3-4 per day) on its Derry-Letterkenny-Falcarragh-Dungloe route. The **Hill Hostel ❶** is 3 mi. from Crolly, the next town inland. Buses drop off in Crolly, and calling ahead saves a trek, though those who hike the whole length past two reservoirs, a quarry, and flocks of sheep are rewarded with a big bowl of soup, airy dorms, and whitewashed, batik-furnished doubles. The hostel is an excellent and personable departure point for the mountains, though ramblers may never leave the glens behind the house. (☎954 8593. Dorms €12.50; doubles €15.) Campers rest easy at **Sleepy Hollow's Campsite ❶**, a 2min. walk past Tabbairne Leo. This clean, charming campsite is family-friendly, and has so many amenities tent-heads won't believe they're camping. (☎954 8272; http://homepage.eircom.net/~sleepyhollow. Showers. Laundry €3. **Internet** €3 per hr. Babysitting available. 2-person tent €12, additional people €1.) Travelers seeking luxury B&B pampering head to **Danny Minnie's ❹**. All rooms come complete with bath and gorgeous antique furniture, creating a comfortable and cozy contemporary abode. (☎954 8201. €45.) Downstairs, enjoy a superb candlelit meal in the hotel's elegant **restaurant ❺** (mains €20-35). In addition to their storytelling and fine dining, the outskirts of Annagry hold some well-respected trad institutions. About 500 yd. south of the village, in a big beige building on top of a hill to the left of the road, is **Teác Jack's** (☎954 8113) pub and restaurant. Although better known for genre-defying pub food (€3.50-4.75), Jack's also hosts congregations of talented local musicians on weekend nights in the summer. Three miles west of town is the (in)famous **Tabbairne Leo** (☎954 8143). Leo is the father of voice guru **Enya** and the family group **Clannad**, and he's certainly not shy about it—beyond hanging their silver, gold, and platinum records from the walls, Leo has cobbled together an entire lounge act centered around his role as humble *paterfamilias*. For a more feasible (and surprisingly impressive) musical experience, head to **Teác Tessie**, across the street, where a rotating cast of locals and musical pilgrims gathers for fine, spontaneous trad on weekends and whenever the spirit rises. (☎954 8124. Food served noon-8pm.)

GWEEDORE (GAOTH DUBHAIR)

The coastal parish of Gweedore must be among the most beautiful parts of Ireland. Visitors are dwarfed by the surrounding glens, and the romantic (and wealthy) follow the Guinness family's lead and look for property in this sparse and amazing terrain. The parish serves as a gateway to the inland mountains that guard its border with Cloghaneely. Errigal Mountain, the legendary Poison Glen on gorgeous Dunlewy Lake, the Bloody Foreland with its Mars-red hue, and Gleneveagh National Park are the most famous sights in this beautiful expanse of bog, rock, and sea. Because it is situated between the Rosses to the southwest and Cloghaneely to the east, Gweedore fulfills another, more socially relevant role as the weekend amusement center for *gaeltacht* youth, who flood Derrybeg's discos on weekend nights. Tory Island, off Gweedore's northern coast, *is* a world apart from Ireland, with its own elected king and freedom from Irish taxes.

DUNLEWY AND ERRIGAL MOUNTAIN   ☎075

A mile north of the small town of **Crolly**, N56 and the coastal road diverge. N56 turns inland and reaches R251 after about 5 mi. This road leads east through the village of **Dunlewy** *(Dún Lúiche)*, past the conical **Errigal Mountain**, and on to **Glenveagh National Park.** Dunlewy, which straddles the border of Gweedore and Cloghaneely parishes, makes a great base for exploring the pristine heaths of the **Derryveagh Mountains.** An interlocking web of trails for hikers of varying abilities extend over the region. These are often hard to follow, even with a map; hikers should grab the *Ordnance Survey Discovery Series #1* and *6,* and always inform someone of their plans before setting off. The town itself has its own set of scenic trails, including the ascent to Errigal, a ramble through the **Poison Glen,** and the numerous paths in Glenveagh National Park (see p. 429).

Buses only come as close as Crolly, 1 mi. south. **Feda O'Donnell** (☎075 48114) provides a daily coach service to and from Galway and Donegal Town; **John McGinley Coaches** (☎074 35201) makes Crolly its starting point for a Dublin journey; **O'Donnell Trans-Ulster Express** (☎48356) goes by on its way to Belfast via Letterkenny and Derry; and **Swilly** (Dungloe ☎21380, Derry ☎7126 2017) passes through on its Dungloe-Derry route. To get from Crolly to Dunlewy necessitates a **taxi** ride: **Charlie Mac** (☎087 26037) and **Popeye's** (☎075 32633) do the job.

The two hostels in Dunlewy are along R251. The warden of the **Errigal Youth Hostel (An Óige/HI) ❶**, only 1 mi. from the foot of Errigal, next to a service station, has modernized the clean, basic facilities of this aging hostel. The brisk enjoy their freezing showers. (☎953 1180. Lockout 10am-5pm. Curfew 1am. June-Sept. dorms €11; bunked private rooms €14.50. Oct.-May €9.50/€13.) A few hundred yards down the road to the west, away from the mountain, is the new **Backpackers Ireland**

FROM THE ROAD

"UNSETTLED WEATHER"

One month into my Irish travels, I hadn't had a single day in which there was not at least a brief spell of rain. I had long since given up on checking the forecast: the weather in Ireland is terminally "unsettled," as the meteorologists euphemistically label the reliable mixture of rain and rain. I had nearly forgotten what my skin looked like, as my raincoat had become the quintessential fixture of my wardrobe. When my editors back in sweltering Boston asked if I had been renting bikes to get around I scoffed, "you do realize that you can't hold an umbrella and ride a bike at the same time?" Nor did those in Ireland offer any solace, as the daily reminders that this was the worst summer they had seen in three, five, even 50 years did little to buoy my spirits (though they might offer the 2004 reader more hope!). What I wanted to hear was that the clouds would somehow "run out" of rain, and that the remainder of my summer would be bone dry. No such luck; I instead was told that rainy Junes precede rainy Julys.

With this in mind, I was less than excited by the approach of the 4th of July, the American day of independence that is typically celebrated with cookouts, fireworks, and trips to the beach. My plan for the 4th did include a trip to the beach—Bundoran—but a beach in 50° weather is somehow not quite the same. I was

(cont. on next page)

Lakeside Hostel ❶, which lacks the regulations of its neighbor. (☎953 2133. Dorms €10; private rooms €13.) For a real treat, turn off the road toward the Poison Glen to reach **Radharc an Ghleanna B&B ❸**, which has such a superior view of the lake and surrounding mountains that you'll beg to move in. (☎953 1835. Singles €30; doubles €26.) Hungry chefs should stock up in advance, as the only store within walking distance is the Top service station next to the Errigal Hostel.

A few minutes up the road toward the mountain is a turnoff to **Dunlewy Lake** and the **Poison Glen**. A misnomer to be sure, the glen's name was a mistranslation of the similar sounding "Heavenly Glen." Within the glen is the former **manor** of an English aristocrat, now one of the Guinness family's many holiday homes. In an open spot next to the lake stands his **abandoned church;** its decaying, roofless exterior makes a spooky addition to the myth-laden surroundings. Along the paved road around a few curves lies an unmarked carpark that signals the beginning of the trail up **Errigal Mountain** (at 2466 ft., Ireland's 2nd-highest peak). The mountain is a wet bog partly covered in rocks and loose scree, so plan accordingly; stick to the grass for as long as possible, since the rocks make for bad traction and not-so-cushy falls. Expect the challenging scramble to take 3hr. round-trip. Keep an eye on the clouds—they've been known to congregate suddenly around the mountaintop, and if visibility drops too much, the trip back down could be shortened by several hours, in a very bad way. That said, the view from the narrow ridge leading to the tip is breathtaking, sweeping over several counties and even more lakes.

Back in Dunlewy proper, just before the Lakeside Hostel, the **Ionad Cois Locha Dunlewy,** or Dunlewy Lakeside Centre, offers 30min. boat tours on Dunlewy Lake, paddle boats for the independent, weaving demonstrations, a craft shop, a playground, resident red deer, enough info on the area to stand as a tourist office, and a fire-warmed cafe. (☎953 1699. Open Easter-Oct. M-Sa 10:30am-6pm, Su 11am-7pm. Boat trip or weaving cottage tour €5, students and seniors €4.50, children €3.50, family €12.50. Combined ticket €8/€7.50/€6/€20. Playground €3.50, children €3, family €10.) The center also provides interested ramblers with an excellent packet of walks in Dunlewy. Two routes go through the Errigal Mountains: the "tourist route" (3 mi., ascending 1716 ft.; 2-2½hr.) and the more rugged northwest ridge route (2 mi., 1860 ft.; 2-2½hr.); each route leads to the summit (which is, incidentally, the smallest in the country at only a few feet across). The center also hosts trad on Tuesdays at 8:30pm in July and August with a craft workshop to entertain the kids (tickets €6-10), and music workshops year-round.

🔲 DAYTRIPS FROM DUNLEWY

On the eastern side of the Derryveagh Mountains, **Gartan Parish** is the most rural of the *gaeltacht* parishes. As a result, there are few towns and even fewer accommodations. Nevertheless, Gartan is home to some of the *gaeltacht*'s greatest attractions. Aesthetically-minded visitors find much to treasure here, whether in the scenic beauty of **Glenveagh National Park** or the eclectic collection of **Glebe House.** Most travelers base themselves in Dunlewy or daytrip from Letterkenny via **Bus Éireann's** "Hills of Donegal" Tour. (☎074 912 1309. €7.60 return.)

GLENVEAGH NATIONAL PARK. From the hostels in Gweedore, it's an 8 mi. hike into Glenveagh National Park's 37 sq. mi. of forest glens, bogs, and mountains. One of the largest herds of red deer in Europe roams the park; deer-watching is best at dusk and in winter, when the deer come down to forage in the valley. Badgers, endangered Golden Eagles, sandpipers, and other species round out the all-star wildlife cast. Despite Glenveagh's status as the second most popular national park in Ireland and an important Heritage Site, it's easy to forget other humans along the park's wide-open spaces. Though the solitude can be intoxicating, hold onto that map. Park rangers lead **guided nature walks** and more strenuous **hill walks.** The **visitors center** has information about these as well as self-guided routes, and prepares hikers with several exhibits, a 25min. video on the park's wildlife and history, and a €7-9 meal at its cafeteria-style **restaurant.** The Park Guide (€6.35) and *Ordnance Survey #6* (€4.95) are available at the visitors center on R251 east of Dunlewy (☎*074 913 7090; www.heritageireland.ie. Open Mar.-Nov. daily 10am-6pm; car park gates don't close until 8pm. Call ahead for info or to schedule a walk.)*

Summertime tourists can take the minibus from the park's entrance to **Glenveagh Castle,** 2½ mi. away. Altough it was only built in 1870, Glenveagh Castle looks like a medieval keep with its thick walls, battle-ready rampart, turrets, and round tower. *(Minibus from park entrance runs every 10-15min.; last departure 1½hr. before closing. €2, students €1. Castle open for guided tours only; last tour 1¼hr. before closing. €2.50, students €1.20.)* The surrounding **gardens** brighten the bleak history of the castle; they were designed by a later owner, American Henry McIlhenny, who left the estate to the government upon his death. Free **tours** of the grounds depart from the castle courtyard. *(July-Aug. Tu and Th 2pm.)* A mile up the incline behind the castle, **View Point** provides a glimpse of the park's vast expanse.

also scheduled to check out the somewhat nearby Errigal Mountain. Decision one was somewhat embarrassing: I decided that I would see *Spiderman* (which I had heard contained moments of sentimental American patriotism) at night, after eating at McDonald's (which I don't even particularly like). Decision two was that I would actually climb Errigal Mountain, rain or shine.

Waking up to rain (surprise!) that morning, I decided to splurge a bit and take a taxi to Dunlewy. As I hiked through the village, the rain continued unabated, and as I set out for Errigal, with water beginning its ascent from my soaked-jean legs, I wasn't entirely sure I would resist calling the cab again if I ran across a pay phone. Luckily, my hour and a half stroll afforded me no such "wuss out" opportunities, and by the time I reached the foot of the mountain, my resolve to reach its pinnacle was strong. I knew that it probably wasn't entirely wise to climb a mountain by myself on a rainy day; *Let's Go* would certainly not recommend doing so. But with each step I took, pressing into the wet wind, I felt better and better, and there was no way that I was turning back before reaching the top. Halfway up my umbrella busted entirely, having flipped inside out too many times. I laughed out loud as suspicious sheep eyed the wet and wild-haired madwoman I had become. No more would I fight or fear the rain, I loved it. And when I reached the summit and circled the cairn, my head literally in the clouds I had so often cursed, I had to marvel at the beauty of having that moment to myself, on top of the world.

GLEBE GALLERY AND GLEBE HOUSE. The delicately manicured 20-acre plot on the northern shore of Gartan Lough, 11 mi. east of Dunlewy, is another Irish Heritage Site, bequeathed to the state in 1981 by the English-cum-Irish painter Derek Hill. The site houses two radically different art spaces. The **Glebe Gallery,** formerly Hill's own display space, displays rotating exhibits of contemporary art in a gallery with wood floors, track lighting, and all the other modern trappings. ◪**Glebe House,** Hill's former residence, is another beast altogether. The house contains over 300 paintings and an assortment of craft objects, preserved as they were when Hill lived there. The wildly colored wallpaper and equally colorful artifacts give visitors a glimpse of life inside a box of paints. The collection lies somewhere between the ridiculous and the sublime—Renoirs and Picassos command attention, but the whole house is so animated that even the bathroom merits a stop on the tour. Works by Hill's contemporaries (including the Tory Island "primitive" painters) complete the cluttered collection. The gallery and house are on R251, 5 mi. southeast of Glenveagh National Park's visitor's center. (☎074 913 7071. *Open Easter week and late May to late Sept. M-Th and Sa-Su 11am-6:30pm; 45min. tours leave about every 30min. 11:30am-5:30pm. €2.75, seniors €2, students and children €1.25, family €7.)*

ST. COLMCILLE HERITAGE CENTRE. St. Colmcille (AD 521-597), famed for taking Christianity from Ireland to Scotland, once resided near the shores of Gartan Lough. The countryside around the lough is punctuated with Colmcillian ruins. The newly opened St. Colmcille Heritage Centre, across Gartan Lough from Glebe House, is devoted to his legacy, and has permanent exhibits about the development of Christianity in Donegal, with a focus on Colmcille's life and martyrdom in Iona, Scotland. (☎074 913 7306 or 913 7021. *Open Apr.-Sept. M-Sa 10:30am-6:30pm, Su 1-6:30pm. €2, students and seniors €1.50, children €1.)* It also functions as an unofficial tourist office; handouts provide lucid directions to other saintly sights, including **Colmcille's Birthplace, Abbey,** and **Bed of Loneliness.** This giant stone slab, on the southeastern corner of the lake, was the site where the saint meditated and slept the night before he began his exile in Scotland. Since then, prospective emigrants have lain on the stone overnight to ward off future loneliness.

BUNBEG AND DERRYBEG   ☎075

Where N56 moves inland to Dungloe, R257 continues along the coast to Bunbeg *(An Bun Beag)*. With little traffic, this scenic stretch of road is perfect for cyclists. Hitchers tend to stay on N56, where cars are more common. **Bunbeg Harbour,** the smallest enclosed harbor in Ireland, was a main exit and entry point during the height of British occupation, and period relics—military barracks, grain stones, look-out towers— line the harbor. The mile of R257 between Bunbeg and **Derrybeg** *(Doirí Beaga)* is facetiously called "the Golden Mile" by locals; unlike the rest of the region, this stretch has not escaped the touch of tourism.

Bunbeg's harbor is one of two docking places for **Donegal Coastal Cruises** (a.k.a. **Turasmara;** ☎953 5061 or 953 1991), the ferry service for Tory Island, which departs from R257 at the edge of town once a day at 9am (see **Transportation,** p. 431). Boats also sail from Bunbeg to **Gola Island,** which claims deserted beaches and beautiful views. (☎953 2487 or 087 293 4895. 25min.; 6 per day; €10.15, under 12 €6.35.) Halfway between Bunbeg and its harbor, a single stone pillar marks a rough path leading to the banks of the **Clady River,** where salmon friends fish. **Teach Tomáis** (☎31054), the oldest shop in the parish, specializes in Irish books and crafts, but also offers a small and brilliantly-selected collection of English-language works. (Open M-F 10am-6pm. If shop is locked, knock at the kitchen door to its right.)

North of Derrybeg on R257, the **Bloody Foreland,** a short length of rough scarlet rock, juts into the sea. At sunset on clear evenings, the sea reflects the deep red hue of the rocks and sea, composing one of Ireland's most famous views. An old legend holds that the sea is colored with the blood of sailors who perished in the wrecks of Spanish galleons. Farther west, the headland at **Meenlaragh (Magher-aroarty)** stretches for miles of unspoiled beaches. A **holy well** remains full of fresh water despite tidal rushes twice a day.

To reach Derrybeg by **bus**, try **Swilly's** (☎ 074 912 2863), whose Donegal-Derry service stops in town (2-3 per day). Derrybeg's streets have several banks, but only the **AIB** has both a **bureau de change** and an **ATM. Gweedore Chemists** (☎ 953 1254) is housed in a white building across the street and a few yards up from Hudi Beag's pub. The local **post office** takes care of the mail. (☎ 953 1165. Open M-F 9am-1pm and 2-5:30pm.)

Budget accommodations are no longer in Bunbeg or Derrybeg; these are primarily stop-by-and-stock-up towns for the budget traveler. However, several reasonable, lovely B&Bs and a couple of hotel options await in town. The left immediately after the AIB leads to **An Teach Bán ❸**, run by amiable owners Linda and Paul, who serve the best Irish breakfast around. Clean, cheerful rooms have beautiful bay views, and the new conservatory fosters a refreshing sense of community rare in B&Bs. (☎ 953 2359 or 953 1569; pmcgill@iol.ie. Singles €24-32; shared rooms €25.) The **Bunbeg House ❸**, of *Round Ireland With Fridge* fame (see p. 430), is found on the waterfront and greets guests with quiet, serenely colored rooms. (☎ 953 1305; www.bunbeghouse.com. €30.)

For the healthy set, **Organic Bean and Wholefoods** faces the pharmacy. (☎ 956 0698. Open M-Sa 10am-6pm.) At the west end of Derrybeg, the green building across from Hudi Beag's is **Teach Niocáin**—not only a **grocery** with a fantastic hot bar and sandwich shop, but also a **laundrette**. (☎ 953 1065. 5 sausage rolls for €1.30. Wash and dry €6.35. Open daily 8am-10pm.) Derrybeg's best option for takeaway is **Pepper's Diner ❶**, stocked with a wide selection of the three basic food groups—pizza, ice cream, and deep-fried. (☎ 953 1110. Open daily noon-12:30am.) The irresistible ▪**Hudi Beag's** pub (☎ 953 1016), a two-story white building at the western entrance to town, is the epicenter for half of Derrybeg's musical tradition. On Monday nights, only the truly tone-deaf could pass up their intense sessions, with 10-25 musicians jamming (10pm-1am).

TORY ISLAND (OILEÁN THORAIGH)   ☎ 074

Bare Tory Island, only 8 mi. off shore, is visible from the Bloody Foreland. Named for its many *tors* (hills), the island provides minimal footing for its weather-beaten cottages and eccentric local characters. The independent islanders refer to the mainland as "the country," and still elect a **"Rí na nóileán"** (king of the island) to a life-time position that usually entails his becoming the island's PR man—currently, his name is Patsy Dan. The island gained mythical status as the home of the demonic Formorians—the original Tory Island pirates who regularly invaded the mainland. Its age-old reputation as a haven for pirates prompted people to equate the word "Tory" with "pirate" or "rascal." The use of "Tory" to mean "Conservative" derives from this Irish slang. (A Whig, incidentally, was originally a Scottish horse thief.) Tory's reputation for swashbuckling and buccaneering was accurate as recently as last century, when the island thrived on illegal *poitín;* the inaccessibility of the island thwarted British efforts to control its trade (see **Love Poitín #9,** p. 418). All six layers of the island's turf were burned in *poitín* production; as a result, today's Tory appears sandier and grassier than the mainland. Only one tree survives in the island's harsh conditions; please stop by and give it a hug. The eastern end of the island breaks apart into a series of jagged sea cliffs.

Most of Tory's sights are decrepit at best, but a little informed imagination can do wonders. Pick up a free copy of *Tory Island*, by Jim Hunter, at the hotel to read up. A right off the pier, **Gailearai Dixon** (Dixon Gallery) showcases the work of the Tory Primitives, a group of local artists promoted by Derek Hill of Glebe House fame (see p. 430). The group's work, typically painted using donkey-hair brushes, usually depicts the natural scenery of the island drenched in color. (☎ 913 5011 or 086 351 7160. Call on Anton Meenan up the road at cottage #6 if the facility is shut.) The island's historical sights include the **ruins** of the monastery that St. Colmcille founded in the 6th century, the **Tau**

FROM THE ROAD

ROAD WARRIOR

In Ireland, you'll always find a helpful hand from the locals—this is something I've learned all too well. One day, while on my way to Tory Island, I found myself on a somewhat perilous, unmarked single-car road. After about 3 mi. of unposted driving I lost faith in the Irish transit authorities, as one is wont to do when faced with a dearth of signs encouraging you along your uncertain way. As fate or karma would have it, I soon paid for my lack of faith when my trusty Nissan Micra became stuck in a veritable ditch. After 20min. of wheel-spinning, mud flying, and some ingenious attempts at self-extraction via plywood planks, I was almost resigned to a roadside fate and a night in the car. Beaten, but not broken, I instead hiked back to the nearest farmhouse only to have a family greet me with excited, knowing smiles. Apparently, I was not the first casualty of this road. The previous week they had pulled out some Slovakians from the very same ditch, and the year before was a record one, with nearly a dozen such stranded visitors. It was decided that the car would not budge from mere pushing, so another local was called, and he brought with him the might of a tractor. I took pictures of the successful extraction, and I promised to send a shot back to my saviors. They declined my offer of monetary payment, wisely acknowledging that I could someday return the favor if they ever found themselves in a ditch in California.

—KIRA WHELAN

Cross by the pier, and a **torpedo** that washed ashore during WWII and was erected in the middle of the road, dividing east and west Tory; all three contribute to Tory's quirky and alien feel.

Island legend claims that a stone on one of Tory's hills has the power to fulfill wishes. Dreamers with good aim who throw three pebbles onto the stone, which sits on the tip of the island's east end (20min. from the pier) on an unapproachable perch, will be granted a wish. In addition to the **wishing stone,** the island features a **cursing stone.** (The location of the latter has been concealed by local elders to prevent its misuse.) The cursing stone has been credited with the 1884 shipwreck of the aptly named *HMS Wasp,* which British officials had sent to collect taxes. The islanders still pay no taxes. Bird buffs crow with joy at the free and informal **Tory Mor** (bird sanctuary) near the wishing stone, home to swans, puffins, and seagulls.

Donegal Coastal Cruises (a.k.a. Turasmara; ☎ 075 31320 or 075 31340; see Bunbeg and Derrybeg, p. 430) runs boats from Bunbeg (1½hr.; June-Oct. 1 daily, Nov.-May 5 per wk.) and, more frequently, from Meenlaragh (a.k.a. Magheroarty) beyond Bloody Foreland on R257. (1hr.; June and Sept. daily 11:30am and 5:30pm, July-Aug. daily 11:30am, 1:30, 5pm.) Call ahead to check departure times and arrive on time—unlike most things in Donegal, the ferry is extremely punctual. The crossing is choppy in the clearest of weather, and storms have stranded travelers here for days in summer and even weeks in winter. (Bunbeg dock ☎ 075 31991, Meenlaragh ☎ 074 913 5061. All crossings €22 return, students €19, under 15 €10, under 5 and bicycles free.) On the island, **bikes** can be hired from Patrick Rodgers, next to Teach Billie's. (Open all day June-Sept. €7-8 per day, deposit €6.35.)

Tory tourists have several options for accommodations, the cheapest being the newly reopened **Teach Billie's ①.** Turn left off the ferry and walk 200 yd. along the shore, past the tower; it's the unmarked, bright yellow house with green trim, just after the seawall. The ensuite rooms and modern self-catering kitchen have plenty of sun, and sea views. (☎ 916 5145. Call in advance. Open June-Sept. €20.) **Óstan Thóraig ④,** in a white building with bright sky-blue trim in front of the pier, has airy, sweet-smelling hotel rooms with baths and TVs. The knowledgeable staff compensates for Tory's lack of a tourist office. (☎ 913 5920; www.toryhotel.com. Breakfast included. Open Apr.-Oct. Singles €70, shared rooms €55; June-Aug., Easter, and Bank Holidays €75/€60. Children 5-12 half-price, under 5 free. Inquire for specials.) The hotel's **restaurant ⑤** is expensive (open 6:30-9:30pm; mains €18.50-23), but its **bar ②** has daytime and evening menus (food served 8:30-10am, 12:30-4pm and 6:30-9:30pm; mains €7.25-10.50) and an enormous stained-glass underwater scene. **Club Thoraighe,** beyond the cafe, features Tory Island trad, which has a slightly stronger rhythmic emphasis than mainland music, and *céilís* (KAY-lees), probably the most popular nighttime option…maybe the only option short of playing chicken with the sea. (☎916 5121 or 913 5502. Open year-round 8:30pm-late.)

CLOGHANEELY

East of Gweedore lies the parish of Cloghaneely. Thanks to its *gaeltacht* schools, white sand beaches, and excellent weather, in summertime it's inundated with visitors from the North and English-speaking Irish teens learning Irish. Yet, as Galway is to musicians, so is Cloghaneely to artists and poets. The presence of great 20th-century Ulster poet Cathal O Searcaigh and other visiting poets and artists ensures a bohemian population and nice, mellow *craic*. Judging from the area's year-round natural beauty, from Horn Head to the Ards Forest Park, it's no wonder that many visitors stay on longer than expected. The **Samhain International Poetry Festival** in July and master classes at the Poet's House also lend a hand.

FALCARRAGH (AN FÁL CARRACH)   ☎074

Amidst the silvery strands that stretch along the coast northeast of the Bloody Foreland, and the rocky landscape found further inland, rests one of the busiest Irish-speaking villages in the *gaeltacht*. Falcarragh, like many of the settlements in this region, offers little to do in the town during the day; it does, however, serve as a colorful stop for those heading to the beaches beyond Dunfanaghy. The towering sand dunes at **Ballyness,** 3 mi. out of town, are Falcarragh's primary attraction; to reach them, follow the signs for "Trá" (beach) at the south end of town.

■ 冠 TRANSPORTATION AND PRACTICAL INFORMATION. Several private **bus** companies stop in Falcarragh: **Feda O'Donnell** (☎48114) traces the West Coast, running from Crolly through Donegal Town to Sligo and Galway; **McGinley** (☎35201 or 01 451 3809) passes through on a Donegal-Dublin trek; **O'Donnell Trans Ulster Express** hits Falcarragh as it cuts a swath from Dungloe to Belfast via Letterkenny and Derry; and **Swilly** (☎912 2863 in Letterkenny, ☎913 5995 in Falcarragh) drops in on its way from Donegal to Derry. Hitching is reportedly quite common in this area. For travel over shorter distances, **Joe's Taxi** is ready to help (☎916 5017 or 916 5018). At Magheraroarty Strand off the main road to the south, the wee port of **Magheraroarty** sends ships to **Tory** and **Inishbofin Islands.** (To Inishbofin: 5min.; call ahead to Teach Johnny's at ☎075 31320 or 9135061. To Tory Island: June and Sept. daily 11:30am and 5:30pm; July-Aug. daily 11:30am, 1:30, 5:30pm.) A brand new **An tSean Bheairic (visitor centre)** keeps a craft center and coffee shop, and gives guided tours, a short audio-visual presentation, and reading material about the town and region in two languages. (☎918 0888; www.falcarraghvisitorscentre.com. Open Apr.-Oct. M-F 9am-5pm, Sa-Su noon-5pm.) The **Bank of Ireland** on Main St. has an **ATM** and **bureau de change.** (☎35484. Open M and W-F 10am-12:30pm and 1:30-4pm, Th until 5pm.) As **work opportunities** are concerned, **Maggie Din's** is always keen to hire musicians, traditional or otherwise, for accommodation and a small salary per gig. (Contact Milo at ☎916 0800.) The anonymous **Laundrette** on Main St., across from the post office, keeps odd hours but also keeps clothes clean. (☎913 5794. Open M-Tu and F-Sa 10am-5pm with breaks for lunch, dinner, and tea.) **Flynn's Pharmacy** vends medicines. (☎913 5778. Open M-F 9:30am-6pm, Sa 10am-6pm.) Falcarragh's **post office,** Main St., delivers mail. (☎913 5110. Open M-F 9am-1pm and 2-5:30pm, Sa 9am-1pm.)

⌐ ⊏ ⊠ ACCOMMODATIONS, FOOD, AND PUBS. The **Shamrock Lodge Hostel (IHH) ❶,** above the pub on Main St., has been restored to its former glory after being ravaged by fire in 2002. Dorms with framed art and basic bunks house poets and artists who descend for the International Poetry Festival and summer conferences at the Poet's House. (☎913 5959. Dorms €14.) Across from the post office, **Barrett's B&B ❷** welcomes guests with frilly, fluffy beds and floral wallpaper for a fiscally sound price. (☎913 5583. Singles €25; doubles €50.)

Across from the visitor's center, the simply decorated, simply delicious **Fulacht Fiadh Cafe ❶** ("ancient cooking site" in Irish) satisfies bohemians with bohemian purses. (☎918 0683. Breakfast €3.50, panini €5. Open M-Sa 10am-5:30pm.) The focus at **Damian's ❶**, at the top of Main St., is the delicious food they serve. Cramped benches and plain white walls conceal better-than-average chipper fare. (☎916 5613. Mains €3.75-11. Open M-Th 10am-7:30pm, F-Sa 'til 9:30 pm; summer also open Su noon-7pm.) The **Gweedore Bar ❷**, Main St., carries favor with lunching local businessmen and vacationers sunning themselves in the makeshift beer garden. (☎913 5293. Lunch specials €5.50; served 12:30-2:30pm. W bar quiz, F-Su live rock music.) **Centra** provides a good selection of produce, and alcoholic libations in its off-license. (☎35529. Open M-Sa 8:30am-9pm, Su 9am-7pm.)

Visitors to the **Shamrock Lodge** (*Lóistín na Seamróige*), in the center of town, are greeted by cartoon paintings of Celtic warriors on the pub's facade. Inside, the front room is a traditional pub with a *céilí* room for trad and plenty of typical GAA paraphernalia; in back, the pool room and the authentic swinging doors of the "Mexican" saloon allow dramatic entrances. (☎913 5859. Th rock and country, Sa trad. Open M-Th 11:30am-11:30pm, F-Sa until 1am.) On Ballyconnell Rd., just off Main St. at the northern end of town, the **Loft Bar's** purple facade conceals a cave-like interior, a collection of old mugs, flowery upholstery, and colorful regulars to match. (☎913 5992. Occasional music in summer.)

Gortahork (Gort a'Choirce), 1 mi. south of Falcarragh on the N56, offers excellent beds, food, and *craic* beyond the ordinary. **Ostán an Bear Mór ❹** keeps its pine-furnished rooms pristine, and equipped with red bathtubs. A classy restaurant and bar top it off. (☎916 5400; www.anbearmore.com. Open July-Aug. €45, off season €35.) ▧**Maggie Dan's** is more a cultural institution than a bistro. The establishment's patriarch, Milo, hosts music events all summer long including a Monday night piano bar, a tearoom, and an upstairs theater space with monthly poetry recitals. Helpful staff offer deals on accommodations, tours, and daring love advice. (☎916 5630; www.maggiedans.ie. Light entrees €2-5. Open 6pm-midnight.) For the best pint in Donegal Co., seasoned drinkers seek out **Teach Billie's Pub** next to Maggie Dan's. Trad sessions on Wednesday nights sweeten the deal.

◙ ⚲ **SIGHTS AND ACTIVITIES.** Festivals and concerts revolve around **Maggie Dan's**, in Gortahork (see above), and **The Poets' House,** 2km outside Falcarragh toward the Muckish Gap. At Maggie Dan's a **Jazz and Blues Festival** draws crooners and swingers during Easter week, starting Easter Sunday. The mid-July **Gaelic Festival** celebrates the best of Gaelic culture with performances, readings, and music in Irish and English. The equal-opportunity **Women's Festival** kicks off the second week in August with intriguing international females, such as Bernadette Devlin, the Republican protester and youngest woman elected to the House of Commons. Around Halloween, €5000 goes to the winner of the **Samhain International Poetry Festival,** hosted by Cathal O Searcaigh and emphasizing Irish language and culture. (www.samhainpoetry.com; all other event info through Maggie Dan's.) The Poets' House hosts an MA program in Creative Writing and summer conferences, workshops, and performances in July and August. (☎916 5470; www.poetshouse.ie.)

NEAR FALCARRAGH: INISHBOFIN ISLAND

Just a five minute motorboat ride from Magheraroarty beach, it's a wonder that Inishbofin remains the same untouched island fishing settlement it has been for ages. Introduced to tap water in April 2003 and running electricity the year before, the village houses 40 people, two tractors, three jeeps, and four dogs, all living on one side of the 3 mi. island. The crescent white sand beach is littered with smooth rocks and inundated with rabbits, whose presence more than doubles the population. Large rock outcroppings are brutalized daily by the sea. A stone arch is fabled to break if tread upon by a family or a pair of lovers. Serenity is a selling point, though a stay in the island's only hostel engulfs the traveler in an ad hoc community, formed of islanders and their international guests.

■**Teach Johnny** keeps a pristine white house with airy dorms, firm matresses, and fluffy spreads. The dining room is heated by a wood-burning stove and lit by candles in the evening. The ambience and open setup fosters conversation, and a liquor license loosens even the shyest tongues. Saturday nights unleash mighty *craic* from islanders and visitors, who save up all week. Fishing, island tours, and boat trips can be arranged. Call ahead to Tony for pickup at Magheroarty. (☎916 2970 or 087 2100129; www.teachjohnny.com. Boat, bed, and breakfast included. Laundry €5. Open St. Patrick's Day through Oct. July-Aug. €25; off season €20.)

DUNFANAGHY (DÚN FIONNACHAIDH)   ☎074

Seven miles north of Falcarragh, Dunfanaghy is a pleasant beach town with a distinctly Anglicized character; it serves as a summer refuge for Northern Irish tourists seeking to avoid marching season. The **Dunfanaghy Workhouse Heritage Centre**, a few hundred yards southwest of town, is a former poorhouse transformed since Famine days. An exhibit on the effects of the Great Hunger in Northwest Donegal is both grisly and deeply moving. (☎913 6540. Open Mar.-Oct. M-Sa 10am-5pm, Su noon-5pm. €4, seniors €2.85, children €2, family €10.) The natural attractions within a 5 mi. radius of Dunfanaghy and Falcarragh are easily accessible by foot, cycle, or car, and hitching is common. The helpful *Walking Donegal: Dunfanaghy* (€3) is available throughout the region, and stocked en masse at Carcreggan Hostel—the proprietor wrote it. **Horn Head,** signposted on the way into Dunfanaghy, invites long rambles around its pristine beaches, megalithic tombs, and gorse-covered hills. Tireless hikers who make the 8½ mi. (3½hr., 4½hr. in spring) trek to the northern tip of Horn Head from Dunfanaghy reach some of the most spectacularly high sea cliffs in Ireland. The lazy can drive all but the last 1½ mi. **Ards Forest Park,** a couple miles past Dunfanaghy on N56, features a number of nature trails (1½-8 mi.). Pristine beaches only accessible on foot lie nearby. (Open July-Aug. daily 10:30am-9pm; Easter-June and Sept. Sa-Su 10:30am-4pm. Parking €4.) About 5 mi. south of town on N56, **New Lake**—so called because it was formed in 1912 after a massive storm blocked an estuary—features a world-famous ecosystem and frisky otters. Beach bums enjoy the spectacular ■**Tramore Strand,** a 25min. walk through dunes from the Horn Head Bridge. Turning your back to the sea anywhere in Dunfanaghy brings the expanse of **Muckish Mountain** into view.

Those interested in climbing Muckish Mountain have two options. The first, more difficult route takes 4hr. and covers 7 mi. It's best to bring along *Ordinance Map #2* (€6.35) and a compass. To reach the path, drive from Dunfanaghy toward Creeslough, turn right when the graveyard is on the left, and continue for 3 mi. to where the grassy track crosses the road. Park here and walk uphill on the road to the two foundations. The path begins to the right of the upper foundation, across a narrow steam. Once you reach the quarry, the path to the summit is to the right. *Let's Go* advises hikers not to attempt the mountain in low visibility, as there are some huge drops. For those with less time, or less energy, the second and easier route to the summit takes only 2hr. Drive to Muckish Gap (marked by a shrine), follow the path northeast for half a mile, then turn northwest to reach the summit. **Dunfanaghy Stables** (☎913 6208), behind Arnold's Hotel in Dunfanaghy town, leads rides over the dried up lake and through Ards Forest Park.

Transportation to Dunfanaghy is as sparse as in the rest of the region. Buses serving the area include **Feda O'Donnell's** (☎914 8114) route from Donegal south to Galway and Sligo and **McGinley's** (☎913 5201) service between Donegal and Dublin. There is an **ATM** in **Ramsay's,** but it only takes local cards. Non-locals should hit Falcrannagh for funds. In the **work opportunities** department, **Corcreggan Mill Hostel** frequently looks for administrative and gardening help, for which it provides accommodation, food, and €40 per week. (Contact Brendan Rohan at ☎913 6902.) **Internet** hides out in **Muck 'n Muffins** (€2 per 15min., €7 per hr.).

Just over 1 mi. south of Dunfanaghy toward Falcarragh, the **図Corcreggan Mill Hostel (IHH, IHO)** ❶ sits by the side of the road in a complex that consists of a kiln house and a railway car. Owner Brendan converted an old train into comfortable 4-bed dorms and private doubles with mahogany floors and walls, and equipped the former kiln house with bunks and loft doubles. Most buses stop at the door; just ask to get off. (☎913 6902; www.corcreggan.com. Laundry €3 with line dry. Kiln house dorms €11; loft doubles €28. Railway dorms €14; doubles €32. **Camping** €6 per person.) The **Corcreggan Mill House B&B** ❸ is run by a separate group that leases from the hostel. The modern facilities include conference rooms, a **restaurant** (early-bird 3-course €15, mains €17-30), and the **Sulas Centre of Healing and Life Renewal** (☎913 6940), with meditation, dance, and relaxation courses. (Call hostel for B&B bookings. Doubles €60.) In town, the 3-star B&B accomodations at the **Carrig Rua Hotel** ❹ are a more upscale alternative. (☎913 6133. €45-58.)

Ramsay's Store, on the parking lot in the center of town, stocks food items. (☎913 6120. Open M-Sa 7:30am-9:30pm, Su 8am-10:30pm.) In the main square, **Muck n' Muffins** ❶ is a purveyor of pottery, pastry, light meals, and lovely bay views. (☎913 6780. Open M-Sa 10am-5pm, Su 11am-5pm.) The **Carrig Rua Hotel** ❸ contains a steep bistro and the elegant **Sheephaven Fine Dining Room.** (☎36133. Bistro mains €7-13. Open daily 12:30-9pm. Dining room mains €12.95-21. Open daily 7-9pm.) A local pearl of fun, **The Oyster,** in **McGilloway's,** attracts *craic*-seekers on Thursdays with trad, and on weekends with a live rock band. (Open M-Th noon-11pm, F-Su noon-late.) **Michael's,** the first building on the right into town from Falcarragh, won the Best Traditional Music Pub in Ireland in 2002; it's a diamond in the rough of traditional pub life with a cheery beer garden and mature crowd.

FANAD PENINSULA

The Fanad Peninsula, which juts into the Atlantic between Lough Swilly and Mulroy Bay, is a study in contrasts, with the verdant fields of its interior and the clean, sandy beaches running along its edges. Most visitors stick to the eastern coastal villages of **Ramelton, Rathmullan,** and **Portsalon,** which contain colorful old houses and sweeping views across Lough Swilly. These villages may lack the nightlife and cultural offerings of their (relatively) more cosmopolitan neighbors, but wanderers who revel in wide-open spaces know what a treasure the Fanad is. Backpackers enjoy several gentle hikes, either along the northeastern coast or into the **Knockalla Mountains.** The Fanad Peninsula presents a challenge for the car-less—buses are infrequent and road conditions are not ideal for cyclists. Those who do venture into this remote region, however, enjoy lush scenery and a level of isolation unknown on the more touristed Inishowen (see p. 441). The Swilly bus only runs as far as Portsalon once per day; without a car, plan on spending the night.

RATHMULLAN (RÁTH MAOLÁIN)   ☎074

The town of Rathmullan sits 5 mi. north of Ramelton along the main coastal road. Its claim to fame? In 1607, the last powerful Gaelic chieftains, flighty Earls Hugh O'Neill and Red Hugh O'Donnell, fled from Ireland after suffering numerous defeats to British invaders. They and 99 of their closest friends set sail from Rathmullan for Spain to gather military support from the Catholic King Phillip II (see **Feudalism,** p. 58). In more recent Anglo-Irish struggles, Wolfe Tone, champion of Irish independence, was arrested here in 1798 (see **Rebellion,** p. 61). These historical MVPs tell their stories at **"Flight of the Earls" Heritage Centre,** housed in foreboding Martello tower in the town center. The exhibit employs artwork, literature, and wax models to recount Rathmullan's history in detail. (☎915 8131 or 915 8454. Open Apr.-Sept. M-Sa 10am-1pm and 2-5pm, Su noon-5pm. €5, students and seniors €3, children €2.) Around the corner toward Ramelton, the remains of **Rathmullan Priory,** a 14th-century Carmelite monastery, lie shrouded in ivy.

Those interested in **fishing** can beam aboard the *Enterprise 1* full- and half-day excursions. (Contact Angela Crerand at ☎915 8131 after 6pm or 087 248 0132 all day). **Golden Sands Equestrian Centre,** 3 mi. up the Portsalon Rd., encourages landlubbers to trek across the countryside atop grand equine beasts (☎915 8124).

Buses leave from the town grocery to Derry via Letterkenny (M-Sa 8am, Sa only 12:30pm). **Tourist information** of the printed variety is happily dispensed at the heritage center (see above). **Mace Supermarket,** on the coastal road into town, meets basic gastronomic needs. (☎58148. Open daily 8am-10pm.) Up a small alleyway off Main St., hidden from the stark coastal scene below, the ivy-covered ⊠**Knoll B&B ❸** looks more like a dollhouse than a B&B, and shelters itinerants in baby blue and pink rooms. (☎915 8241; call ahead. Singles €35; shared rooms €25.) Next door to the heritage center, the **Beachcomber Bar ❷** offers beach access and pub grub, some of which is vegetarian. One wall is consumed by a gigantic ocean view, and a sandy beer garden opens out back in the summer. (☎915 8125. Meals €7-10. Food served June-Sept. daily noon-9pm.)

NORTHERN AND WESTERN FANAD   ☎074

North of Rathmullan, the road narrows, winding and dipping at the whim of the increasingly wild landscape. These remote roads are discouraging to pedestrians, as sites are few and far between, and to all but the fittest bikers, who breeze down the enormous hill to Portsalon but won't want to go back; hitching is nearly impossible here, as well. The "towns" in this region are generally little more than a group of holiday cottages centered around a post office, but this is also where the peninsula's only budget accommodations lie. Along the coast a little over halfway from Rathmullan to Portsalon and just north of the village of **Glenvar,** a signposted lane leads from the main road to the **Bunnaton House Hostel (IHO) ❶,** on the way to Portsalon. Perched on a cliff in the restored shell of an 1813 coast guard station, the hostel has an incredible view to the east, providing some consolation to travelers who have undertaken the arduous journey there. Basic rooms, kitchen and small sitting area are among the amenities. (☎915 0122; http://homepage.eircom.net/~crishewett. Breakfast €4-6. Dorms €11; private rooms €15.) Continuing north, the main road becomes both mind-bogglingly steep and breathtakingly beautiful. Just before Portsalon, the road crests a hill where the northern tip of the peninsula and **Stocker Strand,** rated second best in the world by a British "beach expert," suddenly appear. Next to the strand and 3 mi. south of Portsalon, the enormous **Knockalla Holiday Centre ❶** buzzes in the summer with an army of campers and caravans. (☎915 3213. Open Mar.-Sept. €17 per family tent, €12 per 2-man tent. Showers €1 per 5min.)

Portsalon (port-SAL-un), a resort town until its hotel burned down three years ago, now has just three shops and a few residences along the water. The scenic riches that justify the trials of visiting the peninsula lie just north of town, though they are circuitously signposted—stopping for directions, even for the most stubborn, proves rewarding. Five miles away lies **Fanad Head,** where the **Great Arch of Doaghbeg** keeps the private, publicly inaccessible **Fanad Lighthouse** company. The arch, a mass of rock over 80 ft. wide detached from seaside cliffs, is visible from above, though not from the main road. Cyclists are advised to approach these sights from the west, on the newer, smoother road. Arch-lovers follow the unmarked walking trail from the 6-acre **Ballydaheen Gardens,** a seaside array of Japanese and English gardens designed to blend into the natural landscape; this trail is the only way to reach the series of coastal caves known as the **Seven Arches.** (☎915 9091. Open May-Sept. M-Sa 10am-3pm. €4.) From Fanad Head, the route down the western side of the peninsula winds along the inlets of

Mulroy Bay. Mrs. Borland's **Avalon Farmhouse ❷**, on Main St. in tiny **Tamney** (also known as Tawney)—also reachable by a road that cuts across the peninsula from Portsalon—has homemade jam and attractive decor. (☎59031. Open Easter-Sept. €25.)

LETTERKENNY (LEITIR CEANAINN) ☎074

Letterkenny is the commercial center of Donegal and, more importantly for travelers, the region's primary transportation hub. Though its heavy traffic may be a civil engineer's nightmare, the town is a surprisingly cosmopolitan breeze in an otherwise rustic atmosphere—the large student population supports a number of hipster cafes and pubs.

▣ TRANSPORTATION

Buses: The almighty **Bus Depot** is on the eastern side of the roundabout at the junction of the Port (Derry) Rd. and Pearse Rd., in front of the shopping center.

Bus Éireann (☎912 1309) "Hills of Donegal" tour to: **Dungloe, Glenveigh National Park,** and **Gweedore** (July-Aug. M-F 11:05am; €20, children €15). Regular service to: **Derry** (30min.; M-Sa 9 per day, Su 3 per day; €6.50, students €5, children €4.20); **Dublin** (4½hr., M-Sa 6 per day, Su 4 per day; €14.50/€13/€9); **Galway** (4¾hr., 4 per day, €16.50/€13/€10.50) via **Donegal Town** (50min.; M-Sa 6 per day, Su 5 per day; €7.20/€6/€4.60); **Sligo** (2hr.; M-Sa 5 per day, Su 4 per day; €11.40/€10.50/€7.50).

Doherty's Travel (☎075 21105). To: **Dungloe** and **Burtonport** (daily 5pm, €6.35), from Dunnes Stores.

Feda O'Donnell Coaches (☎075 48114 or 091 761 656). To: **Crolly** (2 per day, €6.35) via **Dunfanaghy** and **Galway** (2-3 per day, €12.70) via **Donegal Town** (€6.35).

Lough Swilly Buses (☎22863). To: **Derry** (M-Sa 11 per day, €5.60); **Dungloe** (M-Th 2 per day, F 3 per day; €10.20); **Fanad Peninsula** (M-F 3 per day, Sa 4 per day; €8.90); **Inishowen Peninsula** (M-F 4 per day, Sa 3 per day) via **Buncrana** (€5.70), **Cardonagh** (€6.35), and **Moville** (€7).

McGeehan's (☎075 46150). 2 per day to **Glencolmcille** (€11.50) and **Killybegs** (€8.90).

McGinley Coaches (☎35201). 2 per day to **Dublin** (€14) and to **Gweedore** via **Dunfanaghy.**

Northwest Busways (☎077 82619) sends buses around Inishowen (M-F 4 per day, Sa 3 per day), making stops in **Buncrana** (€5.70), **Carndonagh** (€6.35), and **Moville** (€7).

Taxis: Letterkenny Cabs (☎912 7000) offers 24hr. service and handicapped-accessible cabs. **Shilly Cabs** (☎912 1666) are also at your service.

▣ PRACTICAL INFORMATION

Tourist Offices: Bord Fáilte (☎912 1160; www.irelandnorthwest,ie), off the 2nd rotary at the intersection of Port (Derry) Rd. and Blaney Rd., towards Derry; ¾ mi. from town past the bus station. Accommodations bookings and info on Co. Donegal. Open July-Aug. M-Sa 9am-8pm, Su 10am-2pm; Sept.-June M-F 9am-5pm. **Chamber of Commerce Visitors Information Centre,** 40 Port Rd. (☎24866), is closer but has slightly less info. Open M-F 9am-5pm.

Banks: AIB, 61 Upper Main St. (☎912 2877). **Bank of Ireland,** Lower Main St. (☎912 2122). **Ulster Bank,** Main St. (☎912 4016). All open M-F 10am-4pm, Th until 5pm. AIB and Bank of Ireland both have **24hr. ATMs.**

Bookstore: Bookmark, High Rd. Eclectic mix of used books. Open M-Sa 11am-5:30pm.

Laundry: Duds n' Suds, Pearse Rd. (☎912 8303). Load €8.50. Open M-Sa 8am-7pm.

Hospital: Letterkenny General, north off High Rd. past the roundabout (☎912 5888).

Pharmacy: Magee's Pharmacy, Main St. (☎912 1409 or 912 1419). Open M-W and Sa 9am-6:30pm, Th-F 9am-8pm.

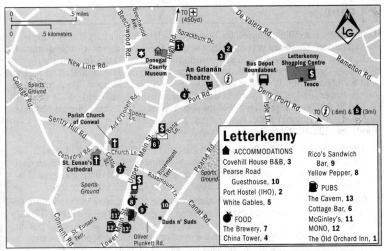

Letterkenny

ACCOMMODATIONS
Covehill House B&B, **3**
Pearse Road
   Guesthouse, **10**
Port Hostel (IHO), **2**
White Gables, **5**

🍴 FOOD
The Brewery, **7**
China Tower, **4**

Rico's Sandwich
   Bar, **9**
Yellow Pepper, **8**

🍺 PUBS
The Cavern, **13**
Cottage Bar, **6**
McGinley's, **11**
MONO, **12**
The Old Orchard Inn, **1**

Internet Access: Letterkenny Central Library, Main St. (☎912 4950). Web-surfing free with (easily obtained) membership; email €2 per hr. Book in advance. Open M, W, and F 10:30am-5:30pm; Tu and Th 10:30am-8pm; Su 10:30am-1pm. **Cyberworld,** Main St. (☎912 0440), in the basement of the Four Lanterns takeaway. €6.35 per hr., students €4.45. Open M-Sa 10:30am-9:30pm.

Post Office: Midpoint of Main St. (☎912 2287). Open M-F 9am-5:30pm, Sa 9am-1pm.

ACCOMMODATIONS

Few options exist for travelers who want to stay in the city center, as most accommodations make their homes on its outskirts. Two B&Bs and one hostel fit the bill, though other options are around the corner.

Covehill House B&B, on a turnoff just before An Grianán Theatre (☎912 1038). Convenient to the town center, the individualized rooms at this B&B are stocked with amenities, and 6 of the 9 have private baths. Singles €25; doubles €50, with bath €56. ❷

Pearse Road Guesthouse (☎912 3002). A 7min. walk down Pearse Rd. from the bus depot; look for a large white house. Cool green, ensuite rooms sweep guests away from the traffic outside. Rub shoulders with Ireland's *artistes*, as all performers in the Earigal Arta Festival reside here in the summer. Singles €35; doubles €60. ❸

The Port Hostel (IHO), Orchard Crest (☎912 5315; www.porthostel.com), past Cove Hill B&B. Letterkenny's only hostel enjoys a central location and budget-friendly price-tag; its facilities are serviceable if a bit drab. The proprietress occasionally leads pub crawls, barbecues, and roadtrips to the beach and Glenveagh (€7.60). Some rooms have balconies. Laundry €4.45. Dorms €14; private rooms €16-28. ❶

White Gables, Dromore (☎912 2583). Head 3 mi. out the Port (Derry) Rd. and take the Dromore turnoff (on the left) from the N13/N14 roundabout; the house is ½ mi. down. Call for pickup from town. Thoroughly pastoral with clean, cheery rooms and a conservatory overlooking flocks of sheep. Singles €35; shared rooms €30, with bath €35. ❷

FOOD

Letterkenny is a culinary haven for budget travelers, particularly if they happen to be vegetarian. There are several quirky options for cheap meals with fresh ingredients. Even the grocery options are unusually extensive. **Tesco,** in the Letterkenny Shopping Centre behind the bus station, has it all, including an **ATM.** (Open M-Tu and Sa 8:30am-7pm, W 8:30am-8pm, Th-F 8:30am-9pm, Su noon-6pm.) **SuperValu,** on the lower level of Courtyard, is well-stocked and central. (☎912 5738. Open M-W and Sa 8:45am-6:15pm, Th-F 8:45am-9pm.) Around the corner, **Simple Simon Living Food,** Oliver Plunkett Rd., has an admirable selection of organic and vegetarian foods. (☎912 2382. Open M-Sa 9am-6pm.)

Rico's Sandwich Bar, 3-4 Oliver Plunkett Rd. (☎912 9808), at the end of Main St. next to Simple Simon. Full breakfasts, desserts, and sandwiches (€2.50-5.50) in an often-frantic and ever-funky coffee shop, with an eclectic collection of lamps and colors. Take-away available. Open M-F 8:30am-5:30pm, Sa until 6pm, Su 11am-5pm. ❶

China Tower, up Main St. after the Theater (☎912 9610), entices with flavors of the Orient and sleek black-and-red decor. From noon 'til 4pm, lunch specials deliver 3 steaming courses (€6); afternoon specials delight the 3-6pm crowd with an appetizer and small entree (€5). Vegetarians have plenty of choices, and night-owls appreciate the restaurant's adherence to the Shanghai timezone. Open daily noon-3am. ❷

The Brewery, Market Sq. (☎912 7330), takes its name seriously and sports barrel tables. Barristers and other young professionals enjoy the town's best pub food (€3.30-10.40), or sit down for an a la carte dinner upstairs from 5:30-10:30pm (€15-22.50). Carvery lunch M-F noon-3pm (€7). Bar food M-F noon-10pm, Sa-Su noon-8pm. ❹

Yellow Pepper, 36 Lower Main St. (☎912 4133), serves savory, sophisticated dishes (stuffed peppers €7.25) in a fragrant yellow interior. Lunch specials (€7.80) change daily, but guarantee at least one vegetarian option. Open M-Sa noon-8:30pm. ❷

 PUBS

McGinley's, 25 Main St. (☎912 1106). Popular student bar in chapel-like upstairs; older-but-still-hip crowd on Victorian ground floor. American bartender blasts his homeland's hip-hop from the top bar Tu nights. W trad at 10:30pm, F-Sa rock and blues.

The Old Orchard Inn, High Rd. (☎912 1615). Despite encroaching popularity of newer establishments, good Ol' Orchard remains the weekend bar of choice, sporting 3 perpetually-packed floors of logwood furniture. Cellar bar hosts occasional trad and other live music (Th-F and Su); upstairs bar defines all things "hep." Bar food daily 12:30-10pm. Disco on the top floor is a local-magnet. Cover €7-8. Disco W-Su until 2am.

Cottage Bar, 42 Main St. (☎912 1338). A kettle on the hearth, artifacts of bygone days on the walls, animated conversation around the bar, and nuns drinking Guinness in the corner. Trad whenever the local band sees fit to show. Open 10:30am-12:30am.

The Cavern, 46 Lower Main St. (☎912 6733; www.thecavern.ie), across from McGinley's, kicks it urban-style with DJs Th-Su. MTV on plasma screens, coffee in the afternoon, and W karaoke keeps you buzzing and entertained all day long. Upstairs, a placid blue bar portrays an equally placid Irish town in stained glass. Open 10:30am-1am.

MONO, next to McGinley's on Main St. (☎917 7911; www.barmono.com). Letterkenny's newest pleasure complex, with 3 action-packed bars. First floor numbs senses with music videos on infinite flat-screen TVs, while the rambunctious practice their moves upstairs. A chiller bar bathed in blue light holds peaceful sway near the dance floor. Tu karaoke, W open mic, Th international charts and techno hits, F-Sa charts disco, Su live alternative rock. 18+. No cover. Open 10:30pm-12:30am, Sa nights 'til 2am.

👁 🏔 SIGHTS AND ACTIVITIES

St. Eunan's Cathedral, perched high above town on Church Ln., looks like the heavenly kingdom when it's lit at night. (Church Ln. is on the right up Main St. away from the bus station.) Proposed as a "resurrection of the fallen shrines of Donegal," the cathedral's construction took 11 years—all years of economic hardship and depression. The story of St. Colmcille is beautifully carved in the arch at the junction of the nave and transept. (☎912 1021. Open daily 8am-5pm, except during Su masses 8-11:15am and 12:30pm. Free.) Across the way, the Church of Ireland's smaller **Parish Church of Conwal** shelters a number of tombstones, some circa 1600. (Su services 8 and 10:30am.)

Renovated during the summer of 1999, the **Donegal County Museum,** High Rd., displays exhibits on all things Donegal. (☎912 4613. Open M-F 10am-12:30pm and 1-4:30pm, Sa 1-4:30pm. Free.) Entering its third year, the **An Grianán Theatre** serves as the primary venue for July's **Earagail Festival** (see p. 404), Co. Donegal's musical, dramatic, comedic, and literary extravaganza (☎074 912 0777; www.donegalculture.com). During the rest of the year, it puts on an eclectic program of music, dance, and visual art. (☎912 0777; www.angrianan.com. Open M-F 9:30am-6pm.)

Those interested in ancient history head to **Grianán Ailigh** (see p. 444) to view the former seat of the ancient Celtic kings. Anglers hook salmon in a number of nearby lakes. Call **Letterkenny Anglers** for more details (☎912 1160). Golfers of all ages perfect their short game at the 18-hole **Letterkenny Pitch & Putt** (☎912 5688 or 912 6000). Those looking to hit the long ball try **Letterkenny Golf Club** (☎912 1150). **Black Horse Stables** (☎915 1327) and **Ashtree Riding Stables** (☎915 3312) have treks and lessons for all experience levels. If horses can't meet the need for speed, rev up at **Letterkenny Indoor/Outdoor Karting Centre** and take to the road a la Mario Andretti. (☎912 9077. Open M-Sa 1-11pm.) Off-road fun abounds at **Letterkenny ATV Co. Ltd.** (☎912 4604). After it all, relax in the sauna, swimming pool, and whirlpool at **Letterkenny Leisure Centre** on High Rd. (☎912 5251).

INISHOWEN PENINSULA

Brochures trumpet the Inishowen as the "crown of Ireland." Indeed, leaving Ireland without visiting this characteristically Donegalian landscape would be a shame. During the week, Inishowen is a relatively unpopulated mosaic of mountains, forests, meadows, and white-sand beaches, including the transcendently beautiful **Malin Head.** Two towns, **Buncrana** and **Carndonagh,** are connected by a winding road that affords sublime views. Sadly, *Let's Go* is not the only organization to have noted these attractive qualities—signs of development abound on the recently untouristed peninsula. Hordes of holiday-makers from Derry and elsewhere in the North rush in on summer weekends, and construction sites for luxury apartments and cottages have cropped up along the coast. Despite all this, the peninsula's attractions merit several days of exploration; visitors traveling by public transportation have no choice but to spend at least this long, and those with cars hardly want to do otherwise.

The nearest Northern Ireland commercial center to Inishowen is Derry. **Lough Swilly Buses** (Derry office ☎028 7126 2017, Buncrana ☎077 61340) runs buses from Derry to points on the Inishowen: Buncrana (35min.; M-Sa 11-13 per day, Su 3 per day; £2.50/€5); Carndonagh (1hr., M-F 5 per day, Sa 3 per day; £4/€7.10); Malin (1hr.; M, W, F 1 per day, Sa 3 per day; £5/€8); Greencastle and Moville (50min., M-Sa 5-6 per day, £3.50/€5.50); and Malin Head (1½hr.; M, W, F 2 per day, Sa 3 per day; £5/€8). Swilly also connects Buncrana directly to Carndonagh (50min.; M-F 4

Inishowen Peninsula

NORTHWEST IRELAND

Hell's Hole • • Banba's Crown
Devil's • • Malin Ballyhillion
Bridge Head • • Portmore Pier
• Wee House of Malin
Slievebane
R242
Knockamany
Bens
Crockalough
Glengad
Head
Five Fingers Strand
Carrickabraghy
Castle
Lagg
Back
Strand
Glengad
Culdaff
Bay Dunmore Head
The Inish Eoghain
100 Scenic Route
Tullagh
Bay
Doagh
Island
Malin
Culdaff
Tremone
Bay
Dunaff
Head
Trawbreaga
Bay
Drumaville
Templemoyle
Kinnagoe
Bay
Ballyliffin
Clonmany
Ballymagaraghy
Lenan
Head
Urris
Raghtin
More Mtn.
Donagh
Cross
Carndonagh
Carrowmena
Inishowen
Head
Shroove
Gap of
Mamore
Effishmore
Gleneely
Craignamaddy
R238
R244
Bredagh Glen
Dunree
Head
Drunfries
Slieve
Snaght
Glentogher
Greencastle
R238
Dunree
Fort
Slieve
Main
Moville
Magilligan
Point
Lough
Swilly
Glenvar
Tullyarvan
Mill
Buncrana
REPUBLIC
OF IRELAND
R240
Whitecastle
Redcastle
Saltpans
R238
Rathmullan
Lisfannon
Grainne's
Gap
Iskaheen
Quigley's
Point
(Carrowkeel)
Lough
Foyle
Fahan
R238
R239
Muff
Inch Island
Burnfoot
Bridgend
A2
Culmore
Eglinton
Airport
Grianán
Ailligh
Derry
NORTHERN
IRELAND
Eglinton

N
LG
0   3 miles
0   3 kilometers

per day, Sa 3 per day), and offers an eight-day "Runabout Ticket" (£20/€32, students £12/€19). **Northwest Buses** (Moville office ☎ 82619) run from Moville through Ballyliffin, Buncrana, Carndonagh, Clonmany, Culdaff, Fahan, and Letterkenny (M-Sa 3 per day, €6.35); Shrove to Derry via Moville (1hr., M-Sa 2 per day, €4.70); Derry to Culdaff (M-Sa 2 per day, €2.50); Moville-Letterkenny express bus (M-Sa 2 per day, €6.35); and Carndonagh to Derry (M-Sa 3-4 per day, €4.70).

Drivers follow the well signposted **Inish Eoghain 100** road that navigates the peninsula's perimeter over the course of almost exactly 100 mi.; hitchers report an easy time finding rides on this road. Ambitious **bikers** enjoy miles of smooth, if sometimes inclined, roads; cycling can be difficult near the **Gap of Mamore,** due to ferocious northwesterly winds and hilly terrain. The map published by the Inishowen Tourism Society, available at the Carndonagh tourist office, and the *Ordnance Survey Discovery Series #3,* help explorers navigate the peninsula; the former is more schematic and easier to read, while the latter provides more detailed topographical information useful for pedestrians.

BUNCRANA (BUN CRANNCHA)   ☎ 077

Long Slieve Snaght looms over Buncrana, at Inishowen's southeastern edge. While not terribly exciting in itself, the town is the peninsula's most common entry point, offering beds and conveniences to northbound explorers. Each July, the town swells with revelers during the **Buncrana Music Festival.**

TRANSPORTATION AND PRACTICAL INFORMATION. The **Swilly Bus Service** (☎61340) at the bus depot in Buncrana travels to: Carndonagh (M-F 6 per day, Sa 3 per day), Derry (M-F 11 per day, Sa 13 per day, Su 3 per day), and Letterkenny (M-F 8:35am, 12:35, and 4:30pm, F also 2:30pm). The **tourist office,** on St. Oran's Dr., a 7min. walk down Main St., dispenses peninsular information, including a book of waymarked hikes. (☎62600; www.irelandnorthwest.ie. Open Tu-W 11am-4pm, Th-F until 5pm, Sa until 3pm.) **AIB,** 8 Market Sq. (☎61087; open M-F 10am-12:30pm and 1:30-4pm, Th until 5pm), and **Bank of Ireland,** Main St. (☎61795; open M-F 10am-4pm, Th until 5pm), have 24hr. **ATMs. ValuClean,** Lower Main St., washes dirty clothes. (☎62570. Laundry from €8. Open M-Sa 9am-6pm.) **E. Tierney Chemist's,** 42 Lower Main St., is the local pharmacy. (☎62412. Open M-F 9:30am-6:30pm, Sa 9:30am-6pm.) **Job Club** on St. Oran's Rd. has **Internet** access. (☎61376. €3 per hr. Open M-F 9am-5pm.) Or, try the **library** on Lower Main St. (☎61941. Surfing free; email €2 per hr., students and children €1. Open Tu and F 10:30am-5:30pm, W and Th until 8pm, Sa 10:30am-12:30pm and 1:30-4pm.) The **post office,** Main St., is also a newsagent. (☎61010. Open M-F 9am-1:15pm and 2:15-5:30pm, Sa 9am-1pm.)

ACCOMMODATIONS, FOOD, AND PUBS. Accommodations in the town center don't exist, but travelers stay nearby in the few but high quality B&Bs off Main St. **Tudor House ❸,** Causeway Rd., off Main St. on the northern end of town, has large rooms with TVs, baths, polished wood cabinets, and lovely pastel duvets. (☎61692. €25, children €12.) Mrs. Anna McCallion's **Ross na Ri House ❸,** at the end of Main St. a left off the Buncrana Rd. after the Tullyarvan Mill, sets off the austere wood-panelled sitting room with bright and airy chambers. (☎936 1271. Singles €30; doubles €46.) **O'Donnell's Supermarket,** also at the north end of Main St., sells sundry staples. (☎61719. Open daily 7am-11pm.) **Food for Thought** sells health food and raw materials for an ethnic feast. (☎63550. Open M-Sa 10am-6pm.) **O'Flaitbeartais** (o-FLAH-her-tees) ❷, Main St., resembles a hunting lodge but attracts a varied crowd for noontime feedings and the town's best trad. (☎61305. Mains €5. Lunch served noon-3pm. W trad.) The black-clad waitresses at **Town Clock Restaurant ❷** contrast with the menu of home-style favorites, from toasties to kebabs. (☎63279. Mains €5. Open daily 8:15am-9pm.) **West End Bar,** Upper Main St. (☎61564), has a copper bar that shines like a lucky penny, unlike the low-lit lounge in back. The mostly-local crowd arrives on weekends around 10pm.

SIGHTS AND ACTIVITES. Buncrana's primary attractions stretch along the river north of the town. Behind a youth activity center, peaceful, pretty **Swan Park** is overlooked by two castles: stately Queen Anne-era **Buncrana Castle,** where Wolfe Tone was imprisoned after the French "invasion" of 1798 failed (see **Rebellion,** p. 61), and the 1430 **O'Doherty Keep,** a castle that resembles a derelict mansion. Both are closed to the public. To reach the park, walk up Main St. toward the shorefront and follow Castle Ave. from the roundabout next to the West End Bar and Cinema. The park is beyond the Castle Bridge, which arcs 100 yd. to the right. A **coastal walk** begins at Castle Bridge, passes the keep, turns left at the castle, and ascends the hill. **Ned's Point Fort,** also along the coast, built in 1812, seems jarringly modern. The path passes **Porthaw Bay** and culminates in sandy **Sragill Strand. Friar Hegarty's Rock,** beyond the beach, witnessed the friar's murder during Penal times.

Outside the northern edge of the park on Dunree Rd. (a continuation of Main St.) is the community-owned and operated **Tullyarvan Mill.** This renovated corn mill presents a mixture of exhibits on textile history, tracing Buncrana's transition from hand-weaving in 1739 to Fruit-of-the-Looming in 1999. The mill also houses a **craft shop** and **coffee shop,** and its riverside benches make a nice spot for picnics. (☎ 61613. Open M-Sa 10am-5pm.) **Inishowen Geneaology Centre,** Alleach Rd. along the shorefront, draws on a multitude of documents from Co. Donegal and Derry to find long lost roots. (☎ 63998. Open 9am-6pm though unorthodox hours can be arranged with a phone call.) **Buncrana Leisure Centre** keeps kids and others entertained with swimming and tennis (☎ 61000. M, W, F 9am-10pm; Tu and Th 7:45am-10pm; F 9am-10pm; Sa 10am-10pm; Su 10am-10pm, last admission 1 hr. before closing.) Those looking to golf head to the **Buncrana Golf Club** for a relaxing 9-hole game or four. (☎ 20749. Open Tu-Su 8:30am-12:30pm and 2-6pm.)

⬧ DAYTRIP FROM BUNCRANA

GRIANÁN AILIGH. At the bottom of the peninsula, 10 mi. south of Buncrana and 3 mi. west of Derry (see p. 544), the hilltop ringfort Grianán Ailigh (GREEN-in ALL-ya) is an excellent place to start or finish a tour of Inishowen. This site—which provides 360° views of the surrounding countryside—has been a cultural center for at least 4000 years: first as a Druidic temple at the grave site of Aedh, son of The Dagda, divine king of the Túatha De Dannan; then as a seat of power for the northern branch of the Uí Néill clan, who ruled Ulster and moved here after their chieftain married Princess Aileach of Scotland; and finally as a Mass rock for secret Catholic worship during Penal times. Much of the present stone structure is a 19th-century reconstruction, but the bottom section of the circular wall is original. Beyond the fort, a cross marks a **healing well**, holy since pre-Christian times and supposedly blessed by St. Patrick.

Grianán Ailigh is just west of the junction of R238 and N16; the 300-year-old **Burt Woods** grow alongside. From Buncrana, follow the Inish Eoghian 100 south to Burnfoot, continue onto Bridgend, and follow the signs to Burt Woods; the ringfort is a mile to the southeast. To reach the fort from Letterkenny, follow N13 past the turnoff for R265 and R237, and follow the signs that point the way. Two miles down N13 from Bridgend is the Catholic **Burt Circular Chapel,** a replica of the ancient fort. To reach the fort from the Chapel, take the 2 mi. road to the top of the hill. Past the Chapel is the **Grianán Ailigh Heritage Centre,** inside a former Church of Ireland. The center prepares visitors for the 2 mi. journey with mind-bending displays of wax figures, garbled commentary about the fort, and Irish food from its **cafe.** (☎ 077 68000; www.grianailigh.ie. Lunch specials €7; served noon-3pm. Restaurant open daily noon-10pm. Center open May-Oct. 10am-6pm; Nov.-Apr. 10am-4pm. €3.50, children €3. Site admission free.) **Swilly buses** (☎ 074 952 2373) pass on Derry-Buncrana and Derry-Letterkenny routes. Ask to stop at the visitor's center.

WESTERN INISHOWEN

From Buncrana, the Inish Eoghain 100 runs through Dunree Head and the Mamore Gap, while R238 cuts through the interior directly to Clonmany and Ballyliffin. Spectacular beaches, marvelous mountainsides, and complete isolation await the traveler who dares venture this deep into the peninsula.

DUNREE HEAD AND THE MAMORE GAP   ☎ 077

Fort Dunree and the Mamore Gap were the last areas of the Republic occupied by the British, who handed over the fort keys to the Irish army in 1938. **Dunree Head** juts into Lough Swilly 6 mi. northwest of Buncrana. Peaks rise against the ocean, buffered by the occasional bend of sandy, smooth beach. At the tip of the head, **Fort Dunree** hides in the jagged sea cliffs. Today the fort holds a military museum and is a superb vantage point for admiring the sea-carved landscapes of the Inishowen and Fanad peninsulas. One of the six **Guns of Dunree,** built during the 1798 Rebellion to defend Lough Swilly against Napoleonic invaders, is among the museum's displayed weaponry. The exhibits also include copies of German Intelligence maps of the Inishowen from WWII. The fort's location overlooking the lough is a boon for birdwatchers. (Open June-Sept. M-Sa 10:30am-6pm, Su 1-6pm; Oct.-May M-F 10:30am-4:30pm, Sa-Su 1-6pm. Fort and walks €4, students €2.)

Farther north along the Inish Eoghain 100 toward Clonmany, a sign points left up a hill to the edge of the **Mamore Gap**. Eighty feet above sea level, the pass meanders between Mamore Hill and Urris. The pass's eastern face affords otherworldly views over the mountains to the Atlantic. The sharply inclined road through proves difficult but worthwhile for hikers and cyclists. It's only a 30min. climb uphill; most bikers are forced to walk. Driving is easier, although the hairpin turns over the sea are sometimes quite frightening. Queen Mebdh of Connacht, Cú Chulainn's diva archenemy (see **Legends and Folktales**, p. 73), is supposedly buried here—and at Knocknarea, Co. Sligo, and a few other places.

The road descends from the gap onto wave-scoured northern beaches. The Inish Eoghain 100 proceeds to **Urris, Lenan Head**, and inviting **Lenan Strand**. Once known for its prodigious—even for Donegal—*poitín* production (See **Love Poitín #9**, p. 418), Urris was the last area in Inishowen to relinquish spoken Irish. The subdivided flat-bed farms along the road reveal the enduring influence of Famine-era farming practices. Heading north, the road passes over **Dunaff Head**, through **Rockstown Harbour**, and ends at a stunning beach, the aforementioned Lenan Strand.

CLONMANY, BALLYLIFFIN, AND DOAGH ISLAND   ☎074

North of the Gap, the two tiny villages of **Clonmany** (*Cluain Maine*) and **Ballyliffin** (*Baile Lifin*) are separated by a single mile. Travelers with the resources to hire a car and stay in a B&B find them a restful spot to spend a night; Ballyliffin has plenty of beds and long sandy strands, while Clonmany provides the pubs.

Ballyliffin's highlights are its three long miles of golden sands on **Pollen Strand** and its world-famous **golf course;** Nick Faldo and Fred Daly are among the many pros who have played the greens of the **Ballylifin Golf Club**. Grassy dunes connect the village with **Doagh Island**, where **Carricksbrahy Castle**, a former seat of the Mac-Faul and O'Donnell clans, is a wave-battered ruin at the end of a 2½ mi. beach walk. Area signs point to Doagh Island and the **Doagh Visitors Centre**, which houses a collection of makeshift exhibits discussing poverty and starvation in Ireland. (☎937 8078. Open Easter-Sept. daily 10am-5:30pm. Admission includes tea and guided tour. Tours every 45min. €5, children €3.50.)

Many of the golfers visiting Ballyliffin stay at ⬛**Rossaor House** ❹, near the entrance to town. Though more expensive than other B&Bs, Rossaor pampers guests with a garden, fantastic views of the Strand and Malin Head, and smoked salmon and scrambled egg breakfasts. (☎937 6498; www.ballyliffin.com/rossaor.htm. Singles €45; doubles €70.) Alternatively, wanderers stay in the spacious, well-furnished rooms of **Castlelawn House** ❸, behind Strand Hotel. (☎937 6600. All rooms with bath and TV. €30-33; singles €45.) Though no individual restaurants exist in Ballyliffin, several of the hotels host decent meal deals on certain nights. **The Strand Hotel** ❸ feeds the hungry on Monday and Wednesday nights with a five-course dinner for two (€13.95 per person). **The Ballyliffin Hotel** ❸ offers the same deal on Tuesday and Thursday nights. In Clonmany, the best and possibly only bet for a bite is **Village Diner** ❷, an unrepentant chipper and takeaway with an all-day Irish breakfast for €5. (☎78887. Open M-W 9am-10pm, Th 9am-10:30pm, F and Su 9am-midnight, Sa 9am-1:30am.) Weekend country music and occasional trad fill the air in and around **McFeeley's**, on Main St. (☎937 6122. Open 1pm-midnight.) Bright red and bustling **Briney's Bar,** across from McFeeley's (☎937 6415), has a beer garden, weekend live music, and summer barbeques. During the first full weekend in August, all the pubs in the Square are saturated with trad for the **Clonmany Festival**. (Contact Hugo Boyce ☎937 6477; www.clonmany.com.)

NORTHERN INISHOWEN

From the southeastern coast, R240 cuts straight up the middle of the peninsula to commercial Carndonagh, an important stocking-up point. North of Carndonagh, R238 veers east to Culdaff. Going north on R242 leads to Malin Head, the northernmost tip of the island. The northern half of the Peninsula is the most friendly to budget travelers, containing the largest tracts of unspoiled scenery and the region's only hostels, all of which happen to be superlative.

CARNDONAGH (CARN DOMHNACH)   ☎ 074

Two miles south of Trawbreaga Bay, Carndonagh (known locally as "Carn") is Inishowen's main market town—the peninsula's farmers swarm here on alternate Mondays to hawk their hoofed creatures. Predictably, commercial Carn has but one sight to offer: the old Church of Ireland that hulks 10min. down Bridge St. Outside its walls, **Donagh Cross**, a 7th-century Celtic cross, is the sole remnant of the monastery founded by St. Patrick when he brought Christianity to the peninsula. Two shorter pillars flank the cross: one depicts David playing his harp, and the other displays Christ's crucifixion. The **church's bell** supposedly came from the Spanish Armada ship *Trinidad de Valoencera*, which went down in **Kinnagoe Bay.**

Carn Cabs, the Diamond (☎74580), provides taxis for late-night jaunts. **McCallion's Cycle Hire**, 3 mi. from town on the Ballyliffin Rd., collects and delivers bikes anywhere on the peninsula. (☎74084. €9 per day, €40 per wk.) **Inishowen Tourism**, Chapel St., off the Diamond, is non-Bord Fáilte approved, but books accommodations and provides limited info. (☎74933; www.visitinishowen.com. Open Sept.-May M-Th 9am-5:30pm, F 9am-4:30pm; June-Aug. also Sa-Su 11am-4pm.) **AIB**, the Diamond, is the only bank in town with a 24hr. **ATM.** (☎74388. Open M-F 10am-12:30pm, 1:30-4pm; M until 5pm.) Headed out of town from the Diamond on the Moville road, **The Book Shop** sells used books, with a huge selection for Irish history enthusiasts. (☎389 086 or 607 6905. Open M-Tu and Th-Su 2-6pm.) **ValuClean**, Bridge St., washes and dries for €5.40. (☎74150. Open M-Sa 9am-6pm.) **McAteer's**, the Diamond, is the local **pharmacy.** (☎74120. Open M-Sa 10am-6pm.) **Internet** is at the modern **library** past Arch Bar in the Council Services building on Malin St. (Surfing free for members; email €1, adults €2 per hr.) The **post office** meters mail on Bridge St. (☎74101. Open M-F 9:30am-1:30pm, 2:30-5:30pm; Sa 9:30am-1pm.)

Less than a 5min. walk from the Diamond, Chapel St. becomes Millbrae as it passes **Dunshenny House B&B ❸**, where dainty-flowered wallpaper sets a dainty-flowered mood. (☎74292. All rooms with bath. Coffee- and tea-making facilities. Singles €30; shared rooms €25.) Down Chapel St. from the church, the house of **Oregon B&B ❷** has stood since 1911; except for a few modern fixtures, the antique rooms haven't changed much. (☎74113. Shared rooms €21.) **G&S Coscutters,** in Cardonagh Shopping Centre on Bridge St., stocks an array of food. (☎74124. Open M-Sa 9am-9pm, Su 10am-7pm.) **Sandwich Mill ❶** at **Arch Inn**, the Diamond, sells sandwiches on baps, panini, and ciabatta, all under €4. (☎73029. Open M-Sa 10:30am-6pm.) **The Quiet Lady,** Main Rd., gets noisy at night when she plays hits for a local crowd of fancy-footers. During the day she has filling meals. (☎74777. Roasted meats and vegetables €5. Food served 10:30am-9pm. F karaoke.)

CULDAFF (CÚI DAPBHCHA). The area around Culdaff on the eastern side of the peninsula holds a variety of ancient monuments. The "Bronze Age triangle" above Bocan Parochial House, a mile from Culdaff toward Moville, includes the **Bocan Stone Circle, Temple of Deen,** and **Kindroyhead** with evidence of a prehistoric field and fort system. A 12 ft. **high cross** stands next to **Cloncha Church,** a signposted 1½ mi. from Culdaff toward Moville. The village hosts the annual **Charles Macklin Festival** (☎937 9104), the second weekend in October, with performances of the 17th-century playwright's plays, poetry competitions, and a slew of trad sessions.

Culdaff Strand, a short walk east, is the darling of Inishowen beaches and best seen at daybreak or dusk. Those who want to spend the night find upscale lodging with a jovial air at ◪**McGrory's** ❹, a comfort-laden, family-run guesthouse with exposed stone walls and rustic wood furniture. (☎937 9104; www.mcgrorys.ie. Singles €50-60; shared rooms €45-50. Call for special deals.)

MALIN HEAD (CIONN MÁLAINN)   ☎077

Inishowen's most popular attraction is Malin Head, Ireland's northernmost peninsula. Aside from its latitude, the stretch is remarkable for its rocky, wave-tattered coast and sky-high sand dunes, reputedly the highest in Europe. Inish Eoghain 100 continues east from Cardonagh to Malin Head, passing through the tiny, tidy town of **Malin** on its way. Five miles from Culdaff, R242 coincides with the Inish Eoghain 100 and winds toward Lagg, where the five standing rocks of **Five Fingers Strand** jut into the ocean. The water, though tempting, is icy cold and dangerous. Turn left above the little, white church and look for the signs. High above the beach, the **Knockamany Bens** provide fantastic views of the whole peninsula and even Tory Island on a clear day. Meteorologists have repeatedly recorded Malin Head as the ◪**sunniest spot in Ireland.** Yes, sunshine and Ireland can coexist.

The scattered town of **Malin Head** includes **Bamba's Crown**, a tooth of dark rock rising from the ocean spray, noteworthy for being the peninsula's northernmost tip. Until the 19th century, Malin Head was the site of an annual pilgrimage in which young men and women "frisked and played in the water all stark naked" to celebrate the sea god's affair with the goddess of the land. On a clear day, the Head offers a view of Scotland, and perhaps an opportunity to hear the call of the **corncrake,** a near-extinct bird indigenous to the area. Written in white-washed stones on a nearby lower cliff, and legible from thousands of feet above, "S. S. EIRE" (*Saor Stát Éire*; "Irish Free State") identified Ireland as neutral territory to Nazi would-be bombers. People have removed many of the stones to announce their own identities, but "EIRE" is still intact. A path to the left of the carpark skirts the cliff face and leads to **Hell's Hole,** a 250 ft. chasm that roars with the incoming tide. Farther down the coast is the (super) naturally formed **Devil's Bridge.** The ◪**raised beaches** around Malin Head, the result of glaciers that ripped through the region millions of years ago, are covered with semi-precious stones; walkers sifting through the sands may find jasper, quartz, small opals, or amethysts. The **Atlantic Circle** is a 5 mi. circuit of the Inish Eoghain 100 that tours the peninsula's tip.

The area around Malin Head teems with affordable accommodations. To reach ◪**Sandrock Holiday Hostel (IHO/IHH)** ❶, Port Ronan Pier, take the left fork off the Inish Eoghain 100, before Crossroads Inn (also a bus stop). On the water with potential opportunities to see passing seals and dolphins, the hostel also boasts an extensive movie collection and musical instruments for impromptu jam sessions. (☎937 0289; www.inishowenonline.com/sandrock. **Bike rental** €9 per day. Sheets €1.25. Laundry wash €4, dry €2. 10-bed dorms €10.) Five miles past Malin on the way into Malin Head, ◪**Druin Doo B&B** ❷ has standard rooms and a wonderful wooden loft for the weary. (☎937 0287; www.angelfire.com/me5/druimdoo/index.html. €24.) On the Inish Eoghain 100, after the phone booth across from the post office, **Malin Head Hostel (IHO/IHH)** ❶ welcomes guests with an open fire, reflexology (€35), aromatherapy (€45), and fresh, cheap veggies from Mary's garden. (☎937 0309. **Bike rental** €9 per day. Wash €3.50, dry €2.50. 5-bed dorms €12; doubles €30.) Both Malin Head and Sandrock hostel provide **bike rental** from **McCallion's Cycle Hire** in Carn. (☎937 4084. €9 per day.)

All of Malin Head's pubs have licensed fishermen's late hours and sell groceries. Country-rock, fishing tackle, and revitalizing brew are found at **Farren's,** Ireland's northernmost pub. (☎937 0128. Music nightly July-Aug.) **Seaview Tavern and Restau-**

rant, commonly called "Vera Dock's" after long-gone owners, pours pints beneath shelves of corn flakes and motor oil. (☎937 0117. Open 8am-1am.) The **restaurant** ❷ serves local seafood and takeaway. (Food from €6.30; served 10am-9:15pm.)

EASTERN INISHOWEN

Though overshadowed by its northern neighbor Malin Head, **Inishowen Head** draws hundreds of beach-bathers to the natural beauty of its **Shroove Strand.** On the northernmost beaches, which look over Lough Foyle, small crowds gather on the handful of hot days in an Irish summer. A delightful "shore walk" runs about 6 mi. between the small thumb of Inishowen Head through Greencastle and Moville. Any local can direct shore-explorers to **Port a Doris,** a delightful little cove accessible only at low tide and littered with semi-precious Shroove pebbles. **Tunn's Bank,** a huge sandbank a few hundred yards offshore, is reputedly the resting place of Manannan McLir, the Irish sea god whose children were turned into swans.

MOVILLE AND GREENCASTLE ☎074

Tiny Moville *(Bun an Phobail)* straddles the intersection of R239 (from Derry) and R238 (from Culdaff). Even smaller Greencastle *(An Caislean Nua)* hides 3 mi. north along R239. During the summer, both towns are swamped with upscale Derryites searching for the beach and a game of golf.

⁊ PRACTICAL INFORMATION. Though there's no tourist office, the **library,** in the back corner of the carpark next to Susie's Bar, has free material on the peninsula. The car park also contains a sign with information from a practical and historical perspective. In Moville, an **AIB** with a 24hr. **ATM** is on Main St. (☎82050. Open Tu-F 10am-12:30pm and 1:30-4pm, M until 5pm.) **Ulster Bank,** Main St., also has a 24hr. cash box. **Foyle's,** Main St., works it as only a **pharmacy** can. (☎82929. Open M-Sa 9:30am-6pm.) Surf the **Internet** for free at the **library** with a membership (free and easy to obtain in Donegal), or check email for a small fee (€2 per hr., students €1). Book 1hr. session in advance. (☎918 5110. Open Tu 2-4:30pm and 5-8pm, W-Th 10:30-12:30pm and 1:30-5:30pm, Sa 10:30-2pm.) The **post office** is on Malin Rd. where it intersects Main St. (☎82016. Open M-F 9am-1pm and 2-5:30pm, Sa 9am-1pm.) **McLaughlin's taxi** (☎938 1500) is a call away for sojourners.

⁊⬛⬛ ACCOMMODATIONS, FOOD, AND PUBS. For a good night's rest, try Mrs. McGuinness's **Dunroman B&B ❸,** off the Derry road across from the football field, where breakfast is served in a sunny conservatory overlooking the River Foyle. A choice of green, blue, or peach bedrooms complete the splendid setting. (☎82234. Singles €30; shared rooms €25 per person.) **Mace Grocery,** Main St., sells groceries, oddly enough. (☎82045. Open daily 7am-9pm.) The local budget traveler's haven, **Barron's Cafe ❷,** Main St., serves heaps of food cooked in the kitchen of the family house behind the storefront. (☎82472. All-day breakfast €5, burgers around €3, mains €5-11. Open daily 9:30am-8pm.) Everyone keeps time to the music at the **Town Clock Pub,** in the car park on Main St. The high vaulted ceilings and light wood interior lend a decidedly light mood to the traditional Irish pub motif...or maybe it's just the Guinness. DJ plays top-40 hits on Friday and Saturday nights. (☎85815. Bar menu items €3.50-5.25. More substantial fare of the grilled meat persuasion €8.95-11.95. Open daily noon-11pm.) **Eggman's,** on Main St., sports benches and tables low enough for the wee people, but gathers an older local crowd in its front rooms and a younger set in back. (☎82183. Open M-W 10:30am-11:30pm, Th-Sa 10:30am-12:30am, Su 12:30-11pm. F-Su disco; no cover.)

From Inishowen Head, the road leads south to **Greencastle,** a village that throws some spice (or sea salt, at least) into the one-street Irish-village mix as the main drag is situated along the shoreline. Even beyond that, its blue flag **Stroove Strand** pulls visitors to the end of the peninsula. Travelers on the go welcome Greencastle's newest addition, **Lough Foyle Ferry Co.'s** frequent service from the town's dock to Magilligan, on Northern Ireland's Antrim Coast. (☎81901; info@loughfoyle-ferry.com. 15min.; every 20min. April-Sept. 7:20am-9:50pm, Su 9am-9:50pm; Oct-Mar. 7:20am-7:50pm, Su 9am-7:50pm; €1.60, children €0.80, with car €8.) Greencastle's **castle,** built by the Red Earl of Ulster, is now an ivy-covered ruin. The Irish government maintains a training center for professional fisherfolk next to the ruins. Relics of life on the seas are in the spotlight at the **Greencastle Maritime Museum** on the shorefront. Housed in an old coast guard station, the museum's impressive collection includes a traditional but newly built Fanad *curragh,* an Armada room, ship models, photographs, and a 19th-century rocket cart for rescuing passengers of wrecked ships. The brand new **planetarium** has daily laser light shows covering a breadth of subjects, from the cosmos to a more local Irish-themed laser show set to traditional music. (☎81363. Open Apr.-Nov. M-Sa 10am-6pm, Su noon-6pm; call ahead for off season hours. €4; students, seniors, and children €2; family €10. Combined museum-planetarium pass €8/€4/€20. Hourly laser light shows 1-5pm; included in museum admission.)

In a secluded mansion overlooking Lough Foyle, Mrs. Anna Wright warmly welcomes guests to the high-ceilinged, aristocratic **Manor House ❸.** From Main St., head out of town toward the castle. Turn right at the first gravel drive after the town, follow it to the end, and make a right at the signs for the B&B. (☎81010. €30.) Next to the Maritime Museum, the **Brooklyn Cottage ❸** is a modest but intimate whitewashed house with two bedrooms and a wall-to-wall loughview from its magnificent glass conservatory. (☎81087. Open Mar.-Nov. Singles €32.50; doubles €55.) To satisfy fresh fish cravings, head to **Wild Atlantic Salmon,** next to the Maritime Museum, where a whole salmon is about €3.65 per lb. (☎81605. Open M-F 8:30am-5pm.) For the lazily-inclined, **Seamy's Fish and Chips ❸** serves fried fish from its spic 'n' span kitchen, behind an inviting neo-Georgian storefront. (☎81379. All meals under €4. Open M-F noon-1am, Sa-Su 2pm-midnight.) Up the street from the Maritime Museum past the ferry terminal and next to Seamy's, the **Ferryport Bar** is a second home for most of the youth in Greencastle (☎81296. Summer Th-Su chart or trad music. Open M-W 11am-11:30pm, Th-Sa 11am-12:30am, Su 'til 11pm.) **The Drunken Duck** (☎81362), 3 mi. north of Greencastle toward Stroove Strand, may look like the home of a duck enthusiast, but it's really a friendly pub named for a local woman whose beer leaked into her poultry troughs.

NORTHERN
IRELAND

Northern Ireland. The very name conjures images of a violent, and perhaps oppressive society, not unlike Beirut of the past. The calm tenor of everyday life in Northern Ireland has been overshadowed by media headlines screaming about riots and bombs. But acts of violence and extremist fringe groups are less visible than many might expect. There are, however, many observable divisions in civil society, with Protestants and Catholics usually living in separate neighborhoods, attending separate schools, stores, and pubs, and even playing different sports.

The split is sometimes hard for an outsider to discern, especially in rural vacation spots. On the other hand, it would be nearly impossible for a visitor to leave Northern Ireland without seeing curbs in cities and villages painted with the colors of their residents' identity. The 1998 Good Friday Agreement, an attempt to lead Northern Ireland out of its struggles, has itself been an endeavor. It continues to be a bumpy road to peace and greater autonomy. The Assembly, in Sormont in Belfast, has been suspended on a number of occasions and the lack of progress on various emotive issues continues to frustrate. London has had to take the reins again, while all sides have renewed their efforts to make their contry as peaceful as it is beautiful. And Northern Ireland is beautiful.

Fising villages dot the strands of the Ards Peninsula, leading to the rounded peaks of the Mournes and the National Park retreats of Newcastle. To the west lie the easily-accessible Sperrin Mountains and the tidy-walled farms of the Fermanagh Lake District. Industrial Enniskillen rests just north, though travelers would do well to continue onward to Derry/Londonderry, a city rich in both political and historical significance. Nearby lies the Giant's Causeway, a volcanic staircase that extends out into the Atlantic. Hillside forts and castles loom on the cliffs above. On the way to the vibrant nightlife of Belfast you'll pass through the waterfalls and valleys of the glorious Glens of Antrim.

LIFE AND TIMES

MONEY

Legal tender in Northern Ireland is the British pound. Northern Ireland has its own bank notes, which are identical in value to English and Scottish notes of the same denominations but not accepted outside Northern Ireland. Both English and Scottish notes, however, are accepted in the North.

Euros are generally not accepted in the North, with the exception of some border towns which will calculate the exchange rate and add an additional surcharge. UK coins come in denominations of 1p, 2p, 5p, 10p, 20p, 50p, and £1. Most banks are closed on Saturday, Sunday, and all public holidays. On "bank holidays," occurring several times a year in both countries, most businesses shut down. Usual weekday bank hours in Northern Ireland are M-F 9:30am to 4:30pm.

For more comprehensive travel information, see **Essentials**, p. 8.

AUS$1 = £0.35		£1 = AUS$2.73
CDN$1 =£0.42		£1 = CDN$2.18
NZ$1 = £0.30		£1 = NZ$3.34
ZAR1=£0.09		£1 = ZAR11.74
US$1 = £0.71		£1 = US$1.42
€1= £0.62		1 = €1.61

BRITISH POUND

> The information in this book was researched in the summer of 2003. Inflation and the Invisible Hand may raise or lower the listed prices by as much as 20%. You can find up-to-date exchange rate information in major newspapers or on the web at www.oanda.com.

NORTHERN IRELAND

SAFETY AND SECURITY

Much work has taken place within Northern Ireland in the past years to overcome these difficulties and the turmoil is certainly not what it was previously. Although sectarian violence is dramatically less common than in the height of the Troubles, some neighborhoods and towns still experience unrest during sensitive political times. It's best to remain alert and cautious while traveling in Northern Ireland, especially during **Marching Season,** which reaches its height July 4-12. The 12th of August, when the **Apprentice Boys** march in Derry/Londonderry, is also a testy period when urban areas should be traversed with much circumspection. The most common form of violence is property damage, and tourists are unlikely targets (beware of leaving a car unsupervised, however, if it bears a Republic of Ireland license plate). In general, if traveling in Northern Ireland during marching season, be prepared for transport delays, and for some shops and services to be closed. Vacation areas like the Glens and the Causeway Coast are less affected by the parades. In general, use common sense in conversation and, as in dealing with any issues of a different culture, be respectful of locals' religious and political perspectives. Overall, Northern Ireland has one of the lowest tourist-related crime rates in the world.

Border checkpoints have been removed, and armed soldiers and vehicles are less visible in Belfast and Derry. Do not take **photographs** of soldiers, military installations, or vehicles; the film will be confiscated and you may be detained for questioning. Taking pictures of political murals is not a crime, although many people feel uncomfortable doing so in residential neighborhoods. Unattended luggage is always considered supicious and worthy of confiscaiton. It is generally unsafe to hitch in Northern Ireland. *Let's Go* never recommends hitchhiking.

> Northern Ireland is reached by using the UK **country code 44;** from the Republic dial **048.** The **phone code** for every town in the North is **028.**

HISTORY AND POLITICS

Ireland has had a turbulent history, and this is especially true of Northern Ireland. The people of Northern Ireland have remained steadfast in their determination to retain their individual cutural and political identities, even at the cost of lasting peace. Many continue to defend the lines that define their differences, whether ideological divisions across the chambers of Parliament or actual streets marking the end of one culture and the beginning of the next. Generally, the 950,000 Protes-

NORTHERN IRELAND

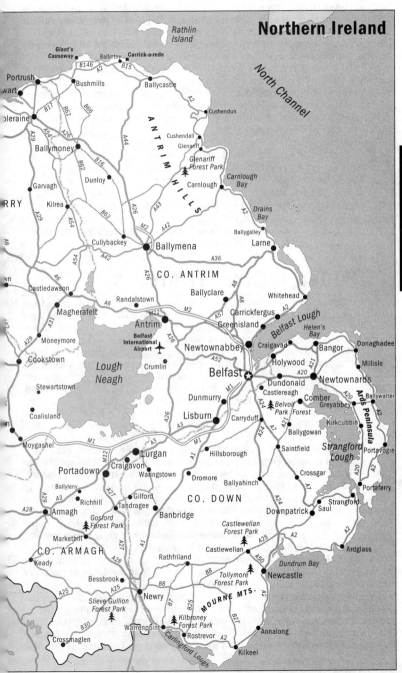

Northern Ireland

Rathlin Island

North Channel

Giant's Causeway • Ballintoy • Carrick-a-rede
Portrush
wart
Bushmills • Ballycastle
• Cushendun
oleraine
Cushendall
Ballymoney • Glenariff
Glenariff Forest Park
Garvagh • Dunloy • Carnlough Bay
Kilrea • Carnlough
RRY
Drains Bay
Cullybackey • Ballymena • Ballygalley
vn • Larne
Castledawson
Magherafelt • Randalstown • CO. ANTRIM
Antrim • Ballyclare
Moneymore • Belfast International Airport • Carrickfergus • Whitehead
Cookstown • Newtownabbey • Greenisland • Belfast Lough
Stewartstown • Crumlin • Craigavad • Helen's Bay
Lough Neagh • Belfast • Holywood • Bangor • Donaghadee
Coalisland • Dundonald • Newtownards • Millisle
Dunmurry • Castlereagh • Comber • Ballywalter
Moygashel • Lisburn • Belvoir Park Forest • Greyabbey
Lurgan • Carryduff • Ballygowan • Kirkcubbin
Portadown • Craigavon • Waringstown • Ballyahinch • Saintfield • Strangford Lough • Portavogie
Ballyleny • Dromore • Crossgar • Portaferry
Richhill • Gilford • Tandragee • Banbridge • CO. DOWN • Strangford
Armagh • Gosford Forest Park • Downpatrick • Saul
Markethill • Castlewellan Forest Park • Ardglass
CO. ARMAGH • Castlewellan • Dundrum Bay
Keady • Rathfriland • Newcastle
Bessbrook • Tollymore Forest Park
Slieve Gullion Forest Park • Newry • MOURNE MTS. • Annalong
Crossmaglen • Kilbroney Forest Park
Warrenpoint • Rostrevor • Kilkeel
Carlingford Lough

NORTHERN IRELAND

tants are **Unionists,** who want the six counties of Northern Ireland to remain in the UK; the 650,000 Catholics tend to identify with the Republic of Ireland, not Britain, and many are **Nationalists,** who want the six counties to be part of the Republic. The more extreme, and generally working class, on either side are known as **Loyalists** and **Republicans,** respectively, groups who tend to prefer defending their turf with rocks and petrol bombs. In 1998, the world felt a stirring of optimism with the signing of the Good Friday Peace Accord and subsequent opening of the Assembly in Belfast, but continued tensions over disarmament of extremist factions and recent political victories by hardliners have kept peace just out of reach.

For more information about Ireland before the break between the North and South in 1920, see **Life and Times,** p. 56.

> The history of Northern Ireland is complex and controversial. In composing this brief history, we have tried to remain neutral and report only facts and significant events. However, each side tells a different version of the events, neither of which is less valid. This makes for a sharp edge that we have tried to walk. We encourage all to read more on Northern Ireland from both perspectives. Some excellent works are *Hope against History: the Course of Conflict in Northern Ireland* by Jack Holland and *The Narrow Ground: Aspects of Ulster, 1609-1969* by A.T.Q. Stewart. Online, CAIN (Conflict Archive on the INternet) http://cain.ulst.ac.uk/.

A DIVIDED ISLAND: IT STARTS

The first human residents of the province of Ulster came over a land bridge from Scotland in the Mesolithic period. It existed largely in a clan system, with wars breaking out between clans as the population grew. This all began to change when St. Patrick arrived in what is now Northern Ireland in 432, bringing Christianity with him. Ireland evolved into a system of High Kings, Brian Ború being the most famous, but the real struggles began with the arrival of the Normans in 1116. Over the next six decades a steady stream of British and Norman invaders waged war for control of the island. In 1171 the English King Henry II arrived, heralding the involvement of England in Ireland's affairs. During the following centuries the English would take control of Ireland, with King Henry VIII declaring himself King of Ireland in 1541. The Irish rose up on various occasions, often siding with England's enemies, the French and Spanish. This encouraged King James I to begin a series of plantations in six of the nine counties of **Ulster.** English law was enforced throughout Ireland from 1603 and, although various parts of Ireland had been settled previously, the Scottish settlers were "planted" in the Ards Peninsula area of Ulster in large numbers from 1606 onwards. In 1641, 59% of Ireland's land was owned by Catholics, who formed the majority of the native Irish, but by 1688 this was down to 22%, and reduced to 7% by 1714. Two of the main events commemorated by Protestants in Northern Ireland took place during this period, although neither was actually of great significance in the struggle. In 1688 the gates of walled Derry/Londonderry shut against the troops of Catholic James II (commemorated each August by the **Apprentice Boys of Derry**), while in 1690 William III defeated James II at the **Battle of the Boyne** (commemorated in July by the **Orange Order**).

Over the following two centuries, many merchants and wolking-class immigrants from nearby Scotland settled in northeast Ulster. Institutionalized religious discrimination may have limited Catholic access to land ownership and other basic rights, but made it also made Northern Ireland quite an attractive destination for Scots Protestants, who profited from the cheap land options. The British

EARLY EMIGRATION The Scots Irish, as they are called in the US, descended from settlers on the Ulster plantation. In Northern Ireland, Protestants affectionately refer to this group as the Ulster-Scots. It is also a matter of tremendous pride that 5 of the US's early presidents were Ulster-Scots. The most famous was President Buchanan, who said "My Ulster blood is my most priceless heritage."

brought the smokestacks of progress to Counties Antrim and Down while the rest of the island remained agrian. By the end of the 19th century, Belfast was a booming industrial center with thriving textile mills and ship-building factories, most of which refused to hire Catholic workers.

Yet, as in present-day Northern Ireland, the division between Protestants and Catholics had much gray area. Despite tremendous discrimination against Catholics, it is actually **Wolfe Tone**, a Protestant Presbyterian, who is considered the Father of Republicanism. He founded the **Society of United Irishmen,** a predecessor of the modern IRA, in Belfast during 1791; the Orange Order was formed in County Armagh in 1795. The following year, the first march commemorating the Battle of the Boyne occured. In 1798 Wolfe Tone instigated an uprising.

In the late 19th century, Republicanism continued to develop in pockets in the south, resulting in the formation of **Sinn Fein** under Arthur Griffith in 1905. The picture looked very different in the Northeast. During its 300-year tenure, the Ulster Plantation had created a working- and middle-class population in Ulster that identified with the British Empire and did not support Irish Home Rule. The **Orange Order's** local lodges served to provide structure to Protestant struggle against Home Rule. The Order's constituency and radicalism continued to grow despite legislative disapproval—it quietly gained momentum, culminating in its explosive opposition to the first **Home Rule Bill in 1886.**

Lawyer and politician **Edward Carson,** with trusty sidekick **James Craig,** advocated against Home Rule and sought to make the British elite better understand the arguments against it. In 1912, when Home Rule seemed more likely, Carson held a mass meeting, and approximately 447,000 Unionists signed the **Ulster Covenant of Resistance to Home Rule.** Home Rule continued to appear even more likely, so the **Ulster Volunteer Force** was formed and armed itself by smuggling guns in through Larne in 1913. This act prompted the formation of the **Irish Citizen Army** and the **Irish National Volunteers,** who in turn armed themselves by sneaking their own guns in through Howth. As Ireland, and what would become Northern Ireland in particular, raced towards armed conflict, WWI began.

Two days after the guns arrived in Dublin for the Irish Volunteers, Austria declared war on Serbia. The immediate effect of Britain's entry into WWI, on August 4, 1914, was, on the surface, to defuse the recent tensions over independence. However, a minority in Ireland merely drove their activities underground. While the political wheeling and dealing continued, the patriotism of many people across Ireland became paramount as men enlisted. It is estimated that during WWI some 70,000 men from the future Northern Ireland alone voluntarily enlisted to serve for the British army; not all of these volunteers were Unionist.

A process facilitated by the British War Office created the **36th (Ulster) Division** specifically for members of the UVF, although this change encouraged many Catholics to join the predominantly Protestant force. The 36th fought bravely and is renowned for its role at the Battle of Somme. While WWI continued, the **Irish Republican Brotherhood** decided that "England's difficulty is Ireland's opportunity." The Easter Rising had no chance of military success. Shortly after noon, the Dublin battalions rushed in and occupied the General Post Office, the Four

Courts, three of the railway terminals, and a number of other important points circling the center of Dublin. Although the uprising only lasted a week, Easter 1916 began another period of resistance against the English. In 1920, a series of meetings between Irish leaders and the British Government led to the signing of the **Government of Ireland Act.** This allowed for the creation of two self-governing units, one based on the 28 counties and the other on six counties of northeast Ireland, soon to be Northern Ireland.

The newly constituted statelet of Northern Ireland, included only six of the nine counties of Ulster, leaving predominately Catholic **Donegal, Monaghan,** and **Cavan** to their own devices. This arrangement suited the one million Protestants in the six counties, yet it threatened the half-million Catholic Nationalists living within the new Ulster. Protestant groups controlled politics, and the Catholic minority boycotted elections in protest of their "imprisonment within the North." Anti-Catholic discrimination was widespread. The IRA continued sporadic campaigns in the North through the 1920s and 1930s with little result. In the Republic, the IRA was gradually suppressed.

The 1930s sent the Northern economy into the dumps, requiring more and more British subsidies, while the **Stormont Cabinet** aged and withered. During **WWII** the Republic stayed neutral and stayed out, but Northern Ireland welcomed Allied troops, ships, and airforce bases. The need to build and repair warships raised employment in Belfast and allowed Catholics to enter the industrial workforce for the first time. Toward the end of the war the Luftwaffe firebombed Belfast, making it one of the UK's most damaged cities and earning Churchill's public commendation. In 1949 the Republic was officially established and the **Ireland Act** guaranteed the position of Northern Ireland within the UK.

Over the following two decades, a grateful British Parliament poured money into loyal Northern Ireland. The standard of living in Northern Ireland stayed higher than in the Republic, but discrimination and joblessness persisted for the working class, especially for Catholics. The government at Stormont neglected to institute social reform, and parliamentary districts were painfully and unequally drawn to favor middle class Protestants. Religious rifts reinforced cultural divides between and even within neighborhoods. After a brief, unsuccessful attempt at school desegregation, Stormont granted subsidies to Catholic schools. As the Republic gained a surer footing, violence (barring the occasional border skirmish) receded on the island. Between 1956-1962, the IRA waged a campaign of attacks on the border, but this ended for lack of support in 1962 and the New York Times bid the IRA a formal, eulogistic farewell. **Capt. Terence O'Neill,** who became the third Stormont Prime Minister in 1963, tried to enlarge the economy and soften discrimination, meeting in 1965 with the Republic's Prime Minister, Sean Lemass. O'Neill summed up the liberal Unionist view of the time, "If you treat Roman Catholics with due kindness and consideration, they will live like Protestants."

THE TROUBLES

The economy grew, but the bigotry festered along with the Nationalist community's resentment at their forced unemployment and lack of political representation. In 1966, for fear of this resentment, Protestant Unionists founded the **UVF** and issued a statement: "Known IRA men will be executed mercilessly and without hesitation." Both the UVF and the IRA actively bombed the opposition throughout 1966. The American civil rights movement inspired the 1967 founding of the **Northern Ireland Civil Rights Association (NICRA),** a religiously mixed organization aiming to end discrimination throughout Northern Ireland. NICRA leaders tried to distance the movement from constitutional concerns, although many of their followers didn't get the message. Many Protestants, including those in power, began to fear NICRA as a cover for the IRA, and while the first NICRA march was raucous it was nonviolent. The second, however, held in Derry in 1968, was a bloody mess disrupted by Unionists and then by the **Royal Ulster Constabulary's** water cannons. The Troubles had begun.

Catholic **John Hume** and Protestant **Ivan Cooper** formed a new civil rights committee in Derry/Londonderry but were overshadowed by Bernadette Devlin's radical, student-led **People's Democracy (PD).** The PD encouraged, and NICRA opposed, a four-day march from Belfast to Derry/Londonderry starting on New Year's Day, 1969. On the fourth and final day of the march, seven miles from its destination, the marchers were ambushed and attacked but a mob of some 200 at Burntollet Bridge. As the march entered Derry/Londonderry it was again attacked at Irish Street, a mainly Protestant area of the city. The march was finally broken up by RUC in the center of the city, an action which sparked wide-spread and serious rioting. It became so serious that police could no longer enter parts of some cities, Derry/Londonderry, in particular, where 'Free Derry' became infamous.

Civil rights concessions were granted in the hope of calming everyone down, but this began to cause tensions with Unionism. On August 12, 1969, Catholics based in Free Derry threw rocks at the annual Apprentice Boys parade along the city walls. The RUC attacked the Bogside residents, and a two-day siege ensued. Free Derry retained its independence, but the violence showed that the RUC could not maintain order alone. The British Army arrived to regain order.

Between 1970 and 1972, leaders alternated concessions and crackdowns to little effect. The rejuvenated IRA split in two, with the "Official" faction giving way to the new **Provisional IRA,** or **Provos** (the IRA we talk about today), who took over with less ideology and more guns. British troops became their main target. In 1970, John Hume founded the **Social Democratic and Labor Party (SDLP),** with the intention of bringing about social change through the support of both Catholics and Protestants; by 1973, it had become the moderate political voice of Northern Irish Catholics. British policies of **internment** (imprisonment without trial) outraged Catholics and led the SDLP to withdraw from government. The pattern was clear: any concessions to the Catholic community might provoke Protestant violence, while anything that seemed to favor the Unionists risked an explosive IRA response.

On January 30, 1972, British troops fired into a crowd of protesters in Derry; **Bloody Sunday,** and the ensuing perceived reluctance of the British government to investigate, increased Catholic outrage. Fourteen Catholics were killed—the soldiers claimed they had not fired the first shot, while Catholics said the soldiers shot at unarmed, fleeing marchers. Only in 1999 did official re-examination of the event begin; the inquiry is ongoing and will likely take several more years.

On February 2, 1972, the British embassy in Dublin was burned down. Soon thereafter, the IRA bombed a British army barracks. After further bombings in 1973, Stormont was dissolved and replaced by the **Sunningdale Executive,** which

NORTHERN IRELAND

TROUBLED LANGUAGE As with the Republic, language is very important in Northern Ireland. It is often a means of defining oneself. Several contentious terms include:

-Derry/Londonderry: Because the renaming of Derry by the British during the establishment of Ulster plantations is associated with the taking of land and resources from the native Irish, calling the "maiden city" Derry demonstrates a more Catholic bent, while calling it Londonderry is generally associated with the Protestants. Though both sides say Derry most often, it is a contentious term.

-Ulster: Originally the province consisted of nine counties. Referring to Northern Ireland as Ulster is typically a Protestant expression of pride in their roots in the country.

split power between Catholics and Protestants, but also developed links with the Republic of Ireland. As this power sharing began to take shape, a general workers strike was instigated due mainly to the links with the Republic of Ireland. This strike lasted 14 days and brought the end of the executive. A policy of direct British rule from Westminster began initially for four months.

Two pieces of legislation, one in 1976 and one in 1978, removed special status for prisoners charged with paramilitary, terrorist, or political offences. In 1978, prisoners in the **Maze Prison** began a campaign to have their special category as political prisoners restored. This campaign included blanket protests, dirty protests, and climaxed when Republican prisoners in H-Block went on **hunger strike** in 1981. Republican leader **Bobby Sands** was elected to Parliament from a Catholic district in Tyrone and Fermanagh while leading the hunger strike. He was the first to die. Sands died after 66 days and became a symbol of resistance; his face appears on murals throughout Northern Ireland. Nine more protestors followed him to their deaths. During the protest Margaret Thatcher, then Prime Minister of the United Kingdom, said, "We are not prepared to consider special category status for certain groups of people serving sentences for crime. Crime is crime is crime, it is not political." The remaining prisoners officially ended the hunger strike on October 3, seven months and two days after it began. The hunger strikes galvanized Nationalists, and support for **Sinn Fein,** the political arm of the IRA, surged in the early 80s.

With the increase in support for Sinn Fein and violence continuing, British Prime Minister Margaret Thatcher and Taoiseach Garret FitzGerald had a series of meetings. The **Anglo-Irish Agreement** was signed in 1985, with the first part stating, "The two Governments affirm that any change in the status of Northern Ireland would only come about with the consent of a majority of the people of Northern Ireland." However, the Agreement only granted the Republic a "consultative role," no legal authority in the governance of Northern Ireland. It improved relations between London and Dublin but infuriated extremists on both sides; Republicans were outraged by the principle of the 'consent of the majority of people' in a state they believed to be invalid, while Unionists were enraged by the involvement of the Republic. A protest, organized by Unionism used the slogan, "Ulster says NO" which would be seen around Northern Ireland for many years.

Protestant paramilitaries went on to attack "their own" RUC, while the IRA continued its bombing campaigns in England. Through 1991 and 1992, the Brooke Initiative led to the first multi-party talks in Northern Ireland in over a decade. The **Downing Street Declaration** was issued at the end of 1993 by Prime Minister John Major and Taoiseach Albert Reynolds, and served as a foundation upon which the peace process could be built.

1994 CEASEFIRE

On August 31, 1994, the IRA announced a, "complete cessation of military activities." Then on October 13, 1994, the **Combined Loyalist Military Command,** speaking on behalf of all Loyalist paramilitary organizations, offered "to the loved ones of all innocent victims…abject and true remorse" as they announced their ceasefire. Unionist leaders bickered over the meaning of the IRA's statement; in their opinion, it did not go far enough—only disarmament could signify a commitment to peace. Nonetheless, **Gerry Adams,** Sinn Fein's leader, defended the statement. The peace held for over a year.

In February 1995, John Major and Irish Prime Minister John Bruton issued the **joint framework** proposal. The document suggested the possibility of a new Northern Ireland Assembly that would include the "harmonizing powers" of the Irish and British governments and the right of the people of Northern Ireland to choose their own destiny. Subsequently, the British government began talks with both Loyalists and Sinn Fein. Disarmament was the most prominent problem in the 1995 talks—both Republican and Loyalist groups refused to put down their guns.

The IRA ended their ceasefire on February 9, 1996, with the bombing of an office building in London's Docklands. Despite this setback, the stalled peace talks, to be chaired by US diplomat **George Mitchell,** were slated for June 10. Ian Paisley, leader of the extreme **Democratic Unionist Party (DUP),** objected to Mitchell's appointment, calling it a "dastardly deed," but did not boycott the talks. The talks proceeded sluggishly and precariously. Sinn Fein initially refused to participate because it did not agree to the **Mitchell Principles,** which included the total disarmament of all paramilitary organizations. Sinn Fein's popularity had been growing in Northern Ireland, but its credibility was seriously jeopardized on June 15, 1996, when a blast in a Manchester shopping district injured more than 200 people.

As the peace process pressed forward, the Orangemen's July and August marches grew more contentious. Parades through Catholic neighborhoods incited violence by marchers and residents. The government created a **Parades Commission** to oversee the re-routing of parades and encourage the participation of both sides in negotiations. Protestants believe the Commission's decisions infringe on their right to practice their culture. Catholics argue that the marches are a form of harassment and intimidation from which they deserve protection. **A march in 1996** saw another burst of violence after the Parades Commission banned an Orange Order march through **Garvaghy Road** in Portadown, Co. Armagh. Unionists reacted by chucking petrol bombs, bricks, and bottles at police, who replied with plastic bullets. After four days of violence, police allowed the marchers to go through, but this time Catholics responded with a hail of debris. Similarly, the nightlife in Belfast and Derry consisted mostly of those rioting and those avoiding rioters.

In May of 1997, the Labour party swept the British elections and **Tony Blair,** riding high on hopes of peace, became Prime Minister. Sinn Fein made its most impressive showing yet: **Gerry Adams** and **Martin McGuinness** (who has recently admitted to being second-in-command of the IRA during Bloody Sunday) won seats in Parliament but refused to swear allegiance to the Queen and were barred from taking their places. The government ended its ban on talks with Sinn Fein. However, hopes for a renewed ceasefire were dashed when the car of a prominent Republican was bombed; in retaliation, the IRA shot two members of the RUC.

GOOD FRIDAY AGREEMENT

The 1997 marching season gave Mo Mowlam, the British government's Northern Ireland Secretary, a rough introduction to her new job. The Orange Order started their festivities a week early in Portadown. More than 80 people were hurt in the ensuing rioting and looting, and Mowlam came under scrutiny for allowing the parade without considering the consequences. On July 10, the Orange Order called off and re-routed a number of contentious parades, offering hope for peace. For the most part, the marches went peacefully—police fired a smattering of plastic bullets at rioters in Derry/Londonderry and Belfast, but there were no casualties. On July 19, the IRA announced an "unequivocal" ceasefire to start the next day.

In September 1997, Sinn Fein joined the peace talks. Members of the **Ulster Unionist Party (UUP),** the voice of moderate Protestants, joined shortly thereafter and were disparaged by Paisley and the DUP for sitting with terrorists. UUP leader **David Trimble** assured Protestants that he would not negotiate directly with Sinn Fein. Catholic Monica McWilliams and Protestant Pearl Sagar, co-founders of the recently formed, religiously mixed **Northern Ireland Women's Coalition,** brought a human rights agenda and a commitment to peace to the talks, and found themselves next in line for Paisley's derisive attacks.

NORTHERN IRELAND

The peace process, despite its noble aspirations, did not enjoy universal support. In January 1998, another dozen lives were lost. After two Protestants were killed by Catholic extremists in early February, Unionist leaders charged Sinn Fein with breaking its pledge to support only peaceful actions toward political change and tried to oust party leaders from the talks. Representatives from Britain, Ireland, and the US continued to push for progress, holding the group to a strict deadline in April. Mowlam expressed her commitment by visiting Republican and Loyalist prisoners in the maximum-security Maze prison to encourage their participation in the peace process.

After a long week of negotiations, the delegates approved a draft of the **1998 Northern Ireland Peace Agreement** in the wee hours of Saturday, April 11—the **Good Friday Agreement.** The pact emphasized that change in Northern Ireland could come about only with the consent of a majority of the people of Northern Ireland. It declared that the "birthright" of the people is to choose whether to identify personally as Irish, British, or both; even as the status of Northern Ireland changes, the Agreement says, residents retain the right to hold Irish or British citizenship.

On Friday, May 22, in the first island-wide vote since 1918, residents of Northern Ireland and the Republic voted the Agreement into law. A resounding majority (71% of Northern Ireland and 94% of the Republic) voted "yes" to the Agreement, which divided governing responsibilities of Northern Ireland into three strands. The new main body, a 108-member **Northern Ireland Assembly,** assigns committee posts and chairs proportionately to the parties' representation. Voices of moderation on both sides, David Trimble of the UUP and Seamus Mallon of the SDLP were elected First Minister and Deputy First Minister. The second strand of the new government, a **North-South Ministerial Council,** serves as the cross-border authority. At least 12 possible areas of focus are still under consideration, including social welfare issues such as education, transportation, urban planning, tourism, and EU programs. The final strand, the **British-Irish Council,** approaches similar issues, but operates on a broader scale, concerning itself with all British Isles.

While many felt that a lasting peace was finally in reach, a few controversial issues remained unresolved. Calls were made for the disbandment of the largely Protestant RUC, decommissioning of paramilitary weapons, and reductions in troop numbers, among other things. Blair declared that the RUC would continue to exist, but appointed Chris Patten, the former governor of Hong Kong, to head a small one-year commission to review the RUC's recruiting, hiring, training practices, culture, and symbols.

And then it was marching season again. In the end of May 1998, a march by the **Junior Orange Order** provoked violence on Portadown's **Garvaghy Road,** an area still smarting from the unrest in 1996. In light of this disturbance, the Parades Commission hesitated to grant the Orange Day marching permits. On June 15, the Parades Commission rerouted the Tour of the North, banning it from entering the Cliftonville Rd.-Antrim Rd. areas in Belfast. Aside from two short standoffs with the RUC, the parade proceeded without conflict. But the day after the assembly elections, Nationalists and policemen at a parade in West Belfast started the familiar dance of destruction. Early July saw a wave of violence that included hundreds of bombings and assaults.

Other parades passed peacefully, but a stand-off began over the fate of the July 4 **Drumcree** parade, which was forbidden from marching down war-torn Garvaghy Rd. Angered by the decision but encouraged by a history of indecision by the British government, thousands of people participated in a week-long standoff with the RUC. Rioting occurred in Portadown and elsewhere, and Protestant marchers were angered by what they saw as the disloyalty of their own police force. Neither the Orangemen nor the Parade Commission would budge, and the country looked with anxiety toward July 12. On the night of July 11, however, a Catholic home in

Ballymoney was firebombed in a sectarian neighborhood, and three young boys were killed. Marches still took place the following day. Due to the universal condemnation of the deaths of the Quinn boys, the **Drumcree Sandoff** gradually lost it numbers, and the Church of Ireland publicly called for its end. Although some tried to distance the boys' deaths from the events at Drumcree, the deaths led to a reassessment of the Orange Order and a new sobriety about the peace process.

Then, on August 15, a bombing in the religiously mixed town of **Omagh** left 29 dead and 382 injured. A splinter group calling itself the **"Real IRA"** claimed responsibility for the attack. The terrorists' obvious motive for one of the worst atrocities of the Troubles was to undermine the Good Friday Agreement. The US has now outlawed the Real IRA and inducted them into the Terrorist Hall of Infamy.

In October of 1998, Nationalist John Hume and Unionist David Trimble received the Nobel Peace Prize for their participation in the peace process. The coming year, however, was full of disappointments. The formation of the **Northern Ireland Assembly,** a fundamental premise from Good Friday, ended up in failure. Two major provisions of the Agreement highlighted serious rifts between Nationalist and Unionist politicians: the gradual decommissioning of all paramilitary groups' arms, and the early release of political prisoners. Disagreement over the **Northern Ireland (Sentences) Bill** fanned the flames and split the UK Parliament for the first time during the talks. The bill required the release of all political prisoners, including those convicted of murder, by May 2000. Dissenters feared that the bill did not sufficiently link the release of prisoners to their organizations' full disarmament, which was the greatest concern for most Unionists: the military wings of political parties, most notably Sinn Fein, were expected to disarm themselves in time for the June elections. The Agreement, unfortunately, lacked a time frame for decommissioning.

CURRENT EVENTS

December 1999—A power-sharing government was formed, under the leadership of Trimble and Mallon, but the IRA's hidden weapon caches remained a central conflict and threatened the collapse of the new assembly.

In late January 2000, Trimble gave the IRA an ultimatum to put its weapons "beyond use," and predicted political responsibility being returned to Westminster in London. The IRA's unwillingness to comply hamstrung the February peace talks, and just to make things a little more interesting, the dissident Continuity IRA bombed a rural hotel in Irvinestown. Every Northern Irish political group, including Sinn Fein, condemned the attack. Though the blast injured no one, it was an unwelcome reminder of the past in the midst of a stalled peace process. Britain suspended the power-sharing experiment just 11 weeks after its implementation and reintroduced direct British rule.

On midnight of May 29, 2000, Britain restored the power-sharing scheme after the IRA promised to begin disarmament. In June, they allowed two ambassadors to inspect their secret weapon caches.

The long, slow path to disarmament points to a safer future—the IRA still drags its heels, but has allowed international diplomats a third visit to their secret arms dumps. The inspectors confirmed that the weapons (rumored to be enough to keep a small country in the war-making business for a decade) are unused. Then, in 2002, the IRA broke new ground when they destroyed a small payload of their weapons, marking the first time they had ever voluntarily destroyed any of their resources. Though the public's reaction was not as grand as they had hoped, the concession proved to be conducive to continued peaceful discussion. In 2000 the last political prisoners in **Maze Prison** walked free under the highly criticized Good Friday provisions. Supporters gave them heroes' welcomes, but other civilians and

> **ALSO FROM THE NORTH** Many famous people and inventions have come from Northern Ireland. C.S. Lewis was born in Belfast, as was Van Morrison. Liam Neeson was born in Ballymena and Sam Neill was born in Omagh. The most notable northern creations are tires (or tyres), tractors, and of course *The Titanic*.

relatives of the deceased found the early release of convicted murderers, some carrying life sentences, appalling. Many of the released men expressed remorse and stated that their war was over, but others refused to apologize. Her Majesty has not yet declared what is to be done with Her Prison.

In 2003 life remains much the same in Northern Ireland—the Assembly is currently suspended (though efforts continue to have elections and get 'ordinary' politics up and running again), and political squabbling at the negotiation tables and on the floors of various Parliaments continues, punctuated now and then by bombs or plastic bullets on the streets. Both sides are making efforts to repair the past—the **Bloody Sunday Inquiry** continues with testimony from British Military and IRA figures, and RUC has been reformed into the **Police Service of Northern Ireland.**

LITERARY VOICES

The literature of Northern Ireland deals largely with the divided Catholic and Protestant cultures. Many Northern writers attempt to create works of relevance to members of both communities. Poet **Louis MacNeice** (1907-63) infused his lyric poems with a Modernist concern for struggle and social upheaval, but he took no part in the sectarian politics. **Derek Mahon** tried to focus on the common elements that people of all cultures share. Contemporary poet **Frank Ormsby** addresses larger social concerns through the lens of the everyday, and has collected and edited the works of many other Northern Irish poets. Novelist **Brian Moore's** *The Emperor of Ice Cream* (1965) is a coming-of-age story set in wartime Belfast. Born in rural Co. Derry/Londonderry, **Seamus Heaney** (famous Seamus) won the Nobel Prize in 1995 and is the most prominent living Irish poet. Although Heaney's tone is highly lyrical, his mode is anti-pastoral. His subject matter ranges from bogs to skunks to archaeological remains, and his fourth book, *North* (1975), tackles the Troubles directly. His recent translation of *Beowulf* (2000) has given Grendel and his mother a popularity they haven't seen in centuries. Heaney was part of the **Field Day Movement,** led by Derry poet and critic **Seamus Deane,** which produced what was billed as the definitive anthology of Irish writing. One of Heaney's contemporaries, **Paul Muldoon,** occupies himself more with self-skepticism and an ear for weird rhyme than with politics.

BELFAST (BÉAL FEIRSTE)

Despite the violent associations conjured by the name Belfast, the North's capital feels more urbane and neighborly than most international, and even Irish, visitors expect. The second-largest city on the island, Belfast (pop. 330,000) is the focus of Northern Ireland's cultural, commercial, and political activity. For several hundred years it has been a cosmopolitan, booming center of mercantile activity, in brazen contrast to the rest of the island (that is, until the "Celtic Tiger" began roaring). Renowned writers and the annual arts festival maintain Belfast's reputation as an up-and-coming artistic center, with galleries, coffee houses, and black-clad sub-cultural connoisseurs to prove it. Luminaries such as Nobel Prize-winning Seamus Heaney roamed the halls of Belfast's esteemed Queen's College, while Samuel Beckett taught English to the young men of Campbell College. The Belfast bar scene, a mix of Irish-British pub culture and international trends, entertains locals, foreigners, and a student population as lively as any in the world.

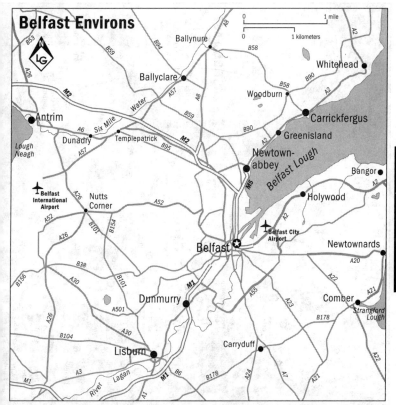

Belfast Environs

0   1 mile
0   1 kilometers

B53
A3
Ballynure
B58
Whitehead
B59
B94
B90
B58
Ballyclare
A57
A8
Woodburn
A2
B59
B90
Carrickfergus
M2
Water
Six Mile
A6
M2
A2
Greenisland
Antrim
Dunadry
Templepatrick
B95
Newtown-
abbey
Belfast Lough
Bangor
Lough
Neagh
A57
A52
M5
A2
Holywood
Belfast
International
Airport
Nutts
Corner
A52
B101
B154
A26
Belfast City
Airport
A2
Belfast
Newtownards
A20
B38
A55
A22
A21
B156
A30
B101
M1
A23
Comber
Dunmurry
A501
Strangford
Lough
B178
A26
A30
Carryduff
A22
B104
A24
A7
A21
Lisburn
A3
M1
B6
B178
M1
River Lagan
A1

Belfast was founded as the capital of the 17th-century "Scots-Irish" Presbyterian settlement and was William of Orange's base during his battles against Catholic King James II (see **The Protestant Ascendancy,** p. 60). In the 19th century, Belfast became the most industrial part of Ireland, with world-famous factories and shipyards. By 1900, Belfast had gathered enough slums, smoke, flax mills, Victorian architecture, and social theorists to look more British than Irish. The ship-building industry drew Scottish laborers across the channel for jobs, securing the region's allegiance to the UK. During the Troubles (see p. 458), armed British soldiers patrolled streets, frequent military checkpoints slowed all traffic, and stores advertised "Bomb Damage Sales."

Those days are now gone, and, due to extensive renovations of Belfast's downtown commercial district, the unobservant could remain oblivious to the city's former history. Indeed, the Belfast of today is really many cities: the City Centre, with its stately City Hall, hums with hurried shoppers, briefcase-toters, and mohawked teens during the day; the industrial docks now hold The Odyssey, Northern Ireland's newest, most extravagant entertainment complex; south of Shaftesbury Square, college hipsters idle nights away in cafes and keep the streets alive moving between clubs; in West and East Belfast, Catholics and Protestants separate in ideology and geography, paint their stories on the walls, depicting fascinating, if sometimes grim, living history. These parts comprise a surprisingly accessible, stimulating capital with an interesting traditional and modern population whose way of life is revealed to the visitors who remain in Belfast.

Belfast

♦ ACCOMMODATIONS

All Season's B&B, **57**
The Ark (IHH), **44**
Arnie's Backpackers (IHH), **46**
Avenue Guest House, **55**
Belfast Hostel (HINI), **31**
Botanic Lodge, **42**
Camera Guest House, **50**
Eglantine Guest House, **54**
The George, **52**
The Linen House Youth Hostel (IHH), **1**
Liserin Guest House, **53**
Marine House, **51**
Queen's University Accomodations, **58**

♠ FOOD AND DRINK

Archana Balti House and Little
    India, **29**
Azzura, **10**
Beachroom, **47**
Benedict's, **32**
Bewley's, **8**
Blinkers, **5**
Bookfinders, **45**
Café Clementine, **56**
Caffè Casa, **17**
Clements, **2, 4, 22 & 41**
Esperanto, **36**
Feasts, **28**
Maggie May's Belfast Cafe, **37**
The Moghul, **38**
Oscar's Champagne Cafe, **19**
The Other Place, **39 & 49**
Pizza Express, **25**
Spuds, **35**
Thai Village, **30**
Windsor Dairy, **14**

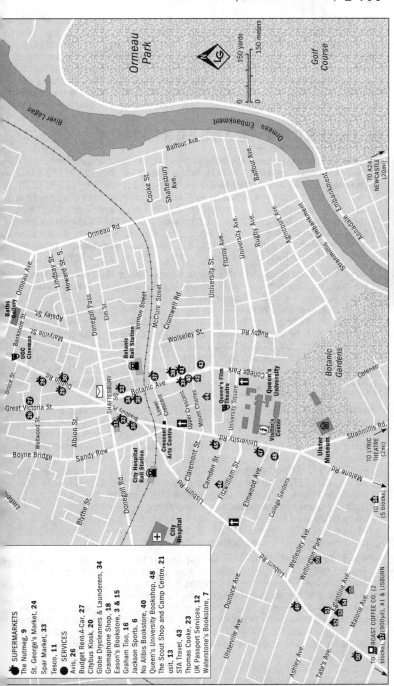

NORTHERN IRELAND

Ormeau Park

Golf Course

River Lagan

Ormeau Embankment

Balfour Ave.

Cooke St.

Shaftesbury Ave.

Balfour Ave.

TO A24, NEWCASTLE (20mi)

Ormeau Rd.

Strandmillis Embankment

Annadale Embankment

University Ave.

Fitzroy Ave.

Rugby Ave.

Agincourt Ave.

Lindsay St.

Howard St. S.

Donegall Pass

Elm St.

Vernon Street

University St.

Baths Gallery

Banknore St.

Maryville St.

Apsley St.

Botanic Rail Station

McClure Street

Cromwell Rd.

UGC Cinemas

Wolseley St.

Rugby Rd.

Botanic Gardens

Bruce St.

Dublin Rd.

Botanic Ave.

College Park

Queen's University

Colenso

Great Victoria St.

SHAFTESBURY SQ.

Bradbury Pl.

Queen's Film Theatre

University Square

Strandmillis Rd.

Wellwood St.

Albion St.

Lower Crescent

Upper Crescent

Mount Charles

Visitor's Center

Ulster Museum

TO LYRIC THEATRE (2mi)

Boyne Bridge

Sandy Row

Crescent Arts Centre

University Rd.

Camden St.

Claremont St.

Blythe St.

Donegall Rd.

City Hospital Rail Station

Lisburn Rd.

Fitzwilliam St.

Elmwood Ave.

College Gardens

Malone Rd.

TO 58 (5 blocks)

Linfield

City Hospital

Dunluce Ave.

Wellesley Ave.

Wellington Park

Eglantine Ave.

TO ROAST COFFEE CO. (2 blocks), (900yd), A1 & LISBURN

Ulsterville Ave.

Ashley Ave.

Tate's Ave.

Lisburn Rd.

Malone Ave.

LG

150 yards
150 meters

During the first week of July through around July 12, or "Marching Season" (also known by some locals as "the silly season"), the murals of anger and mourning gain their greatest pertinence. This is when the "Orangemen," Protestants celebrating William's victory over James II, parade through Northern Ireland's streets wearing orange sashes and bowler hats. These marches usually meet with Nationalist (pro-Republic) protests, and violence can ensue. If in Belfast during this week, exercise common-sense safety measures and expect delays in transportation and availability of services, as many restaurants and stores temporarily close.

◪ INTERCITY TRANSPORTATION

Airports: Belfast International Airport (☎9448 4848; www.belfastairport.com) in Aldergrove. **Aer Lingus** (☎0845 973 7747); **British Airways** (☎0845 722 2111); **British European** (☎9045 7200); **BMI** (☎9024 1188); and **Easyjet** (☎0870 600 0000; www.easyjet.com) land here. **Airbus** (☎9066 6630) runs to Laganside and Europa bus stations, in that order, in city center (40 min., M-Sa every 30min. 5:45am-10:30pm, about every hr. Su 6:15am-9:30pm; £6, £9 return). **Taxis** (☎9448 4353) do the same for £22. **Belfast City Airport** (☎9093 9093; www.belfastcityairport.com), at the harbor, holds **Manx Airlines** (☎0845 7256 256) and **British European. Trains** run from City Airport **(Sydenham Halt)** to Central Station (M-Sa 25-33 per day, Su 12 per day; £1).

Trains: For info on trains and buses, contact **Translink.** (☎9066 6630; www.translink.co.uk. Inquiries daily 7am-10pm.) All trains arrive at Belfast's **Central Station,** E. Bridge St. Some also stop at **Botanic Station** on Botanic Ave. in the center of the University area, or at **Great Victoria Station,** next to Europa Hotel. To: **Bangor** (33min.; M-F 39 per day, Sa 25 per day, Su 9 per day; £3.10, with ISIC card £2); **Derry** (2hr.; M-F 9 per day, Sa 6 per day, Su 3 per day; £8.20/£4); and **Larne** (M-F 21 per day, Sa 17 per day, Su 6 per day; £3.90/£3.30). Trains to **Dublin** (2hr.; M-Sa 9 per day, Su 5 per day; £20) leave from Central Station. To get to Donegall Sq. from Central Station, turn left and walk down East Bridge St. Turn right on Oxford St., then left on May St., which runs into Donegall Sq. For those with luggage the **Centrelink** bus service is free with rail tickets (see **Local Transportation,** p. 468).

Buses: Belfast has 2 main stations. Buses traveling to and from the west, north coast, and the Republic operate out of **Europa Station** off Great Victoria St., behind Europa Hotel (☎9066 6630; inquiries daily 7am-10pm). To: **Cork** (10hr., M-Sa 1 per day, £20, with ISIC card £16); **Derry** (1¾hr.; M-Sa 19 per day, Su 7 per day; £7.50/£5); **Donegal** (4hr.; M-Sa 10 per day, Su 4 per day; £12.70/£10); **Dublin** (3hr.; M-Sa 7 per day, Su 6 per day; £12/£10); **Galway** (6¾hr.; M-Th 7 per day, F 3 per day, Sa 2 per day, Su 1 per day; £18/£14.30). Buses to and from Northern Ireland's east coast operate out of **Laganside Station,** off Donegall Quay (☎9066 6630; inquiries daily 7am-10pm). To reach city center from the station, turn left exiting the terminal onto Queen's Sq. and walk past the clock tower. Queen's Sq. becomes High St. and runs into Donegall Pl.; a left here goes to City Hall and Donegall Sq. **Centrelink** bus connects both stations with city center (see **Local Transportation,** p. 468).

Ferries: To reach city center from **Belfast SeaCat terminal** (☎08705 523 523; www.seacat.co.uk), off Donegall Quay, there are 2 options. Late at night or early in the morning, a **taxi** is the best bet, as the docks are rather isolated. If on foot, take a left when exiting the terminal onto Donegall Quay. Turn right onto Albert Sq. about 2 blocks down at Customs House (a large Victorian stone building). After 2 more short blocks, turn left on Victoria St. (not Great Victoria St.). Turn right again at the clock tower onto High St., which runs into Donegall Pl. Here, a left leads to the City Hall and Donegall Sq. (at the end of the street), where a **Centrelink** bus stops (see **Local Transportation,** p.

468). **SeaCat** departs for: **Heysham** in England (4hr., Apr.-Nov. 1-2 per day); **Isle of Man** (2¾hr.; Apr.-Nov. M, W, F 1 per day); and **Troon** in Scotland (2½hr., 2-3 per day). £10-30 without car, cheapest if booked 4 wk. in advance. **Norse Merchant Ferries** (☎0870 600 4321; www.norsemerchant.com) runs to **Liverpool** in England (8hr.). **P&O Irish Ferries** in Larne (☎0870 242 4777) run to **Cairnryan** in Scotland, to **Fleetwood**, and many other locations in Ireland, England, and France. **Stena Line** (☎0870 570 7070; www.stenaline.com), farther up Lagan River has the quickest service to Scotland, docking in **Stranraer** (1 ¾ hr.). For information on ferries and hovercraft to Belfast from **England** and **Scotland**, see **By Ferry, p. 33.**

Car Rental: Budget, 96-102 Great Victoria St. (☎9023 0700). Economy £51 per day, £185 per wk. Ages 23-75. Open M-F 9am-5pm, Sa 9am-12pm. Or look into **AVIS,** across Great Victoria St. (☎0870 606 0100 for central reservations; www.avis.co.uk). Other Budget offices at **Belfast International Airport Office** (☎9442 3332; Open daily 7am-11pm) and **Belfast City Airport Office** (☎9045 1111; www.belfastcityairport.com; Open M-Sa 7:30am-9:30pm, Su 9am-9:30pm). At **Belfast International Airport** also look for **Dan Dooley** (☎9445 2522 or use the courtesy phone right at the end of the hall past other rental car kiosks); **Hertz** (☎9442 2533; Open M-F 7:30am-10:30pm); **Europcar** (☎9442 3444; www.europcar.ie); and **National** (☎9442 2285). Dan Dooley alone rents to 21-23 year-olds. At **Belfast City Airport** also find **Alamo** (☎9073 9400) and **Hertz** (☎9073 2451), among others.

Hitching: Hitchhiking is notoriously hard around Belfast and particularly inadvisable in the weeks around Marching Season. Most people take the bus out as far as Bangor or Larne before they stick out a thumb.

ORIENTATION

Buses arrive at Europa bus station on **Great Victoria Street** near several landmarks: Europa hotel, Crown Liquor Saloon, and the Opera House. To the northeast is **City Hall** in **Donegall Square.** A busy shopping district extends north for four blocks between City Hall and enormous Castlecourt Shopping Centre. Donegall Pl. turns into **Royal Avenue** and runs from Donegall Sq. through the shopping area. In the eastern part of the shopping district is **Cornmarket**, where pubs in their narrow **entries** (small alleyways) and centuries-old buildings hold their ground amongst modern establishments. **Laganside Bus Centre,** with service to Northeast Ireland, is, indeed, alongside the River Lagan, on Queen's Sq., northeast of Cornmarket. South of Europa bus station, Great Victoria St. meets **Dublin Road** at **Shaftesbury Square.** The stretch of Great Victoria St. between the bus station and Shaftesbury Sq. is known as the **Golden Mile** for its highbrow establishments and Victorian architecture. **Botanic Avenue** and **Bradbury Place** (which becomes **University Road**) extend south from Shaftesbury Sq. into **Queen's University's** turf, where cafes, pubs, and budget accommodations await. In this southern area, the busiest neighborhoods center around **Stranmillis, Malone,** and **Lisburn Roads.** The city center, Golden Mile, and the university are quite safe. Though locals advise caution in the East and West, central Belfast is generally safer for tourists than most European cities.

Westlink Motorway divides working class **West Belfast,** historically more politically volatile than the city center, from the rest of Belfast. A sharp division remains between sectarian neighborhoods: the Protestant district stretches along **Shankill Road,** just north of the Catholic neighborhood, centered around **Falls Road.** The **peace line** separates them. **River Lagan** splits industrial **East Belfast** from Belfast proper. The shipyards and docks extend north on both sides of the river as it grows into **Belfast Lough.** During the week, the area north of City Hall is essentially

> **"THE RAPE OF THE FALLS"** The area stretching from Divis Tower to Cavendish Sq. is known as the **Lower Falls**. This area was sealed off by the British Army for 35 hours in July 1970, in an episode known as the **Rape of the Falls**. Soldiers, acting on a tip that arms were hidden in some of the houses, searched homes at random while residents were forbidden to leave the area, even for milk or bread. It is estimated that before this event, there were only 50 Republicans in the area. After the incident, however, over 2000 people turned to the IRA. Many regard this raid as the biggest tactical mistake ever made by the British Army in Northern Ireland.

deserted after 6pm. Though muggings are infrequent in Belfast, it's wise to use taxis after dark, particularly near clubs and pubs in the northeast. West Belfast's murals are best seen by day. Ask the tourist office or local hostels for more information on where and when to exercise the most caution.

M1 and M2 motorways join north of Belfast's city center. A1 branches off from M1 around **Lisburn** and heads south to **Newry,** where it becomes N1 and continues through **Drogheda** to **Dublin**. M2 merges into A6 then heads northwest to **Derry**. **Larne** is connected to Belfast by A8. A third motorway, **M3**, runs east from the city, becoming A2 and leading to **Bangor** and **Ards Peninsula**.

⊡ LOCAL TRANSPORTATION

Local Transportation: The red **Citybus Network** (☎9066 6630; www.translink.co.uk) is supplemented by **Ulsterbus's** "blue buses" to the suburbs. Travel within the city center £1.10, concessions (under 16) 55p. Citysaver fares available M-F 9:30am-2pm (90p/45p). Generally, Citybuses going south and west leave from Donegall Sq. E. Those going north and east leave from Donegall Sq. W. 5-journey tickets £5.50-9.75/£3.38-5.50 depending on which zones of the city will be accessed. 10-day journey passes are £9.75-18.25/£5.50-9.75. All transport cards and tickets can be bought from the kiosks in Donegall Sq. W. (M-F 8am-6pm, Sa 8:30 am-5:30pm) and around the city. **Centrelink** bus connects all major areas of Belfast over its cloverleaf-shaped route: Donegall Sq., Europa, Castlecourt Shopping Centre, Central Train Station, and Laganside Bus Stations. The buses can be caught at any of 24 designated stops (every 12min.; M-F 7:25am-9:15pm, Sa 8:36am-9:15pm; £1.10, free with bus or rail ticket). Late **Nightlink** buses shuttle the tipsy from Donegall Sq. W. to various towns outside of Belfast. (F-Sa 1 and 2am. £3, payable on board or at the Donegall Sq. W. kiosk.)

Taxis: 24hr. metered cabs abound: **Value Cabs** (☎9080 9080); **City Cab** (☎9024 2000); and **Fon a Cab** (☎9023 3333 or 9032 0000).

Bike Rental: McConvey Cycles, 183 Ormeau Rd. (☎9033 0322; www.mcconvey.com). Locks supplied. £10 per day, £40 per wk., F-M £20. Open M-Sa 9am-6pm, except Th 9am-8pm. A threatened £50 deposit, but they just photocopy a credit card. Panniers £15 per wk. **Life Cycles,** 36-37 Smithfield Market (☎9043 9959; www.lifecycles.co.uk) offers bikes for hire (£9 per day) and **bicycle city tours** (see **Tours,** p. 480).

🛂 PRACTICAL INFORMATION

TOURIST AND FINANCIAL SERVICES

Tourist Office: Belfast Welcome Centre, 47 Donegall Pl. (☎9024 6609; www.gotobelfast.com). Has a very helpful, comprehensive free booklet on Belfast and info on surrounding areas. Books reservations in Northern Ireland and the Republic (£2). Open June-Sept. M 9:30am-7pm, Tu-Sa 9am-7pm, Su noon-5pm; Oct.-May M 9:30am-

5:30pm, Tu-Sa 9am-7pm. **Irish Tourist Board (Bord Fáilte),** 53 Castle St. (☎9032 7888). Has info, books accommodations in the Republic, and answers Irish passport inquiries. Open June-Aug. M-F 9am-5pm, Sa 9am-12:30pm; Sept.-May M-F 9am-5pm.

Travel Agency: usit, College St., 13b The Fountain Centre (☎9032 7111), near Royal Ave. Sells ISICs, European Youth Cards, TravelSave stamps (£7), and virtually every kind of bus or rail pass imaginable. Books ferries and planes, and compiles round-the-world itineraries. Open M-F 9:30am-5:30pm. Additional office at Queen's University **Student Union** (☎9024 1830). Open M-F 10am-5pm. **StaTravel,** 92-94 Botanic Ave. (☎9024 1469; www.statravel.co.uk), does all the same duties from its convenient location. Open M-Tu, Th-F 9am-5:30pm; W 10am-5:30pm; Sa 11am-5pm.

Hostelling International Northern Ireland (HINI): 22 Donegall Rd. (☎9032 4733; www.hini.org.uk). Books HINI hostels free, international hostels for £2.80. Sells HI membership cards to NI residents (£10, under 18 £6).

Embassies: For an extensive list of embassies and consulates, see **Essentials,** p. 8.

Banks: Banks and **ATMs** are plentiful: **Bank of Ireland,** 54 Donegall Pl. (☎9023 4334); **First Trust,** 92 Ann St. (☎9032 5599); **Northern Bank,** 14 Donegall Sq. W. (☎9024 5277); **Ulster Bank,** Donegall Sq. E. (☎9027 6000). Most open M-F 9am-4:30pm.

Currency Exchange: Thomas Cook, 10 Donegall Sq. W. (☎9088 3800). No commission on cashing Thomas Cook travelers cheques, others 2%. Open M-F 8am-6pm, Sa 10am-5pm. **Belfast International Airport office** (☎9448 4848; www.belfastairport.com). Open May-Oct. M-Th 5:30am-8:30pm, F-Sa 5:30am-11pm; Nov.-Apr. daily 6am-8pm.

Work Opportunities: The Ark (see **Accommodations,** p. 471) regularly hires travelers to work at the hostel; workers often live in hostel's long-term housing. Flexible payment/accommodation arrangements. **The Linen Youth Hostel** (see **Accommodations** p. 471) often has openings and posts temporary work throughout the city and Ireland. Those with catering experience may contact Sharon at **Azzura** (see **Food,** p. 473). This friendly, eclectic restaurant hires workers for a minimum 2mo. For a formally arranged temp position, inquire at **Industrial Temps,** 87/91 Great Victoria St. (☎9032 2511); **Adecco,** 38 Queen St. (☎9024 4660); or one of the city's top agencies, **Lynne Recruitment,** 48-50 Bedford St. (☎9023 4324; www.lynnerecruitement.co.uk).

LOCAL SERVICES

Luggage Storage: For security reasons, there is no luggage storage at airports, bus stations, or train stations. **Belfast Welcome Centre** (see p. 468) stores luggage for 4hr. (£2) or longer (£4). All 4 **hostels** hold bags during the day for guests, and **the Ark** holds bags during extended trips for former guests (see **Accommodations,** p. 471).

Bookstores: Waterstone's, 8 Royal Ave. (☎9024 7355) and 44-46 Fountain St. (☎9024 0159), has a large selection, including a section on Northern Ireland, and a helpful staff. Open M-W, F-Sa 9am-6pm; Th 9am-9pm; Su 1-6pm. **Eason's,** Donegall Pl. and Castlecourt Shopping Centre (☎9023 5070). Large Irish section; lots of travel guides. Open M-W, F-Sa 8:30am-5:30pm; Th 9am-9:30pm. **Queen's University Bookshop,** 91 University Rd. (☎9066 6302), has Irish history textbooks and a renowned collection of Beat generation manuscripts. Open M-F 9am-5:30pm, Sa 9am-5pm. For gumshoes-in-training, **No Alibies Bookstore,** 83 Botanic Ave. (☎9031 9607), specializes in crime, mystery, and American studies. Open M 10am-4:30pm, Tu-Sa 10am-6pm. Second-hand bookstores abound; a walk in the university area is sure to turn up several. **The Gramophone Shop,** 16 Donegall Sq. N. facing City Hall (☎9043 8435; www.carolinemusic.com) offers a 10% student discount on CDs and books (Open M-W 9am-5:30pm, Th 9am-9pm, F-Sa 9am-5:30pm, Su 1pm-5:30pm.)

Libraries: Belfast Central Library, 122 Royal Ave. (☎9050 9150). Open M, Th 9am-8pm; Tu-W, F 9am-5:30pm; Sa 9am-1pm. Belfast residents get 30min. **free Internet** per day. £1.50 per 30min. for non-residents; not always strictly enforced. **Linen Hall**

Library, 17 Donegall Sq. North, enter via 52 Fountain St., around the corner (☎9032 1707; www.linenhall.com.) Extensive genealogy, used books, and info on the Troubles. Many activities, especially for children, in May-Aug. Free Irish language courses Sept.-May. Open M-F 9:30am-5:30pm, Sa 9:30am-4pm. (See **Sights, p. 481.**)

Irish Cultural Centre: 216 Falls Rd. (☎9096 4180; oifigfailte@irelandclick.com). Arts center celebrating the Irish language, including performances with English translation. Open daily 9am-5pm, later on performance nights.

Women's Resources: Women's Resource and Development Agency, Mount Charles (☎9023 0212).

Bisexual, Gay, and Lesbian Information: Rainbow Project N.I., 33 Church Ln. (☎9031 9030), provides mental and emotional support to gay and bisexual men including counseling and drop-in HIV center. Open M-F 10am-5:30pm. **Lesbian Line** (☎9023 8668). Open Th 7:30-10pm. **Cara Friends Homosexual Hotline** (☎9032 2023) has resources and information for homosexual men and women. Open M-W 7:30am-10pm.

Disability Services: Disability Action (☎9029 7880). Open M-Th 9am-5pm, F 9am-1pm.

Laundry: Globe Drycleaners & Launderers, 37-39 Botanic Ave. (☎9024 3956). About £4-5 per load. Open M-F 8am-9pm, Sa-Su noon-6pm.

Camping Equipment: Graham Tiso, 12-14 Cornmarket (☎9023 1230), offers 3 floors of everything to survive the great outdoors. Notice boards and flyers sometimes advertise hiking, climbing, and water-related trips. Open M-W, F-Sa 9:30am-5:30pm; Th 9:30am-8pm. **The Scout Shop and Camp Centre,** 12-14 College Sq. E. (☎9032 0580). Ring bell for entry. Vast selection, though light on women's sizes and models. Open M-Sa 9am-5pm. **Jackson Sports,** 70 High St. (☎9023 8572) has good brand diversity for mountain and water sports. M-F 9:15am-5:30pm, Th 9:15am-8pm, Sa 9:15am-5pm.

EMERGENCY AND COMMUNICATIONS

Emergency: ☎999; no coins required. Police: 65 Knock Rd. (☎9065 0222).

Counseling and Support: Samaritans (☎9066 4422). 24hr., 7 days per wk. hotline lends a kind ear to any topic. **Rape Crisis Centre,** 29 Donegall St. (☎9024 9696, free-phone 0800 052 6813). Open M-F 10am-6pm. **Contact Youth,** 139 Raven Hill Rd. (☎9045 7848. Open M-F 9:30am-5pm. Toll-free ☎0808 808 8000; Line open M-F 4-9pm.) Offers one-on-one counseling appointments for youths 11-25 yrs.

Pharmacy: Boot's, 35-47 Donegall Pl. (☎9024 2332). Open M-W, F-Sa 8:30am-6pm; Th 8:30am-9pm; Su 1-6pm. Also on Great Victoria St. and Castle Pl.

Hospitals: Belfast City Hospital, 9 Lisburn Rd. (☎9032 9241). From Shaftesbury Sq. follow Bradbury Pl. and take a right at the fork. **Royal Victoria Hospital,** 12 Grosvenor Rd. (☎9024 0503). From Donegall Sq., take Howard St. west to Grosvenor Rd.

Internet Access: Belfast Central Library (see **Local Services,** p. 469) has email access £1.50 per 30min., with photo ID. Wheelchair-accessible. **Revelations Internet Cafe,** 27 Shaftesbury Sq. (☎9032 3337). £4 per hr., students and hostelers £3 per hr. Open M-F 10am-10pm, Sa 10am-6pm, Su 11am-7pm. **The Kremlin** (see **Gay and Lesbian Nightlife,** p. 480), offers **free Internet** to paying customers during the day; the service is extended only to gay clientele during late-night club hours. **Belfast Welcome Centre,** 47 Donegall Pl., the most central. £1.25 for 15min., students £1. Open M-Sa 9:30am-7pm, Su noon-5pm. **Friends Cafe,** 109-113 Royal Ave. (☎9024 1096). £3 per hr.; £10 card for 5hr. Open M-F 8am-5pm, Sa 9am-3pm. Near the south of the city in B&B territory, **Roast Coffee,** 407 Lisburn Rd., has **Internet** for £1.40 per 20 min.

Post Office: Central Post Office, 25 Castle Pl. (☎9032 3740). Open M-Sa 9am-5:30pm. *Poste Restante* mail comes here (see **Mail,** p. 26). Postal code: BT1 1NB. Branch offices: **Botanic Garden,** 95 University Rd., across from the university (☎9038 1309; **postal code:** BT7 1NG); 1-5 **Botanic Ave.** (☎9032 6177; **postal code:** BT2 7DA). Both open M-F 8:45am-5:30pm, Sa 10am-12:30pm.

⚑ ACCOMMODATIONS

Despite a competitive hostel market, Belfast's fluctuating tourism and rising rents have shrunk the number of available cheap digs. Nearly all lie near Queen's University, south of city center; convenient to pubs and restaurants and a short walk or bus to city center, this area is by far the best place to stay. If hindered by baggage, catch **Citybus** #69, 70, 71, 83, 84, or 86 from Donegall Sq. to areas in the south. A walk to these accommodations takes 10-20min. from bus or train stations. Reservations are highly recommended in summer, as hostels and B&Bs can be busy.

HOSTELS AND UNIVERSITY HOUSING

⚑ **Arnie's Backpackers (IHH),** 63 Fitzwilliam St. (☎9024 2867). From Europa Bus Station on Great Victoria St., take a right through Great Northern Mall, exit and go through Shaftsbury Sq. to Bradbury Pl.; go right onto Fitzwilliam, diagonal to Queen's University. On the right 200 yd. down the road. Relaxed, friendly, in the comfort of an antiqued building. Amusing triple-bunked beds in Crayola-colored rooms. Impressively clean despite Jack Russell staffers Rosy and Snowy. Library of travel info includes bus and train timetables. Luggage storage during the day. 8-bed dorms £7; 4-bed £9.50. ❶

Belfast Hostel (HINI), 22 Donegall Rd. (☎9031 5435; www.hini.org.uk), off Shaftesbury Sq., a right at the KFC on the corner of Donegall Rd. and Great Victoria St. Walking their stairs is a physical and mental exercise; try to recognize the neo-Warholian portraits of famed Northern Irish citizens including Sam Neil (Jurassic Park) and Jabba the Hut (the guy in the suit was born in Belfast). Clean and inviting interior is highlighted by colorful floors and rooms. Simple, modern 2- to 6-bed rooms. Large common room popular with large groups; can get slightly loud. Book ahead for weekends. **Books tours** of Belfast and Giant's Causeway. Breakfast (£2) served in a Giant's Causeway lounge. Wheelchair-accessible. **Internet** £1 per 20min. Laundry £3. 24hr. reception. Dorms £8.50-10.50; singles £17; triples £33. Expect slightly higher prices on weekends.❶

The Ark (IHH), 18 University St. (☎9032 9626). A 10min. walk from Europa bus station on Great Victoria St. Follow the street through Shaftsbury Sq., taking Botanic Ave. and a right on University St. before Queen's University. Look for the blue grating on the right. Unsuspecting building across from Queen's University holds a functional 4 stories of dorm rooms, a bustling, well-stocked kitchen (with free tea and coffee), and a staff of former guest MVPs. Staff provides info on finding work; more spacious long-term housing nearby (£40 per wk. or so). **Books tours** of Belfast (£8) and Giant's Causeway excursions (single-day £16). **Internet** £1 per 20min. Weekend luggage storage. Laundry £4. Curfew 2am. Coed 4- to 6-bed dorms £8.50-9.50; doubles £32. ❶

The Linen House Youth Hostel (IHH), 18-20 Kent St. (☎9058 6400; www.belfasthostel.com), bordering West Belfast. Across from main entrance to City Hall, turn left onto Donegall Pl., which becomes Royal Ave. Take a left onto Kent St. before Belfast Library. Converted 19th-century linen factory now houses scores of weary travelers (about 130 beds) packed into bare rooms. Basement common room (open until 1am) with foosball and ping-pong tables, but impersonal feel. Downtown location is a mixed blessing, depending on season and time of night. **Books tours:** black cab (£7); Giant's Causeway (£16). 24hr. reception. Hires guests on occasion and posts area employment opportunities. **Internet** £2 per hr. Bike and luggage storage 50p. Towels 50p. Laundry £3. 20-bed male dorms or 18-bed female dorms £6.50-7; 6- to 10-bed dorms £8.50-9; singles £15-20; doubles £24-30. ❶

Queen's University Accommodations, 78 Malone Rd. (☎9038 1608; www.qub.ac.uk). Take bus #71 from Donegall Sq. E.; 35min. trek on foot from Europa. University Rd. runs into Malone Rd.; residence halls are down a long driveway on the left. Institutional dorms make spacious singles or twin rooms with sinks and desks. Free laundry. Open June-Sept. 10, Christmas and Easter vacations. Singles UK students £8.75, with bath £12.40; international students £10.30/£14.90; non-students £12.80/£22. ❶

THE LOCAL STORY

An interview with Danny Devenny, painter of West Belfast murals and former designer for Sinn Fein:

LG: When did murals first appear in the neighborhood?

A: They started in the Loyalist community about the turn of the century. In the Nationalist community, if you had even dared to put a slogan on a wall, you would have been at least beaten up or at worst, put in prison. So, the murals in the Nationalist community didn't appear until well into the late 70s, 80s.

LG: What changed in the 80s?

A: The British recognized that this was a political conflict, and that the people who were arrested and put in prison were doing so for political purposes. Longcash (prison) was seen as a university of liberation, so people on the outside who were activists were using the time in prison to educate themselves on history and politics and probably also about the military aspects of a war. The British decided they couldn't have this, so they took away the prisoners' political status. The prisoners were angered, so they refused to comply with the prison regime, which led on to the hunger strikes, as a last resort. During that period people on the outside felt so close to these people that they just defied the British state and painted images on the walls.

LG: How have the murals developed over time?

A: The first murals that went up were about censorship. They were depicting the brutality which the British media were denying was taking

(cont. on next page)

BED AND BREAKFASTS

The B&B universe, south of Queen's University between Malone and Lisburn Rd., is one of healthy competition and close (sometimes familial) camaraderie. Occupying every other house on the block, they tend to be surprisingly similar in price, quality, and decor. Most offer free tea and coffee. Calling ahead is generally a good idea; most owners, however, will refer travelers to other accommodations.

Camera Guesthouse, 44 Wellington Park (☎9066 0026; camera_gh@hotmail.com). Pristine, light-filled, family-run guest house. Breakfasts delight with a wide selection of organic options and herbal teas. Caters to specific dietary concerns. Singles £25, with bath £40; doubles £48/£55. Lower rates in July. MC/V. ❸

Botanic Lodge, 87 Botanic Ave. (☎9032 7682), the corner of Mt. Charles Ave. Comfort surrounded by many eateries and a short walk to city center. All rooms with sinks and TVs. Singles £25, with bath £35; doubles £40/£45. Small charge if paying with V. ❸

Marine House, 30 Eglantine Ave. (☎9066 2828; www.marineguesthouse.com). Mansion gracefully overcomes alienating implications of its size. Having seen the airy interior, *Let's Go* can almost assure it's not haunted. Housekeeping standards as high as the ceilings. Esteemed position as a 3-star guest house. All rooms with TVs, baths, and phones. Singles £38; doubles £48; triples £66. MC/V. ❹

All Seasons B&B, 356 Lisburn Rd. (☎9068 2814; www.allseasonsbelfast.com). Comfy roost especially great for drivers; secure parking free. Amazingly hospitable owners and super-strength showers round out the deal. Singles £25; doubles £40; triples £55. ❸

Avenue Guest House, 23 Eglantine Ave. (☎9066 5904; steve.kelly6@nt1world.com). Large rooms with excellent beds, a modern decor, and expansive window views. All rooms with bath, TV, and direct dial phone. Singles £35; doubles £45. ❹

The George, 9 Eglantine Ave. (☎9068 3212). Fresh fruit at breakfast and saloon-appropriate leather couches in common room entice guests to stay on. All rooms with bath. Singles £22; doubles £44. MC/V with an extra £1 charge. ❹

Liserin Guest House, 17 Eglantine Ave. (☎9066 0769). Comfy beds and homey lounge make an inviting abode. Watch TV while showering. Sky-lit upper rooms. Singles £23; doubles £40; triples £55. ❸

Eglantine Guest House, 21 Eglantine Ave. (☎9066 7585.) Small but comfortable rooms for slightly less than competition. TV in each room. Guests enjoy in-room sinks, but must share bathrooms. Singles £22; doubles £40; triples £60. ❸

☐ FOOD

Dublin Rd., Botanic Ave., and the Golden Mile, all around Shaftsbury Sq., have the highest concentration of restaurants. Bakeries and cafes dot the shopping areas; nearly all close by 5:30pm, though on Thursdays most of city center stays open until 8:45pm. For dinner in city center, head to a pub for cheap grub, or to a bar for more upscale fare (see **Pubs,** p. 548). Huge **Tesco Supermarket,** at 2 Royal Ave., in an old bank building, is one of the few groceries and its prices are better than most of the city's convenience stores. (☎9032 3270. Open M-W and Sa 8am-7pm, Th 8am-9pm, F 8am-8pm, Su 1-5pm.) **Spar Market** at the top of Botanic Ave. is open 24hr.; order food through a service window at night. For farmer's-market-quality fruits and vegetables, plunder lively **St. George's Market,** E. Bridge St., in the enormous warehouse between May and Oxford St. (Open F 8am-2pm, Sa 6am-noon.) **The Nutmeg,** 9A Lombard St. (☎9024 9984), supplies health and wholefoods, including organic foods, vitamins, and pastries. (Open M-Sa 9:30am-5:30pm.)

QUEEN'S UNIVERSITY AREA

The University area brims with every type of student-filled eatery. Beyond, in B&B territory, a few establishments stand out.

Bookfinders, 47 University Rd. (☎9032 8269). Stuffy, dusty bookstore/cafe resembles an untidy professor's office with mismatched dishes, counter-culture paraphernalia, and occasional poetry readings. Right door may be a gateway to Narnia. Art gallery upstairs features student work. Soup and bread £2.75, sandwiches under £3; extensive vegetarian options, and even a few for woebegone vegans. Open M-Sa 10am-5:30pm. ❶

The Moghul, 62A Botanic Ave. (☎9032 6677), overlooking the street from 2nd fl. corner windows. Outstanding Indian lunch. Thali for carnivores or vegetarians M-Th noon-2pm (£2.99), or all-you-can-eat buffet F noon-2pm (£4.99). Open for dinner M-W 5-11pm, Th-Sa 5-midnight, Su 5-11pm. Takeaway available. ❷

Cafe Clementine, 245 Lisburn Rd. (☎9038 2211.) Pricey meals are supplanted by a "Beat the Clock" special that offers substantial and elegant meals at a price based on the time ordered (Tu-Sa 5-7pm). Open M-Sa 11:30am-3pm, 5pm-10:30pm. ❸

Maggie May's Belfast Cafe, 50 Botanic Ave. (☎9032 2622). Hip dive with nostalgic murals of yesteryear's Belfast. Relax with a cuppa and newspaper, or any one of the floating arts publications; order when inspired to,

place within the prison camps. The second batch of murals went up when the prison struggle was resolved, celebrating the IRA people themselves. And with the peace process, I think they purposefully went out to change the style of the murals because in conflict resolution we need to compromise. The murals started to say, "Yes, okay, we're responsible here. Let's find a brighter future." But simultaneously, there was a politicization within our communities, looking at the broader issue: at who we are culturally and at what colonialism has meant. That's why you now have the Celtic imagery going up.

LG: How do you go about painting a mural in West Belfast?

A: You just up and get a set of brushes and paint and go. No one will stop you and, in fact, people will stop and admire it and discuss it with you, and they'll ask you if you want cigarettes or food. The people in the community are so overcome and overjoyed by the murals in their area that they actually vie with each other (for one).

LG: What do you want your murals to teach your community?

A: We're teaching our younger generation about our history. The history taught in the schools was of a totally British bias, so you don't really learn about your own history until you sit down and study, and most of us didn't have that opportunity until we were in prison. We don't want the next generation to have to go to prison to learn about this. So, I think we're using the murals to try to get them interested and find out for themselves what this last 30, 80, or 3000 year period was all about.

but don't expect to be served anytime soon. Breakfast served all day. Toasted pancakes with maple syrup £1.75. Dinners £4-8. Heaps of veggie options. Open M-Sa 8am-10:30pm, Su 10am-10:30pm. ❷

Esperanto, 35 Botanic Ave. (☎9059 1222) and 158 Lisburn Rd. (☎9059 0888). Kebab Specialists. Budget protectors. Most meals £3. Botanic location open 11am-1am; Lisburn 4:30pm-1am. ❷

The Other Place, 79 Botanic Ave. (☎9020 7200), 133 Stranmillis Rd. (☎9020 7100), and 537 Lisburn Rd. (☎9020 7300). All-day breakfast (£3-4) with chalkboard specials. Huge servings and an array of ethnic foods. Open Tu-Su 8am-10pm. ❷

Beachroom, 1 Elmwood Ave. (☎9032 4803), in University Student Union. Cafeteria-style food served in a cafeteria. Beachroom closed mid-May to Sept.; **Cloisters** opens instead, serving basic panini and sandwiches (£2). Both open M-F 8:30am-4:30pm. ❶

THE GOLDEN MILE AND DUBLIN ROAD

We at *Let's Go* always try for a classy meal, but when late-night Guinness-induced munchies strike, Dublin Rd. and the latter portion of Golden Mile, especially Bradbury Pl., are the places to go. Beside the establishments listed, it has the highest density of takeaways in Belfast, ranging from Chinese to Indian to Mediterranean.

Benedict's, 7-21 Bradbury Pl. (☎9059 1999; www.benedicts.hotel.co.uk), straight through Shaftsbury Sq., immediately on the right heading toward Queen's University. Those sick of sandwiches and pizza take refuge in this swanky hotel restaurant. Its "Beat the Clock" meal deal offers fine meals from 5:30pm-7:30pm with the time ordered as price. Curried chicken, seafood, and vegetarian options. Open M-Sa 7-10am, lunch 12-2:30pm, (regular) dinner 5:30-10:30pm; Su dinner 5:30-9pm. ❸

Pizza Express, 25-27 Bedford St. (☎9032 9050). Sounds like the typical franchise, but the spiral staircase and Tuscan decor suggest otherwise. Actually serves good pizza. 1- to 2-person pies £6-7. Open M-Sa noon-11:30pm. ❷

Archana Balti House and Little India Vegetarian Restaurant, 53 Dublin Rd. (☎9032 3713; www.archana.info). Cozy joint. Upstairs Belfast's only Balti House; downstairs only vegetarian Indian restaurant. Thankfully, pioneering doesn't inflate prices. Downstairs Thali lunch £2.50 from noon-2pm, dinner £8.50; upstairs £4.95/£7.95 and up. Lunch M-Sa noon-2pm; dinner M-Th 5-11:30pm, F-Sa 5pm-midnight, Su 5-10:30pm. ❸

Feasts, 39 Dublin Rd. (☎9033 2787). Pleasant street-side cafe, serving Irish and international farmhouse cheeses in sandwiches (£3.95, takeaway £2.95) and other dishes. Makes pasta on the premises (£5-7). Open M-F 9am-6pm, Sa 10am-6pm. ❷

Thai Village, 50 Dublin Rd. (☎9024 9269). One of the few, the proud, the only Thai restaurants in Northern Ireland. Tofu dishes and other veggie options (under £5). 2-course lunch £6.95. Open M-Sa noon-2:30pm, 6-11pm; Su 5:30-10pm. ❸

Spuds, 23 Bradbury Pl. (☎9033 1541). Stereotype of Irish fast-food. Spuds stuffed with anything from bacon, cheese to chicken curry (most £2.50). Especially busy with post-pub crowd on weekends. Open M-W 9am-2am, Th-Sa 9am-3am, Su 9am-1am. ❶

NORTH OF DONEGALL SQUARE

Some lunch spots reside in the shopping district north of City Hall, but an economic meal here or one after 5:30pm, requires ducking into a historic pub. Late night, the hungry are better off strolling Golden Mile, south of Donegall Sq.

🔳 **Azzura,** 8 Church Ln. (☎9024 2444). Tiny cafe about as good as it gets for foodies—gourmet pizzas, pastas, soups, and sandwiches arrive warm from the oven (under £4). Pick peppers from those present, freshly grown by the owners. Seemingly psychic chef Sharon knows orders before they're placed. Intriguing and delicious options abound for both veggies and meat-lovers. Open M-Sa 9am-5pm. ❷

Windsor Dairy, 4 College St. (☎9032 7157). This takeaway bakery delights with piles of pastries for 30-50p and daily specials that satiate for around £2. Hot food runs out by 3pm, due to hungry locals in the know. Open M-Sa 7:30am-5:30pm. ❶

Blinkers, 1-5 Bridge St. (☎9024 3330). Well-worn diner—cluttered ashtrays and all—with authentic prices. True local haunt among the ultra-modern and ultra-pricey cafes that engulf the area. ¼ lb. burger £2.30. Open M-W 9am-7pm, Th-Sa 9am-9:30pm. ❶

Clements, 37-39 Rosemary (☎9032 2293). More locations at 4 Donegall Sq. W., 66-68 Botanic Ave., 131-133 Royal Ave., and 139 Stanmillis. Each has programmed modern interior; standard array of soups, bagels, panini, and desserts (£1-4). Chocoholics melt tasting hot chocolate (£1.80); everyone feels good drinking Fair Trade Coffee. Open F-W 8am-6pm, Th 8am-8pm. Botanic and Stranmillis open daily 'til midnight. ❶

Caffe Casa, 12-14 College St. (☎9031 9900). Early arrival in the new crop of swanky cafes, it boasts Belfast's best coffee. In good weather, windows are opened, spilling tables onto the sidewalk. Sandwiches (£4), entrees (£4.50), and sumptuous desserts (£1-2.50). Open M-W and F-Su 8am-5:30pm, Th 8am-7:30pm. ❷

Oscar's Champagne Cafe, 11 Chichester St. (☎9043 9400). Voguish take on a Tuscan countryside cafe. Upscale and thus expensive menu. Wild boar foccaccia £4.50; steak bocata £5.25. Wine, beer, and champagne available. Open M-Sa 9am-5pm. ❸

Bewley's, Rosemary St. (☎9023 4955), inside Donegall Arcade. For those missing Dublin, Bewley's is a replica of the original Japanese tea room. Newspapers and magazines upstairs. Takeaway save about a third. Open M-Sa 8am-5:30pm. ❷

◼ PUBS

Pubs were prime targets for sectarian violence at the height of the Troubles. As a result, most of the popular pubs in Belfast are new or restored. Those in the city center and university area are now quite safe. *Bushmills Irish Pub Guide*, by Sybil Taylor, relates the history of Belfast pubs (£6.99; available at local book stores). So without further ado, *Let's Go* proudly presents the **Belfast Pub Crawl** from North of the city to its southern end (Pub Crawl Map included.) Since city center closes early and can feel deserted late at night, we recommend beginning early in the traditional downtown, moving to Cornmarket's historic entries, then partying until closing near the university. The city's pub/clubbing schedule builds in intensity from Thursday night, culminating in blow-out Saturday nights during the university term. The student free months (June-Aug.) are notably toned down, but by no means dead. People start their night early, around 9pm as most bars must stop serving liquor at 1am, though they can remain open after that. Many bars have an "official" age policy, though looking the part goes just as far as an extra birthday or two (or four.) With this in mind, most bars and clubs are "smart casual," meaning slightly dressy, though presentable does the job. More casual pubs are come-as-you-are. Because of potential sectarian problems, football jerseys, baseball caps, and politically charged, visible tattoos are generally outside the dress code. Sports bars at game time are a valid exception. For a full list of entertainment options at each pub or club grab a free copy of "The List" or visit www.wheretonight.com.

NORTH BELFAST

Given that the city center clears out after 6pm, pubs in this area should be the starting point. After dark, take a cab to the pubs near the docklands.

◼ **The Duke of York,** 7-11 Commercial Ctr. (☎9024 1062). From City Hall, go up Donegal Pl., take a right onto Castle Pl., then a left on Waring with a quick left on Donegall St.; pub through a small entry marked "Duke of York" in large letters. Students make the long journey from Queen's for good *craic* with a mixed crowd and old-timey, traditional

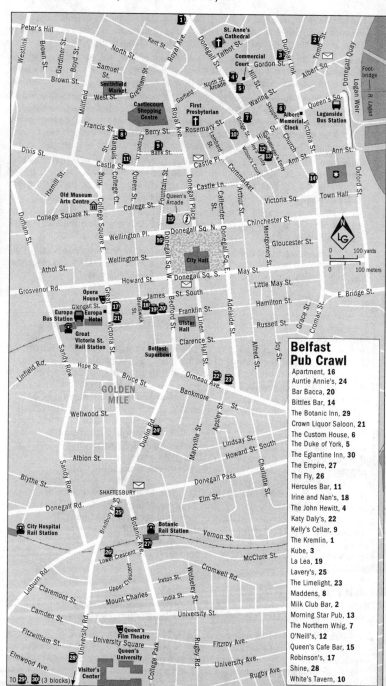

Belfast Pub Crawl

Apartment, **16**
Auntie Annie's, **24**
Bar Bacca, **20**
Bittles Bar, **14**
The Botanic Inn, **29**
Crown Liquor Saloon, **21**
The Custom House, **6**
The Duke of York, **5**
The Eglantine Inn, **30**
The Empire, **27**
The Fly, **26**
Hercules Bar, **11**
Irine and Nan's, **18**
The John Hewitt, **4**
Katy Daly's, **22**
Kelly's Cellar, **9**
The Kremlin, **1**
Kube, **3**
La Lea, **19**
Lavery's, **25**
The Limelight, **23**
Maddens, **8**
Milk Club Bar, **2**
Morning Star Pub, **13**
The Northern Whig, **7**
O'Neill's, **12**
Queen's Cafe Bar, **15**
Robinson's, **17**
Shine, **28**
White's Tavern, **10**

feel. Old boxing venue turned Communist printing press, rebuilt after being bombed by IRA in 60s; now home to city's largest selection of Irish whiskeys. 18+. Th trad at 10pm, Sa disco featuring rock and £4 cover. Open M noon-9pm, Tu noon-1am, W noon-midnight, Th-F noon-2am, Sa noon-3am.

▨ **The Northern Whig,** 2 Bridge St. (☎9050 9888; www.thenorthernwhig.com.) Although prominent statues used to grace top of Communist Party Headquarters in Prague, clientele has more capitalistic leanings. Young professionals pack in during hopping lunch hours and return at night to "give back" to economic underdog—alcohol. If staying outside city, bar arranges for reasonable overnight stays in town. Lunch £6. Food 10am-6pm. 21+. Bar open M-Sa 10am-1am, Su 1pm-midnight. DJ Th-Sa nights.

The John Hewitt, 51 Lower Donegall St. (☎9023 3768), up street from the Duke, through tunnel connecting it to Donegall St. Named after the late Ulster poet. Run by the Unemployment Youth Resource Centre, to which half the profits go, so drink up. Tu, W, Sa trad, Th live bands, F jazz. Music starts around 9:30pm. 18+. Open M 11:30am-11pm, Tu-F 11:30am-1am, Sa noon-1am, Su 6pm-midnight.

White's Tavern, 2-4 Winecellar Entry (☎9024 3080), between Lombard and Bridge St.; a left off High St. Belfast's oldest tavern, serving since 1630. Excellent for afternoon pint. W gay-friendly night (£5 after 10pm). Live trad Th-Sa. Open M-Sa 11:30am-11pm.

CORNMARKET AND VICINITY

Here stand Northern Ireland's oldest and most inviting. Expect local crowds in most of the establishments, and authentic *craic* in all.

▨ **Morning Star Pub,** 17-19 Pottinger's Entry (bar ☎9032 3976; restaurant ☎9023 3986), between Ann and High St. Victorian wrought-iron bracket above the entry. Classy with excellent U-shaped bar and wooden snugs for closer chats. Hugely mixed crowd: families enjoy all-you-can-stuff-onto-a-plate buffet (M-Sa 11:45am-3:30pm, £3.95), old men watch horseracing, homesick Aussies supplement pints with croc and ostrich meat (£7-11) courtesy of Australian half-owner. Open M-Sa 11am-11pm, Su noon-6pm.

Bittles, 70 Upper Church Ln. (☎9033 3006.) Heading through Cornmarket toward river, take a right onto Victoria St.; block down on the right and shaped like a smoothing iron. Drink a pint in this serene Guinness-colored bar with comical portrait of 6 Irish writers. Owner John Bittles presides over bar and understands need for *craic* in every man's soul. Food from noon-2:30pm. 23+ on weekend nights. Cover £5 after midnight. Open M-Th 11am-11pm; F-Sa 11am-3am.

O'Neill's, Joy's Entry (☎9032 6711; oneillsbar@dney.co.uk), off High St. Rght off High St., away from post office, on the left through Hoy's entry. A pub during the week; on weekends it transforms into wild club. Features house music on Th and some weekends drum and bass. 21+. Cover F-Sa £7. Open M-Th noon-9pm, F-Sa noon-3am.

NORTH OF DONEGALL SQUARE

Although patrons in pubs North of Donegall Sq. are as friendly as any other, this area tends to get rather deserted at night; pub-crawlers should practice extra caution in these parts.

▨ **Queen's Cafe Bar,** 4 Queen's Arcade (☎9024 9105), between Donegall Pl. and Fountain St. A buzzing yet friendly, casual day bar in a glitzy shopping arcade off Donegall Pl. Popular with city center workers. Open M-W 11:30am-9pm, Th-Sa 11:30am-11pm.

Hercules Bar, 61-63 Castle St. (☎9032 4587). Pub pulls in best musicians local soil produces; avidly promotes local culture and ethos. F-Sa trad sessions ; largely instrumental; Su 9:30pm sessions get up to 20 musicians, instrumental and vocal. Open M-W 11:30am-11pm, Th-Sa 11:30am-1am, Su noon-8pm.

Madden's, 74 Berry St. (☎9024 4114; www.maddensbar.com). Buzz to be let in. Old wooden bar with musical instruments on the walls. Attracts sizeable crowds with traditional Irish bands (M-Tu; upstairs F-Sa) and traditional blues and folk (downstairs F-Sa). No cover. Open M-Tu noon-midnight, W noon-11pm, F-Sa noon-1am. 18+.

Kelly's Cellars and **Kavanagh's,** 30 Bank St. (☎9032 4835), From Donegall Pl., make a left before Tesco; it's right in front. Oldest pub in Belfast, that hasn't been fully renovated, with the downstairs unchanged since 1720. Draws a mixed bohemian and traditional crowd thanks to overflow into next door's **Kavanagh's...**and its lax closing policy. Stay until 1am or beyond, but once you exit the "lock-in" policy won't let you come a-knockin' as insiders keep a-rockin'. No dress code, but customers warn against wearing white as it inevitably gets partied on. 18+. Trad Th-Sa, occasional live bands, including folk and rock. Open M-W 11:30am-10pm, Th-Sa 11:30am 'til the wee hours.

CITY CENTER AND SOUTH

In a move to reclaim the city's center after decades of unease from the Troubles, many a fancy and fun bar have appeared for young movers, shakers, and those more comfortable sitting with a pint.

🏠 **Katy Daly's Pub,** 17 Ormeau Ave. (☎9032 5942). Go straight behind City Hall, heading toward Queen's; a left on Ormeau. High-ceilinged, wood-paneled, antique pub; young relaxed crowd exuding modern *craic*. Local bands Tu; singer/songwriters W-Th, Sa.

Bar Bacca, 48 Franklin St. (☎9023 0200; www.barbacca.com), from Queen's University area, a left off Bedford St. after passing Ulster Hall. Dark, Morroccan bar smells of incense and young professionals, complete with small open fires set in wall cubbies, helped to win 2002 Bar of the Year honors for Ireland and the UK. Homey, if raised in posh apartment in Marrakesh. 21+. Open Sa 11am-1am, Su 6pm-midnight.

Apartment, 2 Donegall Sq. W. (☎9050 9777). Facing City Hall, to the right. Where Belfast's beautiful people, and occasionally their uncles, come for pre-clubbing cocktails (a reasonable £3.50.) Spacious, modern layout promotes "urban living, made easy" with a cafe/bar/bistro downstairs and upscale upstairs lounge in the evenings. Garnered many accolades, including 2002's Best Classic Bar, Best UK Bartender, Best UK Bar Manager and most illustriously Canon Hygiene's "Best Loo 2002" for women's bathroom. Arrive before 9:30pm on weekends and dress smart—jeans and sneakers not allowed. 21+ after 6pm. Open M-F 8am-1am; Sa 9am-1am; Su noon-midnight.

Irine and Nan's, 12 Brunswick St. (☎9023 9123; www.irineandnans.com). Around the corner from Bar Bacca. An instant hit, drawing a standing-room only, smartly-dressed, casual but cool crowd who might have been born when the so-tacky-its-hip 70s decor was made. DJs from 9pm. 23+. Open M-Sa 11am-1am, Su noon-midnight.

THE GOLDEN MILE AND THE DUBLIN ROAD

An interesting mix of chilled out, pint-toting Belfast residents and posh London imports with a fair share of young venues. Drink up, and drink long.

Auntie Annie's, 44 Dublin Rd. (☎9050 1660). Entertaining live music on both floors and a calm atmosphere have won this bar a faithful following among all ages (18+). M-W live rock music. Downstairs features a more pubby, relaxed vibe (Open M-Sa noon-1am, Su 6pm-midnight), while upstairs, darkly-dressed 20-somethings dance and nod to enjoyable indie rock (Open Th-Sa 10pm with £3-5 cover as the weekend wears on).

Crown Liquor Saloon, 46 Great Victoria St. (☎9024 9476). This, the only National Trust-owned pub, had its windows blown in from a bomb attack on the Europa Hotel, but pubbers'd never know it; the stained glass, gas lamps, and impressive Victorian snugs, each with its own door, were restored to their original splendor. Where old Belfast meets new, the old bar features a webcam accessible via www.belfasttelegraph.co.uk. May be filled with tourists, but due to its renown, any celeb in town is bound to pop in. Open M-F 8:30am-midnight, Su 12:30-10pm.

Robinson's, 38-40 Great Victoria St. (☎9024 7447). Four floors of themed bars, but is most renowned for **Fibber McGee's** in the back, which hosts incredible trad sessions all week at 10:30pm. Nightclubs **BT1** and **mezza(nine)** on top 2 fl. F 80s night. Cover F £5, Sa £8. Open M-Sa 11:30am-1am, Su noon-midnight.

Lavery's, 12 Bradbury Pl. (☎9087 1106; laverys@utvinternet.com). Three floors, each dimmer than the last. 1st fl. offers unpretentious chill sessions for 20somethings, while upstairs the **Gin Palace** teeny bops to Top 40 at the disco (Th-Sa £2-4 cover). Ascend to the 3rd fl. **Heaven** club (Sa £5 cover. 18+). Open until 1am; upstairs until 2am.

QUEEN'S UNIVERSITY AREA

Close the books and rally the troops—this is where the children come to play.

The Botanic Inn, 23 Malone Rd. (☎9066 0460). Through Shaftsbury Sq. past Queen's University, on the right on Malone Rd. "The Bot" is a huge and hugely popular student bar, packed nightly from wall to wall. The original "meal deal" (3pm-8pm), a meal with a pint for under £5. Be ready to queue during the school year (Sept. to early June) unless arriving before 9pm. 20+. Cover £2. Open daily 11:30am-1am.

The Empire, 42 Botanic Ave. (☎9024 9276; www.belfastpubs-n-clubs.com). This 120-year-old building was once a church, but its 2 stories were entirely revamped to resemble Belfast's Victorian music halls. Once a student-only hang-out, but returning alums mix things up. Sept.-June Tu comedy (£5), Th-Su live bands, featuring Sa "Glamarama" with over-the-top glam rock. W trad night 8pm-1am. 18+. Cover F-Sa £3-5.

The Eglantine Inn, 32 Malone Rd. (☎9038 1994). Almost an official extra-curricular, "The Eg" is the admitted playground for those too young to get into The Bot. W-Sa shake it upstairs with the DJ. Open M-Sa until 1am, Su until 6pm.

🅿 CLUBS

For information on the city's nightlife, most clubbers consult *The List*, a biweekly newsletter available at the tourist office, hostels, and certain restaurants around town. To savor some history with a pint, take one of the very popular **historical pub tours** of Belfast (see **Tours** p. 480.) Ask the staff at the Queen's University Student Union about the latest night spots.

The Fly, 5-6 Lower Crescent (☎9050 9750). Popular with a young set of partiers. Extensive entomological decor geared toward its namesake (read: this place has a lot of big bugs; fake ones.) 1st fl. bar for the pints, 2nd for mingling and dancing, and a flavored vodka shooter bar with some 60 flavors of vodka—from garlic to coffee to Starburst—in test-tube shots on the 3rd. Win a keg of Harp at W's "game show night," or free perfume at F "ladies' night." Tu "Tag and Shag" singles night rounds out the frequent theme nights, including Alice in Wonderland and Grease. 18+/20+ on weekends. No cover. Open M-Th 9pm-1:30am, F-Sa 9pm-1:45am.

La Lea, 48 Franklin St. (☎9023 0200; www.lalea.com), directly next door to Bar Bacca, off Bedford St. A 2-floor gay-friendly club with a strong post-pub crowd that features all forms of house music all week, save M night's classy and popular jazz session. Club 23+. Cover £2-10. Open M-Su 9:30-3am, closed Tu.

Milk Bar Club, 10-14 Tomb St. (☎9027 8876; www.clubmilk.com). A left at the Albert Sq. Clock onto Tomb Street. This up-and-coming club indulges in the best kind of fun possible: cheesy. Pop and club hits to gyrate to while filling up at the luminous bar. All week noon-3am, with things really moving by 11pm.

The Limelight, 17 Ormeau Ave. next door to Katy Daly's Pub (☎9032 5942; www.the-limelight.co.uk.) Dark, gritty, smoky, strobe-filled nightclub entices young faces. Tu student night (£2), F "Disco A Go-Go" (£4), Sa alternative music (£5). Open 10pm-2am.

Kube, 2-6 Dunbar St. (☎9023 4520; www.kubeonline.com.) A new dance club whose location outside the city center keeps guest moving into the early morning. Eat dinner (£7-12), stay for dancing with a very gay-friendly crowd. Every kind of music that can get a crowd going. Students £4, others £5. 18+. Open M-Su 9pm-3am.

Shine, Queen's University Student Union (☎9032 4803; www.kubeonline). Hot club spot, pulsating with top-notch DJ every Sa. Gets exceptionally hot once monthly. Cover £5-12. Open Sa 10pm-3am.

▼ GAY AND LESBIAN NIGHTLIFE

On Wednesday nights, **White's Tavern,** the oldest pub in Belfast, becomes one of the most progressive (see **Cornmarket,** p. 477), and **Milk** hosts a gay night on Mondays and **Kube,** while not explicitly a gay bar, was recently Parliament Bar, Belfast's first and foremost gay club and still retains the heritage (see **Clubs** p. 479.)

The Kremlin, 96 Donegall St. (☎9080 9700; www.kremlin-belfast.com). Look for the imposing statue of Stalin above the entrance. Belfast's newest, hottest, and friendliest gay and lesbian nightspot with too many different venues to list, from foam parties to internationally renowned drag queens. Gelled and beautiful girls and boys sip and flirt in the sliver of a bar until they spill into the dance area 'round 10:30pm. **Free Internet** upstairs is undermined by free condoms for any lucky party people. Come by 1am as doors close to the outside while the party heats up inside. Tight security. F theme night. Cover varies, but free Su, M, and before 9pm. Bar open M-Th 4pm-3am, F-Su 1pm-3am.

The Custom House, 22-28 Skipper St. (☎9024 5588), off High St. 1 block west of the Albert Memorial Clock. A more relaxed bar during the week that gets wild on weekends—Sa hosts a DJ, karaoke, and live band in separate rooms. Mixed-age crowd, mostly male. W DJ and movie lounge. 18+. Sa £3 cover.

⬛ TOURS

▨ BLACK CAB TOURS. The one thing in this city everyone must do: take a black cab tour of West Belfast. The tours provide a fascinating commentary highlighting the murals, paraphernalia, and sights on both sides of the Peace Line. Most drivers come from the communities and have been touched personally by their histories, but make pains to avoid bias. Almost every hostel books these tours with their favored **black cab** operators, some their own, usually for £7-8. **Original Belfast Black Taxi Tours** give impassioned yet even-handed commentary and one of the five Protestant and five Catholic drivers will answer any question. (☎0800 032 2003 or 077 6393 6704 for Laurence, one of the owners; www.tobbtt.com. 1½hr. £55 for groups of 3.) Michael Johnston of **Black Taxi Tours** has made a name for himself with his witty, objective presentations. (☎0800 052 3914; www.belfast-tours.com. £9 per person for groups of 3 or more.)

▨ BAILEYS HISTORICAL PUB TOURS OF BELFAST. For a break from recreational pubbing, this tour is a primer in Pint Studies as the effervescent Judy Crawford guides visitors through seven or more of Belfast's oldest and best pubs with a little city sightseeing and history in between. (☎9268 3665; www.belfastpubtours.com. 2 hrs. £6, £5 for groups of 10 or more, excluding drinks, though a tumbler of Bailey's Irish Cream is complimentary with the tour.)

BIKE TOURS. In addition to bike hire, **Life Cycles** (see **Bike Rental,** p. 468) offers tours of Belfast for £15 per day, as does **Irish Cycle Tours,** 27 Belvoir View Park (☎9064 2222; www.irishcycletours.com.)

CITYBUS. Citybus provides several tours that hit the city's major sights, both glitzy and gritty. The **Belfast City Tour** introduces visitors to the landmarks of downtown Belfast. **Belfast Living History Tour** is their answer to the numerous black cab tours of West Belfast. (☎9045 8484. Both tours 1½hr. May-Sept. M-Tu and Th-Sa, 11am. All tours leave from Castle Place, in front of the post office. £5, students £8, children and seniors £4, family £13.)

◎ SIGHTS

DONEGALL SQUARE

Donegall Sq. marks the northern boundary of the Golden Mile and the southern end of the pedestrian-only Cornmarket district. Belfast's old city center, the Square is dominated by City Hall, once a favorite target for IRA bombers.

BELFAST CITY HALL. The most dramatic and impressive piece of architecture in Belfast is fittingly its administrative and geographic center. Removed from the crowded streets by a grassy square, its green copper dome (173 ft.) is nonetheless visible from nearly any point in the city. Inside, a grand staircase ascends to the second floor, portraits of the city's Lord Mayors somberly line the halls, and glass and marble shimmer in three elaborate reception rooms. The City Council's oak-paneled chambers, only used once a month, are deceptively austere, considering the Council's reputation for rowdy meetings (fists are known to fly). Directly in front of the main entrance, an enormous marble Queen Victoria statue stares down at visitors with her trademark formidable grimace, while bronze figures representing Shipbuilding and Spinning kneel at her feet. A more sympathetic figure of womanhood stands on East grounds, commemorating the fate of the *Titanic* and her passengers. An inconspicuous pale gray stone column in front remembers the 1942 arrival of the US Expeditionary Force, whose soldiers were stationed here to defend the North from Germany; it was rededicated after President Clinton's visit to Belfast in 1995. The interior of City Hall is accessible only by guided tour. (☎9027 0456. 1hr. tours June-Sept. M-F 11am, 2, and 3pm, Sa 2:30pm; also Oct.-May M-F 11am, 2:30pm, Sa 2:30pm. Free.)

OTHER SIGHTS. One of Belfast's oldest establishments is the **Linen Hall Library;** the red hand of Ulster decorates the top of its street entrance. The library contains a famous collection of political documents relating to Northern Ireland. Devoted librarians scramble to get their hands on every Christmas card, handbill, and newspaper article related to Belfast's political history. (Enter via 52 Fountain St.☎9032 1707. Free tours available, but call ahead. Open M-F 9:30am-5:30pm, Sa 9:30am-4pm.) Nearby, the **Scottish Provident Institution,** built in 1902, displays a decadent facade glorifying virtually every profession that has contributed to industrial Belfast. (Across the street from City Hall, on the corner of Donegall Sq. N. and East Bedford St.) For a taste of Irish craftsmanship, head to **Craftworks.** Collections include leather goods, knitwear, ceramics, and jewelry. (Bedford St. ☎9024 4465. Open M-Sa 9:30am-5:30pm.)

CORNMARKET AND ST. ANNE'S CATHEDRAL

Just north of the city center, a bustling shopping district engulfs eight blocks around Castle St. and Royal Ave. Castle St. was named for the old city castle, whose place has been usurped by the Golden Arches. Although the Cornmarket area is dominated by modern buildings, relics of old Belfast remain in the tiny alleys, or **entries,** that connect the major streets.

ST. ANNE'S CATHEDRAL. Belfast's newspapers set up shop around St. Anne's, also known as the **Belfast Cathedral.** This Church of Ireland cathedral was begun in 1899, but to keep from disturbing regular worship, it was built around a smaller church already on the site; upon completion of the new exterior, builders extracted the earlier church brick by brick. Each of the cathedral's 10 interior pillars name one of Belfast's fields of professionalism: Science, Industry, Healing, Agriculture, Music, Theology, Shipbuilding, Freemasonry, Art, and "Womanhood." Note the mosaics—Gertrude Stein made them. In a small enclave called the **Chapel of Peace**, visitors pray for the healing of world strife. (Donegall St., a few blocks from the city center. Open M-Sa 10am-4pm.)

THE ENTRIES. Between Ann and High St. runs **Pottinger's Entry,** which contains the **Morning Star Pub** and its award-winning food (see **Pubs,** p. 475). **Joy's Entry,** farther down Ann St., is where the Unionist *Belfast News Letter* was printed for over 100 years; the only establishment still in the entry, the **Globe Tavern,** is disappointingly modern inside. Off Lombard and Bridge St., **Winecellar Entry** is the site of Belfast's oldest pub, **White's Tavern,** serving since 1630 (see **Pubs,** p. 475).

OTHER SIGHTS. By European standards, most of Belfast's buildings are young, yet the city's oldest public building, **The Old Stock Exchange,** on the corner of North and Waring St., is no spring chicken. Tireless Charles Lanyon designed a new facade for the building in 1845 when the original was deemed not grand enough. Just a block west on Rosemary St. sits the **First Presbyterian Church of Belfast,** the city's oldest church, founded in 1644. (☎9032 5365. Su service 10:30am.)

THE DOCKS AND EAST BELFAST

Although the docks were once the beating heart of Belfast, commercial development made the area more suitable for industrial machinery than people. However, the **Odyssey,** on the east bank amidst reminders of the city's shipbuilding glory days, promises to reclaim the hordes. **Harland & Wolff,** the most famous of the shipyards, proudly claims the *Titanic* as its magnum opus. The shipyards figure in numerous poems and novels, notably at the end of Paul Muldoon's "7, Middagh St." Today the twin cranes **Samson** and **Goliath** towering over the Harland & Wolff shipyard are the most striking part of the docks' skyline.

ODYSSEY. Belfast's newest mega-attraction is a huge entertainment center that houses five distinct attractions. (2 Queen's Quay. ☎9045 1055; www.theodyssey.co.uk.) The **Odyssey Arena,** with 10,000 seats, is the largest indoor arena in Ireland. Home to the Belfast Giants ice hockey team, big name performers such as Destiny's Child house-sit when the players are away. (Performance box office ☎9073 9074; www.odesseyarena.com. Hockey ☎9059 1111; www.belfastgiants.com.) The ▧**W5 Discovery Centre** is a top-of-the-line science and technology museum that beckons geeks of all ages (as well as the suave and sophisticated *Let's Go* reader) to play with pulley chairs, laser harps, robots, and the Fire Tornado. (☎9046 7700; www.w5online.co.uk. Workshops run throughout the summer. Wheelchair-accessible. Open M-Sa 10am-6pm, Su noon-6pm; last admission 5pm. £5.50, students and seniors £4, children £3.50, family £15.) The **Sheridan IMAX Cinema** shows both 2D and 3D films on its enormous 62 by 82 ft. screen, while **Warner Village Cinemas** shows Hollywood blockbusters on its 14 normal-sized screens. (IMAX ☎9046 7000; www.belfastimax.com. £5, students M-Th £4.50, children M-Th £4. Multiplex ☎9073 9234. £5/£3.70/£3.20.) A mall-esque **Pavilion** contains the usual shops, bars, and restaurants—including that tourist mecca, the Hard Rock Cafe. (Hard Rock Cafe ☎9076 6990. Open M-Sa noon-1am, Su noon-midnight.)

LAGAN LOOKOUT AND LAGAN WEIR. The £14-million weir was built to eliminate the Lagan's drastic tides, which once exposed stinking mud flats during ebb. Depending on the day and weather, the undertaking may or may not seem fully successful. The Lookout, refurbished in 2002, has a near 360° view and a room of displays on the history of Belfast and the purpose of the weir. Both structures are part of a huge development project that includes the **Laganside Trail** along the far side of the river and **Waterfront Hall**, a concert hall with an uncanny resemblance to a sponge cake. *(Donegall Quay, across from the Laganside bus station. ☎ 9031 5444; look-out@laganside.com. Lookout open Apr.-Sept. M-F 11am-5pm, Sa noon-5pm, Su 2-5pm; Oct.-Mar. Tu-F 11am-3:30pm, Sa 1-4:30pm, Su 2-4:30pm. £1.50, students and seniors £1, children 75p.)*

SINCLAIR SEAMEN'S CHURCH. Who says Herman Melville was being silly when he wrote about his Nantucketers' nautical chapel? Here, the minister delivers his sermons from a pulpit carved in the shape of a ship's prow, collections are taken in miniature lifeboats, and an organ with port and starboard lights taken from a Guinness barge carries the tune. The exterior was designed by the prolific Charles Lanyon, who was also responsible for the Custom House and almost every other notable 19th-century building in Belfast—except the Albert Memorial Clock Tower. Boy, was he angry about that! *(Corporation St., down from the SeaCat terminal. ☎ 9071 5997. Open W 2-5 and Su service.)*

OTHER SIGHTS. The stately **Custom House**, Lanyon's 1857 baby, stands between Queen Sq. and Albert Sq., approaching the river from the clock tower. Designed in an E-shape, it rests on an elaborate pediment of Lady Britannia, Salty Neptune, and Mercury, the god of trade. Belfast also has its own leaning tower of Pisa and Big Ben, in one compact piece: the **Albert Memorial Clock Tower**, where Oxford St. runs beside the Lagan. Named for Victoria's prince consort and designed in 1865 by W. J. Barre, the tower slouches precariously at the entrance to the docks, because of all the young ladies leaning on one side of the clock while awaiting their special sailors, or so the story goes. On New Year's, the locals run to the clock at the first stroke of midnight and try to reach it by the last toll, smashing their glasses around it to ring in the New Year.

THE GOLDEN MILE

"The Golden Mile" refers to a strip along Great Victoria St. that is encrusted with many of the jewels in Belfast's crown. Because it drew a number of powerful Englishmen to its glittering establishments and was funded largely by the British-based government, The Golden Mile was once a target for IRA bombers. Today it occupies safe territory within the city center.

GRAND OPERA HOUSE. The city's pride and joy, the opera house was cyclically bombed by the IRA, restored to its original splendor at enormous cost, and then bombed again. Top opera and musical theater allow visitors today to enjoy the current calm in high fashion, while tours on Saturday allow a look behind the ornate facade. *(See Theatre, p. 490. ☎ 9024 1919. Office open M-Sa 8:30am-6pm. Tours begin across the street at the office Sa 11am. £3, seniors and children £2.)*

THE CROWN LIQUOR SALOON. The National Trust restored this highly frequented pub as a showcase of carved wood, gilded ceilings, and stained glass. Doored snugs fit groups of two to 10 comfortably. Once upon a time hitting the buzzer in the booth would order another round, but now pubbers stagger to the bar. *(See Pubs, p. 478.)*

EUROPA HOTEL. Having suffered 32 attacks, the Europa has the dubious distinction of being "Europe's most bombed hotel." In March of 1993, the hotel installed shatterproof windows; luckily, they haven't been tested yet and likely won't be anytime soon. "Enjoy your stay."

QUEEN'S UNIVERSITY AREA

Though the students largely empty out in the summer, their turf, with its city garden oasis, is fun to explore year-round. The walk from the city center only takes 15-20min., but Citybuses #69 and 71 go there as well.

NORTHERN IRELAND

QUEEN'S UNIVERSITY BELFAST. Charles Lanyon designed the beautiful Tudor-revival brick campus in 1849, modeling it after Magdalen College, Oxford. The **Visitors Centre,** in the Lanyon Room to the left of the main entrance, offers Queen's-related exhibits and merchandise. A new gallery keeps aesthetes on their toes with rotating shows. (*University Rd. Visitors Centre ☎9033 5252; www.qub.ac.uk/vcentre. Open May-Sept. M-F 10am-4pm, Sa 10am-4pm; Oct.-Mar. M-F 10am-4pm. Gallery open M-F 9am-5pm, Sa 10am-4pm.*)

BOTANIC GARDENS. Birds do it, bees do it, and on warm days, the majority of the student population does it. Do it with them—bask in Belfast's occasional sun behind the university, that is. Meticulously groomed, the gardens offer a welcome green respite from the traffic-laden city streets. Inside the gardens lie two 19th-century greenhouses, the toasty **Tropical Ravine House,** and the more temperate Lanyon-designed **Palm House.** Summertime visitors should be sure to stop and smell Europe's most fragrant blooms in the rose gardens. (*☎9032 4902. Open daily 8am-dusk. Tropical House and Palm House open Apr.-Sept. M-F 10am-noon and 1-5pm, Sa-Su 2-5pm; Oct.-Mar. M-F 10am-noon and 1-4pm, Sa-Su 2-4pm. Free.*)

ULSTER MUSEUM. This museum has developed a variety of disparate exhibits to fill its halls, including Irish and modern art, local history, dinosaur bones, and 18th-century fashion. Most popular are the blackened, shriveled Mummy of Tak-abuti and the treasure salvaged from the *Girone*, a Spanish Armada ship that sank off the Causeway Coast in 1588. (*In the Botanic Gardens, off Stranmillis Rd. ☎9038 3000. Open year-round M-F 10am-5pm, Sa 1-5pm, Su 2-5pm. Free, except for certain exhibitions.*)

SOUTH BELFAST

Riverside trails, ancient ruins, and idyllic parks south of Belfast make it hard to believe that it's only a few minutes from the city center. The area can be reached by bus #71 from Donegall Sq. E., though it's still a bit of a hike from the drop-off. The **Belfast City Council Parks Section** can provide further information; they have a guide-map at most parks, the Welcome Centre, and Belfast Castle.

SIR THOMAS AND LADY DIXON PARK. The most stunning of the parks, sitting pretty on Upper Malone Rd. 20,000 rose bushes of every variety imaginable bloom here each year. The gardens were founded in 1836 and include stud China roses, imported between 1792 and 1824. (*Open M-Sa 7:30am-dusk, Su 9am-dusk.*)

GIANT'S RING. Four miles north along the tow path near Shaw's Bridge lies an earthen ring with a dolmen in the middle, remarkable for being older than dirt (birthdate 2500 BC or thereabouts). Little is known about the 600 ft. wide circle, but experts speculate that it was built for the same reasons as England's Stonehenge. Those clever experts quickly leave the room when it's mentioned that no one knows too much about Stonehenge, either. (*Always open. Free.*)

NORTH BELFAST

The sights of North Belfast cluster in and around **Cave Hill Forest Park.** A sunny and unhurried day is best for visiting, as walking is the primary mode of transportation after taking Antrim Rd. or Citybuses #45-51 to the park.

BELFAST ZOO. Set in the hills alongside Cave Hill Forest Park, the zoo's best attribute is its natural setting, where animals from the world over struggle to look at home. The recommended route passes elephants, giraffes, camels, zebras, and the ever-entertaining, acrobatic spider monkey. (*5 mi. north of the city on Antrim Rd.;*

take Citybus #9 or any one between #45 and 51. ☎9077 6277. Open Apr.-Sept. daily 10am-5pm; Oct.-Mar. 10am-2:30pm. Apr.-Sept. £6, children £3, family £16.50. Oct.-Mar. £5/£2.50/£13. Seniors, children under 4, and the disabled always free.)

BELFAST CASTLE. The Earl of Shaftesbury presented this building to the city in 1934, a few years after the castle-building craze had gone out of fashion. The castle lacks the history and majesty of older castles; nevertheless, its location, atop **Cave Hill,** long the seat of Ulster rulers, makes for fabulous views. The ancient King Matudan had his McArt's Fort here, where the more modern United Irishmen plotted rebellion in 1795. Marked trails lead north from the fort to five **caves** in the area, thought by historians to be ancient mines; only the lowest is accessible. For those on foot, the small path to the right of the gate makes for a far shorter and prettier walk than the road. *(☎9077 6925; www.belfastcastle.co.uk. Open M-Sa 9am-10:30pm, Su 9am-6pm. Free.)*

NORTHERN IRELAND

WEST BELFAST AND THE MURALS

The neighborhoods of West Belfast have historically been at the heart of political tensions in the North. The Catholic area (centered on **Falls Road**) and the Protestant neighborhood (centered on the **Shankill**) are separated by the **peace line,** a grim, gray, seemingly impenetrable wall. Along the wall, abandoned houses with boarded-up windows point to a tumultuous history and an uneasy future. Yet now, one bit of the peace line, near **Lanark Way,** connecting Falls and Springfield roads, contains peace paintings and signatures—painted mostly by tourists—indicating hope for the future. The Falls and Shankill embody both the raw sentiment that drives the Northern Irish conflict and the casual calm with which those closest to the Troubles approach daily life. West Belfast is not a tourist attraction in the tra-

> It is important for the visitor to note that the neighborhoods described are not necessarily divided upon lines of religion. The Shankill Rd. is almost exclusively Protestant, both Unionists and Loyalists, while the Falls Rd. area, though largely Catholic, tends to be mixed Nationalist and Republican.

ditional sense, though the walls and houses along the area's streets display political **murals** which speak to Belfast's religious and political divide. These murals are the city's most popular and interesting attraction.

Those traveling to these sectarian neighborhoods often take **black taxis,** community shuttles that whisk residents to the city center, picking up and dropping off passengers along their set routes. Some black taxis and **black cabs** can also be booked for tours of the Falls or Shankill (see **Tours,** p. 480). *Let's Go* offers two **neighborhood maps** (see **The Insider's City**) of the Protestant and Catholic murals, allowing individuals to explore the murals for themselves.

It is best to visit the Falls and Shankill during the day, when the neighborhoods are full of locals and, more importantly, when the murals can be seen. The Protestant Orangemen's Marching Season, in the weeks around July 12, is a risky time to visit the area—the parades are underscored by mutual antagonism that can lead to violence (see **History and Politics,** p. 458). Because the area around the peace line is desolate in areas, due to the proximity to either side, travelers are advised not to wander from one neighborhood over to the other, but to return to the city center between visits to Shankill and the Falls, as misunderstandings could arise. If they should wish to cross over without returning to city center, a good place, calm and crowded because of extensive construc-

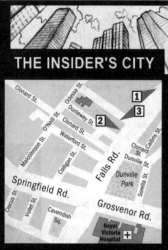

THE INSIDER'S CITY

THE CATHOLIC MURALS

The murals of West Belfast are the city's most intriguing attractions. The following is a list of Catholic Belfast's more famous and important; also included are those buildings most related to the Troubles.

1 Mural illustrating ten of the protesters during **The Hunger Strikes of 1981.** The current Sein Féin office. The premier political organization for the Republican movement. Since the 80s splinter factions and new parties have come to existence and influence.

2 Portrayal of **Bobby Sands,** found on Sevastopol St. on the side of the Sinn Féin Office. Sands was the first hunger striker to die. He was elected to British Parliament during this time and is remembered as the North's most famous martyr.

3 Formerly known as Northern Ireland's National RUC Headquarters, this building has the honor of being the most bombed police station in England, the Republic, and the North. Its fortified, barb-wired facade is found on Springfield St.

tion, is the gate where Workman Ave. crosses Lanark way.

The murals in the Falls and Shankill change constantly, so the sections below and the neighborhood maps describe but a few. For a guide to the mural's iconography, consult our glossary of common mural symbols (see **The Mural Symbols of West Belfast,** p. 489). While it is tacky to gawk at and photograph these walls, they *are* partly intended as propaganda, and many tourists take snap-shots. However, before taking a camera, ask hostel or B&B owners about the current political climate and cautions. An air of inquiry rather than judgement is well received by many Belfast natives who recognize that the Troubles may pique interest in outsiders. During the time leading up to Marching Season, tension sometimes builds, and picture-taking may not be well received. Photography is always acceptable on black cab tours, however, as drivers have agreements with the communities. But **do not take photographs of military installations,** as film may be confiscated.

THE FALLS. This Catholic and Republican neighborhood is larger than Shankill, moving from city center west following Castle St. As Castle St. continues across A12/Westlink, it becomes **Divis Street.** A highrise apartment building marks **Divis Tower,** an ill-fated housing development built by optimistic social planners in 1960s. The project soon became an IRA stronghold and saw some of the worst of Belfast's Troubles in 1970s. The British Army still occupies the top floors.

Continuing west, Divis St. turns into **Falls Road.** The **Sinn Fein** office is easily spotted: one side of it is covered with an enormous portrait of Bobby Sands (see **The Troubles,** p. 458, and **Belfast Murals,** p. 458) and an advertisement for the Sinn Fein newspaper, *An Phoblacht.* Continuing down Falls Rd. one passes a number of murals, which are generally on side streets. In the past both the Falls and the Shankill contained many representations of paramilitaries (IRA in the Falls, UVF and UDA in the Shankill) with armed men in ballyclavas; this and commemorative murals were the main subjects in the past, however, both communities have focused on historical and cultural representations for the newest string, even replacing many older murals. The newest Falls murals recall the ancient Celtic heritage of myths and legends, and depict The Great Hunger, as Northern Catholics refer to the Famine. Earlier militant murals certainly exist and a few that depict the Republican armed struggle remain in the Lower Falls.

The Falls Rd. soon splits into **Andersontown Road** and **Glen Road,** one of the few urban areas with a predominately Irish-speaking population. On the left are the Celtic crosses of **Milltown Cemetery,** the resting place of many Republican dead. Inside the entrance, a memorial to Republican casualties is bordered by a low, green fence on the right; the grave of Bobby Sands can be found here. Another mile along Andersontown Rd. lies the street's namesake—a housing project that was formerly a wealthy Catholic neighborhood—and more murals. The Springfield Rd. Police Service of Northern Ireland station, previously named the RUC station, was the **most-attacked police station in Ireland and the UK.** It was recently demolished, perhaps as a sacrifice to the peace process. Its charred defenses were formidable, and the **Andersonstown Barracks,** at the corner of Glen and Andersonstown Rd. are still heavily fortified.

SHANKILL. Shankill Rd. begins at the Westlink and turns into Woodvale Rd. as it crosses Cambrai St. The Woodvale Rd. intersects the **Crumlin Road.** at the Ardoyne roundabout, and can be taken back into city center. The **Shankill Memorial Garden** honors 10 people who died in a bomb attack on Fizzel's Fish Shop in October 1993; the garden is on the Shankill Rd. facing Berlin St. On the Shankill Rd., farther toward city center, is a mural of James Buchanan, the 15th President of the United States (1857-1861), who was of Ulster Scots descent (in the US they're referred to as the Scots-Irish). Other cultural murals depict the 50th Jubilee of the coronation of Queen Elizabeth in 1952 and the death of the Queen Mother in 2002. These are at the beginning of the Shankill on the road near the Rex bar. Historical murals include a memorial to the UVF who fought at the Battle of the Somme in 1916 during WWI (see **A Divided Island,** p. 454), also near the Rex Bar. In the **Shankill Estate,** streets off to the left of the road, some murals represent Cromwell putting down the 1741 Rebellion against the Protestant plantation owners. The densely decorated **Orange Hall** sits on the left at Brookmount St. McClean's Wallpaper, on the right, was formerly Fizzel's Fish Shop. Through the estate, Crumlin Rd. heads back to the city center, passing an army base, the courthouse, and the jail.

SANDY ROW AND NEWTOWNARDS RD. The Protestant population is growing steadily, partly due to the redevelopment of the Sandy Row area, and also because of too many working-class residents leaving the Shankill. This stretch is a turn off Donegall Rd. at Shaftesbury Sq. An orange arch topped with King William once marked its start. Nearby murals show the Red Hand of Ulster, a bulldog, and William crossing the Boyne. East Belfast is a secure Protestant enclave that is also

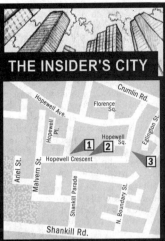

THE INSIDER'S CITY

THE PROTESTANT MURALS

The Protestant murals found in the Shankill area of West Belfast, tend to be of a more overtly militant nature. The following is a guide to the area's more well-known. These murals are all found near Hopewell St. and Hopewell Cresent, to the north of Shankill Rd., down Shankill Parade. Best reached by going South from Crumlin Rd.

1 Painting of a **Loyalist martyr,** killed in prison in 1997. The mural remembers those who have died fighting for British-Ulster rule.

2 Depiction of the **Grim Reaper,** with gun and British flag. Beside him on the painting lie crosses with the names of three IRA men, still at large, who set off a bomb in the Shankill area in 1993.

3 A collage of illustrations that represent Northern Ireland's Loyalist militant groups. Included are: the **UFF, UDU,** and the **UDA.**

Much of Belfast has changed dramatically since the 1994 ceasefires and the 1998 peace agreement. Signs of the conflict that engulfed Northern Ireland for 30 years have nearly vanished from the city center, where cozy cafes, swanky new bars, and bustling shoppers have replaced the army jeeps, battle-scarred buildings, and grim desolation downtown Belfast was once known for. The peace process has been good for business, but take the time to venture just beyond the commercial center, and you'll find that in many neighborhoods at the frontlines of the conflict, the peace dividend never arrived.

Belfast remains a divided city, and the numerous walls (innocently referred to as 'peace lines') built along the city's internal frontiers are by far the most visible indication of persistent sectarian divisions. The city is a patchwork of single-identity communities; the 2001 census revealed that two-thirds of the city's population live in areas that are either more than 90% Catholic or 90% Protestant. A peace-line marks the dividing line of interface—the area where a majority Catholic/nationalist community runs up against a majority Protestant/unionist community. Residential segregation has actually increased since the peace process began and in some areas construction on the walls continues—new ones built and old ones lengthened and heightened, divisions solidified and rigidified amidst the decade-long peace process.

The walls were constructed over the course of the Troubles to separate warring communities, prevent attacks, and sometimes create a buffer zone. Many of the peace-lines in place today stand on ground that has been brutally contested for decades. Tensions run high in areas of such close contact, and attacks on the other community are easily launched from the safety of one's own. Long before the modern Troubles began, there was a history of interface communities building barricades during times of conflict. Riots broke out in Belfast periodically in the first half of the century—during the 1920s with the Anglo-Irish War and subsequent Irish Civil War, and throughout the Depression in the 1930s. In areas affected by the violence, local residents erected barricades to guard their streets from marauding mobs and, in some cases, the security forces.

When parts of Belfast descended into chaos in the late 1960s and early 70s, many communities constructed barricades to protect themselves from the violence sweeping the city. In the early years much of this was concentrated in the borderland between Catholic/nationalist Falls and Protestant/Unionist Shankill. British troops arrived in August of 1969, and within a month they assembled the first official peaceline between the two areas to try to prevent some of the rioting. The army's wall ran along the same line as some community barricades, replacing and institutionalizing them with a permanent structure. Originally intended to be a temporary response, what began as a simple fence became fortified, elongated, and elevated to the 1.5 mile brick wall standing today.

The peace-line solution became an increasingly acceptable (and sought after) solution to intercommunal conflict at interface areas. Walls, fences, and official roadblocks were constructed throughout Belfast—with community activists from across the divide sometimes working together to lobby for their construction. By the year 2000, the Northern Ireland Office (NIO) Civil Representative's Office reported a total of 27 separate walls or fences across the city.

Mysteriously, none of these walls appear on most Belfast maps. Standing next to one, it's hard to imagine how such a dominant and obstructive fixture on the urban landscape could be disregarded. The walls forcefully demarcate not only space but identity as well. As they fortify and contain those within, they identify and guard against those beyond. Some look much like the war wounds they are—looming expanses of corrugated metal sprayed with graffitti epithets and crowned with thick coils of barbed wire. Others demonstrate the NIO's recent creative efforts to make the walls less of an eyesore—red and yellow brick with discreet security cameras and tasteful wrought iron accessories.

Designed to blend more readily into the environment, these new additions achieve a different sense of permanence. This worries some community members who live in interface areas. In recent debates over whether to build new walls and expand others in flashpoint areas, some have argued that once you begin building walls, they're very hard to take down. Once you go to the effort to make them pretty, the chances they will ever be removed become even more remote.

For the last three years, Brenna Powell has worked at the Stanford Center on Conflict and Negotiation on projects in partnership with grass-roots organizations in Northern Ireland.

growing with redevelopment, and as in the other areas be careful when traveling in this area around Marching season. A number of murals line Newtownards Rd. One mural depicts the economic importance of the shipyard and the industrial history. On the Ballymacart Rd., which runs parallel to New-

THE MURAL SYMBOLS OF WEST BELFAST

PROTESTANT MURALS

Blue, White, and Red: The colors of the British flag; often painted on curbs and signposts to demarcate Unionist murals and neighborhoods.

The Red Hand: The crest of Ulster Province, the central symbol of the Ulster flag, which includes a red cross on a white background, used by Unionists to emphasize the separateness of Ulster from the Republic. Symbolizes the hand of the first Norse King, which he supposedly cut off and threw on a Northern beach to establish his primacy. (The crest also appears on Catholic murals which depict the four ancient provinces; evidence of the overlap in heritage.)

King Billy/William of Orange: Sometimes depicted on a white horse, crossing the Boyne to defeat the Catholic King James II at the 1690 Battle of the Boyne. The Orange Order was later founded in his honor.

The Apprentice Boys: A group of young men who shut the gates of Derry to keep out the troops of James II, beginning the great siege of 1689. They have become Protestant folk heroes, inspiring a sect of the Orange order in their name. The slogan **"No Surrender,"** also from the siege, has been appropriated by radical Unionists, most notably Rev. Ian Paisley.

Lundy: The Derry leader who advocated surrender during the siege; now a term for anyone who wants to give in to Catholic demands.

Scottish Flag: Blue with a white cross; recalls the Scottish-Presbyterian roots of many Protestants whose ancestors were part of the Ulster Plantation (see **Cromwell,** p. 60).

CATHOLIC MURALS

Orange and Green: Colors of the Irish Republic's flag; often painted on curbs and signposts in Republican neighborhoods.

The Irish Volunteers: Republican tie to the earlier (nonsectarian) Nationalists.

Saoirse: Irish for "Freedom"; the most common term found on murals.

Éireann go bráth: "Ireland forever"; a popular IRA slogan.

Tiocfaidh ár lá: (CHOCK-ee-ar-LA) "Our day will come."

Slan Abhaile: (Slawn ah-WAH-lya) "Safe home"; directed at the primarily Protestant RUC police force.

Phoenix: Symbolizes united Ireland rising from the ashes of British persecution.

Lug: Celtic god, seen as the protector of the "native Irish" (Catholics).

Green Ribbon: IRA symbol for "free our POWs."

Bulldog: Britain.

Bowler Hats: A symbol for Orangemen.

MORE ON THE MURALS

For further information on the Troubles and the murals try these books by Bill Polston:

Drawing Support 2: Murals of War and Peace. Belfast, Beyond the Pale Publications, 1995.

Drawing Support 3: Murals and Transitions in the North of Ireland. Belfast, Beyond the Pale Publications, 2003.

Or, visit the **Conflict Archive** online at **http://cain.ulst.ac.uk.**

townards Rd, is a mural of *The Lion, the Witch, and the Wardrobe* by C.S. Lewis, who was from the area. One likens the UVF to the ancient hero, Cúchulainn, Ulster's defender.

◪ ARTS AND ENTERTAINMENT

Belfast's many cultural events and performances are covered in the monthly *Arts Council Artslink*, free at the tourist office. Daily listings appear in the daily *Belfast Telegraph* (which also has a Friday Arts supplement) and in Thursday's issue of the *Irish News*. For more extensive information on pub entertainment, grab the biweekly, two-page bulletin *The List*, available free at the tourist office, hostels, and many pubs. The **Crescent Arts Centre,** 2 University Rd., supplies general arts info, but mostly specific news about their own exhibits and concerts, which take place September through May. They also host three seasonal terms of eight-week courses in yoga, writing, traditional music, dance, theater, and drawing. (☎9024 2338. Classes £36. Open M-Sa 10am-10pm.) **Fenderesky Gallery,** 2 University Rd., inside the Crescent Arts building, hosts contemporary shows all year. (2 University Rd. ☎9023 5245. Open Tu-Sa 11:30am-5pm.) The **Old Museum Arts Center,** 7 College Sq. N., is Belfast's largest venue for contemporary artwork. (☎9023 5053; www.oldmuseumartscentre.org. Open M-Sa 9:30am-5:30pm.) Besides exhibits, it features workshops and a variety of dance, theater, and music performances. (Tickets ☎9023 3332. Most tickets £6-8, students and concessions £3.) A word of warning to summer travelers: July and August are slow months for Belfast arts; around July 12, the whole city shuts down.

THEATER

The truly **Grand Opera House,** 4 Great Victoria St., shows a mix of opera, ballet, musicals, and drama. (☎9024 0411; www.goh.co.uk.) Tickets for most shows can be purchased either by phone until 9pm or in person at the box office. (☎9024 1919; 24hr. info line ☎9024 9129. Tickets from £12.50, with occasional student concessions. Open M-W 8:30am-6pm, Th 8:30am-9pm, F-Sa 8:30am-6pm.) **The Lyric Theatre** mixes Irish plays and international works. (55 Ridgeway St. ☎9038 1081; www.lyrictheatre.co.uk. Box office open M-Sa 10am-7pm. Tickets M-Th £10, F-Sa £12.50.) The **Group Theatre** produces comedies and farces in the Ulster Hall from September to May. (Bedford St. ☎9032 9685. Box office open M-F noon-3pm. Tickets £4-8.) The **Old Museum Art Centre** presents avant-garde contemporary works. (7 College Sq. North. ☎9023 5053. Tickets £3-8.)

MUSIC

Ulster Hall brings Belfast everything from classical to pop (Bedford St. ☎9032 3900.) Try independent box offices for tickets: **Our Price** (☎9023 0262) or the **Ticket Shop** at Virgin (☎9032 3744). **The Grand Opera House** (see **Theater,** p. 490) resounds with classical vocal music. **Waterfront Hall** is one of Belfast's newest concert centers, hosting a series of performances from classical to pop throughout the year. (2 Lanyon Pl. ☎9033 4400. Tickets £10-35, student discounts usually available.) The **Ulster Orchestra** plays concerts at Waterfront Hall and Ulster Hall. (☎9066 8798; www.ulster-orchestra.org.uk. Tickets £5-23, with the cheapies behind the stage.)

FILM

There are two major movie theaters in Belfast, besides the new one at the Odyssey (see **Sights,** p. 482). Commercial films are shown at **UGC Cinemas,** 14 Dublin Rd.; most movies arrive a few months after their US release. (24hr. info ☎0870 155 5176. £4.40, students and seniors £2.75, children £2.55; before 5pm £2.75.) **Queen's Film Theatre,** in a back alley off Botanic Ave., draws a more artsy crowd. (☎9024 4857. £2-3.80. "Meal and movie" discounts for certain restaurants.)

FESTIVALS

QUEEN'S UNIVERSITY BELFAST FESTIVAL. Belfast reigns supreme in the art world for three weeks between October and November, during the university's annual festival. Over 300 performances of opera, ballet, film, and comedy invade venues across the city, drawing internationally acclaimed groups. Tickets for the most popular events sell out months ahead of time, but there's always something to see without planning ahead. (✆ *Box office 9066 5577; www.belfastfestival.com. For advance schedules, write to: The Belfast Festival at Queens, 25 College Gardens, Belfast BT9 6BS. Tickets sold by mail and phone from mid-Sept. through the festival's end. Prices £2.50-£25.)*

WEST BELFAST ARTS FESTIVAL (FÉILE AN PHOBAIL). This week-long series of events, held the second week of August, is the high point of the year for Falls residents. The Nationalist festivities celebrate Irish traditional culture, bringing in both big name trad groups and indebted rockers. (*437 Falls Rd.,* ✆ *9031 3440; www.feilebelfast.com.)*

THE BELFAST FILM FESTIVAL. In its fifth year, this film festival presents a full schedule of film screenings from cult to classic, with a particular emphasis on Irish filmmakers and film as a political medium. The event draws world renowned actors and directors to Belfast. This year's festival is scheduled for March 2004. (✆ *9032 5913; www.belfastfilmfestival.org.)*

⚑ SPORTS AND ACTIVITIES

The state-of-the-art **Belfast Superbowl** doesn't offer football, but it does have 20 glow-in-the-dark bowling lanes. (4 Clarence St. ✆9033 1466. Open M-Sa 10am-midnight, Su noon-midnight.) **Lagan Valley LeisurePlex** is one of the biggest family-fun facilities in all of Ireland, and comes complete with a huge galleon, master-blasters, and thrilling water rides. (Lisburn. ✆9267 2121. 8 mi. from Belfast.) Dominating the skyline just north of Belfast, **Cave Hill** offers adventure sports of a different kind. The **Cave Hill walk** starts from the parking lot of the **Belfast Zoo**, trails the Ulster Way for a short distance, and then branches off on its own on a straight shot toward **McArt's Fort** (1100ft.), which sits at the summit. During the 3hr. climb, hikers pass **caves** that were carved into the hill many years ago by Neolithic wanderers searching for shelter. Hikers will also be granted panoramic views of Belfast and its port. (Call ✆9032 1221 for more info.) On the 9 mi. **Lagan Valley Towpath Walk,** travelers also temporarily join with the Ulster Way for part of their journey along the canal towpaths to **Sir Thomas and Lady Dixon Park.** (✆9023 1221 for info.)

Rather sit and watch than walk and run? Take a cab to the **Odyssey Arena** to catch the **Harp Larger Belfast Giants** battle it out with county competitors. (✆9059 1111; www.belfastgiants.com.) **Soccer** fanatics always nab a game or two at the **Windsor**

BUT DOC, A CAR WITH GULL WINGS?!!!

In 1978, John Z. de Lorean, then the Vice President of General Motors, raised the hopes of many Belfastians by deciding to construct his new car factory just outside the city. With a pair of cowboy boots and a heap of great salesmanship, de Lorean gathered $200 million from investors and earned the status of savior among Northern Ireland's unemployed population. There was reason, however, not to believe the hype. In 1982, the factory shut down after producing just 10,000 cars, due to consistently high and unrealistic sales projections. Fast-talkin' de Lorean was arrested the same year on drug charges. His dream car—with its "gull wings" and sleek design—lives on in popular memory as Marty McFly's time-traveling vehicle in the *Back to the Future* series.

Park pitch. (Donegall Ave. ☎9024 4198.) **Gaelic Footballers** run to Andersonstown, West Belfast, to enjoy the Sunday afternoon matches. (Call the GAA at ☎9038 3815.) **Horseracing** goes down at the Maze (Lisburn. ☎9262 1256.) Located just 10 mi. from Belfast, the premier racecourse has a dozen meetings throughout the year, including the **Mirror May Day** fixture and the **Ulster Harp Derby** in June. **Rugby** can be viewed and played at **Ravenhill Stadium.** (☎9064 9141.)

▶ DAYTRIPS FROM BELFAST

ULSTER FOLK MUSEUM AND TRANSPORT AND RAILWAY MUSEUMS

The Museums stretch across 176 acres in the town of Holywood. Take the Bangor road (A2) 7 mi. east of Belfast. Buses and trains stop here on the way to Bangor. ☎9042 8428; www.magni.org.uk. Open July-Sept. M-Sa 10am-6pm, Su 11am-6pm; Mar.-June M-F 10am-5pm, Sa 10am-6pm, Su 11am-6pm; Oct.-Feb. M-F 10am-4pm, Sa 10am-5pm, Su 11am-5pm. Folk Museum £4.50, students and seniors £2.50, family day ticket £12. Transport Museum £4.50/£2.50/£12. Combined admission £6/£3/£16.

Established by an Act of Parliament in the 1950s, the ◪**Folk Museum** aims to preserve the way of life of Ulster's farmers, weavers, and craftspeople. The Museum contains over 30 buildings from the past three centuries divided into a town and rural area, the latter containing cottages from all nine Ulster counties, including the usually overlooked Monaghan, Cavan, and Donegal in the Republic. All but two of the buildings are transplanted originals. All have been artfully integrated into a landscape befitting their regional origin, creating an amazing air of authenticity. Unobtrusive attendants in period costume stand nearby to answer questions. No cheesy historical scenes or written explanations interrupt the visitor's own imaginative roleplay. Ballydugan Weaver's House is worth particular attention as John the Weaver, a fourth generation weaver, operates the only working linen loom in Ireland there. In addition to the functional printer's press on Main St., a sawmill from Fermanagh and a cornmill will soon be added. The museum hosts special events, including trad sessions, dance performances and workshops, storytelling festivals, and textile exhibitions. Call ahead for details.

The Transport Museum and the Railway Museum are across from the Folk Museum. Inside the **Transport Museum,** horse-drawn coaches, bicycles, cars, and airplane and ship models tell the history of vehicles in motion. The motorcycle exhibition is extensive, following the evolution of the vehicle from the bicycle to Harley-mania with a life-size 1950s diner installation, and even a nod to biker fashions from 60s to 90s. Below lies the car exhibition, replete with stylish and bizarre cars, including a model of de Lorean's ill-fated vehicle (see **But Doc...,** p. 491). A *Titanic* exhibit includes original blueprints, china, photographs, and letters from passengers on board as it traces the fate of the Belfast-built ship. "The Flight Experience" focuses on airborne travel with a life-sized airplane cabin and hands-on displays explaining the physics involved, while the hangar-shaped **Railway Museum** stuffs in 25 old railway engines, including the largest locomotive built in Ireland.

NEAR BELFAST

ISLE OF MAN   ☎01624

Isle of Man Steam Packet Company (☎646 645; www.steam-packet.com) runs ferries to **Douglas** *from the SeaCat Terminal, Donegall Quay, in Belfast (2¾hr.; Apr.-Oct. 2 per week, usually M and F, July-Aug. also W; £27-30, students £19-30). Public transportation is run by* **Isle of Man Transport** *(☎663 366); the* **Travel Shop,** *by the Douglas bus station, has* *maps and schedules. (☎ 662 525. Open M 10am-12:30pm and 1:30-5:45pm, Tu-F 8am-5:45pm, Sa 8am-3:30pm.)* **Isle of Man Bus Tour Company**, *Central Promenade (☎ 674 301), in Douglas, operates the popular "Round the Island" tour (W and Su; £15).*

When the grit and grime of Belfast city proves too much, the Isle of Man offers a welcome retreat. Belfast and Dublin locals often vacation to the Isle to take advantage of its coastal vistas and isolated hiking opportunities. But be warned: Though it may appear as simply a droplet of land in the Irish Sea, the Isle of Man is actually its own tiny independent nation. It has its own currency, though Northern Irish currency can be used, and its international dialing code (44) is shared with Britain.

Douglas, the small island's capital city (town), is home to the **Manx Museum,** which chronicles Man's history. (☎ 648 000. Open M-Sa 10am-5pm. Free.) Past the Villa Marina Gardens on Harris Promenade sits the **Gaiety Theatre.** Designed in 1900 and recently restored, the theater shone during Douglas's seaside resort days. (☎ 625 001. 1½hr. tours leave Sa 10:15am. £4, children £2). For a place to stay, check at the friendly **Devonian Hotel ❷,** 4 Sherwood Terr., a Victorian townhouse off the Promenade. (☎ 674 676. £18-22, with bath £25). Or, try the **Grandstand Campsite ❶.** (☎ 696 330; open mid-June to mid-Aug. and Sept; £5.50 per person). At **Brendann O'Donnell's** pub, 16-18 Strand St., Guinness posters and Irish music point to the owner's loyalties. (☎ 621 566. Open Su-Th noon-11pm, F-Sa noon-midnight.) Paramount City, on Queens Promenade, houses the city's biggest and best nightclubs: **Director's Bar** and **Dark Room.** (☎ 622 447. Open F-Sa 10pm-3:30am.)

Peel is a beautiful fishing town on the west coast. ▧**Peel Castle,** on St. Patrick's Isle, is reached by a causeway from the Quay. (Open Easter-Oct. daily 10am-5pm; winter hours vary. Last admission 1hr. before closing. £3, children £1.50, family £7.50.) Across the harbor, the **House of Manannan** emphasizes the role of the sea in Manx history. (☎ 648 000. Open daily 10am-5pm, last admission 3pm. £5, children £2.50.) Buses (☎ 662 525) from Douglas come to the station on Atholl St. The **Tourist Centre** is in the Town Hall, Derby Rd. (☎ 842 341. Open M-Th 8:45am-5pm, F 8:45am-4:30pm.) Pitch tents at **Peel Camping Park ❶,** Derby Rd., which has laundry facilities and showers. (☎ 842 341. Open Easter-Sept. £4 per person. Electricity £1.50.)

Hiking on Man is excellent. The 90 mi. Raad ny Foillan ("Road of the Gull") trail winds around the island; the spectacular 12 mi. ▧**Port Erin to Castletown route** highlights the south; and Bayr ny Skeddan ("The Herring Road") runs 14 mi. between Peel and Castletown, overlapping the Millennium Way, 28 mi. from Castletown to Ramsey along the 14th-century Royal Highway. All tourist centers on the island can provide you with the appropriate maps and guides.

The first two weeks of June turn Man into a motorcycling beast for the **T.T. (Tourist Trophy) Races;** the respected **International Cycling Week** occurs around the same time. The **Manx language** is heard when laws are proclaimed on July 5, during the **Manx Heritage Festival**. Find other events at www.isleofman.com.

COUNTIES DOWN AND ARMAGH

Locals flock to this sleepy but scenic area to take advantage of the seaside—the coast of Down and the Ards Peninsula are covered with fishing villages, holiday resorts, and 17th-century ruins. The Mourne Mountains, almost directly south of Belfast and just a *lough* away from the Irish Republic, rise above the town of Newcastle, the largest seaside resort in Co. Down. An inland county surrounded by rivers and lakes, Armagh is set on the rolling hills of Northern Ireland's Drumlin Belt. The best time to visit Co. Armagh is during apple blossom season in May, when the

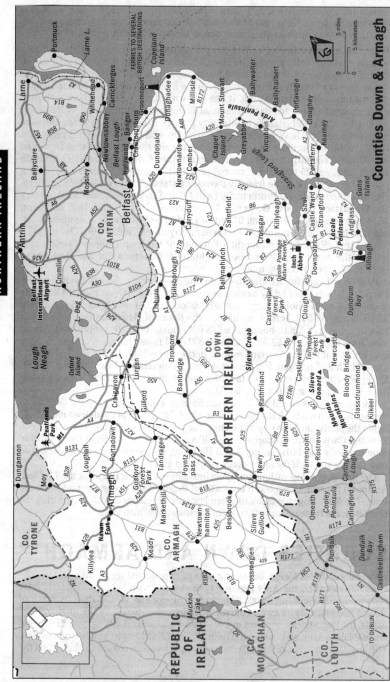

Counties Down & Armagh

countryside, known as the "Orchard of Ireland," is covered in pink. Armagh town is an ecclesiastical center of great historical interest; traces of human habitation at Navan Fort date back to 5500 BC. Armagh's other population centers, Craigavon and Portadown, near Lough Neagh, are industrial centers of less interest to tourists, although Craigavon does host the Lough Neagh Discovery Centre's acres of feathered friends and wooded park land.

BANGOR (BEANNCHOR)

Bangor found a place on early medieval maps of Ireland with its famous Abbey, but this pious era ended in the 9th century, when Vikings ran rampant. By the Victorian era, the town had become eminent again, this time as the seaside see-and-be-seen for Belfast residents. Today, hilly Bangor is one of the top destinations on the Ards Peninsula, and hosted the Olympic torch for the Special Olympics in 2003. While the town caters to families and older vacationers during the week, its nightlife draws Belfast twenty-somethings on the weekends. Such traffic does not affect the serene air about the town, however, and its location makes it an inevitable (and enjoyable) stop on the way down the Ards Peninsula.

▐ TRANSPORTATION

Trains: Abbey St. (☎9127 1143; www.translink.co.uk), at the south end of town. To: **Belfast** (40min.; M-F 39 per day, Sa 25 per day, Su 11 per day; £3.10, with ISIC card £2).

Buses: Abbey St. (☎9127 1143), joined to the train station. To: **Belfast's** Laganside Bus Station (45min.; M-F 14 per day, Sa 27 per day, Su 8 per day; £2.70, with ISIC card £2.20). All **Ards Peninsula** towns must be accessed via Newtownards Station (☎9181 2391).

Taxis: Atlastaxi (☎9145 6789; £3 min.); **LA Cabs** (☎9127 0848).

▐ ▐ ORIENTATION AND PRACTICAL INFORMATION

The road from Belfast runs south-north through town, changing names several times along the way—**Abbey Street** becomes **Main Street** at a roundabout that curves to the right at the waterfront to (briefly) become **Bridge Street**, then **Quay Street,** and finally **Seacliff Road.** Turning to the left at the waterfront marina leads to B&B lined **Queens Parade.** The train and bus stations are next to each other where Abbey St. becomes Main St. From there, Main St. intersects three important roads: **Castle Park Road** becomes restaurant-filled **Dufferin Avenue** as it crosses Main St.; **Hamilton Rd.** becomes **Central Avenue** and leads to Crawfordsburn and its park; and pub-intensive **High Street,** divides miniscule Bridge St. and Quay St.

Tourist Office: Tower House, 34 Quay St. (☎9127 0069; www.northdown.gov.uk, and www.bangorgoesglobal.com). Books accommodations and provides a **bureau de change.** Open July-Aug. M 10am-7pm, Tu-F 9am-7pm, Sa 10am-4pm, Su noon-6pm; Sept. and June M 10am-5pm, Tu-F 9am-5pm, Sa 10am-4pm, Su 1-5pm; Jan.-May and Oct.-Dec. M 10am-5pm, Tu-F 9am-5pm, Sa 10am-4pm.

Banks: First Trust, 85 Main St. (☎9127 0628). Open M-F 9:30am-4:30pm, W open 10am. **Northern Bank,** 77 Main St. (☎9127 1211). Open M 10am-5pm, Tu-F 10am-3:30pm, Sa 9:30am-12:30pm. All have 24hr. **ATMs.**

Pharmacy: Boots Pharmacy, 79-83 Main St. (☎9127 1134). Open M-Sa 9am-5:30pm.

Work Opportunities: The Marine Court Hotel, 18-20 Quay St. (☎9145 1100; www.marinecourthotel.net). Will hire travelers to work in its restaurant for a minimum of 2 mo. Experience is preferred. Minimum wage.

Emergency: ☎999; no coins required. **Police:** Castle Park Ave. (☎9145 4444). **Bangor Hospital,** Hamilton Rd. (☎9147 5120), treats minor injuries.

Internet Access: The **Bangor Library** (☎9127 0591). Coming into the city, take a right off Main St. onto Hamilton Rd. Library is on the right past a park. £1.50 per 30min.; members free. Open M-W 10am-8pm, F 10am-5pm, Sa 10am-1pm and 2-5pm.

Post Office: 143 Main St. (☎9146 3000), on the corner of Dufferin Ave. Open M-Sa 9am-5:30pm. **Postal code:** BT20.

ACCOMMODATIONS

Although Bangor lacks a hostel or a campground, it teems with B&Bs; check the tourist office window for details. Often the 'No Vacancy' signs in windows are left up by mistake—inquire with the B&B owner if interested. "En suite" or private-bath rooms are few, but there for the asking for anyone willing to dole out a few more pounds. B&B's cluster along coastal Seacliff Rd. and inland Princetown Rd., Dufferin Ave.'s extension. Choosing between them can be a challenge, as all are cozy, homey, and on the small side. Those on Seacliff Rd. are recommended for their spectacular sea views.

Cairn Bay Lodge, 278 Seacliff Rd. (☎9146 7636; www.cairnbaylodge.com). A longer walk and a bit more money earn visitors one of the most beautiful accommodations in town. This turn-of-the-century B&B includes elegant guest lounges decorated to historic Victorian perfection and large rooms with sitting areas. Certified proprietress Jenny willing to give spa treatments to weary travelers (£18-50). Singles £30-35; doubles £55-60. ❸

The Anchorage, 36 Seacliff Rd. (☎9146 1326). Larger than the cramped B&B room trend, these stately digs come with excellent showers and large breakfast plates. £17, with bath £22.50. ❷

The Dolly Rocks Guest House, 72 Seacliff Rd. (☎9172 72644). Though no sea view graces any of the beautiful, snug rooms, an excellent visitor's lounge obliges those with a look-don't touch attitude toward waves. £16. ❷

Anglers Rest B&B, 24 Seacliff Rd. (☎9127 4870). Equipped with a friendly owner and big TVs in every room, as well as 1 enviable room with bath. £16. ❷

Hebron House, 59 Queens Parade (☎9146 3126; www.hebron-house.com). Marble fireplaces in the sitting area, sunny bedrooms with outstanding views, and a full-course dinner for £10. Complimentary coffee and tea served in front. Strictly non-smoking. Singles £25; doubles £30-45; family room £55. ❸

Pierview, 28 Seacliff Rd. (☎259 146 3381). A guesthouse with an eclectic approach to decoration, Pierview invites guests to lounge in the lovely family room in front. Singles £16; doubles £35-40. ❷

FOOD AND PUBS

Like any great resort town, Bangor has no shortage of places to eat. Every third shop on Main St. has baked goods and sandwiches, and every pub in town serves grub. Pubs and clubs gather along High St. and the waterfront.

Piccola Pizzeria, 3 High St. (☎9145 3098). Turkish management serves kebabs, burgers, and the town's best takeaway pizza for £2.90-4.70. Watch for lines as scavengers pick up their late night nibbles. Open daily 4:30pm-late. ❷

Ava Bar, 132 Main St. (☎9146 5490; paul.hillen@ukonline.co.uk), across from the bus and train station. It may look like the average mahogany and velvet snug bar, but the unbeatable meal deal scores a main course and a pint for £3.95. Unlike those at other bars, this deal includes dinner hours. Bar open daily 11:30am-11:30pm; meal deal noon-2:30pm and 5-9pm. ❷

The Diner Cafe, 8 Dufferin Ave. (☎9146 4586). A strong bastion of budget bites, providing filling, inexpensive fish, chips, and other kids-meal faves in a no-frills setting. All-day breakfast £2.50. Open M-Sa 8am-5:30pm, Su 10am-4pm. ❶

Brazilia Cafe, Bridge St. (☎9127 2763). White-washed halls and colorful paintings whisk diners away to an Irish designer's vision of Brazil. Chef serves Amazon-inspired sandwiches (£2.80-5) and omelettes (£5). Open 9am-4:30pm. ❷

Fealty's, 35 High St. (☎9146 0088; www.fealtys.com). The bar marked "Ormeau Arms" has always been known as Fealty's, a popular hangout renowned for spreading turf on its floor for rugby season's most important games (those involving Ireland, Australia, and New Zealand). Come for the 6 Nations Championship in February, or F-Sa for trad music. Live music 9:30pm. Open M-Sa 11:30am-1am, Su 12:30pm-midnight.

Jenny Watts, 41 High St. (☎9127 0401). Draws an older crowd, except during Su jazz, when younger chill-mongers converge (1-3pm). Low-ceilinged underpass feels like the cave where the pub's namesake, a 18th century smuggler and overall rogue, is fabled to have hid from the authorities. Kids eat free Sa-Su noon-3pm. For the older crowd, DJs spin at the 23+ club upstairs F-Sa from 10pm-1am, and folk music features Tu and Th. Cover £2. Bar open M 11:30am-11pm, Tu-Sa 11:30am-1am, Su 12:30pm-12am.

Bar Mocha, 18-20 Quay St. (☎9145 1100), on a little alley off Quay. Difficult to find, but many Belfast natives brave the search. 21+ age requirement generates a 25-35 crowd. Cover F-Sa £3. Open W-Sa 8pm-late.

🔍 📷 SIGHTS AND ACTIVITIES

North Down Visitors and Heritage Centre, adjoining Town Hall on Castle Park, is on the grounds where the castle of the Hamilton family, who once owned all the land around Bangor, once stood. The site now houses collected photographs and artifacts of Bangor history. (☎9127 1200; www.northdown.gov.uk/heritage. Open July-Aug. Tu-Sa 10:30am-5:30pm, Su 2-5:30pm; Sept.-June Tu-Sa 10:30am-4:30pm, Su 2-4:30pm. Free.) The rest of the Hamilton Estate consists of 129 sometimes-wooded, sometimes-grassy acres that now comprise the public **Castle Park.** Nearby, 37 acre **Ward Park,** up Castle St. or Hamilton Rd. from Main St., entices with tennis courts, bowling greens, a cricket pitch, a pitch-and-putt, and a string of lakes harboring a wildlife sanctuary. Contact the **Bangor Leisure Centre** to reserve plots. (☎9127 0271 and 9145 8773. Tennis courts £3.90 per hr.; rackets £1.60. Bowls £4.05; children, students, and seniors £3. Pitch-and-putt £2.65/£1.85. Centre open M-F 7:30am-10pm, Sa 7:45am-6pm, Su 2-6pm.) Additionally, the Leisure Centre provides a swimming pool (£1.85/£1.35), a gym and spa (£2.15-4.50), and squash courts (£3.65-4.95). Like any good port town, Bangor has its share of aquatic options. **Fishing** enthusiasts relish herring or deep-sea fishing, or perhaps a short sea cruise or a foray to observe Irish sea birds. Trips depart from the North Pier on the Purple Heather across from the tourist office. (☎077 960 0607 or 070 5060 8036; www.bangorboat.com. Fishing trips July-Aug. 9:30am-noon and 7:20-9:30pm. £7, children £5. Sea cruises July-Aug. afternoons; weekends in spring and autumn. £2.50/£1.50. Birdwatching in June. £8/£5.) The **North Down Coastal Path** forays 15 mi. along the bay's edge from Holywood through Bangor and Groomsport to Orlock Point. Along the way lie abandoned WWII lookouts, Helen's Bay (a popular bathing spot), Crawfordsburn Country Park, **Greypoint Fort** (an old fort with a massive gun), and a giant redwood. Bikes are not allowed on the path. The region is recognized for its colonies of **black guillemots,** more widely known as the Bangor penguins.

THE BIG SPLURGE

HIGHER AND HIGHER

Is anything lovelier than the shoreline of the Ards, or the Giant's Causeway at sunset? Could it get any better than gazing at the placid Mourne Mountains? For those who don't suffer from vertigo and are willing to leave the idyllic behind, it could get a lot more interesting: the pilots at **Ulster Helicopter Hire** are primed to show you how, and **Ulster Flying Club** is fool enough to put you at the helm.

Ulster Helicopter Hire straps thrill-seekers into the backseat of a helicopter and takes them for a joyride 1500 ft. in the air, soaring over the Ards Peninsula and as far as Belfast, the Northern Antrim Coast, and the Mourne Mountains. The helicopters hug each knoll and glen of the Northern Irish landscape, close enough for photo opps and good old-fashioned fear...um...fun.

Overconfident control freaks might do better paying **Ulster Flying Club** a visit. Accompanied by a professional pilot, the intrepid take off on trial flights over the Ards and the Mournes. If the flight reveals a life's passion, hours flown count toward a Private Pilot's License (PPL), though it should be stressed that only practice makes perfect.

Both fly from Ards Airport, 1 mi. outside Newtownards down the Comber Rd. **Ulster Helicopter Hire** *(☎9182 0028; www.helicoptercentre.co.uk). 30min. £10.50, 1hr. £141, 1½hr. £211.50. Open Mar.-Oct. Sa-Su 9am-5pm.* **Ulster Flying Club** *(☎9181 3327). 30min. £70, 45min. £100, 1hr. £130.*

The path also passes through the picturesque village of Crawfordsburn, 3 mi. from Bangor and home to Ireland's oldest hotel. **The Old Inn,** Main St., dates from 1614 and maintains many of its original wood decorations. The Inn has been visited by celebrities ranging from Peter the Great of Russia to C.S. Lewis, and serves affordable food in its **Parlour Bar ❷.** (☎9185 3255. Mains £3-10. Food served M-Sa 12:30-2:30pm and 7-9:30pm; high tea Su 5-7pm.) The **Crawfordsburn Country Park,** off B20 (A2) at Helen's Bay, offers coastal paths, forests, and a waterfall. To walk there, turn onto the easily missed footpath just before the Texaco station. (Open Apr.-Sept. 9am-8pm; Oct.-Mar. 9am-4:45pm.) Inside the park, a **Visitors Centre** provides info on trails and natural history. (☎9185 3621. Open M-Sa 9am-5pm, Sa-Su 10am-5pm.) The Bangor **bus** and **train** both run through Crawfordsburn.

Bangor claims to be the **festival** capital of Northern Ireland, hosting many events throughout the year. The hills are alive in April for the **Bangor International Choral Festival,** and all the world's a stage that same month as the town's weeklong **Drama Festival** attracts hordes. The **Ultimate Bank Holiday Weekend** sweeps through town in August—£15 gains access to foam machines, trapeze artists, and DJs galore. In September, crowds gather for four days of **Aspects,** one of Ireland's premier literary festivals. Seamus Heaney has been known to make an appearance. Contact the tourist office for details.

ARDS PENINSULA

The Ards Peninsula is bounded on the west by tranquil Strangford Lough, and the east by the agitated Irish Sea. The shore of the lough from Newtownards to Portaferry is crowded with historic houses, crumbling ruins, and spectacular lake views. Several wildlife preserves announce the lough as an area of particular scientific and environmental interest—the area sees 80% of all the species found along Ireland's coast. On the Irish Sea side of the Ards, each fishing village seems tinier than the last.

Ulsterbus leaves Laganside Station in **Belfast** to traverse the peninsula, stopping in almost every town. **Trains** roll no farther than Bangor. From the south, a **ferry** crosses frequently between Strangford and Portaferry (see p. 503). **Biking** is another excellent and fairly painless way to see the Ards Peninsula.

NEWTOWNARDS

At the head of the Strangford Lough lies Ards borough's capital city. As such, Newtownards offers the traveler a conveniently situated locale for further exploration of the Ards Penninsula, and many an interesting site of its own. Though invaluable as the premier source of information about its down coast neighbors, Newtownards manages to distance itself from the tourist throngs.

TRANSPORTATION

Buses: 33 Regent St., next to the tourist office (☎9081 23910; www.translink.co.uk). To **Belfast** (30min.; 6:40am-9pm every 5min.) and all **Ards Peninsula** towns, including **Portaferry** (75min.; M-F 9 per day, Sa 8 per day, Su 5 per day). All buses stop at Gibson's Lane between Regent St. and Mill St.

Taxis: Call **Ards Cabs,** 5 Gibson's Lane (☎9181 1617); **A&G,** Lower Mary St. (☎9181 0360); or the wheelchair-accessible **Rosevale Taxis,** Unit 11 North St. (☎9181 1440 or 9182 1111). Taxis also operate from the bus station at Regent St.

ORIENTATION AND PRACTICAL INFORMATION

Two main streets surround Newtownards' center at **Conway Square,** home to the town hall and a small pedestrian area. Running north to south on either side of the square are **Church Street,** which becomes **Regent Street** and then **Frances Street** as it progresses north to Donaghadee, and **High Street,** which becomes **Mill Street.** Between the two main streets toward the tourist office is **Gibson's Lane,** where all buses stop and leave.

Tourist office: 31 Regent St. (☎9182 6846; www.ards-council.gov.uk). Books accommodations and, unlike most Ards tourist offices, stays open all year. Open Sept.-June M-F 9:15am-5pm, Sa 9:30am-5pm; July-Aug. M-Th 9am-5:15pm, F-Sa 9am-5:30pm.

Banks: Bank of Ireland, 12 Conway Sq. (☎9181 4200). Open M-F 9:30am-4:30pm, W 10am-4:30pm. **Northern Bank,** 35 High St. (☎9181 2220). Open M 10am-5pm, Tu-F 10am-3:30pm, Th 9:30am-5pm, Sa 9:30am-12:30pm. **Abbey National,** 15 High St. (☎5765 4321). Open M-F 9am-5pm, Th 10am-3pm, Sa 9am-noon.

Pharmacy: Boots, 12-14 Regent St. (☎9181 3359). Open M-Sa 9am-5:30pm.

Work opportunities: Contact **Grafton Recruitment,** 13 High St. (☎9182 6353), or other numerous recruitment agencies in town.

Emergency: ☎999. No coins required.

Hospital: Ards Hospital, Church St. (☎9151 0110), treats minor injuries. Emergencies and children under 4 yr. go to **Ulster Hospital,** Upper Newtownards Rd. in **Dondonald** (☎9048 4511).

Internet access: The **Newtownards Library,** on Regent St. a few doors from the tourist office toward Conway Sq., provides Internet at £1.50 per 30min. (☎9181 4732. Open M-W 10am-8pm, F 10am-5pm, Sa 10am-1pm, 2-5pm.) The **Ards Development Bureau** is farther up Regent St. past Conway Sq. at 43-45 Frances St., and provides access for an unheard-of £1 per hr. (☎9181 4625. Open M-Th 9am-5pm, F 9am-4:30pm.)

Post Office: 8 Frances St. (☎9181 3800). Open M-F 9am-5:30pm, Sa 10am-12:30pm. There is also an office at **Ards Shopping Center** (☎9182 0203). Open M-F 9am-1pm and 2-5:30pm, Sa 9am-1pm. **Postal code:** BT23.

ACCOMMODATIONS

Despite its centrality and accessibility to the rest of the Ards, Newtownards itself does not have a developed accommodation market. Only one hotel is in town, but a short (5-10min.) cab or car ride outside the city delivers a plethora or B&B options. The closest are listed here.

Strangford Arms Hotel, 92 Church St. (☎9181 4141; info@strangford.co.uk). Finally a legitimate reason to indulge, as the town's only hotel just happens to be a three-star oasis in a land of B&Bs. £24.50-29.50. ❸

Linden Lodge, 264 Bangor Rd. (☎9181 2078; www.kingdomsofdown.com/linden-lodge). A 5min. drive on the Bangor Rd. heading toward, well, Bangor leads to a cozy getaway in a 3-bedroom bungalow with free tea, coffee, TVs and Internet access. Parking available. Singles £20-25; doubles £20-22.50. ❷

Rockhaven, 79 Mountain Rd. (☎9182 3987; www.kingdomsofdown.com/rockhaven). A modern home with 2 comfortable rooms lies a 5min. drive toward Crawfordsburn (A2). Parking available. Singles £25; doubles £22. ❸

🄯🄼 FOOD AND PUBS

Many a culinary delight awaits on the streets around Conway Sq. The most prominent delicacy is the sandwich, while pubs serve up familiar pub grub. A **Tesco** and **Safeway** lie at the edge of town in a shopping center off Church St., after the Strangford Arms Hotel. Bakeries and fruit stands are found on the stretch of Regent St. between Frances St. and the tourist office, and in Conway Sq.

Regency Restaurant, 5A Regent St. (☎9181 4347). This bakery/restaurant welcomes the hungry with reputed country cooking in the restaurant (grills £4.95-8.35) and soda sandwiches (£1.25-1.55) to take away. Wake up to the "Ulster Fry" breakfast special (sausage, bacon, eggs, and bread for £1.80; 8:30-10:45am). Open M-F 7:30am-5pm, Sa 7:30am-7pm. ❶

The Blue Room, 12 Frances St. (☎9182 0609). Focaccia, bagels, croissants, and wraps round out their roster of sandwich all-stars. An assortment of fillings encourages further creativity. Feel free to byob to dinner Th-Sa. Open M-Th 10am-4pm, F 10am-4:30pm, Sa 9am-4:30pm, Su 9:30am-3pm. ❷

JD Wetherspoons, 54-56 Regent St. (☎9182 4270). Pub grub of all kinds (£2.95-5.75) caters to adults while miniature versions of similar foods are touted as a children's menu (£2-4). Wheelchair-accessible. Open M-W 10am-9:45pm, Th-Sa 10am-midnight, Su 12:30-10:30pm. MC/V. ❷

👁🄽 SIGHTS & ACTIVITIES

Besides the access to the many Ards towns, Newtownards is the closest hub to the much-visited **Scrabo Tower and Country Park,** 203A Scrabo Rd., the site of one of Northern Ireland's most recognizable landmarks. To reach the tower and park, head north out of Newtownards taking Blair Maine Rd. from Newtownards Shopping Center roundabout, then make a right at Scrabo Rd. and the second left on that road. The 200 ft. tower was erected as a memorial to Charles William Steward, Third Marquess of Londonderry (1778-1854), in comemoration of his concern for his tenants during the Great Famine. The adjoining park includes quarries whose stones were used to build **Greyabbey,** down the road (see p. 501), and the Albert Clock in Belfast, and welcomes ramblers and bird-watchers into **Killyneater Wood,** home to many wooded walks. Visitors are also treated to an exhibition about the tower's history and an audio-visual presentation. (☎9181 1491; www.ehsni.gov.uk. Open daily Easter to Sept. 30 10am-4pm. Free.)

Six miles from Newtownards (and 12 from Belfast), the Wildfowl and Wetlands Trust maintains **Castle Espie,** 78 Ballydrain Rd., a wetlands preserve that serves as a protective home for endangered birds. From Newtownards, take the C2 toward Comber, then the A22 toward Killyleagh. Take the first left at Ballydrain Rd. An emphasis on conservation and environmental education govern the site's woodland walks, children's activities, sustainable garden, and art gallery. Activity is especially high in autumn and winter months when migrating flocks from the Arctic take refuge in Northern Ireland's comparatively temperate climate. (☎9187 4146; www.wwt.org.uk. Open Mar.-Oct. M-Sa 10:30am-5pm, Su 11:30am-5:30pm; Nov.-Feb. M-F 11am-4pm, Sa-Su 11am-4:30pm.) At **The Ark Open Farm,** 296 Bangor Rd., right off A3 leaving Newtownards, visitors are encouraged to return to their agrarian roots and milk a cow, feed red deer, pet a lama, or ride on a tractor. Following the conservation-minded example set by Castle Espie, the working farm specializes in preserving and caring for endangered species of domestic animals on their 40 acres of land. (☎9182 0045. £3.10, children £2.50, family £10.90. Open Mar.-Oct. M-Sa 10am-6pm, Su 2-6pm; Nov.-Feb. M-Sa 10am-4pm, Su 2-4pm.) Fishermen and women can look to the **Movilla Trout Fishery,** to catch their own dinner or practice a little catch and release fishing. Fly fishing takes place on Movilla Lake, 4 mi. down Donaghadee Rd. (B172) from Newtownards, on Movilla Rd. (☎9181; TrevorWest2002@aol.com. 1 fish £12, 2 fish £14; catch and release £10. Open year-round 9am-dusk.) Note that a rod license is necessary and can be purchased at **Country Sports,** across from the bus station on Regent St.

DV Diving, 138 Mount Steward Rd., provides a profound experience with dives in Belfast and Strangford lochs as well as other points of the peninsula. To reach their headquarters, leave Newtownards on Portaferry Rd. (E4) and pass Ards Sailing Club, making a left onto Mount Steward Rd. The BS-AC and PADI certified instructors provide equipment and guidance, including diving qualification courses for £40 per day with equipment. (☎9146 4671; dive center 9186 1686; www.dvdiving.co.uk.) Land and lough lovers alike delight in the double-whammy bike and kayak hire offered at **Mike the Bike,** 53 Francis St. (☎9181 1311; www.mikethebike.net. Bikes £10 per day, kayaks £15 per day.) For an aeronautical thrill look into **flight lessons** or **helicopter hire** from the **Ards Airport** (see The Big Splurge, p. 498). Ards Tourist Information organizes occasional tours from Easter through September, ranging from historical guided walking tours of Newtownards to a folklore- and fairy-themed jaunt. Contact the Tourist Board for schedules.

Festivals throughout the peninsula are de rigeur, but Newtownards hosts its own in August when **The Creative Penninsula** showcases artists and crafts-people's work at the **Ards Arts Gallery** in the Tourist Center. The same gallery is a stage for budding musicians who hold free concerts on Saturdays throughout September, culminating in the **No Stairway Guitar Concert** competition at the end of the month. Led Zeppelin fans need not attend. Late September presents the Ards-wide **Festival of the Peninsula,** when musicians, dramatists, dancers, storytellers, and other performers come from Donegal, Scotland, and all over Ireland to entertain visitors.

South of Newtownards, gnat-sized fishing villages buzz along the eastern shoreline. **Doneghadee, Millisle, Ballywalter, Ballyhalbert, Portavogie, Cloughey,** and **Kearney** make good stops on an afternoon's drive, but none merits a special visit. **Doneghadee** has a lifeboat and still-operational lighthouse. **Portavogie** is famous for its prawns, and **Millisle** is home to the **Ballycopeland Windmill.** A2 runs the length of the shore, where hitching is reportedly easy, but *Let's Go* doesn't recommend it.

MOUNTSTEWART AND GREYABBEY

Fifteen miles southeast of Belfast on A20 sits ▨**Mountstewart House and Gardens.** To reach Mountstewart from Belfast, take the Portaferry **bus** from Laganside Station and ask the driver to stop at Mount Stewart (1hr.; M-F 16 per day, Sa 14 per

THE BIG SPLURGE

GRACE NEILL'S PUB AND BISTRO

To say there are a lot of pubs in Ireland would be a pitiful understatement. It's no false stereotype that pints are the life-blood of many an Irish village, town, and city. Because there are so many, though, it can sometimes be tricky to weed out the good from the bad, and to make worthwhile distinctions between the often similar establishments. But Grace Neill's Pub and Bistro in Donaghadee stands out from the crowd as the **oldest pub in Ireland,** at least according to the *Guinness Book of World Records*. Originally opened as "The King's Arms" in 1611, and renamed for a former landlady just last century, Grace Neill's has allegedly catered to the likes of Peter the Great and Oliver Cromwell during its 390-year lifespan.

Luckily, a world-class chef keeps the award-winning menu in pace with the times—with nightly specialties ranging from Thai to Italian dishes—while still offering up more traditional Irish fare. Of course, it will cost you to dine amidst history: while the "pub" aspect of Grace Neill's may only set you back £3.30 for a pint, the "bistro" asks £21 for its tasty yet steep prix-fixe meal. Tempting treats include local artichoke soup, risotto of chorizo and squid, and baked mango and white chocolate cheesecake. The prices might be a lot to stomach, but think of the bragging rights!

Grace Neill's Bistro, 33 High St., Donaghadee (☎9188 4595; www.graceneills.co.uk).

day, Su 4 per day; £2.60). From Newtownards take the Portaferry Rd. (C4). Held by many a Marquess of Londonderry, the house was perfected Lady Edith, First Viscount of Chaplin, who brought Mountstewart to its current splendor as an upper-crust Shangri-La in the 1920s-40s. Both house and garden are now National Trust property, though Lady Edith's daughter Lady Mairi Stewart resides in the house. Many of the trappings of the stately 18th-century **Mountstewart House** are well-worn, belying the care-free summer visits paid by the likes of Winston Churchill, George Bernard Shaw, and European royalty. Among the treasures are George Stubbs' life-sized painting of Stewart family horse and race champion, Hambletonian—one of the Royal Academy of Painting's Top Ten British Paintings. Other artifacts drew the BBC's "Antiques Roadshow" in July 2003. (☎4278 8387. Open May-June M and W-F 1-6pm, Sa-Su noon-6pm; July-Aug. daily noon-6pm; Sept. M and W-Su noon-6pm; Oct. Sa-Su noon-6pm; and Mar.-Apr. Sa-Su and bank holidays noon-6pm. Tours every 30min.; 1st tour at noon, last tour 5pm. House, garden, and temple £4.95, children £2.35, family £10.15.)

Mountstewart's **gardens,** covering 80 acres, are a more enticing attraction than the house itself; they are currently nominated as a UNESCO World Heritage Site. A penchant for rare and wild plants prompted Lady Edith to take advantage of Ireland's temperate climate and finance the great plant hunters to gather flowers, shrubs, and trees from as far as Africa and Australia. Her **Dodo Terrace** contains a menagerie of animal statues representing the members of her upper-crust circle of friends dubbed "the Ark Club." Each member adopted an animalian alter-ego, with Lady Edith, the group's matriarch, named "Circe the Sorcerer" after the character in the *Odyssey* who turned Ulysses' men into swine. Other elite critters include Winston "the Warlock" Churchill and Nelson "the Devil" Chamberlain. The **Shamrock Garden,** whose name belies its shape, contains a Red Hand of Ulster made of begonias, and a topiary Irish Harp planted, appropriately enough, over a cluster of the Emerald Isle's shamrocks. The Lake Walk leads to **Tir Nan Og** ("the land of the ever young"), the beautiful family burial ground above the lake. The gardens also host the wildly popular **Summer Garden Jazz Series** on the last Sunday of each month from April through September, as well as murder mystery evenings and car and railway engine shows. Check website for details. (☎4278 8387; www.nationaltrust.org.uk. Open Mar. Sa-Su 10-4pm and St. Patrick's Day; Apr. and Oct. daily 10am-6pm; May-Sept. daily 10am-8pm. Garden

£3.90, children £2.10, family £8.85.) Based on The Tor of the Winds in Athens, the **Temple of the Winds,** used by Mountstewart's inhabitants for "frivolity and jollity," sits atop a hill with a superb view of Strangford Lough. To reach the temple from Mountstewart House, turn left on the main road and go about ¼ mi. (Open Apr.-Oct. Sa-Su and bank holidays 2-5pm.)

A few miles down from Mountstewart through the town of **Greyabbey** lies its famous ruined Cistercian abbey. Founded in AD 1193 by Affreca, wife to Norman conqueror John de Courcey, who also built Inchabbey near Downpatrick, the abbey was the first fully Gothic building in Ireland. The beautiful ruins have an adjoining cemetery and a medieval ▧**"physick" garden,** where healing plants were cultivated to cure such common monastic ailments as melancholy, flatulence, lunacy, and even breast-feeding. Visitors can touch and taste the plants, and even take some home for self-medication. A medieval vegetable garden grows "elephant garlic," kale, and white carrots, which graced monks' meals before their orange counterparts came into existence in 1500. (☎9054 4278. Open Apr.-Sept. Tu-Sa 10am-6pm, Su 2-6pm; Oct.-Mar. Sa 10am-4pm, Su 2-4pm. Free.) After a day of touring, abandon the ascetic life and have a pint or generous meal in Greyabbey's **Wildfowler Inn,** 1-3 Main St. (☎4278 8260).

PORTAFERRY (PORT AN PHEIRE)   ☎028

Portaferry lies on the southern tip of Ards Peninsula and peers at Strangford town across the waters of Strangford Lough. Tourists stop in this lovely seaside town to relax, explore the southern Ards, and enjoy its aquatic offerings, including Northern Ireland's largest aquarium. Portaferry's claim to fame is ▧**Exploris,** Northern Ireland's only public aquarium and one of the UK's best. Near the pier next to the ruins of unimpressive **Portaferry Castle,** Exploris holds first-rate exhibits on local marine ecology. The journey begins in the shallow waters of Strangford Lough, proceeds through the Narrows, and ends in the depths of the Irish Sea, where Europe's largest tank houses sharks and other large fish whose feeding times (M, W and F 2-4pm; Sa-Su 2:30-3:30pm) amaze onlookers. Touch tanks and interactive displays keep kids educated and engaged. At the building's center, an open-air sanctuary welcomes injured seals and their young admirers. Pupping season (Apr.-June) provides most opportunities for seal sightings. (☎4272 8062; www.exploris.org.uk. Open Apr.-Aug. M-F 10am-6pm, Sa 11am-6pm, Su noon-6pm; Sept.-Mar. M-F 10am-5pm, Sa 11am-5pm, Su 1-5pm. £5.40; seniors and children £3.20; family £11-15; under 5 free.) Traditional sailing yachts called "Hookers," like European versions of Chinese *junks*, take to the seas in June, bound for the **Galway Hooker Festival.** July brings the massive **Gala Week** of boatraces, crowds, performers, drink, and general revelry (www.portaferrygala.com). Another Portaferry celebration is the **Seafood Festival** in early September.

To reach Strangford Lough from the bus stop, follow either **Ferry Street** or **Castle Street** downhill for about 100m. **Ulsterbuses** from Belfast drop off visitors at **The Square** in the center of town. (1½hr.; M-F 19 per day, Sa 16 per day, Su 9 per day; £4.50.) **Ferries** leave Portaferry's waterfront at 15 and 45min. past the hour for a 10min. chug to Strangford, returning on the hour and half-hour. (☎4488 1637. £1, seniors free, children 50p, car and driver £4.20.) To reach the **tourist office** from the bus stop, take **Castle Street** downhill toward the lough. The tourist office is on the corner of Castle St. and **The Strand,** the shoreline's official name, in front of crumbling **Portaferry Castle.** Beyond the usual brochures and a **bureau de change,** it also has a 12min. video on the medieval "tower houses" of Co. Down, precursors of the grand estates. (☎4272 9882. Open July-Aug. M-Sa 10am-5:30pm, Su 1:30-6pm; Easter-June and Sept. M-Sa

10am-5pm, Su 2-6pm.) **Portaferry Health Centre,** 44 High St., is on the north side of town. (☎4272 8429; tourism@ards-council.gov.uk. Open M-F 8:30am-6pm.) Near the bus station is **Northern Bank,** The Square (☎4272 8208; open M 10am-5pm; Tu-W, F 10am-3:30pm; Th 9:30am-3:30pm; closed daily 12:30-1:30pm; 24hr. **ATM**), and the **post office,** 28 The Square (☎4272 8201; open M-W and F 9am-1pm and 2-5:30pm, Th 9am-1pm, Sa 9am-12:30pm). **Postal code:** BT22.

A peaceful stay awaits at ▧**Portaferry Barholm Youth Hostel ❶,** 11 The Strand, across from the ferry dock. Defying hostel stereotypes, Barholm is supremely accommodating and ideally located right on Strangford Lough, with single and double bedrooms, full baths shared by a few hall-mates, a conservatory dining room, and excellent views. However, the management is often scarce and has limited office hours. Weekend reservations are necessary. (☎4272 9598. Wheelchair-accessible. Breakfast Sa-Su £3.70. Laundry £3. Apr.-Sept. £13; Oct.-Mar. £11.50.) For beds closer to the pubs, the digs at **Fiddler's Green B&B ❸,** located above the pub on Church St., are unbeatable. Hardwood floors, private baths, and airy rooms with matching bedsheets and curtains add that extra touch of class. Call ahead, as it fills up on weekends. (☎4272 8393. Singles £25, with bath £30; doubles £44/£55.)

Numerous fresh fruit and veggie **markets** and convenience stores are scattered around High St. and The Square. Every Saturday from Easter through the end of September, Market House in the Square welcomes a **country market** (10am-noon). For a quick bite, **Ferry Grill ❶,** on High St. across from Spar Market, stays open until 1am on weekends and serves various burger-and-fries configurations as well as locally fished and fried fish and chips. (☎4272 8568. Food less than £2.50. Take away only. Open M-F 11am-2pm, 5-9pm; Sa 11am-1am; Su 2-9pm.) For dinner, wander down to **Cornstore ❷,** Castle St., before Exploris and Portaferry castle. Well-cooked seafood, traditional plates, and a wealth of vegetarian options (peppers filled with bbq risotto and mozzarella £5.25) are served in a "country" atmosphere. (☎4272 9000. Open daily noon-9pm.) Duck into **The Shambles Coffee Shop ❶,** 3 Castle St., through the crafts shop, for homemade muffins and soup. (☎4272 9675. Open M-Sa 10am-5pm, Su 11am-5pm.)

At night, everyone stumbles to **Fiddler's Green,** Church St., where publican Frank and his sons lead rowdy sing-alongs, encouraging musicians to join in the festivities. The amazingly friendly atmosphere stands testament to their plaque: "There are no strangers here. Just friends who have not yet met." (Open M-Sa 11:30am-11pm, Su noon-10pm.) Across the street, John Wayne memorabilia decks the walls of **The Quiet Man,** commemorating the Duke's silver screen jaunt south in the Republic. On weekends, the pub plays music ranging from disco to live bands, while patrons amuse themselves with karaoke and billiards. (☎4272 9629. Open daily 11:30am-11pm; bar until 1am.) **M.E. Dumigan's,** Ferry St., is up from the waterfront. This tiny pub is so crammed with locals that *craic* is guaranteed. (Open M-Sa 11:30am-midnight, Su 12:30pm-midnight.)

LECALE PENINSULA

Called by some "The Island of Lecale," the region spans the west coast of Strangford Lough from the village of Strangford to Downpatrick, then continues inland to Ballynahinch in the north and Dundrum in the west. It was once bound entirely by bodies of water, including the Irish Sea, Strangford Lough, and a series of streams and ponds, until these waterways were re-routed for mills and hydro-centered agricultural pursuits. Industrialization passed Catholic Lecale by, concentrating on the wealthier Protestant populated areas of Co. Down, leaving the area culturally isolated. Today, animals are raised on its rolling green hills, as the rocky farmland can't support heavy cultivation. Beautiful parks, lavish estates, and St. Patrick-related sites/sightings draw visitors from afar.

STRANGFORD (BAILE LOCH CUAN)

This tiny harbor village lies just across the Lough from Portaferry, northeast of Downpatrick on A25 and north of Ardglass on A2. Strangford has limited (as in, one) accommodation; its tourist appeal lies in its proximity to the ■Castle Ward House and Estate (see p. 505). Its isolated serenity also appeals to over-tired travelers. **Buses** to Downpatrick leave from the center of town, called The Square (25min.; M-F 10 per day, Sa 5 per day; £2.20). **Ferries** leave for Porta-ferry every 30min. (M-F 7:30am-10:30pm, Sa 8am-11pm, Su 9:30am-10:30pm; £1, cars £4.80.) The **Castle Ward Caravan Park ❶** stands on the Castle Ward National Trust property; headed out of town, take a right off the road to Downpatrick. (☎4488 1680. Open mid-Mar. to Sept. Warden's cottage closed daily 1-2pm and 5-6pm. £5.50 per small tent; caravans £10.50. Free showers.) At the cozy old **Cuan Bar and Restaurant ❹**, The Square, enjoy a warm welcome, quality pub grub, and a room-temperature Guinness. (☎4488 1222. Broccoli & walnut lasagna £7.10, 2-course meal £16. Open M-Sa noon-9:30pm, Su noon-9pm. Live music on weekends.) The Cuan pulls triple duty as the **Cuan B&B ❹**. Its hard-wood floors, cushy big beds, and tidy en-suite bathrooms recommend it...along with its status as the only accommodation in Strangford proper. (All rooms with bath and TV. Singles £35-40; doubles £60-70.)

Back in town, a small 16th-century tower house optimistically called **Strangford Castle** stands to the right of the ferry dock as you disembark. Wander into its dark, spooky interior and find a humbling view from the third floor. (Gate key available from Mr. Seed, 39 Castle St., across from the tower house's gate, daily 10am-7pm.)

CASTLEWARD HOUSE AND ESTATE

To get to Castleward House and Estate by car or bus (request to be dropped off there) from Strangford, take A25 toward Downpatrick. The entrance is about 2 mi. up the road on the right. Pedestrians seeking a safe and pleasant stroll along a shady and cool path should take the **Loughside Walk** (see **Strangford,** p. 505). This 18th-century estate, once owned by Lady Anne and Lord Bangor and now the property of the National Trust, lies atop a verdant hill with a spectac-ular view of the Lough. The house, built between 1760 and 1768, stands as an architectural landmark. It is split lengthwise down the middle—one wing is classical, which satisfied Lord Bangor, and the other is Gothic, to suit Lady Anne's fancy. Alas, the couple split, but left the house intact and spared its curious artifacts, including a **"living cartoon"** of two stuffed squirrels duking it out in a boxing ring in the Morning room. Charles Stewart Parnell, a relation by marriage, claims a bed in one of the guest suites. As an artifact of English land-lord life, the 800-acre estate features a stable, Victorian laundry room, and kitchen, and its greater lands hold a rectangular lake, restored corn mill, two tower houses, and a "Victorian Pastimes Centre" for children. (☎4488 1204; www.ntni.org.uk. Grounds open Oct.-Apr. daily 10am-4pm; May-Sept. daily 10am-8pm. House and Wildlife Center open 15 Mar.-Apr. daily noon-6pm; May W-M noon-6pm; Aug. daily noon-6pm; Sept.-Oct. Sa-Su noon-6pm. House tours on the hr.; last leaves at 5pm. Grounds only £3.10, children £1.30, family £7.30. House, grounds, and wildlife center £4.70/£1.80/£9.90.)

The **Strangford Lough Wildlife Centre** is located on the estate and provides infor-mation on the natural environment of the lough, and fun with microscopes! On foot, follow A25 past the causeway and take an immediate sharp right, which leads to the entrance to the Castle Ward Caravan Park (see p. 505). Follow the driveway to the right fork and go through the brown gate on the right. This leads to the **Loughside Walk**, a 30min. stroll along the coastline to the Centre. Step lively, or risk stepping on one of the many birds scuttling across the path. (☎4488 1411. Same hours as estate.) During the first three weeks of June, the **Castle Ward Opera**

(☎9066 1090) performs here to a tuxedoed and tiara-ed crowd. (Tickets £45.) From March through September, **Jazz in the Garden** sounds every second Sunday of the month. Occasional piano recitals culminate in a **music festival** the first weekend in August as trad, rock, and country-western bands regale the public.

DOWNPATRICK (DÚN PÁDRAIG)

Rumored to be the final resting place of St. Paddy himself, with a burial plot to substantiate the claim, Downpatrick is the county's administrative center and capital. Though nights here can be slow, by day the town's streets are filled with shoppers, school children, and heavy traffic, as young and old alike flock to town from nearby villages to shop or learn. The surrounding countryside, peppered with St. Patrick-related sites, is best seen in a daytrip by car or bike.

■ TRANSPORTATION

Buses: 83 Market St. (timetable inquires ☎4461 2384). To: **Belfast** (1hr.; M-F 30 per day, Sa 12 per day, Su 6 per day; £4.10, children £2.05); **Newcastle** (30min.; M-F 21 per day, Sa 12 per day, Su 5 per day; £2.60, children £1.30); **Strangford** (25min.; M-F 9 per day, Sa 5 per day; £2.30, children £1.15).

Taxis: Downpatrick Taxis, 96 Market St. (☎4461 4515), runs early to late.

Bicycles: Down Discount Cycles, 45b Church St. (☎4461 4990), next to the Texaco station, runs an informal operation from June-Aug. Be sure to call ahead. Rentals £5 per day. Open M-Sa 9:30am-5:30pm.

■ ORIENTATION AND PRACTICAL INFORMATION

Market Street, the town's main avenue, is flanked by the bus station and connections to other significant streets. From the station, the first right is **St. Patrick's Avenue.** Farther on, Market St. meets **Irish Street** on the right and **English Street** on the left, spelling out the town's geopolitical divide. Market St. becomes **Church Street** and continues straight. **Scotch Street** lies between Church and Irish St.

Tourist Office: 53a Market St. (☎4461 2233; www.downdc.gov.uk), in the **Heritage Centre,** books accommodations and provides useful info about the area and county. Open July-Aug. M-Sa 9:30am-6pm, Su 2-6pm; Sept.-June M-Sa 10am-5pm.

Banks: Northern Bank, 58-60 Market St. (☎4461 4011). Open M 9:30am-5pm, Tu-F 10am-3:30pm. **Bank of Ireland,** 80-82 Market St. (☎4461 2911). Open M-Tu and Th-F 9:30am-4:30pm, W 10am-4:30pm. Both have 24hr. **ATMs.**

Laundry: Crawford's Dry Cleaners, 16 St. Patrick's Ave. (☎4461 2284). £5-6 per load. Open M-Sa 9am-5:30pm.

Emergency: ☎999; no coins required. **Police:** Irish St. (☎4461 5011).

Pharmacy: Foy's Chemist, 16 Irish St. (☎4461 2032). Open M-F 9am-1pm, 2-5:30pm. **Deeny Pharmacy,** 30a St. Patrick's Ave. (☎4461 3807). Open M-Sa 9am-5:30pm.

Hospital: Downe Hospital, Pound Ln., off Irish St. (☎4461 3311).

Internet Access: e-Learn Shop, 102 Market St. (☎4461 1500), across from the bus stop. £1 per hr. Open M and W 9am-9pm, Tu and Th-F 9am-5pm, Sa 10am-1pm. The **Tourist Office** has **Internet** £1.50 per 30min., with a bottomless cup of coffee or tea. **Downpatrick Library,** 79 Market St. (☎4461 2895), next to the bus stop. Internet £1.50 per 30min. Open M-Tu and Th 10am-8pm, W and F-Sa 10am-5pm.

Post Office: 65 Market St. (☎4461 2061), inside the SuperValu shopping center. Open M-F 9am-5:30pm, Sa 9am-5pm. **Postal code:** BT30.

ACCOMMODATIONS

With pricey B&Bs, often located on the outskirts of town, visitors to Downpatrick usually stay at one of Portaferry or Newcastle's hostels, or the caravan parks near Strangford. The closest campground is **Castle Ward,** near Strangford (see p. 505).

Dunleath House, 33 St. Patrick's Dr. (☎4461 3221). Turn off Market St. onto St. Patrick's Ave., take the first right onto St. Patrick's Dr., then left onto Mourne View Ct. 3 luxurious rooms, 1 with private bath. A superbly hospitable proprietress stays current on the town's events. Breakfast included. Singles £25; doubles £40. ❸

Hillside B&B, 62 Scotch St. (☎4461 3134). Follow Market St. to its end and turn right after the Arts Centre. Comfortable rooms, convenient location, and relatively low prices await at this large B&B. Singles £18; doubles £35; triples £50. ❷

Denvir's Hotel, 14-16 English St. (☎4461 2012), a left onto English St. from Market St. This homey 6-room tavern, with private baths, has slept the likes of Jonathan Swift and Daniel Day Lewis. Breakfast included. Singles £32.50; doubles £55. ❸

FOOD AND PUBS

Downpatrick's eateries surpass those of many nearby towns in both quality and quantity. For unsurpassable takeaway sandwiches made from fresh ingredients, try the deli in **Hanlon's Fruit and Veg,** 26 Market St. (☎4461 2129; open M-Sa 8am-5:45pm), or the supermarkets surrounding the bus station for picnic supplies. Finding a square meal after the locals' workday proves more difficult. At night full-blown restaurants or pubs ease grumbling stomachs.

Daily Grind Coffee Shop, 21a St. Patrick's Ave. (☎4461 5949), a right of Market St. toward the town's center. Basic, wee cafe serves tasty sandwiches (£2-3), salads (£3-4), and rich desserts (£2) in cheery yellow and blue interior. Open M-Sa 10am-5pm. ❶

Denvir's Restaurant and Pub, 14 English St. (☎4461 2012). Honest Irish cooking with a slice of history to help it down. Pub dates from 1642. United Irishmen fighting for Home Rule in the 1768 rebellion met here as a literary society (see p. 62). Rumored to have served Thomas Russell, the revolutionary rabble-rouser, his last meal. Thankfully, the prices haven't matured with age. Restaurant serves pub food. Pub hosts live music Th and Sa. Lunch (£3-6) served M-Sa noon-2:30pm. Dinner (£5-9) served M-Th and Su 7-8pm, F-Sa 7-9pm. ❸

Abbey Cafe, 36 Market St. (☎4461 3039). Inexpensive lunches and themed specials, such as the Abbey Belly-Buster, a bulked-up burger dressed to impress or ingest (£5). Vegetarian options also available. Open M-Sa 9:30am-5:30pm. ❷

Oakley Fayre's, 52 Market St. (☎4461 2500). Join Downpatrick's old ladies for tea and scones or their hearty grandchildren for full meals in a diner-esque seating area. Restaurant through bakery. Lasagna or cottage pie £4. Open M-Sa 9am-5:15pm. ❷

Mullans Pub, 48 Church St. (☎4461 2227). A little out of the way, but good *craic* on weekends justify the walk. F live band, Sa blues (10pm-1am) and Su tea time (6pm) trad sessions close out the weekend. Open daily noon-1am.

Hogan's, 78 Market St. (☎4461 2017; www.hogans-bar.com), directly opposite the tourist office, appeases drinkers and dancers with a bar on the ground floor and a club above. Food served noon-8pm. 18+. Pub and club cover £5. Open M-Th noon-11:30pm, F-Sa 11:30am-1am, Su 11:30am-2am.

👁 🚶 SIGHTS AND ACTIVITIES

The state-of-the-art ▧**Saint Patrick Center,** 53a Market St., tells everything you always wanted to know but never cared enough to ask about Ireland's patron saint. An incredible interactive biographical tour goes from St. P's early capture by Irish pirates through his later teachings and enduring legacy, including the center's pièce de résistance: a 20min. cinematic field trip to all the sites in Ireland associated with the saint. Signs outside the auditorium warn of possible motion sickness, but those with strong constitutions will be enthralled. A rooftop garden, craft shop, art gallery, and **Internet** cafe (see **Practical Information,** p. 506) also await, as does the local **tourist office.** (☎ 4461 9000; www.saint-patrickcentre.com. Open June-Aug. M-Sa 9:30am-6pm, Su 1-6pm; Apr.-May and Sept. M-Sa 9:30am-5:30pm, Su 1-5:30pm; Oct.-Mar. M-Sa 10am-5pm. Last admission 1½hr. before closing. Exhibit £4.50, students and seniors £3, children £2.25. Garden and art gallery free.)

Past the carpark to the right of the St. Patrick's Center is the **Downpatrick Railway Museum,** which features restored trains, a replica of a turn-of-the century Belfast and County Down railway station, and behind-the-scenes tours of train operation and restorations. On weekends from July-Sept. trains run around the site from 2-5pm, though trips to Inch Abbey, a restored cornmill, and Viking King Magnus's grave will be added in the next two years. (☎ 4461 5779; www.ukhrail.uel.ac.uk/drm/drm.html. Tours available June-Sept. M-Sa 11am-2pm.)

Down County Museum and Historical Gaol, at the end of English St., offers effusive regional history. Housed in the jail where Thomas Russell, early father and martyr of Irish republicanism, was hanged, the museum displays artifacts from Co. Down, St. Patrick, and a wax gang of 19th-century prisoners. Once up on the history, visit the courtyard for a game of gigantic chess or checkers. (☎ 4461 5218; www.downcoutymuseum.com. Open M-F 10am-5pm, Sa-Su 1-5pm.) Beside the museum is the Church of Ireland **Down Cathedral** (☎ 4461 4922). A Celtic monastery until the 12th century, the cathedral went Benedictine under the Norman conqueror John de Courcey and was demolished in the 1316 invasion by Edward de Bruce of Scotland. Rebuilt in 1818, the present cathedral incorporates stone carvings from its medieval predecessor and houses the only private pew boxes still used in Ireland. The entrance proudly proclaims 1500 years of Christian heritage, beginning with St. Patrick's settlement in nearby Saul (see below). In the cemetary, a stone commemorates the **grave of St. Patrick,** though most believe the saint rests in peace beneath the church itself, joined by the remains of **St. Brigid** and **St. Colmcille** (a.k.a. St. Columba). Choral Evensong showcases its world class organ every third Sunday of the month at 3:30pm. (Open M-Sa 1-5pm, Su 2pm-5pm. Free.)

The top of **Mound of Down,** behind the Down Co. Museum, affords a beautiful view. By car, head down English St. away from the museum or Down Cathedral and turn left on Mt. Cresent. This Bronze Age hill fort was once known as Dunlethglaise, or "fort on the green hill." Later, in the Iron Age, an early Christian town flourished on the mound until Anglo-Norman invaders under John de Courcey defeated the Irish chief MacDunleavy. Today, visitors are hard-pressed to find signs of the fort or the city, but the green hill remains a lovely spot for a ramble. (☎ 9054 3034. Open daily dawn-dusk.) Downpatrick also boasts a number of green fields perfect for sporting events. In town, on Saturday mornings (9am-noon) from February to October, **Gaelic** or **soccer matches** are played at Dunleath Park, next to the **Down Leisure Center** (☎ 4461 3426), past the bus stop on Market St.

FESTIVALS

In Downpatrick, festivals commemorate the obvious (St. Patrick's day, anyone?) and the more obscure. The days leading to St. P's big day, March 17, mark the **St. Patrick's Festival and Cross-Community Parade.** Children's entertainment, guided historical walks, music, theater, and storytelling vary with the annual theme (☎4461 2233; www.st-patricksdayfestival.com). **The Magnus Barelegs Viking Festival** ransacks Downpatrick and County Down, celebrating the town's Viking King Magnus Barelegs, with reenacted battles, fierce longships, and other Norse pastimes. Taking its cue from the Castleward Opera season, Downpatrick lifts the red velvet curtain for the **Fringe Opera Festival** (www.downartscentre.com/fringe). Info for all festivals is available from the tourist office (☎4461 2233; events@downdc.gov.uk).

⚡ DAYTRIPS FROM DOWNPATRICK

SAUL AND THE STRUELL WELLS

Follow the signs on the Saul Rd. for 2 mi. past Downpatrick and a golf course to reach Saul Church, on the site where St. Patrick is believed to have landed in the 5th century. Bus to Raholp stops here on request. Church ☎4461 4922. Open daily until 5pm. Su services 10am. Other sites always open to the public. Free.

Co. Down reveres anything touched by St. Patrick's sweet, sweet hands; **Saul** may be the most beloved sight of all. After being converted to Christianity, local chieftain Dichu gave Patrick the barn *(sabhal)* that later became the first parish church in Ireland. Replicas of an early Christian church and round tower commemorate Big Paddy's arrival from Scotland. A little over a mile farther down Saul Rd., on the summit of Slieve Patrick, stands **St. Patrick's Shrine.** The monument consists of a huge granite statue of St. Patrick, bronze panels depicting his life, and an open-air temple. The statue sports mismatched footwear, and contains the wedding rings of the sculptors and many townspeople, donated as tributes to the saint. Indecisive about Pat's shoe choice, the sculptors gave the saint a boot and a sandal, one on each foot to cover their historical bases. Even nonbelievers appreciate the 360° panorama of the lough, the mountains, and, on a clear day, the Isle of Man. At the **Struell Wells,** southeast of Downpatrick on the Ardglass road (B1), healing waters run through underground channels from one well to the next until they reach the 200-year-old bath houses at the base of the hill. Belief in their curative powers originated long before Christianity arrived on the scene.

INCH ABBEY AND THE QUOILE PONDAGE NATURE RESERVE

The Abbey lies 1 mi. from Downpatrick on the Belfast Rd. (A7). The bus to Belfast stops at nearby Abbey Lodge Hotel on request. Nature Reserve is 1 mi. from Downpatrick off Strangford Rd. ☎4461 5520. Open Apr.-Aug. daily 11am-5pm; Sept.-Mar. Sa-Su 1-5pm.

The **Cistercian Inch Abbey,** the earliest standing Gothic ruin in Ireland, was founded in 1180 by the Norman conqueror John de Courcey to make amends for his destruction of the Eneragh monastery a few years earlier. The Abbey, which was closed off to Irishmen for some 400 years until it closed in 1541, is near the marshes of the River Quoile. Though only low foundation walls remain, the Abbey's enchanting grounds, which are always open, make an excellent picnic site. The **Quoile Pondage Nature Reserve** offers hiking and bird-watching around a manmade pond, created in 1957 when a tidal barrier was erected to prevent the flooding of Downpatrick. The barrier has attracted an unusual assortment of vegetation, fish, and insects. The **Quoile Countryside Centre** provides ample information.

NEWCASTLE (AN CAISLEÁN NUA)

The numerous arcades, joke shops, and waterslide parks of Newcastle's main drag stand in dramatic contrast to the majestic Mourne Mountains rising from the south end of town. On weekends, packs of kids prowl the streets in search of fun, while July and August bring the rest of the family to sunbathe on the beach. With its hostel and numerous B&Bs, Newcastle is often used by travelers as an inexpensive base for exploration of the nearby parks and the Mourne Mountains.

▐ TRANSPORTATION

Buses: Ulsterbus, 5-7 Railway St. (☎4372 2296), end of Main St. away from the mountains. To: **Belfast** (80min.; M-F 19 per day, Sa 17 per day, Su 10 per day; £5.30, child £2.65); **Downpatrick** (43min., express 20min.; M-F 15 per day, Sa 10 per day, Su 5 per day; £2.60/£1.30); **Dublin** via Newry (3hr.; M-Sa 4 per day, Su 2 per day; £9.70/£4.85); **Newry** (37min.; M-F 12 per day, Sa 7per day, Su 2 per day; £3.80/£1.90).

Taxis: Donard Cabs (☎4372 4100 or 4372 2823). **Shimna Taxis** (☎4372 6030).

Bike Rental: Wiki Wiki Wheels, 10b Donard St. (☎4372 3973), a right from the bus station, up Railway St. on the left. £10 per day, £50 per wk.; children £5 per day. ID deposit. Open M-Th and Sa 9am-6pm, F 9am-8pm, Su 2-6pm.

✦ ☷ ORIENTATION AND PRACTICAL INFORMATION

Newcastle's main road runs parallel to the waterfront; initially called **Main Street** (where it intersects with **Railway Street**), its name subsequently changes to **Central Promenade** and then to **South Promenade** as it approaches the Mournes.

Tourist Office: 10-14 Central Promenade (☎4372 2222), 10min. down the main street from the bus station. Free map and visitor's guide. Mildly frustrating 24hr. touch-screen computer in front provides basic information about traveling in Northern Ireland. Open July-Aug. M-Sa 9:30am-7pm, Su 1-7pm; June and Sept. M-Sa 10am-5pm, Su 2-6pm.

Banks: First Trust Bank, 28-32 Main St. (☎4372 3476). Open M-F 9:30am-4:30pm, W open 10am. **Ulster Bank,** 115-117 Main St. (☎4372 3276). Open M-F 9:30am-4:30pm. Both have 24hr. **ATMs.**

Work Opportunities: Anchor Bar hires international waitstaff and bartenders for a min. of 2 mo. No experience necessary. Pays about £5 per hr. Call ☎4372 3344.

Camping Equipment: Hill Trekker, 115 Central Promenade (☎4372 3842). Mourne trail maps, hiking tips, info on guided tours, and boot rentals (£2.50 per day; deposit £10). Open Tu-Su 10am-5:30pm.

Bookshop: Smyth's Musique, 4 Railway St. (☎4372 2831; smyths.musique@btinternet.com), has maps and paperbacks. Open M-Sa 9am-6pm, Su 2-6pm.

Laundry: Crystal Clear Dry Cleaner, Main St. (☎4372 3863). Open M-Sa 8:30am-5:30pm.

Emergency: ☎999. **Police:** S. Promenade (☎4372 3583).

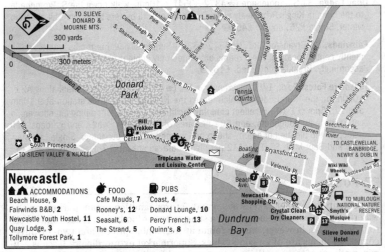

Newcastle

ACCOMMODATIONS	FOOD	PUBS
Beach House, 9	Cafe Mauds, 7	Coast, 4
Fairwinds B&B, 2	Rooney's, 12	Donard Lounge, 10
Newcastle Youth Hostel, 11	Seasalt, 6	Percy French, 13
Quay Lodge, 3	The Strand, 5	Quinn's, 8
Tollymore Forest Park, 1		

Pharmacy: Gordon's, Railway St. (☎4372 2724). Open M-F 9am-6pm, Sa 9:30am-5pm. **Thornton's,** 49 Central Promenade (☎4372 3248). Open M-Sa 9am-6pm.

Internet Access: The **Anchor Bar** (see **Pubs,** p. 512) has unlimited web access, customer or no. To avoid repeating past drunken email experiences, use **Newcastle Library,** 141-143 Main St. (☎4372 2710). £1.50 per 30min. Open M-Tu 10am-8pm, W and F 10am-5pm, Sa 10am-1pm and 2pm-5pm.

Post Office: 33-35 Central Promenade (☎4372 2418). Open M-W and F 9am-12:30pm and 1:30-5:30pm; Th and Sa 9am-12:30pm. **Postal Code:** BT33.

ACCOMMODATIONS AND CAMPING

B&Bs crowd this seaside town like 13-year-old boys around a new arcade game. The tourist office happily provides a list of them (the B&Bs, not the games). The many self-catering accommodations, some in the town center, are generally meant to be booked for at least a week. A lone hostel rounds out the accommodation portfolio. Of the area's campsites, Tollymore Forest Park is probably the most scenic, but the Mournes themselves are a free and legal alternative.

Newcastle Youth Hostel (HINI), 30 Downs Rd. (☎4372 2133; leave a message for reservations). Walking away from the bus stop, go left along Railway St. and right onto Downs Rd. at the parking lot in front of the waterfront. The central, seaside location is about 45 sec. from the bus station, and light streams in through huge windows. Large, well-furnished kitchen. Lockers 50p. Laundry £2. Check-in 5-11:30pm. Dorms £12, under 18 £10; 6-person apartment £45. ❶

Beach House, 22 Downs Rd. (☎4372 2345). Welcomes guests twice-over: from the smiling baker statuette on the porch to the acorns (symbolizing hospitality) intricately carved into the amazing staircase inside. The antique claw-foot bathtub uncovered by the discerning proprietress is a treasure. Singles £40; doubles £60. ❹

Quay Lodge, 31 S. Promenade (☎4372 3054), a 10min. walk down the S. Promenade to the bend in King's Rd. Cheery yellow town house with owners to match. Call ahead in winter. Single £25, double £45. ❺

Fairwinds, 86 Bryansford Rd. (☎4372 6839.) Simple seviceable rooms with a conveniently central location. The 3 rooms are rented only in high season (May-Aug.), so plan accordingly. Breakfast included. £16. ❷

Tollymore Forest Park, 176 Tullybrannigan Rd. (☎4372 2428), a 2 mi. walk along A2 or 10min. on the "Rural Rover," which leaves the Newcastle Ulsterbus station at 9:10am and 12:25pm (£1.10). Excellent **camping** facilities include clean, piping hot showers, a cafe with tasty doughnuts, and 584 hectares of well-marked walks and gardens. Fall asleep to the bleating of nearby sheep or a snoring old age pensioner. Single tent May-June and Sept M-Th £8, F-Su £12 per night. Caravan space £12. Electricity £1.50. ❷

🗲 FOOD

The density of burger takeaways, candy stores, and ice cream parlors on the waterfront leaves greasemongers in a state or sweet-tooths in a sugar coma. Well-rounded meals, however, can be found at reasonable prices, and two- or three-course set meals are often good values. Supermarket extraordinaire **Tesco** is a 10 min. walk out of town on Railway St. or toward Castle welles on the A50. Fruit and veggie vendors tote their natural wares on Main St. near the bus station.

▨ **Seasalt,** 51 Central Promenade (☎4372 5027; www.seasaltfood.com). Mod interior in sleek neutral colors. Create dream panini from gourmet fillings (£3-4). Go epicurean with pâté (£3.50) or local crab (£6.50). F-Sa nights, it transforms into a reservations-only 3-course bistro (£19.50). Accommodates special dietary needs. Open M-W and Su 9am-5pm, Th-Sa 9am-midnight. Bistro begins 6pm. Closed M Sept.-May. ❷

Cafe Mauds, 106 Main St. (☎4372 6184). Order a personal pizza (£5), crepe (£3.25-5.25), or panini (£3.75) at the classy cafeteria counter and enjoy it on the terrace overlooking the water, or on a squishy couch inside. Open M-Su 9am-9:30pm. ❷

Rooney's, corner of Railway St. and Downs Rd. (☎4372 3822). Fusion menu features ostrich (£13), New Zealand mussels (£4.50), and delightful veggie options. Romantics request table 105, on a private balcony. Open Su-Th noon-9pm, F-Sa noon-10pm. ❹

The Strand, 53-55 Central Promenade (☎4372 3472; www.strand.net). Popular family restaurant serves filling dinners (£5-7), each with tea and plentiful scones. Seek snacks at the Bakery (£3-5). Open daily June-Aug. 8:30am-11pm; Sept.-May 9am-6pm. ❸

🗏🍸 PUBS AND CLUBS

With a few exceptions, the pubs of Newcastle cater largely to the older set on all but karaoke night when young thangs crowd in for their chance in the spotlight. Check signs in windows for karaoke nights to know what to expect.

Donard Lounge, Main St. (☎4372 2614), by the Donard Hotel. Karaoke Th popular with 20-somethings; mixed crowd swills pints all week watching football. 18+. Cover £2 after 11pm on Th. Open M-W 11am-11pm, Th-Sa 11am-1am, Su 11am-midnight.

Quinn's, 62 Main St. (☎4372 6400). A 20s-style interior with dark green snugs, to lose the crowd. Th student night, F karaoke, Sa-Su cover bands. Open M-W 11:30am-midnight, Th-Su 11:30am-1:30am.

Percy French (☎4372 3175), right outside the Slieve Donard Hotel where Railway meets the sea. Classy drinks and older crowd in spacious lodge setting. French was a popular late 19th-century Irish songwriter whose flowery lyrics adorn the bar's frosted mirrors. Tu karaoke. Cover bands F-Sa, June-Aug. Su. 18+. Open M-Th 11:30am-11pm, F-Sa 11:30am-1am, Su 12:30-10pm.

Coast, 121 Central Promenade (☎4372 4100; www.oharesloungebars.com), behind O'Hare's Front Bar; enter through Bryansford Rd. carpark. The popular new kid on the clubbing block. Cover £5 after 11pm. Club open Sept.-June F (18+) and Sa (officially 21+) 10pm-1:30am; July and Aug. nightly with cover M-Th £3. **Front Bar,** with backroom pool and karaoke W. Open daily 11:30am-2am.

🎥 🎿 SIGHTS AND ACTIVITIES

Hikers find paradise in the majestic Mournes (see **Hiking: The Mourne Mountains,** p. 514), while equestrians choose between beach or forest for riding. Three parks managed by the Department of Agriculture are just a hop, skip, and jump from Newcastle. **Tollymore Forest Park** lies just 2 mi. west of town at 176 Tullybrannigan Rd. A magical entrance lined with gigantic, gnarled trees leads toward ancient stone bridges, rushing waters, and well-marked trails. The **Shimna River** runs from east to west and cuts the park in half. From the four main trails, which range in length from 1-8 mi., hikers encounter diverse wildlife including deer, foxes, badgers, and otters (if they're quiet and well-behaved). The "Rivers Trail" hike (3 mi.) encompasses most of the park and is highly recommended, as is the hike (3½ mi.) to the Curraghard viewpoint overlooking the Irish sea. (☎4372 2428. Open daily 10am-9pm. Cars £4.) The park is amply equipped with a campground (see **Accommodations,** p. 512), ranger station complete with brochures and trail info, visitors center, cafe, and impressive outdoor arboretum. If you're not up for the rambling walk to Tollymore, take one of Ulsterbus's "Rural Rover" shuttles from the Newcastle bus station (10min.; every hr. 10am-noon and 2-5pm; £1.10). Excursions into the Tollymore forest can be arranged through **Tollymore Mountain Center** (☎437 22158), a left out of the exit onto the Newry Rd. Apart from deals on hiking, canoeing, and camping equipment, an indoor climbing wall awaits.

Castlewellan Forest Park spreads over the hills north and east of the Mournes. From the Newcastle bus station take Castlewellan Rd. into town, turn left on Main St. at the roundabout, and continue for 400m. The entrance is at the top of the main street in Castlewellan, and the campground is opposite the library. (☎4377 8664. Open daily 10am-sunset. £4 per car. Call M-F 9am-5pm for info and site booking. **Camping:** Single tent July-Aug. and Oct.-Apr. £12; May-June and Sept. M-Th £8. Caravan space £12. Electricity £1.50.) The park contains easily accessible attractions: a Scottish **baronial castle** (now a Christian Conference Centre not open to the public but visible from across the park), an impressive **Sculpture Trail** (2.5 mi. of sculptures made from natural materials), and the North's **National Arboretum.** The park's lake, around which the hearty can delight in a mile walk, overflows with trout; fishing permits are available at the **ranger station,** the first building on the right near the lake, from April through mid-October. Buses run from Newcastle to Castlewellan (10min.; M-F 25 per day, Sa 16 per day, Su 6 per day; £1.50).

At the opposite end of town is the **Murlough National Nature Reserve,** on the Dundrum Rd. (A24) toward Belfast. Home to sand dunes and woodlands, Murlough boasts marvelous swimming (for the polar bear crowd), and seal-watching during the summer/fall molting season. In July, upwards of 150 seals stretch out on the sands. Plenty of critters can be seen throughout the year, including badgers, foxes, skylarks, meadow pipits, and the endangered European insect species of marsh fritillary (a checkered little bugger). To get there, take the Downpatrick or Belfast bus from Newcastle and get off at Murlough. (☎4375 1467. Beach and walks open in daytime. May-Sept. £3 per car; free other times.)

Mount Pleasant Riding and Trekking Center, a cozy, family-run riding center on 15 Bannonstown Rd. in Castlewellan, leads forest or beach rides for all experience levels. (☎4377 8651. £11 per hr., helmet provided. 5+. Open daily 10am-4:30pm.) More experienced riders head to **Mourne Trail Riding Centre,** in Castlewellan at 96 Castlewellan Rd., for 2hr. rides in Tollymore Forest Park. (☎4372 4351; £10 per hr., helmet included. 10+. Open daily, first ride at 11am. Ring ahead for other ride times. Advanced booking required.) For the less equestrian, the **Tropicana Water and Leisure Center,** 10-14 Central Promenade, back in town, has a heated outdoor swimming pool, water slides, swan boats, and a pitch-and-putt. Tuesday nights are reserved for **Tropicana-rama** when the centre gets festive and hosts a disco for the wee ones. (☎4372 5034. Swimming £2.50, children under 8 £2. Tropicana-rama 6-8pm. Open M and W-F 11am-6:45pm, Tu 11am-4pm, Sa 11am-5:45pm, Su 1-5:30pm.)

🅝 HIKING: THE MOURNE MOUNTAINS

Before heading for the hills from Newcastle, stop at the **Mourne Countryside Centre** and **Mourne Heritage Trust,** 87 Central Promenade (☎4372 4059). A friendly and knowledgeable staff leads hikes and offers a broad selection of guides to the mountains. Those planning short excursions can purchase *Mourne Mountain Walks* (£6), which describes 10 one-day hikes, while those planning to camp in the Mournes overnight should buy the *Mourne Country Outdoor Pursuits Map* (£4.95), a detailed topographical map. (Open year-round M-F 9am-5pm.) If the Centre is closed, get maps at the Newcastle tourist office and information at **Hill Trekker** (see **Practical Information,** p. 495). Seasoned hikers looking for company can join the **Mourne Rambling Group,** which sends gangs into the Mournes each Sunday. (Call the group's secretary, Mari Doran, ☎4372 5827, for meeting locations. Walks generally 4½-5 hr., at varying levels.) Shuttle buses run between Silent Valley and Ben Crom Reservoirs. (☎4372 2296. June and Sept. Sa-Su 1 per day, 1pm; July-Aug. daily 3 per day. £2.15.) In late June, join in the **Mourne International Walking Festival** for planned group walks along designated trails of varying lengths and difficulties. (☎4176 9965; www.mournewalking.com.)

The **Mourne Wall,** built between 1904 and 1923, was a landlord's idea of a barrier, though at an unimpressive 3 ft., one wonders why the mountains wouldn't do. It encircles 12 of the mountains just below their peaks. Following the length of the 22 mi. wall takes a strenuous 8hr.; many people break it up with a night under the stars. The Mournes' highest peak, **Slieve Donard** (850m), towers above Newcastle. The trail up is wide, well-maintained, and paved in many places with flagstones and cobblestones (5hr. return). **Donard Park,** on the corner of Central Promenade and Bryansford Rd., provides the most direct access to the Mournes from Newcastle. (Always open. Free.) It's convenient to both Slieve Donard and **Slieve Commedagh,** both 3 mi. from town. Follow the dirt path behind the carpark as it crosses two bridges. It eventually joins the Glen River Path for about 1½ mi. to reach the Mourne Wall. At the wall, turn left for Slieve Donard or right for Slieve Commedagh. Those seeking a more remote trek might try **Slieve Bernagh** (739m) or **Slieve Binnian** (747m), most easily accessed from **Hare's Gap** (430m) and **Silent Valley,** respectively. The two craggy peaks, both with tremendous views, can be combined into a 12 mi. half-day hike. Hare's Gap is accessible through a carpark known to savvy locals. From Newcastle pass Tollymore Park, making a right on Trassey Road at a sign marked **Meelmore Amenity Area.** The carpark is the closest to the track and it's a 1min. walk up the **Trassey Track** to Hare's Gap. The ascent crosses the **Ulster Way,** a walking trail that runs east to west. Most of the land in and around the Mournes is privately owned, so campers should be wary of treading on a none-too-benign landlord's turf. Bearing this in mind, trekkers should feel free but treat the environs with respect. Close those sheep gates!

Wilderness **camping** in designated forest areas is legal and popular. (Contact Catherine McAleenan for more info at ☎417 69825.) Common spots include the **Annalong Valley, Lough Shannagh,** and **Trassey River. Hare's Gap** and the shore of **Blue Lough** at the foot of Slievelamagan are good places to pitch a tent. While camping around the Mourne Wall is allowed, camping in the forest is strictly prohibited due to the risk of forest fires. Remember to bring warm clothing; the mountains get cold and windy at night, and Irish weather conditions are known to change suddenly. A local volunteer **Mountain Rescue** team (☎999) is available in emergencies.

NEWRY ☎028

Though on the scene for thousands of years, it is only in the past two years that the up-and-coming town has arrived. In honor of the Queen's Golden Jubilee Celebration in 2002, Newry was declared an official town by the Queen mum. With a royal word, Newry jumped to attention as a city between the Mournes and the Ring of Gullion, bordering Co. Antrim and Down, and a none too distant neighbor to the Republic. Another boon—the Euro—has ushered Newry into prominence. The frugal of the Republic hop over to Newry for its famed shopping centers and independent stores, which are a steal due to excellent exchange rates.

▐ TRANSPORTATION. A mile out the Camlough Rd., to the northeast of town resides the **train station** (☎3026 9271). Accessible by a quick taxi ride, shuttle buses also make the trip into town regularly. To: Dublin (70min.; M-Sa 9 per day, Su 4 per day; £14.50, child £7.25) and Belfast (55min.; M-F 12 per day, Sa 9 per day, Su 5 per day; £6.30/£3.15). **Buses** run from the Ulsterbus depot on the Mall, which runs parallel to Mill St. To: Belfast (1½hr.; M-F 16 per day, Sa 12 per day, Su 6 per day; £5.90/£2.95); Downpatrick (1hr.; M-F 16 per day, Sa 15 per day, Su 2 per day; £5.90/£2.95); Dublin (2hr.; M-Sa 7 per day; Su 5 per day; £9.30/£4.65). **ABC** (☎3025 2511) and **ACE** (☎3026 2666) run 24hr. **taxis.**

▐▐ ORIENTATION AND PRACTICAL INFORMATION. Newry has two main streets which run parallel to each other and the **Newry Canal,** which flows between them. From the tourist office, **Hill Street** moves into town and changes to **John Mitchell Place,** while farther north, **Merchant's Quay** moves alongside the canal and shopping area to become **Buttercrane Quay.** Connecting the two streets is **Mill Street,** which becomes **Francis Street** as it crosses the canal. The **tourist office,** at the end of Hill St. in the town hall, books accommodations and provides information about Newry, its surroundings, and the Republic. (☎3026 8877; www.seenewryandmourne.com. Open Apr.-June M-F 9am-5pm, Sa 10am-4pm; July-Sept. M 9am-5pm, Tu-F 9am-7pm, Sa 10am-4pm; Oct.-Mar. M-F 9am-5pm.) **McCumiskey** holds the **car hire** monopoly (☎3088 8598). **Camping equipment** as well as hunting

NORTHERN IRELAND

and horse tack can be purchased at **Smyths Tack Bo,** 5-9 Kildare St. in front of the tourist office (☎3026 5303; www.smythsports.co.uk. Open M-Sa 9am-6pm.) **First Trust Bank,** 42-44 Hill St. (☎3026 6221), and other banks on Hill St. have **ATMs.** The **library,** 79 Hill St., has **Internet** access. (☎3026 4683. £1.50 per 30min. Open M and F 9:30am-6pm, Tu and Th 9:30am-8pm, W and Sa 9:30am-5pm.) The **post office** is also on Hill St. (Open M-F 9am-5:30pm, Sa 9am-12:30pm.) **Postal code:** BT34 1JD.

⌂🍴🍺 ACCOMMODATIONS, FOOD, AND PUBS. A few fancy hotels mark Newry as the mover and shaker it claims to be. However, cheaper and more personable B&Bs lie just outside of town on the Belfast Rd. by the tourist office. ▓**Belmont Hall ❹,** 18 Downshire Rd., envelops visitors in enormous rooms with great oak beds, high ceilings, fluffy comforters, big windows, private baths, and coffee-making facilities. A large apartment through the greenhouse sleeps 10-12 in a plush dark oak interior with velvet couches and a fireplace. (☎3026 2163; www.bellmonthall.co.uk. Singles £30; doubles £60 with breakfast; apartment £120 without breakfast.) **Marymount B&B ❸,** on Windsor Ave., up a steep hill a 7min. walk from town on the Belfast Rd., is a pleasant white house with beautifully airy rooms. Large windows let whatever light the weather allows flood in. (☎3026 1099. Breakfast included. Singles €25, doubles £40.) **Clanrye House B&B ❸,** 24 Belfast Rd., yards past the turn-off for Marymount. A little farther from the center of town, but still within walking distance, the three front rooms in this small house offer light and hospitality, especially from the youngest proprietess Lauren—a charming, wee colleen. (☎3026 2384. Singles €25; doubles €40, with bath €45.)

A **Supervalu** on Hill St. sells groceries. (Open M-W and Sa 8:30am-6pm, Th-F 8:30am-9pm.) Also on Hill St., **The Shelbourne Bakery ❷** entices the working lunch crowd and the old ladies on errands with fresh baked goods (£0.35-0.50) and sandwiches (£2.25-3). Eat at the cafe or takeaway. (☎3026 2002. Heaping specials £5-7. Open M-Sa 8am-6pm.) For a spot of chai tea (£1.35) in a world of Earl Grey and scones, check out **Jay Cee's ❷,** 1b Francis St., a left off Buttercrane Quay. Piping hot panini and soup prevail in this cafe. (☎3026 7113. Open M-W and Sa 8:30am-5pm, Th-F 8:30am-8pm, Su 10am-6pm.)

Pubs also serve decent meals. A popular and reasonable carvery meal of assorted meats and side dishes (served daily noon-3pm, £6.50) is on at the Canal Court Hotel's **Granary Bar,** Merchants Quay. Many of the city's residents and visitors wash down the feast with pints to 80s-90s music in the enormous, elegant bar and party on weekends at the upstairs disco **The Millers Suit.** (☎3025 1234; www.canalcourthotel.com. Su karaoke. Bar 18+. Club 23+. Cover £9. Bar open M-Sa 11:30am-1am, Su noon-12:30am. Club open Sa 9:30pm-2am.) The area's young professionals hand over their bills to the **Bank Bar** and its corresponding **Vault Club,** 2 Trevor Hill, diagonal to the tourist office before the Belfast Rd. A swank bar on the ground floor is eclipsed by an enormous club area with more sound and light equipment than a U2 concert. A projector above the dance floor lets those gettin' jiggy check their moves on the big screen. (☎3083 5501; www.thebanknewry.com. Live cover band F-Sa. F "Time Warp" plays 70-90s hits. Sa "Club Classics" pumps mainstream jams. 20+. Cover £7. Bar open daily 9am-1am. Club open 10pm-2am.) The even younger, wiley set get their kicks at **O'Dowds,** 17-19 Francis St. The bar spills into the newly refurbished Gothic revival **Club Velvet,** where the sacrilegious pray to the porcelain god after a night at the five gothic triptych bars under the fake fires of gilded candelabras. (☎6936 6926. Cover F-Sa £6, Th and Su £4. Bar open daily 11am-1am. Club open June-Aug. Th-Sa 10:30pm-1:30am.)

🖼 ⚠ SIGHTS AND ACTIVITIES. The tourist office is terribly ready to expound on this newly christened town's potential. A free guide to the "Newry Town Trail" highlights most of the city's historic sites including **St. Patrick's Church,** the first Reformation church in Ireland, begun in 1578. **Newry Canal Way** is a marked trail from Portadown to Newry with ancient monuments, wildlife, and bird-watching along the way. In the Arts Centre, next to the tourist office, **Newry and Mourne Museum** exhibits the town's expansive history. Its newest display details the recent castle excavation site nearby. (☎3026 6232; museum@newryand-mourne.gov.uk.) Newry's **shopping** is locally renowned, with **Quays Shopping Centre** on Bridge St. off Buttercrane Quay where the equally large **Buttercrane Shopping Centre** resides. Boutiques line the area between Hill and Merchants St. The town hosts some of the most unique festivals in Northern Ireland. The year kicks off in January with the annual **pantomime,** a funny political satire based on a traditional yarn or fairy-tale. (Call town hall ☎3026 6232.) March introduces Newry to 10 plays on 10 consecutive nights as theater troops from all over the Republic and the North compete to advance to the **All Ireland Drama Festival.** (Contact Miss Eileen Mooney ☎3026 6407. Admission to each play £5, children £3.) **Newry Musical Feis** (FESH) sees Irish and contemporary dancers, choirs, and classical musicians compete for a creative two weeks. (Contact Mary Goss ☎3026 2849; a.m.goss@bt.internet.com.) **Newry Agricultural Show** starts the summer in late June when dog and livestock shows, vintage cars, pig races, and homemade crafts deck the lawn of Derrymore House, a landed estate 2½ miles from town. (Contact the show office ☎3026 2059.)

WARRENPOINT (AN POINTE)

A few miles down the coast from Newcastle, on the north side of Carlingford Lough, lies the harbor town of Warrenpoint. It first gained fame as a resort town in the 1800s, when merely having a half-decent beach satisfied tourists. Today, a fortuitous gulf stream keeps Warrenpoint several significant degrees warmer than its neighbors, though nearby Rostrevor is a larger part of Warrenpoint's appeal. Rostrevor draws annual crowds for the **Fiddler's Green Festival,** making Warrenpoint an important source of accommodations. The end of the pier provides an unparalleled view of the Cooley and Mourne Mountains, whose proximity makes it hard to believe that they're technically in a different country—the Republic. While lough and mountain views are Warrenpoint's only in-town sights, **Narrow Water Castle** is a 2 mi. walk or drive on A2 toward Newry; bus drivers stop on request. The 16th-century structure is one of the best-preserved tower houses in Ireland and was built for defense and toll collection. In the 19th century, it became a dog kennel. A more tragic event in recent years resonates with locals who recall the **IRA bombing** of a British army lorry on August 27, 1979. A 29-year-old onlooker from the opposite shore, William Hudson, was mistaken for the bomber and shot by the survivors. Across the shore in the Republic, a commemorative stone enshrines the slain boy. Hundreds tip their glasses on August 1st in celebration of the **Feast of the Immaculate Conception** with a small parade, family activities, and a fun fair in the square. Since 1990, mid-August is ruled by the **Maiden of the Mournes Festival,** for which lasses from Ireland, Europe, and the US gather to display their personalities and prodigious talents. Bookies accept bets a week before, but the **Junior Miss Maiden of the Mournes** competition, involving 7- to 8-year-olds, is left to sidebetters.

The bus drop-off is in **The Square;** facing the water, the street bordering the Square and parallel to the lough coast becomes **Church Street** on the left and **Charlotte Street** on the right. Euphemistically named **"ferries"** (tiny motorboats) land at the other end of the waterfront and putt-putt over to Omeath in the Republic. The

tourist office, two blocks right from the bus stop when facing away from the water, offers a town map and armloads of free glossy regional guides. (Open M-F 9am-1pm and 2-5pm.) **Ulster Bank,** 2 Charlotte St., **Northern Bank** on Queen St., and **First Trust** on the Square have 24hr. **ATMs. Red Star Passenger Ferry** (☎4177 3070) runs a sporadic service (weather and tides permitting) across the lough to Omeath in the Republic. (June-Sept.; £3 return.) **Rent bikes** at **Stewart's Cycles,** 14 Havelock Pl., beside the Surgery Clinic on Marine Parade. (☎4177 3565. Also does repairs. £8 per day, £40 per wk. Open M-F 2-6pm, Sa 10am-6pm.) In an **emergency** dial ☎999, no coins required. **Walsh's Pharmacy** is at 25 Church St. (☎4175 3661. Open M-Sa 9am-6pm.) The **post office** sits at 9 Church St. (☎4175 2225. Open M-Tu, Th 8:30am-5:30pm; W 8:30am-1pm; F 9am-5:30pm; Sa 9am-12:30pm.) **Postal code:** BT34.

Whistledown and Finn's ❹, 6 Seaview, on the waterfront next to a playground at the end of Church St., has hotel-quality, TV-laden rooms at B&B prices. The Victorian townhouse also houses a modern bar and restaurant. As there is no real front desk, talk to the bartender to book rooms. (☎4175 4174. Breakfast included. Singles £30; doubles £55.) **Lough View ❸,** 10 Osborne Promenade, along the lough leading out of town, has cozy B&B rooms for comfortable prices. (☎4177 3067. Singles £25; doubles £40.) Most of Warrenpoint's eateries offer takeaway, ideal for eating with your feet dangling from the pier. **Diamonds Restaurant ❶,** the Square, is famed for the best food at the best price and is always packed with locals and their wee ones devouring burgers, seafood, pasta, and the only Mexican food available this side of the Rio Grande. (☎4175 2053. Entrees £3.75-8. Open M-Th 10am-7pm, F-Su noon-10pm.) **Genoa Cafe ❶,** the Square, has served fish and chips to Warrenpoint since 1910. Practice made them perfect and won several local chipper competitions. Don't pass up the smooth vanilla ice cream (£0.70), the Italian owners' family recipe. (☎4175 3688. Open M-F 11am-11pm, Sa-Su noon-11pm.) On Church St., **Jenny Black's ❶** coffee bar serves simple hot sandwiches (£2-3.50) and desserts (£1-2.50) amidst up-and-coming local art. (☎4177 3775. Open M-Sa 9am-5:30pm.) **Vecchia Roma ❹,** 1 Marine Parade, on the corner of the Square and Marine Parade, serves carnivorous and vegetarian Italian fare and a plethora of wine under a decorative trellis. (☎4175 2082. Pizzas £4.45-7.45; other entrees £7-15. Open M-Th 5-10pm, F-Sa 5-11pm, Su 12:30-2:30pm and 5-9:30pm.)

Though quite a few locals go into Newry at night, enough seek *craic* in Warrenpoint to maintain a decent nightlife. **Jack Ryan's,** the Square, serves eats (most dishes £2-5), has live music at its huge two-tiered bar Friday and Saturday at 9pm, and passes the mic with karaoke on Thursday and Sunday at 10pm. (☎4175 2001. Food served M-F 12:30-2:30pm; Sa-Su 12:30-8pm.) At **The Square Peg,** 14 The Square, 20- and 30-somethings pour in after 11:30pm. (☎4175 3429; www.squarepeg.co.uk. Live music F-Sa nights. Occasional weekend cover up to £7. Open M-Sa 11:30am-1am, Su 12:30pm-12:30am.)

MY MONUMENT IS BIGGER THAN YOUR MONUMENT

Hidden by trees about halfway between Rostrevor and Warrenpoint stands a dull, massive gray spike. The unadorned monument stands in honor of Trevor Ross, who led the commandeering and burning of the United States White House in 1814. Seizing the President's home during an official banquet, General Ross evacuated the house and set it ablaze—but only after polishing off the meal with the help of his battallion. The General's hometown has honored him not only with the great pointer (whose uncannily phallic resemblance to the Washington Monument may or may not be intentional), but also by taking his name, Rostrevor.

ROSTREVOR (CAISLEAN RUAIRI)

The tiny village of Rostrevor, which lies 3 mi. from Warrenpoint along the A2, has a "downtown" of one sharply sloped block (the #39 **bus** from Newry to Kilkeel frequently makes the journey). At its bottom, a short bridge ends at **Fairy Glen,** a small park with a bike path that runs along a pretty stream. A hundred yards farther are the rolling hills of the much larger **Kilbroney Park.** In addition to a cafe and some wonderful climbing trees, Kilbroney holds the town's crown jewel **Rostrevor Forest,** one of the few remaining virgin Irish Oak forests in Ireland. An easy walk up the main gravel path from the carpark and a jaunt down the small left arching path reveals a sweeping view of the lough below and the Cooley Mountains across and a huge, anomalous hunk of sandstone. Locals swear that the suspicious stone was thrown by an Irish-smashing giant from Scotland. It is only fitting that an ancient act of ire inspires lovers to carve their immortal love into the rock's side. (Open daily dawn-9pm. Free.) Aside from its idyllic parks, Rostrevor is known for its annual **Fiddler's Green Festival.** During this late July extravaganza, fans and performers gather to enjoy traditional Irish music, poetry readings, storytelling, and dancing in the streets. (Call tourist information ☎4175 2256; www.fiddlersgreen-festival.com.) As a wee colleen, former President of the Republic and Rostrevor native Mary Robinson tipped her half-pints at her father's **Corner House Bar,** the big, red barn-like building at the top of the town's steep main drag. (1 Bridge St. ☎4173 8236. Tu and F trad 10pm. Open daily 11:30am-1am, later on weekends.) **The Glenside Inn,** 33 Bridge St. at the bottom of Main St. hill, draws scores to its excellent trad sessions (F-Su), especially during the Fiddler's Green Festival when it fills with the drunk, the dancing, and those who just can't find the exit.

ARMAGH (ARD MACHA)

Armagh challenges Downpatrick's claim, calling itself "City of St. Patrick." In the 5th century, St. Patrick ostensibly based his saintly mission on the hill *Druim Saileach.* Today, the Church of Ireland's St. Patrick's Cathedral rests where the original church was built in AD 445. On a facing hilltop, St. Patrick's Roman Catholic Cathedral also overlooks town. In the 19th century, the city was further shaped by Archbishop Robinson, who filled Armagh with Georgian architecture, including the observatory, the district council office, and the Robinson Library—formerly his palace. Only Dublin parallels such architecture; unsurprisingly, Robinson also had a hand in that city. Under the watch of the two ancient behemoths, the town shops, enjoys the arts, and greets visitors with a lively pub scene.

▊ TRANSPORTATION

Buses: Ulsterbus station, Lonsdale Rd. To: **Belfast** (70min.; M-F 22 per day, Sa 15 per day, Su 7 per day; £5, child £2.95) and **Enniskillen** via **Monaghan** (2hr.; Sept.-July 2 per day, Oct.-June M-Sa 1 per day; £7/£3.50). Armagh is also a stop for the "Cross-Border Service" from **Portrush** to **Dublin** (3hr.; M-Sa 2 per day, Su 1 per day; £9.30/£4.65). **Local buses** to areas like **Markethill** and **Newry** stop along the Mall West. Check the station on College St. or the tourist office for schedules.

Taxis: Eurocabs (☎3751 1900) is the largest 24hr. cab company in the city.

▣ ▜ ORIENTATION AND PRACTICAL INFORMATION

English Street, Thomas Street, and **Scotch Street** comprise Armagh's city center. Just to the east lies **the Mall,** a former racecourse that became a grassy park after betting was deemed offensive to the city's sanctity. To the west, two cathedrals sit on

NORTHERN IRELAND

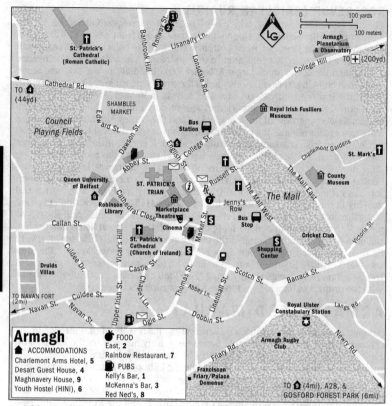

Armagh

🏠 ACCOMMODATIONS
Charlemont Arms Hotel, **5**
Desart Guest House, **4**
Maghnavery House, **9**
Youth Hostel (HINI), **6**

🍴 FOOD
East, **2**
Rainbow Restaurant, **7**

🍺 PUBS
Kelly's Bar, **1**
McKenna's Bar, **3**
Red Ned's, **8**

neighboring hills: the Catholic Cathedral rears its neo-Gothic spires, while a medieval-looking tower represents the Church of Ireland. North of Shambles marketplace is a primarily **Nationalist area;** the city's **Protestant neighborhood** lies south and east of Scotch St. While most of the busy city center is safe, the area on the Mall West has been known to spawn weekend brawls amongst concerned factions.

Tourist Office: Old Bank Building, 40 English St. (☎3752 1800). Booking service 10% plus £2. *Armagh Miniguide* covers the city's sights and attractions. Pious pedestrians can grab the *Armagh Pilgrim's Trail* (£1), a walking tour of holy sites. Open M-Sa 9am-5pm; Sept.-June also Su 2-5pm; July-Aug. also Su 1-5pm.

Banks: First Trust, English St. (☎3752 2025. Open M-Tu and W 10am-4:30pm, Th-F 9:30am-4:30pm.); **Ulster Bank,** Market St. (☎3752 2053); **Northern Bank,** Thomas St. (☎3752 2004). All have 24hr. **ATMs.**

Emergency: ☎999; no coins required. **Police:** Newry Rd. (☎3752 3311).

Pharmacy: J.W. Gray, at the corner of Russell St. and English St. (☎3752 2092). Open M-Sa 9am-6pm. Rotating Su schedule for prescriptions.

Hospital: Armagh Community Hospital, Tower Hill (☎3752 2381), off College Hill.

Internet Access: Armagh Computer World, 43 Scotch St. (☎3751 0002), inside the Best Buy and up the stairs. Open M-Sa 9am-5:30pm. £3 per hr. In 2004 expect Internet at the **Armagh Branch Library** (☎3752 4072), on Market St., as it is undergoing installation. Open M and F 9:30am-6pm, Tu and Th 9:30am-8pm, W and Su 9:30am-5pm.

Post Office: 31 Upper English St. (☎3751 0313), through a convenience store. *Poste Restante* mail across the street at 46 Upper English St. (☎3752 2079). Beat lines at 5 Ogle St. office. Open M-F 9am-5:30pm, Sa 9am-12:30pm. **Postal code:** BT6 17AA.

ACCOMMODATIONS

Travelers not toting tents find refuge at Armagh's in-town hostel and B&Bs outside the city center; the more rugged camp near **Gosford Forest Park** (see p. 524).

Armagh Youth Hostel (HINI), next to Queen's University campus (☎3751 1800). Facing away from the tourist office, turn left twice and follow Abbey St. for 2 blocks. Go through the carpark; the entrance is in a small alley. Huge and squeaky clean, if a little sterile, with superb, under-used facilities such as a kitchen, TV room, and lounge. Excellent security. Handicapped-accessible. Wash and dry £1.50 each. Reception 8-11am and 5-11pm. Dorms £12.75; private rooms £13.50. Under 18 £2 less. ❷

Desart Guest House, 99 Cathedral Rd. (☎3752 2387), a 7min. walk from the city center and a right onto Desart Ln. The 2nd building on the left. A formidable mansion with sunny rooms and, in the hall, embalmed birds. A bastion of character among legions of "quaint" B&Bs. Children welcome. Singles £20; doubles £35. ❸

Maghnavery House, 89 Gosford Rd., Markethill (☎3755 2021; www.maghnavery-house.co.uk). Seven miles out of town past Gosford Forest Park, across from a go-kart course. 19th-century farmhouse offers only a few rooms, but is a restful base for drivers to explore Armagh, Newry, and Gosford Forest Park. Singles £25-30; doubles £40-50. ❸

Charlemont Arms Hotel, 57-65 Upper English St. (☎ 3752 2028; www.charlemontarms-hotel.com), across from tourist office. Family-run hotel with 30 large standardized rooms with TVs and tea/coffee facilities. Attached bar **Turner's** and restaurant **downstairs@turner's** ensure guests don't go to bed hungry. Singles £45; doubles £60-65. ❺

FOOD AND PUBS

Finding affordable grub is a challenge. The best bet is to get groceries at **Sainsbury's** in the Mall Shopping Centre, Mall West (☎3751 1050; open M-W and Sa 8:30am-8pm, Th-F 8:30am-9pm) or at **Emerson's** on Scotch St. (☎3752 2846; open M 9am-6pm, Tu-W 8am-8pm, Th-F 8am-9:30pm, Sa 8am-6:30pm). Armagh's nightlife is a strange beast—like the rest of the town scene, it's segregated along sectarian lines. Visitors should orient themselves with the help of locals (such as hostel workers) before hittin' the town.

downstairs@turners, under Turner's bar, attached to Charlemont Arms Hotel (☎3752 2719). Even the subterranean location can't hide Armagh's best, most popular restaurant from its public. The restaurant manager recommends the fish (salmon £13.75). Call ahead for dinner. Lunch M-Sa noon-3pm, dinner Th-Sa only 5:30pm-9:30pm. ❺

East, 143-147 Railway St. (☎3752 8288), above Kelly's Bar. Far and away the town's favorite Chinese restaurant. Extensive vegetarian menu makes it dear to the health conscious. 3-course lunch special M-F noon-1:45pm (£5). Night-owls hoot for late night hours. Absolutely book ahead for Sa dinner. Open M-Th noon-1:45pm and 5pm-midnight; F noon-1:45pm and 5pm-1am; Sa 5pm-1am; Su 5pm-midnight. ❸

Rainbow Restaurant, 13 Lower English St. (☎3752 5391). Buffet-style lunches in a cheery location with decor that thankfully doesn't take its name to heart. Student hangout during term. Lunch from £3. Open M-F 8:45am-5:30pm, Sa 8:45am-9pm. ❷

Turner's, 56-57 Upper English St. (☎3752 2028), attached to Charlemont Arms Hotel. Though open for over a year, still the newest hot spot; comfortable drinking in a mixed crowd. 20-somethings clique off and gossip to the strains of a live cover band on F-Sa. 18+. Open M-Th and Su 11:30am-11:30pm, F-Sa 11:30am-1am.

Red Ned's, 27 Ogle St. (☎3752 2249), following English through to Market and Thomas St. Formally "O'Neil's," but informal locals have used the pseudonym for 3 generations since red-headed Edward O'Neil opened it. The business is a family affair; everyone is next of kin for trad every other W and Gaelic football matches on the thin plasma telly. 18+. Open M-Sa 11:30am-1am, Su 12:30pm-midnight.

Kelly's Bar, 147 Railway St. (☎3752 2103). Cluttered bar attracts Armagh's youngest for a full weekend. Karaoke Th and Su, disco F-Sa. Pool table battlefield for Sa tournaments where winner takes all. Open M–Sa 11:30am-1am, Su 11:30am-midnight.

McKenna's Bar, 21 Upper English St. (☎3752 2645). Popular with betters. Football and other sports distract the racetrack crowd as does trad on Sa 10:30pm. Open M-Sa 11:30am-1am, Su 11:30am-midnight.

🧭 SIGHTS

THE ROMAN CATHOLIC CATHEDRAL OF ST. PATRICK. Armagh's cathedrals watch over the city from opposing hills. To the north on Cathedral Rd. sits the 1873 Roman Catholic **Cathedral of St. Patrick.** The imposing exterior and exquisite mosaic interior contrast mightily with the ultra-modern granite sanctuary, which seems to have been designed by a federation of pagans and Martians. (☎3752 2802; www.armagharchdiocese.org. Open daily until dusk. Free.)

THE CHURCH OF IRELAND CATHEDRAL OF ST. PATRICK. South of the city is the Protestant incarnation. Authorities claim that the 13th-century church rests upon the site where St. Paddy founded his main place o' worship in AD 445. The cathedral is also the final resting place of great 10th-century Irish King Brian Ború. (☎3752 3142; www.stpatrickscathedralarmagh.org. Open daily Apr.-Oct. 9:30am-5pm; Nov.-Mar. 9:30am-4pm. Tours June-Aug. M-Sa 11:30am and 2:30pm. Free.)

ST. PATRICK'S TRIAN. In the center of town, ■**St. Patrick's Trian** shares a building with the tourist office. Most exhibits emphasize St. Pat's role in Armagh, although his link to the town is historically dubious. The **Armagh Story** is a walk-through display and audio-visual presentation where plaster Vikings, priests, and pagan warriors relate the lengthy history of the town. **Patrick's Testament** introduces the curious to the patron saint's writings, most pertinently "The Book of Armagh." A smaller, fanciful display, geared toward the little people, recreates **Swift's Land of Lilliput.** (☎3752 1801; www.visit-armagh.com. Open M-Sa 10am-5pm, Su 2-5pm. £4, students and seniors £3, children £2, family £9.50.)

ARMAGH OBSERVATORY AND PLANETARIUM. Up College Hill, north of the Mall, is the **Armagh Observatory,** founded and designed in 1790 by Archbishop Robinson, architect of Armagh and Dublin's Georgian buildings. The star-struck observe a modern weather station and an 1885 refractory telescope. Ireland's largest public telescope reaches for the stars and is free to families and small groups during dark nights from Oct-April. (☎3752 2928. By appt. only, though the grounds are open 9:30am-4:30pm.) More celestial wonders await in the nearby **Planetarium,** which displays a few centimeters of Mars. The whole solar system is scaled down to human level in the outdoor **Astropark.** (☎3752 3689; www.armaghplanet.com. 45min. shows July-Aug. 3-5 times per day; Apr.-June M-F 1 per day. Open M-F 10am-4:45pm, Sa-Su 1:15-4:45pm. Seating limited; book ahead. £3.75, students £2.75.)

PALACE DEMESNE. Palace Demesne (dah-MAIN) sprawls south of the town center. The palace, chapel, and stables were another of the Archbishop of Armagh's efforts to rebuild the city. The County Council now occupies the main building, relegating the public to the **Palace Stables Heritage Centre,** where a multimedia show presents "A Day in the Life" of the closed palace; in the three-dimensional world, Georgian characters enact tradional tasks. A **Franciscan Friary** occupies a peaceful corner of the grounds. (☎3752 9629; www.visit-armagh.com. Open May-Aug. M-Sa 10am-5:30pm, Su 1-5pm; Sept.-Apr. M-Sa 10am-5pm, Su 2-5pm. £3.75, children £2.)

OTHER SIGHTS. Visitors can peek at a first edition of **Gulliver's Travels**—covered with Swift's own scrawled comments—at the **Armagh Public Library.** (43 Abbey St. ☎3752 3142; www.armaghrobinsonlibrary.org. Open M-F 10am-1pm and 2-4pm. Access to rare books by appointment.) **Cardinal Thomas O'Fiaich Memorial Library and Archive** contains materials pertaining to Irish history, diaspora, sport, and language based on the eponymous Cardinal's collection. (15 Moy Rd. ☎3752 2981; www.ofiach.ie. Open M-F 9:30am-1pm and 2-5pm.) Computerised genealogical resources unite to present families with their ancestors at the **Armagh Ancestry Genealogical Centre.** The records focus on Co. Armagh and trace back past 1900. (38a English St. ☎3752 1802; www.armagh.gov.uk. Open M-F 11am-4pm. Search fees based on extent of request.) Bargain-hunters fill the walled **Shambles marketplace.** Regular "car boot" sales dredge up old records, Jackie Collins best-sellers, and other "antiques"; a farmers market makes an irregular appearance. (At the foot of the hill where Cathedral Rd., Dawson St., and English St. meet. ☎3752 8192. Open Tu, F, and alternate Sa 9am-noon.) The **Armagh County Museum,** on the east side of the Mall, displays a panoply of 18th-century objects—old wedding dresses, photographs, stuffed birds, jewelry, and militia uniforms. (☎3752 3070. Handicapped-accessible. Open M-F 10am-5pm, Sa 10am-1pm and 2-5pm. Free.)

🎵 ENTERTAINMENT

Armaghnian aesthetes enjoy a varied program of theater, music, dance, and visual arts within the white-tiled confines of the **Marketplace Theatre and Arts Centre,** on Market Sq. The theater also organizes the **Music in Armagh Festival** in September. (☎3752 1821; www.marketplacearmagh.com. Open M-Sa 9am-5pm, performance nights 9am-7pm.) Around the first week of June, Armagh holds an annual **Comhaltas Ceoltori Traditional Music Festival** (for info call Liz Watson ☎3752 5353). In mid-August, the Ulster **Road Bowls Finals** (see **Sports,** p. 80) are held on highways and byways throughout the county (for info call Sammy Gilespie ☎3752 5622). The **Apple Blossom Festival,** the second week of May, brings a number of events to the city, such as craft shows and blossom tours in Armagh and Moy, culminating in a lavish **May Ball** (contact the tourist office for info and schedules). On March 17, the **St. Patrick's Day** revels bring people together from far away to celebrate Big Paddy. *Céilí* dancing at St. Patrick's Parochial Hall on Cathedral Rd. demonstrates the Irish precursor to a hoe-down. (Th 9-10pm. Contact Brendan Kirk or Seamus McDonagh ☎3752 6088.) **Set dancing** also welcomes visitors on Monday nights at the **Pearse Og Social Club** on Dalton Rd. (contact Pat Prunty ☎3755 18414).

🏅 SPORTS AND ACTIVITIES

The area surrounding Armagh contains a multitude of outdoors activities. **Angling** is popular; daily permits are available from GI Stores, including the one on Dobbin St. (☎3752 2335). **Loughall County Park** promises a 37-acre fishery with daily permits for £3; yearly permits are only £25. (☎3889 2900; www.armagh.gov.uk.) Break out the 9-iron at the 18-hole **County Armagh Golf Club.** (☎3752 2501. BYO-clubs. Non-members £12-18. Open daily 8am-dark.) For more horsepower than a golf cart, head to **Moy**

Riding School, where an equine escort awaits. The school presents **show jumping** on Friday nights. (☎8778 4440. £8 per hr.) **Gosford Karting** satisfies the truly fast and furious. (☎3755 1248; www.gosfordkarting.co.uk. £5 per 7-10min.; £10 per 10-15min.)

◆ DAYTRIPS FROM ARMAGH

NAVAN FORT

On Killylea Rd. (A28), 2 mi. west of Armagh. ☎3752 1800; www. visit-armagh.com. Fort open daily dawn-dusk. £3.95, students £3.

On the outskirts of Armagh, the mysterious Navan Fort, also called *Emain Macha* (AHM-win maka), hosted the capital of the Kings of Ulster for 800 years. This may look like a grassy mound of dirt, but the imaginative see extensive fortifications and elaborate religious paraphernalia strewn across the site. In 94 BC, a huge wooden structure 40 yd. in diameter was constructed where the mound now stands; it was filled with stones, burnt to the ground in a religious rite, and covered with soil. Queen Macha (see **Legends and Folktales,** p. 73) is said to have founded the fort, although it is also associated with St. Patrick, who probably chose *Ard Macha* (Armagh, for those who weren't paying attention earlier) as a Christian center because of its proximity to this pagan stronghold. Following a series of tragic circumstances beginning with fire and ending with bankruptcy, the once-famous Navan Centre is now closed until further notice.

LOUGH NEAGH AND OXFORD ISLAND

Route A3 runs northeast from Armagh to loughside Craigavon and Lurgan. Discovery Centre ☎3832 2205; www.oxfordisland.com. Open Apr.-Sept. M-Sa 10am-6pm, Su 10am-7pm; Oct.-Mar. W-Su 10am-5pm. Last admission 1hr. before closing. Audio-visual displays £1.50.

Birdwatching and various aquatic activities are the principle amusements in the towns around Lough Neagh. A small paddling pool and play area interest the young. The lough's **Kinnego Marina** offers boat trips aboard the *Master Mc'Gra.* (Every Sa-Su between Apr-Oct. ☎3832 7573.) The lough's shores are also seen by car during daytrips from Belfast or Armagh. Some say that a giant once scooped a prime heap of Ulster out of the ground and hurled it into the Irish sea, creating not only the Isle of Man but also Lough Neagh, the UK's largest lake. The **Lough Neagh Discovery Centre,** on the **Oxford Island National Nature Reserve** in **Craigavon,** contains acres of wooded parkland for exploration. Audio-visual displays inside the center detail the lake's ecosystem and wildlife. **Boat rides** to the island run June to August. The **Kinnego Caravan Park,** on the Kinnego Marina in Lurgan, hosts hundreds of species of wild campers. (☎3832 7573. £6 per 2-person tent.)

GOSFORD FOREST PARK

Take A28 for about 7 mi. or hop #40 bus to Markethill. ☎3755 1277 or 3755 2169. Open daily 8am-sunset. £1.50, children £0.50, €3 per car. Youth site £1.80 per tent; May-June and Sept. £6.50 per tent, £8 per caravan; July-Aug. tent or caravan £10.

The Gosford Forest Park, 7 mi. southeast of Armagh, cordially invites all to spend a nice day with its castle, old walled garden, and miles of nature trails. **Horse-riding** and **golf** are also in the area. Visitors are welcome to **camp** in the Gosford Forest. Ten miles north of Armagh on the A29, the Moy Rd., lies **The Agory,** Derryclaw Rd., Moy. This small estate house remains as it was left, stylish without electricity. Original gas fixtures, central stove heating, and a Victorian laundry room illustrate such life and times. (☎8778 4753; www.nationaltrust.org. Handicapped-accessible. Open Mar.15-May 31 and Sept. Sa-Su noon-6pm; June-Aug. daily noon-6pm. £2.10 per car, grounds and house £4.10, children £2, family £10.40.)

Conversing with the People of Northern Ireland

One of the greatest draws of Northern Ireland, even for the short-term visitor, is that history lives in the present. It is written on walls, mourned in song, debated and celebrated on the street. However, its beauty lies in its complexity and depth, which can at times be confusing and intimidating.

But if you find understanding the situation in Northern Ireland difficult, you're not alone. During the darkest days of the Troubles, someone sprayed a message on a Belfast wall: "If you think you know what's going on, you don't know anything at all." Even those who have spent their lives at the frontlines have a hard time making sense of the conflict that was chaotic and contradictory even as it oversimplified things.

Given this, it might be tempting to forsake the history lesson, pack a picnic, and head for the spectacular scenery of the Antrim coast or the Mourne Mountains. With misty lakes, ruined castles, and pristine beaches never more than half an hour away, all you need for a great afternoon is a bottle of Guinness, an Irish cheddar sandwich, and a scoop of Maude's famous Pooh Bear honeycomb ice cream. (Maude's ice cream shops can be found across the province and are definitely worth seeking out.)

But wherever you go, chances are the local lore is rich, and it's worth spending a little time getting to know the area's history and people. Stories and histories hover like ghosts in every pub and along every hedgerow. Uncovering them is the greatest joy of traveling in Northern Ireland. Fortunately for visitors, folks here are some of the world's most gifted talkers. It would be cliché to expound on the warmth of an Irish welcome, but hospitality in the north is exceptional. In fact, Northern Ireland may be one of the last places in Western Europe where locals are actually glad to see tourists. Good conversation (*craic*) is a highly revered pastime, and when approached respectfully, folks are pleased to share their wit, wisdom, and personal experience with the open-minded.

So strike up a conversation with the taxi driver, the woman in line at the bakery, or the bartender pouring a pint, and get to know the people whose daily lives and raucous humor

tell the story of Northern Ireland better than any history book. As you do, it will become clear that for any question, there are a hundred answers. Often the best answer is "all of the above." In Northern Ireland, there is often truth in contradiction.

Try to pin down when the Troubles began, for example, and you'll find that even the standard 400-year timeline of British-Irish antagonism doesn't capture the full complexity of Northern Ireland's past. The province can be understood as much through the essentially entangled nature of its people's history, as through the legacies of division.

For centuries the twelve-mile stretch of sea between Ireland and Scotland provided a steady migration back and forth of people, language, culture, and folklore. The first humans to settle on Ireland actually arrived via Scotland, across this narrow section of the Northern Channel. The land was even united under the ancient maritime kingdom of Dalriada, stretching from Antrim to the Mull of Kintyre in Scotland.

This shared and ancient past is often overlooked, and the Troubles are characterized as the result of two distinct peoples in conflict over the future of the state. And in a way, this is true. Unionists feel British and want to be British. Nationalists feel Irish and want to be Irish. Left out of this picture are the many people in Northern Ireland who feel that they're a bit of both. (Even more problematic are the people that nobody wants to talk about, the folks that don't really think they care one way or the other.)

Regardless of what each person feels, their individual stories and complex identities are all true, and all an equal piece of the puzzle. The impassioned and the ambivalent alike are responsible for driving the course of events in Northern Ireland.

There aren't any easy answers to explain the violent conflict that has engulfed Northern Ireland for the past 30 years, and giving up on finding any is a good first step to experiencing the place. Start instead with real experts, the people themselves. Only these individual stories, memories, and experiences fully capture the meaning and beauty of Northern Ireland.

For the last three years, Brenna Powell has worked at the Stanford Center on Conflict and Negotiation on projects in partnership with grass-roots organizations in Northern Ireland.

ANTRIM AND DERRY

The A2 coastal road skitters along the edge of Antrim and Derry, connecting the scenic attractions of both counties. West of Belfast, stodgy and industrial Larne gives way to lovely seaside villages. The nine Glens of Antrim give scenery fiends plenty of excitement. Near the midpoint of the northern coast, the Giant's Causeway spills its geological honeycomb into the ocean; this mid-section of the coast road is a cyclist's paradise. Urban sprawl reappears past the Causeway with the carnival lights of Portrush and Portstewart. The road terminates at the turbulent, walled city of Derry, the North's second largest city.

LARNE (LATHARNA) ☎028

Though it claims aristocratic roots—Prince Lathar lent his name to the original settlement of *Latharna*—today's Larne is a working man's town whose major attractions are its ferries to and from Scotland, Britain, and France. The town also serves the surrounding rural communities with a **livestock fair** on Fridays in the Market Yard. **P&O Ferries** (☎087 0242 4777; www.poirishsea.com) operates boats from Larne to Cairnryan, Scotland (1hr.; generally 7-10 per day; £15-24 based when booked, students £12-18, child £8-12, cycles free); Troon (2hr., Apr.-Sept. only travelers with cars); Fleetwood, England (8hr., daily 10am and 10pm, M-F 4pm; car and driver £68-78, additional adults £17-30, child £11-20). The **train station** is adjacent to a roundabout, down the street from the tourist office on Narrow Gauge Rd. (☎9066 6630; www.translink.co.uk. Open daily 7:30am-5:30pm.) Trains chug from Central Station in Belfast to Larne Town and Larne Harbour, a 15min. walk from town (50min.; M-Sa 17-20 per day, Su 6 per day; £3.60). The **bus station** is south of town, on the other side of the A8. (☎2827 2345. Open M-F 9am-5:15pm.) Buses depart from Station Rd. for Laganside Station in Belfast (1½hr., express 50min.; M-Sa 14 per day, Su 4 per day in summer; £3.20) and stops along the Antrim coast.

To reach the town center from the harbor, take the first right outside the ferryport. As the road curves left, it becomes **Curran Road,** and then **Main Street.** It's best to take a cab in the evening, as the route passes through a fairly rough Unionist neighborhood. The **tourist office,** Narrow Gauge Rd., books accommodations and has a free town map. (☎2826 0088; www.larne.gov.uk. Open Easter-Sept. M-F 9am-6pm, Sa 9am-5pm; Oct.-Easter M-Sa 9am-6pm.) **Internet** beams from the **library** on Pound St. at the top of High St. (☎2827 7047. £1.50 per 30min., Members free. Open M and Th 10am-8pm; Tu-W, F 10am-5:30pm; Sa 10am-5pm.) **Northern Bank,** 19 Main St. (☎2827 6311) has 24hr. **ATMs.** The **post office** is at 98 Main St. inside a bookshop. (☎2826 0489. Open M-F 9am-5:30pm, Sa 9am-12:30pm.) **Postal code:** BT40.

Larne's not a town where people linger. For comfort and safety's sake, avoid crashing at the harbor near the ferry. Instead, **Glenarm** and **Curran Road** spring from Main St. toward the terminal and hold a more affluent area closer to town lined with B&Bs. **The Aardvark ❷,** 21 Curran Rd., close to the ferry, has beautifully decorated, spacious rooms with TVs and tea/coffeemakers. (☎2827 0898. £16-17.) **Inverbann ❷,** at 7 Glenarm Rd., demands attention with satellite TVs and en suite rooms. (☎2827 2524. £15.) **Curran Caravan Park ❶,** 131 Curran Rd., between the harbor and town, is a congested campground. (☎2827 5505. £1.50 per person; £5 per tent.) The giant **Co-op Superstore** is on Station Rd., next to the bus station. (☎2826 0737. Open M-W 9am-9pm, Th-F 9am-10pm, Sa 9am-8pm, Su 1-6pm.) For fresher fare—fruits, veggies, fish, knock-off designer gear—hit the **farmer's market,** in the Market Yard. (W between 8am-noon.) Larne's main street is littered with cheap sandwich shops. **Caffe Spice ❶,** 7 Dunluce St., is popular with the younger crowd. (☎2826 9633. Open M-W 10am-5pm, Th-Sa 10am-10pm.) Fans of substance over style enjoy **The Big Sandwich Company ❶,** 27 Point St., on the corner of Narrow Gauge St., up from the tourist office, where an assembly line manufactures filling lunches. (☎2826 0410. Sandwiches around £2. Open M-Sa 9am-5pm.) **Chekker's Wine Bar ❷,** 33 Lower Cross St., serves a broad selection of bistro food in a leisurely atmosphere. (☎2827 5305. Mains £5; food served daily noon-9pm.) Smoky, lamp-lit **Bailie,** 111-113 Main St., pours congratulatory pints for brave ocean voyagers. (☎2827 3947. Entrees £4-5. Food served daily 11:30am-2:30pm and 5-8pm.)

GLENS OF ANTRIM

During the Ice Age, glaciers ripped through the mountainous coastline northeast of Antrim, leaving nine deep scars in their wake. Over the years, water collected in these valleys, spurring the growth of trees, ferns, and other lush flora not usually found in Ireland. The A2 coastal road connects the mouths of these glens and provides entry to roads inland, allowing weekenders easy access to the area. The glens and their mountains and waterfalls can best be seen on daytrips inland from the coastal villages of Glenarm, Waterfoot, and Cushendall.

Most visitors travel the glens by car, but two **Ulsterbus** routes serve the area year-round (Belfast ☎9032 0011; Larne ☎2827 2345). Bus #156 from Belfast stops in Larne, Ballygally, Glenarm, and Carnlough (summer M-Sa 6-7 per day; Su 3 per day; off season M-Sa 5-7 per day, Su 1 per day; £2.80-5.20) and sometimes continues to Waterfoot, Cushendall, and Cushendun (summer M-F 4 per day, Sa-Su 2 per day; off season M-F 2 per day). Bus #150 runs between Ballymena and Glenariff (M-Sa 5 per day, £2.60) then to Waterfoot, Cushendall, and Cushendun (M-F 5 per day, Sa 3 per day; £4.30). The **Antrim Coaster** (#252) runs year-round, following the road from Belfast to Coleraine and stopping at every town along the way (2 per day, £7.50). **Cycling** the glens is fabulous. The **Ardclinis Activity Centre** in Cushendall **rents bikes** (see p. 528). The coastal road from Ballygally to Cushendun is both scenic and flat. Once the road leaves Cushendun, though, it becomes hilly enough to make even motorists groan. Crossroads are the best places to find a lift, but like dodgy Indian food, *Let's Go* does not recommend it.

GLENARIFF

Mirror, mirror, on the wall, who's the fairest Glen of all? The answer is the beautiful, broad, Glenariff. Guarded from any wicked stepmothers by the village of **Waterfoot,** the glen is 9 mi. up the coast from Glenarm. Thackeray dubbed this area "Switzerland in miniature" because of the steep, rugged landscape. An introduction to the natural zone, **Red Castle,** atop **red arch,** is an Irish lookout to scout toward Scotland for marauding Englishmen. Following A43 toward Ballymena, past Waterfoot, leads to the large **Glenariff Forest Park,** where the glen lies. The **bus** between Cushendun and Ballymena (#150) stops at the official park entrance (M-Sa 3-5 per day). If walking from Waterfoot, however, enter 1½ mi. downhill by taking the road that branches left toward the Manor Lodge Restaurant. (☎2175 8769 or 2177 1796. Open daily 10am-dusk. £3 per car, £1.50 per pedestrian.) Once inside the park, trails range in length from half a mile to 5 mi. All paths pass the Glenariff and Inver rivers and the three waterfalls that feed them. The awesome 3 mi. ◼**Waterfall Trail,** marked by blue triangles, follows the cascading, fern-lined Glenariff River from the park entrance to the Manor Lodge. The entrance to the **Moyle Way,** a 17 mi. hike from Glenariff to Ballycastle, is directly across from the park entrance. All the walks begin and end at the carpark and the **Glenariff Tea House ❷.** This bay-windowed restaurant has fresh snacks (sandwiches ₤2), exotically seasoned meals (₤5-8), and a gorgeous view. The attached shop has **free maps** of the park's trails. (☎2565 8769. Open Easter-Sept. daily 11am-6pm.)

Those wishing to commune with beautiful Glenariff for longer than an afternoon lodge in Waterfoot. **Lurig View B&B ❷,** at 4 Lurig View on Glen Rd., off Garron Rd. about half a mile past town toward Larne on the waterfront, provides big, comfy beds and big, tasty breakfasts. (☎2177 1618. ₤18.) **Glenariff Forest Park Camping ❶,** 98 Glenariff Rd., is self-explanatory. (☎2175 8232. Tents ₤7-10 and park entrance.) Stock up at **Kearney's Costcutter,** 21 Main St., before treking into the waterfall wilderness. (☎2177 1213. Open daily 7am-10pm.) Run out of a family home, **Angela's Restaurant and Bakery ❷,** 32 Main St., serves meals (₤4-7) of fried, curried, or sweet-and-soured chicken. The back patio has grand views of Lurigethan Hill to the left and Garron Point to the right. (☎2177 1700. Takeaway available all day. Open M-W 10am-8pm, Th-Su 10am-11pm.) **The Saffron Bar,** 4-6 Main St. (☎2177 2906), is wild about hurling. The owners seek to infuse this mellow pub with new life through an indoor bar and outdoor beer garden. **Cellar Bar,** downstairs, has live music ranging from country to trad on weekends. **The Mariners' Bar,** 7 Main St. (☎2177 1330), has a variety of live music on Friday and Saturday nights.

CUSHENDALL (BUN ABHANN DALLA)

Cushendall is nicknamed the capital of the Glens, probably for its sheer proximity to the natural wonders. The four streets in the town center house a variety of goods, services, and pubs unavailable anywhere else in the region. The town's proximity to Glenaan, Glenariff, Glenballyeomon, Glencorp, and Glendun supplement its importance as a commercial center. Unfortunately, the closing of its hostel may mean Cushendall's days as a budget travel mecca are over, though the camping barn outside town seeks to fill the gap.

■ **TRANSPORTATION AND PRACTICAL INFORMATION. Ulsterbus** (☎9033 3000) stops at the Mill St. tourist office where the current bus times are posted. Bus #162 has limited service from Belfast (₤6.20) via Larne (₤5.20) and Cushendall, then north to Cushendun (July-Aug. M-F 5 per day, Sa-Su 2 per day; Sept.-June M-F 2 per day). #252 (a.k.a. the **Antrim Coaster**) goes coastal from Belfast to Coleraine, stopping in Cushendall and most everywhere else (July-Aug. 2 per day; Sept.-June M-Sa only with fewer stops). #150, from Belfast via Ballymena, stops in Glenariff (a.k.a. Waterfoot; M-Sa 5 per day, ₤2.60). **Ardclinis Activity Centre,** 11 High St., **rents bikes** and provides advice and equipment for hill-walking, canoeing, cycling, rafting, gorge-walking, and other outdoor pursuits. (☎2177 1340; www.ardclinis.com. Mountain bikes ₤10 per day; deposit ₤50. Wetsuits ₤5 per day.)

The busiest section of Cushendall is its crossroads. From the center of town, **Mill Street** turns into **Chapel Road** and heads northwest toward Ballycastle; **Shore Road** extends south toward Glenarm and Larne. On the north side of town, **Hill Street** leads uphill from **Bridge Road,** a section of the **Coast road** (an extension of the A2) that continues toward the sea at Waterfoot. The **tourist office** hands out info at 25 Mill St., near the bus stop at the northern (Cushendun) end of town. (☎2177 1180. Open July-Sept. M-F 10am-1pm, 2-5:30pm; Sa 10am-1pm, 2-4:30pm. Oct. to mid-Dec., Feb.-June Tu-Sa 10am-1pm.) **Cushendall**

Development Office, behind the tourist office, has **Internet.** (☎2177 1378. £1.50 per 30min.; students and seniors £1. Open M-F 9am-1pm, 2-5pm. When that's closed, access at the tourist office (£1 per 15min.). The **library** across from the tourist office happily obliges its members for free or charges those outside the coven £1.50 per 30min. **Northern Bank,** 5 Shore Rd., has a **24hr. ATM.** (☎2177 1243. Open M 9:30am-12:30pm, 1:30-5pm; Tu-F 10am-12:30pm, 1:30-3:30pm.) **Numark Pharmacist,** 8 Mill St., heals ills. (☎2177 1523. Open M-Sa 9am-6pm.) The **post office** is inside the Spar Market on Coast Rd. (☎2177 1201. Open M, W-F 9am-1pm, 2-5:30pm; Tu, Sa 9am-12:30pm.) **Postal code:** BT44.

⌂☐☑ ACCOMMODATIONS, FOOD, AND PUBS. Ballyeamon Camping Barn ❶, 6 mi. south of town on the B14, is Cushendall's last bastion of budget travel, with homey facilities, renowned storytelling owners, friendly pets, and views of Glenariff Forest Park. It's far from town, but only a few hundred yards from the Moyle Way. (☎2175 8451; www.taleteam.demon.co.uk. Blankets £2. Dorms £7. Book ahead and call for pickup.) B&Bs occupy every other house on Cushendall's radiating roads. South of town overlooking the sea, Mrs. Mary O'Neill warmly welcomes guests to **Glendale ❷,** 46 Coast Rd., with huge rooms and colorful company. Tea, coffee, biscuits, and baths are in each room. (☎2177 1495. £18.) The town's caravan parks aren't particularly suited to tents, but campers in need can find a bit of earth. Strong winds can make camping "rugged" at **Cushendall Caravan Park ❶,** 62 Coast Rd., adjacent to Red Bay Boat yard. (☎2177 1699. No kitchen. 2-person tent £6.50; family tent £10.50. Free showers. Wash free, dry £1.50 per 15min.)

Spar market, 2 Coast Rd., past Bridge Rd., has plenty of fruits and veggies. (☎2177 1763. Open daily 7am-10pm.) **Arthur's ❶,** Shore St., brings princely, fresh sandwiches to the masses, and slips in a little history, as the family has run a business on-site for over a century. (☎2177 1627. Panini £3. Open daily 10am-5pm.) Fish are on the menu and smiles are on all faces at **Harry's ❸,** 10-12 Mill St. Inventive, delicious permutations of salmon, trout, and other fresh fins. (☎2177 2022. Bar food served daily noon-9:30pm; a la carte dinner 6-9:30pm.) One of the Isle's best pubs, **◪Joe McCollam's (Johnny Joe's),** 23 Mill St. (☎2177 1876), features impromptu ballads, fiddling, and slurred limericks. It's exciting most nights of the week, but musicians are guaranteed to gather on weekend nights. Come for pints and stay for *craic* at **An Camán,** 5 Bridge St., an inconspicuous off-white building across from the Half Door. (☎2177 1293. Sa night and Su afternoon live bands.)

◙ SIGHTS. The sandstone **Curfew Tower** in the center of town, on the corner of Mill St. and High St., was built in 1817 by the eccentric and slightly paranoid Francis Turley. This Cushendall landlord made a fortune in China, and when he returned he eagerly wanted to protect his riches. He built the tower with features like openings for pouring boiling oil onto non-existent attackers. The bell on the tower was co-opted by the British forces during the Irish Revolution (see **History and Politics,** p. 454) and sounded at the designated curfew after which Catholics were would be shot if out—hence the tower's name. Today, the structure is privately owned and closed to the public. The extensive remnants of **Layde Church,** a medieval friary, lie along Layde Rd. When it was established in 1306, the church was valued at 20 shillings. Its ruins are noteworthy for their surrounding graveyard, spectacular seaviews, and the pretty **seaside walks** that begin at its carpark. (Always open. Free.) The graveyard includes **Cross Na Nagan,** a pagan holestone used for marriage ceremonies and Christianized into a Celtic cross with four clever strokes. **Tieveragh Hill,** half a mile up High St., is known locally as Faery Hill for the otherworldly "little people" who supposedly reside in the area. Though it would make a rare patch of farmland, locals still refuse to cut the hedgerows, the wee folk's reputed dwelling. **Lurigethan Hill** (1153 ft.), more commonly "Lirig Mountain," would soar above town, if only its summit weren't flattened on the way up. Locals have clocked 26min. (men) and 38min. (women) racing up the hill for a "Lurig Run" during the **Heart of the Glens** festival. The less eager wander up in about 45min. The festival is a 10-day affair starting the second week of August and building to a giant block party. (Contact the development office ☎2177 1378.) **Ossian's Grave** (O-shan's) rests a few miles away on the lower slopes of **Tievebulliagh Mountain.** Actually a neolithic burial cairn dating from around 4000 BC, it is linked by tradition with the Ulster warrior-bard Ossian, who was supposedly buried here 'round AD 300. The A2 leads north from Cushendall toward Ballymoney and the lower slopes of Tievebulliagh, where a sign points to the grave. The steep walk up the southern slope of **Glenaan** rewards with views of the lush valley. The Glens of Antrim **Rambling Club** plans a series of walks throughout the year. Contact the chairman (Liam Murphy ☎2565 6079) or the tourist office for details.

CUSHENDUN (BUN ABHANN DUINNE)   ☎028

In 1954, the National Trust bought the tiny, picturesque seaside village of Cushendun, 5 mi. north of Cushendall on the A2; since then, the Trust has protected the town's "olde," squeaky-clean image. Its white-washed, black-shuttered buildings lie next to a vast beach perforated by wonderful, murky **caves** carved into red seacliffs. The largest cave, located south of town off the Coast road, serves as the only entrance to **Cave House,** built in 1820 but now occupied by the Mercy religious order and closed to the public. From behind what used to be the hotel, an excruciatingly steep path leads to the clifftop. Other less painful walks meander around the **historic monuments** in town and in nearby **Glendun,** a preserved village and a fine example of Cornish architecture. The **"Maud Cottages"** lining the main street were built by Lord Cushendun for his wife in 1925; tourist information signs in town remind visitors not to mistake them for almshouses.

    Buses pause on the Coast road at Cushendun's grocery shop on their way to Waterfoot via Cushendall (#162; July-Aug. 2-4 per day; Sept.-June M-F 2 per day). West of town on the A2 is ▨**Drumkeerin,** 201a Torr Rd., signposted from the main drag, where visitors choose between immaculate all white **B&B ❸** rooms and **camping barn ❶** (hostel) facilities with very basic sleeping cubicles and flimsy foam matresses. Each boasts a gorgeous view of Cushendun and the rest of the coast. Owners Mary and Joe also teach **painting courses** for improving talents, or developing talents yet undiscovered. Mary was named Landlady of the Year for the whole of the UK in 2002; it's no wonder—she makes her own bread and jams, and offers eggs from her hens. Mary's husband leads **hill walks** and **historical tours.** (☎2176 1554; www.drumkeerinbedandbreakfast.co.uk. Blankets, sheets, and towels £2. Camping barn £8. B&B with bath singles £20; doubles £35.) Camping at **Cushendun Caravan Site ❶**, 14 Glendun Rd., 50 yd. from the end of the beach, is cheap and presents the exciting possibility of lounging in a TV/game-room. (☎2176 1254. No kitchen. Laundry £2. Open Mar.-Sept. £6.50 per small tent.) The town's most popular attraction is also its only real pub: **Mary McBride's,** 2 Main St., used to be in the *Guinness Book of World Records* as the smallest bar in Europe. The original bar remains, but has been vigorously expanded to create a lounge, seemingly designed for viewing GAA matches (see **Sports,** p. 80). Cushendun's characters leave the bar only when musicians start a session in the lounge. (☎2176 1511.

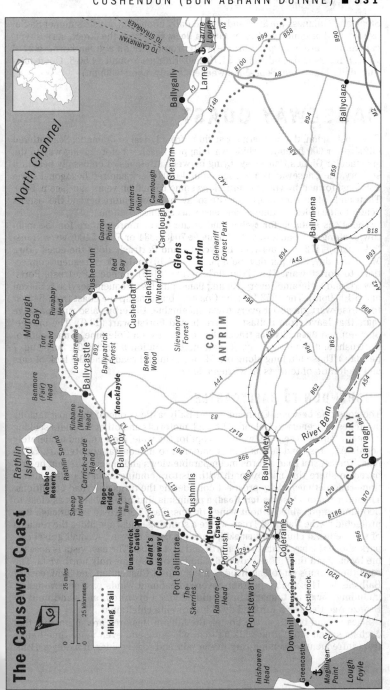

The Causeway Coast

Hiking Trail

0 ────── 25 miles
0 ────── 25 kilometers

North Channel

TO CAIRNRYAN
TO STRANRAER

Larne Lough
Larne
Ballygally
Ballyclare
Ballymena

Glenarm
Carnlough Bay
Carnlough
Hunters Point
Garron Point
Glens of Antrim
Glenariff Forest Park

Cushendun
Red Bay
Glenariff (Waterfoot)
Cushendall
Silevanora Forest
CO. ANTRIM

Murlough Bay
Runabay Head
Torr Head
Loughareema
Ballypatrick Forest
Breen Wood

Benmore (Fair) Head
Ballycastle
Knocklayde

Kinbane (White) Head

Rathlin Island
Kebble Reserve
Sheep Island
Rathlin Sound
Carrick-a-rede Island
Rope Bridge
White Park Bay
Ballintoy
Bushmills
Dunseverick Castle
Giant's Causeway
Dunluce Castle
Port Ballintrae
The Skerries
Portrush
Ramore Head
Portstewart
Coleraine
Downhill
Mussenden Temple
Castlerock

Ballymoney
River Bann
CO. DERRY
Garvagh

Inishowen Head
Greencastle
Magilligan Point
Lough Foyle

Steak and Guinness pie £5. Food served daily noon-9pm. Music summer Sa-Su; usually trad or country.) **Cushendun Tea Room ❷,** across the street, serves typical chipper fare in atypical ornate white iron chairs on a green lawn. (☎2176 1506. Burgers and sandwiches £1.70-2.50. Entrees around £4.50-8. Open July-Aug. daily 11am-7pm; Sept.-June weekends only, noon-6:30pm.)

CAUSEWAY COAST

Past Cushendun, the northern coast shifts from lyrical to dramatic. Sea-battered cliffs tower 600 ft. above white, wave-lapped beaches before giving way to the spectacular Giant's Causeway. Lying between stretches of colossally beautiful scenery, the Causeway is a hopscotch of 40,000 black and red hexagonal stone columns, formed by volcanic eruptions some 65 million years ago (see p. 540). Thousands of visitors swarm the site today, but few venture beyond the visitors center to the miles of stunning and easily-accessible coastline.

The A2 is suitable for **cycling** and is the major thoroughfare for the main towns along the Causeway. **Ulsterbus** (☎7043 3334 or 7032 5400; www.translink.co.uk) #172 runs between Ballycastle and Portrush along the coast (1hr.; M-F 6 per day, Sa 4 per day, Su 5 per day; £4.10) and makes frequent connections to Portstewart. The "Triangle" service (#140) connects Portrush, Portstewart, and Coleraine (every 10min., 9am-5pm, less frequent service 6:55-9am and 5-10:30pm). The #252 "Antrim Coaster" bus runs up the coast from Belfast to Portstewart via about every town imaginable. Ulsterbus also runs package **tours** that leave from Belfast, Portrush, and Portstewart (£3-9). The orange, open-topped **Bushmills Bus** traces the coast between Coleraine, 5 mi. south of Portrush, and the Causeway. (Coleraine bus station ☎7043 3334. July-Aug. 7 per day.) Those hitching along the A2 or the inland roads find the lack of cars and high ratio of tourists slows them down.

CUSHENDUN TO BALLYCASTLE

The coastline between Cushendun and Ballycastle is one of the most famous stretches of scenery in Ireland. Although motorists and other travelers seeking a speedy trip between the two towns opt for the wide, modern, and moderately scenic A2, this road seems tame compared to its coastal counterpart, ▨**Torr road.** The coastal road affords incomparable views and sheer cliffs, but be prepared to share this narrow path with visitors coming from the other direction—a sometimes tricky prospect considering the turns and road conditions. The most famous vista is **Torr Head,** a peninsula that brings visitors as close to Scotland as possible without wings or fins. Past Torr Head is **Murlough Bay,** protected by the National Trust, where a stunning landscape hides the remains of the medieval church **Drumnakill,** once a pagan holy site. A small gravel carpark above the bay leads to the north and east vistas. The east vista is accessible by car, and thus more crowded than the pedestrians-only north vista. The road then bumps on to **Fair Head,** 7 mi. north of Cushendun and 3 mi. east of Ballycastle. This rocky, heather-covered headland winds past several lakes, including **Lough na Cranagh;** in its middle sits a *crannog,* an island built by Bronze Age Celts as a fortified dwelling for elite chieftains.

Bikes should be left at the hostel: the hills in this area are so horrific that cyclists spend more time walking than wheeling and even more time hiding from infrequent, oncoming cars in the rain and fog; besides, it's only a 1½hr.

hike from Ballycastle. Drivers should head straight for this splendid stretch of road, but they seldom do, and the lack of autos translates into poor hitching conditions; *Let's Go* believes there are no other kind. Taking the A2, the official bus route, straight from Cushendun to Ballycastle has its advantages—the road passes its own set of attractions and is more manageable for cyclists, with only one long climb and an even longer descent from a soft boggy plain.

A few miles northeast of Cushendun, a high hollow contains a vanishing lake called **Loughareema** (or **Faery Lough**), which during the summer can appear and disappear into the bog in less than a day. When it's full, the lake has fish in it. When it empties, they take refuge in caverns beneath the porous limestone. Farther along, part of the plain was drained and planted with evergreens. The result is secluded **Ballypatrick Forest,** with a forest drive and pleasant, pine-scented walks. **Camping** is allowed with a permit from the ranger or **Forest Office** at 155 Cushendall Rd., 2 mi. toward Ballycastle on the A2. (☎2076 2301. Park open daily 10am-sunset. ₤5 per tent.) Before Ballycastle town, **Ballycastle Forest** contains eminently climbable, 1695 ft. **Knocklayde Mountain,** whose base is approximately a mile into the woods.

BALLYCASTLE (BAILE AN CHAISIL)

The Causeway Coast leaves behind the sleepy Glens at Ballycastle, a bubbly seaside town shelter for Causeway-bound tourists. Friendlier than many of its neighbors, Ballycastle makes a nice base for budget travelers exploring the coast.

⌖ TRANSPORTATION. Buses stop at Marine Hotel at the end of Quay Rd. **Ulsterbus** rruns to: #131 to Belfast via Ballymena (3hr., M-Sa 5-6 per day, ₤6.10); #171 to Coleraine via Ballymoney (1hr.; M-F 4 per day, Sa 3 per day; ₤3.80); #162A to Cushendall via Cushendun (50min., M-F 1 per day, ₤3); #172 to Portrush (1hr.; M-F 7 per day, Sa 2 per day, Su 3 per day; ₤3.50). The #252 Antrim Coaster runs from Glens of Antrim and Larne to Belfast (4hr., 2 per day). **Argyll and Antrim Steam Packet Co.** (☎08705 523 523) hopes to resume service in 2004. In the past, **ferries** have run between Campbeltown, Scotland (on Kintryre Peninsula), and Ballycastle (3hr.; Feb.-Dec. 2 per day; ₤20-25, car or caravan ₤80-105). **Castle** (☎2076 8884) and **Grab-a-Cab** (☎2076 9034) run **taxis** in Ballycastle. **Cushleake B&B,** Quay Rd. **rents bikes.** (☎2076 3798 or 079 8095 9887. ₤6 per day.)

⌖ ⚐ ORIENTATION AND PRACTICAL INFORMATION. The town's main street runs perpendicular to the waterfront, starting at the ocean as **Quay Road,** becoming **Ann Street,** and turning into **Castle Street** as it passes **the Diamond.** Most restaurants and shops cluster along Ann St. and Castle St. As Quay Rd. meets the water, it takes a sharp left onto **North Street,** where more stores and food await. East of Quay Rd. are tennis courts, the tourist office, and the town strand on **Mary Road.** B&Bs nest on **Quay Rd.** The **tourist office,** Sheskburn House, 7 Mary St. (☎2076 2024; ballycastle@hotmail.com), has info on the Antrim coast and a free brochure on *Ballycastle Heritage Trial.* The office books accommodations for ₤2 and holds baggage for free. The 24hr. computerized info kiosk outside has limited information. (Open July-Aug. M-F 9:30am-7pm, Sa 10am-6pm, Su 2-6pm; Sept.-June M-F 9:30am-5pm.) **First Trust Bank,** Ann St. (☎2076 3326; Open M-F 9:30am-4:30pm, W open 10am) and **Northern Bank,** 24 Ann St. (☎2076 2238. Open M-F 9:30am-12:30pm, 1:30-3pm; F until 5pm.) have 24hr. ATMs. **McMullan's NuMark,** 63 Castle St. handles all pharmacetical needs. (☎2076 3135; Open M-Sa 9am-6pm, alternating Su noon-1pm) The **police** are stationed on Ramoan Rd. (☎2076 2312 or 2076 3125). In an

emergency dial ☎999, no coins required. The **library** (☎2076 2566), corner of Castle St. and Leyland St. has **Internet**. (£2.50 per hr., members free. Open M, F 10am-1pm, 2-5:30pm; Tu, Th 6-8pm; Sa closes 5pm.) **Herald's**, 22 Ann St., has one terminal for public use. (☎2076 9064. £1 per 30min.) Tourist office hopes to go cyber by 2004. The **post office** 3 Ann St. sorts mail for the **postal code** BT54. (☎2076 2519. Open M-Tu and Th-F 9am-1pm and 2-5:30pm, W 9am-1pm and Sa 9am-12:30pm.)

⌐⌐⌐ ACCOMMODATIONS, FOOD, AND PUBS. Most of Ballycastle's housing cluster around the harbor at the northern end of town. Plan for the **Ould Lammas Fair** (see **Sights and Festivals**, p. 535) held the last Monday and Tuesday in August—B&Bs fill almost a year in advance, and hostels fill weeks before the fair. **Castle Hostel (IHH) ❶**, 62 Quay Rd., just in town from shore on Quay Rd., next to Marine Hotel, is a 40-bed hostel with a relaxed, welcoming atmosphere and fair facilities. (☎2076 2337; www.castlehostel.com. Wash £2, dry £2. Dorms £7.50; private rooms £10.) **Ballycastle Backpackers (IHO) ❶**, North St., is also next to Marine Hotel. The view of the strand's sunrises makes up for a somewhat absentee management. (☎2076 3612 or 077 7323 7890. Dorms £7.50; singles £10, with bath £12.50-15.) Although the house is one of Ballycastle's oldest, **Fragrens' ❷**, 34 Quay Rd., renovations brought a modern sheen to the immaculate and better-than-hotel-quality rooms. Fresh fruit at breakfast is a welcome change from greasy meat. (☎2076 2168; http://members.aol.com/JGreene710. £17-18.) **Marine Hotel ❺**, 1-3 North St. Beautiful views, spacious rooms, and on-site dining. (☎2076 2222; www.marinehotel.com. Singles £40-50; doubles £70-90.)

Friendly local **SuperValu**, 54 Castle St., is a 10min. walk from the hostels. (☎2076 2268. Open M-Sa 8am-10pm, Su 9am-10pm.). Yet, splurging on a proper meal is in order as Ballycastle's gastronomic offerings surpass those in most Irish towns. **Flash-in-the-Pan ❶**, 74 Castle St. , pretends to be a humble chipper, but the £3 fried-fish-fiesta suggests otherwise. (☎2076 2251. Open Su-Th 11am-midnight, F-Sa 11am-1am.) **Wysner's ❹**, 16 Ann St., caters to a sophisticated palate, and prides itself on using local ingredients to make dishes of Mediterranean, Asian, and Mexican influence. (☎2076 2372. Lunch around £5, dinner special £6-15. Open daily June-Aug. lunch 12:30-2:30pm, dinner 6:30-8pm; Sept.-May 8am-8pm.) The black-clad gourmet sandwich technicians at **Park Deli ❸**, Auay Rd., serve fast, fresh creations (£1.89-4.49). Friday and Saturday nights' four-course (£12.99) menu is hot, fancy, and tasty, but BYO bottle. Book ahead for weekend dinner. Takeaway during the day cuts the price. (☎2076 8563. Open M-Th and Su 9am-6pm, F-Sa 9am-6pm and 7:30-9:40pm. **Herald's ❷**, 22 Ann St., serves huge, fleshy portions and pasta dishes at cheap prices. The wonderful staff is icing on the cake. (☎2076 9064. **Internet** £1 per 30min. Su roast and potatoes £4.95. Entrees £4-8. Open daily 8am-9pm.) **The Cellar ❸**, the Diamond., has yummy homemade pizza (£3-7) to eat in or takeaway. Gourmands try the more daring Italian offerings like crab linguine for £7.50. (☎2076 3037. Mains £7-12.50. Open daily noon-10pm.)

Trad can be hard to come by in the North, even in tourist-subservient areas. Not so in Ballycastle, where pubs satiate the masses with frequent summertime sessions. **House of McDonnell,** 71 Castle St. (☎2076 2975), draws tourists for trad Friday, folk Saturday, and the more elusive Spontaneous Trad, which pops up sporadically during the week. **Central Bar,** 12 Ann St. (☎2076 3877), hosts musical fun ranging from impromptu piano sing-alongs to karaoke on Tuesday and Saturday to the ever-popular trad on Wednesday. The first Monday of each month is "Black Nun night," when an odd mix of serious fans and tourists listen to trad upstairs. On Saturdays, Central pumps tunes for dancing 20-somethings in the upstairs disco. **O'Connor's Bar,** 7 Ann St. (☎2076 2123), is the place for reels and jigs on Friday and one- or two-piece bands Saturday nights, with a beer garden out back for more relaxed guzzlers. A quiet pint by day in simple, serene **Boyd Arms,** 4 the Diamond (☎2076 2364) becomes many, and a wild night.

◙ ※ SIGHTS AND FESTIVALS. The Holy Trinity Church of Ireland—a.k.a. Boyd Church—is responsible for the bizarre octagonal spire. Built by 18th-century landlord Hugh Boyd—who also brought Quay Rd., Ann St. (named for his wife), and local industrialization—the improvements fell into ruin when industrial profiteering lost its groove. Half a mile out of town on the Cushendall Rd., the 15th-century Bonamargy Friary sits in the middle of a golf course, complimenting its graveyard and climbable priory with a par-3 hole. (Always open. Free.)

For those who'd rather *do* than *see,* **Moyle Sightseeing Tours** hosts fishing and sightseeing tours, and sells local fishing licenses. (Contact Dan McCauley ☎2076 9521. One-day license £11, 8-day £23.50.) For **boat hire,** charter the *Lady Linda* for fishing (☎2076 9665 or 077 1216 7502); or, for sea fishing contact **Ballycastle Charters** (☎2076 2074. M, W, F evenings. £10 per person.) The **◙Ould Lammas Fair,** Northern Ireland's oldest and most famous fair, has been held in Ballycastle for 413 years. Originally a week-long fiesta, the festival is now crammed into two frenzied days, August's last Monday and Tuesday. Following the traditions of the ancient Celtic harvest festival, the fair jams Ballycastle's streets with vendors of cows, sheep, crafts, and baked goods, as trad musicians pack pubs. (Contact the tourist office for info, or the Environmental Health Agency ☎2076 2225.)

NEAR BALLYCASTLE: RATHLIN ISLAND (REACHLAINN)

Off the coast of Ballycastle, bumpy, boomerang-shaped Rathlin Island ("Fort of the Sea") offers the ultimate escape for 20,000 puffins, the odd golden eagle, 100 human beings, and four daily ferries of tourists. Its windy surface supports few trees, but does harbor an eco-paradise of orchids, purple heather, and seabirds. The contrast between the white chalk and black basalt cliffs that encircle the island led the novelist Charles Kingsley to compare Rathlin to a "drowned magpie." During 20 years of Famine, the island's population dwindled from 1000 to 500; most of Rathlin's emigrants sailed for America and created a community in Maine. Even though electricity only arrived in Rathlin in 1992, the island holds a unique place in the history of technology: in 1898, the Italian scientist Marconi sent the first wireless telegraph message from here to Ballycastle.

A leaflet from the Ballycastle **tourist office,** on Mary St. by the shore, contains a decent map and description of the island's walks and sights. For a more complete presentation of its intricately intertwined history and myths, visit the island's **Boat House Heritage Centre** (a.k.a. the Rathlin Island Visitors Centre), a right exiting the ferry, for birdwatching advice, books, and maps. (☎2076 2225; www.moyle-council.org. Open May-Aug. daily 10am-4pm, other months by arrangement. Free.) **Irene's minibus** service (☎2076 3949) shuttles from the ferry docks to **Kebble Bird Sanctuary,** at the western tip of the island, 4½ mi. from the harbor (20min., every 45min., £2.50). Peak bird-watching season lasts from May to mid-July. The **lighthouse** is the best place to view the enormous colony of puffins, guillemots, and gulls nesting in the cliffs, but it's accessible only with the warden's supervision. (Call in advance ☎2076 3948.) A walk to **Rue Point,** 2½ mi. from the harbor, site of a classic black and white lighthouse, allows visitors to marvel at the crumbled remains of **Smuggler's House,** whose wall cavities once hid contraband during the days when pirates and smugglers fueled Rathlin's economy. **Fair Head** and its frolicking **seals** loom a few miles from Rue Point.

Caledonian MacBrayne runs a **ferry** service to the island from Ballycastle. In the summer, the ferry runs four times daily from the pier at Ballycastle, on Bayview Rd., up the hill from Quay Rd. and by the harbor. The small MacBrayne office at the Ballycastle pier opens before each departure to sell tickets, but buying at the central office ensures a timely return. (☎2076 9299. 45min.; June-Sept. M-F 10am, noon, 4:50pm, F only 7pm; Oct.-May 2 per day; £8.40 return, children £4.20.)

For a break from it all, **Kinramer Camping Barn (ACB) ❶**, a 4½ mi. hike from the harbor, has clusters of bunks isolated by plywood partitions. (☎2076 3948. Dorms or camping beds £5.75.) A far more civilized alternative is **Manor House ❸**, directly in front of the ferry terminal, a late Georgian gentleman's abode so historical the National Trust owns it. The individualized rooms vary in style. Evening meals can be arranged in advance. (☎2076 3964; uravfm@grp-wse.ntrust.org.uk. Singles £23-27; doubles £42.) **Soerneog View Hostel ❶** is a simple, functional option closer to the bustle of the ferry landing. To get there, take a right from the dock and turn left at the side road before the pub. At the top of the road, turn right; the hostel is ¼ mi. down on the left. Call ahead for pickup and to reserve one of six beds. (☎2076 3954. **Bike rental** £7 per day. Wash £3, dry 50p. 2-bunk private dorms £8.) Gourmands and picnickers buy groceries on the mainland, as **McCuaig's Bar ❷** is the island's only food source. It's also the sole entertainment center for the entire island. (☎2076 3974. Sometimes allows free **camping** on its grounds. Sandwiches, toasties, burgers £2-4; limited entrees £4-6. Food served 9am-9pm.)

BALLINTOY, CARRICK-A-REDE ISLANDS, AND ROPE BRIDGE

Five miles west of Ballycastle on the B15, the modest village of **Ballintoy** *(Baile an Tuaighe)* consists of a church, harbor, hostel, and fisherman's bridge that is one of the most frequented tourist destinations in all of Northern Ireland. The **Causeway Rambler** connects Bushmills to Carrick-a-Rede bridge with a stop in Ballintoy. (☎7032 5400 or 9066 6630; www.translink.co.uk.) Two diminutive but remarkable islands, Sheep and Carrick-a-rede, put Ballintoy on the map. Visible from Ballintoy village, **Sheep Island** is home to puffins, razor bills, kittiwakes, and the largest cormorant colony in Ireland. Even smaller but better-known **Carrick-a-rede Island** lies offshore east of Ballintoy. Meaning "rock in the road," Carrick-a-rede presents a barrier to migrating salmon returning to their home rivers. Since 1624, fishermen annually cast their nets in the salmon's path, stringing a **rope bridge** between the mainland and the island from April to September to retrieve their haul. Due to depleted salmon populations, fishing has stopped now, but the bridge remains as a popular tourist attraction, carefully rebuilt by engineers each summer. Crossing the shaky, 48 in. wide, 67 ft. long bridge over the dizzying 100 ft. drop to rocks and sea can be a harrowing experience, but it's much safer than it used to be. Wardens are on site during opening hours, and the bridge closes in windy weather. A sign about ½ mi. east of Ballintoy on the Coast road marks the turnoff for the bridge; the carpark is a ¼ mi. farther, and the bridge is less than 1 mi. beyond that.

The walk to the bridge leads courageous crossers along the heights of the limestone **Larrybane sea cliffs,** nesting place of the unusual black-and-white razor bill, the quirky brown- and white-bellied guillemot, and the mundane gull. The National Trust's leaflet, available from a warden upon entrance, has a map of the area's geological notables. A shell of a fishing hut totters on the eastern side of the island. The **tearoom** by the carpark sells snacks, posts information, and gives local advice. For 50p, they'll also distribute certificates for successfully crossing the bridge. **Free camping** can be arranged with the wardens. Carpark access is zealously protected by National Trust employees.

(☎2076 2178 or 2076 2178. Bridge open Mar.-Sept. 10am-6pm; July-Aug. 9:30am-7:30pm. Last entry 30min. before closing. Carpark closes 8pm. Tea room open July-Sept. daily 10am-8pm. £3 per car.)

Quiet Ballintoy provides beds and grub for Carrick-a-rede's daredevils. Aptly-named **Sheep Island View Hostel (IHH)** ❶, 42A Main St., has functional, bunked rooms and an enormous kitchen. Management makes an effort to mention the admittedly few town events. Call for pickup from anywhere between Ballycastle and Portrush. (☎2076 9391; www.sheepislandview.com. Wheelchair-accessible. Continental breakfast £3, Ulster fry £4.50. Laundry £2. Dorms with bath £10. **Camping** £5 per person.) In town, **Fullerton Arms** ❸ serves pub food behind frosted windows, and has three-star **B&B** rooms. (☎2076 9613; www.fulertonarms.co.uk. Pub food £5-7. Served 12:30-9pm. Open M-F 6-9pm, Sa-Su all day. B&B £25.) Across the street, **Carrick-a-rede Pub** is cheaper and less ostentatious, food- and music-wise. (☎2076 2241. Food £3.50-5.50; served noon-9pm. Tu, F, and Su trad.)

Three miles west along the coast road from Ballintoy is the **Whitepark Bay Youth Hostel (HANI)** ❶. Its out-of-the-way setting, overlooking one of the most famous—and least swimmable—beaches on the Antrim Coast, is either a blessing or bane, depending on car possession. It has clean, clinical facilities in primary colors. Portrush-Ballycastle bus (#172) or Antrim Coaster (#252) will stop 200 yd. from the hostel, but there are no shops or pubs for miles. (☎2073 1745; www.hini.org.uk. Breakfast £2.50. 4-bed dorms £11; doubles £13. Under 18 £1 less.)

PORTRUSH (PORT RUIS)   ☎028

Portrush's name should be taken quite literally: in the fall, when the universities reopen, students flood the city center; in July, when their summer holidays begin, they race back out again to make room for an even more vicious influx of tourists. The streets boil over on summer days with families flocking to amusements and carnival rides. In the evenings, teeny elements swamp the town's discos. Despite its flaws—or charms, depending on taste—Portrush remains the town most convenient to the region's major attractions.

▉ TRANSPORTATION. Trains run from Eglinton St. (☎7082 2395) in the center of town (Open July-Aug. M-F 11am-8pm; Sept.-June 7:45am-3:30pm.) To: Belfast (2hr.; M-F 6 per day, Sa 7 per day, Su 4 per day; £5.30) and Derry via Colraine (1hr.; M-F 3 per day, Sa 7 per day, Su 3 per day; £5.90). Most causeway-bound **buses** stop in town at Dunluce Ave. Ulster-bus #140 ("Triangle Service") runs to Coleraine via Portstewart (30min., every 10min. 6:55am-10:30pm). #402, "The Causeway Rambler" runs along the coast to Bushmills (20min., 5-6 per day); Giant's Causeway (25min.); Ballintoy (40min.); and Ballycastle

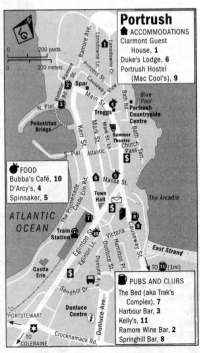

Portrush

🏠 ACCOMMODATIONS
Clarmont Guest House, **1**
Duke's Lodge, **6**
Portrush Hostel (Mac Cool's), **9**

🍎 FOOD
Bubba's Café, **10**
D'Arcy's, **4**
Spinnaker, **5**

🍺 PUBS AND CLUBS
The Bed (aka Trak's Complex), **7**
Harbour Bar, **3**
Kelly's, **11**
Ramore Wine Bar, **2**
Springhill Bar, **8**

(1hr.). #252, "The Antrim Coaster" ends in Belfast after stopping at every sight along the Antrim coast, from Bushmills, Ballycastle, and each glen, through to Larne (M-Sa 3 per day, Su 2 per day). For night-owls, **Radio Taxis** (☎0800 032 339 or 7035 5055) provides eight-seater cabs. **Cromore Cabs** (☎7083 4550) are also an efficient service. **Rent a bike** at **Thompson Cycles**, 77b Lower Main St. (☎7082 9606. £7 per day; ID deposit. Open daily 10am-5pm; after closing return bikes to the hostel.)

7 PRACTICAL INFORMATION. The **tourist office**, in the Dunluce Centre off Sandhill Dr. south of the town center, has a **bureau de change** and books accommodations for a 10% commission. (☎7082 3333. Open mid-June to Aug. daily 9am-7pm; Apr.-June and Sept. M-F 9am-5pm, Sa-Su noon-5pm; Mar. and Oct. Sa-Su noon-5pm.) For more money services try **First Trust**, 25 Eglinton St. (☎7082 2726. Open M-F 9:30am-4:30pm, W open 10am.) The **post office** is on Eglinton St. (☎7082 3700. Open M-Tu, Th-Sa 9am-12:30pm and 1:30-5:30pm; W 9am-1pm.) **Postal code:** BT56.

▢◧ ACCOMMODATIONS AND FOOD. The Irish hordes that appear on summer weekends make booking any B&Bs along the sea coast tough. If the recommended B&Bs are full, a stroll down **Kerr, Mark,** and **Main Streets** in town could prove fruitful. For more remote lodgings, **Landsdowne Crescent** and **Ramore Avenue,** north of the city centre, are tucked away up the peninsula's end. The one hostel, **Portrush Hostel (Mac-Cool's)** ❶, 35 Causeway St., down the street from the library, shelters a few hearty travelers in an intimate, simple facility. The new owners are enthusiastic and attentive, ready with a cup of tea and advice on touring the coast. (☎7082 4845; www.portrush-hostel.com. Laundry £3. **Internet** available. Dorms £10, private rooms £13.) **Duke's Lodge** ❷, 6-7 Kerr St., keeps clubbers happy with ominibus service to and from Portrush's clubs for £1. The seven en suite rooms, family rooms and access for the disabled make it a popular destination. Ask for an ocean view. (☎7082 4354; www.dukeslodge.com. Doubles Oct.-Mar. £30, Apr.-Sept. £35, with bath £40.) **Clarmont Guest House** ❸, 10 Landsdowne Crescent, caters to a tamer breed of holiday maker. Its placid white exterior fits the leisurely mood, with rooms that nestle visitors in fluffy blankets. (☎7082 2397; www.clarmont.com. Singles £25; doubles Mar.-Sept. £50, Oct.-Apr. £40.)

Portrush's abundant chippers and pricey eateries are spurred by a tiny **Spar**, 106 Lower Main St. (☎7082 5447. Open daily 7am-11pm.) The new management at ▧**D'Arcy's** ❹, Main St., has a reputation for intimate dinners of ambitious cuisine—mint almond pesto, ostrich filets. (☎7082 2063. Lunches £4-6, dinners £8-14. Open daily noon-9:30pm, F-Sa until 10pm.) Lonely wenches rebounding from plate after plate of greasy chips find solace in the fishy arms of **Spinnaker** ❸, 25 Main St., where the spoils of the sea are broiled, grilled, sauteed, and otherwise smothered in butter. (☎7082 2348. Specials £5-7.) **Bubba's Cafe** ❷, Eglinton St., is the sister restaurant to Coleraine's student fave. The excellent waitstaff does pizza and pasta proud; late night, hungry, "happy" crowds from the nightclubs might not. (☎7082 2000. Mains £3.90-6.90. Open daily 9:30am-11pm; F-Su takeaway 'til 3am.)

▥◧ PUBS AND CLUBS. The nightlife scene in this once-and-future metropolis has increasingly consolidated into a collection of multi-venue complexes, with pubs feeding directly into live music clubs and discos. Although bar crowds remain mixed, the (very) young set seems to prevail on disco nights. The newest such multiplex tops the North Pier, off Harbour Rd. **Harbour Bar,** 5 Harbour Rd. (☎7082 2430), tries its darndest to remain a sailor pub with bands rocking on Wednesday, Friday, and Saturday nights, but **Ramore Wine Bar** (☎7082 4313), at the top of the hill, aspires to a more lofty, well-heeled clientele. A quieter pint at **Springhill Bar,** Causeway St., across from the library accompanies the best trad on Tuesday nights, and free food occasionally showered on hungry college students. The upstairs lounge has pool and darts, and hosts a 60-80s themed disco Friday and Saturday nights. Summertime brings all-you-can-eat barbeques Wednesday nights at 8:30pm for £1. (☎7082 3361. Handicapped-accessible. Open M-Sa 11am-1am; Su noon-midnight.) The crowd at **Bed** (aka **Trak's**

Complex) remains more consistently inconsistent; **Station Bar** feeds relative innocents to the hard-techno **Trak's Nightclub** and relative oldsters to the live-music **Shunter's.** (☎ 7082 2112; www.traks-complex.com. Nightclub cover ₤7; open M and Th-Sa. Music cover ₤3-5; open summer Tu-Sa, winter Th-Sa.) **Kelly's** (officially **Beetle's Bar and Disco;** ☎ 7082 2027), outside of town on the Bushmill's Rd., is the Original King of Nightlife, with 10 bars and three clubs, including the main disco and jailbait wholesaler **Lushi.** Overwhelmingly tacky, this behemoth has a niche for every type of teenager.

◙ **SIGHTS AND ACTIVITES.** Portrush's best-advertised attraction is **Dunluce Centre,** in Dunluce Arcade, a kiddie ride of a heritage sight. Perfect for families, it hosts the largest soft-play area in Ireland, an interactive computer Treasure Hunt, and **Turbo Tours Hydraulic Movie Room.** (☎ 7082 4444. Open July-Aug. daily 10:30am-7pm; Sept.-Mar. noon-5pm; Apr.-May Sa-Su noon-7pm; June M-F 10am-5pm, Sa-Su noon-7pm. Turbo tours ₤2.50, whole enchilada ₤5.) The yin to Dunluce Centre's yang is **Portrush Countryside Centre,** 8 Bath Rd., next to East Strand. The displays, which cater to the same kiddies but with less exclusivity, include wildlife exhibits and a tidal pool with sea urchins and starfish. (☎ 7082 3600; www.nics.gov.uk/ehs. Open June-Sept. daily 10am-6pm; June by pre-booking only. Free.)

Beyond all the amusement-park silliness, **East Strand Beach** stretches 1½ mi. from town toward the **Giant's Causeway** (see p. 539). At the far end of the beach is a carpark; from here, it's another 1½ mi. along the main road to **Dunluce Castle,** a surprisingly intact 16th-century fort. The castle was built close to the cliff's edge—so close that one day the kitchen fell into the sea. (₤2, students ₤1. Open Apr.-Sept. M-Sa 10am-6pm, Su 2-6pm; June-Aug. M-Sa 10am-6am, Su noon-6pm; Oct.-Mar. Tu-Sa 10am-4pm, Su 2-4pm. Last admission 30min. before closing.) Near the edge of the castle, the mouth of a **sea cave** opens to the water. Getting down can be quite slippery, but the adventurous are rewarded with outstanding sea views.

The best **surfing** on the North Antrim coast is at **Portballintree Beach,** where the waves soar almost as high as the nearby castle. Outfit a surfing excursion at **Trogg's,** 88 Main St. (☎ 7082 5476. Open July-Aug. daily 10am-9pm; Sept.-June 11am-6pm.) Before hitting the amazing Antrim waves, make sure to check the **surf report** (☎ 0906 133 7770). **Gareth Becket** teaches the timid to conquer the surf and hang ten like a pro. (☎ 028 7032 9468 or 078 8430 67951. ₤25 per 2hr. session, equipment included.) After a hard day of surfing, retire to **Waterworld's Pirate's Cove,** where two water slides, a water playground, and a swimming area await. When sick of liquid, **Pirate Bowl bowling lanes** is a good way to dry. (Pirate's Cove ☎ 7082 2001; Open July-Aug. M-Sa 10am-8pm, Su noon-8pm; May and Sept. Sa 10am-7pm, Su noon-7pm; June M-Sa 10am-7pm, Su noon-7pm. Last tickets sold 1hr. before closing. Pirate Bowl ☎ 7082 2334. Open July-Aug. M-Sa 10am-8pm, Su noon-10pm; Sept. F 6-10pm, Sa noon-10pm, Su noon-10pm; June M-Sa 10am-10pm, Su noon-10pm.)

Portrush's **Summer Theatre** stage, St. Patrick's Hall, Causeway St., is a venue for several Northern Irish theater companies. (☎ 7082 2500; www.audf.org.uk/portrush.html. Shows W-Sa 8pm. Tickets ₤4, child ₤3. Box office open W-Sa 11am-noon and 6-8pm.) For festive family fun, May's **Portrush Raft Race Weekend** (☎ 7034 7234) incorporates street theatre, music, and a big raft race. Scots and their adoring fans flock to town in mid-August for the **Scottish Dance and Music Festival,** featuring competitions in bagpipes, drumming, dancing, and ribaldry. (☎ 7034 7234 for info, George Ussher to compete ☎ 9265 1576 or 3839 5160.)

▌ DAYTRIPS FROM PORTRUSH

THE GIANT'S CAUSEWAY

The Causeway is always open and free to pedestrians. Ulsterbuses #172 to Portrush, the #252 Antrim Coaster, the "Causeway Rambler," and the Bushmills Bus drop visitors at Giant's Causeway Visitors Centre (in the shop next to the carpark). The Causeway Coaster minibus

THE LOCAL STORY

ROCK YOUR SOCKS OFF: THE REAL STORY OF THE GIANT'S CAUSEWAY

A graduate of *Rocks for Jocks*, *Let's Go* is proud to dispel any myths about the Giant's Causeway that leprechauns, fairies and giants may have been feeding into your wee head. The truth of the matter is that 60 million years ago, in the short interlude between the death of the dinosaurs and the appearance of man, the earth's plates began to separate into what would become the present continents. As the geographic schisms occurred, lava rose through the cracks, hardening into basalt rock.

The scene remained the same for two million years, with little addition to the cooling lava. Over the centuries, the lava returned to its deep red color, but in the form of a condensed red soil which any Irish farmer would delight to have in his field. As the soil dried it cracked into hexagonal shapes, forming the causeway steps.

The end of the second Ice Age, some 15 thousand years ago, created the dramatic shoreline now associated with the causeway's coast. As the ice melted, sea levels rose around the steps and its surrounding cliffs.

Though the Causway is the only place in Ireland where such a geological anomaly appears, the tourist office prefers to omit the fact that similar structures are found in Israel, Thailand and New Zealand. They just don't have the giants to blame for them.

runs to the columns. (☎9066 6630; www.translink.co.uk. 2min., every 15min., £1.20.) The Giant's Causeway and Bushmills Railway runs between the sites, dropping passengers 3min. downhill from the centre (☎2073 2594; www.giantscausewayrailway.org. 15min. Open Mar.-Dec., irregularly; June-Sept. daily 11am-4pm, 2 per hr. £3.50, child £2.) Centre info ☎2073 1855; www.northantrim.com. Open June daily 10am-6pm; July-Aug. 10am-7pm; Sept.-Oct. M-F 10am-5pm, Sa-Su 10am-5:30pm; May daily 10am-5:30pm. Parking £5. To avoid the fee park at nearby Heritage Railway Centre's free car-park, a 2min. walk away.

Geologists believe the unique rock formations found at ▨**Giant's Causeway** were formed some 60 million years ago, through gradual chemical reactions **(see feature)**. Though locals have different ideas **(see other feature)**, everyone agrees that the Causeway is an awesome sight to behold. Comprised of over 40,000 perfectly symmetrical hexagonal basalt columns, it resembles a large descending staircase leading from the cliffs to the ocean's floor. While most simply enjoy the causeway proper, several other formations stand within the Great Causeway: **The Giant's Organ, The Wishing Chair, The Granny, The Camel,** and **The Giant's Boot.** Advertised as the eighth natural wonder of the world, the Giant's Causeway is Northern Ireland's most famous sight, so don't be surprised if 2000 other travelers picked the same exact day to visit. Visiting after the center closes drastically reduces the number.

Once travelers reach the visitors center, they have two options: the more popular low road, which directly swoops down to the causeway from the center (20min.); and the more rewarding high road, which takes visitors the 4½ mi. to the overwhelmingly romantic Iron Age ruins of **Dunseverick Castle,** high above on a sea cliff. Bus #172 and the #252 Antrim Coaster stop in front of the castle, from which it's 4½ mi. farther to Ballintoy. Coach potatoes kick back and enjoy the center's audiovisual presentation. If forging outside, the trail is well-marked and easy to follow, but those looking for additional help should consult the free map available at the visitors center. Two miles west of the Causeway, **Bushmills** (of distillery fame) is the next place to check out (see p. 540).

BUSHMILLS DISTILLERY

The distillery and its Bushmills are 3 mi. east of Portrush and 2 mi. west of the Causeway, at the intersection of A2 and B17; they are served by The Causeway Rambler bus (☎7032 5400 or 9066 6630; www.translink.co.uk; daily 10:15am-5pm) and the Bushmills bus. The Giant's Causeway and Bushmills' Railway connects the two. ☎2073 2594; www.giantscausewayrailway.org. Open Mar.-Dec. irregularly; June-Sept. 11:15am-4:30pm, every 15min. and 30min. after the hr. £5, child £3.50. Distillery ☎2073 1521; www.whiskeytours.ie. Open M-

Sa 9:30am-5:30pm; last tour 4pm. Closed around Christmas. Tours Apr.-Oct. when enough people accumulate; Nov.-Mar. daily at 10:30, 11:30am, 1:30, 2:30, and 3:30pm. £3.95, students and seniors £3.50.

Ardently Protestant Bushmills has been home to the **Old Bushmills Distillery,** creator of Bushmills Irish Whiskey, since 1608, making it the oldest licensed whiskey producer in the world. Travelers have been stopping here since ancient days, when it lay on the route to Tara from castles Dunluce and Dunseverick. When the plant is operating, the tour shows whiskey being thrice-distilled; during the three weeks in July when production stops for maintenance, the far-less-interesting experience is redeemed only by the free sample at its end. Serious whiskey fans (and who isn't these days?) should shoulder their way to the front as the tour winds down and volunteer when the guide makes his cryptic request for "help."

PORTSTEWART (PORT STÍOBHAIRD) ☎028

The twin ports of Portstewart and Portrush have enough in common to have developed a friendly rivalry. Although it's as crowded as Portrush, Portstewart feels far less claustrophobic. 'Stewart's crowds remain more affluent, lending the town a more refined, ice-cream-parlor-rather-than-fast-food aesthetic, but recent overcrowding in 'Rush has pushed some of its famous nightlife over the border, allowing 'Stewart's visitors to couple their beachy fun with lusty clubbing.

▐▌ TRANSPORTATION AND PRACTICAL INFORMATION. Buses stop in the middle of **the Promenade.** Ulsterbus #140 ("The Triangle") connects Portstewart, Portrush, and Coleraine (M-Sa 21-28 per day, Su 9 per day). Portstewart's **tourist office,** in the red-brick library/town hall complex, sits on the crescent at the southern end of the Promenade before the Diamond. (Open July-Aug. M-Sa 10am-4:30pm. Closed for lunch 1-2pm.) **First Trust,** 13 the Promenade, offers financial services inside and out with a 24hr. **ATM.** (☎7083 3273. Open M-F 9:30am-4:30pm, W open 10am.) **McElhone's Pharmacy,** 22A the Promenade, has prescriptions and essentials. (☎7083 2014. Open M-Sa 9am-5:30pm.) The **library** provides **Internet** for £1.50 per 30min. (☎7083 2286. Open M and W-F 10am-5:30pm, Tu 10am-8pm, Sa 10am-5pm. Closed 1-2pm.) The **post office,** 90 the Promenade, awaits inside the Spick and Span cleaners. (☎7083 2001. Open M-Tu and Th-F 9am-1pm and 2-5:30pm, W 9am-1pm, Sa 9am-12:30pm.) **Postal code:** BT55.

▐▐▌ ACCOMMODATIONS, FOOD, AND PUBS. The Victoria Terr. area, on the left heading out of town on the Portrush Rd., has beds galore. **Rick's Causeway Coast Independent Hostel (IHH/IHO) ❶,** 4 Victo-

THE LOCAL LEGEND

THE REAL MACCOOL

If the geological explanation of the Giant's Causeway seems all too prosaic, a little story time is in order. One of the best known yarns in the Irish oral tradition tells that the Giant's Causeway was formed when the famed giant Finn MacCool (*Finn mac Cumaill*), leader of the warrior clan *Fianna,* found himself, as warrior giants are wont to be, in a row with his hulking Scottish counterpart, Benandonner. Enthusiastic at the prospect of a fight, Finn cavalierly built the honeycomb-esque stairs to Big Ben's home on Staffa Island off the Scottish coast.

Upon hearing rumors of Benandonner's massive corpulence and his approaching presence, the deflated Finn did what any good leader of a warrior clan of giants would do: he asked his wife, Oonagh, to hide him. In turn, Oonagh did what every fine lady giant would do: dress her husband up as a baby and place him in a huge cradle in plain sight.

When the Scot arrived and got a load of the size of that baby, he imagined how big the father must have been and quickly turned back to Scotland in mortal fear, ripping up the Causeway as he fled to ensure that Pap Finn wouldn't be able to pursue. The nearby Giant's boot was Benandonner's cast-off, lost in his haste back to Scotland.

ria Terr., keeps its airy rooms sparkling and inviting with high-ceilings and sea-blue duvets. (☎7083 3789; rick@causewaycoasthostel.fsnet.co.uk. Barbeque available. Laundry £4, free if staying for more than one night. Key deposit £2. Dorms £7.50; doubles £18-22.) **Wanderin' Heights ❷**, 12 High Rd., near Victoria Terr., is a modern, upscale B&B, with stellar sea views from some of its clear, bright rooms. (☎7083 3250. All rooms with bath. Singles £25; shared rooms £20-25.) The centrally located **Anchorage Inn ❹**, of Skipper's Wine Bar fame, makes the morning stumble back to luxury rooms as short as possible. (☎7083 4401. All rooms with bath. Singles £35; doubles £60.)

Portstewart cultivates good cooks and a tradition of superb ice cream. **Centra** supermarket, 70 the Promenade, has an impressive selection of cheeses. (☎7083 3203. Open daily 7am-midnight.) ▨**Morelli's Sundae Garden ❶**, 55-58 the Promenade, provides Portstewart's indispensable gustatory experience—the remarkable waffle cone sundae. (☎7083 2150. Open July-Aug. daily 9am-11pm; Sept.-June variable weekend hours only.) **Smyth's Restaurant ❸** is up the hill through the Promenade and to the left of the Diamond by the Church on Lever Rd.; it serves delightful culinary concoctions. Even the food in the upstairs bar exhibits worldliness, featuring Chinese, Irish, and Mexican options. (☎7083 3564. Steak £2.25-6.99. Bar food Tu-F and Su noon-3pm and 5:30-8:30pm, Sa noon-3pm.) **Ecosse Restaurant ❹**, Atlantic Circle, serves dinners with lovely ocean views. (☎7083 5822. A la carte dinner F-Sa 6-10pm, Su 6-8:30pm £8-15. Su brunch £6-8.)

Portstewart's two major entertainment monoliths, **O'Hara's** and **The Anchor**, are at the southern end of the Promenade, uphill from the shore. Each is comprised of a few bars and a music club/venue. **Anchor Pub**, 87 the Promenade, provides unpretentious pints. Upstairs houses a live music venue and a disco Tuesday and Thursday nights for the college crowd, as does the nearby **Skipper's Wine Bar.** Both The Anchor and Skipper serve food, though the food at Skipper's is a bit more expensive. (☎7083 2003. M and Th-Su live music.) Across the street, **O'Hara's** public bar has as mixed a crowd as the multiplexes get, with a pool table and a cool lounge for the kids; **Shenanigan's** serves sophisticated and adventurous fare to a thumpin' dance beat; **Bar 7** courts a mature see-and-be-seen crowd with upscale, up-price whiskeys; **Chaines** is the weekend disco for youngsters. (☎7083 6000. Restaurant open noon-2:30pm and 5-9:30pm. Disco F-Sa.) Breaking out of these pleasure domes requires a simple walk to **Smyth's** (☎7083 3564), where the owner actualized many a teen's dream and turned his old bedroom into a small, mod bar with low couches and wacky bar food (see **Restaurants**, p. 541).

🔲 🎿 **SIGHTS AND ACTIVITIES.** Beachcombers have a full day in store on the 6½ mi. coastal path that leads east from Portstewart Strand, on the west side of town, toward Portrush. The path passes sea cliffs, blow holes, an ancient hermit's house, and plenty of other odd sights that a free map from the tourist office helps identify. **Portstewart Strand,** less than a mile west of town, is owned and preserved by the National Trust. (Site open year-round. Visitors facilities open Mar.-Sept. daily 10am-6pm; Oct. Sa-Su 10am-5pm. £4 per car, free after 6pm.) The **Port-na-happle rock pool,** between the town and beach, is ideal for bathing. A small but dedicated group of surfers call these waters home; the town's two surf shops exist to serve them. Surfers, beginner or expert, should check the surf report for the height and temperature of waves, time of tides, and other useful info. (Updated daily 8am. ☎0906 133 7770.) **Troggs,** 20 the Diamond, rents wetsuits, surfboards, bodyboards, and wild things. (☎7083 3361; www.troggs.com. Equipment £3-10 per day. Open July-Aug. daily 10am-6pm; Apr.-June Sa-Su 10am-6pm.) **Ocean Warriors,** at 80 the Promenade and on the Strand, rents similar equipment. (☎7083 6500. Open daily 10am-6pm.) Both have sister stores in Portrush. According to locals, the best waves hit the shore from September to March and reach 5-6 ft. **Fishing** is possible aboard the *M.F.V. Boy Matthew.* (☎7083 4734. Sails daily June-Aug. at 2 and 6pm). **Scuba** lovers indulge with **Portstewart Sub Aqua** (☎0150 476 5169 or 01504 301 409.) **Aquahol-**

ics, 14 Portmore Rd., across from Wandering Heights B&B, leads night-time dives. (☎7083 2584 or 079 6816 4748; www.aquaholics.org. 1 dive without equipment £20. Open daily 9am-6pm. After 6pm ring mobile.) **Flowerfield Arts Centre,** 185 Coleraine Rd., shelters traveling art exhibits and holds lectures on subjects from local history and folklore to the royal family. (☎7083 3959. Open M-F 9am-1pm and 2-5pm.) For a week in late-July, Portstewart paints the town during the **Red Sails Festival** with bands, karaoke, fishing, and fireworks (☎7083 3005).

DOWNHILL   ☎028

The land between Castlerock and Downhill once belonged to the Earl Bishop Frederick Hervey, Earl of Bristol and Derry, who will long be remembered as one of the wackiest members of British aristocracy ever to tamper with the Irish landscape. His construction of **Downhill Castle** in the late 18th century challenged the coast's stoic sea cliffs with the heavy hand of human decadence. Alas, it suffered a disastrous fire and was abandoned after WWII. The residence was later bought by a Yankee Doodle Dandy, who gutted it and sold the windows, chandeliers, furnishings, and even the roof, leaving behind only the stone shell of a former palace.

On the cliffs in front of the castle, **Musendun Temple** all but teeters over a precipitous drop to the sea. This circular library was based on the Temples of Vesta in Italy and was named after the niece with whom locals speculated Earl Bishop Fred had an affair. Behind the castle sit the remains of another of Hervey's architectural frivolities—the **mausoleum** he built for his brother, which sings a cautionary song. Ignoring warnings that the windy clifftop would not long support the structure he had planned, Herv erected a monument twice the height of the one that now stands. Needless to say, a second tier and the statue atop it toppled in a windstorm. (☎7084 8728; www.nationaltrust.org.uk. Temple and castle open June-Aug. daily 11am-7:30pm; Mar.-May and Sept.-Oct. 11:30am-6pm. £3.50 per car.) On the road from Downhill to Castlerock, **Hezlett House** is a 17th century thatched cottage cum-Victorian-mini-museum. (☎7084 8567. Mar. 15-May Sa-Su noon-6pm; June-Aug. W-M noon-6pm. Tours £3.50, child £2, family £7.) **Downhill Forest,** on the same road, features waterfalls, streams, wonderous wildfowl, and paths through the lush forest for hikers and bikers. (Open dawn-dusk. Free.) **Downhill Beach,** one of the most gorgeous on the Northern coast, lies below in front of the hostel.

Getting to Downhill is surprisingly easy. **Bus** #134 from Coleraine to Limavady swings right by (7-8 per day); ask the driver to stop at the hostel, which is a 2min. walk straight ahead. The **train** (☎9066 6630; www.translink.co.uk) stops at Castlerock on its way to and from Belfast to Derry (M-F 8 per day). From there the hostel retrieves guests for free if they call ahead. Otherwise it's a beautiful 30min. walk out of Castlerock. From Co. Donegal the ferry from Greencastle on the Inishowen Peninsula sails straight to Magilligan, 10 mi. away. (☎778 1901; info@loughfoyleferry.com. 10min.; Apr.-Sept. M-Sa 7:20am-9:50pm, Su 9am-9:50pm; Oct.-Mar. M-Sa 7:20am-7:50pm, Su 9am-7:50pm.) Cyclists and lucky car owners are almost there; pedestrians can catch one of **Tony's Taxis** (☎7084 8147 or 079 7626 8076) from Magilligan and anywhere in and around Downhill. Leaving may be more difficult— ◪**Downhill Hostel's ❶** gentle embrace proves mighty addictive. This dreamhouse has a beach out front, cliffs out back, and a rocky stream flowing along its border. High bunks, hand-sewn quilts, and a luxurious shower provide more reasons to stick around. The hostel houses a working pottery studio; guests are invited to paint and decorate their own. Call ahead for pickup from town. (☎7084 9077; www.downhillhostel.com. Pottery painting £6-25 depending on piece. Wetsuit £6 and boogie board rental £4 per day. Laundry £3.50. Dorms £8; private rooms £12.) The closest food source other than Downhill's pub is the grocery store 2 mi. away in **Castlerock,** so shop before arriving. In the nearby **library,** on the road into town across the railroad tracks toward the shore, are books galore and **Internet.** (☎7084 8463. Open Tu 2-5pm and 6-8pm, W and F 2-5:30pm, Sa 10:30am-1pm and 2-5pm.)

DERRY (DOIRE CHOLM CILLE)

Derry became a major commercial port under the Ulster Plantation of the 17th century (see p. 60). Under the English feudal system, the city was the outpost of London's authority, which changed its name from the Irish "Diore" to Derry and finally to Londonderry. (Phone books and the minority Protestant population use this official title, but many Republican Northerners and informal Protestants refer to the city as Derry.) The past three centuries of Derry's history have given rise to the iconography used by both sides of the sectarian conflict. The city's troubled history spans from the siege of Derry in 1689, when the now-legendary Apprentice Boys closed the city gates on the advancing armies of the Catholic King James II (see p. 60), to the civil rights turmoil of the 1960s, when protests against religious discrimination against Catholics exploded into violence publicized worldwide. In 1972, the Troubles reached their pinnacle on Bloody Sunday, a tragic public massacre in which British soldiers shot into a crowd of peaceful protesters. None of the soldiers were ever convicted, and Nationalists are still seeking redress from the British government (see **The Troubles**, p. 458). Hearings into the Bloody Sunday Massacre were recently reopened, and are being held in Derry's Guildhall, with a brief relocation to London in summer 2003. As of September 2003, the hearings were back in Derry and open to public viewing.

Present-day Derry is far more relaxed since things seem to be getting back to a state of normalcy not enjoyed for decades. The citizenry and government pride themselves on the leaps the city has made in its clean and cohesive appearance, as well as the emotional and practical compromises made by both sides of the political and religious divide. Perhaps due to the town's previous reputation, Derry natives are quick to stand up for their beautiful and intimate city. Despite these advances, visitors have often stayed away, shielding Derry from a different kind of disturbance. Far from shunning intruders, Derry's population makes the visitors that do journey here feel welcomed and engaged.

✖ INTERCITY TRANSPORTATION

Airport: Eglinton/Derry Airport, Eglinton (☎7181 0784). 7 mi. from Derry. Flights to **Dublin, Glasgow, London-Stanstead,** and **Manchester.**

Trains: Duke St., Waterside (☎7134 2228), on the east bank. A free **Rail-Link bus** connects the bus station to the train station. Call the rail or bus station to find the corresponding bus. Trains from Derry go east to: **Belfast** via **Castlerock, Coleraine, Ballymoney, Ballymena,** and **Lisburn** (2½hr.; M-F 9 per day, Sa 7 per day, Su 4 per day; £8.20). Connections may be made from Coleraine to **Portrush.**

Buses: Most stop at the Ulsterbus depot on Foyle St. between the walled city and the river. **Ulsterbus** (☎7126 2261) serves all destinations in the North and a few in the Republic. #212 to: **Belfast** (1½-3hr.; M-Sa 14-16 per day, Su 6 per day; £8); #234 to **Coleraine** (M-F 4 per day, Su 1 per day; £5.40); #275 to Donegal (90min., M-Sa 1 per day at noon); #274 to **Dublin** via **Omagh** (4-6 per day, £10.31); #296 to **Galway** via Longford and **Athlone** (7hr., M-Sa at 9am); #273-4 to **Omagh** (M-Sa 13 per day, Su 9 per day; £5.40). **Lough Swilly** bus service (☎7126 2017) heads to the **Fanad Peninsula,** the **Inishowen Peninsula,** and **Letterkenny,** and other parts of northwest Donegal. Buses to: **Buncrana** (35min.; M-Sa 10-12 per day, Su 4 per day; £3); **Letterkenny** (1hr.; M-F 10 per day, Sa 13 per day; £4); **Malin Head** (1½hr.; M, W, and F 1 per day, Sa 3 per day; £5). **Northwest Busways** (Republic ☎077 82619) heads to: **Inishowen** from Patrick St. opposite the Multiplex Cinema and to **Buncrana** (M-Sa 9 per day, £2.50), **Carndonagh** (M-Sa 7 per day, £3.20), and **Malin Head** (2 per day, £4.20).

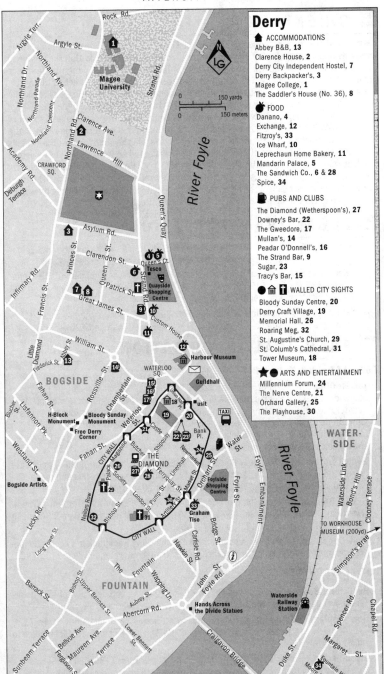

Derry

⌂ ACCOMMODATIONS
Abbey B&B, **13**
Clarence House, **2**
Derry City Independent Hostel, **7**
Derry Backpacker's, **3**
Magee College, **1**
The Saddler's House (No. 36), **8**

🍎 FOOD
Danano, **4**
Exchange, **12**
Fitzroy's, **33**
Ice Wharf, **10**
Leprechaun Home Bakery, **11**
Mandarin Palace, **5**
The Sandwich Co., **6** & **28**
Spice, **34**

🍺 PUBS AND CLUBS
The Diamond (Wetherspoon's), **27**
Downey's Bar, **22**
The Gweedore, **17**
Mullan's, **14**
Peadar O'Donnell's, **16**
The Strand Bar, **9**
Sugar, **23**
Tracy's Bar, **15**

● 🏛 🛈 WALLED CITY SIGHTS
Bloody Sunday Centre, **20**
Derry Craft Village, **19**
Memorial Hall, **26**
Roaring Meg, **32**
St. Augustine's Church, **29**
St. Columb's Cathedral, **31**
Tower Museum, **18**

★ ● ARTS AND ENTERTAINMENT
Millennium Forum, **24**
The Nerve Centre, **21**
Orchard Gallery, **25**
The Playhouse, **30**

NORTHERN IRELAND

◈ ORIENTATION

Derry straddles the **River Foyle** just east of Co. Donegal's border. The **city center** and the **university area** both lie on the Foyle's western banks. The old city, within the medieval walls, is Derry's downtown. At the center lies **The Diamond,** from which radiate four main streets: **Shipquay Street** to the northeast (downhill), **Butcher Street** to the northwest, **Bishop Street** to the southwest (uphill), and **Ferryquay** to the southeast. Outside the city walls, Butcher St. intersects **Waterloo Street,** which comprises the pedestrian shopping district. **Magee University** is to the north off **Strand Road,** the northern extension of Waterloo St. The famous Catholic **Bogside** neighborhood that became Free Derry in the 70s (see **The Troubles,** p. 458) is west of the city walls. On the south side of the walls is the tiny Protestant enclave of the **Fountain.** The residential areas of the Foyle's western bank are almost entirely Catholic, while most of Derry's Protestant population lives on the eastern bank, in the housing estates commonly referred to as **Waterside.** The train station is on the east side of the river and can be reached from the city center by way of the double-decker **Craigavon Bridge,** or via a free shuttle at the bus station.

◈ LOCAL TRANSPORTATION

Bike Rental: Rent-A-Bike, 245 Lone Moor Rd., a 20min. walk from the city center (☎7128 7128; www.happydays.ie). £9 per day, £35 per wk. ID deposit.

Car Rental: Europcar, City of Derry Airport (☎7181 2773; www.europcar.ie). 23+. Economy cars £35 per day, £165 per wk. Open M-F 8:30am-5:30pm, Sa 8:30am-1pm, but will meet flights and deliver at other times.

Taxis: Derry Taxi Association (☎7126 0247). Also offers tours of the city center (1hr.) and as far as Portrush and Donegal for up to 7-8 people for around £20.

◈ PRACTICAL INFORMATION

TOURIST AND FINANCIAL SERVICES

Tourist Office: 44 Foyle St. (☎7126 7284; www.derryvisitor.com), inside the Derry Visitor and Convention Bureau. Be sure to ask for the useful *Derry Visitor's Guide* and *Derry Visitor's Map.* 24hr. computerized info kiosk. Books accommodations and runs a **bureau de change.** Runs guided walking tours of the city. **Bord Fáilte** (☎7136 9501) keeps a desk here, too. Open July-Sept. M-F 9am-7pm, Sa 10am-6pm, Su 10am-5pm; Nov.-Easter M-F 9am-5pm; Easter-June and Oct. M-F 9am-5pm, Sa 10am-5pm.

Budget Travel: usit, 4 Shipquay Pl. (☎7137 1888; www.usitnow.com). ISICs, TravelSave stamps, and the like. Books accommodations worldwide, and sells bus and plane tickets and rail passes. Open M-F 9:30am-5:30pm, Sa 10am-1pm.

Banks: Bank of Ireland, Shipquay St. (☎7126 4992). Open M-F 9:30am-4:30pm. **Northern Bank,** Guildhall Sq. (☎7126 5333). Open M-W and F 9:30am-3:30pm, Th 9:30am-5pm, Sa 9:30am-12:30pm. All have 24hr. **ATMs.**

Work Opportunities: Derry Independent Hostel and **Derry Backpacker's** accept temporary help, and offer housing and a small salary. Contact Steve and Kylie ☎7137 7989.

LOCAL SERVICES

Bookstore: Bookworm, 18 Bishop St. (☎7128 2727). A good selection of Irish books and travel guides. Open M-Sa 9:30am-5:30pm.

Gay, Lesbian, and Bisexual Information: Foyle Friend, 32 Great James St. (☎7126 3120). Info and support for all of Northern Ireland. Open M-F noon-5pm. Closed June to mid-July.

Disability Resources: Disability Action, 52 Strand Rd. (☎7136 0811). Serves the physically and mentally disabled. Open M-Th 9am-1pm and 2-5pm, F until 4pm.

Laundry: Duds 'n' Suds, 141 Strand Rd. (☎ 7126 6006). Wash £1.80, dry £2; students £1.25 for each. Open M-F 8am-9pm, Sa 8am-6pm. Last wash 1½hr. before closing.

Camping Equipment: Graham Tiso, 2-4 Carlisle Rd. (☎ 7137 00546), outside Ferryquay Gate, has two floors of stylin' outdoor equipment. Open M-Sa 9:30am-5:30pm.

EMERGENCY AND COMMUNICATIONS

Emergency: ☎ 999; no coins required. **Police:** Strand Rd. (☎ 7136 7337).

Pharmacy: Gordon's Chemist, 3a-b Strand Rd. (☎ 7126 4502). Open M-Th and Sa 9am-5:30pm, F 9am-8pm.

Hospital: Altnagelvin Hospital, Glenshane Rd. (☎ 7134 5171).

Internet Access: Central Library, 35 Foyle St. (☎ 7127 2300). £3 per hr. Open M and Th 9:15am-8pm, Tu-W and F-Sa 9:15am-5pm. **bean-there.com,** 20 The Diamond (☎ 7128 1303; www.bean-there.com). £2.50 per 30min.; coffee, cake, and 30min. of Internet £3.50. Open M-F 9am-7pm, Sa 10am-6pm, Su 2-6pm.

Post Office: 3 Custom House St. (☎ 7136 2563). Open M-F 8:30am-5:30pm, Sa 9am-12:30pm. **Postal code:** BT48. Unless addressed to 3 Custom House St., *Poste Restante* letters will go to the **Postal Sorting Office** (☎ 7136 2577) on the corner of Great James and Little James St.

◪ ACCOMMODATIONS

Derry provides a number of excellent accommodation options for travelers, from a friendly hostel and a self-catering townhouse to a plethora of B&Bs.

▩ **Derry City Independent Hostel,** 44 Great James St. (☎ 7137 7989 or 7137 0011). Down Strand Rd. and a left up Great James, 5min. from city center. Welcome to the Derry Vortex; it may be hard to leave this go-with-the-flow chiller's nirvana (and 5th night's free...). Owner filled this hostel with various items from his own travels to exotic locales, alongside an eclectic assortment of music and books. Free breakfast, **free Internet,** and frequent all-you-can-eat bbqs for £2. Organizes trips to Giant's Causeway in summer (£16). Near-identical **Derry Backpacker's** (aka **Steve's Backpacker's**), 4 Asylum St., a 2min. walk down Princes St. and a left up Asylum, has the same owners and the same list of services. Dorms £9; singles £13; doubles £26. ❶

▩ **The Saddler's House (No. 36),** 36 Great James St. (☎ 7126 9691; www.thesaddlershouse.com). Friendly, knowledgeable owners welcome guests into their lovely Victorian home. French coffee, fresh fruit, and homemade jam in excellent breakfasts. Same family runs **The Merchant's House,** an award-winning, restored Georgian townhouse with fluffy beds. Both houses singles £25; doubles £45. ❸

Abbey B&B, Abbey St. (☎ 7127 9000; abbey.accom@ntlworld.com). From Waterloo Sq. up William St. through the roundabout and a left at Abbey St. Close to the city center and in the Bogside neighborhood, this B&B greets visitors with a "cuppa" and spacious peach rooms. £20. Reduced rates for families. ❷

Clarence House, 15 Northland Rd. (☎ 7126 5342; www.clarenceguesthouse.co.uk). Accommodating owner pleases all with a range of breakfast offerings and quality rooms stocked with phones, hair dryers, TVs, irons, and bottled water. £20, with bath £25. Reduced prices for longer stays. ❷

Magee College, on the corner of Rock and Northland Rd. (☎ 7137 5255; www.bunk.com). Walk ½ mi. up Strand Rd. and turn left onto Rock Rd.; Magee College is atop of the hill on the left. Housing Office is on the ground floor of Woodburn House, a red brick building just past the main building. Rooms with desk, drawers, and sink. Wheelchair-accessible. Wash and dry £1 each. Mandatory reservations by phone or Internet M-Th 9am-5pm, F 9am-4pm. Available mid-June to Sept. Singles in 5-bedroom flats £20, students £16.45-18.45; 6- to 8- person flat £52.30 per wk. ❷

◘ FOOD

Tesco supermarket, in the Quayside Shopping Centre, is a few minutes' walk from the walled city along Strand Rd. (Open M-Th 9am-9pm, F 8:30am-9pm, Sa 8:30am-8pm, Su 1-6pm.)

Exchange, Queens Quay (☎ 7127 3990), down Great James toward the River Foyle and a right at the Derry City Hotel. It's a swank attack at this sleek restaurant, with big circular booths for you and your entourage. The slim-conscious will appreciate the celiac-friendly menu. Dinner £8.50-13.75. Open M-Sa noon-10pm, Su 5-9:30pm. ❹

Ice Wharf, Strand Rd. across from The Strand nightclub. This link in Wetherspoon's restaurant chain smacks of capitalist standardization. However, 2 meals for the price of 1 all day and a €4.70 carvery roast noon-3pm on Su make it attractive and affordable to follow Adam Smith and enrich the British economy. Open M-Sa noon-8:30pm. ❸

Spice, 162 Spencer Rd. (☎ 7134 4875), on E. bank. Cross Craigavon Bridge and continue as it turns into Spencer. Rumored to be the best food in Derry. Appetizers £3-4. Daily veggie specials £7.95; sesame seed pork with ginger dressing £8.50; seabass with tomato and coriander salsa £11.50. Open 12:30-2:30pm and 5:30-10pm. ❸

The Sandwich Co., The Diamond (☎ 7137 2500), and 61 Strand Rd. (☎ 7126 6771). A choice of breads stuffed with a wide range of tasty fillings, though there's no choice about the matching black-and-white interiors of both locations. Journey to the Strand location at lunch to avoid queues. Sandwiches £2-3. Both open M-F 8:30am-5pm. ❶

Fitzroy's, 2-4 Bridge St. (☎ 7126 6211), next to Bishop's Gate. Modern cafe culture and filling meals, from simple chicken breast to mango lamb. Don't let the eerie green light from the illuminated staircase ruin your appetite. During the day most meals £4-6; dinners £7-12. Open M-Tu 9:30am-8pm, W-Sa 9:30am-10pm, Su noon-8pm. ❸

Mandarin Palace, Queen's Ct., Lower Clarendon (☎ 7137 3656). A stylish Chinese restaurant with a suspiciously bamboo-colored wooden interior that looks onto the River Foyle. Adjacent takeaway is cheaper, with most meals £5-6, and always open until midnight. Restaurant open Su-Th 4:30-11pm, F-Sa 4:30pm-midnight. ❸

Danano, 2-4 Lower Clarendon St. (☎ 7126 9034). A tasty Italian restaurant where the hungry can watch their pizzas (£4-6) form or see their lobsters pushed into the only wood-burning oven in Northern Ireland. Anticipation is half the pleasure. Adjoining takeaway offers pizzas, pastas, and salads for slightly less; call ahead if you're in a hurry. Ask about promotions on M-Tu. Open daily 5pm-midnight. ❸

Leprechaun Home Bakery, 21-23 Strand Rd. (☎ 7136 3606). The standard eclairs, buns, cakes, and whatnot; sandwiches (£3), salads (£3), and meals (£4). Home-made marmalade and bread set it apart. Open M-Sa 9am-5:30pm. ❷

⚉ ⚐ PUBS AND CLUBS

Most pubs line Waterloo and the Strand, though a growing number are popping up within the walls. Trad and rock can be found almost any night of the week, and all age groups keep the pubs lively until the 1am closing time. Many bars have cheap drink promotions on weeknights; just read the chalkboards out front.

⚐ **Mullan's,** 13 Little James St. (☎ 7126 5300), on the corner of William and Rossville St. Incredible pub with idiosyncratically lavish decor, from stained-glass ceilings and bronze lion statues to flat-screen TVs. Drink up and don't worry if the stodgy portraits seem to be staring. Hosts excellent jazz W nights and Su afternoon. A disproportionate number of women at M night karaoke. Open M-Sa 10am-2am, Su noon-12:30am.

Peadar O'Donnell's, 53 Waterloo St. (☎7137 2318). Named for the famous Donegal Socialist who organized the Irish Transport and General Workers Union and took an active role in the 1921 Irish Civil War. Celtic and Orangeman paraphernalia hang beside chalkboards of drink specials. Trad Su. Open M-Sa 11am-1am, Su 7pm-midnight.

The Gweedore, 59-61 Waterloo St. (☎7126 3513). The back door has connected to Peadar's since Famine times. An intimate venue where crowds listen attentively to rock, bluegrass, and funk bands nightly. Open M-Sa 4:30pm-1am, Su 7pm-midnight.

The Diamond (Wetherspoon's), The Diamond (☎7127 2880). Cheap meals of the chicken and meat variety (£2-4) and even cheaper drinks of the alcoholic sort make this a good place to start the night before moving onto pubs with more character. Frequent promotions stretch a few quid a long way. Food until 10pm. Open M-W 11:30am-11pm, Th and Su 11:30am-midnight, F-Sa 11:30am-1am.

The Strand Bar, 31-35 Strand Rd. (☎7126 0494). 3 floors of decadently decorated space pull in young partiers, especially on F when DJs occupy every floor, spinning dance faves from Top 100 to electronica. The downstairs has live music Tu-Th and the top floor is a nightclub. Cover £4-6. Open M-Sa 11:30am-1am, Su noon-midnight.

Tracy's Bar, 51 Waterloo St. (☎7126 9770). Locals circle the straw-ringed central bar nightly; bands play Th-Su. Open M-Sa 11:30am-12:45am, Su 12:30-11:45pm.

Downey's Bar, 33 Shipquay St. (☎7126 0820). 20-somethings people this bar to play pool on purple tables and pretend that they can hear each other over the pulsing pop music. In nice weather, the ceiling over the bar opens up. Tu karaoke, W-Sa DJs.

Sugar, 33 Shipquay St. (behind Downey's). Downey's sweaty cousin and the newest nightclub in Derry. Big-name DJs drop in on weekends. Th 18+, F-Sa 21+. Cover £3-5.

⬛ TOURS

THE DERRY VISITOR AND CONVENTION BUREAU GUIDED TOURS. Walking tours are an excellent way to see many of the city's sights while getting an introduction to its history-laden geography. Most walks circle the top of the city walls, stepping down to visit various sights. The Derry Visitor and Convention Bureau Guided Walking Tours leave from the tourist office and take visitors around the city walls, including a brief tour of St. Columb's Cathedral. Other tours look at narratives ranging from the Siege of 1689 to Emigration. (☎7126 7284. 1½hr. tours. July-Aug. M-F 11:15am and 3:15pm; Sept.-June M-F 2:30pm. £4; students, seniors, and children £3.)

THE BOGSIDE ARTISTS' TOURS. Guests are invited to tour the Bogside murals under the informed tutelage of the artists who created them. The guides pick up groups of eight or more people in the city center and work their way through the 11 murals painted in the open air gallery in Meenan Sq., around the Free Derry Corner. The 1½hr. tours finish in the studio—which doubles as a youth reconciliation center by night—for a question and answer session with the murals' creators. (☎7128 4123 or 7135 7781; www.bogsideartists.com. M-Sa 10am-5pm. £4.)

CITY TOURS. Highly acclaimed City Tours urges the curious to lace their walking shoes and pound the pavement for close to 2hr. Flexibility allows for other tours through the Sperrins or Literary and Cultural tours throughout Northern Ireland. French and German language interpreters are available. (11 Carlisle Rd. ☎7127 1996 or 7127 1997; www.irishtourguides.com. Depart daily at 10am, noon, 2pm. Book ahead. £4.)

FOYLE CRUISES. Daily and weekly sailing trips along the Foyle reveal the city's beauty from a nautical perspective. Daytime ships float over to Culmore Bay while nighttime cruises sail to Greencastle in Co. Donegal and include a live band. (☎7136 2857. Boats leave from the Harbour Museum daily at 2pm and 4pm. 75min. £6, concessions £4, family £18. Evening rides leave at 8pm. 4hr. £10/£7/£30.)

◎ SIGHTS

Derry was once the main emigration point in Ireland—massive numbers of Ulster Catholics and Scottish Presbyterians fled the area's religious discrimination. In fact, Derry was the only point of immigration to Australia, a journey of 26 sea-sick weeks. Around the time of the Famine, many Catholics gave up on emigration and settled in the peatbog area outside the city walls, now called the **Bogside** neighborhood. The creation of the Republic made Derry a border city, and a Catholic majority made it a headache for Unionist leaders; it became the site of blatant civil rights violations, including gerrymandering and religious discrimination. The civil rights marches that sparked the Troubles originated here in 1968. The following became powerful touchstones for Catholics in Derry and for Nationalists everywhere: **Free Derry,** the western, Catholic part of the city, seized and controlled by the IRA in retaliation against the constant siege the neighborhood experienced at the hands of the British, and an effective "no-go" area for the army from 1969 to 1972; **Bloody Sunday,** January 30, 1972, when British troops fired on demonstrators and killed 14 (see p. 458); and **Operation Motorman,** the July 1972 army effort to penetrate Free Derry and arrest IRA leaders. Although the city-scape was once razed by years of bombings, Derry has since been rebuilt and looks sparklingly new. Through the cooperative efforts of Unionists and Republicans, no violent incidents have erupted for the past five years, even during Marching Season and other contentious sectarian events.

■ **THE CITY WALLS.** Derry's city walls, 18 ft. high and 20 ft. thick, were erected between 1614 and 1619. They have never been breached, hence Derry's nickname "the Maiden City." However, such resilience did not save the city from danger; during the **Siege of 1689,** 600 mortar bombs sent from the nearby hills by fleeing English King James II and his brigade of Catholic Frenchmen went over what they could not go through, devastating the 30,000 Protestants crowded inside. This sad irony has caused some to quip, "The first planned city, the first planned mistake." A walk along the top of its mile-long perimeter affords a far-reaching view of Derry from its self-contained early days to its present urban sprawl. Seven **cannons**—donated by Queen Elizabeth I and the London Guilds who "acquired" the city during the Ulster Plantation—are perched along the northeast wall between Magazine and Shipquay Gates. A plaque on the outside of this section of wall marks the water level in the days when the Foyle ran along the walls (now 300 ft. away). The 1.5 mi. walk around the city walls leads past most of Derry's best-known sights, including the raised portion of the stone wall past New Gate that shields **St. Columb's Cathedral,** the symbolic focus of the city's Protestant defenders. The same area also affords a perfect view of the red, white, and blue painted Unionist **Fountain** neighborhood. Stuck in the center of the southwest wall, **Bishop's Gate** received an ornate face-lift in 1789, commemorating the victory of Protestant William of Orange 100 years earlier. The southwest corner supports **Roaring Meg,** a massive cannon donated by London fishmongers in 1642 and used in the 1689 siege. The sound of the cannon alone was rumored to strike fear into the hearts of enemies. This corner affords a sprawling view of the **Bogside** neighborhood, and access to all 11 murals.

ST. COLUMBA'S CATHEDRAL. Named after the former chieftain-cum-monk St. Columba, whose monastery was the foundation on which Derry was built, the cathedral was constructed between 1628 and 1633 and was the first Protestant cathedral in Britain or Ireland (all the older ones were confiscated Catholic cathedrals). The spire of the cathedral, in the southwest corner of the walled city, is visible from almost anywhere in Derry. Today's steeple is the church's third. The original wooden spire burnt down after being struck by lightning, while the second (a leaden and rounded replacement) was smelted into bullets and cannonballs during the siege. The same fate did not befall the cathedral itself, as it was designed to double as a fort with six-inch-thick walls and a

HERE, KITTY-KITTY... In the last century, Derry's statesmen and merchants bought opulent homes within the city walls, and their wealthy wives would order fashionable dresses from London. When the frilly frocks arrived, the ladies donned them and met to stroll about on the city walls. The residents of the Bogside, looking up at the wall-wenches from their own poverty-stricken neighborhood, were enraged at the decadent lifestyle on display. On one occasion, several Bogsiders took it upon themselves to write a letter of complaint to the London papers about the parading "cats." The press in London was so amused by the nickname for Derry's finest ladies that it stuck, and the phrase "cat walk" fell into common usage.

walkway for musketeers to shoot from the spire. The interior is fashioned of roughly hewn stone and holds an exquisite Killybegs altar carpet, an extravagant bishop's chair dating from 1630, and 214 hand-carved Derry-oak pews, of which no two are the same. A tiny, museum-like **chapterhouse** at the back of the church displays the original locks and keys of the four main city gates, relics from the 1689 siege. Cecil Francis Alexander, author of the children's hymn "All Things Bright and Beautiful," smiles from a picture that is half photo, half drawing, created when early subjects of photography still sought the beautifying treatment of traditional portraiture. More fun, however, is comparing the photograph and portrait of her husband, Rev. William Alexander. The official portrait shows an abundant and pompous figure while the photograph of the posing man shows the diminutive reality. In the **graveyard** outside, the tombstones flat on the ground were leveled during the siege to protect the graves from Jacobite cannonballs. The small **Mound of Martyrs**, in the back left corner toward the walls, contains the 5000 dead previously buried in the cellars of the nearby houses, transplanted here during the city's redesigning efforts. (London St., off Bishop St. in the southwest corner of the city. ☎ 7126 7313; www.stcolumbscathedral.org. Open Easter-Oct. M-Sa 9am-5pm; Nov.-Mar. M-Sa 9am-4pm. Tours recommended, and available on arrival with no prior notice for the suggested donation of £1.)

MEMORIAL HALL. The Apprentice Boys have had their headquarters here for centuries. Inside the clubhouse there is (supposedly) a museum's worth of historical items dating back to the Apprentices who shut the gates in 1689. Admission is strictly regulated and highly unlikely, except perhaps through the tourist office-run Walled City Cultural Trail in July and August. Membership is open only to Protestant men, but they generously allow women to cook and clean. (Between Royal Bastion and Butcher's Gate. ☎ 7126 3571. Call ☎ 7126 7284 for current information about the Walled City Cultural Trail.)

GUILDHALL. This neo-Gothic building was formerly home to the City Council. First built in 1887, wrecked by fire in 1908, and destroyed by bombs in 1972, today's structure contains replicas of the original stained-glass windows. Among the bountiful rarities is the mayor's chain of office, which was officially presented to the city by William of Orange. Upstairs, the hall houses an enormous organ with over 3000 pipes. The hall also sponsors various concerts, plays, and exhibitions throughout the year. Currently, the hall is home to the public hearings of the Bloody Sunday Inquiry, and to sensitive documents pertaining to the event. Hearings are open to the public and will resume their place in Derry (from a sabbatical in London) in September 2003. They are slated to conclude in March 2004. The ghost of Sam Mackay, a turn-of-the-century superintendent and the sole Guildhall tenant, is rumored to haunt the place and has been seen pacing the viewing gallery. (Shipquay Pl. at Shipquay Gate. ☎ 7137 7335. No tours due to the ongoing Bloody Sunday inquiry, but the council chamber is open Sept.-May M-F 9am-5pm.)

TOWER MUSEUM. Derry's top attraction utilizes engaging walk-through dioramas and audio-visual displays to relay Derry's intriguing history, from its days as an oak grove, through the siege of 1689, 20th-century wars, and the troublesome Troubles. A

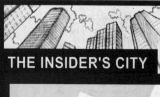

THE INSIDER'S CITY

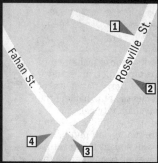

THE BOGSIDE MURALS

1 **The Rioter:** A single rioter holds a bedspring shield against an oncoming British tank during the August 1969 Battle of the Bogside. Citizens of the Catholic enclave, sick of harassment by British troops, barricaded their neighborhood and re-christened it "Free Derry," holding troops at bay for nearly three years.

2 **Bloody Sunday Monument** remembers 14 non-violent protesters who died on January 30, 1972 when British soldiers fired into a crowd of civil rights marchers. British-run Widgery Inquiry found no foul play on the part of British troops. Reopened in 1999, it is on-going.

3 **The H-Block Monument** commemorates the 10 lost to the 1981 hunger strike, which grew out of blanket protests wherein no inmates would wear prison uniforms or bathe.

4 **Bloody Sunday Mural:** The priest depicted, Edward Daly, helps rush gunshot wound victim Jackie Duddy from the crossfire.

series of short videos illustrates Derry's economic, political, and cultural past. The museum does a largely even-handed job at depicting the city's divided history. The whole museum merits at least 1½hr., and is a welcome tutorial for the history quiz at the end of this book. (Union Hall Pl., inside Magazine Gate. ☎7137 2411; www.derry.net/tower. Open July-Aug. M-Sa 10am-5pm, Su 2-5pm; Sept.-June Tu-Sa 10am-5pm. Last entrance 4:30pm. £4.20, students and seniors £1.60, family £8.50.)

WORKHOUSE MUSEUM. Located in a recently restored Victorian building on the east side of the River Foyle. Pass through Simpson's Brae and turn left at Clooney Terrace; then take the first right after Clooney Methodist Church and a left after Glendermott Rd. The museum will be on the right. This workhouse-turned-showplace now houses displays dealing with poverty, health care, and the history of the Famine in Northern Ireland, which it compares with the famine in Somalia. The museum also houses the Atlantic Memorial exhibition that examines the role of the city in WWII. (23 Glendermott Rd. ☎7131 8328. Open July-Aug. M-Sa 10am-4:30pm; Sept.-June M-Th and Sa 10am-4:30pm. Free.)

MAGEE COLLEGE. This neo-Gothic building, found outside the city walls, shines among its clumsier neighbors. The university has changed its affiliation several times: originally a member of the Royal University of Ireland in 1879, by 1909 it was part of Trinity College Dublin. It has been part of the University of Ulster since 1984. (12min. walk east of the city center. ☎7137 1371.)

OTHER SIGHTS. Maritime buffs head to the **Harbour Museum,** which features paintings and artifacts related to Derry's harbor history. (Guildhall St., on the banks of the Foyle. ☎7137 7331. Open M-F 10am-1pm and 2-4:30pm. Free.) The **Bloody Sunday Centre,** though primarily for families and friends of those directly affected by the tragedy, also has a small exhibition space with moving black-and-white photographs and news footage of the marches. (Bank Pl. ☎7136 0880. Open M-F 9:30am-4:30pm. Free.) The **Genealogy Centre** conducts research on ancestry in Co. Derry and Donegal. (14 Bishop St. ☎7126 9792; www.irishroots.net. Open M-F 9am-5pm.) The **Derry Craft Village,** Shipquay St., was built from cast-away building materials by entrepreneurial youth in an abandoned lot in the Bogside. The village encompasses a pleasant courtyard lined with cafes and kitschy craft shops. The **Tower Hotel** is summertime host to Derry's award-winning **Teach Ceoil (Music House).** In July and August, it holds evening performances of Irish music, reading, and dance, as well as "Irish suppers" (tea), with céilí dancing and trad sessions. (Performances Tu-Th 8pm. £6.)

RESIDENTIAL NEIGHBORHOODS AND MURALS

Near the city walls, Derry's residential neighborhoods, both Catholic and Protestant, display brilliant murals. Most pay tribute to historical events. The Bogside murals combine photographs, film clips, and the artists' symbolic touches, while those in the Unionist side focus on Ulster-American heritage and portray para-military casualties and aims. Several murals are visible from points along the city wall. A sculpture at the west side of Craigavon Bridge looks forward optimistically, with two men reaching out to each other across a divide.

WATERSIDE AND THE FOUNTAIN ESTATE. These two neighborhoods are home to Derry's Protestant population. The Waterside, on the east side of the River Foyle, is nearly split in its percentage of Catholics and Protestants, but the Fountain, right outside of the Derry city walls, is almost entirely Protestant. The Fountain is reached from the walled city by exiting through the left side of Bishop's Gate; it is contained by Bishop, Upper Bennett, Abercorn, and Hawkin St. This small area of only 600 residents holds the more interesting Protestant murals, among them a stark whitewashed house with black letters declaring "No Surrender," a slogan carried through from siege days and touted by present-day Protestants. It stands in contrast to the Bogside "Free Derry Corner" of similar motif and motivation. The flat tiled area across from it is a publically designated area for the Orangemen's annual bonfire on July 12. Prior to the city council's acknowledgment of the ritual, the bonfire was carried out impromptu, causing much damage. Though the area is cleared for the 20-30m pile of rubbish that will be lit every July, this too has left scars on the neighborhood as the surrounding lamppost glasses have been warped by the heat. The few Loyalist murals in the Waterside lie along Bonds and Irish St. and portray famous Ulster-descended US Presidents, including George Washington and James Buchanan, beside a likeness of the Queen.

THE BOGSIDE. The Bogside is hard to miss—a huge facade just west of the city walls at the junction of Fahan St. and Rossville Sq. declares "You Are Now Entering Free Derry." Surrounded by other, equally striking, nationalist artistic creations, this area is referred to as Free Derry Corner. The Bogside Artists offer tours of the area, led by the men who painted the murals (see Tours, p. 549). Though *Let's Go* cannot reveal the artistic intentions of their creation, comprehensive information on the symbols and circumstances of the murals and monuments is offered in this edition. Only nine murals are mentioned here, but by Summer 2004 11 murals will have been completed, the last a Peace mural.

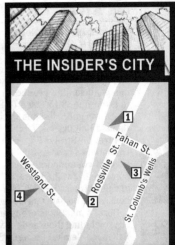

THE INSIDER'S CITY

1 **Free Derry corner** marks the east-side barrier of the sealed-off Bogside outpost. The painted side of the house is not the original facade. In 1972, British troops were ordered to break the wall down, though it was repeatedly rebuilt. A widely recognized symbol of Republican resistance, the monument is untouchable: traffic patterns go around it.

2 **Death of an Innocent** is a portrait of 14 year-old Annette McGavigan, the 100th victim of the Troubles. In 1971 she was caught in crossfire of IRA and British troops on her way home from school, becoming the first child to die due to the cause in Derry.

3 The **British Army headquarters** are on the hill. Though a constant eye is kept on Bogside, it is largely a family neighborhood and now one of the safest areas in Derry.

4 The **Bogside Artists' Studio** holds frequent tours hosted by muralists. It is a youth reconciliation centre where children from both sides come together to resolve issues creatively.

⚡ ARTS AND ENTERTAINMENT

The Millenium Forum, Newmarket St., has a 1000-seat theater that hosts big name performances. (Box office ☎ 7126 4455; www.milleniumforum.co.uk. Performances from £16, concessions often available.) **The Nerve Centre,** 7-8 Magazine St., is Derry's newest venue for local and international performances; it recently welcomed rising star David Gray. Various lessons in music and the arts are also available. A series of independent films are shown in its **cinema.** (☎ 7126 0562; www.nerve-centre.org. Bar, music venue £8-15. Open Th-Su 9pm-1:30am. Films play at 8pm, and sometimes 2pm; £1. Group guitar lessons £5 per class.) For more mainstream films in the city center, **Orchard Hall Cinema,** Orchard St. (☎ 7126 2845) and the **Strand Multiplex,** Quayside Centre, on Strand Rd. (☎ 7137 3900) screen feature films daily. **Orchard Gallery,** Orchard St., is one of the best spots on the Isle for viewing well-conceived exhibitions of contemporary Irish and international art. (☎ 7126 9675. Open Tu-Sa 10am-6pm. Free.) **The Playhouse,** 5-7 Artillery St., showcases the work of young playwrights and performers. (☎ 7126 8027. Tickets £7, students £5.) **St. Columb's Hall,** Orchard St., houses the **Orchard Cinema** (☎ 7126 2945).

Derry's most boisterous and festive time of year is Halloween, when the whole city, including thousands of visitors, dresses up and revels at the **Banks of the Boyle Halloween Carnival** (☎ 7126 7284). The event culminates in a fireworks show over the river. In early June, the **Walled City Festival** turns Derry into "Carnival City," with a weekend that includes a free outdoor concert and various events around the city's walls (☎ 7126 7284). August brings the **Maiden City Festival** (☎ 7134 6677). Organized by the Apprentice Boys, this week-long event features pageantry, drama, and music commemorating the siege of Derry.

⚡ SPORTS AND ACTIVITIES

Sporting events in Derry are as prevalent and exciting as in any big city. **Gaelic football** and **soccer** are played at **Brandywell** on Lone Moor Rd. (Gaelic info ☎ 7126 7142. Games June-Sept. Su afternoon. Tickets £6. Football info ☎ 7128 1337. Games Aug.-May. Tickets £7.) Brandywell also hosts **greyhound racing** (about £5). **Rugby** can be caught at **Judges Rd. pitch.** (☎ 7186 1101. Sept.-Mar. Sa 2:30pm. Tickets £2-5.) For those who want to take part in the fun, **Brooke Park Leisure Centre,** Rosemount Ave., has tennis and squash courts, a fitness room, and exercise and sporting equipment. (☎ 7126 2637. Prices generally £2-7.) The **City Baths,** on William St., promise a swimmingly good time. (☎ 7126 4459. £2. Open M and W 10am-2pm and 6-8pm, Tu and Th 10am-2pm and 6-7pm, F 10am-2pm, Sa noon-4pm.)

⚡ THE SPERRIN MOUNTAINS

The Sperrin Mountains span a 40 mi. arc northeast from **Strabane** to **Milltown** to **Downhill.** The new **Sperrin Way,** an ambitious collection of way-marked trails, aims to make a portion of this land more accessible to outdoors enthusiasts. **Hikers** and **bikers** who embark on the trail can expect rambles through the best preserved high elevation blanket bogs and moorlands in Ireland, as well as some fantastic inland stretches of lush countryside. A number of maps and guided walks to the area are available; for travelers expecting an extended stay in the Sperrins, *Ordnance Survey Discoverer Series #13* is an invaluable guide to the southern part of the range. *Walking in the Western Sperrins* (£3) has concise instructions and miniature maps for five short walks (5-10 mi.) focused on the area around **Gortin,** north of Omagh. *Walk the Sperrins* (£4.95) provides a broader selection of 10 hikes (5-13 mi.) with more detailed narrative descriptions of the routes and focused geological information about the area. Maps and guides are available at the Omagh tourist office (see p. 556) and the Sperrins Heritage Centre (see p. 555).

Hikers can also take advantage of the **Central Sperrins Way,** newly signposted in August 2001. A product of the fragmentation of the former Ulster Way into several more manageable pieces, the Central Way runs 30 mi. through the mountains between the **Glenelly** and **Owenkillew Rivers** in Co. Tyrone. The route can be picked up at any point, but the carpark at **Barnes** (where there is also free **camping**) is a logical starting location. The longest segment of the trail extends northeast from Barnes, following the **Glenelly River** to **Corraltary Hill.** The Way then crosses the mountains and circles back to **Scotch Town,** which is connected to Barnes by a well-trod path. To the west of Barnes and Scotch Town is the Way's shorter loop, which traverses higher elevations and the expansive bogs of **Craignamaddy Hill.** The *Central Sperrins Way* (50p) brochure details the route's segments and sights.

The bounty of the Sperrins is not restricted to pedestrians. **Cyclists** can enjoy the **National Cycle Network,** which connects Derry, Strabane, and Omagh via smooth, low-traffic roads. The route is labeled on *Ordnance Survey* maps and is signposted in most areas. Further options for Sperrin-edification abound. For starters, the **Sperrins Heritage Centre,** 1 mi. east of **Cranagh** on the Plumbridge-Draperstown road, presents some state-of-the-art multimedia ballyhoo, featuring storytelling ghost bartenders, glaciation, and a small stream where the lucky and foolish try their hands at gold prospecting. (☎ 8164 8142. Open Apr.-Oct. M-F 11:30am-5:30pm, Sa 11:30am-6pm, Su 2-6pm. £2.20, seniors and children £1.30, family £6.90.) **Sperrin Guides** (☎ 8164 8157 or 7126 1148), an organization of specialists in local geology, ecology, and archaeology, offers individually tailored local hikes. Visitors to the Sperrins often base themselves in **Gortin** (see p. 559) or **Omagh** (see p. 556), the towns closest to the most heavily traveled stretch of the range. Distant **Dungiven,** on the A6 in Co. Derry, provides access to the less-traveled northeastern region.

DUNGIVEN (DUN GEIMHIN)

Dungiven is located on the main road between Derry and Belfast. Perfectly situated at the foot of the Sperrins, the town also sports sights of its own; the ornate 14th-century tomb of Cooey na Gal, a Chieftan of the O'Cahans, is one of the best preserved tombs in Northern Ireland. The town is also home to two of the North's most interesting accommodations. Though certainly off the beaten path, Dungiven need not be beyond reach. An hourly **bus** service to Derry and Belfast runs M-Sa and stops in front of Dungiven Castle. Inside the castle is a small **tourist enclave** with free reading material on the Sperrins and Roe Valley. Though unmanned, the castle's front desk can help answer additional questions.

Before checking out the local abodes, stock up on food at **Mace** (Main St.; open M-Su 7:30am-11pm) or **Spar** (Main St.; open M-Sa 9am-10:30pm, Su 1-10:30pm). As one of the self-catering options has no refrigerator, a meal out might be in order. **Skippers Take-away ❶,** Main St. (☎ 7774 0370), a chipper and so much more, fills bellies with hamburgers, fish, and sandwiches (all under £4. Open M-Sa 9:15am-10:15pm, Su 5-10:30pm.) **Northern Banks** (☎ 7774 1215) has a 24hr. **ATM** on Main St. And don't forget to send some postcards home from the **post office,** Main St. (Open M-W and F 9am-12:30pm and 1:30-5:30pm, Th and Sa 9am-12:30pm.)

Whether you're heading to the peaks or simply passing between major cities, the ▓**Flax Mill Hostel (IHH) ❶,** just outside of town, is an anachronistic treasure. Take the first right after passing through Dungiven toward Derry; or if coming from Derry, take a left immediately before the sign announcing Dungiven town. The German owners, Hermann and Marion, charm visitors with their pastoral utopia; they mill flour for delicious homemade bread, grow organic vegetables, and make jam, cheese, and muesli. Despite being without electricity much of the time, the hostel facilities remain top-notch thanks to the ingenuity of the owners: gas lamps glow throughout the building, and gas heating warms water for showers or dips in the incredible bath. The hostel also hosts a variety of cultural programs, including weaving demonstrations and trad sessions, the biggest of which is the **Yard Session**

Festival, a weekend of world-renowned trad and tasty food launched on the second Saturday of September. (☎7774 2655. Call for pick-up from town. Festival suggested donation £10. Book far in advance if planning to attend. Breakfast £2—and well worth it. Dorms £5.80. **Camping** £3.80.) For travelers with a taste for modern amenities, the **Dungiven Castle ❶** has a wide range of "budget accommodation" facilities that bear a striking resemblance to those of a hostel, though it prefers to avoid the name. The castle grounds are surrounded by 22 acres of betrailed land that hovers somewhere between wilderness and domestication, and all of the rooms afford great inland views. (☎7774 2428; www.dundivencastle.com. 1 wheelchair-accessible room. Laundry wash £2, dry £1. Dorms £12; doubles £32; family rooms £16 per person, children £7.)

COUNTY TYRONE

As lakes are to Fermanagh, forests are to Co. Tyrone. Moving toward the Sperrin Mountains, which Tyrone shares with Londonderry, ordered, protected woodlands are followed by forest wilds too unruly to contain. The only thing the county is more proud of than its forests is its history of emigration; the Ulster American Folk Park is a paean to Ulstermen who made it in America. Omagh is a large town that provides bus access to the rest of Ireland; it's also the last chance to pick up supplies before heading to Gortin Glen Forest Park, a scant 8 mi. from town.

OMAGH (AN OMAIGH)

On August 15, 1998, a bomb ripped through Omagh's busy downtown area, killing 29 people and injuring hundreds more. Later, "The Real IRA," a splinter group of the Provisional IRA, took responsibility for the act. Despite persistent memory of this tragedy, the town's sloping main street is once again a center for frenzied commercial activity. Tourists rarely stay in Omagh for long, and most often simply see the bus station and river in the rear view mirror as they head to the Ulster American Folk Park, the nearby forests, and the mountains to the North.

TRANSPORTATION. Ulsterbus runs from the station on Mountjoy Rd. (☎8224 2711. Open M-F 8:30am-5:45pm, Sa 7:30am-12:30pm, Su 3:30-7:15pm. Closed Sa-Su in July-Aug.) Buses go to: Belfast (2hr.; M-Sa 11 per day, Su 5 per day; £7.50, chilren £3.75); Derry (1hr.; M-Sa 11 per day, Su 5 per day; £6/£3); Dublin (3hr.; M-Sa 6 per day, Su 5 per day; £12/£6); Enniskillen (1hr., M-Sa 6 per day, £5.10/£2.30). **Taxis** await at the bus depot, or can be contacted at ☎8229 1010. Cabs have fixed fares to all destinations in the town center (£3), the hostel (£5), and the Folk Park (£6).

ORIENTATION AND PRACTICAL INFORMATION. Omagh's buildings cluster to the south of the **River Strule.** The town center, across the bridge from the bus depot, is bounded by one street with three names as it marches uphill to the town courthouse: **Market, High,** and finally **George Street.** At the top of the hill, High St. splits into pub-lined **John Street.** Warm welcomes and town maps, including the *Historical Walks of Omagh Guide,* are free at the **tourist office** at 1 Market St., but that lovingly detailed *Ordnance Survey* (#13) of the Sperrin Mountains costs £6. Accommodations bookings cost £2. **Internet** access (£1.50 per hr.) is a new addition. (☎8224 7831; www.omagh.gov.uk/tourism/htm. Open Apr.-June, Sept. M-Sa 9am-5pm; July-Aug. M-Sa 9am-5:30pm; Oct.-Mar. M-F 9am-5pm.) Nab cash from the 24hr. **ATM** at **First Trust,** 8 High St., next to the tourist office. (☎8224 7133. Open M-F 9:30am-4:30pm, W open 10am.) **Boots** pharms out prescriptions at 47 High St. (☎8224 5455. Open M-Sa 9am-5:30pm.) To **get 'netted,** walk downhill on Market St.

Counties Tyrone & Fermanagh

and turn right onto the Dublin Rd; the **library** is at 1 Spillars Pl. Their 40 terminals rarely require waiting. (☎8224 4821. £2.50 per hr., free M-F 9:15am-1pm. Open M, W, and F 9:15am-5:30pm;

Tu and Th 9:15am-8pm, Sa 9:15am-1pm and 2-5pm.) If a visit to the Folk Park is in the cards, its **Centre for Migration Studies** offers **free Internet**. The **post office** is at 7 High St. (☎8224 2015. Open M-F 9am-5:30pm, Sa 10am-12:30pm.) **Postal code:** BT78 1AB.

⌂◨▨ ACCOMMODATIONS, FOOD, AND PUBS. Indulge in a three-in-one combination at **Hawthorne House,** 72 Old Mountfield Rd. The hotel, bar, and restaurant has some of the nicest food in town, and the convenience of being one of the only accommodations clos(er) to the town center (a 15min. walk). Spacious rooms with all the amenities of a fancy home make it hard to resist. (☎8225 2005; www.hawthornhouse.co.uk. Singles £40; doubles £60.) The **Omagh Hostel ❶,** 9a Waterworks Rd., perches atop a remote hill overlooking the town, sharing its space with several cattle and sheep. The building itself is plain and clean, but has been expanded to include a small conservatory perfect for sipping tea and watching the sun set. Call the owners for pickup or head north from town on the B48; turn right and follow the signs that start about a mile out of town. Expect a 15min. ride through cow country. (☎8224 1973; www.omaghhostel.co.uk. Laundry £3. £7 per person. 2hr. of clean-up around the hostel scores a free night's stay.) At the **4 Winds ❷,** 10min. from town at 63 Dromore Rd., the owner (a former chef) provides

THE LOCAL STORY

An interview with Paddy Fitzgerald of the Ulster American Folk Museum.

LG: Being from the North, how do you define your "Irish identity?"

PF: Ah, right. It's a very important question. I think it's an issue that everyone in Northern Ireland, and probably all of Ireland, are obsessed with. I think we spend most of our time belly-button gazing trying to define ourselves. My own identity fluctuates. I used to tell myself that I was "Bri-rish" to negotiate my dual identities. And that's not just a cute way of saying something or nothing at all. The word "Bri-rish" addressed the fact that I was an Ulster Protestant, that I have areas culturally and so on where I feel attached to the British heritage, but that I also have areas where I would see myself relating to an Irish Catholic culture, or an Irish Gaelic culture if you want to use those terms. The word is a way to negotiate the two. I tend to see myself as Irish, even though I am also an Ulster Protestant. Let me give you an example: Gaelic rugby football is something I've played since I was a kid. I often find meself screaming in joy at the TV in Belfast when the Irish score against England. So I see meself as Irish, even though I'm also a 'Proddie.' I mean, there have been people who played on the Irish team and had UVF tattoos. That should give you a good sense of the multi-faceted cultures and identities in the North. I mean, I'm a Northern Irish Protestant named Paddy Fitzgerald. If that doesn't explain the torn identities in Northern Ireland, I don't know what will.

a filling Irish breakfast and packs lunches on request. Call for pickup or directions. (☎8224 3554; www.fourwinds.org.uk. £18, £20 with bath.) Pitch a tent 8 mi. north of Omagh at **Glen Caravan and Camping Park ❶**, on the Gortin road (B48). The facility includes special rates to the Omagh Leisure Complex and its pool, sauna, gym, and tennis courts. (☎8164 8108. **Bike hire** £7 per day. £4-9 per tent.)

Grant's (aka **Ulysses S. Grant's**) ❸, 29 George St., reminds visitors of that proud Irish-American link by letting them raze their way through a menu of pasta, steak, and seafood, all printed on Lady Liberty's visage. Dinner is pricey (£8.95-15.95), but lunch (about £5) and the evening special (£5-7.50) fit most budgets. (☎8225 0900. Open M-Th noon-10pm, F-Sa noon-10:30pm, Su 5-10pm.) The **Riverfront Coffeehouse ❶**, 38 Market St., lures the lunch swarms with swank blue lights and an industrial-strength sandwich bar. (☎8225 0011. Sandwiches £2, daily special £4. Open M-Sa 9am-5:15pm.) **Dragon Castle ❷**, High St., captures its maidens with affordable, tried-and-true takeaway. For what it's worth, it's the oldest Chinese restaurant in Omagh, though age has not necessarily translated to beauty as the hypercolor scenes of Shanghai attest. Lunch specials Th-F £5-6. (☎8224 5208. Open M-Th 5-11:45pm, F-Sa 5pm-12:45am, Su 5-11:45pm.) **McElroy's ❷**, on Castle St., serves up sandwiches, chicken nuggets, and seafood at reasonable prices. (☎8224 4441. Club sandwich £3.50.) **Sally O'Brien**, cowering down the street from the Dragon, began as a tea merchant in the 1880s but has since moved on to stronger brews. Drink among the old tins and decrepit boxes nestled into well-oiled cubbies and hearken back to the days when the place resembled a country store more than a meet-and-greet. W karaoke, Th trad, F-Su live music, with mostly cover bands and country-western on Su. On weekend nights, clubbers shake it in the back at **Eden**, a club in full color to contrast with the gray night's monochrome. (☎8224 2521. Bar 18+, club 20+. Cover £5-6.) Other gotta-dance youngsters join the throngs at **McElroy's**. (☎8224 4441. Cover £4-6. Open Sa.)

◪ **SIGHTS.** The 🏛**Ulster American Folk Park**, 5 mi. north of Omagh on the Strabane road (A5), proudly chronicles the experiences of the two million folk who left Ulster in the 18th and 19th centuries, including exhibits on Andrew Jackson, Davy Crockett, and Ulysses S. Grant. The indoor museum has full-scale tableaux of a Famine cottage and a New York City tenement. The open air museum is spread around the Mellon (of Mellon Bank and Carnegie-Mellon fame) homestead, the only building in its original location.

The buildings in the rest of the park were transplanted from all over Ulster. Seafaring types relish the journey from a reconstructed Irish port town, onto the Brig Union sailing ship, and straight to the streets of Boston...all in only 10min. Frequent special events include July 4th celebrations on the weekend nearest the 4th, an Appalachian and Bluegrass Festival in September, and occasional farming demonstrations and craft workshops. The Omagh-Strabane bus (M-Sa 5-7 per day, Su 2 per day; £1.75) runs directly to the Park. (☎8224 3292; www.folkpark.com. Open Apr.-Sept. M-Sa 10:30am-6pm, Su 11am-6:30pm; Oct.-Mar. M-F 10:30am-5pm. Last admission 1½hr. before closing. £4, seniors and children £2.50, family £10. Joint ticket with History Park £6.50/£4.)

Next door is the **Centre for Migration Studies,** which includes an extensive collection of books on Irish-Americana and emigration, and has **free Internet** access. (☎8225 6315; www.qub.ac.uk/cms. Open M-F 9:30am-4:30pm.) The **Ulster History Park,** 7 mi. out of town on the Gortin Rd., is a precursor to the Folk Park. The open air museum seeks to trace the millenia leading to emigration. The many replicas include a *dolmen* (megalithic tomb), an early monastery, a *crannog* (island fort), and a Plantation settlement. The park hosts periodic special events, such as St. Patrick's Day festivities and a craft fair in August. The Omagh-Gortin bus stops here. (☎8164 8188; www.omagh.gov.uk/historypark.htm. Open July-Aug. daily 10am-6:30pm; Apr.-June and Sept. 10am-5:30pm; Oct.-Mar. M-F 10am-5pm. Last admission 1hr. before closing. Tours at 12:30pm, 2pm, and 3:30pm are highly recommended to suss out the mysterious megalithic rock piles. £3.75, students £2.50; joint ticket with Folk Park £6.50/£4. HINI members receive 10% discount.)

The **Gortin Glen Forest Park,** brimming with deer, nature trails, and breathtaking views, is a 3min. walk to the left as you leave the History Park. (☎8167 0666; www.forestserviceni.gov.uk. Open daily 8am-8pm. Cars £2.50.) **Take A Walk on the Wild Side,** 137 Donaghadee Rd., leads simple strolls, and rock climbing and abseiling (rappeling) expeditions for the wilder ones (☎8275 8452; www.walkwithmarty.com). The annual **Omagh Agricultural Show** is held the first Saturday of July on the Gillygoolly Rd. beyond the Derry Rd. and is a veritable family day out with barnyard animals, music, tractor rides, and great carnival food. Archaeology enthusiasts should check out Ireland's answer to Stonehenge: on the A505 between Omagh and Cookstown, **An Creagán** has 44 well-preserved Neolithic monuments. (☎8076 1112; www.ancreagan.com. Open Apr.-Sept. daily 11am-6:30pm; Oct.-Mar. M-F 11am-4:30pm. £2, students £1.50.) The first weekend in May, born-again Celts descend on the village of **Creggan** for the **Bealtaine Festival,** an ancient rite of fertility and fun.

NEAR OMAGH: GORTIN

Ten miles north of Omagh on the B48, one-street, two-hostel Gortin provides access to the walking trails of the **Central Sperrins Way** and the **Gortin Forest Park** (see **Sights,** p. 559). Despite its ideal location right on the edge of the **Sperrin Mountains,** Gortin feels largely undiscovered. Short walks surround the town—the **Gortin Burn Walk,** for instance, offers a gentle 2 mi. meander along a riverbank toward the forest park. The trailhead is up a gravel road just before the post office. For **guided walks** of the Sperrins, contact Oonagh McKenna anytime at **Sperrin Trails,** 29 Crocknaboy Rd. or in Badony Tavern, on the main drag; her brother Pete will happily track her down. (☎8164 8157 or 079 5081 4602; www.sperrintrails.com.) Details of walking routes and guides can be found at the **Gortin Activity Centre**, 62 Main St. (☎8164 8346 or 8164 8390). **Fishing permits** can be purchased with sausages at **Treanor Meats,** 56 Main St. (☎8164 8543; £10 per day).

Gortin is easily reached by **bus** from Omagh (30min., 4 per day, £2), or on the **Gortin Rambler** (Sa-Su 5 per day). The **Ulster Bank** has a **24hr. ATM.** (Open M-F 9:30am-12:30pm and 1:30-4:30pm.) An anonymous **pharmacy** at the end of Main St. relieves maladies. (☎8164 8020. Open M-F 9:30am-1pm and 2-6pm, Th-Sa 9:30am-1pm.)

The **Gortin Accommodation Suite and Activity Centre ❶**, 62 Main St., is modern and child-friendly, with a number of accommodations from 6-8 person self-catering apartments (£55-60 per night) to family rooms (£30-34 per night). Kitchen, laundry, and aclounge with a fireplace can't compete with the playground out back. (☎8164 8346; www.gortin.net. Dorm rooms £8.50.) That renovated schoolhouse on the Omagh road is actually the **Gortin Hostel ❶**, 198 Glenpark Rd., uphill on Main St. across from the Church of Ireland. The comfort of the beds in the lofty rooms is matched by the hearthside chairs. Relaxed owners lend bikes bikes with only visitors' word as a deposit. (☎8164 8083; if no answer, ring the warden who lives next door at ☎8164 8087. Dorms £6.50.) Pitch a tent in a forest plot at the **Gortin Glen Caravan Park ❶**, 2 mi. south of town on the Omagh road. (Contact the tourist office at ☎8224 7831 for bookings. Laundry £1.60. 2-person tent £4.50 per night, £26 per wk.) **McSwiggen's Costcutters** sells groceries. (☎8164 8810. Open M-F 8am-9pm, Sa 8am-10:30pm, Su 9am-8pm.) **Glenview ❶**, down the street, fries up takeaway goodies. (☎8164 8705. Open Su-Th 5-11:30pm, F-Sa 5pm-1:30am.) **Badoney Tavern,** the town's only pub, complements its pints with cheap pub grub and a heaping of *craic*. (☎8164 8157. Food served noon-10pm.)

FERMANAGH LAKE DISTRICT

Crossing the border into Co. Fermanagh from Sligo is a jarring experience due to rough southern roads. Heading inland, the landscape changes dramatically, as hills become peppered with trees and placid cattle. In Fermanagh, fields are tidy and walled, with firm rectangular boundaries; everything here seems slightly more ordered than in neighboring counties to the south. Eventually, hills descend into small valleys filled with wide lakes. Along with Upper and Lower Lough Erne, a number of smaller lakes intertwine into a matrix of waterways, whose placid streams creep from Sligo in the west, across Enniskillen, and south into Co. Cavan. Vacationers, mostly from Northern Ireland, crowd into this, the "Lake District of Northern Ireland," in July and August.

ENNISKILLEN (INIS CEITHLEANN)

Busy. Clean. Industrious. Enniskillen seems best captured in single words, so fast is the pace of life in this tidy market town compared to its country neighbors. The major transportation hub between Northern Ireland and the Republic, Enniskillen is nonetheless relatively manicured and neighborly, and its abundant shops and services make it a thoroughly pleasant base for explorations of the Lake District. The town center's shops and pubs rest on an island between Upper and Lower Lough Erne, connected to the mainland by five traffic-choked bridges. Though undetectable on its neat streets or in the faces of its people, Enniskillen still bears the emotional scars of an IRA bombing on Remembrance Day 1987, which killed 11 and injured 61. In 2001, the Clinton Centre, named and inaugurated by the former US President and Fermanagh Co. descendant, was finished on the site of the bombing. The futuristic edifice, a working monument to peace, houses the youth Hostel, cafes, and conference rooms.

▐▀ TRANSPORTATION

Buses: Wellington Rd. (☎6632 2633), across from tourist office. Open M-F 8:45am-5:15pm, Sa 8:45am-2:45pm. To: **Belfast** (2½hr.; M-F 13 per day, Sa 12 per day, Su 8 per day; £8.20.); **Derry** via **Omagh** (3hr.; M-F 8 per day, Sa 3 per day, Su 4 per day; £7.80); **Dublin,** from Donegal (3hr.; M-Sa 5 per day, Su 4 per day; €11.40); **Galway** (5hr.; M-Sa 3 per day, Su 1 per day; €18.50); **Sligo** (1hr., M-Sa 3 per day, €10.20).

Taxis: Speedy Cabs (☎6632 7327; toll-free ☎0800 855 327).

Bike Rental: Lakeland Canoe Centre. Bikes £10 per day.

✦ ⚡ ORIENTATION AND PRACTICAL INFORMATION

Enniskillen's primary streets run laterally across the island: **Queen Elizabeth Road.** borders the town to the north, while **Ann, Darling, Church, High, Townhall,** and **East Bridge Streets** are the six segments of the schizophrenic middle street after Queen Elizabeth and before **Wellington Road** to the south.

Tourist Office: Fermanagh Tourist Information Centre, Wellington Rd. (☎6632 3110; www.fermanagh-online.com), across from the bus station. Accommodations booking, bureau de cha4nge, and a 24hr. touch screen information system. Open July-Aug. M-F 9am-7pm; Sept.-June M-F 9am-5:30pm.

Banks: Bank of Ireland, Townhall St. (☎6632 2136). Open M-Tu, Th-F 9:30am-4:30pm; W 10am-4:30pm. **Ulster Bank,** Darling St. (☎6632 4034). Open M-F 9:30am-4:30pm.

Luggage Storage: Ulsterbus Parcel-link (☎6632 2633), at the bus station. 50p per bag. Open M-F 9am-5:30pm; no overnight storage. Closed on bank holidays.

Pharmacy: Gordon's, High St. (☎6632 2393). Open M-Sa 9am-5:30pm. Rotating Su hours.

Emergency: ☎999; no coins required. **Police:** Queen St. (☎6632 2823).

Internet Access: Intech Centre (☎6632 2556), the orange building on E. Bridge St. across from the youth hostel. £2 per hr. Open M-F 9am-5pm. Book ahead for Internet at the **Library,** Queen Elizabeth Rd. (☎6632 2886). £1.50 per 30min. Open M, W, F 9:15am-5:15pm; Tu and Th 9:15am-7:30pm; Sa 9:15am-1pm.

Post Office: E. Bridge St. (☎6632 4525), at the back of the Spar. Open M-F 8am-5:30pm, Sa 9am-5:30pm. **Postal code:** BT7 47BW.

▌ ACCOMMODATIONS AND CAMPING

Backpackers have a couple of hostel options in Enniskillen, while quality B&Bs are surprisingly scarce and farther from the town center. Those blessed with wheels may want to check out the **HINI ❶** hostel 10 mi. north of town on the B82 in **Castle Archdale Country Park,** in a historic 1773 farmhouse on the shores of Lough Erne. (☎6862 8118; www.hini.org.uk. Open Mar.-Oct. Dorms £9.50; doubles £23.)

▨ **The Bridges (HINI),** Belmore St. (☎6634 0110; www.hini.org.uk). 5min. walk from bus depot. Turn right on Wellington Rd., take 1st left after Erneside Shopping Centre. Turn right onto E. Bridge St.; futuristic building at the end. Shiny new hostel is clean, spacious, and environmentally friendly (1st building in Ireland to use both photo voltaic cells *and* solar panels for energy). Friendly staff and comfy beds recommend the place. Kitchen closes at 10:30pm, but TV, dining, and quiet rooms open all night. **Internet** access £0.50 per 5min. Laundry £3. 2- to 6-bed dorms £12.50, under 18 £10. ❷

Sharvedda, Dublin Rd. (☎6632 2659), a 10min. walk from town. Guests are lodged in private converted stables behind the main house, though pristine interiors are in no way sties. Pillowy bedspreads are comfort itself. Singles £25; doubles with bath £45. ❸

Railway Hotel, 34 Forthill St. (☎6632 2084), a left off Belmore St. out of town. A cheery yellow building with blue trim. Staying here is an excercise in convenience with TVs, direct dial phones, and private baths in big rooms. More comfort in a downstairs restaurant and bar. Book ahead for weekends. Singles £32.50; doubles £60. ❹

◖ ▨ FOOD AND PUBS

The most budget conscious option for gustation is scavenging through the grocery stores lining the main streets; **Dunnes,** Belmore St., is the largest. (☎6632 5132. Open M-Tu and Sa 9am-6pm, W-F 9am-9pm, Su 1-6pm). Proper restaurants feed a dinner crowd and cafes in the city's center tide over lunch crowds.

NORTHERN IRELAND

Kenny's, Forthill St. (☎6632 3376), a left off Belmore away from town's center. Locals rave about fish and chips and chicken fillet burger. £3 buys most anything. Sit-in open M-F 10am-11pm, Sa 10am-10:30pm. Takeaway noon-11pm. ❶

Scoffs Restaurant, 17 Belmont St. (☎6634 2622). After an afternoon cavorting with sheep, an amazing leg of lamb (£11.50) can be indulgingly consumed here in the warm dark-wooded interior. Entrees £9-14. Open daily 5pm-11pm. ❹

Kamal Mahal, 1 Water St. (☎6632 5045; www.kamal-mahal.com), a left onto Water St. toward town from Queen Elizabeth's Rd. Portions large enough to sate an army of carnivores or a cadre of vegetarians. Lunch buffet £4.95, served M-Sa noon-3pm. Takeaway or sit-down. Dinner served daily 5pm-midnight. ❷

World Cafe, 1 Middleton St. (☎6632 2264), past Buttermarket toward High St. Trendy cafe serves wraps and cappuccino at passable prices. Real deal is shoe store above, where independent designer shoes sell for appetizing prices. Chicken Tikka Wrap £3.95. Black slingback £17. Open M-Sa 9:30am-5pm. ❶

Oscar's, Bemore St. (☎6632 7037; www.oscars-restaurant.co.uk). A Mediterranean-influenced menu in a unique pub/library. In homage to Oscar Wilde (who attended Enniskillen's Portora Royal School), books line the walls. Upstairs, the candlelit **Writer's Room** allows smoking. Most meals £8-12. Veggie menu. Open daily 6-10pm. ❹

▨ **Blake's of the Hollow,** 6 Church St. (☎6632 2143; blakesofthehollow@utvinternet.com). Ancient, red facade reads "William Blake." Door leads to dark front pub with gated snugs, modern pub upstairs, airy beer garden out back, Greco-Roman wine bar in the cellar; and mod 60s club to top the building. Trad F. Club cover Sa £3, F after midnight £2-3. Club open W-Su 10:30pm-late. Bar M-Sa 11:30am-1am, Su noon-midnight.

Pat's Bar, 1-5 Townhall St. (☎6632 7462; www.pats.bar@virgin.net). Live music weekends, from trad to rock, with nightly acts in summer. Sa is big with band downstairs and one upstairs. Popular club pulses above. 18+. Open M-Sa 9:30am-1am, Su noon-1am.

The Crowe's Nest, 12 High St. (☎6632 5252;www.crows-nest.net). Gas masks and swords decorate this central pub/grill. Nightly music at 10pm, from country to trad. W and Sa nights especially bumpin'. 18+. Upstairs, **Thatch Niteclub** runs the musical gamut, including slow songs for lovers. 21+. No cover W and Su; disco F £4, Sa £5.

⊙ 🎿 SIGHTS AND ACTIVITIES

At the end of Wellington Rd., the jumbled buildings of **Enniskillen Castle** were home to the fearsome Gaelic Maguire chieftains in the 15th century before becoming Elizabethan barracks; these days they house two separate museums. The castle's **heritage center** presents a comprehensive look at rural Fermanagh, beginning with a pottery display and culminating in a large-scale tableau of an 1830s kitchen. The **Museum of the Royal Inniskilling Fusiliers,** in the castle keep, is a militarophile's playground, with guns, uniforms, and row upon row of medals. (☎6632 5000; www.enniskillencastle.co.jk. Open Oct.-Apr. M 2-5pm, Tu-F 10am-5pm; May-Sept. also Sa 2-5pm; July-Aug. also Su 2-5pm. £2.)

One and a half miles south of Enniskillen on A4, **Castle Coole** rears up in Neoclassical pride, with a hauteur justified by the £7 million the National Trust spent restoring it. Prolific British architect James Wyatt completed this impressive mansion in 1798; while Italian marble craftsman Bartoli designed its numerous scagioli columns (hollow columns encased by fine marble but not used to support the roofs). A less celebrated feature delights gadget-lovers: the face of the **French clock** in the dining room turns while the hands remain immobile. Other artifacts of interest include the **sate room,** outfitted for King George IV's visit with royal luxuries. The saloon holds a **wedgewood piano** with plaques embedded in its body. Only three are known to exist; the other two reside in U.S. museums. The castle grounds are 10min. along the Dublin road; the castle itself appears at the end of a 20min. hike up the driveway, though the savvy note a second parking lot mere meters from the entrance. (☎6632 2690; www.national-trust.org.uk. Open July-Aug. daily noon-6pm; June W-M noon-6pm; mid-Mar. to May and Sept. Sa and Su noon-6pm. Last tour 5:15pm. Admission to house by guided tour only. £3.50, children £1.75, family £8.50.) Diagonally across from the castle, the **Ardho-wen Theatre** poses by the shore, satisfying dance, drama, music, and comedy enthusi-asts. (☎6632 5440; www.ardhowentheatre.com. Performances generally Th-Sa. Box office open M-Sa 10am-4:30pm, until 7:30pm performance nights. Tickets £7-15.)

Fermanagh Lakeland Forum, behind the tourist office, has squash, badminton, and tennis courts, and a swimming pool. (☎6632 4121; www.fermanagh-online.com. Open M-F 8am-10:30pm, Sa 10am-6pm, Su 2-6pm. Tennis £3 per hr. Racket rental 50p. Pool £2.) The 18-hole **Enniskillen Golf Club,** Castle Coole Rd., is within walking distance of town. (☎6632 5250. M-F £15, Sa and Su £18.) For watersports, make waves at the **Drumrush Watersports Center,** Boa Island. (☎9693 1578. Open June-Sept. daily 10am-6pm. Sailing £20 per hr.; £100 per day. Waterskiing £30 per 30min. Jet skiing £35 per 30min. Canoes £7.50 per hr. Paddleboats £10 per hr. Powerboats £30 per 30min.) Slightly cheaper **waterskiing** is available at **Tudor Farm,** also on Boa Island. (☎6863 1943. Open daily 11am-7pm. £15 per 25min. lesson. Experienced skiers £10 per run.) The **Castle Archdale Marina** rents boats. An extra £25 gets the boat overnight and free **camping** on one of the islands. The marina also **rents bikes** (£6 per half day, £10 per day), sells **fishing rods** and bait (£30), and runs **pony trek-king** expeditions. (☎6862 1892. Boats £50 per day; £25 per 2hr. Fishing rod and bait £5.) A **GAA Pitch** lies on Factory Rd. Experienced spelunkers rock it to **Correlea** in Belcoo (☎6638 6668) or **Gortatole** in Florencecourt (☎6634 8888) for planned trips into the Marble Arch Caves. The **Speleological Union of Ireland** (www.cavingire-land.org) has information about sites outside the Lake District.

▶ DAYTRIPS FROM ENNISKILLEN

FLORENCE COURT AND FOREST PARK. Florence Court, which once housed the Earls of Enniskillen, is a mid-18th-century Georgian mansion built by Sir John Cole, though he never lived to see its completion. The third Earl left behind his fos-sil collection for visitors' delectation; the rocks have been supplemented by the return of much of the original artwork and furniture in recent years. To reach the castle and its artwork, take the Sligo road (A4) out of Enniskillen, then turn left onto the A32 (Swanlinbar Rd.) and follow the signs. (☎6634 8249. Open June-Aug. daily noon-6pm; Apr.-May and Sept. Sa-Su noon-6pm. £4, children £2, family £10.)

MARBLE ARCH CAVES. Four miles farther down the road from Florence Court to Belcoo, and easily combined with Florence Court as a comfortable daytrip from Enniskillen, are the Marble Arch Caves, a subterranean labyrinth of hidden rivers and strangely sculpted limestone. An underground boat trip begins the 1¼hr. tour, which leads to exalted creations carved by nature's weird hand over thousands of years. The winding trip is all too short. A good imagination presents angels, ele-phants, bacon, cauliflower, and other real-life objects in rock form. The reflections of stalactites in the river are a sight to behold. The subterranean trip gets chilly, so wear warm clothes and, as limestone is quite soluble, shoes with good grip soles. The adjacent **geopark** is free and open to the public. It is the actual spot of the **mar-ble arch** through which water flows. To reach the caves, take the Sligo bus to Bel-coo and follow the 3 mi of signposts. A £12 taxi ride is the only alternative. (☎6634 8855; www.marblearchcaves.net. Open Mar.-Oct. daily 10am-4:30pm. Tours every 20min. £6, students and seniors £4. Book ahead. Tours may be canceled due to heavy rain.)

CUILCAH MOUNTAIN PARK. Farther down the road from Florence Court and the Marble Caves, 5min. by car, lies a rugged piece of protected peatland, home to grazing cows and sheep. The **Legnabrocky Trail** from the mountain park's road leads to a stupendous mountain overlook. Trekkers are advised to allow 6hr. for the long, rough climb and to bring proper gear as weather can change drastically in the area. (☎ 6634 8855; mac@fermanagh.gov.uk.)

BELLEEK. Belleek lies 25 mi. from Enniskillen on the A46. Buses run there six times per day (1hr.) from Enniskillen. At the northern tip of Lower Lough Erne, tiny Belleek would go unnoticed were it not for its famously delicate china. Tours of the **Belleek Pottery Factory** tell the story of young John C. Bloomfield's quest to turn a humble toilet manufacturer into the powerhouse of kitsch it is today. (☎ 6865 8501. Open Mar.-Oct. Sa 10am-6pm, Su 2-6pm; Nov.-Feb. M-F 9am-5:30pm. 2 tours per hr. Last tour 4:15pm. £3, seniors £2.)

DEVENISH ISLAND. Today the ruins on Devenish mostly serve as a children's playpen, but they can also provide insight into the culture of early Irish monastic life; St. Molaise founded a monastery here in the 6th century. Today all that remain are **St. Molaise's House,** an oratory; an 81 ft. **round tower** dating from the 12th century; and St. Mary's 15th-century Augustinian **priory.** To reach the island, friendly **Devenish Ferries** pushes off from Trory Point, 4 mi. from Enniskillen on Irvinestown Rd. or a 1 mi. walk to the left from the Trory ferry bus stop on the Pettigoe route. (☎ 07702 052873. 4 boats run Apr.-Sept. daily 10am-5pm. £2.25.)

LONDON

Tourists often travel to or from London on their way to Dublin or Belfast. What follows is enough information to find a good place to sleep and plan a short stay. This is the bare-bones highlights of the majestic city; for more detailed information on sights, museums, shopping, restaurants, nightlife, and more, pick up a copy of *Let's Go: London 2004.*

☞ TRANSPORTATION

Airports: Heathrow Airport (www.baa.co.uk/main/airports/heathrow). The cheapest and best way to get to central London is the **Tube:** Heathrow is in Zone 6, on the Piccadilly Line (40-60min. to Zone 1; every 4-5min. M-Sa 5am-11:34pm, Su 6am-10:43pm; £3.40, under 16 £1.50). The fast but expensive **Heathrow Express** (www.heathrowexpress.co.uk) travels to **Paddington Station** in 15min., every 15min. (5:10am-11:40pm, £14). **Gatwick Airport** is farther from London but has good transport links (www.baa.co.uk/main/airports/gatwick). Trains to London leave from the **South Terminal. Gatwick Express** (☎08705 850 1530; www.gatwickexpress.co.uk) and the cheaper **Connex** (☎0870 603 0405; www.connex.co.uk) both run to **Victoria Station;** Connex takes 7min. longer. (Gatwick Express: 35min., every 15min. 4:30, 5am, then every 15min. until midnight. £11. Connex: 42min., every 15-20min. 5am-midnight and every 30-60min. through the night. £8.20.) Don't even think about taking a taxi from either airport—the trip will take over an hour and will cost a fortune.

Public Transportation: The **24hr. help line** (☎020 7222 1234) helps plan travel. London's subway system is divided into 6 concentric transport zones; fares depend on the distance of the journey and the number of zones crossed (central London £1.60). The **Underground** (or **Tube**) is fast, efficient, and crowded; note that most Tube stations have steep staircases. (Open 6am-approx. midnight.) Buying a **Travelcard** allows unlimited trips—on the Underground, regular buses, British Rail, and the Docklands Light Railway—within certain zones. Available from any station in 1-day, weekend, 1-week, and 1-month increments. If you're doing any amount of sightseeing, you'll almost definitely save money with a Travelcard. The **bus** network is divided into 4 zones. 1-way fares range 70p-£1; a 1-day bus pass is £2. **Night buses** (the "N" routes) run throughout London 11:30pm-6am. All pass through Trafalgar Sq. Pick up free maps and guides at **London Transport's Information Centres** (look for the lower-case "i" logo on signs) at the following Tube stations: Euston, Victoria, King's Cross, Liverpool St., Oxford Circus, Piccadilly, and Heathrow Terminals 1, 2, and 4.

Taxis: A light signifies an available taxi. Fares are steep, and 10% tip is standard.

⏺ PRACTICAL INFORMATION

TOURIST AND LOCAL SERVICES

London Visitor Centres (www.londontouristboard.com): **Heathrow Terminals 1,2,3:** In the Tube station. Open Oct.-Aug. daily 8am-6pm; Sept. M-Sa 9am-7pm, Su 8am-6pm. **Liverpool St.:** In the Tube station. Open June-Sept. M-Sa 8am-7pm, Su 8am-6pm; Oct.-May daily 8am-6pm. **Victoria Station:** Open Easter-Sept. M-Sa 8am-8pm, Su 8am-6pm; Oct.-Easter daily 8am-6pm. **Waterloo Int'l.:** Open daily 8:30am-10:30pm.

Embassies and Consulates: For a full list of those in London, see p. 7.

Gay, Lesbian, and Bisexual: Boyz (www.boyz.co.uk) and **Gingerbeer** (www.ginger-beer.co.uk) are gay and lesbian web portals respectively with listings of clubs, bars, and restaurants. **GAY to Z** (www.gaytoz.co.uk): directory of gay resources and gay-friendly businesses in Britain.

Disability Resources: RADAR, 12 City Forum, 250 City Rd., EC1V 8AF (☎020 7250 3222; www.radar.org.uk), is a network of 500 charities that offer info and support.

Pharmacies: Most "chemists" keep regular store hours; late at night, try: **Bliss,** 5-6 Marble Arch (☎020 7723 6116). Tube: Marble Arch. Open daily 9am-midnight. **Zafash Pharmacy,** 233 Old Brompton Rd. (☎020 7373 2798). Tube: Earl's Court. Open 24hr.

EMERGENCY AND COMMUNICATIONS

Emergency: ☎999; no coins required. ☎112 from a mobile (cell) phone.

Hospitals: The following have 24hr. walk-in A&E departments: **Charing Cross Hospital,** Fulham Palace Rd. (entrance St. Dunstan's Rd.; ☎020 8846 1234; Tube: Baron's Ct. or Hammersmith); **St. Thomas's Hospital,** Lambeth Palace Rd. (☎020 7928 9292; Tube: Waterloo); **University College Hospital,** Grafton Way (☎020 7387 9300; Tube: Warren St.).

Internet Access: easyEverything (☎020 7241 9000; www.easyeverything.com). 5 locations: 9-16 Tottenham Court Rd. (Tube: Tottenham Court Rd.); 456/459 Strand (Tube: Charing Cross); 358 Oxford St. (Tube: Bond St.); 9-13 Wilson Rd. (Tube: Victoria); 160-166 Kensington High St. (Tube: High St. Kensington). From £1 per hr.; min. charge £2. Open 24hr.

Royal Mail (www.royalmail.co.uk). Delivers twice a day M-F, once Sa. Rates within the UK: 1st class letter (next business day) 28p, 2nd class letter (3 business days), 20p. Airmail letters 38p within Europe, 47p intercontinental. Offices all over London.

▐ ACCOMMODATIONS

Accommodations in London cost 2-3 times more than in Ireland. Family rooms often offer good deals. The area near Victoria station (Westminster) is convenient for major sights and transportation. Bloomsbury, near the British Museum, has affordable accommodations. In West London, posh Kensington and less-so Bayswater offer reasonably priced B&Bs. Book well in advance, especially in summer.

WESTMINSTER

▨ **Alexander Hotel,** 13 Belgrave Rd., SW1V 1RB (☎020 7834 9738; www.alexanderhotel.co.uk). Tube: Victoria. Rooms are eclectically and lavishly furnished with quality fittings, oak dressers, comfy beds, and satellite TV. A halberd-wielding suit of armor keeps order in the sunny and pleasant breakfast room. Prices vary according to demand. Singles £45; doubles £65; triples from £75; quads and quints £120. MC/V. ❹

▨ **Melbourne House,** 79 Belgrave Rd. (☎020 7828 3516; www.melbournehousehotel.co.uk). Tube: Pimlico. A clean, well-kept, and recently refurbished establishment with a superbly friendly staff. Non-smoking rooms all with TV, phone, coffee-maker, and kettle; the pride and joy is the luxurious basement double with a triangular bathtub large enough for 2. Continental breakfast included. Reserve 2 weeks ahead; 48hr. cancellation policy. Singles £30, with bath £55; doubles with bath £75; triples with bath £95; quad with bath £110. MC/V (payment on arrival; cash preferred). ❸

BLOOMSBURY

▨ **The Generator,** Compton Pl., off 37 Tavistock Pl. (☎020 7388 7655; www.the-generator.co.uk). Tube: Russell Sq. or King's Cross. The ultimate party hostel. Under-14s not allowed, under-18s restricted to the quieter private rooms upstairs. Mixed-sex dorms, a hopping bar, and well-equipped common rooms have earned this former police barracks a reputation for excellence. All rooms have mirrors and washbasins; private doubles have tables and chairs. Continental breakfast included. Luggage storage, lockers (free—bring your own lock), towels and linens (free and changed on request), laundry. Internet access. Reserve 1 week ahead for weekends. Single-sex dorms available. 8-bed dorms £15 per person; 6-bed £16; 4-bed £17, and cheaper weekly rates apply. Mar.-Oct. singles £42; doubles £53; triples £67.50; quads £90; quints £112.50. Discounts for long stays and online booking. Credit card required with reservation. MC/V. ❷

■ **Ashlee House,** 261-265 Gray's Inn Rd. (☎020 7833 9400; www.ashleehouse.co.uk). Tube: King's Cross St. Pancras. Clean, brightly painted rooms crammed with blue steel bunks. It's "backpackers only," and the enthusiastic staff work hard to ensure a quiet, friendly atmosphere. The crowd is friendly, young, and diverse. King's Cross location may not be the most pleasant, but it's massively included. Lift, TV room, continental breakfast included. Luggage room, safe (free), linen included, towels £1, laundry, kitchen. No lockers, but all rooms lock. 2-week max. stay. Internet access. May-Sept. 16-bed dorms £15; 8- to10-bed £17; 4- to 6-bed £19. Singles £36; doubles £48. Oct.-Apr. dorms £13/£15/£17; singles £34; doubles £44. MC/V. ❷

■ **Jenkins Hotel,** 45 Cartwright Gdns., entry on Barton Pl. (☎020 7387 2067; www.jenkinshotel.demon.co.uk). Tube: Euston or King's Cross St. Pancras. Airy, pleasant rooms with large windows and antique-style furniture have a bright, summery feel whatever the weather. Guests can use the tennis courts in Cartwright Gardens. All rooms have TV, kettle, phone, fridge, hair dryer, and safe. English breakfast included. Completely non-smoking. Reserve 1-2 months ahead. Singles £52, with bath £72; doubles with bath £85; triples with bath £105. MC/V. ❺

■ **The Langland Hotel,** 29-31 Gower St. (☎020 7636 5801; www.langlandhotel.com). Tube: Goodge St. Family atmosphere, wood-framed beds, solid furniture, and plenty of spacious, sparkling baths (cleaned twice daily) help this B&B stand out from its neighbors. Garden and a comfortable lounge with satellite TV. All rooms have TV, kettle, and fan, and have been recently refurbished. English breakfast included. Singles £40, with bath £55; doubles £50/£75; triples £70/£90; quads £90/£110; quint (no bath) £100. Discounts available for longer stays, for students, and in winter. AmEx/MC/V. ❹

KENSINGTON

■ **Oxford Hotel,** 24 Penywern Rd. (☎020 7370 1161; www.the-oxford-hotel.com). Large, bright rooms with enormous windows that let in tons of light. Sparkling-clean baths. Furnishing is minimal but high-quality, with comfortable beds, TV, kettle, safe, chair, and clothes rail. Continental breakfast included. Reserve 2-3 weeks ahead for June. Singles with shower only £36, with bath £50; doubles £57/£67; triples £69/£79; quads £87/£93; quints £105/£115. Discount on stays over 1 week. AmEx/MC/V. ❹

■ **Five Sumner Place Hotel,** 5 Sumner Pl. (☎020 7584 7586; www.sumnerplace.com). Tube: South Kensington. Sumner Place boasts all the amenities of a luxury hotel with the charm of the converted Victorians in the area. All accessible by lift, the spacious rooms have elegant ceiling moldings and large windows; all have private bath, TV, fridge, phone, and hair dryer. English breakfast served in the beautiful conservatory dining room. 14-day cancellation policy; book 1 month ahead in summer. Singles £85; doubles £130. AmEx/MC/V. ❺

■ **Swiss House Hotel,** 171 Old Brompton Rd. (☎020 7373 2769; www.swiss-hh.demon.co.uk). Tube: Gloucester Rd. or South Kensington. On a quiet, shady part of Old Brompton Rd. All of the large, wood-floored rooms have TV, phone, fan, and bath. Book 1 month ahead for summer. Continental breakfast included; English breakfast £6.50. Singles £71, with shower only £51; doubles £89-104; triples £120; quads £134. 5% discount for stays over 7 nights and cash payments. AmEx/MC/V. ❺

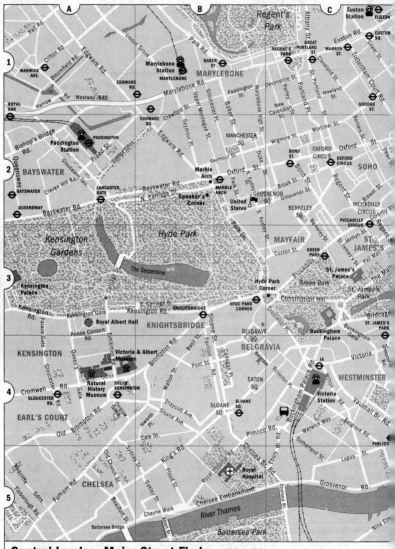

Central London: Major Street Finder (Map 26)

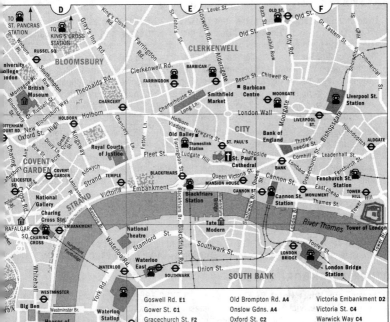

LONDON

Eccleston Pl. **C4**
Edgware Rd. **A1**
Euston Rd. **C1**
Exhibition Rd. **A4**
Farringdon Rd. **E1**
Fenchurch **F2**
Fleet St. **E2**
Fulham Rd. **A5**
Gloucester Pl. **B1**
Gloucester Rd. **A4**

Goswell Rd. **E1**
Gower St. **C1**
Gracechurch St. **F2**
Gray's Inn Rd. **D1**
Gt. Portland St. **C1**
Gt. Russell St. **D1**
Grosvenor Pl. **C3**
Grosvenor Rd. **C5**
Grosvenor St. (Upr.) **C2**
Haymarket **D3**
Holborn/High/Viaduct **D1**
Horseferry Rd. **C4**
Jermyn St. **C3**
Kensington Rd. **A3**
King's Cross Rd. **D1**
King's Rd. **B5**
Kingsway **D2**
Lambeth Rd. **D4**
Lancaster Pl. **D2**
Leadenhall St. **F2**
Lisson Grove **A1**
Lombard St. **F2**
London Wall **E1**
Long Acre/Gt. Queen St. **D2**
Long Ln. **E1**
Ludgate Hill **E2**
Marylebone High St. **B1**
Marylebone Rd. **B1**
Millbank **D4**
Montague Pl. **D1**
Moorgate **F1**
Mortimer St. **C2**
New Cavendish St. **C1**
Newgate St. **E2**
Nine Elms Ln. **C5**
Oakley St. **B5**
Old St. **F1**

Old Brompton Rd. **A4**
Onslow Gdns. **A4**
Oxford St. **C2**
Paddington St. **B1**
Pall Mall **C3**
Park Ln. **B3**
Park Rd. **B1**
Park St. **B2**
Piccadilly **C3**
Pont St. **B4**
Portland Pl. **C1**
Praed St. **A2**
Queen St. **E2**
Queen Victoria St. **E2**
Queen's Gate **A4**
Queensway **A2**
Redcliffe Gdns. **A5**
Regent St. **C3**
Royal Hospital Rd. **B5**
St. James's St. **C3**
Seymour Pl. **B2**
Seymour St. **B2**
Shaftesbury Ave. **D2**
Sloane St. **B3**
Southampton Row **D1**
Southwark Bridge Rd. **E3**
Southwark St. **E3**
Stamford St. **E3**
Strand **D2**
Sydney St. **A5**
Thames St. **F2**
The Mall **C3**
Theobalds Rd. **D1**
Threadneedle St. **F2**
Tottenham Court Rd. **C1**
Tower Hill **F2**
Vauxhall Br. Rd. **C4**

Victoria Embankment **D2**
Victoria St. **C4**
Warwick Way **C4**
Whitehall **D3**
Wigmore St. **C2**
Woburn Pl. **D1**
York Rd. **D3**

RAILWAY STATIONS
Barbican **E1**
Blackfriars **E2**
Cannon St. **F2**
Charing Cross **D3**
City Thameslink **E2**
Euston **C1**
Farringdon **E1**
King's Cross **D1**
Liverpool St. **F1**
London Bridge **F3**
Marylebone **B1**
Moorgate **F1**
Old St. **F1**
Paddington **A2**
St. Pancras **D1**
Victoria **C4**
Waterloo **D3**
Waterloo East **E3**

BRIDGES
Albert **B5**
Battersea **A5**
Blackfriars **E2**
Chelsea **C5**
Hungerford Footbridge **D3**
Lambeth **D4**
London Bridge **F2**
Millennium **E2**
Southwark **E2**
Tower Bridge **F3**
Waterloo **D2**
Westminster **D3**

BAYSWATER

Hyde Park Hostel, 2-6 Inverness Terr. (☎020 7229 5101; www.astorhostels.com). Tube: Queensway or Bayswater. Despite flimsy mattresses and cramped quarters (though the big dorms are relatively spacious), this colorful, backpacker-friendly hostel is tons of fun. The jungle-themed basement bar and dance space hosts DJs and theme parties (open W-Sa 8pm-3am). Continental breakfast and linen included. Kitchen, laundry, TV lounge, secure luggage room. Ages 16-35 only. Reserve 2 weeks ahead for summer; 24hr. cancellation policy. Internet access. Online booking with 10% non-refundable deposit. 10- to 12-bed dorms £11-13.50; 8-beds £14.50-15.50; 6-beds £15.50-16.50; 4-beds £16.50-17.50; twins £42-45. 10% ISIC discount. MC/V. ❶

Quest Hostel, 45 Queensborough Terr. (☎020 7229 7782; www.astorhostels.com). Tube: Bayswater or Queensway. Another in the Astor chain, but with more comfortable, snazzy bunkbeds and more space than the Hyde Park Hostel (see above). Dorms are mostly mixed-sex, and many have baths; those that don't could be 2 floors from a shower. Laundry, kitchen available. Continental breakfast, linen, and lockers included. 4- to 8-bed dorms £14-16; twins £40. MC/V. ❷

Admiral Hotel, 143 Sussex Gdns. (☎020 7723 7309; www.admiral-hotel.com). Tube: Paddington. Beautifully kept family-run B&B, with bath, TV, and kettle, decorated in summer colors. Some baths are linoleum—ask for a room with tiled baths. Non-smoking. English breakfast included. Call 10-14 days ahead in summer; 4-day cancellation policy. Singles £45; doubles £65; triples £90; quads £100; quints £120. MC/V. ❹

OTHER NEIGHBORHOODS

▨ **Westminster House Hotel,** 96 Ebury St. (☎020 7730 7850; www.westminsterhousehotel.co.uk). Tube: Victoria. Extreme cleanliness, prime location, and a charming family staff make this a standout. The spotless rooms have TV, tea, coffee and hot chocolate, and almost all have private bath. English breakfast included. 48hr. cancellation policy. Singles £55, with bath £60; doubles £75/£85; triples with bath £95; quad with bath £105. AmEx/MC/V. ❺

▨ **Travel Inn County Hall,** Belvedere Rd. (☎020 0870 238 3300; www.travelinn.co.uk). Tube: Westminster or Waterloo. Seconds from the South Bank and Westminster. All rooms are clean and modern with bath and color TV. Facilities include elevator, restaurant, and bar. Prices by the room make it a great deal for families. Reserve at least 1 month ahead; cancel by 4pm on day of arrival. Continental breakfast £5, English £6, Singles/doubles and family rooms (2 adults and 2 children) M-Th £83, F-Su £80. AmEx/MC/V. Family ❷, individual ❺.

▨ **High Holborn Residence,** 178 High Holborn (☎020 7379 5589; www.lse.ac.uk/vacations). Tube: Holborn. One of the nicest university dorms that converts into a hostel during the summer, with a great location. Accommodations are clustered into 4-5 rooms, each with phone and shared kitchen and bath; rooms with private bath are much larger, though all are decent-sized. Some rooms wheelchair-enabled. Bar, elevator, laundry, TV room, and games room. Continental breakfast included. Open July 5-Sept. 29 in 2004. Singles £30; twins £48, with bath £58; triples with bath £68. MC/V. ❸

◉ 🖭 TOP SIGHTS & MUSEUMS

Although it may sound hackneyed, a good city tour has its advantages: it offers a quick overview of London's major sights and historic neighborhoods, and while few venture off the beaten path, sightseeing from the top of a bus will give you a better sense of London's geography than point-to-point excursions by Tube. **The Big Bus Company,** 48 Buckingham Palace Rd. (☎020 7233 9533; www.bigbus.co.uk) runs 3 routes, with buses every 5-15min.; £17, children £8.

BUCKINGHAM PALACE. Originally built for the Dukes of Buckingham, Buckingham House was acquired by George III in 1762, and converted into a full-scale palace by George IV. The Palace opens to visitors every August and September while the Royals are off sunning themselves; call for details. The **Changing of the Guard** takes place daily around 11:30am Apr.-Oct., every other day Nov.-Mar., provided the Queen is in residence, it's not raining too hard, and there are no pressing state functions. To witness the spectacle, show up well before 11:30am and stand directly in front of the palace, or on the steps of the Victoria Memorial. *(At the end of the Mall. Tube: St. James's Park, or Victoria.* ☎ *020 7839 1377; www.royal.gov.uk.)*

THE HOUSES OF PARLIAMENT. The Houses of Parliament have been at the heart of English governance since the 11th century, when St. Edward the Confessor established his court here. The current building was designed by classicist Charles Barry and Gothic champion Augustus Pugin, resulting in a masterful combination of both styles of architecture. Both houses are open to all while Parliament is in session (Oct.-July. M-W), but afternoon waits can be over 2hr. *(Parliament Sq. Enter at St. Stephen's Gate, between Old and New Palace Yards. Tube: Westminster. Commons Info Office* ☎ *020 7219 4272; www.parliament.uk. Lords Info Office* ☎ *020 7219 3107; www.lords.uk.)*

WESTMINSTER ABBEY. Almost nothing remains of St. Edward's 1065 Abbey: Henry III's 13th-century Gothic reworking created most of the grand structure you see today. Every ruler since 1066 has been crowned here; many were married and buried here. Alongside dead royals lie such greats as Chaucer and T.S. Eliot. *(Parliament Sq.; access from Dean's Yd. Tube: Westminster.* ☎ *020 7222 5152; www.westminster-abbey.org. Open M-Tu and Th-F 9:30am-3:45pm, W 9:30am-7pm, Sa 9:30am-1:45pm, Su open for services only. £6, concessions and ages 11-15 £4, under 11 free, family £12. Services free.)*

ST. PAUL'S CATHEDRAL. Christopher Wren's masterpiece is the fifth cathedral to occupy the site; the original was built in AD 604 shortly after St. Augustine's mission to the Anglo-Saxons. The stout of heart can climb to the top of St. Paul's dome. 530 steps lead past the Whispering Gallery and the Stone Gallery to the Golden Gallery at the base of the lantern. *(St. Paul's Churchyard. Tube: St. Paul's.* ☎ *020 7246 8348; www.stpauls.co.uk. Open M-Sa 8:30am-4:30pm, last admission 4pm; dome open M-Sa 9:30am-4pm. £6, concessions £5, children £3.)*

THE TOWER OF LONDON. The Tower of London has served as palace, prison, and living museum for over 900 years. The excellent ◩**Yeoman Warder Tours** detail the history and legends associated with the Tower. If want to see the **crown jewels** in Jewel House, get there early or prepare to queue—in the afternoon, the wait can be over an hour. *(Tower Hill. Tube: Tower Hill.* ☎ *020 7709 0765; www.hrp.org.uk. Open Mar.-Oct. M-Sa 9am-6pm, Su 10am-6pm; last entry 5:30pm; Nov.-Feb. all closing times 1hr. earlier, and on M opens at 10am. Yeoman Warder Tours (free) meet near entrance; 1hr., every 90min. M-Sa 9:30am-2:30pm, Su 10am-2:30pm. £12, concessions £9, ages 5-15 £7.80, under 5 free, family £36. Tickets also sold at Tube stations; buy them in advance, as queues at the door are horrendous.)*

BRITISH MUSEUM. With 50,000 items, the magnificent collection is somewhat undermined by a chaotic layout and poor labeling. To avoid getting lost, take a free tour (see the Info desk for details), or purchase the color map available at the entrance (£2). Room 4 houses the Rosetta Stone, while the rest of the enormous Egyptian collection is in rooms 61-68. Rooms 41-42 hold the Sutton Hoo treasure and the stunning Lewis Chessmen. Other exhibits include objects from Africa, Mexico, Japan, and everyplace in between. *(Great Russell St. Tube: Tottenham Court Rd. or Russell Sq.* ☎ *020 7323 8000; www.thebritishmuseum.ac.uk. Open daily 10am-5:30pm; some galleries open later Th-F. Free.)*

NATIONAL GALLERY. One of the world's best art collections. The new Sainsbury Wing holds a stunning collection of Medieval and Renaissance art, including the *Wilton Diptych* and works by Van Eyck, Vermeer, and Leonardo. Room 23 boasts 18 Rembrandts. Room 45 holds Van Gogh's *Sunflowers;* room 44 contains a brilliant set of paintings by Seurat as well as work by Manet, Monet, and Renoir. *(Trafalgar Sq. Tube: Charing Cross. ☎ 020 7747 2885; www.nationalgallery.org.uk. Open M-Tu and Th-Sa 10am-6pm, W 10am-9pm. Free.)*

TATE MODERN. The largest modern art museum in the world (until New York's MOMA re-opens in 2005), its most striking aspect is Giles Gilbert Scott's mammoth building, formerly the Bankside power station. The seventh floor offers amazing panoramic views of London. By grouping works according to themes such as "Subversive Objects," the Tate has turned itself into a work of conceptual art. Picasso, Cézanne, Monet, Miró, Magritte, and Ernst are all on display, along with some brilliant claymation by Jan Svankmajer and any number of temporary exhibits. *(Holland St., Bankside. Tube: Southwark or Blackfriars. ☎ 020 7887 8000; www.tate.org.uk. Open Su-Th 10am-6pm, F-Sa 10am-10pm. Free.)*

VICTORIA & ALBERT MUSEUM. The V&A's five *million* square meters of galleries house the best collection of Italian Renaissance sculpture outside Italy, the largest array of Indian art outside India, and a gallery of fashion from the 16th century to the latest designer collections. Dedicated to displaying "the fine and applied arts of all countries, all styles, all periods," the V&A comes awfully close, with galleries of objects from Medieval Europe, modern Japan, and everything in between. *(Cromwell Rd. Tube: South Kensington. ☎ 020 7942 2000; www.vam.ac.uk. Open Su-Tu and Th-Sa 10am-5:45pm, W plus last F of month 10am-10pm. Free.)*

▓▢ NIGHTLIFE & SHOPPING

London is one of the world's top cities for **clubbing.** *Time Out* (£2.20) is published weekly and lists many of the special nights on offer in the city. **Brixton** is the current club hot spot, with dozens of clubs and bars attracting partiers from all over the world. From Tube: Brixton, turn left and follow the streams of clubbers to **Tongue&Groove,** 50 Atlantic Rd. (☎ 020 7274 8600) and **Bug Bar,** in the crypt of St. Matthew's Church (☎ 020 7738 3184). South London's undisputed megaclub is the **Ministry of Sound,** 103 Gaunt St. (☎ 020 7378 6528; Tube: Elephant and Castle), which is one of the top clubs in the world. **Fabric,** 77a Charterhouse St. (☎ 020 7336 8898; Tube: Farringdon), is among the best nightclubs north of the Thames.

When it comes to shopping, you can't beat the West End. **Oxford Street** (Tube: Oxford Circus) is an amazing sight: thousands of shoppers pack the streets every day. Department stores line the main street, while trendy and edgy boutiques line the side streets. If the Oxford St. crowds are too much for you, **High Street Kensington** (Tube: High St. Kensington) is filled with mainstream chain stores, and leads right to Kensington Gardens and Hyde Park. If you're looking to blow a cool thousand, head to ultra-exclusive **Sloane Street** and **King's Street** (Tube: Sloane Sq.). One would hardly guess that these streets, filled with the poshest of chains from D&G to Armani, once gave birth to both the miniskirt and the Sex Pistols.

APPENDIX

TIME DIFFERENCES

Ireland and the UK are on **Greenwich Mean Time (GMT)**; thus, they are: 1hr. behind (most of) continental Europe; 5hr. ahead of New York (EST); 6hr. ahead of Hibbing, Minnesota (CST); 7hr. ahead of Phoenix, Arizona (MST); 8hr. ahead of Los Angeles, California (PST); 8, 9½, and 10hr. behind Australia; and 12hr. behind Auckland, New Zealand.

MEASUREMENTS

MEASUREMENT CONVERSIONS

1 foot (ft.) = 0.30 m	1 meter (m) = 3.28 ft.
1 yard (yd.) = 0.914m	1 meter (m) = 1.09 yd.
1 mile = 1.61km	1 kilometer (km) = 0.62 mi.
1 acre (ac.) = 0.405ha	1 hectare (ha) = 2.47 ac.
1 square mile (sq. mi.) = 2.59km^2	1 square kilometer (km^2) = 0.386 sq. mi.

TEMPERATURE AND CLIMATE

°CELSIUS	-5	0	5	10	15	20	25	30	35	40
°FAHRENHEIT	23	32	41	50	59	68	77	86	95	104

To convert from °C to °F, multiply by 1.8 and add 32. For a rough approximation, double the Celsius and add 25. To convert from °F to °C, subtract 32 and multiply by 0.55. For a rough approximation, subtract 25 from Fahrenheit and cut it in half.

AVERAGE TEMPERATURE AND RAINFALL

Avg. Temp. (low/high), Precipitation	January			April			July			October		
	°C	°F	mm	°C	°F	mm	°C	°F	mm	°C	°F	mm
Dublin	2/7	37/46	63	5/11	41/52	48	12/18	54/66	66	7/12	46/55	73
Cork	3/7	38/46	124	4/11	40/52	66	11/18	53/65	68	7/12	46/65	106
Belfast	4/7	40/45	83	6/10	44/51	51	13/17	56/63	79	8/11	47/52	85
London	2/7	36/45	60	5/12	41/55	43	13/22	56/72	45	7/14	46/58	78

INTERNATIONAL CALLING CODES

To call internationally without a calling card anywhere in Ireland, dial the international access number ("00") + country code (for the destination country) + number. For operator-assisted and calling card calls, dial the international operator: 114 in the Republic and 155 in the North. For directory assistance, dial 11818 in the Republic and 153 in the North.

CITY CODES		COUNTRY CODES	
Dublin	01	**Australia**	61
Belfast	01232	**Canada**	1

CITY CODES		COUNTRY CODES	
Cork	021	France	33
Galway	091	Ireland	353
Killarney	064	New Zealand	64
Letterkenny	074	Northern Ireland from the Republic	048
Londonderry/Derry	01504	South Africa	27
Limerick	061	Switzerland	41
Sligo	071	U.K.	44
Waterford	051	U.S.	1

DISTANCE (IN MILES)

Distances may vary depending on the type of transportation used and the route traveled. The national speed limit in Ireland is 55mph; in urban areas it is 30mph and 70mph on motorways. However, as there are few large motorways and a bounty of country roads, expect to go about 40mph.

	Ath-lone	Belfast	Cork	Donegal	Dublin	Galway	Limerick	London-derry/Derry	Port-laoise	Water-ford
Athlone		141	136	114	78	58	75	130	46	108
Belfast	141		264	112	104	190	201	73	157	207
Cork	136	264		250	160	130	65	266	108	78
Donegal	114	112	250		138	127	184	250	160	222
Dublin	78	104	160	138		136	123	147	52	98
Galway	58	190	130	127	136		65	169	93	137
Limerick	75	201	65	184	123	65		204	71	80
London-derry/Derry	130	73	266	250	147	169	204		175	238
Portlaoise	46	157	108	160	52	93	71	175		62
Waterford	108	207	78	222	98	137	80	238	62	

GLOSSARY

For a brief history of the Irish language, see **The Irish Language,** p. 73. On the left side of this table is a list of Gaelic/Irish words (or English words marked by a distinct Irish dialect). The glossary on the right side of the table should help sort things out. Spelling conventions do not always match English pronunciations: for example, "mh" sounds like "v," "dh" like "g" and "ai" like "ie."

IRISH	PRONUNCIATION	(AMERICAN) ENGLISH
	Getting to know the locals	
Ba mháich liom point.	ba WHY-lum pee-yunt	I would like a pint.
Cann eille led' thoil.	cahn EYE-leh led-TOIL	Another one, please.
Conas tá tú?	CUNN-us taw too	How are you?
dia dhuit	JEE-a dich	Good day, hello
dia's muire dhuit	Jee-as MWUR-a dich	The reply to "good day"
fáilte	FAHL-tshuh	Welcome
go raibh maith agat	guh roh moh UG-ut	Thank you
mór	more	Big, great
oíche mhaith dhuit	EE-ha woh dich	Good night
sláinte	SLAWN-che	Cheers, to your health

IRISH	PRONUNCIATION	(AMERICAN) ENGLISH
slán agat	slawn UG-ut	Goodbye
Tá sé fluic.	tah SHAY fluck	It's raining.
Tá sé trim!	tah SHAY trim!	It's not raining!
tóg é go bog é	TOG-ah BUG-ay	Take it easy
tuigim	tiggum	I understand
Sleeping and Living		
bedsit		One-room apartment, sometimes with kitchen
biro		Ball point pen
caravan		RV, trailer
dust bin		Trash can
fir	fear	Men
first floor		First floor up from the ground floor (second floor)
flat		Apartment
ground floor		First floor (are you confused yet?)
half-ten, half-nine, etc.		Ten-thirty, nine-thirty, etc.
hoover		Vacuum cleaner
lavatory, lav		Bathroom
leithras	LEH-hrass	Toilets
loo		Bathroom
mná	min-AW	Women
Oifig an Phoist	UFF-ig un fwisht	Post office
to queue up, "the Q"	CUE	Waiting line
teach	chock	House
torch		Flashlight
siopa	SHUP-ah	Shop
Locations and Landmarks		
An Lár	on lahr	City center
Baile Átha Cliath	BALL-yah AW-hah CLEE-ah	Dublin
drumlin		Small hill
Éire	AIR-uh	Ireland; official name of the Republic of Ireland
gaeltacht	GAYL-tokt	A region where Irish is the everyday language
inch, innis		island
quay	key	A waterside street
slieve or sliabh	shleev	Mountain
sraid	shrawd	Street
strand		Beach
trá	thraw	Beach
Getting Around		
coach		Bus (long distance)
hire		Rental
left luggage		Luggage storage
a lift		A ride
lorry		Truck
motorway		Highway
petrol		Gasoline
roundabout		Rotary road interchange
self-drive		Car rental

APPENDIX

IRISH	PRONUNCIATION	(AMERICAN) ENGLISH
single ticket		One-way ticket
Sightseeing		
Bord Fáilte	Bored FAHL-tshuh	Irish Tourist Board
concession		Discount on admission for seniors and students
dolmen		Chamber formed by huge stones
dún	doon	Fort
gaol	jail	Jail
kil	kill	Church; monk's cell
ogham	Oh-um	Early Irish, written on stones
rath	rath *or* rah	Earthen fort
tumulus		Stone burial mound
Money Please		
cheap		Inexpensive (not shoddy)
dear		Expensive
fiver		€5 note (used to mean £5 punts)
sterling		British pound
tenner		€10 note (used to mean £10 punts)
Civic and Cultural		
chemist		Pharmacist
garda, Garda Siochána	GAR-da SHE-och-ANA	Police
OAP		Old age pensioner, "senior citizen"
RTÉ		Radio Telefis Éireann, the Republic's broadcasting authority
RUC		Royal Ulster Constabulary, the police force of Northern Ireland
Please Sir, May I Have Another		
bangers and mash		Sausage and mashed potatoes
bap		A soft round bun
bill		Check (in restaurants)
biscuit		Cookie
candy-floss		Cotton candy
carvey		Meal of meat, potatoes, and carrots/vegetables
chips		French fries
chipper		Fish and chips vendor
crisps		Potato chips
rashers		Irish bacon
takeaway		Take-out, "to go"
Pubs & Music		
bodhrán	BOUR-ohn	Traditional drum
brilliant		Great, "awesome"
busker		Street musician
céilí	KAY-lee	Irish dance
to chat up		To hit on
concertina		Small, round-button accordian
craic	krak	Good cheer, good pub conversation, a good time
faders	FOD-ers	Party poopers who go to bed early
fag		A cigarette
feis	fesh	An assembly or Irish festival

IRISH	PRONUNCIATION	(AMERICAN) ENGLISH
fleadh	flah	A musical festival
knakered		Exhausted and very tired
off-license		Retail liquor store
pissed		Drunk
poitín	pa-CHEEN	Moonshine; sometimes toxic homemade liquor
pub grub		Quality bar food
publican		Barkeep
to slag		To tease and ridicule
to snog		To kiss
to take the piss out		To make fun of in a joking way
trad		Traditional Irish music
uilleann pipes	ILL-in	"Elbow pipes," a form of bagpipes
táim	thaw im	I am...
súgach	SOO-gakh	Tipsy
ar meisce	uhr MEH-shka	Drunk
caoch ólta	KWEE-ukh OLE-ta	"Blind drunk"
Sports		
football		Gaelic football in the Republic, soccer in the North
GAA		Gaelic Athletic Association; organizes Gaelic sports
peil	pell	Football
snooker		A game similar to pool
Politics in the Republic		
Dáil	DOY-il	House of Representatives in the Republic
dole, on the dole		Welfare or unemployment benefits
Fianna Fáil	FEE-in-ah foil	"Soldiers of Destiny," political party in Éire
Fine Gael	FINN-eh gayl	"Family of Ireland," political party in Éire
Seanad	SHAN-ud	The Irish Senate
Taoiseach	TEE-shukh	Irish Prime Minister
Oireachtas	OR-uch-tus	Both houses of the Irish Parliament
Politics in the North		
Bobby Sands		The first IRA member to die during the 1980s hunger strikes; also a member of British parliament
Catholic		Someone of the Roman Catholic faith: usually implies loyalty to the Republic of Ireland
DUP		Democratic Unionist Party; right-wing NI party led by extremist Ian Paisley
INLA		Irish National Liberation Army, an IRA splinter group
IRA (Provisional IRA)		Irish Republican Army; a Nationalist paramilitary group
Loyalist		Pro-British Northern Irish (see Unionists)
Nationalists		Those who want Northern Ireland and the Republic united (see Republicans)
Orangemen		A widespread Protestant Unionist secret order
Protestant		Someone of the Anglican Protestant faith: usually implies allegiance with the British Crown
Provos		Slang for the Provisional IRA

IRISH	PRONUNCIATION	(AMERICAN) ENGLISH
Real IRA		Small splinter group of radicals who claimed responsiblity for the 1998 Omagh bombing
Republicans		Northern Irish who identify with the Republic (see Nationalists)
SDLP		Social Democratic and Labor Party; moderate Nationalist Party in the North
Sinn Féin	shin fayn	"Ourselves Alone," Northern political party; affiliated with the IRA
Sunday, Bloody Sunday		Refers to 30 January 1970, when 13 Catholic civilians were gunned down by the British Army
the Troubles		The period of violence in the North that started in 1969 and continues today
UDA		Ulster Defense Association; Unionist paramilitary group
UFF		Ulster Freedom Fighters (synonymous with UDA)
Unionists		Those who want Northern Ireland to remain part of the UK (see Loyalists)
UUP		Ulster Unionist Party; the ruling party in the North
UVF		Ulster Volunteer Force; Unionist paramilitary group

2004 BANK HOLIDAYS

Government agencies, post offices, and banks are closed on the following days, and businesses may have shorter hours. Sights are more likely to remain open

DATE	HOLIDAY	AREAS
January 1	New Year's Day	Republic of Ireland and Northern Ireland
March 17	St. Patrick's Day	Republic of Ireland and Northern Ireland
April 9	Good Friday	Republic of Ireland and Northern Ireland
April 12	Easter Monday	Republic of Ireland and Northern Ireland
May 3	May Day Bank Holiday	Republic of Ireland and Northern Ireland
May 31	Spring Bank Holiday	Northern Ireland
June 7	First Monday in June	Republic of Ireland
July 12	Battle of the Boyne (Orangeman's Day)	Northern Ireland
August 2	Summer Bank Holiday	Republic of Ireland
August 30	Summer Bank Holiday	Northern Ireland
October 25	Halloween Weekend (last Monday in October)	Republic of Ireland
December 25	Christmas Day	Republic of Ireland and Northern Ireland
December 26	Boxing Day/St. Stephen's Day	Republic of Ireland and Northern Ireland
December 27	Christmas Holiday (carried over)	Northern Ireland
December 28	Boxing Day (carried over)	Northern Ireland

INDEX

I N D E X

INDEX

Map Index

MAP LEGEND

Hospital	Airport	Museum
Police	Bus Station	Hotel/Hostel
Post Office	Train Station	Camping
Tourist Office	Lighthouse	Food & Drink
Bank	Ferry Landing	Shopping
Embassy/Consulate	Church	Nightlife
Site or Service	Monastery	Pubs
Pharmacy	Castle	Internet Café
Theater	Mountain	Service
Library	Park	Pedestrian Zone

Park

Beach

Water

The Let's Go compass always points NORTH.